946	1947	1948	1949	1950	1951	1952	1953	1954	1955	1956	1957	1958	
43.8	$161.7	$174.8	$178.1	$192.0	$207.1	$217.1	$229.7	$235.8	$253.7	$266.0	$280.4	$289.5	1
30.7	34.0	45.9	35.3	53.8	59.2	52.1	53.3	52.7	68.4	71.0	69.2	61.9	2
27.5	25.5	32.0	38.4	38.5	60.1	75.6	82.5	75.8	75.0	79.4	87.1	95.0	3
7.6	11.6	6.5	6.2	1.9	3.8	2.4	.6	2.0	2.2	4.3	6.1	2.5	4
09.6	232.8	259.1	258.0	286.2	330.2	347.2	366.1	366.3	399.3	420.7	442.8	448.8	5
13.9	17.2	20.3	21.9	23.9	27.6	29.6	31.6	33.1	35.3	38.9	42.0	44.0	6
95.7	215.6	238.8	236.1	262.3	302.6	317.6	334.5	333.2	364.0	381.8	400.8	404.8	7
17.4	21.0	19.8	23.4	26.1	30.3	31.8	34.8	34.1	36.0	34.9	38.5	40.8	8
78.3	194.6	219.0	212.7	236.2	272.3	285.8	299.7	299.1	328.0	346.9	362.3	364.0	9
6.1	5.8	5.4	5.9	7.1	8.5	9.0	9.1	10.1	11.5	12.9	14.9	15.2	10
9.1	11.3	12.4	10.2	17.9	22.6	19.4	20.3	17.6	22.0	22.0	21.4	19.0	11
1.9	4.6	9.6	9.6	6.9	7.0	7.5	6.4	7.9	12.3	9.9	9.2	7.1	12
16.1	17.0	16.9	18.5	21.8	19.4	20.5	22.1	24.6	26.4	28.8	32.5	36.7	13
77.3	189.8	208.5	205.6	226.1	253.7	270.4	286.1	288.2	308.8	330.9	349.3	359.3	14
18.7	21.4	21.1	18.5	20.6	28.9	34.0	35.4	32.5	35.4	39.6	42.4	42.2	15
58.6	168.4	187.4	187.1	205.5	224.8	236.4	250.7	255.7	273.4	291.3	306.9	317.1	16
77.0	468.3	487.7	490.7	533.5	576.5	598.5	621.8	613.7	654.8	668.8	680.9	679.5	17
14.7	− 1.8	4.1	.6	8.7	8.1	3.8	3.9	− 1.3	6.7	2.1	1.8	− .2	18
374	3249	3326	3289	3504	3722	3799	3882	3764	3946	3960	4031	3885	19

46	1947	1948	1949	1950	1951	1952	1953	1954	1955	1956	1957	1958	
58.5	66.9	72.1	71.4	72.1	77.8	79.5	80.1	80.5	80.2	81.4	84.3	86.6	20
35.0	39.4	41.1	38.8	44.9	48.7	50.6	54.8	51.9	58.5	61.1	61.9	57.9	21
10.0	113.1	111.5	111.2	116.2	122.7	127.4	128.8	132.3	135.2	136.9	135.9	141.1	22
41.4	144.1	146.6	149.2	152.3	154.9	157.5	160.2	163.0	165.9	168.9	172.0	174.9	23
57.5	59.3	60.6	61.3	62.2	62.0	62.1	63.0	63.6	65.0	65.5	66.9	67.6	24
2.3	2.3	2.3	3.6	3.3	2.1	1.9	1.8	3.5	2.9	2.8	2.9	4.6	25
3.9	3.9	3.8	5.9	5.3	3.3	3.0	2.9	5.5	4.4	4.1	4.3	6.8	26
8.4	11.6	14.4	17.4	21.5	22.7	27.5	31.4	32.5	38.8	42.3	45.0	45.1	27

(Continued on back cover)

SEVENTH EDITION

ECONOMICS

Principles, Problems, and Policies

CAMPBELL R. McCONNELL

Professor of Economics
University of Nebraska-Lincoln

McGRAW-HILL BOOK COMPANY

New York   St. Louis   San Francisco   Auckland   Bogotá   Düsseldorf   Johannesburg
London   Madrid   Mexico   Montreal   New Delhi   Panama   Paris   São Paulo
Singapore   Sydney   Tokyo   Toronto

TO MEM

ECONOMICS

234567890   DODO   78321098

This book was set in Century Schoolbook by York Graphic Services, Inc. The editors were J. S. Dietrich, Marjorie Singer, and Edwin Hanson; the text was designed by Merrill Haber, with cover and part openings designed by Betty Binns; the production supervisor was John F. Harte. The drawings were done by E. H. Technical Services. R. R. Donnelley & Sons Company was printer and binder.

Library of Congress Cataloging in Publication Data

McConnell, Campbell R
    Economics: principles, problems, and policies.

    First ed. published in 1960 under title: Elementary economics.
    Bibliography: p.
    Includes index.
    1. Economics. I. Title.
HB171.5.M139   1978   330   77-22684
ISBN 0-07-044913-9

CONTENTS

PREFACE   **xvi**

THREE SUGGESTED OUTLINES FOR ONE-SEMESTER COURSES   **xxiii**

PART 1

AN INTRODUCTION TO AMERICAN CAPITALISM

1 THE NATURE AND METHOD OF ECONOMICS   1

THE AGE OF THE ECONOMIST Economics for citizenship Personal applications
METHODOLOGY Descriptive economics Economic theory Policy economics
TWO CHEERS FOR ECONOMISTS
PITFALLS TO STRAIGHT THINKING Terminology Bias and preconceptions
Fallacy of composition: macro and micro Prosperity and depression Cause and
effect Effect of expectations Intentions versus realizations Logical explanations
and social practice Economic quackery
LAST WORD TOWARD A CRITIQUE OF ECONOMICS

2 AN INTRODUCTION TO THE ECONOMIZING PROBLEM   23

THE FOUNDATION OF ECONOMICS Unlimited wants Scarce resources
ECONOMICS DEFINED Full employment and full production Production
possibilities table Production possibilities curve Optimum product-mix Law of
increasing costs
FURTHER IMPLICATIONS Unemployment and underemployment A growing
economy Present choices and future possibilities
ECONOMIZING: FIVE FUNDAMENTAL QUESTIONS What is to be produced
Organizing production Distributing output Level of resource use Flexibility
THE ''ISMS''
LAST WORD BOMBS OR BREAD FOR INDIA?

3 PURE CAPITALISM AND THE CIRCULAR FLOW   44

CAPITALIST IDEOLOGY Private property Freedom of enterprise and choice Role
of self-interest Competition Markets and prices Limited government
OTHER CHARACTERISTICS Extensive use of capital goods Specialization
Specialization and comparative advantage Use of money
CIRCULAR FLOW OF INCOME Circular flow models Limitations
LAST WORD SPECIALIZATION AND THE ALIENATED WORKER

4 THE MECHANICS OF INDIVIDUAL PRICES: DEMAND AND SUPPLY   **61**

DEMAND Law of demand The demand curve Individual and market demand Determinants of demand Changes in demand Changes in quantity demanded
SUPPLY Law of supply The supply curve Determinants of supply Changes in supply Changes in quantity supplied
SUPPLY AND DEMAND: MARKET EQUILIBRIUM Rationing function of prices Changes in supply and demand The resource market "Other things equal" revisited
A POWERFUL TOOL Applicability Interference: legal prices Novel uses
LAST WORD THE DEMAND FOR BASKETBALL GAMES

5 THE FIVE FUNDAMENTAL QUESTIONS AND THE PRICE SYSTEM   **84**

FRAMEWORK OF THE PRICE SYSTEM
ECONOMIC CHOICES, SCARCITY, AND SUBSTITUTABILITY Scarcity Substitutability Choice
OPERATION OF THE PRICE SYSTEM Determining what is to be produced Organizing production Distributing total output Providing for flexibility Competition and control: the "invisible hand"
AN EVALUATION OF THE PRICE SYSTEM The case for the price system The case against the price system Relevance, realism, and the price system
LAST WORD PRODUCER, NOT CONSUMER, SOVEREIGNTY

6 MIXED CAPITALISM AND THE ECONOMIC FUNCTIONS OF GOVERNMENT   **105**

ECONOMIC FUNCTIONS OF GOVERNMENT
LEGAL AND SOCIAL FRAMEWORK FOR THE PRICE SYSTEM
MAINTAINING COMPETITION
REDISTRIBUTION OF INCOME
REALLOCATION OF RESOURCES Spillovers or externalities Social goods and services Allocating resources to social goods
STABILIZATION
EVALUATING GOVERNMENT'S ROLE Desirability of functions Benefit-cost analysis
PUBLIC SECTOR FAILURE? Special interests Clear benefits, hidden costs Nonselectivity Bureaucracy and ineffeciency Imperfect institutions
THE ISSUE OF FREEDOM The conservative position The liberal stance
LAST WORD CAPITALIST DOMINATION OF THE STATE

7 THE FACTS OF AMERICAN CAPITALISM: THE PRIVATE SECTOR   **128**

HOUSEHOLDS AS INCOME RECEIVERS Functional distribution of income Personal distribution of income
HOUSEHOLDS AS SPENDERS Personal taxes Personal saving Personal consumption expenditures Consumer protection
THE BUSINESS POPULATION Plants, firms, and industries Diversity and fluidity
LEGAL FORMS OF BUSINESS ENTERPRISES Sole proprietorship Partnership Corporation To incorporate or not to incorporate
INDUSTRIAL DISTRIBUTION OF THE BUSINESS POPULATION
BIG BUSINESS IN AMERICAN CAPITALISM Extent of bigness Means and

incentives for bigness   Should big business be feared?
LAST WORD   BIG CORPORATIONS: THE VIEW FROM WEST VIRGINIA

**8   THE FACTS OF AMERICAN CAPITALISM:
THE PUBLIC SECTOR**   **148**
PUBLIC SECTOR GROWTH   Some causes   Purchases versus transfers
FEDERAL FINANCE   Federal expenditures   Federal receipts   Federal tax loopholes
STATE AND LOCAL FINANCE   State expenditures and receipts   Local
expenditures and receipts
REVENUE SHARING
APPORTIONING THE TAX BURDEN   Benefits received versus ability to
pay   Progressive, proportional, and regressive taxes   Shifting and incidence of
taxes   The American tax structure
LAST WORD   THE AMERICAN WAY OF TAX

PART **2**

NATIONAL INCOME, EMPLOYMENT, AND FISCAL POLICY

9   NATIONAL INCOME ACCOUNTING   **167**
MEASURING THE ECONOMY'S PERFORMANCE
GROSS NATIONAL PRODUCT   GNP is a monetary measure   Adjusting GNP for
price changes   Inflating and deflating   Double counting   GNP excludes
nonproductive transactions   GNP and social welfare   Two sides to GNP
THE EXPENDITURES APPROACH TO GNP   Personal consumption expenditures
(C)   Government purchases of goods and services (G)   Gross private domestic
investment (I_g)   Net exports (X_n)
THE INCOME APPROACH TO GNP   Depreciation: capital consumption
allowance   Indirect business taxes   Compensation of employees   Rents
Interest   Proprietors' income   Corporate profits
OTHER SOCIAL ACCOUNTS   Net national product (NNP)   National income (NI)
Personal income (PI)   Disposable income (DI)   Relationships between major social
accounts
LAST WORD   NATIONAL INCOME: VOLUNTARY AND INVOLUNTARY
EXPENDITURES

10   THE BUSINESS CYCLE: UNEMPLOYMENT AND INFLATION   **191**
THE MACROECONOMIC TRILOGY
TOTAL DEMAND, EMPLOYMENT, AND THE PRICE LEVEL   Range 1:
unemployment and price stability   Range 2: premature inflation   Range 3: full
employment and pure inflation   Nonreversibility
UNEMPLOYMENT   Frictional unemployment   Structural unemployment   Cyclical
unemployment   Defining ''full employment''   Economic costs of unemployment
Noneconomic costs
PRICE INSTABILITY: INFLATION AND DEFLATION   Redistributive effects   Output
effects   Creeping inflation
THE BUSINESS CYCLE   Noncyclical fluctuations   Cyclical impact: durables and
nondurables
BUSINESS CYCLES SINCE 1920   The twenties: prosperity   The thirties: the Great

Depression   The forties: prosperity and inflation   The war years (1940 to 1945)
The postwar years (1946 to 1949)   The fifties: economic kaleidoscope   The sixties:
a mixed bag   The turbulent seventies: Four observations
PROSPECTS FOR STABILITY
LAST WORD   INFLATION IN JAPAN: UP, UP AND AWAY

**11   THE BACKGROUND AND ANALYTICAL TOOLS OF
     EMPLOYMENT THEORY**   **222**
THE CLASSICAL THEORY OF EMPLOYMENT   Say's Law   Price-wage flexibility
Classical theory and laissez faire
KEYNESIAN ECONOMICS   The unlinking of saving and investment plans   The
discrediting of price-wage flexibility
TOOLS OF MODERN EMPLOYMENT THEORY
CONSUMPTION AND SAVING   Income-consumption and income-saving
relationships   The consumption schedule   The saving schedule   Average and
marginal propensities   Nonincome determinants of consumption and saving   Shifts
and stability
INVESTMENT   Expected rate of net profits   The interest rate   Investment-demand
curve   Shifts in investment demand   Investment and income   Instability of
investment
LAST WORD   POVERTY AMIDST PLENTY

**12   THE EQUILIBRIUM LEVELS OF OUTPUT,
     EMPLOYMENT, AND INCOME**   **248**
AGGREGATE DEMAND-AGGREGATE SUPPLY APPROACH   Tabular analysis
Graphic analysis
LEAKAGES-INJECTIONS APPROACH   Tabular analysis   Graphic analysis
PLANNED VERSUS ACTUAL SAVING AND INVESTMENT   Disequilibrium and
inventories   Achieving equilibrium
CHANGES IN EQUILIBRIUM NNP AND THE MULTIPLIER   The multiplier effect
Paradox of thrift
EQUILIBRIUM VERSUS FULL-EMPLOYMENT NNP   Recessionary gap   Inflationary
gap   Premature inflation
LAST WORD   LOOKING A GIFT HORSE IN THE MOUTH

13   FISCAL POLICY AND THE PUBLIC DEBT   **269**
BUDGET PHILOSOPHIES   Annually balanced budget   Cyclically balanced
budget   Functional finance
EMPLOYMENT ACT OF 1946 AND THE CEA
DISCRETIONARY FISCAL POLICY   Simplifying assumptions   Government spending
and equilibrium NNP   Taxation and equilibrium NNP   The budget impact
Balanced-budget multiplier   Fiscal policy over the cycle
NONDISCRETIONARY FISCAL POLICY: BUILT-IN STABILIZERS   Built-in stability
Qualifications and subtleties
TWO REFINEMENTS   Financing deficits and disposing of surpluses   Types of
expenditures and taxes
SOME COMPLICATIONS   Problems of timing   Political problems   State and local
finance
THE PUBLIC DEBT   Dimensions of debt   Two myths   Real burden of the debt
Positive role of debt
LAST WORD   THE IMPOTENCE OF FISCAL POLICY

PART 3

MONEY, MONETARY POLICY, AND ECONOMIC STABILITY

14 MONEY AND BANKING IN AMERICAN CAPITALISM   **295**
THE FUNCTIONS OF MONEY
MONEY IN AMERICAN CAPITALISM   Money defined: M_1 Near-monies and M_2
WHAT "BACKS" THE MONEY SUPPLY?   Money as debt   Value of money   Money and prices   Managing money   Recap
INSTITUTIONAL FRAMEWORK OF THE AMERICAN BANKING SYSTEM   Need for centralization   Structure of the Federal Reserve System   Functions of the Federal Reserve System
LAST WORD   A DIALOGUE ON MONEY

15 HOW BANKS CREATE MONEY   **313**
THE BALANCE SHEET OF A COMMERCIAL BANK
A SINGLE COMMERCIAL BANK IN A BANKING SYSTEM   Formation of a commercial bank   Recap   Money-creating transactions of a commercial bank   Profits and liquidity
THE BANKING SYSTEM: MULTIPLE-DEPOSIT EXPANSION   The banking system's lending potential   The monetary multiplier   Some modifications
LAST WORD   THE GREAT CASH MYSTERY

16 THE FEDERAL RESERVE BANKS AND MONETARY POLICY   **333**
OBJECTIVES OF MONETARY POLICY   Cause-effect chain   Monetary policy and investment
CONSOLIDATED BALANCE SHEET OF THE FEDERAL RESERVE BANKS   Assets   Liabilities
MONETARY POLICY: MAJOR QUANTITATIVE CONTROLS   The reserve ratio   Open-market operations   The discount rate   Reserve Bank credit   Easy money and tight money
MONETARY POLICY: MINOR QUALITATIVE CONTROLS   Selective credit controls   Moral suasion
RELATIVE IMPORTANCE OF CONTROLS
MONETARY POLICY: GRAPHIC RESTATEMENT
EFFECTIVENESS OF MONETARY POLICY   Shortcomings of monetary policy   Strengths of monetary policy
EMPLOYMENT THEORY AND POLICY: RECAPITULATION   Consumption   Investment   Government spending   Fiscal and monetary policy   Complexities and problems
LAST WORD   PROBLEMS IN CONTROLLING THE MONEY SUPPLY

17 MONETARISM: AN ALTERNATIVE VIEW   **356**
PHILOSOPHICAL-IDEOLOGICAL DIFFERENCES   Keynesians: political liberalism   Monetarists: laissez faire and conservativism
THE BASIC EQUATIONS   Spotlight on money   The fiscal policy debate   The monetary rule
VELOCITY: STABLE OR UNSTABLE?   Empirical evidence   Velocity and the demand for money   Monetarists: V is stable   Keynesians: V is unstable   Monetary

policy revisited   A continuing debate
LAST WORD   INFLATION: A MONETARY PHENOMENON?

**18   UNEMPLOYMENT AND INFLATION: NEW PROBLEMS AND
NEW POLICIES**   **371**
DEMAND-PULL INFLATION
THE PHILLIPS CURVE: PREMATURE INFLATION   Logic of the Phillips Curve   The
wage rate–productivity nexus   Stabilization policy dilemma
NEW POLICY OPTIONS   Market policies   Wage-price policies
STAGFLATION: THE AWKWARD SEVENTIES   The 1960s: stimulus and
demand-pull   The Nixon ''game plan''   Severe cost-pull shocks   Why stagflation?
THE PHILLIPS CURVE REVISITED   The accelerationist view   Keynesian position
Policy implications
LESSONS AND ISSUES   Lessons of the 1970s   Keynesianism and planning
LAST WORD   THE SLOW ROAD TO FULL EMPLOYMENT

PART 4

ECONOMIC GROWTH: ANALYSIS AND POLICY

19   THE SIMPLE ANALYTICS OF ECONOMIC GROWTH   **397**
GROWTH ECONOMICS   Two definitions   Importance of growth   Arithmetic of
growth
INGREDIENTS OF GROWTH: A FIRST LOOK
GROWTH: A MORE SOPHISTICATED VIEW   Law of diminishing returns   The
production possibilities curve and diminishing returns   Diminishing returns:
arithmetic example   Optimum population   Malthus and misery   Rising productivity
and growth
AGGREGATE DEMAND AND GROWTH   Keeping pace with capacity
Full-employment growth model
ALLOCATIVE EFFICIENCY AND GROWTH
LAST WORD   POPULATION AND THE GROWTH MYSTIQUE

20   ECONOMIC GROWTH: FACT AND CONTROVERSY   **415**
GROWTH RECORD OF THE UNITED STATES
SOURCES OF UNITED STATES GROWTH   Natural resources   Human resources
Technological advance   Capital formation: investment   Instability and growth
Allocative efficiency   Relative importance
IS GROWTH DESIRABLE?   The case against growth   In defense of growth
THE DOOMSDAY MODELS
NEW HORIZONS?   Fun and games with numbers?   Role of technology   Feedback
mechanisms
LAST WORD   SUMMER OF '73

21   GROWTH AND THE UNDERDEVELOPED NATIONS   **435**
UNDERSTANDING UNDERDEVELOPMENT   Low per capita income   Dimensions of
inequality   Implications   Viewpoint of underdeveloped nations   Dubious lessons of
history
BREAKING THE POVERTY BARRIER   Natural resources   Employment of human

resources   Capital accumulation   Technological advance   Sociocultural and institutional factors
THE VICIOUS CIRCLE: A SUMMING UP
CRUCIAL ROLE FOR GOVERNMENT
ROLE OF THE ADVANCED NATIONS   Expanding trade   Private capital flows
Foreign aid: public loans and grants
NEOCOLONIALISM?
THE FUTURE
LAST WORD   THE THUNDER OF TINY FEET

PART 5

THE ECONOMICS OF THE FIRM AND RESOURCE ALLOCATION

22 THE MARKET STRUCTURES OF AMERICAN CAPITALISM   459
FOUR BASIC MARKET MODELS   Pure competition   Pure monopoly   Monopolistic competition   Oligopoly   Imperfect competition
THE BUYER'S SIDE OF THE MARKET
OTHER COMPETITIVE DIMENSIONS   Geographic factor   Interindustry competition   Nonprice competition   Technological advance
DETERMINANTS OF MARKET STRUCTURE   Legislation and government policy
Business policies and practices   Technology   Capitalistic institutions
LAST WORD   GALBRAITHIAN ECONOMICS

**23 DEMAND, SUPPLY, AND ELASTICITY:
SOME APPLICATIONS**   476
DEMAND, SUPPLY, AND MARKET PRICE
ELASTICITY OF DEMAND   The elasticity formula   Refinement: midpoints formula
The total-revenue test   Characteristics   Determinants of elasticity of demand   Some practical applications   Elasticity of supply
APPLICATIONS OF SUPPLY AND DEMAND ANALYSIS   Legal prices   Tax incidence   Demand from the individual firm's viewpoint
LAST WORD   RENT CONTROLS: A SELF-FULFILLING PROPHECY

**24 FURTHER TOPICS IN THE THEORY OF
CONSUMER DEMAND**   500
TWO EXPLANATIONS OF THE LAW OF DEMAND   Income and substitution effects   Law of diminishing marginal utility
THEORY OF CONSUMER BEHAVIOR   Consumer choice and budget restraint
Utility-maximizing rule   An algebraic restatement
MARGINAL UTILITY AND THE DEMAND CURVE
CRITICISMS: THE TIME DIMENSION   The value of time   Some implications
LAST WORD   DOES MONEY BUY HAPPINESS?

25 THE COSTS OF PRODUCTION   513
ECONOMIC COSTS   Explicit and implicit costs   Normal profits as a cost
Economic, or pure, profits   Short run and long run
PRODUCTION COSTS IN THE SHORT RUN   Law of diminishing returns   Fixed, variable, and total costs   Per unit, or average, costs   Marginal cost

PRODUCTION COSTS IN THE LONG RUN Economies and diseconomies of scale Significance of economies and diseconomies of scale
LAST WORD ECONOMIES OF SCALE AT AMERICAN MOTORS

26 PRICE AND OUTPUT DETERMINATION: PURE COMPETITION   531

PURE COMPETITION: CONCEPT AND OCCURRENCE
PROFIT MAXIMIZATION IN THE SHORT RUN Total-receipts–total-cost approach Marginal-revenue–marginal-cost approach Short-run competitive pricing Firm and industry: equilibrium price
PROFIT MAXIMIZATION IN THE LONG RUN Entry of firms eliminates profits Exodus of firms eliminates losses Long-run supply for a constant-cost industry Long-run supply for an increasing-cost industry
AN EVALUATION OF COMPETITIVE PRICING Efficient allocation of resources Shortcomings of the competitive price system
LAST WORD TECHNOLOGY AND COMPETITION

27 PRICE AND OUTPUT DETERMINATION: PURE MONOPOLY   559

PURE MONOPOLY: CONCEPT AND OCCURRENCE
BARRIERS TO ENTRY Economies of scale Public utilities: natural monopolies Ownership of essential raw materials Patents and research Unfair competition Economies of being established Two implications
PRICE AND OUTPUT DETERMINATION Monopoly demand Cost data Equating marginal revenue and marginal cost Misconceptions concerning monopoly pricing Possible restraints upon profit maximization
PRICE DISCRIMINATION Conditions Desirability
ECONOMIC EFFECTS Price, output, and resource allocation Income distribution Technological advance
REGULATED MONOPOLY Socially optimum price ''Fair-return'' price Dilemma of regulation
LAST WORD MONOPOLY IN PROFESSIONAL BASKETBALL

28 PRICE AND OUTPUT DETERMINATION: MONOPOLISTIC COMPETITION   578

MONOPOLISTIC COMPETITION: CONCEPT AND OCCURRENCE Relatively large numbers Product differentiation Entry conditions Illustrations
PRICE AND OUTPUT DETERMINATION The firm's demand curve The short run: profits or losses The long run: break-even
WASTES OF MONOPOLISTIC COMPETITION
NONPRICE COMPETITION Product differentiation and product development Advertising Monopolistic competition and economic analysis
LAST WORD BEER: TROUBLE BREWING

29 PRICE AND OUTPUT DETERMINATION: OLIGOPOLY   592

OLIGOPOLY: CONCEPT AND OCCURRENCE Fewness Underlying causes Mutual interdependence
ANALYTICAL COMPLEXITIES
PRICE-OUTPUT BEHAVIOR Noncollusive oligopoly and price rigidity Collusion: joint-profit maximization Obstacles to collusion
OLIGOPOLY AND GAMES The profits-payoff table Interdependence of behavior Price rigidity Collusion and merger

ROLE OF NONPRICE COMPETITION
OLIGOPOLY AND ECONOMIC EFFICIENCY Restrictive oligopoly Progressive
oligopoly Countervailing power Oligopoly: tentative appraisal
LAST WORD AUTO RENTALS: TRYING TOO HARD?

**30 PRODUCTION AND THE DEMAND FOR ECONOMIC
RESOURCES**   **614**
SIGNIFICANCE OF RESOURCE PRICING
COMPLEXITIES OF RESOURCE PRICING
MARGINAL PRODUCTIVITY THEORY OF RESOURCE DEMAND Resource demand
as a derived demand Marginal revenue product (MRP) Rule for employing
resources: MRP = MRC MRP is a demand schedule Resource demand under
imperfect competition Market demand for a resource
CHANGES IN RESOURCE DEMAND Changes in product demand Productivity
changes Prices of other resources
ELASTICITY OF RESOURCE DEMAND
A FIRM'S DEMAND FOR SEVERAL RESOURCES The profit-maximizing
combination of resources The least-cost combination of resources Modifications
for imperfect competition
LAST WORD PUSH-BUTTON WARFARE

**31 THE PRICING AND EMPLOYMENT OF RESOURCES:
WAGE DETERMINATION**   **631**
MEANING OF WAGES
GENERAL LEVEL OF WAGES Role of productivity Real wages and
productivity Secular growth Recent slowdown?
WAGES IN PARTICULAR LABOR MARKETS Competitive model Monopsony
model Some union models Bilateral monopoly model The minimum-wage
controversy Do unions raise wages?
WAGE DIFFERENTIALS Noncompeting groups Equalizing differences Market
imperfections
INVESTMENT IN HUMAN CAPITAL The concept The investment decision
Explanatory value Recent criticism
LAST WORD WHY DOCTORS EARN SO MUCH

**32 THE PRICING AND EMPLOYMENT OF RESOURCES:
RENT, INTEREST, AND PROFITS**   **656**
ECONOMIC RENT Land rent is a surplus A single tax on land? Productivity
differences and alternative uses
INTEREST Range of rates The money market: liquidity preference theory The
demand for money Supply of money and equilibrium
BUSINESS PROFITS AND ECONOMIC PROFITS Economic profits and the
entrepreneur Sources of economic profit Functions of profits
INCOME SHARES Current shares Historical trends
LAST WORD LAND RENT GOES APE

**33 GENERAL EQUILIBRIUM: THE PRICE SYSTEM AND
ITS OPERATION**   **676**
PARTIAL AND GENERAL EQUILIBRIUM
MARKET INTERRELATIONSHIPS: AUTOMOBILES
GENERAL EQUILIBRIUM: A TWO-INDUSTRY MODEL Behind the

curves   Short-run adjustments   Long-run adjustments   Further adjustments
ECONOMIC WELFARE AND THE PRICE SYSTEM
THE REAL WORLD AND IMPERFECT COMPETITION
OUTPUT, INCOME, AND ETHICS   Allocative activities of government   Government
and distributive justice
GENERAL EQUILIBRIUM: INPUT-OUTPUT ANALYSIS   Input-output
table   Interdependencies
GENERAL EQUILIBRIUM AND ECONOMIC UNDERSTANDING   Some
illustrations   Forecasting and planning
LAST WORD   THE ENGLISH COTTON FAMINE

PART 6

CURRENT ECONOMIC PROBLEMS

**34   THE MONOPOLY PROBLEM: THE SOCIAL CONTROL
OF INDUSTRY**   **691**

BIG BUSINESS AND MONOPOLY
MONOPOLY: GOOD OR EVIL?
THE CASE FOR MONOPOLY   "Workable competition"   Technological determinism:
a new industrial state?   Other defenses: stability and responsibility
THE CASE AGAINST MONOPOLY   Inefficiency and inequality   Obstacle to
progress?   Instability   Political dangers   Character of society   Empirical evidence
PUBLIC POLICY TOWARD MONOPOLY   Legislation and policies restricting
monopoly   The regulation of natural monopolies   Antitrust legislation   Legislation
and policies promoting monopoly
FUTURE POLICY ALTERNATIVES   Maintaining the status quo   Toward public
regulation and ownership   Restoring vigorous competition
LAST WORD   THE ANTITRUST CHARADE

35   RURAL ECONOMICS: THE FARM PROBLEM   **713**

HISTORY OF THE FARM PROBLEM
FARM INCOMES
CAUSES OF THE FARM PROBLEM   The long-run problem   The short-run
problem   A restatement   Agriculture and growth
RATIONALE FOR PUBLIC POLICY   Costs-of-progress argument   Market-power
argument
FARM POLICY: NEW AND OLD
TRADITIONAL POLICY: PARITY   Price supports   Surplus controls   Evaluation
THE SEVENTIES: WINDFALL OR WATERSHED?   A new era?   A new farm
program   Consequences and implications
LAST WORD   FARMING: THE GOOD LIFE?

36   URBAN ECONOMICS: THE PROBLEMS OF THE CITIES   **733**

WHY CITIES DEVELOP   In general: where to produce?   In particular: economies of
agglomeration   Demand considerations   Deglomerative forces
THE FLIGHT TO THE SUBURBS: URBAN SPRAWL   Political fragmentation
Economic imbalance
THE URBAN TRANSPORTATION PROBLEM
IMPROVING URBAN TRANSPORTATION   The short run: user charges and peak

pricing   The long run: mass transit
THE POLLUTION PROBLEM: THE EFFLUENT SOCIETY?   Dimensions of the
problem   Causes: materials balance approach   Antipollution policies
THE GHETTOS: APARTHEID AMERICAN STYLE   The human aspect: alleviating
ghetto poverty   The physical aspect: housing and urban renewal
SOLVING URBAN PROBLEMS: THE PREREQUISITES   Political consolidation   The
larger fiscal problem   New cities
LAST WORD   THE GHETTO AS AN ECONOMIC SUBSYSTEM

37   THE ECONOMICS OF INCOME DISTRIBUTION:
INEQUALITY AND POVERTY   **760**
INCOME EQUALITY   Causes of income inequality   Trends in income inequality   Of
taxes, time, and transfers   The case against income inequality   The case for
income inequality
THE DISMAL ECONOMICS OF POVERTY   Who are the poor?
DISCRIMINATION AND POVERTY   Dimensions of discrimination   The "invisible"
poor   Costs of discrimination
TWO PHILOSOPHIES   Personal shortcomings? Social victims?   The evidence
SOCIAL SECURITY SYSTEM   OASDI   Unemployment compensation   SSI and
AFDC   Food stamp program   Medicare and medicaid   "The welfare mess"
NEGATIVE INCOME TAX (NIT)   Illustration   Goals and conflicts
THE BIG TRADE-OFF
LAST WORD   DANGERS OF THE WELFARE STATE

38   UNIONISM, COLLECTIVE BARGAINING, AND WOMEN
AT WORK   **783**
BRIEF HISTORY OF AMERICAN UNIONISM   Repression phase: 1790 to 1930
Encouragement phase: 1930 to 1947   Intervention phase: 1947 to date   Labor
unity   The postmerger era: stagnation?
COLLECTIVE BARGAINING   The bargaining process   The work agreement
CONTRACT AND AGREEMENT   Sample agreement   Basic contract areas   Three
implications
WOMEN IN THE LABOR MARKET   Increased participation rate   Economic status
of women   Occupational discrimination: a simple model   Conflicting explanations
LAST WORD   WORK AND ALIENATION

39   THE ECONOMICS OF WAR AND DEFENSE   **808**
SIZE OF THE WAR INDUSTRY   Measurement problems   Other implications
ECONOMIC COSTS   Alternative to unemployment?   Prosperity without arms
The issue restated
ALLOCATIVE ASPECTS   The military establishment and the firm   War goods
procurement   "Pentagon capitalism"   The costs of military procurement
The military in the labor market   Case for a volunteer army   Objections   Other
manpower problems
AGGREGATIVE ASPECTS   Defense spending and stability   Détente and
disarmament   The current malaise
IN DEFENSE OF DEFENSE   Guns and butter?   Technological-organizational
spillovers   Is war inherently inflationary?   Cost overruns; are they inevitable?
Survival in a nuclear age
THE NATIONAL PRIORITIES DEBATE
LAST WORD   APOLLO: A TECHNOLOGICAL SUPERSTUNT

40 THE RADICAL CRITIQUE: THE ECONOMICS OF DISSENT 829

THE MARXIAN HERITAGE: THE "OLD LEFT" The class struggle Private property and the exploitation of labor Capital accumulation and its consequences Increasing degradation of the working class Monopoly capitalism and imperialism Revolution and socialism
ORTHODOX AND RADICAL ECONOMICS: BASIC DIFFERENCES Harmony or conflict? Disciplinary narrowness
THE RADICAL CONCEPTION OF CAPITALISM Corporate or monopoly capitalism Domination of the state Dynamics of capitalist expansion Exploitation Inequality Alienation The irrational society: production for waste Imperialism Socialist visions
THE ORTHODOX REBUTTAL Invalid perceptions Nonobjectivity Importance of ideology Viable options
LAST WORD MONOPOLY CAPITALISM AT WORK

PART 7

INTERNATIONAL ECONOMICS AND THE WORLD ECONOMY

41 INTERNATIONAL TRADE AND COMPARATIVE ADVANTAGE 851

IMPORTANCE OF WORLD TRADE Quantitative aspects Unique aspects
THE ECONOMIC BASIS FOR TRADE
INTERNATIONAL SPECIALIZATION AND COMPARATIVE ADVANTAGE Two isolated nations Specialization according to comparative advantage Terms of trade The gains from trade Increasing costs
MICROECONOMIC EFFECTS OF WORLD TRADE Resource allocation and output Product prices Resource prices Other considerations
MACROECONOMIC EFFECTS OF WORLD TRADE Net exports and aggregate demand Exports, imports, and NNP Open-economy multiplier
LAST WORD IMPERIALISM AND WORLD TRADE

42 THE ECONOMICS OF FREE TRADE AND PROTECTION 869

THE CASE FOR FREE TRADE
TRADE BARRIERS Protective tariffs and import quotas Motivations Economic impact of tariffs
THE CASE FOR PROTECTION: A CRITICAL REVIEW Military self-sufficiency argument Protect domestic living standards Increase domestic employment Diversification for stability Infant-industry argument The diffusion-of-technology argument A summing up
INTERNATIONAL TRADE POLICIES Reciprocal Trade Act and GATT Economic integration: the Common Market The Kennedy Round A new initiative: the Geneva Round United States-Communist trade
LAST WORD PETITION OF THE CANDLEMAKERS, 1845

43 THE BALANCE OF PAYMENTS AND EXCHANGE RATES 887

FINANCING INTERNATIONAL TRADE American export transaction American import transaction

THE INTERNATIONAL BALANCE OF PAYMENTS Exports and imports of goods
and services Remittances Government transactions Net capital movements
Errors and omissions Financing transactions A peculiar deficit
INTERNATIONAL DISEQUILIBRIUM An analogy Autonomous and accommodating
transactions
RESTORING INTERNATIONAL EQUILIBRIUM Freely floating exchange rates
Changing price and income levels Public controls
LAST WORD ARE FLOATING EXCHANGE RATES DESIRABLE?

**44 INTERNATIONAL TRADE AND FINANCE:
PROBLEMS AND POLICIES**   **904**

A BACKWARD GLANCE World trade in the thirties World War II: disruption of
trade Postwar problems
REBUILDING THE EUROPEAN ECONOMY
THE BRETTON WOODS MONETARY SYSTEM IMF and adjustable pegs
Correcting disequilibria International monetary reserves
UNITED STATES PAYMENTS DEFICIT Causes Cures: basic measures Controls:
a cure? Flexible rates: a new system
DEMISE OF THE BRETTON WOODS SYSTEM The reserves problem The
adjustment problem Shattering of the system
EMERGENCE OF FLOATING RATES The "managed float" Liquidity and special
drawing rights Demonetization of gold? Evaluation and options
COMPATIBILITY OF DOMESTIC AND INTERNATIONAL POLICIES
LAST WORD MULTINATIONAL CORPORATIONS: FOR GOOD OR EVIL?

45 THE ECONOMIC SYSTEM OF SOVIET RUSSIA   **923**

INSTITUTIONS OF THE COMMAND ECONOMY State ownership Central
economic planning Circumscribed freedom
CENTRAL PLANNING Planning goals Basic planning problem: coordination
Coordination techniques Executing the plan: control agencies Incentives
Planning and prices
RECENT PROBLEMS AND REFORMS Microeconomic problems Reforms:
Libermanism
SOVIET ECONOMIC GROWTH Growth comparisons Sources of Soviet
growth Retarding factors Future growth
GENERAL EVALUATION Accomplishments Shortcomings
THE CONVERGENCE HYPOTHESIS
LAST WORD THE TESTIMONY OF AVRAHAM SHIFRIN

INDEX   **945**

PREFACE

One of the less obvious benefits of authoring a text which has met the test of the market is the opportunity for revision. Although it is a highly demanding and sometimes dreary undertaking, revision affords the chance for improvement—to delete the archaic and install the novel, to rectify errors of omission or commission, to rephrase potentially misleading statements, to introduce more relevant illustrations, to bring more pertinent data to bear, to upgrade organizational logic—in short, to build constructively upon a tested framework of ideas. Much of my time these past two years has been devoted to the preparation of this seventh edition of *Economics*. I hope and trust that those who examine this new edition will agree that I have exploited fully the opportunity afforded me.

Although the seventh edition bears only a modest resemblance to the first, the basic purpose remains the same: to introduce the beginning economics student to those principles essential to an understanding of fundamental economic problems and the policy alternatives society may utilize to contend with these problems. It is hoped that the ability to reason accurately and objectively about economic matters and the development of a lasting interest in economics will be two valuable byproducts of this basic objective. Furthermore, my intention remains that of presenting the principles and problems of economics in a straightforward, logical fashion. To this end great stress has been put upon clarity of presentation and organization.

THE SEVENTH EDITION

This edition incorporates many extensive changes. Let me briefly summarize some of the more important ones.

□ Two New Chapters

Although the total number of chapters has not changed, I can say with only slight exaggeration that two chapters are new. First, Chapter 17 is a new chapter on Monetarism. The scattered references to Monetarism found in the sixth edition have now been brought together and fleshed out to provide a systematic comparison with Keynesianism. The contrast encompasses not only analytical and policy differences, but also variance of ideological perspectives. The monetarist-Keynesian debates over fiscal policy, the efficacy of the monetary rule, and the stability of the velocity of money are all considered in some detail. Second, Chapter 18 is substantially new, although it appropriately retains some material on wage-price policies from the previous edition. The focal point is the awkward events of the 1970s. The macroeconomic record of the past decade is presented and explained; the challenges stagflation has raised for Keynesian economics are laid out. Accelerationist and Keynesian interpretations of the 1970s are both presented as is a brief pro-and-con consideration of the rejuvenated debate over central economic planning.

◻ Other Major Changes

Let us consider briefly other major changes, roughly in order of their appearance.

Chapter 4 includes a new section on various applications of the supply and demand model. In Chapter 6 the old material on social balance has been supplanted by a new discussion of the theory of public choice. Public choice theory provides a rationale for public sector failure, that is, it explains the apparent inability of government to resolve various socioeconomic problems. Also, the benefit-cost illustration has been rewritten for greater clarity. Chapters 7 and 8 on the private and public sectors have been tightened and improved; for example, the section on business accounting has been dropped and a better illustration of the mechanics of the personal income tax provided. Chapters 11 and 12 on macrotheory embody a number of changes. The classical theory has been reworked for greater clarity. The Keynesian ex ante inequality of saving and investment has been clarified by introducing changes in the money supply and money balances as explanatory factors. The investment demand curve has been introduced, making the discussion of investment theory more precise and tying it more closely to monetary policy. Greater emphasis is placed upon unintended inventory changes in explaining the equilibrium level of national output. Chapters 14 to 16 on money and banking have been reassessed for the purpose of tightening and sharpening the discussion throughout. For example, in Chapter 15 the discussion of the lending ability of a monopoly bank has been dropped. Chapter 16 now ties monetary policy explicitly to Keynesian theory through investment demand and

saving-investment diagrams. This chapter now ends with the synopsis of Keynesian theory and policy which was the core of Chapter 17 in the sixth edition. Chapter 20 on growth has been extensively reworked and updated; the material on the Doomsday debate has been revitalized. Chapter 21 now embodies pertinent new empirical data on the degree of inequality between the industrialized and the less developed countries, and the discussions of natural resources and sociocultural factors in growth have been redone. Material on the trade-aid role of advanced nations has been rewritten as has the section on neocolonialism. Three scenarios of possible future interrelationships between advanced and underdeveloped nations are introduced. In Chapter 23 the discussion of the determinants of the elasticity of demand has been entirely rewritten. Chapter 24 now includes a short section at its close introducing the Becker-Linder analysis which takes time into account and generalizes the theory of consumer behavior. A new section on price discrimination has been added to Chapter 28 which tends to increase its relevance. There are two major changes in Chapter 31 on wages: first, consideration is given to the recent slowdown in the rate of productivity growth; and, second, recent criticisms of human capital theory are considered. The interest rate section of Chapter 32 is entirely new, shifting from the loanable funds to the liquidity preference approach. This change allows the discussion of interest rate determination to be tied explicitly to both Keynesian theory and monetary policy. Chapter 34 embodies a modest rewrite with more discussion of regulation and related problems. Chapter 35 on agriculture has been rather substantially reworked. Distinction is now made between traditional farm policy and policies of the 1970s. The consequences and implications of market-oriented farm programs are considered. Chapter 37 on inequality has been revised thoroughly to reflect the new ideas and research of Rawls, Browning, Jencks, and Okun. The discussion of existing income maintenance programs has been rewritten and the chapter now concludes with a synopsis of Okun's "big tradeoff" theme. In Chapter 38 the section on sex discrimination has been restructured and a simple supply and demand model of occupational discrimination added. In Chapter 40 the radical view of imperialism has been improved and extended; new material on the theory of dual labor markets has been added as a part of the explanation of poverty; and the orthodox rebuttal has been partly rewritten. The basic comparative advantage example of Chapter 41 has been recast and rephrased for greater clarity. In Chapter 42 the Trade Reform Act of 1974 and the Geneva Round of negotiations are considered and the section of East-West trade has been reworked. The historical material of Chapter 44 has been tightened and the sections on the "managed float" and special drawing rights have been rewritten. Brief comment on the "vicious circle" theory of inflation has been appended. Finally, in Chapter 45 the section on future prospects for Soviet growth has been recast and shortened.

It is to be emphasized that the above recitation of seventh edition changes is *not* comprehensive. Users of the sixth edition will be aware of many other alterations. It is safe to assert that no chapter has escaped some rewriting, revision of content, organizational improvement, or updating. The extensiveness of the revision is necessitated by the novel and troublesome changes in the economic milieu of recent years, the solicited and volunteered criticisms of users of the sixth edition, and, in no small measure, by the increased competition evident in the market for principles texts.

□ "Last Word" Minireadings

The built-in minireadings introduced in the sixth edition were enthusiastically received by most users. These "Last Word" selections serve several purposes: some provide meaningful real-world applications of economic concepts; others reveal "human interest" aspects of economic problems; and still others challenge the concepts and interpretations of mainstream economics. The minireadings are purposely placed at the end of each chapter so as not to interrupt the continuity of the text material. Approximately 20 percent of the "Last Words" are new in the seventh edition.

□ Pedagogical Improvements

Aside from extensive content revision, the seventh edition of *Economics* embodies at least two pedagogical improvements worthy of comment. First, feedback over the years suggests that the organizational structure of *Economics* has been an important factor in explaining its market acceptance. With this is mind, I have made it a point to use subheads—particularly third- and fourth-order subheads—more liberally in the new edition to highlight the organizational framework for the student. Second, the first question found at the end of each chapter in the new edition is a list of the basic terms and concepts encountered in that particular chapter. Because any introductory course is heavily imbued with terminology, this listing should be helpful.

■ PRODUCT DIFFERENTIATION

In terms of content I feel this text embraces a number of departures in content and organization which distinguish it from other books in the field.

1 The principles course usually fails to provide students with a comprehensive and meaningful definition of economics. To remedy this shortcoming, one complete chapter (Chapter 2) is devoted to a careful statement and development of the economizing problem and an exploration of its implications. The foundation thereby provided should be helpful in putting the many particular subject areas of economics into proper perspective.

2 For better or worse, government is obviously an integral and increasingly important component of modern capitalism. Its economic role, therefore, should not be treated piecemeal or as an afterthought. This text introduces the economic functions of government early and accords them systematic treatment (Chapters 6 and 9).

3 This volume puts considerable emphasis upon the crucial topic of economic growth. Chapter 19 summarizes growth theory. Chapter 20 discusses American growth, the growth controversy, and the Doomsday models. Chapter 21 draws upon the conceptual framework of Chapter 19 in treating the obstacles to growth which plague the underdeveloped countries. An important segment of Chapter 45 concerns the growth record and prospects of Soviet Russia's command economy. Beyond this it will be found that the chapters on price theory pay special attention to the implications that the various market structures have for technological progress.

4 It is understandable that the elusiveness of general equilibrium analysis eminently qualifies this topic for omission at the principles level. The result, however, is a grievous shortcoming of most introductory courses. A sincere effort is made in this book to remedy the deficiency. Specifically, an entire chapter (Chapter 5) is devoted to the notion of the price system, and another chapter (Chapter 33) explicitly outlines the nature and significance of general equilibrium analysis.

5 I have purposely given considerable attention to microeconomics in general and to the theory of the firm in particular. There are two reasons for this emphasis. In the first place, the concepts of microeconomics are difficult for most beginning students. Short expositions usually compound these difficulties by raising more questions than they answer. Secondly, I have coupled analysis of the various market structures with a discussion of the social implications of each. The impact of each market arrangement upon price and output levels, resource allocation, and the rate of technological advance is carefully assessed.

6 Part 6 provides a broad spectrum of chapters on current socioeconomic problems. As most students see it, this is where the action

is. I have sought to guide the action along logical lines through the application of appropriate analytical tools. My bias in Part 6 is in favor of inclusiveness; each instructor can effectively counter this bias by omitting those chapters he feels to be less relevant for his particular students.

ORGANIZATION AND CONTENT

In terms of organization, this book has been written with the conviction that the basic prerequisite of an understandable economics text is the logical arrangement and clear exposition of subject matter. This concern with organization is most evident in Part 1, which centers upon the step-by-step development of a comprehensive and realistic picture of American capitalism. This coherent group of introductory chapters is substituted for the traditional smattering of more or less unrelated background topics that ordinarily introduce the student to the study of economics.

Throughout this volume the exposition of each particular topic and concept is directly related to the level of difficulty which in my experience the average student is likely to encounter. It is for this reason that national income accounting, microeconomics, and to a lesser degree, employment theory are purposely accorded comprehensive and careful treatments. Simplicity in these instances is correlated with comprehensiveness, not brevity. Furthermore, my experience suggests that in the treatment of each basic topic—employment theory, money and banking, international economics, and so forth—it is highly desirable to couple analysis and policy. A three-step development of basic analytical tools is employed: (1) verbal description and illustration, (2) numerical examples, and (3) graphic presentation based upon these numerical illustrations.

The material is organized around seven basic topics: (1) an introduction to American capitalism; (2) national income, employment, and fiscal policy; (3) money and monetary policy; (4) economic growth; (5) economics of the firm and resource allocation; (6) current economic problems; and (7) international economics and the Soviet economy.

Part 1 is designed to introduce the method and subject matter of economics and to develop the ideological framework and the factual characteristics of American capitalism. This group of chapters develops in an orderly fashion the overall picture of how our economy operates. After an introduction to the methodology of economics in Chapter 1, an entire chapter is devoted to defining and explaining the economizing problem. Chapters 3 to 5 develop the capitalistic ideology and the notion of the most fundamental institution of capitalism—the price system. Early emphasis upon the price system is designed to provide the necessary orientation for the detailed treatment of pricing found in Part 5 and to contribute to an understanding of the national income analysis of Part 2 and, more specifically, the topics of inflation and deflation. Chapter 6 introduces government as a basic economic component of modern capitalism; government's economic functions are systematically explained and evaluated. Upon this superstructure of a mixed public-private economy, Chapters 7 and 8 add the factual information concerning the private and public sectors of the economy, thereby making our mixed capitalism model much more realistic. However, instructors who wish to minimize institutional material may choose to omit Chapters 7 and 8.

Part 2 treats national income analysis and fiscal policy. Chapter 9 on national income accounting reflects my conviction that this difficult topic merits detailed treatment. Chapter 10 employs the national income measures in describing the last six decades of American business cycle experience. The next three chapters are devoted to neo-Keynesian employment theory, fiscal policy, and the public debt.

Part 3 emphasizes the balance sheet approach to money and banking. This approach seems most in accord with the goal of providing the student with an analytical tool needed in reasoning through, as opposed to memorizing, the economic impact of the various basic banking transactions. Just as fiscal policy is linked directly to income theory in Part 2, monetary policy immediately follows the discussion of money and banking. Monetarism is portrayed as an alternative to Keynesianism and this is followed by a rather detailed look at the distressing macroeconomic events of the 1970s. The first half of the book is completed with Part 4 on economic growth in both the United States and the underdeveloped nations and problems related thereto.

For reasons already noted, the treatment of pricing and resource allocation in Part 5 is purposely detailed. Throughout Chapters 26 to 29 emphasis is placed upon the social implications of the various market structures. What is the significance of each market structure for price and output levels, resource allocation, and technological progress? Emphasis in the discussion of distribution—Chapters 30 to 32—is generally in accord with the relative quantitative importance of the various market shares in our economy. I have not belabored the analysis of interest, rent, and profits where, it seems to me, economic analysis is rather tentative. Chapter 33 provides a simple and, it is hoped, revealing discussion of general equilibrium and an introduction to input-output analysis.

Part 6 deals largely with domestic issues: the monopoly problem, the farm problem, the problems of the cities, the economics of inequality and poverty, labor relations and collective bargaining, the economic problems associated with war and defense, and the radical critique. Excepting Chapter 40, in each of these chapters an attempt has been made to (1) describe the historical and factual background of the problem, (2) analyze its causes and effects, (3) explore government policy, and (4) offer a thought-provoking discussion of public policy alternatives. As noted, instructors may choose to use the chapters of Part 6 selectively.

The first four chapters of Part 7 survey international trade and finance with some rigor. Finally, Chapter 45 offers a relatively comprehensive discussion of the Soviet economy, emphasizing its planning processes and its growth prospects.

End-of-chapter summaries provide a concise, pointed recapitulation of each chapter. Much thought has gone into the end-of-chapter questions. Though purposely intermixed, these questions are of three general types. Some are designed to highlight the main points of each chapter. Others are "open-end" discussion or thought questions. Wherever pertinent, numerical problems which require the student to derive and manipulate key concepts and relationships are employed. Numerical problems are stressed in those chapters dealing with national income accounting and analysis, money and banking, and price theory. Some optional "advanced analysis" questions accompany certain theory chapters. These problems usually involve the stating and manipulation of certain basic concepts in equation form. The bibliographical references at the end of each chapter are designed to provide both breadth and depth for the ambitious student. Yet care has been taken to see that these references are not beyond the grasp of the average college sophomore.

ORGANIZATIONAL ALTERNATIVES

Though economics instructors are in general agreement as to the basic content of a principles of economics course, there are considerable differences of opinion as to what particular arrangement of material is best. The structure of this book is designed to provide considerable organizational flexibility. And I am happy to report that users of prior editions have informed me that they accomplished substantial rearrangements of chapters with little sacrifice of continuity. Though I have chosen to move from macro- to microeconomics, there is no reason why the introductory material of Part 1

cannot be followed immediately by the microanalysis of Part 5. Similarly, in my judgment money and banking can best be taught after, rather than before, national income analysis. Those who disagree will encounter no problems by preceding Chapter 9 with Chapters 14, 15, and 16. Furthermore, some instructors will prefer to intersperse the microeconomics of Part 5 with the problems chapters of Part 6. This is easily accomplished. Chapter 35 on the farm problem may follow Chapter 26 on pure competition; Chapter 34 on the social control of monopoly may follow Chapters 27 to 29 on imperfect competition. Chapter 38 on labor unions and collective bargaining may either precede or follow Chapter 31 on wages, and Chapter 37 on income inequality may follow Chapters 31 and 32 on the distributive shares of national income.

Those who teach the typical two-semester course and who feel comfortable with the book's organization will find that, by putting the first four parts in the first semester and Parts 5 through 7 in the second, the material is divided both logically in terms of content and quite satisfactorily in terms of quantity and level of difficulty between the two semesters. For a course based on three quarters of work I would suggest Chapters 1 through 13 for the first quarter, 14 through 33 for the second, and 34 through 45 for the third. Finally, those interested in the one-semester course will be able to discern several possible groups of chapters that will be appropriate to such a course. Tentative outlines for three one-semester courses, emphasizing macroeconomics, microeconomics, or a survey of micro and macro theory, follow this preface on page xxiii.

SUPPLEMENTS

The seventh edition of *Economics* is accompanied by a wide range of useful supplements, making it perhaps the most complete instructional package available for the principles course.

The fifth edition of *Economic Issues: A Book of Readings* remains available as a supplement for this or any other mainstream textbook.

Professor Robert C. Bingham of Kent State University has prepared two valuable supplements. First, students have found his *Study Guide* to be an indispensable aid. The new seventh edition features an extensive glossary and a chapter-by-chapter statement of instructional objectives. Second, his *Economic Concepts* provides carefully designed programmed materials for all the key analytical areas of the principles course.

The *Personalized System of Instruction* prepared by Professor Jerry Petr of the University of Nebraska–Lincoln for the sixth edition is also available. This system of self-paced instruction offers instructors and their students an exciting new pedagogical option.

My *Instructor's Manual* includes some comments of a pedagogical character and, more important, is a reservoir of objective and essay questions. The seventh edition of the *Manual* has been substantially expanded with the addition of some 300 new multiple-choice questions. Furthermore, answers to all of the text's quantitative end-of-chapter questions are now provided for the convenience of instructors.

The *Test File* of questions which was introduced with the fourth edition is also available in enlarged form. The file contains the multiple-choice questions from the *Instructor's Manual* which can be arranged in any desired sequence and efficiently employed in constructing an examination. The *Test File* has been received enthusiastically by instructors, but somewhat less ecstatically by the publisher, who provides the *File* without charge to users of *Economics*. I am particularly pleased that other authors have accorded the *Test File* the most sincere form of flattery.

Color transparencies and black-and-white enlarged transparency masters for overhead projectors are available to those desiring these classroom aids.

DEBTS

The publication of this seventh edition extends the life of *Economics* to almost two decades. The acceptance of *Economics,* which was generous from the outset, has expanded with each edition. This surprising reception has no doubt been fostered by the many teachers and students who have been kind enough to give me the benefit of their suggestions and criticisms.

This seventh edition has benefited from comprehensive reviews by the following scholars: Professors Robin Barlow, University of Michigan; Robert J. Carbaugh, University of Wisconsin at Eau Claire; Richard M. Friedman, California State University at Northridge; Wendy L. Gramm, Texas A & M University; James B. Heisler, College of Wooster; Henry A. Knopf, Essex Community College; Randolph C. Martin, University of South Carolina; Vincent R. McDonald, Howard University; W. Arthur Parrish, Belleville Area College; and Alvin C. White, Knox College.

Professor W. H. Pope of Ryerson Polytechnical Institute, who is preparing a Canadian adaptation of *Economics,* has made many helpful suggestions. My colleagues at the University of Nebraska–Lincoln continue to be most generous in giving me both assistance and encouragement.

I am greatly indebted to the many professionals at McGraw-Hill—Stephen Dietrich, Edwin Hanson, et al.—for their expertise in the production of this book. My greatest debt is to Marjorie Singer who has been especially helpful in easing the task of revision.

Last, but not least, my daughter Lauren has again undertaken the demanding job of preparing the index.

Given this myriad of assistance, I see no compelling reason why the author should assume full responsibility for errors of omission or commission. But I bow to tradition.

Campbell R. McConnell

THREE SUGGESTED OUTLINES FOR ONE-SEMESTER COURSES

OPTION ONE: One-Semester Course Emphasizing Macroeconomics

1 THE NATURE AND METHOD OF ECONOMICS

2 AN INTRODUCTION TO THE ECONOMIZING PROBLEM

3 PURE CAPITALISM AND THE CIRCULAR FLOW

4 THE MECHANICS OF INDIVIDUAL PRICES: DEMAND AND SUPPLY

5 THE FIVE FUNDAMENTAL QUESTIONS AND THE PRICE SYSTEM

6 MIXED CAPITALISM AND THE ECONOMIC FUNCTIONS OF GOVERNMENT

7 THE FACTS OF AMERICAN CAPITALISM: THE PRIVATE SECTOR

8 THE FACTS OF AMERICAN CAPITALISM: THE PUBLIC SECTOR

9 NATIONAL INCOME ACCOUNTING

10 THE BUSINESS CYCLE: UNEMPLOYMENT AND INFLATION

11 THE BACKGROUND AND ANALYTICAL TOOLS OF EMPLOYMENT THEORY

12 THE EQUILIBRIUM LEVELS OF OUTPUT, EMPLOYMENT, AND INCOME

13 FISCAL POLICY AND THE PUBLIC DEBT

14 MONEY AND BANKING IN AMERICAN CAPITALISM

15 HOW BANKS CREATE MONEY

16 THE FEDERAL RESERVE BANKS AND MONETARY POLICY

17 MONETARISM: AN ALTERNATIVE VIEW

18 UNEMPLOYMENT AND INFLATION: NEW PROBLEMS AND NEW POLICIES

19 THE SIMPLE ANALYTICS OF ECONOMIC GROWTH

20 ECONOMIC GROWTH: FACT AND CONTROVERSY

21 GROWTH AND THE UNDERDEVELOPED NATIONS

Three Suggested Outlines for One-Semester Courses

OPTION TWO: One-Semester Course
Emphasizing Microeconomics

1 THE NATURE AND METHOD OF ECONOMICS

2 AN INTRODUCTION TO THE ECONOMIZING PROBLEM

3 PURE CAPITALISM AND THE CIRCULAR FLOW

4 THE MECHANICS OF INDIVIDUAL PRICES: DEMAND AND SUPPLY

5 THE FIVE FUNDAMENTAL QUESTIONS AND THE PRICE SYSTEM

6 MIXED CAPITALISM AND THE ECONOMIC FUNCTIONS OF GOVERNMENT

7 THE FACTS OF AMERICAN CAPITALISM: THE PRIVATE SECTOR

8 THE FACTS OF AMERICAN CAPITALISM: THE PUBLIC SECTOR

23 DEMAND, SUPPLY, AND ELASTICITY: SOME APPLICATIONS

24 FURTHER TOPICS IN THE THEORY OF CONSUMER DEMAND (OPTIONAL)

25 THE COSTS OF PRODUCTION

26 PRICE AND OUTPUT DETERMINATION: PURE COMPETITION

35 RURAL ECONOMICS: THE FARM PROBLEM (OPTIONAL)

27 PRICE AND OUTPUT DETERMINATION: PURE MONOPOLY

28 PRICE AND OUTPUT DETERMINATION: MONOPOLISTIC COMPETITION

29 PRICE AND OUTPUT DETERMINATION: OLIGOPOLY

34 THE MONOPOLY PROBLEM: THE SOCIAL CONTROL OF INDUSTRY (OPTIONAL)

30 PRODUCTION AND THE DEMAND FOR ECONOMIC RESOURCES

31 THE PRICING AND EMPLOYMENT OF RESOURCES: WAGE DETERMINATION

38 UNIONISM, COLLECTIVE BARGAINING, AND WOMEN AT WORK (OPTIONAL)

32 THE PRICING AND EMPLOYMENT OF RESOURCES: RENT, INTEREST, AND PROFITS

37 THE ECONOMICS OF INEQUALITY AND POVERTY (OPTIONAL)

33 GENERAL EQUILIBRIUM: THE PRICE SYSTEM AND ITS OPERATION

OPTION THREE: One-Semester Survey
of Micro and Macro Theory

1 THE NATURE AND METHOD OF ECONOMICS

2 AN INTRODUCTION TO THE ECONOMIZING PROBLEM

3 PURE CAPITALISM AND THE CIRCULAR FLOW

4 THE MECHANICS OF INDIVIDUAL PRICES: DEMAND AND SUPPLY

23 DEMAND, SUPPLY, AND ELASTICITY: SOME APPLICATIONS

25 THE COSTS OF PRODUCTION

26 PRICE AND OUTPUT DETERMINATION: PURE COMPETITION

27 PRICE AND OUTPUT DETERMINATION: PURE MONOPOLY

28 PRICE AND OUTPUT DETERMINATION: MONOPOLISTIC COMPETITION

29 PRICE AND OUTPUT DETERMINATION: OLIGOPOLY

30 PRODUCTION AND THE DEMAND FOR ECONOMIC RESOURCES

31 THE PRICING AND EMPLOYMENT OF RESOURCES: WAGE DETERMINATION

32 THE PRICING AND EMPLOYMENT OF RESOURCES: RENT, INTEREST, AND PROFITS

33 GENERAL EQUILIBRIUM: THE PRICE SYSTEM AND ITS OPERATION

9 NATIONAL INCOME ACCOUNTING

10 THE BUSINESS CYCLE: UNEMPLOYMENT AND INFLATION

11 THE BACKGROUND AND ANALYTICAL TOOLS OF EMPLOYMENT THEORY

12 THE EQUILIBRIUM LEVELS OF OUTPUT, EMPLOYMENT, AND INCOME

13 FISCAL POLICY AND THE PUBLIC DEBT

14 MONEY AND BANKING IN AMERICAN CAPITALISM

15 HOW BANKS CREATE MONEY

16 THE FEDERAL RESERVE BANKS AND MONETARY POLICY

17 MONETARISM: AN ALTERNATIVE VIEW

18 UNEMPLOYMENT AND INFLATION: NEW PROBLEMS AND NEW POLICIES

PART ONE

AN INTRODUCTION
TO AMERICAN CAPITALISM

The Nature and Method of Economics

Man, unfortunate creature, is plagued with wants. He wants, among other things, love, social recognition, and the material necessities and comforts of life. Man's striving to improve his material well-being, to "make a living," is the concern of economics. More specifically, economics is the study of man's behavior in producing, exchanging, and consuming the material goods and services he wants. Most of us think of economics in terms of specific problems—balancing the household budget, labor disputes, taxes, debt, inflation, unemployment, poverty, the energy crisis, and so forth. Although limited, this thinking is not incorrect. These individual problems are fragments or signs of the larger problem of man's attempt to satisfy his material wants.

It is tempting to seek out immediately answers and solutions to the obvious problems of current interest. But this would be precipitate; certain preliminary matters must be discussed first. In particular, we must know the answers to these questions:

1 Of what importance or consequence is the study of economics?

2 How should we study economics—what are the proper procedures? Stated in more technical terms, what is the character of the methodology of economics?

3 What specific problems, limitations, and pitfalls might we encounter in studying economics?

These topics will occupy our attention in this introductory chapter.

1

THE AGE OF THE ECONOMIST

Is economics a discipline of consequence? Is the study of economics an endeavor worthy of one's time and effort? Some four decades ago John Maynard Keynes (1883–1946)—clearly the most influential economist of this century—offered a telling response:

> The ideas of economists and political philosophers, both when they are right and when they are wrong, are more powerful than is commonly understood. Indeed the world is ruled by little else. Practical men, who believe themselves to be quite exempt from any intellectual influences, are usually the slaves of some defunct economist.

The ideologies of the modern world which compete for the minds of men have been shaped in substantial measure by the great economists of the past—Adam Smith, John Stuart Mill, David Ricardo, Karl Marx, and John Maynard Keynes.[1] And it is currently commonplace for world leaders to receive and invoke the advice and policy prescriptions of economists; "the political economist is now a fixture in the high councils of government."[2] To illustrate: The President of the United States benefits from the ongoing counsel of his Council of Economic Advisers. The broad spectrum of economic issues with which political leaders must contend, and on which they must assume some tenable posture, is suggested by the contents of the annual *Economic Report of the President:* unemployment and inflation, economic growth and productivity, taxation and public expenditures, poverty and income maintenance, the balance of payments and the international monetary system, labor-management relations, manpower development and training, pollution, discrimination on the basis of race and sex, competition and antitrust, to enumerate only a few of the areas covered.

□ Economics for Citizenship

These comments correctly imply that a basic understanding of economics is essential if we are to be well-informed citizens. Most of the specific problems of the day have important economic aspects, and as voters, we can influence the decisions of our political leaders in coping with these problems. Should America permanently maintain price and wage controls to stop inflation? Should we make a national commitment to the development of new sources of energy? Should we attempt to break up the huge corporations which seem to dominate certain segments of our economy? What can be done to reduce unemployment? Are existing welfare programs effective and justifiable? Should we continue to subsidize farmers? Is there any justification for protecting certain industries from foreign competition? Should income be distributed more equally? What are the economic implications of war? And of disarmament? What are the advantages and disadvantages of alternative economic systems? Is our economy due for major institutional surgery? Since the answers to such questions are determined by our elected officials, intelligence at the polls requires that we have a basic working knowledge of economics.

□ Personal Applications

Economics is also a vital discipline for somewhat more mundane and immediate reasons. Economics is of practical value in business. An understanding of the overall operation of the economic system puts the

---

[1] Either of the following two volumes—Robert Heilbroner, *The Worldly Philosophers,* 4th ed. (New York: Simon and Schuster, Inc., 1972), or Daniel R. Fusfeld, 3d ed., *The Age of the Economist* (Chicago: Scott, Foresman and Company, 1977)—will provide the reader with a fascinating introduction to the historical development of economic ideas.

[2] Walter W. Heller, *New Dimensions of Political Economy* (New York: W. W. Norton & Company, Inc., 1967), p. 14.

businessman in a better position to formulate his policies. For example, if he understands the causes and consequences of inflation, he is better equipped during inflationary periods to make intelligent decisions concerning his enterprise than he might be otherwise. Indeed, more and more economists are appearing on the payrolls of large corporations. Their job? To gather and interpret economic information upon which rational business decisions can be made. Also, economics gives the individual as worker and income receiver some insights as to how he might make himself more secure against the effects of inflation and unemployment. How can one "hedge" against the reduction in the purchasing power of the dollar which accompanies inflation? What occupations are most immune to unemployment?

In spite of its practical benefits, however, the reader must be forewarned that economics is an academic, not a vocational, subject. Unlike accounting, advertising, corporation finance, and salesmanship, economics is not primarily a how-to-make-money area of study.[3] A knowledge of economics may be helpful in running a business or in managing one's personal finances, but this is not its primary objective. In economics, problems are examined from the social, not from the individual, point of view. The production, exchange, and consumption of goods and services are discussed from the viewpoint of society as a whole, not from the standpoint of one's own bankbook.

■
METHODOLOGY

What do economists do? What are their goals? What procedures do they employ? The title of this volume—*Economics: Principles, Problems, and Policies*—contains a thumbnail

[3] An economist has been defined as an individual with a Phi Beta Kappa key on one end of his watch chain and with no watch on the other.

answer to the first two questions. Economists are concerned with the derivation of economic *principles* which are useful in the formulation of *policies* designed to solve economic *problems*. The procedure employed by the economist is summarized in Figure 1-1. The economist must first ascertain and gather the facts which are relevant to consideration of a specific economic problem. This aspect of his job is sometimes called "descriptive economics." The economist then puts his collection of facts in order and summarizes them by "distilling out" a principle, that is, by generalizing about the way individuals and institutions actually behave. Deriving principles from facts is called "economic theory" or "economic analysis." Fi-

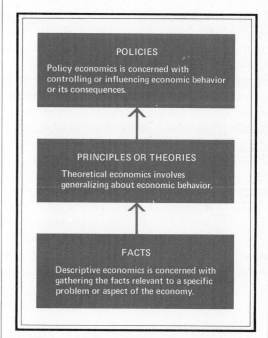

FIGURE 1-1 THE RELATIONSHIP BETWEEN FACTS, PRINCIPLES, AND POLICIES IN ECONOMICS

In studying any problem or segment of the economy, the economist must first gather the relevant facts. These facts must then be systematically arranged, interpreted, and generalized upon. These generalizations are useful not only in explaining economic behavior, but also in predicting and therefore controlling future events.

nally, the general knowledge of economic behavior which economic principles provide can then be used in formulating policies, that is, remedies or solutions, for correcting or avoiding the problem under scrutiny. This final aspect of the field is sometimes called "applied economics" or "policy economics."

Still using Figure 1-1 as a point of reference, let us now examine this three-step procedure in more detail.

☐ Descriptive Economics

All sciences are empirical. All sciences are based upon facts, that is, upon observable and verifiable behavior of certain data or subject matter. In the physical sciences the factual data are inorganic. As a social science, economics is concerned with the behavior of individuals and institutions engaged in the production, exchange, and consumption of goods and services.

The first major step, then, in investigating a given problem or a specific segment of the economy is to gather the facts. This can be an infinitely complex task. The world of reality is cluttered with a myriad of interrelated facts. The economist therefore must use discretion in fact gathering. He must distinguish economic from noneconomic facts and then determine which economic facts are relevant and which are irrelevant for the particular problem under consideration. But even when this sorting process has been completed, the relevant economic facts may appear diverse and unrelated.

☐ Economic Theory

A conglomeration of facts is relatively useless; mere description is not enough. To be meaningful, facts must be systematically arranged, interpreted, and generalized upon. This is the task of economic theory or analysis. Principles and theories—the end result of economic analysis—bring order and meaning to a number of facts by tying these facts to-

gether, putting them in correct relationship to one another, and generalizing upon them. "Theories without facts may be barren, but facts without theories are meaningless."[4]

The interplay between the levels of fact and theory is more complex than Figure 1-1 indicates. Principles and theories are meaningful statements drawn from facts, but facts, in turn, serve as a constant check on the validity of principles already established. Facts—how individuals and institutions actually behave in producing, exchanging, and consuming goods and services—change with time. This makes it essential that economists continuously check existing principles and theories against the changing economic environment. The history of economic ideas is strewn with once-valid generalizations about economic behavior which were rendered obsolete by the changing course of events.

Terminology A word on terminology is essential at this juncture. Economists talk about "laws," "principles," "theories," and "models." These terms all mean essentially the same thing: generalizations, or statements of regularity, concerning the economic behavior of individuals and institutions. The term "economic law" is a bit misleading because it implies a high degree of exactness, universal application, and even moral rightness. So, to a lesser degree, does the term "principle." And some people incorrectly associate the term "theory" with idle pipe dreams and ivory-tower hallucinations, divorced from the facts and realities of the world. The term "model" has much to commend it. A model is a simplified picture of reality, an abstract generalization of how the relevant data actually behave. In this book these four terms will be used synonymously. The choice of terms in labeling any particular generalization will be governed by custom or convenience here. Hence, the rela-

[4]Kenneth E. Boulding, *Economic Analysis: Microeconomics,* 4th ed. (New York: Harper & Row, Publishers, Incorporated, 1966), p. 5.

tionship between the price of a product and the quantity consumers purchase will be called the "law" of demand, rather than the theory or principle of demand, because it is customary so to designate it.

These comments on terminology raise two points which merit further consideration: First, economic principles (laws, theories, or models) are *generalizations,* and second, they are *abstractions.*

Generalizations Economic principles are generalizations and, as such, subject to exceptions and to quantitatively imprecise statement. Economic facts are usually diverse; some individuals and institutions act one way and some another way. Hence, economic principles are frequently stated in terms of averages or statistical probabilities. For example, when economists say that the average household earned an income of about $16,500 in 1976, they are making a generalization. It is recognized that some households earned much more and a good many others much less. Yet this generalization, properly handled and interpreted, can be very meaningful and useful. Or an economist may conclude that 95 percent of the time—95 chances out of 100—consumers will increase their purchases of a product when its price falls. Five percent of the consumers constitute an exception to the general rule.

The main reason for the inexactness of economic principles is that economists cannot conduct controlled experiments—they do not have a laboratory in which they can create simplified and controlled conditions. The laboratory of the social sciences is the real world, where the specific aspects of human behavior we wish to examine cannot be readily isolated from the social and cultural milieu. Chemists can "make other things equal" in their controlled experiments; economists cannot.

The "Other Things Equal" Assumption Unable to make other things equal in their analyses, economists do the next best thing:

They *assume* other things are equal in isolating certain data for analysis. To illustrate: In analyzing the relationship between the price of product X and the amount of X purchased, economists assume that of all the factors influencing the amount of X purchased, only its price varies. To cut the problem down to size, they must assume that all other factors which might influence the amount of X purchased are unchanged or "equal." In this way economists can isolate the relationship between price and quantity demanded from all sorts of real-world complications. However, in applying the resulting generalization—consumers buy more of X at a low price than they do at a high price—to a real-world situation, exceptions may be encountered. Why? Because other things usually are not equal in the real world. For example, an increase in incomes—another consideration which, in addition to a price change, will cause the amount of X purchased to alter—may complicate the application of the general conclusion about the relationship between the price of X and the amount of X purchased. The economist may find that, although the price of X has risen, the quantity demanded has *increased* contrary to his generalization. This does not make the generalization invalid, but, rather, means that peculiar circumstances—higher incomes—have entered this particular application of the principle to upset its accuracy. It is merely an exception to the rule, and in economics such exceptions may be rather frequent. Economics is admittedly an inexact science.

Abstractions Economic principles, or theories, are necessarily abstractions. They do not embody the full bloom of reality. The very process of sorting out noneconomic and irrelevant facts in the fact-gathering process involves abstracting from reality. Unfortunately, the abstractness of economic theory prompts the uninformed to identify theory as something which is impractical and unrealistic. This is nonsense! As a matter of fact, economic theories are practical for the simple reason that they are abstractions. The level of reality is too complex to be very meaningful. Economists theorize in order to give meaning to a maze of facts which would otherwise be confusing and useless and to put facts into a more usable, practical form. Thus, to generalize is to abstract; generalization for this purpose is practical, and therefore so is abstraction. An economic theory is a model—a simplified picture or map—of some segment of the economy. This model enables us to better understand reality *because* it avoids the details of reality. Finally, theories—*good* theories— are grounded on facts and therefore are realistic. Theories which do not fit the facts are simply not good theories.

Graphic Expression   Theories, or models, can be expressed in many ways. For example, the physicist and the chemist illustrate their theories by building Tinker-Toy arrangements of multicolored wooden balls that represent protons, neutrons, and so forth, held in proper relationship to one another by wires or sticks. Economists are not so lucky as to have theories that lend themselves to such tangible demonstrations. *Economic models may take the form of verbal description, numerical tables, mathematical equations, or graphs.* The last are particularly helpful and will be used throughout this book. Most of the principles we shall encounter will explain the relationship between just two sets of economic facts, for example, the relationship between the price of a specific product and the quantity of it which consumers buy. Simple two-dimensional graphs are a convenient and clear way of summarizing and manipulating these relationships.

As shown in Figure 1-2, graphs are drawn on squared paper divided into four quarters, or quadrants, by a horizontal axis and a vertical axis, which intersect at right angles. The point of intersection is called the *origin*. Each axis has a scale of numerical values. On the vertical axis, all values above the origin are positive,

FIGURE 1-2 ECONOMIC PRINCIPLES CAN BE EXPRESSED GRAPHICALLY

Two-dimensional graphs are a convenient way of presenting and manipulating relationships between data. The relationship between two sets of economic data with positive numerical values is shown in the northeast quadrant of the chart.

and all values below are negative. On the horizontal axis, values to the right of the origin are positive; those to the left are negative. The point of intersection, that is, the origin, designates zero. Though the vertical and horizontal scales in Figure 1-2 measure the same numerical values, this need not be the case. Each unit on the vertical axis may measure $1, while the same distance on the horizontal axis may denote 1000 bushels of corn.

In elementary economics we are virtually always concerned with the relationship between two sets of economic facts the values of which are positive. Hence, we are concerned with the upper right-hand (northeast) quadrant where both scales measure positive values.

Now let us explore an example or two to illustrate the construction and interpretation of graphs. Suppose detailed factual investigation reveals that, other things being equal, the relationship between the price of corn per bushel and the amount farmers are willing to produce and offer for sale per year is as shown in Table 1-1.

How can this be shown graphically? Simply by putting the two sets of facts—product price and quantity supplied—on the two axes of the chart and locating the five combinations of price-quantity supplied as shown in Table 1-1. Convention or convenience dictates which set of facts goes on the vertical axis and which on the horizontal axis. By convention, economists put "price" on the vertical and "quantity" on the horizontal axis, as indicated in Figure 1-3. The five price-quantity combinations are plotted on the chart by drawing perpendiculars from the appropriate points on the two axes. For example, in plotting the $5–12,000-bushel combination, perpendiculars must be drawn across from the vertical (price) axis at $5 and up from the horizontal (quantity-supplied) axis at 12,000 bushels. Their point of intersection locates the $5–12,000-bushel combination on the graph. The same procedure locates the other four price-quantity combinations. If it is assumed that the same general relationship between price and quan-

Table 1-1   THE QUANTITIES OF CORN FARMERS WILL SUPPLY AT VARIOUS PRICES (*hypothetical data*)

Price per bushel	Bushels supplied per year
$5	12,000
4	10,000
3	7,000
2	4,000
1	1,000

tity supplied will prevail at all points between the five graphed, a line or curve can be drawn to connect these points. In this instance the two sets of data are *directly related*; that is, price and quantity supplied move in the same direction. As price increases, the quantity supplied increases. As price declines, so does the quantity supplied. When two sets of data are directly related, they will always graph as an *upsloping* line or curve, such as *SS* in Figure 1-3.

Now suppose fact gathering reveals that the price of corn and the quantity which consumers will buy per year are related in the manner shown in Table 1-2. These data indicate that consumers will demand more corn

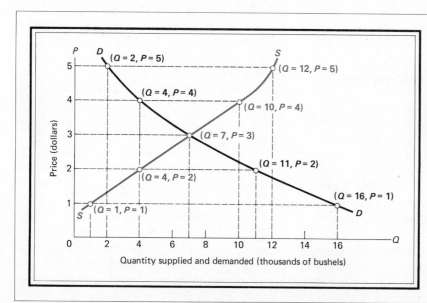

FIGURE 1-3 GRAPHING DIRECT AND INVERSE RELATIONSHIPS

Two sets of economic data which are directly related, such as price and quantity supplied, graph as an upsloping curve (*SS*). Two sets of data which are inversely related, such as price and quantity demanded, graph as a downsloping curve (*DD*).

Table 1-2   THE QUANTITIES OF CORN CONSUMERS
WILL PURCHASE AT VARIOUS PRICES (*hypothetical
data*)

Price per bushel	Bushels demanded per year
$5	2,000
4	4,000
3	7,000
2	11,000
1	16,000

when its price is low than they will when the price is high; that is, price and quantity are *inversely related*. If price increases, the amount purchased will decline. If price declines, the quantity purchased will increase. An inverse relationship will always graph as a *downsloping* line or curve, such as *DD* in Figure 1-3.

Anticipating Chapter 4, we note in passing that Figure 1-3 constitutes a basic economic model of a market. That is, by combining the direct relationship between price and quantity supplied—called the *law of supply*—and the inverse relationship between price and quantity demanded—labeled the *law of demand*—we have constructed a simple economic model. Hence, we will find in Chapter 4 that the intersection of these two curves identifies the market price ($3 in this case) and the quantity of the product (7000 bushels) which will be bought and sold. Although this model is very simple, it has wide applicability and great explanatory power. For example, it will prove useful in explaining not only how product prices and outputs are determined (Figure 4-5), but also wage rates and rents (Figures 31-3 and 32-1), exchange rates among foreign currencies (Figure 43-4), the economic impacts of both price controls and supports (Figures 23-5 and 23-6), the consequences of sales taxes and tariffs (Figures 23-7 and 42-1), and so forth.

Induction and Deduction   Our discussion thus far describes the *inductive* or empirical method. Here we begin with an accumulation of facts which are then arranged systematically and analyzed so as to permit the derivation of a generalization or principle. Induction moves from facts to theory, from the particular to the general. We must now note that, in terms of Figure 1-1, economists can set about their task by beginning at the level of theory and proceed to the verification or rejection of this theory by an appeal to the facts. This is the *deductive* or hypothetical method. Thus, economists may draw upon casual observation, insight, or intuition to frame a tentative, untested principle called a *hypothesis*. For example, they may conjecture, on the basis of "armchair logic," that consumers will buy more of a product when its price is low than they will when its price is high. The validity of this hypothesis must then be tested by the systematic and repeated examination of relevant facts. The deductive method goes from the general to the particular, from theory to facts. Most economists view deduction and induction as complementary, rather than opposing, techniques of investigation. Hypotheses formulated by deduction provide guidelines for the economist as he gathers and systematizes empirical data. Conversely, a casual understanding of factual evidence—of the "real world"—is prerequisite to the formulation of meaningful hypotheses.

Dangers of Models   When properly constructed and interpreted, economic models are invaluable tools. But we must be aware of certain potential dangers in deriving and applying these models.

1 The fundamental danger in constructing an economic model or principle is that the economist might fail to distinguish correctly between relevant and irrelevant facts. If the economist "boils out" some relevant facts, the resulting principle may be a disjointed, misleading, and, at best, incomplete analytical tool. A related difficulty stems from the possibility that an overzealous economist might

abstract from too many facts and construct a model which is hyperabstract and truly out of touch with reality.

2 In applying economic models, we must always recognize them for what they are—useful first approximations. It is easy, but dangerous, to slip into the practice of becoming so enamored of the logical clarity of a model that we forget it is only a rough outline of reality. There may be many omissions between a simplified economic model and reality.

3 We must be on guard in applying economic models so as not to impute any ethical or moral qualities to them. Economic models are the analytical tools of the economist and, as such, they are ethically neutral. Because they are constructed of facts, economic models afford general statements about "what is," not indications of "what ought to be." Figure 1-3 does not tell us that farmers *should* supply more corn at higher prices than at lower prices, but, rather, that they *actually do*. Economic models are not tin gods to be worshiped as an end in themselves, or as a compendium of ethically desirable results. Instead, they should be recognized for what they are—a means to an end, a summary of factual data.

□ **Policy Economics**

Of what value are economic principles? The answer is twofold.

1 There is first the matter of explanation for explanation's sake—economic principles help to explain to us why certain events occur the way they do. Through economic principles we can comprehend why prices change, how surpluses and shortages of products arise, what causes depression and unemployment, and so forth. Our curiosity concerning these and similar phenomena can be satisfied through the development of economic principles to serve as tools for the understanding of reality.

2 More importantly, economic theory is the basis for *economic policy;* that is, our un-

derstanding of economic principles can be applied in resolving specific problems and in furthering the realization of society's overall goals. Economic principles are extremely valuable as predictive devices. And accurate prediction is obviously required if we want to alter some event or outcome. More specifically, if some undesirable event (such as unemployment or inflation) can be predicted or understood through economic theory, we may then be able to influence or control that event. Or, if we cannot control an outcome, at least we gain from prediction invaluable time to prepare for adjusting to its consequences. Ability to predict a rainstorm does not give us control over the weather, but it does permit us to prepare for it by carrying a raincoat and an umbrella.

Values It is evident that value judgments—opinions as to what is desirable or undesirable—come into the picture at this juncture. Descriptive economics and economic theory are both concerned with facts—the former immediately and the latter once removed. Policy economics necessarily entails value judgments as to the desirability of certain events. When operating at this level, economists are no longer functioning as scientists per se, but, rather, as policy makers. They are dealing not only with facts, but also with values.

An example or two will help at this point. Our previously noted law of demand is the basis for one illustration: "Consumers generally buy more of a product at a low price than they do at a high price." Suppose a clothing merchant finds that he is greatly overstocked with summer clothing at a time when shipments of fall and winter clothing are due. The merchant has the problem of ridding himself of his undesired surplus stock of summer wear. Our law of demand helps the merchant to solve this problem by predicting for him how consumers will react to price changes. In particular, the principle predicts that the merchant will be able to increase his sales and "move" the surplus by lowering prices. The merchant, formulating his price policies accordingly, "runs a sale." The surplus disappears.

A second example, of greater consequence to the economy as a whole, involves the fundamental principle that, within certain limits, there is a direct relationship between total spending and the level of employment in the economy. "If total spending increases (decreases), the volume of employment will rise (fall)." This principle can be invaluable to government in determining its economic policies. For example, if government economists note that available statistics indicate an actual slackening of total expenditures, the principle will permit them to predict the undesirable consequence of unemployment. Aware of this anticipated result, public officials are now in a position to set in motion certain government policies designed to bolster total spending and head off expected unemployment. In short, we must be able to predict in order to effectively control. Economic principles help make prediction possible.

Economic Goals   It is important at this point that we note, and reflect upon, a number of economic goals or values which are widely, though not universally, accepted in our society and, indeed, in many other societies. These goals may be briefly listed as follows:

1   Economic growth   The production of more and better goods and services, or, more simply stated, a higher standard of living, is desired.

2   Full employment   Suitable jobs should be available for all who are willing and able to work.

3   Price stability   Sizable upswings or downswings in the general price level, that is, inflation and deflation, should be avoided.

4   Economic freedom   Businessmen, workers, and consumers should enjoy a high degree of freedom in their economic activities.

5   An equitable distribution of income   No group of citizens should face stark poverty while others enjoy extreme luxury.

6   Economic security   Provision should be made for those who are chronically ill, disabled, handicapped, aged, or otherwise dependent.

Now this list of widely accepted goals provides the basis for several significant points. First, note that this or any other statement of basic economic goals inevitably entails problems of interpretation. What are "sizable" changes in the price level? What is a "high degree" of economic freedom? What is an "equitable" distribution of income? Although most of us might accept the above goals as generally stated, we might also disagree very substantially as to their specific meanings and hence as to the types of policies needed to attain these goals. It is noteworthy that, although goals 1 to 3 are subject to reasonably accurate measurements, the inability to quantify goals 4 to 6 undoubtedly contributes to any controversy over their precise meaning.

Second, certain of these goals are complementary in that to the extent one goal is achieved, some other goal or goals will also tend to be realized. For example, the achieving of full employment (goal 2) obviously means the elimination of unemployment, a basic cause of low incomes (goal 5) and economic insecurity (goal 6). Furthermore, considering goals 1 and 5, it is generally agreed that the sociopolitical tensions which may accompany a highly unequal distribution of income are tempered to the extent that most incomes rise absolutely as a result of economic growth.

Third, some goals may be conflicting or mutually exclusive. Some economists argue that those forces which further the attainment of economic growth and full employment may be the very same forces which cause inflation. In fact, the apparent conflict between goals 2 and 3 has been at the forefront of economic research and debate in recent years. Later, we will undertake an extended discussion of the prospects for making full employment and price stability compatible goals (Chapter 18). Other economists feel that to some extent economic growth and full employment (goals 1 and 2) may conflict with economic freedom (goal 4). They contend that rapid growth and continuous full employment may require an expanding role for government and that this role will inevitably impinge upon the free choices of businessmen, workers, and consumers.

This leads us to a fourth point: When basic goals do conflict, society is forced to develop a system of priorities for the objectives it seeks. To illustrate: If full employment and price stability are to some extent mutually exclusive, that is, if full employment entails some inflation and price stability entails some unemployment, society must decide upon the relative importance of these two goals. Suppose the relevant choice is between, say, a 4 percent annual increase in the price level accompanied by full employment on the one hand, and a perfectly stable price level with 6 percent of the labor force unemployed on the other. Which is the better choice? Or how about a compromise goal in the form of, say, a 2 percent increase in the price level each year with 5 percent of the labor force out of work? There is obviously ample room for disagreement here.

There would admittedly be disagreement among individuals in our society as to the priorities to be assigned these six goals, or, for that matter, as to whether this is a "correct" list in the first place.[5] Furthermore, other societies can, and do, have substantially different priorities. Soviet society—or perhaps more accurately the Soviet state—puts relatively greater emphasis upon goals 1 and 2 and, our experts tell us, has at times done a better job of

achieving these goals than we have (Chapter 45). A good part of the explanation of the success of the Soviet Union in achieving rapid growth and full employment is that it attaches a much lower priority than we do to other goals. In particular, Soviet disregard for economic freedom allows the use of policies for achieving full employment and rapid growth which would be completely unacceptable in our society. In short, other societies assign different weights or priorities to various goals, and their differing priorities may permit those societies to do a better job in achieving certain of these objectives.

Formulating Economic Policy   The creation of specific policies designed to achieve the broad economic goals of our society is no simple matter. A brief examination of the basic steps in policy formulation is in order.

1 The first step is to make a clear statement of goals. If we say that we have "full employment," do we mean that everyone between, say, 16 and 65 years of age has a job? Or do we mean that everyone who wants to work has a job? Should we allow for some "normal" unemployment caused by workers' voluntarily changing jobs?

2 Next we must state and recognize the possible effects of alternative policies designed to achieve the goal. This entails a clear-cut understanding of the economic impact, benefits, costs, and political feasibility of alternative programs. Thus, for example, economists currently debate the relative merits and demerits of fiscal policy (changing government spending and taxes) and monetary policy (altering the supply of money) as alternative means of achieving and maintaining full employment (Chapter 17).

3 We are obligated to both ourselves and future generations to look back upon our experiences with chosen policies and evaluate their effectiveness; it is only through this type of evaluation that we can hope to improve policy applications. Did a given change in taxes or

[5] For example, we will discover in Part 7 that the realization of balance in our international trade and finance is an important national goal. Furthermore, the improvement of the physical environment is a goal of increasing significance (Chapter 36).

the supply of money alter the level of employment to the extent originally predicted? If not, why not?

One final point: The formulation of economic policy is greatly complicated by the fact that our economy is a dynamic, changing organism. We must therefore not expect once-and-for-all answers to basic economic problems, but, rather, short-run adjustments which may rapidly become obsolete. What is correct policy today may be rendered inappropriate tomorrow by a rapidly changing economic milieu.

■——————————————

TWO CHEERS FOR ECONOMISTS

How successful have economists been in formulating economic principles and applying them to economic problems? What is the current "state of the art"? This is a broad and complex question to which there are no simple, unqualified answers.

There is, on the one hand, substantial evidence that economics has achieved rapid and significant progress in recent decades. The flow of scholarly articles, monographs, and treatises on a vast spectrum of economic questions has been "swelling like a tidal wave," reflecting a knowledge explosion in the discipline. Furthermore, economists take considerable pride in that their discipline is the only social science for which the Swedish Academy of Science awards a Nobel Prize. And, as noted at the outset of this chapter, the counsel and advice of economists are systematically sought and applied by governments at all levels and of all ideologies.

Yet, there is an undercurrent of dissatisfaction with the accomplishments of economics. As one critic has put it, the light of economic understanding "is curiously uneven. Some parts of the social machinery are brilliantly lit. Other parts are left shadowy or

totally dark."[6] Although interrelated and somewhat overlapping, the criticisms of economics run along the following lines.

1 The ability of economists to "theorize" in the sense of reasoning abstractly has outrun the base of factual data. Because of the application of mathematics to economics and the availability of computers, economists can construct and manipulate highly complex models involving in some instances hundreds of equations. But, it is argued, the economic relationships shown in these equations are often *assumed* or based upon sketchy and questionable empirical evidence. To a degree, economics has lost touch with reality in that it is often difficult, if not impossible, to verify or reject economic theories in the light of reliable empirical facts.

2 In their desire to maintain scientific objectivity, economists have generally tended either to avoid, or to approach timidly, those problems or issues which are immersed in subjective value judgments. Stated differently, economics has increasingly limited itself to quantifiable aspects of human behavior and has skirted qualitative questions in the name of scientific purity. Notable example: Economists have had little to say concerning the highly relevant question of how income ought to be distributed. The reason: There is no scientific way of calculating the gain to person B and the loss to person A as dollars are shifted from A to B. These gains and losses are subjective and nonmeasureable. Consequently, economists have largely dodged the question of income redistribution.

3 This avoidance shades into a third point. In their effort to be pure scientists, economists have failed to interpret the problems of the day within a sufficiently broad context. Real-world problems are multidisciplinary in character; that is, in addition to

[6]Robert L. Heilbroner, "On the Limited 'Relevance' of Economics," *The Public Interest,* Fall 1970, p. 81.

economics these problems entail social, political, cultural, historical, and psychological aspects. As a result, the purely economic analysis of these problems entails a limited and unrealistic understanding of them and, consequently, ineffective and misguided policy recommendations. First example: Many studies of the problems of the less developed countries have resulted in ineffective growth policies for these nations, not because of faulty economic analyses, but because of a failure to grasp the sociocultural milieu, the historical background, the political institutions, and the attitudinal characteristics of the country. Second example: It is contended that the insistent inflation of the 1970s is *not* explainable in terms of accepted economic theory (as presented in Part 2), but, rather, in terms of political decisions and the exertion of *power*. In particular, the formation of the oil cartel by the Organization of Petroleum Exporting Countries (OPEC) caused a dramatic power shift internationally, the immediate consequence of which was a quadrupling of the price of oil. And the political exigencies of détente resulted in massive grain sales to the Soviet Union, thereby reducing food supplies and raising food prices domestically. Similarly, despite an economic environment uncongenial to price increases, large corporations exerted their market power to substantially increase their prices and contribute to overall inflation.[7]

4 Radical (Marxian) economists of the New Left contend that orthodox economists have become apologists for the capitalist system. Orthodox economists stress the harmony of interests among individuals, institutions, and classes; they couch their analyses in terms of gradual or marginal changes; and, perhaps most important, they take the basic institutions of the capitalistic system—for example, private property and the market system—for granted. To the radical economists the workings of the capitalist system can better be understood in terms of conflicts of interest and disruptive, nongradual change. Furthermore, the radicals hold that the resolution of the fundamental problems or "contradictions" of capitalism can be resolved only through basic institutional changes, for example, the abolition of private property. The Last Word segment of this chapter elaborates the radical criticism.

PITFALLS TO STRAIGHT THINKING

Our discussion of the economist's procedure has, up to this point, skirted some of the specific problems and pitfalls frequently encountered in deriving and applying economic principles. Some of these difficulties—for example, problems of terminology and bias—are almost self-evident. Indeed, they are so obvious that we tend to overlook them, which makes explicit comment imperative. Other difficulties, particularly those which take the form of logical pitfalls, are rather complex and most conducive to faulty economic reasoning.

□   **Terminology**

It is extremely important in studying any science to understand its terminology, but this is particularly so in the social sciences. There are three specific reasons why a clear, objective grasp of relevant terms will prove to be half the battle in understanding many aspects of economics:

[7]See Robert Lekachman, *Economists at Bay* (New York: McGraw-Hill Book Company, 1976), particularly chap. 1, and John Kenneth Galbraith, "Power and the Useful Economist," *American Economic Review,* March 1973, pp. 1–11. The ideas expressed in these first three criticisms of orthodox economics are associated with an alternative conception of the economy known as "institutional economics" or "evolutionary economics." The interested reader should consult Allan G. Gruchy, *Contemporary Economic Thought* (Clifton, N.J.: Augustus M. Kelley, Publishers, 1972).

1 Emotionalism The economic terminology to which we are exposed in newspapers and popular magazines is sometimes emotionally loaded. The writer—or more frequently the particular interest group he represents—may have a cause to further or an ax to grind, and his terms will be slanted to solicit the support of the reader. Hence, we may find a governmental flood-control project in the Great Plains region called "creeping socialism" by its opponents and "intelligent democratic planning" by its proponents. We must be prepared, therefore, to discount such terminology in achieving objectivity in the understanding of important economic issues.

2 Dual Terminology It is embarrassing to admit that economists are often guilty of dual terminology—the unfortunate practice of using two or more labels to designate the same thing. In part, this is a matter of historical accident. It is also the result of economic inquirers' not discovering immediately that two seemingly different theories or explanations are actually the same. The dual labels persist after the theories have been merged. For example, the terms "economic resources," "productive services," and "factors of production" have identical meanings. Similarly, in probing the causes of economic depression, we hear some authorities laying the blame at the door of "underconsumption," while others cite "oversaving" as the villain. The beginner who is not familiar with the definitions of these terms may envision a basic conflict of views. Actually, "oversaving" and "underconsumption," properly defined, refer essentially to the same phenomenon.

3 Definitions It is important to keep in mind that no scientist is obligated to use commonsense or man-in-the-street definitions of his terms. He may find it convenient and essential to define his terms in such a way that they are clearly at odds with the definitions held by laymen in everyday speech. So long as the economist is explicit and consistent in his definitions, he is on safe ground. A typical example: The term "investment" to John Q. Citizen is associated with the buying of bonds and stocks in the securities market. How often have we heard someone talking of "investing" in General Motors stock or government bonds? But to the economist, "investment" means the purchase of real capital assets such as machinery and equipment, or the construction of a new wing on a factory building, not the purely financial transaction of swapping cash or part of a bank balance for a neatly engraved piece of paper. As a matter of fact, we shall discover in Chapter 9 that what the layman calls "investment" is a swapping of assets or a form of saving, as the economist sees it.

□ **Bias and Preconceptions**

The beginning student in chemistry or physics traditionally knows little or nothing about the subject matter of these fields at the outset. He starts from scratch with a blank, but supposedly clear, mind. Not so in the social sciences in general or in economics in particular. For a variety of reasons the budding economist ordinarily launches into his field of study with a bundle of preconceptions about the operation of our economy and its component parts. Such issues as the energy crisis, inflation, the public debt, the legitimate functions of labor unions, big business versus competition, the nature and operation of our tax system, and the like are everyday topics of conversation. Unless we live in a void, most of us have some *preconceived notions* on these issues. Unfortunately, all too often these preconceptions are flatly wrong or, at best, partially true; in other cases, they are hopelessly biased. Thus, as neophyte economists—in contrast with physicists or chemists—we start at a disadvantage in our search for truth, and our task in learning economics is doubled: we must recognize and "unlearn" misguided preconceptions, and we must supplant these inaccuracies with valid concepts and generalizations.

These observations contain an urgent plea for objectivity in studying economics. Economic principles can become a vice rather than a valuable analytical tool if, in using them, we are obsessed with a "point of view." By approaching them from the angle or viewpoint of, say, management or labor, we jeopardize much of the value these principles hold for us. Dissociating ourselves from any particular viewpoint—whether that of the workingman, the businessman, or the farmer—will pay us dividends, because such associations can undermine our reasoning and hopelessly color our conclusions. *Objectivity is an obvious prerequisite to the successful pursuit of scientific truth.* This objectivity is most likely to be achieved when a *social point of view* is embraced. "How does this policy or action affect the economy (society) as a whole and *all* its relevant parts?" is a question much superior to "How does this policy or action affect me as a businessman or laborer?" We must keep an open mind in pursuing economic knowledge.

□ **Fallacy of Composition: Macro and Micro**

Many of the false preconceptions people have about economics are attributable to the fallacy of composition. This is the fallacy of contending that "what is true for the individual or part is necessarily also true for the group or whole." This is a logical fallacy; it is not correct. The validity of a particular generalization for an individual or part does not necessarily ensure its accuracy for the group or whole.

A noneconomic example may help: You are watching a football game on a sunny autumn afternoon. The home team executes an outstanding play. In the general excitement, you leap to your feet to get a better view. *Generalization:* "If you, *an individual,* stand, then your view of the game is improved." But does this also hold true for the group—for everyone watching the game? Certainly not!

If everyone stands to watch the play, everyone—including you—will probably have the same or even a worse view than when seated!

Consider an example or two from economics: A wage increase for Smith is desirable because, given product prices, it increases his purchasing power and hence his standard of living. But if everyone realizes a wage increase, product prices will rise, that is, inflation will occur. Therefore, Smith's standard of living may be unchanged as higher prices offset his larger salary. Second illustration: An *individual* farmer who is fortunate enough to realize a bumper crop is likely to find that his resulting income is larger than usual. This is a correct generalization. Does it apply to farmers as a *group?* Possibly not, for the simple reason that to the individual farmer, crop prices will not be influenced (reduced) by his bumper crop, because each farmer is producing a negligible fraction of the total farm output. But to farmers as a group, prices vary inversely with total output.[8] Thus, as all farmers realize bumper crops, the total output of farm products rises, thereby depressing prices. If price declines overbalance the unusually large output, farm incomes *fall.*

In a sense, these comments on the fallacy of composition boil down to this: There are two essentially different levels of analysis at which the economist may derive laws concerning economic behavior. The level of *macroeconomics* is concerned either with the economy as a whole or with the basic subdivisions or aggregates—such as the government, household, and business sectors—which make up the economy. An aggregate is a collection of specific economic units which are treated *as if* they were one unit. Thus, we might find it convenient to lump together the 74 million households in our economy and treat them as if they were one huge unit. In dealing with aggregates, macroeconomics is concerned with

---

[8]This assumes there are no government programs which fix farm prices.

obtaining an overview, or general outline, of the structure of the economy and the relationships among the major aggregates which constitute the economy. No attention is given to the specific units which make up the various aggregates. It is not surprising, then, to find that macroeconomics entails discussions of such magnitudes as *total* output, the *total* level of employment, *total* income, *total* expenditures, the *general* level of prices, and so forth, in analyzing various economic problems. The problems of unemployment and inflation, by the way, are the primary topics of macroeconomics. In short, macroeconomics examines the forest, not the trees. It gives us a bird's-eye view of the economy.

On the other hand, *microeconomics* is concerned with *specific* economic units and a *detailed* consideration of the behavior of these individual units. When operating at this level of analysis, the economist figuratively puts an economic unit, or very small segment of the economy, under the microscope to observe the details of its operation. Here we talk in terms of an individual industry, firm, or household and concentrate upon such magnitudes as the output or price of a *specific* product, the number of workers employed by a single firm, the revenue or income of a particular firm or household, the expenditures of a given firm or family, and so forth. In microeconomics we examine the trees, not the forest. Microeconomics is useful in achieving a worm's-eye view of some very specific component of our economic system.

The basic point is this: The fallacy of composition reminds us that *generalizations which are valid at one of these levels of analysis may or may not be valid at the other.*

□   **Prosperity and Depression**

Closely related to the fallacy of composition is the fact that notions or ideas which are valid during prosperity may be invalid during depression, or vice versa. Some economic principles rest upon a specific presupposition concerning the phase of the business cycle; the validity of a given principle may depend upon the existence of good times or bad times. For example, the economist deems thrift or saving as economically beneficial and therefore desirable during periods of prosperity involving sharp inflation. Why? Because, as we shall discover, a high level of saving will tend to reduce inflationary pressure. Yet, during periods of depression, the economist is equally correct in generalizing to the effect that saving is an economic vice, the reason being that too much saving is the immediate cause of unemployment or depression.

□   **Cause and Effect**

The discovery of cause-and-effect relationships is an important and difficult part of any science. The absence of controlled experimentation adds significantly to the woes of the social scientist in isolating such cause-effect relationships. It is therefore exceedingly important to warn against grasping at straws in constructing cause-effect sequences. In particular, beware of the *post hoc, ergo propter hoc,* or "after this, therefore, because of this," fallacy—the incorrect notion that simply because one event precedes another, the first is necessarily the cause of the second.

A classic example clearly indicates the fallacy inherent in such reasoning. Suppose that early each spring the medicine man of a native tribe performs his ritual by cavorting around the village in a green costume. A week or so later the trees and grass turn green. Can we safely conclude that event A, the medicine man's gyrations, has caused event B, the landscape's turning green? Day follows night, but this doesn't mean that night is the cause of day!

It is especially important in analyzing various sets of empirical data *not* to confuse correlation with causation. *Correlation* is a technical term which indicates that two sets of data are associated in some systematic and dependable way; for example, we may find that when X increases, Y also increases. But this does not necessarily mean that X is the cause of Y. The relationship could be purely coincidental or determined by some other factor, Z, not included in the analysis. Example: Economists have found a positive correlation between education and income. In general, people with more education earn higher incomes than do people with less education. Common sense prompts us to label education as the cause and higher incomes as the effect; more education suggests a more productive worker and such workers receive larger monetary rewards. But, on second thought, might not causation run the other way? That is, do people with higher incomes buy more education, just as they buy more automobiles and more steaks? Or is the relationship explainable in terms of still other factors? Are education and income positively correlated because the bundle of characteristics—ability, motivation, personal habits—required to succeed in education are the same characteristics required to be a productive and highly paid worker? Upon reflection, seemingly simple cause-effect relationships—"more education results in more income"—may prove to be suspect or perhaps flatly incorrect.

Furthermore, causation in economics rarely resides in a simple, single event. Example: Many people believe that the stock market crash of 1929 caused the Great Depression of the 1930s. Although there is an element of accuracy in this statement, it is basically incorrect. The Depression and the stock market crash itself were the *results* of a number of more fundamental forces within the economy (see Chapter 10).

In short, cause-and-effect relationships are typically not self-evident in economics; the economist must look carefully before he leaps to the conclusion that event A caused event B. Certainly the simple fact that A preceded B is not sufficient to warrant any such conclusion.

□ **Effect of Expectations**

The anticipations, or expectations, of consumers and businesses are frequently of great importance in economics. This is so because the widespread anticipation of an event can prompt behavior which may cause the expected event to become a reality. For example, if consumers and businessmen suspect that inflation lies on the economic horizon, they may increase their current levels of spending to "beat" expected higher prices. But increased outlays are likely to cause the anticipated inflation to materialize. Conversely, if the economy expects a siege of unemployment, its natural reaction is to retrench on spending. Building a nest egg of savings seems to be a logical means of financing ourselves through an anticipated economic slump. But increasing savings means less spending, and this is likely to cause expected unemployment to become a reality. Similarly, if speculators expect the price of a stock to dip, they will attempt to sell that stock before the decline occurs. The resulting increased offerings of that stock relative to the demand for it will then cause the value of that stock to nosedive.

In short, what people think will happen has a vital influence upon what actually does occur in the economy.

□ **Intentions versus Realizations**

It is also important to recognize that what consumers or business firms attempt or intend to do may be considerably at odds with what they are actually able to accomplish or realize. You may plan to wage a campaign of hard work and frugality each summer vacation in order to provide adequate finances for school expenses, but at summer's end you find you have managed to save considerably less than originally planned. Events can drastically alter plans. As a matter of fact, the very attempt to achieve a given goal may create certain circumstances which prevent the attainment of that objective. For example, we shall find in Chapter 12 that if the economy attempts to achieve too high a rate of saving, unemployment will result. But unemployment means lower incomes, and this in turn undermines the ability to save. The attempt to save too much may create a situation in which the economy can actually save little or nothing at all. Plans, on the one hand, and accomplishments, on the other, may be quite different things.

□   Logical Explanations and Social Practice

Economics is concerned with both describing and explaining human behavior. Explanations in economics, however, occasionally fall short of logical standards. Thus, some explanations in the following chapters will not be "logical" but will, nevertheless, expound the actual operation of our economic units in terms of current social or business practice. For example, we might consider a more logical system of practices and regulations under which our monetary and banking system could operate than that currently employed. Despite the fact that our logically superior system might be valuable as a guide to reform, it would be misleading not to discuss our money and banking arrangements as they exist and function in the real world. In brief, we will occasionally find ourselves relying upon that's-the-way-it-is explanations in which logic is subservient to business or social practice. Fortunately, this kind of explanation is not encountered with great frequency.

□   Economic Quackery

A final general warning: The field of economics is, and always has been, a fertile ground for quacks and charlatans. Although few feel capable of offering aid and advice to the nuclear physicist or research chemist, a great many people envision themselves as unrecognized geniuses in economics and politics. The world abounds with self-styled economists who stand ready to cure the world's ills with seemingly simple changes in the structure, legal framework, or ideology of our economy. Some half-baked schemes are frequently appealing in their directness and simplicity, and the task of undermining such schemes is not easy. Usually the ideas of the quack chemist or physicist can be taken to the laboratory and quickly tested for validity. But no clear-cut testing ground is available for rapidly exposing the remedies of economic quacks. (However, one quite obvious earmark of a quack is an eagerness to engage in the highly unscientific practice of generalizing from a single, isolated case rather than from a carefully gathered broad base of empirical evidence.)

The economist's job is made even more difficult by the fact that hard scraping and manipulating will uncover statistics that "prove" just about any point desired![9] Thus, quack schemes often achieve considerable popular support before they are exposed and relegated to the scrap heap as nonsense or half-truths.

We would be foolish to accept medical advice for the treatment of cancer from our plumber or corner grocer. We ought to be equally hesitant to accept the economic analyses and remedies offered by untrained but highly vocal amateurs. Let us remember that answers to major economic problems are rarely self-evident or clear-cut. If they were, the given problem would in all likelihood have been solved and forgotten long ago. The best answers to complex economic problems rarely present themselves in terms of blacks and whites, but rather as varying shades of gray. Easy answers do not often go hand in hand with complex questions.

---

[9]One can spend a profitable and highly entertaining evening with Darrell Huff's *How to Lie with Statistics* (New York: W. W. Norton & Company, Inc., 1954).

Summary

1 Economics is studied for several reasons: **a.** It provides valuable knowledge concerning man's social environment and his behavior; **b.** it equips a democratic citizenry to render fundamental decisions intelligently; **c.** although not a vocational discipline, economics may provide the businessman with valuable information.

2 Economics is based upon facts concerning the activities of individuals and institutions in producing, exchanging, and consuming goods and services. The task of descriptive economics is the gathering of those economic facts which are relevant to a particular problem or specific segment of the economy.

3 These facts are then studied, arranged, and generalized upon. The resulting generalizations are called "principles," "theories," or "models." The derivation of these principles is the task of economic theory.

4 Economic principles have several noteworthy characteristics. First, they are generalizations and, as such, are subject to exceptions and elude quantitatively precise statement. Further, economic principles are models of reality and are hence abstract; their usefulness depends upon this abstraction. Finally, economic principles often can be conveniently expressed on two-dimensional graphs.

5 In deriving and applying principles, the economist must **a.** not omit any relevant facts, **b.** recognize that principles are simplified models of reality, and **c.** take care not to impute any moral qualities to these principles.

6 Economic principles are particularly valuable as predictive devices; they are the bases for the formulation of economic policy designed to solve problems and control undesirable events.

7 Economic growth, full employment, price stability, economic freedom, equity in the distribution of income, and economic security are all widely accepted economic goals in our society. Some of these goals are complementary; others are mutually exclusive.

8 There are numerous pitfalls in studying economics which the beginner may encounter. Some of the more important chuckholes strewn along the road to economic understanding are **a.** terminological difficulties, **b.** biases and erroneous preconceptions, **c.** the fallacy of composition, **d.** the fact that the validity of some economic ideas may depend upon the stage of the business cycle, **e.** the difficulty of establishing clear cause-effect relationships, **f.** the fact that expectations may influence actual events, **g.** the fact that intentions and accomplishments may be at odds, **h.** possible discrepancies between logic and social practice, and finally, **i.** the ever-present threat of economic quackery.

Questions and Study Suggestions

1 Key terms and concepts to remember: descriptive economics; economic theory; policy economics; generalizations or principles; "other things equal" assumption; direct and inverse relationships; induction and deduction; value judgments; economic goals; fallacy of composition; macroeconomics and microeconomics; *post hoc, ergo propter hoc* fallacy; correlation and causation; expectations.

2 Explain in detail the interrelationships between economic facts, theory, and policy. Critically evaluate: "The trouble with economics is that it is not practical. It has too much to say about theory and not enough to say about facts."

3   Analyze and explain the following quotation:[10]

Facts are seldom simple and usually complicated; theoretical analysis is needed to unravel the complications and interpret the facts before we can understand them . . . the opposition of facts and theory is a false one; the true relationship is complementary. We cannot in practice consider a fact without relating it to other facts, and the relation is a theory. Facts by themselves are dumb; before they will tell us anything we have to arrange them, and the arrangement is a theory. Theory is simply the unavoidable arrangement and interpretation of facts, which gives us generalizations on which we can argue and act, in the place of a mass of disjointed particulars.

4   "As is the case with other sciences, economics is not content with merely descriptive knowledge. Economics tries to discern general patterns of uniformity in human behavior." Explain.

5   Of what significance is the fact that economics is not a laboratory science? What problems may be involved in deriving and applying economic principles?

6   "Like all scientific laws, economic laws are established in order to make successful prediction of the outcome of human actions."[11] Explain.

7   "Abstraction . . . is the inevitable price of generality . . . indeed abstraction and generality are virtually synonyms."[12] Explain.

8   Briefly explain the use of graphs as a means of presenting economic principles. What is an inverse relationship? How does it graph? What is a direct relationship? How does it graph? Graph and explain the relationships one would expect to find between **a.** the number of inches of rainfall per month and the sale of umbrellas, **b.** the amount of tuition and the level of enrollment at a university, and **c.** the size of a university's athletic scholarships and the number of games won by its football team. In each case cite and explain how considerations other than those specifically mentioned might upset the expected relationship. Is your second generalization consistent with the fact that, historically, enrollments and tuition have both increased? If not, explain any difference.

9   To what extent would you accept the six economic goals stated and described in this chapter? What priorities would you assign to them? It has been said that we seek simply four goals: progress, stability, justice, and freedom. Is this list of goals compatible with that given in the chapter?

10   Analyze each of the following specific goals in terms of the six general goals stated on page 10, and note points of conflict and compatibility: **a.** Conservation of natural resources and the lessening of environmental pollution; **b.** increasing leisure; and **c.** protection of American producers from foreign competition. Indicate which of these specific goals you favor and justify your position.

11   Interpret and explain the following quotation.[13] Do you agree with this view?

[10] Henry Clay, *Economics for the General Reader* (New York: The Macmillan Company, 1925), pp. 10–11.
[11] Oskar Lange, "The Scope and Method of Economics," *Review of Economic Studies,* vol. 13, 1945–1946, p. 20.
[12] George J. Stigler, *The Theory of Price* (New York: The Macmillan Company, 1947), p. 10.
[13] Henry C. Wallich, *The Cost of Freedom* (New York: Harper & Row, Publishers, Incorporated, 1960), p. 48.

In comparison with the free economy, the Russian system shows elements of decided strength. Its power to . . . carry out plans without opposition gives it an advantage that may overcome grave handicaps in other respects. If we reject this system, as we most decidedly do, we must found our rejection on our attachment to freedom, not on economic grounds. . . . We want freedom, and we are willing to pay an economic price for it, by sacrificing the larger output that we might have in a forced draft economy.

12   Interpret the solid curve in Figure 18-2 on page 376, indicating the nature of the public policy dilemma it illustrates. Which of the choices posed by the curve do you prefer? Why?

13   Explain and give an illustration of **a.** the fallacy of composition, and **b.** the "after this, therefore, because of this" fallacy. Why are cause-and-effect relationships difficult to isolate in the social sciences?

14   "Economists should never be popular; men who afflict the comfortable serve equally those who comfort the afflicted and one cannot suppose that American capitalism would long prosper without the critics its leaders find such a profound source of annoyance."[14] Interpret and evaluate.

Selected References

Boulding, Kenneth E.: *Economics as a Science* (New York: McGraw-Hill Book Company, 1970).

Gurley, John G.: "The State of Political Economics," *American Economic Review,* May 1971, pp. 53–62.

Helppie, Charles, James Gibbons, and Donald Pearson: *Research Guide in Economics* (Morristown, N.J.: General Learning Press, 1974).

Hough, Robbin R.: *What Economists Do* (New York: Harper & Row, Publishers, Incorporated, 1972).

Keynes, J. N.: *The Scope and Method of Political Economy,* 4th ed. (New York: The Macmillan Company, 1930).

Lange, Oskar: "The Scope and Method of Economics," *Review of Economic Studies,* vol. 13, 1945–1946, pp. 19–32.

Lekachman, Robert: *Economists at Bay* (New York: McGraw-Hill Book Company, 1976).

Stigler, George J.: *The Theory of Price* (New York: The Macmillan Company, 1947), chap. 1.

Ward, Benjamin: *What's Wrong with Economics?* (New York: Basic Books, Inc., Publishers, 1972).

[14]John Kenneth Galbraith, *American Capitalism,* rev. ed. (Boston: Houghton Mifflin Company, 1956), p. 49

Last Word
Toward a Critique of Economics

Radical economists argue that the method of orthodox economics emphasizes harmony of interests and gradual change, thereby making it an "apologetic ideology." Paul M. Sweezy contends that Marxian economics is much more relevant in that it stresses conflict, power, and disruptive change.

Orthodox economics takes the existing social system for granted, much as though it were part of the natural order of things. Within this framework it searches for harmonies of interest among individuals, groups, classes, and nations; it investigates tendencies toward equilibrium; and it assumes that change is gradual and nondisruptive. I don't think I need to illustrate or support these propositions beyond reminding you that the foundation of all orthodox economics is general and/or partial equilibrium (the two, far from being incompatible, really imply each other). And as for the point about gradualism, I need only recall that printed on the title page of Alfred Marshall's *magnum opus, Principles of Economics,* is the motto *natura non facit saltum*—nature makes no leaps.

It might perhaps be plausibly argued that equilibrium and gradualism provided a workable axiomatic base for a real social science at a certain time and place—the time being roughly the half-century before the First World War, and the place being Britain and a few other countries of advanced capitalism. For my part, I do not believe this was true even then. I think economics by the time of what may be called the "marginalist revolution" of the 1870s had already practically ceased to be a science and had become mainly an apologetic ideology. Putting harmony, equilibrium, and gradualism at the center of the stage was dictated not by the scientific requirement of fidelity to reality, but by the bourgeois need to prettify and justify a system which was anything but harmonious, equilibrated, and gradualistic.

It was almost at the same time as the marginalist revolution, when economics (as distinct from classical political economy) was being born as an apologetic ideology, that Karl Marx put forward a radically different and opposed mode of analyzing the dominant economic systems. In place of harmony he put conflict. In place of forces tending toward equilibrium, he stressed forces tending to disrupt and transform the status quo. In place of gradualism he found qualitative discontinuity. *Natura facit salta* could well have been imprinted on the title page of *Das Kapital*.

It seems to me that from a scientific point of view the question of choosing between these two approaches—the orthodox or the Marxian—can be answered quite simply. Which more accurately reflects the fundamental characteristics of the social reality which is under analysis? I have already indicated my own view that orthodox economics does not reflect that reality but rather serves as an apologetic rationalization for it. Similarly it seems to me that Marxism *does* reflect capitalist reality. Or, to put the matter in other terms, the world we live in is not one of harmonies of interest, tendencies to equilibrium, and gradual change. Rather, it is a world dominated by conflicts of interest, tendencies to disequilibrium, and recurring breaks in the continuity of development. A would-be science which starts with a false or irrelevant conception of reality cannot yield very significant results, no matter how refined and sophisticated its methods may be. The answers a scientist gets depend, first and foremost, not on the methods he uses but on the questions he asks.

2

An Introduction to the Economizing Problem

The primary objective of this chapter is to introduce and explore certain fundamental considerations which constitute the foundation of economic science.

But we must be more specific. We shall first introduce a more sophisticated definition of economics. No longer can we content ourselves with the mere statement that economics is concerned with man's behavior in making a living, or that economics has to do with the production, exchange, and consumption of goods and services. These accurate, but not particularly revealing, assertions concerning the nature of economics must give way to a comprehensive understanding of the economizing problem. To this end, we shall illustrate, extend, and modify the sophisticated definition of economics by the use of so-called production possibilities tables. We shall then restate and discuss the economizing problem in terms of certain practical questions. Finally, we shall survey briefly the different ways in which institutionally and ideologically diverse economies go about "solving" or responding to the economizing problem.

THE FOUNDATION OF ECONOMICS

Two fundamental facts provide a foundation for the field of economics. It is imperative that we carefully state and fully understand these two facts, since everything that follows in our study of economics depends directly or indirectly upon them. The first fact is this: *Society's material wants, that is, the material wants of its citizens and institutions, are virtually unlimited or insatiable.* Second: *Economic resources are limited or scarce.*

□   **Unlimited Wants**

Let us systematically examine and explain these two facts in the order stated. In the first statement, precisely what do we mean by "material wants"? We mean, first, the desires of consumers to obtain and use various *goods* and *services* which give pleasure or satisfaction.[1] An amazingly wide range of products fills the bill in this respect: houses, automobiles, toothpaste, pencils, onions, sweaters, and the like. In short, innumerable products which we sometimes classify as *necessities* (food, shelter, clothing) and *luxuries* (perfumes, yachts, mink coats) are all capable of satisfying human wants. Needless to say, what is a luxury to Smith may be a necessity to Jones, and what is a commonplace necessity today may have been a luxury a few short years ago.

But services may satisfy our wants as much as tangible products. A repair job on our car, the removal of our appendix, a haircut, and legal advice have in common with goods the fact that they satisfy human wants. On reflecting, we realize that we indeed buy many goods, for example, automobiles and washing machines, for the services they render. The differences between goods and services are often less than they seem to be at first.

Material wants also include those which businesses and units of government seek to satisfy. Businesses want factory buildings, machinery, trucks, warehouses, and other things that assist them in realizing their production goals. Government, reflecting the collective wants of its citizenry or goals of its own,

seeks highways, schools, hospitals, and military hardware.

As a group, these material wants are, for practical purposes, *insatiable,* or *unlimited.*[2] This means that material wants for goods and services are incapable of being completely satisfied. A simple experiment will help to verify this point: Suppose we are asked to list those goods and services we want but do not now possess. If we take time to ponder our unfilled material wants, chances are our list will be impressive. And over a period of time, our wants seem to multiply so that, as we fill some of the wants on the list, at the same time we add new ones. Material wants, like rabbits, have a high reproduction rate. This is particularly so in the United States, where the seemingly rapid introduction of new products whets our appetites, and extensive advertising tries to persuade us that we need countless items we might not otherwise consider buying. Not too many years ago, the desire for color television, air conditioners, portable cassette recorders, and tubeless tires was nonexistent. Furthermore, we often cannot stop with simple satisfaction: the acquisition of a Pinto or Vega has been known to whet the appetite for a Porsche or Jaguar.

In summary, we may say that at any given time the individuals and institutions which constitute society have innumerable unfulfilled material wants. Some of these wants—food, clothing, shelter—have biological roots. But some are also influenced by the conventions and customs of society: the specific kinds of food, clothing, and shelter we seek are frequently determined by the general social and cultural environment in which we live. Over

---

[1]This definition leaves a variety of wants—recognition, status, love, and so forth—for the other social sciences to worry about.

[2]It should be mentioned in passing that the fallacy of composition is relevant here. Our wants for a *particular* good or service can obviously be satisfied; that is, over a short period of time we can get sufficient amounts of toothpaste or beer. Certainly one appendicitis operation is par for the course. But goods *in general* are another story. Here we do not, and presumably cannot, get enough. We shall say more about the satisfying of wants for specific goods in Chapter 24.

time, wants change and multiply, abetted by the development of new products and by extensive advertising and sales promotion.

Finally—although we may be getting ahead of ourselves—let us emphatically add that the overall end or objective of all economic activity is the attempt to satisfy these diverse material wants.

□ **Scarce Resources**

Consider now the second fundamental fact: *Economic resources are limited or scarce.* What do we mean by "economic resources"? In general, we are referring to all the natural, human, and man-made resources that go into the production of goods and services. This obviously covers a lot of ground: factory and farm buildings and all sorts of equipment, tools, and machinery used in the production of manufactured goods and agricultural products; a variety of transportation and communication facilities; innumerable types of labor; and, last but not least, land and mineral resources of all kinds. There is an apparent need for a simplified classification of such resources, which we shall meet with the following categories: (1) *property* resources—land or raw materials and capital; (2) *human* resources—labor and entrepreneurial ability.

Resource Categories What does the economist mean by *land?* Much more than the layman. Land refers to all natural resources—all "free gifts of nature"—which are usable in the productive process. Such resources as arable land, forests, mineral and oil deposits, and water resources come under this general classification. What about *capital?* Capital, or investment goods, has a variety of meanings attached to it. The one that is correct for our purposes refers to all man-made aids to production, that is, all tools, machinery, equipment, and factory, storage, transportation, and distribution facilities used in produc-

ing goods and services and getting them to the ultimate consumer. Capital goods ("tools") differ from consumer goods in that the latter satisfy wants directly, whereas the former do so indirectly by facilitating the production of consumable goods. We should note especially that the term "capital" as here defined does *not* refer to money. True, businessmen and economists often talk of "money capital," meaning money which is available for use in the purchase of machinery, equipment, and other productive facilities. But money, as such, produces nothing; hence, it is not to be considered as an economic resource. *Real capital*—tools, machinery, and other productive equipment—is an economic resource; *money* or *financial capital* is not.

Labor is a broad term which the economist uses in referring to all man's physical and mental talents usable in producing goods and services (with the exception of a special set of human talents—entrepreneurial ability—which, because of their special significance in a capitalistic economy, we choose to consider separately). Thus the services of a ditch-digger, retail clerk, machinist, teacher, professional football player, and nuclear physicist all fall under the general heading of labor.

Finally, what can be said about this special human resource which we label *entrepreneurial ability,* or, more simply, *enterprise?* We shall give the term a specific meaning by assigning four related functions to the entrepreneur.

1 The entrepreneur takes the initiative in combining the resources of land, capital, and labor in the production of a good or service. Both a sparkplug and a catalyst, the entrepreneur is at once the driving force behind production and the agent who combines the other resources in what he hopes will be a profitable venture.

2 The entrepreneur has the chore of making basic business-policy decisions, that is, those nonroutine decisions which set the course of a business enterprise.

3 The entrepreneur is an innovator—the person who attempts to introduce on a commercial basis new products, new productive techniques, or even new forms of business organization.

4 The entrepreneur is obviously a risk bearer. This is apparent from a close examination of his other three functions. The entrepreneur in a capitalistic system has no guarantee that he will make a profit. The reward for his time, efforts, and abilities may be attractive profits *or* immediate losses and eventual bankruptcy. In short, the entrepreneur risks not only his time, effort, and business reputation, but his invested funds and those of his associates or stockholders.

Resource Payments We shall see shortly how these resources are provided for business institutions in exchange for money income. The income received from supplying property resources—raw materials and capital equipment—is called *rental* and *interest income.* The income accruing to those who supply labor is called *wages* and includes salaries and various wage and salary supplements in the form of bonuses, commissions, royalties, and so forth. Entrepreneurial income is called *profits,* which, of course, may be a negative figure— that is, losses.

These four broad categories of economic resources, or *factors of production* as they are often called, leave room for debate when it comes to classifying specific resources. For example, suppose you receive a dividend on some General Motors stock which you may own. Is this an interest return for the capital equipment which the company was able to buy with the money you provided in buying GM stock? Or is this return a profit which compensates you for the risks involved in purchasing corporate stock? What about the earnings of a one-man general store where the owner is both the entrepreneur and the labor force? Are his earnings to be considered as wages or

profit income? The answer to both queries is "some of each." The important point is this: Although we might quibble about classifying a given flow of income as wages, rent, interest, or profits, all income can be listed without too much arbitrariness under one of these general headings.

Relative Scarcity All economic resources, or factors of production, have one fundamental characteristic in common: *Economic resources are scarce or limited in supply.* Without a doubt, our economy possesses extremely large amounts of arable land, mineral deposits, capital equipment, and labor. These are, however, not infinitely large supplies; they have limits. A civilian labor force of 95 million workers may seem extremely large, but it is not an infinite amount. World War II, for example, reminded us of just how scarce labor actually is. Critical shortages of semiskilled and skilled labor constituted a formidable obstacle in the production of vitally needed armaments. More recently, elaborate computer models have been used to predict that natural resource limitations, on the one hand, and current rates of population and output growth, on the other, are on a "collision course"; the controversial forecast is that the living standards of advanced countries such as the United States will have to be curtailed (Chapter 20). Finally, the popular press continually features discussions on the possibility that intensifying energy shortages will impede economic progress.

One additional point: These economic resources—land, labor, capital, and entrepreneurial ability—are obviously the *means* by which we produce goods and services in trying to satisfy material wants. Consumption in the broadest sense of the term—that is, fulfilling the material wants of the institutions and individuals which make up society—is the objective of economic activity. We are now pointing out that the means of attaining the goal of consumption are our available supplies of various economic resources. And these resources, though perhaps abundant in the absolute sense, are scarce relative to the demand for them in the production of goods and services.

ECONOMICS DEFINED

Given that wants are unlimited and resources are scarce, economics can be defined as *the social science concerned with the problem of using or administering scarce resources (the means of producing) so as to attain the greatest or maximum fulfillment of society's unlimited wants (the goal of producing)*. Economics is concerned with "doing the best with what we have." If our wants are virtually unlimited and our resources are scarce, we cannot conceivably satisfy all society's material wants. The next best thing is to achieve the greatest possible satisfaction of these wants. Economics is a science of efficiency—efficiency in the use of scarce resources.

Precisely what is meant by *efficiency* as economists use the term? It means something akin to, but not identical with, the term "efficiency" as used in engineering. The mechanical engineer tells us that a steam locomotive is only "60 percent efficient" because a large part—some 40 percent—of the energy in its fuel is not transformed into useful power but is wasted through friction and heat loss. The maximum output of usable power is not derived from the inputs of fuel.

Economic efficiency is also concerned with *inputs* and *outputs*. Specifically, it is concerned with the relationship between the units of scarce resources which are put into the process of production and the resulting output of some wanted product; economic efficiency deals with inputs of scarce resources and outputs of useful products.

☐   **Full Employment and Full Production**

Economic efficiency is achieved when full employment and full production are realized or, stated negatively, when unemployment and underemployment are avoided. A worker is clearly unemployed when involuntarily out of work. This is the individual who is "on welfare" or receiving unemployment compensation payments. This is a case of *apparent unemployment* or simply *unemployment;* the worker obviously has no job connection. On the other hand, a worker may have a job but in a sense still be "unemployed." For example, a farmer who is harvesting wheat with a scythe rather than a combine and a lawyer who is employed as a court reporter are both "partially unemployed." So is an accountant or a social worker who is working, say, as a retail clerk. In these cases, however, it is a matter of *disguised unemployment* or, more simply, *underemployment*. The worker has a job but is not being employed efficiently. The *unem*ployed worker who has no job and the *under*employed worker who has a job but is producing in a highly inefficient manner or, alternatively, is failing to use his talents to best advantage, differ more in degree than in kind. Both entail the relatively inefficient use of resources. The point is this: There are two major aspects of economic efficiency. On the one hand, there is the *full-employment* problem—the problem of providing jobs for all who are able and willing to work. On the other hand, there is the closely related *full-production* or resource-allocation problem—the problem of using employed resources in the most efficient manner. These two facets of economic efficiency are of such importance as to merit further comment.

Eliminating Unemployment Economic efficiency requires, first, that available resources be actually utilized in the production of goods and services rather than allowed to lie idle. An unused locomotive is of zero efficiency. The same can be said for unemployed resources. Unutilized resources—both human and property—obviously mean waste and inefficiency. Unemployment is the height of economic inefficiency; when society fails to put its available resources into the productive process, it obviously realizes no output at all.

Note that we specify that all *available* resources should be employed. Each society has certain established customs and practices which determine what particular resources are available for employment. For example, legislation and custom provide that children and the very aged should not be employed. Also, we should not employ all our farmland every year; it is desirable for productivity to allow land to lie fallow periodically. Furthermore, society wants to avoid complete utilization and rapid exhaustion of particularly scarce resources in order to apportion their use efficiently through time. In short, society wants to employ only those resources that are available for employment and whose current employment is desirable.

In Part 2 we shall discover that in a capitalistic economy it is the volume of total spending which determines the level at which resources are employed. If buyers are willing and able to spend in large amounts in satisfying their wants, entrepreneurs will respond by employing large quantities of resources in producing goods and services to fulfill these wants. Conversely, a meager volume of spending will mean unemployment.

Eliminating Underemployment   But the full employment of all available resources is not sufficient for the attainment of economic efficiency. Society also seeks full production; that is, the production of goods must be carried out with a proper assignment or allocation of available resources and with use of the best available production techniques. In other words, society wants to get the maximum amount of goods and services produced with its

limited inputs of employed resources. For example, if society's wants include both wheat and space probes, it would obviously entail an inefficient or uneconomical allocation of resources to assign astrophysicists and mathematicians to farming and experienced farmers to space research centers. Nor should we want Iowa's farmland planted to cotton and Alabama's to corn when experience indicates that the opposite assignment would provide the nation substantially more of both products from the same amount of land. We also want to use the best production methods; for example, other things being equal, a given volume of resources will produce more corn when crop rotation is employed as a technique of production. To plant the same acres to corn year after year will wear out the soil and eventually result in a relatively small output. By employing the same amounts of land, capital, labor, and entrepreneurial resources and by practicing the technique of crop rotation, a larger output of corn can be realized.

□   **Production Possibilities Table**

The nature of the economizing problem can be brought into even clearer focus by the use of a production possibilities table.[3] This ingenious device reveals the core of the economizing problem: *A full-employment, full-production economy cannot have an unlimited output of goods and services.*

Assumptions   We make several specific assumptions to set the stage for our illustration.

1 The economy is operating at full employment and achieving full production. Neither *un*employment nor *under*employment exists.

2 The available supplies of the factors of production are fixed. But, of course, they can

[3]Paul A. Samuelson, *Economics*, 10th ed. (New York: McGraw-Hill Book Company, 1976), pp. 19–22.

be shifted or reallocated, within limits, among different uses; for example, a relatively un-skilled laborer can work on a farm, on an automobile assembly line, or in a gas station.

3 The state of the technological arts is constant; that is, technology does not change during the course of our analysis.

The second and third assumptions are another way of saying that we are looking at our economy at some specific point in time, or over a very short period of time. Over a relatively long period it would clearly be unrealistic to rule out technological advances and the possibility that resource supplies might vary. In short, we assume full employment and full production, fixed resources, and a fixed technology.

4 To simplify our illustration further, let us suppose that our economy is producing just two products—for example, drill presses and bread—instead of the innumerable goods and services actually produced. Bread is symbolic of *consumer goods,* that is, those goods and services which directly satisfy our wants; drill presses are symbolic of *capital goods,* that is, those goods which satisfy our wants *indirectly* by permitting more efficient production of consumer goods.

Necessity of Choice Now, is it not evident from the assumptions we have made that our economy is faced with a very fundamental choice? Our total supplies of resources are limited. Thus the total amounts of drill presses and bread that our economy is capable of producing are limited. *Limited resources mean a limited output.* A choice must be made as to what quantities of each product society wants produced. Since resources are limited in supply and fully employed, any increase in the production of drill presses will necessitate the shifting of resources away from the production of bread. And the reverse holds true: If we choose to step up the production of bread, needed resources must come at the expense of drill-press production. *Society cannot have its*

cake and eat it, too. Facetiously put, there's no such thing as a "free lunch." This is the essence of the economizing problem.

Let us generalize by noting in Table 2-1 some alternative combinations of drill presses and bread which our economy might conceivably choose. Though the data in this and ensuing tables are hypothetical, the points illustrated are of tremendous practical significance. At alternative A, our economy would be devoting all its resources to the production of drill presses, that is, capital goods. At alternative E, all available resources would be devoted to the production of bread, that is, consumer goods. Both these alternatives are clearly unrealistic extremes; any economy typically strikes a balance in dividing its total output between capital and consumer goods. As we move from alternative A to E, we step up the production of consumer goods (bread). How? By shifting resources away from capital goods production. When we remember that consumer goods directly satisfy our wants, any movement toward alternative E looks tempting. In making this move, society increases the current satisfaction of its wants. But there is a cost involved. This shift of resources catches up with society over time as its stock of capital goods dwindles—or at least ceases to expand at the current rate—with the result that the efficiency of future production is impaired. In short, in moving from alternative A toward E, society is in effect choosing "more now" at the expense of "much more later." In moving from E toward A, society is choosing to forgo cur-

Table 2-1 PRODUCTION POSSIBILITIES OF BREAD AND DRILL PRESSES WITH FULL EMPLOYMENT, 1978 (*hypothetical data*)

Type of product	Production alternatives				
	A	B	C	D	E
Bread (in hundred thousands)	0	1	2	3	4
Drill presses (in thousands)	10	9	7	4	0

rent consumption. This sacrifice of current consumption frees resources which can now be used in stepping up the production of capital goods. By building up its stock of capital in this way, society can anticipate more efficient production and, therefore, greater consumption in the future.

The critical idea is this: *At any point in time, a full-employment, full-production economy must sacrifice some of product X to obtain more of product Y.* The basic fact that economic resources are scarce prohibits such an economy from having more of both X and Y.

□   **Production Possibilities Curve**

To ensure our understanding the production possibilities table, let us view these data graphically. We employ a simple two-dimen-

FIGURE 2-1 THE PRODUCTION POSSIBILITIES CURVE

Each point on the production possibilities curve represents some maximum output of any two products. Society must choose which product-mix it desires: more drill presses means less bread, and vice versa.

sional graph, putting the output of drill presses (capital goods) on the vertical axis and the output of bread (consumer goods) on the horizontal axis, as in Figure 2-1. Following the plotting procedure discussed in Chapter 1, we can locate the "production possibilities" or "transformation"[4] curve, as shown in Figure 2-1.

□   **Optimum Product-mix**

We know that each point on the production possibilities curve represents some maximum output of the two products. To realize the various combinations of bread and drill presses which fall on the production possibilities curve, society must achieve full employment and full production. All combinations of bread and drill presses on the curve represent maximum quantities attainable only as the result of the most efficient use of all available resources.

But now a final question arises: If all outputs on the production possibilities curve reflect full employment and full production, which combination will society prefer? This is a subjective question—a moral issue—and the economist as a social scientist possesses no superior judgment or insight on this matter. Consider, for example, points *B* and *D* in Figure 2-1. Which output-mix is superior or "best"? This, to repeat, is a nonscientific matter; it reflects the values of society as expressed by its control group—the dictatorship, the party, the electorate, the citizenry, the individual institutions, or some combination thereof. What the economist can say is that if a society's production possibilities are as in Table 2-1 *and* if that society seeks the product-mix indicated by, say, alternative B, it is using its resources inefficiently if it realizes a total output

[4]Why "transformation"? Because in moving from one alternative to another, say from *B* to *C*, we are in effect transforming drill presses into bread by shifting resources from the production of the former to the production of the latter.

comprised only of $8\frac{7}{8}$ units of drill presses and $\frac{9}{10}$ unit of loaves of bread. And the economist can also say that the society cannot hope to achieve a national output of $9\frac{1}{2}$ units of drill presses and $1\frac{3}{8}$ units of loaves of bread with its available resources. These are quantitative, objective, matters. But, although he may have opinions as an individual, the economist as a social scientist cannot say that combination B is "better" or "worse" than combination D. This is purely a qualitative matter.

□   **Law of Increasing Costs**

We have stressed that resources are scarce relative to the virtually unlimited wants which these resources can be used to satisfy. As a result, choices among alternatives must be made. Specifically, more of X (bread) means less of Y (drill presses). *The amount of other products which must be forgone or sacrificed to obtain a unit of any product is called the opportunity cost of that good.* In our case the amount of Y (drill presses) which must be forgone or given up to get another unit of X (bread) is the opportunity cost, or simply the cost, of X. Hence, in moving from possibility A to B in Table 2-1, we find that the cost of 1 unit of bread is 1 unit of drill presses. But, as we now pursue the concept of cost through the additional production possibilities—B to C, C to D, and so forth—an important economic principle is revealed to us. In moving from alternative A to alternative E, the sacrifice or cost of drill presses involved in getting each additional 100,000 units of bread *increases.* Hence, in moving from A to B, just 1 unit of drill presses is sacrificed for 1 more unit of bread; but going from B to C involves the sacrifice of 2 units of drill presses for 1 more of bread; then 3 of drill presses for 1 of bread; and finally 4 for 1.

Graphically, the law of increasing costs is reflected in the shape of the production possibilities curve. Specifically, the curve is *concave* or bowed out from the origin. Why? Because,

as verified by the dashed lines in Figure 2-1, when the economy moves from A toward E, it must give up successively larger amounts of drill presses (1, 2, 3, 4) as shown on the vertical axis to acquire equal increments of bread (1, 1, 1, 1) as shown on the horizontal axis. Technically, this means that the slope of the production possibilities curve becomes steeper as we move from A to E and such a curve, by definition, is concave as viewed from the origin.

What is the economic rationale for the law of increasing costs? *Why* does the sacrifice of drill presses increase as we get more bread? The answer to this query is rather complex. But, simply stated, it amounts to this: *Economic resources are not completely adaptable to alternative uses.* As we attempt to step up bread production, resources which are less and less adaptable to agriculture must be induced, or "pushed," into that line of production. If we start at A and move to B, we can first pick resources whose productivity of bread is greatest in relation to their productivity of drill presses. But as we move from B to C, C to D, and so on, those resources which are highly productive of bread become increasingly scarce. To get more bread, resources whose productivity in drill presses is great in relation to their productivity in bread will be needed. It will obviously take more and more of such resources—and hence an increasingly great sacrifice of drill presses—to achieve a given increase of 1 unit in the production of bread. This lack of perfect flexibility, or interchangeability, on the part of resources and the resulting increase in the sacrifice of one good that must be made in the acquisition of more and more units of another good are sometimes termed the *law of increasing costs,* costs in this case being stated as sacrifices of goods and not in terms of dollars and cents.

The reader should verify that (1) under the unrealistic assumption of perfect adaptability of resources the production possibilities would be a straight line, implying *constant* opportunity costs, and (2) in Table 2-1 and

Figure 2-1 the law of increasing costs holds true in moving from alternative E to alternative A.

FURTHER IMPLICATIONS

It is important to understand what happens when the three assumptions underlying the preceding explanation are released.

□   Unemployment and Underemployment

The first assumption was that our economy is characterized by full employment and full production. How would our analysis and conclusions be altered if idle resources were available or if employed resources were used inefficiently? With full employment and full production, our five alternatives represent a series of maximum outputs; that is, they illustrate what combinations of drill presses and bread might be produced when the economy is operating at its full capacity. With *un*employment or *under*employment, the economy would obviously be producing less than each alternative shown in Table 2-1.

Graphically, a situation of unemployment or underemployment can be illustrated by a point *inside* the original production possibilities curve, which has been reproduced in Figure 2-2. Point *U* is such a point. Here the economy is obviously falling short of the various maximum combinations of bread and drill presses reflected by all the points *on* the production possibilities curve. The broken arrows in Figure 2-2 indicate three of the possible paths back to full employment and full production. A movement toward full employment and full production will obviously entail a greater output of one or both products. And there are points *outside* the production possibilities curve, like point *W*, which would be superior to any point on the curve; but such

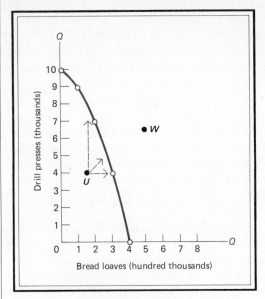

FIGURE 2-2   UNEMPLOYMENT AND THE PRODUCTION POSSIBILITIES CURVE

Any point inside the production possibilities curve, such as *U*, indicates unemployment or underemployment. By moving toward full employment and full production, the economy can produce more of either or both of the two products, as the arrows indicate. Point *W* is unattainable.

points are unobtainable, given the current supplies of resources and technology. The production barrier of full employment prohibits the production of any combination of capital and consumer goods lying outside the production possibilities curve.

It is interesting to note that in beginning to produce war goods for World War II, the United States found itself with considerable unemployment. Hence, our economy was able to accomplish the production of an almost unbelievably large quantity of war goods and at the same time increase the volume of consumer goods output.[5] The Russians, on the other hand, entered World War II at almost capacity production; that is, they were operat-

---

[5] There did occur, however, rather acute shortages of specific types of consumer goods.

ing close to full employment. Therefore, their military preparations entailed a considerable shifting of resources from the production of civilian goods and a concomitant drop in the standard of living.[6]

☐ A Growing Economy

What happens to the production possibilities curve when we drop the remaining assumptions that the quantity and quality of resources and technology are fixed? The answer is: The production possibilities curve will shift position; that is, the potential total output of the economy will change.

Expanding Resource Supplies Now let us abandon the simplifying assumption that our total supplies of land, labor, capital, and entrepreneurial ability are fixed. Common sense tells us that over a period of time the growing population in the United States will bring about increases in the supplies of labor and entrepreneurial ability.[7] Historically, our stock of capital has increased at a significant, though unsteady, rate. And although we are depleting some of our energy and mineral resources, new sources are constantly being discovered. The drainage of swamps and the development of irrigation programs add to our supply of arable land. Assuming continuous full employment and full production, the net result of these increased supplies of the factors of production will be the ability to produce more of both drill presses and bread. Thus in, say, 1998, the production possibilities of Table 2-1 may be obsolete, having given way to those shown in Table 2-2. Observe that the greater

[6]Needless to say, it is sheer folly to leap to the conclusion that this contrast illustrates the desirability of unemployment at the outbreak of hostilities!

[7]This is not to say that population growth as such is always desirable. In Chapter 21 we shall discover that overpopulation can be a constant drag upon the living standards of many underdeveloped countries. In advanced countries overpopulation can have adverse effects upon the environment and the quality of life.

Table 2-2 PRODUCTION POSSIBILITIES OF BREAD AND DRILL PRESSES WITH FULL EMPLOYMENT, 1998 (*hypothetical data*)

Type of product	Production alternatives				
	A′	B′	C′	D′	E′
Bread (in hundred thousands)	0	2	4	6	8
Drill presses (in thousands)	14	12	9	5	0

abundance of resources results in a greater output of one or both products at each alternative; economic growth, in the sense of an expanded total output, has occurred.

But note this important point: Such a favorable shift in the production possibilities curve does not guarantee that the economy will operate at a point on that new curve. The economy might fail to realize its new potentialities. Some 95 million jobs will give us full employment at the present time, but ten years from now our labor force, because of a growing population, will be much larger, and 95 million jobs will not be sufficient for full employment. In short, the production possibilities curve may shift, but the economy may fail to produce at a point on that new curve.

Technological Advance Our final simplifying assumption is a constant or unchanging technology. Observation tells us that technology has progressed with amazing rapidity over a long period. What does an advancing technology entail? New and better goods and improved ways of producing these goods. For the moment, let us think of technological advance as entailing merely improvements in capital facilities—more efficient machinery and equipment. How does such technological advance alter our earlier discussion of the economizing problem? In this way: Technological advance, by improving productive efficiency, allows society to produce more goods with a fixed amount of resources. As with increases in resource supplies, technological advance permits the production of more drill presses *and* more bread.

What happens to the production possibilities curve of Figure 2-2 when the supplies of resources increase or an improvement in technology occurs? The curve shifts outward and to the right, as illustrated by the brown curve in Figure 2-3. *Economic growth can be defined as a rightward shift of the production possibilities curve; it is the result of increases in resource supplies and technological progress.* The consequence of growth is that our full-employment economy can enjoy a greater output of both bread and drill presses.

On Figure 2-2 the student should pencil in two new production possibilities curves: one to show the situation where a better technique for producing drill presses has been developed, the technology for producing bread being unchanged, and the other to illustrate an improved technology for bread, the technology for producing drill presses being constant.

□   **Present Choices and
Future Possibilities**

You may have anticipated this important point in the foregoing paragraphs: *An economy's current choice of position on its production possibilities curve is a basic determinant of the future location of that curve.* To illustrate this notion, let us designate the two axes of the production possibilities curve as "goods for the future" and "goods for the present," as in Figure 2-4a and b. By "goods for the future" we refer to such things as capital goods, research and education, and preventive medicine, which obviously tend to increase the quantity and quality of property resources, enlarge the stock of technological information, and improve the quality of human resources. It is, as we have already seen, "goods for the future" which are the ingredients of economic growth. By "goods for the present" we mean pure consumer goods in the form of foodstuffs, clothing, transistor radios, automobiles, power mowers, boats, and so forth.

Now suppose there are two economies, Alphania and Betania, which at the moment are identical in every respect except that Alphania's current (1978) choice of position on its production possibilities curve strongly favors "present goods" as opposed to "future goods." The dot in Figure 2-4a indicates this choice. Betania, on the other hand, renders a current (1978) choice which stresses large amounts of "future goods" and lesser amounts of "present goods" (Figure 2-4b). Now, all other things being the same, we can expect the future (1998) production possibilities curve of Betania to be farther to the right than that of

FIGURE 2-3   ECONOMIC GROWTH AND THE PRODUCTION POSSIBILITIES CURVE

The expanding resource supplies and technological advances which characterize a growing economy move the production possibilities curve outward and to the right. This permits the economy to enjoy larger quantities of both types of goods.

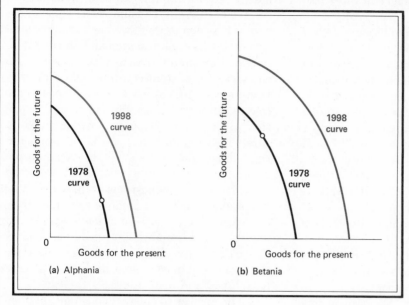

FIGURE 2-4 AN ECONOMY'S PRESENT CHOICE OF POSITION ON ITS PRODUCTION POSSIBILITIES CURVE HELPS DETERMINE THE CURVE'S FUTURE LOCATION

A current choice favoring "present goods," as rendered by Alphania in (a), will cause a modest rightward shift of the curve. A current choice favoring "future goods," as rendered by Betania in (b), will result in a greater rightward shift of the curve.

Alphania. That is, by currently choosing an output which is more conducive to technological advance and to increases in the quantity and quality of property and human resources, Betania will tend to achieve greater economic growth than will Alphania, whose current choice of output places less emphasis upon those goods and services which cause the production possibilities curve to shift rightward.

ECONOMIZING: FIVE FUNDAMENTAL QUESTIONS

In order to provide a broad understanding of the essence of the economizing problem, the preceding discussion is pitched at a fairly abstract level. Let us now be more practical and examine some of the specific questions or problems that any economic system must answer in attempting to use its scarce resources to achieve the maximum satisfaction of society's material wants. Basically, there are Five Fundamental Questions which must be answered in attempting to achieve and maintain efficiency in the use of scarce resources.

☐ What Is to Be Produced

Society must somehow decide what collection of goods and services will most fully satisfy its wants. This decision concerning the composition of total output is obviously constrained by the production possibilities currently facing the economy. Choosing a combination of capital and consumer goods lying *inside* the production possibilities curve entails economic inefficiency in the form of unemployment. Seeking a combination *outside* the current production possibilities curve is unrealistic; society is obviously setting its sights on an unattainable target.

Actually, the basic question of determining what is to be produced can be divided into two closely related subquestions: First, what goods and services are to be produced? Second, in what quantities does society want these goods produced?

Consider the first subquestion: What goods and services should be produced? Answering this entails, in effect, the setting up of a list of goods and services which society deems important enough to produce. How should society apportion its scarce resources among those products which it is capable of producing? Should our list include bread? Drill presses? Fords? Cadillacs? Highways? Color television? Textbooks? Mink coats? Buggy whips? Football stadiums? An ICBM system? Society must somehow decide what items to include in—and what items to exclude from—the list of goods that are to be produced.

But this decision is only half the battle. Once society has decided what to produce, somehow it must then assign proper weights to each of the items on the list. Without asking how this decision has been reached, suppose society has decided that bread, drill presses, Fords, and football stadiums are the items from the above list which it actually wants to produce. The fact that resources are scarce tells us that society cannot produce unlimited amounts of the goods on this list. Society must now decide *how many* loaves of bread, *how many* drill presses, *how many* Fords, and *how many* football stadiums it wants in its total output. Society must not only decide the relative amounts of capital and consumer goods to be produced—the question posed in our production possibilities illustrations—but it must also determine the specific quantities of each type of capital goods and each type of consumer goods that will best fulfill society's material wants. Even in relatively primitive economies these decisions can become complex.

Remember, too, that in deciding the relative amounts of capital and consumer goods to be produced, society is of necessity weighing the relative merits of future, as opposed to current, want fulfillment. More resources devoted to technological research and to the expansion of the economy's capital facilities means fewer available for the production of goods for current consumption. The choice here is between more now or much more later. By cutting back on research and on the expansion of our productive facilities, society can enjoy greater current consumption. But sacrificing some current consumption in order to free resources for research and capital expansion will mean an expanded output in the future. There is, in other words, an important time dimension to the question, What to produce?

These two subquestions—what goods shall we produce? in what quantities?—have been considered in a very simplified way in our analysis of the production possibilities tables. We solved—or dodged!—the first by assuming the economy had somehow decided to produce only bread and drill presses.

The answer to the second subquestion entails society's choosing which one of the five alternatives—A, B, C, D, or E—yields the highest level of satisfaction. Thus the perennial question of consumer goods versus capital goods is part of the larger question of deciding the specific composition of the total output. The vital question of civilian versus war goods, dramatically portrayed in the Last Word section of this chapter, falls under the same general heading.

□   **Organizing Production**

Hand in glove with our decision as to the composition of total output is another query: *How should this total output be produced?* This major question can also be broken into parts.

1 How does society steer resources into industries producing goods that we want produced and, conversely, keep resources away from industries producing goods wanted in very small amounts or not at all?

2 What firms in the various industries are to do the producing, and how are they to obtain the needed resources?

3 What is the most efficient combination of resources for each firm to use in producing a given level of output? More subtly, what is the best technology to use in production?

All these questions center upon the goal of achieving full production from society's available resources. A reminder: Although the question of organizing production is spelled out here in terms of an industrially advanced economy, similar questions would be pertinent for a primitive or underdeveloped economy.

☐ **Distributing Output**

The third basic decision comes close to home: *How is society to divide or ration the total output among the various economic units which comprise our economic system?* How should the total output of consumer goods be shared by the various households in our economy? Should output be distributed on the basis of need? Or on the basis of one's contribution to production? What degree of inequality in the sharing of output is necessary or desirable? Similarly, how should any additions to our stock of capital equipment included in our total output be apportioned to the various industries and the individual firms in those industries? What part of total output should be given over to government? In short, the question of how the total output is to be distributed among households, businesses, and government must somehow be answered by society. Obviously, these questions involve not only economics but also politics and ethics.

☐ **Level of Resource Use**

Society is obligated to determine the degree to which its economic resources are to be utilized. This decision is more complex than it first appears. Two related subquestions are involved:

1 To what degree is society *willing* to utilize its human and property resources?

2 To what extent is society actually *able* to employ its resources?
Let us briefly explore these subquestions in the order stated.

A society which seeks to maximize the immediate fulfillment of its material wants must be willing to utilize its human and property resources to a very high degree. For human resources, this means that both men and women must enter the labor force at an early age, retire at a very old age, and work long hours with few holidays and vacations in the intervening span of years. This obviously means little leisure. And leisure, after all, is a source of satisfaction—a part of our standard of living. What good is a stereo set or golf clubs if one has no time to use them? In all economies the decision as to how the time at the disposal of human resources is to be divided between production and leisure is influenced by sociocultural factors. The mores and customs of society are important in determining what percentage of the population is to work, the number of work hours, and even the intensity of labor.

The problem of resource conservation is primary in discussing the willingness of society to utilize its property resources currently. The nature of this decision can best be envisioned in terms of nonrenewable natural resources such as petroleum, natural gas, and a host of mineral deposits. The current rapid exploitation of these resources makes for a high output now but at the same time lessens the ability of the economy to produce in the future. A lower current rate of utilization would spread more evenly over time the output of goods and services whose production is dependent upon these resources. A less obvious facet of the conservation problem has to do with the overall deterioration of the physical environment; high levels of resource use—high levels of industrial production—are a serious challenge to nature's limited capacity to absorb wastes.

Having determined the level of resource utilization which it desires, society must then achieve that level of resource use. Society must avoid the involuntary idleness of its human and property resources. Involuntary idleness is the height of economic inefficiency. To be efficient, any economic system must somehow provide for high and stable levels of employment. We shall discover in Part 2 of this book that one of the basic defects of modern capitalism lies in the fact that it does not guarantee economic stability—full employment accompanied by a stable level of prices. Unemployment—actual or potential—is generally recognized as one of the crucial domestic problems which American capitalism currently faces. Inflation can be an equally potent adversary.

In a primitive Robinson Crusoe economy, there is no problem of achieving full employment. The consumer and the producer are one and the same. Thus the producer, if he so desires, can spend all his waking hours in an effort to fulfill his material wants. Though we cannot pause at this point for lengthy explanations, the problem of achieving full employment is not so simple a task in such modern industrial societies as American capitalism. Here producers and consumers—sellers and buyers—have different identities, and their decision making is linked only imperfectly by the use of money in buying and selling both goods and resources. Hence, although consumers on the one hand and producers on the other both desire full employment, their nonidentity raises the possibility that inconsistencies in their spending and producing decisions may lead to unemployment. If the spending of buyers is deficient in amount, producers will not find it advantageous to employ all the economy's available resources. Why hire resources to produce goods that no one will buy? Conversely, too much spending will result in price inflation. The point is this: Nothing guarantees that an industrially advanced economy—particularly a capitalistic economy—will operate at a point on its production possibilities curve. Finally, it is also worth

recalling that an economy with an expanding population and a growing labor force must provide more and more jobs each year to sustain full employment; the status quo with respect to the level of employment is not enough in a growing economy.

□   **Flexibility**

To achieve the maximum fulfillment of society's material wants over time, the economy must be flexible and adaptable to change. Modern industrialized economies are far from static, unchanging things. Indeed, their basic feature is *change*. What changes? Several things: consumer tastes, the supplies of resources, and technology. Why does our basic objective of efficiency in the use of scarce resources demand that the economy be adaptable to such changes? Because a changing technology, changes in consumer tastes, and variations in resource supplies necessitate significant reallocations of our resources in order to preserve efficiency in their use. The collection of goods and services which maximizes consumer satisfactions today will fail to do so tomorrow if consumer wants have changed in the meantime. The collection of goods and services which pleased your grandparents in the 1930s will simply not be acceptable to you in the 1980s. Put more bluntly, we should not be particularly happy if today's output provided for large quantities of buggy whips and mustache cups at the expense of stereophonic phonographs, transistor radios, and ballpoint pens. Similarly, changing resource supplies and the development of improved techniques of production will call for changes in the combinations of resources used in the production of given products if efficiency is to be maintained.

We should keep constantly in mind that scarcity of economic resources lurks behind all five of these Fundamental Questions and their component parts; the Five Questions are merely a breakdown of the basic economizing problem of scarce resources and unlimited wants. Also, the apparent interrelatedness of these questions is almost self-evident, as we shall see in the following chapters, where we shall attempt to describe in detail how a capitalistic economy answers these questions. Indeed, it is difficult to treat the Five Questions independently of one another—they demand simultaneous treatment.

THE "ISMS"

If we lived in an isolated, one-man economy—a Robinson Crusoe economy—the answers we would provide to our Fundamental Questions would be relatively simple. But when millions of diverse and interdependent economic units exist, no easy answers to these queries present themselves. Is it possible for our society, for example, to strike a tolerable balance between the business tycoon's demand for a Cadillac, the black's demand for improved housing, the schoolchild's demand for bubble gum and roller skates, and the housewife's demand for an automatic washer? Certainly no simple answer can be expected. And, to complicate matters, we know that answers which are acceptable today may not be acceptable tomorrow. The preferences of economic units change over time, and so do productive techniques, supplies of resources, and standards of equity in distributing output. In short, there are no final, once-and-for-all answers of a universal nature to the questions which constitute the economizing problem.

Furthermore, we must recognize that *various societies have established different output goals and utilize different institutions and methods of organizing their resources in trying to fulfill these goals.* Generally speaking, a survey of modern, industrially advanced economies suggests there are two fundamentally different philosophies concerning the means of achieving the best answers to the Five Fundamental Questions. At the one extreme, emphasis is put upon private ownership of resources, the freedom of individual economic units to make those choices which they feel are most appropriate in terms of their own specific objectives, and the use of a market system as a coordinating mechanism. The other extreme stresses public ownership of property resources and central economic planning by government as the mechanism of coordination, the presumption being that the exercise of authoritarian power by the state in the functioning of the economy will result in greater efficiency and equity than the sum of free economic choices by individual economic units. The former philosophy crudely describes the core of *pure, or laissez faire, capitalism;* the latter, the basic tenet of *authoritarian socialism,* or *communism.* The United States economy has a fairly strong capitalistic orientation, while the Soviet Union is the standard example of authoritarian socialism. But it must be emphasized that private ownership and reliance on the market system do not always go together; nor do central planning and public ownership. For example, although Nazi Germany's economy was subject to a high degree of government control and direction, property was still privately owned. And in today's Yugoslavia, property resources are largely publicly owned, but individual economic units are rather highly market-oriented. In short, there is theoretically an unlimited number of "isms," each of which has different ownership and decision-making patterns.

Table 2-3 summarizes the fundamental assumptions, institutional characteristics, and basic methods employed in achieving efficiency in the use of resources which are associated with pure capitalism, communism, and an intermediate hybrid—*liberal socialism.* Although students of comparative economic systems might quibble a bit about these descriptions, all would agree with the basic point emphasized by the table. And that point is: There are no unique or universally accepted answers to the Five Fundamental Questions.

Table 2-3   THE "ISMS" AND THE ECONOMIZING PROBLEM

Economic system	Underlying assumption	Institutional characteristics	Method of solving economizing problem
Pure, or laissez faire, capitalism	Each economic unit decides what choices and policies are best for it; such choices will prove to be in the social interest.	Private ownership of resources and business institutions; freedom of choice for consumers, resource suppliers, and enterprisers.	Emphasis upon a system of free, competitive markets—virtually no governmental planning or control.
Liberal, or democratic, socialism	Some governmental intervention is needed to improve upon the choices and policies of individual economic units.	Mixture of public and private ownership and public and private decision making.	Mixture of loose governmental planning and regulation of basic industry; reliance on system of markets and prices in other segments of economy.
Communism, or authoritarian socialism	The state is in the best position to know what choices and policies are beneficial for the economy as a whole and for its component parts.	Public ownership and control of the bulk of industry and agriculture; severe restriction of individual choices when in conflict with state-determined objectives.	Governmental plans are established by central planning authority; heavy reliance on government directives; some reliance on a price system to implement the plans.

Various societies, having different cultural and historical backgrounds, different mores and customs, and contrasting ideological frameworks—not to mention resources which differ both quantitatively and qualitatively—supply significantly different answers to the Five Questions. Russia, the United States, and Great Britain, for example, are all—in terms of their accepted goals, ideology, technologies, resources, and culture—attempting to achieve efficiency in the use of their respective resources. The best method for answering the Five Questions in one economy may be inappropriate for another economic system.

Table 2-3 is couched in terms of industrially advanced or "mature" economies. We shall discover in Chapter 21 that many nations of the world have underdeveloped economies. These *traditional* or *customary* economies are often characterized by feudalistic remnants of the Middle Ages. In these systems answers to the Five Fundamental Questions are shrouded in custom, habit, and tradition, all of which tend to perpetuate the status quo. In pursuing economic development, traditional economies must face the basic question as to which model in Table 2-3 will result in growth and simultaneously be consistent with other economic and noneconomic goals.

The ensuing four chapters undertake to explain how, in the so-called *mixed capitalism* of the United States, which stands at some intermediate position between pure capitalism and liberal socialism in Table 2-3, decisions are made about the objectives of the economy, how production is to be organized, and how output is to be distributed. Chapter 3 discusses the institutional framework of capitalism and provides a very general picture of the operation of pure, or laissez faire, capitalism. Chapter

4 explains the mechanics of supply and demand as price- and output-determining forces. The role of markets and prices in answering the Five Fundamental Questions is the topic of Chapter 5. Government is brought into the picture in Chapter 6, enlarging our picture of pure capitalism to one of mixed capitalism.

Summary

1   The science of economics centers upon two basic facts: First, human material wants are virtually unlimited; second, economic resources are scarce.

2   Economic resources may be classified as property resources—materials and capital—or as human resources—labor and entrepreneurial ability.

3   Economics is concerned with the problem of administering scarce resources in the production of goods and services for the fulfillment of the material wants of society. Both the full employment and the full production of available resources are essential if this administration is to be efficient.

4   At any point in time a full-employment, full-production economy must sacrifice the output of some types of goods and services to achieve increased production of others. Because resources are not equally productive in all possible uses, the shifting of resources from one use to another is subject to the law of increasing costs; that is, the production of additional units of product X entails the sacrifice of increasing amounts of product Y.

5   Over time, technological advance and increases in the quantity and quality of human and property resources permit the economy to produce more of all goods and services. Society's choice as to the composition of current output is a determinant of the future location of the production possibilities curve.

6   The Five Fundamental Questions are an elaboration of the economizing problem.

7   The various economic systems of the world differ in their ideologies and also in their approaches in answering the Five Fundamental Questions.

Questions and Study Suggestions

1   Terms and concepts to remember: economizing problem; land, labor, capital, the entrepreneurial ability; full employment; full production; production possibilities table (curve); law of increasing costs; economic growth; the Five Fundamental Questions; laissez faire capitalism; communism; liberal socialism.

2   "Economics is the study of the principles governing the allocation of scarce means among competing ends when the objective of the allocation is to maximize the attainment of the ends."[8] Explain. Why is the problem of unemployment a part of the subject matter of economics?

3   "Wants aren't insatiable. I can prove it. I get all the coffee I want to drink every morning at breakfast." Critically analyze. Explain: "Goods and services are scarce because resources are scarce." Analyze: "It is the nature of all economic problems that absolute solutions are denied us."

[8]George J. Stigler, *The Theory of Price* (New York: The Macmillan Company, 1947), p. 12.

4   What are economic resources? What are the major functions of the entrepreneur? "Economics is . . . neither capitalist nor socialist: it applies to every society. Economics would disappear only in a world so rich that no wants were unfulfilled for lack of resources. Such a world is not imminent and may be impossible, for time is always limited."[9] Carefully evaluate and explain these statements. Do you agree that, conceptually, time is an economic resource?

5   Comment on the following statement from a newspaper article: "Our junior high school serves a splendid hot meal for 55 cents without costing the taxpayers anything, thanks in part to a government subsidy."

6   The following is a production possibilities table for war goods and civilian goods:

Type of product	Production alternatives				
	A	B	C	D	E
Automobiles (in millions)	0	2	4	6	8
Guided missiles (in thousands)	30	27	21	12	0

a.   Show these production possibilities data graphically. What do the points on the curve indicate? How does the curve reflect the law of increasing costs? Explain.

b.   Label point *G* inside the curve. What does it indicate? Label point *H* outside the curve. What does this point indicate? What must occur before the economy can attain the level of production indicated by point *H?*

c.   Upon what specific assumptions is the production possibilities curve based? What happens when each of these assumptions is released?

d.   Suppose improvement occurs in the technology of producing guided missiles but not in the production of automobiles.

7   "The present choice of position on the production possibilities curve is a major factor in economic growth." Explain.

8   State and thoroughly discuss the Five Fundamental Questions which all economies face. Why must an economy be adaptable to change in order to maintain efficiency in the use of scarce resources? Contrast the means by which pure capitalism, democratic socialism, and communism attempt to answer the Five Questions.

Selected References

Heilbroner, Robert L.: *The Worldly Philosophers,* 4th ed.(New York: Simon & Schuster, Inc., 1972), chap. 2.

Knight, Frank H.: *The Economic Organization* (New York: Harper & Row, Publishers, Incorporated, 1965), chap. 1.

Mundell, Robert A.: *Man and Economics* (New York: McGraw-Hill Book Company, 1968), chap. 1.

[9]Joseph P. McKenna, *Intermediate Economic Theory* (New York: Holt, Rinehart and Winston, Inc., 1958), p. 2.

Last Word
Bombs or Bread For India?

India illustrated vividly the economizing problem in the form of the "guns or butter" issue by exploding its first atomic bomb in May of 1974.

The Indian government woke up Sunday as the sixth nation in the world with a nuclear capability. Rakhal and millions of his countrymen woke up hungry.

The 40-year-old laborer hadn't even heard of his country's first atomic test blast. When he was told the device exploded Saturday in the Rajastan Desert, he showed little interest.

"It's beyond my intelligence to know anything about a bomb," he told a visitor to his streetside camp. "My only ambition is to feed my children and my wife."

Some of the higher levels of Indian society were jubilant over the underground explosion, which put India alongside the United States, the Soviet Union, Britain, France and China as nations which have exploded nuclear devices.

Politicians and newspapers from the Moscow-leaning Patriot to the right-wing Motherland hailed the blast as a grand national achievement. "Indian genius triumphs," headlined the middle-of-the-road Hindustan Times. "Nation is thrilled."

But some young educated Indians, speaking at a Saturday night gathering, questioned the wisdom of Prime Minister Indira Gandhi's decision to devote resources to nuclear explosions when millions of Indian poor like Rakhal can't get enough to eat.

There are about 580 million people in India; an estimated 30% live in poverty, earning less than $30 a year. Nearly 80% of the nation's children are said to be malnourished; more than 70% of the country's people are illiterate.

"We may be hungry," one young Indian celebrant said in a typical comment. "But now at least we're someone to be reckoned with."

The Hindustan Times said the nuclear test proves "India has the talent, the resources and the infrastructure that makes for high achievement capability."

"Our knowledge in nuclear science has raised our status not only in Southeast Asia but in the whole world," said defense minister Jagjivan Ram.

But as newspaper readers were learning details of the explosion, Rakhal and his wife were giving their five children a chunk of bread for breakfast.

"Look at the oven there," Rakhal said, gesturing at a small hole flanked by rocks. "There is no fire in it because there is nothing to cook. The children are crying because they don't have enough to eat."

Rakhal brought his family to New Delhi from Bihar in eastern India on a public promise of land redistribution.

That was four months ago. Since then he's been working as a day laborer when he can. When there is no work, he goes to government offices to claim the land he thinks he is due.

"They don't give me any hope," he said. "For the past four days I have not had any jobs. If this continues I will go back home."

Accurate estimates are unavailable of how much was spent for the blast, which the government insists will not be used to develop nuclear weapons. But experts say the cost of equipping the country with a modest nuclear retaliatory force would range from $3 billion over 10 years to $1 billion over five years.

"Atomic Test Raises India's Clout; Poor Remain Hungry," *Lincoln Evening Journal,* May 29, 1974.

CHAPTER

3

Pure Capitalism and the Circular Flow

The task of the present chapter is to describe the capitalist ideology and to explain how pure, or laissez faire, capitalism would operate. Strictly speaking, pure capitalism has never existed and probably never will. Why, then, do we bother to consider the operation of such an economy? Because it gives us a very rough *first approximation* of how modern American capitalism functions. And approximations or models, when properly handled, can be very useful. In other words, pure capitalism constitutes a simplified model which we shall then modify and adjust to correspond more closely to the reality of American capitalism.

In explaining the operation of pure capitalism, we shall discuss:

1 The institutional framework and basic assumptions which make up the capitalist ideology.

2 Certain institutions and practices common to all modern economies.

3 Capitalism and the circular flow of income.

4 How product and resource prices are determined.

5 The market system and the allocating of economic resources.

The first three topics constitute the present chapter; the latter two will be the subject matter of Chapters 4 and 5.

CAPITALIST IDEOLOGY

Unfortunately, there is no neat and universally accepted definition of capitalism to aid us in our present task. We are therefore required to examine in some detail the basic tenets of capitalism to acquire a comprehensive understanding of what pure capitalism entails. In short, the framework of capitalism embodies the following institutions and assumptions: (1) private property, (2) freedom of enterprise and choice, (3) self-interest as the dominant motive, (4) competition, (5) reliance upon the price system, and (6) a limited role for government.

□   Private Property

Under a capitalistic system, the means of production—that is, scarce resources—are owned by private individuals and private institutions rather than by government. Private property, coupled with the freedom to negotiate binding legal contracts, permits private persons or businesses to obtain, control, employ, and dispose of economic resources as they see fit. The institution of private property is sustained over time by the *right to bequeath,* that is, by the right of a property owner to designate the recipient of his property at the time of death.

Needless to say, there are broad legal limits to this right of private ownership. For example, the use of one's resources for the production of narcotics is prohibited by legislation. Nor is public ownership nonexistent. Even in pure capitalism, recognition is given to the fact that public ownership of certain "natural monopolies" may be essential to the achievement of efficiency in the use of resources.

□   Freedom of Enterprise and Choice

Closely related to private ownership of property is freedom of enterprise and choice. Capitalism charges its component economic units with the responsibility of making certain choices, which are registered and made effective through the free markets of the economy.

Freedom of enterprise means that under pure capitalism, private business enterprises are free to obtain economic resources, to organize these resources in the production of a product of the firm's own choosing, and to sell this product in the markets of their choice. No artificial obstacles or restrictions imposed by government or other producers block an entrepreneur's choice to enter or leave a particular industry.

Freedom of choice means that owners of property resources and money capital can employ or dispose of these resources as they see fit. It also means that laborers are free to enter any of those lines of work for which they are mentally and physically qualified. Finally, it means that consumers are at liberty, within the limits of their money incomes, to buy that collection of goods and services which they feel is most appropriate in satisfying their wants. Freedom of consumer choice may well be the most profound of these freedoms. The consumer is in a particularly strategic position in a capitalistic economy; in a sense, the consumer is sovereign. The range of free choices for suppliers of human and property resources is circumscribed by the choices of consumers. The consumer ultimately decides what the capitalistic economy should produce, and resource suppliers must make their free choices within the boundaries thereby delineated. Resource suppliers and businesses are not really "free" to produce goods and services consumers do not desire.

Again, broad legal limitations prevail in the expression of all these free choices.

□   Role of Self-Interest

Since capitalism is individualistic, it is not surprising to find that the primary driving force of such an economy is the promotion of one's self-interest; each economic unit attempts to do what is best for itself. Hence, entrepreneurs aim at the maximization of their firms' profits or, as the case might be, the minimization of losses. And, other things being equal, owners of property resources attempt to achieve the highest price obtainable from the rent or sale of these resources. Given the amount and irksomeness of the effort involved, those who supply human resources will also attempt to obtain the highest possible incomes from their employment. Consumers, in purchasing a given product, will seek to obtain it at the lowest price. In short, capitalism presumes self-interest as the fundamental *modus operandi* for the various economic units as they express their free choices. The motive of self-interest gives direction and consistency to what might otherwise be an extremely chaotic economy.

Although self-interest is the basic motive underlying the functioning of capitalism, there are exceptions to the rule: Businesses and individuals do not always act in their own self-interest. Altruistic motives are part of the makeup of economic units. Yet, self-interest is the best single statement of how economic units actually behave.

□   **Competition**

Freedom of choice exercised in terms of promoting one's own monetary returns provides the basis for competition, or economic rivalry, as a fundamental feature of capitalism. Competition, as economists see it, entails:

1 The presence of large numbers of independently acting buyers and sellers operating in the market for any particular product or resource.

2 The freedom of buyers and sellers to enter or leave particular markets.

Let us briefly explore these two related aspects of competition:

Large Numbers   The essence of competition is the widespread diffusion of economic power within the two major aggregates—businesses and households—which comprise the economy. Specifically, when a large number of buyers and sellers are present in a particular market, no one buyer or seller will be able to demand or offer a quantity of the product sufficiently large to noticeably influence its price. Let us examine this statement in terms of the selling or supply side of the product market.

We have all observed that when a product becomes unusually scarce, its price will rise. For example, an unseasonable frost in Florida may seriously curtail the output of citrus crops and sharply increase the price of orange juice. Similarly, *if* a single producer, or a small group of producers acting together, can somehow control or restrict the total supply of a product, he can raise the price to his own advantage. By controlling supply, the producer can "rig the market" on his own behalf. Now the essence of competition is that there are so many sellers that each, *because he is contributing an almost negligible fraction of the total supply,* has virtually no control over the supply or, therefore, over the product price.

For example, suppose there are 10,000 farmers, each of whom is supplying 100 bushels of corn in the Kansas City grain market at some particular time when the price of corn happens to be $4 per bushel. Could a single farmer who feels dissatisfied with the existing price cause an artificial scarcity of corn and thereby boost the price above $4? The answer is obviously "No." Farmer Jones, by restricting output from 100 to 75 bushels, exerts virtually no effect upon the total supply of corn. In fact, total supply is reduced only from 1,000,000 to 999,975 bushels. This obviously is not much of a shortage! Supply is virtually unchanged, and, therefore, the $4 price persists. In brief, competition means that each seller is providing a drop in the bucket of total supply. Individual sellers can make no noticeable dent in total supply; hence, a seller cannot *as an individual producer*[1] manipulate product price. This is what is meant when it is pointed out that an individual competitive seller is "at the mercy of the market."

The same rationale applies to the demand side of the market. Buyers are plentiful and act independently. Thus no single buyer can manipulate the market to his advantage.

The important point is this: *The widespread diffusion of economic power underlying competition controls the use and limits the potential abuse of that power.* Economic rivalry prevents economic units from wreaking havoc upon one another as they attempt to further their self-interests. Competition imposes limits upon expressions of self-interest by buyers and sellers. Competition is a basic regulatory force in capitalism.

Entry and Exit Competition also assumes that it is a simple matter for producers to enter (or leave) a particular industry; there are no artificial legal or institutional obstacles to prohibit the expansion (or contraction) of specific industries. This aspect of competition is prerequisite to the flexibility which is essential if an economy is to remain efficient over time. Freedom of entry is necessary if the economy is to adjust appropriately to changes in consumer tastes, technology, or resource supplies. This matter will receive detailed treatment in Chapter 5.

□ **Markets and Prices**

Private property, freedom of choice, and self-interest are all basic features of capitalism. But the basic coordinating mechanism of such an economy is the market or price sys-

tem. *Capitalism is a market economy.* The decisions rendered by the buyers and sellers of products and resources are made effective through a system of markets. The preferences of sellers and buyers are registered on the supply and demand sides of various markets, and the outcome of these choices is a system of product and resource prices. These prices are guideposts upon which resource owners, entrepreneurs, and consumers make and revise their free choices in furthering their self-interests. Just as competition is the controlling mechanism, so a system of markets and prices is a basic organizing force. The price system is an elaborate communication system through which innumerable individual free choices are recorded, summarized, and balanced against one another. Those who obey the dictates of the price system are rewarded; those who ignore it are penalized by the system. Through this communication system, society renders its decisions concerning what the economy should produce, how production can be efficiently organized, and how the fruits of productive endeavor are to be distributed among the individual economic units which make up capitalism.

Not only is the price system the mechanism through which society renders decisions concerning how it allocates its resources and distributes the resulting output, but it is through the price system that these decisions are carried out. However, a word of caution: Economic systems based upon the ideologies of socialism and communism also depend upon price systems, but not to the same degree or in the same way as does pure capitalism. Socialistic and communistic societies use markets and prices primarily to implement the decisions made wholly or in part by a central planning authority. In capitalism, the price system functions both as a device for rendering innumerable choices of free individuals and businesses *and* as a mechanism for carrying out these decisions.

---

[1]Of course, if a number of farmers simultaneously restricted their production, the resulting change in total supply could no longer be ignored, and price would rise. Competition (a large number of sellers) implies the impossibility of such collusion.

In Chapters 4 and 5 we shall analyze the mechanics and the operation of a capitalistic price system.

□ Limited Government

A competitive capitalist economy is thought to be conducive to a high degree of efficiency in the use or allocation of its resources. Hence, there is allegedly little real need for governmental intervention in the operation of such an economy beyond its aforementioned role of imposing broad legal limits upon the exercise of individual choices and the use of private property. The historical development of the concept of pure capitalism as a self-regulating and self-adjusting type of economy precludes any significant economic role for government. As we shall see shortly, capitalism in practice has not been self-regulating to the degree economists once supposed. But for the moment, at least, our analysis will exclude government. Chapter 6 will elaborate the functions of government in present-day mixed capitalism.

■ OTHER CHARACTERISTICS

Private property, freedom of enterprise and choice, self-interest as a motivating force, competition, and reliance on a price system are all institutions and assumptions which are more or less exclusively associated with pure capitalism. In addition, there are certain institutions and practices which are characteristic of all modern economies. They are (1) the use of an advanced technology and large amounts of capital goods, (2) specialization, and (3) the use of money. Specialization and an advanced technology are prerequisites to the efficient employment of any economy's resources. The use of money is a permissive characteristic which allows society more easily to practice

and reap the benefits of specialization and of the employment of advanced productive techniques.

□ Extensive Use of Capital Goods

All modern economies—whether they approximate the capitalist, socialist, or communist ideology—are based upon an advanced technology and the extensive use of capital goods. Under pure capitalism it is competition, coupled with freedom of choice and the desire to further one's self-interest, which provides the means for achieving a rapid rate of technological advance. The capitalistic framework is felt to be highly effective in harnessing incentives to develop new products and improved techniques of production. Why? Because the monetary rewards derived therefrom accrue directly to the innovator. Pure capitalism therefore presupposes the extensive use and rapid development of complex capital goods: tools, machinery, large-scale factories, and facilities for storage, transportation, and marketing.

Why are the existence of an advanced technology and the extensive use of capital goods important? Because the most direct method of producing a product is usually the least efficient.[2] Even Robinson Crusoe avoided the inefficiencies of direct production in favor of "roundabout production." It would be ridiculous for a farmer—even a backyard farmer—to go at production with bare hands. Obviously, it pays huge dividends in terms of more efficient production and, therefore, a more abundant output, to fashion tools of production, that is, capital equipment, to aid in the productive process. There is a better way of getting water out of a well than to dive in after it!

But there is a catch involved. As we recall

---

[2] Remember that consumer goods satisfy wants directly, while capital goods do so indirectly through the more efficient production of consumer goods.

our discussion of the production possibilities curve and the basic nature of the economizing problem, it is evident that, with full employment and full production, resources must be diverted from the production of consumer goods in order to be used in the production of capital goods. We must currently tighten our belts as consumers to free resources for the production of capital goods which will increase productive efficiency and permit us to have a greater output of consumer goods at some future date.

□ **Specialization**

The extent to which society relies upon specialization is astounding. The vast majority of consumers produce virtually none of the goods and services they consume and, conversely, consume little or nothing of what they produce. The hammer-shop laborer who spends his life stamping out parts for jet engines may never "consume" an airplane trip. The assembly-line worker who devotes eight hours a day to the installation of windows in Chevrolets may own a Ford. Few households seriously consider any extensive production of their own food, shelter, and clothing. Many farmers sell their milk to the local creamery and then buy oleomargarine at the Podunk general store. Society learned long ago that self-sufficiency breeds inefficiency. The jack-of-all-trades may be a very colorful individual, but he is certainly lacking in efficiency.

In what specific ways might human specialization—*the division of labor*—enhance productive efficiency? First, specialization permits individuals to take advantage of existing differences in their abilities and skills. If caveman A is strong, swift afoot, and accurate with a spear, and caveman B is weak and slow, but patient, this distribution of talents can be most efficiently utilized by making A a hunter and B a fisherman. Second, even if the abilities of A and B are identical, specialization may prove to be advantageous. Why? Because by

devoting all his time to a single task, the doer is more likely to develop the appropriate skills and to discover improved techniques than when apportioning his time among a number of diverse tasks. One learns to be a good hunter by hunting! Finally, specialization—devoting all one's time to, say, a single task—obviously avoids the loss of time which is entailed in shifting from one job to another. For all these reasons the division of labor results in greater productive efficiency in the use of human resources.

Specialization also is desirable on a regional basis. Oranges could be grown in Nebraska, but because of the unsuitability of the land, rainfall, and temperature, the costs involved would be exceedingly high. Florida could probably achieve some success in the production of wheat, but for similar reasons, such production would be a relatively costly business. As a result, Nebraskans produce those products—wheat in particular—for which their resources are best adapted, and Floridians do the same, producing oranges and other citrus fruits. In so doing, both produce surpluses of their specialties. Then, very sensibly, Nebraskans and Floridians swap some of their surpluses. Specialization permits each area to put its best foot forward, that is, to turn out those goods which its resources can most efficiently produce. In this way both Nebraska and Florida can enjoy a larger amount of both wheat and oranges than would otherwise be the case. In short, human and geographical specialization are both essential in achieving efficiency in the use of resources.

□ **Specialization and Comparative Advantage**[3]

These simple illustrations make very plausible the axiom that specialization is economically desirable because it results in more

---

[3]This section may be skipped by instructors who wish to defer any detailed treatment of comparative advantage to Part 7 on international economics.

Table 3-1 NEBRASKA PRODUCTION POSSIBILITIES
TABLE (*hypothetical data; in tons*)

Product	Production alternatives			
	A	B	C	D
Wheat	0	20	40	60
Oranges	15	10	5	0

efficient production. Indeed, the point is almost self-explanatory. But, because the concept of specialization is so vital to an understanding of the production and exchange processes of modern economies, let us tackle a couple of more exacting illustrations of the gains which accrue from specialization. Our examples will be simplified to make the principles involved as clear as possible.

Comparative Costs   Let us pursue our Nebraska-Florida example of specialization at a more sophisticated level, relying upon an already familiar concept—the production possibilities table—as a basic analytical device. Suppose production possibilities data for the Nebraska and Florida economies are as in Table 3-1 and 3-2, respectively.

You will immediately sense that these production possibilities tables are "different" from those of Chapter 2 in that we here assume *constant costs* rather than increasing costs. In other words, each state must give up a constant, rather than an increasing, amount of one product in securing constant increments of the other product. This simplification will expedite our discussion without impairing the overall validity of our conclusions. The effects

of increasing costs will be noted later (Chapter 41) when we discuss international specialization.

The basic truth which we wish to reveal is that *specialization and trade are mutually beneficial or "profitable" to the two states (individuals, regions, nations) if the comparative costs of the two products within the two states differ.* What is the comparative cost of oranges and wheat in Nebraska? Table 3-1 tells us that 5 tons of oranges must be forgone or sacrificed to produce 20 tons of wheat. Or more simply, it costs 1 ton of oranges to get 4 tons of wheat in Nebraska ($1O = 4W$). Remember that because of our constant-cost assumption, this comparative-cost relationship will not change as we expand the output of either product. Similarly, we find in Table 3-2 that at a cost of 10 tons of oranges, Floridians can obtain 30 tons of wheat, that is, in Florida the comparative-cost ratio for the two products is: $1O$ equals $3W$. The comparative cost of the two products within the two states is clearly different. Economists describe this situation by saying that Florida has a comparative-cost advantage, or more simply, comparative advantage, in oranges; that is, Florida must forgo less wheat (3 tons) to get 1 ton of oranges than is the case in Nebraska where 1 ton of oranges costs 4 tons of wheat. Comparatively speaking, oranges are cheap in Florida. Nebraska, on the other hand, has a comparative (cost) advantage in wheat. Whereas it costs $\frac{1}{3}$ ton of oranges to get 1 ton of wheat in Florida, by comparison 1 ton of wheat only costs $\frac{1}{4}$ ton of oranges in Nebraska. Comparatively speaking, wheat is cheap in Nebraska. Given these comparative-cost differences, we now want to demonstrate that if both states specialize according to their comparative advantage, they can achieve a larger total output of oranges and wheat than otherwise! That is, they can get a larger total output with the same total input of resources through specialization and thereby obviously will be allocating their scarce resources more efficiently.

Table 3-2 FLORIDA PRODUCTION POSSIBILITIES
TABLE (*hypothetical data; in tons*)

Product	Production alternatives			
	A	B	C	D
Wheat	0	30	60	90
Oranges	30	20	10	0

Terms of Trade   Given Florida's cost ratio of 1*O* equals 3*W,* it stands to reason that Floridians would be pleased to specialize in oranges, if they could obtain *more than* 3 tons of wheat for a ton of oranges through trade with Nebraska. Similarly, recalling Nebraska's 1*O* equals 4*W* cost ratio, it will be advantageous to Nebraskans to specialize in wheat, provided they can get 1 ton of oranges for *less than* 4 tons of wheat. Suppose through negotiation the two states agree upon an exchange rate of 1 ton of oranges for $3\frac{1}{2}$ tons of wheat.[4] Note that these *terms of trade* will be mutually beneficial in that both states can "do better" through trade than they can at home. Floridians get $3\frac{1}{2}$ tons of wheat by sending 1 ton of oranges to Nebraska, whereas they can get only 3 tons of wheat by reallocating resources from oranges to wheat production at home. It would cost Nebraskans 4 tons of wheat to obtain 1 ton of oranges by reallocating their domestic resources, whereas 1 ton of oranges can be obtained through trade with Florida at the smaller cost of only $3\frac{1}{2}$ tons of wheat.

Gains from Specialization and Trade   In order to pinpoint the size of the gains in total output from specialization and trade, let us assume that before specialization and trade, production alternative B was the optimum product-mix for each state. That is, Nebraskans preferred 20 tons of wheat and 10 tons of oranges (Table 3-1) and Floridians preferred 30 tons of wheat and 20 tons of oranges (Table 3-2) to all other alternatives available within the respective state economies. Both states now specialize according to comparative advantage, Nebraska producing 60 tons of wheat and no oranges (alternative D) and Florida producing no wheat and 30 tons of oranges (alternative A). Utilizing our 1*O* equals $3\frac{1}{2}W$ terms of trade, assume that Ne-

braska exchanges 35 tons of its wheat for 10 tons of Florida oranges. Nebraskans will now have 25 tons of wheat and 10 tons of oranges, while Floridians will thus obtain 35 tons of wheat and 20 tons of oranges. As compared with their optimum product-mixes prior to specialization and trade, both states now enjoy the same amount of oranges and 5 additional tons of wheat! These extra 10 tons of wheat, equally divided between the two state economies in this instance,[5] represent the *gains from specialization and trade.*

The crucial point is that *resource allocation has been improved through specialization according to comparative advantage.* This is obviously so, because the same total inputs of resources have resulted in a larger total output. By having Nebraska and Florida allocate all their resources to wheat and oranges respectively, the same total inputs of resources have given rise to more output, indicating that resources are being more efficiently utilized or allocated.

We might envision the gains from trade from a slightly different vantage point. In Chapter 2 we learned that an expansion of resource supplies or technological progress would permit an economy (state or national) to penetrate its current production possibilities boundary and obtain an output superior to any that was currently available to it. *Although the domestic production possibilities boundaries of the two states have not actually been pushed to the right, we have in specialization and trade discovered a means of circumventing the constraints of the production possibilities curve. In short, the economic effects of specialization and trade between states (regions, nations) are tantamount to having more or better resources or to achieving technological progress.*

Technical postscript: The absolute levels

---

[4]In Chapter 41 we will find that market forces—supply and demand—will determine the rate at which the two products are exchanged.

[5]We will discover in Chapter 41 that different terms of trade would result in a different division of the 10 tons of wheat between the two states.

of real costs are not important to this analysis and its conclusions. For example, we might compare the prespecialization optimum product-mixes for Nebraska and Florida (the B alternatives in Tables 3-1 and 3-2) and find that the resulting outputs are being produced with the same total inputs of resources in the two states. This obviously suggests that Florida's resources are absolutely more productive in both oranges *and* wheat. Despite this, specialization and trade will still be advantageous to both parties. All that matters is that the comparative-cost ratios differ!

It should be emphasized that specialization and an advanced technology go hand in hand. Specialization and technological advance reinforce one another. Nebraskans and Floridians are more likely to discover better techniques for producing wheat and oranges when specializing than they would if each state divided its resources between the two products. Specialization encourages technological advance, and technological advance in turn stimulates greater specialization.

Disadvantages   One final word: Serious reflection on this matter of geographical and human specialization reveals certain drawbacks. For example, the monotony and drudgery of specialized work are well known. Imagine the boredom of our previously mentioned assembly-line worker who is still putting windows in Chevrolets. The Last Word segment of this chapter dramatizes this point. Second, specialization and mutual interdependence vary directly with one another. The less each of us produces for oneself, the more we are dependent upon the output of others. The less wheat produced in Florida, the greater is that state's dependence upon Nebraska wheat. For the economy as a whole, it is not surprising to discover what profoundly serious consequences may stem from a transportation strike or, on a more localized basis, from the breakdown of an assembly line. A third problem centers upon the exchanging of the surpluses which speciali-

zation entails. An examination of this problem leads us into a discussion of the use of money in the economy.

□   Use of Money

Virtually all economies, advanced or primitive, are money-using. Money performs a variety of functions (see Chapter 14), but first and foremost it is a medium of exchange.

In our Nebraska-Florida example, it was necessary for Nebraskans to trade or exchange 35 tons of wheat for 10 tons of Florida's oranges if both states were to share in the benefits of specialization. If trade were prohibited for some reason, gains from specializing according to comparative advantage might be lost to society. Why? Because consumers want a wide variety of products and, in the absence of trade, would tend to devote their human and material resources to many diverse types of production. If exchange could not occur or was very inconvenient to transact, Nebraska and Florida would be forced to be more self-sufficient, and the advantages of specialization would not be realized. *In short, a convenient means of exchanging goods is a prerequisite of specialization.*

Now exchange can, and sometimes does, occur on the basis of *bartering,* that is, swapping goods for goods. But bartering as a means of exchange can pose serious problems for the economy. Specifically, exchange by barter requires a *coincidence of wants* between the two transactors. In our example, we assumed that Nebraskans had excess wheat to trade and that they wanted to obtain oranges. And we assumed Floridians had excess oranges to swap and that they wanted to acquire wheat. So exchange occurred. But if this coincidence of wants did not exist, trade would be stymied. Let us pose such a problem.

Suppose Nebraska does not want any of Florida's oranges but is interested in buying potatoes from Idaho. Ironically enough, Idaho wants Florida's oranges but not Nebraska's wheat. And, to complicate matters, suppose that Florida wants some of Nebraska's wheat but none of Idaho's potatoes. The situation is summarized in Figure 3-1.

In no case do we find a coincidence of wants. Trade by barter would be difficult. To overcome such a stalemate, modern economies use *money,* which is simply a convenient social invention for facilitating the exchange of goods and services. Historically, cattle, cigarettes, shells, stones, pieces of metal, and many other diverse commodities have been used, with varying degrees of success, as a medium for facilitating exchange. But to be money, an item needs to pass only one test: *It must be generally acceptable by buyers and sellers in exchange.* Money is socially defined; whatever society accepts as a medium of exchange is money. Most modern economies, for reasons made clear in Chapter 14, find it convenient to use pieces of paper as money. We shall assume that this is the case with the Nebraska-Florida-Idaho economy; they use pieces of paper which they call "dollars" as money. Can the use of paper dollars as a medium of exchange overcome the stalemate we have posed?

Obviously it can, with trade occurring in this way:

1 Floridians can exchange money for some of Nebraska's wheat.

2 Nebraskans can take the money realized from the sale of wheat and exchange it for some of Idaho's potatoes.

3 Idahoans can then exchange the money received from the sale of potatoes for some of Florida's surplus oranges.

These transactions are shown by the arrows in Figure 3-1.

The willingness to accept paper money (or any other kind of money, for that matter) as a medium of exchange has permitted a three-way trade which allows each state to specialize in one product and obtain the other product(s) its residents desire, despite a noncoincidence of wants. Barter, resting as it does upon a coincidence of wants, would have impeded this exchange and in so doing would have induced the three states not to specialize. Of course, the efficiencies of specialization would then have been lost to those states. Strange as it may first seem, two exchanges—surplus product for money and then money for a wanted prod-

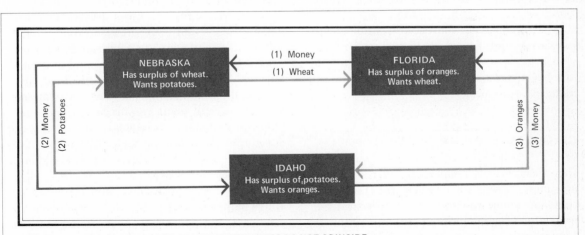

FIGURE 3-1 MONEY FACILITATES TRADE WHERE WANTS DO NOT COINCIDE

By the use of money as a medium of exchange, trade can be accomplished, as indicated by the arrows, despite a noncoincidence of wants. By facilitating exchange, the use of money permits an economy to realize the efficiencies of specialization.

uct—are simpler than the single product-for-product exchange which bartering entails! Indeed, in this example, product-for-product exchange would not be likely to occur at all.

A final example: Imagine a Detroit laborer producing crankshafts for Oldsmobiles. At the end of the week, instead of receiving a brightly colored piece of paper endorsed by the company comptroller, or a few pieces of paper neatly engraved in green and black, the laborer receives from the company paymaster four Oldsmobile crankshafts. Inconvenient as this is, and with no desire to hoard crankshafts, the laborer ventures into the Detroit business district, intent upon spending his hard-earned income on a basket of food, a suit of clothes, a baseball game, and a haircut. Needless to say, he is faced with some inconvenient and time-consuming trading, and he may not be able to negotiate any exchanges at all. Finding a clothing merchant who has a suit which meets his approval and who happens to be in the market for an Oldsmobile crankshaft is a formidable task. And, even if he locates a barber in need of a crankshaft, how is the barber going to make change for the laborer's haircut? Examples such as this demonstrate that money is one of the great social inventions of civilization!

To recapitulate: The use of technologically advanced capital goods, a high degree of specialization in production, and the use of money are basic institutional characteristics of all modern economies.

CIRCULAR FLOW OF INCOME

Our discussion has pointed out the role of markets and prices as a mechanism for the tabulation and communication of the decisions of individual economic units. In pure capitalism, the free decisions of businesses and households concerning what the economy should produce, how production should be organized, and how total output should be distributed are thus rendered effective through a system of markets and prices.

The next logical step in this discussion is to examine in some detail the nature of markets and prices. The remainder of this chapter is devoted to a general overview of the market system of pure capitalism for the purpose of pinpointing the two basic types of markets of pure capitalism and noting the character of the transactions which occur therein. Chapter 4 presents a rather detailed examination of how specific prices are actually determined in pure capitalism. Then Chapter 5 provides a more rigorous discussion of how pure capitalism goes about answering the Five Fundamental Questions through the workings of the price system.

□ Circular Flow Models

How does pure capitalism work? Several answers can be offered, depending upon the amount of detail one desires.

Real Flows   In a barter economy, households, which directly or indirectly (through their ownership of business corporations) own all economic resources, supply these resources to businesses, as is shown in the upper loop of Figure 3-2. (Let us for the moment think of businesses simply as organizational charts, that is, institutions on paper apart from the capital, raw materials, labor, and entrepreneurial ability which breathe life into them and make them "going concerns.") Businesses, of course, will want resources, because these are the means by which goods and services are produced. In return for making their resources available for use by businesses, households will receive payments in kind; that is, they will be paid in terms of the goods and services they have helped produce. This flow of payments is shown in the lower loop of Figure 3-2. Of course, households, being paid in terms of crankshafts, shoes, doughnuts, and so forth, will face some difficult exchange problems in swapping goods for goods with one another in

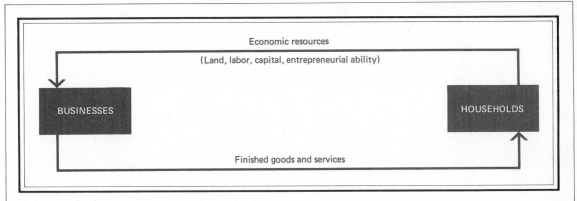

FIGURE 3-2 THE OPERATION OF A BARTER ECONOMY

In a nonmonetary, or barter, economy, households supply their economic resources (upper loop) and receive finished goods and services (lower loop) in return.

seeking to satisfy their various wants. In any event, this simple picture of the economy does accurately locate the main *real* flows, that is, the flow of resources and the flow of goods and services which occur in a capitalistic economy.

Money Flows   To circumvent problems of inconvenience in bartering, virtually all economies are money-using. How does our circular flow picture change as we progress from a barter to a monetary economy? The fact that money is a medium of exchange suggests that money is used as a go-between to facilitate the exchanges of resources and products which occur between businesses and households. In Figure 3-3, the upper loop shows a counterclockwise flow of resources accompanied by a clockwise flow of money payments of income in the form of wages, rent, interest, and profits. These income payments are made in the acquisition of resources and are looked upon as costs to the business firms making them. Note, incidentally, that in economics we treat profits—the expense involved in retaining the firm's supply of entrepreneurial ability—as a cost of production.

But money income received from the sale of resources does not, as such, have real value.

Consumers cannot eat or wear coins and paper money. Households will want to obtain a share of the fruits of production by spending their money incomes. Indeed, money income received by a household for the resources it supplies constitutes dollar claims against the total output it helped produce. Households exercise these claims by spending their money incomes—all their incomes, let us assume—on the goods and services of their choice. The clockwise flow of consumption expenditures and the counterclockwise flow of goods and services shown in the lower loop of Figure 3-3 reflect the exchange of income for products. From the viewpoint of businesses, the flow of consumption expenditures coming from households is receipts or revenue.

To summarize: In a monetary economy, households, as resource owners, sell their resources to businesses and, as consumers, spend the money income received therefrom in buying goods and services. Businesses must buy resources in order to produce goods and services; their finished products are then sold to households in exchange for consumption expenditures or, as businesses view it, receipts. The net result is a counterclockwise real flow of economic resources and finished goods and

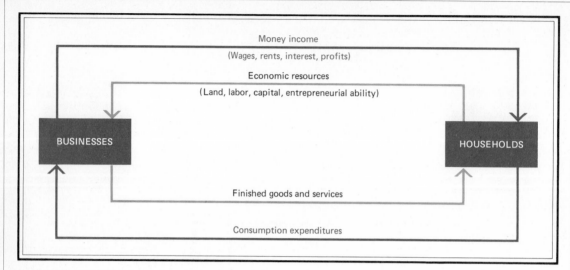

FIGURE 3-3   THE OPERATION OF A MONETARY ECONOMY

In a money-using economy, households exchange their economic resources for money income (upper loop), which can then be spent on finished goods and services (lower loop).

services and a clockwise money flow of income and consumption expenditures. These flows are simultaneous and repetitive.

Real Flows, Money Flows, and Markets

Figure 3-4 adds a final step to our circular flow picture. The cost-income and resource flows of the upper loop and the goods-expenditure flows of the lower loop of Figure 3-3 pass through markets where money is exchanged for resources and for goods and services. In the upper loop of Figure 3-4, income payments and resources flow through *resource markets*. Here, households supply resources at certain existing market prices and receive money income in return from businesses that buy or demand these resources. Obviously, the amount of money income flowing through the resource markets and into the hands of households will depend upon the quantities of the various resources supplied by households and the prices at which they are sold. Similarly, in the lower loop, consumer expenditures and goods and services pass through *product markets*. The

size of these consumption flows will depend upon the quantities of the various goods and services purchased and the prices at which they sell. In other words, there are two basic types of markets in a capitalistic economy— resource markets and product markets. Businesses are on the buying or *demand* side of the resource markets, and households, as resource owners and suppliers, are on the selling or *supply* side. In the product market, these positions are reversed; households, as consumers, are on the buying or demand side, and businesses are on the selling or supply side. Each group of economic units both buys and sells.

Note that the specter of scarcity haunts these transactions. Because households have only limited amounts of resources to supply to businesses, the money incomes of consumers will be limited. This means that each consumer's income will go only so far. A limited number of dollars obviously will not permit the purchase of all the goods and services which the consumer might like to buy. The consumer, being handicapped by limited money

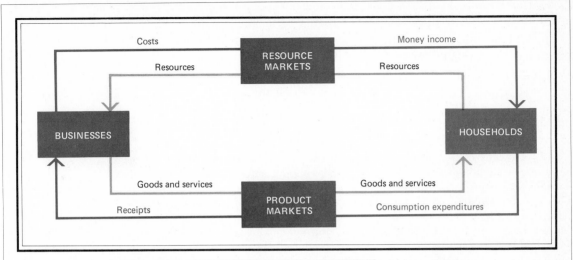

FIGURE 3-4 RESOURCE AND PRODUCT MARKETS IN A MONETARY ECONOMY

The prices paid for the use of land, labor, capital, and entrepreneurial ability are determined in the resource market shown in the upper loop. Businesses are on the demand side and households on the supply side of this market. The prices of finished goods and services are determined in the product market located in the lower loop. Households are on the demand side and businesses on the supply side of this market.

income, necessarily operates under a *budget restraint*. Similarly, because resources are scarce, the output of finished goods and services is also necessarily limited. Scarcity permeates our entire discussion.

□ Limitations

There are certain noteworthy shortcomings and omissions inherent in the circular flow overview of the workings of pure capitalism:

1 This simple model ignores the transactions which occur *within* the business and household sectors of the economy. For example, the sales of processed materials to manufacturers, parts to fabricators, and finished products to wholesalers and then to retailers are all ignored. This is not a crucial defect, however. At this stage of our discussion, these intrabusiness and intrahousehold transactions are not vital to our understanding of how pure capitalism operates.

2 We must acknowledge that the circular flow model does not reflect the myriad of facts and details about specific households, specific businesses, and specific resource and product markets. Indeed, the main virtue of the circular flow model is that it lays bare the fundamental operations of pure capitalism without ensnaring the viewer in a maze of details. We seek here a view of the whole forest; the examination of specific trees will come later.

3 The circular flow model makes no mention of the economic role of government. The reason? The institutions of pure capitalism would allegedly give rise to a self-contained, self-regulating economy in which government's role would be minor. In Chapter 6 the circular flow will be modified to reflect the economic functions of government in the mixed capitalism which now characterizes the American economy.

4 This model assumes that households spend exactly all their money income and that, therefore, the flows of income and expenditure are constant in volume. In real terms this means that the levels of output and employment are constant. Part 2 of this book is concerned with the causes and effects of fluctuations in income and output flows.

5 Our discussion of the circular flow assumes the existence of certain resource and product prices, but it does not explain how resource and product prices are actually deter-mined. This is the task to which we turn in the ensuing chapter: How are resource and product prices determined in a purely capitalistic economy?

Summary

1 The capitalistic system is characterized by the private ownership of resources and the freedom of individuals to engage in the economic activities of their choice as a means for advancing their material well-being. Self-interest is the driving force of such an economy, and competition functions as a regulatory or control mechanism. Capitalistic production is not organized in terms of a government plan, but rather features the price system as a means of organizing and making effective the myriad of individual decisions which determine what is produced, the methods of production, and the sharing of output. Indeed, government plays a minor and relatively passive role.

2 Specialization according to the principle of comparative advantage and an advanced technology based on the extensive use of capital goods are features common to all modern economies. Functioning as a medium of exchange, money circumvents the problems entailed in bartering and thereby permits greater specialization.

3 An overview of the operation of the capitalistic system can be gained through the circular flow of income. This simplified model locates the product and resource markets and presents the major income-expenditure flows and resources-output flows which constitute the lifeblood of the capitalistic economy.

Questions and Study Suggestions

1 Key terms and concepts to remember: private property; freedom of choice; freedom of enterprise; self-interest; competition; roundabout production; specialization and division of labor; comparative cost; comparative advantage; terms of trade; barter; money as a medium of exchange; circular flow of income.

2 "Capitalism may be characterized as an automatic self-regulating system motivated by the self-interest of individuals and regulated by competition."[6] Explain and evaluate.

3 Explain how the price system is a means of communicating and implementing decisions concerning the allocation of the economy's resources.

4 What advantages result from "roundabout" production? What problem is involved in increasing a full-employment, full-production economy's stock of capital goods? Illustrate this problem in terms of the production possibilities curve. Does an economy with unemployed resources face the same problem?

5 What are the advantages of specialization in the use of human and material resources? Be specific.

[6]Howard R. Bowen, *Toward Social Economy* (New York: Holt, Rinehart and Winston, Inc., 1948), p. 249.

6 Foreigners frequently point out that, comparatively speaking, Americans are very wasteful of food and other material goods and very conscious of, and overly economical in, their use of time. Can you provide an explanation for this observation?

7 The following are production possibilities tables for Japan and Hawaii. Assume that prior to specialization and trade, the optimum product-mix for Japan is alternative B and for Hawaii alternative D.

Product	Japan's production alternatives					
	A	B	C	D	E	F
Radios (in thousands)	30	24	18	12	6	0
Pineapples (in tons)	0	6	12	18	24	30

Product	Hawaii's production alternatives					
	A	B	C	D	E	F
Radios (in thousands)	10	8	6	4	2	0
Pineapples (in tons)	0	4	8	12	16	20

a. Are comparative-cost conditions such that the two nations should specialize? If so, what product should each produce?

b. What is the total gain in radio and pineapple output which results from this specialization?

c. What are the limits of the terms of trade? Suppose the actual terms of trade are 1 unit of radios for $1\frac{1}{2}$ units of pineapples and that 4 units of radios are exchanged for 6 units of pineapples. What are the gains from specialization and trade for each nation?

d. Can you conclude from this illustration that specialization according to comparative advantage results in the more efficient use of world resources? Explain.

8 What problems does barter entail? Indicate the economic significance of money as a medium of exchange. "Money is the only commodity that is good for nothing but to be gotten rid of. It will not feed you, clothe you, shelter you, or amuse you unless you spend or invest it. It imparts value only in parting."[7] Explain this statement.

9 Describe the operation of pure capitalism as portrayed by the circular flow of income. Emphasize the fact of scarcity throughout your discussion.

Selected References

Bowen, Howard R.: *Toward Social Economy* (New York: Holt, Rinehart and Winston, Inc., 1948), chaps. 1–5.

Ebenstein, William: *Today's Isms,* 7th ed. (Englewood Cliffs, N.J.: Prentice-Hall, Inc., 1973), chap. 3.

Loucks, William N., and William G. Whitney: *Comparative Economic Systems,* 9th ed. (New York: Harper & Row, Publishers, Incorporated, 1973), chap. 2.

Monsen, R. Joseph, Jr.: *Modern American Capitalism: Ideologies and Issues* (Boston: Houghton Mifflin Company, 1963).

Romano, Richard, and Melvin Leiman (eds.): *Views on Capitalism,* 2d ed. (Beverly Hills, Calif.: Glencoe Press, 1975).

[7] Federal Reserve Bank of Philadelphia, "Creeping Inflation," *Business Review,* August 1957, p. 3.

Last Word

Specialization and the Alienated Worker

Although specialization is a fundamental means of increasing productivity, it makes for monotonous and boring jobs. Gary Brynner, President of UAW Local 1112 at GM's Lordstown, Ohio, Vega assembly plant, airs his views.

"Alienation" is, I guess, a good term. There are symptoms of the alienated worker in our plant where we specialize, where I am president. Absentee rate has gone continually higher. Turnover rate is enormous. The use and turning to alcohol and drugs is becoming a bigger and bigger problem, and apathy—apathy within our union movement toward union leaders and to the Government.

I think those lead from the alienation of the worker. In our plant we make 101.6 Vegas an hour, the fastest line speed in the country. A guy has about 36 seconds to do an operation. The jobs are so fragmented that he is offered very little as far as input to that project. He cannot associate with it or he does not realize what he is doing to it.

Conveyor lines in our plant, the heights, and every movement of the conveyor line is determined to make the guy a little more efficient, to take movement of the bending and stretching, to make him more efficient.

The arbitrary rights of management tend to alienate the worker. The number of hours he works in a day, the number of days he works in a week, are all determined by arbitrary management, their decision, no recourse by the employee.

The job assignments within the plant in the same classification are solely the right of management, no say for the employee. The job content, and there is not much to that because when you have 36 seconds you do not have much of a job to do, and all we are left with is the dead end jobs, as you pointed out, jobs that offer little challenge to the more educated worker, little chance for advancement, and hardly any chance to participate as a worker. We have more educated workers, as everybody knows, and that creates a problem in our plant. He is brought into the plant and his orientation session ends and starts with his papers on insurance and his assignment to a foreman who immediately puts his warm body on the line. He is introduced to a gentleman or a brother and told this is your operation and in 15 or 20 minutes or an hour or 3 hours, whatever, as quickly as they can get away, that is his job. That is what he looks forward to day in and day out, 10 hours a day, 11 hours a day, 6 or 7 days a week, as in our case.

From *Worker Alienation, 1972:* Hearings before the Subcommittee on Employment, Manpower, and Poverty, U.S. Senate, 92d Congress, 2d Session, Washington, p. 10, abridged.

The Mechanics of Individual Prices: Demand and Supply

"Teach a parrot to say, 'Demand and supply,' and you have an economist!" There is a strong element of truth in this quip because, in fact, the simple tools of demand and supply can take one far in understanding not only specific economic issues, but also the operation of the entire economic system.

The much-simplified analysis of the operation of pure capitalism presented at the conclusion of Chapter 3 assumed that resources and goods and services sell for certain given prices. This permitted us to sidestep the fundamental question to which we now turn: How are prices "set," or determined, in pure capitalism? The answer is easy to state but a bit more difficult to understand. In short, prices are determined in the product market by the interaction of the supply decisions of competing businesses and the demand decisions of competing households. In the resource market, the demand decisions of competing businesses, coupled with the supply decisions of competing households, determine prices. Our immediate objective is to verify these answers. In doing so, we shall concentrate on the product market, then shift our attention later in the chapter to the resource market. The immediate task is to explain the mechanics of prices. How does the interaction of demand and supply decisions determine product and resource prices?

DEMAND

The term "demand" has a very definite meaning to the economist. *Demand* is defined as *a schedule which shows the various amounts of a product which consumers are willing and able to purchase at each specific price in a set of possible prices during some specified period of time.*[1] Demand simply portrays a series of alternative possibilities which can be set down in tabular form. As our definition indicates, we usually view demand from the vantage point of price; that is, we read demand as showing the amounts consumers will buy at various possible prices. It is equally correct and sometimes more meaningful to view demand from the reference point of quantity. That is, instead of asking what quantities can be sold at various prices, we can ask what prices can be gotten from consumers for various quantities of a good. Table 4-1 is a hypothetical demand schedule for a single consumer who is purchasing bushels of corn.

This tabular portrayal of demand reflects the relationship between the price of corn and the quantity that our mythical consumer would be willing and able to purchase at each of these prices. Note that we say willing and *able,* because willingness alone is not effective in the market. I may be willing to buy a Cadillac, but if this willingness is not backed by the ability to buy, that is, by the necessary dollars, it will not be effective and, therefore, not reflected in the market. In Table 4-1, if the price of corn in the market happened to be $5 per bushel, our consumer would be willing and able to buy 10 bushels per week; if it were $4, he would be willing and able to buy 20 bushels per week; and so forth.

The demand schedule in and of itself does not tell us which of the five possible prices will actually exist in the corn market. As we have

Table 4-1   AN INDIVIDUAL BUYER'S DEMAND FOR CORN (*hypothetical data*)

Price per bushel	Quantity demanded per week
$5	10
4	20
3	35
2	55
1	80

already said, this depends on demand *and supply*. Demand, then, is simply a tabular statement of a buyer's plans, or intentions, with respect to the purchase of a product.

Note that, to be meaningful, the quantities demanded at each price must relate to some specific time period—a day, a week, a month, and so forth. To say that "a consumer will buy 10 bushels of corn at $5 per bushel" is vague and meaningless. To say that "a consumer will buy 10 bushels of corn *per week* at $5 per bushel" is clear and very meaningful.

□   Law of Demand

A fundamental characteristic of demand is this: As price falls, the corresponding quantity demanded rises, or, alternatively, as price increases, the corresponding quantity demanded falls. In short, there is an *inverse* relationship between price and quantity demanded. Economists have labeled this inverse relationship the *law of demand.* Upon what foundation does this law rest? There are many levels on which the case can be argued, but it is sufficient for present purposes to rest the case on common sense and simple observation.[2] People ordinarily *do* buy more of a given product at a low price than they do at a high price. To consumers, price is an obstacle which deters them from buying. The higher this obstacle, the less of a product they will buy; the lower the price obstacle, the more they will buy. In other words, a high price discourages con-

---

[1] In adjusting this definition to the resource market, merely substitute the word "resource" for "product" and "business" for "consumer."

[2] Common sense and simple observation will give way to more sophisticated explanations in Chapter 24.

sumers from buying, and a low price encourages them to buy. The plain fact that businessmen have "sales" is concrete evidence of their belief in the law of demand. "Bargain days" are based on the law of demand.

The law of demand can also be explained in terms of the substitutability of products for one another. There are usually (but not always) a number of reasonably good substitutes for any particular product. Hence, an increase in the price of this product will make consumers substitute other products for it. A decline in the price of the given product will induce customers to substitute it for other products. To be more specific, if the price of butter goes up, consumers substitute oleomargarine and therefore purchase less butter at the higher price. If the price of butter declines, consumers substitute butter for oleomargarine, thereby purchasing more butter at the lower price.

□   The Demand Curve

This inverse relationship between product price and quantity demanded can be presented on a simple two-dimensional graph measuring quantity demanded on the horizontal axis and price on the vertical axis.[3] From Chapter 1, we recall that the process involved is merely that of locating on the graph those five price-quantity possibilities shown in Table 4-1. We do this by drawing perpendiculars from the appropriate points on the two axes. Thus, in plotting the "$5-price–10-quantity-demanded" possibility, we must draw a perpendicular from the horizontal (quantity) axis at 10 to meet a perpendicular drawn from the vertical (price) axis at $5. If this is done for all five possibilities, the result is a series of points as shown in Figure 4-1. Each of these points represents a specific price and the corresponding quantity

which the consumer will choose to purchase at that price. Now, assuming the same inverse relationship between price and quantity demanded at all points between the ones graphed, we can generalize on the inverse relationship between price and quantity demanded by drawing a curve to represent *all* price-quantity-demanded possibilities within the limits shown on the graph. The resulting curve is called a *demand curve* and is labeled *DD* in Figure 4-1. It slopes downward and to the right because the relationship it portrays between price and quantity demanded is inverse. The law of demand—people buy more at a low price than they do at a high price—is reflected in the downward slope of the demand curve.

What is the advantage of graphing our demand schedule? After all, Table 4-1 and Figure 4-1 contain exactly the same data and reflect the same relationship between price and quantity demanded. The advantage of graphing is that it permits us to represent clearly a given relationship—in this case the law of demand—in a much simpler way than we could if we were forced to rely upon verbal and tabular presentation. A single curve on a graph, if understood, is simpler to state *and to manipulate* than tables and lengthy verbal presentations would be. Graphs are invaluable tools in economic analysis, as has been previously indicated. They permit clear expression and handling of ofttimes complex relationships.

□   Individual and Market Demand

Until now we have been dealing in terms of just one consumer. The assumption of competition makes us consider a situation in which a large number of buyers are in the market. The transition from an *individual* to a *market* demand schedule can be accomplished easily by the process of summing the quantities demanded by each consumer at the various possible prices. If there were just three buyers in the market, as is shown in Table 4-2, it would be an easy chore to determine the total quan-

---

[3]Putting price on the vertical axis and quantity demanded on the horizontal axis is a matter of convention; we do it for the same reason that a red traffic light means "Stop" and a green one means "Go."

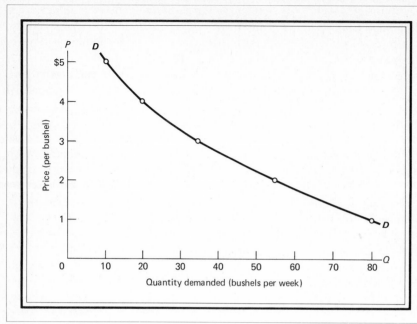

FIGURE 4-1 AN INDIVIDUAL BUYER'S DEMAND CURVE FOR CORN

An individual's demand schedule graphs as a downsloping curve such as *DD*, because price and quantity demanded are inversely related. Specifically, the law of demand generalizes that consumers will buy more of a product as its price declines.

tities demanded at each price. Figure 4-2 shows the same summing procedure graphically, using only the $3 price to illustrate the adding-up process. Note that we are simply summing up the three individual demand curves *horizontally* to derive the total demand curve.

Competition, of course, entails many more than three buyers of a product. So—to avoid a lengthy addition process—let us suppose there are 200 buyers of corn in the market, each of whom chooses to buy the same amount at each

of the various prices as our original consumer does. Thus, we can determine market demand by multiplying the quantity-demanded data of Table 4-1 by 200, as in Table 4-3. Curve D_1 in Figure 4-3 indicates this market demand curve for the 200 buyers.

☐ **Determinants of Demand**

When the economist constructs a demand curve such as D_1 in Figure 4-3, he makes the assumption that price is the most important

Table 4-2 MARKET DEMAND FOR CORN, THREE BUYERS (*hypothetical data*)

Price per bushel	Quantity demanded, first buyer		Quantity demanded, second buyer		Quantity demanded, third buyer		Total quantity demanded per week
$5	10	+	12	+	8	=	30
4	20	+	23	+	17	=	60
3	35	+	39	+	26	=	100
2	55	+	60	+	39	=	154
1	80	+	87	+	54	=	221

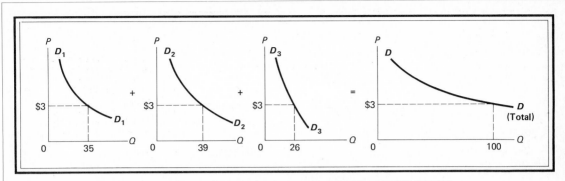

FIGURE 4-2   THE MARKET DEMAND CURVE IS THE SUM OF THE INDIVIDUAL DEMAND CURVES

Graphically the market demand curve (*D* total) is found by summing horizontally the individual demand curves (D_1, D_2, and D_3) of all consumers in the market.

determinant of the amount of any product purchased. But he is aware that factors other than price can and do affect purchases. Thus, in locating a given demand curve such as D_1, the economist must also assume that "other things are equal"; that is, the *nonprice determinants* of the amount demanded are conveniently assumed to be constant. When these nonprice determinants of demand do in fact change, the location of the demand curve will

shift to some new position to the right or left of D_1.

What are the major nonprice determinants of market demand? The basic ones are (1) the tastes or preferences of consumers, (2) the number of consumers in the market, (3) the money incomes of consumers, (4) the prices of related goods, and (5) consumer expectations with respect to future prices and incomes.

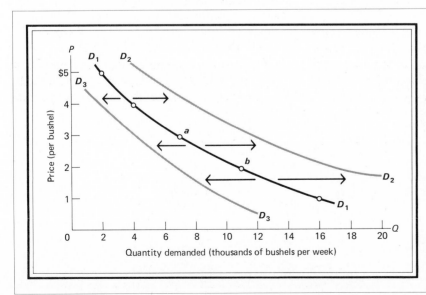

FIGURE 4-3   CHANGES IN THE DEMAND FOR CORN

A change in one or more of the determinants of demand—consumer tastes, the number of buyers in the market, money incomes, the prices of other goods, or consumer expectations—will cause a change in demand. An increase in demand shifts the demand curve to the right, as from D_1D_1 to D_2D_2. A decrease in demand shifts the demand curve to the left, as from D_1D_1 to D_3D_3. A change in the quantity demanded involves a movement, caused by a change in the price of the product under consideration, from one point to another—as from *a* to *b*—on a fixed demand curve.

☐ **Changes in Demand**

What happens if one or more of the determinants of demand should change? We know the answer: A change in one or more of the determinants will change the demand schedule data in Table 4-3 and therefore the location of the demand curve in Figure 4-3. Such a change in the demand schedule data, or, graphically, a shift in the location of the demand curve, is designated as a *change in demand*.

More specifically, if consumers become willing and able to buy more of this particular good at each possible price than is reflected in column 4 of Table 4-3, an *increase in demand* has occurred. In Figure 4-3, this increase in demand is reflected in a shift of the demand curve to the *right,* for example, from D_1 to D_2. Conversely, a *decrease in demand* occurs when, because of a change in one or more of the determinants, consumers buy less of the product at each possible price than is indicated in column 4 of Table 4-3. Graphically, a decrease in demand entails a shift of the demand curve to the *left,* for example, from D_1 to D_3 in Figure 4-3.

Let us now examine the effect upon demand of changes in each of the aforementioned nonprice determinants.

1   Tastes   A change in consumer tastes favorable to this product—possibly prompted by advertising or fashion changes—will mean that more will be demanded at each price; that is, demand will increase. An unfavorable change in consumer preferences will cause demand to decrease, shifting the curve to the left.

2   Number of Buyers   It is equally obvious that an increase in the number of consumers in a market—brought about perhaps by improvements in transportation or by population growth—will constitute an increase in demand. Fewer consumers will be reflected by a decrease in demand.

3   Income   The impact of changes in money income upon demand is a bit more complex. For most commodities, a rise in income will cause an increase in demand. Consumers typically buy more shoes, steaks, stereos, and Scotch as their incomes increase. Conversely, the demand for such products will decline in response to a fall in incomes. Commodities whose demand varies *directly* with money income are called *superior,* or *normal,* goods.

Although most products are normal goods, there are a few exceptions. Examples: As incomes increase beyond some point, the amounts of bread or potatoes or cabbages purchased at each price may diminish because the higher incomes now allow consumers to buy more high-protein foods, such as dairy products and meat. Similarly, rising incomes may cause the demands for hamburger and oleomargarine to decline as wealthier consumers switch to T-bones and butter. Goods whose

Table 4-3   MARKET DEMAND FOR CORN, 200 BUYERS (*hypothetical data*)

(1) Price per bushel	(2) Quantity demanded per week, single buyer		(3) Number of buyers in the market		(4) Total quantity demanded per week
$5	10	×	200	=	2,000
4	20	×	200	=	4,000
3	35	×	200	=	7,000
2	55	×	200	=	11,000
1	80	×	200	=	16,000

demand varies *inversely* with a change in money income are called *inferior* or "poor man's" goods.

4   Prices of Related Goods   Whether a given change in the price of a related good will increase or decrease the demand for the product under consideration will depend upon whether the related good is a substitute for, or a complement to, it. For example, butter and oleomargarine are *substitute,* or competing, goods. When the price of butter rises, consumers will purchase a smaller amount of butter, and this will cause the demand for oleomargarine to increase. Conversely, as the price of butter falls, consumers will buy larger quantities of butter, causing the demand for oleomargarine to decrease. To generalize: When two products are substitutes, the price of one good and the demand for the other are *directly* related. So it is with Schlitz and Budweiser, sugar and saccharin, Chevrolets and Fords, tea and coffee, ice cream and apple pie, and so forth.

But other pairs of products are *complementary* goods; they "go together." If the price of gasoline falls and, as a result, you drive your car more, this extra driving will increase your demand for motor oil. Conversely, an increase in the price of gasoline will diminish the demand for motor oil. Thus gas and oil are jointly demanded; they are complements. And so it is with ham and eggs, Scotch and soda, phonographs and records, golf clubs and golf balls, cameras and rolls of film, and so forth. When two commodities are complements, the price of one good and the demand for the other are *inversely* related.

Many pairs of goods, of course, are not related at all—they are *independent* goods. For such pairs of commodities as, for example, butter and golf balls, potatoes and automobiles, bananas and wristwatches, we should expect that a change in the price of one would have little or no impact upon the demand for the other.

5   Expectations   Consumer expectations of higher future prices may prompt them to buy now in order to "beat" the anticipated price rises, and, similarly, the expectation of rising incomes may induce consumers to be less tightfisted in their current spending. Conversely, expectations of falling prices and income will tend to decrease the current demand for products.

We might summarize by saying that an increase in the demand for product X—the decision of consumers to buy more of X at each possible price—can be caused by (1) a favorable change in consumer tastes, (2) an increase in the number of buyers in the market, (3) a rise (fall) in income if X is a normal (inferior) good, (4) an increase (decrease) in the price of related good Y if Y is a substitute for (complement to) X, and (5) expectations of future increases in prices and incomes. Conversely, a decrease in the demand for X can be associated with (1) an unfavorable change in tastes, (2) a decrease in the number of buyers in the market, (3) a rise (fall) in income if X is an inferior (normal) good, (4) an increase (decrease) in the price of related good Y if Y is complementary to (a substitute for) X, and (5) expectations of future price and income declines.

□   **Changes in Quantity Demanded**

A "change in demand" must not be confused with a "change in the quantity demanded." We have noted that a *change in demand* refers to a shift in the entire demand curve either to the right (an increase in demand) or to the left (a decrease in demand). The consumer's state of mind concerning his purchases of this product has been altered. The cause: a change in one or more of the determinants of demand. As used by economists, the term "demand" refers to a schedule or curve; therefore, a "change in demand" must mean that the entire schedule has changed or that the curve has shifted its position.

In contrast, a *change in the quantity demanded* designates the movement from one point to another point—from one price-quantity combination to another—on a fixed demand curve. The cause of a change in the quantity demanded is a change in the price of the product under consideration. In Table 4-3 a decline in the price asked by suppliers of corn from $5 to $4 will increase the quantity of corn demanded from 2000 to 4000 bushels.

Figure 4-3 is helpful in making the distinction between a change in demand and a change in the quantity demanded. The shift of the demand curve D_1 to either D_2 or D_3 entails changes in demand. But the movement from point a to point b on curve D_1 is a change in the quantity demanded.

The reader should decide whether a change in demand or a change in the quantity demanded is involved in each of the following illustrations:

1 Consumer incomes rise, with the result that more jewelry is purchased.

2 A barber raises the price of haircuts and experiences a decline in volume of business.

3 The price of Fords goes up, and, as a consequence, the sales of Chevrolets increase.

■
SUPPLY

Supply may be defined as *a schedule which shows the various amounts of a product which a producer is willing and able to produce and make available for sale in the market at each specific price in a set of possible prices during some specified time period.*[4] This schedule portrays a series of alternative possibilities, such as those shown in Table 4-4 for a single producer. Let us suppose, in this case, that our

[4] In talking of the resource market, our definition of supply reads: a schedule which shows the various amounts of a resource which its owners are willing to supply in the market at each possible price in a series of prices during some specified time.

Table 4-4 AN INDIVIDUAL PRODUCER'S SUPPLY OF CORN (*hypothetical data*)

Price per bushel	Quantity supplied per week
$5	60
4	50
3	35
2	20
1	5

producer is a farmer producing corn, the demand for which we have just considered. Our definition of supply indicates that supply is usually viewed from the vantage point of price. That is, we read supply as showing the amounts producers will offer at various possible prices. It is more useful and quite correct in some instances to view supply from the reference point of quantity. Instead of asking what quantities will be offered at various prices, we can ask what prices will be required to induce producers to offer various quantities of a good.

□   **Law of Supply**

It will be immediately noted that Table 4-4 shows a *direct* relationship between price and quantity supplied. As price rises, the corresponding quantity supplied rises; as price falls, the quantity supplied also falls. This particular relationship is called the *law of supply.* It simply tells us that producers are willing to produce and offer for sale more of their product at a high price than they are at a low price. Why? This again is basically a commonsense matter.

Price, we recall, is a deterrent from the consumer's standpoint. The obstacle of a high price means that the consumer, being on the paying end of this price, will buy a relatively small amount of the product; the lower the price obstacle, the more the consumer will buy. The supplier, on the other hand, is on the receiving end of the product's price. To him, price is an inducement or incentive to produce and sell a product. The higher the price of the product, the greater the incentive to produce and offer it in the market.

You will also remember that the law of demand was explainable on the basis of product substitution. When the price of product X rises, consumers tend to substitute other goods for it, therefore buying less of X. When the price of X declines, consumers buy more of X, substituting it for other products. The direct relationship between price and quantity supplied can also be explained on the basis of substitutability. In many instances the resources and productive techniques used by a supplier are readily adaptable to a variety of products. A farmer's land and capital, for example, may be of about equal efficiency in producing corn, wheat, soy beans, milo, and so forth. As the market price of one of these products—say, corn—rises, the farmer will shift his resources from other commodities to corn because it pays him to produce more corn when the price goes up.

A simple example may help at this point. Suppose a farmer has just 2 acres of land. He finds from experience that these 2 acres are equally prolific in the production of corn and wheat. Specifically, he has found that each acre is capable of producing *either* 20 bushels of wheat *or* 20 bushels of corn. Suppose, too, that no matter how our farmer decides to apportion his 2 acres between wheat and corn, his total costs of production are always the same—say $25. To begin, let us say that the price of corn is $1 per bushel and that of wheat is $2 per bushel. The farmer will obviously plant all his land to wheat, producing 40 bushels. Total revenue will be $80 (= 40 × $2) and profits will be $55 (= $80 − $25). The output of corn, the crop in which we are particularly interested, will be zero. To plant any corn at a price of $1 per bushel will necessarily result in profits of less than $55. But what if the market price of corn rises to $3, while the price of wheat remains at $2? It would now be profitable for the farmer to shift all his resources to

corn, that is, to substitute corn for wheat production. By doing so, his total revenue will be increased to $120 (= 40 × $3) and his profits to $95 (= $120 − $25). Although this example is greatly simplified, the basic point is clear: It is profitable to substitute the production of relatively high-priced goods for the production of relatively low-priced ones by shifting resources accordingly. Given the $2 price of wheat, no corn will be produced when its price is $1 per bushel, but 40 bushels will be forthcoming when its price is $3. Product substitution explains this direct relationship between the price of corn and the quantity supplied.

In practice, this substitution may be more complex and time-consuming than our illustration implies: very different products whose production requires radically different methods and resources may be involved. The process may well necessitate the shifting of resources among different producers. The basic conclusion, however, still holds true.

□ **The Supply Curve**

As in the case of demand, it is convenient to present graphically the concept of supply. Our axes in Figure 4-4 are the same as those in Figure 4-3, except for the obvious change of "quantity demanded" to "quantity supplied." The graphing procedure is the same as that previously explained, but of course the quantity data and relationship involved are different. The market supply data graphed in Figure 4-4 as S_1 are shown in Table 4-5, which assumes there are 200 suppliers in the market having the same supply schedules as the producer previously portrayed in Table 4-4.

□ **Determinants of Supply**

In constructing a supply curve, the economist assumes that price is the most significant determinant of the quantity supplied of any product. But, as with the demand curve, the supply curve is anchored on the "other things

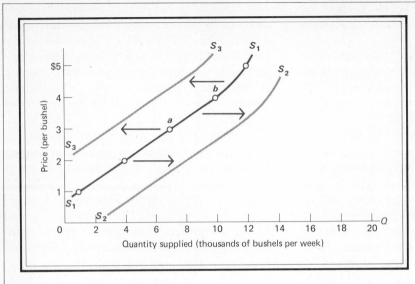

FIGURE 4-4 CHANGES IN THE SUPPLY OF CORN

A change in one or more of the determinants of supply—productive techniques, resource prices, the prices of other goods, price expectations, or the number of sellers in the market—will cause a change in supply. An increase in supply shifts the supply curve to the right, as from S_1S_1 to S_2S_2. A decrease in supply is shown graphically as a movement of the curve to the left, as from S_1S_1 to S_3S_3. A change in the quantity supplied involves a movement caused by a change in the price of the product under consideration, from one point to another—as from a to b—on a fixed supply curve.

are equal" assumption. That is, the supply curve is drawn on the supposition that certain nonprice determinants of the amount supplied are given and do not change. If any of these nonprice determinants of supply do in fact change, the location of the supply curve will be altered.

The basic nonprice determinants of supply are (1) the technique of production, (2) resource prices, (3) prices of other goods, (4) price expectations, (5) the number of sellers in the market, and (6) taxes and subsidies. To repeat: A change in any one or more of these determinants will cause the supply curve for a product to shift to either the right or the left. A shift to the *right,* from S_1 to S_2 in Figure 4-4, designates an *increase in supply:* producers are now offering more of the product at each possible price. A shift to the *left,* S_1 to S_3 in Figure 4-4, indicates a *decrease in supply:* suppliers are offering less at each price.

□   **Changes in Supply**

Let us consider the effect of changes in each of these determinants upon supply.

1 and **2** The first two determinants of supply—technology and resource prices—are

Table 4-5   MARKET SUPPLY OF CORN, 200 PRODUCERS (*hypothetical data*)

(1) Price per bushel	(2) Quantity supplied per week, single producer		(3) Number of sellers in the market		(4) Total quantity supplied per week
$5	60	×	200	=	12,000
4	50	×	200	=	10,000
3	35	×	200	=	7,000
2	20	×	200	=	4,000
1	5	×	200	=	1,000

the two components of production costs. And the relationship between production costs and supply is an intimate one. (In Chapter 26, in fact, we shall find that cost and supply data are synonymous.) For our present purposes, it is sufficient to note that anything which serves to lower production costs, that is, a technological improvement or a decline in resource prices, will increase supply. With lower costs, businessmen will find it profitable to offer a larger amount of the product at each possible price. An increase in the price of resources (a deterioration of technology being unlikely) will cause a decrease in supply; that is, the supply curve will shift to the left.

3 Changes in the prices of other goods can also shift the supply curve for a product. A decline in the price of wheat may cause a farmer to produce and offer more corn at each possible price. Conversely, a rise in the price of wheat may make farmers less willing to produce and offer corn in the market.

4 Expectations concerning the future price of a product can also affect a producer's current willingness to supply that product. It is difficult, however, to generalize concerning the way the expectation of, say, higher prices will affect the present supply curve of a product. Farmers might withhold some of their current corn harvest from the market, anticipating a higher corn price in the future. This will cause a decrease in the current supply of corn. On the other hand, in many types of manufacturing, expected price increases may induce firms to expand production immediately, causing supply to increase.

5 Given the scale of operations of each firm, the larger the number of suppliers, the greater will be market supply. As more firms enter an industry, the supply curve will shift to the right. The smaller the number of firms in an industry, the less the market supply will be. This means that as firms leave an industry, the supply curve will shift to the left.

6 Finally, we will discover later (Chapters

6 and 23) that certain taxes, such as sales taxes, add to production costs and therefore reduce supply. Conversely, subsidies lower costs and increase supply.

□ **Changes in Quantity Supplied**

The distinction between a "change in supply" and a "change in the quantity supplied" parallels that between a change in demand and a change in the quantity demanded. A *change in supply* is involved when the entire supply curve shifts. An increase in supply shifts the curve to the right; a decrease in supply shifts it to the left. The cause of a change in supply is a change in one or more of the determinants of supply. The term "supply" is used by economists to refer to a schedule or curve. A "change in supply" therefore must mean that the entire schedule has changed or that the curve has shifted.

A *change in the quantity supplied,* on the other hand, refers to the movement from one point to another point on a stable supply curve. The cause of such a movement is a change in the price of the specific product under consideration. In Table 4-5 a decline in the price of corn from $5 to $4 decreases the quantity of corn supplied from 12,000 to 10,000 bushels.

Shifting the supply curve from S_1 to S_2 or S_3 in Figure 4-4 obviously entails changes in supply. The movement from point *a* to point *b* on S_1, however, is merely a change in the quantity supplied.

The reader should determine which of the following involves a change in supply and which entails a change in the quantity supplied:

1 Because production costs decline, producers sell more automobiles.

2 The price of wheat declines, causing the number of bushels of corn sold per month to increase.

3 Fewer oranges are offered for sale because their price has decreased in retail markets.

SUPPLY AND DEMAND: MARKET EQUILIBRIUM

We may now bring the concepts of supply and demand together to see how the interaction of the buying decisions of households and the selling decisions of producers will determine the price of a product and the quantity which is actually bought and sold in the market. In Table 4-6, columns 1 and 2 reproduce the market supply schedule for corn (from Table 4-5), and columns 2 and 3, the market demand schedule for corn (from Table 4-3). Note that in column 2 we are using a common set of prices. We assume competition—the presence of a large number of buyers and sellers.

Now the question to be faced is this: Of the five[5] possible prices at which corn might sell in this market, which will actually prevail as the market price for corn? Let us derive our answer through the simple process of trial and error. For no particular reason, we shall start with an examination of $5. Could this be the prevailing market price for corn? The answer

[5] Of course, there are many possible prices; our example shows only five of them.

Table 4-6 MARKET SUPPLY AND DEMAND FOR CORN (*hypothetical data*)

(1) Total quantity supplied per week	(2) Price per bushel	(3) Total quantity demanded per week	(4) Surplus (+) or shortage (−) (arrows indicate effect on price)
12,000	$5	2,000	+10,000↓
10,000	4	4,000	+ 6,000↓
7,000	3	7,000	0
4,000	2	11,000	− 7,000↑
1,000	1	16,000	−15,000↑

is "No," for the simple reason that producers are willing to produce and supply to the market some 12,000 bushels of corn at this price while buyers, on the other hand, are willing to take only 2000 bushels off the market at this price. In other words, the relatively high price of $5 encourages farmers to produce a great deal of corn, but that same high price discourages consumers from taking the product off the market. Other products appear as "better buys" when corn is high-priced. The result in this case is a 10,000-bushel *surplus* of corn in the market. This surplus, shown in column 4, is the excess of quantity supplied over quantity demanded at the price of $5. Practically put, corn farmers would find themselves with unwanted inventories of output.

Could a price of $5—even if it existed temporarily in the corn market—persist over a period of time? Certainly not. The very large surplus of corn would prompt competing sellers to bid down the price in order to encourage buyers to take this surplus off their hands. Suppose price gravitates down to $4. Now the situation has changed considerably. The lower price has encouraged buyers to take more of this product off the market and, at the same time, has induced farmers to use a smaller amount of resources in producing corn. The surplus, as a result, has diminished to 6000 bushels. However, a surplus still exists and competition among sellers will once again bid down the price of corn. We can conclude, then, that prices of $5 and $4 will be unstable because they are "too high." The market price for corn must be something less than $4.

To avoid letting the cat out of the bag before we fully appreciate how supply and demand determine product price, let us now jump to the other end of our price column and examine $1 as the possible market price for corn. It is evident that at this price, quantity demanded is in excess of quantity supplied by 15,000 units. This relatively low price discourages farmers from devoting their resources to corn production; the same low price encourages consumers to attempt to buy more corn than would otherwise be the case. Corn is a "good buy" when its price is relatively low. In short, there is a 15,000-bushel *shortage* of corn. Can this price of $1 persist as the market price? No. Competition among buyers will bid up the price to something greater than $1. In other words, at a price of $1, many consumers who are willing and able to buy at this price will obviously be left out in the cold. Many potential consumers, in order to ensure that they will not have to do without, will express a willingness to pay a price in excess of $1 to ensure getting some of the available corn. Suppose this competitive bidding up of price by buyers boosts the price of corn to $2. This higher price obviously has reduced, but not eliminated, the shortage of corn. For $2, farmers are willing to devote more resources to corn production, and some buyers who were willing to pay $1 for a bushel of corn will choose not to buy corn at a price of $2, deciding to use their incomes to buy other products or maybe to save more of their incomes. But a shortage of 7000 bushels still exists at a price of $2. We can conclude that competitive bidding among buyers will push market price to some figure greater than $2.

By trial and error we have eliminated every price but $3. So let us now examine it. At a price of $3, *and only at this price,* the quantity which farmers are willing to produce and supply in the market is identical with the amount consumers are willing to buy. As a result, there is neither a shortage nor a surplus of corn at this price. We have already seen that a surplus causes price to decline and a shortage causes price to rise. With neither a shortage nor a surplus at $3, there is no reason for the actual price of corn to move away from this price. The economist calls this price the *equilibrium price,* equilibrium meaning "in balance" or "at rest." At $3, quantity supplied and quantity demanded are in balance; hence $3 is the only stable price of corn under the supply and demand conditions shown in Table 4-6. Or, stated differently, the price of corn will be established where the supply decisions of producers and the demand decisions of buyers are mutually consistent. Such decisions are consistent with one another only at a price of

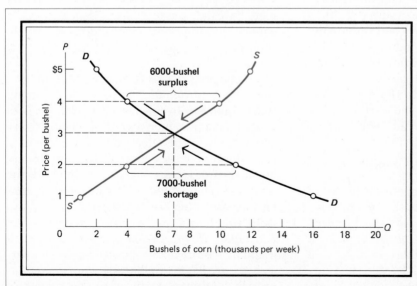

FIGURE 4-5 THE EQUILIBRIUM PRICE AND QUANTITY FOR CORN AS DETERMINED BY MARKET DEMAND AND SUPPLY

The intersection of the down-sloping demand curve *D* and the upsloping supply curve *S* indicates the equilibrium price and quantity, $3 and 7000 bushels in this instance. The shortages of corn which would exist at below equilibrium prices, for example, 7000 bushels at $2, drive price up, and in so doing, increase the quantity supplied and reduce the quantity demanded until equilibrium is achieved. The surpluses which above-equilibrium prices would entail, for example 6000 bushels at $4, push price down and thereby increase the quantity demanded and reduce the quantity supplied until equilibrium is achieved.

$3. At any higher price, suppliers want to sell more than consumers want to buy; at any lower price, consumers want to buy more than producers are willing to offer for sale. Discrepancies between supply and demand intentions of sellers and buyers, respectively, will prompt price changes which subsequently will bring these two sets of plans into accord with one another.

A graphic analysis of supply and demand should yield the same conclusions. Figure 4-5 puts the market supply and market demand curves for corn on the same graph, the horizontal axis now reflecting both quantity demanded and quantity supplied. A close examination of this diagram clearly indicates that at any price above the equilibrium price of $3, quantity supplied will exceed quantity demanded. This surplus will cause a competitive bidding down of price by sellers eager to relieve themselves of their surplus. The falling price will cause less corn to be offered and will simultaneously encourage consumers to buy more. Any price below the equilibrium price will entail a shortage; that is, quantity demanded will exceed quantity supplied. Competitive bidding by buyers will push the price up toward the equilibrium level. And this rising price will simultaneously bring forth a greater supply from producers and ration buyers out of the market, thereby causing the shortage to vanish. Graphically, the intersection of the supply curve and the demand curve for the product will indicate the equilibrium point. In this case, as we know, equilibrium price and quantity are $3 and 7000 bushels.

☐   Rationing Function of Prices

The ability of the competitive forces of supply and demand to establish a price where supply and demand decisions are synchronized is sometimes called the *rationing function* of prices. In this case, the equilibrium price of $3 clears the market, leaving no burdensome surplus for the sellers and no inconvenient short-

age for the potential buyers. The composite of freely made individual buying and selling decisions sets this price which clears the market. In effect, the market mechanism of supply and demand says this: Any buyer who is willing and able to pay $3 for a bushel of corn will be able to acquire one; those who are not, will not. Similarly, any seller who is willing and able to produce bushels of corn and offer them for sale at a price of $3 will be able to do so successfully; those who are not, will not. As we will see shortly, were it not that competitive prices automatically bring supply and demand decisions into consistency with one another, some type of administrative control by government would be necessary to avoid or control the shortages or surpluses which might otherwise occur.

☐   Changes in Supply and Demand

It was noted earlier that demand might change because of fluctuations in consumer tastes or incomes, changes in consumer expectations, or variations in the prices of related goods. On the other hand, supply might vary in response to changes in technology or in resource prices. Our analysis would be incomplete if we did not stop to consider the effect of changes in supply and demand upon equilibrium price.

Changing Demand   Let us first analyze the effects of a change in demand, assuming that supply is conveniently constant. Suppose now that demand increases, as shown in Figure 4-6*a*. What is the effect upon price? Noting that the new intersection of the supply and demand curves is at a higher point on both the price and quantity axes, we can conclude that an increase in demand, other things (supply) being equal, will have a *price-increasing effect* and a *quantity-increasing effect*. (The value of graphic analysis now begins to become apparent; we need not fumble with columns of figures in determining the effect on price and

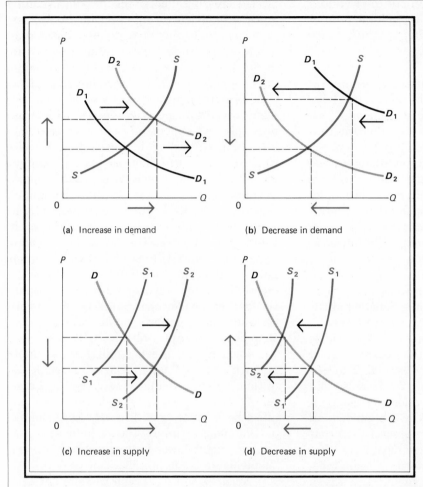

FIGURE 4-6 CHANGES IN DEMAND AND SUPPLY AND THE EFFECTS ON PRICE AND QUANTITY

The increase in demand of **(a)** and the decrease in demand of **(b)** indicate a direct relationship between a change in demand and the resulting changes in equilibrium price and quantity. The increase in supply of **(c)** and the decrease in supply of **(d)** show an inverse relationship between a change in supply and the resulting change in equilibrium price, but a direct relationship between a change in supply and the accompanying change in equilibrium quantity.

(a) Increase in demand

(b) Decrease in demand

(c) Increase in supply

(d) Decrease in supply

quantity but only compare the new with the old point of intersection on the graph.) A decrease in demand, as illustrated in Figure 4-6*b,* reveals *price-decreasing* and *quantity-decreasing effects.* Price falls, and quantity also declines. *In brief, we find a direct relationship between a change in demand and the resulting changes in both equilibrium price and quantity.*

Changing Supply Let us reverse the procedure and analyze the effect of a change in supply on price, assuming that demand is con-

stant. If supply increases, as in Figure 4-6*c,* the new intersection of supply and demand is obviously at a lower price; equilibrium price falls. Equilibrium quantity, however, increases. If supply decreases, on the other hand, this will tend to increase product price. Figure 4-6*d* illustrates this situation. Here, price increases but quantity declines. In short, an increase in supply has a *price-decreasing* and a *quantity-increasing effect.* A decrease in supply has a *price-increasing* and a *quantity-decreasing effect. There is an inverse relationship between a change in supply and the resulting* *change in equilibrium price, but the relationship between a change in supply and the resulting change in equilibrium quantity is direct.*

Complex Cases   Obviously, a host of more complex cases might arise, involving changes in both supply and demand. Two cases are possible when it is supposed that supply and demand change in *opposite directions.* Assume first that supply increases and demand decreases. What effect does this have upon equilibrium price? This example couples two price-decreasing effects, and the net result will be a price fall greater than that which would result from either change taken in isolation. How about equilibrium quantity? Here the effects of the changes in supply and demand are opposed: The increase in supply tends to increase equilibrium quantity, but the decrease in demand tends to reduce the equilibrium quantity. The direction of the change in quantity depends upon the relative sizes of the changes in supply and demand. The second possibility is for supply to decrease and demand to increase. Two price-increasing effects are involved here. We can predict an increase in equilibrium price greater than that caused by either change taken separately. The effect upon equilibrium quantity is again indeterminate, depending upon the relative size of the changes in supply and demand. If the decrease in supply is relatively larger than the increase in demand, the equilibrium quantity will be less than it is initially. But if the decrease in supply is relatively smaller than the increase in demand, the equilibrium quantity will increase as a result of these changes. The reader should trace through these two cases graphically to verify the conclusions we have outlined.

What if supply and demand change in the *same direction?* Suppose first that supply and demand both increase. What is the effect upon equilibrium price? It depends. Here we must compare two conflicting effects on price—the price-decreasing effect of the increase in supply and the price-increasing effect of the increase in demand. If the increase in supply is of greater magnitude than the increase in demand, the net effect will be for equilibrium price to decrease. If the opposite holds true, equilibrium price will increase. The effect upon equilibrium quantity is certain: Increases in supply and in demand both have quantity-increasing effects. This means that equilibrium quantity will increase by an amount greater than that which either change would have entailed in isolation. In the second place, a decrease in both supply and demand can be subjected to similar analysis. If the decrease in supply is greater than the decrease in demand, equilibrium price will rise. If the reverse holds true, equilibrium price will fall. Because decreases in supply and demand both have quantity-decreasing effects, it can be predicted with certainty that equilibrium quantity will be less than that which prevailed initially.

Incidentally, the possibility that supply and demand will both change in a given period of time is not particularly unlikely. As a matter of fact, a single event might simultaneously affect both supply and demand. For example, a technological improvement in cheese production might lower both the supply of, and the demand for, fluid milk.

Needless to say, special cases might arise where a decrease in demand and a decrease in supply, on the one hand, and an increase in demand and an increase in supply, on the other, cancel out. In both these cases, the net effect upon equilibrium price will be zero; price will not change. The reader should again work out these more complex cases in terms of supply and demand curves to verify all these results.

□   **The Resource Market**

What about the shape of the supply and demand curves in the resource market? As in the product market, resource supply curves are typically upsloping, and resource demand curves are typically downsloping. Why?

Resource supply curves generally slope upward, that is, they reflect a *direct* relationship between resource price and quantity supplied, because it is in the interest of resource owners themselves to supply more of a particular resource at a high price than at a low price. High income payments in a particular occupation or industry encourage households to supply more of their human and property resources. Low income payments discourage resource owners from supplying resources in this particular occupation or industry and, as a matter of fact, encourage them to supply their resources elsewhere.

On the demand side, businesses tend to buy less of a given resource as its price rises, and they tend to substitute other relatively low-priced resources for it. Entrepreneurs will find it profitable to substitute low- for high-priced resources. More of a particular resource will be demanded at a low price than at a high price. The result? A downsloping demand curve for the various resources.

In short, just as the supply decisions of businesses and the demand decisions of consumers determine prices in the product market, so the supply decisions of households and demand decisions of businesses set prices in the resource market.

☐   **"Other Things Equal" Revisited**

Recall from Chapter 1 that as a substitute for their inability to conduct controlled experiments, economists invoke the "other things being equal" assumption in their analyses. We have seen in the present chapter that a number of forces bear upon both supply and demand. Hence, in locating specific supply and demand curves, such as D_1 and S in Figure 4-6a, the economist is isolating the impact of what he judges to be the most important determinant of the amounts supplied and demanded—that is, product price. In thus representing the laws of demand and supply by downsloping and upsloping curves respectively, the economist assumes that all the nonprice determinants of demand (incomes, tastes, and so forth) and supply (resource prices, technology, and other factors) are constant or unchanging. That is, price and quantity demanded are inversely related, *other things being equal.* And price and quantity supplied are directly related, *other things being equal.*

By failing to remember that the "other things equal" assumption is requisite to the laws of demand and supply, one can encounter confusing situations which *seem* to be in conflict with these laws. For example: Suppose General Motors sells 200,000 Vegas in 1977 at an average price of $3500; 300,000 at an average price of $3800 in 1978; and 400,000 in 1979 at an average price of $4100. Price and the number purchased vary *directly,* and these real-world data seem to be at odds with the law of demand. But is there really a conflict here? The answer, of course, is "No." These data do *not* refute the law of demand. The catch is that the law of demand's "other things equal" assumption has been violated with the passage of time. Specifically, because of, for example, growing incomes, population growth, and rising gasoline prices which increase the attractiveness of compact cars, the demand curve for Vegas has simply increased over the years— shifted to the right as from D_1 to D_2 in Figure 4-6a—causing price to rise and, simultaneously, a larger quantity to be purchased.

Conversely, consider Figure 4-6d. Comparing the original S_1D and the new S_2D equilibrium positions, we note that *less* of the product is being sold or supplied at a higher price; that is, price and quantity supplied seem to be *inversely* related, rather than *directly* related as the law of supply indicates. The catch again is that the "other things equal" assumption underlying the upsloping supply curve has been violated. Perhaps production costs have gone up or a special tax has been levied on this product, shifting the supply curve from S_1 to S_2. These examples clarify the importance of our earlier distinction between a "change in the quantity demanded (or supplied)" and a "change in demand (supply)."

■─────────────────────────────

A POWERFUL TOOL

It should be stressed that the competitive market, or "supply and demand," model is an extremely powerful and versatile tool for economic understanding. Anticipating a number of topics which will be considered in more detail in later chapters, let us briefly note (1) the wide applicability of the model, (2) some implications of governmental interference with the competitive market, and (3) some novel applications of the model to current problems.

□   Applicability

We have seen in the present chapter that the supply and demand model applies to both product and resource markets. But our treatment of resource markets has been most general. Later we will discover how the model can be applied in modified forms to explain wage rates, rents, and interest rates (see Figures 31-3, 32-1, and 32-2 and the accompanying discussions). The model is also very helpful in explaining exchange rates among foreign currencies (Figure 43-4) and in predicting the effects of sales taxes (Figures 23-7 and 23-8). Similarly, the model is most instructive in delineating the economic implications of tariffs on imported products (Figure 42-1). It would not be difficult to cite additional examples.

□   Interference: Legal Prices

A thorough understanding of the market model is helpful in forecasting the effects of legal prices, that is, of governmentally established prices which are higher (price supports) or lower (price ceilings or controls) than equi-

librium prices. Consider, first, *price supports*. In the product market, price supports for certain agricultural products result in surpluses. Price supports—designed to subsidize farm incomes—rob the price mechanism of its rationing ability, making it necessary for government to buy and store surplus output (Figure 35-4 and accompanying discussion). In the labor market, the minimum wage creates surpluses of labor; that is, the minimum wage tends to cause unemployment (Figure 31-7 and discussion). Conversely, *price ceilings* upset the rationing function of prices in the opposite direction by causing product and resource shortages (see Chapter 18's discussion of wage-price controls). In this case, government must introduce some sort of bureaucratic mechanism to ration products and resources which are in short supply at the controlled (below-equilibrium) prices.

The tone of the above comments suggests that legal prices are undesirable. Actually, their desirability is a matter of debate. Proponents of price supports in agriculture, the minimum wage, and wage-price controls make forceful equity or income distribution arguments to justify the use of such legal prices. Perhaps the most telling criticism is that interference with the competitive market model to achieve equity objectives may be in conflict with the efficiency of the free market in bringing buyers and sellers together, that is, in assuring that the market is cleared. Let us look at a further example to underscore this point. Some economists have pointed out that the equity-efficiency tradeoff is dramatically evident in the case of rent controls as practiced in New York City since World War II. Controls were originally imposed to deal with the equity aspects of the wartime housing shortage, that is, to prevent landlords from "gouging" tenants. But as the general price level has increased since the war and rent controls have persisted, landlords have found it increasingly unprofitable to maintain their buildings and private construction has declined sharply.

This has contributed to blighted and decaying neighborhoods and, ironically, to an intensification of the housing shortage. In brief, free-market proponents contend that rent controls have been counterproductive; rent controls have intensified the housing shortage and, curiously, the persistence of the shortage has tended to "justify" and perpetuate the application of rent controls![6]

□ Novel Uses

Some economists advocate new applications of the market model to solve problems which we are currently trying—with varying degrees of success—to resolve through the public bureaucracy. Consider two illustrations. First, it is argued that the imposition of legal prohibitions or special taxes upon pollutors gives rise to endless legal wrangling and costly bureaucracies for enforcement. It would allegedly be more efficient (less costly) and more effective to establish a market for "pollution rights." The supply of these rights should be equal to the amount of pollutants that, say, a lake can recycle or absorb naturally. Demand will then determine the price of these rights. Potential pollutors will now be confronted with a direct monetary incentive *not* to pollute. Desirable side effects may also occur: the market price for pollution rights may stimulate incentives to develop more efficient (cheaper) means for waste disposal; the revenue from the sale of the rights may be used to

[6]Milton Friedman, *An Economist's Protest* (New Jersey: Thomas Horton and Company, 1972), pp. 157–158.

finance environmental improvements; conservationists may buy up and not use some of the rights, thereby contributing to an even cleaner environment; and so forth. (For further details consult Figure 36-2 and the accompanying discussion.)

Second example: Some economists hold that the use of "peak pricing" might effectively deal with temporary problems of congestion. (Congestion, by the way, is one form of pollution.) To illustrate, on certain days and at certain hours, airports become congested with the landings and takeoffs of unusually large numbers of aircraft. This congestion problem during peak traffic hours can be dealt with in several ways. One solution is to expand airport facilities (increase supply). But critics say this is an overly costly and therefore inefficient solution because the new facilities, not to mention a portion of existing facilities, will be underutilized during off-peak hours. Another option is queuing, that is, forcing planes to be stacked in a circling pattern until landing space becomes available. This imposes costs upon passengers in the form of delays in reaching their destinations and increased risk of accidents. The final solution—of particular interest to us—is to use peak pricing, that is, to increase landing fees during the peak hours and thereby create a monetary incentive for some airlines to shift their flights away from peak hours. In the short run, this shift will obviously decrease the demand for airport facilities during peak periods—the peaks will tend to be evened out—*and* airports will realize additional revenue to expand facilities as justified by the long-term growth of air travel.

Summary

1 Demand refers to a schedule which summarizes the willingness of buyers to purchase a given product during a specific time period at each of the various prices at which it might be sold. According to the law of demand, consumers will ordinarily buy more of a product at a low price than they will at a high price. Therefore, the relationship between price and quantity demanded is inverse and demand graphs as a downsloping curve.

2 Changes in one or more of the basic determinants of demand—consumer tastes, the number of buyers in the market, the money incomes of consumers, the prices of related goods, and consumer expectations—will cause the market demand curve to shift. A shift to the right is an increase in demand; a shift to the left, a decrease in demand. A change in demand is to be distinguished from a change in the quantity demanded, the latter involving the movement from one point to another point on a fixed demand curve because of a change in the price of the product under consideration.

3 Supply is a schedule showing the amounts of a product which producers would be willing to offer in the market during a given time period at each possible price at which the commodity might be sold. The law of supply says that producers will offer more of a product at a higher price than they will at a low price. As a result, the relationship between price and quantity supplied is a direct one, and the supply curve is upsloping.

4 A change in production techniques, resource prices, the prices of other goods, price expectations, or the number of sellers in the market will cause the supply curve of a product to shift. A shift to the right is an increase in supply; a shift to the left, a decrease in supply. In contrast, a change in the price of a given product will result in a change in the quantity supplied, that is, a movement from one point to another on a given supply curve.

5 Under competition, the interaction of market demand and market supply will adjust price to that point at which the quantity demanded and the quantity supplied are equal. This is the equilibrium price. The corresponding quantity is the equilibrium quantity.

6 The ability of market forces to synchronize selling and buying decisions so as to eliminate potential surpluses or shortages is sometimes termed the "rationing function" of prices.

7 A change in either demand or supply will cause equilibrium price and quantity to change. There is a direct relationship between a change in demand and the resulting changes in equilibrium price and quantity. Though the relationship between a change in supply and the resulting change in equilibrium price is inverse, the relationship between a change in supply and equilibrium quantity is direct.

8 The concepts of supply and demand are also applicable to the resource market.

Questions and Study Suggestions

1 Key terms and concepts to remember: demand schedule (curve); law of demand; normal (superior) good; inferior good; complementary goods; substitute (competing) goods; supply schedule (curve); law of supply; change in demand (supply) versus change in the quantity demanded (supplied); equilibrium price and quantity; rationing function of prices.

2 Explain the law of demand. Why does a demand curve slope downward? What are the determinants of demand? What happens to the demand curve when each of these determinants changes? Distinguish between a change in demand and a change in the quantity demanded, noting the cause(s) of each.

3 Critically evaluate: "In comparing the two equilibrium positions in Figure 4-6a, I note that a larger amount is actually purchased at a higher price. This obviously refutes the law of demand."

4   Explain the law of supply. Why does the supply curve slope upward? What are the determinants of supply? What happens to the supply curve when each of these determinants changes? Distinguish between a change in supply and a change in the quantity supplied, noting the cause(s) of each.

5   Explain the following news dispatch from Hull, England: "The fish market here slumped today to what local commentators called 'a disastrous level'—all because of a shortage of potatoes. The potatoes are one of the main ingredients in a dish that figures on almost every café menu—fish and chips."

6   Suppose the total demand for wheat and the total supply of wheat per month in the Kansas City grain market are as follows:

Thousands of bushels demanded	Price per bushel	Thousands of bushels supplied	Surplus (+) or shortage (−)
90	$4.40	70	_____
85	4.60	72	_____
80	4.80	73	_____
75	5.00	75	_____
70	5.20	77	_____
65	5.40	79	_____
60	5.60	81	_____
55	5.80	83	_____

a.   What will be the market or equilibrium price? What is the equilibrium quantity? Using the surplus-shortage column, explain why your answers are correct.

b.   Using the above data, graph the demand for wheat and the supply of wheat. Be sure to label the axes of your graph correctly. Label equilibrium price *"P"* and equilibrium quantity *"Q."*

c.   Why will $4.60 not be the equilibrium price in this market? Why not $5.60?

d.   Now suppose that the government establishes a ceiling price of, say, $4.80 for wheat. Explain carefully the effects of this ceiling price. Demonstrate your answer graphically. What might prompt government to establish a ceiling price?

e.   Assume now that the government establishes a supported price of, say, $5.40 for wheat. Explain carefully the effects of this supported price. Demonstrate your answer graphically. What might prompt the government to establish this price support?

f.   "Legally fixed prices strip the price mechanism of its rationing function." Explain this statement in terms of your answers to 6*d* and 6*e*. "Surpluses drive prices up; shortages drive them down." Do you agree?

7   What effect will each of the following have upon the demand for product B?
a.   Product B becomes more fashionable.
b.   The price of product C, a good substitute for B, goes down.
c.   Consumers anticipate declining prices and falling incomes.
d.   There is a rapid upsurge in population growth.

8   What effect will each of the following have upon the supply of product B?
a.   A technological advance in the methods of producing B.
b.   A decline in the number of firms in industry B.
c.   An increase in the prices of resources required in the production of B.
d.   The expectation that the equilibrium price of B will be lower in the future than it is currently.

e. A decline in the price of product A, a good whose production requires substantially the same techniques and resources as does the production of B.

9 Explain and illustrate graphically the effect of:

a. An increase in income upon the demand curve of an inferior good.

b. A drop in the price of product S upon the demand for substitute product T.

c. A decline in income upon the demand curve of a normal good.

d. An increase in the price of product J upon the demand for complementary good K.

10 "In the corn market, demand often exceeds supply and supply sometimes exceeds demand." "The price of corn rises and falls in response to changes in supply and demand." In which of these two statements are the terms "supply" and "demand" used correctly? Explain.

11 How will each of the following changes in demand and/or supply affect equilibrium price and equilibrium quantity in a competitive market; that is, do price and quantity *rise, fall,* or *remain unchanged,* or are the answers *indeterminate,* depending upon the magnitudes of the shifts in supply and demand? You should rely on a supply and demand diagram to verify answers.

a. Supply decreases and demand remains constant.

b. Demand decreases and supply remains constant.

c. Supply increases and demand is constant.

d. Demand increases and supply increases.

e. Demand increases and supply is constant.

f. Supply increases and demand decreases.

g. Demand increases and supply decreases.

h. Demand decreases and supply decreases.

12 "Prices are the automatic regulator that tends to keep production and consumption in line with each other." Explain.

13 Explain: "Even though parking meters yield little or no net revenue, they should nevertheless be retained because of the rationing function they perform."

14 Many states have usury laws which stipulate the maximum interest rate which lenders (commercial banks, savings and loan association, and so forth) can charge borrowers. Indicate in some detail what would happen in the loan market during those periods when the equilibrium interest rate exceeds the stipulated maximum? On the basis of your analysis, do you favor usury laws?

15 *Advanced analysis:* Assume that the demand for a commodity is represented by the equation $Q_d = 12 - 2P$ and supply by the equation $Q_s = 2P$, where Q_d and Q_s are quantity demanded and quantity supplied, respectively, and P is price. Using the equilibrium condition $Q_s = Q_d$, solve the equations to determine equilibrium price. Now determine equilibrium quantity. Graph the two equations to substantiate your answers.

Selected References

Boulding, Kenneth E.: *Economic Analysis: Microeconomics,* 4th ed. (New York: Harper & Row, Publishers, Incorporated, 1966), chaps. 8, 10, 11.

Brue, Stanley L., and Donald R. Wentworth: *Economic Scenes: Theory in Today's World* (Englewood Cliffs, N.J.: Prentice-Hall, Inc., 1976), chap. 4.

Henderson, Hubert: *Supply and Demand* (Chicago: The University of Chicago Press, 1958), chap. 2.

Last Word
The Demand for Basketball Games

Given an average ticket price of $4.50, what nonprice factors are most important in determining the number of tickets that will be demanded for professional basketball games?

It is important to be able to assess quantitatively the effect on team attendance of factors such as the quality of the team, the size of the team's home city, ticket prices, competition from alternative forms of entertainment, and the number of games played. From knowledge of the importance of these factors, one can predict the likely success of a team, and whether teams in certain areas are likely to be much more financially successful than teams in other areas . . .

(1) Population is a significant factor in team success. Each additional 1 million population in a team's home area is worth 58,000 additional spectators. At the average ticket price of $4.50, this translates into at least $250,000 in revenues, not including income from concessions.

(2) The playing success of the team is also important. Winning 60 percent of the games played is worth nearly 100,000 fans more than winning 40 percent.

(3) Competition from other sports is also a factor in attendance. For every professional sports team in the city, regardless of the sport, basketball attendance declines by 66,000.

(4) If every team in both leagues played one more home game during a season, the average increase in team attendance for the season would be 4,000; the actual attendance at the extra game might be higher, of course, but some of this attendance would be a switch from other games.

(5) All other things being equal (including the playing record of the teams), a team that has played in a city 10 years will draw 7,000 fewer fans during the season than a team playing its first year in a new city.

(6) We define a superstar as any player who has made a league all-star team five times or, in the case of players with only a few years of professional experience, one who is obviously a dominant player in the game—e.g., a Kareem Abdul-Jabbar or an Issel. Using this definition, having a superstar on the team is worth 25,000 attendance during the season. This figure, of course, is an average for all teams and for all 17 players in the two leagues classified as superstars by our criteria. Still using the $4.50 average ticket price, this means that about 17 professional basketball players produce about $100,000 a year in gross revenues for their teams beyond whatever contribution these talented athletes make to the won-lost record of the team.

Including the contribution a superstar makes to his team's winning percentage, the results suggest that basketball superstars are worth salaries exceeding $100,000 a year, as measured by the contribution they make to team revenues. Furthermore, a player such as Kareem Abdul-Jabbar is probably worth much more. If he is the difference between winning and losing in 20 percent of his team's games and if he is twice the fan attraction of the average of our 17 superstars, then, by himself, he accounts for nearly $500,000 a year in gate receipts. . . .

Statement of Dr. Roger G. Noll in *Professional Basketball,* Hearings before the Subcommittee on Antitrust and Monopoly of the Committee on the Judiciary, U.S. Senate, 92d Congress, 1st Session, Washington, 1971, pp. 343–345, abridged.

5

The Five Fundamental Questions and the Price System

We saw in Chapter 3 that the capitalist ideology makes clear the importance of freedom of enterprise and choice. Consumers are at liberty to buy what they choose; businesses, to produce and sell what they choose; and resource suppliers, to make their property and human resources available in whatever occupations they choose. Upon reflection, we might wonder why such an economy does not collapse in complete chaos. If consumers want bread, businesses choose to produce automobiles, and resource suppliers want to offer their services in manufacturing shoes, production would seem to be deadlocked because of the obvious inconsistency of these free choices.

Fortunately, two other features of capitalism—a system of markets and prices and the force of competition—provide the coordinating and organizing mechanisms which overcome the potential chaos posed by freedom of enterprise and choice. *The competitive price system is a mechanism both for communicating the decisions of consumers, producers, and resource suppliers to one another and for synchronizing those decisions toward consistent production objectives.*

Armed with an understanding of individual markets and prices gained from Chapter 4, we are now in a position to analyze the operation of the price system. More specifically, in this chapter we first want to understand how the price system operates as a mechanism for communicating and coordinating individual free choices. Deferring the full-employment question until Part 2, we want to see how the price system answers the other four Fundamental Questions. How does the price system (1) determine what is to be produced, (2) organize production, (3) distribute total output, and (4) adapt itself to change? Then, secondly, we want to evaluate the operation of the market economy.

FRAMEWORK OF THE PRICE SYSTEM

If we could suddenly "freeze" a purely capitalist economy at some point in time, here is what we should find:

1 Households, as consumers, have a variety of material wants. For all practical purposes, these wants are unlimited. Possessing a limited money income derived from the sale of limited amounts of resources at its disposal, each household seeks to purchase that combination of goods and services which will give it the greatest satisfaction. These various consumer wants in effect are tallied on the demand side of the product market. The demand schedule or curve for each product communicates to producers how much competing consumers would purchase of that product at various prices. The demand curve for each product is downsloping, because consumers find it to their advantage to substitute low-priced for high-priced products. Because of the large number of consumers buying each product, no one significantly influences actual product prices.

2 Competing business institutions stand on the supply side of the product market. Their goal is to maximize profits. In so doing, they must decide what product will be most profitable to produce, in what quantity it will be most profitable to produce it, and what combination of resources will produce the desired output at the least cost. For the business sector as a whole, these decisions, which in effect indicate the willingness of businesses to produce and offer various products, are reflected in product supply curves. These supply curves are upsloping, indicating that, other

things being equal, businesses will profit by substituting the production of high-priced goods for the production of low-priced ones. Together with the product demand curves which mirror consumer preferences, these supply curves will establish an equilibrium price for all those products which consumers might want and which businesses might be willing to supply.

3 Businesses require resources in accomplishing production. As we noted in Chapter 4, businesses will minimize their costs and, other things being equal, maximize their profits by substituting low-priced resources for high-priced resources; this means that resource demand curves will be downsloping. These resource demand curves will communicate to resource suppliers how much of each resource businesses will be willing to employ at various possible resource prices.

4 Finally, households as resource suppliers offer the land, labor, capital, and entrepreneurial talents which they own to businesses. The decisions of competing resource suppliers are reflected in resource supply curves. These curves are generally upsloping, reflecting the fact that households seek the greatest return from the sale of their resources. The upsloping nature of these curves implies that households not only want, but within limits are able, to shift resources from low-paying to high-paying lines of employment.

In brief, the product demand intentions of households and the product supply decisions of businesses will determine a series of product prices. Similarly, the resource demand decisions of businesses and the resource supply decisions of households will establish a series of resource prices. Our simple circular flow model of Figure 3-4 implied all these relationships.

ECONOMIC CHOICES, SCARCITY, AND SUBSTITUTABILITY

It is evident that our picture of the price system merely envisions a series of interrelated choices on the part of households as consumers and resource suppliers and businesses as producers and resource users. These choices are based upon the fact of scarcity and influenced by considerations of substitutability.

□   **Scarcity**

Society is faced with the problem of making economic choices because resources are scarce. If resources were infinitely abundant in relation to the demand for them, the economizing problem would dissolve in a sea of affluence. Consumers would *not* have to choose between various products; abundance would enable every consumer to have any type and any amount of goods and services he desired. The same would be true for businesses in their use of resources to carry on production. But, unfortunately, this describes economic utopia, not economic reality; in real life, resources, and therefore products, are relatively scarce. Hence, consumers with money incomes limited by their sales of scarce resources are forced to choose between relatively scarce commodities. And businesses, possessing limited money receipts from the sale of relatively scarce products, must choose between scarce resources in carrying on their productive efforts. Indeed, the presence of the basic theme of scarcity in our picture of the price system is mirrored in the very fact that products and resources have price tags on them! Only when something is scarce in relation to the demand for it will it command a price in the market.

□   **Substitutability**

How does substitutability come into the picture? Within limits, both resources and products are versatile. Consumer wants can usually be satisfied with various goods. The want for a trip from New York to Chicago can be satisfied by driving there by car or by buying a train ticket, a plane ticket, or a bus ticket. Hunger can be satisfied by a wide variety of foods—a bowl of rice, a hamburger, or a sirloin steak. And so it is with producing spe-

cific products. Resources, within limits dictated by technology, are substitutable for one another. Various resource combinations can be employed in the production of most products. The nature of both the supply and demand choices in a market economy is strongly influenced by substitutability. The demand curve for a product is downsloping because consumers will substitute other products for any particular product whose price happens to rise. And producers tend to substitute alternative resources for that resource whose price rises. Upsloping product and resource supply curves also imply substitutability. Producers tend to substitute high-priced for low-priced products in formulating their production intentions. And resource suppliers shift their human and property resources from low-paying to high-paying employments.

This, of course, is not to say that substitutability is perfect. It obviously is not. A bowl of rice is not a perfect substitute for a sirloin steak. Yet, within limits, the possibility of substitution exists in both the product and the resource market. Indeed, if substitutability did not exist, businesses would have no choices to make in hiring resources to produce specific goods. And if resources were not versatile, households would have no choices to make in supplying them. Similarly, if various products were not substitutable, households would have no problem of choice in spending their incomes.

□   **Choice**

Thus we may say that economic choices must be rendered because resources, and therefore products, are scarce. The particular choices rendered by businesses and households depend upon:

1 The prices of resources and products as indicators of relative scarcities.

2 The possibilities of substituting between resources, on the one hand, and products, on the other.

The interrelationship between scarcity and substitution is even more intimate than we have suggested. For example, if a product becomes particularly scarce, its price as an index of its relative scarcity will rise. This will signal buyers to substitute other products for the now higher-priced product. This substitution will rechannel consumer purchases away from this particularly scarce product toward others less scarce. Substitution eases this particularly acute scarcity by, in effect, transferring consumer purchases to other substitutable products. Through substitutability, society alters its choices so as to use less of particularly scarce products and resources and more of less scarce ones. By substituting, society conserves most on those products and resources which are most scarce.

OPERATION OF THE PRICE SYSTEM

Now, with this point-in-time picture of the price system before us and with the significance of scarcity and substitutability in the making of economic choices clearly in mind, let us examine in some detail the manner in which the competitive price system would answer the Fundamental Questions.

☐ Determining What Is to Be Produced

Given the product and resource prices established by competing buyers and sellers in both the product and resource markets, how would a purely capitalistic economy decide the types and quantities of goods to be produced? Remembering that businesses are motivated to seek profits and avoid losses, we can generalize that those goods and services which can be produced at a profit will be produced and those whose production entails a loss will not. And what determines profits or the lack of them? Two things:

1 The total receipts which a firm gets from selling a product.

2 The total costs of producing it.

Both total receipts and total costs are price-times-quantity figures. Total receipts are found by multiplying product price by the quantity of the product sold. Total costs are found by multiplying the price of each resource used by the amount employed and summing the costs of each.

Economic Profits   To say that those products which can be produced profitably will be produced and those which cannot will not is only an accurate generalization if the meaning of economic costs is clearly understood. In order to grasp the full meaning of costs, let us once again think of businesses as simply organizational charts, that is, businesses "on paper," distinct and apart from the capital, raw materials, labor, and entrepreneurial ability which make them going concerns. In order to become actual producing concerns, these "on paper" businesses must secure all four types of resources. The payments which must be made to secure and retain the needed amounts of these resources are *economic costs*. The per unit size of these costs—that is, resource prices—will be determined by supply and demand conditions in the resource market. The point to note is that—like land, labor, and capital—entrepreneurial ability is a scarce resource and consequently has a price tag on it. Costs therefore must include not only wage and salary payments to labor and interest and rental payments for capital and land, but also payments to the entrepreneur for the functions he performs in organizing and combining the other resources in the production of some commodity. The cost payment for these contributions by the entrepreneur is called a *normal profit*. Hence, a product will be produced only when total receipts are large enough to pay wage, interest, rental, and normal profit costs. Now if total receipts from the sale of a product more than cover all production costs, including a normal profit, the remainder will accrue to the entrepreneur as the risk taker and organizing force in the going concern. This return above costs is called a *pure,* or *economic, profit*. It is *not* an economic cost, because it need not be realized in order for the business to acquire and retain entrepreneurial ability.

Profits and Expanding Industries

A few hypothetical examples will explain more concretely how the price system determines what is to be produced. Suppose that the most favorable relationship between total revenue and total cost in producing product X occurs when the firm's output is 15 units. Assume, too, that the best combination of resources to use in producing 15 units of X entails 2 units of labor, 3 units of land, 1 of capital, and 1 of entrepreneurial ability, selling at prices of $2, $1, $3, and $3, respectively. Finally, suppose that the 15 units of X which these resources produce can be sold for $1 per unit. Will firms enter into the production of product X? Yes, they will. A firm producing product X under these conditions will be able to pay wage, rent, interest, and normal profit costs of $13 $[= (2 \times \$2) + (3 \times \$1) + (1 \times \$3) + (1 \times \$3)]$. The difference between total revenue of $15 and total costs of $13 will be an economic profit of $2.

This economic profit is evidence that industry X is a prosperous one. Such an industry will tend to expand as new firms, attracted by these above-normal profits, are created or shift from less profitable industries. But the entry of new firms will be a self-limiting process. As new firms enter industry X, the market supply of X will increase relative to the market demand. This will lower the market price of X to the end that economic profits will in time disappear. The market supply and demand situation prevailing when economic profits become zero will determine the total amount of X produced.

Losses and Declining Industries

But what if the initial market situation for product X were less favorable? Suppose conditions in the product market initially were such that the firm could sell the 15 units of X at a price of just 75 cents per unit. Total revenue would be

$11.25 $(= 15 \times 75$ cents). After paying wage, rental, and interest costs of $10, the firm would yield a below-normal profit of $1.25. In other words, *losses* of $1.75 $(= \$11.25 - \$13)$ would be incurred. Certainly, firms would not be attracted to this unprosperous industry. On the contrary, if these losses persisted, entrepreneurs would seek the normal or economic profits offered by more prosperous industries. This means that, in time, existing firms in industry X would go out of business entirely or migrate to other industries where normal or better profits prevail. However, as this happens, the market supply of X will fall relative to the market demand, thereby raising product price to the end that losses will eventually disappear. Industry X will then stabilize itself in size. The market supply and demand situation that prevails at that point where economic profits are zero will determine the total output of product X.

"Dollar Votes"

The important role of consumer demand in determining the types and quantities of goods produced must be emphasized. Consumers, unrestrained by government and possessing money incomes from the sale of resources, spend their dollars upon those goods which they are most willing and able to buy. These expenditures are in effect "dollar votes" by which consumers register their wants through the demand side of the product market. If these votes are great enough to provide a normal profit, businesses will produce that product. An increase in consumer demand, that is, an increase in the dollar votes cast for a product, will mean economic profits for the industry producing it. These profits will signal the expansion of that industry and increases in the output of the product. A decrease in consumer demand, that is, fewer votes cast for the product, will result in losses and, in time, contraction of the adversely affected industry. As firms leave the industry, the output of the product declines. In short, the dollar votes of consumers play a key role in determining what products profit-seeking businesses will produce. As noted in Chapter 3, the capitalistic system is sometimes said to be characterized by *consumer sovereignty* because of the strategic role of consumers in determining the types and quantities of goods produced. Be aware, however, that the real-world relevance of consumer sovereignty has been questioned by some economists, as this chapter's Last Word section attests.

Market Restraints on Freedom From the viewpoint of businesses, we now see that firms are not really "free" to produce what they wish. The demand decisions of consumers, by making the production of some products profitable and others not, restrict the choice of businesses in deciding what to produce. Businesses must synchronize their production choices with consumer choices or face the penalty of losses and eventual bankruptcy.

Much the same holds true with respect to resource suppliers. The demand for resources is a *derived demand*—derived, that is, from the demand for the goods and services which the resources help produce. There is a demand for auto workers only because there is a demand for automobiles. More generally, in seeking to maximize the returns from the sale of their human and property resources, resource suppliers are prompted by the price system to make their choices in accord with consumer demands. If only those firms which produce goods wanted by consumers can operate profitably, only those firms will demand resources. Resource suppliers will not be "free" to allocate their resources to the production of goods which consumers do not value very highly. The reason? There will be no firms producing such products, because consumer demand is not sufficient to make it profitable to do so. In short, consumers register their preferences on the demand side of the product market, and producers and resource suppliers respond appropriately in seeking to further their own self-interests. The price system communicates the wants of consumers to business and resource suppliers and elicits appropriate responses.

Organizing Production

How is production to be organized in a market economy? This fundamental question, we recall, is composed of three subquestions:

1 How should resources be allocated among specific industries?

2 What specific firms should do the producing in each industry?

3 What combinations of resources—what technology—should each firm employ?

Production and Profits The preceding section has answered the first subquestion. The price system steers resources to those industries whose products consumers want badly enough to make their production profitable. It simultaneously deprives unprofitable industries of scarce resources. If all firms had sufficient time to enter prosperous industries and to leave unprosperous industries, the output of each industry would be large enough for the firms to just make normal profits. If total industry output at this point happens to be 1500 units and the most profitable output for each firm is 15 units, as in our previous example, the industry will obviously be made up of 100 competing firms.

The second and third subquestions are closely intertwined. In a competitive market economy, the firms which do the producing are those which are willing and able to employ the economically most efficient technique of production. And what determines the most efficient technique? Economic efficiency depends upon:

1 Available technology, that is, the alternative combinations of resources or inputs which will produce the desired output.

2 The prices at which the needed resources can be obtained.

Least-Cost Production The combination of resources which is most efficient economically depends not only upon the physical or engineering data provided by available technology but also upon the relative worth of the required resources as measured by their market prices. Thus, a technique which requires just a few physical inputs of resources to produce a given output may be highly *in*efficient economically if the required resources are valued very highly in the market. In other words, economic efficiency entails getting a given output of product with the smallest input of scarce resources, when both output and resource inputs are measured in dollars-and-cents terms. In short, that combination of resources which will produce, say, $15 worth of product X at the lowest possible money cost is the most efficient.

Table 5-1 will help illustrate these points. Suppose there are three different techniques by which the desired $15 worth of product X can be produced. The quantity of each resource required by each technique and the prices of the required resources are shown in Table 5-1. By multiplying the quantities of the various resources required by the resource prices in each of the three techniques, the total cost of producing $15 worth of X by each technique can be determined. It can be concluded that technique No. 2 is economically the most efficient of the three, for the simple reason that it is the least costly way of producing $15 worth of X. Technique No. 2 permits society to obtain $15 worth of output by using up a smaller amount of resources—$13 worth—

than would be used up by the two alternative techniques. Technique No. 2 is the most efficient, because it gives society $15 worth of output for an input of $13 worth of resources; the alternative techniques entail an input of $15 worth of resources for the same amount of output.

But what guarantees that technique No. 2 will actually be used? After all, techniques No. 1 and No. 3 entail a normal profit and thereby will permit firms to survive, at least for the moment. The answer to this question can be stated as follows.

1 Technique No. 2 allows the user an economic profit of $2. And firms seeking to further their own interests can be expected to employ techniques which permit them to realize the greatest profits. Firms will *want* to use the most efficient technique; it yields the greatest profit.

2 Competition will literally *force* firms to use the most efficient technique. The firm that fails to employ the least costly method of production will find that other existing firms or new firms coming into the industry will adopt the least costly technique. This leads to an increase in supply and hence to a reduction in the price of X. This will turn the normal profits of the inefficient firm into losses unless it switches to the most efficient technique. Thus, the competitive price system makes the adoption of the most efficient production techniques a condition of survival.

We must emphasize that a change in *either* technology *or* resource prices may cause the firm to shift from the technology now em-

Table 5-1 TECHNIQUES FOR PRODUCING $15 WORTH OF PRODUCT X (*hypothetical data*)

Resource	Technique No. 1	Technique No. 2	Technique No. 3	Price per unit of resource
Labor	4	2	1	$2
Land	1	3	4	1
Capital	1	1	2	3
Entrepreneurial ability	1	1	1	3
Total cost of $15 worth of X	$15	$13	$15	

ployed. For example, if the price of labor falls to 50 cents, technique No. 1 will be superior to technique No. 2. That is, businesses will find that they can lower their costs by shifting to a technology which involves the use of more of that resource whose price has fallen. This shift in techniques illustrates why resource demand curves are downsloping. In this case, a decline in the price of labor prompts businesses to shift to a technique employing more labor and less land. The reader should verify that a new technique involving 1 unit of labor, 4 of land, 1 of capital, and 1 of entrepreneurial ability will be preferable to all three techniques listed in Table 5-1, assuming the resource prices given there.

Postscript: There is a geographic or locational aspect to the question of organizing production which we ignore at this point. The question "*Where* to produce?" will be considered in detail in Chapter 36.

☐ Distributing Total Output

The price system enters the picture in two ways in solving the problem of distributing total output. Generally speaking, any given product will be distributed to consumers on the basis of their ability and willingness to pay the existing market price for it. If the price of X is $1 per unit, those buyers who are able and willing to pay that price will get a unit of this product; those who are not, will not. This, we recall, is the rationing function of equilibrium prices.

What determines a consumer's ability to pay the equilibrium price of X and other available products? The size of his money income. And money income in turn depends upon the types and quantities of the various property and human resources which the income receiver supplies and the prices which they command in the resource market. Thus, resource prices play a key role in determining the size of each household's claim against the total output of society. Within the limits of a consumer's money income, his willingness to pay

the equilibrium price for X determines whether or not some of this product is distributed to him. And this willingness to buy X will depend upon his preference for X in comparison with available close substitutes for X and their relative prices. Thus, product prices play a key role in determining the expenditure patterns of consumers.

We should emphasize that there is nothing particularly ethical about the price system as a mechanism for distributing the output of pure capitalism. Those households which manage to accumulate large amounts of property resources by inheritance, through hard work and frugality, through business acumen, or by crook will receive large incomes and thus command large shares of the economy's total output. Others, offering unskilled and relatively unproductive labor resources which elicit low wages, will receive meager money incomes and small portions of total output. In fact, we shall find in later chapters that one's money income, and hence one's slice of the economy's output, depends not simply upon the quantity and quality of resources provided, but also upon such factors as race, sex, and the ability to exert both market and political power. The point to stress at this juncture is that the price system is an impersonal and amoral mechanism, and if money incomes are very unequally distributed, a very unequal distribution of the fruits of production will follow (see Chapter 37).

☐ Providing for Flexibility

In order to ensure efficiency in the administration of its resources over a period of time, an economy must be flexible. That particular allocation of resources which is *now* the most efficient for a *given* pattern of consumer tastes, for a *given* range of technological alternatives, and for *given* supplies of resources can be expected to become obsolete and inefficient as consumer preferences change, new techniques of production are discovered, and resource supplies alter over time. Can the market economy negotiate adjustments in resource uses appropriate to such inevitable changes and thereby remain efficient? Furthermore, in addition to being permissive of, or adaptable to, such changes, is the market economy conducive to changes in technology and the stock of capital which are crucial to economic growth and a higher standard of living?

Is the Price System Adaptable to Change?   Let us suppose a change occurs in consumer tastes. Specifically, let us say that consumers decide they want more shoes and fewer shirts than the economy is currently providing. Will the price system communicate this change to businesses and resource suppliers and prompt appropriate adjustments?

The assumed change in consumers' tastes will be communicated to producers through an increase in the demand for shoes and a decline in the demand for shirts. This means that shoe prices will rise and shirt prices will fall. Now, assuming firms in both industries are enjoying precisely normal profits prior to these changes in consumer demand, higher shoe prices will mean economic profits for the shoe industry, and lower shirt prices will entail losses for the shirt industry. Self-interest induces new competitors to enter the prosperous shoe industry. Losses will in time force firms to leave the depressed shirt industry. As a matter of fact, some firms leaving the shirt industry might enter the shoe industry. But, in all probability, most firms entering the shoe industry will be newly created and those leaving the shirt industry will become permanently defunct.

In any event, the prosperous shoe industry will expand, and the unprosperous shirt industry will contract. But these adjustments, we recall, are both self-limiting. The expansion of the shoe industry will continue only to the point at which the resulting increase in the market supply of shoes brings shoe prices back down to a level at which normal profits again prevail. Similarly, contraction in the shirt industry will persist until the accompanying decline in the market supply of shirts brings shirt

prices up to a level at which the remaining firms can receive a normal profit. The crucial point to note is that these adjustments in the business sector are completely appropriate to the assumed changes in consumer tastes. Society—meaning consumers—wants more shoes and fewer shirts, and that is precisely what it is getting as the shoe industry expands and the shirt industry contracts. This discussion, incidentally, portrays the concept of consumer sovereignty at work.

But this analysis proceeds on the assumption that resource suppliers are agreeable to these adjustments. Will the price system prompt resource suppliers to reallocate their human and property resources from the shirt to the shoe industry, thereby permitting the output of shoes to expand at the expense of shirt production? The answer is "Yes."

The economic profits which initially follow the increase in demand for shoes will not only provide that industry with the inducement to expand but will also give it the added receipts with which to obtain the resources essential to its growth. Higher shoe prices will permit firms in that industry to pay higher prices for resources, thereby drawing resources from what are now less urgent alternative employments. Willingness and ability to employ more resources in the shoe industry will be communicated back into the resource market through an increase in the demand for resources. Substantially the reverse occurs in the adversely affected shirt industry. The losses which the decline in consumer demand initially entails will cause a decline in the demand for resources in that industry. Workers and other resources released from the contracting shirt industry can now find employment in the expanding shoe industry. Furthermore, the increased demand for resources in the shoe industry will mean higher resource prices in that industry than those being paid in the shirt industry, where declines in resource demand have lowered resource prices. The resulting differential in resource prices will provide the incentive for resource owners to further their self-interests by reallocating their resources from the shirt to the shoe industry. And this, of course, is the precise shift needed to permit the shoe industry to expand and the shirt industry to contract.

The ability of the price system to communicate changes in such basic data as consumer tastes and to elicit appropriate responses from both businesses and resource suppliers is sometimes called the *directing* or *guiding function* of prices. By affecting product prices and profits, changes in consumer tastes direct the expansion of some industries and the contraction of others. These adjustments carry through to the resource market as expanding industries demand more resources and contracting industries demand fewer. The resulting changes in resource prices guide resources from the contracting to the expanding industries. In the absence of a price system, some administrative agency, presumably a governmental planning board, would have to undertake the task of directing business institutions and resources into specific lines of production.

Analysis similar to that just outlined would indicate that the price system would adjust appropriately to similar fundamental changes—for example, to changes in technology and changes in the relative supplies of various resources.

Is the Price System Conducive to Change? Adjusting to given changes is one thing; inducing changes, particularly desirable changes, is something else again. Is the competitive price system congenial to technological improvements and capital accumulation, the interrelated changes which lead to greater productivity and a higher level of material well-being for society? This is not an easy question to answer. We state our reply at this point without stopping for qualifications and modifications (see Chapter 29).

Technological advance The ideology of pure capitalism, with its emphasis upon the competitive price system, is quite a fertile environment for technological advance. Compe-

tition provides the *opportunity* for entrepreneurs to introduce new techniques and new products, unimpeded by the artificial barriers which a noncompetitive environment might entail. The competitive price system also furnishes the *incentive* for technological advance. The introduction of cost-cutting techniques provides the innovating firm with a temporary advantage over its rivals. Lower production costs mean economic profits for the pioneering firm. By passing a part of its cost reduction on to the consumer through a lower product price, the innovating firm can achieve a sizable increase in sales and lucrative economic profits at the expense of rival firms. And remember, because the monetary rewards of the successful introduction of a new technique will accrue to the innovating firm, the price system will be very effective in harnessing individual incentives in the cause of technological advance.

Looking at technological advance from the social point of view, we should note that the innovating firm's economic profits will be a temporary phenomenon. Other firms can also adopt the new cost-reducing technique. Indeed, as we have seen, they will be forced to do so. Why? Because, by price cutting, the innovating firm will turn the once-normal profits of its competitors into losses. This is of considerable significance: It is in this fashion that the competitive price system communicates or diffuses the technological improvements of one firm to all other firms in that industry. Rivals must follow the lead of the most progressive firm or suffer the immediate penalty of losses and the eventual pain of bankruptcy.

We should note that the lower product price which the technological advance permits will cause the innovating industry to expand. This expansion may be the result of existing firms' expanding their rates of output or of new firms entering the industry under the lure of the economic profits initially created by a technological advance. This expansion, that is, the diversion of resources from nonprogressive to progressive industries, is as it should be.

Sustained efficiency in the use of scarce resources demands that resources be continually reallocated from industries whose productive techniques are relatively less efficient to those whose techniques are relatively more efficient.

Capital accumulation But technological advance typically entails the use of increased amounts of capital goods. Can the price system provide the capital goods upon which technological advance relies? More specifically, can the entrepreneur as an innovator command through the price system the resources necessary to produce the machinery and equipment upon which technological advance depends?

Obviously, the entrepreneur can. If society registers dollar votes for capital goods, the product market and the resource market will adjust to these votes by producing capital goods. In other words, the price system acknowledges dollar voting for both consumer and capital goods. Indeed, the relative sizes of these two types of dollar voting determine how a market economy will divide its total output between consumer goods, which satisfy wants directly, and capital goods, which satisfy wants indirectly through the more efficient production of consumer goods.

But who will register votes for capital goods? First, the entrepreneur as a receiver of profit income can be expected to apportion a part of his income to the accumulation of capital goods. By so doing, he can achieve an even greater profit income in the future if his innovation proves successful. Furthermore, by paying a rate of interest, entrepreneurs can borrow portions of the incomes of other households and use these borrowed funds in casting dollar votes for the production of more capital goods.

In practice, the process of technological advance and capital accumulation is much more complex than envisioned here (see Chapter 11). The important point for present purposes is that the market economy provides the opportunity and incentive for technological advance and the means for providing the capital goods which such advance typically presumes.

□   **Competition and Control:
The "Invisible Hand"**

Though the price system is the organizing mechanism of pure capitalism, it is essential to recognize the role of competition as the mechanism of control in such an economy. The market mechanism of supply and demand communicates the wants of consumers (society) to businesses and through businesses to resource suppliers. It is competition, however, which forces businesses and resource suppliers to make appropriate responses. To illustrate: The impact of an increase in consumer demand for some product will raise that good's price above the wage, rent, interest, and normal profit costs of production. The resulting economic profits in effect are a signal to producers that society wants more of the product. It is competition—in particular, the ability of new firms to enter the industry—that simultaneously brings an expansion of output and a lowering of price back to a level just consistent with production costs. However, if the industry was not competitive, but was dominated by, say, one huge firm which was able to prohibit the entry of potential competitors, that firm could enjoy economic profits by preventing the expansion of the industry.

But competition does more than guarantee responses appropriate to the wishes of society. It is competition which forces firms to adopt the most efficient productive techniques. In a competitive market, the failure of some firms to use the least costly production technique means their eventual elimination by other competing firms who do employ the most efficient methods of production. Finally, we have seen that competition provides an environment conducive to technological advance.

A very remarkable aspect of the operation and the adjustments of a competitive price system is that a curious and important identity is involved—the identity of private and social interests. That is, firms and resource suppliers, seeking to further their own self-interest and operating within the framework of a highly competitive market system, will simultaneously, as though guided by an "invisible hand,"[1] promote the public or social interest. For example, we have seen that given a competitive environment, business firms use the least costly combination of resources in producing a given output because it is in their self-interest to do so. To act otherwise would be to forgo profits or even to risk bankruptcy over a period of time. But, at the same time, it is obviously also in the social interest to use scarce resources in the least costly, that is, most efficient, manner. Not to do so would be to produce a given output at a greater cost or sacrifice of alternative goods than is really necessary. Furthermore, in our more-shoes–fewer-shirts illustration, it is self-interest, awakened and guided by the competitive price system, which induces the very responses appropriate to the assumed change in society's wants. Businesses seeking to make higher profits and to avoid losses, on the one hand, and resource suppliers pursuing greater monetary rewards, on the other, negotiate the very changes in the allocation of resources and therefore the composition of output which society now demands. The force of competition, in other words, controls or guides the self-interest motive in such a way that it automatically, and quite unintentionally, furthers the best interests of society.

AN EVALUATION OF THE PRICE SYSTEM

Is the price system the best means of deciding how total output is to be determined, how production of that output should be organized,

[1] Adam Smith, *The Wealth of Nations* (New York: Modern Library, Inc., originally published in 1776), p. 423.

and how total output should be distributed? This is a complex question; any complete answer necessarily leaps the boundary of facts and enters the realm of values. This means there is no scientific answer to the query. The very fact that there exist many competing ways of allocating scarce resources—that is, many different kinds of economic systems (Table 2-3)—is ample evidence of disagreement as to the effectiveness of the price system.

☐ **The Case for the Price System**

The virtues of the price system are implicit in our discussion of its operation. Two merit emphasis.

Allocative Efficiency   The basic economic argument for the price system is that it leads to an efficient allocation of resources. The competitive price system, it is argued, guides resources into the production of those goods and services most wanted by society. It forces the use of the most efficient techniques in organizing resources for production, and it is conducive to the development and adoption of new and more efficient production techniques. In short, proponents of the price system argue that the "invisible hand" will in effect harness self-interest so as to provide society with the greatest output of wanted goods from its available resources. This, then, suggests the maximum economic efficiency. It is this presumption of allocative efficiency which makes most economists hesitant to advocate governmental interference with, or regulation of, free markets.

Freedom   The major noneconomic argument for the price system is its great emphasis upon personal freedom. One of the fundamental problems of social organization is how to coordinate the economic activities of large numbers of individuals and businesses. We recall from Chapter 2 that there are basically two ways of providing this coordination: one is central direction and the use of coercion; the other is voluntary cooperation through the price system. Only the price system can coordinate economic activity without coercion. The price system permits—indeed, it thrives upon—freedom of enterprise and choice. Entrepreneurs and workers are not herded from industry to industry to meet the production targets established by some omnipotent governmental agency. On the contrary, they are free to further their own self-interests, subject, of course, to the rewards and penalties imposed by the price system itself.

> So long as effective freedom of exchange is maintained, the central feature of the market organization of economic activity is that it prevents one person from interfering with another in respect of most of his activities. The consumer is protected from coercion by the seller because of the presence of other sellers with whom he can deal. The seller is protected from coercion by the consumer because of other consumers to whom he can sell. The employee is protected from coercion by the employer because of other employers for whom he can work, and so on. And the market does this impersonally and without centralized authority.[2]

To summarize: the competitive price system is allegedly conducive to both allocative efficiency and freedom.

□   **The Case against the Price System**

The case against the price system is somewhat more complex. Critics of the market economy base their position on the following points.

Demise of Competition   Critics argue that capitalistic ideology is permissive of, and even conducive to, the demise of its main controlling mechanism—competition. The alleged

weakening of competition as a control mechanism comes from two basic sources.

1 Though desirable from the social point of view, competition is most irksome to the individual producer subject to its rigors. It is allegedly inherent in the free, individualistic environment of the capitalistic system that the profit-seeking entrepreneur will attempt to break free of the restraining force of competition in trying to better his position. Combination, conspiracy, and cutthroat competition are all means to the end of reducing competition and escaping its regulatory powers. As Adam Smith put the matter two centuries ago: "People of the same trade seldom meet together but the conversation ends in a conspiracy against the public, or in some diversion to raise prices."

2 Some economists believe that the very technological advance which the price system fosters has contributed to the decline of competition. Modern technology typically requires (*a*) the use of extremely large quantities of real capital; (*b*) large markets; (*c*) a complex, centralized, and closely integrated management; and (*d*) large and reliable sources of raw materials. Such an operation implies the need for producers who are large scale not only in the absolute sense but also in relation to the size of the market. In other words, the achievement of maximum productive efficiency through the employment of the best available technology often requires the existence of a small number of large firms rather than a large number of small ones.

To the degree that competition declines, the price system will be weakened as a mechanism for efficiently allocating resources. Producers and resource suppliers will be less subject to the will of consumers; the sovereignty of producers and resource suppliers will then challenge and weaken the sovereignty of consumers. The "invisible hand" identity of private and social interests will begin to lose its grip. Furthermore, the protection from coercion which the market system provides is predicated upon the widespread dispersion of economic power. The concentration of economic

[2]Milton Friedman, *Capitalism and Freedom* (Chicago: The University of Chicago Press, 1962), pp. 14–15.

power which accompanies the decline of competition permits the possessors of that power to engage in coercive acts.

Wasteful and Inefficient Production Critics also challenge the assertion that the price system provides the goods most wanted by society. We have just encountered one facet of the critics' position: To the extent that a weakening of competition lessens consumer sovereignty, the price system becomes less proficient in allocating resources in precise accord with the wishes of consumers. But there are other reasons for questioning the efficiency of the price system.

Unequal income distribution Critical socialists contend that the price system allows the more efficient, or more cunning, entrepreneurs to accumulate vast amounts of property resources, the accumulation process being extended through time by the right to bequeath. This, in addition to differences in the amount and quality of human resources supplied by various households, causes a highly unequal distribution of money incomes in a market economy. The result is that families differ greatly in their ability to express their wants in the market. The wealthy have more dollar votes than the poor. Hence, it is concluded that the price system allocates resources to the production of frivolous luxury goods for the rich at the expense of the output of necessities for the poor. A country that

> . . . spends money on champagne before it has provided milk for its babies is a badly managed, silly, vain, stupid, ignorant nation. . . . The only way in which such a nation can make itself wealthy and prosperous is by good housekeeping: that is by providing for its wants in order of their importance, and allowing no money to be wasted on whims and luxuries until the necessities have been thoroughly served.[3]

[3]George Bernard Shaw, *The Intelligent Woman's Guide to Socialism and Capitalism* (New York: Brentano's, Inc., 1928), pp. 50–55. Used by permission of the Public Trustee and the Society of Authors.

The point is that the claim of "efficiency" in the allocation of resources has a hollow ring if the distribution of income and therefore of output does not meet some reasonable standards of fairness or equity. And the unmodified income distribution of the market economy, as socialists see it, is far from equitable (Chapter 40). Indeed, many orthodox economists have deep concerns about the degree of income inequality in American capitalism.

Market failure: Externalities Critics cite two important cases of market failure. First, the price system may fail to register all the benefits and costs associated with the production and consumption of certain goods and services. That is, some benefits and costs are external to the market in that they accrue to parties other than the immediate buyer and seller. Such benefits and costs are called *spillover* or *external* benefits and costs. For example, consumer demand as registered in the market embodies only the satisfactions which accrue to individual consumers who purchase goods and services; it does not reflect the fact that the purchase of such services as polio shots and chest x-rays yields widespread benefits or satisfactions to the community (society) as a whole. Similarly, the supply decisions of producers are based upon the costs which the market obligates them to bear and do not reflect external costs, that is, costs borne by society at large as various forms of environmental pollution. The point is this: Where demand and supply do not accurately reflect all the benefits and all the costs of production, that is, where external benefits and costs exist, the price system cannot be expected to bring about an allocation of resources which best satisfies the wants of society. In Chapter 6 we examine policies to correct such malallocations of resources.

Market failure: Social goods Second, the price system tabulates only individual wants. There are many wants involving goods and services which cannot be financed by individuals through the market. For example, such goods and services as education, highways, flood-control programs, and national defense cannot be purchased in desired amounts by households on an individual basis. They can only be consumed economically on a social, or collective, basis. The price system, it is argued, is incapable of registering such social, or collective, wants.

Resource immobilities   The price system has also been criticized for its failure to adjust fully and within a reasonable period of time to changes in society's production objectives. There is allegedly a persistent time lag between society's production targets and the actual pattern of resource allocation provided by the price system. Even in a highly competitive market economy, the occupational and geographic mobility of human resources will be far from perfect. Laborers are hesitant to sever social ties and move to a strange community to take a new job. Such a move may also be costly, particularly if the worker must acquire new skills. The existence of discrimination based upon race, sex, or ethnic origin is a particularly serious obstacle to the realization of an allocation of labor based upon ability and productivity. And property resources are usually reallocated through the price system with even less rapidity. In short, the exodus of resources from declining industries and their entry to expanding industries is a time-consuming and imperfect process. This tardy adjustment of the pattern of resource use to changes in the structure of demand is a persistent source of inefficiency.

Unemployment   Finally, the price system is widely recognized as an imperfect mechanism for providing the continuous full employment of the economy's resources. The problem of unemployment will be analyzed in detail in Part 2.

Which of these two positions—one for, and the other against, the price system—is correct? To a degree both are. The several criticisms of the market economy are reasonably accurate and certainly too serious to ignore. On the other hand, we cannot judge an issue

by the number of arguments pro and con. The basic economic argument for the price system—that it tends to provide an efficient allocation of resources—is not easily undermined. In practice, the price system is—or at least can be—reasonably efficient.

□   **Relevance, Realism, and the Price System**

Does the price system of American capitalism function in the same fashion as the price system discussed in this chapter? In principle, yes; in detail, no. Our discussion of the price system provides us with a working model—a rough approximation—of the actual price system of American capitalism. Our analysis presents a much simplified, yet useful, picture of the real thing. The competitive price system also gives us a norm, or standard, against which the real-world economy can be compared.

Specifically, there are two basic differences between the price system as pictured in this chapter and the actual price system of American capitalism.

Bigness   In many product and resource markets, competition clearly has been supplanted by a few giant business corporations and huge labor unions. Competition is simply not as vigorous in practice as our discussion of the price system assumed. This means that the decisions of businesses and resource suppliers are less than perfectly synchronized with those of consumers, and that changes in the production goals of society are less precisely communicated throughout the economy. Giant business and labor groups in American capitalism have the power to resist the dictates of consumer sovereignty and, as a matter of fact, will usually find it personally advantageous to do so.

Government   Another major difference between our model price system and the market system of American capitalism lies in the economic role of government in the latter. In contrast with the passive, limited government envisioned in the ideology of pure capitalism, the government of American capitalism is an active and integral component of the economy. In particular, the economy of the United States has taken cognizance of the important elements of truth which permeate the noted criticisms of the price system. Through government, society has taken steps to correct these shortcomings. Therefore, government pursues policies designed not only to preserve and bolster competition, but also to adjust certain inequities fostered by the price system, to hasten the reallocation of resources, to meet collective wants, and to help maintain full employment. It is with these and related eco-

nomic functions of government that the ensuing chapter is concerned.

Is our analysis of the price system realistic? Does it provide a workable description of the price system of American capitalism? One scholar has responded to these questions as follows:

> For all the new quality of twentieth-century industrial society, the great principles of self-interest and competition, however watered down or hedged about, still provide basic rules of behavior which no economic organization can afford to disregard entirely . . . the laws of the market can be discerned . . . if we look beneath the surface.[4]

[4] Robert L. Heilbroner, *The Worldly Philosophers,* 3d ed. (New York: Simon & Schuster, Inc., 1967), pp. 53–54.

Summary

1 In a market economy, the interacting decisions of competing buyers and sellers will determine a system of product and resource prices at any given point in time.

2 The relative scarcity of economic resources makes the operation of any economy a matter of choosing between alternatives. At any point in time, these choices depend upon the relative scarcity of resources and products. Over time, the degree to which these choices are altered in a market economy as product and resource prices change depends upon the willingness and ability of consumers to make substitutions among products and the willingness and ability of producers to make substitutions among resources. Substitutability tends to relieve particular scarcities of resources and products.

3 Those products whose production and sale yield total receipts sufficient to cover all costs, including a normal profit, will be produced. Those whose production will not yield a normal profit will not be produced.

4 Economic profits designate an industry as prosperous and signal its expansion. Losses mean an industry is unprosperous and result in a contraction of that industry. Industrial expansion and contraction are self-limiting processes. As expansion increases market supply relative to market demand, the price of a product falls to the point where all economic profits disappear. As contraction decreases market supply relative to market demand, the resulting increase in product price eliminates losses and makes the industry normally profitable once again.

5 Consumer sovereignty dominates a competitive market economy. The penalty of losses and the lure of profits force both businesses and resource suppliers to channel their efforts in accordance with the wants of consumers.

6 Competition forces firms to use the least costly, and therefore the most economically efficient, productive techniques.

7   The price system plays a dual role in distributing total output among individual households. The prices commanded by the quantities and types of resources supplied by each household will determine the number of dollar claims against the economy's output each household receives. Given consumer tastes, product prices are of fundamental importance in determining consumer expenditure patterns. Within the limits of each household's money income, consumer preferences and the relative prices of products determine the distribution of total output.

8   The competitive price system can communicate changes in consumer tastes to resource suppliers and entrepreneurs, thereby prompting appropriate adjustments in the allocation of the economy's resources. The competitive price system also provides an environment conducive to technological advance and capital accumulation.

9   Competition, the primary mechanism of control in the market economy, will foster an identity of private and social interests; as though directed by an "invisible hand," competition harnesses the self-interest motives of businesses and resource suppliers so as to simultaneously further the social interest.

10   The basic virtue of the price system is its continuing emphasis upon efficiency. It produces what consumers want through the use of the most efficient techniques. Operation and adjustments of the price system are automatic in the sense that they are the result of individual, decentralized decisions, not the centralized decisions of government.

11   Criticisms of the price system are several: *a.* The controlling mechanism, competition, tends to weaken over time; *b.* inherent income inequalities, inability to register collective wants, and the presence of external benefits and costs prevent the price system from producing that collection of goods most wanted by society; *c.* the price system reallocates resources sluggishly and imperfectly to changes in the structure of demand; *d.* the competitive price system does not guarantee continued full employment.

12   The price system of American capitalism differs from the competitive price system in that the former is characterized by *a.* giant corporations and unions in certain product and resource markets, and *b.* government intervention in the economy to correct the major defects of the price system. Yet, the competitive price system does provide a working model whereby we can understand the price system of American capitalism.

Questions and Study Suggestions

1   Key terms and concepts to remember: economic versus normal profits; expanding versus declining industries; consumer sovereignty; least-cost production technique; directing (guiding) function of prices; "invisible hand"; market failure.

2   Describe in detail how the price system answers the Five Fundamental Questions. Why must economic choices be made? How do scarcity and substitutability influence the rendering of economic choices? Be specific. Explain: "The capitalistic system is a profit and loss economy."

3   "Production methods which are inferior in the engineering sense may be the most efficient methods in the economic sense." Explain.

4   Evaluate and explain the following statements:

a.   "The most important feature of capitalism is the absence of a central economic plan."

b. "Competition is the indispensable disciplinarian of the market economy."

5 Explain fully the meaning and implications of the following quotation.[5]

The beautiful consequence of the market is that it is its own guardian. If output or prices or certain kinds of remuneration stray away from their socially ordained levels, forces are set into motion to bring them back to the fold. It is a curious paradox which thus ensues: the market, which is the acme of individual economic freedom, is the strictest taskmaster of all. One may appeal the ruling of a planning board or win the dispensation of a minister; but there is no appeal, no dispensation, from the anonymous pressures of the market mechanism. Economic freedom is thus more illusory than at first appears. One can do as one pleases in the market. But if one pleases to do what the market disapproves, the price of individual freedom is economic ruination.

6 Assume that a business firm finds that its profits will be at a maximum when it produces $40 worth of product A. Suppose also that each of the three techniques shown in the following table will produce the desired output.

Resource	Technique No. 1	Technique No. 2	Technique No. 3	Price per unit of resource
Labor	5	2	3	$3
Land	2	4	2	4
Capital	2	4	5	2
Entrepre- neurial ability	4	2	4	2

a. Given the resource prices shown, which technique will the firm choose? Why?

b. Assume now that a new technique, technique No. 4, is developed. It entails the use of 2 units of labor, 2 of land, 6 of capital, and 3 of entrepreneurial ability. Given the resource prices in the table, will the firm adopt the new technique? Explain your answer.

c. Suppose now that the price of labor falls to $1.50 per unit, all other resource prices being unchanged. What technique will the producer now choose? Explain.

d. "The price system causes the economy to conserve most in the use of those resources which are particularly scarce in supply. Resources which are scarcest relative to the demand for them have the highest prices. As a result, producers use these resources as sparingly as is possible." Evaluate this statement. Does your answer to question 6c bear out this contention? Explain.

7 Interpret and explain the following quotation in terms of Table 5-1.[6]

Soviet industrialization has taken place against the background of an abundance of manpower. . . . It was therefore economically sensible for them to use labor lavishly, substituting it whenever possible for capital goods, and bringing in more

[5] Ibid., p. 42.
[6] Robert W. Campbell, "Problems of United States–Soviet Economic Comparisons," in Joint Economic Committee, *Comparisons of the United States and Soviet Economies* (Washington: Government Printing Office, 1960), p. 26.

workers whenever it was possible by doing so to squeeze a bit more output out of existing enterprises. The result of such a policy was to make output per worker low, but it was still the correct thing to do in the light of the abundance of labor.

Output per Soviet worker is considerably lower than output per American worker. Does this necessarily mean that the Soviet economy is inefficient and wasteful as compared with the United States economy? Explain.

8   What are the major criticisms of the price system? Carefully evaluate these criticisms. Analyze in detail: "No allocation of resources can be termed 'efficient' unless we define the 'optimum' distribution of income."

Selected References

Boulding, Kenneth E.: *Economic Analysis: Microeconomics,* 4th ed. (New York: Harper & Row, Publishers, Incorporated, 1966), chap. 6.

Fels, Rendigs, and Robert G. Uhler: *Casebook of Economic Problems and Cases* (St. Paul: West Publishing Company, 1976), parts 1–3.

Heilbroner, Robert L.: *The Worldly Philosophers,* 4th ed. (New York: Simon & Schuster, Inc., 1972), chap. 3.

Klaasen, Adrian (ed.): *The Invisible Hand* (Chicago: Henry Regnery Company, 1965).

Leeman, Wayne A. (ed.): *Capitalism, Market Socialism, and Central Planning* (Boston: Houghton Mifflin Company, 1963), chaps. 1, 2, 9–11.

Last Word
Producer, Not Consumer, Sovereignty

Harvard's John Kenneth Galbraith argues that the concept of consumer sovereignty must be replaced by the notion of producer sovereignty. He contends that the failure to make this substitution diverts attention from a clear understanding of the socioeconomic and political problems of our society.

The assumption that economics must now abandon . . . is that of consumer sovereignty—and, in light of the role of the modern state in the economy, what might also be called "citizen sovereignty." If this is not done, the discipline will serve, indeed is now serving, not as an elucidation of social phenomena but as a design for suppressing inconvenient social conclusions and action.

It is hard to believe that the uncommitted reader will find the case for producer sovereignty . . . wholly implausible. The case is perhaps strongest for public goods; there can be few men of available mind who have recently looked at the process by which the national defense is provided without wondering if the conventional view of ultimate citizen sovereignty is acceptable. This is not a detail; it is half the federal budget. And many must have wondered if the conventional view, indistinct as it is, might not be serving to divert attention from the disenchanting reality—if it did not accord the public the mythology of power while giving the military bureaucracy and associated industries the reality of power. But in the large-scale consumer goods industries the case is not greatly less convincing. There is the massive outlay on persuading the consumer. There is also the general increase in the persuasive effort paralleling the development of increasingly complex technology and organization. It is a tenet of the more developed consumer goods industries that products must be selected, designed, and produced with a view to what lends itself to persuasion. Accordingly, it involves an exercise of imagination to suppose that the taste so expressed originates with the consumer. What the consumer deems to be a desirably shaped and chromatically compelling automobile is substantially different this year from what it was five years ago. But few would wish to argue that this represented a change in the consumer's intrinsic and improving vision of a vehicle—that, indeed, it was other than something accomplished with no slight skill, art and expense by the automobile producers. It is not necessary to argue that the management of the consumer by the producer is complete, only that it makes consumer behavior conform in broad contours to producer need and intent. This is plausibly in accord with everyday observation of marketing practice and the commonplace claims of its practitioners. Nor will many resist the idea that these industries can bring the state to the support of their efforts in creating and managing consumer wants—that the automobile companies can get the highways that are essential for a consumer preference for automobile transportation. . . .

The first and by far the most important matter that thus becomes clear concerns the relation of the individual to industrial society in the largest sense. In the accepted economics, no general conflict can arise here. The individual or citizen is sovereign. . . . The individual is ultimately and fundamentally in command; he cannot be at war with himself.

When producer sovereignty is assumed, the result is very different. This sovereignty is exercised, we have seen, by large and complex organizations. This exercise of power is to serve their own goals—goals that include the security of the organization and its growth, convenience, prestige, commitment to technological virtuosity as well as its profits. There is every probability that these goals will differ from the aggregate expression of individual goals. Individuals are then accommodated to these goals, not the reverse.

The consequence of economic development, so viewed, is not of harmony between the individual and economic institutions but of conflict. . . . This conflict is sharply at odds with accepted economic (and political) interpretations of the reality. But it is not at odds with the reality. If there is an agreed diagnosis of contemporary discontent both in the United States and the other industrial societies, it is that the individual feels himself in the grip of large, impersonal forces whose purposes he senses to be hostile and in relation to which he feels helpless. The Pentagon pursues wars and builds weapons systems in accordance with an inner dynamic. Similarly NASA. So the Department of Transportation in relation to the SST. So General Motors as a producer of automobiles that threaten to smother cities and as a sponsor of highways that have already gone far to devour them. So industry generally as it subsumes countryside, water and air.

. . . the notion of consumer and citizen sovereignty is diverting attention from fundamental problems of the economic and political system in a fashion that serves to strengthen the very producer sovereignty that the discipline denies. . . .

If the mix of goods being produced at any given time seems unsatisfactory—if there are too many automobiles, too little mass transport—consumer sovereignty holds that this reflects the dominant consumer will. Similarly, if housing is scarce and poor, housing appliances abundant and efficient. The person who expresses doubt is seeking, in undemocratic elitist fashion, to substitute his taste for that of a majority. But if producer sovereignty is assumed the product mix will be the expression of its comparative power. If there appear to be too many automobiles, insufficient intercity or commuter rail service, or urban rapid transit, this will plausibly be because the automobile industry exercises its sovereignty (including its power to persuade people that they want automobiles more) more effectively than do the producers of alternative transport. We have more appliances than houses because General Electric is more powerfully sovereign than the house builders. Except to the exceptionally devout, none of this, I venture to think, will seem unreasonable. But economics as it is taught, by emphasizing consumer sovereignty, makes itself a shield for the exercise of producer sovereignty by the automobile industry. For by making questions about too many automobiles an elitist and undemocratic interference with consumer choice, it effectively excludes questions about the power of the automobile industry to impose its preference. In effect, it gives high moral sanction to social indifference.

Consumer sovereignty allows of no question as to a socially desirable upper limit to the consumption either in general or in particular products. The consumer wants more; theirs not to reason why, theirs but to satisfy that want. With producer sovereignty the level of consumption is seen to be a derivative of producer goals including the producer commitment to growth. Consumer attitudes are seen to be substantially formed by producer persuasion on behalf of goods. The question must then arise as to whether General Motors is the proper agency to decide the proper level of consumption for its products. And since the matter is not decided by the collective inner will of the public the question also arises as to the optimal upper level of production and consumption in general. This question should, perhaps, have been faced before now. For a host of reasons, including the effect on environment, it is unlikely that we can continue to increase physical output at recent past rates for the next (say) twenty years. It is easy to see how, once again, economics has rendered conservative service. By holding this matter to be resolved by the inner collective will of the public, it has effectively banned from public discussion all question as to how much a community should produce or consume.

John Kenneth Galbraith, *Economics, Peace and Laughter* (Boston: Houghton Mifflin Company, 1971), pp. 64, 73, 75–79. Copyright © 1971 by John Kenneth Galbraith. Reprinted by permission of the publisher, Houghton Mifflin Company.

6

Mixed Capitalism and the Economic Functions of Government

We now begin the move from our abstract working model of pure capitalism to a discussion of American capitalism. In so doing we inject a significant dose of reality into our analysis.

All real-life economies are "mixed"; government and the price system share the function of answering the Five Fundamental Questions. Yet, the various economies of the world differ drastically in the particular blend of government direction and market direction which they embody (see Table 2-3). The economy of Soviet Russia, the topic of the final chapter of this book, leans heavily toward a centrally planned economy. American capitalism, on the other hand, is predominantly a market economy. At the same time, the economic functions of government—Federal, state, and local—are of very considerable significance. In American capitalism a number of strategic economic decisions are rendered, not by individuals as such, but collectively through government. A rough indicator of the relative importance of the market and government in American capitalism is the fact that currently about four-fifths of the total output of the economy is provided by the market system, the remaining one-fifth being produced under the sponsorship of government. In short, the economy of the United States can be accurately described as *mixed capitalism*. Our economy holds *generally* to the capitalist ideology outlined in Chapter 3 and relies primarily upon the price system, the rudiments and functioning of which were outlined in Chapters

4 and 5. Government, however, assists and modifies the functioning of the price system in a variety of significant ways.

ECONOMIC FUNCTIONS OF GOVERNMENT

The economic functions of government are many, and they are varied. In fact, the economic role of government is so broad in scope that it is virtually impossible to establish an all-inclusive list of its economic functions. We shall employ the following breakdown of government's economic activities as a pattern for our discussion, recognizing that some overlapping is unavoidable.

First, some of the economic functions of government are designed to strengthen and facilitate the operation of the price system. The two major activities of government in this area are:

1 Providing the legal foundation and a social environment conducive to the effective operation of the price system.

2 Maintaining competition.

Through a second group of functions, government supplements and modifies the operation of the price system. There are three major functions of government here. They involve:

3 Redistributing income and wealth.

4 Adjusting the allocation of resources so as to alter the composition of the national output.

5 Stabilizing the economy, that is, controlling unemployment and inflation caused by the business cycle and promoting economic growth.

While this fivefold breakdown of government's functions is a useful way of analyzing its economic role, we shall find that most government activities and policies have *some* impact in all these areas. For example, a program to redistribute income to the poor affects the allocation of resources to the extent that the poor buy somewhat different goods and services from those that wealthier members of society buy. A decline in, say, government military spending for the purpose of lessening inflationary pressures also tends to reallocate resources from public to private uses.

Let us briefly consider the first two functions of government and then analyze the redistributive, allocative, and stabilization roles of government in more detail.

LEGAL AND SOCIAL FRAMEWORK FOR THE PRICE SYSTEM

Government assumes the task of providing the legal framework and certain basic services prerequisite to the effective operation of a market economy. The necessary legal framework involves such things as providing for the legal status of business enterprises, defining the rights of private ownership, and providing for the enforcement of contracts. Government also establishes legal "rules of the game" to govern the relationships of businesses, resource suppliers, and consumers with one another. Through legislation, government is enabled to referee economic relationships, detect foul play, and exercise authority in imposing appropriate penalties. The basic services provided by government include the use of police powers to maintain internal order, provision of a system of standards for measuring the weight and quality of products, and establishment of a monetary system to facilitate the exchange of goods and services.

The Pure Food and Drug Act of 1906 and its various amendments provide an excellent example of how government has strengthened the operation of the price system. This act sets rules of conduct to govern producers in their relationships with consumers. It prohibits the sale of adulterated and misbranded foods and drugs, requires the net weights and ingredients of products to be specified on their containers, establishes quality standards which must be stated on the labels of canned foods, and prohibits deceptive claims on patent-medicine labels. All these measures are designed to prevent fraudulent activities on the part of producers and, simultaneously, to increase the public's confidence in the integrity of the price system. In later chapters we shall discuss similar legislation pertaining to labor-management relations and the relations of business firms to one another.

It is worth noting that resource allocation will be altered and, in general, improved upon by this type of government activity. Supplying a medium of exchange, ensuring the quality of products, defining ownership rights, and enforcing contracts tend to increase the volume of exchange. This widens markets and permits greater specialization in the use of both property and human resources. Such specialization, we saw in Chapter 3, means a more efficient allocation of resources.

MAINTAINING COMPETITION

Competition is the basic regulatory mechanism in a capitalistic economy. It is the force which subjects producers and resource suppliers to the dictates of buyer or consumer sovereignty. With competition, it is the supply and demand decisions of *many* sellers and buyers which determine market prices. This means that individual producers and resource suppliers can only adjust to the wishes of buyers as tabulated and communicated by the price system. Profits and survival await the competitive producers who obey the price system; losses and eventual bankruptcy are the lot of those who deviate from it. With competition, buyers are the boss, the market is their agent, and businesses are their servant.

The growth of monopoly drastically alters this situation. What is monopoly? Broadly defined, it is the situation wherein the number of sellers becomes small enough for each seller to influence total supply and therefore the price of the commodity being sold. What is its significance? Simply this: When monopoly supplants competition, sellers can influence, or "rig," the market in terms of their own self-interests and to the detriment of society as a whole. Through their ability to influence total supply, monopolists can create artificial shortages of products and thereby enjoy higher prices and, very frequently, persistent economic profits. This is obviously in direct conflict with the interests of consumers. Monopolists are not regulated by the will of society as competitive sellers are. Producer sovereignty supplants consumer sovereignty to the degree that monopoly supplants competition. The result is that resources are allocated in terms of the profit-seeking interests of monopolistic sellers rather than in terms of the wants of society as a whole. In short, monopoly tends to cause a misallocation of economic resources.

In the United States the government has attempted to control monopoly primarily in two ways. First, in the case of "natural monopolies"—that is, in industries wherein technological and economic realities rule out the possibility of competitive markets—the government has created public commissions to regulate prices and service standards. Transportation, communications, and electric and other utilities are illustrations of regulated industries. At local levels of government, public ownership of electric and water utilities is quite common. But, second, in the vast majority of markets, efficient production can be attained with a high degree of competition. The Federal government has therefore enacted a series of antimonopoly or antitrust laws, beginning with the Sherman Act of 1890, for the purpose of maintaining and strengthening competition as an effective regulator of business behavior. The regulatory commissions and antitrust laws will be examined critically in Chapter 34.

Even if the legal foundation of capitalistic institutions is assured and competition is maintained, there will still be a need for certain additional economic functions on the part of government. *The market economy at its best has certain biases and shortcomings which compel government to supplement and modify its operation.*

REDISTRIBUTION OF INCOME

The price system is an impersonal mechanism, and the distribution of income to which it gives rise may entail more inequality than society desires. The market system yields very large incomes to those whose labor, by virtue of inherent ability and acquired education and skills, commands high wages. Similarly, those who possess—by virtue of hard work or easy inheritance—valuable capital and land receive large property incomes. But others in our society have less ability and have received modest amounts of education and training. And these same people typically have accumulated or inherited no property resources. Hence, their incomes are very low. Furthermore, many of the aged, the physically and mentally handicapped, and husbandless women with dependent children earn only very small incomes or, like the unemployed, no incomes at all through the price system. In short, the price system entails considerable inequality in the distribution of money income and therefore in the distribution of total output among individual households. Although progress has been made, poverty amidst overall plenty in American capitalism persists as a major economic and political issue.

Government has assumed the responsibility for ameliorating income inequality in our society. This responsibility is reflected in a variety of policies and programs. *Public assistance or welfare programs* provide relief to the destitute, aid to the dependent and handicapped, and unemployment compensation to the unemployed. These programs bring income to households which would otherwise have little or none. They achieve this goal by altering the income distribution which the price system provides. Our social security and

Medicare programs provide financial support for the retired and aged sick. Other programs involve *direct market intervention,* in which the government alters income distribution by modifying the prices established by the forces of supply and demand. Price supports for farmers and minimum-wage legislation both involve government price fixing designed to aid those whose incomes would otherwise be meager. Finally, the Federal *income tax* is designed to take a greater proportion of the incomes of the rich than of the poor and therefore has a kind of Robin Hood effect upon income distribution. The currently debated *negative income tax* proposal holds that those individuals and families whose incomes fall below specified "poverty levels" should receive payments *from* the government sufficient to bring them up to the poverty line. Despite these and other programs designed to lessen income inequality, we will find in Chapter 37 that there is considerable debate about whether government has sufficiently reduced income inequality and provided a minimum standard of living for all its citizenry.

REALLOCATION OF RESOURCES

The price system of pure capitalism operates in response to decisions made by *individual* consumers and *individual* business firms. In deciding what is to be produced and not produced, the price system reacts to the summation of individual wants and satisfactions. And the specific amounts of various goods produced will depend upon the costs which individual firms must bear in acquiring the resources necessary for production.

Now, as we saw in Chapter 5, competitive markets result in an efficient allocation of resources. For example, in Figure 6-1*a* the resulting equilibrium equates the willingness of consumers to pay for additional units of a good (as reflected in the demand curve) and the cost of producing extra units of the good (as re-

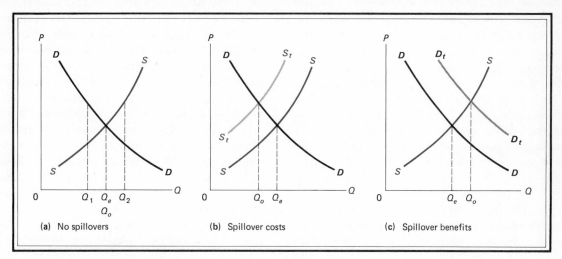

FIGURE 6-1 SPILLOVERS AND THE ALLOCATION OF RESOURCES

Without spillovers **(a)** the equilibrium output Q_e is also the most efficient, or optimal, output Q_o. But with spillover costs **(b)** resources are overallocated to production; that is, the equilibrium output exceeds the optimum output. Conversely, spillover benefits **(c)** cause an underallocation of resources in that the optimum output exceeds the equilibrium output.

flected in the supply curve). That is, at equilibrium the extra or marginal *benefit* (satisfaction) derived from consuming the last unit of output is just equal to the extra or marginal *cost* of producing that last unit. To produce some output short of the equilibrium output Q_e would mean that society is forgoing some output of product X, the benefits from which are worth more than their cost. That is, the production of Q_1 units of output would involve an underallocation of resources to product X; there is a net gain or benefit to society in producing all units of X between Q_1 and Q_e. This is so because for these units of output the demand curve (reflecting extra benefits) lies above the supply curve (reflecting extra costs). This net gain is obviously forgone if production involves only Q_1 units of output. Similarly, the production of each unit of output in excess of Q_e—for example, all the units between Q_e and Q_2—entails extra or marginal costs in excess of extra or marginal benefits. We know this from the fact that the supply curve (reflecting marginal costs) lies above the demand curve (reflecting marginal benefits) for units in

excess of Q_e. The production of units in excess of Q_e would impose net costs upon society. Here the problem is clearly an overallocation of resources to the production of X. The basic point is that in a competitive market system, production will take place at that output where the amount of resources allocated to X is "just right" or, more technically put, efficient or optimum. At Q_e there is neither an underallocation (Q_1) nor an overallocation (Q_2) to the production of X. It follows that if all markets are competitive, an efficient or optimum allocation of resources among all alternative uses will result. Hence, we equate the equilibrium output (Q_e) in Figure 6-1a with the optimum output (Q_o).

□   **Spillovers or Externalities**

But this analysis and its conclusion that competitive markets automatically bring about allocative efficiency rest upon the hidden assumption that all the benefits and costs associated with the production and consumption of each product are fully reflected in the market demand and supply curves. Stated differently, it is assumed that there are no *spillovers* or *externalities* associated with the production or consumption of any good or service. A *spillover*[1] occurs when some of the benefits or costs associated with the production or consumption of a good spill over to third parties, that is, to parties other than the immediate buyer or seller. Spillovers are also termed externalities because they are benefits and costs accruing to some individual or group external to the market transaction.

Spillover Costs   When the production or consumption of a commodity inflicts costs upon some third party without compensation, there exists a spillover cost. The most obvious examples of spillover or social costs involve environmental pollution. When a chemical manufacturer or meat-packing plant dumps its wastes into a lake or river, swimmers, fishermen, and boaters—not to mention communities which seek a usable water supply—suffer spillover costs. When a petroleum refinery pollutes the air with smoke or a paint factory creates distressing odors, the community bears spillover costs for which it is not compensated.

How do spillover or social costs affect the allocation of resources? Figure 6-1b tells the story. When spillover costs occur—when producers shift some of their costs onto the community—their production costs are lower than would otherwise be the case. That is, the supply curve does not include or "capture" all the costs which can be legitimately associated with the production of the good. Hence, the producer's supply curve, SS, understates the total costs of production and therefore lies below the supply curve which would include all costs, S_tS_t. That is, S_tS_t includes the production costs which the polluting firm must bear *plus* the additional costs it would incur if it had properly disposed of its wastes. It is obvious

that with S_tS_t the firm would find it profitable to produce output Q_o. This is the optimum output for reasons previously explained. But by polluting, that is, by creating spillover costs, the firm enjoys lower costs and the supply curve SS. The result is that the equilibrium output Q_e is larger than the optimum output Q_o. In short, resources are overallocated to the production of the commodity; each unit of output between Q_o and Q_e entails costs (including spillover costs) in excess of benefits; S_tS_t lies above DD for all units of output between Q_o and Q_e. Output Q_e fulfills the interest of producers in maximizing profits, but it exceeds output Q_o, which fulfills society's interest in allocating resources efficiently.

Spillover Benefits   But spillovers may also take the form of benefits. The production or consumption of certain goods and services may confer social or spillover benefits on third parties or the community at large for which payment or compensation is not required. For example, chest x-rays and polio immunization shots result in direct benefits to the immediate consumer. But an early diagnosis of tuberculosis and the prevention of a contagious disease yield widespread and substantial spillover benefits to the entire community. Education is another standard example of spillover benefits. Education entails benefits to individual consumers: "more educated" people generally achieve higher incomes than do "less educated" people. But education also confers sizable benefits upon society; for example, the economy as a whole benefits from a more versatile and more productive labor force, on the one hand, and smaller outlays in the areas of crime prevention, law enforcement, and welfare programs, on the other. Significant, too, is the fact that political participation correlates positively with the level of education; for example, the percentage of persons who vote increases with educational attainment.

Figure 6-1c shows the impact of spillover benefits upon resource allocation. The existence of spillover benefits simply means that

---

[1]Spillovers may go by other names—for example, external economies and diseconomies, neighborhood effects, and social benefits and costs.

the market demand curve, which reflects only private benefits, understates total benefits. The market demand curve fails to capture all the benefits associated with the provision and consumption of goods and services which entail spillover benefits. Thus DD in Figure 6-1c indicates the benefits which private individuals derive from education; D_tD_t is drawn to include these private benefits *plus* the additional spillover benefits accruing to society at large. Thus, while market demand DD and supply SS would yield an educational output of Q_e, this output would be less than the optimum output Q_o. That is, if the market took all benefits—private and spillover or external—into account, the output of education would be greater than the market would provide. Comparing D_tD_t and SS, we find that for all units of output between Q_e and Q_o, the extra or marginal benefits shown by the demand curve exceed the extra or marginal costs embodied in the supply curve. Hence, there is a net benefit to society in having this additional output.

Our discussion of spillover costs and benefits yields two generalizations—two instances of "market failure":

1 When spillover *costs* are significant, the market will *overallocate* resources to the production of that good or service. The equilibrium output will exceed that output which entails allocative efficiency.

2 When spillover *benefits* are important, the market will *underallocate* resources to that commodity. The equilibrium output will fall short of the optimum output.

Corrective Government Policy   What actions might government take to correct the overallocations and underallocations of resources associated with spillover costs and benefits? In both instances government attempts to "internalize" the external costs and benefits; that is, government follows certain policies designed to cause the market to take into account spillover costs and benefits.

Consider, first, the case of spillover costs.

Two basic courses of action are common: corrective legislation and special taxes.

1 Looking at our examples of air and water pollution, we find that the most direct action is simply to pass *legislation* against it. Cities may pass ordinances which prohibit or control pollution. Such legislation forces potential polluters to bear the costs of more properly disposing of industrial wastes; for example, firms must buy and install smoke-abatement equipment or facilities to purify water which has been contaminated by manufacturing processes. Such action forces potential offenders, under the threat of legal action, to bear *all* the costs associated with their production. In short, legislation can shift the supply curve SS toward S_tS_t in Figure 6-1b, tending to bring the equilibrium and optimum outputs into equality.

2 A second and less direct action is for government to levy a *special tax* which approximates the spillover costs per unit of output. In effect, through this tax, government attempts to shove back onto the offending firm those external or spillover costs which private industry would otherwise avoid. With the added tax costs we again find that producers will have to get a higher price at each possible level of output. This means a decline in supply relative to demand. It is profitable for firms to produce smaller outputs, and resources are freed for alternative uses. The net result will be an improved allocation of resources—an allocation more consistent with the *total* costs of production. By again shifting the SS curve toward S_tS_t, the existing overallocation of resources to this product will be corrected; Q_e will move toward Q_o.

What policies are appropriate for the case of spillover benefits? In the first place, assuming that the spillover or social benefits are not inordinately large when compared with the benefits received by individual purchasers, government can encourage the production of such goods and services by subsidizing their output. *Subsidies* are simply special taxes in reverse; taxes impose an extra cost on producers, whereas subsidies provide extra revenue. A unit of government may thus provide an outright bounty to firms for each unit of output they produce. The effect is to internalize the spillover benefits by shifting the *DD* curve of Figure 6-1*c* toward D_tD_t, bringing the equilibrium output into accord with the optimum output. Public subsidization of mass immunization programs and public health clinics are cases in point.

A second policy option arises if spillover benefits are extremely large: Government may simply choose to finance or, in the extreme, to own and operate such industries. This option leads us into a discussion of social goods and services.

□ **Social Goods and Services**

Why is it that we purchase bread, shoes, Fords, stereo receivers, and sweaters from private producers through the market system, while national defense, lighthouses, space exploration, and flood-control and insect-abatement programs are provided through the public sector? Why are the former *private goods* and the latter *social or public goods?* The answer hinges largely on the following two points.

Applicability of the Exclusion Principle The so-called *exclusion principle* applies to private goods, but not to public goods. That is, in the case of private products, those who are willing to pay the price get the product, but those who are unwilling to pay are excluded from the benefits provided by the product. The exclusion principle applies to private goods in that producers can effectively withhold the product from those who are unwilling to pay for it. But there are certain kinds of goods and services to which the exclusion principle does *not* apply; that is, there is no practical and effective way of excluding individuals from the benefits provided by some goods if they refuse to pay. The classic example is a

lighthouse on a treacherous coast or a harbor. Once in operation, its warning light is a guide to *all* ships. There is no practical way to exclude certain ships from its benefits. And why should any ship owner voluntarily pay for the benefits he receives from the light? The light is there for all to see, and a ship captain cannot be excluded from seeing it if the owner chooses not to pay. Furthermore, given the inapplicability of the exclusion principle, there is obviously no economic incentive for private enterprises to supply lighthouses. If the services of the lighthouse cannot be priced and sold, it will clearly be unprofitable for private firms to devote resources to lighthouses. In short, here is a service which yields substantial benefits but for which the market would allocate no resources. National defense, flood-control programs, and the other public goods mentioned earlier have this same characteristic. Hence, if society is to enjoy such goods and services, they must be provided by the public sector and financed by compulsory charges in the form of taxes.

Large Spillover Benefits While the inapplicability of the exclusion principle rather sharply sets off public from private goods, a variety of other goods and services are provided by government even though the exclusion principle *could* be applied. In particular, such goods and services as education, streets and highways, police and fire protection, preventive medicine, and sewage disposal could be subject to the exclusion principle, that is, they could be priced and provided by private producers through the market system. But, as noted earlier, these are all services which entail substantial spillover benefits and therefore would be grossly underproduced by the market system. Therefore, government undertakes or sponsors their provision to avoid the underallocation of resources which would otherwise occur. Such goods and services are sometimes called *quasi-public goods.* One can readily understand the long-standing controversies surrounding the status of medical care and housing. Are these private goods to be provided through the market system, or are they quasi-public goods to be provided by government?

☐   **Allocating Resources
to Social Goods**

Given that the price system would fail to allocate resources for public goods and would underallocate resources for quasi-public goods, what is the mechanism by which such goods get produced?

Social goods are purchased through the government on the basis of group, or collective, choices, in contrast to private goods, which are purchased from private enterprises on the basis of individual choices. More specifically, the types and quantities of the various social goods produced are determined in a democracy by political means, that is, by voting. The quantities of the various social goods consumed are a matter of public policy.[2] These group decisions, made in the political arena, supplement the individual choices of households and businesses in answering the Five Fundamental Questions.

Assuming these group decisions have been rendered, precisely how are resources reallocated from the production of private goods to the production of social goods? In a full-employment economy, government is faced with the task of freeing resources from private employment to make them available for the production of social goods. The obvious means of releasing resources from private uses is to reduce private demand for them. This is ac-

complished by levying taxes on businesses and households, thereby diverting some of their incomes—some of their potential purchasing power—out of the income-expenditure streams. With lower incomes, businesses and households will be forced to curtail their investment and consumption spending. *In short, taxes tend to diminish private demand for goods and services, and this decrease in turn prompts a drop in the private demand for resources.* By diverting purchasing power from private spenders to government, taxes free resources from private uses. Government expenditure of the tax proceeds can then reabsorb these resources and provide social goods and services. For example, corporation and personal income taxes release resources from the production of investment goods—drill presses, boxcars, warehouses—and consumer goods—food, clothing, and television sets. Government expenditures tend to reabsorb these resources in the production of guided missiles, military aircraft, and new schools and highways. Government purposely reallocates resources to bring about significant changes in the composition of the economy's total output.

STABILIZATION

The primary purpose of the governmental functions considered thus far is to alter the allocation of resources or, in other words, to change the composition of the national output. Historically, the most recent and in some ways the most important function of government is that of stabilizing the economy—assisting the private economy to achieve both the full employment of resources and a stable price level. Part 2 of this book examines in detail the determinants of employment and the price level in a capitalistic economy. Hence, at this point we pause only to outline and assert (rather than fully explain) the stabilization function of government.

---

[2]There are obvious differences between *dollar voting,* which dictates output in the private sector of the economy, and *political voting,* which determines output in the public sector. The rich person has many more votes to cast in the private sector than does the poor person. In the public sector, each—at least in theory—has an equal say. Furthermore, the children who cast their votes for bubble gum and comic books in the private sector are banned by virtue of their age from the registering of social choices.

The key point is that the level of output depends directly upon total spending or aggregate demand. A high level of total demand means it will be profitable for the various industries to produce large outputs, and this condition, in turn, will necessitate that both property and human resources be employed at high levels. But we shall find in Part 2 that there are no mechanisms in the capitalistic system to ensure that aggregate demand will be at that particular level which will provide for full employment. Two unhappy possibilities might arise:

1   Unemployment   The level of total demand in the private sector may be too low for full employment. The government's obligation is to augment private demand so that total demand—private *and* public—will be sufficient to generate full employment. How can government do this? The answer is, by using the same techniques—government spending and taxes—as it uses to reallocate resources to the production of social goods. Specifically, government should increase its own spending on social goods and services on the one hand, and reduce taxes in order to stimulate private spending on the other.

2   Inflation   The second possibility is that the economy may attempt to spend in excess of its productive capacity. If aggregate demand exceeds the full-employment output, the excess demand will have the effect of pulling up the price level. Excessive aggregate demand is inflationary. Government's obligation here is to eliminate the excess spending. It does this primarily by cutting its own expenditures and by raising taxes so as to curtail private spending.

Caution: The real world, unfortunately, is more complex than our discussion implies. Hence, the lamentable situation of simultaneous unemployment and inflation which has plagued the 1970s is not susceptible to such simple and self-evident remedies. We deal with these complexities in Chapter 18.

EVALUATING GOVERNMENT'S ROLE

Thus far we have been content to state the major economic functions of government and to indicate the overall impact of their performance upon the economy. We now turn to the problem of evaluating the economic role of government. Unfortunately, government's economic role is extremely difficult to assess. There are no simple quantitative standards by which the scope and quality of government's performance can be gauged. Any evaluation of the public sector quickly pushes us beyond the boundaries of economic science and into the larger realms of political theory and philosophy. Nevertheless, let us consider the following three questions:

1 To what extent is there agreement upon the legitimacy of the five stated governmental functions?

2 Do guidelines exist for determining the appropriate scope of public sector activities?

3 Given that there are certain deficiencies or failures in private decision making through the market system, are there analogous failures involved in collective decision making in the public sector?

□   Desirability of Functions

Should government perform the five economic functions we have just discussed? All things considered, there is general and widespread agreement that these functions entail tasks which legitimately devolve on government. And, in fact, with the exception of the stabilization function, government has performed all these functions to a greater or lesser degree throughout American economic history. True, a small minority within the United States espouses the philosophy of "that government is best which governs least." At the other extreme, there are those who look upon an expansion of the functions of government as a panacea for any and all the ills of society. Though these groups are often highly vocal, it

must be emphasized that they are small minorities. The vast majority of people is in
fairly close agreement that government has
some obligation in each of the areas we have
discussed.

Men of goodwill may agree that all five of
the stated functions of government are legitimate, but they may seriously disagree about
the extent to which these functions should be
pursued and whether a specific project or program falls within the public sector. Few would
question that government has *some* role to
play in providing national defense, education,
and highways. But there may be substantial
disagreement about the size of the public
budget for each of these purposes. And there
may be controversy about whether certain
particular projects—the provision of medical
care or electric power, for example—should be
within the public sector at all. Such controversy is not surprising. One's view of the
proper scope of government is ultimately a
matter of personal values and ideology. The
relative size of the private and public sectors is
only partially an economic question; one's
judgment here depends upon one's "politics,"
in addition to one's conception of the relative
efficiency of the private and public sectors.

☐ **Benefit-Cost Analysis**

Economics can provide some guidance to
efficient decision making in the public sector.
This guidance takes the form of *benefit-cost
analysis.*

Suppose government is contemplating
some specific project, for example, a flood-control project. The basic nature of the economizing problem (Chapter 2) tells us that any
decision to use more resources in, say, the public sector will involve both a benefit and a cost.
The benefit is the extra satisfaction resulting
from the output of more social goods; the cost
is the loss of satisfaction associated with the
concomitant decline in the production of private goods. Should the resources under consideration be shifted from the private to the
public sector? The answer is "Yes" *if* the benefits from the extra social goods exceed the cost
resulting from having fewer private goods. The
answer is "No" *if* the value or cost of the forgone private goods is greater than the benefits
associated with the extra social goods.

But benefit-cost analysis can do more
than merely indicate whether a public program
is worth undertaking. It can also provide guidance concerning the extent to which a given
project should be pursued. Economic questions, after all, are not simply questions to be
answered by "Yes" or "No," but rather, matters of "how much" or "how little." Consider
the case of flood control. We note first that the
benefits from a flood-control project are largely
spillovers and that the exclusion principle is
not readily applicable. That is, a flood-control
project is basically a social good. Now, should
government undertake a flood-control project
in a given river valley? And, if so, what is the
proper size or scope for the project?

Table 6-1 provides us with the answers.
Here we list a series of increasingly ambitious
and increasingly costly flood-control plans. To
what extent, if at all, should government undertake flood control? The answers depend
upon costs and benefits. Costs in this case are
largely the capital costs of constructing and
maintaining levees and reservoirs; benefits
take the form of reduced flood damage.

In the first place, a quick glance at all the
plans indicates that in each instance total benefits (column 4) exceed total costs (column 2),
indicating that a flood-control project on this
river is economically justifiable. But a second
question remains: What is the optimum size or
scope for this project? The answer is determined by comparing the additional, or *marginal,* costs and the additional, or *marginal,*
benefits associated with each plan. The guideline is formalized common sense: Pursue an
activity or project so long as the marginal benefits (column 5) exceed the marginal costs
(column 3). Stop the activity or project at, or
as close as possible to, that point at which
marginal benefits equal marginal costs. In this

Table 6-1   BENEFIT-COST ANALYSIS FOR A FLOOD-CONTROL PROJECT

(1) Plan	(2) Total annual cost of project	(3) Extra or marginal cost	(4) Total annual benefit (reduction in damage)	(5) Extra or marginal benefit
Without protection	$ 0		$ 0	
A: Levees	3,000	$ 3,000	6,000	$ 6,000
B: Small reservoir	10,000	7,000	16,000	10,000
C: Medium reservoir	**18,000**	8,000	**25,000**	9,000
D: Large reservoir	30,000	12,000	32,000	7,000

Source: Adapted from Otto Eckstein, *Public Finance,* 3d ed. (Englewood Cliffs, N.J.: Prentice-Hall, Inc., 1973), p. 23. Used with permission.

case Plan C—the medium-sized reservoir—is the best plan. Plans A and B are too modest; in both cases marginal benefits exceed marginal costs. Plan D entails marginal costs ($12,000) in excess of marginal benefits ($7000) and therefore cannot be justified. Plan D isn't economically justifiable; it involves an overallocation of resources to this flood-control project. Plan C is closest to the optimum; it "pushes" flood control so long as marginal benefits exceed marginal costs. Regarded from a slightly different vantage point, the marginal benefit–marginal cost rule will determine which plan entails the maximum excess of total benefits over total costs or, in other words, the plan which yields the largest *net* gain to society.

Some Implications   This elementary discussion of benefit-cost analysis implies several points which are helpful in our thinking about the appropriate scope of the public sector.

1 Benefit-cost analysis explodes the myth that "economy in government" and "reduced government spending" are synonymous. "Economy" is concerned with efficiency in resource use. If a government program yields marginal benefits which are less than the marginal benefits attainable from alternative private uses—that is, if costs exceed benefits— then the proposed public program should *not* be undertaken. But if the reverse is true—if benefits exceed costs—then it would be uneconomical or "wasteful" *not* to spend on that governmental program. Economy in govern-

ment does *not* mean the minimization of public spending; rather, it means allocating resources between the private and public sectors until no net benefits can be realized from additional reallocations.

2 A special point must be made with respect to the stabilization function of government. One can argue that if the economy is experiencing substantial unemployment, public programs can be initiated which benefit society, on the one hand, but entail no costs, on the other. That is, we might construct a production possibilities curve similar to Figure 2-2, with social goods on the vertical axis and private goods on the horizontal axis, and put the economy at some unemployment point inside the curve. Now increases in government spending on public projects which move the economy vertically from the unemployment point to a point on the curve entail an increased output of social goods *without* any decline in the availability of private goods. Thus many of the New Deal make-work programs of the Great Depression of the 1930s were labeled as grossly inefficient and wasteful. What could be more inefficient than putting men to work raking leaves, planting trees, and manicuring the roadside at a time when poverty and hunger were widespread? Yet, the New Deal projects were quite efficient in the sense that benefits were large as compared with the cost of forgone output. The alternative to New Deal employment during much of the 1930s was unemployment; hence, employment on government projects entailed no real cost in the sense of forgone private production.

3 The application of the benefit-cost principle to the problem of the relative size of the private and public sectors is basically no different than the automatic benefit-cost comparisons which the market makes with respect to the composition of output within the private sector. In our earlier discussion we noted that in the absence of spillovers, the competitive market would result in an optimum output of each private good. That is, each private good would be produced so long as the benefits associated with an extra unit exceeded the accompanying costs. In Figure 6-1a the market automatically applies benefit-cost analysis and negotiates the production of the optimum output Q_o.

Limitations and Problems Benefit-cost analysis is extremely helpful in promoting clear thinking about the public sector and is in fact very useful in actual studies involving projects such as flood control and highway construction. But we must acknowledge that many attempts to apply benefit-cost analysis encounter severe problems and limitations.

Measurement In the first place, benefit-cost analysis—as demonstrated in Table 6-1—assumes that benefits and costs can be measured with reasonable accuracy. To the extent that this is not the case, the reliability of benefit-cost analysis as a guide to public spending is diminished. Now the problem is that most of the programs appropriate for the public sector are those which entail large spillover effects. For social goods per se, the benefits are almost entirely in the form of spillovers and, in addition, the exclusion principle is inapplicable. In short, benefits are widely diffused and not automatically measured by the dollar yardstick of the market. How does one quantify in dollar terms the decline in the loss of crops and livestock due to flood control? What is the value of the recreational benefits associated with the construction of a reservoir? How does one quantify the total cost of

putting, say, several thousand acres of productive farmland under water? What might be the spillover cost of the reservoir in terms of damage to the ecology of the area?

Consider the possible benefits and costs associated with the construction of a new freeway in a major metropolitan area. In addition to estimating the obvious costs—land purchase and construction costs—the responsible agency must also estimate the spillover cost of additional air pollution which results from an enlarged flow of traffic. Furthermore, more traffic may call for increased expenditures for traffic police. What about benefits? Improved transportation means a widening of markets, more competition, and a greater opportunity for the community to specialize according to comparative advantage. But what is the monetary value of this benefit? And the freeway may help make more jobs accessible to the central city poor. Again, what is the dollar value of these benefits? Given the suggested difficulties in estimating all the costs and benefits associated with such relatively tangible undertakings as highway and reservoir construction, one can imagine the enormous obstacles in applying benefit-cost analysis to space exploration, foreign aid, or a vocational training program for disadvantaged youths. The point is that the full costs and benefits associated with government programs are not easily calculated, and benefit-cost analysis is frequently difficult, if not impossible, to apply.

Interactions Secondly, we must recognize that in practice the allocative, redistributional, and stabilization functions of government are all closely intertwined. A government policy or action specifically designed, say, to reallocate resources from private to public uses will almost invariably affect the distribution of income and have implications for output and price level stabilization. These interactions complicate the making of rational decisions. Consider, once again, our flood-control project. Its purpose is primarily allocative—to increase the output of a specific social good which is worth more than alternative private goods. But the project might have adverse effects in terms of society's distributional and stabilization objectives. Suppose that the taxes to be collected in financing the project are of such a kind that they are paid disproportionately by low-income people. And suppose that the resulting benefits accrue chiefly to wealthy farmers and prosperous businessmen. *If* greater equality in income distribution is a high-priority policy objective of society, then presumably the adverse redistributional effects of the project should be taken into account. But how? How can the "cost" of the redistributional impact be measured?

A similar conflict might arise with respect to the stabilization function. Assume the economy is experiencing quite severe inflation as a result of excess aggregate spending. Now, despite the desirability of the flood-control project as indicated by benefit-cost analysis, should the project be initiated in view of the fact that the added spending on flood control will intensify inflationary pressures and promote price level instability? The point is that if a social goods project has adverse implications with respect to society's distributional and stabilization goals, the case for the project is less clear than if these implications were favorable or, at least, substantially neutral. In the context of such possible dilemmas, the rendering of rational public policy decisions becomes complex indeed.

■
PUBLIC SECTOR FAILURE?[3]

For much of this century the view was widely held that government was somehow blessed with the capacity to resolve otherwise intractable problems. But this conception of the

public sector has undergone a substantial transition in the past decade and there now exists considerable disenchantment with, and even distrust of, government. This change in sentiment has diverse roots, but it stems largely from the apparent failure of costly government programs to resolve socioeconomic ills. For example, it is argued that foreign aid programs have contributed little or nothing to the economic growth of the less developed nations. Similarly, critics of the war on poverty programs point to the persistence of poverty, particularly in the urban ghettos. We hear reports that well-financed state and Federal school enrichment programs have had no perceptible impact upon the educational attainment of students. Some programs have allegedly fostered the very problems they were designed to solve: our farm programs were originally designed to save the family farm, but in fact have heavily subsidized large corporate farms which in turn have driven family farms out of business. There are also charges that government agencies have become mired in a blizzard of paperwork. The popular press tells us that social workers in New York City spend 70 to 80 percent of their time doing paperwork, leaving only 20 to 30 percent of their time for their clients. It is alleged that the public bureaucracy embodies great duplication of effort; that obsolete programs persist; that various agencies work at cross purposes, and so on.

Coincident with this popular disenchantment, there has evolved a body of literature on the *theory of public choice* which alleges that, just as certain limitations or failures are embodied in the private sector's price system, so there are also more-or-less inherent deficiencies in the political processes and bureaucratic agencies which comprise the public sector. Hence, we might agree that government has a legitimate role to play in dealing with instances of market failure; that is, government should make adjustments for spillover costs and benefits, provide social goods and services, temper income inequality, and so forth. We might also accept benefit-cost anal-

[3]This section is based upon the excellent discussion of public sector failure found in James D. Gwartney, *Economics: Private and Public Choice* (New York: Academic Press, 1976), chap. 30. The interested reader should also consult Richard B. McKenzie and Gordon Tullock, *The New World of Economics* (Homewood, Ill.: Richard D. Irwin, Inc., 1975), chap. 17.

ysis as an important guide to economically efficient decision making in the public sector. But a more fundamental question remains: Are there inherent problems or shortcomings within the public sector which constrain governmental decision making as a mechanism for promoting economic efficiency? In fact, casual reflection suggests that there may be significant divergence between "sound economics" and "good politics." We know that the former calls for the public sector to pursue various programs so long as marginal benefits exceed marginal costs. Good politics, however, suggests that politicians should support those programs and policies which will maximize their chances of getting elected and retained in office.

Let us now briefly consider some possible reasons for public sector failure, that is, some reasons why the public sector may function inefficiently in an economic sense.

□   Special Interests

Ideally, public decisions promote the general welfare or, at least, the interests of the vast majority of the citizenry. Indeed, government presumably protects society at large from abuse by powerful economic interest groups. Example: government should protect the consumer from natural monopolies. But it is contended that, in fact, government often promotes the goals of small interest groups to the detriment of the public at large. Stated differently, efficient public decision making is often impaired by a *special-interest effect.*

How can this happen? In part the answer is inherent in the definition of a special-interest issue: this is an issue, program, or policy from which a small number of people individually will receive *large* gains at the expense of a large number of persons who individually suffer *small* losses. The small group of potential beneficiaries will be well informed and highly vocal on this issue, pressing politicians for approval. The large numbers who face small losses will generally be uninformed and indif-

ferent on this issue; after all, they have little at stake. Crudely put, the politician feels he will clearly lose the support of the small interest group which supports the program if he votes against it. But he will *not* lose the support of the large group of uninformed voters who will evaluate him on other issues in which they have a stronger interest. Furthermore, the politicians' inclination to support special-interest legislation is enhanced by the fact that such groups are often more than willing to help finance the campaigns of "right-minded" politicians. The result is that the politician will support the special-interest program, even though that program may *not* be economically desirable from a social point of view.

Examples of special-interest groups realizing legislation and policies which are unjustified on the basis of efficiency or equity considerations are manifold: tariffs on foreign products which limit domestic competition and raise prices to consumers (Chapter 42); tax loopholes which benefit the very rich (Chapter 8); "pork-barrel" public works programs; and so forth. Incidentally, the Last Word segment of this chapter presents a Marxist view of the impact of special-interest groups. It envisions the political state as an instrument through which large corporations (the capitalist class) exploit the working class.

□   Clear Benefits, Hidden Costs

It is also contended that the vote-seeking politician will not *objectively* weigh all the costs and benefits of various programs, as economic rationality demands, in deciding which to support and which to reject. Rather, the vote-seeking politician will tend to favor programs which entail immediate and clear-cut benefits, on the one hand, and vague, difficult-to-identify, or deferred, costs, on the other. Conversely, politicians will look askance at programs which embody immediate and easily identifiable costs along with future benefits which are diffuse and vague. The point here is that such biases in the area of public choice can lead politicians to reject economically justifiable programs and to accept programs which are economically irrational. Example: A proposal to construct and expand mass transit systems in large metropolitan areas may be economically rational on the basis of objective benefit-cost analysis. But if (1) the program is to be financed by immediate increases in highly visible income taxes *and* (2) benefits will accrue only a decade hence when the project is completed, the vote-seeking politician may decide to oppose the program. Assume, on the other hand, that a proposed program of Federal aid to municipal police forces is *not* justifiable on the basis of objective benefit-cost analysis. But if costs are concealed and deferred through deficit financing, the program's modest benefits may loom so large that it gains political approval.

□   Nonselectivity

Public-choice theorists also argue that the nature of the political process is such that citizens are forced to be less selective in the choice of public goods and services than they are in the choice of private goods and services. In the market sector, the citizen *as consumer* can reflect his personal preferences very precisely by buying certain goods and forgoing others. However, in the public sector the citizen *as voter* is confronted with two or more candidates for office, each of whom represents different "bundles" of programs (social goods and services). The critical point is that in no case is the bundle of social goods represented by any particular candidate likely to precisely fit the wants of the particular voter. For example, voter Smith's favored candidate for office may endorse national health insurance, the development of nuclear energy, subsidies to tobacco farmers, and tariffs on imported automobiles. Citizen Smith votes for this candidate because the bundle of programs he endorses comes closest to matching Smith's preferences, even

though Smith may oppose tobacco subsidies and tariffs on foreign cars. The voter, in short, must take the good with the bad; in the public sector, one is forced to "buy" goods and services one does not want. It is as if, in going to a clothing store, you were forced to buy an unwanted pair of slacks to get a wanted pair of shoes. This is obviously a situation wherein resources are *not* being allocated efficiently so as best to satisfy consumer wants. In this sense, the provision of social goods and services is held to be inherently inefficient.

□   Bureaucracy and Inefficiency

Finally, it is contended that private businesses are inherently more efficient than public agencies. The reason for this is *not* that lazy and incompetent workers somehow end up in the public sector, while the ambitious and capable gravitate to the private sector. Rather, it is held that the market system creates incentives and pressures for internal efficiency which are absent in the public sector. More specifically, the managers of private enterprises have a strong personal incentive— increased profit income—to be efficient in their operation. Whether a private firm is in a competitive or monopolistic environment, lower costs through efficient management contribute to enlarged profits. There is no tangible personal gain—a counterpart to profits—for the bureau chief who achieves efficiency within his domain. In brief, there is simply less incentive to be cost-conscious in the public sector. Indeed, in a larger sense the market system imposes an explicit test of performance of private firms—the test of profits and losses. A firm which is efficient is profitable and therefore successful; it survives, prospers, and grows. An enterprise which is inefficient is unprofitable and unsuccessful; it declines and in time goes bankrupt and ceases to exist. But there is no similar, clear-cut test by which one can assess the efficiency or inefficiency of public agencies.

How can one determine whether TVA, a state university, a local fire department, the Department of Agriculture, or the Bureau of Indian Affairs is operating efficiently?

Cynics argue that, in fact, a public agency which uses its resources inefficiently may be in line for a budget increase! In the private sector, inefficiency and monetary losses lead to the abandonment of certain activities—the discontinuing of certain products and services. But government, it is contended, is loath to abandon activities in which it has failed. "Indeed, the typical response of government to the failure of an activity is to double its budget and staff." [4] This obviously means that public sector inefficiency may be sustained on a larger scale. Furthermore, returning to our earlier comments regarding special-interest groups, it has been pointed out that public programs spawn new constituencies of bureaucrats and beneficiaries whose political clout causes programs to be sustained or expanded after they have fulfilled their goals or, alternatively, even if they have failed miserably in their mission. Relevant bureaucrats, school administrators, and teachers may become a highly effective special-interest group for sustaining inefficient programs of Federal aid to education or for causing these programs to be expanded beyond the point at which marginal benefits equal marginal costs.

Postscript: Some specific suggestions have been offered recently to deal with the problems of bureaucratic inefficiency. Benefit-cost analysis, of course, is one suggested approach. It has also been proposed that all legislation establishing new programs contain well-defined performance standards so the public can better judge efficiency. Further, the suggestion has been made that expiration dates be written into all new programs, thereby forcing a thorough periodic evaluation which might indicate the need for program abandonment.

□ **Imperfect Institutions**

One might argue that these criticisms of public sector efficiency are overdrawn and too cynical. Perhaps this is so. On the other hand, they are sufficiently persuasive to shake one's faith in a simplistic concept of a benevolent government responding with precision and efficiency to the wants of its citizenry. We have seen that the market system of the private sector is by no means perfectly efficient; indeed, government's economic functions are attempts to correct the price system's shortcomings. But now we find that the public sector may also be subject to important deficiencies in fulfilling its economic functions. "The relevant comparison is not between perfect markets and imperfect governments, nor between faulty markets and all-knowing, rational, benevolent governments, but between inevitably imperfect institutions." [5]

One of the important implications of the fact that the market system and public agencies are both imperfect institutions is that, in practice, it can be exceedingly difficult to determine whether some particular activity can be performed with greater success in the private or the public sector. [6] It is easy to reach agreement on polar cases: national defense must lie in the public sector, whereas wheat production can best be accomplished in the private sector. But what about health insurance? The provision of parks and recreation areas? Fire protection? Housing? Education? The point is that it is very hard to assess each type of good or service and to say unequivocally that its provision should be assigned to either the public or the private sector. Evidence that this is so is reflected in the fact that all the goods and services mentioned above are provided in part by both private enterprises and public agencies.

[4] Peter F. Drucker, "The Sickness of Government," *The Public Interest,* Winter 1969, p. 13.

[5] Otto Eckstein, *Public Finance,* 3d ed. (Englewood Cliffs, N.J.: Prentice-Hall, Inc., 1973), p. 17.

[6] Our survey of the "isms" in Chapter 2 is indicative of the diversity of judgments on this question internationally.

THE ISSUE OF FREEDOM

Finally, let us consider an important, but elusive, question: What is the nature of the relationship between the role and size of the public sector, on the one hand, and freedom, on the other? Although no attempt is made here to explore this issue in depth, it is relevant to indicate the outlines of two divergent views on this question.

□ The Conservative Position

Many conservative economists feel that, in addition to the economic costs involved in any expansion of the public sector, there is also a cost in the form of diminished individual freedom. Two basic points constitute this position. First, there is the "power corrupts" argument.[7] "Freedom is a rare and delicate plant. . . . history confirms that the great threat to freedom is the concentration of power. . . . by concentrating power in political hands, [government] is . . . a threat to freedom." Secondly, one can practice selectivity in the market system of the private sector, using one's income to buy precisely what one chooses and rejecting unwanted commodities. But in the public sector—even assuming a high level of political democracy—conformity and coercion are inherent. If the majority decides in favor of certain governmental actions—to build a reservoir, to establish an old-age insurance program, to provide a guaranteed annual income—the minority must conform. Hence, the "use of political channels, while inevitable, tends to strain the social cohesion essential for a stable society."[8] To the extent that decisions can be rendered selectively by individuals through markets, the need for conformity and coercion is lessened and this "strain" reduced. Proponents of this view argue that (1) the

[7] Milton Friedman, *Capitalism and Freedom* (Chicago: The University of Chicago Press, 1962), p. 2.
[8] Ibid., p. 23.

scope of government should be strictly limited, and (2) government power should be decentralized.

□ The Liberal Stance

But liberal economists are skeptical of the conservative position. They hold that the conservative view is based upon what we shall call the *fallacy of limited decisions*. That is, the conservatives implicitly assume that during any particular period of time there is a limited, or fixed, number of decisions to be made in connection with the operation of the economy. Hence, if government makes more of these decisions in performing its stated functions, the private sector of the economy will necessarily have fewer "free" decisions or choices to make. This is held to be fallacious reasoning. By sponsoring the production of social goods, government is, in fact, *extending* the range of free choice by permitting society to enjoy goods and services which would not be available in the absence of governmental provision. One can cogently argue that it is in large measure through the economic functions of government that we have been striving to free ourselves in some measure from ignorance, poverty, disease, crime, discrimination, and other ills. Note, too, that in providing most social goods, government does not typically undertake production itself, but rather, purchases these goods through private enterprise. When government makes the decision to build an interstate highway, private concerns are given the responsibility for making a myriad of specific decisions and choices in connection with the carrying out of this decision.

Finally, it should be noted that during a depression, the number of choices made by private businesses and households is greatly restricted. Why? Because production has been slowed and incomes have been drastically curtailed. The businessman has fewer choices to make concerning, for example, the types of products and combinations of resources he may use. Indeed, some firms will have to close down and make no decisions at all. The consumer has fewer decisions to make in disposing of his income, because his income is now very small or conceivably nonexistent. Now if government, by increased participation and intervention in the economy, can correct or even alleviate a depression, the number of decisions and choices open to both businesses and consumers will increase. That is, government, by making more decisions concerning the operation of the economy, might restore prosperity, permitting the number of private decisions to increase also. Hence, the number of private and public decisions made in the operation of the economy may, *within limits,* vary in the same direction. A larger number of governmental decisions may or may not mean a smaller number of private decisions.

One of America's leading economists has summarized the liberal view in these pointed words:[9]

> Traffic lights coerce me and limit my freedom. Yet in the midst of a traffic jam on the unopen road, was I really "free" before there were lights? And has the algebraic total of freedom, for me or the representative motorist or the group as a whole, been increased or decreased by the introduction of well-engineered stop lights? Stop lights, you know, are also go lights. . . . When we introduce the traffic light, we have, although the arch individualist may not like the new order, by cooperation and coercion created for ourselves greater freedom.

[9] Paul A. Samuelson, "Personal Freedoms and Economic Freedoms in the Mixed Economy," in Earl F. Cheit (ed.), *The Business Establishment* (New York: John Wiley & Sons, Inc., 1964), p. 219.

Summary

1 The American economy can be described as mixed capitalism. It is primarily a market economy, yet government influences the operation of the price system in a variety of ways.

2 The basic economic functions of government entail **a.** providing a legal and social framework appropriate to the effective operation of the price system, **b.** maintaining competition, **c.** redistributing income, **d.** reallocating resources to adjust for spillovers and provide social goods and services, and **e.** stabilizing the economy.

3 Society generally condones government activity in the five areas outlined above. Benefit-cost analysis can provide useful guidance as to the economic desirability and most efficient scope of social goods output.

4 Public choice theorists cite a number of reasons why government might be inefficient in providing social goods and services. **a.** There are strong reasons for politicians to support special-interest legislation. **b.** Public choice may be biased in favor of programs with immediate and clear-cut benefits and difficult-to-identify costs *and* against programs with immediate and easily identified costs and vague or deferred benefits. **c.** Citizens as voters have less selectivity with respect to social goods and services than they do as consumers in the private sector. **d.** Government bureaucracies have less incentive to operate efficiently than do private businesses.

5 There is substantial disagreement as to the relationship between the size of the public sector and individual freedom.

Questions and Study Suggestions

1   Key terms and concepts to remember: mixed capitalism; monopoly; spillover costs and benefits; social good; exclusion principle; benefit-cost analysis; public choice theory; special-interest effect; nonselectivity of social goods; bureaucracy.

2   Why is the American economy called "mixed capitalism"? Enumerate and briefly discuss the main economic functions of government.

3   Explain why, in the absence of spillovers, equilibrium and optimum outputs are identical in competitive markets. What divergences arise between equilibrium and optimum output when *a.* spillover costs and *b.* spillover benefits are present? How might government correct for these discrepancies?

4   What are the basic characteristics of social goods? Explain the significance of the exclusion principle. By what means does government provide social goods?

5   The following table shows the total costs and total benefits in billions for four different antipollution programs of increasing scope. Which program should be undertaken? Why?

Program	Total cost	Total benefit
A	$ 3	$ 7
B	7	12
C	12	16
D	18	19

6   Carefully evaluate this statement: "The public, as a general rule . . . gets less production in return for a dollar spent by government than from a dollar spent by private enterprise." [10]

7   "The conclusion seems inescapable that pure capitalism . . . would be subject to grave deficiencies and inconsistencies. Such a system would have little chance of survival." [11] Do you agree? Why?

8   "It is conceivable that the Federal government can contribute materially to economic stability and greater efficiency in the use of resources without interfering in the details of business and personal life." Do you agree? Explain.

9   Carefully evaluate the following statement, and contrast its philosophy with that in question 6.[12]

The admitted functions of government embrace a much wider field than can be easily included within the ring fence of a restrictive definition . . . it is hardly possible to find any ground of justification common to them all, except the comprehensive one of general expediency; nor to limit the interference of government by any universal rule, save the simple and vague one that it should never be admitted but when the case of expediency is strong.

[10] National Association of Manufacturers, *The American Individual Enterprise System* (New York: McGraw-Hill Book Company, 1946), p. 952.
[11] Howard R. Bowen, *Toward Social Economy* (New York: Holt, Rinehart and Winston, Inc., 1948), p. 321.
[12] John Stuart Mill, *Principles of Political Economy* (New York: Appleton-Century-Crofts, Inc., 1878), vol. II, p. 392.

10 Interpret and evaluate the following quotation:[13]

> Plan or no plan? Everyone believes in planning in the literal sense of the word: and, for that matter, everyone believes that national governments should execute some plans for economic life. No one favors bad planning. Plan or no plan is no choice at all; the pertinent questions turn on particular techniques: Who shall plan, for what purposes, in what conditions, and by what devices? Free market or regulation? Again, this issue is badly posed. Both institutions are indispensable.

What do you feel are the virtues, if any, of government planning? How does the price system "plan"? Explain.

11 What are the possible sources of public sector failure, that is, of government actions which are uneconomic? Do you think the private sector or the public sector is more efficient? Justify your response.

Selected References

Carson, Robert B., Jerry Ingles, and Douglas McLaud (eds.): *Government in the American Economy* (Lexington, Mass.: D. C. Heath and Company, 1973).

Eckstein, Otto: *Public Finance,* 3d ed. (Englewood Cliffs, N.J.: Prentice-Hall, Inc., 1973), chaps. 1, 2.

Gwartney, James D.: *Economics: Private and Public Choice* (New York: Academic Press, 1976), chaps. 28–30.

Haveman, Robert Henry: *The Economics of the Public Sector* (New York: John Wiley & Sons, Inc., 1970), chaps. 1–5.

McKean, Roland N.: *Public Spending* (New York: McGraw-Hill Book Company, 1968).

Musgrave, Richard A., and Peggy B. Musgrave: *Public Finance in Theory and Practice,* 2d ed. (New York: McGraw-Hill Book Company, 1976), chaps. 1–5.

Phelps, Edmund S. (ed.): *Private Wants and Public Needs,* rev. ed. (New York: W. W. Norton & Company, Inc., 1965).

[13] Robert A. Dahl and Charles E. Lindblom, *Politics, Economics and Welfare* (New York: Harper & Row, Publishers, Incorporated, 1953), p. 5.

Last Word

Capitalist Domination of the State

Orthodox economists generally envision an essentially benevolent public sector which protects and promotes the general welfare. Radical or Marxian economists argue that in fact the political state is dominated by, and an instrument of, the capitalist class.

The development and operation of capitalist institutions divides society into classes. First, class division is a prerequisite for the effective organization of the institutions: most of the population must be reduced to worker status while simultaneously a capitalist elite is created and its existence justified. Second, the basic institutions function so as to augment the wealth, power, and privilege of that elite. . . .

If, as according to our hypothesis, the state is dominated by the capitalist class, then the operations of the state should reflect the needs of the capitalist class. In modern capitalist states, when the basic institutions have been thoroughly established, the maintenance and preservation of these institutions upon which the structure of class and privilege depends is of the greatest importance to the capitalist class. The uninhibited operation of the economic institutions will continue to bestow power, wealth, and prestige upon the capitalists. They do not need the state to enhance their position, only to assure it.

The system-preserving function of the state is evident in several areas. A continued threat to capitalism has been the failure of the economy autonomously to generate adequate aggregate demand. This failure has brought recurring crises with substantial unemployment. In spite of once seemingly inviolable ideological objections to the contrary, the state has assumed the function of demand regulator. Such regulation does not eliminate unemployment but simply reduces it to levels which are not system threatening.

A second system-preserving function of the state has been its decisive role in obfuscation and suppression of class conflict. This is accomplished through suppressing system-threatening groups (e.g., the Wobblies, Black Panthers), by deflecting their demands for structural changes into acceptable material demands (e.g., labor union economism, black capitalism), or through ameliorative programs. . . .

The enormous military establishment provides another example of system-preserving state operations; as such, it performs a dual function. First, it provides the rationale for huge expenditures which serve to maintain aggregate demand without threatening the security or position of any group in the ruling class. For example, social welfare measures often do threaten such groups. Second, as the capitalist system becomes increasingly an international system, the military directly protects the far-flung parts of that system.

The response of the state to changes in the process of production which require more highly developed labor, illustrates a second priority of the state; namely, the creation of new institutions. The rise of mass education in the United States has occurred in response to the need by industry for a skilled work force. Because workers are not tied to particular employment, individual capitalists cannot invest in the general training of workers and expect to appropriate the returns. Thus, capitalists turn to the state to provide a skilled work force. When education is handled by the state and portrayed as social welfare, it is paid for by general tax revenue rather than by the capitalists themselves.

The primacy of the roles of the state in preserving the system and in developing new institutions to meet changing circumstances should not obscure the fact that the state also intervenes directly in the economy to benefit immediate interests of capitalists. The most significant realm—in quantitative terms—where the state intervenes is in military and space spending, which we discussed above.

Another example of direct intervention, one which illustrates the case particularly well, is the government's relation to the agricultural sector. The general picture of what has happened in agriculture is well known. Wages in agriculture have remained low and unemployment high. Subsistence farmers have been unable to survive. The rural poor have been forced into the urban ghettos, supplying the low-cost labor force for industrial expansion. All the while, large farmers have received subsidies, price supports, and protection.

Richard C. Edwards and Arthur MacEwan, "A Radical Approach to Economics: Basis for a New Curriculum," *American Economic Review,* May 1970, pp. 357, 359–360, abridged. Reprinted by permission.

The Facts of American Capitalism: The Private Sector

This and the next chapter are designed to put meat on our bare-boned model of mixed capitalism. We have discussed the three major aggregates of mixed capitalism—business, households, and government—on a very general and somewhat abstract basis. We must now add color to our crude sketch by painting in the factual characteristics of these transactors as they function in our American brand of mixed capitalism. In short, we must breathe reality into our abstract model by adding "the facts" of American economic life. The present chapter contributes factual information pertinent to the *private sector,* that is, households and businesses. The following chapter does the same for the governmental, or *public, sector.*

HOUSEHOLDS AS INCOME RECEIVERS

The household sector of American capitalism is currently composed of some 74 million households. These households play a dual role: they are the ultimate suppliers of all economic resources and simultaneously the major spending group in the economy. Hence, we shall consider households first as income receivers and second as spenders.

There are two related approaches to studying the facts of income distribution. The *functional distribution* of income is concerned with the manner in which society's money income is divided among wages, rents, interest, and profits. Here total income is distributed according to the function performed by the income receiver. Wages are paid to labor, rents and interest compensate property resources, and profits flow to the owners of corporations and unincorporated businesses. The *personal distribution* of income has to do with the way in which the total money income of society is apportioned among individual households. A basic understanding of both the functional and the personal distribution of income is essential to understanding the role of households in American capitalism.

□   Functional Distribution of Income

The distributive shares of the national income for 1976 were as shown in Table 7-1.[1]

Clearly the largest source of income for households are the wages and salaries paid to workers by the businesses and governmental units hiring them. Wages and salaries tend to be quite stable over time as a percentage of the national income. Proprietors' income—that is, the incomes of doctors, lawyers, small businessmen, farmers, and other unincorporated enterprises—is in fact a combination of wage, profit, rent, and interest incomes. As a percentage of total income, this income share has tended to decline somewhat over the years, reflecting the growing significance of corporate enterprises and the historic decline in the rela-

[1] The section entitled "Income shares" in Chapter 32, focusing upon Table 32-1, is relevant to this discussion and is recommended reading at this point.

Table 7-1   THE SOURCES OF INCOME, 1976

	Billions of dollars	Percent of total
Wages and salaries	$1028	76
Proprietors' income	97	7
Corporate profits	118	9
Interest	82	6
Rents	24	2
Total income	$1349	100

Source: U.S. Department of Commerce, *Survey of Current Business,* March 1977. Details may not add to totals because of rounding.

tive importance of farming. Corporate profits have fluctuated substantially in both absolute and relative terms; over the past two decades, they have varied from 6 to 12 percent of the national income. The variability of profits reflects the risk-bearing function of the entrepreneur (Chapter 2) and the fact that profits are a residual share. Interest and rent are earnings received by households from the money capital and real property resources which they possess. Interest and rent have constituted relatively small shares of total income over an extended period. Incidentally, in absolute terms, all components of total income tend to expand during prosperity and to contract during depression.

Perhaps the remarkable thing about the functional distribution of income in our capitalistic system is that the bulk of the national income goes to labor and not to "capital." If we make the reasonable estimate that about two-thirds of proprietors' income is, in fact, wages and salaries and the remainder is capitalist income, we find that approximately four-fifths of total income is received by labor resources and only about one-fifth as capitalist incomes.

□   Personal Distribution of Income

A quick glance ahead at Table 37-1 will reveal that there is considerable inequality in the distribution of income among individual households. But we defer examination of empirical details and policy issues relevant to the personal distribution of income until Chapter 37 to concentrate on this question: Why is the personal distribution of money income—the way income is apportioned among households—important in understanding the operation of American capitalism? What impact does the distribution of money income among households have upon the operation of the economy? The answer is that the manner in which income is distributed among families affects both the *size* and the *composition* of output.

1   Size of Output   The personal distribution of income is a major determinant of how society divides its money income between consumption and saving. We will discover in Chapters 11 and 12 that this division is of utmost significance in determining the levels of output and employment in the economy. Consumption, being a form of spending, induces production and employment. Saving, defined by economists as that part of current income which is not consumed, does not account for production and employment. It follows that a distribution of income which results in a large volume of saving in relation to consumption *may* be conducive to declining levels of production and employment. On the other hand, a distribution which entails a very small volume of saving in relation to consumption will promote high levels of production and employment.

2   Composition of Output   The personal distribution of money income goes a long way toward determining the pattern of consumer spending in the economy. A highly unequal distribution of income among individual households results in an expenditure pattern much different from that entailed in a more nearly equal distribution. Generally speaking, the more unequal the distribution of a given total money income, the greater will be the demand for, and the output of, luxury goods. Businesses, as we have seen, usually find it to their advantage to adjust their outputs to consumer demands. As a consequence, the economy's product-mix is largely geared to the composition of consumer expenditures. And in turn, the economy's product-mix obviously determines the manner in which scarce resources are allocated.

To repeat, the personal distribution of income has direct and significant consequences for the two major aspects of economics: (1) the level of resource use, and (2) the allocation of resources among alternative uses.

Determinants   What determines the amount of money income received by an individual household in, say, a year? Common sense tells us that (1) the quantities of the various human and property resources which a household is able and willing to supply to businesses, (2) the prices which these resources command in the resource market, and (3) the actual level of employment of these resources are the immediate determinants of a household's money income. For the majority of American households, labor service is the only resource supplied. Thus by taking, for example, 2000 hours of labor service at a wage rate of $5 per hour, total money income for the year is found to be $10,000. But the third determinant poses a possible qualification: Though the household may be willing and able to supply 2000 hours of labor service per year, there is no guarantee that businesses will purchase this amount. Money income depends on the extent to which businesses are willing to employ available supplies of resources. If businesses are only able to use profitably 1500 of the hours offered, the workers' money income will obviously decline accordingly.

Income and Productivity   In capitalistic economies, money income is roughly based upon the contribution which a household's resources make to the total production of the economy. Households earn money incomes which are generally in accord with the value of their contributions to total output. If the resources in a household's possession are capable of efficiently producing goods which consumers want, the income earned will be high; if not, it will be low. The prices established by the forces of supply and demand in the resource market roughly gauge the relative worth or "productivity" of the various resources. If a business enterprise pays $4 an hour for unskilled labor and $8 an hour for highly skilled labor, it implies that the skilled labor is twice as productive as unskilled labor. If the market places a high value on the contributions of a resource to production, the supplying household receives a large income. If the market puts a low value on a resource's contribution, the supplying household's income tends to be low.

It is obvious that a distribution of income based upon productivity can result in considerable inequality. The quantity and quality of resources owned by various households and the prices they can command in the resource market can and do vary quite widely. Furthermore, the relationship between income and productivity is in fact only a very rough approximation. Some resource suppliers receive incomes substantially in excess of, and others receive incomes substantially less than, their productivity. Why is this so? Because monopolistic forces in both product and labor markets in the form of huge corporations and strong labor unions can distort prices so they do not accurately reflect productivity. Similarly, barriers to mobility—for example, discrimination on the basis of race and sex which arbitrarily keeps qualified blacks and women out of high-productivity–high-wage occupations—also distort the link between productivity and incomes. Hence, the personal distribution of income is actually more unequal than it would be if the economy were more competitive and discrimination did not exist.

■_____

HOUSEHOLDS AS SPENDERS

Having briefly discussed households as income receivers, we shall now examine the other side of the coin by viewing households as disposers of income. How do households dispose of the income which they receive? In general terms, the answer is simple: A part is given to government in the form of personal taxes, and the remainder is divided between personal consumption expenditures and personal saving.

Specifically, the way in which households disposed of their total income in 1976 is shown in Table 7-2.[2]

□   Personal Taxes

Personal taxes, of which the Federal personal income tax is the major component, have risen sharply in both absolute and relative terms since 1941. In 1929, households paid $2.6 billion, or about 3 percent of their $85.9 billion personal income, in personal taxes. In 1976, $194 billion, or about 14 percent of that year's $1350 billion total income, flowed to government as personal taxes. The high levels of government spending associated with World War II, the Korean war, and the war in Vietnam; the expanded provision of nonmilitary social goods and services, such as highways and education; the rapid growth of antipoverty and other income-maintenance programs; and population growth have all been major factors contributing to rising tax bills (Chapter 8).

Economists define saving as "not spending"; hence, households have just two choices with their incomes after taxes—to consume or to save.

[2]Technical note: As we will find in Chap. 9, the income concepts used in Tables 7-1 and 7-2 are different and this accounts for the slight quantitative discrepancy in "total income" in the two tables.

Table 7-2   THE DISPOSITION OF INCOME, 1976

	Billions of dollars	Percent of total
Personal taxes	$ 194	14
Personal consumption expenditures	1080	80
Personal saving	76	6
Total income	$1350	100

Source: U.S. Department of Commerce, *Survey of Current Business,* March 1977.

□ **Personal Saving**

Let us first consider the saving component of after-tax income. Saving is defined as that portion of current (this year's) income which is not paid out in taxes or in the purchase of consumer goods, but rather, flows into bank accounts, insurance policies, bonds and stocks, and other financial assets.

Why do households want to save? After all, it is ultimately goods and services which satisfy consumer wants, not the pieces of paper which we call checkbooks, savings account books, certificates of deposit, and bonds. The reasons for saving are many and diverse, but they center around *security* and *speculation*. Households save to provide a nest egg for unforeseen contingencies—sickness, accident, unemployment—for retirement from the work force, or simply for the overall financial security of one's family. On the other hand, saving might well occur for speculation. One might channel a part of one's income to the purchase of securities, speculating as to increases in their monetary value.

The desire or willingness to save, however, is not enough. This willingness must be accompanied by the *ability* to save. And, as we shall discover later (Table 11-1), the ability to save depends basically upon the size of one's income. If income is very low, households may *dissave;* that is, they may consume in excess of their after-tax incomes. They manage to do this by borrowing and by digging into savings which they may have accumulated in years when their incomes were higher. However, both saving and consumption vary directly with income; as households get more income, they divide it between saving and consumption. Actually, the bulk of the personal saving that occurs in our economy is done by those households in the $50,000, $100,000, or higher income brackets. The top 10 percent of the income receivers account for most of the personal saving in our society.

□ **Personal Consumption Expenditures**

Table 7-2 clearly shows that the bulk of total income flows from income receivers back into the business sector of the economy as personal consumption expenditures.

Since the size and composition of the economy's total output depend to a very considerable extent upon the size and composition of the flow of consumer spending, it is imperative that we examine how households divide their expenditures among the various goods and services competing for their dollars. Consumer expenditures may be classified in several ways. For example, they may be divided into services and products; and products in turn may be subdivided on the basis of their durability. Thus the U.S. Department of Commerce classifies consumer spending as (1) expenditures on nondurables, (2) expenditures on durables, and (3) expenditures on services. If a product generally has an expected life of one year or more, it is called a "durable good"; if its life is less than one year, it is labeled "nondurable." Automobiles, refrigerators, washing machines, television sets, and most furniture are good examples of consumer durables. Most food and clothing items are nondurables. Services, of course, refer to the services which lawyers, barbers, mechanics, and others provide to consumers.

Table 7-3 shows that of the $1080 billion spent by consumers in 1976, $440 billion was for nondurables, $157 billion for durables, and $483 billion for services. This threefold breakdown is of considerable importance because it reminds us that a good many consumer outlays are discretionary or postponable. During good times, durable, or "hard," goods are typically traded in or scrapped before they become utterly useless. This is ordinarily the case with automobiles and most major household appliances. But if bad times threaten or begin to materialize, consumers may forgo expenditures on durables, choosing to put up with an old model car and outdated household appliances.

When depression threatens, the desire to conserve dollars for the nondurable necessities of food and clothing may cause a radical shrinkage of expenditures on durables. Much the same is true of many services. True, one cannot postpone an operation for acute appendicitis. But education, dental work, and a wide variety of less pressing services can be deferred or, if necessary, forgone entirely. In brief, the durable goods and services segments of personal consumption expenditures are subject to considerably more variation over time than are expenditures on nondurables. As is true of saving, many types of spending on durables and services are postponable during an economic recession.

□ Consumer Protection

In the past decade we have witnessed a burgeoning interest in consumer protection and knowledge. Consumer ignorance is basically an obstacle to effective competition. If consumers do not know the characteristics and qualities of different products or are unaware of the range of alternative products available

to them, they are likely to make inefficient choices. If consumers buy pie and pantyhose—not to mention such complex products as drugs and stereo components—out of ignorance or under the influence of misleading advertising, they will foster a misallocation of resources from quality to shoddy products and thereby experience a decline in their real incomes. Furthermore, as Ralph Nader's efforts have sometimes dramatically illustrated, certain products may pose a hazard to the immediate consumer and to others either directly or indirectly through adverse environmental effects.

The Federal government has a long history of involvement in consumer protection. The 1906 Pure Food and Drug Act and the Fair Packaging and Labelling Act of 1969 are obvious and important illustrations. A major purpose of the Federal Trade Commission is to take action against fraudulent and misleading advertising. The 1969 Truth in Lending Act is designed to protect the consumer as a debtor. The act requires lenders to state in concise and uniform language the costs and terms of consumer credit. In particular, the total dollar

Table 7-3   THE COMPOSITION OF PERSONAL CONSUMPTION EXPENDITURES, 1976

Types of consumption	Amount (billions of dollars)		Percent of total
Durable goods		$ 157	15
Motor vehicles and parts	$ 71		7
Furniture and household equipment	63		6
All others	23		2
Nondurable goods		440	41
Clothing and shoes	75		7
Food	224		21
Gasoline and oil	42		4
Fuel oil and coal	12		1
All others	87		8
Services		483	45
Household operations	72		7
Housing	166		15
Transportation	38		3
Personal services, recreation, and others	207		19
Personal consumption expenditures		$1080	100

Source: U.S. Department of Commerce, *Survey of Current Business,* February 1977. Details may not add to totals because of rounding.

amount of finance charges on a loan (including interest, investigation fees, credit insurance, and so on) must be explicitly indicated, and interest must be stated as an annual percentage rate.

One can make a good case for the government to establish and enforce standards of quality and safety for potentially hazardous products. Indeed, Federal safety standards for new automobiles have been imposed. In some cases—recall the thalidomide tragedy and the environmental questions surrounding DDT—government has prohibited or restricted product sales. But some economists envision possible problems in proposals to have government establish product standards on a broad front:[3]

> Despite their beneficial intent, their adoption could in some cases have the undesirable effect of lessening competition among producers— and thus breaching one of the consumer's most effective defenses. The consumer's interest may not be served if so much reliability is required that it adds heavily to the cost. Another possible disadvantage in these restrictions is their effect on the development of new products. Producers may be uncertain about how well potential new products or services can meet published standards requiring reliable performance and freedom from other defects. Such uncertainty, together with the threat of costly damage suits, confiscation of goods, or time-consuming delays in satisfying a multitude of Federal requirements, may inhibit the development of new products and the entry of new firms into the market to compete with established companies.

THE BUSINESS POPULATION

Businesses constitute the second major aggregate of the private sector.

[3]*Economic Report of the President, 1970,* pp. 97–98.

□   Plants, Firms, and Industries

To avoid any possible confusion, we preface our discussion of the business population with some comments concerning terminology. In particular, one must distinguish among a plant, a firm, and an industry. A *plant* is a physical establishment in the form of a factory, farm, mine, retail or wholesale store, or warehouse which performs one or more specific functions in the fabrication and distribution of goods and services. A business *firm,* on the other hand, is the business organization which owns and operates these plants. Although most firms operate only one plant, many firms own and operate a number of plants. Multiplant firms may be "horizontal," "vertical," or "conglomerate" combinations. For example, without exception each of the large steel firms of our economy—United States Steel, Bethlehem Steel, Republic Steel, and the others—are vertical combinations of plants; each firm owns ore and coal mines, limestone quarries, coke ovens, blast furnaces, rolling mills, forge shops, foundries, and, in some cases, fabricating shops. The large chain stores in the retail field—for example, A&P, Kroger, Safeway, J. C. Penney—are horizontal combinations in that each plant is at the same stage of production. Other firms are conglomerates; that is, they comprise plants which operate across many different markets and industries. For example, International Telephone and Telegraph, apart from operations implied by its name, is involved through affiliated plants on a large-scale basis in such diverse fields as automobile rentals, hotels, baking products, education materials, and insurance (Chapter 34).

An *industry* is a group of firms producing the same, or at least similar, products. Though an apparently uncomplicated concept, industries are usually difficult to identify in practice. For example, how are we to identify the automobile industry? The simplest answer is, "All firms producing automobiles." But automobiles are heterogeneous products. While

Cadillacs and Buicks are similar products, and Buicks and Fords are similar, and Fords and Vegas are similar, and Vegas and Volkswagens are similar, it is clear that Volkswagens and Cadillacs are very dissimilar. At least most buyers think so. And what about trucks? Certainly, small pickup trucks are similar in some respects to station wagons. Is it better to speak of the "motor vehicle industry" rather than of the "automobile industry"? This matter of delineating an industry becomes all the more complex when it is recognized that most enterprises are multiproduct firms. American automobile manufacturers are also responsible for such diverse products as diesel locomotives, buses, refrigerators, guided missiles, and air conditioners. We pose these questions, not with a view to resolving them, but merely to note that industry classifications are rarely clear-cut and always somewhat arbitrary.

□ **Diversity and Fluidity**

If we were able to stand back and achieve a broad overview of the business sector of American capitalism, we should be amazed by the phenomenal diversity of its approximately 13.6 million component firms. Indeed, no two business enterprises are exactly alike. At one extreme, you would be impressed by a giant corporation such as General Motors, which in 1975 owned total assets of $22 billion, employed 681,000 people, and realized annual sales of about $36 billion. At the other end of the scale, you could not help being astonished by the extremely large number of "shoestring" enterprises in the form of neighborhood beaneries and small specialty shops with gross sales of less than $100 or $150 per day, and maybe one or two employees and some relatively worthless showcases or counters as their only real capital assets.

The American business population is also very fluid; "here today, gone tomorrow" is a fitting slogan for it. New firms are constantly entering and old firms leaving the business

population. In recent years, it has been common for some 450,000 to 500,000 new firms to come into existence each year and a somewhat smaller number—say 400,000 or 425,000—to fail every year. Each year—even during periods of prosperity—thousands upon thousands of enterprises fail. And thousands of new ones are started. Average age of all operating firms? About seven or eight years. Although the lion's share of the failures is among the "shoestring" enterprises, it is not uncommon for firms of significant size to slip into the sea of bankruptcy, for example, the Penn Central Railroad and the W. T. Grant retail chain. Some people interpret such statistics with alarm. All things considered, however, it is amazing that so many of the "shoestring" enterprises which are started every year survive and thrive as well as they do.

The fluidity of the business sector is often due to such a mundane factor as incompetent business management. But fundamental economic forces—changes in consumer tastes, technological change, changes in resource supplies—are often at work. Some examples: Historically, expenditures for food have increased proportionately less than incomes, causing agriculture to become relatively less important and the number of farms to decline (Chapter 35). The recession of the mid-1970s caused many households to forgo or curtail vacation travel, resulting in adverse effects upon the airline and hotel-motel industries. The recent development of digital watches poses a serious competitive threat to conventional watchmakers. Similarly, the development of low-cost hand calculators has seriously undermined the market for slide rules.

LEGAL FORMS OF
BUSINESS ENTERPRISES

The very diverse nature of the business population makes it imperative that we do some classifying. There are many bases for classifying business firms—legal structure, type of product, and size are common criteria. We shall use all three of these, in varying degrees.

The present emphasis, however, is upon the basic legal forms which businesses might assume: (1) sole proprietorship, (2) partnership, and (3) the corporation. Let us define and outline the advantages and disadvantages associated with each.

□   Sole Proprietorship

A sole proprietorship is literally an individual in business for himself. It is typically "a one-man show." The proprietor owns or obtains the materials and capital equipment used in the operation of his business and personally supervises its operation. Responsibility for the efficient coordination of the resources he owns or can command rests directly upon the proprietor's shoulders.

Advantages   Obviously, this extremely simple type of business organization has certain distinct advantages:

1 A sole proprietorship is very easy to organize—there is virtually no legal red tape or expense. The businessman merely acquires the needed facilities and is "in business."

2 The proprietor is his own boss and has very substantial freedom of action. Since his own profit income depends upon his enterprise's success, there is a strong and immediate incentive for him to manage the affairs of his business wisely.

Disadvantages   The sole proprietorship looks very rugged and individualistic. And it clearly is. But the disadvantages of this form of business organization are great:

1 With rare exceptions, the financial resources of a sole proprietorship are insufficient to permit the firm to grow into a large-scale enterprise. Specifically, finances are usually limited to what the proprietor has in his bank account and to what he is able to borrow.

Since the mortality rate is very great for proprietorships, commercial banks are not overly eager to extend much credit to them.

2 Being in complete control of an enterprise forces the proprietor to carry out all basic management functions. The proprietor must be a jack-of-all-trades and must make all basic decisions concerning, for example, buying, selling, and the acquisition and maintenance of personnel, not to mention the technical aspects which might be involved in producing, advertising, and distributing the product. In short, the potential benefits of specialization in business management are usually inaccessible to the typical small-scale proprietorship.

3 Most important of all, the proprietor is subject to *unlimited liability*. This means that individuals in business for themselves risk not only the assets of the firm but also their personal assets. Should the assets of an unsuccessful proprietorship be insufficient to satisfy the claims of creditors, those creditors can file claims against the proprietor's personal property. The stakes are high insofar as individual proprietorships are concerned.

□   Partnership

The partnership form of business organization is more or less a natural outgrowth of the sole proprietorship. As a matter of fact, partnerships were developed in an attempt to overcome some of the major shortcomings of proprietorships. A partnership is almost self-defining. It is a form of business organization wherein two or more individuals agree to own and operate a business. Usually they pool their financial resources and their business acumen. Similarly, they share the risks and the profits or losses which may accrue to them. There are innumerable variations. In some cases, all partners are active in the functioning of the enterprise; in others, one or more partners may be "silent"—that is, they contribute their finances but do not actively participate in the management of the firm.

Advantages What are the advantages of a partnership arrangement?

1 Like the sole proprietorship, it is easy to organize. Although a written agreement is almost invariably involved, legal red tape is not great.

2 Greater specialization in management is made possible, because there are more participants. Managerial functions can be apportioned among the partners in terms of their abilities and training, with increased efficiency as the potential result.

3 Again, because there are several participants, the odds are that the financial resources of a partnership will be less limited than those of a sole proprietorship. Partners can pool their money capital and are usually somewhat better risks in the eyes of bankers.

Disadvantages But the disadvantages cannot be minimized. The partnership often does less to overcome the shortcomings of the proprietorship than first appears and, indeed, raises some new potential problems which the sole proprietorship does not entail.

1 Whenever there are several people participating in management, this division of authority can lead to inconsistent, divided policies or to inaction when action is required. Worse yet, partners may flatly disagree on basic policy. For all these reasons, management in a partnership may be very unwieldy and cumbersome.

2 The finances of partnerships are still limited, although generally superior to those of a sole proprietorship. The financial resources of three or four partners may be such as to restrict severely the potential growth of an enterprise.

3 The continuity of a partnership is very precarious. The withdrawal or death of a partner generally entails the dissolution and complete reorganization of the firm. Needless to say, this may severely disrupt the firm's operations.

4 Finally, unlimited liability plagues a partnership, just as it does a proprietorship. In fact, each partner is liable for all business debts incurred, not only as a result of his own management decisions, but also as a consequence of the actions of any other partner. A wealthy partner risks all his riches on the prudence of his less affluent partners.

☐ **Corporation**

Corporations are legal entities, distinct and separate from the individuals who own them. As such, these governmentally designated "legal persons" can acquire resources, own assets, produce and sell products, incur debts, extend credit, sue and be sued, and carry on all those functions which any other type of enterprise performs.

Advantages The advantages of the corporate form of business enterprise have catapulted this type of firm into a dominant position in modern American capitalism.

1 The corporation is by far the most effective form of business organization for raising money capital. The corporation features new methods of finance—the selling of stocks and bonds—which allow the firm to tap the savings of untold thousands of households. Through the securities market, corporations can pool the financial resources of extremely large numbers of people. Financing by the sale of securities also has decided advantages from the viewpoint of the purchasers of these securities. First, households can now participate in enterprise and share the expected monetary reward therefrom without having to assume an active part in management. And, in addition, an individual can spread his risks by buying the securities of a variety of corporations. Finally, it is usually easy for the holder of corporate securities to dispose of his holdings. Organized stock exchanges facilitate the transfer of securities among buyers and sellers. Needless to say, this increases the willingness of savers to buy corporate securities. Furthermore, corporations ordinarily have easier access to bank credit than do other types of business organi-

zation. This is the case not only because corporations are better risks but also because they are more likely to provide banks with profitable accounts.

2 Corporations have the distinct advantage of *limited liability*. The owners (stockholders) of a corporation risk only what they paid for the stock purchased. Their personal assets are not at stake if the corporation founders on the rocks of bankruptcy. Creditors can sue the corporation as a legal person, but not the owners of that corporation as individuals. Once again, this limitation eases the corporation's task in acquiring money capital.

3 As a legal entity, the corporation has a life independent of its owners and, for that matter, of its individual officials. Proprietorships are subject to sudden and unpredictable demise, but, legally at least, corporations are immortal. The transfer of corporate ownership through the sale of stock does not disrupt this continuity which the corporation boasts. In short, corporations have a certain permanence which is lacking in other forms of business organization. This permanence is conducive to long-range planning and growth.

4 Corporations, because of their strategic position in acquiring money capital, typically have the ability to obtain more specialized, and therefore more efficient, management than can proprietorships and partnerships.

5 Last but not least is the possible tax advantage which incorporation may give for an enterprise whose net profits are sizable. As we shall find in Chapter 8, the maximum 48 percent marginal tax rate facing a corporation is preferable to the maximum 70 percent marginal rate of the personal income tax.

Disadvantages The corporation's advantages are of tremendous significance and typically override any accompanying disadvantages. Yet the drawbacks of the corporate form of organization merit mentioning.

1 There are some red tape and legal expense in obtaining a corporate charter.

2 From the social point of view, it must be noted that the corporate form of enterprise lends itself to certain abuses. Because the corporation is a legal entity, unscrupulous business owners sometimes can avoid personal responsibility for questionable business activities by adopting the corporate form of enterprise. And, despite legislation to the contrary, the corporate form of organization has been a cornerstone for the issue and sale of worthless securities. Note, however, that these are potential abuses of the corporate form, not inherent defects.

3 A further possible disadvantage of corporations has to do with the taxation of corporate income. Briefly, that part of corporate income which is paid out as dividends to stockholders is taxed twice—once as a part of corporate profits and again as a part of the stockholders' personal incomes. This disadvantage must be weighed against the previously noted fact that the maximum tax rates on corporate enterprises are less than those which may apply to unincorporated firms.

4 In the sole proprietorship and partnership forms, those who own the real and financial assets of the firm also manage or control those assets.[4] Most observers agree that this is as it should be. But, in larger corporations where the ownership of common stock is widely diffused over thousands or tens of thousands of stockholders, a fundamental cleavage between ownership and control will arise. This divorce of corporate ownership and control is intriguing because, in theory at least, corporations are organized democratically. Each share of common stock has one vote in electing the firm's board of directors, which has ultimate authority for the operation of the enterprise. The more shares of common stock you own, the more votes you have in selecting the corporation's officials.

How, then, do ownership and control come to be separated? The roots of the cleavage lie in the lethargy of the typical stockholder. Most stockholders simply do not exercise their

---

[4]The silent-partner arrangement is the exception.

voting rights or, if they do, merely sign these rights over by proxy to the corporation's present officers. And why not? The average stockholder knows little or nothing about the efficiency with which "his" corporation is being managed. So long as his dividends are regular and comparable in size to those received by the other members of his golf foursome who also hold common stock in various concerns, he is not troubled by the question of efficient management. And, after all, since the typical stockholder may own only 100 of 150,000 shares of common stock outstanding, his vote "really doesn't make a bit of difference"! Not voting, or the automatic signing over of one's proxy to current corporate officials, typically has the effect of making those officials self-perpetuating.

The separation of ownership and control is of no fundamental consequence so long as the actions of the control (management) group and the wishes of the ownership (stockholder) group are in accord. The catch lies in the fact that the interests of the two groups are not always identical. For example, management, seeking the power and prestige which accompanies control over a *large* enterprise, may favor unprofitable expansion of the firm's operations, or a conflict of interest can easily develop with respect to current dividend policies. What portion of corporate earnings after taxes should be paid out as dividends, and what amount should be retained by the firm as undistributed profits? More obviously, corporation officials may vote themselves large salaries, pensions, bonuses, and so forth, out of corporate earnings which might otherwise be used for increased dividend payments.

There is no doubt that separation of ownership and control raises important and intriguing questions about the distribution of power and authority, the accountability of corporate managers, and the possibility of intramural conflicts between managers and shareholders. But perhaps a more fundamental question is whether the separation of ownership and control has undesirable conse-

quences for society as a whole. In fact, there is no compelling evidence to suggest that this separation per se is economically harmful: "It would appear . . . that ownership–management separation has no significant economic impact, that is, it affects imperceptibly or not at all the allocation of resources, the rate of capital formation, and the distribution of income."[5]

□   **To Incorporate or Not to Incorporate**

Which legal form of enterprise—proprietorship or corporation—is best? Probably the basic determinant of the legal form of enterprise is the amount of funds which a given line of production requires. For example, the corner magazine stand or the small curio or gift shop will have very modest money capital requirements. The only fixed assets which tie up some money capital are a few, relatively inexpensive display counters. And the volume of business is so small that the need for "working capital" (funds which bridge the gap between costs and sales receipts) is also minimal. Why go to the cost and trouble of incorporating such a firm when the primary advantage of incorporating—the accessibility of large amounts of money capital through the sale of securities—is actually of little relevance? In contrast, modern technology and a much larger dollar volume of business make incorporation imperative in many lines of production. For example, in most branches of manufacturing—automobiles, steel, fabricated metal products, electrical equipment, household appliances, and so forth—very substantial money requirements for investment in fixed assets and for working capital are involved. The typical concern in the United States has about $27,000 worth of capital equipment *per worker!* Given these circumstances, there is often little choice. To exist is to incorporate. In brief, the

[5]Morton S. Baratz, *The American Business System in Transition* (New York: Thomas Y. Crowell Company, 1970), p. 53.

best legal form of business enterprise varies from industry to industry, and the primary determinant of legal form is the money capital requirement of the particular industry.

Actually, the American business population is distributed among the three legal forms in the manner indicated in Table 7-4. It is strikingly clear that the proprietorship form is numerically dominant. Yet corporations, though small in number, are frequently large in size and scale of operations. In fact, they account for about two-thirds of the output of all private business enterprises.

INDUSTRIAL DISTRIBUTION OF THE BUSINESS POPULATION

What do the 13.6 million firms which compose the business sector of our economy produce? Table 7-5 measures in several different ways the significance of the various industry classi-

Table 7-4 THE BUSINESS POPULATION BY FORM OF LEGAL ORGANIZATION

Form	Number of firms	Percent of total
Sole proprietorships*	10,648,000	78
Partnerships	1,039,000	8
Corporations	1,905,000	14
Total	13,592,000	100

*Includes farmers and professional people in business for themselves.
Source: U.S. Department of Commerce. Data are for 1973.

fications. Column 2 indicates the numerical and percentage distribution of the business population among the various industries. Column 3 shows in both absolute and relative terms the portion of the national income originating in the various industries. Column 4 indicates the absolute and relative amounts of employment provided by each industry. Several points in Table 7-5 are noteworthy:

1 The relatively small number of firms in manufacturing account for about one-fourth of

Table 7-5 INDUSTRY CLASSES: NUMBER OF FIRMS, NATIONAL INCOME ORIGINATING, AND EMPLOYMENT PROVIDED*

(1) Industry	(2) Number of private businesses		(3) Contribution to national income		(4) Full-time workers employed	
	Thousands	Percent	Billions	Percent	Thousands	Percent
Agriculture, forestry, and fisheries	3,586	26	$ 44.7	4	3,476	4
Mining	86	1	16.4	1	767	1
Construction	1,099	8	57.9	5	3,595	4
Manufacturing	449	3	303.1	25	18,704	23
Wholesale and retail trade	2,945	22	201.1	16	17,388	21
Finance, insurance, and real estate	1,576	12	139.0	11	4,266	5
Transportation, communications, and public utilities	434	3	94.6	8	4,489	5
Services	3,367	25	167.3	14	14,342	18
Government			197.1	16	14,855⎱	18
Rest of world	——	—	10.5	1		
Total	13,542	100	$1231.6	100	78,121	100

*Column 2 is for 1975; 3 for 1975; and 4 for 1976.
Source: Statistical Abstract of the United States, 1976, pages 399, 507, and *Survey of Current Business.*

national income and total employment. These figures correctly suggest that the American capitalist economy is highly industrialized, characterized by gigantic business corporations in its manufacturing industries.

2 The wholesale and retail industries and the service industries (hotels, motels, personal services, and so forth) are heavily populated with firms and are simultaneously very important sources of employment and incomes in the economy.

3 Note, too, the large number of firms engaged in agriculture but the relative insignificance of agriculture as a provider of incomes and jobs.

4 Table 7-5 reminds us that not all the economy's income and employment originate in private domestic enterprises. Government and foreign enterprises account for about 17 percent of the economy's national income and employ about 18 percent of the labor force.

BIG BUSINESS IN AMERICAN CAPITALISM

In terms of employees, the vast majority of business firms are relatively small; over 80 percent of the total number of business firms in the United States hire fewer than 10 workers. But the relatively few firms which are large are extremely important, and for this reason American capitalism is sometimes labeled a "big business" economy.

The major questions to be faced in connection with the existence of big businesses in American capitalism are these:

1 To what degree does big business prevail in the American economy?

2 Why and through what means have businesses sought "bigness"; that is, what are a firm's incentives for and means of growth?

3 What dangers, if any, are posed by the existence of giant business firms?

☐ Extent of Bigness

To what degree does big business prevail in our economy? Casual evidence suggests that many of our major industries are dominated by corporate giants which enjoy assets and annual sales revenues calculated in billions of dollars, employ hundreds of thousands of workers, have a hundred thousand or more stockholders, and earn annual profits after taxes running into hundreds of millions of dollars. We have already cited the vital statistics of General Motors, America's second largest corporation, for 1975: sales, about $36 *billion;* assets, about $22 *billion;* employees, about 681,000. Remarkably, there are only 18 or 20 nations in the world with annual national outputs in excess of GM's annual sales! Our largest corporation is Exxon (formerly Standard Oil of New Jersey) with sales of $45 billion and assets of $33 billion in 1975. In that year some 102 industrial corporations enjoyed annual sales of over $2 billion; a total of 203 industrial firms realized sales in excess of $1 billion. By comparison, only 12 state governments had revenues in excess of $2 billion in the same year. More generally, the fact that corporations, constituting only 14 percent of the business population, produce two-thirds of total business output hints at the dominant role of large corporations in our economy.

But the dominance of giant corporations varies significantly from industry to industry. Big business dominates manufacturing and is pronounced in the transportation, communications, power utilities, and banking and financial industries. At the other extreme are some 3 million farmers whose total sales are less than the economy's four largest industrial corporations! In between are a wide variety of retail and service industries wherein relatively small firms are characteristic.[6] More specifi-

---

[6]See John Kenneth Galbraith, *Economics and the Public Purpose* (New York: New American Library, 1973), pp. 42–43. For a capsule view of Galbraith's conception of

cally, a look ahead at Table 28-1 reveals a list of industries wherein economic concentration is quite modest. Table 29-1, on the other hand, indicates a number of very basic manufacturing industries wherein economic power is highly concentrated.

Historical data on the concentration of economic power do not reveal an unambiguous trend. For example, we note in Table 7-6 that the share of manufacturing assets held by the 100 largest manufacturing firms rose from about 38 percent in 1929 to 44 percent in 1974. In fact, today the 100 largest firms hold about the same share of total manufacturing assets as the 200 largest firms did some forty-five years ago. Observe, however, that concentration seems to have diminished in the 1968–1974 period. It should be emphasized that economists debate the meaning and relevance of these and similar data to the issue of concentration; some highly respected economists believe that concentration has not been increasing or, if it has, it has been "at the pace of a glacial drift." It is generally agreed that the American economy is highly concentrated and that this concentration will persist.

We shall return to the issues of big business and government policy in later chapters. Let it suffice to say at this point that large corporations do dominate the American business landscape and reasonable grounds do exist for labeling the United States a "big business" economy.

□   **Means and Incentives for Bigness**

The means by which once-small firms have evolved into huge industrial giants are essentially twofold. In a relatively few cases—for example, Ford Motor Company and Alcoa (Aluminum Company of America)—gigantic business enterprises have developed primarily through *internal growth,* that is, through the reinvestment of the firm's earn-

Table 7-6   SHARE OF MANUFACTURING ASSETS HELD BY THE 100 LARGEST AND 200 LARGEST CORPORATIONS

Year	Share of 100 largest corporations	Share of 200 largest corporations
1929	38.2%	45.8%
1941	38.2	45.1
1950	38.4	46.1
1955	43.0	51.6
1960	45.5	55.2
1965	45.9	55.9
1968	48.8	60.4
1974	44.4	56.7

Source: Senate Subcommittee on Antitrust and Monopoly, *Economic Concentration,* part 8a (Washington, 1969), p. 173, and *Statistical Abstract of the United States.*

ings and the acquisition of additional funds for expansion by floating new issues of securities. However, most of the firms now classified as "big businesses" have relied basically upon some form of business *combination*—mergers, consolidations, or the formation of trusts and holding companies—in achieving their present positions of dominance in their respective industries.

What motivates business to grow? The incentives are complex and to some extent overlapping.

1 The desire to achieve greater *productive efficiency* has undoubtedly played a role in the growth of big business. Large firms are frequently in a better position to realize "mass-production economies" than are their small-scale brethren. Yet, it seems that the production economies of many mergers—particularly of the conglomerate type—are nil. Furthermore, empirical research indicates that in many important industries the degree of economic concentration has gone beyond the point necessary to attain technically efficient plants.[7]

2 The search for *power* and *prestige* by business leaders has been a factor in the

[7] See in particular Joe S. Bain, "Economies of Scale, Concentration, and the Condition of Entry in Twenty Manufacturing Industries," *American Economic Review,* March 1954, pp. 15–39.

American industry, the reader should consult Chapter 23's Last Word section.

growth of big business. Being the largest employer or controlling the largest quantity of real capital assets in a given industry carries a certain amount of prestige that is generally recognized and much sought for in the business world.

3 *Security* and *assurance of long-run survival* have been factors in the growth of big business. Combination is often effected to "diversify the product line" of a firm as a safeguard against seasonal and cyclical fluctuations in business activity. Diversification also affords some measure of protection against the risk of unfavorable changes in consumer tastes. A multiproduct firm, by not putting all its eggs in one basket, is in a better position to survive the fickleness of consumers. And, of course, the goal of long-run survival prompts firms to branch out into newly developed industries where the prospects of future growth seem to be good. Similarly, combination may serve to ensure a firm of steady and continuing supplies of raw materials, semifinished goods, and product parts.[8]

4 The seeking of *greater financial rewards* has been the dominant factor in the growth of big business. One aspect of this profit seeking has to do with the windfall gains, or promoter's profits, immediately resulting from the combination of several corporations. But of greater significance in the long pull is the enhancement of prospective profits through the demise of competition which combination typically entails.

Given that big business is a fact of American economic life, it is highly relevant to probe briefly the implications of bigness.

□ **Should Big Business Be Feared?**

This is a knotty question, permitting honest differences of opinion. Two basic schools of thought exist on this issue. We summarize these views here and defer a detailed analysis to Chapter 34.

One school of thought holds that big business is a natural and necessary outgrowth of a progressive industrial economy. In particular, it is argued that modern technology requires (1) the use of extremely large quantities of real capital; (2) wide markets; (3) a complex, closely integrated management; and (4) large and reliable sources of raw materials. Such an operation implies the need for large-scale producers. In short, the achievement of maximum productive efficiency through the employment of the best available technology often presupposes the concentration of economic power. Efficient production is attainable only when business units are large.

Equally competent observers view this situation much differently. Though efficiency may require "bigness" up to a point, it is argued that many American businesses have grown far beyond the size necessary for the achievement of maximum productive efficiency. Indeed, it is pointed out that some industrial giants are inefficient because they are too large; bureaucratic red tape has made them inflexible and unresponsive to fundamental changes in the economy. Furthermore, it is contended that bigness and monopoly power frequently go together. If control of the means of production rests in the hands of a relative few, then the concept of consumer sovereignty may be eroded or substantially supplanted by "producer sovereignty," to the end that resources are no longer allocated in terms of consumer wants. Stated differently, the internal logic of the circular flow model, as introduced in Chapter 3 and developed in Chapter 5, will be disrupted. The "invisible hand" will now fail to function effectively in identifying the private and social interest. The Last Word segment of Chapter 5, you may recall, is pertinent to this line of reasoning.

Even more serious is the contention that an ominous interdependence has evolved between big business and big government. It is argued that political leaders need the financial

---

[8] The quest for security is a major theme of John Kenneth Galbraith's widely read book, *The New Industrial State* (Boston: Houghton Mifflin Company, 1967).

support of big business to achieve and maintain power; furthermore, government also depends upon big business for military goods which are the source of international power. In return, government provides a favorable environment for profitable business operations by maintaining prosperity, subsidizing the education of the managers and technicians needed by big business, and providing a host of social goods and services of which large corporations are the major beneficiaries. Those who maintain that such a tacit partnership has been evolving feel that it has altered the American economic and political systems so that they function more and more to promote the interests of corporate enterprise and the political leadership and less and less to further the general socioeconomic welfare. This line of thought is a sweeping indictment of American capitalism and will merit more detailed treatment in Chapter 40. Closer at hand, this chapter's Last Word section is a highly critical commentary upon the activities of large coal corporations in West Virginia.

Summary

1   The functional distribution of income shows how society's total income is divided among wages, rents, interest, and profits; the personal distribution of income shows how total income is divided among individual households. The distribution of income is an important determinant of the level and composition of total output.

2   Households divide their total incomes among personal taxes, saving, and consumer goods. Consumer expenditures on durables and some services are discretionary and therefore postponable.

3   The business population of American capitalism is both heterogeneous and fluid. Sole proprietorships, partnerships, and corporations are the major legal forms which business enterprises may assume. Though proprietorships dominate numerically, the bulk of total output is produced by corporations. Corporations have grown to their position of dominance in the business sector primarily because they are *a.* characterized by limited liability, and *b.* in a superior position to acquire money capital for expansion.

4   Manufacturing accounts for a larger percentage of national income and employment in American capitalism than does any other industrial classification. The wholesale, retail, and service industries are also major sources of income and employment.

5   Many basic industries in our economy are dominated by a small number of large corporations. Major incentives underlying the growth of these big businesses are *a.* the desire to achieve greater productive efficiency, *b.* the search for power and prestige by business leaders, *c.* security and the assurance of a long-run survival, and *d.* the pursuit of greater financial rewards. Big businesses have developed by means of internal growth and by combination. Economists disagree on the desirability of big businesses.

Questions and Study Suggestions

1   Key terms and concepts to remember: functional and personal distribution of income; durable and nondurable goods; horizontal and vertical combinations; sole proprietorship; partnership; corporation; limited liability; separation of ownership and control.

2   What implications does the personal distribution of income have for the size and composition of the economy's total output? For resource allocation? Explain.

3   What happens to the volumes of consumption and saving as disposable income rises? What is "dissaving"? When is dissaving most likely to occur?

4   Why is the demand for consumer durable goods less stable than that for nondurables?

5   Explain the relationship between "consumer protection" and allocative efficiency.

6   Distinguish clearly between a plant, a firm, and an industry. Why is an "industry" difficult to define in practice?

7   What are the major legal forms of business organization? Briefly state the advantages and disadvantages of each. How do you account for the dominant role of corporations in our economy?

8   Explain and evaluate the separation of ownership and control which characterizes the corporate form of business enterprise.

9   What are the major industries in American capitalism in terms of *a.* the number of firms in operation, and *b.* the amount of income and employment provided?

10   What factors have motivated the growth of big business in the United States? What are the pros and cons of big business?

11   Explain and evaluate the following statements:

a.   "It is the consumer, and the consumer alone, who casts the vote that determines how big any company should be."

b.   "The very nature of modern industrial society requires labor, government, and businesses to be 'big' and their bigness renders impossible the functioning of the older, small-scale, simpler, and more flexible capitalist system."[9]

c.   "The legal form which an enterprise assumes is dictated primarily by the financial requirements of its particular line of production."

d.   "If we want capitalism, we must also accept inequality of income distribution."

Selected References

Baratz, Morton S.: *The American Business System in Transition* (New York: Thomas Y. Crowell Company, 1970).

Boulding, Kenneth E.: *Economic Analysis: Microeconomics,* 4th ed. (New York: Harper & Row, Publishers, Incorporated, 1966), chaps. 15, 16.

Cheit, Earl F. (ed.): *The Business Establishment* (New York: John Wiley & Sons, Inc., 1964).

Reid, Samuel Richardson: *The New Industrial Order* (New York: McGraw-Hill Book Company, 1976), introduction and part 1.

Swagler, Roger M.: *Caveat Emptor!* (Lexington, Mass.: D. C. Heath and Company, 1975).

Trebing, Harry M. (ed.): *The Corporation in the American Economy* (Chicago: Quadrangle Books, Inc., 1970).

[9]Eugene O. Golob, *The Isms* (New York: Harper & Row, Publishers, Incorporated, 1954), p. 53.

Last Word
Big Corporations: The View from West Virginia

Big business—good or bad? Here a coal miner sets forth his views on the impact of large coal corporations on life in his state.

I started to work in the coal mines at the age of 13. I worked in the summer months and went to school in the winter months. When times were really rough I worked during school months also. In spite of this, I can look back on my childhood and recollect many fond memories.

I can remember swimming and fishing in the clear, clean rivers and streams. I hunted in the mountains and valleys. I breathed the fresh, clean air and felt that it was great to be alive and to live in such beautiful surroundings.

It was in the late 1930's that the people in my county and surrounding ones began to get alarmed at what was happening to our environment. The streams became polluted; the fish disappeared; the mountains became scarred and barren; and the roads were ruined by overloaded coal trucks. Huge gob piles burned and are still burning, thus destroying trees and endangering animal and human life. None of these things happened until the days of the big corporations.

I, and other citizens I have talked with from West Virginia, indict the big corporations which have come into our State and have virtually destroyed its beauty and the dignity of its people. I have learned the hard way that these corporations do not worry or care about treating people fairly. They take millions of dollars worth of coal, timber, and gas out of the State and leave nothing in return except barren mountains, bad roads, polluted streams, and people who have been robbed of their birthright.

The people of West Virginia are determined to use whatever means they can to stop this and to see that a fair share of the extracted wealth is left in the State. Up to the present time, all we have been getting is the refuse. Our State is being used as a garbage dump for out-of-State interests who could not care less for the State or its people. These big corporations make coal a curse rather than an asset to the State. As they operate now, West Virginia would be better off if coal had never been discovered there.

Following are some of the ways in which these corporations are destroying West Virginia:

1 Destruction of the environment. Land is stripped that is impossible to reclaim. Steep mountains are stripped of timber and coal with no regard as to where they are located in relation to people's homes, private property, and streams. Thus, homes are destroyed, streams are polluted, and mountainsides are eroded, causing slides and floods.

2 Cutting down the job market. These corporations feel no obligation to the people. Their sole purpose is to make money. The first way they think of is to cut down on jobs and keep production high. They do this through mechanization. They are willing to spend large sums of money on upkeep and repairs, but they never feel obligated to make more money by employing more people.

3 The use of discriminatory practices. The companies would hire white workers who lived 50 to 60 miles away in order not to hire local black workers. This has happened in some instances that I know of personally. My own father was denied a job because of this practice.

4 Unfair labor practices. In some instances, local people are hired, but the main work force usually lives in other communities some distance away or even in other States. This cuts down on union activity by keeping the men apart.

5 Absentee land ownership. The corporations buy up the land and the mineral rights and hold it in reserve. They will not sell it for homesites, and they do not let others develop it. They also pay very low taxes on it. If this land could be obtained by other people, perhaps small local industries could be started and developed, thus helping the economic development of the area.

6 They tend to control agencies. I have known mines that were unsafe and whenever the mine inspectors would come around they would be notified beforehand so they could get things seemingly safe for 1 day and when they did not get them safe, the mining inspector would not go inside but certify the mine as being safe anyway. They would cause people to not receive unemployment compensation by saying there was work available when there was not. They try to stop pensions connected with the coal industry such as black lung, social security, and miner's welfare, and workmen's compensation. They conspire to shut down small businesses. With their money and power they make a joke of the free enterprise system. They finance political campaigns, and in a lot of instances get their own people elected to office.

I know that the beauty of bygone days is lost forever, but I feel that there is something still left to salvage. Therefore, I ask that the plunder and pillage of large corporations stop now.

From *Controls or Competition,* Hearings before the Subcommittee on Antitrust and Monopoly of the Committee on the Judiciary, U.S. Senate, 92d Congress, 1st Session, Washington, 1972, pp. 143–144.

8

The Facts of American Capitalism: The Public Sector

The basic goal of this chapter is to get acquainted with some factual aspects of the public sector. Specifically, what kinds of taxes are used by Federal, state, and local governments? For what purposes and programs are their tax revenues disbursed? Persistent controversy surrounding the scope of government's economic role makes it particularly important that the facts of government be clearly understood and placed in proper perspective. Two points must be made at the outset.

1 Although, as Chapter 6 revealed, there are many ways in which government affects economic life, it is through taxation and expenditures that the functions of government are most directly felt. Indeed, changes in the size and composition of government spending and the volume of tax revenues reflect with a fair degree of accuracy any changes in the size and character of government's role in the economy. It is with the public sector's role as a transactor, that is, as a receiver and disposer of "income," that this chapter is concerned.

2 There is a significant difference between the transactions of the private and public sectors of the economy: the former are *voluntary,* and the latter *compulsory.* The receipts and expenditures of households and businesses are the result of voluntary decisions by those two aggregates in buying and selling goods and resources. Government tax revenues are the result of compulsory levies: households and businesses have no choice but to pay taxes. To a lesser degree, this compulsion appears on the expenditure side of government's transactions.

148

While no one is compelled to use governmentally provided highways, libraries, or health clinics, all physically and mentally capable children who are within stated age brackets must consume public education or its equivalent.

PUBLIC SECTOR GROWTH

By any reasonable measure, the public sector's role in the economy has expanded both *absolutely* and *relatively*. Figure 8-1 portrays the absolute increases in government spending

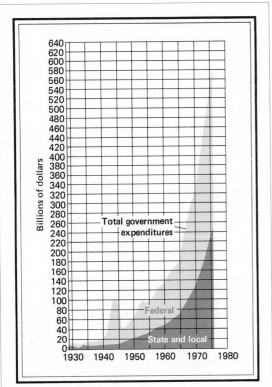

FIGURE 8-1 FEDERAL, STATE, AND LOCAL EXPENDITURES, 1929-1976

Government expenditures have grown both absolutely and as a percentage of total output. Hot and cold wars, population growth, urbanization, income maintenance programs, and inflation are some of the more important factors underlying this growth. Government tax collections have also increased significantly over time, roughly matching the increases in government spending. (*Economic Report of the President, 1976.*)

since 1929. In relative terms, government expenditures claimed only 8 percent of total output in 1929; by 1976 government spending was almost 22 percent of national output! In 1975, public spending was financed by an average tax bill of $2255 presented to every man, woman, and child in the United States. Or, from a slightly different vantage point, in 1976 the average taxpayer will spend 2 hours and 39 minutes of an 8-hour workday to pay taxes!

□   Some Causes

Recall from Chapter 6 that the desire of the citizenry to correct or alleviate the instability, inefficiency, and inequities which the price system may foster provides a basic rationale for the public sector. Consider now an admittedly incomplete list of some specific factors which account for the spectacular growth of government spending and taxes.

1   War and Defense   Hot and cold wars have tended to sustain Federal expenditures at high levels for the past three decades. War, national defense, and military-space research are among the major causes of the phenomenal growth of government spending and taxation which has occurred since 1940. In 1976, expenditures by the Department of Defense were on the order of $93 billion.

2   Population Growth   The growth of population has been rapid; there are about twice as many Americans today as there were a scant fifty-five years ago. This obviously means there are more people for whom social goods and services must be provided. Stated differently, even with a constant level of government spending per person, total government spending would have increased dramatically in recent decades.

3   Urbanization and the Demand for Social Goods   Not only has the size of our population been an important factor underlying the growth of government, but so has the geographic location of the population. In particular, the increasing urbanization of our economy has necessitated massive expenditures on streets, public transportation facilities, police and fire protection, sewers, and so forth. Furthermore, the public has demanded more and better social goods and services to "match" the rising standard of living provided by the private sector of the economy. We want bigger and better highways to accommodate more and better automobiles. We want more and better educational facilities to upgrade the labor force for the more demanding jobs of private industry.

4   Environmental Quality   Population growth and urbanization have contributed to serious and well-publicized problems of environmental quality. In particular, society has become highly aware that the production and consumption of vast quantities of goods can give rise to serious social or spillover costs in the form of air, water, and land pollution. Government has inherited a central role in coping with these environmental problems.

5   Egalitarianism   Since the mid-1960s there has occurred a sharp expansion of programs designed to alleviate poverty and reduce income inequality. Social security, unemployment compensation, welfare, Medicare, food stamps, and public housing are examples. These programs accounted for about 3 percent of national output twenty years ago; now they require over 10 percent.

6   Inflation   A rising price level accounts for a considerable portion of the historical rise in government spending. Because of inflation, government has had to spend larger and larger amounts for given quantities of goods and services. Indeed, the prices of the goods and services purchased by government have increased more rapidly than have the prices of private consumer and investment goods.

As with the business and household sectors of the economy, the receipt and the expenditure of government income need not match in any particular year or period of years. Surpluses and deficits—the latter in particular—are not at all uncommon insofar as public finance is concerned. Nevertheless, with the exception of large-scale deficit financing during World War II, a graph of government tax collections would rather closely follow the trend of spending shown in Figure 8-1.

☐   **Purchases versus Transfers**

Going beyond the trend of government spending, we must also distinguish between two fundamentally different types of governmental outlays.

Purchases   Government purchases of goods and services are virtually self-defining. This concept refers to such ordinary governmental purchases as paper clips, typewriter ribbons, automobiles, and school buildings, as well as to such uniquely social goods as jet fighters, atomic submarines, superhighways, and space capsules. Purchases of services include the hiring of clerks, schoolteachers, judges, service personnel, and so forth. Government purchases are often called *exhaustive* in that they directly absorb or employ resources, and the resulting production contributes to the national output.

Transfers   Transfer payments, on the other hand, are disbursements for which government currently receives no products or services in return. Most government insurance and income-maintenance programs fall in this classification: for example, social security payments to the aged, unemployment compensation, welfare payments, and aid to the handicapped. Some transfer payments, called "subsidies," go to businesses: for example, certain payments to farmers under our agricultural programs. Because transfer payments rechannel tax revenues back to households and businesses, these payments in effect are "negative taxes." Transfers are frequently labeled *nonexhaustive* because, as such, they do not directly absorb resources or account for production.

A Distinction   There is a noteworthy difference between transfer payments and government purchases of goods and services. Through government spending on goods, society tends to reallocate resources from private to social goods consumption. Through transfers, government changes the composition of the output of private goods. If government taxes amount to $10, we can expect purchases of private goods and services to decline by roughly that amount. In purchasing social goods and services with this $10 worth of tax revenue, individuals or groups within the economy, working through government, are in effect negotiating a substitution of social for private goods. Transfer payments are different: Instead of increasing social goods at the expense of private goods, transfers merely tend to "rearrange" private consumption. Though $10 in tax revenues will reduce the private goods consumption of taxpayers by about that amount, households to whom this $10 is transferred can be expected to increase their expenditures on private goods by about $10. But,

in all probability, the recipients will purchase somewhat different goods from those bought by the taxpayers. Hence, transfers alter the composition of private goods production.

This distinction between government purchases and transfer payments is relevant for our discussion of the growth of government. One can argue that transfer payments involve a lesser degree of government intervention in the economy than do government purchases. Because transfers in recent years have been growing more rapidly than government purchases, Figure 8-1 may tend to overstate in a sense the expanding role of the public sector.

■
FEDERAL FINANCE

Let us now disaggregate the public sector into Federal, state, and local units of government in order to compare the character of their expenditures and taxes. Table 8-1 tells the story for the Federal government.

□   **Federal Expenditures**

Although Table 8-1 reveals a wide variety of Federal expenditures, two important areas of spending stand out: *income security and*

Table 8-1   THE FEDERAL BUDGET, 1976

Tax receipts	Billions of dollars	Percent of total	Expenditures	Billions of dollars	Percent of total
Personal income taxes	$131	43	Income security and health	$161	43
Payroll taxes	93	31	National defense	93	25
Corporate income taxes	40	13	Veterans' services	19	5
Excise taxes	17	6	Interest on public debt	35	9
Estate and gift taxes	5	2	International affairs	6	2
All other	12	4	Science, space, and technology	4	1
			Education and manpower	19	5
			Commerce and transportation	18	5
Total receipts	$298	100	Natural resources, environment, and energy	12	3
			All other	7	2
			Total expenditures	$374	100

Source: Economic Report of the President. Because of rounding, figures may not add up to totals. Data are estimates.

health and *national defense.* The first category reflects the myriad of previously mentioned income-maintenance programs which assist the aged, the disabled, the unemployed, the handicapped, the medically indigent, families with no breadwinner, and so forth. The national defense category understates the economic costs of wars and military preparedness because the ensuing four classifications are closely associated with the military. *Veterans' services*—which include GI Bill payments, medical care, disability pay, and pensions to veterans and their dependents—obviously are expenditures associated with past wars. And, since a large portion of the Federal debt was incurred in financing past wars, the annual payment of *interest on the public debt* also can be considered as a war-born outlay. Furthermore, *international affairs* involve expenditures for the economic and technological development of foreign countries and the costs of administering our foreign affairs. In part, these outlays stem from altruistic motives. But a selfish reason dominates: These expenditures are designed to keep foreign countries from turning to communism. Finally, outlays for science and space research clearly have important implications for national security. As a group, these five expenditure categories account for about $157 billion, or about 42 percent, of total Federal outlays. War and military preparedness carry extremely high price tags. The remaining categories of spending listed in Table 8-1 are largely self-explanatory.

□   **Federal Receipts**

The receipts side of Table 8-1 makes it clear that the personal income tax, payroll taxes, and the corporate income tax are the basic Federal revenue getters, accounting for 43, 31, and 13 cents of each tax dollar collected.

Personal Income Tax   The personal income tax is the kingpin of our national tax system and it therefore deserves rather extended comment. This tax is levied on *taxable income,* that is, on the incomes of households and unincorporated businesses after certain exemptions and deductions have been taken into account.[1]

Mechanics   Table 8-2 gives us a general picture of the mechanics of the personal income tax. Although the figures are hypothetical, the actual tax rates shown correspond closely to those which now prevail. Column 2 shows the absolute amount of taxes which

[1]The major deductions and exemptions from gross income in determining taxable income are (1) business costs and expenses incurred in earning income, (2) gifts to charitable institutions, (3) interest payments, (4) certain state and local tax payments, and (5) a $750 exemption for the taxpayer and each of his dependents.

Table 8-2   A PROGRESSIVE PERSONAL INCOME TAX (*hypothetical data*)

(1) Total taxable income	(2) Total tax	(3) Average tax rate, (2) ÷ (1)	(4) Change in income, Δ(1)	(5) Change in taxes, Δ(2)	(6) Marginal tax rate, (5) ÷ (4)
$ 1,000	$ 0	0%			
3,000	150	5	$ 2,000	$ 150	7.5%
6,000	600	10	3,000	450	15
10,000	1,500	15	4,000	900	22.5
20,000	5,000	25	10,000	3,500	35
50,000	20,000	40	30,000	15,000	50
100,000	50,000	50	50,000	30,000	60
500,000	300,000	60	400,000	250,000	62
1,000,000	650,000	65	500,000	350,000	70

must be paid at each income level shown in column 1. The *average tax rate* in column 3 is merely the total tax paid divided by taxable income. Thus, at a taxable income of $3000, the average tax rate is 5 percent (= $150 ÷ $3000); at $6000, it is 10 percent (= $600 ÷ $6000); and so on. By definition, any tax—such as our personal income tax—whose average tax *rate* increases as income increases is called a *progressive tax.*

The *marginal tax rate* is the tax rate paid on additional or incremental income. By definition, it is the *increase* in taxes paid as additional income is obtained divided by that increase in income. Columns 4 and 5 provide the data needed to calculate the marginal tax rate. Thus we observe that if a family's taxable income is $1000, it pays no taxes. But if its income rises to $3000, it will be required to pay $150 (column 5) on the $2000 increase in its income (column 4). The marginal tax rate is therefore 7.5 percent (= $150 ÷ $2000). On the next $3000 increment of taxable income which takes the family from the $3000 to the $6000 level, it must pay additional taxes of $450, so the marginal tax rate on this extra income is 15 percent (= $450 ÷ $3000). Note that as income increases, the marginal tax rate rises rather sharply. Indeed, it is the fact that each increment of income is taxed at a higher marginal tax rate which pulls up the average tax rate.[2] For the United States, the top marginal tax rate is 70 percent. This obviously means that you can never be made worse off by earning an extra dollar; at least 30 cents of it will be yours to keep.[3]

Economic aspects The economic implications of the personal income tax merit brief comment. Recall from Chapter 6 that three basic functions of government are to provide social goods and services, stabilize the economy, and redistribute income. The personal income tax can be employed very effectively in pursuing these goals. First, it is obviously capable of bringing in large amounts of revenue to finance social goods and services, as Table 8-1 clearly indicates. Indeed, the progressive tax rates make tax collections very responsive to the long-run growth of the national income. A second and less obvious point is that a progressive income tax can help to stabilize the economy. For example, during prosperity, money incomes rise and total demand tends to outrun productive capacity so that inflation occurs. The fact that income tax rates are progressive means that tax collections will rise at a more rapid rate than incomes. These rising tax collections have the effect of diverting income from the expenditures stream, thereby lessening inflationary pressures. Conversely, as the economy backslides into recession and total demand is inadequate to maintain full employment, tax collections decline at a more rapid rate than does income. This decrease tends to bolster the income-expenditures stream and to cushion the recession. In short, the *automatic* changes in tax collections which accompany a progressive income tax add an element of *built-in stability* to the economy (Chapter 13). Finally, the personal income tax obviously has considerable potential for redistributing income. Given its progressivity as revealed by Table 8-2, the tax contributes to greater income equality. But we must be cautious on this point: we shall find momentarily that a variety of tax loopholes have eroded the income tax base and that its progressivity is substantially less than the table suggests.

Despite these virtues, critics of the personal income tax contend that its high marginal tax rates may discourage incentives to work, invest, and assume risks. But it is difficult to determine whether these harmful effects have in fact occurred. Consider work. A rising marginal tax rate means a worker gets a smaller after-tax wage rate for each hour of

[2]The theory is the same as one you may have encountered in school. You must get a score on an additional or "marginal" examination which is higher than your existing average grade in order to pull your average up!

[3]Maybe more! If all the family's income is "earned" income (from wages, salaries, and professional fees), the maximum marginal tax rate is 50 percent, rather than 70 percent.

work. Hence, because work is less and less rewarding, he may decide to work *fewer* hours. On the other hand, if he is motivated to earn a target income of, say, $15,000 per year, the progressive tax rates may spur him to work *more* hours to achieve that income. The consensus of empirical studies on this matter is that the effect of income taxes on work habits is small.

Payroll Taxes   Social security contributions, or payroll taxes, are the premiums paid on the compulsory insurance plans, for example, old age insurance and Medicare, provided for by existing social security legislation. These taxes are paid by both employers and employees. Improvements in, and extensions of, our social security programs, plus growth of the labor force, have resulted in very significant increases in payroll taxes in recent years.

Corporate Income Tax   The corporate income tax has a relatively simple structure. The first $25,000 of taxable profits is taxed at a 20 percent rate; the next $25,000 is taxed at 22 percent; any profits in excess of $50,000 are taxed at 48 percent. For example, a corporation realizing a taxable income of $75,000 would pay $22,500 in corporate income taxes—$5000 (20 percent of the first $25,000) *plus* $5500 (22 percent of the second $25,000) plus $12,000 (48 percent of the remaining $25,000).

The corporate income tax, as mentioned in Chapter 7, entails a highly controversial problem—"double taxation." That particular part of the income stream which takes the form of dividends is taxed twice, while other forms of income are taxed but once. All corporate net income is first taxed under the corporate income tax as described in the last paragraph. In addition, that portion of corporate earnings which flows to stockholders is taxed for a second time as personal income. This double taxation of dividends is felt by many economists to be a glaring inequity in the present structure of income taxes. The inequity, however, is at least partially offset by the fact that retained corporate earnings are not subject to tax rates higher than 48 percent.

Sales, Excise, and Other Taxes   Commodity or consumption taxes may take the form of sales taxes or excise taxes. The difference between the two is basically one of degree. Sales taxes fall on a wide range of products, whereas excises are taxes on a small, select list of commodities.

As Table 8-1 indicates, the Federal government collects excise taxes imposed upon such commodities as alcoholic beverages, tobacco, gasoline, and tires. However, the Federal government does *not* levy a general sales tax; sales taxes are the bread and butter of most state governments.

□   **Federal Tax Loopholes**

The progressive rates of the personal and corporate income taxes imply that the Federal tax system makes the distribution of income more nearly equal. But in fact, these taxes contain a number of important legal loopholes, that is, provisions which give favorable tax treatment to certain kinds of income. Because these loopholes generally favor high-income recipients, the after-tax distribution is less nearly equal than would otherwise be the case. In particular, the personal income tax in practice is significantly less progressive than Table 8-2 suggests. For example, Treasury Department data show that people falling in tax brackets where the average tax rate of Table 8-2 is, say, 40 or 50 percent, actually pay taxes at a rate of 30 or 35 percent. Indeed, the widely publicized fact that many rich and superrich Americans—some of whom realize annual incomes of $1 million or more—have legally manipulated their financial affairs so as to pay no taxes at all led to provisions in the Tax Reform Act of 1969 which "catch" ultrahigh income receivers, albeit at low tax rates.

Skirting technical details, let us briefly mention a few of the more important loopholes.

1   Tax-exempt Securities   Interest income on the bonds of state and local governments is exempt from the Federal income tax. Many high-income people can reduce their income tax liabilities very substantially by availing themselves of this loophole. For example, people in the highest personal income tax bracket can reduce the tax rate on their interest income from 70 to zero percent by switching from savings deposits or corporate bonds to state and local bonds.

2   Capital Gains   An individual realizes a capital gain when he sells either securities or property at a higher price than he paid. Provided the gain is long term, that is, that the securities or property have been held for six months or more, one-half the value of the capital gain is tax exempt and the remainder is taxed as ordinary income *or,* at the taxpayer's discretion, the capital gain is taxed at one-half the rate which applies to ordinary income. Because the maximum tax rate on ordinary income is 70 percent, this means that capital gains are taxed at half that rate or, in other words, at 35 percent.[4]

3   Other Tax Breaks   A variety of other means exist by which the taxable portion of personal and corporate incomes can be reduced. Homeowners—who increasingly are upper-income people—can deduct interest charges and property taxes in determining their taxable incomes. By making deposits in certain retirement programs, high-income people can defer tax payments on those deposits until retirement when their incomes—and therefore their tax rates—will probably be lower. Corporations currently enjoy an investment tax credit by which they can deduct 10 percent of their expenditures for capital

goods from their tax bills. Business executives can receive compensation in several forms—for example, annuities and pension funds—which are not currently taxable. Multinational corporations pay no taxes on the profits of their overseas subsidiaries until (and if) these profits are brought home to the United States.

The basic point to be emphasized is that these and other tax loopholes are means by which high-income people are able to reduce their tax liabilities. The result is that the Federal personal and corporate income taxes are, in practice, much less effective in leveling incomes than might first appear.

■ ———————————————————

STATE AND LOCAL FINANCE

While the Federal government finances itself largely through personal and corporate income taxation and payroll taxes, state and local governments rely heavily upon sales and property taxes, respectively. And although there is considerable overlapping in the types of expenditures made by the three levels of government, income security and national defense account for the majority of Federal expenditures, whereas education, highways, and public welfare lead at state and local levels.

□   State Expenditures and Receipts

Note in Table 8-3 that the basic sources of tax revenue at the state level are sales and excise taxes, which account for about 54 percent of all state tax revenues. State personal income taxes, which entail much more modest rates than those employed by the Federal government, run a poor second. Taxes on corporate income, property, inheritances, and a variety of licenses and permits constitute the remainder of state tax revenue. On the expenditure side of the picture, the major outlays of state governments are for (1) education, (2) highway maintenance and construction, and (3) public welfare.

It is important to note that the budget

[4]Furthermore, the first $50,000 of capital gains are taxed at only 25 percent!

Table 8-3   CONSOLIDATED BUDGET OF ALL STATE GOVERNMENTS, 1975

Tax receipts	Billions of dollars	Percent of total	Expenditures	Billions of dollars	Percent of total
Sales, excise, and gross receipts taxes	$43.3	54	Education	$22.9	26
Personal income taxes	18.8	23	Highways	17.5	20
Corporate income taxes	6.6	8	Public welfare	14.3	17
Property taxes	1.5	2	Health, hospitals	10.1	12
Death and gift taxes	1.4	2	Natural resources	3.6	4
Licenses, permits, and others	8.5	11	All others	17.9	21
Total receipts	$80.1	100	Total expenditures	$86.3	100

Source: Bureau of the Census, *State Government Finances in 1975.* Because of rounding, figures may not add up to totals.

statement shown in Table 8-3 contains aggregated data and therefore tells us little about the finances of individual states. States vary tremendously in the types of taxes employed. Thus, although sales and personal income taxes are the major sources of revenue for all state governments combined, four states have no general sales tax and four do not use the personal income tax. Furthermore, great variations in the size of tax receipts and disbursements exist among the states.

☐ **Local Expenditures and Receipts**

The receipts and expenditures shown in Table 8-4 are for all units of local government, including counties, municipalities, townships, and school districts. One major source of revenue and a single basic use of revenue stand out: the bulk of the revenue received by local government comes from property taxation; the bulk of local revenue is spent for education. Other, less important sources of funds and types of disbursements are self-explanatory.

The gaping deficit shown in Table 8-4 is largely removed when nontax resources of income are taken into account: In 1975 the tax revenues of local governments were supplemented by some $62 billion in intergovernmental grants from Federal and state governments. Furthermore, local governments received an additional $10 billion as proprietary income, that is, as revenue from government-owned liquor stores and utilities.

Table 8-4   CONSOLIDATED BUDGET OF ALL LOCAL GOVERNMENTS, 1975

Tax receipts	Billions of dollars	Percent of total	Expenditures	Billions of dollars	Percent of total
Property taxes	$50.0	81	Education	$ 65.0	45
Sales and excises	6.5	11	Police, fire, and general government	14.2	10
Personal and corporate income taxes	2.6	4	Public welfare	9.7	7
Licenses, permits, and others	2.2	4	Health and hospitals	9.9	7
Total receipts	$61.3	100	Highways	8.3	6
			All others	36.0	25
			Total expenditures	$143.1	100

Source: Bureau of the Census, *Government Finances in 1974–1975.* Because of rounding, figures may not add up to totals.

REVENUE SHARING

A serious fiscal mismatch has evolved in recent years between the Federal government, on the one hand, and state and local governments, on the other. Federal tax revenues, derived heavily from personal and corporate income taxes, are very sensitive to changes in the economy. As growth increases the national income, sizable increases in Federal tax revenues automatically occur. State and local tax revenues, based primarily on sales and property taxes, are less responsive to growth. At the same time, population growth and urbanization have necessitated substantial increases in state and local expenditures for education, streets and highways, public welfare, police protection, and other public services. Furthermore, the costs of state and local governments have been pushed up rapidly as a result of the unionization of many state and municipal workers. In short, despite substantial increases in sales and property tax rates, state and local governments have been faced with serious fiscal problems. The well publicized financial problems of New York City are a dramatic case in point.

Historically, this fiscal imbalance has been redressed by a growing volume of intergovernmental grants flowing from the Federal government to state and local governments. Until 1972 this aid took the form of *categorical grants,* that is, grants which are earmarked to such specific programs as highway construction, education, and health care *and* are contingent upon matching state and local funds. A major departure from this pattern came in 1972 with the passage of the State and Local Fiscal Assistance Act, more commonly known as the Revenue Sharing Act. The essence of this act is that the Federal government will make unrestricted or "block" grants without the requirement of matching funds. The states retain one-third of their grants and must pass the remaining two-thirds on to local units of government. The formula for allocating Fed-

eral monies to the states takes into account such factors as (1) state and local tax efforts, (2) per capita incomes, and (3) population. Inclusion of the first factor is to provide relatively more aid to those states which display an interest in meeting their own problems *and* to discourage states from using the grants to "finance" tax cuts. Per capita income and population size are used in the grant formula to provide relatively more aid to states with large populations and low per capita incomes, thereby tending to redistribute income among the states. The act, as extended by 1976 congressional action, provides approximately $6 billion of aid per year to states and localities.

APPORTIONING THE TAX BURDEN

The very nature of social goods and services (see Chapter 6) makes it exceedingly difficult to measure precisely the manner in which their benefits are apportioned among individuals and institutions in the economy. It is virtually impossible to determine accurately the amount by which John Doe benefits from military installations, a network of highways, a public school system, and local police and fire protection.

The situation is a bit different on the taxation side of the picture. Statistical studies reveal rather clearly the manner in which the overall tax burden is apportioned. Needless to say, this is a question which affects each of us in a vital way. Although the average citizen is concerned with the overall level of taxes, chances are he is even more interested in exactly how the tax burden is allocated among individual taxpayers.

☐   **Benefits Received versus Ability to Pay**

There are two basic philosophies on how the economy's tax burden should be apportioned.

Benefits-received Principle   The *bene-fits-received principle* of taxation asserts that households and businesses should purchase the goods and services of government in basically the same manner in which other commodities are bought. It is reasoned that those who benefit most from government-supplied goods or services should pay the taxes necessary for their financing. Some social goods are financed essentially on the basis of the benefits principle. For example, gasoline taxes are typically earmarked for the financing of highway construction and repairs. Those who benefit from good roads pay the cost of those roads. Difficulties immediately arise, however, when an accurate and widespread application of the benefits principle is considered:

1 How does one go about determining the benefits which individual households and businesses receive from national defense, education, and police and fire protection? Recall (Chapter 6) that social goods entail widespread social or spillover benefits and that the exclusion principle is inapplicable. Even in the seemingly tangible case of highway finance we find it difficult to measure benefits. Individual car owners benefit in different degrees from the existence of good roads. And those who do not own cars also benefit. Businesses certainly benefit greatly from any widening of their markets which good roads will encourage.

2 The shortcomings of the benefits principle become even more apparent when certain government welfare programs are considered. Welfare payments and payments to the physically handicapped would be self-defeating if they were financed on the benefits principle. It would be ridiculous to think of taxing unemployed workers to finance the unemployment compensation payments which they receive. In short, government activities designed to redistribute income preclude the use of the benefits principle in their financing.

Ability-to-pay Principle   The *ability-to-pay principle* of taxation stands in sharp contrast to the benefits principle. Ability-to-pay taxation rests on the idea that the tax burden should be geared directly to one's financial position. As the ability-to-pay principle has come to be applied in the United States, it contends that individuals and businesses with larger incomes should pay more taxes—both absolutely and relatively—than those with more modest incomes.

What is the rationale of ability-to-pay taxation? Proponents argue that each additional dollar of income received by a household will yield smaller and smaller amounts of satisfaction. It is argued that, because consumers act rationally, the first dollars of income received in any period of time will be spent upon basic high-urgency goods; that is, upon those goods which yield the greatest benefit or satisfaction. Successive dollars of income will go for less urgently needed goods and finally for trivial goods and services. This means that a dollar taken through taxes from a poor man who has few dollars constitutes a greater sacrifice on his part than does a dollar taken by taxes from the rich man who has many dollars. Hence, to balance the sacrifices which taxes impose on income receivers, it is contended that taxes should be apportioned according to the amount of income one receives.

This is appealing, but problems of application exist here, too. In particular, although we might agree that the household earning $25,000 per year has a greater ability to pay taxes than the household receiving a paltry $5000, exactly *how much more* ability to pay does the first family have as compared with the second? Should the rich man simply pay the *same percentage* of his larger income—and hence a larger absolute amount—as taxes? Or should the rich man be made to pay a *larger fraction* of his income as taxes? The problem is that there is no scientific way of measuring one's ability to pay taxes. Thus, in practice, the answer hinges upon guesswork, the tax views of the political party in power, expediency, and the urgency with which government needs revenue. As we shall discover in a few moments, the tax structure of our economy is somewhat more in tune with the ability-to-pay principle than with the benefits-received principle.

□ **Progressive, Proportional, and Regressive Taxes**

Any discussion of the ability-to-pay and the benefits-received principles of taxation leads ultimately to the question of tax rates and the manner in which tax rates change as one's income increases.

Definitions   Taxes are ordinarily classified as being progressive, proportional, or regressive.

1 A tax is *progressive* if its rate *increases* as income increases. Such a tax claims not only a larger absolute amount, but also a larger fraction or percentage of income as income increases.

2 A *regressive* tax is one whose rate *declines* as income increases. Such a tax takes a smaller and smaller proportion of income as income increases. A regressive tax may or may not take a larger absolute amount of income as income expands.

3 A tax is *proportional* when its rate *remains the same,* regardless of the size of income.

Let us illustrate in terms of the personal income tax. Suppose the tax rates are such that everyone pays 10 percent of his income in taxes, regardless of the size of his income. This would obviously be a proportional income tax. But suppose the rate structure is such that the household with an annual taxable income of less than $1000 pays 5 percent in income taxes, the household realizing an income of $1000 to $2000 pays 10 percent, $2000 to $3000 pays 15 percent, and so forth.[5] This, as we have already explained, would obviously be a *progressive* income tax. The final case is where the rates decline as taxable income rises: you pay 15 percent if you earn less than $1000; 10 per-

cent if you earn $1000 to $2000; 5 percent if you earn $2000 to $3000; and so forth. This is a *regressive* income tax. Generally speaking, progressive taxes are those which bear down most heavily on the rich; regressive taxes are those which hit the poor hardest.

Applications   What can we say about the progressivity, proportionality, or regressivity of the major kinds of taxes used in the United States? We have already stressed the progressive features of the Federal *personal income tax.* Recall, however, that in practice various exemptions, deductions, and tax loopholes dampen its overall progressivity.

At first glance a *general sales tax* with, say, a 3 percent rate would seem to be proportional. But in fact it is regressive. The reason for its regressivity is that a larger portion of a poor man's income is exposed to the tax than is the case with a rich man; the latter avoids the tax on the part of his income which he saves, whereas the former is unable to save. Example: "Poor" Smith has an income of $6000 and spends it all. "Rich" Jones has an income of $12,000 but spends only $8000 of it. Assuming a 3 percent sales tax applies to the expenditures of each individual, Smith will obviously pay $180 (3 percent of $6000) in sales taxes, and Jones will pay $240 (3 percent of $8000). Note that whereas *all* of Smith's $6000 income is subject to the sales tax, only two-thirds of Jones's $12,000 income is taxed. Thus, while Smith pays $180, or 3 percent, of his $6000 income as sales taxes, Jones pays $240, or just 2 percent, of his $12,000 income. Hence, we conclude that the general sales tax is regressive.

The Federal *corporate income tax* appears to be progressive and is generally regarded as such; after all, tax rates rise from 20 to 48 percent as corporate profits rise. But this assumes that corporation owners (shareholders) bear the tax. Some tax experts argue that at least a part of the tax is passed through to consumers in the form of higher product prices. To the extent that this occurs, the tax tends to be regressive, like a sales tax.

[5]We refer here to average or effective tax rates, not to marginal tax rates.

Property taxes and payroll taxes are regressive. The *property tax* is regressive for two reasons. First, property owners add the tax to the rents which tenants are charged. Second, property taxes, as a percentage of income, are higher for poor families than for rich families because the poor must spend a larger proportion of their incomes for housing. *Payroll taxes* are regressive because they apply to only a fixed absolute amount of one's income. For example, in 1977, payroll tax rates were 5.85 percent, but this figure applies only to the first $16,500 of one's wage income. Thus a person earning exactly $16,500 would pay $965, or 5.85 percent of his wage income, while someone with twice that income, or $33,000, would also pay $965—only 2.92 percent of his wage income. Note, too, that this regressivity is enhanced because the payroll tax excludes nonwage income. If our individual with the $33,000 wage income also received $16,500 in nonwage (dividend, interest, rent) income, then his payroll tax would only be 1.95 percent (= $965 ÷ $49,500) of his total income.

☐ **Shifting and incidence of Taxes**

Suppose society has decided how it wants the current tax burden to be apportioned among specific households and businesses. Now a complicating factor arises. Taxes do not always stick where the government puts them. Some taxes can be *shifted* among various parties in the economy. It is therefore necessary to locate as best we can the final resting place or *incidence* of the major types of taxes.

Personal Income Tax   The incidence of the personal income tax generally falls on the individual upon whom the tax is levied; little chance exists for shifting. But there might be exceptions to this. Individuals and groups who can effectively control the price of their labor services may be able to shift a part of the tax. For example, doctors, dentists, lawyers, and other professional people who can readily increase their fees may do so because of the tax.

Unions might regard personal income taxes as part of the cost of living and, as a result, bargain for higher wages. If they are successful, they may shift a portion of the tax from workers to employers. Generally, however, we can conclude that the individual upon whom the tax is initially levied bears the burden of the personal income tax. The same ordinarily holds true of inheritance taxes.

Corporate Income Tax   We have already suggested that the incidence of the corporate income tax is much less certain. The traditional view has it that a firm which is currently charging the profit-maximizing price and producing the profit-maximizing output will have no reason to change price or output when a corporate income tax is imposed. That price and output combination which yields the greatest profit before the tax will still be the most profitable after government takes a fixed percentage of the firm's profits in the form of income taxes. According to this view, the company's stockholders must bear the incidence of the tax in the form of lower dividends or a smaller amount of retained earnings. On the other hand, some economists argue that the corporate income tax is shifted in part to consumers through higher prices and to resource suppliers through lower prices. In modern industry, where a small number of firms may control a market, producers may not be in the profit-maximizing position initially. The reason? By fully exploiting their market position currently, monopolistic firms might elicit adverse public opinion and governmental censure. Hence, they may await such events as increases in tax rates or wage increases by unions to provide an "excuse" or rationale for price increases with less fear of public criticism. When this actually occurs, a portion of the corporate income tax may be shifted to consumers through higher prices.

Both positions are plausible. Indeed, the incidence of the corporate income tax may well be shared by stockholders and the firm's customers and resource suppliers.

Sales and Excise Taxes   Sales and excise taxes are the "hidden taxes" of our economy. They are hidden because such taxes are typically shifted by sellers to consumers through higher product prices. There may be some difference in the shiftability of sales taxes and excises, however. Because a sales tax covers a much wider range of products than an excise, there is little chance for consumers to resist the price boosts which sales taxes entail by reallocating their expenditures to untaxed products.

Excises, however, fall on a relatively short, select list of goods. Therefore, the possibility of consumers turning to substitute goods and services is greater. For example, an excise tax on theater tickets which does not apply to other types of entertainment might be difficult to pass on to consumers via price increases. Why? Because price boosts might result in considerable substituting of alternative types of entertainment by consumers. From the seller's point of view, the higher price will cause such a marked decline in sales that he will be better off to bear all, or a large portion of, the excise rather than the sharp decline in sales. With many excises, however, modest price increases have little or no effect on sales. Excises on gasoline, cigarettes, and alcoholic beverages are cases in point. Here there are few good substitute products to which consumers can turn as prices rise. For these commodities, the seller is in a better position to shift the tax.

In general, it is safe to say that the bulk of a sales or excise tax will generally be shifted to the consumer through higher product prices. Later (Chapter 23) we will employ supply and demand analysis as a basis for more sophisticated generalizations as to the shifting and incidence of sales taxes.

Property Taxes   Many property taxes are borne by the property owner for the simple reason that there is no other party to whom they can be shifted. This is typically true in the case of taxes on land, personal property, and owner-occupied residences. For example, even when land is sold, the property tax is not likely to be shifted. The buyer will tend to discount the value of the land to allow for the future taxes which he will be required to pay on it, and this expected taxation will be reflected in the price he is willing to offer for the land.

Taxes on rented and business property are a different story. Taxes on rented property can be, and usually are, shifted wholly or in part from the owner to the tenant by the simple process of boosting the rent. Business property taxes are treated as a business cost and therefore are taken into account in establishing product price; thus such taxes are ordinarily shifted to the firm's customers.

Table 8-5 summarizes this discussion of the shifting and incidence of taxes.

□   **The American Tax Structure**

As we have seen, the Federal, state, and local governments of the United States employ a variety of taxes. We have concluded that

Table 8-5   THE PROBABLE INCIDENCE OF TAXES

Type of tax	Probable incidence
Personal income tax	The household or individual upon which it is levied.
Corporate income tax	Disagreement. Some economists feel the firm on which it is levied bears the incidence; others conclude the tax is shifted, wholly or in part, to consumers.
Sales and excise taxes	With exceptions, consumers who buy the taxed products.
Property taxes	Owners in the case of land and owner-occupied residences; tenants in the case of rented property; consumers in the case of business property.

some of these taxes—the personal and corporate income taxes and inheritance taxes—are progressive, whereas others—sales taxes, excises, and property taxes—are for the most part regressive. What is the total picture? A recent estimate—and these figures must be very rough because of the uncertainty of tax incidence—is shown in Table 8-6.

Employing family income as the tax base, column 2 of this table tells us the percentage of income taken by Federal taxes in each of the nine income classes. The progressivity found here reflects the important role of the personal and corporate income taxes at the Federal level. Column 3 presents similar data for state and local taxes. Regressivity is evident here, reflecting the predominance of sales and property taxes at the state and local levels. Column 4 sums the two preceding columns and shows the percentage of income taken in Federal, state, and local taxes combined from each of the listed income groups.

Column 4 tells us that aside from the highest and lowest income classes, the overall tax structure is roughly proportional. Only for the highest "$50,000 and over" income class do we find strong evidence of progressivity. And, conversely, for the very poor "under $2000" class, the tax structure is highly regressive.

Given that the overall tax system takes roughly one-third of income in taxes from a very large proportion of income receivers, we can conclude that, except for the noted extremes, the tax system per se is generally neutral in its impact upon the distribution of income.

But columns 5 and 6 remind us that tax revenues are used in part to finance transfer payments. Transfers are in effect "taxes in reverse" or "negative taxes." While taxes flow from households to government, transfers flow from government to households. We note in columns 5 and 6 that direct government transfers to families are highly progressive. For example, although the families in the "under $2000" class pay 50 percent of their income as taxes, they receive transfer benefits equal to 106 percent of their incomes. Hence, net taxes—that is, taxes and transfers combined—augment the incomes of these families by 56 percent. Similarly, families in the "$2000–$4000" class receive transfers in excess of their taxes, so that their incomes are supplemented by about 14 percent. All higher-income classes pay taxes in excess of transfers and therefore are "net contributors" to, rather than "net recipients" from, the total tax-transfer system. The conclusion to be drawn

Table 8-6 ESTIMATED TAX RATES BY INCOME LEVELS (*taxes as a percentage of income*)

(1) Family income	(2) Federal taxes	(3) State and local taxes	(4) All taxes, or (2) + (3)	(5) Government transfer payments	(6) Net taxes, or (4) − (5)
Under $2,000	22.7%	27.2%	50.0%	106.5%	−56.5%
$2,000–$4,000	18.7	15.7	34.6	48.5	−13.9
$4,000–$6,000	19.0	12.1	31.0	19.6	11.4
$6,000–$8,000	19.4	10.7	30.1	8.6	21.5
$8,000–$10,000	19.1	10.1	29.2	5.5	23.7
$10,000–$15,000	19.9	9.9	29.8	3.9	25.9
$15,000–$25,000	20.7	9.4	30.0	3.0	27.0
$25,000–$50,000	25.0	7.8	32.8	2.1	30.7
$50,000 and over	38.4	6.7	45.0	0.4	44.7
Total tax on all income	21.7%	9.9%	31.6%	6.9%	24.6%

Source: Roger A. Herriot and Herman P. Miller, "The Taxes We Pay," *Conference Board Record,* May 1971, p. 40.

from column 6 is that the impact of the combined tax-transfer system is quite progressive.

A final point: Table 8-6 is an incomplete picture of the redistributive effect of total governmental activities for the simple reason that it excludes government purchases of goods and services. As mentioned earlier in regard to households and businesses, determining the extent to which each income class benefits from the various types of Federal, state, and local expenditures shown in Tables 8-1, 8-3, and 8-4 is extremely difficult. Therefore, the overall progressivity or regressivity of total public sector activity—including taxes, transfers, and government purchases of goods and services—is anything but clear.[6]

[6]The ambitious reader should consult Richard A. Musgrave and Peggy B. Musgrave, *Public Finance in Theory and Practice,* 2d ed., (New York: McGraw-Hill Book Company, 1976), chap. 16.

Summary

1   Historically, government tax receipts and expenditures have grown rapidly both in absolute amounts and in relation to the size of the national income. Wars and national defense, population growth, urbanization, environmental problems, egalitarianism, and inflation have been among the more important causes underlying the growth of government.

2   The main category of Federal spending is for "income security and health" and "national defense"; revenues come primarily from the personal income, payroll, and corporate income taxes. The primary sources of revenue for the states are sales and excise taxes; education, highways, and welfare are the major state expenditures. At the local level, most revenue comes from the property tax, and education is the most important expenditure. State and local tax revenues are supplemented by Federal revenue sharing.

3   The ability-to-pay principle of taxation is more evident in the American tax structure than is the benefits-received philosophy.

4   Taxes on personal income and inheritance taxes are progressive. The corporate income tax is probably progressive. General sales, excise, payroll, and property taxes tend to be regressive.

5   Sales and excise taxes are likely to be shifted; personal income taxes are not. There is disagreement as to whether corporate income taxes are shifted. The incidence of property taxes depends primarily upon whether the property is owner- or tenant-occupied.

6   Over the income range which includes the bulk of American households, the overall tax structure is roughly proportional. The combined tax-transfer system, however, is quite progressive.

Questions and Study Suggestions

1   Key terms and concepts to remember: transfer payments; personal income tax; marginal and average tax rates; payroll tax; corporate income tax; double taxation; sales and excise taxes; property tax; revenue sharing; benefits-received principle; ability-to-pay principle; progressive tax; proportional tax; regressive tax; tax shifting; tax incidence.

2   Describe and account for the historical growth of the public sector of the economy. Why might it be significant to distinguish between "transfer payments" and

"government purchases of goods and services" in evaluating the impact of the growth of government expenditures?

3   What are the most important source of revenue and the major type of expenditure at the Federal level? At the state level? At the local level?

4   Briefly describe the mechanics of the Federal personal income tax. Explain why the average or effective personal income tax rate is less than the marginal tax rate.

5   What is revenue sharing? Why has it occurred? Briefly describe the State and Local Fiscal Assistance Act of 1972. If you were in charge of distributing $10 billion per year among the states, what considerations would you include in your distribution formula?

6   Distinguish clearly between the benefits-received and the ability-to-pay principles of taxation. Which philosophy is more evident in our present tax structure? Justify your answer. To which principle of taxation do you subscribe? Why?

7   Precisely what is meant by a progressive tax? A regressive tax? A proportional tax? Comment upon the progressivity or regressivity of each of the following taxes, indicating in each case your assumption concerning tax incidence:

a.   The Federal personal income tax

b.   A 3 percent state general sales tax

c.   A Federal excise tax on playing cards

d.   A municipal property tax on real estate

e.   The Federal corporate income tax

What is likely to be the incidence of each of these taxes?

8   Comment in detail on the overall progressivity or regressivity of *a.* the American tax structure and *b.* the tax-transfer structure.

9   Explain and evaluate each of the following statements:

a.   "No tax on income can be a just tax unless it leaves individuals in the same relative condition in which it found them."

b.   "Because there is no sure definition of the limits to progression, no firm basis of its 'reasonable' use, no protection against its unconscionable abuse, those who uphold the system as a revenue device are playing into the hands of the group that would use progressive taxation as the means of destroying private capitalism and ushering in the collectivist state."

c.   "Even tho it be an open question whether all inequality in wealth and income be unjust, such great degrees of inequality as the modern world shows are regarded as not consonant with canons of justice. Very rich persons should be called to pay taxes not only in proportion to their incomes but more than in proportion."

Selected References

Break, George F., and Joseph A. Pechman: *Federal Tax Reform: The Impossible Dream?* (Washington: The Brookings Institution, 1975).

Maxwell, James A., and J. Richard Aronson: *Financing State and Local Government,* 3d ed. (Washington: The Brookings Institution, 1977).

Musgrave, Richard A., and Peggy B. Musgrave: *Public Finance in Theory and Practice,* 2d ed. (New York: McGraw-Hill Book Company, 1976), particularly part 3.

Pechman, Joseph A.: *Federal Tax Policy,* 3d ed. (Washington: The Brookings Institution, 1977).

Steiner, George A., and John F. Steiner (eds.): *Issues in Business and Society,* 2d ed. (New York: Random House, 1977).

Last Word
The American Way of Tax

The tax system can have curious effects upon behavior and decision making.

The Tax Man was very cross about Figg. Figg's way of life did not conform to the way of life several governments wanted Figg to pursue.

"What's the idea of living in a rental apartment over a delicatessen in the city, Figg?" he inquired.

Figg explained that he liked urban life. In that case, said the Tax Man, he was raising Figg's city sales and income taxes. "If you want them cut, you'll have to move out to the suburbs," he said.

Figg gave up the city and rented a suburban house but the Tax Man was not satisfied. He squeezed Figg until beads of blood popped out along the seams of Figg's wallet.

"Mercy, good Tax Man," Figg gasped. "Tell me how to live so that I may please my government, and I shall obey."

The Tax Man told Figg to quit renting and buy a house. The government wanted everyone to accept large mortgage loans from bankers. If Figg complied, it would cut his taxes.

Figg bought a house, which he did not want, in a suburb where he did not want to live, and he invited his friends and relatives to attend a party celebrating his surrender to a way of life that pleased his governments.

"I have had enough of this, Figg," the Tax Man declared. "Your government doesn't want you entertaining friends and relatives. This will cost you plenty."

Figg immediately threw out all his friends and relatives, then asked the Tax Man what sort of people his government wished him to entertain. "Business associates," said the Tax Man. "Entertain plenty of business associates, and I shall cut your taxes."

To make the Tax Man and his government happy, Figg began entertaining people he didn't like in the house he didn't want in the suburb where he didn't want to live.

Then was the Tax Man enraged indeed. "Figg!" he thundered, "I will not cut your taxes for entertaining straw bosses, truck drivers and pothole fillers."

"Why not?" said Figg. "These are the people I associate with in my business."

"Which is what?" asked the Tax Man.

"Earning my pay by the sweat of my brow," said Figg.

"Your government is not going to bribe you for performing salaried labor," said the Tax Man. "Don't you know, you imbecile, that tax rates on salaried income are higher than on any other kind?"

And he taxed the sweat of Figg's brow at a ferocious rate.

"Get into business, or minerals, or international oil," warned the Tax Man, "or I shall make your taxes as the taxes of 10."

Figg went into business, which he hated, and entertained people he didn't like in the house he didn't want in the suburb where he did not want to live, and the Tax Man and all the governments and the nation were happy, except for a rising incidence of divorce, tax forms, madness, fatuity, loneliness and suicide.

At length the Tax Man summoned Figg for an angry lecture. He demanded to know why Figg had not bought a new plastic factory to replace his old metal and wooden plant. "I hate plastic," said Figg.

"Your government is sick and tired of metal, wood and everything else that smacks of the real stuff, Figg!" roared the Tax Man, seizing Figg's purse. "Your depreciation is all used up."

There was nothing for Figg to do but go to plastic, and the Tax Man rewarded him with a brand new depreciation schedule plus an investment credit deduction from the bottom line.

Thanks to the money the Tax Man granted him for living in a suburb where he didn't want to live and for entertaining people he didn't like in a house he didn't want while engaging in work he wasn't interested in with plastic equipment he hated, Figg began to make a profit. The Tax Man was outraged.

"What's the idea of making a profit, Figg?" he demanded, placing his iron grip on Figg's bank account.

"Spare me," Figg pleaded.

"Only if you sell your business!" roared the Tax Man.

"After forcing me to get into business, the Government now wants me to get out of business?" asked Figg.

"Exactly" said the Tax Man. "Sell, and I'll tax the profit from the sale at a delightfully low capital-gain rate of only 25 percent. Otherwise, I'll take the meat ax to those profits."

Figg sold. Having nothing to do with his time, he decided to die. The Tax Man was furious. "Just try it," he said, "and I'll strip your estate down to the stalk." So Figg changed his mind.

This is why people are living so much longer nowadays. The government needs a large supply of people over 65 to keep the Social Security tax rising.

National Income Accounting

Throughout Part 1 of this book we have made the flat statement that American capitalism does not consistently provide for the full employment of available resources. It has also been noted that the levels of employment and production depend upon the size of certain flows of expenditures and income. Part 2 now deals at length with the problem of measuring, explaining, and using public policy to manage, if need be, the volumes of employment, production, and income in the economy. Specifically, in this chapter we seek an understanding of certain accounting techniques which assist us in gauging the level of production achieved by the economy. In Chapter 10 we examine the historical record of American capitalism as reflected in these accounts in order to appraise the past performance of our economy. Then in Chapters 11 and 12 we seek to explain those factors which determine the levels of employment and production in American capitalism. Finally, in Chapter 13 we explore the problems involved in deriving and applying public policies designed to stabilize output, employment, and the price level.

■ MEASURING THE ECONOMY'S PERFORMANCE

The present task is that of defining and understanding a group of so-called social or national income accounting concepts which have been designed to measure the overall production performance of the economy. Why do we bother with such a project? Because social accounting does for the economy as a whole what private accounting does for the individual business enterprise or, for that matter, for the household. The individual businessman is vitally interested in knowing how he is doing in his operations, but the answer is not always immediately discernible. Measurement of the firm's flows of income and expenditures is needed to assess the firm's operations for the current year. With this information before him, the businessman can gauge the economic health of his firm. If things are going well, he can use his accounting data to explain his success. He might find that costs are down or that sales and product prices are up, resulting in large profits. If things are going badly, he can also look to his accounting measures to discover the immediate cause of his plight. And by examining his accounts over a period of time, the businessman can detect growth or decline for his firm and indications of the immediate causes. All this information is invaluable in helping the businessman make intelligent policy decisions.

A system of national income accounting does much the same thing for the economy as a whole: It allows us to keep a finger on the economic pulse of the nation. The various measures which make up our social accounting system permit us to measure the level of production in the economy at some point in time and explain the immediate causes of that level of performance. Further, by comparing the national income accounts over a period of time, we can plot the long-run course which the economy has been following; the growth or stagnation of the economy will show up in the national income accounts. Finally, the information supplied by the national income accounts provides a basis for the formulation and application of public policies designed to improve the performance of the economy; without the national income accounts, economic policy would be based upon guesswork. In short, national income accounting allows us to

keep tab on the economic health of society and to formulate intelligently policies which will improve that health.

GROSS NATIONAL PRODUCT

There are many conceivable measures of the economic well-being of society. It is generally agreed, however, that the best available indicator of an economy's health is its annual total output of goods and services or, as it is sometimes called, the economy's aggregate output. The basic social accounting measure of the total output of goods and services is called the *gross national product* or, simply, GNP. It is defined as *the total market value of all final goods and services produced*[1] *in the economy in one year.* Our definition of GNP is very explicit and merits considerable comment.

□   GNP is a Monetary Measure

Note, first, that GNP measures the market value of annual output. GNP is a monetary measure. Indeed, it must be if we are to compare the heterogeneous collections of goods and services produced in different years and get a meaningful idea of their relative worth. Put simply, if the economy produces three oranges and two apples in year 1 and two oranges and three apples in year 2, in which year is society better off? There is no answer to this question until price tags are attached to the various products as indicators of society's evaluation of their relative worth. The problem is resolved in Table 9-1, where it is assumed that the money price of the oranges is 10 cents and the price of apples is 15 cents. It can be concluded that year 2's output is superior to that of year 1. Why? Because society

---

[1] We shall see that all goods *produced* in a particular year may not be *sold;* some may be added to inventories. Any increase in inventories must be included in determining GNP, since GNP measures all current production regardless of whether or not it is sold.

Table 9-1   COMPARING HETEROGENEOUS OUTPUTS BY USING MONEY PRICES (*hypothetical data*)

Year	Annual outputs	Market value
1	3 oranges and 2 apples	3 at 10 cents + 2 at 15 cents = 60 cents
2	2 oranges and 3 apples	2 at 10 cents + 3 at 15 cents = 65 cents

values year 2's output more highly; society is willing to pay more for the collection of goods produced in year 2 than of goods produced in year 1.

□   Adjusting GNP for Price Changes

But you might well object. You have read of inflation in the newspapers. Does this not mean that money prices and therefore the value of the dollar itself will change? You are quite right. The money value of different years' outputs can be accurately compared only if the value of money itself does not change because of inflation or deflation.

Stated differently, inflation or deflation complicates gross national product because GNP is a prices-times-quantity figure. The raw data from which the national income accountants estimate GNP are the total sales figures of business firms; these figures obviously embody changes in *both* the quantity of output *and* the level of prices. This means that a change in either the quantity of total physical output or the price level will affect the size of GNP. However, it is the quantity of goods produced and distributed to households

which affects their standard of living and not the size of the price tags which these goods bear. The hamburger of 1965 which sold for 30 cents yielded the same satisfaction as will an identical hamburger selling for 80 cents in 1978. The problem, then, is one of adjusting a price-times-quantity figure so it will accurately reflect changes in physical output, not changes in prices.

Fortunately, national income accountants have been able to resolve this difficulty: they deflate GNP for rising prices and inflate it when prices are falling. These adjustments give us a picture of GNP for various years *as if* prices and the value of the dollar were constant.

□   Inflating and Deflating

Some examples will help us understand how GNP figures are adjusted for price changes. First, an exceedingly simple example: Assume our economy produces only one good, product X, and in the amounts indicated in Table 9-2 for years 1, 2, and 3. An examination of columns 1 and 2 tells us that the *money* GNPs for years 2 and 3, as shown in column 4,

Table 9-2   DEFLATING MONEY GNP (*hypothetical data*)

Year	(1) Units of output	(2) Price of X	(3) Price index, percent (Year 1 = 100)	(4) Unadjusted, or money, GNP (1) × (2)	(5) Adjusted, or real, GNP
1	5	$10	100	$ 50	$50 (= $ 50 ÷ 1.00)
2	7	20	200	140	70 (= 140 ÷ 2.00)
3	8	25	250	200	80 (= 200 ÷ 2.50)
4	10	30	_____	_____	_____
5	11	28	_____	_____	_____

greatly overstate the increases in *real* output occurring in those two years. That is, the monetary measure of production (money GNP) does not accurately reflect the actual changes which have occurred in physical output (real GNP). Considerable portions of the sharp increases in money GNP in years 2 and 3 are due to the drastic inflation shown in column 2, the remainder being due to the changes in physical output shown in column 1. Both increases in physical output and price increases are reflected in the money GNP.

Now the situation facing our social accountants is this: In gathering statistics from the financial reports of businesses and deriving GNP for years 1, 2, and 3, governmental accountants come up with the figures for money GNP shown in column 4. They will not know directly to what extent changes in price, on the one hand, and changes in quantity of output, on the other, have accounted for the given increases in money GNP. Social accountants will not have before them the data of columns 1 and 2, but only the data of column 4. Being resourceful individuals, they attempt to adjust the money GNP figure for price changes. They do this by deriving a general price index which estimates overall changes in the price level. By expressing this price index as a decimal and dividing it into money GNP, one can obtain real GNP. In our example, wherein we are dealing with only one product, a simple single-price index number is all that is required. Such a price index is nothing more than *a percentage comparison from a fixed point of reference.* This point of reference, or bench mark, is called the *base year.* By comparing prices in previous and ensuing years with prices in the base year, we can tell how much prices have increased or decreased *relative to* what they were in the base year. Suppose product X sells for $10 in year 1, $20 in year 2, and $25 in year 3, as shown in Table 9-2. Selecting year 1 as the base year, we can express the prices of product X in years 2 and 3 relative to X's price in year 1 through the formula

$$\text{Price index} = \frac{\text{price in any given year}}{\text{price in base year}} \times 100$$

We multiply the price comparison by 100 in order to express it as a percentage. Using year 2 as the given year, we find that

$$\text{Price index} = \frac{\$20}{\$10} \times 100 = 200 \text{ percent}$$

and for year 3,

$$\text{Price index} = \frac{\$25}{\$10} \times 100 = 250 \text{ percent}$$

For year 1 the index must be 100 percent, since the given year and the base year are identical. In this case,

$$\text{Price index} = \frac{\$10}{\$10} \times 100 = 100 \text{ percent}$$

These index numbers tell us that the price of product X in the year 2 was 200 percent of what it was in year 1 and in year 3 it was 250 percent of year 1's price. The index numbers of column 3 can now be used to deflate the inflated money GNP figures of column 4. As already noted, *the simplest and most direct method of deflating is to express these index numbers as hundredths, that is, in decimal form, and divide them into the corresponding money GNP.*[2] Column 5 shows the results. These real GNP figures measure the value of total output in years 1, 2, and 3 *as if* the price of product X had been constant at $10 throughout the three-year period. Real GNP thus shows the market value of each year's output measured in terms of constant dollars, that is, dollars which have the same value, or purchasing power, as in the base year. Real GNP is clearly superior to money GNP as an indicator of the economy's productive performance over a period of time.

To ensure his understanding of the deflating process, the reader is urged to complete Table 9-2 for years 4 and 5. Second, it is rec-

[2]This yields the same result as the more complex procedure of dividing money GNPs by the corresponding index number and multiplying the quotient by 100.

Table 9-3   ADJUSTING GNP FOR CHANGES IN THE PRICE LEVEL (*selected years, in billions of dollas*)

(1) Year	(2) Money, or unadjusted, GNP	(3) Price level index,* percent (1972 = 100)	(4) Real, or adjusted, GNP, 1972 dollars
1946	$ 209.6	44.06	$ 475.7 (= 209.6 ÷ 0.4406)
1951	330.2	57.27	_____
1958	448.9	66.06	$ 679.5 (= 448.9 ÷ 0.6606)
1964	635.7	72.71	_____
1968	868.5	82.57	$ 1051.8 (= 868.5 ÷ 0.8257)
1972	1171.1	100.00	$ 1171.1 (= 1171.1 ÷ 1.0000)
1974	1406.9	116.20	
1975	1498.9	126.37	$ 1186.1 (= 1498.9 ÷ 1.2637)

* U.S. Department of Commerce implicit price deflators.
Source: U.S. Department of Commerce data.

ommended that you rework the entire deflating procedure, using year 3 as the base year. You will find, by the way, that in this case you must inflate some of the money GNP data, just as we have deflated it in our examples.

Table 9-3 provides us with a "real-world" illustration of the inflating and deflating process. Here we are taking actual money GNP figures for selected years and adjusting them with an index of the general price level to obtain real GNP. Note that the base year is 1972. Because the long-run trend has been for the price level to rise, the problem is one of increasing, or *inflating,* the pre-1972 figures. This upward revision of money GNP acknowledges that prices were lower in years prior to 1972 and, as a result, money GNP figures understated the real output of those years. Column 4 indicates what GNP would have been in all these selected years if the 1972 price level had prevailed. However, the rising price level has caused the money GNP figures for the post-1972 years to overstate real output; hence, these figures must be reduced, or *deflated,* as in column 4 in order for us to gauge what GNP would have been in 1974, 1975, and so on, if 1972 prices had actually prevailed. In short, while the *money* GNP figures reflect both output and price changes, the *real* GNP

figures allow us to make a better estimate of changes in real output, because the real GNP figures, in effect, hold the price level constant. The reader should trace through the computations involved in deriving the real GNP figures given in Table 9-3 and also determine real GNP for years 1951, 1964, and 1974, for which the figures have been purposely omitted.[3]

[3]Technical footnote: While this discussion of Table 9-3 provides an intuitive understanding of the process of inflating or deflating GNP with appropriate index numbers, a thorough grasp of the rationale for dividing money GNP by an appropriate index to get real GNP calls for further comment. Suppose we want to adjust money GNP for 1976 to real GNP (in 1972 prices) so we can determine the growth of real GNP between 1972 and 1976. We know, first, that money GNP for 1976 (GNP_{1976}) is equal to the physical output in 1976 (Q_{1976}) times the prices (P_{1976}) at which the output sold. That is,

$$GNP_{1976} = Q_{1976} \cdot P_{1976}$$

We also know from the text's discussion of index numbers that the price index for 1976, using 1972 as the base year, equals the ratio of prices in 1976 to prices in 1972. Thus

$$1976 \text{ price index} = P_{1976}/P_{1972}$$

The text also directs us to divide money GNP for 1976 by this 1976 price index to get real GNP for 1976, that is, 1976's output measured at 1972 prices:

$$\frac{GNP_{1976}}{P_{1976}/P_{1972}} = \frac{Q_{1976} \cdot P_{1976}}{P_{1976}/P_{1972}}$$

(Continued on following page.)

□ **Double Counting**

To measure total output accurately, all goods and services produced in any given year must be counted once, but not more than once. Most products go through a series of production stages before reaching a market. As a result, parts or components of most products are bought and sold many times. Hence, to avoid counting several times the parts of products that are sold and resold, GNP includes only the market value of final goods and ignores transactions involving intermediate goods.

By *final goods* we mean goods and services which are being purchased for final use and not for resale or further processing or manufacturing. Transactions involving *intermediate goods,* on the other hand, refer to purchases of goods and services for further processing and manufacturing or for resale. The sale of final goods is *included* and the sale of intermediate goods is *excluded* from GNP. Why? Because the value of final goods includes all the intermediate transactions involved in their production. The inclusion of intermediate transactions would involve double counting and an exaggerated estimate of GNP.

An example will clarify this point. Suppose there are five stages of production in getting a Hart, Schaffner & Marx suit manufactured and into the hands of a consumer who, of course, is the ultimate or final user. As Table 9-4 indicates, firm A, a sheep ranch, provides

$40 worth of wool to firm B, a wool processor. Firm A pays out the $40 it receives in wages, rents, interest, and profits. Firm B processes the wool and sells it to firm C, a suit manufacturer, for $65. What does firm B do with this $65? As noted, $40 goes to firm A, and the remaining $25 is used by B to pay wages, rents, interest, and profits for the resources needed in processing the wool. And so it goes. The manufacturer sells the suit to firm D, a clothing wholesaler, who in turn sells it to firm E, a retailer, and then, at last, it is bought for $160 by a consumer, the final user of the product. At each stage, the difference between what a firm has paid for the product and what it receives for its sale is paid out as wages, rent, interest, and profits for the resources used by that firm in helping to produce and distribute the suit.

The basic question is this: How much should we include in GNP in accounting for the production of this suit? Just $160, the value of the final product! Why? Because this figure includes all the intermediate transactions leading up to the product's final sale. It would be a gross exaggeration to sum all the intermediate sales figures and the final sales value of the product in column 2 and add the entire amount, $460, to GNP. This would be a serious case of double counting, that is, counting the final product and the sale and resale of its various parts in the multistage productive process.

There is an alternative means of determining the $160 figure which is to be included in GNP. And this is by the *value-added* method—that is, by summing the value added to the total worth of the product at each step in the productive process. Column 3 summarizes this procedure. Note that this measures the total income derived from the production and sale of the suit. As you might expect, it is easier for the national income accountants to count only final goods than to pursue the value-added method of deriving GNP.

Inverting and multiplying by the fraction or ratio which represents the 1976 index, we get

$$\frac{\text{GNP}_{1976}}{P_{1976}/P_{1972}} = (Q_{1976} \cdot P_{1976}) \cdot \frac{P_{1972}}{P_{1976}}$$

The P_{1976} expressions cancel, leaving

$$\frac{\text{GNP}_{1976}}{P_{1976}/P_{1972}} = Q_{1976} \cdot P_{1972}$$

That is to say, by dividing the 1976 money GNP (GNP_{1976}) by the 1976 price index (P_{1976}/P_{1972}) we derive real GNP for 1976 or, more specifically, the 1976 output (Q_{1976}) measured in terms of 1972 prices (P_{1972}).

Table 9-4 VALUE ADDED IN A FIVE-STAGE PRODUCTIVE PROCESS
(*hypothetical data*)

(1) Stage of production	(2) Sales value of materials or product	(3) Value added
Firm A, sheep ranch	$ 40	$ 40
Firm B, wool processor	65	25
Firm C, suit manufacturer	85	20
Firm D, clothing wholesaler	110	25
Firm E, retail clothier	160	50
Consumer, the final user		$160

□ GNP Excludes Nonproductive Transactions

GNP attempts to measure the annual production of the economy. In so doing, the many nonproductive transactions which occur each year must be carefully excluded. Nonproductive transactions are of two major types: (1) purely financial transactions, and (2) secondhand sales.

Financial Transactions Purely financial transactions in turn are of three general types: public transfer payments, private transfer payments, and the buying and selling of securities. We have already mentioned public transfer payments (Chapter 8). These are the social security payments, welfare payments, and veterans' payments which government makes to particular households. The basic characteristic of these disbursements is that recipients make no contribution to *current* production in return for them. Thus, to include them in GNP would be to overstate this year's production. Private transfer payments—for example, a university student's monthly subsidy from home or an occasional gift from a wealthy relative—do not entail production but simply the transfer of funds from one private individual to another. Security transactions, that is, the buying and selling of stocks and bonds, are also excluded from GNP. Stock market transactions involve merely the swapping of paper assets. As such, these transactions do not directly involve current production. It should be noted, however, that by getting money from the hands of savers into the hands of spenders, some of these security transactions may indirectly give rise to spending which does account for output.

Secondhand Sales The reason for excluding secondhand sales from GNP is fairly obvious: Such sales either reflect no *current* production, or they involve double counting. For example, suppose you sell your 1973 Ford to a neighbor. This transaction would be excluded in determining GNP because no current production is involved. The inclusion of the sales of goods produced some years ago in this year's GNP would be an exaggeration of this year's output. Similarly, if you purchased a brand new Ford and resold it a week later to your neighbor, we should still want to exclude the resale transaction from the current GNP. Why? Because when you originally bought the new car, its value was included in GNP. To include its resale value would be to count it twice.

□ GNP and Social Welfare

GNP is a reasonably accurate and extremely useful measure of national economic performance. It is not, and was never intended to be, an index of social welfare. GNP is merely a measure of the annual volume of market-oriented activity. And, while GNP may yield a workable impression of material well-being, it is a far cry from being a meaningful indicator of social welfare:[4]

> . . . any number of things could make the Nation better off without raising its real GNP as measured today: we might start the list with peace, equality of opportunity, the elimination of injustice and violence, greater brotherhood among Americans of different racial and ethnic backgrounds, better understanding between parents and children and between husbands and wives, and we could go on endlessly.

There is, nevertheless, a widely held assumption that there should be a strong positive correlation between real GNP and social welfare, that is, greater production should move society toward "the good life." Hence, it is important to understand some of the shortcomings of GNP—some reasons why GNP might understate or overstate real output and why more output will not necessarily make society better off.

1 Nonmarket Transactions There are certain productive transactions which do not appear in the market. Hence, GNP as a measure of the market value of output fails to include these productive transactions. Standard examples include the productive services of the housewife, the efforts of the carpenter who repairs his own home, or the work of the erudite professor who writes a scholarly but nonremunerative article. Such transactions are *not* reflected in the profit and loss statements of business firms and therefore escape the national income accountants, causing GNP to be understated. However, some very

important nonmarket transactions, such as that portion of a farmer's output which the farmer consumes himself, are estimated by national income accountants.

2 Leisure Over a long period of years, leisure has increased very significantly. The current average workweek is about 39 hours, as compared with 53 hours at the turn of the century. The expanded availability of paid vacations and holidays, particularly since World War II, has significantly reduced work time. Increased leisure has added immeasurably to our well-being. Hence, our system of social accounting understates our well-being by not directly taking cognizance of this. Nor do the accounts reflect the satisfaction—the "psychic income"—which one might derive from one's work.

3 Improved Product Quality GNP is a quantitative rather than a qualitative measure. It does not accurately reflect improvements in the quality of products. This is a shortcoming: Quality improvement obviously affects economic well-being every bit as much as does the quantity of goods. To the extent that product quality has improved over time, GNP understates improvement in our material well-being.

4 The Composition and Distribution of Output Changes in the composition and the allocation of total output among specific households may influence economic welfare. GNP, however, reflects only the size of output and does not tell us anything about whether this collection of goods is "right" for society. A switchblade knife and a Beethoven LP record, both selling for $5.95, are weighted equally in the GNP. And, although the point is a matter for vigorous debate (see Chapter 37), some economists feel that a more equal distribution of total output would increase national economic well-being. If these economists are correct, a future trend toward a more nearly equal distribution of GNP would enhance the eco-

---

[4] Arthur M. Okun, "Social Welfare Has No Price Tag," *The Economic Accounts of the United States: Retrospect and Prospect* (U.S. Department of Commerce, July 1971), p. 129.

nomic welfare of society. A less nearly equal future distribution would have the reverse effect. In short, GNP measures the size of total output but does not reflect changes in the composition and distribution of output which might also affect the economic well-being of society.

5   GNP and the Environment There are undesirable and much publicized "gross national by-products" which accompany the production and growth of the GNP. These take the form of dirty air and water, automobile junkyards, congestion, noise, and various other forms of environmental pollution. Although we shall defer detailed discussion of the economics of pollution to Chapter 36, it is quite clear that the costs of pollution affect our economic well-being adversely. These spillover costs associated with the production of the GNP are not now deducted from total output and, hence, GNP overstates our national economic welfare. Ironically, as GNP increases, so does pollution and the extent of this overstatement. As put by one economist, "The ultimate physical product of economic life is garbage."[5] A rising GNP means more garbage—more environmental pollution. In fact, under existing accounting procedures, when a manufacturer pollutes a river and government spends to clean it up, the cleanup expense is added to the GNP while the pollution is not subtracted! This line of thought is explored further in the Last Word segment of the present chapter.

6   Per Capita Output For many purposes the most meaningful measure of economic well-being is per capita output. Because GNP measures the size of total output, it may conceal or misrepresent changes in the standard of living of individual households in the economy. For example, GNP may rise significantly, but if population is also growing rapidly, the per capita standard of living may be relatively constant or may even be declining. The Last Word segment of Chapter 21 is pertinent.

□ **Two Sides to GNP**

Recognizing the characteristics and the shortcomings of GNP as a measure of output, we now raise this question: How can the market value of total output—or for that matter, any single unit of output—be measured? How can we measure, for example, the market value of a cashmere sweater?

In two ways: First, we can just look at how much a consumer, as the final user, spends in obtaining it. Second, we can add up all the wage, rental, interest, and profit incomes created in the production of the sweater. This is simply the value-added approach we spoke of earlier. These are, indeed, two ways of looking at the same thing. *What is spent on a product is received as income by those who contributed to its production.* Indeed, Chapter 3's circular flow model is based upon this notion. If $35 is spent on the sweater, that is necessarily the total amount of income derived from its production. This equality of the expenditure for a product and the income derived from its production is guaranteed, because profit income serves as a balancing item. Profit—or loss—is the income which remains after wage, rent, and interest incomes have been paid by the producer. If the wage, rent, and interest incomes which the firm must pay in getting the sweater produced are less than the $35 expenditure for the sweater, the difference will be the firm's profits.[6] Conversely, if wage, rent, and interest incomes exceed $35, profits will be negative, that is, losses will be realized, to balance the expenditure on the product and the income derived from its production.

The same line of reasoning is also valid for the output of the economy as a whole. There

---

[5] See the delightful and perceptive essay "Fun and Games with the Gross National Product" by Kenneth E. Boulding, in Harold W. Helfrich, Jr. (ed.), *The Environmental Crisis* (New Haven: Yale University Press, 1970), p. 162.

[6] The term "profits" is used here in the accounting sense so as to include both normal profits and economic profits as defined in Chapter 5.

are two different ways of looking at GNP: One is to look at GNP as the sum of all the expenditures involved in taking that total output off the market. This is called the *output,* or *expenditures, approach.* The other is to look at it in terms of the income derived or created from the production of the GNP. This is called the *earnings,* or *income,* or *allocations, approach* to the determination of GNP. A closer analysis of these two approaches will reveal that they amount to this: *GNP can be determined either by adding up all that is spent on this year's total output or by summing up all the incomes derived from the production of this year's output.* Putting this in the form of a simple equation, we can say that

$$\left.\begin{array}{l}\text{The amount}\\\text{spent on this}\\\text{year's total}\\\text{output}\end{array}\right\} = \left\{\begin{array}{l}\text{the money income}\\\text{derived from the}\\\text{production of this}\\\text{year's output}\end{array}\right.$$

As a matter of fact, this is more than an equation: it is an identity. Buying—that is, spending money—and selling—that is, receiving money income—are actually two aspects of the same transaction. *What is spent on a product is income to those who have contributed their human and property resources in getting that product produced and to market.*

For the economy as a whole, we can expand the above identity to read as in Table 9-5. This summary statement simply tells us that all final goods produced in the American economy are purchased either by the three domestic sectors, households, government, and

businesses, or by foreign nations. It also shows us that the total receipts which businesses acquire from the sale of total output are allocated among the various resource suppliers as wage, rent, interest, and profit income. Later we shall explain two additional nonincome allocations of total receipts. Using this summary as a point of reference, let us point out in some detail the meaning and significance of the various types of expenditures and the incomes derived therefrom.

THE EXPENDITURES APPROACH TO GNP

To determine GNP through the expenditures approach, one must add up all types of spending on finished or final goods and services. But our national income accountants have much more sophisticated terms for the different types of spending than the ones we have employed in Table 9-5. We must therefore familiarize ourselves with these terms and their meanings.

□ Personal Consumption Expenditures (*C*)

What we have called "consumption expenditures by households" is "personal consumption expenditures" to the national income accountants. It entails expenditures by households on durable consumer goods (automobiles, refrigerators, gas ranges, and so forth),

Table 9-5 THE INCOME AND OUTPUT APPROACHES TO GNP

Output, or expenditures, approach		Income, or allocations, approach
Consumption expenditures by households plus Government purchases of goods and services plus Investment expenditures by businesses plus Expenditures by foreigners	= GNP =	Wages plus Rents plus Interest plus Profits plus Nonincome charges or allocations

nondurable consumer goods (bread, milk, beer, cigarettes, shirts, toothpaste), and consumer expenditures for services (of lawyers, doctors, mechanics, barbers). We shall use the letter C to designate the total of these expenditures.

☐ Government Purchases of Goods and Services (G)

This classification of expenditures includes all governmental spending, Federal, state, and local, on the finished products of businesses and all direct purchases of resources—labor, in particular—by government. However, it excludes all government transfer payments, because such outlays, as previously noted, do not reflect any current production but merely transfer governmental receipts to certain specific households. The letter G will be used to indicate government purchases of goods and services.

☐ Gross Private Domestic Investment (I_g)

This seemingly complicated term refers to all investment spending by American business firms. What is included as investment spending? Basically three things: (1) all final purchases of machinery, equipment, and tools by business enterprises; (2) all construction; and (3) changes in inventories. This obviously entails more than we have imputed to the term "investment" thus far. Hence, we must explain why each of these three items is included under the general heading of gross private domestic investment.

The reason for inclusion of the first group of items is apparent. This is simply a restatement of our original definition of investment spending as the purchase of tools, machinery, and equipment. The second item—all construction—merits some explanation. It is clear that the building of a new factory, warehouse, or grain elevator is a form of investment. But why include residential construction as investment rather than consumption? The reason is

this: Apartment buildings are clearly investment goods because, like factories and grain elevators, they are income-earning assets. Other residential units which are rented are for the same reason investment goods. Furthermore, owner-occupied houses are classified as investment goods because they could be rented out to yield a money income return, even though the owner does not choose to do so. For these reasons all residential construction is considered as investment. Finally, why are changes in inventories counted as investment? Because an increase in inventories is, in effect, "unconsumed output," and that precisely is what investment is!

Inventory Changes as Investment Remembering that GNP is designed to measure total current output, we must certainly make an effort to include in GNP any products which are produced *but not sold* this year. In short, if GNP is to be an accurate measure of total output, it must include the market value of any additions to inventories which accrue during the year. Were we to exclude an increase in inventories, GNP would understate the current year's total output. If businessmen have more goods on their shelves and in their warehouses at the end of the year than they had at the start, the economy has produced more than it has consumed during this particular year. This increase in inventories obviously must be added to GNP as a measure of *current* production.

What about a decline in inventories? This must be subtracted in figuring GNP, because in such a situation the economy sells a total output which exceeds current production, the difference being reflected in an inventory reduction. Some of the GNP taken off the market this year reflects not current production but, rather, a drawing down of inventories which were on hand at the beginning of this year. And the inventories on hand at the start of any year's production represent the production of previous years. Consequently, a decline in inventories in any given year means that the economy has consumed more than it has produced during the year; that is, society has consumed all of this year's output plus some of the inventories inherited from previous years' production. Remembering that GNP is a measure of the current year's output, we must omit any consumption of past production, that is, any drawing down of inventories, in determining GNP.

Noninvestment Transactions We have discussed what investment is; it is equally important to emphasize what investment is not. Specifically, investment does not refer to the transfer of paper assets or secondhand tangible assets. The buying of stocks and bonds is excluded from the economist's definition of investment, because such purchases merely transfer the ownership of existing assets. The same holds true of the resale of existing assets. Investment is the construction or manufacture of *new* capital assets. It is the creation of such earning assets that gives rise to jobs and income, not the exchange of claims to existing capital goods.

Gross versus Net Investment We have broadened our concepts of investment and investment goods to include purchases of machinery and equipment, all construction, and changes in inventories. Now let us focus our attention on the three modifiers, "gross," "private," and "domestic," which national income accountants see fit to use in describing investment. The second and third terms simply tell us, respectively, that we are talking about spending by private business enterprises as opposed to governmental (public) agencies and that the firms involved are American—as opposed to foreign—firms.

The term "gross," however, cannot be disposed of so easily. *Gross private domestic investment* includes the production of *all* investment goods—those which are to replace the machinery, equipment, and buildings used up in the current year's production plus any

net additions to the economy's stock of capital. In short, gross investment includes both replacement and added investment. On the other hand, we reserve the term *net private domestic investment* to refer only to the added investment which has occurred in the current year. A simple example will make the distinction clear. In 1976 our economy produced about $240 billion worth of capital goods. However, in the process of producing the GNP in 1976, the economy used up some $180 billion worth of machinery and equipment. As a result, our economy added $60 (or $240 minus $180) billion to its stock of capital in 1976. Therefore, *gross* investment was $240 billion in 1976, but *net* investment was only $60 billion. The difference between the two is the value of the capital used up or depreciated in the production of 1976's GNP.

Net Investment and Economic Growth
The relationship between gross investment and depreciation provides a good indicator of whether our economy is expanding, static, or declining. Figure 9-1 illustrates these three cases.

1 Expanding economy When gross investment exceeds depreciation, as in Figure 9-1a, the economy is obviously expanding in the sense that its productive capacity—as measured by its stock of capital goods—is growing. More simply, net investment is a positive figure in an expanding economy. For example, as noted above, in 1976 gross investment was $240 billion, and $180 billion worth of capital goods were consumed in producing that year's GNP. This meant that our economy ended 1976 with $60 billion more capital goods than it had on hand at the start of the year. Increasing the supply of capital goods, you will recall, is a basic means of expanding the productive capacity of the economy (see Figures 2-3 and 2-4).

2 Static economy A stationary or static economy reflects the situation in which gross investment and depreciation are equal. This posely diverted from the production of capital goods for nonessential industries, and even in essential industries resources were used sparingly for the production of capital goods. Why? Because the wartime emergency demanded astonishing amounts of finished war goods, and the lion's share of our available resources was directed toward attaining that goal. Therefore, it is not surprising that in 1942 gross investment and depreciation were approximately equal at $10 billion. This meant that at the end of 1942 our stock of capital was about the same as at the start of that year. In other words, *net* investment was about zero. Our economy was a stationary one in the sense that its productive facilities failed to expand. Figure 9-1*b* represents the case of a static economy.

3 Declining economy The unhappy case of a declining economy arises whenever gross investment is less than depreciation, that is, when the economy consumes more capital in a year than it manages to produce. Under such circumstances net investment will be a negative figure—the economy will be "disinvesting." Depressions foster such circumstances. During bad times, when production and employment are at a low ebb, the nation has a greater productive capacity than it is currently utilizing. Hence, there is little or no incentive to replace depreciated capital equipment, much less add to the existing stock. Depreciation is likely to outweigh gross investment, with the result that the nation's stock of capital is less at the end of the year than it was at the start. This was the case during the heart of the Great Depression. In 1933, for example, gross investment was only $1.4 billion, while the capital consumed during that year was $6.9 billion. Net disinvestment was therefore $5.5 billion. Figure 9-1*c* illustrates the case of a disinvesting, or declining, economy.

We shall use the symbol I to refer to domestic investment spending and attach the subscript g when referring to gross and n when referring to net investment.

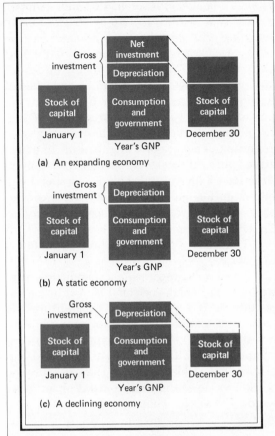

FIGURE 9-1 EXPANDING, STATIC, AND DECLINING ECONOMIES

In an expanding economy (a), gross investment exceeds depreciation, which means that the economy is making a net addition to its stock of capital facilities. In a static economy (b), gross investment precisely replaces the capital facilities depreciated in producing the year's output, leaving the stock of capital goods unchanged. In a declining economy (c), gross investment is insufficient to replace the capital goods depreciated by the year's production. As a result, the economy's stock of capital declines.

means the economy is standing pat; it is producing just enough capital to replace what is consumed in producing the year's output—no more and no less. In 1942, as the United States attempted to push its production of military goods into high gear, our economy approximated this situation. Resources were pur-

☐   **Net Exports (X_n)**

How do American international trade transactions enter into national income accounting? We can best explain it in this way: First, remember that we are trying to add up all spending in American markets which accounts for or induces the production of goods and services in the American economy. A bit of reflection will lead you to the conclusion that spending by foreigners on American goods will account for American output just as will spending by Americans. Hence, we want to add in what foreigners spend on American goods and services—that is, we want to add in the value of American exports—in determining GNP by the expenditures approach. On the other hand, what about spending by Americans on goods and services brought into American markets by foreigners? Obviously this spending induces the output of foreign goods and services. Thus, in determining the GNP for the United States by the expenditures approach, we should want to subtract the value of American imports from total expenditures. Why? Because it accounts for no domestic production.

Rather than treat these two items— American exports and imports—separately, our national income accountants merely take the difference between the two. Hence, *net exports of goods and services* or, more simply, *net exports is the amount by which foreign spending on American goods and services exceeds American spending on foreign goods and services.* For example, should foreigners buy $9 billion worth of American exports and Americans buy $7 billion worth of foreign imports in a given year, net exports would be *plus* $2 billion. It must be emphasized that our definition of net exports might result in a negative figure. If foreigners spend $10 billion on American exports and Americans spend $12 billion on foreign imports, our "excess" of foreign spending over American spending is *minus* $2 billion.

The letter X_n will be used to designate net exports.

The four categories of expenditures that we have discussed—personal consumption expenditures (C), government expenditures on goods and services (G), gross private domestic investment (I_g), and net exports (X_n)—are comprehensive. They include all possible types of spending. Added together, they measure the market value of the year's output or, in other words, the GNP. That is,

$$C + I_g + G + X_n = \text{GNP}$$

For 1976 (Table 9-6):

$$\$1080 + \$240 + \$365 + \$7 = \$1692$$

Table 9-6   THE INCOME STATEMENT FOR THE ECONOMY, 1976 (*in billions of dollars*)

Receipts: expenditures approach		Allocations: income approach	
Personal consumption expenditures (C) . . .	$1080	Capital consumption allowance	$ 180
Government purchases of goods and		Indirect business taxes	163
services (G)	365	Compensation of employees	1028
Gross private domestic investment (I_g) . . .	240	Rents	24
Net exports (X_n)	7	Interest	82
		Proprietors' income	97
		Corporate income taxes	65
		Dividends	35
		Undistributed corporate profits	18
Gross national product	$1692	Gross national product	$1692

Source: U.S. Department of Commerce data. Because of rounding, figures may not add up to totals.

THE INCOME APPROACH TO GNP

How was this $1692 billion of expenditures allocated or distributed as income? It would be most convenient if we could simply say that the total expenditures upon the economy's annual output flow to households as wage, rent, interest, and profit incomes. Unfortunately, the picture is complicated somewhat by two nonincome charges against the value of total output, that is, against GNP. These are (1) a capital consumption allowance, and (2) indirect business taxes.

□ Depreciation: Capital Consumption Allowance

The useful life of most capital equipment extends far beyond the year of purchase. Actual expenditures for capital goods and their productive life are not synchronized in the same accounting period. Hence, to avoid gross understatement of profit and therefore of total income in the year of purchase and overstatement of profit and of total income in succeeding years, individual businesses estimate the useful life of their capital goods and allocate the total cost of such goods more or less evenly over the life of the machinery. The annual charge which estimates the amount of capital equipment used up in each year's production is called "depreciation." Depreciation is essentially a bookkeeping entry designed to provide a more accurate statement of profit income and hence total income provided by a firm in each year.

If profits and total income for the economy as a whole are to be stated accurately, a gigantic depreciation charge for the economy as a whole must be made against the total receipts of the business sector. This depreciation charge is called a "capital consumption allowance." Why? Because that is exactly what it is—an allowance for capital goods which have been "consumed" in the process of producing this year's GNP. It is this huge depreciation charge which constitutes the previously noted difference between I_g and I_n. For present purposes, the significance of this charge lies in the fact that it claims a part of the business sector's receipts which is, therefore, not available for income payments to resource suppliers. In real terms, that is, in terms of physical goods and services, the capital consumption allowance tells us in effect that a portion of this year's GNP must be set aside to replace the machinery and equipment used up in accomplishing its production. In other words, all of GNP cannot be consumed as income by society without impairing the economy's stock of productive facilities.

□ Indirect Business Taxes

The second complicating nonincome charge arises from the presence of government. Government levies certain taxes—in particular, general sales taxes, excise and business property taxes, license fees, and customs duties—which business firms treat as costs of production and therefore add to the prices of the products they sell. These taxes, as a matter of fact, are called "indirect business taxes" because sales taxes and excises are not levied directly upon the corporation, partnership, or proprietorship as such but, rather, upon their products or services. Businessmen, knowing the sizes of such levies, pass them on to the consumer in the form of higher prices. We can think of it in this way: A firm produces a product designed to sell at, say, $1. As we have seen, the production of this item creates an equal amount of wages, rental, interest, and profit income. But now government, in need of revenue to finance its activities, imposes a 3 percent sales tax on all products sold at retail. The retailer merely adds this 3 percent to the price of the product, raising its price from $1 to $1.03 and thereby shifting the burden of the sales tax to consumers.[7]

---

[7] In Chap. 23 we shall use supply and demand analysis to find that the shifting of a sales tax is not quite this simple.

Obviously, this 3 percent of total receipts which reflects the tax must be paid out to government before the remaining $1 can be paid to households as wage, rent, interest, and profit incomes. Government, in effect, is a preferred creditor. Furthermore, this flow of indirect business taxes to government is not earned income, because government contributes nothing directly to the production of the good in return for these sales tax receipts. As a matter of fact, in the cases of sales and excise taxes the finished product is being handed to the consumer at the time the tax is levied. In short, we must be careful to exclude indirect business taxes when figuring the total income earned in each year by the factors of production.

Capital consumption allowances and indirect business taxes account for the nonincome allocatons listed in Table 9-5. As just noted, what remains is wages, rents, interest, and profits. But, for a variety of reasons, national income statisticians need a more sophisticated breakdown of wages and profits than we have employed thus far in this discussion.

□   Compensation of Employees

This largest income category comprises primarily the wages and salaries which are paid by businesses and government to suppliers of labor. It also includes an array of wage and salary supplements, in particular payments by employers into social insurance and into a variety of private pension, health, and welfare funds for workers. These wage and salary supplements are a part of the employer's cost of obtaining labor and therefore are treated as a component of the firm's total wage payments.

□   Rents

Rents are almost self-explanatory. They consist of income payments received by households which supply property resources.

□   Interest

Interest refers to money income payments which flow from private businesses to the suppliers of money capital. For reasons to be noted later, interest payments made by government are excluded from interest income.

□   Proprietors' Income

What we have loosely termed "profits" is also broken into two basic accounts by national income accountants: One part is called *proprietors' income* or income of unincorporated businesses, and the other, *corporate profits*. The former account is largely self-defining. It refers to the net income of sole proprietorships, partnerships, and cooperatives. On the other hand, corporate profits cannot be dismissed so easily, because corporate earnings may be distributed in several ways.

□   Corporate Profits

Generally speaking, three things can be done with corporate profits: First, a part will be claimed by, and therefore flow to, government as *corporate income taxes*. Second, a part of the remaining corporate profits will be paid out to stockholders as *dividends*. Such payments flow to households, which, of course, are the ultimate owners of all corporations. What remains of corporate profits after both corporate income taxes and dividends have been paid is called *undistributed corporate profits*. These retained corporate earnings, along with capital consumption allowances, are invested currently or in the future in new plants and equipment, thereby increasing the real assets of the investing businesses.

Table 9-6 summarizes our detailed discussions of both the expenditure and income approaches to GNP. The reader will recognize that this is merely a gigantic income statement for the economy as a whole. The left-hand side tells us what the economy produced in 1976 and the total receipts derived from that production. The right-hand side indicates how the income derived from the production of 1976's GNP was allocated. One can determine GNP either by adding up the four types of expenditures on final goods and services or by adding up the nine categories of income and nonincome changes which stem from that output's production. Because output and income are two sides of the same coin, the two sums will necessarily match.

OTHER SOCIAL ACCOUNTS

Our discussion thus far has centered upon GNP as a measure of the economy's annual output. However, there are certain related social accounting concepts of equal importance which can be derived from GNP. To round out our understanding of social accounting, it is imperative that we trace through the process of deriving these related concepts. This procedure will also enhance our understanding of how the expenditure and income approaches to GNP dovetail one another. Our plan of attack will be to start with GNP and make a series of adjustments—subtractions and additions—necessary to the derivation of the related social accounts.

□   **Net National Product (NNP)**

GNP as a measure of total output has an important defect: It tends to give us a somewhat exaggerated picture of this year's production. Why? *Because it fails to make allowance for that part of this year's output which is necessary to replace the capital goods consumed in the year's production.*

Two examples will help make this point clear: First, suppose a farmer starts the year by planting 20 bushels of wheat, realizing a total output of 400 bushels at the end of the year. Is it correct to represent his output for the year as 400 bushels? Certainly not. He would have had 20 bushels available if he had planted

nothing at all. His net output for the year is 400 minus 20, or 380 bushels. This is a more accurate measure of the production that has actually occurred this year than is 400 bushels. Second, using hypothetical figures, suppose that on January 1, 1978, the economy had $100 billion worth of capital goods on hand. Assume also that during 1978, $40 billion worth of this equipment and machinery is used up in producing a GNP of $800 billion. Thus, on December 31, 1978, the stock of capital goods on hand stands at only $60 billion. Is it fair to say that the GNP figure of $800 billion accurately measures this year's output? No. It would be much more accurate to subtract from the year's GNP the $40 billion worth of capital goods which must be used to replace the machinery and equipment consumed in producing that GNP. This leaves a *net* output figure of $800 minus $40, or $760 billion.

In short, a figure for *net* output is a more accurate measure of a year's production than is *gross* output. In our system of social accounting, we derive a figure for *net national product* (NNP) by subtracting the capital consumption allowance, which measures the value of the capital used up in a year's production, from GNP. Hence, in 1976:

	Billions
Gross national product	$1692
Capital consumption allowance	−180
Net national product	$1512

NNP, then, is GNP adjusted for depreciation charges. It measures the total annual output which the entire economy—households, businesses, and governments—might consume without impairing our capacity to produce in ensuing years.

It is a simple matter, by the way, to adjust Table 9-6 from GNP to NNP. On the income side we just strike out capital consumption allowance. The other eight allocations should add up to an NNP of $1512 billion. On the expenditure side, one must change *gross* private domestic investment to *net* private domestic investment by subtracting replacement investment as measured by the capital consumption allowance from the former figure. In 1976, a gross investment figure of $240 billion less a depreciation charge of $180 billion results in a net private domestic investment figure of $60 billion and therefore an NNP of $1512 billion.

□ **National Income (NI)**

In analyzing certain problems, we are vitally interested in how much income is *earned* by resource suppliers for their contributions of land, labor, capital, and entrepreneurial ability which go into the year's net production or, alternatively stated, how much it costs society in terms of economic resources to produce this net output. The only component of NNP which does not reflect the current productive contributions of economic resources is indirect business taxes. It will be recalled that government contributes nothing directly to production in return for the indirect business tax revenues which it receives; government is not considered to be a factor of production. Hence, to get a measure of total wage, rent, interest, and profit incomes earned from the production of the year's output, we must subtract indirect business taxes from NNP. The resulting figure is called the *national income*. From the viewpoint of resource suppliers, it measures the incomes they have earned for their current contributions to production. From the viewpoint of businesses, national income measures factor or resource costs; national income reflects the market costs of the economic resources which have gone into the creation of this year's output. In 1976:

	Billions
Net national product · · · · · · · · · · · · · · ·	$1512
Indirect business taxes · · · · · · · · · · · · ·	−163
National income · · · · · · · · · · · · · · · ·	$1349

A glance at Table 9-6 shows that national income can also be obtained through the income approach by simply adding up all the allocations with the exception of capital consumption allowances and indirect business taxes. The seven allocations of GNP which remain after the two nonincome charges have been subtracted constitute the national income.

□ **Personal Income (PI)**

Income *earned* (national income) and income *received* (personal income) are likely to differ for the reason that some income which is earned—social security contributions (payroll taxes), corporate income taxes, and undistributed corporate profits—is not actually received by households, and, conversely, some income which is received—transfer payments—is not currently earned. Transfer payments, you may recall, are made up of such items as (1) old age and survivors' insurance payments and unemployment compensation, both of which stem from our social security program, (2) welfare payments, (3) a variety of veterans' payments, for example, GI Bill of Rights and disability payments, (4) payments out of private pension and welfare programs, and (5) interest payments paid by government and by consumers.[8]

Obviously, in moving from national income as a measure of income earned to personal income as an indicator of income actually received, we must subtract from national income those three types of income which are earned but not received and add in income received but not currently earned. This is done as follows:

[8] Why include interest payments on government bonds as income *not* currently earned, particularly when interest on the bonds of private firms is included in national income as earned income? The rationale underlying the exclusion is this: Much of the debt has been incurred in connection with (1) war and defense and (2) recessions. Furthermore, unlike public deficits to finance airports or highways, deficits stemming from the military and recessions yield no productive assets (services) to the economy. Hence, interest paid on such debt does *not* reflect the generation of any current output or income. Similar reasoning underlies the inclusion of interest payments by consumers as a part of transfer payments.

	Billions
National income (income earned)	$1349
Social security contributions	−123
Corporate income taxes	−65
Undistributed corporate profits	−18
Transfer payments	+232
Personal income (income received)	$1375

During reasonably prosperous periods, national income exceeds personal income. But when unemployment is above normal, as has been the case in recent years, personal income tends to exceed national income. Note that this was the case in 1976. The reason PI exceeds NI during recessions is the simple fact that the three subtracted items tend to be small and the added item is large. Can you explain why this is the case?

☐ Disposable Income (DI)

Disposable income is simply personal income less personal taxes. *Personal taxes* are comprised of personal income taxes, personal property taxes, and inheritance taxes, the first of the three being by far the most important. This adjustment is as follows:

	Billions
Personal income (income received before personal taxes)	$1375
Personal taxes	−193
Disposable income (income received after personal taxes)	$1182

Disposable income is the amount of income which households have to dispose of as they see fit. Basically, the choices are two. Remembering that economists conveniently define saving as "not spending," or better, "that part of disposable income which is not spent on consumer goods," it follows that households divide their disposable income between consumption and saving. On rare occasions—deep depressions in particular—households will consume in excess of their disposable incomes by borrowing or drawing down past accumulations of savings. Such was the case in 1933, for example, when saving was a *minus* $0.9 billion.

☐ Relationships between Major Social Accounts

We have derived four new social accounting concepts from GNP: (1) net national product (NNP), the market value of the annual output net of capital consumption allowances; (2) national income (NI), income *earned* by the factors of production for their current contributions to production, or the factor costs entailed in getting the year's total output produced; (3) personal income (PI), income *received* by households before personal taxes; and (4) disposable income (DI), income received by households less personal taxes. The relationships between these concepts are summarized in Table 9-7.

Table 9-7 THE RELATIONSHIPS BETWEEN GNP, NNP, NI, PI, AND DI IN 1976

	Billions
Gross national product (GNP)	$1692
Capital consumption allowance	−180
Net national product (NNP)	$1512
Indirect business taxes	−163
National income (NI)	$1349
Social security contributions	−123
Corporate income taxes	−65
Undistributed corporate profits	−18
Transfer payments	+232
Personal income (PI)	$1375
Personal taxes	−193
Disposable income (DI)	$1182

Summary

Figure 9-2 embodies a comprehensive summary and synthesis of all the social accounting measures discussed in this chapter. As a more realistic and more complex expression of the circular flow model of the economy (discussed in Chapter 3), this figure merits careful study by the reader. Starting at the GNP rectangle in the upper left-hand corner, the expenditures side of GNP is shown to the left. For simplicity's sake, we have assumed net exports to be zero. Immediately to the right of the GNP rectangle are the nine income components of GNP and then the various additions and subtractions which are needed in the derivation of NNP, NI, and PI. In the household sector we see the flow of personal taxes out of PI and the division of DI between consumption and personal saving. In the government sector the flows of revenue in the form of four basic types of taxes are denoted on the right; on the left, government disbursements take the form of purchases of goods and services and transfers. To simplify, a balanced budget is assumed in the public sector. The position of the business sector is such as to emphasize, on the left, investment expenditures and, on the right, the three major sources of funds for business investment.

The major virtue of Figure 9-2 is that it simultaneously portrays the expenditure

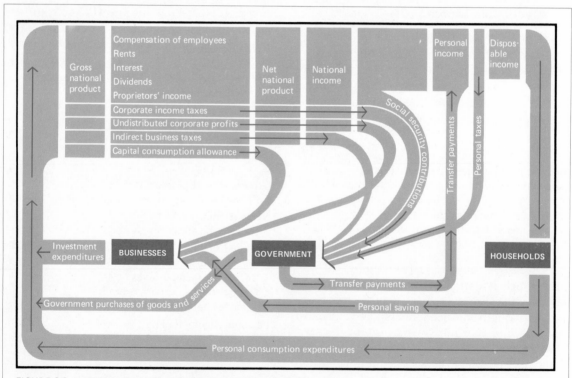

FIGURE 9-2 NATIONAL OUTPUT AND THE FLOWS OF EXPENDITURE AND INCOME

This figure is an elaborate circular flow diagram which fits the expenditures and allocations sides of GNP to one another. The reader should trace through the income and expenditures flows, relating them to the five basic national income accounting measures.

and income aspects of GNP, fitting the two approaches to one another. This figure correctly indicates that these flows of expenditure and income are part of a continuous, repetitive process. Cause and effect are intermingled: expenditures give rise to income, and out of this income arise expenditures which again flow to resource owners as income, and so forth.

Finally, the following concise definitions of the most important measures of the economy's performance should be thoroughly understood in studying Figure 9-2:

1   *Gross national product* (GNP) refers to the market value of all final goods and services produced in the economy in a given year.

2   *Net national product* (NNP) is gross national product minus capital consumption allowances (depreciation). NNP may also be found by summing personal consumption expenditures, *net* private domestic investment, government purchases of goods and services, and net exports.

3   *National income* (NI) is the total income *earned* by resource suppliers for their contributions to the production of GNP. National income also measures the costs of the resources used up in producing GNP. Its magnitude can be derived by subtracting indirect business taxes from NNP or by summing compensation of employees, rents, interest, proprietors' income, corporate income taxes, dividends, and undistributed corporate profits.

4   *Personal income* (PI) is the total income *received* by households during a given year. PI is determined by subtracting from national income that income which is earned but not received (social security contributions, corporate income taxes, and undistributed corporate profits) and adding that income which is received but not earned (transfer payments).

5   *Disposable income* (DI) is the portion of personal income which remains after the payment of personal taxes.

Questions and Study Suggestions

1   Key terms and concepts to remember: gross national product; inflating and deflating; final and intermediate goods; double counting; value added; expenditure and income approaches; gross and net private domestic investment; net exports; net national product; national income; personal income; disposable income.

2   "National income statistics are a powerful tool of economic understanding and analysis." Explain. "An economy's output is its income." Do you agree?

3   Why do national income accountants compare the market value of the total outputs in various years rather than actual physical volumes of production? Explain. What problem is posed by any comparison over time of the market values of various total outputs? How is this problem resolved?

4   Why do national income accountants include only final goods in measuring total output? How do GNP and NNP differ?

5   What is the difference between gross private domestic investment and net private domestic investment? If you were to determine net national product through the expenditures approach, which of these two measures of investment spending would be appropriate? Explain.

6   Why are changes in inventories included as a part of investment spending? Suppose inventories declined by $1 billion during 1978. How would this affect the size of gross private domestic investment and gross national product in 1978? Explain.

7   Use the concepts of gross and net investment to distinguish between an expanding, a static, and a declining economy. "In 1933 net private domestic invest-ment was minus $5.5 billion. This means in that particular year the economy pro-duced no capital goods at all." Do you agree? Explain: "Though net investment can be positive, negative, or zero, it is quite impossible for gross investment to be less than zero."

8 Define net exports. Suppose foreigners spend $7 billion on American exports in a given year and Americans spend $5 billion on imports from abroad in the same year. What is the amount of America's net exports?

9 The following is a list of national income figures for a given year. All figures are in billions. The ensuing question will ask you to determine the major national income measures by both the expenditure and income methods. The answers derived by each approach should be the same.

Personal consumption expenditures	$245
Transfer payments	12
Rents	14
Capital consumption allowance (depreciation)	27
Social security contributions	20
Interest	13
Proprietors' income	31
Net exports	3
Dividends	16
Compensation of employees	221
Indirect business taxes	18
Undistributed corporate profits	21
Personal taxes	26
Corporate income taxes	19
Corporate profits	56
Government purchases of goods and services	72
Net private domestic investment	33
Personal saving	16

   a.   Using the above data, determine GNP and NNP by both the expenditure and income methods.

   b.   Now determine NI (1) by making the required subtractions from GNP, and (2) by adding up the types of income which comprise NI.

   c.   Make those adjustments for NI required in deriving PI.

   d.   Make the required adjustments from PI (as determined in 9c) to obtain DI.

10   Given the following national income accounting data, compute **a.** GNP, **b.** NNP, and **c.** NI. All figures are in billions.

Compensation of employees	$194.2
U.S. exports of goods and services	13.4
Capital consumption allowance	11.8
Government purchases of goods and services	59.4
Indirect business taxes	12.2
Net private domestic investment	52.1
Transfer payments	13.9
U.S. imports of goods and services	16.5
Personal taxes	40.5
Personal consumption expenditures	219.1

11 The following table shows money GNP and an appropriate price index for a group of selected years. Compute real GNP. Indicate in each calculation whether you are inflating or deflating the money GNP data.

Year	Money GNP, billions	Price level index, percent (1972 = 100)	Real GNP, billions
1947	$ 232.8	49.70	$_____
1956	420.7	62.90	$_____
1967	796.3	79.02	$_____
1973	1306.3	105.92	$_____

12 Which of the following are actually included in deriving this year's GNP? Explain your answer in each case.
  a. Interest on an AT&T bond
  b. Social security payments received by a retired factory worker
  c. The services of a painter in painting the family home
  d. The income of a dentist
  e. The money received by Smith when he sells a 1974 Chevrolet to Jones
  f. The monthly allowance which a college student receives from home
  g. Rent received on a two-bedroom apartment
  h. The money received by Wilson when he resells this year's model Plymouth to Wilcox
  i. Interest received on government bonds
  j. A two-hour decline in the length of the workweek
  k. The purchase of an AT&T bond
  l. A $2 billion increase in business inventories
  m. The purchase of 100 shares of GM common stock
  n. The purchase of an insurance policy
  o. Wages paid to a domestic servant
  p. The market value of a housewife's services
  q. The purchase of a Renaissance painting by a public art museum

13 Explain: "A man diminishes the national income by marrying his cook."

Selected References

Abraham, William I.: *National Income and Economic Accounting* (Englewood Cliffs, N.J.: Prentice-Hall, Inc., 1969).

Dernburg, Thomas F., and Duncan M. McDougall: *Macroeconomics,* 5th ed. (New York: McGraw-Hill Book Company, 1976), chaps. 1–3.

Shapiro, Edward: *Macroeconomic Analysis,* 3d ed. (New York: Harcourt Brace Jovanovich, Inc., 1974), chaps. 2–5.

U.S. Department of Commerce: *The Economic Accounts of the United States: Retrospect and Prospect* (Washington, 1971).

———: *The National Income and Product Accounts of the United States, 1929–1974* (Washington, 1976).

———: *Survey of Current Business.* July issues contain annual national income data.

Last Word
National Income: Voluntary and Involuntary Expenditures

Professor Robert Lekachman of City University of New York contends that our voluntary expenditures on national output often necessitate involuntary expenditures. While the former enhance our economic well-being, the latter clearly do not.

At its simplest, my argument claims that current conventions in vogue among the income estimators suffer from an aggregative fallacy: the requirement that the statistician lump together voluntary and involuntary expenditures. In the realm of common sense at least, is it not strange to count according to their respective dollar values both the market sales of cigarettes and the medical expenditures by the victims of cigarette-induced maladies such as lung cancer, emphysema, tuberculosis, and coronaries? With an equally weird agnosticism, the national income expert totals not only the value of the oil pumped up from the Santa Barbara channel or the Gulf coast but also the expenses of cleaning up beaches and salvaging fishing grounds in the wake of oil-well blowouts. There are other peculiar triumphs of theory over reality. The statistician joins together the value of Consolidated Edison's sales of electrical energy in metropolitan New York and its customers' additional spending upon soaps and cleansers to restore their clothing, windows, household goods, and persons from the damage caused by air pollution. By current criteria, gross national product rises when auto sales increase, regardless of what may be happening to the quality of the enjoyments that these arrogant chariots generate or the variety of adverse side effects for which they are responsible. The gross national product records the sales of distilled liquor and the expenditures upon the treatment of alcoholics. And so on and on. Generically, the fault is a refusal to distinguish between spending that implements the tastes and desires of the spender and defensive expenditures forced upon him by his environment.

Probably the best that can be said for conventional statistics is that so long as the composition of output between the pluses of pleasure and the minuses of repair and treatment remains roughly the same, intertemporal comparisons convey meaning. That is to say, if in 1972 as in 1962 two-thirds of what Americans buy represents uncoerced choice and the remaining third is an effort to defend themselves against the side effects of harmful goods and careless misuse of the environment, sensible comparisons are possible of such magnitudes as per capita gross national product. Totally unanswered, however, because unmeasured, is the central query about the key assumption: Have these percentages in fact remained constant? Many believe that they have not, that in truth defensive spending is steadily rising both in absolute amount and as a share of total expenditure.

Robert Lekachman, *National Income and the Public Welfare* (New York: Random House, Inc., 1972), pp. 7–8.

CHAPTER

10

The Business Cycle: Unemployment and Inflation

Emphasis in Part 1 of this book was upon the essentially microeconomic problem of full production. To facilitate our discussion of how American capitalism allocates resources, we assumed that resources would be fully employed. But actual experience indicates that full employment cannot be taken for granted. Hence, in Parts 2 and 3 we seek to explore the problem of achieving and maintaining full employment in American capitalism.

The goals of the present chapter are fourfold. First, we introduce the "macroeconomic trilogy" of growth, full employment, and price stability. Next, we discuss total spending as the immediate determinant of the levels of employment and prices. Thirdly, the meanings and implications of unemployment and price instability are explored. Finally, the major characteristics of the American business cycle are discussed and its history is sketched.

■
THE MACROECONOMIC TRILOGY

Society seeks economic growth *and* full employment *and* price level stability along with other less quantifiable goals (Chapter 1). The broad spectrum of American economic history reflects quite remarkable economic growth. Technological progress, rapid increases in productive capacity, and a standard of living which is among the highest in the world are strategic facets of the dynamic character of our economy. But our long-run economic growth has not been steady. Rather, it has been inter-

191

rupted by periods of economic instability. Periods of rapid economic expansion have sometimes been marred by inflation, that is, price instability, and at other times, expansion has given way to recession and depression, that is, instability in employment and output. Indeed, on a few occasions—most notably in the 1970s—we have had the unhappy experience of a rising price level and abnormally high unemployment simultaneously. In short, secular economic growth has been interrupted and complicated by both unemployment and inflation.

The extent to which the United States economy has been successful in realizing this macroeconomic trilogy is depicted in detail by the historical record embodied in the national income statistics (see tables inside covers). A glance ahead at Figure 10-4 gives us a bird's-eye view of the ups and downs of the economy over the past century. Aside from a few comments in our historical discussion of the business cycle, we defer any detailed treatment of economic growth until Part 4. In Parts 2 and 3 we concentrate upon the problems involved in achieving full employment and price stability.

TOTAL DEMAND, EMPLOYMENT, AND THE PRICE LEVEL

We begin with a rough approximation: Generally speaking, the levels of output and employment, on the one hand, and the level of prices, on the other, have a common determinant— the level of total spending or demand.[1] In a market-directed economy such as ours, businesses produce only those goods which can be sold profitably. Crudely stated, if total demand is low, many businesses will not find it

profitable to produce a large volume of goods and services. Hence, output, employment, and the level of incomes will all be low. A higher level of total demand will mean that more production will be profitable; hence, output, employment, and incomes will all be higher also. Finally, the economy may attempt to spend beyond its capacity to produce; that is, it may seek some point like W in Figure 2-2. The business sector cannot respond to this excess demand by expanding real output for the obvious reason that all available resources are fully employed. Therefore, this excess demand will bid up the prices of the fixed real output, causing what economists term *demand-pull inflation*.

But the relationship between total demand, on the one hand, and output, employment, and the price level, on the other, is more complex than these terse comments suggest. Figure 10-1 is helpful in unraveling these complications.

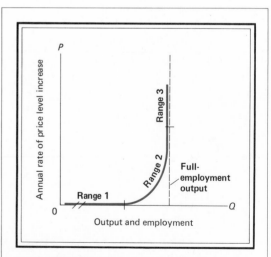

FIGURE 10-1 THE PRICE LEVEL AND THE LEVEL OF EMPLOYMENT

The price level generally begins to rise before full employment is reached. At full employment, additional spending tends to be purely inflationary.

---

[1] Later in this chapter and in Chapter 18 we shall discover that in the 1970s, economists are paying more and more attention to supply and cost considerations in explaining inflation.

Range 1: Unemployment and Price Stability

Suppose initially that the economy is in a serious recession with large amounts of unemployed labor and idle machinery. Assume, too, that for some reason total demand increases. Now, under the recession conditions specified, we can expect the increase in total demand will increase employment and output but that the price level will remain virtually constant. Why so? Most obviously, there are large amounts of virtually all types of human and property resources which can be readily employed by firms *at current resource prices* to expand their outputs. Alternatively, our simple demand-and-supply analysis of Chapter 4 suggests this outcome: The price-raising effects of the assumed increases in demand are offset by the price-reducing effects of increases in supply. The increases in supply are possible because idle resources are available and the additional production is profitable. The net result is large output-increasing effects and no price-increasing effects.

Range 2: Premature Inflation

As total spending continues to rise, however, this picture will begin to change. As production expands, supplies of unemployed resources will not vanish simultaneously in the various industries and sectors of the economy. For example, the full employment of labor and capital may be realized in industry X, while industry Y has excess capacity and unemployed workers. Supply is therefore quite fixed in industry X and increases in demand will have substantial price-increasing effects. In industry Y, increases in demand elicit offsetting supply responses and prices are constant. In short, because the full employment of resources is not achieved simultaneously in all industries, prices in *some* industries will rise as the economy *approaches* overall full employment. The resulting inflation is called "premature" simply because it occurs before the economy in the aggregate reaches full employment.

Range 3: Full Employment and Pure Inflation

If we assume still further increases in total demand, then all sectors and industries will ultimately realize full employment. Industries in the aggregate can no longer respond to increases in demand with increases in supply. Therefore, increases in demand for products will result in price increases, that is, in inflation. In other words, at full employment the economy encounters the production barrier of scarce resources; the economy will be operating at capacity at a point *on* its production possibilities curve. Businesses as a group cannot respond to increases in spending by expanding real output. Total demand in excess of society's productive capacity pulls the price level upward; that is, the previously mentioned demand-pull inflation occurs. Higher levels of total spending will bid up the prices of a fixed real output. At full employment, increases in spending will cause "pure" inflation to set in.

Chapter 9 drew a distinction between money and real GNP that is helpful at this point. So long as the price level is constant (range 1), increases in money and real GNP are identical. But with premature inflation (range 2), money GNP is rising faster than real GNP, so money GNP must be "deflated" to measure changes in physical output. With pure inflation (range 3), money GNP is rising—perhaps rapidly—but real GNP is constant.

Nonreversibility

The relationship expressed in Figure 10-1 is only partially reversible. That is, many product and resource prices which are flexible upward as the economy approaches the full-employment output become relatively rigid and inflexible when declines in total spending result in reductions in output and employment. This is primarily the result of monopolistic power—the ability to influence prices—which many businesses and unions possess. Unions can usually resist wage cuts and sometimes secure modest wage boosts even though the total level of spending and therefore output and employment are falling. Monopolistic businesses are equally able to forestall reductions in product prices. Prices that go up during periods of full employment do not necessarily come down—at least all the way—when spending declines and unemployment ensues. It is not surprising that the long-run trend of the price level in American capitalism has been upward. The significance of the downward inflexibility of prices will become evident in Chapter 11.

We shall examine the premature inflation range of Figure 10-1 in detail in Chapter 18. Our immediate task, however, is to assess more carefully the meaning and significance of both unemployment and price instability.

UNEMPLOYMENT

"Full employment" is an elusive concept to define. One might initially interpret it to mean that everyone who is in the labor market—100 percent of the labor force—is employed. But such is not the case. Some unemployment is regarded as normal or warranted.

□ Frictional Unemployment

Given freedom of occupational and job choice, at any point in time some workers will be "between jobs." That is, some workers will be in the process of voluntarily switching jobs. Others will have job connections but will be temporarily laid off because of seasonality (for example, bad weather in the construction industry) or model changeovers (as in the automobile industry). And there will be some workers, particularly young people, looking for their first jobs.

Economists use the term *frictional unemployment* for the group of workers who are unemployed for these kinds of reasons. Frictional unemployment is regarded as inevitable and, at least in part, desirable. Why desirable? Because workers typically move from low-paying, low-productivity jobs to higher-paying, higher-productivity positions. This means more income for the workers and a better allocation of labor resources—and therefore a larger real output—for the economy as a whole.

□ Structural Unemployment

Frictional unemployment shades into a second category, called *structural unemployment*. Important changes occur over time in the structure of consumer demand and in technology, which in turn alter the structure or the composition of the total demand for labor. Unemployment results because the composition of the labor force does not respond quickly or completely to the new structure of demand. As a result, some workers find that they have no readily marketable talents; their skills and experience have been rendered obsolete and unwanted by changes in technology and consumer demand. Examples: Years ago, highly skilled glassblowers were thrown out of work by the invention of bottlemaking machines. More recently, unskilled and inadequately educated blacks have been dislodged from agriculture in the South as a result of the mechanization of agriculture. Many of these workers have migrated to the ghettos of northern cities and have suffered prolonged unemployment because of insufficient skills.

The distinction between frictional and structural unemployment is hazy. The difference essentially is that frictionally unemployed workers have salable skills, whereas structurally unemployed workers are not readily reemployable without retraining, additional education, and possibly geographic movement.

Cyclical Unemployment

By cyclical unemployment we obviously mean unemployment caused by the business cycle, that is, by a deficiency of aggregate or total demand. As the overall level of business activity decreases, unemployment increases; as business activity increases, unemployment declines. Cyclical unemployment at the depth of the Great Depression in 1933 reached about 25 percent of the labor force!

Defining "Full Employment"

Economists regard some frictional and structural unemployment as unavoidable; hence, "full employment" is defined as something less than employment of 100 percent of the labor force. It has become customary in recent years to estimate this unavoidable minimum of unemployment to be 4 percent of the labor force. Therefore, full employment is said to exist when 96 percent of the labor force is employed. In 1976, for example, full employment would exist when up to approximately 3.8 million of the 95 million persons in the civilian labor force were out of work.

Caution: There is disagreement here. Some economists, looking back to the unemployment figures of the prosperous period from 1966 to 1969 and to the substantially lower unemployment rates of various Western European nations, argue that unavoidable unemployment is only about 3.0 or 3.5 percent. More recently, government economists have argued that the full-employment unemployment rate should be revised upward to 5 or $5\frac{1}{2}$ percent. They point out that certain groups, in particular women and young workers who traditionally have quite high unemployment rates, are becoming more important in the labor force. Furthermore, our unemployment compensation program, which has expanded both in terms of numbers of workers covered and size of benefits, allows unemployed workers to seek reemployment at a more leisurely pace. We will settle for a 4 percent figure,

recognizing that it is a matter of considerable debate.

Complication: Official unemployment statistics can be misleading. For example, statistics for 1975 indicate that 8.5 percent of the civilian labor force—7.8 million workers—were out of work. But these figures understate the unemployment problem. First, there were another 3.5 million workers who were working part time because full-time employment was not available to them. Second, another group of workers, estimated in excess of 1 million, unsuccessfully sought employment and, discouraged by their efforts, dropped out of the labor force. (One must be actively seeking work to be counted as unemployed in government figures.) Thus, the actual rate of unemployment, derived by adding part-time and "discouraged workers" to those officially unemployed, was roughly 11.5 percent, significantly higher than the 8.5 percent official rate.

Economic Costs of Unemployment

Regardless of the exact interpretation one gives to these statistics, above-normal or "true" unemployment entails great economic and social costs. The economic cost of unemployment is obviously forgone output—the goods and services which society could have produced but didn't. For example, the high 8.5 percent rate of unemployment in 1975 probably cost the American economy $175 to $185 billion in forgone production.

The cost of a prolonged depression can be astronomical. One scholar has estimated the cost of the Great Depression of the 1930s in these terms:[2]

A full-employment output for the 1930s would have produced $650 billion additional goods and services in terms of the 1956 price level. Such a sum would have been higher than the material cost of World War II. It would have meant roughly $5000 more in income for each

[2] Sherman J. Maisel, *Fluctuations, Growth, and Forecasting* (New York: John Wiley & Sons, Inc., 1957), p. 18.

individual in the United States in that decade, or $20,000 more for the average family. If all resources had been fully employed in this manner, every family could have had a new house, several new cars, and most of the other durable goods it desired.

GNP Gap   Government economists measure the cost of unemployment in terms of a *GNP gap*. This gap is simply the amount by which the *actual GNP* falls short of *potential GNP*. Potential GNP is determined by assuming that full employment (defined as 4 percent unemployment) is achieved and projecting the economy's "normal" growth rate. Figure 10-2 shows the GNP gap for recent years and underscores the close correlation between the unemployment rate and the GNP gap. Unemployment is indeed costly. The gap between

potential and actual GNP in 1975 was about $175 billion (measured in 1972 prices) of forgone production!

Unequal Burdens   Aggregate figures conceal the fact that the cost of unemployment is unequally distributed. An increase in the unemployment rate from 4 to, say, 6 percent would be more tolerable if every worker's hours of work and wage income were reduced proportionately. But, in fact, unemployment is borne heavily by teenagers, by women workers, and particularly by minority groups. For example, data show that in 1976 the unemployment rate was 7.7 percent for the labor force as a whole. But the breakdown of this figure revealed startling inequities. The unemployment rate for Negroes and other minorities was 13.1 percent, compared with 7.0 percent for

FIGURE 10-2 POTENTIAL AND ACTUAL GNP (a) AND THE UNEMPLOYMENT RATE (b)

The difference between potential and actual GNP is the GNP gap. The GNP gap measures the output which the economy sacrifices because it fails to utilize fully its productive potential. Note that a high unemployment rate means a large GNP gap. (*Economic Report of the President* and *Business Conditions Digest*.)

(a) The GNP gap

(b) Unemployment rate

whites. Unemployment among male workers 20 years of age and over was only 5.9 percent, compared with 7.4 for females. Among all teenagers of labor-force age, the unemployment rate was 19 percent. For black teenagers, the figure was about 37 percent.

□ Noneconomic Costs

Unemployment is much more than an economic catastrophe; it is a social catastrophe as well. Depression means idleness. And idleness means loss of skills, loss of self-respect, a plummeting of morale, family disintegration, and sociopolitical unrest. Consider the following two commentaries on the Great Depression from Studs Terkel's revealing book *Hard Times*.[3] First, the comments of a young woman who was fortunate enough to attend college:

> When I attended Berkeley in 1936, so many of the kids had actually lost their fathers. They had wandered off in disgrace because they couldn't support their families. Other fathers had killed themselves, so the family could have the insurance. Families had totally broken down. Each father took it as his personal failure. These middle-class men apparently had no social sense of what was going on, so they killed themselves.
>
> It was still the Depression. There were kids who didn't have a place to sleep, huddling under bridges on the campus. I had a scholarship, but there were times when I didn't have food. The meals were often three candy bars.

Second, the reminiscences of a craftsman's son:

> One of the most common things—and it certainly happened to me—was this feeling of your father's failure. That somehow he hadn't beaten the rap. Sure things were tough, but why should I be the kid who had to put a piece of cardboard into the sole of my shoe to go to school? It was not a thing coupled with re-

sentment against my father. It was simply this feeling of regret, that somehow he hadn't done better, that he hadn't gotten the breaks. Also a feeling of uneasiness about my father's rage against the way things are. . . .

> Remember, too, the shock, the confusion, the hurt that many kids felt about their fathers not being able to provide for them. This reflected itself very often in bitter quarrels between father and son. . . .

> We had bitter arguments about new ideas. Was Roosevelt right in making relief available? Was the WPA a good idea? Did people have the right to occupy their farms and hold them by force? The old concept that there was something for everybody who worked in America went down the drain with the Great Depression. This created family strains. A lot of parents felt a sense of guilt. . . .

> My father led a rough life: he drank. During the Depression, he drank more. There was more conflict in the home. A lot of fathers—mine, among them—had a habit of taking off. They'd go to Chicago to look for work. To Topeka. This left the family at home, waiting and hoping that the old man would find something. And there was always the Saturday night ordeal as to whether or not the old man would get home with his paycheck. Everything was sharpened and hurt more by the Depression.

It is no exaggeration to say that:[4]

> A job gives hope for material and social advancement. It is a way of providing one's children a better start in life. It may mean the only honorable way of escape from the poverty of one's parents. It helps to overcome racial and other social barriers. In short . . . a job is the passport to freedom and to a better life. To deprive people of jobs is to read them out of our society.

History makes it all too clear that severe unemployment is conducive to rapid and

---

[3]Studs Terkel, *Hard Times* (New York: Avon Books, 1971), pp. 131, 398.

[4]Henry R. Reuss, *The Critical Decade* (New York: McGraw-Hill Book Company, 1964), p. 133.

sometimes violent social and political change. Witness the movement to the left of American political philosophy during the Depression of the 1930s. The Depression-inspired New Deal was a veritable revolution in American political and economic thinking. Witness also Hitler's ascent to power against a background of unemployment. Furthermore, there can be no question that the heavy concentration of unemployment among blacks and other minorities has been an important cause of the unrest and violence which have plagued American cities in recent years.

PRICE INSTABILITY: INFLATION AND DEFLATION

Inflation is feared by all of us, criticized by most of us, but not clearly understood by many of us. Indeed, the problems posed by inflation are more subtle than those of unemployment.

What is inflation? Why is it to be feared? *Inflation is a rising general level of prices.* This does not mean, of course, that *all* prices are necessarily rising. Even during periods of acute inflation, some specific prices may be relatively constant and others actually falling. Nor does inflation mean that prices rise evenly or proportionately. Indeed, one of the major sore spots of inflation lies in the fact that prices tend to rise very unevenly. Some spring upward; others rise at a more leisurely pace; others do not rise at all. Although the causes of inflation are diverse, the traditional source of inflation is excess demand. Figure 10-3 gives us an historical overview of inflation in the United States. Note the more-or-less continuous rise in the price level since the start of World War II.

Deflation is substantially the reverse of

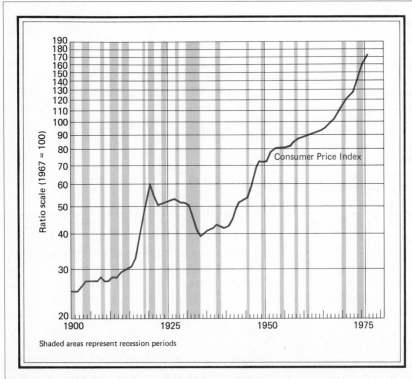

FIGURE 10-3 PRICE LEVEL BEHAVIOR IN THE UNITED STATES SINCE 1900

The price level has generally risen since the turn of the century. Three particularly sharp periods of increase are evident: the World War I period, the immediate post-World War II period (1945-1948), and the period 1966 to the present. Note that periods of deflation generally correspond with recession years as shown by the shaded areas.

Ratio scale (1967 = 100)

Consumer Price Index

Shaded areas represent recession periods

inflation—a falling general level of prices. Once again, deflation does not mean that all prices are falling evenly. Falling prices accompany severely declining levels of output and employment; the cause is a deficiency of total spending.

☐ Redistributive Effects

In practice, output and the price level may move together; inflation is often, but certainly not always, associated with an expanding real output. And, on those infrequent occasions wherein deflation occurs, it is typically accompanied by a shrinking real output. But in order to isolate the effects of a changing price level upon the distribution of income, let us for the moment imagine that real output is constant and at the full-employment level. Assuming the size of the income pie is fixed, how does inflation affect the size of the slices going to different income receivers? At the close of our analysis, we shall release this fixed-output assumption and modify our conclusions accordingly.

Any analysis of the redistributive impact of inflation and deflation demands that we first distinguish carefully between real and money income. *Money income* is simply the number of dollars one receives in his or her pay envelope. *Real income,* on the other hand, is the amount of goods and services which a consumer can obtain with his or her money income. A moment's reflection will make clear that your real income depends upon (1) your money income, and (2) the prices which you must pay for the goods and services you purchase.

Fixed Money Income Groups   With this distinction in mind, it is easy to see why inflation arbitrarily penalizes people living on relatively fixed money incomes. Those households whose money incomes lag behind the rising level of product prices will find that their real incomes will deteriorate because of inflation. The purchasing power of each dollar's worth of

income they receive will fall as prices rise. And, because they receive about the same number of dollars in their pay envelopes, their standard of living must decline accordingly.

Who are these people? The most obvious cases are pensioners, white-collar workers, some public employees, people living on welfare and other transfer payments which remain fixed over substantial periods. In particular, elderly people who receive modest and inflexible pensions are the victims of inflation. Note, however, that the adverse redistributive effect of inflation upon social security recipients has been offset in recent years by substantial increases in the size of benefits; in fact, social security benefits are now tied to the consumer price index to prevent erosion from inflation.

People living on flexible incomes may benefit from inflation. The money incomes of such households may spurt ahead of the price level, or cost of living, with the result that their real incomes are enhanced. Workers employed in expanding industries and represented by vigorous unions may keep their wage incomes apace with, or ahead of, the rate of inflation. However, some wage earners are hurt by inflation. Those situated in declining industries or without the benefit of strong, aggressive unions may find that the price level skips ahead of their money incomes. Businessmen and other profit receivers might benefit from inflation. *If* product prices rise faster than resource prices, business receipts then will grow at a faster rate than will costs. Thus some profit incomes will outdistance the rising tide of inflation.

Debtors and Creditors   Inflation also redistributes income by altering the relationship between debtors and creditors. Specifically, inflation tends to benefit debtors at the expense of creditors. Suppose you borrow $1000 from a bank, which you are to repay in two years. If in that period of time the general level of prices were to double, the $1000 which you repay will have only half the purchasing power of the $1000 originally borrowed. True, if we ignore interest charges, the same number of dollars is repaid as was borrowed. But because of inflation, each of these dollars will now buy only half as much as it did when the loan was negotiated. As prices go up, the value of the dollar comes down. Thus, because of inflation, the borrower is given "dear" dollars but pays back "cheap" dollars.

Empirical research suggests that, since World War II, inflation has brought about a massive redistribution of wealth from the household to the public sector of the economy. The reason is that governments have incurred very large debts and, to a considerable extent, government bonds have been held by households. That is, governments are large debtors and households have been their creditors. The postwar inflation has consequently shifted wealth from households to government. Incidentally, skeptics suggest that, given these redistributive consequences, we should not expect government to be particularly zealous in its efforts to halt inflation. Furthermore, debtor status is undoubtedly important in assessing the redistributive impact of inflation upon the various income classes. Data suggest that inflation seems to hit the very poor and the very rich the hardest, while providing some benefit for middle and upper-middle income receivers. Explanation: The poor have few debts because no one will lend to them; the rich have relatively few debts because they are rich! Thus, neither the poor nor the rich benefit as debtors from inflation. But the middle and upper-middle income classes are heavily in debt and they do benefit from inflation. Finally, the relative importance of indebtedness suggests that inflation tends to transfer wealth from the elderly to the young. The former owe little, whereas the latter are heavily in debt as the result of "setting up households, borrowing heavily to buy houses, cars, furniture, and the like, and to finance their children's education."[5]

[5]See G. L. Bach, "Inflation: Who Gains and Who Loses?" *Challenge,* July–August 1974, pp. 48–55. The above paragraph is based upon Bach's research.

Savers   Inflation also casts its evil eye upon savers. As prices rise, the real value, or purchasing power, of a nest egg of liquid savings will deteriorate. Savings accounts, insurance policies, annuities, and other fixed-value paper assets which were once adequate to meet rainy-day contingencies or to provide for a comfortable retirement decline in real value during inflation. Mortgage holders and bondholders will be similarly affected. A household's accumulated claims upon the economy's output are worth less and less as prices rise.

On the other hand, these two important exceptions should be noted. First, stock values are flexible and determined by current market conditions; hence, savings in this form will tend to increase in value with, or in some cases ahead of, the general level of prices. Second, so long as the interest rate on savings exceeds the rate of inflation, the purchasing power of savings will increase rather than diminish. For example, the purchasing power of a $1000 savings account will increase if the annual interest rate is, say, 5 percent and the annual increase in the price level only 3 percent.

Summary and Addenda   To summarize: Inflation arbitrarily "taxes" those who receive relatively fixed money incomes and "subsidizes" those who receive flexible money incomes. Inflation benefits debtors at the expense of creditors. Finally, inflation arbitrarily penalizes savers. It should come as no surprise that the effects of deflation are substantially the reverse. *Assuming no change in total output,* those with fixed money incomes will find their real incomes enhanced. Creditors will benefit at the expense of debtors. And savers will find that the purchasing power of their savings has grown as a result of falling prices.

Two final points must be appended to this discussion. First, the fact that any given family is likely to be an income earner, a holder of financial assets, and an owner of real assets simultaneously is likely to cushion the redistributive impact of inflation. For example, if the family owns fixed-value monetary assets (savings accounts, bonds, and insurance policies), inflation will lessen their real value. But that same inflation is likely to increase the real value of any property assets (a house, land) which the family owns. In short, many families are simultaneously hurt and benefited by inflation. All these effects must be considered before we can conclude that the family's net position is better or worse because of inflation.

The second point to be reemphasized is that the redistributive effects of inflation *are* arbitrary in that they occur without regard to society's goals and values. Inflation lacks a social conscience and takes from some and gives to others, regardless of whether they be rich, poor, young, old, healthy, or infirm.

□   Output Effects

We have assumed thus far that the economy's real output is fixed at the full-employment level. As a result, the redistributive effects of inflation and deflation have been in terms of some groups gaining absolutely at the expense of others. If the size of the pie is fixed and inflation causes some groups to get larger slices, other groups must necessarily get smaller slices. This is obviously modified somewhat when inflation is accompanied by an expanding real output, as would be the case when the economy is approaching, but has not yet attained, the full-employment output (Range 2 of Figure 10-1). When the pie is growing, the gains which inflation brings to some will exceed the losses which it imposes upon others. In brief, the redistributive impact of a given amount of inflation will tend to be less adverse when inflation is accompanied by an expansion of real output.

Although mild inflation may be accompanied by an expanding real total output, extreme inflation—"hyperinflation"—might well have adverse effects upon the level of production. There are two main reasons for this. In the first place, as we shall note shortly, hyperinflation may undermine the functioning of the monetary system, forcing the economy to rely upon exchange by barter. And barter, you recall (Chapter 3), inhibits specialization and thereby fosters inefficient production and a declining real output. Secondly, severe inflation encourages speculative, as opposed to productive, activity. Rather than invest in capital equipment, business managers and savers find that the hoarding of goods and materials and the purchase of nonproductive wealth—jewels, precious metals, real estate, and so forth—are good hedges against inflation and hence more lucrative outlets for one's money.

Furthermore, some economists have examined the economic milieu of the 1970s—an unfortunate combination of abnormally high unemployment and quite rapid inflation—and have suggested that inflation can be an important *cause* of unemployment. They argue that the inflation of the 1970s has originated largely on the cost or supply side, rather than from an excess of demand. That is, worldwide shortages of certain raw materials have increased their costs; the members of the Organization of Petroleum Exporting Countries (OPEC) have exerted market power to more than quadruple the price of oil; strong labor unions and big businesses have used their market power to boost wages and prices, and so forth. This cost or supply inflation reduces the amount of real output that any given level of money demand will buy; hence, real output and employment will fall.

What about deflation? Falling prices typically go along with depression and a declining total output. Hence, with a rapidly shrinking pie, virtually all groups will get a smaller slice. It is true that those on relatively fixed incomes *who are able to hold their jobs* will find that their real incomes rise as a result of deflation. But many of these people may lose their jobs and all their income. Creditors *who are fortunate enough to collect from debtors* will gain. But many debts may not be collectible. And those *who are able to hold on to their savings* as the economy backslides into depression will find the purchasing power of their savings enhanced by lower prices. But, again, some may lose their savings as stock market prices tumble and financial institutions go bankrupt. In short, during deflation, fixed money income receivers, creditors, and savers are not likely to be better off in an absolute sense, because in all probability total output will be falling too. But they may be "less worse off" than flexible-income receivers, debtors, and nonsavers.

☐ **Creeping Inflation**

Virtually all economists condemn a sharply rising price level. Economists are divided, however, on the merits and demerits of mild or "creeping" inflation—that is, a 2, 3, or 4 percent annual increase in the price level.

The Case for Creeping Inflation Despite the arbitrary redistributive effects of inflation, some respected economists feel that creeping inflation may very well be desirable because of its expansionary effect upon the economy.[6] Product prices, it is argued, tend to increase ahead of resource prices as the economy approaches full employment. This stimulates money profits and is conducive to additional investment spending, which, in turn, brings the economy closer to full employment. Furthermore, the larger stock of investment goods causes a favorable shift in the production possibilities curve, and economic growth is the result. It is concluded that only under the pressure of a high, inflation-causing level of aggregate demand does American capitalism realize full employment, capacity production, and its maximum growth potential. Mild inflation is allegedly a small price to pay for the attainment of these objectives. It is recognized that mild inflation will tread on the toes of fixed-income receivers, creditors, and savers. But any arbitrary redistributive effects will be more than offset by the benefits which infla-

tion-born increases in output and employment will bring to the economy as a whole. More fixed-income employees will have jobs, creditors will be more certain of repayment, and prosperity will permit more households to enjoy the luxury of saving. The alternatives, as these economists see it, are full employment and growth, accompanied by creeping inflation *or* price stability, accompanied by unemployment and the failure of the economy to realize its growth potential. The former choice, they conclude, is far superior to the latter.

The Case against Creeping Inflation But other competent authorities[7] take a dim view of this position. They make two major arguments against creeping inflation. First, they contend that when compounded over the years, the redistributive impact of mild or creeping inflation can be very severe. Given the annual rate of inflation, the *"rule of 70"* allows one to quickly calculate the number of years required for a doubling of the price level. Specifically, the number of years necessary for the price level to double is found by dividing 70 by the annual rate of inflation. For example, a 3 percent annual rate of inflation will double the price level in about 23 ($= 70 \div 3$) years. An 8 percent annual rate of inflation will double the price level in about 9 ($= 70 \div 8$) years! The point is that a rather innocent annual rate of inflation, when compounded, can cause dramatic changes in the absolute level of prices in fairly short periods of time.

Second, it is argued that creeping inflation may readily snowball into hyper- or "galloping" inflation. It is felt that as the economy draws close to the full-employment level, individual segments of the economy will exert pressure to keep their incomes rising ahead of the creeping inflation. But this pressure will cause creeping inflation to get up and run. It happens something like this: As prices persist in creeping upward, people come to expect

---

[6] For classic arguments in favor of this position, see Alvin H. Hansen, *The American Economy* (New York: McGraw-Hill Book Company, 1957), pp. 45–47, and Sumner H. Slichter, "How Bad Is Inflation?" *Harper's Magazine,* August 1952.

[7] In recent years the monetary authorities in the United States have generally been opposed to creeping inflation.

them to rise further. So, rather than let their idle savings and current incomes depreciate, people are induced to "spend now" to beat anticipated price rises. Businesses do the same in buying capital goods. Action on the basis of this "inflationary psychosis" intensifies the pressure on prices, and inflation feeds upon itself. Furthermore, as the cost of living rises, labor demands and gets higher money wages. Indeed, unions may seek wage increases sufficient not only to cover last year's price level increase but also to compensate for the inflation anticipated during the future life of their new collective bargaining agreement. Prosperity is not a good time for business firms to risk strikes by resisting such demands. Business managers recoup their rising labor costs by boosting the prices they charge consumers. And for good measure, businesses are likely to jack prices up an extra notch or two to be sure that profit receivers keep abreast or ahead of the inflationary parade. As the cost of living skips merrily upward as a result of these price increases, labor once again has an excellent excuse to demand another round of substantial wage increases. Unions will bargain to recoup declines in real wage incomes resulting from past inflation *and* in anticipation of future rises in the price level. But this triggers another round of price increases. The net effect is a cumulative *wage-price inflationary spiral.* Money-wage and price rises feed upon each other, and this helps creeping inflation burst into galloping inflation. Thus, many economists feel that the trouble with a small dose of inflation is that it is not likely to remain small.

But, aside from capricious and disruptive effects upon the distribution of income, why is such hyperinflation to be feared? The answer, curiously enough, is that hyperinflation can lead to a depression. As prices shoot up sharply and unevenly, normal economic relationships are disrupted. Business owners do not know what to charge for their products. Consumers do not know what to pay. Money becomes "hot," because inflation is rapidly diminishing the purchasing power of the dollar.

In the extreme case, inflation may become so severe as to render money virtually worthless. Resource suppliers will want to be paid in kind. Creditors will avoid debtors to escape the repayment of debts with cheap money. Money will cease to do its job as a medium of exchange and a standard of value. Nor will people want to store their wealth in the form of money. The economy will literally be thrown into a state of barter. As inflation increases in severity, businesses may find it more profitable to hoard both materials and finished products, awaiting further price increases. But, by further restricting the availability of materials and products relative to the demand for them, such action will merely tend to intensify inflationary pressures. Production and exchange grind toward a halt, and the net result is economic, social, and very possibly political chaos. Hyperinflation has precipitated monetary collapse, depression, and sociopolitical disorder. The conclusion? Mild inflation is a very risky foundation for achieving healthy economic progress.

Which view is correct? It is hard to say. Both have proved accurate in specific instances. American economic history does reveal that many periods of healthy economic growth have entailed mild inflation. On the other hand, other nations of the world have had mild inflation that got out of control—particularly during wartime—and broke into galloping inflation with disastrous results.[8]

The inflation in Hungary exceeded all known records of the past. In August, 1946, 828 octillion (1 followed by 27 zeros) depreciated pengös equaled the value of 1 prewar pengö. The price of the American dollar reached a value of 3×10^{22} (3 followed by 22 zeros) pengös. . . . In Germany of 1923 a larger box was needed to carry money to the grocery store than to bring back the groceries bought. . . . Prices rose some 116 times in Japan, 1939 to 1948.

[8]Theodore Morgan, *Income and Employment,* 2d ed. (Englewood Cliffs, N.J.: Prentice-Hall, Inc., 1952), p. 361.

We must settle for the conclusion that creeping inflation can be expansionary but that such inflation may expose the economy to the real risk of galloping inflation.

THE BUSINESS CYCLE

What is the record of American capitalism in providing for stability in output, employment, and the price level? The record is a spotty one. At times, the economy has suffered from prolonged periods of underspending. The consequences of such periods have been widespread unemployment, low incomes, and a depressed GNP. At other times, the economy has overspent; that is, it has spent in excess of its capacity to produce. The result has been full employment and a high GNP, on the one hand, but inflation—that is, a rising level of prices—on the other. In fact, on a few occasions we have encountered the worst of all possible economic worlds; as noted, much of the 1970s has been characterized by simultaneous inflation and high levels of unemployment.

Generally speaking, the term "business cycle" refers to the recurrent ups and downs in the level of economic activity which extend over a period of several years. Individual business cycles vary tremendously in detail. Yet all embody common phases which are variously labeled by different economists. Thus some economists talk of prosperity, recession, depression, and recovery as being the four phases of the business cycle. Others simply distinguish between the phases of expansion and contraction, with upper and lower turning points to divide the two. Still other economists are content to talk merely in terms of the "upswing" and "downswing" of the business cycle.

Despite common phases, specific business cycles vary greatly. (Indeed, some economists prefer to talk of business *fluctuations,* rather than *cycles,* because the latter term implies regularity and the former does not.) In particular, cycles vary in duration and intensity. The Great Depression of the 1930s seriously undermined the level of business activity for an entire decade. By comparison, the business declines of 1924 and 1927 were minor in both intensity and duration, as most of our post-World War II recessions also have been. Figure 10-4 provides ample historical evidence as to the existence of the business cycle and its irregularity in duration and intensity.

☐   **Noncyclical Fluctuations**

It must not be concluded that all changes in business activity are due to the business cycle. On the one hand, there are *seasonal*

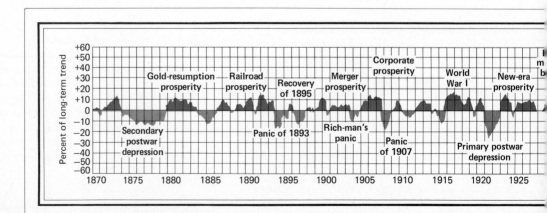

variations in business activity. For example, the pre-Christmas and pre-Easter buying rushes cause considerable fluctuations each year in the tempo of business activity, particularly in the retail industry. Agriculture, the automobile industry, construction—indeed, virtually all industries are subject to some degree of seasonality. These seasonal variations complicate the measurement of cyclical fluctuations in business activity. For example, an upswing in retail sales in December may or may not be evidence of a cyclical upswing in business activity. To speak with any degree of certainty, one would have to compare the increase in this December's retail sales with the increase in sales which statistical records for previous Decembers indicate as being normal. If retail sales normally double in December, a tripling of sales in December 1978 would suggest a cyclical upswing in business activity. Conversely, if retail sales for the month fall short of doubling, a cyclical downswing is implied.

Business activity is also subject to a *secular trend*. The secular trend of an economy is its expansion or contraction over a long period of years, for example, 25, 50, or 100 years. We simply note at this juncture that the long-run secular trend for American capitalism has been one of rather remarkable expansion (Chapter 20). For present purposes, the importance of this long-run expansion is that the business cycle involves fluctuations in business activity around a long-run growth trend. Note that in Figure 10-4 cyclical fluctuations are measured as deviations from the secular growth trend. Needless to say, the long-run trend may influence the duration and intensity of particular phases of the business cycle.

□ **Cyclical Impact: Durables and Nondurables**

The business cycle is pervasive; it is felt in virtually every nook and cranny of the economy. The interrelatedness of the economy allows few, if any, to escape the cold hand of depression or the fever of inflation. Yet we must keep in mind that various individuals and various segments of the economy are affected in different ways and in different degrees by the business cycle.

Insofar as production and employment are concerned, those industries producing capital goods and consumer durables are typically hit hardest by recession. The construction industry is particularly vulnerable. Output and employment in nondurable consumer goods industries are less sensitive to the cycle. Industries producing housing and commercial buildings, heavy capital goods, farm implements, automobiles, refrigerators, gas ranges,

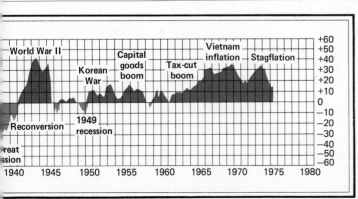

FIGURE 10-4 AMERICAN BUSINESS-CYCLE EXPERIENCE

The American economy has encountered periods of prosperity and depression. Post-World War II recessions have been modest as compared with the Great Depression of the 1930s. (Cleveland Trust Company.)

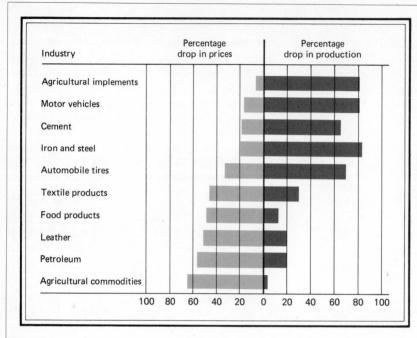

FIGURE 10-5 RELATIVE PRICE AND PRODUCTION DECLINES IN TEN INDUSTRIES, 1929-1933

The high-concentration industries shown in the top half of this figure were characterized by relatively small price declines and large declines in output when the economy entered the Great Depression. In the low-concentration industries of the bottom half, price declines were relatively large, and production fell by relatively small amounts. [Gardiner C. Means, *Industrial Prices and Their Relative Flexibility* (Washington, 1953), p. 8.]

and similar products bear the brunt of bad times. Conversely, these "hard goods" industries seem to be stimulated most by expansion. Two facts go far to explain the vulnerability of these industries to the cycle.

1 Postponability Within limits, the purchase of hard goods is postponable. Hence, as the economy slips into bad times, producers forestall the acquisition of more modern productive facilities and the construction of new plants. The business outlook simply does not warrant increases in the stock of capital goods. In all probability the firm's present capital facilities and buildings will still be usable and in excess supply. Except in bad times, capital goods are usually replaced before they are completely depreciated; when recession strikes, however, business firms will patch up their outmoded equipment and make it do. As a result, investment in capital goods will decline sharply. Chances are that some firms, having excess plant capacity, will not even bother to

replace all the capital which they are currently consuming. Net investment may be a negative figure.

Much the same holds true for consumer durables. When recession rolls around and the family budget must be trimmed, it is likely that plans for the purchases of durables will first feel the ax. You decide to make repairs on your old car rather than buy a new model. Concluding that your present black-and-white television set is "good enough," you defer plans to purchase a color TV.

Food and clothing—consumer nondurables—are a different story. A family must eat and must clothe itself. These purchases are much less postponable. True, to some extent the quantity and most certainly the quality of these purchases will decline. But not so much as is the case with durables.

2 Monopoly Power Most industries producing capital goods and consumer durables are industries of high concentration, wherein a relatively small number of firms dominate the market. As a result, these firms have sufficient monopoly power to resist lowering prices by restricting supply in the face of a declining demand. Consequently, the impact of a fall in demand centers primarily upon production and employment. The reverse holds true in nondurable, or soft, goods industries, which are for the most part highly competitive and characterized by low concentration. Price declines cannot be resisted in such industries, and the impact of a declining demand falls to a greater extent on prices than upon the levels of production. Figure 10-5 is informative on this point. It shows the percentage declines in price and quantity which occurred in ten selected industries as the economy fell from peak prosperity in 1929 to the depth of depression in 1933. Speaking very generally, high-concentration industries make up the top half of the table and low-concentration industries the bottom half. Note the drastic production declines and relatively

modest price declines of the high-concentration industries on the one hand, and the large price declines and relatively small output declines which took place in the low-concentration industries on the other.

■───────────────────────────
BUSINESS CYCLES SINCE 1920[9]

Let us now apply our rudimentary understanding of the business cycle to survey the cyclical experiences of American capitalism since 1920. Such a summary gives us many valuable insights into both the causes and effects of economic fluctuations. The emphasis is upon variations in the different components of total spending.

We shall employ Table 10-1 to substantiate our description of the 1920s. Official U.S. Department of Commerce national income

[9]To the instructor: This descriptive section may be omitted without seriously impairing continuity.

Table 10-1 GNP, THE PRICE LEVEL, UNEMPLOYMENT, AND PRODUCTIVITY IN THE 1920s

(1) Year	(2) GNP, billions of current dollars	(3) Real GNP, billions of 1972 dollars	(4) Unemployment, millions	(5) Index of output per man-hour in manufacturing, percent (1947 = 100)	(6) Consumer price index, percent (1967 = 100)
1920	$ 91.6	$217.0	0.6	44.6	60.0
1921	70.0	197.8	4.8	51.3	53.6
1922	74.3	225.8	2.9	56.2	50.2
1923	85.5	254.2	0.7	55.2	51.1
1924	85.1	254.4	2.0	58.9	51.2
1925	93.6	277.2	0.8	62.8	52.5
1926	97.8	291.7	0.5	64.5	53.0
1927	95.8	292.7	1.6	66.2	52.0
1928	98.3	297.2	1.9	69.7	51.3
1929	104.4	314.7	1.6	72.5	51.3

Sources: Columns 2, 3, and 6 are from The National Industrial Conference Board, *The Economic Almanac, 1958* (New York: Thomas Y. Crowell Company, 1958), pp. 71, 394. Columns 4 and 5 are from U.S. Bureau of the Census, *Historical Statistics of the United States: Colonial Times to 1970* (1975) pp. 211, 950.

statistics are available starting with 1929 and provide a factual backbone for our discussion of the ensuing five decades. These figures are presented in the inside covers of the book.

□ The Twenties: Prosperity

Aside from a sharp but brief depression in 1921 and minor bouts with unemployment in 1924 and 1927, the 1920s were years of booming prosperity. This prosperity was reflected in an expanding GNP and in a level of unemployment which never exceeded 2 million workers in the 1923–1929 period. Furthermore, this growth was cloaked in general price stability (see columns 3, 4, and 6 of Table 10-1).

The major driving force underlying this period of prosperity was a high and prolonged level of investment spending on capital equipment and construction. The following are prominent among the many interrelated causal factors that contributed to this high rate of investment:

1 The Strong Demand for Capital Goods World War I had created a backlog of demand for investment goods. Resources simply could not be spared from the production of armaments during the war for the production of investment goods to replace or expand the nation's stock of capital. As a result, the need for capital goods to replace those worn out and rendered obsolete during the war persisted into the 1920s. Investment in machinery and equipment was bolstered by a residential housing boom in the early 1920s.

2 The Development of New Products and Industries The spectacular rise of a group of new and important industries provided both direct and indirect stimuli to investment spending during the twenties. The development of the automobile, the electric power, radio, telephone, and electric refrigerator industries all called for tremendous amounts of investment spending in these and related industries. The most notable of these

vigorous new developments was the automobile industry. Widespread acceptance of the automobile—annual production increased from 2.2 million in 1920 to 5.5 million by 1929—induced tremendous expansion in the industry. Of greater importance, however, were the secondary effects which the manufacture of the automobile had upon a host of related industries. The petroleum, rubber, steel, glass, and textile industries all expanded their facilities enormously to feed parts and materials into the booming auto industry. In addition, an estimated $10 billion was spent on roads and highways during the twenties.

3 Declining Labor Costs and Business Optimism The development of mass-production techniques and simultaneous increases in specialization sharply boosted the productivity of labor during the 1920s (see Table 10-1, column 5). Teamed with the relative ineffectiveness of labor unions in boosting wage rates during this era, these productivity increases caused labor costs per unit of output to decline. The resulting expansion of profit margins created an environment of business optimism, which in turn was conducive to further investment spending. Moreover, the stock market boom which accompanied the good times of the decade inflated stock prices, thereby creating conditions very favorable for business borrowing and investing.

But the end of the decade brought an abrupt halt to this vigorous economic growth.

□ The Thirties: The Great Depression

In October of 1929 the stock market collapsed, ushering in the most severe and prolonged depression of modern times. GNP plummeted from $103.4 billion in 1929 to a low of $55.8 billion in 1933. Unemployment rose from 1.6 million to 12.8 million in the same period (lines 5 and 25 of the table on the inside covers). Recall that unemployment was an incredible 25 percent of the labor force in 1933.

Just as a high level of investment spending

was the backbone of the booming twenties, so a low and sagging level of investment was the major weight that pulled American capitalism into the economic chaos of the thirties. Gross investment spending contracted from $16.2 billion in 1929 to $1.4 billion in 1933 (line 2 of the table)—a 90 percent decline! To a considerable degree, the reasons behind this decline in investment spending have their roots in those factors which underlay the high level of investment of the booming twenties.

1 Excess Industrial Capacity The new industries whose growth underscored the prosperity of the 1920s reached maturity late in that decade. The rapid expansion of these adolescent industries had occurred at a rate which could not be indefinitely maintained. The markets for these new consumer durables were becoming saturated. Hence, the rate of investment in the automobile and related industries began to level off and decline in the early 1930s. Much the same pattern applied to other industries whose growth had been vigorous in the 1920s. Overexpansion in the previous decade came home to roost in the 1930s.

2 The Decline in Residential Construction The 1920s was also an era of overbuilding. The high level of construction was partially war-deferred construction; building occurred at a rapid rate in the 1920s to make up for the construction that was forgone during the emergency of World War I. And in part the decline in construction was due to a decline in the rate of population growth during the late twenties. In any event, spending on construction began to level off as early as 1926, residential construction leading the decline. By the late twenties, the construction industry had virtually collapsed.

3 The Heavy Hand of Debt Indebtedness expanded rapidly and became abnormally large as the economy burgeoned in the 1920s. This indebtedness assumed three basic forms: consumer credit, mortgage credit, and indebtedness for stock purchases. The growth of consumer credit—installment buying—had accompanied the development of the various new industries producing consumer durables in the 1920s. The building boom of the 1920s gave rise to heavy mortgage commitments on residential housing and commercial real estate.

The result of this tremendous growth in indebtedness was that, by the late twenties, much of the income of businesses and households was committed for the payment of interest and principal on past purchases, and hence not available for current expenditures. As expenditures declined, so did incomes and prices. And income declines prompted creditors to liquidate their claims as readily as possible. This was evidenced in a rising tide of business failures and mortgage foreclosures.

4 The Stock Market Crash The most dramatic facet of the Great Depression was the stock market crash of October 1929.[10] The optimism of the prosperous twenties had elevated stock market speculation to something of a national pastime. This speculation had bid up stock prices to the point where they were decidedly out of touch with reality; that is, the prices of stocks were far beyond the profit-making potentials of the issuing firms. The necessary downward adjustment came with a vengeance in 1929. It was sudden, violent, cumulative.[11]

> In that awful last week of October, 1929, the market collapsed. . . . The grim jokes of the period speak for themselves: it was said that with every share of Goldman Sachs you got a complimentary revolver, and that when you booked a hotel room the clerk inquired, "For sleeping or jumping?"

As already noted, many stock purchases had been made on credit. Speculators found them-

---

[10] For a fascinating account of this aspect of the Great Depression, read John Kenneth Galbraith's *The Great Crash 1929* (Boston: Houghton Mifflin Company, 1961).
[11] Robert L. Heilbroner, *The Worldly Philosophers*, 4th ed. (New York: Simon & Schuster, Inc., 1972), p. 242.

selves hopelessly in debt, with only pieces of now worthless paper as reward for their efforts.

The stock market crash had significant secondary effects. Most important was the accompanying unfavorable psychological repercussions; the buoyant optimism of the 1920s gave way to a wave of crippling pessimism. In particular, the crashing of stock prices created most unfavorable conditions for acquiring additional money capital for investment or for any other purpose.

5 Shrinking of the Money Supply
Closely allied with the stock market crash and the rapid contraction of indebtedness was a very sharp reduction in the money supply in the early years of the Depression. The money supply of $26.4 billion of 1929 shrunk to $19.8 billion by 1933 (line 22 of the table on the inside covers). This shrinkage was the result of certain complex forces operating both at home and abroad. In part, the shrinkage was tied to the stock market crash and its effect upon the value of bank-held assets. In part, it was the result of faulty policies invoked by the monetary authorities. In part, it stemmed from the very structure of the banking system—a large number of small and relatively weak banks. The important point for our purposes is that this drastic reduction in the supply of money contributed to the sharp decline in the volume of spending which characterized the early 1930s.

6 Other Considerations Though we have touched upon the major considerations underlying the Great Depression, many other factors also entered the picture. For example, the enactment of restrictive tariffs, designed to shield domestic workers and their jobs from the rigors of international competition, backfired, dealing a death blow to the already declining volume of international trade. Rather than preserve jobs, higher tariffs only reduced trade and further intensified unemployment. Moreover, drought conditions added materi-

ally to the woes of the agricultural segment of the economy in the mid-thirties. All these factors and more combined to turn the booming twenties into the stagnant thirties.

An outstanding feature of the Great Depression was its length. Some economists felt it marked the beginning of an era of "secular stagnation." The dynamic, expansive forces of American capitalism were allegedly losing their force, to the end that persistent unemployment was to be the lot of the United States. But darkening war clouds in Europe were soon to resolve the persistent unemployment of the 1930s.[12]

□ **The Forties: Prosperity and Inflation**

Prosperity and inflation were the economic bywords of the 1940–1949 decade. The mobilization of 1940 and 1941 and the all-out war effort of 1942 to 1945 paved the way for a vivid economic contrast with the depressed thirties. War has one great economic virtue—it creates jobs for the unemployed. But governmental expenditures in financing World War II did more than create jobs and boost output; they also gave rise to considerable inflationary pressure. Although this pressure was repressed by direct governmental controls during the war, it broke loose at the cessation of hostilities to boost the price level sharply in the postwar era. We divide this decade into the war years (1940 to 1945) and the postwar years (1946 to 1949). Although prosperity was a main feature of both periods, underlying causal factors differed.

□ **The War Years (1940 to 1945)**

The root causes of prosperity in the early forties contrast vividly with those which produced good times in the twenties:

---

[12] The 1930 depression continues to have a special fascination for economists. See Lester V. Chandler, *America's Greatest Depression: 1929–1941* (New York: Harper & Row, Publishers, Incorporated, 1970).

1 The Upsurge of Military Spending

Sharp increases in government military spending underlay the upsurge in output and employment which characterized the 1940–1945 period. As line 3 of the table on the inside covers clearly indicates, government spending boomed from $14.2 billion in 1940 to a peak of $97 billion by 1944. This tremendous expansion in armaments expenditures took many a worker out of the breadline and put them in the production line of a defense plant.

2 Rising Incomes and Consumer Spending

With employment and incomes rising as a result of increased government spending, we should not be surprised to find that consumption spending increased during the war years. It did: the $71 billion consumption level of 1940 rose steadily to $119.5 billion by 1945 and was destined to increase even more sharply in the postwar years (line 1 of the table on the inside covers).

3 The Rise and Forced Decline of Investment Spending

The role of investment spending provides an interesting contrast. Investment spurted significantly in 1940 and 1941, basically in response to the increased demand for war goods. By 1943, "overfull" employment was achieved; in 1944, the unemployment rate reached an unheard-of low of 1.2 percent (lines 25 and 26 of the table on the inside covers). Full employment meant that further expansion in the production of war and consumer goods had to come at the expense of the production of investment goods. This is precisely what happened. Nonessential investment spending bore the brunt of this cutback. *Net* private domestic investment was negative throughout the height of the war effort in order to free as many resources as possible for the immediate production of war goods (lines 2 and 6 of the table). The nation "lived off its capital" during the 1942–1945 period, as was evidenced by a decline in its accumulated stock of capital.

4 Expansion of the Money Supply

Monetary factors played a significant role in the wartime boom. In the six years between 1939 and 1945 the nation's supply of money almost tripled! The 1939 money supply of about $36.2 billion rose to $102.4 billion by 1945 (line 22). This expansion made possible the tremendous increase in economic activity which the war necessitated.

5 Wartime Inflationary Pressures

By 1943, the American economy had clearly hit the production barrier of full employment. But the total level of spending continued to rise, government and consumption spending leading the way. The inevitable result of spending more and more dollars on a relatively fixed amount of goods is inflation. And war is highly inflationary: it pours money into the pockets of civilians and military personnel but fails to turn out civilian goods at a matching rate (Figure 39-3).

During the war, however, this inflationary pressure was repressed with considerable success by a bevy of government controls. Price and wage controls were aimed directly at holding the lid on inflation. At the same time, tax increases and intensive war-bond campaigns tried to drain off excessive purchasing power to reduce spending and thereby relieve the pressure on prices. All things considered, these programs were quite successful in postponing inflation until the postwar era. After the war, significant increases in the general price level did occur.

☐ The Postwar Years (1946 to 1949)

As the war drew to a successful close, forecasts of a severe postwar depression clouded the air. Drastic declines in government military spending were expected to precipitate such a crisis. But, aside from a mild setback in 1945–1946, prosperity and economic growth persisted into the postwar era. The reasons once again lay in the components of total demand. The drastic $55.3 billion *decline* in government spending which occurred between 1945 and 1946 (line 3 of the table on the inside covers) was largely offset by a $52.6 billion *increase* in private (consumption, investment, and foreign) spending (lines 1, 2, and 4). Aside from a brief recession in 1949, the levels of consumption and investment spending increased in the immediate postwar years to the extent that rather serious inflation resulted.

1 The Investment Backlog, Reconversion, and the Housing Shortage The desire to replace capital facilities used up during the war years created a large backlog of demand for capital goods. The need to modernize existing capital facilities, plus the reconversion to civilian production, added to this high level of demand for investment goods. Furthermore, the chronic problem of a housing shortage had reached acute proportions, with the result that the postwar era unleashed a sharp increase in residential construction activity.

2 Government and the Climate for Investment At the war's end, the Federal government passed the Employment Act of 1946, expressing a readiness to take positive steps to correct any serious deviations from full employment. This assurance undoubtedly provided a favorable psychological climate for the resulting high level of investment.

3 Net Exports and Postwar Aid Net exports also jumped sharply in the postwar era as foreign nations, flush with American loans and Marshall Plan dollars, eagerly sought American goods to aid in the reconstruction of their war-torn economies (line 4 of the table).

4 The Postwar Consumption Boom The lion's share of the drop in government military spending was filled by an abrupt increase in consumer spending. As line 1 of the table on the inside covers indicates, consumer spending jumped by over $24 billion between 1945 and 1946.

A host of factors contributed to the high level of consumption spending which persisted in the postwar years. First, the wartime unavailability of consumer durables meant that consumers emerged from the war with a backlog of demands for automobiles, washing machines, refrigerators, and so forth. Second, consumers had the means of financing a high volume of expenditures. Not only were current money incomes at record levels, but consumers had accumulated a huge volume of savings in the form of government bonds and other highly liquid assets during the war. This purchasing power was supplemented by (1) a hasty cut in personal taxes (line 15 of the table), (2) a significant increase in government transfer payments to veterans (line 13), and (3) rapid growth in the volume of consumer credit (line 27). Finally, on top of all this, prices were already rising and showed little sign of falling; it seemed sensible therefore to "spend now" before further price increases occurred. All these factors contributed to a consumer spending orgy.

5 Postwar Inflation High levels of spending not only maintained full employment in the postwar era; they also brought rather sharp inflation. Government was able to do a fair job of repressing inflationary pressure during the war. But it was politically impossible to hold the lid on the inflationary kettle once hostilities ended. Wartime wage and price controls met a sudden death in 1946, and the field was clear for open inflation to move into the economic spotlight. Successive rounds of wage and price increases were the order of the day, and the cost of living spiraled upward. As a result, the consumer price index, which stood at a relatively innocent 53.9 percent in 1945, had soared to 72.1 percent by 1948 (line 20 of the table). This spending spree leveled off in 1949, and the result was a mild recession. But the Korean conflict in 1950 quickly pushed the vision of depression to one side. Specifically, the Korean hostilities bolstered both government spending and consumer spending—the former because of the need for increased military outlays and the latter because households anticipated and wanted to "beat" war-born inflation and product shortages. As American capitalism entered the fifties, inflation was still the major economic problem of the day.

□   The Fifties: Economic Kaleidoscope

The decade of the 1950s is not easily assessed. On the one hand, the period was generally characterized by overall prosperity and the attainment of an unprecedented level of affluence. On the other hand, there was some inflation, two troublesome recessions, and a weakening of the growth rate late in the decade. Again, the general picture is explainable in terms of the major components of total spending.

The Korean Conflict and the 1954 Recession   We have already noted that the invasion of South Korea in 1950 stimulated anticipatory buying by consumers and business managers, most of whom expected shortages of goods and materials and inflated prices to result. This was followed in 1951 by a substantial increase in armament spending by the Federal government. The result was a buoyant, expanding economy in the 1950–1953 period. Total spending was high enough to induce substantial increases in real GNP and, in the 1951–1953 period, an unemployment rate of approximately 3 percent of the labor force (lines 17 and 25 of the table). In fact, total spending was sufficiently strong to cause significant inflation; the consumer price index rose from 72.1 in 1950 to 79.5 by 1952 (line 20).

But then came a readjustment. The war-born upsurge in consumer spending was too great to be sustainable, and in 1953 and 1954 consumption expenditures leveled off. Businesses, having geared their production to the 1951–1952 high levels of consumption, found themselves with overlarge inventories of goods. The resulting cutback in production, coupled with a gradual reduction in Federal military spending as the Korean conflict drew to a close, paved the way for the relatively mild "inventory recession" in 1954.

The 1955–1957 Durable Goods Boom   The 1954 recession might have been much more severe in duration and intensity were it not for the fact that long-term investment spending on machinery, equipment, and construction held up during this period. There were several factors which contributed to the stability of long-term investment:

1 Technological advances and continued long-term growth in population and incomes bolstered business investment in plant and equipment.

2 Population growth and governmental provision of favorable credit policies sustained the postwar demand for residential construction.

3 The expenditures of state and local governments on schools, highways, and similar social goods continued to expand steadily.

These investment-stimulating factors teamed with a rapidly expanding demand for consumer durables (particularly automobiles) to make 1955 a year of vigorous economic expansion. Substantial growth in consumer credit in 1954 and 1955 (line 27) and the increased demand for furniture and appliances which accompanied the high rate of residential construction were factors in this expansion of consumer spending on durables. Real GNP surged from $614 to $655 billion between 1954 and 1955. In 1956 and 1957, expenditures for residential housing and automobiles fell rather significantly, and, despite continued strong expenditures for plant and equipment and growing expenditures by state and local governments, the economy plateaued. As a result, although prosperity was sustained in 1956 and 1957, these were years of only modest economic growth. Note (line 26 of table) that unemployment hovered slightly above the full-employment mark of 4 percent in the entire 1955–1957 period.

The 1958 Recession and Recovery

Though the 1958 recession was brief—lasting less than a year—it was also the most severe of the post-World War II recessions thus far encountered. Note (line 17 of table) that real GNP actually fell by more than $1 billion between 1957 and 1958. Unemployment rose to 6.8 percent of the labor force—clearly the highest figure since the end of the war (line 26). The basic cause of this recession was a substantial decline in business investment in machinery and equipment—a decline which was in part a reaction to the leveling of consumer spending in 1956 and 1957. In addition, the enactment of restrictive credit policies by the government in seeking to restrain the price level probably contributed to the downturn by also restraining purchases of housing and consumer durables. Furthermore, the automobile industry simultaneously encountered both market saturation and strong foreign competition.

Increased spending on consumer durables, an expansion of residential construction (aided by governmentally eased credit conditions), and increased government spending all underlay recovery in 1959. Increases in state and local government spending stemmed from continually expanding outlays on school and highway construction, whereas increases in Federal spending reflected an intensification of the cold war and, in no small measure, a reaction to Russia's orbiting of Sputnik I.

Lagging Growth   One of the most distressing features of the fifties was the slowing down of the growth rate during the latter part of the decade. While the average annual growth rate in real GNP in the early postwar period had been on the order of $4\frac{1}{2}$ percent, this figure fell to about $2\frac{1}{2}$ percent in the later 1950s. This sluggishness of the economy was reflected in a rising unemployment rate (lines 25 and 26) and in a widening GNP gap (Figure 10-2). Virtually all other industrially advanced economies of the world were achieving growth rates superior to that of the United States.

Many explanations were offered for this slowing down of the economy. Some held that the high growth rates of earlier years were a consequence of economic stimuli associated with World War II and Korea, and that, in the late fifties, the economy was readjusting to a normal and lower growth rate. Others felt that insufficient investment—the result of high interest rates and declining profits—was the cause of the problem. Still others contended that, ironically, the character and pace of technological progress were creating a growing problem of structural unemployment; automation was creating blocs of technologically unemployed blue-collar workers whose training and skills were inappropriate for reemployment in new, expanding white-collar industries. And, finally, others held that the fiscal system of the Federal government—the economy's primary stabilization device—was actually exerting a contractionary effect on the economy, keeping unemployment above, and growth below, desired rates. The argument here was that the progressiveness of the Federal tax system was resulting in the withdrawal of more and more purchasing power from the economy each year as the national income expanded; this withdrawal made it increasingly difficult to achieve a level of total spending high enough to maintain full employment and a rapid growth rate (Chapter 13). The point to note at this juncture is that the related problems of slow growth and above-normal unemployment were major concerns as the economy entered the sixties.

☐   The Sixties: A Mixed Bag

Marred in 1959 by the longest steel strike in American history, the recovery from the 1958 recession was neither rapid nor complete. Each of the postwar recessions seemed to leave a larger and larger residue of unemployed workers. Newspaper headlines which had lamented "creeping inflation" in the early 1950s were speaking of "creeping unemployment" as the 1960s began. Thus, in 1960, the economy was marking time in another recession.

The Long Expansion   But then, in early 1961, the economy began an unprecedented period of expansion which was to last most of the decade. As is typically the case, several causal factors can be identified.

Perhaps the major factor in this long expansion was the economic policies which occurred under the Kennedy-Johnson administrations. In brief, these policies called for government to manipulate its tax collections and expenditures in such a way as to stimulate total demand, thereby reducing unemployment and increasing the rate of growth. For example, in 1962 legislation was enacted which provided for a 7 percent tax credit on investment in new machinery and equipment, thereby strengthening incentives to invest. However, the major government stimulus to the economy came in 1964 when taxes were cut by some $11 billion. This boosted corporate profits and personal income, stimulating investment and consumer spending in turn. Unemployment fell from 5.2 percent in 1964 to 4.5 percent in 1965.

At this point, a second major expansionary force came into play: the escalation of the war in Vietnam. Expenditures for national defense rose from $50 billion in 1965 to $70 billion in 1967. A further $10 billion increase followed in 1968. Simultaneously, the draft claimed more and more young people from the ranks of the unemployed.

There were undoubtedly other factors which contributed to the long expansion. The spending of state and local governments rose steadily and substantially in the 1960s, reflecting acute problems in education, highway construction, urban renewal, and the like. In the private sector, the crucial automobile industry continued to enjoy record-breaking years as the result of suburban growth and the increasing numbers of young people who were reaching driving age. Business investment was

stimulated not only by the 1964 tax cut, but also by a rapid rate of technological progress.

As a result of all these stimulative forces, the economy achieved full employment and a high rate of economic growth. The unemployment rate remained below 4 percent during the entire 1966–1969 period.

A Stubborn Inflation   Prior to the upsurge of military spending in 1965, economic expansion entailed only modest inflation. The consumer price index (line 20 of the table on the inside covers) rose from 89.6 in 1961 to only 92.9 in 1964. But then, as unemployment fell below 4 percent, price inflation began to accelerate. In fact, the economic demands of Vietnam, imposed upon an already booming economy, brought about the worst inflation in nearly two decades. The consumer price index jumped from 97.2 in 1966 to 116.3 in 1970 (line 20). Initially, this inflation was of a "demand-pull" character; that is, rising total demand—spearheaded by government military spending—pulled up the price level. But rising prices and the accompanying low level of unemployment generated growing pressure for wage increases. The resulting boosts in wage costs were passed on by businesses to consumers in the form of higher prices, and inflation began to assume more of a "cost-push" character.

□   **The Turbulent Seventies**

Thus the 1970s began on a sour economic note. In response to the rather alarming inflation of 1966–1969, the Federal government undertook policies in 1969 to restrict total demand and thereby curtail the rate of price increases. But the inflation proved stubborn and difficult to contain. In fact, the unexpected impact of the government's demand-restricting policies was to increase unemployment. In December 1969, the unemployment rate was a mere 3.5 percent; exactly a year later, the rate had climbed to 6.1 percent and it hovered near 6 percent all through 1971 and into early 1972. Worse yet, the price level continued to rise; the consumer price index jumped from 116.3 in 1970 to 125.3 in 1972.

Stagflation and Controls Thus the early 1970s seemed to embody the worst of all macroeconomic worlds—high unemployment rates and a rapidly rising price level. This combination of stagnation in the growth of real output, coupled with inflation, has been dubbed *stagflation*. The basic dilemma confronting the Nixon administration was how to stimulate employment and growth without accelerating (and, it was hoped, ameliorating) the rate of inflation. President Nixon's response to this awkward state of affairs was contained in his New Economic Policy (NEP), announced on August 15, 1971. To stimulate employment and growth, the administration proposed a package of tax reductions, including an increase in the income tax exemption, a special tax credit for business investment in new machinery and equipment, and elimination of the existing excise tax on automobiles.

Problem: What would prevent the increases in private spending, induced by these tax reductions, from being translated into additional inflation rather than into increases in employment and real output? *Solution:* the imposition of mandatory wage and price controls. Unprecedented in peacetime, these controls began with a 90-day freeze on wages, prices, and rents which was followed by a far-reaching system of wage and price controls administered by the Cost of Living Council. The longer-term purpose of the freeze and the ensuing controls was to undermine the inflationary expectations—the "inflationary psychosis"—which seemed to underlie the persistent wage-price inflationary spiral. The controls were liberalized over time and expired in the spring of 1974. The rates of wage and price increases did diminish somewhat in 1972, but economists disagree as to whether the decline was attributable to the controls or to other forces, for example, the continuance of above-normal levels of unemployment.

The Mid-Seventies: A Bad Scene The Nixon policies not only brought about economic expansion in time for the 1972 election; they also set the stage for a dramatic reassertion of inflationary pressures in the 1973–1975 period. Consider the unlikely mixture of inflation-causing forces which were at work. First, a series of worldwide agricultural shortfalls—combined with rapidly rising foreign incomes—increased the demand for American farm products. The result was sharp increases in food prices in the United States. Second, the OPEC oil cartel became effective in late 1973 and crude oil prices quadrupled. The ensuing increases in energy prices quickly permeated the economy. Third, to cope with our increasingly acute balance of payments problem (Chapter 44), the United States effectively devalued the dollar, that is, we made the dollar cheaper to foreigners. This obviously meant that United States goods were less expensive and more attractive to foreigners. Hence, foreign demand for our exports boomed (see line 4 of the cover table), adding to the inflationary pressure. Fourth, as these inflationary forces filtered through the economy, they triggered wage- and price-push pressures. Workers bargained aggressively for money-wage increases to keep up with, or push ahead of, the rising price level. Businesses, confronted with rising costs, used their market power to raise product prices. Finally, government efforts to protect the environment were contributing to inflation by internalizing spillover costs (Chapter 6). For example, automobile manufacturers were forced to improve their emission systems, but the improvements raised the costs and prices of cars substantially. The net result of the convergence of all these forces was the most rapid inflation since World War II. The percentage increase in the consumer price index was almost 9 percent in 1973; in 1974 we experienced double-digit inflation of over 12 percent!

The most remarkable and disconcerting fact, however, was that this inflation was accompanied by our most severe postwar recession. The unemployment rate of 4.9 percent in 1973 rose to 5.6 percent in 1974 and onward to 8.5 percent in 1975 (see line 26 of the cover table). Real GNP actually *declined* in 1974 and 1975. Why would inflation and recession occur simultaneously? After all, Figure 10-1 suggests that a rising price level should be associated with high and rising levels of output and employment. The basic complication in the 1973–1975 case was that the inflation was caused, *not* by a rising or excessive level of demand as is assumed in Figure 10-1, but by forces operating on the supply or cost side of the market. Hence, many economists agree, when the Federal government used restrictive fiscal and monetary policies to fight the inflation, the result was counterproductive: the restricted demand caused output to fall and unemployment to rise, but inflation—fueled by forces largely divorced from total demand—continued unabated. Bluntly stated, the recession was in some measure the result of a serious policy blunder. Furthermore, the downswing was largely a "consumer recession" in that the rapid inflation eroded the real income or purchasing power of consumers. The sharp increase in oil prices, for example, was tantamount to a gigantic excise tax—estimated at $35 billion in 1974—with the OPEC countries as "tax collectors." This meant less income was available to spend on autos, housing, television sets, and so forth. Recall, too, that personal and corporate income taxes *usually* function as a built-in stabilizer in that as real and money incomes increase during an expansionary period, tax payments automatically rise and thereby constrain the boom (Chapter 8). But in this case the inflation caused *money* incomes and tax payments to rise even though *real* income was falling. The added tax payments simply reduced after-tax real incomes further, tending to curtail consumer spending and intensify the recession. We will have much more to say later in Chapter 18 about the turbulent and unexpected economic events of the 1970s.

□ **Four Observations**

Our historical examination of the economic ups and downs of American capitalism yields several noteworthy points:

1 Complexity The business cycle is clearly a complex phenomenon. In particular, the factors which cause or contribute to prosperity and depression are most diverse. Though the immediate cause of the business cycle is change in the volume of spending, we find that a host of different factors influences the course of total spending. Such diverse considerations as innovations, changes in the volume of indebtedness, productivity changes, business and consumer expectations, wars, droughts, population changes, and governmental policies at home and abroad all make for variations in total spending and, hence, in the level of economic activity.

2 Variability of Investment The variability of investment spending as a component of total spending also deserves mention. A surging level of investment was the backbone of the prosperous twenties. Similarly, a declining volume of investment ushered in the prolonged depression of the thirties. Sharp increases in investment helped fill the gap left by declining governmental spending at the close of World War II. Our review of recent business-cycle experience strongly suggests that the forces which contribute most to economic instability are those which bear upon the decisions of business executives to invest.

3 Money Changes in the money supply have a substantial effect upon the level of economic activity. The catastrophic depression of the 1930s was intensified by a sharp contraction of the money supply; in contrast, the burgeoning prosperity of World War II was accompanied by rapid monetary expansion. Part 3 focuses upon the money supply and its relationship to employment, output, and the price level.

4 Multiplier Effect Finally, our discussion suggests that, within limits, upswings and downswings in business activity tend to be cumulative. To illustrate: When the nation is at less than full employment, increases in, say, investment spending give rise to increases in output and employment. A higher level of employment means rising incomes, which prompt further increases in spending. Further increases in spending mean still further increases in output, employment, and incomes. The reverse interactions tend to occur as an initial decline in total spending causes the economy to backslide from a full-employment level of performance. Later (Chapter 12) we shall formalize this cumulative character of business fluctuations in the *multiplier* concept.

PROSPECTS FOR STABILITY

In the late 1960s economists viewed our postwar economic experience with both satisfaction and confidence; some talked in terms of a "depression-proof economy." Indeed, the historical record seemed to indicate that the economy was now less vulnerable to cyclical fluctuations than in earlier times. And it was not difficult to cite a variety of reasons to explain the greater stability. (1) The economy now contains a number of "built-in stabilizers" which automatically tend to dampen changes in the level of economic activity. In particular, recall from Chapter 8 that the progressive income tax automatically increases tax revenues during inflation and trims tax bills during recession. To the same end, unemployment compensation helps maintain the incomes and consumption levels of temporarily unemployed workers. (2) Our banking and financial systems have been strengthened not only through improved policies, but also because of better systems of insurance and public supervision. (3) The occupational structure of the labor force has changed historically from cyclically volatile industries to jobs which are sheltered from unemployment. (4) The fact that the public sector has expanded both absolutely and relatively has also contributed to economic stability for the simple reason that government expenditures are not geared to expected profits. (5) The science of economics has made important strides during the postwar period. In particular, new knowledge has been developed concerning how to manipulate government spending and tax revenues (fiscal policy) and the supply of money (monetary policy) in such a way as to influence total spending and therefore total output and the price level.

But the disquieting stagflation of the 1970s has seriously diminished the confidence of economists in themselves and in the stability of the economy. The 1973–1976 period encompassed both the highest rates of inflation *and* the highest rates of unemployment of the entire postwar era. Thus economists now find themselves questioning existing theories of inflation and unemployment and the associated policy prescriptions. This agonizing reappraisal of economic thought will be detailed in Chapter 18. For the moment, let us merely stress that economists, political leaders, and the general public are all decidedly less certain than they were a decade ago that the roaring lion of the business cycle has been transformed into a gentle lamb.

Summary

1 The level of spending determines the levels of output, employment, and incomes in American capitalism. Demand-pull inflation becomes increasingly severe as the economy approaches full employment; an increase in total spending at full employment tends to boost the price level sharply. The general price level is more flexible upward than downward.

2   It is considered normal for some 4 percent of the labor force to be unemployed in our economy. The economic cost of unemployment, as measured by the GNP gap, consists of the goods and services which society forgoes when its resources are involuntarily idle. Unemployment is also conducive to a deterioration of national morale and to social and political unrest.

3   Inflation—a rising general level of prices—is usually caused by excessive spending, although in recent years supply (cost) factors have become increasingly important. Deflation is caused by a deficiency of total spending. Inflation redistributes income at the expense of fixed-income receivers, creditors, and savers. Deflation has substantially the reverse effects.

4   Economists disagree as to the effect which mild inflation may have upon the level of performance achieved by the economy. Some argue that modest inflation is essential in achieving full employment and maximum economic expansion. Another group feels that, over time, mild inflation has substantial and undesirable redistributive effects and that it is likely to precipitate hyperinflation and economic collapse by causing a breakdown in the monetary system and diverting otherwise productive energies to speculative activities.

5   Although characterized by common phases—recession, depression, recovery, and prosperity—business cycles vary greatly in duration and intensity.

6   All sectors of the economy are affected by the business cycle, but in varying ways and degrees. The cycle has greater output and employment ramifications in the capital goods and durable consumer goods industries than it does in nondurable goods industries. Over the cycle, price fluctuations are greater in competitive than in monopolistic industries.

7   Historically, American capitalism has fostered both vigorous expansion and stagnation. An examination of our business cycle experience suggests that *a.* the factors which bear upon total spending and hence output, employment, and the price level are many and varied; *b.* variations in investment play a crucial role in cyclical fluctuations; *c.* changes in the money supply affect economic activity; and *d.* within limits, prosperity and depression are cumulative.

Questions and Study Suggestions

1   Key terms and concepts to remember: macroeconomic triology; demand-pull inflation; premature inflation; pure inflation; frictional, structural, and cyclical unemployment; full employment; GNP gap; inflation and deflation; money and real income; creeping and hyperinflation; rule of 70; inflationary psychosis; business cycle; seasonal variation; secular trend; stagflation.

2   Carefully describe the relationship between total spending and the level of resource utilization. Explain the relationship between the price level and increases in total spending as the economy moves from substantial unemployment to moderate unemployment and, finally, to full employment. What is the significance of this relationship? "Inflation is a friend on the journey to full employment, but an enemy once the destination is reached." Evaluate and explain. Explain how severe inflation might lead to unemployment.

3   Carefully define "full employment." Why is it difficult to distinguish between frictional, structural, and cyclical unemployment? Why is unemployment an economic problem? What are the consequences of the "GNP gap"? What are the noneconomic effects of unemployment?

4   Explain how an *increase* in your money income and a *decrease* in your real income might occur simultaneously.

5   Evaluate as accurately as you can the manner in which each of the following individuals would be affected by fairly rapid inflation:

a.   a pensioned railroad worker

b.   a department-store clerk

c.   a UAW assembly-line worker

d.   a heavily indebted farmer

e.   a retired businessman whose current income comes entirely from interest on government bonds

f.   the owner of an independent smalltown department store

6   A noted television comedian once defined inflation as follows: "Inflation? That means your money today won't buy as much as it would have during the depression when you didn't have any." Is his definition accurate?

7   What are the major phases of the business cycle? How long do business cycles last? How do seasonal variations and secular trends complicate measurement of the business cycle? Why does the business cycle affect durable goods industries more severely than industries producing nondurables?

8   Briefly outline the major factors which contributed to the prosperity of the 1920s. Now explain the basic considerations underlying the Great Depression of the 1930s. What relationships, if any, can you cite between the causes of the booming twenties and the depressed thirties?

9   Explain the extended period of overall prosperity which we enjoyed after World War II. How do you account for the "long expansion" of the 1960s? What is the likelihood of another Great Depression?

10   Can you reconcile the stagflation of the mid-1970s with Figure 10-1?

Selected References

Bach, G. L.: "Inflation: Who Gains and Who Loses?" *Challenge,* July–August 1974, pp. 48–55.

Economic Report of the President (Washington, D.C.). Published annually.

Gordon, Robert Aaron: *Economic Instability & Growth: The American Record* (New York: Harper & Row, Publishers, Incorporated, 1974).

Lekachman, Robert: *Inflation: The Permanent Problem of Boom and Bust* (New York: Random House, Inc., 1973).

U.S. Department of Commerce: *Survey of Current Business.* January issues survey the economy's performance in the preceding year.

Last Word
Inflation in Japan: Up, Up and Away

The following excerpt dramatizes the impact of inflation upon a Japanese working-class family.

Last year at this time, Kinichi Kurihara was sitting pretty. As a driller at Tokyo's giant Ishikawajima-Harima shipyard, the 35-year-old Kurihara was pulling down $394 a month plus overtime and bonuses. He lived with his wife and their two small children in a tiny but comfortable apartment that they rented from his company for only $10 a month. Signs of modest affluence were all around. They had a new Sony color TV and a piano, and had recently begun buying a small vacant lot on which to build their own home. Even with all this, they were able to put a little money in the bank each month—and were looking forward this year to a Hawaiian vacation. But in the final months of 1973, life for the Kuriharas turned very sour. As prices soared higher by the day, their family budget plunged frighteningly into the red. The Kuriharas suddenly decided they could do without new winter coats, banished all thought of Honolulu and abandoned their plans to build a bungalow of their own. "Our dreams," Mrs. Kurihara lamented last week, "have been ruined by inflation."

The Kuriharas are hardly alone. In recent weeks, the bubble of the postwar economic miracle has burst for millions of other Japanese as the cost of living climbed at the fastest rate since the government began keeping tabs on it in 1952. In the first ten days of December, the wholesale price index jumped an astounding 3.5 per cent—and figures due out shortly are expected to show almost a 30 per cent rise in the index for the whole of 1973 (compared with an estimated 17 per cent in the U.S. during the same period). What's more, major Japanese banks predict that prices will increase at the same rate for at least the next year. Adding to the squeeze on wage earners is the dramatic slowdown—aggravated by Arab oil cutbacks—of what a year ago was regarded as the "unstoppable" Japanese economy. . . .

While prices have been soaring across the entire spectrum of the Japanese economy, nowhere has inflation been felt more keenly than in the supermarket. In the first three weeks of November, Mrs. Kurihara spent $47 on food. In the first three weeks of December, she spent $81—even though the Kuriharas were forced to give up eating meat entirely. Huge price hikes are noticeable not just from week to week, but even from hour to hour. "I paid 53 cents for a carton of milk one morning this week," Mrs. Kurihara said, "and six hours later they had marked it up to 72 cents." In an effort to keep up with food prices, Mrs. Kurihara has taken to going down to the supermarket two or three times a day. "I feel like a fool," she said, "but we all do it."

With prices rising so rapidly, many Japanese have turned to hoarding. With considerable embarrassment, Mrs. Kurihara pulled up the woven-reed tatamis on her floor and revealed a cache of 55 pounds of potatoes, 50 pounds of onions, 66 pounds of sugar, six large cartons of hand soap, a dozen light bulbs and 30 rolls of toilet paper. "During the war, people used to do this secretly," she said. "Now, they do it openly." The hoarding has created a number of shortages, and Mrs. Kurihara and her neighbors tip each other off when they spot hard-to-find items. "Some of my neighbors," she said, "even use ham radios to pass the word."

While runaway inflation has forced the Kuriharas to scale down their standard of living, they are still managing to get by. But there are signs that things may get considerably tougher in the months ahead. During the boom times, Kurihara came to count on earning an extra $72 to $108 a month in overtime pay. Last week, the shipyard informed him that there would be no more overtime until further notice. Yet for all the gloomy projections, Japanese are continuing to spend as freely as ever. "My brother-in-law just came back from Guam," Mrs. Kurihara said, "with a fancy cigarette lighter he paid $107 for. It was a good buy, he told us, because in Japan it would cost $180." And then, more reflectively, she added: "Isn't that crazy? I feel like we are living the last days of Rome—with the Prime Minister playing the violin like Emperor Nero while Tokyo burns."

"Japan: Up, Up and Away," *Newsweek*, Jan. 7, 1974, pp. 35–36. Copyright Newsweek, Inc. 1974 reprinted by permission.

The Background and Analytical Tools of Employment Theory

This and the following chapter are concerned with assessing the ability of a capitalistic economy to achieve the full employment of its resources. If the price system can provide for a reasonably efficient allocation of resources, what is to prevent it from providing for the full utilization of society's available resources?

More specifically, the objectives of the present chapter are threefold: In the first place, we want to understand why for many years economists thought capitalism was capable of providing for virtually uninterrupted full employment. Involved here is a discussion of the so-called classical theory of employment. Second, the shortcomings of the classical theory will be noted and analyzed. Then, finally, the tools of modern employment theory will be introduced and explained. In Chapters 12 and 13 we shall employ these tools to analyze the equilibrium levels of output and employment and extend our analysis to indicate the effects of government policies upon output and employment.

Three simplifying assumptions will greatly facilitate the achievement of these stated objectives:

1 A "closed economy" will be assumed. That is, our discussion will deal with the domestic economy, deferring the complications arising from international trade transactions until later chapters.

2 Government will be ignored until Chapter 13, thereby permitting us in Chapters 11 and 12 to determine whether or not laissez

faire capitalism is capable of achieving full employment.

3 Although saving actually occurs in both the business and household sectors of the economy, we shall speak as if all saving were personal saving.[1]

Two implications of these assumptions are noteworthy. First, assumptions 1 and 2 mean that we are omitting net exports, X_n, and government purchases, G, from our total spending equation of Chapter 9. Thus, for the time being, total spending or "aggregate demand" is comprised simply of consumption, C, and investment, I. Second, assumptions 2 and 3 permit us to treat NNP, NI, PI, and DI as being equal to one another for the simple reason that all the items which in practice distinguish them from one another are due to government (taxes and transfer payments) and business saving (see Table 9-7). This means that we can readily shift our discussion among these various output and income measures without encountering serious complications which would otherwise arise.

Now the ground is cleared to rephrase our basic question: Is capitalism able to achieve and maintain a full-employment, noninflationary total output?

THE CLASSICAL THEORY OF EMPLOYMENT

Answers to this question have varied historically. Until the Great Depression of the 1930s, many prominent economists—now called classical economists[2]—felt that the price system

[1]When using NNP as our measure of total output, it is accurate to assume that the bulk of the economy's saving is done by households. Personal saving was $78 billion and undistributed corporate profits were $18 million in 1976. If GNP were employed, however, capital consumption allowances of $180 billion would have to be included as a part of business saving, making business saving almost three times as great as personal saving.

[2]Most notable among the classical economists are John Stuart Mill, F. Y. Edgeworth, Alfred Marshall, and A. C. Pigou.

was capable of providing for the full employment of the economy's resources. It was acknowledged that now and then abnormal circumstances would arise in such forms as wars, political upheavals, droughts, speculative crises, gold rushes, and so forth, to push the economy from the path of full employment (see Figure 10-4). But it was contended that when these deviations occurred, automatic adjustments within the price system would soon restore the economy to the full-employment level of output. Though the classical theory of employment is now rejected by the vast majority of economists (including some who earlier were leaders in this school of thought), an analysis of classical thinking will lay a firm foundation for understanding modern employment theory.

The classical theory of employment was grounded on two basic notions. First, it was argued that underspending—that is, a level of spending insufficient to purchase a full-employment output—was most unlikely to occur. Second, even if a deficiency of total spending were to arise, price-wage adjustments would occur so as to ensure that the decline in total spending would not entail declines in real output, employment, and real incomes.

□ Say's Law

The classical economists' denial of the possibility of underspending was based upon their faith in Say's Law. Say's Law is the disarmingly simple notion that the very act of producing goods generates an amount of income exactly equal to the value of the goods produced. That is, the production of any output would automatically provide the wherewithal to take that output off the market. *Supply creates its own demand.*[3] The essence of Say's Law can be envisaged most easily in terms of a barter economy. A shoemaker, for

[3]Attributed to the nineteenth-century French economist J. B. Say.

example, produces or *supplies* shoes as a means of buying or *demanding* the shirts and stockings produced by other craftsmen. The shoemaker's supply of shoes *is* his demand for other goods. And so it allegedly is for other producers and for the entire economy: demand must be the same as supply! In fact, the circular flow model of the economy and national income accounting both suggest something of this sort. The income generated from the production of any level of total output would, *when spent,* be just sufficient to provide a matching total demand. Assuming that the composition of output is in accord with consumer preferences, all markets would be cleared of their output. It would seem that all that business owners need do to sell a full-employment output is to produce that output; Say's Law guarantees that there will be sufficient consumption spending for its successful disposal.

Saving: A Complicating Factor   However, there is one obvious omission in this simple application of Say's Law. Although it is an accepted truism that output gives rise to an identical amount of money income (Chapter 9), there is no guarantee that the recipients of this income will spend it all. Some income might be saved (not spent) and therefore not reflected in product demand. Saving would constitute a break, or "leakage," in the income-expenditure flows and therefore would undermine the effective operation of Say's Law. Saving is a withdrawal of funds from the income stream which will cause consumption expenditures to fall short of total output. If households saved a given portion of their incomes, supply would not create its own demand. Saving would cause a deficiency of consumption. The consequences? Unsold goods, cutbacks in production, unemployment, and fal''ng incomes.

Saving, Investment, and the Interest Rate   But the classical economists were reluctant to bow to those economists who suggested

that such a virtuous act as saving could give rise to underspending and the calamity of depression. Instead, they argued that saving would not really result in a deficiency of total demand, because each and every dollar saved would be invested by businesses. Investment would allegedly occur to compensate for any deficiency of consumer spending; that is, investment would fill any consumption gap caused by saving. Business firms, after all, do not plan to sell their entire output to consumers but, rather, to produce a considerable portion of total output in the form of capital goods for sale to one another. In other words, investment spending by businesses is a supplement or an addition to the income-expenditure stream which may fill any consumption gap arising from saving. Thus, if businesses as a group intend to invest as much as households want to save, the levels of national output and employment will remain constant. Whether or not the economy could achieve and sustain a level of spending sufficient to provide a full-employment level of output and income therefore would depend upon whether businesses were willing to invest enough to offset the amount households want to save.

The classical economists argued that capitalism contained a very special market—the *money market*—which would guarantee an equality of saving and investment plans and therefore full employment. That is, the money market—and, more specifically, the *interest rate* (the price paid for the use of money)—would see to it that dollars which leaked from the income-expenditure stream as saving would automatically reappear as dollars spent on investment goods. The rationale underlying the saving and investment equating adjustments of the interest rate was simple and, if not too carefully scrutinized, very plausible. The classical economists contended that, other things being equal, households normally prefer to consume rather than to save. The consumption of goods and services satisfies human wants; idle dollars do not. Hence, it was reasoned that consumers would save only if someone would pay them a rate of interest as a reward for their thriftiness. The greater the interest rate, the more dollars saved; that is, the saving (supply-of-dollars) curve of households would be upsloping, as shown by *S* in Figure 11-1. And who would be inclined to pay for the use of saving? None other than investors—business owners who seek (demand) money capital to replace and enlarge their plants and their stocks of capital equipment. Because the interest rate is a cost to borrowing businessmen, they will be more willing to borrow and invest at low than at high interest rates. This means that the investment (demand-for-dollars) curve of businesses is downsloping, as shown by *I* in Figure 11-1.

Classical economists concluded that the money market, wherein savers supply dollars and investors demand dollars, would establish an equilibrium price for the use of money—an equilibrium interest rate—at which the quantity of dollars saved (supplied) would equal the number of dollars invested (demanded). Saving, said the classicists, does not really constitute a break in the income-expenditure stream or a fatal flaw in Say's Law, because the money market or, more specifically, the interest rate will guarantee that each and every dollar saved will get into the hands of investors and be spent on capital equipment. Therefore, an increase in thriftiness is not a cause for social concern, because this simply shifts the supply-of-saving curve to the right. Although saving will momentarily exceed investment and perhaps cause some temporary unemployment, the surplus of saving will drive the interest rate down to a new and lower equilibrium level. And this lower interest rate will expand the volume of investment spending until it again equals the amount of saving, thereby preserving full employment. In short, changes in the interest rate would guarantee the operation of Say's Law even in an economy in which substantial saving occurs. As the classical economists saw it, the economy was analogous to a gigantic bathtub wherein the volume of water measured the levels of output and employment. Any leakage down the drain of saving would be returned to the tub through the spigot of investment. This had to be the case, because the interest rate connected the drainpipe and the spigot!

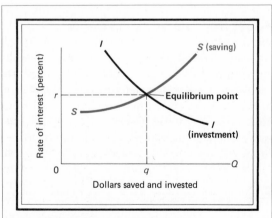

FIGURE 11-1   CLASSICAL VIEW OF THE MONEY MARKET

The classical economists believed that the saving plans of households would be reflected in a supply-of-dollars curve *S* and the investment plans of businesses in a demand-for-dollars curve *I* in the money market. The equilibrium interest rate *r*, the price paid for the use of money, would equate the amounts households and businesses planned to save and invest, thereby guaranteeing a full-employment level of spending.

□   **Price-Wage Flexibility**

The classical economists bolstered their conclusion that full employment is the norm of capitalism with a second basic argument. They argued that the level of output which business producers can sell depends not only upon the level of total spending but also upon the level of product prices. This meant that even if the interest rate should somehow temporarily fail to equate the amounts which households wanted to save with the investment intentions of businesses, any resulting decline in total spending would be offset by proportionate declines in the price level. That is, $20 will buy four shirts at $5, but $10 will buy the same number of shirts only if their price should fall to $2.50. Hence, if households somehow managed to succeed in saving more than businesses were willing to invest, the resulting decline in total spending would not result in a decline in real output, real income, and the level of employment *if* product prices declined in proportion to the decline in expenditures.

And, according to the classical economists, this is precisely what would happen. Competition among sellers would guarantee it! As declines in product demand became general, competing producers would lower their prices to dispose of accumulating surpluses. In other words, the result of saving would be to lower prices; and lower prices, by increasing the value of the dollar, would permit nonsavers to obtain more goods and services with their current money incomes. Saving would therefore lower prices, but not output and employment.

"But," ever-present skeptics have asked, "doesn't this ignore the resource market? Although businesses can sustain their sales in the face of a declining demand by accepting lower product prices, won't they find it unprofitable to do so? As product prices decline, won't resource prices—particularly wage rates—have to decline significantly to permit businesses to produce *profitability* at the now lower prices?" The classical economists replied that wage rates must and would decline. General declines in product demand would be mirrored in declines in the demand for labor and other resources. The immediate result would be a surplus of labor, that is, unemployment, at the wage rate prevailing prior to these declines in the demand for labor. However, though not willing to employ all workers at the original wage rates, producers would find it profitable to employ additional workers at lower wage rates. The demand for labor, in other words, is downsloping; those workers unable to locate employment at the old higher wage rates could find jobs at the new lower wage rates.

Would workers be willing to accept lower wage rates? Competition among unemployed workers, according to the classical economists, would guarantee it. In competing for scarce jobs, idle workers would bid down wage rates until these rates (wage costs to employers) were so low that employers would once again find it profitable to hire all available workers. This would happen at the new lower equilibrium wage rate. The classical economists therefore concluded that *involuntary unemployment* was impossible. Anyone who was willing to work at the market-determined wage rate could readily find employment. Competition in the labor market ruled out involuntary idleness.

□ **Classical Theory and Laissez Faire**

Strictly speaking, each of these price system adjustments—fluctuations in the interest rate on the one hand, and price-wage flexibility on the other—seemed fully capable of maintaining full employment in a capitalistic economy. Working together, the classical economists felt, the two adjustment mechanisms made full employment a forgone conclusion. The classical economists came to embrace capitalism as a self-regulating economy wherein full employment was regarded as the norm. Capitalism was capable of "running itself." Government assistance in the operation of the economy was deemed unnecessary—nay, harmful. In an economy capable of achieving both full production and full employment, governmental interference could only be a detriment to its efficient operation.

■
KEYNESIAN ECONOMICS

One embarrassing fact persistently denied the validity of the classical theory of employment—recurring periods of prolonged unemployment and inflation. While one might explain a minor depression, such as the brief downswings of 1924 and 1927, in terms of wars and similar external considerations, serious and prolonged downswings, such as the Great

Depression of the 1930s, were not so easily rationalized. There is a remarkable inconsistency between a theory which concludes that unemployment is virtually impossible and the actual occurrence of a ten-year siege of very substantial unemployment.[4] And so various economists came to criticize both the rationale and the underlying assumptions of classical employment theory. They tried to find a better, more realistic explanation of those forces which determine the level of employment.

Finally, in 1936 the renowned English economist John Maynard Keynes (pronounced "canes") came forth with a new explanation of the level of employment in capitalistic economies. In his *General Theory of Employment, Interest, and Money*,[5] Keynes virtually knocked the props out from under the classical view and, in doing so, touched off a major revolution in economic thinking on the question of unemployment. Although Keynes fathered modern employment theory, many others have since refined and extended his work. In this and the following chapters, we are concerned with modern employment theory, or "Keynesian economics," as it stands today.

Modern employment theory contrasts sharply with the classical position. Its blunt conclusion is that capitalism simply does not contain any mechanisms capable of guaranteeing full employment. The economy, it is argued, might come to rest—that is, reach an aggregate output equilibrium—with either considerable unemployment or severe inflation. Full employment accompanied by a relatively stable level of prices is more of an accident than a norm. Capitalism is *not* a self-regulating system capable of perpetual

prosperity; capitalism cannot be depended upon to "run itself." Furthermore, depressions should not be associated exclusively with external forces such as wars, droughts, and similar abnormalities. Rather, the causes of unemployment and inflation lie to a very considerable degree in the failure of certain fundamental economic decisions—in particular, saving and investment decisions—to be completely synchronized in a capitalistic system. Internal, in addition ω external, forces contribute to economic instability.

Modern employment theorists back these sweeping contentions by rejecting the very mechanisms upon which the classical position is grounded—the interest rate and price-wage adjustments.

☐   **The Unlinking of Saving and Investment Plans**

Modern employment theory rejects Say's Law by seriously questioning the ability of the interest rate to synchronize the saving and investment plans of households and businesses. The fact that modern capitalism is amply endowed with an elaborate money market and a wide variety of financial institutions does not diminish this skepticism about the interest rate as a mechanism capable of connecting the saving drain and the investment spigot. Most untenable is the classical contention that business firms would invest more when households increased their rates of saving. After all, does not more saving mean less consumption? Can we really expect business planners to expand their capital facilities as the markets for their products shrink? More generally, the modern view holds that savers and investors are essentially distinct groups that formulate their saving and investment plans for different reasons which, in each instance, are largely unrelated to the rate of interest.

1   Savers and Investors Are Different Groups   Who decides the amounts to be saved

---

[4]It is interesting to note that most of the classical economists stuck to their theoretical guns during the 1930s, arguing that (1) the reluctance of union and business monopolies to accept price and wage cuts, (2) misguided New Deal policies which sought to prevent price-wage declines, and (3) government policies in the area of money and banking which interfered with the operation of the interest rate prevented a quick recovery from the cyclical downswing of the early 1930s.

[5]New York: Harcourt, Brace & World, Inc., 1936.

and invested in a capitalistic economy? (We continue to ignore government in our discussion.) Business organizations of all kinds and descriptions, and, in particular, corporations, make the vast majority of investment decisions. And who makes the saving decisions? Here the picture is a bit more cluttered. In a wealthy economy such as that of American capitalism, households save substantial amounts—at least when prosperity prevails. It is true, of course, that business corporations also do a considerable amount of saving in the form of undistributed corporate profits. The important point is that to a significant degree, saving and investment decisions are made by different groups of individuals (see footnote 1 of this chapter).

2 Savers and Investors Are Differently Motivated The nonidentity of savers and investors would not necessarily be fatal to the classical theory if their decisions were motivated and synchronized by some common factor such as the interest rate. But this is not the case. Saving decisions are motivated by diverse considerations. Some save in order to make large purchases which exceed any single paycheck; households save to make down payments on houses and to buy automobiles or television sets. Some saving is solely for the convenience of having a pool of liquid funds readily available to take advantage of any extraordinarily good buys which one may chance upon. Or saving may occur to provide for the future needs of an individual and his family: households save to provide for the future retirement of the family breadwinner or to expose the offspring to the rigors of a college education. Or saving may be a precautionary, rainy-day measure—a means of protecting oneself against such unpredictable events as prolonged illness and unemployment. Or saving may be merely a deeply ingrained habit that is practiced on an almost automatic basis with no specific purposes in mind. Much saving is highly institutionalized or contractual: for example, payments for life insurance and

annuities or participation in a "bond-a-month" program. The basic point is that none of these diverse motives for saving is particularly sensitive to the interest rate. In fact, one can readily pose a situation wherein, contrary to the classical conception (Figure 11-1), saving is *inversely* related to the interest rate. To illustrate: If a family requires an annual retirement income of $3000 from saving, it will need to save $100,000 if the interest rate is 3 percent, but only $50,000 if the interest rate is 6 percent!

What, in the Keynesian view, does determine the level of saving? The primary determinant is the level of national income. In particular, a higher level of income will mean a high volume of both saving and consumption for households individually and as a group. When income is low, households must spend their entire incomes to achieve an acceptable standard of living; indeed, low incomes may give rise to dissaving. Higher incomes, however, permit households to increase both consumption and the level of saving.

Why do businesses purchase capital goods? The motivation for investment spending, as we shall discover in a few pages, is complex. The interest rate—the cost of obtaining money capital with which to invest—undoubtedly is a consideration in formulating investment plans. But the interest rate is not the most important factor. The rate of profit which business firms expect to realize on the investment is the really crucial determinant of the amounts they desire to invest. In fact, some economists argue that the investment plans of businesses are generally rather insensitive to changes in the interest rate. Furthermore, during the downswing of the business cycle, profit expectations will be so bleak that the level of investment will be low and possibly declining despite substantial reductions in the interest rate. Interest rate reductions are not likely to stimulate investment spending when increases in saving (declines in consumption) make it most sorely needed.

3 Money Balances and Banks Modern employment theory envisions the classical conception of the money market (Figure 11-1) as being oversimplified and therefore incorrect in another sense. Specifically, the classical money market assumes that current saving is the only source of funds for the financing of investment. Keynesian economics holds that there are two other sources of funds which can be made available in the money market: (1) the accumulated money balances held by households, and (2) commercial banks. Modern employment theory stipulates that the public holds money balances not merely to negotiate day-to-day transactions, but also as a form of accumulated wealth. Now the important point for present purposes is that, by drawing down or decumulating a portion of these money balances and offering these dollars to investors, a supply of funds in excess of current saving can be made available in the money market. Similarly, as we will find in Chapter 15, when commercial banks make loans, they add to the money supply. Bank lending, therefore, is also a means of augmenting current saving as a source of funds for investment. The consequence is that a reduction in the money balances held by households *and* bank lending can give rise to an amount of investment which is in excess of current saving. This implies that Say's Law is invalid and that output, employment, and the price level can fluctuate. More specifically, we shall soon discover that an excess of investment over saving results in an increase in total spending which has an expansionary effect on the economy. If the economy is initially in a recession, output and employment will increase; if the economy is already at full employment, the added demand will be inflationary.

Conversely, classical theory is incorrect in assuming that all current saving will appear in the money market. If (1) households add some of their current saving to their money balances rather than channel it into the money market, or (2) some current saving is used to retire outstanding bank loans, then the amount of funds made available in the money market will be less than that shown by the classical saving curve in Figure 11-1. This suggests that the amount of current saving will exceed the amount invested. Again, Say's Law does not hold and macroeconomic instability will result. In this case the excess of saving over investment will mean a decline in total demand which is contractionary; output and employment will tend to fall.[6]

[6]Technical footnote: It is a relatively simple matter to portray these Keynesian criticisms in terms of the classical conception of the money market. In the first case (Figure *a*), funds are shifted by households from their money balances to the money market *and* banks create funds (money) by lending. Adding these amounts horizontally to current saving S, we get the supply of funds curve F_1. At

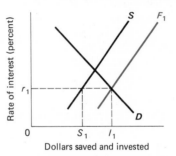

(a) Decreased money balances and bank lending

(b) Increased money balances and bank loan retirement

the resulting equilibrium interest rate r_1, investment is I_1 and obviously in excess of current saving S_1. In the second case (Figure *b*), the supply-of-funds curve, F_2, is less than current saving S, because portions of current saving have been added to the money balances of households *and* used to retire bank debt. These portions of current saving have been subtracted horizontally from the S curve to derive the F_2 curve. At the relevant equilibrium interest rate r_2, investment is only I_2 while current saving is obviously more at S_2. The conclusion is that the money market does not

To summarize: The modern position is that saving and investment plans can be at odds and thereby can result in fluctuations in total output, total income, and the volume of employment. It is largely a matter of chance that households and businesses will desire to save and invest identical amounts. Modern economists have proved themselves better plumbers than their classical predecessors by recognizing that the saving drain and the investment spigot are not connected.

☐ **The Discrediting of Price-Wage Flexibility**

But what of the second aspect of the classical position—the contention that downward price-wage adjustments will eliminate the unemployment effects of a decline in total spending?

1 Price-wage flexibility, modern theorists argue, simply does not exist to the degree necessary for ensuring the restoration of full employment in the face of a decline in total spending. The price system of modern capitalism is no longer a perfectly competitive one; rather, it is riddled by market imperfections and circumscribed by practical and political obstacles which work against downward price-wage flexibility. To be specific, monopolistic producers, dominating many important product markets, will have both the ability and the desire to resist falling product prices as demand declines. And in the resource markets, strong labor unions are equally persistent in holding the line against wage cuts. In this endeavor they are ably assisted by minimum-wage legislation, public opinion as to what are reasonable and "customary" wage rates, and practical-minded politicians who are well aware of the power of labor at the polls. In short, as a practical matter, downward price-

wage flexibility cannot be expected to offset the unemployment effects of a decline in total spending.

2 Furthermore, even if price-wage declines accompanied a contraction of total spending, it is doubtful that these declines would help reduce unemployment. The reason? The volume of total money demand cannot remain constant as prices and wages decline. That is, lower prices and wages necessarily mean lower money incomes, and lower money incomes in turn entail further reductions in total spending. The net result is likely to be little or no change in the depressed levels of output and employment.

The modern view points out that the classicists were tripped up in their reasoning by the fallacy of composition. Because any particular group of workers typically buys only a small amount of what they produce, the product and therefore labor demand curves of a single firm can be regarded as independent of any wage (income) changes accorded its own workers. In other words, it is correct to reason that a decline in its wage rate will move a *single firm* down its stable labor demand curve and result in more workers hired, that is, more employment. But the same reasoning, argue modern economists, is not applicable to the economy as a whole, to general wage cuts. Why? Because wages are the major source of income in the economy. Widespread wage declines will therefore result in declines in incomes and in the demand for both products and the labor used in producing them. The result is that employers will hire little additional labor after the general wage cuts (conceivably, less labor than they did before). What holds true for a single firm—a wage cut for its employees will not adversely affect labor demand—is not true for the economy as a whole—general wage cuts will lower money incomes and cause the demand for products and labor to decline generally.

Recapitulation: Modern theorists argue, in the first place, prices and wages are in fact

---

ensure the equality the saving and investment, Say's Law is therefore invalid, and the economy is subject to macroeconomic instability.

not flexible downward and, second, even if they were, it is doubtful that price-wage declines would alleviate widespread unemployment.

TOOLS OF MODERN EMPLOYMENT THEORY

By rejecting the analysis of the classical economists, we are in effect recognizing that there is no automatic mechanism with the capacity to make full employment the normal state of affairs in a capitalistic system. Yet the question remains: How are the levels of output and employment determined in modern capitalism?

The touchstone of any meaningful answer is that *the amount of goods and services produced and therefore the level of employment depend directly upon the level of total spending.* Subject to the economy's productive potential as determined by the scarce resources available to it, businesses will produce that level of output which they can profitably sell. Men and machinery are idled when there are no markets for the goods and services they are capable of producing. Total spending, on the one hand, and total output and employment, on the other, vary directly. Therefore, in explaining the economy's output-employment levels, we must obviously begin by examining the consumption and investment components of total spending.

CONSUMPTION AND SAVING

In terms of absolute size, consumption is the main component of total spending (Chapter 9). It is therefore of obvious importance to understand the major determinants of consumption spending. Recall (from Chapter 9) that economists define personal saving as "not spending" or "that part of DI which is not consumed"; in other words, disposable income equals consumption plus saving. Hence, in

examining the determinants of consumption we are also indirectly exploring the determinants of saving.

☐ **Income-consumption and Income-saving Relationships**

There are many considerations which influence the level of consumer spending. But common sense and available statistical data both suggest that the most important determinant of consumer spending is income—in particular, disposable income. And, of course, since saving is that part of disposable income which is not consumed, DI is also the basic determinant of personal saving.

Consider some recent historical data. In Figure 11-2 each dot indicates the consumption–disposable income relationship for each year since 1950 and the thick line is fitted to these points. Note, most obviously, that consumption is directly related to disposable income and, indeed, households clearly spend most of their income. But we can say more. The thin 45-degree line is added to the diagram as a point of reference. Because this line bisects the 90-degree angle formed by the vertical and horizontal axes of the graph, each point on the 45-degree line must be equidistant from the two axes. We can therefore regard the vertical distance from any point on the horizontal axis to the 45-degree line as either consumption *or* disposable income. If we regard it as disposable income, then the amount (the vertical distance) by which the actual amount consumed in any given year falls short of the 45-degree guideline indicates the amount of saving in any particular year. For example, in 1976 consumption was $1080 billion, and disposable income was $1182; hence, saving in 1976 was $102 billion. That is, disposable income less consumption equals saving. By observing these vertical distances as we move to the right on Figure 11-2, we note that saving also increases, as does the level of disposable income. In fact, not shown on Figure 11-2 is

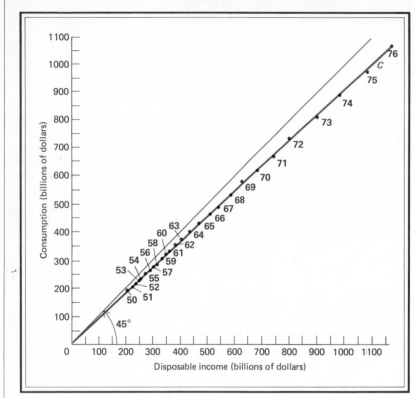

FIGURE 11-2 CONSUMPTION AND DISPOSABLE INCOME, 1950–1976

Each dot in this figure shows consumption and disposable income in a given year. The *C* line generalizes upon the relationship between consumption and disposable income. It indicates a direct relationship and that households consume the bulk of their incomes.

the fact that in years of very low income, for example, some of the worst years of the Great Depression, consumption exceeded disposable income. The dots for these years would obviously be located *above* the 45-degree line. Households actually consumed in excess of their current incomes by *dissaving,* that is, by going into debt and liquidating previously accumulated wealth.

To summarize: Figure 11-2 suggests that (1) households consume most of their disposable income and (2) both consumption and saving are directly related to the level of income.

☐   **The Consumption Schedule**

Figure 11-2 embodies historical data; it shows us how much households *actually did consume* (and save) at various levels of DI over

a period of years. For analytical purposes we need an income-consumption relationship—a consumption schedule—which shows the various amounts households *plan* or *intend* to consume at various possible levels of disposable income which might conceivably prevail at some specific *point in time.* A hypothetical *consumption schedule* of the type we require for analysis is shown in columns 1 and 2 of Table 11-1. It is plotted in Figure 11-3*a*. This consumption schedule reflects the consumption–disposable income relationship suggested by the empirical data of Figure 11-2, and it is consistent with a variety of empirical family budget studies. The relationship is direct—as common sense certainly would suggest—and, in addition, we note that households will spend a larger *proportion* of a small disposable income than of a large disposable income.

Table 11-1   THE CONSUMPTION AND SAVING SCHEDULES (*hypothetical data; columns 1 through 3 in billions*)

(1) Level of output and income (NNP = DI)	(2) Consump- tion	(3) Saving, or (1) − (2)	(4) Average propensity to consume (APC) (2)/(1)	(5) Average propensity to save (APS) (3)/(1)	(6) Marginal propensity to consume (MPC) $\Delta(2)/\Delta(1)$	(7) Marginal propensity to save (MPS) $\Delta(3)/\Delta(1)$
$370	$375	$−5	1.01	−.01		
390	390	0	1.00	.00	.75	.25
410	405	5	.99	.01	.75	.25
430	420	10	.98	.02	.75	.25
450	435	15	.97	.03	.75	.25
470	450	20	.96	.04	.75	.25
490	465	25	.95	.05	.75	.25
510	480	30	.94	.06	.75	.25
530	495	35	.93	.07	.75	.25

□   **The Saving Schedule**

It is a simple task to derive a *saving schedule*. Because disposable income equals consumption plus saving, we need only subtract consumption from disposable income to find the amount saved at each level of DI. Hence, columns 1 and 3 of Table 11-1 constitute the saving schedule. This schedule is plotted in Figure 11-3*b*. Note that there is a direct relationship between saving and DI but that saving constitutes a smaller proportion of a small DI than it does of a large DI. If households consume a smaller and smaller proportion of DI as DI goes up, they must save a larger and larger proportion.

Remembering that each point on the 45-degree line indicates an equality of DI and consumption, we see that dissaving would occur at the relatively low DI of $370 billion; that is, households will consume in excess of their current incomes by drawing down accumulated savings or by borrowing. Graphically, the vertical distance of the consumption schedule *above* the 45-degree line is equal to the vertical distance of the saving schedule *below* the horizontal axis at the $370 billion level of output and income (see Figure 11-3*a* and *b*). In this instance, each of these two vertical distances measures the $5 billion of *dissaving* which occurs at the $370 billion in-

come level. At the $390 billion income level, households will "break even" by spending their entire incomes. Graphically, the consumption schedule cuts the 45-degree line, and the saving schedule cuts the horizontal axis at this income level. At all higher incomes, households will plan to save a portion of their income. The vertical distance of the consumption schedule *below* the 45-degree line measures this saving, as does the vertical distance of the saving schedule *above* the horizontal axis. For example, at the $410 billion level of income, both these distances indicate $5 billion worth of saving (see Figure 11-3*a* and *b*).

□   **Average and Marginal Propensities**

Columns 4 to 7 of Table 11-1 point up additional characteristics of the consumption and saving schedules.

APC and APS   That fraction, or percentage, of any given total income which is consumed is called the *average propensity to consume* (APC), and that fraction of any total income which is saved is called the *average propensity to save* (APS). That is,

$$APC = \frac{consumption}{income}$$

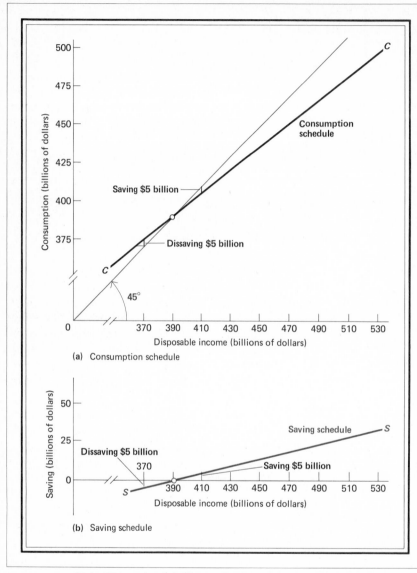

FIGURE 11-3 CONSUMPTION (a) AND SAVING (b) SCHEDULES

The two parts of this figure show the income-consumption and income-saving relationships graphically. Each point on the 45-degree line in **(a)** indicates an equality of DI and consumption. Therefore, because saving equals DI minus consumption, the saving schedule in **(b)** is found by subtracting the consumption schedule vertically from the 45-degree guideline. Consumers "break even," that is, consumption equals DI (and saving therefore equals zero) at $390 billion for these hypothetical data.

and

$$\text{APS} = \frac{\text{saving}}{\text{income}}$$

For example, at the $470 billion level of income in Table 11-1, the APC is 45/47, or about 96 percent, while the APS is obviously 2/47, or about 4 percent. By calculating the APC and APS at each of the nine levels of DI shown in Table 11-1, we find that the APC falls and the

APS rises as DI increases. The fraction of total DI which is consumed declines as DI rises, a movement that makes it necessary for the fraction of DI which is saved to rise as DI rises.

MPC and MPS   The fact that households consume a certain portion of some given total income—for example, 45/47 of a $470 billion disposable income—does not guarantee that they will consume the same proportion of any *change* in income which they might receive. The proportion, or fraction, of any change in income which is consumed is called the *marginal propensity to consume* (MPC), marginal meaning "extra." Or, alternatively stated, the MPC is the ratio of a *change* in consumption to the *change* in income which brought the consumption change about; that is,

$$MPC = \frac{change\ in\ consumption}{change\ in\ income}$$

The fraction of any change in income which is saved is called the *marginal propensity to save* (MPS). That is, MPS is the ratio of a *change* in saving to the *change* in income which brought it about:

$$MPS = \frac{change\ in\ saving}{change\ in\ income}$$

Thus, if disposable income is currently $470 billion and households for some reason find that their incomes rise by $20 billion, we find that they will consume $^{15}/_{20}$, or $^{3}/_{4}$, and save $^{5}/_{20}$, or $^{1}/_{4}$, of that increase in income (see Table 11-1). In other words, the MPC is $^{3}/_{4}$, or .75, and the MPS is $^{1}/_{4}$, or .25. *The sum of the MPC and the MPS for any given change in disposable income must always be 1.* That is, consuming and saving out of extra income is an either-or proposition; that fraction of any change in income which is not spent is, by definition, saved. Therefore the fraction consumed (MPC) plus the fraction saved (MPS) must exhaust the whole increase in income:

$$MPC + MPS = 1$$

In our example .75 plus .25 equals 100 percent, or 1.

Economists are not in complete agreement as to the exact behavior of the MPC and MPS as income increases. For many years it was assumed that the MPC declined and the MPS increased as income increased. That is, it was felt that a smaller and smaller fraction of increases in income would be consumed and a larger and larger fraction of these increases would be saved. Many economists now feel

that the MPC and MPS for the economy as a whole are relatively constant. Statistical data such as those of Figure 11-2 are consistent with this position. We will assume the MPC and MPS to be constant not only because of this statistical evidence but also because a constant MPC and MPS will simplify our analysis considerably. You will note that for each of the eight $20 billion income increases shown in Table 11-1, consumption increases by $15 billion, that is, by $^{15}/_{20}$, or $^{3}/_{4}$, of the increase in income, and saving increases by $5 billion, that is, by $^{5}/_{20}$, or $^{1}/_{4}$, of the increase in income. We assume the MPC and MPS to be constant at $^{3}/_{4}$ and $^{1}/_{4}$, respectively (see columns 6 and 7).[7]

□ **Nonincome Determinants of Consumption and Saving**

The level of disposable income is the basic determinant of the amounts households will consume and save, just as price is the basic

[7] The mathematically inclined reader will recognize that the MPC is the numerical value of the slope of the consumption schedule and the MPS is the numerical value of the slope of the saving schedule. The slope of any line can be measured by the ratio of the vertical change to the horizontal change involved in moving from one point to another point on that line. Thus, in the accompanying diagram, if the vertical change is 15 and the horizontal change is 20 between points *A* and *B*, the slope of the line is $^{3}/_{4}$. Now it is evident in the figure that the slope of the

consumption schedule between any two points is measured by the change in consumption (the vertical change) relative to the change in income (the horizontal change). And this ratio, change in consumption/change in income, is the fraction of any change in income that is spent; that is, it measures the MPC. Similar reasoning tells us that the MPS measures the slope of the saving schedule.

determinant of the quantity demanded of any product. You will recall that changes in determinants other than price, such as consumer tastes, incomes, and so forth (Chapter 4), will cause the demand curve for a given product to shift location. Similarly, there are certain determinants other than income which might cause households to consume more or less at each possible level of DI and thereby change the locations of the consumption and saving schedules.

1 Stocks of Liquid Assets Generally speaking, the greater the amounts of liquid assets—money, private and public bonds, stocks, insurance policies, saving accounts, and so forth—owned by consumers, the greater will be their willingness to consume at each possible level of DI. The ownership of liquid assets makes households feel more secure financially and hence more willing to spend out of current disposable income.

2 Stocks of Durable Goods on Hand If the economy has enjoyed an extended period of prosperity, consumers may find themselves well supplied with various durable goods. That is, the majority of families may own late-model cars, television sets, refrigerators, and other household appliances, all worthy of many years of future service. Hence, for a time many households will be "out of the market" for such products, with the result that consumers are willing to spend less and save more at each possible level of disposable income.

3 Expectations Household expectations concerning future prices, money incomes, and the availability of goods may have a significant impact upon current spending and saving. Expectations of rising prices and product shortages tend to trigger more spending and less saving currently. Why? Because it is natural for consumers to seek to avoid paying higher prices or having to "do without." Expected inflation and expected shortages induce people to "buy now" to escape higher future prices

and bare shelves. The expectation of rising money incomes in the future also tends to make consumers more footloose in their current spending. Conversely, expected price declines, anticipations of shrinking incomes, and the feeling that goods will be abundantly available may induce consumers to retrench on their consumption and build up their savings.

4 Consumer Indebtedness The level of consumer credit can also be expected to affect the willingness of households to consume out of current income. If households are in debt to the degree that, say, 20 or 25 percent of their current incomes are committed to installment payments on previous purchases, consumers may well be obliged to retrench on current consumption in order to reduce their indebtedness. Conversely, if consumer indebtedness is relatively low, households may consume at an unusually high rate by increasing this indebtedness.

5 Attitudes toward Thrift Next, a catchall item: An economy's general attitude toward frugality will help determine the amounts of consumption and saving forthcoming at each possible level of DI. Attitudes toward thrift are governed as much by social and psychological considerations as they are by economic factors. If a society accepts the belief that saving is very virtuous and that "a dollar saved is a dollar earned," saving will tend to be greater and consumption less at each level of disposable income than would be the case where saving was held in lower esteem. There is some evidence to suggest that in the underdeveloped countries attitudes toward thrift are relatively weak, as most households are very anxious to consume in order to emulate the higher living standards of the more advanced nations.

Attitudes toward thrift can be influenced by government policies. During World War II the Federal government waged intensive propaganda campaigns to encourage households to save by buying war bonds. These campaigns—coupled with the hard fact that many consumer durables were unavailable or in scant supply—were fairly successful in boosting the saving schedule and therefore in lowering the consumption schedule. Peacetime government policies may also affect the consumption and saving schedules. By committing itself to policies designed to promote full employment, government may diminish the fear of unemployment and thereby weaken an important motive to save.

6   Taxation   In Chapter 12, where consumption will be plotted against before-tax income, we will find that changes in taxes will shift the consumption and saving schedules. Specifically, we will discover that taxes are paid partly at the expense of consumption and partly at the expense of saving. Therefore, an *increase* in taxes will shift *both* the consumption and saving schedules *downward.* Conversely, a tax reduction will be partly consumed and partly saved by households. Thus a tax *decrease* will shift *both* the consumption and saving schedules *upward.*

□   **Shifts and Stability**

Three final and related points are relevant to our discussion of the consumption and saving schedules.

1 The movement from one point to another on a given stable consumption schedule (for example, A to B on C_0 in Figure 11-4a) is called a *change in the amount consumed.* The sole cause of this change is a change in the level of disposable income. On the other hand, a *change in the consumption schedule* refers to an upward or downward shift of the entire schedule—for example, from C_0 to C_1 or C_2 in Figure 11-4a. A relocation of the consumption schedule is obviously caused by changes in any one or more of the nonincome determinants just discussed. A similar terminological distinction applies to the saving schedule in Figure 11-4b.

2 A related point is that, insofar as the

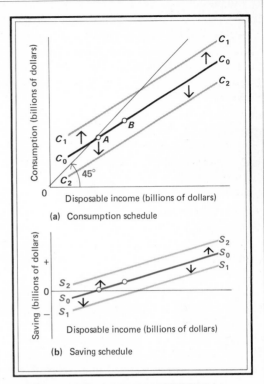

FIGURE 11-4   SHIFTS IN THE CONSUMPTION (a) AND SAVING (b) SCHEDULES

A change in any one or more of the nonincome determinants will cause the consumption and saving schedules to shift. If households consume more at each level of DI, they are necessarily saving less. Graphically this means that an upshift in the consumption schedule (C_0 to C_1) entails a downshift in the saving schedule (S_0 to S_1). Conversely, if households consume less at each level of DI, they are saving more. A downshift in the consumption schedule (C_0 to C_2) is reflected in an upshift of the saving schedule (S_0 to S_2).

first five nonincome determinants of consumption are concerned, the consumption and saving schedules will necessarily shift in opposite directions. If households decide to consume *more* at each possible level of disposable income, this means that they want to save *less,* and vice versa. Graphically, if the consumption schedule shifts upward from C_0 to C_1 in Figure 11-4, the saving schedule will shift downward from S_0 to S_1. Similarly, a downshift in the consumption schedule from C_0 to

C_2 means an upshift in the saving schedule from S_0 to S_2. The exception to this involves the sixth nonincome determinant—taxation. We shall discover in Chapter 13 that households will consume less *and* save less in order to pay higher taxes. Hence, a tax increase will lower *both* the consumption and saving schedules, whereas a tax cut will shift *both* schedules upward.

3 Economists are in general agreement that, aside from deliberate governmental actions designed to shift them, the consumption and saving schedules are quite stable. This may be because consumption-saving decisions are strongly influenced by habit or because changes in the nonincome determinants frequently work in opposite directions and therefore tend to be self-canceling.

INVESTMENT

Let us now turn to investment, the second component of private spending. Recall that investment refers to expenditures on new plants, capital equipment, machinery, and so forth. What determines the level of net investment spending? There are two basic determinants: (1) the expected rate of net profits which businesses hope to realize from investment spending, and (2) the rate of interest.

□ Expected Rate of Net Profits

The level of investment spending is guided by the profit motive; the business sector buys capital goods only when it expects such purchases to be profitable. Consider a simplified example. Suppose the owner of a small cabinetmaking shop is considering investing in a new sanding machine which costs $1000 and has a useful life of only one year. The new machine will presumably increase the firm's output and sales revenue. Specifically, let us suppose that the *net* expected revenue (that is, net of such operating costs as power, lumber, labor, and so forth) from the machine is $1100.

In other words, after operating costs have been accounted for, the remaining expected net revenue is sufficient to cover the $1000 cost of the machine and leave a return of $100. Comparing this $100 return or profit with the $1000 cost of the machine, we find that the expected *rate* of net profit on the machine is obviously 10 percent ($= \$100/\$1000$).

□ The Interest Rate

But there is one important cost associated with investing which our example has ignored. And that, of course, is the interest rate—the financial cost the firm must pay to borrow the *money* capital required for the purchase of the *real* capital (the sanding machine).[8] Our generalization is this: If the expected rate of net profits (10 percent) exceeds the interest rate (say, 7 percent), it will be profitable to invest. But if the interest rate (say, 12 percent) exceeds the expected rate of net profits (10 percent), it will obviously be unprofitable to invest.

□ Investment-Demand Curve

We must now move from our discussion of a single firm's investment decision to an understanding of the total demand for investment goods by the entire business sector. Assume every firm in the economy has estimated the net rate of expected profits from all relevant investment projects and these data have been collected. These estimates can now be cumulated by asking: How many dollars' worth of investment projects entail a net expected rate of profits of, say, 16 percent or more? Of 14 percent or more? Of 12 percent or more? And so on.

Suppose we find that there are no prospective investments which will yield an ex-

---

[8] The role of the interest rate as a cost in investing in real capital is valid even if the firm does not borrow but, rather, finances the investment internally out of funds saved from past profits. By using this money to invest in the sander, the firm incurs a cost in the sense that it forgoes the interest income which it could have realized by lending the funds to someone else.

pected net profit of 16 percent or more. But there are $5 billion of investment opportunities with an expected net profit rate between 14 and 16 percent; an *additional* $5 billion yielding between 12 and 14 percent; still an *additional* $5 billion yielding between 10 and 12 percent; and an *additional* $5 billion in each successive 2 percent range of yield down to and including the 0 to 2 percent range. By *cumulating* these figures we obtain the data of Table 11-2, which are shown graphically by the *investment-demand curve* in Figure 11-5. Note in Table 11-2 that the figure opposite 12 percent, for example, tells us there are $10 billion worth of investment opportunities which will yield an expected net profit of 12 percent *or more;* the $10 billion, in other words, includes the $5 billion of investment which will yield an expected return of 14 percent or more *plus* the $5 billion which is expected to yield between 12 and 14 percent.

Given this cumulated information on expected net profit rates of all possible investment projects, we again introduce the interest rate or financial cost of investing. We know from our sanding machine example that an investment project will be undertaken provided its net expected profit rate exceeds the interest rate. Let us apply this reasoning to Figure 11-5. If we assume that the rate of interest is 12 percent, we find that $10 of investment spending will be profitable, that is, $10 worth

FIGURE 11-5 THE INVESTMENT-DEMAND CURVE

The investment-demand curve for the economy is derived by arraying all relevant investment projects in descending order of their expected rate of net profitability and applying the rule that investment should be undertaken up to the point at which the interest rate is equal to the expected rate of net profits. The investment-demand curve is downsloping, reflecting an inverse relationship between the interest rate (the financial price of investing) and the aggregate quantity of capital goods demanded.

of investment projects entail an expected net profit rate of 12 percent or more. Stated differently, at a financial "price" of 12 percent, $10 billion worth of investment goods will be demanded. Similarly, if the interest rate was lower at, say, 10 percent, then an additional $5 billion of investment projects would become profitable and the total amount of investment goods demanded would be $15 billion (= $10 + $5). At an interest rate of 8 percent, a further $5 billion of investment would become profitable and the total demand for investment goods would be $20 billion. At 6 percent, investment would be $25 billion. And so forth. *By applying the rule that all investment projects should be undertaken up to the point at which the expected rate of net profits equals the interest rate, we discover that the curve of Figure 11-5 is the investment-demand curve.* That is, various possible financial prices

Table 11-2 PROFIT EXPECTATIONS AND INVESTMENT (*hypothetical data*)

Expected rate of net profit (in percent)	Amount of investment (billions of dollars per year)
16%	$ 0
14	5
12	10
10	15
8	20
6	25
4	30
2	35
0	40

of investing (various interest rates) are shown on the vertical axis and the corresponding quantities of investment goods demanded are revealed on the horizontal axis. By definition, any line or curve embodying such data is the investment-demand curve. Consistent with our product and resource demand curves of Chapter 4, observe the *inverse* relationship between the interest rate (price) and the amount of spending on investment goods (quantity demanded).

This conception of the investment decision allows us to anticipate an important aspect of macroeconomic policy. We shall find in our discussion of monetary policy in Chapter 16 that by changing the supply of money, government can alter the interest rate. This is done primarily to change the level of investment spending. Think of it in this way: At any point in time, business firms in the aggregate have a wide variety of investment projects under consideration. If interest rates are high, only those projects with the highest expected rate of net profit will be undertaken. Hence, the level of investment will be small. As the interest rate is lowered, projects whose expected rate of net profits is less will also become commercially feasible and the level of investment will rise.

□ **Shifts in Investment Demand**

In discussing the consumption schedule, we noted that, although disposable income is the key determinant of the amount consumed, there are other factors which affect consumption. These "nonincome determinants," you will recall, cause shifts in the consumption schedule. So it also is with the investment-demand schedule. Figure 11-5 portrays the interest rate as the main determinant of investment. But other factors or variables determine the location of the investment-demand curve. Let us briefly consider several of the more important "noninterest determinants" of investment-demand, noting how changes in these determinants might shift the investment-demand curve.

1 Acquisition, Maintenance, and Operating Costs As our sanding machine example revealed, the initial costs of capital goods, along with the estimated costs of operating and maintaining those goods, are obviously important considerations in gauging the expected rate of net profitability of any particular investment. To the extent that these costs rise, the expected *net* rate of profits from prospective investment projects will fall, shifting the investment-demand curve to the left. Conversely, if these costs decline, expected net profit rates will rise, shifting the investment-demand curve to the right. Note that the wage policies of unions may affect the investment-demand curve because wage rates are a major operating cost.

2 Business Taxes Businessmen look to expected profits *after taxes* in making their investment decisions. Hence, an increase in business taxes will lower profitability and tend to shift the investment-demand curve to the left; a tax reduction will tend to shift it to the right.

3 Technological Change Technological progress—the development of new products, improvements in existing products, the creation of new machinery and new production processes—is a basic stimulus to investment. The development of a more efficient machine, for example, will lower production costs or improve product quality, thereby increasing the expected net rate of profit from investing in the machine. Profitable new products—hand calculators, citizen-band radios, digital watches, and so on—induce a flurry of investment as firms tool up for expanded production. In short, a rapid rate of technological progress shifts the investment-demand curve to the right, and vice versa.

4 The Stock of Capital Goods on Hand Just as the stock of consumer goods on hand affects household consumption-saving decisions, so the stock of capital goods on hand influences the expected profit rate from additional investment in a given industry. To the extent that a given industry is well stocked with productive facilities and inventories of finished goods, investment will be retarded in that industry. The reason is obvious: Such an industry will be amply equipped to fulfill present and future market demand at prices which yield mediocre profits. If an industry has enough, or even excessive, productive capacity, the expected rate of profit from further investment in the industry will be low, and therefore little or no investment will occur. To summarize: Excess productive capacity tends to shift the investment-demand curve to the left; a shortage of capital goods shifts it to the right.

5 Expectations We noted earlier that business investment is based upon *expected* profits. Capital goods are durable—they may have a life expectancy of ten or twenty years—and thus the profitability of any capital investment will depend upon business planners' expectations of the *future* sales and *future* profitability of the product which the capital helps produce. Business expectations may be based upon elaborate forecasts of future business conditions which incorporate a number of "business indicators." Nevertheless, such elusive and difficult-to-predict factors as changes in the domestic political climate, the thrust of foreign affairs, population growth, stock market conditions, and so on, must be taken into account on a subjective or intuitive basis. For present purposes we note that, if businessmen are optimistic about future business conditions, the investment-demand curve will shift to the right; a pessimistic outlook will shift it to the left.

□ **Investment and Income**

In order to add the investment decisions of businesses to the consumption plans of households (Chapter 12), we need to express investment plans in terms of the level of disposable income, or NNP. That is, we want to construct an *investment schedule* showing the amounts

which business firms as a group plan or intend to invest at each of the various possible levels of income or output. Such a schedule will mirror the investment plans or intentions of business owners and managers in the same way the consumption and saving schedules reflect the consumption and saving plans of households.

We shall assume in our analysis that business investment is geared to long-term profit expectations as influenced by such considerations as technological progress, population growth, and so forth, and therefore is autonomous or independent of the level of current income. More specifically, let us suppose that the investment-demand curve is as shown in Figure 11-5 *and* that the current rate of interest is 8 percent. This means that the business sector will find it profitable to spend $20 billion on investment goods. In Table 11-3, columns 1 and 2, we are assuming that this level of investment will be forthcoming at every level of income. The I_n line in Figure 11-6 shows this graphically.

This assumed independence of investment and income is admittedly a simplification. A higher level of business activity may induce additional spending on capital facilities, as suggested by columns 1 and 3 of Table 11-3 and I'_n in Figure 11-6. There are at least two reasons why investment might vary directly with income. First, investment is related to profits;

Table 11-3   THE INVESTMENT SCHEDULE
(*hypothetical data; in billions*)

(1) Level of output and income	(2) Investment, I_n	(3) Investment, I'_n
$370	$20	$10
390	20	12
410	20	14
430	20	16
450	20	18
470	20	20
490	20	22
510	20	24
530	20	26

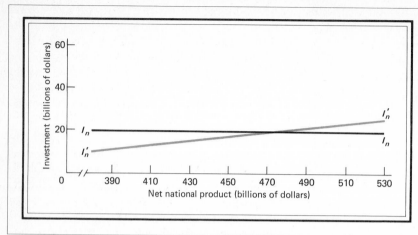

FIGURE 11-6 THE INVESTMENT SCHEDULE: TWO POSSIBILITIES

Our discussion will be facilitated by employing the investment schedule I_n, which assumes that the investment plans of businesses are independent of the current level of income. Actually, the investment schedule may be slightly upsloping, as suggested by I_n'.

much investment is financed internally out of business profits. Therefore, it is very plausible to suggest that as disposable income rises, so will business profits and therefore the level of investment. Second, at low levels of income and output, the business sector will tend to have unutilized, or excess, productive capacity; that is, many industries will have idle machinery and equipment and therefore little incentive to purchase additional capital goods. But, as the level of income rises, this excess capacity disappears and firms are inclined to add to their stock of capital goods. Our simplification, however, is not too severely at odds with reality and will greatly facilitate later analysis.

□ **Instability of Investment**

In contrast to consumption, investment is unstable. Proportionately, investment is the most volatile component of private spending. Some of the more important factors which explain this variability are as follows:

1 Durability Because of their durability, capital goods have a rather indefinite useful life. Within limits, purchases of capital goods are discretionary and therefore postponable. Older equipment or buildings can be scrapped and entirely replaced, on the one hand, or

patched up and used for a few more years, on the other. Optimism about the future may prompt business planners to replace their older facilities, that is, to modernize their plants, and this obviously means a high level of investment. A slightly less optimistic view, however, may lead to very small amounts of investment as older facilities are repaired and kept in use.

2 Irregularity of Innovation We have noted that technological progress is a major determinant of investment. New products and new processes provide a major stimulus to investment. However, history suggests that major innovations—railroads, electricity, automobiles, and so forth—occur quite irregularly, and when they do occur, these innovations induce a vast upsurge or "wave" of investment spending which in time recedes. To illustrate: The widespread acceptance of the automobile in the 1920s not only brought about substantial increases in investment in the automobile industry itself, but, as mentioned in our treatment of the prosperous twenties, also induced tremendous amounts of investment in such related industries as steel, petroleum, glass, and rubber, not to mention public investment in streets and highways. But when investment in these related industries was ultimately completed—that is, when they had created capital facilities sufficient to meet the needs of the automobile industry—total investment leveled off.

3 Variability of Profits We know that business owners and managers invest only when they feel it will be profitable to do so and that, to a significant degree, the expectation of future profitability is influenced by the size of current profits. Current profits, however, are themselves highly variable (line 12 of the table on the inside covers). Hence the variability of profits contributes to the volatile nature of the incentive to invest. Furthermore, the instability of profits may also cause investment fluctuations, because profits are a major source of funds for business investment. American businesses tend to prefer this internal source of financing to increases in external debt or stock issue. In short, expanding profits give business planners both greater incentives and greater means to invest; declining profits have the reverse effects. The fact that actual profits are variable adds to the instability of investment.

4 Variability of Expectations We have already discussed how the durability of capital equipment results in the making of investment decisions upon the basis of *expected* net profits. Now, while there is a tendency for business firms to project current business conditions into the future, it is equally true that expectations are sometimes subject to radical revision when some event or combination of events suggests a significant change in future business conditions. What kinds of events make busi-

ness confidence so capricious? Changes in the domestic political climate, cold-war developments, changes in population growth and therefore in anticipated market demand, court decisions in key labor or antitrust cases, legislative actions, strikes, changes in governmental economic policies, and a host of similar considerations may give rise to waves of business optimism or pessimism.

The stock market merits specific comment in this regard. Business planners frequently look to the stock market as an index or barometer of the overall confidence of society in future business conditions; a rising "bull" market signifies public confidence in the business future, whereas a falling "bear" market implies a lack of confidence. The stock market, however, is a highly speculative market, and initially modest changes in stock prices can be seriously intensified by less informed participants who jump on the bandwagon by buying when prices begin to rise and by selling when stock prices start to fall. Recall our discussion in Chapter 10 of the important psychological repercussions of the 1929 stock market crash. Furthermore, by affecting the relative attractiveness of new capital as opposed to purchasing ownership claims (stock) to existing capital facilities, upsurges and slumps in stock values also affect the level of investment.

For these and similar reasons, it is quite correct to associate most fluctuations in output and employment with changes in investment. In terms of Figure 11-6, we can think of this volatility as being reflected in frequent and substantial upward and downward shifts in the investment schedule.

Summary

1 Classical employment theory envisioned laissez faire capitalism as being capable of providing virtually continuous full employment. This analysis was based on Say's Law and the assumption of price-wage flexibility.

2 The classical economists argued that because supply creates its own demand, general overproduction was impossible. This conclusion was held to be valid even when saving occurred, because the money market, or more specifically, the interest rate, would automatically synchronize the saving plans of households and the investment plans of businesses.

3   Classical employment theory also held that even if temporary declines in total spending were to occur, these declines would be compensated for by downward price-wage adjustments to the end that real output, employment, and real income would not decline.

4   Modern employment theory rejects the notion that the interest rate would equate saving and investment by pointing out that savers and investors are substantially different groups who make their saving and investment decisions for different reasons—reasons which are largely unrelated to the interest rate. Furthermore, because of changes in *a.* the public's holdings of money balances, and *b.* bank loans, the supply of funds may exceed or fall short of current saving to the end that saving and investment will not be equal.

5   Modern economists discredit price-wage flexibility on both practical and theoretical grounds. They argue that *a.* union and business monopolies, minimum-wage legislation, and a host of related factors have virtually eliminated the possibility of substantial price-wage reductions, and *b.* price-wage cuts will lower total income and therefore the demand for labor.

6   The basic tools of modern employment theory are the consumption, saving, and investment schedules, which show the various amounts that households intend to consume and save and that businesses plan to invest at the various possible income-output levels.

7   The locations of the consumption and saving schedules are determined by such factors as *a.* the amounts of liquid assets owned by households; *b.* the stocks of durables consumers have on hand; *c.* expectations of future income, future prices, and product availability; *d.* the relative size of consumer indebtedness; *e.* overall attitudes toward thrift; and *f.* taxation. The consumption and saving schedules are relatively stable.

8   The *average* propensities to consume and save show the proportion or fraction of any level of *total* income that is consumed and saved. The *marginal* propensities to consume and save show the proportion or fraction of any *change* in total income that is consumed or saved.

9   The immediate determinants of investment are *a.* the expected rate of net profits and *b.* the rate of interest. The economy's investment-demand curve can be determined by arraying investment projects in descending order according to their expected net profitability and applying the rule that investment will be profitable up to the point at which the interest rate equals the expected rate of net profits. The investment-demand curve reveals an inverse relationship between the interest rate and the level of aggregate investment.

10   Shifts in the investment-demand curve can occur as the result of changes in *a.* the acquistion, maintenance, and operating costs of capital goods; *b.* business taxes; *c.* technology; *d.* the stocks of capital goods on hand; and *e.* expectations.

11   We make the simplifying assumption that the level of investment determined by projecting the current interest rate off the investment-demand curve does not vary with the level of aggregate income.

12   The durability of capital goods, the irregular occurrence of major innovations, profit volatility, and the variability of expectations all contribute to the high degree of instability of investment spending.

Questions and Study Suggestions

1   Key terms and concepts to remember: classical theory of employment; Say's Law; price-wage flexibility; Keynesian economics; consumption and saving schedules; average propensities to consume and save; marginal propensities to consume and save; investment-demand curve; investment schedule.

2   Explain the classical economists' conclusion that Say's Law would prevail even in an economy where substantial saving occurred. What arguments have modern economists used to undermine the classical view that Say's Law would result in sustained full employment?

3   "Unemployment can be avoided so long as businesses are willing to accept lower product prices, and workers to accept lower wage rates." Critically evaluate.

4   Precisely how are the APC and the MPC different? Why must the sum of the MPC and the MPS equal 1? What are the basic determinants of the consumption-saving schedules? Of your own level of consumption?

5   Explain precisely what relationships are shown by *a.* the consumption schedule, *b.* the saving schedule, and *c.* the investment schedule.

6   Complete the following table:

Level of output and income (NNP = DI)	Consumption	Saving
$240	$_____	$−4
260	_____	0
280	_____	4
300	_____	8
320	_____	12
340	_____	16
360	_____	20
380	_____	24
400	_____	28

   a.   Show the consumption and saving schedules graphically.

   b.   Determine the APS and APC for each level of income.

   c.   Now determine the MPC and MPS for each change in the income level.

   d.   Locate the break-even point. How is it possible for households to dissave at very low income levels?

   e.   If the proportion of total income which is consumed decreases and the proportion which is saved increases as income rises, explain both verbally and graphically how the MPC and MPS can be constant at various levels of income.

7   Explain how each of the following will affect the consumption and saving schedules or the investment schedule:

   a.   A decline in the amount of government bonds which consumers are holding

   b.   The threat of limited, nonnuclear war, leading the public to expect future shortages of consumer durables

   c.   A decline in the interest rate

   d.   A sharp decline in stock prices

   e.   An increase in the rate of population growth

   f.   The development of a significantly cheaper method of manufacturing pig iron from ore

g. The announcement that the social security program is to be expanded in both coverage and size of benefits

h. The expectation that mild inflation will persist in the next decade

i. Expected petroleum shortages

8 Explain why an upshift in the consumption schedule necessarily involves an equal downshift in the saving schedule.

9 What are the basic determinants of investment? Explain the relationship between the interest rate and the level of investment. Why is the investment schedule less stable than the consumption-saving schedules?

10 Assume there are no investment projects in the economy which yield an expected rate of net profit of 25 percent or more. But suppose there are $10 billion of investment projects yielding net expect profits of between 20 and 25 percent; another $10 billion yielding between 15 and 20 percent; another $10 billion between 10 and 15 percent; and so forth. Cumulate these data and present them graphically, putting the expected rate of net profits on the vertical axis and the amount of investment on the horizontal axis. What will be the equilibrium level of aggregate investment if the interest rate is **a.** 15 percent, **b.** 10 percent, and **c.** 5 percent? Explain why this curve is the investment-demand curve.

11 *Advanced analysis:* Linear equations for the consumption and saving schedules take the general form $C = a + bY$ and $S = -a + (1 - b)Y$, where C, S, and Y are consumption, saving, and national income, respectively. The constant a represents the vertical intercept, and b is the slope of the consumption schedule.

a. Use the following data to substitute specific numerical values into the consumption and saving equations.

National income (Y)	Consumption (C)
$ 0	$ 80
100	140
200	200
300	260
400	320

b. What is the economic meaning of b? Of $(1 - b)$?

Selected References

Dernburg, Thomas F., and Duncan M. McDougall: *Macroeconomics,* 5th ed. (New York: McGraw-Hill Book Company, 1976), chaps. 4, 6.

Dillard, Dudley: *The Economics of John Maynard Keynes* (Englewood Cliffs, N.J.: Prentice-Hall, Inc., 1948), chaps. 1, 2, 12.

Lekachman, Robert: *The Age of Keynes* (New York: Random House, Inc., 1966).

Lindauer, John: *Macroeconomics,* 3d ed. (Santa Barbara, Calif.: John Wiley & Sons, Inc., 1976), chaps. 3, 4.

Peterson, Wallace C.: *Income, Employment, and Economic Growth,* 3d ed. (New York: W. W. Norton & Company, Inc., 1974), chap. 4.

Last Word
Poverty Amidst Plenty

Before Keynes' *General Theory* economists did not have a convincing explanation of depression. But intelligent laymen understood that deficient demand was the crux of the problem. Consider the testimony of Mr. Oscar Ameringer, an Oklahoma City newspaper editor, before a Congressional Committee in 1932.

During the last three months I have visited . . . some 20 States of this wonderfully rich and beautiful country. Here are some of the things I heard and saw: In the State of Washington I was told that the forest fires raging in that region all summer and fall were caused by unemployed timber workers and bankrupt farmers in an endeavor to earn a few honest dollars as fire fighters. The last thing I saw on the night I left Seattle was numbers of women searching for scraps of food in the refuse piles of the principal market of that city. A number of Montana citizens told me of thousands of bushels of wheat left in the fields uncut on account of its low price that hardly paid for the harvesting. In Oregon I saw thousands of bushels of apples rotting in the orchards. Only absolute flawless apples were still salable, at from 40 to 50 cents a box containing 200 apples. At the same time, there are millions of children who, on account of the poverty of their parents, will not eat one apple this winter.

While I was in Oregon the Portland Oregonian bemoaned the fact that thousands of ewes were killed by the sheep raisers because they did not bring enough in the market to pay the freight on them. And while Oregon sheep raisers fed mutton to the buzzards, I saw men picking for meat scraps in the garbage cans in the cities of New York and Chicago. I talked to one man in a restaurant in Chicago. He told me of his experience in raising sheep. He said that he had killed 3000 sheep this fall and thrown them down the canyon, because it cost $1.10 to ship a sheep, and then he would get less than a dollar for it. He said he could not afford to feed the sheep, and he would not let them starve, so he just cut their throats and threw them down the canyon.

As a result of this appalling overproduction on the one side and the staggering underconsumption on the other side, 70 percent of the farmers of Oklahoma were unable to pay the interest on their mortgages. Last week one of the largest and oldest mortgage companies in that State went into the hands of the receiver. In that and other States we have now the interesting spectacle of farmers losing their farms by foreclosure and mortgage companies losing their recouped holdings by tax sales.

The farmers are being pauperized by the poverty of industrial populations and the industrial populations are being pauperized by the poverty of the farmers. Neither has the money to buy the product of the other, hence we have overproduction and underconsumption at the same time and in the same country.

. . . I am of the opinion that all this talk about speedy recovery and prosperity being just around the corner is bosh and nonsense. What we are confronted with is not a mere panic like those of 1873 and 1883, but a world-wide economic catastrophy that may spell the end of the capitalistic era—for the cause of it is production for profit instead of production for consumption. The masses can not buy what they have themselves produced; and unless ways and means are found to make cash customers out of some 20,000,000 of unemployed wage earners and bankrupt farmers, there can be no recovery.

I do not believe I have anything further to say.

From *Unemployment in the United States:* Hearings before a Subcommittee of the House Committee on Labor, 72d Congress, 1st Session, Washington, 1932, pp. 98–99, 104–105, abridged.

12

The Equilibrium Levels of Output, Employment, and Income

This chapter is both a continuation and an expansion of Chapter 11. We seek, first, to use the consumption, saving, and investment schedules developed in Chapter 11 to explain the equilibrium levels of output, income, and employment. Next, we analyze changes in the equilibrium level of NNP. Until government is added to our discussion in Chapter 13, we retain the simplifying assumptions of Chapter 11 which permitted us to equate NNP and DI.

We now have before us all the analytical tools necessary to explain the equilibrium levels of output, employment, and income. By *equilibrium output* we refer to that level of total output which, once achieved, will be sustained. It exists where the flow of income created by the production of the output gives rise to a level of total spending sufficient to clear the product market of that output. In pursuing the important task of determining and explaining the equilibrium level of output, two closely interrelated approaches—the *aggregate demand–aggregate supply* (or $C + I_n = $ NNP) approach and the *leakages-injections* (or, in the simplified discussion of this chapter, the $S = I_n$) approach—will be employed. Both will be discussed tabularly and graphically.

AGGREGATE DEMAND–AGGREGATE SUPPLY APPROACH

Let us first discuss the aggregate demand–aggregate supply approach, using both simple arithmetic data and graphic analysis.

□ **Tabular Analysis**

Table 12-1 merely brings together the income-consumption and income-saving data of Table 11-1 and the simplified income-investment data of columns 1 and 2 in Table 11-3.

This table is in many respects similar to Table 4-6, the supply and demand table for a specific product. You will recall that the demand schedule shows the amount consumers plan to purchase, and the supply schedule, the amount producers plan to offer at various prices. The equilibrium price was located at the point where the quantity demanded and the quantity supplied were equal. Barring revisions in the buying plans of consumers or the selling plans of producers, price and the corresponding amount exchanged would not vary from their equilibrium levels. This same general type of reasoning can be applied to *aggregate* demand and *aggregate* supply with three notable differences. First, because total output is composed of heterogeneous goods, it is essential to state total supply in money terms rather than physical units. Second, the equilibrating factor is obviously the level of output and income rather than price. Third, and most important, it is quite accurate to regard the

forces of supply and demand as playing equally important roles in determining the price of an individual product; changes in either supply or demand can alter equilibrium price. But in the case of aggregate equilibrium, it is correct to envision aggregate demand as the crucial determining variable or force to which the level of aggregate supply (NNP) adjusts. We should regard the aggregate supply schedule—the set of production intentions of businesses—as fixed and the actual amount produced by businessmen as responding to shifts in aggregate demand.

Aggregate Supply Column 2 of Table 12-1 is in effect the total, or aggregate, supply schedule for the economy. It indicates the various possible levels of total output—that is, the various possible NNPs—which the business sector of the economy might produce. *Producers are willing to offer each of these nine levels of output on the expectation that they will receive an identical amount of receipts of income from its sale.* That is, the business sector will produce \$370 billion worth of output, thereby incurring \$370 billion worth of wage, rent, interest, and profit costs, only if

Table 12-1 DETERMINATION OF THE EQUILIBRIUM LEVELS OF EMPLOYMENT, OUTPUT, AND INCOME: THE PRIVATE SECTOR (*hypothetical data*)

(1) Possible levels of employment,* millions	(2) Aggregate supply (output and income) (NNP = DI),† billions	(3) Consumption, billions	(4) Saving, billions	(5) Investment, billions	(6) Aggregate demand ($C + I_n$), billions	(7) Unintended investment (+) or disinvestment (−) in inventories	(8) Tendency of employment, output, and incomes
40	\$370	\$375	\$−5	\$20	\$395	\$−25	Increase
45	390	390	0	20	410	−20	Increase
50	410	405	5	20	425	−15	Increase
55	430	420	10	20	440	−10	Increase
60	450	435	15	20	455	−5	Increase
65	**470**	**450**	**20**	**20**	**470**	**0**	**Equilibrium**
70	490	465	25	20	485	+5	Decrease
75	510	480	30	20	500	+10	Decrease
80	530	495	35	20	515	+15	Decrease

*In later chapters on economic growth we will find that employment need not vary proportionately with output.
†If government is ignored and it is assumed that all saving occurs in the household sector of the economy, NNP as a measure of aggregate supply is equal to NI, PI, and DI. This means that households receive a DI equal to the value of total output.

they expect that this output can be sold for $370 billion worth of receipts. Some $390 billion worth of output will be offered if businesses feel this output can be sold for $390 billion. And so it is for all the other possible levels of output.

Aggregate Demand　The total, or aggregate, demand schedule is shown in column 6 of Table 12-1. It shows the total amount which will be spent at each possible output-income level. In dealing with the private sector of the economy, the aggregate demand schedule simply shows the amount of consumption and net investment spending $(C + I_n)$ which will be forthcoming at each output-income level. We use net rather than gross investment because we are employing NNP rather than GNP as a measure of total output.

Equilibrium　Now the question is this: Of the nine possible levels of NNP indicated in Table 12-1, which will be the equilibrium level? That is, which level of total output will the economy be capable of sustaining? The answer is: The equilibrium level of output is that output whose production will actually create total spending just sufficient to purchase that output. In other words, the equilibrium level of NNP is where the total quantity of goods supplied (NNP) is precisely equal to the total quantity of goods demanded $(C + I_n)$. Examination of the aggregate supply schedule of column 2 and the aggregate demand schedule of column 6 indicates that this equality exists only at the $470 billion level of NNP. This is the only level of output at which the economy is willing to spend precisely the amount necessary to take that output off the market. Here the annual rates of production and spending are in balance. There is no overproduction, which results in a piling up of unsold goods and therefore cutbacks in the rate of production, nor is there an excess of total spending, which draws down inventories and prompts increases in the rate of production. In

short, there is no reason for businessmen to vary from this rate of production; $470 billion is therefore the equilibrium NNP.

Disequilibrium　To enhance our understanding of the meaning of the equilibrium level of NNP, let us examine other possible levels of NNP to see why they cannot be sustained. For example, at the $410 billion level of NNP, businesses would find that if they produced this output, the income created by this production would give rise to $405 billion in consumer spending. Supplemented by $20 billion of investment, the total quantity demanded $(C + I_n)$ would be $425 billion, as shown in column 6. The economy obviously provides an annual rate of spending more than sufficient to purchase the current $410 billion rate of production. Because businessmen are producing at a lower rate than buyers are taking goods off the shelves, an unintended decline in business inventories of $15 billion will occur (column 7). Businessmen will adjust to this happy state of affairs by stepping up production. And a higher rate of output will mean more jobs and a higher level of total income. In short, if the total quantity of goods demanded exceeds the total quantity supplied, the latter will be driven upward. By making the same comparisons of NNP (column 2) and $C + I_n$ (column 6) at all other levels of NNP below the $470 billion equilibrium level, it will be found that the economy wants to spend in excess of the level at which businesses are willing to produce. The excess of total spending at all these levels of NNP will drive NNP upward to the $470 billion level.

The reverse holds true at all levels of NNP above the $470 billion equilibrium level. That is, businesses will find that the production of these total outputs fails to generate the levels of spending needed to take them off the market. Being unable to recover the costs involved in producing these outputs, businesses will cut back on their production. To illustrate: At the $510 billion level of output, businessmen will be disappointed to find that there is insufficient spending to permit the sale of that output. Of the $510 billion worth of income which this output creates, $480 billion is received back by businesses as consumption spending. Though supplemented by $20 billion worth of investment spending, the total quantity demanded ($500 billion) falls $10 billion short of the $510 billion quantity supplied. This means that $10 billion of inventories would pile up (column 7), and businesses would react to this unintended accumulation of unsold goods by cutting back on the rate of production. This decline in NNP will mean fewer jobs and a decline in total income. The reader should verify that deficiencies of total spending exist at all other levels of NNP in excess of the $470 billion level.

The equilibrium level of NNP exists where

the total quantity supplied, measured by NNP, and the aggregate quantity demanded, $C + I_n$, are equal. Any excess of total spending over total output will drive the latter upward. Any deficiency of total spending will pull NNP downward.

□   Graphic Analysis

The same analysis can be readily envisioned through a simple graph. In Figure 12-1 the 45-degree line (which was merely a guideline in Chapter 11's discussion of consumption and saving) now represents the economy's aggregate supply schedule. Let us see why this is so. By definition, each point on the aggregate supply schedule will indicate (on the vertical axis) the amount which the business commu-

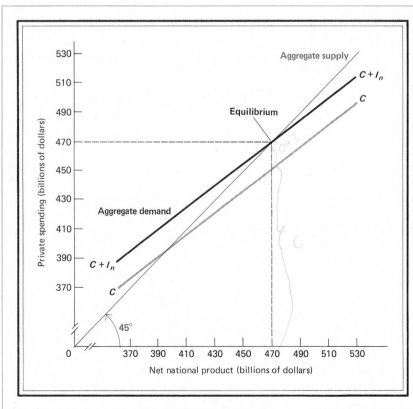

FIGURE 12-1   THE AGGREGATE DEMAND–AGGREGATE SUPPLY APPROACH TO THE EQUILIBRIUM NNP

The aggregate supply schedule is the 45-degree line, because business will produce any given level of NNP only when they expect a level of total spending ($C + I_n$) just sufficient to dispose of that output. The equilibrium level of NNP is determined by the intersection of this aggregate supply schedule with the $C + I_n$, or aggregate demand, schedule. Only at this point are the production and purchasing plans of the economy consistent with one another.

nity must receive back as total spending, or total revenue from business's point of view, in order to be induced or motivated to produce the corresponding level of national output (on the horizontal axis). Now, if we make the quite obvious and realistic assumption that the business community will produce or supply that national output whose value is equal to anticipated spending (receipts), we get a series of points equidistant from the two axes of Figure 12-1—that is, we get the 45-degree line for the aggregate supply schedule. We are simply saying that profit-seeking businessmen in the aggregate will be willing to undertake the production of, for example, a $430 billion national output only if anticipated expenditures are $430 billion. That is, businessmen will offer any level of NNP only if they expect $C + I_n$ to be just sufficient to clear that output off the national market. Similarly, businessmen will produce and offer a $450 billion output if they expect $C + I_n$ to be $450. If businessmen expected total spending to be greater or less than $450 billion, they would find it profitable to offer an equally larger or smaller national output.[1] Thus, a series of points—a line—equidis-

tant from the total output (NNP) axis and the total spending $(C + I_n)$ axis will summarize the aggregate supply plans of business. Being equidistant from the two axes, this line is necessarily the 45-degree line. We conclude that the 45-degree line is the aggregate supply schedule. This schedule shows the various outputs which businesses will offer at each of the various levels of spending that might prevail.

To get the $C + I_n$ or aggregate demand schedule in Figure 12-1, we simply graph the consumption schedule of Figure 11-3a and add to it vertically the constant $20 billion amount from Figure 11-6, which, we assume, businesses will want to invest at each possible level of NNP. More directly, we can plot the $C + I_n$ data of column 6 in Table 12-1.

The question: What is the equilibrium level of NNP? The answer: That NNP at which the aggregate quantity demanded and the aggregate quantity supplied are equal. And this must be where the aggregate supply schedule (the 45-degree line) and the aggregate demand schedule $(C + I_n)$ intersect. Because our graphed schedules are based on the data of Table 12-1, we once again find the equilibrium output to be at the $470 billion level. It is evident from Figure 12-1 that no levels of NNP above the equilibrium level are sustainable, because $C + I_n$ falls short of NNP. For example, at the $510 billion NNP level, $C + I_n$ is only $500 billion. Inventories of unsold goods rise to undesired levels. This unhappy state of affairs will prompt businesses to readjust their production sights downward in the direction of the $470 billion output level. Conversely, at all possible levels of NNP less than the $470 billion level, the economy desires to spend in excess of what businesses are producing. $C + I_n$ exceeds the value of the corresponding output. At the $410 billion NNP, for example, $C + I_n$ totals $425 billion. Inventories decline

---

[1]Quite nonsensical results follow if one experiments with lines lying below or above the 45-degree line. In the accompanying figure, line 1 suggests that the business community would be willing to produce, for example, a $430 billion national output if total expenditures were expected to be only $390 billion! Surely it is ridiculous to suggest that businessmen will purposely produce $40 billion of output in excess of what they anticipate can be sold.

Similarly, line 2 implies that businessmen will produce, for example, only $390 billion of national output when they

anticipate total expenditures of $430 billion. This suggests that the business community will purposely forgo the production of $40 billion of saleable output.

as the rate of spending exceeds the rate of production, prompting businessmen to raise their production sights in the direction of the $470 billion NNP. Unless there is some change in the consumption-saving plans of households or the investment plans of businesses, the $470 billion level of NNP will be sustained indefinitely.

LEAKAGES-INJECTIONS APPROACH

The aggregate demand–aggregate supply approach to the determination of NNP has the advantage of spotlighting total spending as the immediate determinant of the levels of output, employment, and income. Though the leakages-injections approach is less direct, it does have the advantage of giving emphasis to the reason $C + I_n$ and NNP are unequal at all levels of output except the equilibrium level.

The essence of the leakages-injections approach is this: Under our simplifying assumptions we know that the production of any level of national output or aggregate supply will generate an identical amount of income. But we also know a part of that income may be saved—that is, *not* consumed—by households. Saving therefore represents a *leakage,* withdrawal, or diversion of potential spending or demand from the income-expenditures stream. The obvious consequence of saving is that consumption falls short of aggregate output or NNP; hence, by itself consumption is insufficient to take aggregate supply off the market, and this fact would seem to set the stage for a decline in total output. However, the business sector does not intend to sell its entire output to consumers; some of the national output will take the form of capital or investment goods which will be sold within the business sector. Investment can therefore be thought of as an *injection* of spending into the income-expenditure stream which supplements consumption; stated differently, investment is a potential offset to, or replacement for, the leakage of saving.

If the leakage of saving exceeds the injection of investment, then $C + I_n$ will fall short of NNP—aggregate demand will fall short of aggregate supply—and this level of NNP will be too high to be sustainable. In other words, any NNP where saving exceeds investment will be an above-equilibrium NNP. Conversely, if the injection of investment exceeds the leakage of saving, then $C + I_n$ will be greater than NNP and NNP will be driven upward. To repeat: Any NNP where investment exceeds saving will be a below-equilibrium NNP. Only where $S = I_n$—where the leakage of saving is exactly offset by the injection of investment—will aggregate demand equal aggregate supply. And we know that the equality of aggregate demand and aggregate supply defines the equilibrium NNP.

It is important to keep in mind that in the very simple private economy of this chapter, there are only one leakage (saving) and one injection (investment) to worry about. In general terms, a *leakage* is any use of income other than its expenditure on domestically produced output. Hence, in the more realistic models which follow (Chapters 13 and 41), we shall find that the additional leakages of taxes and imports will have to be incorporated into our analysis. Similarly, an *injection* is any supplement to consumer spending on domestic production. So, again, in later models we must add injections of government purchases and exports to our discussion. But for the present, in putting the leakages-injections approach to work, we need only compare the single leakage of saving with the sole injection of investment to assess the impact upon NNP.

□   **Tabular Analysis**

The saving schedule (columns 2 and 4) and the investment schedule (columns 2 and 5) of Table 12-1 are pertinent. Our $C + I_n = $ NNP approach has just led us to conclude that all levels of NNP that are less than $470 billion are unstable because the corresponding $C + I_n$ exceeds these NNPs, driving them upward. A comparison of the amounts households and businesses want to save and invest at each of the below-equilibrium NNP levels explains the excesses of total spending. In particular, at each of these relatively low NNP levels, businesses desire to invest more than households plan to save. For example, at the $410 billion level of NNP, households will save only $5 billion, thereby spending $405 of their $410 billion incomes. Supplemented by $20 billion of business investment, total spending $(C + I_n)$ is obviously $425 billion. Total spending exceeds NNP by $15 billion $(= \$425 - \$410)$ *because* the amount businesses desire to invest at this level of NNP exceeds the amounts households plan to save by $15 billion. It is the fact that a very small "leakage" of saving at this relatively low income level will be more than compensated for by the relatively large injection of investment spending which causes $C + I_n$ to exceed NNP and induce the latter upward.

Similarly, all levels of NNP above the $470 billion level are also unstable, because here NNP exceeds $C + I_n$. The reason for this insufficiency of total spending lies in the fact that at all NNP levels above $470 billion, households will attempt to save in excess of the amount businesses desire to invest. That is, the saving leakage is not replaced or compensated for by the injection of investment. For example, households will choose to save at the high rate of $30 billion at the $510 billion NNP. Businesses, however, will invest only $20 billion at this NNP. This $10 billion excess of saving over investment will cause total spending to fall $10 billion short of the value of total output. And this deficiency will cause NNP to decline.

Again we verify that the equilibrium NNP is at the $470 billion level. It is only at this point that the saving desires of households and the investment plans of businesses are equal. And only when businesses and households attempt to invest and save at equal rates—where the leakages and injections are equal—will

$C + I_n = \text{NNP}$. Only here will the annual rates of production and spending be in balance; only here will unplanned changes in inventories be absent. One can think of it in this way: If saving were zero, consumer spending would always be sufficient to clear the market of any given NNP; that is, consumption would equal NNP. But saving can and does occur, causing consumption to fall short of NNP. Hence, only when businesses are willing to invest at the same rate at which households attempt to save will the amount by which consumption falls short of NNP be precisely compensated for.

□ Graphic Analysis

The leakages-injections approach to determining the equilibrium NNP can be readily demonstrated graphically. In Figure 12-2 we have merely combined the saving schedule of Figure 11-3b and the simplified investment schedule of Figure 11-6. The numerical data for these schedules are repeated in columns 2, 4, and 5 of Table 12-1. It is evident that the equilibrium level of NNP is at $470 billion, where the saving and investment schedules intersect. Only here do households and businesses plan to save and invest at the same rates; therefore, only here will NNP and $C + I_n$ be equal. At all higher levels of NNP, households will attempt to save at a rate higher than businesses are willing to invest. The fact that the saving leakage exceeds the investment injection causes $C + I_n$ to fall short of NNP, driving the latter downward. At the $510 billion NNP, for example, saving of $30 billion will exceed investment of $20 billion by $10 billion, with the result that $C + I_n$ is $500 billion—$10 billion short of NNP. At all levels of NNP below the $470 billion equilibrium level, businesses will desire to invest at a rate in excess of the amount households plan to save. Here the injection of investment exceeds the leakage of saving so that $C + I_n$ exceeds NNP, driving the latter upward. To illustrate: At the $410 billion level of NNP the $5

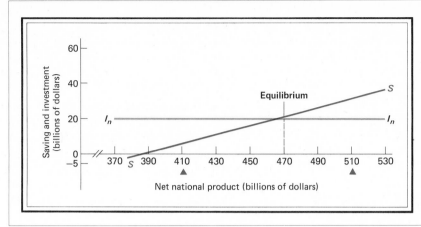

FIGURE 12-2 THE LEAKAGES—INJECTIONS APPROACH TO THE EQUILIBRIUM NNP

A second approach is to view the equilibrium NNP as determined by the intersection of the saving (S) and investment (I_n) schedules. Only at the point of equilibrium will households plan to save the amount businesses want to invest. It is the consistency of these plans which causes NNP and $C + I_n$ to be equal.

billion leakage of saving is more than compensated for by the $20 billion that businesses desire to invest. The result is that $C + I_n$ exceeds NNP by $15 billion, inducing businesses to produce a larger NNP.

PLANNED VERSUS ACTUAL SAVING AND INVESTMENT

We have emphasized that because savers and investors are essentially different groups and are differently motivated, discrepancies in saving and investment can occur and these differences bring about changes in the equilibrium NNP. Now we must recognize that, in another sense, saving and investment must always be equal to one another! This apparent contradiction concerning the equality of saving and investment is resolved when we distinguish between *planned* or *intended* saving and investment (which need not be equal) and *actual* or *realized* saving and investment (which by definition must be equal). The catch essentially is that *actual investment consists of both intended and unintended investment (unintended changes in inventory investment), and the latter functions as a balancing item which always equates the actual amounts saved and invested in any period of time.*

☐ **Disequilibrium and Inventories**

Consider, for example, the $490 billion above-equilibrium NNP (Table 12-1). What would happen if businesses produced this output, thinking they could sell it? At this level, households save $25 billion of their $490 billion DI, so consumption is only $465 billion. *Intended* investment is $20 billion; that is, businessmen want to buy $20 billion worth of capital goods. This means aggregate demand ($C + I_n$) is $485 billion, and sales therefore fall short of production by $5 billion. This extra $5 billion of goods is obviously retained by businesses as an *unintended* or involuntary increase in inventories (column 7). It is unintended because it results from the failure of total spending to take total output off the market. Remembering that, by definition, changes in inventories are a part of investment, we note that actual or *realized* investment of $25 billion ($20 intended or planned *plus* $5 unintended or unplanned) equals *realized* saving of $25 billion, even though *intended* saving exceeds *intended* investment by $5 billion. Businessmen, obviously not anxious to accumulate unwanted inventories at this annual rate, will react by cutting back on production.

Now look at the below-equilibrium $450 billion output (Table 12-1). Because households save only $15 billion of their $450 billion DI, consumption is $435 billion. Businesses want or intend to invest $20 billion, so aggregate demand is $455 billion. That is, sales exceed production by $5 billion. How can this be? The answer is that an unplanned or unintended decline in business inventories has occurred. More specifically, businesses have unintentionally *dis*invested $5 billion in inventories (column 7). Note once again that *realized* investment is $15 billion ($20 intended or planned *minus* $5 unintended or unplanned) and equal to *realized* saving of $15 billion, even though *intended* investment exceeds *intended* saving by $5 billion. This unintended decline in investment in inventories due to the excess of sales over production will induce businessmen to increase the NNP by expanding production.

To summarize: At all *above-equilibrium* levels of NNP (where intended saving exceeds intended investment), realized investment and realized saving are equal because of unintended increases in inventories which, by definition, are included as a part of actual or realized investment. Graphically (Figure 12-2) the unintended inventory increase is measured by the vertical distance by which the (intended) saving schedule lies above the (intended) investment schedule. At all below-equilibrium levels of NNP (where intended investment exceeds intended saving), realized investment will be equal to realized saving because of unintended decreases in inventories which must be subtracted from intended investment to determine actual investment. These unintended inventory declines are shown graphically as the vertical distance by which the (intended) investment schedule lies above the (intended) saving schedule.

◻ **Achieving Equilibrium**

These distinctions are important because they correctly suggest that *it is the equality of intended investment and intended saving which determines the equilibrium level of* *NNP.* We can think of the process by which equilibrium is achieved as follows:

1 A difference between intended saving and intended investment causes a difference between the production and spending plans of the economy as a whole.

2 This difference between aggregate production and spending plans results in unintended investment or disinvestment in inventories.

3 As long as unintended investment in inventories persists, businessmen will revise their production plans downward and thereby reduce the NNP. Conversely, as long as unintended disinvestment in inventories exists, firms will revise their production plans upward and increase the NNP. Both types of movements in NNP are toward equilibrium in that they tend to bring about the equality of intended saving and intended investment.

4 Only where intended saving and intended investment are equal will the level of NNP be stable or in equilibrium; that is, only where intended investment equals intended saving will there be no unintended investment or disinvestment in inventories to drive the NNP downward or upward. Note in column 7 of Table 12-1 that only at the equilibrium NNP is there no unintended investment or disinvestment in inventories.

■
_____

CHANGES IN EQUILIBRIUM NNP AND THE MULTIPLIER

Thus far, we have been concerned with explaining the equilibrium levels of total output and income. But we saw in Chapter 10 that actually the NNP of American capitalism is seldom stable; rather, it is characterized by long-run growth and punctuated by cyclical fluctuations. Let us turn to the questions of *why* and *how* the equilibrium level of NNP fluctuates.

The equilibrium level of NNP will change in response to changes in the investment schedule or the saving-consumption schedules.

Because investment spending generally is less stable than the consumption-saving schedules, we shall assume that changes in the investment schedule occur. The impact of changes in investment can be readily envisioned through Figure 12-3a and b. Suppose the expected rate of net profit on investment rises *or* the interest rate falls and, as a result, investment spending increases by, say, $5 billion. This is indicated in Figure 12-3a as an upward shift in the aggregate demand schedule from $(C + I_n)_0$ to $(C + I_n)_1$, and in Figure 12-3b as an upward shift in the investment schedule from I_{n0} to I_{n1}. In each of these portrayals the

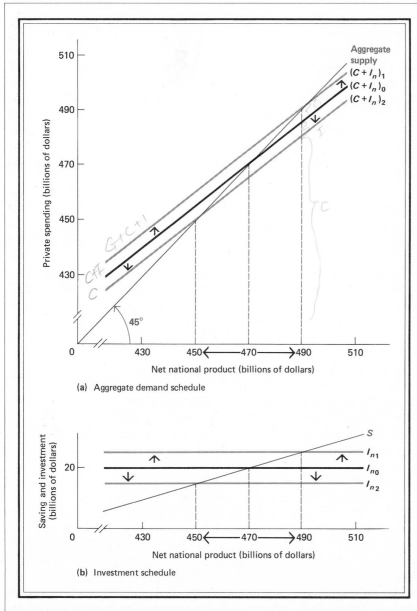

(a)   Aggregate demand schedule

(b)   Investment schedule

FIGURE 12-3 CHANGES IN THE EQUILIBRIUM NNP CAUSED BY SHIFTS IN (a) THE AGGREGATE DEMAND SCHEDULE AND (b) THE INVESTMENT SCHEDULE

An upshift in the aggregate demand schedule from, say, $(C + I_n)_0$ to $(C + I_n)_1$ will increase the equilibrium NNP. Conversely, a downshift in the aggregate demand schedule from, say, $(C + I_n)_0$ to $(C + I_n)_2$ will lower the equilibrium NNP. In the saving-investment figure an upshift in the investment schedule $(I_{n0}$ to $I_{n1})$ will raise, and downshift $(I_{n0}$ to $I_{n2})$ will lower, the equilibrium NNP.

result is a rise in the equilibrium NNP from $470 to $490 billion.

Conversely, if the expected rate of net profits from investment decreases *or* the interest rate rises, a decline in investment spending of, say, $5 billion will occur. This is shown by the downward shift of the investment schedule from I_{n0} to I_{n2} in Figure 12-3b and the aggregate demand schedule from $(C + I_n)_0$ to $(C + I_n)_2$ in Figure 12-3a. In each case, these shifts cause the equilibrium NNP to fall from the original $470 billion level to $450 billion. The reader should verify these conclusions in terms of Table 12-1 by substituting $25 billion and then $15 billion for the $20 billion investment figure given in the table.

Incidentally—and at the risk of getting ahead of ourselves—the indicated $5 billion changes in investment may be the direct result of economic policy. Looking back at Table 11-2, we find that the initial $20 billion level of investment is associated with an 8 percent interest rate. *If* the economy is in a recession, the monetary authorities may purposely negotiate a reduction in the interest rate to 6 percent (by increasing the money supply), causing a $5 billion increase in investment and thereby in aggregate demand to stimulate the economy. Conversely, *if,* with the initial $20 billion of investment, the economy faces a demand-pull inflation problem, the monetary authorities may increase the interest rate to 10 percent (by reducing the money supply), thereby reducing investment and aggregate demand to constrain the inflation. Monetary policy—changing the money supply for the purpose of altering interest rates and aggregate demand—is the subject of Chapter 16.

When changes in the consumption-saving schedules occur, they will have similar effects. If households want to consume more (save less) at each level of NNP, the aggregate demand schedule will shift upward and the saving schedule downward in Figure 12-3a and b, respectively. In either portrayal these shifts will mean an increase in the equilibrium NNP. If households want to consume less (save

more) at each possible NNP, the resulting drop in the consumption schedule and the increase in the saving schedule will in turn reduce the equilibrium NNP.

□ **The Multiplier Effect**

You have undoubtedly detected a curious feature of these examples: A $5 billion change in investment spending has given rise to a $20 billion change in the output-income level. This surprising result is called the *multiplier effect.* It is based upon two seemingly innocent facts. On the one hand, the economy is characterized by repetitive, continuous flows of expenditures and income wherein the dollars spent by Smith are received as income by Jones. On the other hand, any change in income will cause both consumption and saving to vary in the same direction as, and by a fraction of, the change in income. It follows from these two facts that an initial change in the rate of spending will cause a chain reaction which, although of diminishing importance at each successive step, will cumulate to a multiple change in NNP.

Illustration The multiplier effect is illustrated numerically in Table 12-2 for a $5 billion increase in investment spending. We assume that the MPC is three-fourths; the MPS is therefore one-fourth. Also assume that the economy is initially in equilibrium at $470 billion.

The initial increase in investment generates an equal amount of wage, rent, interest, and profit income for the simple reason that spending and receiving income are two sides of the same transaction. How much consumption will be induced by this $5 billion increase in the incomes of households? We find the answer by applying the marginal propensity to consume of three-fourths to this change in income. Thus, the $5 billion income increase causes consumption to rise by $3.75 ($= \frac{3}{4}$ of $5) billion and saving by $1.25 ($= \frac{1}{4}$ of $5) billion. The $3.75 billion which is spent is received by other households as income. They in turn consume three-fourths, or $2.81 billion, of this

6⁷⁰

259

Chapter 12   The Equilibrium Levels of Output, Employment, and Income

Table 12-2 THE MULTIPLIER: A TABULAR ILLUSTRATION
(*hypothetical data; in billions*)

MULTIPLIER TELLS
HOW MUCH CHANGE
GNP PER 100 SPENT

	(1) Change in income	(2) Change in consumption (MPC = $\frac{3}{4}$)	(3) Change in saving (MPS = $\frac{1}{4}$)
Assumed increase in investment	$ 5.00	$ 3.75	$1.25
Second round	3.75	2.81	0.94
Third round	2.81	2.11	0.70
Fourth round	2.11	1.58	0.53
Fifth round	1.58	1.19	0.39
All other rounds	4.75	3.56	1.19
Totals	$20.00	$15.00	$5.00

$3.75 billion and save one-fourth, or $0.94 billion. The $2.81 billion which is consumed flows to still other households as income. Though the spending and respending effects of the initial increase in investment diminish with each successive round of spending, the cumulative increase in the output-income level will be $20 billion if the process is carried through to the last dollar. The assumed $5 billion increase in investment will therefore increase the equilibrium NNP by $20 billion, from $470 to $490 billion.

It is no coincidence that the multiplier effect ends at the point where exactly enough saving has been generated to offset the initial $5 billion increase in investment spending. It is only then that the disequilibrium created by the investment increase will be corrected. In this case, NNP and total incomes must rise by $20 billion to create $5 billion in additional saving to match the $5 billion increase in investment spending. Income must increase by 4 times the initial excess of investment over saving, because households save one-fourth of any increase in their incomes. In this example the multiplier—the number of times the ultimate increase in income exceeds the initial increase in investment spending—is 4.

Characteristics of the Multiplier Two noteworthy characteristics of the multiplier are not sufficiently emphasized by mere illustrations of its mechanics:

1 Remember that a change in any of the components of the aggregate demand schedule will give rise to a multiplier effect. In practice, economists usually associate the multiplier with changes in investment because of the relative instability of the investment schedule as compared with the consumption schedule. But keep in mind that a shift in the consumption schedule or, as we shall see shortly, a shift in the schedule of government spending will also prompt a similar chain reaction.

2 Keep in mind too that the multiplier works in both directions. That is, a small increase in spending can give rise to a multiple increase in NNP, or a small decrease in spending can be magnified into a much larger decrease in NNP by the multiplier. Note carefully the effects of the shift in $(C + I_n)_0$ to $(C + I_n)_1$ or $(C + I_n)_2$ and I_{n0} to I_{n1} or I_{n2} in Figure 12-3*a* and *b*.

The Multiplier and the Marginal Propensities You may have sensed from Table 12-2 that a relationship of some sort must exist between the MPS and the size of the multiplier. There is such a relationship: the fraction of an increase in income which is saved—that is, the MPS—determines the cumulative respending effects of any initial change in I_n, G, or C, and therefore the multiplier. More specifically, *the size of the MPS and the size of the multiplier are inversely related*. The smaller the fraction of any change in income which is saved, the greater the respending at each round and, therefore, the greater the multiplier. If the MPS is one-fourth, as in our example, the multiplier is 4. If the MPS were one-third, the multiplier would be 3. If the MPS were one-fifth, the multiplier would be 5. Look again at Table 12-2 and Figure 12-3*b*. Initially the economy is in equilibrium at the $470 billion level of NNP. Now businessmen increase investment by $5 billion so that intended investment of $25 billion exceeds intended saving of $20 billion at the $470 billion level. That is, $470 billion is obviously no longer the equilibrium NNP. The question is: By how much must net national product or income rise to restore equilibrium? The answer is: By enough to generate $5 billion of additional saving to offset the $5 billion increase in investment. Because households save $1 out of every $4 of additional income they receive (MPS = $\frac{1}{4}$), NNP must obviously rise by $20 billion—4 times the assumed increase in investment—to create the $5 billion of extra saving necessary to restore equilibrium. Hence, a multiplier of 4. If the MPS were one-third, NNP would only have to rise by $15 billion (3 times the increase in investment) to generate $5 billion of additional saving and restore equilibrium, and the multiplier therefore would be 3. But if the MPS were one-fifth, NNP would have to rise by $25 billion in order for an extra $5 billion of saving to be forthcoming and equilibrium to be restored, yielding a multiplier of 5.

We can summarize these and all other possibilities by merely saying that *the multiplier is equal to the reciprocal of the MPS.* The reciprocal of any number is the quotient you obtain by dividing 1 by that number. In short, we can say:

$$\text{The multiplier} = \frac{1}{\text{MPS}}$$

This formula provides us with a shorthand method of determining the multiplier. All we need to know is the MPS to calculate the size of the multiplier quickly. Recall, too, from Chapter 11 that since MPC + MPS = 1, it

follows that MPS = 1 − MPC. Therefore, we can also write our multiplier formula as[2]

$$\text{The multiplier} = \frac{1}{1 - \text{MPC}}$$

Significance of the Multiplier   The significance of the multiplier is self-evident. A relatively small change in the investment plans of businesses or the consumption-saving plans of households can trigger a much larger change in the equilibrium level of NNP. The multiplier magnifies the fluctuations in business activity initiated by changes in spending.

Note that the larger the MPC, the greater will be the multiplier. For example, if the MPC is $\frac{3}{4}$ and the multiplier is therefore 4, a $10 billion decline in investment will reduce the equilibrium NNP by $40 billion. But if the MPC is only $\frac{2}{3}$ and the multiplier is thereby 3, the same $10 billion drop in investment will cause the equilibrium NNP to fall by only $30 billion. This makes sense intuitively: A large MPC means the chain of induced consumption shown in column 2 of Table 12-2 dampens down slowly and thereby cumulates to a large change in income. Conversely, a small MPC causes induced consumption to decline quickly so the cumulative change in income is small.

Incidentally, we will find, in discussing the so-called built-in stabilizers in Chapter 13, that one of the major goals of public policy is to

---

[2] Furthermore, the importance of footnote 7 in Chapter 11 now becomes clear. There we noted that the MPS measures the slope of the saving schedule. In terms of the leakages-injections ($S = I_n$) approach, this means that if the MPS is relatively large (say, one-half) and the slope of the saving schedule is therefore relatively steep (one-half), any given upward shift in investment spending will be subject to a relatively small multiplier. For example, a $5 billion increase in investment will entail a new point of intersection of the S and I_n schedules only $10 billion to the right of the original equilibrium NNP. The multiplier is only 2. But if the MPS is relatively small (say, one-sixth), the slope of the saving schedule will be relatively gentle. Therefore, a $5 billion upward shift in the investment schedule will provide a new intersection point some $30 billion to the right of the original equilibrium NNP. The multiplier is 6 in this case. The reader should verify these two examples by drawing appropriate saving and investment diagrams.

structure a system of taxes and transfer payments which will reduce the MPC and diminish the size of the multiplier, thereby lessening the destabilizing effect of a given change in investment or consumption expenditures.

Generalizing the Multiplier   The multiplier concept as presented here is sometimes called the *simple multiplier* for the obvious reason that it is based upon a very simple model of the economy. In terms of the $\dfrac{1}{\text{MPS}}$ formulation, the simple multiplier reflects only the leakage of saving. But, as noted earlier, in the real world successive rounds of income and spending can also be dampened down by other leakages in the form of taxes and imports. That is, in addition to the leakage into saving, some portion of income at each round would be siphoned off as additional taxes, and another part would be used to purchase additional goods from abroad. The result of these additional leakages is that the $\dfrac{1}{\text{MPS}}$ statement of the multiplier can be generalized by changing the denominator to read "fraction of the change in income which is not spent on domestic output" or "fraction of the change in income which leaks, or is diverted, from the income-expenditure stream." The more realistic multiplier which results when all these leakages—saving, taxes, and imports—are taken into account is called the *complex multiplier*. The Council of Economic Advisers has estimated the complex multiplier for the United States to be about 2.

☐   **Paradox of Thrift**

A curious paradox is suggested by the leakages-injections approach to NNP determination and by our analysis of the multiplier. The paradox is that if society attempts to save more, it may end up actually saving the same amount, or even less. Figure 12-4 is relevant. Suppose I_n and S_1 are the current investment and saving schedules which determine a $470 billion equilibrium NNP. Now assume that households, perhaps anticipating a recession, attempt to save, say, $5 billion more at each income level in order to provide a nest egg against the expected bad times. This attempt to save more is reflected in an upward shift of the saving schedule from S_1 to S_2. But this very upshift creates an excess of planned saving over planned investment at the current $470 billion equilibrium output. And we know that the multiplier effect will cause this small increase in saving (decline in consumption) to be reflected in a much larger—$20 billion ($5 × 4) in this case—*decline* in equilibrium NNP.

There is a paradox here in several different

FIGURE 12-4 THE PARADOX OF THRIFT

Unless offset by an upshift in the investment schedule, any attempt by households to save more (S_1 to S_2) will be frustrated by a multiple decline in the equilibrium NNP.

senses. First, note that at the new $450 billion equilibrium NNP, households are saving the same amount they did at the original $470 billion NNP. Society's attempt to save more has been frustrated by the multiple decline in the equilibrium NNP which that attempt itself caused. Second, this analysis suggests that thrift, which has always been held in high esteem in our economy, can be something of a social vice. From the individual point of view, a penny saved may be a penny earned. But from the social point of view, a penny saved is a penny not spent and therefore causes a decline in someone's income. The act of thrift may be virtuous from the individual's viewpoint but disastrous from the social standpoint because of its undesirable effects upon total output and employment.[3] Third, it is ironic, if not paradoxical, that households may be most strongly induced to save more (consume less) at the very time when increased saving is most inappropriate and economically undesirable, that is, when the economy seems to be backsliding into a recession. An individual fearing the loss of his job will hardly be inclined to go on a spending spree.

The reader should pursue this analysis of the paradox of thrift and the multiplier by substituting an upsloping investment schedule for the simplified investment schedule we have employed. In the case of the paradox of thrift, you should conclude that the attempt of households to save more will not merely be frustrated but will actually give rise to a *decline* in the amount saved. You should also find that a positively sloped investment schedule will increase the size of the multiplier and in effect make it a "supermultiplier."[4]

---

[3] Recall from Chapter 2, however, that an economy which saves and invests a large proportion of its *full-employment output* will tend to achieve a high rate of growth.

[4] *Hints:* (1) Substitute the investment schedule of columns 1 and 3 in Table 11-3 in column 5 of Table 12-1; (2) assume a $5 billion increase in saving; (3) compute (estimate) the new equilibrium point at which intended saving equals intended investment; (4) compare the original and the new amounts saved; and (5) calculate the size of the multiplier. Note that the size of the multiplier is larger because, for

---

EQUILIBRIUM VERSUS FULL–EMPLOYMENT NNP

We now turn from the task of explaining to that of evaluating the equilibrium NNP.

Too much emphasis cannot be placed upon the fact that the $470 billion equilibrium NNP embodied in our analysis (Table 12-1 and Figures 12-1 and 12-2) may or may not entail full employment. Remember: The basic theme of Keynesian economics is that capitalism contains no mechanisms capable of automatically creating that particular level of aggregate demand which will induce businessmen to produce a full-employment noninflationary level of output. For example, if we assume the full-employment noninflationary output to be $490 billion, it would be only by chance that the aggregate demand schedule would be at the $(C + I_n)_0$ level in Figure 12-5 to intersect the aggregate supply schedule at this desired level of output. Aggregate demand might very well lie below this ideal location at, say, the $(C + I_n)_2$ level, or above the full-employment noninflationary output at, say, the $(C + I_n)_1$ level.

□ **Recessionary Gap**

Suppose in Figure 12-5 that the aggregate demand schedule is at $(C + I_n)_2$, which, incidentally, happens to be the aggregate demand

---

each successive round of income, there will occur not only additional consumption as in our simple multiplier, but also additional investment. Not only does the multiplier process involve a marginal propensity to consume (MPC) of .75, but also a marginal propensity to invest (MPI) of .10, the latter defined as the ratio of a change in investment relative to the change in NNP which induced or resulted in that change in investment. Hence, we must add the MPI to the denominator of our $\frac{1}{1 - \text{MPC}}$ formulation of the multiplier, making it $\frac{1}{1 - (\text{MPC} + \text{MPI})}$. In this case the multiplier equals $\frac{1}{1 - (.75 + .10)} = \frac{1}{.15} = 6\frac{2}{3}$.

Question 8 at the end of this chapter provides a further opportunity to work with the "supermultiplier."

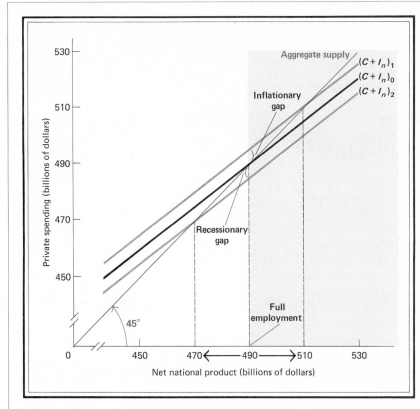

FIGURE 12-5 RECESSIONARY
AND INFLATIONARY GAPS

In a capitalistic system the equilibrium and full-employment NNPs may not coincide. Recessionary and inflationary gaps refer to the deficiency or excess of total spending which may exist at the full-employment NNP. A recessionary gap will cause a multiple decline in the real NNP, whereas an inflationary gap will increase the money NNP.

schedule developed and employed in this chapter. This schedule intersects aggregate supply to the left of the full-employment output, causing the economy's aggregate production to fall $20 billion short of its capacity production. In terms of Table 12-1, the economy is failing to employ 5 million of its 70 million available workers and, as a result, is sacrificing $20 billion worth of output.

The amount by which aggregate demand falls short of the full-employment level of NNP is called the *recessionary gap* simply because this deficiency of spending has a contractionary or depressing impact upon the economy. In this case, note in Table 12-1 that, assuming the full-employment NNP to be $490 billion, the corresponding level of total demand is only $485 billion. Hence, the recessionary gap is $5 billion. Graphically, the deflationary

gap is the *vertical* distance by which the aggregate demand schedule $(C + I_n)_2$ falls short of the full-employment point on the aggregate supply schedule. Caution: The recessionary gap is *not* the $20 billion difference between the equilibrium and the full-employment NNP; this $20 billion difference is the $5 billion recessionary gap *times* the multiplier of 4.

☐   **Inflationary Gap**

If aggregate demand happens to be at $(C + I_n)_1$ in Figure 12-5, an inflationary gap will exist. Specifically, the amount by which aggregate demand exceeds the full-employment level of NNP is called an *inflationary gap*. In this case, a $5 billion inflationary gap is assumed to exist, as shown by the vertical distance between $(C + I_n)_1$ and the full-employment point on the aggregate supply schedule.

The effect of this inflationary gap—this excess demand—will be to pull up the prices on the economy's fixed physical volume of production. Businesses as a whole cannot respond to the $5 billion in excess demand by expanding their real outputs, so *demand-pull inflation* will occur. Now Figure 12-5 suggests that the $5 billion inflationary gap, subject to a multiplier of 4, will cause *money* NNP to rise by $20 billion (to $510 billion) while *real* NNP remains unchanged at $490. This is, in fact, one possible outcome. But the reader should be warned that the inflationary process is dynamic and complex and that equilibrium need not be reestablished at $510 billion. Specifically, the process of inflation may have a feedback effect upon the aggregate demand schedule. For example, the occurrence and anticipation of inflation may shift the consumption schedule upward; rising prices will expand money profits and tend to increase investment spending. In short, inflation might "feed upon itself" and accelerate in a way which cannot be visualized by the simple point-in-time analytics of Figure 12-5. Let us settle for this generalization: NNP changes to the left of the full-employment output (the white area of Figure 12-5) are *real* changes; NNP changes to the right of full-employment output (the brown area) are merely monetary or "paper" changes in NNP:

□   **Premature Inflation**

But, alas, even this generalization must be qualified for the problem of premature inflation. There is substantial evidence to suggest that in advanced capitalist economies the transition from the white (real changes) area to the brown (price changes) area is not abrupt, as in Figure 12-5, but is actually rather blurred. That is, as aggregate demand rises and the economy *approaches* full employment, *both* real NNP *and* the price level will increase (Figure 10-1). If the price level does indeed rise *before* the economy is at full-employment or capacity output, this increase suggests that the ideal goal of "full employment without inflation" may be unattainable. Instead, society may be forced to choose between "full employment with inflation" or "price stability with unemployment." Premature inflation and possible policies to alleviate it will be the focal point of Chapter 18; until then, we embrace the simplification that the price level is constant until full employment is realized.[5]

---

[5] Our discussion ignores another complication: Full employment (or capacity production) itself is something of an elastic concept because a given number of workers can increase their hours of work just by working overtime, or, as a matter of fact, persons who are not ordinarily in the labor force may be induced to offer their services when job opportunities are abundant. The general validity of our analysis is not impaired by ignoring this refinement.

Summary

1   The equilibrium level of NNP is that at which the aggregate quantity demanded and the aggregate quantity supplied are equal or, graphically, where the $C + I_n$ line intersects the 45-degree line. At any NNP greater than the equilibrium NNP, aggregate quantity supplied will exceed the aggregate quantity demanded, resulting in unintended investment in inventories, depressed profits, and eventual declines in output, employment, and income. At any below-equilibrium NNP, the aggregate quantity demanded will exceed the aggregate quantity supplied, thereby resulting in unintended disinvestment in inventories, substantial profits, and eventual increases in NNP.

A complementary leakages-injections approach determines the equilibrium

NNP at the point where the amount households plan to save and the amount businesses plan to invest are equal. This is at the point where the saving and investment schedules intersect. Any excess of planned saving over planned investment will cause a shortage of total spending, forcing NNP to fall. Any excess of planned investment over planned saving will cause an excess of total spending, inducing NNP to rise. These changes in NNP will in both cases correct the assumed discrepancies in investment and saving plans.

3   Shifts in the saving-consumption schedules or in the investment schedule will cause the equilibrium output-income level to change by several times the amount of the initial change in spending. This phenomenon, which accompanies both increases and decreases in spending, is called the *multiplier effect.* The simple multiplier is equal to the reciprocal of the marginal propensity to save.

4   The *paradox of thrift* is the notion that the attempt of society to save more, as reflected in an upshift of the supply schedule, may be frustrated by the multiple decline in the equilibrium NNP which will ensue.

5   The equilibrium level of NNP and the full-employment noninflationary NNP need not coincide. The amount by which aggregate demand falls short of the full-employment NNP is called the recessionary gap; this gap prompts a multiple decline in real NNP. The amount by which aggregate demand exceeds the full-employment NNP is the inflationary gap; it causes demand-pull inflation.

Questions and Study Suggestions

1   Key terms and concepts to remember: aggregate demand; aggregate supply; leakages-injections approach; equilibrium NNP; planned (intended) saving and investment; actual (realized) saving and investment; multiplier effect; paradox of thrift; supermultiplier; recessionary and inflationary gaps.

2   Explain graphically the determination of the equilibrium NNP by *a.* the aggregate demand–aggregate supply approach and *b.* the leakages-injections approach for the private sector of the economy. Why must these two approaches always yield the same equilibrium NNP?

3   Explain why the difference between *planned* saving and investment, on the one hand, and *actual* saving and investment, on the other, is significant. Explain the paradox of thrift, indicating its significance.

4   Critically evaluate:

a.   "It is socially desirable for households to attempt to increase their rate of saving whenever a recession begins. In this way households will be able to accumulate the financial resources to pay their way through bad times."

b.   "The fact that households may try to save more than businesses want to invest is of no consequence, because events will in time force households and businesses to save and invest at the same rates."

5   What is the multiplier effect? What relationship does the MPC bear to the size of the multiplier? The MPS? What will the multiplier be when the MPS is 0, 0.4, 0.6, and 1? When the MPC is 1, $\frac{8}{9}$, $\frac{2}{3}$, $\frac{1}{2}$, and 0? How much of a change in NNP will result if businesses increase their level of investment by \$8 billion and the MPC in the economy is $\frac{4}{5}$? If the MPC is $\frac{2}{3}$? Explain the difference between the simple and the complex multiplier.

6   What effect will each of the changes designated in question 7 at the end of Chapter 11 have upon the equilibrium level of NNP? Explain your answers.

7   Assuming the level of investment is $16 billion and independent of the level of total output, complete the following table and determine the equilibrium level of output and income which the private sector of the economy would provide.

Possible levels of employment, millions	Aggregate supply (NNP = DI), billions	Consumption, billions	Saving, billions
40	$240	$244	$_____
45	260	260	_____
50	280	276	_____
55	300	292	_____
60	320	308	_____
65	340	324	_____
70	360	340	_____
75	380	356	_____
80	400	372	_____

a.   If this economy has a labor force of 70 million, will there exist an inflationary or a recessionary gap? Explain the consequences of this gap.

b.   Will an inflationary or a recessionary gap exist if the available labor force is only 55 million? Trace the consequences.

c.   What are the sizes of the MPC and the MPS?

d.   Use the multiplier concept to explain the increase in the equilibrium NNP which will occur as the result of an increase in investment spending from $16 to $20 billion.

8   Using the consumption and saving data given in question 7, what will the equilibrium level of income be if investment is $2 billion at the $240 billion level of NNP and increases by $2 billion for every $20 billion increase in NNP? Assuming that businessmen decide to invest $4 billion more at each level of NNP, what will be the new equilibrium NNP? What is the size of the "supermultiplier"? Explain why it is larger than the multiplier derived in question 7.

9   Using the consumption and saving data given in question 7 and assuming the level of investment is $16 billion, what are the levels of intended saving and investment at the $380 billion level of aggregate supply? What are the levels of realized saving and investment? What are intended saving and investment at the $300 billion level of aggregate supply? What are the levels of realized saving and investment? Use the concept of unintended investment to explain adjustments toward equilibrium from both the $380 and $300 billion levels of aggregate supply.

10   *Advanced analysis:* Assume the consumption schedule for the economy is such that $C = 50 + 0.8Y$. Assume further that investment is autonomous or exogenous (indicated by I_0); that is, investment is independent of the level of income and in the amount $I = I_0 = 30$. Recall also that in equilibrium the aggregate amount of output supplied (Y) is equal to the aggregate amount demanded $(C + I)$, or $Y = C + I$.

a.   Calculate the equilibrium level of income for this economy. Check your work by putting the consumption and investment schedules in tabular form and determining the equilibrium income.

b.   What will happen to equilibrium Y if $I = I_0 = 10$? What does this tell you about the size of the multiplier?

11   *Advanced analysis:* If $I = I_0 = 50$ and $C = 30 + 0.5Y$, what is the equilibrium level of income? If $I = 10 + 0.1Y$ and $C = 50 + 0.6Y$, what is the equilibrium level of income? What is the multiplier for this economy?

Selected References

Campagna, Anthony S.: *Macroeconomics: Theory and Policy* (Boston: Houghton Mifflin Company, 1974), chaps. 3–5, 8, 9.

Hansen, Alvin: *A Guide to Keynes* (New York: McGraw-Hill Book Company, 1953).

Makin, John H.: *Macroeconomics* (Hinsdale, Ill.: The Dryden Press, 1975), chap. 4.

Peterson, Wallace C.: *Income, Employment, and Economic Growth,* 3d ed. (New York: W. W. Norton & Company, Inc., 1974), chaps. 5–8.

Shapiro, Edward: *Macroeconomic Analysis,* 3d ed. (New York: Harcourt, Brace, Jovanovich, Inc., 1974), chaps. 6–14.

Last Word
Looking a Gift Horse in the Mouth

Humorist Arthur Hoppe interprets the economics of inflation and unemployment.

Woofie Tweeter, the young stockbroker, looked up from the letter he was reading. "Listen to this," he said. "My Uncle Twombley died and left me $1000."

"Oh, Woofie," said his wife Liss, putting down her macrame, "are you sorry he's dead?"

"He was a rich, worthless old coot who never did a lick of work in his life," said Woofie. "But I'm sorry he passed on that $1000. What am I going to do with it?"

"Do with it?" said Liss.

"Well, I suppose I could pay off what we owe on the VW and my hi-fi set," said Woofie thoughtfully. "But I'd still have a couple of hundred left over."

"You could put it in the bank," said Liss.

"What! And fuel the flames of recession?" said Woofie. "This country's in terrible economic trouble, Liss. People are getting too rich."

"I hadn't noticed," said Liss. "Can I get you anything in the kitchen?"

"Now sit down, Liss," said Woofie, frowning. "I know you don't understand economics, but this is important. Do you realize that the national savings rate has leaped from 5.7 to 7.3% of spendable income?"

"No."

"Well, it has. And as a Commerce Department spokesman economist pointed out the other day, people save more in a recession. So they're richer. That's because they're afraid they'll lose their jobs. But when they save more, they buy less. And that causes the recession they fear. So if I save my money, I'll lose my job."

"Maybe you'd better spend it then," said Liss. "You could get that new stereo."

"What! And fuel the flames of inflation?" said Woofie. "Do you realize the inflation rate is now 8.8% and still climbing? We've all got to do our part and stop buying things, Liss, in order to curb the vicious inflationary spiral."

"Well, at least if you spent your money, you'd have what you wanted," said Liss.

"Temporarily," said Woofie, nodding. "But if we spend our money buying the things we want, prices will get so high we won't be able to buy the things we want with the money we already spent. So we'll be poor. Do you see?"

"Oh, sure," said Liss, yawning.

Woofie frowned. "On the other hand, I'm not certain I should even pay off what we owe. After all, it's consumer credit that keeps the economy humming. Let me explain that."

"My," said Liss, glancing at her funky Mickey Mouse wrist watch. "It's bedtime."

"But what am I going to do with the money?" said Woofie. "It's a tough decision."

"It seems simple enough to me," said Liss, rising. "Either you spend it, become poor and can't afford the things you want. Or you put it in the bank, become rich and can't afford the things you want."

"So?"

"So, if we can't afford the things we want anyway," said Liss, "I'd rather be rich."

"I guess you're right," said Woofie with a sigh. "But I hate knowing I'm going to wind up like Uncle Twombley."

"How's that?" asked Liss.

"Rich," said Woofie glumly, "and unemployed."

Fiscal Policy and the Public Debt

CHAPTER

The basic task of Chapter 13 is to add the public sector to the analysis of the equilibrium NNP developed in the two preceding chapters. It is crucial to recall at the outset that the consumption and investment decisions of households and businesses are based upon private self-interest and that the sum of these decisions may result in either a recessionary or an inflationary gap. In contrast, government is an instrument of society as a whole; hence, within limits government's decisions with respect to spending and taxing are designed to influence the equilibrium NNP in terms of the general welfare. In particular, we saw in Chapter 6 that a fundamental function of the public sector is to stabilize the economy. This stabilization is achieved in part through fiscal policy, that is, through the manipulation of the public budget—government spending and tax collections—for the expressed purpose of achieving the full-employment, noninflationary level of NNP. Recall from Chapter 6 that it is appropriate for government to increase its spending and reduce taxes during a recession and to reduce spending and boost taxes to combat inflation.

BUDGET PHILOSOPHIES

As a prelude to discussing modern fiscal policy, it is instructive to examine briefly several budget philosophies and their economic consequences.

269

Annually Balanced Budget

Until the Great Depression of the 1930s, the annually balanced budget was generally accepted without question as a desirable goal of public finance. An incorrect identification of private and public finance and widespread belief in the classical theory of employment both fostered this acceptance.

Upon examination, however, it becomes evident that an annually balanced budget largely rules out government fiscal activity as a countercyclical, stabilizing force. Worse yet, an annually balanced budget actually intensifies the business cycle. To illustrate: Suppose that the economy encounters a siege of unemployment and falling incomes. As we have already noted, in such circumstances tax receipts will automatically decline. In seeking to balance its budget, government must either (1) increase tax rates, (2) reduce government expenditures, or (3) employ a combination of these two. It is obvious that all these policies are deflationary; each one further dampens, rather than stimulates, the level of aggregate demand.

Similarly, an annually balanced budget will intensify inflation. As money incomes rise during the course of inflation, tax collections will automatically increase. To avoid the impending surplus, government must either (1) cut tax rates, (2) increase government expenditures, or (3) adopt a combination of both. It is clear that all three of these policies will add to inflationary pressures.

The basic conclusion, then, is evident: *An annually balanced budget is not economically neutral; the pursuit of such a policy is procyclical, not countercyclical.*

Cyclically Balanced Budget

The Great Depression, general acceptance of Keynesian employment theory, and the recognition that public and private finance are not entirely comparable all contributed to the development of the idea of a cyclically balanced budget. This budget philosophy envisions government exerting a countercyclical influence and at the same time balancing its budget. In this case, however, the budget would not be balanced annually—after all, there is nothing sacred about twelve months as an accounting period—but rather, over the course of the business cycle.

The rationale of this budget philosophy is simple, plausible, and appealing. To offset depression, government should lower taxes and increase spending, thereby purposely incurring a deficit. During the ensuing inflationary upswing, taxes would be raised and government spending slashed. The resulting surplus could then be used to retire the Federal debt incurred in financing the depression. In this way government fiscal operations would exert a positive countercyclical force, and the government could still balance its budget—not annually, but over a period of years.

The basic problem with this budget philosophy is that the upswings and downswings of the business cycle may not be of equal magnitude and duration (Figure 10-4), and hence the goal of stabilization comes into conflict with balancing the budget over the cycle. For example, a long and severe slump, followed by a modest and short period of prosperity, would mean a large deficit during the slump, little or no surplus during prosperity, and therefore a cyclical deficit in the budget.

Functional Finance

Out of the problems associated with any application of the cyclically balanced budget has evolved the idea of functional finance. According to this budget philosophy, the question of a balanced budget—either annually or cyclically—is of secondary importance. The primary purpose of Federal finance is to provide for noninflationary full employment, that is, to balance the economy, not the budget. If the attainment of this objective entails either persistent surpluses or a large and growing public debt, so be it. The problems involved in government deficits or surpluses are relatively minor compared with the highly undesirable alternatives of prolonged depression or severe inflation. The Federal budget is first and foremost an instrument for achieving and maintaining macroeconomic stability. Government should not hesitate to incur any deficits and surpluses required in achieving this goal. In response to those who express concern about the large Federal debt which the pursuit of functional finance might entail, proponents of this budget philosophy offer three arguments. First, they contend that the problems of a large Federal debt are not as burdensome as most people think. In particular, public debt does not involve the same problems as does private debt. Second, given its taxing powers and the ability to create money, the government's ability to finance deficits is virtually unlimited. Finally, as we shall find later, our tax system is such that tax revenues automatically increase as the economy expands. Hence, given government expenditures, a deficit which is successful in stimulating equilibrium NNP will tend to be partially self-liquidating.

EMPLOYMENT ACT OF 1946 AND THE CEA

The evolution of our budgetary philosophy away from the conservative and countercyclical annually balanced budget toward the liberal conception of functional finance has been reflected in Federal legislation. The notion that governmental fiscal actions can exert an important stabilizing influence upon the economy began to gain widespread acceptance during the Depression crisis of the 1930s. As previously noted, Keynesian employment theory played a major role in emphasizing the importance of remedial fiscal measures. In 1946, when the end of World War II recreated the specter of unemployment, the Federal government formalized in law its area of responsibility in promoting economic stability. The Employment Act of 1946 proclaims:

The Congress hereby declares that it is the continuing policy and responsibility of the Federal Government to use all practicable means consistent with its needs and obligations and other essential considerations of national policy, with assistance and cooperation of industry, agriculture, labor and State and local governments, to coordinate and utilize all its plans, functions, and resources for the purpose of creating and maintaining, in a manner calculated to foster and promote free competitive enterprise and the general welfare, conditions under which there will be afforded useful employment opportunities, including self-employment, for those able, willing, and seeking to work and to promote maximum employment, production, and purchasing power.

The Employment Act of 1946 is a landmark in American socioeconomic legislation in that it commits the Federal government to take positive action through monetary and fiscal policy to maintain economic stability.

Responsibility for fulfilling the purposes of the act rests with the executive branch; the President must submit an annual Economic Report which describes the current state of the economy and makes appropriate policy recommendations. The act also established a Council of Economic Advisers (CEA) to assist and advise the President on economic matters, and a Joint Economic Committee (JEC) of the Congress, which has investigated a wide range of economic problems of national interest. In its advisory capacity as "the President's intelligence arm in the eternal war against the business cycle," the CEA and its staff gather and analyze relevant economic data and use them to make forecasts; to formulate programs and policies designed to fulfill the goals of the Employment Act; and to "educate" the President, the Congress, and the general public on problems and policies relevant to the nation's economic health.[1]

[1] Walter W. Heller's *New Dimensions of Political Economy* (New York: W. W. Norton & Company, Inc., 1967) provides an incisive explanation of the functions of CEA and

DISCRETIONARY FISCAL POLICY

Let us first focus attention upon discretionary fiscal policy. *Discretionary fiscal policy* is the deliberate changing of taxes and government spending by the Congress for the purpose of offsetting cyclical fluctuations in output and employment and stimulating economic growth.

□ **Simplifying Assumptions**

To keep a potentially complex discussion as clear as possible, four simplifying assumptions are invoked.

1 We continue to employ the simplified investment schedule, wherein the level of investment is independent of the level of NNP, in our analysis.

2 We shall suppose that the initial impact of government spending is such that it neither depresses nor stimulates private spending. That is, government spending will not cause any upward or downward shifts in the consumption and investment schedules.

3 It will be presumed that the government's net tax revenues[2] are derived entirely from personal taxes. The significance of this is that, although DI will fall short of PI by the amount of government's tax revenues, NNP, NI, and PI will remain equal.

4 Finally, we assume initially that a fixed amount of taxes is collected regardless of the level of NNP. This assumption will be dropped later.

In Figure 13-1a and b we have repeated our equilibrium NNP models for the private sector (Figures 12-1 and 12-2). The intersection of private aggregate demand ($C + I_n$) and aggregate supply in Figure 13-1a indicates the

initial equilibrium NNP, as does the intersection of I_n and S in Figure 13-1b. You will recall from our gap analysis of Chapter 12 that the $470 billion equilibrium NNP is short of the assumed $490 billion full-employment noninflationary NNP.

In our discussion of the private sector of the economy, we implicitly assumed that government purchases of goods and services (G) and tax revenues (T) were both zero. Now let us suppose that G and T both increase from zero to, say, $20 billion, and note the impact of each and then the combined impact of the two. As before, we pursue our analysis both graphically and tabularly.

□ **Government Spending and Equilibrium NNP**

Suppose that government decides to purchase $20 billion worth of goods and services regardless of what the level of NNP might be. By adding this amount of public spending G to the level of private spending, $C + I_n$, in Figure 13-1a, we find that the total spending schedule (public plus private) has been increased to $C + I_n + G$. That is, the aggregate demand schedule now has a third component, which gives us a new and higher aggregate demand schedule. And this means a new and higher equilibrium level of NNP. In particular, Figure 13-1a suggests that the equilibrium level of NNP will increase from $470 to $550 billion.[3] *Increases in public spending, like increases in private spending, will boost the aggregate demand schedule in relation to the aggregate supply schedule and result in a higher equilibrium NNP.* Note, too, that government spending is subject to the multiplier.

Figure 13-1b shows the same change in the equilibrium NNP in terms of the leakages-injections approach. Like investment, government spending is an offset to the leakage of saving. Hence, with G added to our discussion,

---

an intriguing account of the Council's operation under Dr. Heller's chairmanship during the 1961–1964 period. Arthur M. Okun's *The Political Economy of Prosperity* (New York: W. W. Norton & Company, Inc., 1970) is also highly recommended.

[2] By net taxes we mean total tax revenues less negative taxes in the form of transfer payments.

[3] Given our assumption that the full-employment noninflationary NNP is $490 billion, most of this increase will be in *money* rather than *real* NNP.

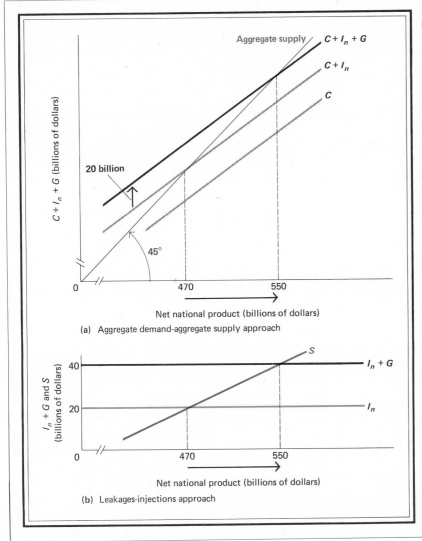

FIGURE 13-1 GOVERNMENT SPENDING AND THE EQUILIBRIUM NNP

(a) *The aggregate demand-aggregate supply approach.* The addition of government expenditures G to our analysis raises the aggregate demand $(C + I_n + G)$ schedule and increases the equilibrium level of NNP as would an increase in C or I_n. Note that changes in government spending are subject to the multiplier effect. **(b)** *Leakages-injections approach.* In terms of the leakages-injections approach, government spending supplements private investment spending $(I_n + G)$, increasing the equilibrium NNP.

(a) Aggregate demand-aggregate supply approach

(b) Leakages-injections approach

the equilibrium level of NNP is now determined at the point where the amount households plan to save is offset exactly by the amount which businesses plan to invest *plus* the amount government desires to spend on goods and services. That is, the equilibrium NNP is determined by the intersection of the S schedule and the $I_n + G$ schedule. Note that either approach indicates the same new equilibrium NNP.

What of the effect of a decline in government spending? Obviously, a decline in G will cause aggregate demand to fall in Figure 13-1a and the $I_n + G$ schedule to fall in Figure 13-1b. In either case the result is a multiple *decline* in the equilibrium NNP.

□ **Taxation and Equilibrium NNP**

But government also collects tax revenues. How do tax collections affect the equilibrium level of NNP? To answer this question in the simplest way, we will assume that government imposes a lump-sum tax of $20 billion on NNP; that is, government now collects $20 billion of taxes at each and every level of NNP.[4] What is the impact of government's increasing tax collections from zero to $20 billion at each level of NNP? The immediate effect will be to lower DI by $20 billion at each NNP level. And, because DI is made up of consumer spending and saving, we can expect a decline in DI to lower both consumption and saving. But by how much will each decline? The MPC and the MPS hold the answer: The MPC tells us what fraction of a decline in DI will come at the expense of consumption, and the MPS indicates what fraction of a drop in DI will come at the expense of saving. Assuming that the MPC equals three-fourths and the MPS equals one-fourth, we can conclude that if government collects $20 billion in taxes at each possible level of NNP, the amount of consumption forthcoming at each level of NNP will drop by $15 billion (three-fourths of $20 billion), and the amount of saving at each level of NNP will fall by $5 billion (one-fourth of $20 billion).

The impact of a $20 billion increase in taxes is shown graphically in Figure 13-2a and b. In Figure 13-2a the $20 billion increase in taxes shows up as a $15 billion *decline* in the aggregate demand $(C + I_n + G)$ schedule. Under our simplifying assumption that all taxes are personal income taxes, this decline in aggregate demand is solely the result of a decline in the consumption component of the aggregate demand schedule. The equilibrium NNP shifts from $550 billion to the $490 billion level as a result of this tax-caused drop in consumption. To generalize: *Increases in taxes will lower the aggregate demand schedule relative to the aggregate supply schedule and cause the equilibrium NNP to fall.*

[4]This is clearly a regressive tax system because the average tax rate, T/NNP, falls as NNP rises. Most industrially advanced economies have proportional or progressive tax systems. The important modifications to which these latter two systems give rise will be noted shortly.

Consider now the leakages-injections approach: The analysis here is slightly more complex because the imposition of $20 billion in taxes has a twofold effect in Figure 13-2b. First, the taxes reduce DI by $20 billion and, with the MPS at one-fourth, cause saving to fall by $5 billion at each level of NNP. In Figure 13-2b this is shown as a shift from S_b (saving before taxes) to S_a (saving after taxes). Then the $20 billion in taxes as such appear as a $20 billion additional leakage at each NNP level which must be added to S_a, giving us $S_a + T$. Equilibrium now exists at the $490 billion NNP, where the total amount which households plan to save plus the amount of taxes government intends to collect are equal to the total amount businesses desire to invest plus the amount government plans to spend. The equilibrium condition for the leakages-injections approach now is $S_a + T = I_n + G$. Graphically, it is the intersection of the $S_a + T$ and the $I_n + G$ schedules which determines the equilibrium NNP.

A decline in existing taxes will cause the aggregate demand schedule to rise as a result of an upward shift in the consumption schedule in Figure 13-2a. In terms of Figure 13-2b a tax cut will cause a decline in the $S_a + T$ schedule. The result in either case is a multiple *increase* in the equilibrium NNP.

□ The Budget Impact

Table 13-1 shows the net impact of government spending and taxation upon the equilibrium NNP in terms of simple arithmetic data. This table is merely Table 12-1 adjusted to allow for $20 billion worth of tax revenues (column 3) and $20 billion of government spending (column 8) at each possible level of NNP. The immediate effect of taxes is shown in column 4: DI is $20 billion less than NNP at each level of NNP. Supposing the MPC and MPS are three-fourths and one-fourth, respectively, we find in columns 5 and 6 that the amounts of consumption and saving forthcoming at each level of NNP are $15 and $5 billion

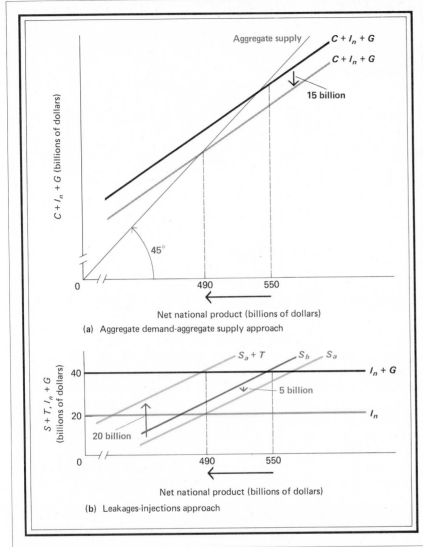

(a) Aggregate demand-aggregate supply approach

(b) Leakages-injections approach

FIGURE 13-2 TAXES AND THE EQUILIBRIUM NNP

(a) *The aggregate demand-aggregate supply approach.* If the MPC is three-fourths, the imposition of $20 billion of taxes will lower the consumption schedule by $15 billion and thereby cause a decline in the equilibrium NNP. **(b)** *The leakages-injections approach.* Here taxes have a twofold effect. First, with an MPS of one-fourth, the imposition of taxes of $20 billion will reduce disposable income by $20 billion and saving by $5 billion at each level of NNP. This is shown by the shift from S_b (saving before taxes) to S_a (saving after taxes). Second, the $20 billion of taxes constitute an additional $20 billion leakage at each NNP level, giving us $S_a + T$. By adding government, the equilibrium condition changes from $S = I_n$ to $S_a + T = I_n + G$.

less, respectively, than the figures in Table 12-1. Thus, for example, before the imposition of taxes, where NNP equaled DI, consumption was $420 billion and saving $10 billion at the $430 billion level of NNP (Table 12-1). After taxes are imposed, DI is $410 billion, obviously $20 billion short of the $430 billion NNP, with the result that consumption is only $405 billion and saving is $5 billion. This is how columns 4, 5, and 6 of Table 13-1 are determined. Column 7 carries over investment from Table 12-1, and column 8 adds government spending.

What is the equilibrium level of output now that taxation and government spending have been brought into the picture? The aggregate demand–aggregate supply, or $C + I_n + G$ = NNP, approach tells us to compare columns 2 and 9. It is apparent that the aggregate amounts demanded and supplied are equal only at the $490 billion NNP. At all higher levels, businesses will attempt to produce in excess of what the economy, including

Table 13-1 DETERMINATION OF THE EQUILIBRIUM LEVELS OF EMPLOYMENT, OUTPUT, AND INCOME: PRIVATE

(1) Possible levels of employment, millions	(2) Possible levels of aggregate supply (NNP = NI = PI), billions	(3) Taxes, billions	(4) Possible levels of disposable income, billions, or (2) − (3)	(5) Consumption, billions
40	$370	$20	$350	$360
45	390	20	370	375
50	410	20	390	390
55	430	20	410	405
60	450	20	430	420
65	470	20	450	435
70	**490**	**20**	**470**	**450**
75	510	20	490	465
80	530	20	510	480

both the private and public sectors, plans to spend. The resulting deficiency of total spending will force these higher levels of NNP back down to the $490 billion level. Conversely, at all levels of NNP below the $490 billion level, the economy will spend at a rate in excess of NNP, inducing businesses to expand NNP. We can conclude that $490 billion is the equilibrium NNP.

Our alternative approach must and does yield the same results. With the public sector added to the private sector, equilibrium will prevail where $S_a + T = I_n + G$. And this is at the $490 billion level. At all lower levels, you should verify that investment and government spending will more than compensate for the saving and taxation leakages, causing $C + I_n + G$ to exceed NNP and thereby inducing the latter to rise. Conversely, at all levels of NNP above the $490 billion level, you should note that the saving and taxation leakages are not offset by investment and government spending, thus causing $C + I_n + G$ to fall short of NNP and forcing declines in NNP.

□ Balanced-budget Multiplier

Note an important and curious thing about our tabular and graphic illustrations. *Equal increases in government spending and taxation increase the equilibrium NNP. That is, if G and T are both increased by $X, the equilibrium level of national output will rise by $X.* The $20 billion increase in G and T causes the equilibrium NNP to increase from $470 to $490 billion. The rationale for this so-called *balanced-budget multiplier* is revealed in our example. The $20 billion increase in personal taxes reduces consumption by only $15 billion, the extra $5 billion in tax revenues coming at the expense of saving. Thus the *net* effect is a $5 billion increase in total spending—the combination of a $20 billion increase in public spending and a $15 billion decline in private spending. Being subject to the multiplier of 4, the $5 billion net increase in spending boosts NNP by $20 billion. *Equal changes in G and T are expansionary.* The reader should experiment to verify that the balanced-budget multiplier is valid regardless of the sizes of the marginal propensities to consume and save.

□ Fiscal Policy over the Cycle

In our illustration—thanks to the net expansionist effect of the balanced-budget multiplier—fiscal policy has moved the economy from the unemployment NNP of $470 billion to the full-employment noninflationary NNP

AND PUBLIC SECTORS (*hypothetical data*)

(6) Saving, billions, or (4) − (5)	(7) Investment, billions	(8) Government expenditures, billions	(9) Aggregate demand $(C + I_n + G)$, billions, or (5) + (7) + (8)	(10) Tendency of employment, output, and income
$−10	$20	$20	$400	Increase
−5	20	20	415	Increase
0	20	20	430	Increase
5	20	20	445	Increase
10	20	20	460	Increase
15	20	20	475	Increase
20	**20**	**20**	**490**	**Equilibrium**
25	20	20	505	Decrease
30	20	20	520	Decrease

of $490 billion. The net $5 billion increase in spending afforded by equal increases in government spending and taxation has closed the initial $5 billion recessionary gap.

More generally, a level of aggregate demand which falls short of the full-employment noninflationary NNP calls for an *expansionary* fiscal policy. An expansionist policy obviously entails (1) increased government spending, (2) lower taxes, or (3) a combination of the two. In other words, if the budget is balanced at the outset, fiscal policy should move in the direction of a government budget *deficit* during a recession or depression to close the existing recessionary gap. Conversely, an excessive level of private spending which threatens to cause inflation, that is, a potential spiraling up of the money GNP, calls for a restrictive or *contractionary* fiscal policy. A contractionary policy is composed of (1) decreased government spending, (2) higher taxes, or (3) a combination of these two policies. Fiscal policy should move toward a *surplus* in the government's budget when the economy is faced with the problem of closing an inflationary gap.[5]

[5]Minor qualification: Because, as we have just noted, a balanced budget is actually expansionary, a relatively small budget surplus might be slightly expansionary rather than deflationary.

NONDISCRETIONARY FISCAL POLICY: BUILT-IN STABILIZERS

The lump-sum tax system described in our discussion of fiscal policy thus far is strong on simplicity but weak on realism. That is, our presentation of the impact of government spending and tax revenues upon the equilibrium NNP has been greatly facilitated by the assumption that the volume of tax revenues is independent of the level of NNP. But such independence is not the case: Virtually all taxes will yield more tax revenue as NNP rises. In particular, personal and corporate income taxes have progressive rates and result in more than proportionate increases in tax collections as NNP expands. Furthermore, as NNP increases and more goods and services are purchased, revenues from sales and excise taxes will increase. And, similarly, payroll tax payments increase as economic expansion creates more jobs. Obviously, when NNP declines, tax receipts from all these sources will decline. Transfer payments (or "negative taxes") behave in precisely the opposite way. Unemployment compensation payments, welfare payments, and subsidies to farmers all *decrease* during economic expansion and *increase* during a contraction. Recalling (from footnote 2) that the term *net taxes* means tax revenues less negative taxes in the form of transfers and subsidies, we are simply saying that *our net tax system is such that net tax revenues vary directly with the level of NNP.*[6] On the table on the inside covers of this book, observe, for example, the declines in personal and corporate income tax receipts (lines 15 and 11) and the increases in transfer payments (line 13) during the 1949, 1954, 1958, and 1970 recessions. Figure 13-3 tells the story in more general terms. Government expenditures G are given and assumed to be independent of the level of NNP; expenditures are decided upon at some fixed level by the Congress. But Congress does *not* determine the *level* of tax revenues; rather, it establishes tax *rates*. Tax revenues then vary directly with the level of NNP which the economy actually realizes. The direct relationship between tax revenues and NNP is shown in the up-sloping T line.

---

[6] From now on, we shall use the term "taxes" in referring to net taxes.

□   **Built-in Stability**

The economic importance of this direct relationship between tax receipts and NNP comes into focus when we remember two things. First, taxes are a leakage or withdrawal of potential purchasing power from the economy. Second, it is desirable from the standpoint of stability to increase leakages or withdrawals of purchasing power when the economy is moving toward inflation and to diminish these withdrawals when the economy is tending to slump. In other words, the kind of tax system portrayed in Figure 13-3 builds some stability into the economy by automatically bringing about changes in tax revenues and therefore in the public budget which tend to counter both inflation and unemployment. Generally speaking, a *built-in stabilizer is anything which tends to increase the government's deficit (or reduce its surplus) during a recession and to increase its surplus (or reduce its deficit) during inflation without requiring explicit action by policy makers.* And, as Figure 13-3 clearly reveals, this is precisely what

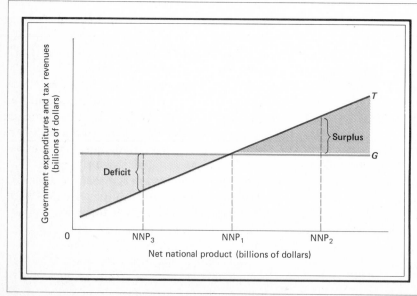

FIGURE 13-3 BUILT-IN STABILITY

If tax revenues vary directly with NNP, then the deficits which will tend to occur automatically during recession will help alleviate that recession. Conversely, the surpluses which tend to occur automatically during expansion will assist in offsetting possible inflation.

our tax system tends to do. As NNP rises during prosperity, tax revenues *automatically* increase and, because they are a leakage, restrain the economic expansion. Stated differently, as the economy moves toward a higher NNP, tax revenues automatically rise and tend to move the budget from a deficit to a surplus. Conversely, as NNP falls during recession, tax revenues *automatically* decline and this reduction in leakages cushions the economic contraction. That is, with a falling NNP, tax receipts decline and tend to move the public budget from a surplus to a deficit. In terms of Figure 13-3, the low level of income NNP_3 will automatically give rise to an expansionary budget deficit; the high and perhaps inflationary income level NNP_2 will automatically generate a contractionary budget surplus. Incidentally, if Congress should alter our tax system so as to make tax revenues even more sensitive to changes in NNP than presumed in Figure 13-3—and this could be done, for example, by putting greater relative dependence upon taxes with progressive rates or by increasing the progressivity of the overall tax structure—then the tax line would be steeper and built-in stability would be more pronounced.

□ Qualifications and Subtleties

There is no question but that the built-in stability provided by our tax system has served the economy well. Yet three significant points must be appended to our discussion.

1 Amelioration, Not Correction The built-in stabilizers are *not* capable of correcting an undesirable change in the equilibrium NNP. All that the stabilizers do is reduce the magnitude or severity of economic fluctuations. Hence, discretionary fiscal action—that is, changes in tax rates, tax structure, and expenditures—by Congress is required to correct an inflation or a recession of any appreciable magnitude. It is estimated that in the United

States the built-in stabilizers are currently strong enough to reduce fluctuations in national income by one-third or more. One recent study suggests that the built-in stabilizers during recent recessions prevented an average of 36 to 52 percent of the income declines which would have occurred in their absence. On the other hand, during recent expansions potential income increases were reduced by as much as 25 to 42 percent.[7]

2 "Fiscal Drag" The presence of a tax system wherein tax revenues vary directly with NNP is not an unmitigated good. Such a tax system may tend to produce a *fiscal drag* in the form of budgetary surpluses which make it difficult to achieve and sustain full employment.

Built-in stability is clearly desirable *if* the economy fluctuates around the full-employment level of NNP. But if the economy is initially in a recession, the same degree of built-in stability can make it more difficult to move to full employment. Consider Figure 13-3 once again. If NNP_1 is the full-employment level of output and the economy is currently enjoying full employment, the built-in stability provided by the T line is clearly desirable in that the tax system will dampen any tendency for the economy to deviate from full employment. But what if the actual output is at some recessionary level, such as NNP_3? In this case the expansionary impact of any increase in $C, I,$ or G will be blunted by the presence of the built-in stabilizers. Some of the stimulating impact of an increase in spending will leak into expanding tax revenues. In short, just as built-in stability is helpful in maintaining full employment once it is achieved, so that same built-in stability tends to maintain unemployment once it exists.

There is also a long-run aspect to the fiscal

[7] Peter Eilbott, "The Effectiveness of the Automatic Stabilizers," *American Economic Review,* June 1966, pp. 450–465.

drag problem. Suppose the full-employment output is at NNP_1 and the economy is actually operating at this level. The budget, you will note, is currently in balance. Now the catch is that ours is a growing economy (Part 3) and that, through time, the full-employment output will shift toward NNP_2. But this growth automatically generates a budget surplus which tends to precipitate a recession and choke off growth. (For example, if the full-employment output expands by 4 percent per year, tax revenues will automatically increase by some $20 to $25 billion per year!) In short, when a time dimension is added to Figure 13-3 to allow for growth, built-in stability may make it difficult to sustain full employment through time. During periods of substantial growth, significant budget surpluses automatically appear and have a contractionary impact. The remedy? The Federal government must use discretionary fiscal policy to cut taxes, increase expenditures, or perhaps increase its revenue-sharing grants to state and local governments to eliminate fiscal drag (Chapter 8).

3   The Full-Employment Budget Built-in stability—the fact that tax revenues vary directly with NNP—makes it hazardous to use the *actual* budget surplus or deficit in any given year as an index of the government's fiscal stance. To illustrate: Suppose the economy is at full employment at NNP_1 in Figure 13-3 and, as we note, the budget is in balance. Now, assume that, during the year, C or I_n declines, causing a recession at NNP_3. The government, let us assume, takes no discretionary fiscal action; therefore, the G and T lines remain in the positions shown in the diagram. Obviously, as the economy moves to NNP_3, tax revenues fall and, with government expenditures unaltered, a deficit occurs. But this deficit is clearly *not* the result of positive countercyclical fiscal actions by the government; rather it is the by-product of fiscal inaction as the economy slides into a recession. The basic point is that one cannot say anything very meaningful about the government's

fiscal posture—whether Congress was appropriately manipulating taxes and expenditures—by looking at the historical record of budgetary deficits or surpluses. Stated differently, given that tax revenues vary with NNP, the fundamental problem of comparing deficits or surpluses in year 1 and year 2 is that the level of NNP may be vastly different in the two years.

Economists have resolved this problem through the notion of a full-employment budget. Simply stated, the *full-employment budget indicates what the Federal budgetary surplus or deficit would be if the economy were to operate at full employment throughout the year.* Figure 13-4 compares the full-employment budget and the actual budget over approximately two decades. Note that, although the actual budget has usually been in deficit, the full-employment budget frequently is in surplus. Consider 1961 and 1962, years of above-normal unemployment and sluggish economic growth. A look at the actual budget deficits in these years implies that government was appropriately engaged in an expansionary fiscal policy. But the full-employment budget data tell us that this was *not* the case. The full-employment budget data indicate that, if the economy had been at full employment, there would have been a budgetary surplus. Our fiscal policy in 1961 and 1962 was in fact contractionary, and this was partially responsible for the less-than-full-employment levels of NNP, the consequent poor tax harvests, and the deficits which occurred in the actual budgets for 1961 and 1962. Our fiscal policy stance in those years? Contractionary as suggested by the full-employment budget, not expansionary as implied by the actual budget.

Let us pursue this discussion into the realm of actual policy making. President Kennedy, when he took office in 1961, was committed to the elimination of the above-normal unemployment and the slow growth which characterized the economy in the early 1960s. The fiscal route he selected was to cut taxes. President Kennedy clearly had the distinction

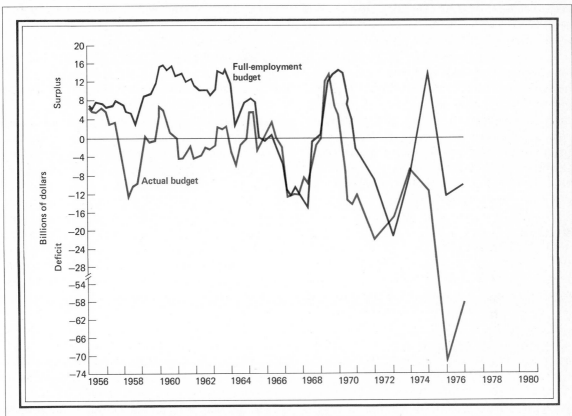

FIGURE 13-4 THE FULL-EMPLOYMENT BUDGET AND THE ACTUAL BUDGET

The full-employment budget surplus or deficit is a better indicator of the government's fiscal posture than is the actual surplus or deficit. The actual budget has been in deficit with much greater frequency than the full-employment budget because NNP has been at less than full employment.

between the full-employment and the actual budget in mind when he offered the following rationale for the massive $11 billion corporate and personal income tax cut of 1964:[8]

It is a paradoxical truth that tax rates are too high today [1962] and tax revenues are too low and the soundest way to raise revenues in the long run is to cut [tax] rates now. . . . And the reason is that only full employment can balance the budget and tax reduction can pave the way to full employment. The purpose of cutting taxes now is not to incur a budget

[8]Speech before the Economics Club of New York, Dec. 14, 1962, printed in *Congressional Record,* Jan. 15, 1963.

deficit, but to achieve the more prosperous, expanding economy which will bring a budget surplus.

The 1964 tax cut was a bold and dramatic application of modern fiscal policy for the specific purpose of stimulating the economy. Did it work? Although the inability to conduct controlled experiments makes it impossible to be absolutely conclusive, available evidence strongly suggests that the tax cut did indeed bring about the predicted expansion of the economy. The CEA has estimated that, by early 1965, the tax cut was responsible for increases in consumption and investment spending totaling over $20 billion; by the end of 1965, these increases in private spending attributable to the tax cut had cumulated to an estimated $30 billion.[9] As a result, the unemployment rate fell and the gap between actual and potential GNP declined significantly in 1964 and 1965 (Figure 10-2). Similarly, as predicted, the economy's growth rate rose perceptibly. And, most relevant for the present discussion, Federal tax collections did increase substantially; observe in Figure 13-4 that in 1965 and 1966 the actual budget was generally in a surplus position.[10]

TWO REFINEMENTS

We must now add two important embellishments to our discussion of fiscal policy.

☐   **Financing Deficits and Disposing of Surpluses**

Given the size of a deficit, its expansionary effect upon the economy will depend upon the method by which it is financed. Similarly, given the size of a surplus, its deflationary impact will depend upon its disposition.

Financing Deficits: Borrowing versus New Money   There are two different ways by which the Federal government can finance a deficit: by borrowing from (selling interest-bearing bonds to) the public, or by issuing new money to its creditors.[11]   The impact upon

aggregate demand will be somewhat different in each case.

1 If the government goes into the money market and borrows, it will obviously be competing with private business borrowers for funds. This added demand for funds will drive the equilibrium interest rate upward. We know from Chapter 11 that investment spending is inversely related to the interest rate. Hence, government borrowing will have a *crowding-out effect;* that is, as government borrows, the interest rate will rise and thereby choke off some private investment spending. The astute reader will note that we are abandoning the second simplifying assumption made at the start of this chapter: the assumption that government spending would neither depress nor stimulate private spending. We are now noting that if government spending is financed by borrowing, the resulting increase in the interest rate can be expected to depress private investment.

2 If deficit spending is financed by issuing new money, the crowding-out effect can be avoided. Government spending can increase without any adverse effect upon investment. Our conclusion is that *the creation of new money is a more expansionary way of financing deficit spending than is borrowing.*

Disposing of a Surplus: Debt Retirement versus an Idle Surplus   Inflation calls for fiscal action by government which will result in a budget surplus. However, the anti-inflationary effect of this surplus depends upon what government does with it. Generally speaking, government can dispose of a surplus in one of two ways. Let us assess these options.

1 Since the Federal government has an outstanding debt of some $620 billion, it is logical that government should use a surplus to retire outstanding debt. The anti-inflationary impact of a surplus, however, may be reduced somewhat by this. In retiring debt held by the general public, the government transfers its surplus tax revenues into the hands of households and businesses that *might* in turn

[9] *Economic Report of the President, 1966,* p. 34.

[10] In Chapter 17 we shall encounter the minority view of the "monetarists" who feel there is no convincing evidence that the 1964 tax cut worked as described here.

[11] This statement implies that government merely prints up new dollar bills to finance its expenditures. Although it could do this, the Treasury accomplishes the same result more subtly by borrowing (obtaining loans) from central (Federal Reserve) banks. The Treasury draws checks against these loans to finance its expenditures and, when the recipients deposit these checks in their own accounts at commercial banks, the supply of demand-deposit or checking account money is increased. The details of this process will be explained in Chapter 16.

spend these funds on consumer and capital goods. But this potential increase in private spending should not be exaggerated. In all probability, a sizable portion of the surplus funds received by households and businesses as their bonds mature will be used to purchase private securities rather than goods and services.

2 On the other hand, government can realize a greater anti-inflationary impact from its budgetary surplus by simply impounding the surplus funds, that is, by allowing them to stand idle. An impounded surplus means that the government is extracting and withholding purchasing power from the income-expenditure stream. If surplus tax revenues are not reinjected into the economy, there is no possibility of the surplus being spent. That is, there is no chance that the funds will create inflationary pressure to offset the deflationary impact of the surplus itself. We conclude that *the impounding of a budgetary surplus is more contractionary than the use of the surplus to retire public debt.*

☐ **Types of Expenditures and Taxes**

The expansionary impact of a deficit and the anti-inflationary significance of a surplus depend in part upon the types of taxes and expenditures employed.

Purchases versus Transfers Generally speaking, there are two types of government disbursements: expenditures on goods and services and transfer payments. The former includes defense spending and what the man in the street terms "public works" projects—the construction of dams, highways, parks, and public buildings. Transfer payments refer to unemployment compensation payments, subsidies to businesses, interest on the public debt, and the like.

Economists agree that government expenditures are subject to a larger multiplier effect and thus stimulate the NNP more than would transfer payments of the same amount.

The reason for this can be seen by referring back to Table 12-2, which describes the multiplier process. In the case of government expenditures, the initial increase in spending of, say, $5 billion obviously gives rise to an increase in output (for example, the construction of highways, parks, and post offices) of $5 billion *and* will also induce another $15 billion increase in consumption. The total increase in output and real income is clearly $20 billion, indicating a multiplier of 4. But in the case of a $5 billion increase in transfer payments, we must remember that, by definition, transfers themselves do *not* give rise to output. For example, if Congress increases social security payments to retired workers by $5 billion, the recipients obviously do not provide $5 billion worth of goods and services in return. However, the $5 billion received by these senior citizens will induce the $15 billion consumption chain reaction, as shown in Table 12-2. Thus the $5 billion transfer payment increases total output by only $15 billion, so the multiplier associated with the transfer payment is only 3.

Caution: The above conclusion that government expenditures will tend to provide a greater stimulus to the economy than would the same volume of transfers assumes that government expenditures will be judicious, in the sense that they will not entail projects which will discourage and displace private investment.

The Deflationary Impacts of Different Taxes What about taxes? Because they tap potential purchasing power from the income-expenditures stream, all taxes tend to be deflationary. But, given the size of government's tax collections, some taxes seem to be more deflationary than others. Most economists feel that consumption taxes—excises and sales taxes—are more deflationary than are personal and corporate income taxes. In other words, regressive taxation is thought to depress private spending more than does progressive taxation. It must be added, however, that this conclusion is not universally accepted. Some authorities contend that, although regressive taxation may dampen consumer spending more than does progressive taxation, heavy taxes on corporate income might entail considerable reduction in business investment. Hence, they conclude that corporate and personal income taxation causes a greater decline in consumption and investment combined than do sales and excise taxes.

■ ─────────────────────────────

SOME COMPLICATIONS

Unfortunately, there is a great deal of difference between fiscal policy on paper and fiscal policy in practice. It is therefore imperative that we examine some specific problems which may be encountered in enacting and applying appropriate fiscal policy.

☐   **Problems of Timing**

Several problems of timing may arise in connection with fiscal policy.

1   Recognition Lag   It is extremely difficult to predict accurately the future course of economic activity. The recognition lag refers to the time which elapses between the beginning of a recession or an inflation and the recognition that it is in fact occurring. The economy may be four or six months into a recession or an inflation before this fact shows up in relevant statistics and is acknowledged.

2   Administrative Lag   The wheels of democratic government are often slow in turning. There will inevitably be a lag between the time that the need for fiscal action is recognized and the time that action is actually taken. The $11 billion tax cut which became law in February of 1964 was first proposed to President Kennedy by the Council of Economic Advisers in 1961, and in turn proposed by him in late 1962! The 1968 surcharge on

personal and corporate incomes was enacted approximately a year after it was requested by President Johnson. Indeed, Congress has on occasion consumed so much time in adjusting fiscal policy that the economic situation has taken a turnabout in the interim, thereby rendering the policy action completely inappropriate.

A frequent proposal is that Congress give the President limited authority to alter tax rates for purposes of countercyclical fiscal policy and thereby circumvent time-consuming congressional debate. Opponents argue that the proposal transfers an important function of the legislative branch to the executive branch of government and disturbs the "balance of power" between the two.

3   Operational Lag   There will also be a lag between the time that fiscal action is taken by Congress and the time that action has an impact upon output, employment, or the price level. Although changes in tax rates can be quickly put into effect, government spending on public works—the construction of dams, interstate highways, and so forth—entails long planning periods and even longer periods of construction. Such spending is of questionable usefulness in offsetting short—for example, six- or eighteen-month—periods of recession.

☐   **Political Problems**

Fiscal policy is created in the political arena. Will political considerations outweigh economic factors in the formation of fiscal policy? Given the general unpopularity of tax increases, can Congress be expected to increase tax rates quickly and sufficiently when severe inflation is encountered? Even if Congress quickly agrees upon needed tax increases, might its efforts founder on disagreement as to what specific types of taxes are to be raised? Can Congress reasonably be expected to reach agreement as to what specific types of expenditures should be trimmed (for example, highway construction, agricultural research, armaments procurement, education) during inflation? More generally put, is the public willing to accept, and the politician to enact, the fiscal cures which inflation and deflation require? There is no simple answer here. But, at a minimum, it must be noted that the democratic political processes do not lend themselves to the making of such decisions quickly and smoothly. "Ineffectual or undesirable changes, or more likely, fiscal inertia, may often result from the interaction of political considerations."[12]

□ State and Local Finance

From the viewpoint of the economy as a whole, it would be desirable for the fiscal policies of all levels of government—Federal, state, and local—to be of a countercyclical nature. Unfortunately, this is not the case. State and local finance often tends to reinforce, rather than alleviate, cyclical fluctuations. State and local governments do most of their spending for schools, libraries, and streets and highways during prosperity. As is true of households and private businesses, they often cut expenditures and sometimes even retire debt during recessions. During the Great Depression of the 1930s, most of the increase in Federal spending was canceled by declines in state and local spending. At the other extreme, state and local governments have on occasion cut taxes during periods of inflationary pressure.

The reasons for the perverse nature of state and local finance are many; the weaker credit standings of state and local governments, the relative instability of state and local tax systems, statutory or constitutional limits on their debts, and a rather widespread belief in the alleged virtues of an annually balanced budget all contribute to the procyclical character of state and local finance.

[12]Joint Economic Committee, *Staff Report on Employment, Growth, and Price Levels* (Washington, 1960), p. 209.

■
THE PUBLIC DEBT

Because modern fiscal policy endorses unbalanced budgets for the purpose of stabilizing the economy, its application will quite possibly lead to a growing public debt. Let us now briefly consider the public debt—its causes, its characteristics, its size, and the burdens and benefits associated with it.

□ Dimensions of Debt

Growth of the public debt, as Table 13-2 indicates, has been substantial since 1929. The public debt is, of course, the accumulation of all past deficits, minus surpluses, of the Federal budget.

Causes Why have these deficits occurred? As Table 13-2 makes clear, a considerable portion of the public debt is attributable to war finance. The public debt grew more than fivefold during World War II and it also increased substantially during the Korean and Vietnam wars. Some deficits have been the result of discretionary fiscal policy designed to offset recession or stimulate growth, for example, the 1964 tax cut. At other times, deficits have been the consequence of built-in stability; for example, above-normal unemployment rates in the 1970s—particularly in the 1974–1976 period—automatically reduced tax collections and tended to cause deficits. Furthermore, in the past ten years various income-maintenance programs—social security, unemployment compensation, food stamps, aid to dependent children, and so forth—have expanded sharply in terms of numbers, coverage, and levels of benefits and have been one of the causes of unbalanced budgets.

Public Debt, Public Credit To whom do we owe the public debt? The answer is: We owe it to ourselves! The vast bulk of our government bonds are held internally, that is, they are owned and held by citizens and

Table 13-2 QUANTITATIVE SIGNIFICANCE OF THE PUBLIC DEBT: THE PUBLIC DEBT AND INTEREST PAYMENTS IN RELATION TO GNP, 1929–1976

(1) Year	(2) Public debt, billions	(3) Gross national product,* billions	(4) Interest payments, billions	(5) Public debt as percentage of GNP, (2) ÷ (3)	(6) interest payments as percentage of GNP, (4) ÷ (3)	(7) Per capita public debt
1929	$ 16.3	$ 103.1	$ 0.7	16%	0.7%	$ 134
1940	50.9	99.7	1.1	51	1.1	382
1946	259.5	208.5	4.2	124	2.0	1827
1950	256.7	284.8	4.5	90	1.6	1689
1954	278.8	364.8	5.0	76	1.4	1404
1958	283.0	447.3	5.6	63	1.3	1617
1962	304.0	560.3	7.2	54	1.3	1626
1967	322.9	796.3	12.6	41	1.6	1625
1972	426.4	1171.1	20.6	36	1.8	2042
1976	620.4	1691.6	34.6	37	2.0	2884

*In current dollars.
Source: Economic Report of the President (Washington, 1977).

institutions—banks, businesses, insurance companies, governmental agencies, and trust funds—within the United States. Thus the public debt is also a public credit. While the public debt is a liability to the American people (as taxpayers), that same debt is simultaneously an asset to the American people (as bondholders). Retirement of the public debt would therefore call for a gigantic transfer payment whereby American individuals and institutions would pay higher taxes and the government in turn would pay out those tax revenues to those same taxpaying individuals and institutions in the aggregate in redeeming the bonds which they hold. Although a redistribution of wealth would result from this gigantic financial transfer, it need not entail any immediate decline in the economy's aggregate wealth or standard of living. The repayment of an internally held public debt entails no leakage of purchasing power from the economy of the country as a whole.

Quantitative Aspects There is no denying it: The absolute size of the public debt is so large—$620 billion in 1976—as to be almost beyond comprehension. But we must not fear large numbers per se. Let us therefore put the size of the public debt in better perspective.

1 Debt and GNP A bald statement of the absolute size of the debt glosses over the fact that the wealth and productive ability of our economy have also increased tremendously over the years. It is safe to say that a wealthy nation has greater ability to incur and carry a large public debt than does a poor nation. In other words, it seems more realistic to measure changes in the public debt *in relation to* changes in the economy's GNP. Column 5 in Table 13-2 presents such data. Note that instead of the twelvefold increase in the debt between 1940 and 1976 shown in column 2, we now find that the *relative* size of the debt has *declined* considerably since 1946. And this ratio of Federal debt to GNP, incidentally, is small when compared with similar ratios for other advanced nations. Note, too, in column 7, that the per capita size of the public debt has not increased spectacularly.

2 Interest charges Many economists feel that the primary burden of the debt is the annual interest charge that accrues as a result of the debt. The absolute size of these interest payments is shown in column 4. Interest charges as a percentage of GNP are presented in column 6. In these latter terms, the burden of the debt is the same as it was in 1946. The failure of this ratio to fall significantly in the last twenty years reflects the phenomenon of rising interest rates much more than a rising debt.

3 Private debt Although the size and growth of public debt are looked upon with awe and alarm, private debt has grown much faster. Private and public debt were of about equal size in 1947. But private debt has grown much faster and is now almost four times as large—about $2380 billion, compared with $620 billion—as the public debt. If you insist upon worrying about debt, you will do well to concern yourself with private rather than public indebtedness.

☐ **Two Myths**

Both the existence and the expansion of the public debt can entail problems. But prior to a discussion of its disadvantages and advantages, let us lay to rest two rather widely held myths.

Going Bankrupt Can a large public debt somehow "bankrupt" the government, making it unable to meet its financial obligations? Given the fact that the government has the power to tax, it is extremely difficult to conceive of a situation wherein the government could become bankrupt. Indeed, there is no reason why the public debt need be reduced, much less eliminated. In practice, as portions of the debt fall due each month, government does not typically cut expenditures or raise taxes to provide funds to *retire* the maturing bonds. (We know that with depressed economic conditions, this would be unwise fiscal policy.) Rather, the government simply *refinances* the debt, that is, it sells new bonds and uses the proceeds to pay off holders of the maturing bonds.

Shifting Burdens Does the public debt impose a burden upon future generations? Was some of the economic burden of World War II, for example, shifted to future generations by the decision to finance military purchases through the sale of government bonds? Again, the answer is "No." Recalling the production possibilities curve, we can see that the economic cost of World War II consisted of the civilian goods which society had to forgo in shifting scarce resources to war goods production. Regardless of whether the financing of this reallocation was achieved through higher taxes or borrowing, the real economic burden of the war would have been essentially the same. In short, the burden of the war was borne by the persons who lived during the war; they were the ones who did without a multitude of consumer goods to permit the United States to arm itself and its allies.[13]

☐ **Real Burden of the Debt**

But we must be careful not to whitewash the public debt. The existence of a large public debt does pose real and potential problems.

External Debt Externally held debt is a burden. This part of the public debt obviously is not "owed to ourselves," and in real terms the payment of interest and principal requires the transfer of a portion of our real output to other nations. However, only 10 or 12 percent of our public debt is externally held.

Incentives Table 13-2 indicates that the present public debt necessitates an annual interest payment of almost $35 billion. With no increase in the size of the debt, this annual interest charge must be paid out of tax reve-

---

[13]Wartime production may cause a nation's stock of capital to cease to grow or to dwindle as precious resources are shifted from the production of capital goods and to the production of war goods. As a result, future generations inherit a smaller stock of capital goods than they otherwise would. This occurred in the United States during World War II (see table on inside covers, line 2). But, again, this shifting of costs is independent of how a war is financed.

nues. These added taxes may tend to dampen incentives to bear risk, to innovate, to invest, and to work. In this indirect way, the existence of a large debt can impair economic growth.

Crowding-out Effect   We have already called attention to the crowding-out effect, that is, the possibility that deficit financing (or the refinancing of existing public debt) will increase the interest rate and reduce private investment spending. If this occurs, future generations will inherit a smaller stock of private capital.

Income Redistribution   The payment of interest on the public debt may rather arbitrarily redistribute income. Many economists argue that the payment of such interest tends to make our net tax system less progressive. That is, bond ownership is concentrated among the wealthier groups in society and the Federal tax structure is basically proportional (Table 8-6). Therefore, payment of interest on the debt contributes to income inequality.[14]

Debt, Liquidity, and Inflation   The very existence of a large debt tends to be inflationary. This is so for at least two reasons:

1 Because they are highly liquid assets, the possession of government bonds makes consumers feel wealthy. This feeling of wealth leads to greater consumption out of their incomes. In short, the existence of a large public debt tends to shift the consumption schedule upward. *If* the economy is already at full employment, this shift will be inflationary.

2 Furthermore, government bonds can be converted into money easily and with little or no risk of loss. Government bonds, therefore, constitute a potential backlog of purchasing

power which can add materially to inflationary fires. During periods of inflation, it is very tempting for consumers to dig into this reserve of purchasing power in an attempt to beat rising prices. Such an attempt to beat inflation will cause more inflation. Something like this happened at the end of World War II; the inflation-causing buying spree of 1946–1947 was financed partially by the cashing in of bonds purchased during the war.

But the contention that a large public debt has an inflationary bias must be qualified. First, *changes* in the size of the public debt have a much greater impact upon employment, output, and the price level than does the *absolute size* of the existing debt. Thus a $15 billion increase in the debt can be expected to exert a much greater expansionary or inflationary effect on the economy than the mere presence of an existing debt of, say, $620 billion. Moreover, remember that deficit spending is inflationary only if it is inappropriate fiscal policy. Deficit spending under full-employment conditions is inflationary; but this is ill-advised fiscal policy. Deficit spending during recession is expansionary; it increases employment and output and is therefore well advised.

Wasteful Government Spending   It is frequently argued that wasteful government expenditures are more likely to creep into the Federal budget when deficit financing is readily available. Politicians are motivated to screen expenditures more carefully when they are faced with the delicate problem of financing such programs currently out of tax increases. The fact that deficit financing gives the illusion of deferring the costs of government expenditures makes it easier for projects of questionable merit to find their way into the budget.

Debt Management and Monetary Policy
In Chapter 16 we shall find that a large public debt may impose a constraint upon effective monetary (interest-rate) policy. The basic di-

[14] However, at least one empirical study suggests that the redistributional impact is not evident and in fact may favor lower income groups. See Donald F. Vitaliano, "The Payment of Interest on the Public Debt and the Distribution of Income," *Journal of Economics and Business,* Spring–Summer 1973, pp. 175–186.

lemma is between the Treasury's desire for *low* interest costs, on the one hand, and the monetary authorities' goal of economic stability, on the other. More specifically, during periods of inflation the monetary authorities should restrict the money supply which will *raise* interest rates and thereby tend to limit investment spending. The higher interest rates will obviously increase the interest charge on a given public debt. In short, low interest charges on the debt and an anti-inflationary monetary policy are conflicting policy goals.

□ **Positive Role of Debt**

But there is a brighter side to the public debt.

Debt Creation, Stability, and Growth We must not forget that debt—both public and private—plays a positive role in a prosperous and growing economy. We know that as income expands, so does saving. Modern employment theory and fiscal policy tell us that if aggregate demand is to be sustained at the full-employment level, this expanding volume of saving or its equivalent must be obtained and spent by consumers, businesses, or government. The process by which saving is transferred to spenders is debt creation. Now, in fact, consumers and businesses do borrow and spend a great amount of saving. Private debt has increased spectacularly—much faster than public debt—since World War II. But if

households and businesses are not willing to borrow and thereby to increase private debt sufficiently fast to absorb the growing volume of saving, an increase in public debt must absorb the remainder or the economy will falter from full employment and fail to realize its growth potential.

Other Advantages Apart from debt creation, in at least three respects the very *existence* of a large debt can be desirable.

1 Because government bonds are highly liquid and virtually risk-free securities, they make an excellent purchase for small and conservative savers. To the extent that the availability of government bonds encourages saving, more resources are freed for investment and economic growth tends to be enhanced.

2 It should also be noted that although a large debt may pose inflationary problems in a full-employment economy, the same debt can cushion a cyclical downswing. A condition that is potentially undesirable in a full-employment economy may be very desirable in a less-than-full-employment economy. A large public debt may prove to be a kind of built-in stabilizer insofar as recessions are concerned.

3 Finally, Chapter 16 will reveal the important role which government bonds play in putting monetary policy into effect. The sale and purchase of government bonds by the economy's central banks influence the money supply, the level of spending, hence the level of economic activity.

Summary

1 Historically, the concept of an annually balanced budget has given ground to that of the cyclically balanced budget and, more recently, to the idea of functional finance.

2 Government responsibility for achieving and maintaining full employment is set forth in the Employment Act of 1946. The Council of Economic Advisers (CEA) was established to advise the President on policies appropriate to fulfilling the goals of the act.

3 Increases in government spending expand, and decreases contract, the equilibrium NNP. Conversely, increases in taxes reduce, and decreases expand, the equilibrium NNP. Appropriate fiscal policy therefore calls for increases in government spending and decreases in taxes—that is, for a budget deficit—to correct for unemployment. Decreases in government spending and increases in taxes—that is, a budget surplus—are appropriate fiscal policy for correcting inflation.

4 The balanced-budget multiplier indicates that equal increases in government spending and taxation will increase the equilibrium NNP.

5 Built-in stability refers to the fact that net tax revenues vary directly with the level of NNP. Therefore, during a recession, the public budget automatically tends toward a stabilizing deficit; conversely, during expansion, the budget automatically tends toward an anti-inflationary surplus. Built-in stability ameliorates, but does not correct, undesired changes in the NNP. Furthermore, the existence of built-in stability creates a "fiscal drag" problem.

6 The full-employment budget indicates what the Federal budgetary surplus or deficit would be *if* the economy operated at full employment throughout the year. The full-employment budget is a more meaningful indicator of the government's fiscal posture than is its actual budgetary surplus or deficit.

7 Financing a government deficit through the creation of new money is more expansionary than financing the same deficit by borrowing. A surplus is more deflationary when impounded by government than it is when used to retire outstanding public debt.

8 The enactment and application of appropriate fiscal policy are subject to certain problems and questions. Some of the most important are these: *a.* Can the enactment and application of fiscal policy be better timed so as to maximize its effectiveness in heading off economic fluctuations? *b.* Can the economy rely upon Congress to enact appropriate fiscal policy? *c.* State and local finance generally works to intensify rather than alleviate the cycle.

9 The public debt is now $620 billion, about 37 percent of the GNP. The public debt is held internally, need not be retired, and does *not* entail a reduced living standard for the economy as a whole when payment of interest or principal is made.

10 A large public debt may *a.* impair incentives to innovate and invest, *b.* "crowd out" private investment, *c.* arbitrarily redistribute income, *d.* add to inflationary pressures, *e.* be conducive to wasteful government spending, and *f.* conflict with monetary policy.

11 Debt creation transfers saving to spenders and thereby plays a positive function in maintaining a high level of output and of employment.

Questions and Study Suggestions

1 Key terms and concepts to remember: fiscal policy; annually balanced budget; cyclically balanced budget; functional finance; Employment Act of 1946; discretionary fiscal policy; built-in stabilizers; balanced-budget multiplier; fiscal drag; full-employment budget; public debt.

2 Explain the three major budget philosophies. To which do you subscribe? Why? Why is an annually balanced budget not economically neutral? "No budget-balancing principle can be as important as maintaining full employment and preventing inflation." Do you agree?

3 Explain graphically the determination of equilibrium NNP through both the aggregate demand–aggregate supply approach and the leakages-injections approach for the private sector. Now add government spending and taxation, showing the impact of each upon the equilibrium NNP.

4 Refer to the tabular data for question 7 at the end of Chapter 12. Now, assuming investment is $16 billion, incorporate government into the table by assuming that it plans to tax and spend $20 billion at each possible level of NNP. Assume all taxes are personal taxes and that government spending does not entail shifts in the consumption and investment schedules. Explain the changes in the equilibrium NNP which the addition of government entails.

5 What is the balanced-budget multiplier? Explain: "Equal increases in government spending and tax revenues of n dollars will increase the equilibrium NNP by n dollars." Does this hold true regardless of the size of the MPS?

6 Explain how discretionary fiscal policy can be used to close inflationary and recessionary gaps. Explain the functioning of the built-in stabilizers. How might the effect of "fiscal drag" be offset? Define the "full-employment budget" and explain its significance.

7 What is the best method of financing a government deficit during depression? What is the best means of disposing of a surplus during inflation? Explain your answers. "If the economy needs $10 billion with which to finance the expansion and improvement of its highways, it should simply print up the needed money to finance the undertaking. In this way we'll get the roads, and no one will be hurt by having to pay higher taxes." Evaluate this suggestion, first under conditions of full employment, and second under depressed conditions.

8 Briefly state and evaluate the major problems encountered in enacting and applying fiscal policy. Which do you feel are the most significant?

9 Comment upon the size and causes of the public debt. How does an internally held public debt differ from an externally held public debt? What would be the effects of retiring an internally held public debt? Distinguish between refinancing and retiring public debt.

10 In what ways might the mere existence of a large public debt contribute to inflationary pressures? "Incurring a public debt is more inflationary than carrying an existing public debt." Do you agree?

11 Explain or evaluate each of the following statements:

a. "Rising prices cause real incomes to fall. In such circumstances all levels of government should cut taxes. This will permit the American people to maintain their standard of living."

b. "A national debt is like a debt of the left hand to the right hand."

c. "Find an individual who is steadily accumulating debt, and you have probably found one who is in trouble; find one who is paying off his debts, and you have probably found one in good economic health. But find a nation whose domestic debts are mounting, whose mortgages year by year are increasing, whose corporate debentures are proliferating, whose state and local and federal bond issues are growing, and chances are that you have found a nation whose rate of growth is high, whose economy is buoyant, whose savings are abundant, whose business is booming."[15]

d. "As a society becomes wealthier, saving increases. If prosperity is to be sustained, the private and public sectors together must borrow and spend an amount sufficient to offset this saving. The expansion of debt is therefore a prerequisite of full employment."

[15] Robert L. Heilbroner and Peter L. Bernstein, *A Primer on Government Spending,* 2d ed. (New York: Vintage Books, Random House, Inc., 1970), p. 45.

12 *Advanced analysis.* Assume that, in the absence of any taxes, the consumption schedule for an economy is as follows:

NNP, billions	Consumption, billions
$100	$120
200	200
300	280
400	360
500	440
600	520
700	600

a. Graph this consumption schedule and note the size of the MPC.

b. Assume now a lump-sum (regressive) tax system is imposed in such a way that the government collects $10 billion in taxes at all levels of NNP. Calculate the tax rate at each level of NNP. Graph the resulting consumption schedule and compare the MPC and the multiplier with that of the pretax consumption schedule.

c. Now suppose a proportional tax system with a 10 percent tax rate is imposed instead of the regressive system. Calculate the new consumption schedule, graph it, and note the MPC and the multiplier.

d. Finally, impose a progressive tax system such that the tax rate is zero percent when NNP is $100, 5 percent at $200, 10 percent at $300, 15 percent at $400, and so forth. Determine and graph the new consumption schedule, noting the effect of this tax system on the MPC and the multiplier.

e. Explain why the proportional and progressive tax systems contribute to greater economic stability, while the regressive system does not. Demonstrate graphically.

13 *Advanced analysis.* We can add the public sector to the private economy model of question 10 at the end of Chapter 12 as follows. Assume $G = G_0 = 28$ and $T = T_0 = 30$. Because of the presence of taxes, the consumption schedule, $C = 50 + 0.8Y$, must be modified to read $C = 50 + 0.8(Y - T)$, where the term $(Y - T)$ is disposable (after-tax) income. Assuming all taxes are on personal income, investment remains $I = I_0 = 30$. Using the equilibrium condition $Y = C + I + G$, determine the equilibrium level of income. Explain why the addition of the public budget with a slight surplus *increases* the equilibrium income. Now substitute $T = 0.2Y$ for $T = T_0 = 30$, and solve again for the level of income.

Selected References

Anderson, William H.: *Financing Modern Government* (Boston: Houghton Mifflin Company, 1973), chaps. 22–29.

Blinder, Alan S.: *Fiscal Policy in Theory and Practice* (Morristown, N.J.: General Learning Press, 1973).

Committee on the Judiciary, *Balancing the Budget* (Washington, 1975).

Economic Report of the President (Washington, published annually).

Heilbroner, Robert L., and Peter L. Bernstein: *A Primer on Government Spending,* 2d ed. (New York: Vintage Books, Random House, Inc., 1970).

Okun, Arthur (ed.): *The Battle against Unemployment,* rev. ed. (New York: W. W. Norton & Company, Inc., 1972), parts 2 and 4.

Last Word
The Impotence of Fiscal Policy

Some economists feel that fiscal policy is an impotent and unpredictable stabilization tool.

The real question is whether or not conventional fiscal policy works as advertised.

If fiscal policy works, and its impact is properly measured by the size of the full employment deficit, then it should be possible to find some correlation between either the level or direction of the full employment budget and some measure of current or subsequent economic activity. George Terborgh tried to find some such link back in 1968, in *The New Economics,* but found only a weak correlation that turned out to be perverse. That is, larger full employment surpluses were associated with faster economic growth. More rigorous tests by economists at the St. Louis Fed, and again at Citibank, had no more luck in uncovering the magical properties of the full employment budget. A sharp shift toward larger full employment deficits did not prevent the recession of 1953–54, for example, nor the mini-recession of 1967. In 1946, a $60 billion reduction of Federal spending (equivalent to $400 billion today) was followed by a vigorous boom, and a combination of tax cuts and higher spending in 1948 (the equivalent of $75 billion today) was followed by a sharp recession.

The theory of fiscal policy is almost as messy as the evidence. If deficit spending is financed by borrowing from the private sector, there is no obvious stimulus—even to that undifferentiated thing called "demand." Whoever buys the government securities surrenders exactly as much purchasing power as is received by the beneficiaries of Federal largess. There would be a net fiscal stimulus only if there were no private demand for the funds needed to cover the added Treasury borrowing. Otherwise, lendable funds are just diverted from market-determined uses to politically determined uses.

There *may* be a stimulus in some circumstances if the deficit is financed by a more rapid increase in the money supply, but this is really a monetary stimulus, not a purely fiscal effect.

In the long run, resources allocated through the government must displace those allocated through markets, and growth of government spending must be at the expense of the private sector. The government has only three sources of revenue—taxes, borrowing, and printing money—and increasing any one of those must reduce the private sector's command over real resources. Although deficit spending may at times be a short-run stimulus to nominal demand, it is also a long-run drag on real supply—siphoning resources from uses that would otherwise augment the economy's productive capacity, and instead diverting those resources into hand-to-mouth consumption through government salaries, subsidies, and transfer payments.

So, the theory and evidence suggests that fiscal policy is essentially impotent, or at least unpredictable, except as a device to promote inflationary monetary policy and/or to reduce investment and growth.

Alan Reynolds, "Full Employment Budget: How Good a Guide to Public Policy?" *Tax Review,* April 1977, pp. 14–15, abridged. Reprinted by permission of the Tax Foundation, Inc.

PART THREE

MONEY, MONETARY POLICY, AND
ECONOMIC STABILITY

14

Money and Banking in American Capitalism

Money—one of the truly great inventions of man—constitutes a most fascinating aspect of economic science.[1]

> Money bewitches people. They fret for it, and they sweat for it. They devise most ingenious ways to get it, and most ingenuous ways to get rid of it. Money is the only commodity that is good for nothing but to be gotten rid of. It will not feed you, clothe you, shelter you, or amuse you unless you spend it or invest it. It imparts value only in parting. People will do almost anything for money, and money will do almost anything for people. Money is a captivating, circulating, masquerading puzzle.

Money is also one of the most crucial elements of economic science. It is much more than a passive component of the economic system—a mere tool for facilitating the economy's operation. When operating properly, the monetary system is the lifeblood of the circular flows of income and expenditure which typify all economies. A well-behaved money system is conducive to both full production and full employment. Conversely, a malfunctioning monetary system can make major contributions to severe fluctuations in the economy's levels of output, employment, and prices.

In this chapter we are concerned with the nature and functions of money and the basic institutions of the American banking system. Chapter 15 looks into the methods by which

[1] Federal Reserve Bank of Philadelphia, "Creeping Inflation," *Business Review,* August 1957, p. 3.

individual commercial banks and the banking system as a whole can vary the money supply. In Chapter 16 we discuss how the central banks of the economy attempt to regulate the supply of money so as to promote full employment and price level stability. Finally, Chapter 17 is devoted to monetarism—an alternative to the Keynesian macroeconomics of Chapters 11 through 13—which contends that the money supply is *the* key determinant of output, employment, and the price level.

The specific objectives of the present chapter are fourfold. We begin with a review of the functions of money. Next, we designate and assess the relative importance of the various types of money used in American capitalism. Third, we pose a query: What "backs" money in the United States? Finally, the institutional structure and the basic functions of the American banking system will be described.

THE FUNCTIONS OF MONEY

What is money? Money is what money does. Anything that performs the functions of money is money. There are three functions of money:

1 First and foremost, money is a *medium of exchange;* that is, money is usable in buying and selling goods and services. As a medium of exchange, money allows society to escape the complications of barter and thereby to reap the benefits of geographic and human specialization (see Chapter 3).

2 Money is also a *standard of value.* Society finds it convenient to use the monetary unit as a yardstick for measuring the relative worth of heterogeneous goods and resources. This has obvious advantages. With a money system, we need not state the price of each product in terms of all other products for which it might possibly be exchanged; that is, we need not state the price of cows in terms of corn, cream, cigars, Chevrolets, cravats, or some other product. This use of money as a common denominator means that the price of each product need be stated *only* in terms of the monetary unit. By dramatically reducing the number of prices in the economy, this use of money permits transactors to readily compare the relative worth of various commodities and resources. Such comparisons facilitate rational decision making. Recall from Chapter 9 the necessity of using money as a standard of value in measuring the GNP. Money is also used as a standard of value for transactions involving future payments. Debt obligations of all kinds are measured in terms of money.

3 Finally, money serves as a *store of value.* Because money is the most liquid of all assets, it is a very convenient form in which to store wealth. Though it does not yield monetary returns such as one gets by storing wealth in the form of real assets (property) or paper assets (stocks, bonds, and so forth), money does have the advantage of being immediately usable by a firm or a household in meeting any and all financial obligations.

MONEY IN AMERICAN CAPITALISM

Historically, such diverse items as whales' teeth, elephant tail bristles, circular stones, nails, slaves, cattle, beer, cigarettes, and pieces of metal have functioned as media of exchange. Currently, the debts of governments and of banks are employed as money.

□ Money Defined: M_1

Economists are not in agreement as to what specific items constitute the economy's money supply. Narrowly defined—and designated as M_1—the money supply is composed of three items: (1) coins, (2) paper money, and (3) demand deposits, or checking accounts. The first two items are debts of government and governmental agencies; the third represents a debt of commercial banks. Table 14-1 gives us an idea of the quantitative importance

Table 14-1 MONEY IN THE UNITED STATES, DECEMBER 1976

Money	Billions of dollars	Percent of total
Coins and paper money	$ 81	26
Demand deposits	231	74
Total M_1	$312	100

Source: Federal Reserve Bulletin, January 1977.

of these items in both absolute and relative terms. Let us comment briefly on each of these components of the money supply.

Coins Ranging from copper pennies to silver dollars, coins constitute the "small change" of our money supply. As Table 14-1 implies, coins constitute a very small portion of our total money supply. Currently about $8 or $9 billion worth of coins are in circulation, amounting to only 2 or 3 percent of the total money supply. Coins are essentially "convenience money" in that they permit us to make all kinds of very small purchases.

It is notable that all coins in circulation in the United States are *token money.* This simply means that the *intrinsic value*—that is, the value of the bullion contained in the coin itself—is less than the face value of the coin. This is purposely the case so as to avoid the melting down of token money for profitable sale as bullion. If our 50-cent pieces each contained, say, 75 cents' worth of silver bullion, it would be highly profitable to melt these coins for sale as bullion. Despite the illegality of such a procedure, 50-cent pieces would tend to disappear from circulation. This is one of the potential defects of commodity money: Its worth as a commodity may come to exceed its worth as money, causing it to cease functioning as a medium of exchange.

Paper Money Much more significant than coins, paper money constitutes about 23 or 24 percent of the economy's money supply. Virtually all this $72 or $73 billion of paper currency is in the form of *Federal Reserve Notes,* that is, notes which are issued by the Federal Reserve Banks with the authorization of Congress. The coin and paper money components of the money supply are frequently lumped together and simply labeled *currency.*

Demand Deposits The safety and convenience of using checks, or bank money, have made demand deposits the most important type of money in the United States. Despite the integrity of our postal employees, one would not think of stuffing, say, $4896.47 in an envelope and dropping it in a mailbox to pay a debt; but to write and mail a check for a large sum is commonplace. A check must be endorsed by the person cashing it; the drawer of the check subsequently receives the canceled check as an endorsed receipt attesting to the fulfillment of his obligation. Similarly, because the writing of a check requires endorsement by the drawer, the theft or loss of one's bankbook is not nearly so calamitous as would be the loss of an identical amount of currency. It is, furthermore, more convenient to write a check in many cases than it is to transport and count out a large sum of currency. For all these reasons, checkbook money has come to be the dominant form of money in American capitalism. Even Table 14-1 belittles the significance of bank money; it is estimated that in dollar value, about 90 percent of all transactions are carried out by the use of checks.

It might seem strange that demand deposits or checking accounts are a part of the money supply. But the reason for their inclusion is clear: Checks, which are nothing more than a means for transferring the ownership of demand deposits, are generally acceptable as a medium of exchange.[2] Furthermore, demand deposits can be immediately converted into paper money and coins on demand; checks drawn upon demand deposits are for all practical purposes the equivalent of currency.

[2] As a stop at any gas station will verify, checks are somewhat less generally acceptable as a medium of exchange than is currency!

In short,

Money, M_1 = demand deposits + currency

Currency is essentially government-created money, and demand deposits, we shall discover in Chapter 15, are bank-created money.

Qualification   A technical qualification of our definition of money must be added: Currency and demand deposits owned by government (the Treasury) and by Federal Reserve or commercial banks are excluded. This exclusion is partly to avoid overstating the money supply and partly because money in the possession of households and businesses—that is, "in circulation"—is more relevant to the level of spending in the economy.[3]

□   **Near-Monies and M_2**

But the line between what we have defined as money and certain other highly liquid assets called "near-monies" is a fine one. *Near-monies* are certain financial assets which, although they do not directly function as a medium of exchange, can be readily converted into currency or demand deposits. The most important near-monies are the various savings and time deposits in commercial banks and a variety of thrift institutions (savings and loan associations, mutual savings banks, credit unions, and so forth). By adding these near-monies to our M_1 definition we obtain a broader and quantitatively enlarged definition of the

money supply which we will label M_2. In December of 1976 these savings and time deposits amounted to $924 billion. Adding these to M_1 yields an M_2 money supply of $1236 billion. Some economists would argue that even M_2 is too narrow a definition of money. They point out, for example, that United States government savings bonds can be redeemed for cash at any time and are therefore as liquid as savings accounts. Hence, they are a near-money and should be included in any definition of the money supply. We shall adopt and employ the narrow M_1 definition in our ensuing discussion and analysis on the grounds that an asset, to be money, must be *directly and immediately* usable as a medium of exchange.

Near-monies are important to our discussion for at least four related reasons.

1 The existence of near-monies points up the fact that the definition of money is somewhat arbitrary. In modern complex economies, there is no clear-cut distinction between money and certain highly liquid assets.

2 The fact that people have such highly liquid assets available affects their consuming-saving habits. Generally speaking, the greater the amount of financial wealth people have in the form of near-monies, the greater is their willingness to spend out of their money incomes.

3 The conversion of near-monies into money or vice versa can affect the stability of the economy. For example, during the prosperity-inflationary phase of the business cycle, a significant conversion of savings and time deposits into demand deposits or currency adds to the money supply and, if not offset, could enhance inflationary pressures.

4 The specific definition of money adopted is important for purposes of monetary policy. For example, the money supply as measured by M_1 might be constant, while money defined as M_2 might be increasing. Now, if the monetary authorities feel it is appropriate to have an expanding supply of money, acceptance of our narrow M_1 definition would call for specific actions to increase cur-

[3] A paper dollar in the hands of John Doe obviously constitutes just $1 of the money supply. But, if we were to count dollars held by banks as a part of the money supply, that same $1 would count for $2 when deposited in a commercial bank. It would count for a $1 demand deposit owned by Doe and also for $1 worth of currency resting in the bank's vault. This problem of double counting can be avoided by excluding currency resting in commercial banks (and currency redeposited in the Federal Reserve Banks or other commercial banks) in determining the total money supply. The exclusion of currency held by, and demand deposits owned by, government is somewhat more arbitrary. The major reason for this exclusion is that it permits us better to gauge the money supply and rate of spending which occurs in the private sector of the economy apart from spending initiated by government policy.

rency and demand deposits. But acceptance of the broader M_2 definition would suggest that the desired expansion of the money supply is already taking place and that no specific policy action is required.

WHAT "BACKS" THE MONEY SUPPLY?

This is a slippery question; any reasonably complete answer is likely to be at odds with the preconceptions many of us hold with respect to money.

☐ Money as Debt

The first point to recognize is that the major components of the money supply—paper money and demand deposits—are simply debts, or promises to pay. Paper money is the circulating debt of the Federal Reserve Banks. Demand deposits are the debts of commercial banks.

Furthermore, paper currency and demand deposits have no intrinsic value. A $5 bill is just a piece of paper, and a demand deposit is merely a bookkeeping entry. And coins, we already know, have an intrinsic value less than their face value. Nor will government redeem the paper money you hold for anything tangible, such as gold. In effect, we have wisely chosen to "manage" our money supply in seeking to provide the amount of money needed for that particular volume of business activity which will foster full employment, price level stability, and a healthy rate of economic growth. Such management of the money supply is eminently more sensible than linking the money supply to gold or any other commodity whose supply might arbitrarily and capriciously change. After all, a substantial increase in the nation's gold stock as the result of mining or importation might increase the money supply far beyond that amount needed to transact a full-employment level of business activity and therefore might result in sharp inflation. Conversely, the historical decline in domestic gold production or the loss of gold in settling international transactions (Chapters 43 and 44) could reduce the domestic money supply to the point where economic activity was choked off and unemployment and a retarded growth rate resulted. The important point is that paper money cannot be converted into gold but is exchangeable only for other pieces of paper money. The government will swap one paper $5 bill for another bearing a different serial number. That is all you can get should you ask the government to redeem some of the paper money you hold. Similarly, demand-deposit money cannot be exchanged for gold but only for paper money, which, as we have just seen, will not be redeemed by the government for anything tangible. The Last Word segment of this chapter merits a careful reading at this point.

☐ Value of Money

If currency and demand deposits have no intrinsic characteristics which give them value *and* if they are not backed by gold or other precious metals, then why are they money? A reasonably complete answer to this question involves three points.

1   Acceptability   Currency and demand deposits are money for the simple reason they are accepted as such. By virtue of long-standing business practice, currency and demand deposits perform the basic function of money; they are acceptable as a medium of exchange. Suppose you swap a $10 bill for a shirt or blouse at a clothing store. Why does the merchant accept this piece of paper in exchange for one of his products? The answer is curious: The merchant accepts paper money because he is confident that others will also be willing to accept it in exchange for goods and services. He knows that he can purchase the services of his clerks, acquire products from wholesalers, pay the rent on his store, and so forth. Each of us accepts paper money in exchange because he has confidence that it will be exchangeable for real goods and services when he chooses to spend it.

2 Legal Tender Our confidence in the acceptability of paper money is partly a matter of law; currency has been designated as *legal tender* by government. This means that paper currency must be accepted in the payment of a debt or the creditor forfeits the privilege of charging interest and the right to sue the debtor for nonpayment. Put more bluntly, the acceptability of paper dollars is bolstered by the fact that government says these dollars are money. The paper money in our economy is basically *fiat money;* it is money because the government says it is, not because of redeemability in terms of some precious metal. The general acceptability of currency is also bolstered by the willingness of government to accept it in the payment of taxes and other obligations due the government.

Lest we be overimpressed by the power of government, it should be noted that the fact that paper currency is generally accepted in exchange is decidedly more important than government's legal tender decree in making these pieces of paper function as money. Indeed, the government has *not* decreed checks to be legal tender, but they nevertheless successfully perform the vast bulk of the economy's exchanges of goods, services, and resources.

3 Relative Scarcity At a more fundamental level, the value of money, like the economic value of anything else, is essentially a supply and demand phenomenon. That is, money derives its value from its scarcity relative to its usefulness. The usefulness of money, of course, lies in its unique capacity to be exchanged for goods and services, either now or in the future. The economy's demand for money thus depends upon its total dollar volume of transactions in any given time period plus the amount of money individuals and businesses want to hold for possible future

transactions. Given a reasonably constant demand for money, the value or "purchasing power" of the monetary unit will be determined by the supply of money. Let us see why this is so.

□ Money and Prices

The real value or purchasing power of money is the amount of goods and services a unit of money will buy. It is obvious, furthermore, that the amount a dollar will buy varies inversely with the price level; stated differently, a reciprocal relationship exists between the general price level and the value of the dollar. Figure 14-1 allows us to visualize this inverse relationship.[4] When the consumer price index or "cost-of-living" index goes up, the purchasing power of the dollar necessarily goes down, and vice versa. Higher prices lower the value of the dollar because more dollars will now be needed to command a given amount of goods and services. Conversely, lower prices increase the purchasing power of the dollar because you will now need fewer dollars to obtain a given quantity of goods and services. If the price level doubles, the value of the dollar will decline by one-half, or 50 percent. If the price level falls by one-half, or 50 percent, the purchasing power of the dollar will double.[5]

You have probably heard or read of situations wherein a nation's currency became worthless and unacceptable in exchange. Indeed, we noted several in Chapter 10. With few

---

[4] Figure 14-1 is called a "ratio" or "semi-log" chart because equal vertical distances measure equal percentage changes rather than equal absolute changes.

[5] The arithmetic of this relationship is slightly more complex than these examples suggest. If we let P equal the price level expressed as an index number and D equal the value of the dollar, then our reciprocal relationship is

$$D = \frac{1}{P}$$

If P equals 1.00, then D obviously is 1.00. But if the price level rises to 1.20, then D will be $.83\frac{1}{3}$. Hence, a 20 percent *increase* in the price level will cause a $16\frac{2}{3}$ percent *decline* in the value of the dollar.

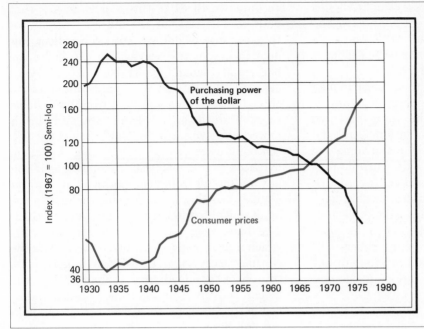

FIGURE 14-1 THE PRICE LEVEL AND THE VALUE OF MONEY

A reciprocal or inverse relationship exists between the general price level and the purchasing power of the dollar.

exceptions these were situations where government issued so many pieces of paper currency that the value of each of these units of money was almost totally undermined. The infamous post-World War I inflation in Germany is a notable example. In December of 1919 there were about 50 billion marks in circulation. Exactly four years later this figure had expanded to 496,585,345,900 billion marks! The result? The German mark in 1923 was worth an infinitesimal fraction of its 1919 value.[6] Inflation, you will recall, is typically the consequence of society's spending beyond its capacity to produce. Other things being equal, increases in the money supply tend to increase total spending. Once full employment is reached and total output becomes virtually fixed, this added spending can only serve to make prices spiral up. The shirt which sold for $10 in our earlier illustration may, after severe inflation, cost $100. This means that the dol-

lar, which was formerly worth one-tenth of a shirt, is now worth just one-hundredth of a shirt. The dollar's value, or purchasing power, has obviously been reduced to 10 percent of its former value by inflation.

How might inflation and the accompanying decreases in the value of the dollar affect the acceptability of paper dollars as money? Households and businesses are willing to accept paper currency as a medium of exchange so long as they know it can in turn be spent by them without any noticeable loss in its purchasing power. But, with spiraling inflation, this is not the case. Runaway inflation, such as Germany faced in the early 1920s, may significantly depreciate the value of money between the time of its receipt and its expenditure. Money will be "hot" money. It is as if the government were constantly taxing away the purchasing power of dollars. Rapid depreciation of the value of the dollar may cause it to cease functioning as a medium of exchange. Businesses and households may refuse to accept paper money in exchange because they do not want to bear the loss in its value which will

[6]Frank G. Graham, *Exchange, Prices and Production in Hyperinflation Germany, 1920–1923* (Princeton, N.J.: Princeton University Press, 1930), p. 13.

occur while it is in their possession. (All this despite the fact that government says the paper currency is legal tender!) Without an acceptable medium of exchange, the economy will revert to inefficient barter.

Similarly, people are willing to use money as a store of value so long as there is no unreasonable deterioration in the value of those stored dollars because of inflation. And the economy can effectively employ the monetary unit as a standard of value only when its purchasing power is relatively stable. A yardstick of value which is subject to drastic shrinkage no longer permits buyers and sellers to establish clearly the terms of trade. When the value of the dollar is declining rapidly, sellers will not know what to charge and buyers will not know what to pay for the various goods and services.

□ Managing Money

The overriding implication of this discussion of the value of money is this: The major "backing" of paper money is the government's ability to keep the value of money reasonably stable. This entails (1) appropriate fiscal policy, as explained in Chapter 13, and (2) intelligent management or regulation of the money supply, as noted above. The acceptability of paper money depends in part upon sound management of the monetary system and in part upon the pursuit of appropriate fiscal measures by government. Businesses and households accept paper money in exchange for goods and services so long as it will command a roughly equivalent amount of goods and services when they in turn spend it. In our economy a blending of legislation, government policy, and social practice serves as a bulwark against any imprudent expansion of the money supply which might jeopardize money's value in exchange.

What we have said with respect to paper currency also applies to demand-deposit money. In this case money is the debt of the commercial banks. If you have a checking account worth $100, this merely means that your commercial bank is indebted to you for that number of dollars. You can collect this debt in one of two ways. You can go to the bank and demand paper currency for your demand deposit; this simply amounts to changing the debts you hold from bank debts to government-issued debts. Or, and this is more likely, you can "collect" the debt which the bank owes you by transferring this claim by check to someone else. For example, if you buy a $100 suit from your clothier, you can pay for it by writing a check, which transfers the bank's indebtedness from you to your clothier. The bank now owes your clothier the $100 which it previously owed to you. Why does the clothier accept this transfer of indebtedness (the check) as a medium of exchange? Because he can convert it into currency on demand or can in turn transfer the debt to others in making purchases of his choice. Thus checks, as means of transferring bank debts, are acceptable as money because of the commercial banks' ability to honor these claims.

In turn, the ability of commercial banks to honor claims against them depends upon their not creating too many of these claims. We shall find in a moment that a decentralized system of private, profit-seeking banks does not contain sufficient safeguards against the creation of too much check money. Hence, the American banking system has a substantial amount of centralization and governmental control to guard against the imprudent creation of check money by commercial banks.

□ Recap

Let us summarize the major points of this section:

1 In the United States and other advanced economies, all money is essentially the debts of government and commercial banks.

2 These debts efficiently perform the functions of money so long as their value, or purchasing power, is relatively stable.

3 The value of money is no longer rooted

in carefully defined quantities of precious metals, but rather, in the amount of goods and services money will purchase in the marketplace.

4 Government's responsibility in stabilizing the value of the monetary unit involves (1) the application of appropriate fiscal policies, and (2) effective control over the supply of money.

INSTITUTIONAL FRAMEWORK OF THE AMERICAN BANKING SYSTEM

We have noted that the major component of the money supply, demand deposits, is created by commercial banks and that government-created money, coins and paper currency, typically comes into circulation through the commercial banks. It is essential, then, that we take a thorough look at the framework of the American banking system prior to a detailed analysis in Chapter 15 of how commercial banks create money.

□ Need for Centralization

It became painfully apparent rather early in American history that, like it or not, centralization and public control were prerequisites of an efficient banking system. Congress became increasingly aware of this about the turn of the twentieth century. Decentralized banking fostered the inconvenience and confusion of a heterogeneous currency, monetary mismanagement, and an inflexible supply of money. The last-mentioned problem was particularly acute. A dynamic and growing economy demands a flexible money supply—one which will respond to the economy's varying needs. The volume of trade expands and contracts unevenly and irregularly; hence, the supply of money must be elastic in meeting the needs of the economy. "Too much" money can precipitate dangerous inflationary problems; "too little" money can stunt the economy's growth by hindering the production and exchange of goods and services. The United States and innumerable foreign countries have learned through bitter experience that a decentralized banking system is not likely to provide that particular money supply which is most conducive to the welfare of the economy as a whole.

An unusually acute money panic in 1907 was the straw that broke Congress's back. A National Monetary Commission was established to study the monetary and banking problems of the economy and to outline a course of action for Congress. The end result was the Federal Reserve Act of 1913.

□ Structure of the Federal Reserve System

The banking system which has developed under the frequently amended Federal Reserve Act is sketched in Figure 14-2. It is important

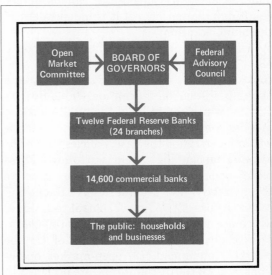

FIGURE 14-2 FRAMEWORK OF THE FEDERAL RESERVE SYSTEM AND ITS RELATIONSHIP TO THE PUBLIC

With the advice and counsel of the Open Market Committee and the Federal Advisory Council, the Board of Governors makes the basic policy decisions which regulate our money and banking systems. These decisions are made effective through the twelve Federal Reserve Banks.

that we understand the nature and functions of the various segments which compose the banking system and the relationships which the parts bear to one another.

Board of Governors The kingpin of our money and banking system is the Board of Governors of the Federal Reserve System. The seven members of this Board are appointed by the President with the confirmation of the Senate. Terms are long—fourteen years—and staggered so that one member is replaced every two years. The intention is to provide the Board with continuity and experienced membership. The Board is staffed by appointment rather than elections in an attempt to divorce monetary policy from partisan politics. An important argument for this philosophy of independence currently is that it is politically expedient for the administration in power to invoke expansionary fiscal policies—tax cuts and pork-barrel spending tend to win votes—and the monetary authorities can offset the resulting inflation only if it is independent of the administration.

The Board of Governors has the responsibility of exercising general supervision and control over the operation of the money and banking system of the nation. The Board's actions, which are to be in the public interest and designed to promote the general economic welfare, determine the basic policies which the commercial banking system is to follow. These basic policy decisions are made effective through the twelve Federal Reserve Banks and entail the use of two sets of control techniques which are at the disposal of the Board. *Quantitative credit controls,* consisting of (1) the reserve requirement, (2) open-market operations, and (3) the discount rate, are designed to negotiate those changes in the money supply which the Board deems most conducive to a stable and expanding economy. From time to time the Board invokes *selective* or *qualitative credit controls* to regulate the availability of certain specific types of credit—for example, consumer credit in the purchase of housing or

durables, and credit in buying securities in the stock market. Much of Chapter 16 will be concerned with a discussion of these two types of credit controls and the manner in which they permit the Board of Governors to influence the activities of commercial banks.

Two important bodies assist the Board of Governors in determining basic banking policy. On the one hand, the Federal Open Market Committee, made up of the seven members of the Board plus five of the presidents of the Federal Reserve Banks, sets the System's policy with respect to the purchase and sale of government bonds in the open market. These open-market operations constitute the most significant technique by which the monetary authorities can affect the money supply (Chapter 16). On the other hand, the Federal Advisory Council is composed of twelve prominent commercial bankers, one selected annually by each of the twelve Federal Reserve Banks. The Council meets periodically with the Board of Governors to voice its views on banking policy. However, as its name indicates, the Council is purely advisory; it has no policy-making powers.

The Twelve Federal Reserve Banks The twelve Federal Reserve Banks have three major characteristics. They are (1) central banks, (2) quasi-public banks, and (3) bankers' banks.

1 Central banks Most Americans are blessed with a more-or-less inherent fear of centralization. As a result, our banking system is less centralized than most of the other advanced economies of the world. As a matter of fact, the Federal Reserve Act was a compromise between exponents of centralization and advocates of decentralization. Hence, instead of creating a single central bank, the act divided the nation into twelve districts and provided for a Federal Reserve Bank to function as a central bank in each of these districts. Figure 14-3 shows these twelve Federal Reserve districts. Geographic considerations were also of significance in the creation of the Fed-

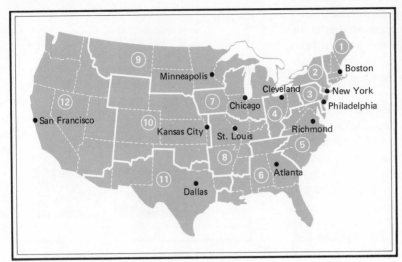

FIGURE 14-3 THE TWELVE FEDERAL RESERVE DISTRICTS

The Federal Reserve System divides the United States into twelve districts, each of which has one central bank and in some instances one or more branches of the central bank. Hawaii and Alaska are included in the twelfth district. (*Federal Reserve Bulletin.*)

eral Reserve Banks. It was felt that a single central bank would be unresponsive to the peculiar economic problems faced by the various regions of the economy. In any event, the net result is that the twelve Federal Reserve Banks make up the central banking system of the economy. It is through these central banks that the basic policy directives of the Board of Governors are made effective. The Federal Reserve Bank of New York City is by far the most important of these central banks. The development of modern communication and transportation facilities has undoubtedly lessened the geographic need for a system of regional banks.

2 Quasi-public banks The twelve Federal Reserve Banks are quasi-public banks. They reflect an interesting blend of private ownership and public control. The Federal Reserve Banks are owned by the member banks in their districts. Upon joining the Federal Reserve System, commercial banks are required to purchase shares of stock in the Federal Reserve Bank in their district. But the basic policies which the Federal Reserve Banks pursue are set by a public body—the Board of Governors. The central banks of American capitalism are privately owned but governmentally controlled.

The fact that the Federal Reserve Banks are essentially public institutions is vitally important to an understanding of their operation. In particular, it must be emphasized that the Federal Reserve Banks are not motivated by profits, as are private enterprises. The policies followed by the central banks are those which tend to promote the economic wellbeing of the economy as a whole. Hence, the activities of the Federal Reserve Banks will frequently be at odds with the profit motive.[7] Furthermore, the Federal Reserve Banks are not in competition with commercial banks. With rare exceptions, the Federal Reserve Banks do not deal with the public, but rather, with the government and the commercial banks.

3 Bankers' banks Finally, the Federal Reserve Banks are frequently called "bankers'

---

[7]Though it is not their basic goal, the Federal Reserve Banks have actually operated profitably, largely as the result of Treasury debts held by them. A part of the profits has been used to pay 6 percent dividends to member banks on their holdings of stock; the bulk of the remaining profits has been turned over to the United States Treasury.

banks." This is a shorthand way of saying that the Federal Reserve Banks perform essentially the same functions for commercial banks as commercial banks perform for the public. Just as commercial banks accept the deposits of and make loans to the public, so the central banks accept the deposits of and make loans to commercial banks. But the Federal Reserve Banks have a third function which commercial banks no longer perform: the function of issuing currency. Congress has authorized the Federal Reserve Banks to put into circulation Federal Reserve Notes, which constitute the economy's paper money supply.

The Commercial Banks The workhorses of the American banking system are its 14,643 commercial banks. The majority of these are *state banks,* that is, private banks operating under state charters. But a good many have received their charters from the Federal government; that is, they are *national banks.* Less than one-half of all existing commercial banks are members of the Federal Reserve System. The 4747 national banks of our economy are required by law to join the Federal Reserve System; the remaining 9896 state banks have the option of joining or declining to do so. As Figure 14-4 indicates, 1029 of the state banks have chosen to join the Federal Reserve System.

These statistics, however, tend to underestimate grossly the significance of the Federal Reserve System. Virtually all the larger commercial banks are members of the System, nonmembers being the smaller "country banks," for the most part. Thus, about 80 percent of all deposits held by the commercial banking system rest in member banks. In addition, nonmember banks can participate on a limited basis in the functioning of the Federal Reserve System. For example, nonmember banks can avail themselves of the Federal Reserve System's program for the efficient collection of checks. Nonmember banks are not entirely disassociated from the Federal Reserve System or immune to its policy decisions.

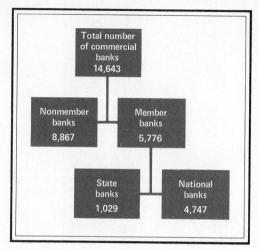

FIGURE 14-4 THE CLASSIFICATION OF COMMERCIAL BANKS, 1976

Less than half of all commercial banks are members of the Federal Reserve System. However, these member banks hold about 80 percent of all commercial bank deposits. (*Federal Reserve Bulletin.*)

Commercial banks, as already noted, have two basic functions. First, they hold the money deposits of businesses and households. Second, commercial banks make loans to the public, and in so doing, increase the economy's supply of money. Detailed analysis of these functions is the main objective of Chapter 15.

Financial Intermediaries Although the present analysis will be concerned only with ordinary commercial banks, it is important to recognize that the commercial banking system is thoroughly supplemented by a diverse group of specialized banking and financial institutions. For example, savings banks and savings and loan associations accept the funds of relatively small savers as time deposits and make these funds available to investors by extending mortgage loans or by purchasing marketable securities. Investment banks, on the other hand, perform the task of marketing the newly issued bonds and stocks of corporations which desire funds for capital expansion. Insurance companies accept huge volumes of savings in the form of premiums on insurance policies and annuities and use these funds, wholly or in part, to buy a variety of private, corporate, and government securities. This listing of banking and financial institutions is not exhaustive.

All banking and financial institutions, including commercial banks, have one point in common: They are all dealers in credit or debt. *These individual institutions lend the funds deposited with them or acquired by them, receiving credit instruments—bonds, stocks, mortgages, or promissory notes—in return.* Hence, these institutions play a significant role in the economy, functioning as *financial intermediaries* between savers and investors. But from the social point of view, you will recall, their operation falls short of perfection. These financial intermediaries do *not* provide for an exact and continuing balance of investment spending and the full-employment volume of saving. Why? Because (1) savers and investors are essentially different groups who make their decisions in response to different motivations; (2) savers may add to or subtract from their money balances; and (3) commercial banks may add to or subtract from the supply of money (Chapter 11).

A Critical Distinction Commercial banks, accepting both time and demand deposits and using the proceeds wholly or in part to acquire income-earning securities, function as intermediaries between savers and investors. But commercial banks also perform an additional function which other banking and financial institutions do not. That unique function is *to create money by extending bank credit—that is, by making loans—to businesses and households.* Other financial institutions can only *transfer* money from savers to spenders. In doing so they do not affect the total supply of money available. Commercial banks, however, can *create* demand-deposit money and make it available for use by potential spenders. Banks are by no means totally dependent upon the

deposits of savers in making money available to spenders. Within limits, commercial banks can create the money which spenders desire. Generally speaking, it works this way: Banks accept the credit of borrowing individuals and businesses (their promissory notes) and give these borrowers bank credit (demand deposits) in return. By exchanging debts that are not money (promissory notes) for debts that are money (demand deposits), commercial banks perform the unique function of increasing the money supply. In retiring bank credit, commercial banks decrease the money supply. The mechanics of these transactions will be studied in some detail in the ensuing chapter. At this juncture, the basic point to recognize is this: *Because of their money-creating and money-destroying abilities, commercial banks are unique and highly strategic institutions in our economy.* Commercial banks play a particularly vital role in affecting the volume of money and hence the levels of spending, output, employment, and prices. Therefore, our attention is centered upon the functioning of commercial banks as opposed to the other financial intermediaries mentioned earlier.

□ **Functions of the Federal Reserve System**[8]

The Federal Reserve System—in particular, the twelve Federal Reserve Banks and the Board of Governors—was established to achieve certain definite objectives. These goals stem largely from the defects inherent in the system of uncoordinated state and national banks which prevailed prior to the passage of the Federal Reserve Act.

Holding the Deposits of Member Banks Federal Reserve Banks hold the deposits, or *reserves,* of member banks. Private businesses and individuals find it convenient to establish

[8]For a more detailed look at the service functions of the Federal Reserve Banks, see Board of Governors of the Federal Reserve System, *The Federal Reserve System: Purposes and Functions,* 6th ed. (1974), chaps. 1, 2, 7.

checking accounts at commercial banks. These accounts are simply reserves of funds which the owner more or less regularly draws upon and occasionally replenishes. In the same manner, member banks keep reserves—that is, money deposits—with the Federal Reserve Bank of their district. When in need of currency, the commercial banks can, within limits, draw upon these reserves. When in possession of surplus cash, commercial banks may deposit this extra currency in their reserves. Or, just as you may buy a bond or fulfill an obligation by drawing a check on your bank account, so may a commercial bank buy a government bond or honor some claim against itself by drawing down its reserves at the Federal Reserve Bank. Much of the daily work of the Federal Reserve Banks is concerned with increasing and decreasing the reserves of commercial banks as routine banking transactions occur.

Supplying the Economy with Paper Currency It is also the responsibility of the Federal Reserve Banks to supply the economy with needed paper currency or, more specifically, Federal Reserve Notes. As the fountainhead of the economy's paper money supply, the Federal Reserve Banks function as a reservoir of cash. When the economy needs more currency, the reservoir is opened and currency spills into the economy. When the economy has more currency than it desires to hold, the excess is channeled back into the reservoir. The commercial banks act as intermediaries between the public and the Federal Reserve Banks in each case. Specifically, it works something like this: During the Christmas buying rush, for example, the public wants more currency in circulation. To get this additional cash, individuals and businesses cash checks at the commercial banks. This lowers the amounts of currency resting in bank vaults. Commercial banks then turn to the bankers' banks and draw checks against their deposits (reserves) with the Federal Reserve

Banks to replenish their vault cash. After the Christmas rush has subsided, less currency is needed. The public deposits this extra currency in their bank accounts. As a result, commercial banks find they have an overabundant stock of currency in their vaults. They deposit their surplus cash in the Federal Reserve Banks, thereby increasing their reserves.

Providing for the Collection of Checks
As previously noted, a check is merely a written order which the drawer may use in making a purchase or paying a debt. A check is collected, or "cleared," when one or more banks negotiate a transfer of part of the drawer's checking account, or demand deposit, to the demand deposit of a recipient of the check. If Jones and Smith have checking accounts in the same commercial bank and Jones gives Smith a $10 check, Smith can collect this check by taking it to the commercial bank, where his account will be increased by $10 and Jones's reduced by $10. In many cases, however, the drawer and the receiver of a check will be located in different towns or different states and therefore have their accounts in commercial banks far distant from one another. An important function of the Federal Reserve Banks is to provide facilities for the rapid collection of checks where the banks of the drawer and the receiver are geographically remote. The mechanics of check collecting and its effect upon the financial position of commercial banks will be outlined in detail in the next chapter.

Acting as Fiscal Agents for Government
The Federal Reserve Banks act as bankers and fiscal agents for the Federal government. The Federal government collects huge sums through taxation, spends equally astronomical amounts, and sells and redeems bonds. Naturally, the government wants to avail itself of banking facilities in carrying out these functions. Hence, the bankers' banks hold a part of

the Treasury's checking accounts, aid the government in collecting various tax revenues, and administer the sale and redemption of government bonds.

Supervising Member Banks   The Federal Reserve Banks supervise the operations of member banks. A banking system stands or falls on the financial soundness of the individual commercial banks of which it is composed. Unsound banking practices can have widespread repercussions, to the point of threatening the financial structure of the entire economy. Since commercial banking is "vested with a public interest," it has been subject to government supervision.

The Federal Reserve has supervisory powers over all member commercial banks.[9] This supervision usually takes the form of periodic, unannounced examinations of the commercial banks. Banks which do not conform to the standards set forth by the Federal Reserve authorities may be denied the privilege of borrowing from the Federal Reserve Banks, and in

[9]The Federal Reserve is not alone in the task of supervision. The individual states supervise all banks which they charter. The Comptroller of the Currency supervises all national banks. Finally, the Federal Deposit Insurance Corporation has the power to supervise all banks whose deposits it insures. Hence, a member national bank which belongs to the FDIC will be subject to three supervisory agencies—the Federal Reserve, the Comptroller of the Currency, and the FDIC.

extreme cases the officers and directors of offending banks may be removed by the Board of Governors.

Regulating the Supply of Money   Finally—and most important of all—the Federal Reserve System has ultimate responsibility for regulating the supply of money. *The major task of the Federal Reserve authorities is to manage the money supply in accordance with the needs of the economy as a whole.* In the dynamic and expanding economy of American capitalism, this task entails making that amount of money available which is consistent with high and steadily rising levels of output and employment and a relatively constant price level. It is through the previously mentioned quantitative and qualitative credit controls that the Federal Reserve authorities attempt to manipulate the supply of money—currency and demand deposits—in terms of short-run stability and long-run economic growth.

Whereas all the other functions are of a more-or-less routine or service nature, the goal of correctly managing the money supply entails the making of basic and unique policy decisions of a nonroutine character. Chapter 16 discusses Federal Reserve monetary policy and its effectiveness in achieving economic stability in a growing economy. But first we must understand how banks create money.

Summary

   1   Anything that functions as *a.* a medium of exchange, *b.* a standard of value, and *c.* a store of value is money.

   2   Most economists define money as demand deposits plus currency (coins and paper money) in circulation (M_1). Demand deposits, the largest component of the money supply, are money because they can be spent by writing checks against them. Some economists feel that savings and time deposits are also money and should be added to currency and demand deposits (M_2).

   3   Money, which is essentially the debts of government and commercial banks, has value because of the goods and services which it will command in the market. Maintenance of the purchasing power of money depends to a considerable degree upon the effectiveness with which government manages the money supply.

4 The American banking system is composed of *a.* the Board of Governors of the Federal Reserve System, *b.* the twelve Federal Reserve Banks, and *c.* some 14,600 commercial banks. The Board of Governors is the basic policy-making body for the entire banking system. The directives of the Board are made effective through the twelve Federal Reserve Banks, which are simultaneously *a.* central banks, *b.* quasi-public banks, and *c.* bankers' banks. The commercial banks of the economy perform the tasks of accepting money deposits and making loans. In lending, commercial banks create demand deposits, and are, therefore, money-creating institutions.

5 The major functions of the Federal Reserve System are *a.* to hold the deposits or reserves of commercial banks, *b.* to supply the economy's needs for paper currency, *c.* to provide facilities for the rapid collection of checks, *d.* to act as fiscal agent for the Federal government, *e.* to supervise the operations of member banks, and *f.* to regulate the supply of money in terms of the best interests of the economy as a whole.

Questions and Study Suggestions

1 Key terms and concepts to remember: medium of exchange; standard of value; store of value; token money; intrinsic value; Federal Reserve Notes; demand deposits; near-monies; M_1 and M_2; fiat money; legal tender; Federal Reserve Banks; Board of Governors; Federal Advisory Council; commercial banks; financial intermediaries; quantitative and qualitative credit controls.

2 Describe how drastic inflation can undermine the ability of money to perform its three basic functions.

3 What are the disadvantages of commodity money? What are the advantages of *a.* paper money and *b.* check money as compared with commodity money?

4 "Money is only a bit of paper or a bit of metal that gives its owner a lawful claim to so much bread or beer or diamonds or motorcars or what not. We cannot eat money, nor drink money, nor wear money. It is the goods that money can buy that are being divided up when money is divided up."[10] Evaluate and explain.

5 Fully evaluate and explain the following statements:

a. "The invention of money is one of the great achievements of the human race, for without it the enrichment that comes from broadening trade would have been impossible."

b. "Money is whatever society says it is."

c. "When prices of everything are going up, it is not because everything is worth more, but because the dollar is worth less."

d. "The difficult questions concerning paper [money] are ... not about its economy, convenience or ready circulation but about the amount of the paper which can be wisely issued or created, and the possibilities of violent convulsions when it gets beyond bounds."[11]

6 What items constitute the money supply in American capitalism? What is the most important component of the money supply? Distinguish between M_1 and M_2. What are near-monies? Of what significance are they? Why is the face value of a coin greater than its intrinsic value?

[10] George Bernard Shaw, *The Intelligent Woman's Guide to Socialism and Capitalism* (New York: Brentano's, Inc., 1928), p. 9. Used by permission of the Public Trustee and the Society of Authors.
[11] F. W. Taussig, *Principles of Economics,* 4th ed. (New York: The Macmillan Company, 1946), pp. 247–248.

7   "In most modern industrial economies of the world the debts of government and of commercial banks are used as money." Explain.

8   What "backs" the money supply in the United States? What determines the value of money? Who is responsible for maintaining the value of money? Why is it important for the money supply to be elastic, that is, capable of increasing or decreasing in size? What is meant by *a.* "sound money" and *b.* a "52-cent dollar"?

9   What is the major responsibility of the Board of Governors? Discuss the major characteristics of the Federal Reserve Banks. Of what significance is the fact that the Federal Reserve Banks are quasi-public?

10   What are the two basic functions of commercial banks? How do commercial banks differ from other financial intermediaries? State and briefly discuss the major functions of the Federal Reserve System.

Selected References

Board of Governors of the Federal Reserve System: *The Federal Reserve System: Purposes and Functions,* 6th ed. (1974), particularly chaps. 1, 2, 7.

Chandler, Lester V., and Stephen M. Goldfeld: *The Economics of Money and Banking,* 7th ed. (New York: Harper & Row, Publishers, Incorporated, 1977), chaps. 1–5, 8, 9.

Cochran, John A.: *Money, Banking, and the Economy,* 3d ed. (New York: The Macmillan Company, 1975), chaps. 1–6.

Gambs, Carl M.: "Money—A Changing Concept in a Changing World," *Monthly Review,* Federal Reserve Bank of Kansas City, January 1977.

Robertson, D. H.: *Money,* 6th ed. (New York: Pitman Publishing Corporation, 1948).

Thorn, Richard S.: *Introduction to Money and Banking* (New York: Harper & Row, Publishers, Incorporated, 1976), chaps. 1–6.

Last Word
A Dialogue on Money

Writing at the close of the Great Depression, the famous British economist Dennis H. Robertson reflected wittily upon the logic of monetary systems.

The British monetary system, as it has emerged from the furnace of the last eight years, is . . . a somewhat eccentric contraption. Between some enquiring Socrates from another planet and an economist instructed to explain its nature some such dialogue as the following might well take place:

Socrates: I see that your chief piece of money carries a legend affirming that it is a promise to pay the bearer the sum of one pound. What is this thing, a pound, of which payment is thus promised?

Economist: A pound is the British unit of account.

Socrates: So there is, I suppose, some concrete object which embodies more firmly that abstract unit of account than does this paper promise?

Economist: There is no such object, O Socrates.

Socrates: Indeed? Then what your Bank promises is to give me another promise stamped with a different number in case I should regard the number stamped on this promise as in some way ill-omened?

Economist: It would seem, indeed, to be promising something of that kind.

Socrates: So that in order to be in a position to fulfil its promises all the Bank has to do is to keep a store of such promises stamped with all sorts of different numbers?

Economist: By no means, Socrates—that would make its balance-sheet a subject for mockery, and in the eyes of our people there resides in a balance-sheet a certain awe and holiness. The Bank has to keep a store of Government securities and a store of gold.

Socrates: What are Government securities?

Economist: Promises by the Government to pay certain sums of money at certain dates.

Socrates: What are sums of money? Do you mean Bank of England notes?

Economist: I suppose I do.

Socrates: So these promises to pay promises are thought to be in some way solider and more sacred than the promises themselves?

Economist: They are so thought, as it appears.

Socrates: I see. Now tell me about the gold. It has to be of certain weight, I suppose.

Economist: Not of a certain weight, but of a certain value in terms of the promises.

Socrates: So that the less each of its promises is worth, the more promises the Bank can lawfully make?

Economist: It seems, indeed, to amount to something of that kind.

Socrates: Do you find that your monetary system works well?

Economist: Pretty well, thank you, Socrates, on the whole.

Socrates: That would be, I suppose, not because of the rather strange rules of which you have told me, but because it is administered by men of ability and wisdom?

Economist: It would seem that that must be the reason, rather than the rules themselves, O Socrates.

Dennis H. Robertson, *Essays in Monetary Theory* (London: Staples Press, Ltd., 1939), pp. 158–159. Reprinted by permission.

How Banks Create Money

In Chapter 14 we saw that the Federal Reserve Banks are the primary source of the economy's paper money. However, we shall find in the present chapter that commercial banks are the fountainhead of the major component of the money system—demand deposits.

More specifically, in this chapter we want to explain and compare the money-creating abilities of (1) a *single* commercial bank which is part of a multibank system, and (2) the commercial banking *system* as a whole.

It will be convenient for us to seek these objectives through the commercial bank's balance sheet. An understanding of the basic items which make up a bank's balance sheet, and of the manner in which various transactions change these items, will provide us with a valuable analytical tool for grasping the workings of our monetary and banking systems.

THE BALANCE SHEET OF A COMMERCIAL BANK

What is a *balance sheet?* It is merely a statement of assets and claims which portrays or summarizes the financial position of a firm—in this case a commercial bank—at some specific point in time. Every balance sheet has one overriding virtue: By definition, it must balance. Why? Because each and every known *asset,* being something of economic value, will be claimed by someone. Can you think of an asset—something of monetary value—which no one claims? A balance sheet balances because assets equal claims. The claims shown on a balance sheet are divided into two groups: the claims of the owners of a firm against the firm's assets, called *net worth,* and the claims of nonowners, called *liabilities.* Thus, it can be said that a balance sheet balances because

$$\text{Assets} = \text{liabilities} + \text{net worth}$$

A balance-sheet approach to our study of the money-creating ability of commercial banks is invaluable in two specific respects: On the one hand, a bank's balance sheet provides us with a convenient point of reference from which we can introduce new terms and concepts in a more or less orderly manner. On the other hand, the use of balance sheets will allow us to quantify certain strategic concepts and relationships which would defy comprehension if discussed in verbal terms alone.

A SINGLE COMMERCIAL BANK IN A BANKING SYSTEM

Our immediate goal is an understanding of the money-creating potential of a single bank which is part of a multibank banking system. What accounts constitute a commercial bank's balance sheet? How does a single commercial bank create and destroy money? What factors govern the money-creating abilities of such a bank?

◻ Formation of a Commercial Bank

The answers to these questions demand that we understand the ins and outs of a commercial bank's balance sheet and how certain, rather elementary transactions affect that balance sheet. We start with the organization of a local commercial bank.

Transaction 1: The Birth of a Bank Let us start from scratch. Suppose some farsighted citizens of the metropolis of Wahoo, Nebraska, decide that their town is in need of a new commercial bank to provide all the banking

services needed by that growing community. Assuming these enterprising individuals are able to secure a state charter for their bank, they then turn to the task of selling, say, $250,000 worth of capital stock to buyers, both in and out of the community. These financing efforts having met with success, the Merchants and Farmers Bank of Wahoo now exists—at least on paper. How does the Wahoo bank's balance statement appear at its birth?

The new owners of the bank have sold $250,000 worth of shares of stock in the bank—some to themselves, some to other people. As a result, the bank now has $250,000 in cash on hand and $250,000 worth of capital stock outstanding. Obviously the cash is an asset to the bank. The cash held by a bank is sometimes dubbed *vault cash* or *till money.* The outstanding shares of stock, however, constitute an equal amount of claims which the owners have against the bank's assets. That is, the shares of stock are obviously the net worth of the bank, though they are assets from the viewpoint of those who possess these shares. The bank's balance sheet would read:

BALANCE SHEET 1: WAHOO BANK

Assets		Liabilities and net worth	
Cash	$250,000	Capital stock	$250,000

Transaction 2: Becoming a Going Concern The newly established board of directors must now breathe life into their infant enterprise. They must get the newborn bank off the drawing board and make it a living reality. The first step will be to acquire property and equipment. Suppose the directors, confident of the success of their venture, purchase a building for $220,000 and some $20,000 worth of office equipment. This simple transaction merely changes the composition of the bank's assets. The bank now has $240,000 less in cash and $240,000 worth of new property assets. Using an asterisk to denote those accounts which are affected by each transaction, we find

that the bank's balance sheet at the conclusion of transaction 2 appears as follows:

BALANCE SHEET 2: WAHOO BANK

Assets		Liabilities and net worth	
Cash*	$ 10,000	Capital stock	$250,000
Property*	240,000		

Note that the balance sheet still balances, as indeed it must.

Transaction 3: Accepting Deposits We have already emphasized that commercial banks have two basic functions: to accept deposits of money and to make loans. Now that our bank is in operation, let us suppose that the citizens and businesses of Wahoo decide to deposit some $100,000 in the Merchants and Farmers Bank. What happens to the bank's balance sheet?

The bank receives cash, which we have already noted is an asset to the bank. Suppose this money is placed in the bank in the form of demand deposits (checking accounts), rather than time deposits (savings accounts). These newly created demand deposits constitute claims which depositors have against the assets of the Wahoo bank. Thus the depositing of money in the bank creates a new liability account—demand deposits. The bank's balance sheet now looks like this:

BALANCE SHEET 3: WAHOO BANK

Assets		Liabilities and net worth	
Cash*	$110,000	Demand	
Property	240,000	deposits*	$100,000
		Capital stock	250,000

You should note that, although there is no direct change in the total supply of money, a change in the composition of the economy's money supply has occurred as a result of transaction 3. Bank money, or demand deposits, have *increased* by $100,000 and currency in circulation has *decreased* by $100,000. Currency held by a bank, you will recall (Chapter

14, footnote 3) is *not* considered to be a part of the economy's money supply.

It is obvious that a withdrawal of cash will reduce the bank's demand-deposit liabilities and its holdings of cash by the amount of the withdrawal. This, too, changes the composition, but not the total supply, of money.

Transaction 4: Joining the Federal Reserve System Being a state bank, the Merchants and Farmers Bank of Wahoo will have the option of joining or not joining the Federal Reserve System. Suppose the directors of the bank decide in favor of joining. To accomplish this, the bank must meet a very specific requirement: It must keep a *legal reserve deposit* in the Federal Reserve Bank of its particular district.

This legal reserve deposit is *an amount of funds equal to a specified percentage of its own deposit liabilities which a member bank must keep on deposit with the Federal Reserve Bank in its district.* Since 1960, banks have been permitted to count vault cash as a part of reserves. As a matter of banking practice, however, the vast bulk of bank reserves are in the form of deposits in the Federal Reserve Banks. We shall simplify our discussion by supposing that our bank keeps its legal reserve *entirely* in the form of deposits in the Federal Reserve Bank of its district.

The "specified percentage" of its deposit liabilities which the commercial bank must deposit in the central bank is known as the *reserve ratio*. Why? Because that is exactly what it is—a ratio between the size of the deposits which the commercial bank must keep in the Federal Reserve Bank and the commercial bank's own outstanding deposit liabilities. This ratio is as follows:

$$\frac{\text{Reserve}}{\text{ratio}} = \frac{\text{commercial bank's required deposit in Federal Reserve Bank}}{\text{commercial bank's demand-deposit liabilities}}$$

Hence, if the reserve ratio were 10 percent, our bank, having accepted $100,000 in deposits from the public, would be obligated to keep $10,000 as a deposit, or reserve, in the Federal Reserve Bank in Kansas City. If the ratio were 20 percent, $20,000 would have to be deposited in the Federal Reserve Bank. If 50 percent, $50,000, and so forth.

How is the exact size of the reserve ratio determined? Upper and lower limits have been legislated by Congress. Within these limits the actual required reserve ratio is established by the Board of Governors of the Federal Reserve System.[1] As Table 15-1 indicates, the Board has set the reserve ratio on a graduated scale based upon the size of a bank's demand deposits. For example, a bank with demand deposits of $10 million would be required to have reserves of $900,000 (= 7 percent of $2 million *plus* 9½ percent of $8 million). To avoid a lot of tedious computations, we shall suppose that the reserve ratio for all banks is 20 percent. This is a nice round figure and is reasonably close to reality. It is to be emphasized that reserve requirements are *fractional,* that is, less than 100 percent. This consideration will be vital in the ensuing analysis of the lending ability of the banking system.

The Wahoo bank will just be meeting the required 20 percent ratio between its deposit in the Federal Reserve Bank and its own deposit liabilities by depositing $20,000 in the Federal

[1]State nonmember banks are required by state laws to keep reserves. These reserves usually take the form of cash and deposits in other commercial banks. Though the reserve ratio varies considerably among the states, 15 percent is about the average.

Table 15-1 RESERVE REQUIREMENTS OF MEMBER BANKS, January 1977

Demand deposits	Reserve requirement
$0–2 million	7 %
$2–10 million	9½
$10–100 million	11¾
$100–100 million	12¾
Over $400 million	16¼

Source: Federal Reserve Bulletin.

Reserve Bank. To distinguish this deposit from the public's deposits in commercial banks, we shall use the term *reserves* in referring to those funds which commercial banks deposit in the Federal Reserve Banks.

But let us suppose that the directors of the Wahoo bank anticipate that their holdings of the public's demand deposits will grow in the future. Hence, instead of sending just the minimum amount, $20,000, they send an extra $90,000, making a total of $110,000. In so doing, the bank will avoid the inconvenience of sending additional reserves to the Federal Reserve Bank each time its own demand-deposit liabilities increase. And we shall see shortly that it is upon the basis of extra reserves that banks can lend and thereby earn interest income.

Actually, of course, the bank would not deposit *all* its cash in the Federal Reserve Bank. However, because (1) banks as a rule hold vault cash only in the amount of 1½ or 2 percent of their total assets, and (2) vault cash can be counted as reserves, we shall find it expedient to assume that all the bank's cash is deposited in the Federal Reserve Bank and therefore constitutes the commercial bank's total reserves. The cumbersome process of adding two assets—"cash" and "deposits in the Federal Reserve Bank"—to determine "reserves" is thereby avoided.

At the completion of this transaction, the balance sheet of the Merchants and Farmers Bank will appear as follows:

BALANCE SHEET 4: WAHOO BANK

Assets		Liabilities and net worth	
Cash*	$ 0	Demand	
Reserves*	110,000	deposits	$100,000
Property	240,000	Capital stock	250,000

There are several points relevant to this transaction which must still be explained:

1 Excess reserves A note on terminology: The amount by which the bank's actual reserves exceed its required reserves is the bank's *excess* reserves. In this case,

Actual reserves	$110,000
Required reserves	−20,000
Excess reserves	$ 90,000

The only reliable way of computing excess reserves is to multiply the bank's demand-deposit liabilities by the reserve ratio ($100,000 times 20 percent equals $20,000) to obtain required reserves, then to subtract this figure from the actual reserves listed on the asset side of the bank's balance sheet. To ensure an understanding of this process, the reader should compute excess reserves for the bank's balance sheet as it stands at the end of transaction 4 on the assumption that the reserve ratio is (*a*) 10 percent, (*b*) 33⅓ percent, and (*c*) 50 percent.

Because the ability of a commercial bank to make loans depends upon the existence of excess reserves, this concept is of vital importance in grasping the money-creating ability of the banking system.

2 Control What is the rationale underlying the requirement that member banks deposit a reserve in the Federal Reserve Bank of their district? One might think that the basic purpose of reserves is to enhance the liquidity of a bank and thereby protect commercial bank depositors from losses; that is, it would seem that reserves constitute a ready source of funds from which commercial banks can meet large and unexpected withdrawals of cash by depositors. But this reasoning does not hold up under close scrutiny. Although, historically, reserves were looked upon as a source of liquidity and therefore protection for depositors, *legal,* or required, reserves cannot be used for the purpose of meeting unexpected cash withdrawals. If the banker's nightmare should materialize—that is, if everyone having a demand deposit in his bank appeared on the same morning to demand his deposits in cash—the banker could not draw upon his required reserves to meet this "bank panic" without violating the legal reserve ratio and thereby incurring the wrath and penalties of the Federal

Reserve authorities. In practice, legal reserves are *not* an available pool of liquid funds upon which commercial banks can rely in times of emergency.[2] As a matter of fact, even if legal reserves were accessible to commercial banks, they would not be sufficient to meet a serious "run" on a bank. Why? Because, as already noted, reserves are *fractional;* that is, demand deposits may be 3, 4, or 5 times as large as a bank's required reserves.

It is not surprising that commercial bank depositors are protected by other means. As noted in Chapter 14, periodic bank examinations are an important device for promoting prudent commercial banking practices. Furthermore, the Federal Deposit Insurance Corporation exists to insure the deposit liabilities of member banks and qualified nonmember banks that voluntarily become members of the FDIC.

If the purpose of reserves is not to provide for commercial bank liquidity, what is their function? *Control* is the basic answer. Legal reserves are a means by which the Board of Governors can influence the lending ability of commercial banks. The next chapter will explain in detail how the Board of Governors can invoke certain policies which either increase or decrease commercial bank reserves and thereby affect the ability of banks to grant credit. The objective is to prevent banks from *over*extending or *under*extending bank credit. To the degree that these policies are successful in influencing the volume of commercial bank

---

[2]This amendment must be added: As depositors withdraw cash from a commercial bank, the bank's demand-deposit liabilities will obviously decline. This lowers the absolute amount of required reserves which the bank must keep, thereby freeing some of the bank's actual reserves for use in meeting cash withdrawals by depositors. To illustrate: Suppose a commercial bank has reserves of $20 and demand-deposit liabilities of $100. If the legal reserve ratio is 20 percent, all the bank's reserves are obviously required. Now, if depositors withdraw, say, $50 worth of their deposits as cash, the bank will only need $10 as required reserves to support the remaining $50 of demand-deposit liabilities. Thus $10 of the bank's actual reserves of $20 is no longer required. The bank can draw upon this $10 in helping to meet the cash withdrawals of its depositors.

credit, the Board of Governors can help the economy avoid the business fluctuations which give rise to bank runs, bank failures, and collapse of the monetary system. It is in this indirect way—as a means of controlling commercial bank credit and thereby stabilizing the economy—that reserves protect depositors, not as a source of liquidity. As we shall see in a moment, another function of reserves is to facilitate the collection or "clearing" of checks.

3 Asset and liability Let us pause to note a rather obvious accounting matter which transaction 4 entails. Specifically, *the reserve created in transaction 4 is an asset to the depositing commercial bank but a liability to the Federal Reserve Bank receiving it*. To the Wahoo bank the reserve is an asset. Why? Because it is a claim which this commercial bank has against the assets of another institution—the Federal Reserve Bank. To the Federal Reserve Bank this reserve is a liability, that is, a claim which another institution—the Wahoo bank—has against it. Just as the demand deposit you get by depositing money in a commercial bank is an asset to you and a liability to your commercial bank, so the deposit or reserve which a commercial bank establishes by depositing money in a banker's bank is an asset to the commercial bank and a liability to the Federal Reserve Bank. An understanding of this relationship is necessary in pursuing transaction 5.

Transaction 5: A Check Is Drawn against the Bank Now let us tackle a very significant and somewhat more complicated transaction. Suppose that Clem Bradshaw, a Wahoo farmer who deposited a substantial portion of the $100,000 in demand deposits which the Wahoo bank received in transaction 3, purchases $50,000 worth of farm machinery from the Ajax Farm Implement Company of Beaver Crossing, Nebraska. Bradshaw very sensibly pays for this machinery by writing a $50,000 check, against his deposit in the Wahoo bank, in favor of the Ajax company. We want to

determine (1) how this check is collected or cleared, and (2) the effect that the collection of the check has upon the balance sheets of the banks involved in the transaction.

To accomplish this, we must consider the Wahoo bank, the Beaver Crossing bank, and the Federal Reserve Bank of Kansas City.[3] Let us suppose that both the commercial banks are members of the Federal Reserve System. And to keep our illustration as clear as possible, we shall deal only with the changes which occur in those specific accounts affected by this transaction.

Let us trace this transaction in three related steps, keying the steps by letters to Figure 15-1.

a. Mr. Bradshaw gives his $50,000 check, drawn against the Wahoo bank, to the Ajax company. The Ajax company in turn deposits the check in its account with the Beaver Crossing bank. The Beaver Crossing bank increases the Ajax company's demand deposit by $50,000 when it deposits the check. (The Ajax company is now paid off.) Bradshaw is elated over his new machinery, for which he has now paid.

b. Now the Beaver Crossing bank has Bradshaw's check in its possession. This check is simply a claim against the assets of the Wahoo bank. How will the Beaver Crossing bank collect this claim? By sending this check—along with checks drawn on other banks—to the Federal Reserve Bank of Kansas City. Here a clerk will clear, or collect, this check for the Beaver Crossing bank by increasing its reserve in the Federal Reserve Bank by $50,000 and by decreasing the Wahoo bank's reserve by a like amount. The check is collected merely by making bookkeeping notations to the effect that the Wahoo bank's claim against the Federal Reserve Bank has been reduced by $50,000 and the Beaver Crossing

---

[3] Actually, the Omaha branch of the Federal Reserve Bank of Kansas City would handle the process of collecting this check.

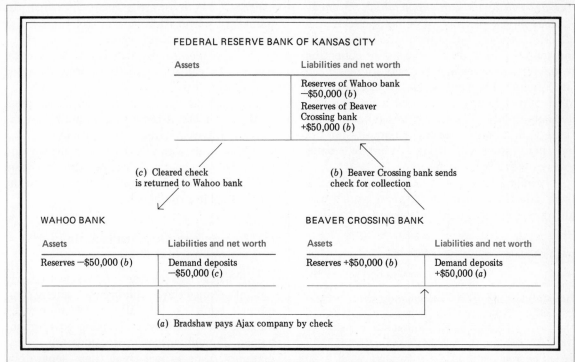

FIGURE 15-1   THE COLLECTION OF A CHECK THROUGH A FEDERAL RESERVE BANK

The bank against which a check is drawn and cleared loses both reserves and deposits; the bank in which the check is deposited acquires reserves and deposits.

bank's claim increased accordingly. Note these changes on the balance sheets in Figure 15-1.[4]

c. Finally, the cleared check is sent back to the Wahoo bank, and for the first time the Wahoo bank discovers that one of its deposi-

[4]Here is an interesting sidelight: The collection of Bradshaw's check by the Beaver Crossing bank through the Federal Reserve Bank involves the same type of procedure as the collection of a check between two individuals who have deposits in the same commercial bank. Suppose you and I both have checking accounts in the Wahoo bank. I owe you $10 and I pay this debt by check. You deposit the $10 check in the bank. Here a bank clerk collects the check for you by noting a "+$10" in your account and a "–$10" in my account. And that's that. The same thing happens at the Federal Reserve Bank of Kansas City when the Beaver Crossing bank clears a $50,000 check against the Wahoo bank. The bankers' bank increases the Beaver Crossing bank's deposit in the Federal Reserve Bank—that is, its reserve—by $50,000 and lowers the Wahoo bank's reserve by the same amount. The check is then cleared.

tors has drawn a check for $50,000 against his demand deposit. Accordingly, the Wahoo bank reduces Mr. Bradshaw's demand deposit by $50,000 and recognizes that the collection of this check has entailed a $50,000 decline in its reserves at the Federal Reserve Bank. Note that the balance statements of all three banks will still balance. The Wahoo bank will have reduced both its assets and its liabilities by $50,000. The Beaver Crossing bank will have $50,000 more in reserves and in demand deposits. The ownership of reserves at the Federal Reserve Bank will have changed, but total reserves will stay the same.

The point we are making is this: *Whenever a check is drawn against a bank and deposited in another bank, the collection of that check will entail a loss of both reserves and deposits by the bank upon which the check is drawn.* Conversely, if a bank receives a check drawn on another bank, the bank receiving the check will, in the process of collecting it, have its reserves and deposits increased by the amount of the check. In our example, the Wahoo bank loses $50,000 in both reserves and deposits to the Beaver Crossing bank. But there is no loss of reserves or deposits for the banking system as a whole. What one bank loses another bank gains.

Bringing all the other assets and liabilities back into the picture, the Wahoo bank's balance sheet looks like this at the end of transaction 5:

BALANCE SHEET 5: WAHOO BANK

Assets		Liabilities and net worth	
Reserves*	$ 60,000	Demand	
Property	240,000	deposits*	$ 50,000
		Capital stock	250,000

The reader should verify that with a 20 percent reserve requirement, the bank's *excess* reserves now stand at $50,000.

Transaction 5 is obviously reversible. If a check drawn against another bank is deposited in the Wahoo bank, the Wahoo bank will receive both reserves and deposits equal to the amount of the check as it is collected.

□   **Recap**

Let us designate here some of the salient conclusions from the first five transactions we have analyzed:

1 When a bank accepts deposits of cash, the composition of the money supply is changed, but the total supply of money is not directly altered.

2 Commercial banks which are members of the Federal Reserve System are required to keep legal reserve deposits, or simply "reserves," equal to a specified percentage of their own deposit liabilities on deposit with the Federal Reserve Bank of their district. The reserve ratio indicates the size of this "specified per-

centage." Reserves are a means by which the monetary authorities can control the lending policies of commercial banks.

3 The amount by which a bank's actual reserves exceed its required reserves is called "excess reserves."

4 Commercial bank reserves are an asset to the commercial bank but a liability to the Federal Reserve Bank holding them.

5 A bank which has a check drawn and collected against it will lose both reserves and deposits equal to the value of the check to the bank receiving the check.

□   **Money-creating Transactions of a Commercial Bank**

The next two transactions are particularly crucial because they explain how a single commercial bank can literally create money by making loans and by purchasing government bonds. Though these transactions are similar in many respects, we treat them separately.

Transaction 6: Granting a Loan   You will recall that in addition to accepting deposits, commercial banks have a basic function of granting loans to borrowers. What effect does commercial bank lending have upon the balance sheet of a commercial bank?

Suppose that the Grisley Meat Packing Company of Wahoo decides that the time is ripe to expand its facilities. Suppose, too, that the company needs exactly $50,000—which, by some unexplained coincidence, just happens to be equal to the Wahoo bank's excess reserves—to finance this project.

The company approaches the Wahoo bank and requests a loan for this amount. The Wahoo bank is acquainted with the Grisley company's fine reputation and financial soundness and is convinced of its ability to repay the loan. So the loan is granted. The president of the Grisley company hands a promissory note—a high-class IOU—to the Wahoo bank. The Grisley company, like all other modern firms, is interested in paying its obligations by check. Hence, instead of receiving a bushel basket full of cash from the bank, the Grisley company will get a $50,000 increase in its demand deposit in the Wahoo bank. From the Wahoo bank's standpoint it has acquired an interest-earning asset (the promissory note) and has created demand deposits to pay for this asset.

In short, the Grisley company has swapped an IOU for the right to draw an additional $50,000 worth of checks against its demand deposit in the Wahoo bank. Both parties are pleased with themselves. The Wahoo bank now possesses a new asset—an interest-bearing promissory note which it happily files under the general heading of "Loans." The Grisley company, sporting a fattened demand deposit, is now in a position to expand its operations.

At the moment the loan is negotiated, the balance sheet of the Wahoo bank's position is shown by balance sheet 6a.

BALANCE SHEET 6a: WAHOO BANK (*when loan is negotiated*)

Assets		Liabilities and net worth	
Reserves	$ 60,000	Demand	
Loans*	50,000	deposits*	$100,000
Property	240,000	Capital stock	250,000

All this looks innocent enough. But a closer examination of the Wahoo bank's balance statement will reveal a startling fact: *When a bank makes loans, it creates money.* The president of the Grisley company went to the bank with something which is not money—his IOU—and walked out with something that is money—a demand deposit.[5] When banks lend, they create demand deposits which are money. By extending credit the Wahoo bank has "monetized" an IOU. The Grisley company and the Wahoo bank have created and then swapped claims. The claim created by the Grisley company and given to the bank is not money; an individual's IOU is not generally acceptable as a medium of exchange. But the claim created by the bank and given to the Grisley company is money; checks drawn against a demand deposit are acceptable as a medium of exchange. It is through the extension of credit by commerical banks that the bulk of the money used in our economy is created.

But there are important forces which circumscribe the ability of a commercial bank to create demand deposits—that is, "bank money"—by lending. In the present case, the Wahoo bank can expect the newly created demand deposit of $50,000 to be a very active account. The Grisley company would not borrow $50,000 at, say, 8 or 10 percent for the sheer joy of knowing the funds were available if needed. Let us assume that the Grisley company awards a $50,000 contract to the Quickbuck Construction Company of Omaha. Quickbuck, true to its name, completes the expansion job and is rewarded with a check for $50,000 drawn by the Grisley company against its demand deposit in the Wahoo bank. The Quickbuck company, having its headquarters in Omaha, does not deposit this check back in the Wahoo bank but instead deposits it in the Fourth National Bank of Omaha. The Fourth National Bank now has a $50,000 claim against the Wahoo bank. This check is collected in the manner described in transaction 5. As a result, the Wahoo bank *loses* both reserves and deposits equal to the amount of the check; the Fourth National Bank *acquires* $50,000 of reserves and deposits. In short, assuming a check is drawn by the borrower for the entire amount of the loan ($50,000) and given to a firm which deposits it in another bank, the Wahoo bank's balance sheet will read as follows *after the check has been cleared against it:*

BALANCE SHEET 6b: WAHOO BANK (*after a check drawn on the loan has been collected*)

Assets		Liabilities and net worth	
Reserves*	$ 10,000	Demand	
Loans	50,000	deposits*	$ 50,000
Property	240,000	Capital stock	250,000

[5] In transaction 3, demand deposits were created, but only by currency going out of circulation. Hence, there was a change in the composition of the money supply but no change in the total supply of money.

You will note immediately that after the check has been collected, the Wahoo bank is just barely meeting the legal reserve ratio of 20 percent. The bank has *no excess reserves*. This poses an interesting question: Could the Wahoo bank have lent an amount greater than $50,000—an amount greater than its excess reserves—and still have met the 20 percent reserve requirement if a check for the full amount of the loan were cleared against it? The answer is "No." For example, suppose the Wahoo bank had loaned $55,000 to the Grisley company. Collection of the check against the Wahoo bank would have lowered its reserves to $5000 (= $60,000 − $55,000) and deposits would again stand at $50,000 (= $105,000 − $55,000). The ratio of actual reserves to deposits would now be only $5000/$50,000, or 10 percent. The Wahoo bank could thus *not* have lent $55,000. By experimenting with other figures in excess of $50,000, the reader will find that the maximum amount which the Wahoo bank could lend at the outset of transaction 6 is $50,000. This figure is identical with the amount of excess reserves which the bank had available at the time the loan was negotiated. We can conclude that *a single commercial bank in a multibank banking system can lend only an amount equal to its initial pre-loan excess reserves.* Why? Because when it lends, it faces the likelihood that checks for the entire amount of the loan will be drawn and cleared against the lending bank. A lending bank can anticipate the loss of reserves to other banks equal to the amount it lends.[6]

If commercial banks create demand deposits—that is, money—when they make loans, it seems logical to inquire whether money is destroyed when the loans are repaid. The answer is "Yes." Using balance sheet 6b, let us see what happens when the Grisley company repays the $50,000 it borrowed.

To simplify, we shall (1) suppose that the loan is repaid not in installments but rather in one lump sum three years after the date of negotiation, and (2) ignore interest charges on the loan. The Grisley company will write a check for $50,000 against its demand deposit, which presumably has been fattened by extra profits resulting from the company's expanded operations. As a result, the Wahoo bank's demand-deposit liabilities decline by $50,000; the Grisley company has given up $50,000 worth of its claim against the bank's assets. In turn, the bank will surrender the Grisley company's IOU which it has been patiently holding these many months. The bank and the company have reswapped claims. But the claim given up by the Grisley company is money; the claim it is repurchasing—its IOU—is not. The supply of money has therefore been reduced by $50,000; that amount of demand deposits has been destroyed, unaccompanied by any increase in the money supply elsewhere in the economy. The Grisley company's IOU has been "demonetized." On the Wahoo bank's balance sheet, demand deposits and loans both fall by $50,000. You will note that the decline in demand deposits increases the bank's holdings of excess reserves; this provides the basis for new loans to be made.

In the highly unlikely event the Grisley company repays the loan with cash, the supply of money will still decline by $50,000. In this case, the Grisley company would repurchase its IOU by handing over $50,000 in cash to the bank. This causes loans to fall on the bank's balance sheet by $50,000 and, obviously, cash to increase by $50,000. Remember that we specifically excluded currency held by banks from the money supply on the ground that to include such cash would be double counting; it is apparent that this constitutes a $50,000 reduction in the supply of money.

Transaction 7: Buying Government Securities When a commercial bank buys gov-

[6]Qualification: If some of the checks written on a loan are redeposited back in the lending bank by their recipients, then that bank will be able to lend an amount somewhat greater than its initial excess reserves.

ernment bonds,[7] the effect is substantially the same as that of lending. New money is created. To illustrate, let us assume that the Wahoo bank's balance sheet initially stands as it did at the end of transaction 5. Now assume that, instead of making a $50,000 loan, the bank buys $50,000 of government securities from a securities dealer. The bank receives the interest-bearing bonds which appear on its balance statement as the asset "Securities" and gives the dealer an increase in its demand-deposit account. The Wahoo bank's balance sheet would appear as follows:

BALANCE SHEET 7: WAHOO BANK

Assets		Liabilities and net worth	
Reserves	$ 60,000	Demand	
Securities*	50,000	deposits*	$100,000
Property	240,000	Capital stock	250,000

The important point is that demand deposits, that is, the supply of money, have been increased by a total of $50,000, as in transaction 6. *Commercial bank bond purchases increase the supply of money in the same way as does lending to the public.* The bank accepts government bonds—which are not money—and gives the securities dealer an increase in its demand deposits—which is money.

Of course, when the securities dealer draws and clears a check for $50,000 against the Wahoo bank, the bank will lose both reserves and deposits in that amount and therefore will just be meeting the legal reserve requirement. Its balance sheet will now read precisely as in 6b except that "Securities" is substituted for "Loans" on the asset side.

Finally, as you undoubtedly suspect, the selling of government bonds by a commercial bank—like the repayment of a loan—will reduce the supply of money. The securities

buyer will pay by check and both "Securities" and "Demand deposits" (the latter being money) will decline by the amount of the sale.

□ **Profits and Liquidity**

The relative importance of the various asset items on a commercial bank's balance sheet is the result of the banker's pursuit of two conflicting goals. One goal is profits. Commercial banks, like any other business, are seeking profits. To this end the bank is desirous of holding loans and securities. These two items are the major earning assets of commercial banks. On the other hand, a commercial bank must seek safety. For a bank, safety lies in liquidity—specifically such liquid assets as cash and excess reserves. Banks must be on guard for depositors' transforming their demand deposits into cash. Similarly, the possibility exists that more checks will be cleared against a bank than are cleared in its favor, causing a net outflow of reserves. Bankers are thus seeking a proper balance between prudence and profits. The compromise that is achieved determines the relative size of earning assets as opposed to highly liquid assets.

THE BANKING SYSTEM: MULTIPLE-DEPOSIT EXPANSION

Thus far we have discovered that a single bank in a banking system can lend dollar for dollar with its excess reserves. Now what of the lending ability of all commercial banks taken as a group? Jumping to our conclusions, we shall find that *the commercial banking system can lend, that is, can create money, by a multiple of its excess reserves. This multiple lending is accomplished despite the fact that each bank in the system can only lend dollar for dollar with its excess reserves.* The immediate task is to uncover how these seemingly paradoxical conclusions come about.

To do this, it is necessary that we keep our analysis as clear as possible. Therefore, we

---

[7] Commercial banks are restrained by law in their purchase of private securities. It is felt that banks should be restricted to the performance of recognized banking functions and not permitted to become holding companies or speculative institutions.

shall rely upon three simplifying assumptions. First, suppose that the reserve ratio for all commercial banks is 20 percent. Second, assume initially that all banks are exactly meeting this 20 percent reserve requirement. No excess reserves exist; all banks are "loaned up." Third, we shall suppose that if any bank becomes able to increase its loans as a result of acquiring excess reserves, an amount equal to these excess reserves will be loaned to one borrower, who will write a check for the entire amount of the loan and give it to someone else, who deposits the check in another bank. This assumption merely means that we are assuming the worst thing possible that can happen to any lending bank—a check for the entire amount of the loan is drawn and cleared against it and in favor of another bank.

□   **The Banking System's Lending Potential**

To get the ball rolling, suppose that one of the twelve Federal Reserve Banks buys a $100 government bond in the open market from a private individual or business firm. The seller of the bond deposits the $100 check he receives in bank A, and this $100 constitutes an addition to the bank's reserves. (We shall find in Chapter 16 that such bond purchases by the central banks are a part of their deliberate policy to increase the excess reserves of commercial banks and ultimately the supply of money through bank lending.) Since we are recording only *changes* in the balance sheets of the various commercial banks, bank A's balance sheet now appears as follows (a_1):

BALANCE SHEET: COMMERCIAL BANK A

Assets		Liabilities and net worth	
Reserves	$+100 \ (a_1)$	Demand	
	$- \ 80 \ (a_3)$	deposits	$+100 \ (a_1)$
Loans	$+ \ 80 \ (a_2)$		$+ \ 80 \ (a_2)$
			$- \ 80 \ (a_3)$

How much *excess reserves* does bank A now have? It has acquired $100 in new reserves, but

in the process it has also acquired $100 in new demand deposits. This means that 20 percent of the new reserves must be earmarked as required reserves to offset the new deposits. In short, $20 of the new reserves will be *required,* freeing the remaining $80 as *excess* reserves. Remembering that a single commercial bank, such as bank A, can lend only an amount equal to its excess reserves, we conclude that bank A can lend a maximum of $80. When a loan for this amount is negotiated, bank A's loans will increase by $80, and the borrower will get an $80 demand deposit. Let us add these figures to bank A's balance sheet (a_2).

But now we must invoke our third assumption: The borrower draws a check for $80—the entire amount of the loan—and gives it to someone who deposits it in another bank, bank B. As we saw in transaction 6, bank A *loses* both reserves and deposits equal to the amount of the loan (a_3). The net result of all the transactions is that bank A's reserves now stand at $20 (= $100 − $80), loans at $80, and demand deposits at $100 (= $100 + $80 − $80). Note that when the dust has settled, bank A is just meeting the 20 percent reserve ratio.

Recalling transaction 5, bank B *acquires* both the reserves and the deposits which bank A has lost. Bank B's balance sheet looks like this (b_1):

BALANCE SHEET: COMMERCIAL BANK B

Assets		Liabilities and net worth	
Reserves	$+80 \ (b_1)$	Demand	
	$-64 \ (b_3)$	deposits	$+80 \ (b_1)$
Loans	$+64 \ (b_2)$		$+64 \ (b_2)$
			$-64 \ (b_3)$

When the check is drawn and cleared, bank A *loses* $80 in reserves and deposits and bank B *gains* $80 in reserves and deposits. But 20 percent, or $16, of bank B's newly acquired reserves must be kept as required reserves against the new $80 in demand deposits. This means that bank B has $64 (= $80 − $16) in excess reserves. It can therefore lend $64 ($b_2$).

When the borrower draws a check for the entire amount and deposits it in bank C, the reserves and deposits of bank B both fall by the $64 ($b_3$). As a result of these transactions, bank B's reserves will now stand at $16 (= $80 − $64), loans at $64, and demand deposits at $80 (= $80 + $64 − $64). Note that after all this has occurred, bank B is just meeting the 20 percent reserve requirement.

We are off and running again. Bank C has acquired the $64 in reserves and deposits lost by bank B. Its balance statement appears as follows (c_1):

BALANCE SHEET: COMMERCIAL BANK C

Assets		Liabilities and net worth	
Reserves	$+64.00 ($c_1$)	Demand	
	−51.20 (c_3)	deposits	$+64.00 ($c_1$)
Loans	+51.20 (c_2)		+51.20 (c_2)
			−51.20 (c_3)

Exactly 20 percent, or $12.80, of this new reserve will be required, the remaining $51.20 being excess reserves. Hence, bank C can safely lend a maximum of $51.20. Suppose it does ($c_2$). And suppose the borrower draws a check for the entire amount and gives it to someone who deposits it in another bank (c_3).

Bank D—the bank receiving the $51.20 in reserves and deposits—now notes these changes on its balance sheet (d_1):

BALANCE SHEET: COMMERCIAL BANK D

Assets		Liabilities and net worth	
Reserves	$+51.20 ($d_1$)	Demand	
	−40.96 (d_3)	deposits	$+51.20 ($d_1$)
Loans	+40.96 (d_2)		+40.96 (d_2)
			−40.96 (d_3)

It can now lend $40.96 ($d_2$). The borrower draws a check for the full amount and deposits it in another bank (d_3).

Now, if we wanted to be particularly obnoxious, we could go ahead with this procedure by bringing banks E, F, G, H, . . . , N into the picture. We shall merely suggest that the student check through computations for banks E,

F, and G, to ensure that he has the procedure firmly in mind.

The nucleus of this analysis is summarized in Table 15-2. Data for banks E through N are supplied so you may check your computations. Our conclusion is a rather startling one: On the basis of the $80 in excess reserves (acquired by the banking system when someone deposited the $100 received from the sale of a government bond in bank A), the *commercial banking system* is able to lend $400. Lo and behold, the banking system is able to lend by a multiple of 5 when the reserve ratio is 20 percent! Yet you will note that each single bank in the banking system is lending only an amount equal to its excess reserves. How do we explain these seemingly conflicting conclusions? Why is it that the *banking system* can lend by a multiple of its excess reserves, but *each individual bank* can only lend dollar for dollar with its excess reserves?

The answer lies in the fact that reserves lost by a single bank are not lost to the banking system as a whole. The reserves lost by bank A are acquired by bank B. Those lost by B are gained by C. C loses to D, D to E, E to F, and so forth. Hence, although reserves can be, and are, lost by *individual* banks in the banking system, there can be no loss of reserves for the banking *system* as a whole. Hence, we reach the curious conclusion that an individual bank can only safely lend an amount equal to its excess reserves, but the commercial banking system can lend by a multiple of its excess reserves. This contrast, incidentally, is a fine illustration of why it is imperative that we keep the fallacy of composition firmly in mind. Commercial banks *as a group* can create money by lending in a manner much different from that of the *individual banks* in that system.

□ **The Monetary Multiplier**

The rationale involved in this *demand-deposit,* or *monetary, multiplier* is not unlike that underlying the income multiplier dis-

Table 15-2 EXPANSION OF THE MONEY SUPPLY BY THE COMMERCIAL BANKING SYSTEM

Bank	(1) Acquired reserves and deposits	(2) Required reserves	(3) Excess reserves, or (1) − (2)	(4) Amount which the bank can lend; new money created = (3)
Bank A	$100.00 (a_1)	$20.00	$80.00	$ 80.00 (a_2)
Bank B	80.00 (a_3, b_1)	16.00	64.00	64.00 (b_2)
Bank C	64.00 (b_3, c_1)	12.80	51.20	51.20 (c_2)
Bank D	51.20 (c_3, d_1)	10.24	40.96	40.96 (d_2)
Bank E	40.96	8.19	32.77	32.77
Bank F	32.77	6.55	26.22	26.22
Bank G	26.22	5.24	20.98	20.98
Bank H	20.98	4.20	16.78	16.78
Bank I	16.78	3.36	13.42	13.42
Bank J	13.42	2.68	10.74	10.74
Bank K	10.74	2.15	8.59	8.59
Bank L	8.59	1.72	6.87	6.87
Bank M	6.87	1.37	5.50	5.50
Bank N	5.50	1.10	4.40	4.40
Other banks	21.97	4.40	17.57	17.57
Total amount of money created				$400.00

cussed in Chapter 12. The income multiplier was based on the fact that the expenditures of one household are received as income by another; the deposit multiplier rests on the fact that the reserves and deposits lost by one bank are received by another bank. And, just as the size of the income multiplier is determined by the reciprocal of the MPS, that is, by the leakage into saving which occurs at each round of spending, so the deposit multiplier D is the reciprocal of the required reserve ratio R, that is, of the leakage into required reserves which occurs at each step in the lending process. In short,

$$D = \frac{1}{R}$$

In this formula, D tells us the maximum number of new dollars of demand deposits which can be created for a *single dollar* of excess reserves, given the value of R. We can easily adjust the formula to show the maximum amount of new deposits which can be created

for *any amount* of excess reserves E, by simply substituting E for 1 in the numerator, so that

$$D = \frac{E}{R}$$

Thus, in our example of Table 15-2,

$$\$400 = \frac{\$80}{.20}$$

But keep in mind that, despite the similar rationale underlying the income and deposit multipliers, the former has to do with changes in income and the latter with changes in the supply of money.

The reader might experiment with these teasers in testing his understanding of multiple credit expansion by the banking system:

1 Rework the preceding analysis (at least three or four steps of it) on the assumption that the reserve ratio is 10 percent. What is the maximum amount of money the banking system could create upon acquiring $100 in

new reserves and deposits? (No, the answer is not $800!)

2 Explain how a banking system which is "loaned up" and faced with a 20 percent reserve ratio might be forced to *reduce* its outstanding loans by $400 as a result of a Federal Reserve Bank's *selling* a $100 bond to a private individual or business.

□ Some Modifications

Our discussion of credit expansion has been conducted in a somewhat rarefied atmosphere. There are certain complications which might modify the quantitative preciseness of our analysis.

Other Leakages Aside from the leakage of required reserves at each step of the lending process, two other leakages of money from the commercial banks might occur, thereby dampening the money-creating potential of the banking system.

1 Currency drains A borrower may request that a part of his loan be paid in cash. Or the recipient of a check drawn by a borrower may present it at his bank to be redeemed partially or wholly in currency rather than added to his account. Thus, if the person who borrowed the $80 from bank A in our illustration asked for $16 of it in cash and the remaining $64 as a demand deposit, bank B would receive only $64 in new reserves (of which only $51.20 would be excess) rather than $80 (of which $64 was excess). This decline in excess reserves reduces the lending potential of the banking system accordingly. As a matter of fact, if the first borrower had taken the entire $80 in cash and if this currency remained in circulation, the multiple expansion process would have stopped then and there. But the convenience and safety of demand deposits make this unlikely.

2 Excess reserves Our analysis of the commercial banking system's ability to expand the money supply by lending is based on the

supposition that commercial banks are willing to meet precisely the legal reserve requirement. In practice, bankers are more prudent than this and arrange to have a "safety margin" of excess reserves to avoid the embarrassment of falling below the legal reserve ratio in the event that an unusually large amount of checks is cleared against them. Therefore bank A, upon receiving $100 in new cash, might choose to add $25, rather than the legal minimum of $20, to its reserves, the extra $5 serving as a buffer, or cushion, against adverse check clearings. The overall credit expansion potential of the banking system would obviously be reduced by such additions to a bank's excess reserves.[8]

Willingness versus Ability to Lend It is only fair to emphasize that our illustration of the banking system's ability to create money rests upon the assumption that commercial banks are willing to exercise their abilities to create money by lending and that households and businesses are willing to borrow. In practice, this need not be the case. Bankers, you will recall, seek a proper balance between prudence and profits. When prosperity reigns, banks may expand credit to the maximum of their ability. Why not? Loans are interest-earning assets, and in good times there is little fear of borrowers' defaulting. But if depression clouds appear on the economic horizon, bankers may hastily withdraw their invitations to borrow, seeking the safety of liquidity even if it involves the sacrifice of potential interest income. Bankers may fear the large-scale withdrawal of deposits by a panicky public and simultaneously doubt the ability of borrowers

[8]Specifically, in our $D = \dfrac{1}{R}$ monetary multiplier, we now add to R, the required reserve ratio, the additional excess reserves which bankers choose to keep. For example, if banks want to hold additional excess reserves equal to 5 percent of any newly acquired demand deposits, then the denominator becomes .25 (equal to the .20 reserve ratio plus the .05 addition to excess reserves). The monetary multiplier is reduced from 5 to 1/.25, or 4.

to repay. It is not too surprising that during some years of the Great Depression of the 1930s, banks had considerable excess reserves but lending was at a low ebb. Obviously, if the amount actually loaned by each commercial bank falls short of its excess reserves, the resulting multiple expansion of credit will be curtailed.

The Need for Control   The fact that bankers may not expand the supply of money to their maximum ability is of more than passing interest. It may be a factor which contributes significantly to business fluctuations. By holding back on credit expansion as the economy begins to slip into a depression, commercial banks may further inhibit total spending and intensify that cyclical downswing. Indeed, as we noted in Chapter 10, a rapid shrinkage of the money supply contributed to the Great Depression of the 1930s. Conversely, by lending and thereby creating money to the maximum of their ability during prosperity, commercial banks may contribute to an excess of total spending and to the resulting inflationary pressures. Chapter 16 will explore the means by which the Board of Governors attempts to influence the lending policies of commercial banks so that they will offset rather than enforce cyclical fluctuations.

Summary

1   Commercial banks create money—that is, demand deposits, or bank money—when they make loans. The creation of demand deposits by bank lending is the most important source of money in American capitalism.

2   The ability of a single commercial bank to create money by lending depends upon the size of its *excess* reserves. Generally speaking, a commercial bank can lend only an amount equal to the size of its excess reserves. It is thus limited because, in all likelihood, checks drawn by borrowers will be deposited in other banks, causing a loss of reserves and deposits to the lending bank equal to the amount which it has loaned.

3   The commercial banking system as a whole can lend by a multiple of its excess reserves because the banking *system* cannot lose reserves, although individual banks can lose reserves to other banks in the system. The multiple by which the banking system can lend is the reciprocal of the reserve ratio. This multiple credit expansion process is reversible.

Questions and Study Suggestions

1   Key terms and concepts to remember: balance sheet; vault cash; legal (required) reserve deposit; reserve ratio; actual and excess reserves; monetary multiplier; leakages.

2   Why must a balance sheet always balance? What are the major assets and claims on a commercial bank's balance sheet?

3   Why are commercial banks required to have reserves? Explain why reserves are assets to commercial banks but liabilities to the Federal Reserve Banks. What are excess reserves? How are they calculated? What is their significance?

4   "Whenever currency is deposited in a commercial bank, cash goes out of circulation and, as a result, the supply of money is reduced." Do you agree? Explain.

5 "When a commercial bank makes loans, it creates money; when loans are retired, money is destroyed." Explain.

6 Explain why a single commercial bank can safely lend only an amount equal to its excess reserves but the commercial banking system can lend by a multiple of its excess reserves. Why is the multiple by which the banking system can lend equal to the reciprocal of its reserve ratio?

7 Assume that Jones deposits $500 in currency in the First National Bank. A half-hour later Smith negotiates a loan for $750 at this bank. By how much and in what direction has the money supply changed? Explain.

8 Suppose the Continental Bank has the following simplified balance sheet. The reserve ratio is 20 percent.

Assets				Liabilities and net worth			
		(1)	(2)			(1)	(2)
Reserves	$22,000	——	——	Demand			
Securities	38,000	——	——	deposits	$100,000	——	——
Loans	40,000	——	——				

a. What is the maximum amount of new loans which this bank can make? Show in column 1 how the bank's balance sheet will appear after the bank has loaned this additional amount.

b. By how much has the supply of money changed? Explain.

c. How will the bank's balance sheet appear after checks drawn for the entire amount of the new loans have been cleared against this bank? Show this new balance sheet in column 2.

d. Answer questions *a, b,* and *c* on the assumption that the reserve ratio is 15 percent.

9 Suppose the National Bank of Commerce has excess reserves of $8,000 and outstanding demand deposits of $150,000. If the reserve ratio is 20 percent, what is the size of the bank's actual reserves?

10 Suppose the following is a simplified consolidated balance sheet for the commercial banking system. All figures are in billions. The reserve ratio is 25 percent.

Assets			Liabilities and net worth		
		(1)			(1)
Reserves	$ 52	——	Demand		
Securities	48	——	deposits	$200	——
Loans	100	——			

a. How much excess reserves does the commercial banking system have? How much can the banking system lend? Show in column 1 how the consolidated balance sheet would look after this amount has been lent.

b. Answer question 10*a* on the assumption that the reserve ratio is 20 percent. Explain the resulting difference in the lending ability of the commercial banking system.

11 The Third National Bank has reserves of $20,000 and demand deposits of $100,000. The reserve ratio is 20 percent. Households deposit $5000 in currency in the bank. This $5000 is added by the bank to its reserves. How much excess reserves does the bank now have?

12 Suppose again that the Third National Bank has reserves of $20,000 and demand deposits of $100,000. The reserve ratio remains at 20 percent. The bank now sells $5000 in securities to the Federal Reserve Bank in its district, receiving a $5000 increase in reserves in return. How much excess reserves does the bank now have? Why does your answer differ (yes, it does!) from the answer to question 11?

13 What are "leakages"? How might they affect the money-creating potential of the banking system? Be specific.

Selected References

Bernstein, Peter L.: *A Primer on Money, Banking, and Gold* (New York: Random House, Inc., 1965).

Chandler, Lester V., and Stephen M. Goldfeld: *The Economics of Money and Banking,* 7th ed. (New York: Harper & Row, Publishers, Incorporated, 1977), chaps. 6, 7.

Duesenberry, James S.: *Money and Credit: Impact and Control,* 3d ed. (Englewood Cliffs, N.J.: Prentice-Hall, Inc., 1972).

Klein, John J.: *Money and the Economy,* 2d ed. (New York: Harcourt Brace Jovanovich, Inc., 1974), chaps. 5–7.

Last Word
The Great Cash Mystery

The convenience of paying by check and the credit card revolution would suggest a declining need for currency. But, curiously, the amount of coins and paper money in circulation has increased significantly.

One of the more intriguing visions put forth by financial "futurists" a while back had to do with a subject of universal interest—money. As they saw it, currency would soon go out of style. Cash would play an ever-smaller role in financing economic activity. A "cashless society," they predicted with much certitude, was just around the corner.

In such a society, people might keep a little folding money and a few coins for trivial transactions or, perhaps, to satisfy nostalgic urges. But for the most part, people would pay for things by bookkeeping entries—via checkbook or the ubiquitous credit card.

Today, a dozen years after such predictions of a currencyless society, the money millenium has yet to arrive. Indeed, the United States has become, if anything, a more-cash-than-ever society.

The amount of paper money and coin in circulation has risen sharply over the past decade and, at nearly $94 billion, stands at a new high. . . .

In per-capita terms, currency outstanding amounts to $436 for each man, woman, and child in the nation—compared with only $182 per capita in 1960. . . .

Actually, there are some clues to help solve the great cash mystery—in part, at least.

Easiest to explain is the sharp rise that has taken place in recent years in coins in circulation. . . .

Behind this rise in coin output, in important part, is operation of one of the oldest principles in economics: Gresham's Law—"bad" money drives out "good." A rising price for silver in the Sixties made the old coins (90% silver, 10% copper *versus* today's 75% copper-25% nickel face, bonded to a copper core) worth more intrinsically than their face value. Silver coins rapidly disappeared into private hoards. . . .

Collectors are contributing in other ways to the rising demand for coins. Some of these collectors do it for sentimental reasons—as for example the demand for the commemorative Kennedy half dollar and the Eisenhower dollar—while others follow numismatic pursuits for fun and profit. And the profits are there, for coins that are scarce and in reasonably good condition. As a random sample, picked from a coin-dealer's catalog, certain 1932 quarters now can command $35 each in the rare-coin market.

The proliferation of local sales taxes, at ever higher rates, has increased the need for coins. So, too, has the trend toward more travel by automobile, which necessitates the paying out of a sackful of coins as a vacationing family moves over toll bridges, through tunnels, and along turnpikes. Meanwhile, a relatively new wrinkle in local transportation in many cities—requiring exact change from riders so the driver will not be a target for robbery—is requiring riders to stock up on coins.

Another major coin user is the vending-machine industry. . . . Not only does it take coins to work the machines but the coins are then immobilized, which reduces their transactions velocity.

Paper money's steep rise—an average of about 6% annually over the past decade—is considerably more difficult to analyze with any degree of certainty. One major reason for the increase, however, is quite obvious—inflation. With prices of practically everything higher these days, more cash is needed to do business.

Tax evasion is believed to be a significant factor in the demand for currency. There is a strong suspicion that some people—from gamblers and racketeers to white-collar professionals and blue-collar "moonlighters"—receive payment in cash so that there is no record. Much of this money, in unquantifiable amounts, winds up—unreported for taxes—in safe deposit boxes, under the mattress, or in fruit jars buried under the old apple tree.

A certain amount of U.S. currency—difficult to quantify—is circulating abroad. Some of these dollars are used, of course, as transactions currencies in foreign lands, where they circulate along with the local money. Then, too, nationals in many foreign nations prefer to hold sums in dollars, trusting U.S. currency more than their own. Beyond these uses, however, there is thought to be a large amount of U.S.-owned currency, in big bills, which derives from illicit operations (e.g., the international drug traffic) or is attempting to evade the tax collector.

Finally, there is a theory, decidedly unscientific yet plausible, which states simply that the U.S., in effect, has grown too big for its old currency britches. The "fit" was quite loose for many years, this theory goes, because of the swift rise in currency during World War II years. . . .

When the war ended millions of people settled down, got married, bought a house, opened a checking and savings account. Growth in the currency levelled off. By the end of the 1950s, however, the country had "grown into" its currency. A bigger size in currency britches became necessary in the 1960s with a growing population, an expanding economy—and a rising price level.

Even the bigger-britches theory of currency leaves many questions unanswered. Currency, after all, is held for two major reasons: to carry on transactions or as a store of value.

As to the first, money substitutes in the form of checks, credit cards, charge accounts, traveler's checks are abundantly available, considerably safer than cash, and usually cheaper for large transactions. . . .

As to the second—a store of value—it is puzzling that many people in the 1960s faced with serious inflation which eroded the value of the dollar and with abundant opportunities to offset inflation's inroads through high interest rates on savings accounts and even higher rates on risk-free market investments, apparently still preferred to build up supplies of cash in sizable amounts. . . .

What seems abundantly clear is that cash money is not about to go out of style. If futurists are holding their breath for a cashless society, surely they will be breathless long before they are cashless.

"Whatever Happened to the Cashless Society?" *The Morgan Guaranty Survey,* February 1972, abridged. Reprinted by permission. Statistics updated by author.

16

The Federal Reserve Banks and Monetary Policy

In Chapter 15 our attention was focused upon the money-creating ability of individual banks and the commercial banking system. Our discussion ended on a disturbing note: Unregulated commercial banking might contribute to cyclical fluctuations in business activity. That is, commercial banks will find it profitable to expand the supply of money during inflationary prosperity and to restrict the money supply in seeking liquidity during depression. It is the task of this chapter to see how the monetary authorities of American capitalism attempt to reverse the procyclical tendencies of the commercial banking system through a variety of control techniques.

More specifically, the goals of the present chapter are these: First, the objectives of monetary policy, the roles of participating institutions, and the route by which monetary policy affects the operation of the economy are detailed. Next, the balance sheet of the Federal Reserve Banks is surveyed, because it is through these central banks that monetary policy is largely implemented. Third, the quantitative and qualitative techniques of monetary control are analyzed in considerable detail. What are the major instruments of monetary control and how do they function? Fourth, the cause-effect chain through which monetary policy functions is restated graphically and the effectiveness of monetary policy is evaluated. Finally, a brief, but important, recapitulation of modern employment theory and policy is presented.

OBJECTIVES OF MONETARY POLICY

Before analyzing the techniques through which monetary policy is put into effect, it is essential that we clearly understand the objectives of monetary policy and locate the institutions responsible for the formulation and implementation of that policy.

Certain key points made in Chapter 14 merit reemphasis at the outset of our discussion. The Board of Governors of the Federal Reserve System has the responsibility of supervising and controlling the operation of our monetary and banking systems. It is this Board which formulates the basic policies which the banking system follows. Because it is a public body, the decisions of the Board of Governors are made in the interests of the general economic welfare of society as a whole. The twelve Federal Reserve Banks—the central banks of American capitalism—have the responsibility of implementing the policy decisions of the Board. You will recall that as quasi-public banks, the Federal Reserve banks are not guided by the profit motive, but rather, they pursue those measures which the Board of Governors recommends.

However, to say that the Board follows policies which "promote the general economic welfare" is not enough. We must pinpoint the goal of monetary policy. It will come as no great surprise that *the fundamental objective of monetary policy is to assist the economy in achieving a full-employment, noninflationary level of total output.* Monetary policy consists of altering the economy's money supply for the purpose of stabilizing aggregate output, employment, and the price level. More specifically, monetary policy entails increasing the money supply during a recession to stimulate spending and, conversely, restricting the money supply during inflation to constrain spending.

☐ Cause-Effect Chain

But precisely how does monetary policy work toward this goal? The process is complicated, but essentially it boils down to this:[1]

1 Excess Reserves By invoking certain control techniques, the Board of Governors and the Federal Reserve Banks can influence the size of both actual and required reserves—and therefore the excess reserves—of commercial banks.

2 Money Supply Because excess reserves are the basis upon which commercial banks can expand the money supply by lending, any manipulations of excess reserves through the control techniques of the Board of Governors will affect the supply of money, that is, the amounts which commercial banks will be able and willing to lend at various possible interest rates.

3 Interest Rate Given the demand for money, changes in the supply of money will affect the cost and availability of money. That is, changes in the supply of money will affect the interest rate and the amount of credit bankers are willing to make available to borrowers.

4 Aggregate Demand Changes in the cost and availability of bank credit will in turn have an impact upon the spending decisions of society, particularly upon investment decisions, and therefore upon the levels of output, employment, income, and prices.

The cause-effect chain between monetary policy and output and employment is summarized in this outline:

Federal monetary policy influences the size of commercial bank reserves

---

[1] We present here the Keynesian interpretation of how monetary policy works. Chapter 17 is devoted to the significantly different "monetarist" view of how monetary policy functions.

which

Influence the supply of money

which

Influences the interest rate (the cost) and the availability of bank credit

which

Influences investment spending, output, employment, and the price level

Let us examine the operation of monetary policy through a simple example. Suppose the economy is operating below the full-employment mark. Sidestepping troublesome complications and qualifications for the moment, we find that monetary policy would work something like this:

1 The Board of Governors will direct the Federal Reserve Banks to pursue certain policies designed to *increase* the (excess) reserves of commercial banks.

2 Finding themselves with abundant excess reserves, commercial banks are now in a position to make available a greater supply of money by granting bank credit. The banking *system* can *expand* the supply of money by a multiple of its excess reserves.

3 With an increase in the supply of money relative to the demand for it, interest rates will *decline,* and the quantity of bank credit (money) taken by borrowers will *increase.*

4 Low interest rates and the ready availability of bank credit will induce *increases* in spending. These increases will be subject to the multiplier effect, driving the equilibrium NNP upward by a multiple of the increase in total spending.

These four comments detail the ideal operation of an *easy money policy.* A *tight money policy* follows the same route, but the procedure is to lower commercial bank reserves, reduce the supply of money, raise the cost and lessen the availability of bank credit, and thereby curtail spending. Tight money should obviously be invoked when an excess of total spending is causing inflation in the economy.

□   **Monetary Policy and Investment**

Economists are in general agreement that the investment component of total spending is more likely to be affected by changes in the interest rate than is consumer spending. The interest rate does not seem to be a very crucial factor in determining how households divide their disposable income between consumption and saving. Indeed, it is not clear whether decreases in the interest rate will tend to increase or decrease the amount of consumption. On the one hand, a lower interest rate may induce some households, particularly those operating small businesses, to save less, because it is now cheap to finance by borrowing. On the other hand, we have noted that those who save to provide a given retirement income or to accumulate funds for the education of their children find that a lower interest rate will mean that a larger volume of saving will be required to earn the needed income. Then, too, the effect of higher interest rates on consumer installment buying is not great, because considerable increases or decreases in the interest rate have little impact on the size of each monthly payment; that is, the consumer is not impressed by the total interest charge but only by how much interest he must pay per month. Furthermore, any tendency for higher interest charges to diminish consumer installment buying can be largely canceled by extending the repayment period from, say, twenty-four to thirty-six months.

The impact of changing interest rates upon investment spending is greater because of the size and long-term nature of such purchases. Capital equipment, factory buildings, warehouses, and so forth, are tremendously expensive purchases. In absolute terms the interest charges on funds borrowed for these purchases will be considerable. Similarly, the interest cost on a house purchased on a long-term contract will be very large: A $\frac{1}{2}$ percent change in the interest rate could easily amount to thousands of dollars on the total cost of a home. It is important to note as well that changes in the interest rate may also affect investment spending by changing the relative attractiveness of capital equipment purchases and bond purchases. If the interest rate rises on bonds, then, given the profit expectations on capital good purchases, businesses will be more inclined to use business savings to purchase securities than to buy capital equipment. Conversely, given profit expectations on investment spending, a fall in the interest rate makes capital purchases more attractive than bond ownership. In short, the impact of changing interest rates will be primarily upon investment spending and, through this channel, upon output, employment, and the level of prices.

So much for the objectives of monetary policy and the cause-effect chain which its application entails. We now seek an understanding of the techniques by which the Board of Governors can manipulate the size of commercial bank reserves.

CONSOLIDATED BALANCE SHEET OF THE FEDERAL RESERVE BANKS

Because monetary policy is implemented by the twelve Federal Reserve Banks, it is essential to consider the nature of the balance sheet of these banks. Some of the assets and liabilities found here are considerably different from those found on the balance sheet of a commercial bank. Table 16-1 is a consolidated balance sheet which shows all the pertinent assets and liabilities of the twelve Federal Reserve Banks as of February 28, 1977.

□   **Assets**

Gold Certificates   Gold certificates are warehouse receipts for the gold bullion held by the Treasury. In settling international payments, the United States Treasury may buy gold from foreign monetary authorities. The Treasury pays for such gold by drawing checks against its deposit in the Federal Reserve Banks. The clearing of these checks reduces Treasury deposits in the Federal Reserve Banks. To replenish these deposits, the Treasury issues gold certificates—claims or warehouse receipts against the newly obtained gold—and deposits them in the Federal Reserve Banks. Treasury sales of gold to foreign monetary authorities have the opposite effect, reducing the Federal Reserve Banks' holdings of gold certificates.

Securities   These securities are the government bonds which the Federal Reserve Banks have purchased. Some of these bonds may have been purchased directly from the Treasury, but most are bought in the open market from commercial banks or the public. Although these bonds are an important source of income to the Federal Reserve Banks, they are not bought and sold purposely for income. Rather, as we shall see, they are bought and sold primarily to influence the size of commercial bank reserves and therefore their ability to create money by lending.

Loans to Commercial Banks   Commercial banks occasionally borrow from the Federal Reserve Banks. The IOUs which the com-

Table 16-1   TWELVE FEDERAL RESERVE BANKS' CONSOLIDATED BALANCE SHEET, FEBRUARY 28, 1977 (*in millions*)

Assets		Liabilities and net worth	
Gold certificates	$11,651	Reserves of member banks	$ 22,788
Securities	95,837	Treasury deposits	12,179
Loans to commercial banks	24	Federal Reserve Notes (outstanding)	81,709
All other assets	17,795	All other liabilities and net worth	8,631
Total	$125,307	Total	$125,307

Source: Federal Reserve Bulletin, March 1977.

mercial banks give to the bankers' banks in negotiating loans are listed as loans to commercial banks. From the Federal Reserve Banks' point of view, these IOUs are assets, that is, claims against the commercial banks which have borrowed from them. To the commercial banks, these IOUs are liabilities. In borrowing, the commercial banks obtain increases in their reserves in exchange for their IOUs.

Before shifting to the liability side of the Federal Reserve Banks' balance sheet, one note on terminology: "Securities" and "Loans to commercial banks" are sometimes called "Reserve Bank credit." These two accounts represent credit which the bankers' banks have extended to (1) the government by buying government securities, and (2) commercial banks by accepting their IOUs in return for increases in their reserves.

☐ **Liabilities**

On the liability side we find three major items:

Reserves of Member Banks   We are already familiar with this account. It is an asset from the viewpoint of the member banks but a liability to the Federal Reserve Banks.

Treasury Deposits   Just as businesses and private individuals find it convenient and desirable to pay their obligations by check, so does the United States Treasury. It keeps deposits in the various Federal Reserve Banks and draws checks on them in paying its obligations. To the Treasury such deposits are obviously assets; to the Federal Reserve Banks, they are liabilities. The Treasury creates and replenishes these deposits by depositing tax receipts, money borrowed from the public or the banks through the sale of bonds, and gold certificates.

Federal Reserve Notes   Virtually all our paper money supply is Federal Reserve Notes.

These notes are issued by the Federal Reserve Banks. When in circulation, these pieces of paper money constitute circulating claims against the assets of the Federal Reserve Banks and are therefore treated by them as liabilities. Just as your own IOU is neither an asset nor a liability to you when it is in your own possession, so Federal Reserve Notes resting in the vaults of the various Federal Reserve Banks are neither an asset nor a liability. Only those notes in circulation are liabilities to the bankers' banks. These notes, which come into circulation through commercial banks, are not a part of the money supply until they are in the hands of the public.

MONETARY POLICY: MAJOR QUANTITATIVE CONTROLS

With this cursory understanding of the Federal Reserve Banks' balance sheet, we are now in a position to explore how the Board of Governors of the Federal Reserve System can influence the money-creating abilities of the commercial banking system. What are the devices that can be employed at the discretion of the Board of Governors to influence commercial bank reserves?

The general, or quantitative, controls of the monetary authorities are three in number: (1) changing the reserve ratio, (2) open-market operations, and (3) changing the discount rate. These controls are general, or quantitative, in that they seek to manipulate the total quantity of bank credit. Later, we shall discuss selective, or qualitative, controls, which are aimed at influencing the volume of specific types of credit.

☐ **The Reserve Ratio**

How can the Board of Governors influence the ability of commercial banks to lend through manipulation of the legal reserve ratio? A simple example will supply a clear answer to this query. Starting with row 2 of

Table 16-2   THE EFFECTS OF CHANGES IN THE RESERVE RATIO UPON THE LENDING ABILITY OF COMMERCIAL BANKS (hypothetical data)

(1) Legal reserve ratio, percent	(2) Demand deposits	(3) Actual reserves	(4) Required reserves	(5) Excess reserves, or (3) − (4)	(6) Money-creating potential of single bank, = (5)	(7) Money-creating potential of banking system
(1) 10	$20,000	$5000	$2000	$ 3000	$ 3000	$ 30,000
(2) 20	20,000	5000	4000	1000	1000	5,000
(3) 25	20,000	5000	5000	0	0	0
(4) 30	20,000	5000	6000	−1000	−1000	−3,333

Table 16-2, suppose a commercial bank's balance sheet shows that reserves are $5000 and demand deposits $20,000. If the legal reserve ratio stands at 20 percent, the bank's *required* reserves are $4000. Since *actual* reserves are $5000, it is apparent that the *excess* reserves of this bank are $1000. On the basis of this $1000 of excess reserves, we have seen that this single bank can lend $1000, but the banking system as a whole could create a maximum of $5000 in new bank money by lending. Now, what if the Board of Governors raised the legal reserve ratio from 20 to 25 percent (row 3)? Required reserves would jump from $4000 to $5000, shrinking excess reserves from $1000 to zero. It is obvious that *raising the reserve ratio increases the amount of required reserves banks must keep. Either banks lose excess reserves, diminishing their ability to create money by lending, or else they find their reserves deficient and are forced to contract the money supply.* In the case just cited, excess reserves are transformed into required reserves, and the money-creating potential of our *single bank* is reduced from $1000 to zero. The banking *system's* money-creating capacity declines from $5000 to zero.

What if the Board of Governors announced a forthcoming increase in the legal reserve requirement to 30 percent (row 4)? The commercial bank would be faced with the embarrassing prospect of failing to meet this requirement. To protect itself against such an eventuality, the bank would be forced to lower its outstanding demand deposits and at the same time to increase its reserves. To reduce its demand deposits, the bank would be disposed to let outstanding loans mature and to be repaid without extending new credit. To increase reserves, the bank might sell some of its holdings of securities, adding the proceeds to its reserves. Both courses of action will reduce the supply of money (see Chapter 15, transactions 6 and 7).

What would be the effect if the Board of Governors lowered the reserve ratio from the original 20 to 10 percent (row 1)? In this case, required reserves would decline from $4000 to $2000, and as a result, excess reserves would jump from $1000 to $3000. We can conclude that *lowering the reserve ratio changes required reserves to excess reserves, thereby enhancing the ability of banks to create new money by lending.*

Table 16-2 reveals that a change in the reserve ratio affects the money-creating ability of the *banking system* in two ways. First, it affects the size of excess reserves. Second, it changes the multiple by which the banking system can lend. Thus, for example, in raising the legal reserve ratio from 10 to 20 percent, excess reserves are reduced from $3000 to $1000, on the one hand, and the demand deposit multiplier is reduced from 10 to 5. Hence, the money-creating potential of the banking system declines from $30,000 (= $3000 × 10) to $5000 (= $1000 × 5).

Although changing the reserve ratio is a

potentially powerful technique of monetary control, it is actually used infrequently. The Board of Governors controls the money supply primarily through open-market operations.

☐   **Open-Market Operations**

The buying and selling of government bonds by the Federal Reserve Banks in the open market—that is, from or to commercial banks and the general public—also affect the excess reserves of commercial banks.

Buying Securities   Suppose the Board of Governors orders the Federal Reserve Banks to buy government bonds in the open market. From whom may these securities be purchased? In general, from commercial banks and the public. In either case the overall effect is basically the same—commercial bank reserves are increased.

Let us trace through the process by which the Federal Reserve Banks buy government bonds *from commercial banks.* This transaction is a simple one.

a. The commercial banks give up a part of their holdings of securities to the bankers' banks.

b. The Federal Reserve Banks pay for these securities by increasing the reserves of the commercial banks by the amount of the purchase.

Just as the commercial bank may pay for a bond bought from a private individual by increasing the seller's demand deposit, so the bankers' bank may pay for bonds bought from commercial banks by increasing the banks' reserves. In short, the consolidated balance sheets of the commercial banks and the Federal Reserve Banks will change as shown in the next column.

The most important aspect of this transaction is that, when Federal Reserve Banks purchase securities from commercial banks, the reserves—and therefore the lending ability—of the commercial banks are increased.

If the Federal Reserve Banks should purchase securities *from the general public,* the

effect on commercial bank reserves would be substantially the same. Suppose that the Grisley Meat Packing Company possesses some negotiable government bonds which it sells in the open market to the Federal Reserve Banks. The transaction goes like this:

a. The Grisley company gives up securities to the Federal Reserve Banks and gets in payment a check drawn by the Federal Reserve Banks on themselves.

b. The Grisley company promptly deposits this check in its account with the Wahoo bank.

c. The Wahoo bank collects this check against the Federal Reserve Banks by sending it to the Federal Reserve Banks for collection. As a result the Wahoo bank receives an increase in its reserves.

Balance-sheet changes are as shown on page 340.

Two aspects of this transaction are noteworthy. First, as with Federal Reserve purchases of securities directly from commercial banks, the reserves and lending ability of the commercial banking system have been increased. Second, in this instance the supply of money is directly increased by the central banks' purchase of government bonds, aside from any expansion of the money supply which may occur as the result of the increase in commercial bank reserves.

You may detect a slight difference between the Federal Reserve Banks' purchases of

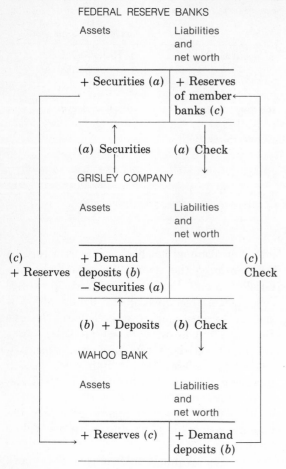

securities from the commercial banking system and from the public. Assuming all commercial banks are "loaned up" initially, Federal Reserve bond purchases from commercial banks will increase the actual reserves and excess reserves of the commercial banks by the entire amount of the bond purchases. Thus a $1000 bond purchase from a commercial bank would increase both the actual and excess reserves of the commercial bank by $1000. On the other hand, Federal Reserve Bank purchases of bonds from the public increase actual reserves but also increase demand deposits. Thus a $1000 bond purchase from the public would increase actual reserves of the "loaned up" banking system by $1000; but with a 20 percent reserve ratio, the excess reserves of the

banking system would only amount to $800. In the case of bond purchases from the public, it is *as if* the commercial banking system had already used one-fifth, or 20 percent, of its newly acquired reserves to support $1000 worth of new demand deposit money.

However, in each transaction the basic conclusion is the same: *When the Federal Reserve Banks buy securities in the open market, commercial banks' reserves will be increased.*

Selling Securities   We should now be highly suspicious that Federal Reserve Bank sales of government bonds will reduce commercial bank reserves. Let us confirm these suspicions.

Suppose the Federal Reserve Banks sell securities in the open market to *commercial banks:*

a.   The Federal Reserve Banks give up securities which the commercial banks obviously acquire.

b.   The commercial banks pay for these securities by drawing checks against their deposits—that is, their reserves—in the Federal Reserve Banks. The Federal Reserve Banks collect these checks by reducing the commercial banks' reserves accordingly.

In short, the balance-sheet changes appear as follows:

FEDERAL RESERVE BANKS

Assets	Liabilities and net worth
− Securities (*a*)	− Reserves of member banks (*b*)
(*a*) Securities	(*b*) − Reserves

COMMERCIAL BANKS

Assets	Liabilities and net worth
− Reserves (*b*) + Securities (*a*)	

Note specifically the reduction in commercial bank reserves.

Should the Federal Reserve Banks sell securities *to the public,* the overall effect would be substantially the same. Let us put the Grisley company on the buying end of government bonds which the Federal Reserve Banks are selling.

a. The Federal Reserve Bank sells government bonds to the Grisley company, the latter paying for these securities by a check drawn on the Wahoo bank.

b. The Federal Reserve Banks clear this check against the Wahoo bank by reducing its reserves.

c. The Wahoo bank returns the Grisley company's check to it, reducing the company's demand deposit accordingly.

The balance sheets change as follows:

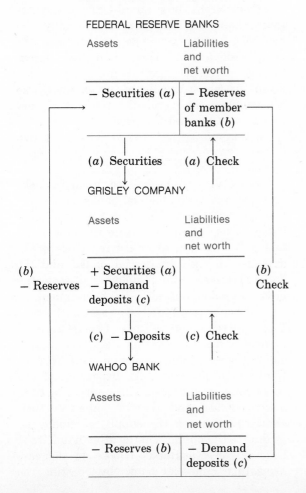

Note that Federal Reserve bond sales of $1000 to the commercial banking system reduce the system's actual and excess reserves by $1000. But a $1000 bond sale to the public reduces excess reserves by $800 because demand-deposit money is also reduced by $1000 by the sale. In the case of bond sales to the public, it is *as if* the commercial banking system had reduced its outstanding demand deposits by $1000 to cushion the decline in excess reserves to the extent of $200.

In each of the two variations of the Federal Reserve bond sale transaction, however, the basic conclusion is the same: *When the Federal Reserve Banks sell securities in the open market, commercial bank reserves are reduced.*

□   **The Discount Rate**

The Federal Reserve Banks perform essentially the same functions for commercial banks as the commercial banks perform for the public. One of these functions is the making of loans. Just as commercial banks extend credit to the public, so the bankers' banks may lend to the commercial banks.

When a commercial bank borrows, it turns over to the Federal Reserve Bank a promissory note or IOU drawn against itself and secured by acceptable collateral—typically United States government securities. Just as commercial banks charge interest on their loans, so do the Federal Reserve Banks charge interest on the loans they grant to commercial banks. This interest rate is called the *discount rate,* the interest on such loans being discounted at the time the loan is negotiated rather than collected at the time the loan is repaid.

Being a claim against the commercial bank, the borrowing bank's promissory note is an asset to the lending Federal Reserve Bank and appears on its balance sheet as "loans to commercial banks." To the commercial bank the IOU is a liability, appearing as "Loans from the Federal Reserve Banks" on the commercial bank's balance sheet. In payment of the loan the Federal Reserve Bank will *increase* the reserves of the borrowing commercial bank. Since no required reserves need be kept against loans from the Federal Reserve Banks, *all* new reserves acquired by borrowing from the Federal Reserve Banks would be excess reserves. These changes are reflected in the balance sheets of the commercial banks and the bankers' banks as follows:

FEDERAL RESERVE BANKS

Assets	Liabilities and net worth
+ Loans to commercial banks	+ Reserves of commercial banks
IOUs	+ Reserves

COMMERCIAL BANKS

Assets	Liabilities and net worth
+ Reserves	+ Loans from the Federal Reserve Banks

It is interesting to note that this transaction is analogous to a private person's borrowing from a commercial bank (see Chapter 15, transaction 6).

The important point, of course, is that *commercial bank borrowing from the Federal Reserve Banks increases the reserves of commercial banks, thereby enhancing their ability to extend credit to the public.*

The Board of Governors of the Federal Reserve System has the power to establish and manipulate the discount rate at which commercial banks can borrow from the Federal Reserve Banks. From the commercial banks' point of view, the discount rate obviously constitutes a cost entailed in acquiring reserves. Hence, a *decrease* in the discount rate encourages commercial banks to build up their reserves by borrowing. Although not obligated to do so, the Federal Reserve Banks usually stand ready to extend credit to borrowing banks which can offer acceptable collateral. But if the discount rate is high, commercial banks which borrow must in turn boost the interest rate at which they lend to the public to make such transactions profitable. If a commercial bank has to pay 7 percent for the attainment of new reserves, it may have to charge 9 or 10 percent for loans made on these new reserves to the public in order to cover administration costs and earn an acceptable profit. Such a high rate discourages the public from increasing the money supply by borrowing from the commercial banks. Conversely, a low discount rate permits commercial banks to acquire new reserves cheaply from the Federal Reserve Banks. This allows the commercial banks to lend profitably at relatively low interest rates to the public, thereby encouraging an expansion in the supply of money.

Apart from these quantitative considerations, changes in the discount rate may well have significant psychological effects upon the credit policies of banks and the public. Changes in the discount rate are a very explicit means by which the Board of Governors can communicate the overall direction of monetary policy to banks and the public.

☐   **Reserve Bank Credit**

Early in this chapter we noted that the sum of loans to commercial banks and securities appearing on the Federal Reserve Banks' balance sheet constitutes Reserve Bank credit. Loans to commercial banks represent credit extended to the commercial banks, and the Federal Reserve Banks' holdings of securities indicate credit granted to the government.

Obviously, when the Federal Reserve Banks increase the volume of loans to commercial banks by lowering the discount rate and buy securities in the open market, Reserve Bank credit increases. An expansion of Reserve Bank credit raises the reserves of commercial banks and thereby enhances their ability to increase the supply of money by lending to the public. On the other hand, if the Federal Reserve Banks choose to decrease loans to commercial banks by boosting the discount rate and sell securities in the open market, Reserve Bank credit will decline. This decline in Reserve Bank credit destroys commercial bank reserves and limits further increases in the supply of money. It may even force a contraction in the money supply. In short, *there is a direct relationship between the volume of Reserve Bank credit and the size of commercial bank reserves.*

□ Easy Money and Tight Money

Suppose the economy is faced with unemployment and deflation. The monetary authorities correctly decide that an increase in the supply of money is needed to stimulate the volume of spending in order to help absorb the idle resources. To induce an increase in the supply of money, the Board of Governors must see to it that the excess reserves of commercial banks are expanded. What specific policies will bring this about?

1 The reserve ratio should be reduced, automatically changing required reserves into excess reserves.

2 The Board of Governors should order the Federal Reserve Banks to buy securities in the open market. This will build up the size of commercial bank reserves.

3 The discount rate should be lowered to induce commercial banks to add to their reserves by borrowing from the Federal Reserve Banks. The second and third policies can be combined merely by saying that Reserve Bank credit should be expanded.

For obvious reasons, this set of policy decisions is called an *easy money policy.* Its purpose is to make credit cheaply and easily available, so as to increase the volumes of spending and employment.

Suppose, on the other hand, an excess of spending is pushing the economy into an inflationary spiral. The Board of Governors should attempt to reduce total spending by limiting or contracting the supply of money. The key to this goal lies in reducing the reserves of commercial banks. How is this done?

1 Increasing the reserve ratio will automatically strip commercial banks of excess reserves.

2 The Federal Reserve Banks should sell government bonds in the open market to tear down commercial bank reserves.

3 A boost in the discount rate will discourage commercial banks from building up their reserves by borrowing at the Federal Reserve Banks. These latter two policies constitute a reduction in Reserve Bank credit.

This group of directives is appropriately labeled a *tight money policy.* The objective is to tighten the supply of money in order to reduce spending and control inflationary pressures.

MONETARY POLICY: MINOR QUALITATIVE CONTROLS

The major techniques of monetary control are (1) changing the reserve ratio, (2) changing the discount rate, and (3) open-market operations. These devices are quantitative controls; they are designed to control the quantity of bank credit generally available. But these instruments of monetary management are supplemented periodically by certain other, less important credit controls in the form of (1) qualitative, or selective, credit controls, and (2) moral suasion.

□ Selective Credit Controls

The monetary authorities also have deemed it advisable to control certain specific types of credit.

1 Stock Market Credit In some instances the overall flow of money and credit in the economy has been fairly serene, and at the same time speculative stock market purchases threaten to precipitate economic difficulties. To thwart this possibility, the Board of Governors has the authority to specify the *margin requirement,* or minimum percentage down payment which purchasers of stock must make. Thus, the current margin requirement of 50 percent means that only 50 percent of the purchase price of a security may be borrowed, the remaining 50 percent being paid "cash on the barrelhead." This rate will be raised when it is deemed desirable to restrict speculative stock purchases and lowered to revive a sluggish market.

2 Consumer and Real Estate Credit Congress occasionally has authorized the Board of Governors to invoke specific restraints on consumer credit. During World War II, money incomes were increasing at a time when the output of civilian goods was declining because of the drastic rechanneling of resources to the production of war goods. The result was sharp inflationary pressure in certain consumer goods industries. To dampen this pressure, Congress gave the Board of Governors temporary authority to specify minimum down payments and maximum repayment periods on loans involving the purchase of real estate and a variety of consumer durables.

☐ **Moral Suasion**

The monetary authorities sometimes use the less tangible technique of moral suasion to influence the lending policies of commercial banks. Moral suasion simply means the employment by the monetary authorities of "friendly persuasion"—policy statements, public pronouncements, or outright appeals—warning that excessive expansion or contraction of bank credit might involve serious consequences for the banking system and the economy as a whole. Such pronouncements are not limited to bank credit in general; they may call for the curtailment of specific types of bank credit. For example, in attempting to relieve inflationary pressures during the Korean conflict in 1951, the public statements and publicity releases of the monetary authorities pleaded for the curtailment of bank lending not essential to the war effort and for the general exercise of voluntary restraint by commercial bankers in creating money by lending. Similarly, in 1966 the Federal Reserve urged banks to limit the expansion of loans to businesses as rising military expenditures began to intensify inflationary pressures. Private bankers' associations often aid the Federal monetary authorities in the application of moral suasion by echoing the pleas of the Board of Governors.

■───────────────────────

RELATIVE IMPORTANCE OF CONTROLS

Of the three major monetary controls, open-market operations clearly have evolved as the most important control mechanism. The reasons for this are worth noting.

The discount rate is less important than open-market operations for at least two reasons. On the one hand, although commercial banks borrow with some frequency from the central banks, only a small portion—perhaps 3 or 4 percent on the average—of commercial bank reserves are obtained by such borrowing. In fact, it is often the effectiveness of open-market operations which prompts the commercial banks to borrow from the Federal Reserve Banks. That is, to the extent that central bank bond sales make commercial banks temporarily short of reserves, the commercial banks will be prompted to borrow from the Federal Reserve Banks. Hence, rather than being a primary tool of monetary policy, discounting occurs largely in response to monetary policy as carried out by open-market operations. A second consideration is that the manipulation of commercial bank reserves through open-market operations and the changing of reserve requirements are accomplished at the initiative of the Federal Reserve System. In comparison, the discount rate, to be influential as an instrument of monetary policy, depends upon the initiative of commercial banks in borrowing from the central banks. And, in fact, many banks choose not to borrow from the Federal Reserve Banks except in extreme emergencies.

What about changes in reserve requirements?[2]

> Because the impact is so powerful, so blunt, so immediate, and so widespread, the Federal Reserve uses its authority to change reserve requirements only sparingly, particularly during tight money periods when increases in reserve requirements would be appropriate. An increase in reserve requirements reduces commercial bank profitability, since banks then must hold a larger percentage of their assets in reserve balances that earn no interest. As membership in the Federal Reserve System is voluntary (except for banks with national charters), the Federal Reserve is not eager to discourage membership by raising reserve requirements too frequently. The "harsh hand of the Fed" is most evident when tight money is executed through higher reserve requirements. Since 1951, reserve requirements against demand deposits have been increased only five times, whereas they have been lowered on nine occasions.

But there are more positive reasons why open-market operations have evolved as the primary technique of monetary policy. This mechanism of monetary control has the advantage of flexibility—government securities can be purchased or sold in large or small amounts—and the impact upon bank reserves is quite prompt. Yet, compared with reserve-requirement changes, open-market operations work subtly and less directly. Furthermore, quantitatively there is no question about the potential ability of the Federal Reserve Banks to affect commercial bank reserves through bond sales and purchases. A glance at the consolidated balance sheet for the Federal Reserve Banks (Table 16-1) reveals very large

holdings of government bonds ($96 billion), the sales of which could theoretically reduce commercial bank reserves from $23 billion to zero!

MONETARY POLICY: GRAPHIC RESTATEMENT

At the beginning of this chapter the cause-effect chain through which monetary policy operates was outlined in a simplified fashion. We are now in a position to restate the relevant cause-effect relationships at a more sophisticated level.

Recalling that monetary (interest rate) policy works primarily through investment, Figure 11-5's downsloping investment-demand curve is reproduced as Figure 16-1a. Assuming the interest rate is initially 8 percent, it will be profitable for businesses to invest $20 billion. In Figure 16-1b this $20 billion of investment is plugged into the simple leakages-injections model for the private economy to determine the equilibrium NNP. *If* this $470 billion equilibrium level of NNP entails unemployment, an *easy money* policy will increase the money supply, lower the interest rate, make a larger volume of investment spending profitable, and thereby expand the equilibrium NNP to, or at least toward, full employment. More concretely, if the full-employment NNP is $490 billion, an increase in the money supply sufficient to reduce the interest rate from 8 to 6 percent would increase investment from $20 to $25 billion, as shown in Figure 16-1a. This $5 billion upshift of the investment schedule from I_{n1} to I_{n2} in Figure 16-1b, subject to the relevant multiplier of 4, will increase equilibrium NNP from $470 billion to the desired $490 billion full-employment level. Conversely, *if* the original $470 billion NNP generates demand-pull inflation, a *tight money* policy will reduce the supply of money, increase the interest rate, cause a decline in investment, and thereby eliminate the inflationary gap. To illustrate: If the full-employment, noninflation-

[2]Lawrence S. Ritter and William L. Silber, *Money,* 2d ed. (New York: Basic Books, Inc., Publishers, 1973), p. 112.

FIGURE 16-1   MONETARY POLICY AND THE EQUILIBRIUM NNP

An easy money policy will lower the interest rate, increase the investment component of aggregate demand, and thereby increase the equilibrium level of NNP. Conversely, a tight money policy will raise the rate of interest, reduce the investment component of aggregate demand, and restrain demand-pull inflation.

ary NNP is $450 billion, an inflationary gap of $5 billion will exist. That is, at the $470 billion level of NNP, planned investment exceeds saving—and therefore aggregate demand exceeds aggregate supply—by $5 billion. A decline in the money supply sufficient to increase the interest rate from 8 to 10 percent will reduce investment from $20 to $15 billion in Figure 16-1a. The consequent $5 billion downshift in Figure 16-1b's investment schedule from I_{n1} to I_{n3} will equate planned investment and saving—and therefore aggregate demand and aggregate supply—at the $450 billion NNP, thereby eliminating the initial $5 billion inflationary gap.[3]

EFFECTIVENESS OF MONETARY POLICY

How well does monetary policy work? Actually, the effectiveness of monetary policy is subject to considerable debate.

[3]To the instructor: If a more rigorous and detailed discussion of monetary policy is desired at this point, students should be assigned the section on "Interest" in Chapter 32.

□   Shortcomings of Monetary Policy

It must be recognized that monetary policy entails certain limitations and encounters a number of real-world complications.

1   Cyclical Asymmetry   If pursued vigorously enough, tight money can actually destroy commercial bank reserves to the point where banks are *forced* to contract the volume of loans. As tight money eliminates excess reserves, banks will be obliged to allow outstanding loans to mature without making offsetting loans to other borrowers. This means a contraction in the money supply. But an easy money policy suffers from a "You can lead a horse to water, but you can't make him drink" kind of problem. An easy money policy can do no more than see to it that commercial banks have the ability—that is, the excess reserves needed—to make loans. It cannot guarantee, however, that loans will actually be negotiated and the supply of money increased. If the public does not want to borrow, or if commercial banks, seeking liquidity, are unwilling to lend, the easy money efforts of the Board of

Governors will be to little avail. An easy money policy can do no more than create excess reserves upon which loans may or may not be made.[4]

Caution: We are *not* suggesting that an easy money policy will not work. Rather, the point is that the power of a tight money policy may be greater than that of an easy money policy. Hence, it might be necessary to increase bank reserves by, say, $2 billion to achieve a given increase in the money supply, whereas only a $1 billion decrease in reserves would bring about an equal decline in the money supply.

2   Velocity and Financial Intermediaries

From a monetary point of view (Chapter 17), total spending or aggregate demand may be regarded as the money supply *multiplied* by the velocity of money, that is, the number of times per year the average dollar is spent on goods and services. Hence, if the money supply is $150 billion, total demand will be $600 billion if velocity is 4, but only $450 billion if velocity is 3. Critics of monetary policy contend that, in fact, velocity has a habit of changing in such a way as to offset or frustrate policy-instigated changes in the money supply. That is, during inflation, when the money supply is restrained by policy, velocity tends to increase. Conversely, when policy measures are taken to increase the money supply during a recession, velocity may very well fall!

But why might velocity behave this way? At least two considerations are relevant. First, the rapidity with which households and businesses spend money depends upon actual and expected changes in the price level. As the economy moves into an inflationary boom with prices currently rising and expected to continue rising in the future, households and businesses will be reluctant to hold money. The

reason: Inflation causes money to depreciate in value (Chapter 10). Hence, money is expended more rapidly and velocity rises. Conversely, during recession with stable or even falling prices, transactors are more willing to hold money as wealth and velocity falls. Second, recall that our economy is characterized by a myriad of financial intermediaries in the form of savings and loan associations, personal finance companies, and so forth. Although they do not create money, these institutions do gather or mobilize savings and make them available by lending to spenders. During economic expansion, for example, these institutions, prompted by rising interest rates, pursue more aggressively and more effectively the task of getting funds from savers into the hands of spenders. To the extent that they are successful, they increase velocity and offset the objectives of a tight money policy. Some economists feel that a more effective monetary policy depends upon making these financial intermediaries directly subject to control by the Board of Governors.

3   Conflict with Treasury Goals   The United States Treasury is the world's greatest, and most renowned, debtor. As such, it is naturally interested in low interest rates: An increase in interest rates of 1 percent on government bonds can cost the Treasury $5 or $6 billion in interest payments each year. But we know that during periods of inflation the Board of Governors is obligated to undertake a tight money policy for the purpose of raising interest rates. Hence, a conflict arises during inflation between the Treasury's desire for low interest rates and the monetary authority's obligation to boost interest rates. During such periods these two agencies attempt to work out an acceptable compromise or "accord" which, as the case may be, can weaken the effectiveness of a tight money policy.

4   Cost-Push Inflation   As is the case with fiscal policy, monetary policy is designed to control inflation by restraining excess total

---

[4] *Qualification:* Remember that Federal Reserve purchases of securities *from the public* directly increase the supply of money apart from any expansion of bank credit which commercial banks may make available on the basis of the reserves they acquire as the result of these bond purchases.

spending. That is, an anti-inflationary monetary policy is geared to alleviate or correct demand-pull inflation. It is *not* very relevant in controlling cost-push inflation, the causes of which lie on the supply or cost side of the market.

5 The Investment Impact Some economists doubt that monetary policy has as much impact upon investment as Figure 16-1 implies. Their position is based upon several points.

First, it is argued that the investment-demand curve is insensitive to the interest rate; that is, the curve of Figure 16-1*a* allegedly has a steep slope so that a given change in the interest rate does *not* elicit a very large change in investment spending. The question of the sensitivity of investment spending to changes in the interest rate is obviously a factual question. But to date empirical studies have not yielded a generally accepted conclusion on this issue.

Second, the operation of monetary policy as portrayed may be complicated, and at least partially offset, by unfavorable changes in the location of the investment-demand curve. For example, the purpose of a tight money policy is to increase the interest rate, move businesses up the investment-demand curve, and thereby restrain aggregate demand and the rate of inflation. However, the very inflationary prosperity which the tight money policy is designed to control may well be accompanied by increasing business optimism or a rapid rate of technological progress which has the effect of *shifting* the investment-demand curve to the *right*. This poses the possibility that investment spending will increase *despite* the higher interest rate. In short, the forces which cause inflation may also generate increases in the demand for investment goods which tend to counter a tight money policy. Conversely, a recessionary environment may undermine business confidence, shift the investment-demand curve to the left, and thereby tend to frustrate an easy money policy.

Finally, large monopolistic firms—the very firms which do the bulk of the investing—are in a position to pass on any increase in interest costs to consumers in the form of higher product prices. Indeed, in many cases monopolistic firms are able to finance substantial portions of their investment programs internally and therefore will not be hindered by the unavailability of credit for investment purposes. However, tight money is likely to have a considerable impact upon smaller firms in competitive industries. This is another criticism of tight money: it discriminates against such firms.

☐ **Strengths of Monetary Policy**

But one should *not* deduce from this discussion of limitations and complications that monetary policy is a weak and ineffectual technique for economic stabilization. Monetary policy *is* an important stabilization device which has proved its worth in helping to offset, for example, the recessions of 1949 and 1958 and to restrain inflation throughout a good portion of the 1950s and, more recently, in the late 1960s. Several specific points can be made on behalf of monetary policy.

1 Speed and Flexibility In comparison with fiscal policy, monetary policy can be quickly altered. We have seen (Chapter 13) that the application of appropriate fiscal policy may be seriously delayed by congressional deliberations. In contrast, the Open Market Committee of the Federal Reserve Board can literally buy or sell securities on a daily basis and thereby influence the money supply and interest rates.

2 Political Acceptability Monetary policy is a more subtle and more politically conservative measure than is fiscal policy. Changes in government spending directly affect the allocation of resources, and, of course, tax changes can have extensive political ramifications. By contrast, monetary policy works by a more subtle route and therefore seems to be more politically palatable.

3 Monetarism In the next chapter we will examine in some detail the current debate over the relative effectiveness of monetary and fiscal policy. Let us merely note here that, although most economists view fiscal policy as a more powerful stabilization technique than monetary policy, there is a group of respected economists who feel that changes in the money supply is the key determinant of the level of economic activity and that fiscal policy is ineffective.

■───────────────────────

EMPLOYMENT THEORY AND POLICY: RECAPITULATION

This is an opportune point at which to recapitulate and synthesize Keynesian employment theory and associated stabilization policies. We want to gain a better understanding of how the many analytical and policy aspects of macroeconomics discussed in this and the seven preceding chapters fit together. Figure 16-2 provides the "big picture" we seek. The overriding virtue of this diagram is that it shows how the many concepts and principles we have discussed relate to one another and constitute a coherent and meaningful theory of what determines the level of resource use in a market economy.

Now let us review the substance of Figure 16-2. Reading from left to right, the key point, of course, is that the levels of output, employment, income, and prices are all directly related to the level of aggregate demand.[5] The decisions of business firms to produce goods and therefore to employ resources depend upon the total amount of money spent on these goods. To discover what determines the level of aggregate spending, we must examine its three major components.[6]

□   **Consumption**

The absolute level of consumption spending depends upon the position of the consumption schedule and the level of net national product or disposable income. Most economists are convinced that the consumption schedule is quite stable. Therefore, the absolute level of consumption spending usually can be thought of as changing in response to changes in NNP brought about by fluctuations in other components in aggregate demand. Furthermore, the slope of the consumption schedule, measured by the MPC (the marginal propensity to consume), is critical in determining the size of the multiplier.

□   **Investment**

Investment spending is a highly volatile component of aggregate demand and therefore likely to be a cause of fluctuations in the levels of output, employment, and prices. The instability of investment lies in its determinants: Business confidence is subject to frequent and substantial revision; technological progress occurs at an uneven rate; and the durability of capital goods makes their purchase postponable. Furthermore, business profits—an increasingly important source of funds for investment—are highly variable.

□   **Government Spending**

The government purchases component of aggregate demand differs from consumption and investment in that it is determined by public policy. Consumption and investment decisions are made in the self-interest of the

───────────────────────

[5] In Chapter 18 we modify this statement in discussing stagflation, that is, inflation accompanied by *rising* unemployment.

[6] We assume a closed economy, that is, net exports are zero. In Chapter 41 we will analyze the effects of exports and imports upon output, income, and employment.

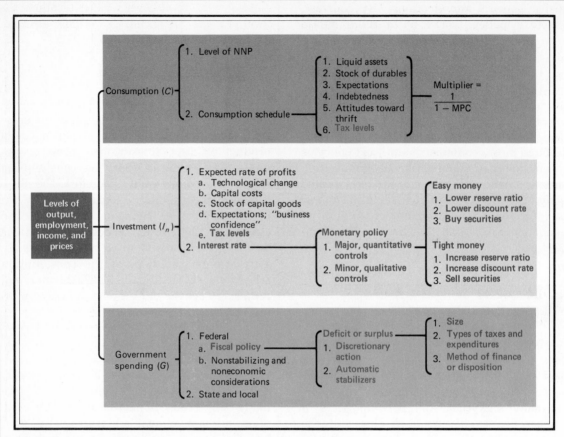

FIGURE 16-2 THE THEORY OF EMPLOYMENT AND STABILIZATION POLICIES

This figure integrates the various components of employment theory and stabilization policy. Note that determinants which constitute, or are strongly influenced by, public policy are shown in brown.

household and business sectors, respectively. Government spending decisions, on the other hand, are made, at least in part, to fulfill society's interest in high levels of output and employment and a stable price level. With this motivational distinction in mind, let us examine the major components and characteristics of stabilization policy.

□ Fiscal and Monetary Policy

Fiscal policy refers, of course, to changes in government spending and tax revenues which are designed to eliminate either an infla-

tionary or a recessionary gap. Figure 16-2 makes the potential stabilizing role of government quite evident; government spending, as one of the three major components of aggregate demand, directly affects output, employment, and the price level. Tax policy, on the other hand, works indirectly through the other two major components of total spending; taxation is a determinant of both consumption and investment.[7] In particular, reductions in the personal income tax tend to shift the con-

[7]In our earlier tabular (Table 13-1) and graphic (Figure 13-2) models of the economy, we made the simplifying assumption that all taxes were personal taxes.

sumption schedule upward; tax increases tend to shift it downward. Cuts in the corporation income tax or other business taxes tend to improve profit expectations, shift the investment-demand curve to the right, and stimulate investment; tax increases weaken profit expectations and reduce the willingness to invest.

Fiscal policy is both *discretionary* and *automatic*. The automatic or built-in stabilizers—the progressiveness of the net tax structure—cause tax collections to vary directly with the level of national income. Discretionary policy consists of the changing of spending levels and the manipulation of tax rates or the tax structure by Congress for the explicit purpose of achieving greater stability in the economy.

The functioning of monetary policy was just detailed in the discussion of Figure 16-1.

□ **Complexities and Problems**

Although Figure 16-2 is a revealing overview of Keynesian theory and policy, it conceals a number of complexities and problems which merit at least brief comment.

1 Employment–Price Level Trade-off Recall (Figure 10-1) that unemployment and inflation may occur simultaneously. Chapter 18 will be concerned with this trade-off problem and the possibility that unemployment and inflation may have causes other than an inappropriate level of aggregate demand.

2 Noneconomic and Microeconomic Factors Figure 16-2 presents a *macroeconomic* theory and, as such, fails to consider the possible impacts of noneconomic and microeconomic considerations. For example, an unfortunate turn of international politics can create serious and prolonged macroeconomic disturbances. The OPEC oil cartel and the Vietnam war immediately come to mind. Furthermore, government spending and taxing decisions are not made on purely macroeconomic grounds. For example, a political party's com-

mitment to relieve certain social problems—to ameliorate economic inequality and the poverty problem—may call for changes in spending or the tax structure that destabilize the economy. More generally stated, government expenditure and taxation policies are used not only to achieve macroeconomic stability, but also to achieve reallocations of resources and to redistribute income.

3 Quantification Aside from the troublesome stagflation problem, it is usually quite simple to identify the appropriate direction for changes in fiscal and monetary policy. Recession, for example, calls for a public deficit and an easy money policy. What we do *not* know—or at least do not know with great accuracy—is the *size* of the deficit needed or the *amount* by which the money supply should be increased. An important consequence is that it is simply not realistic to expect stabilization policy to work perfectly so as to provide continuous full employment and price stability. "Fine tuning" of the economy through stabilization policies has proven most difficult to achieve.

4 Policy Coordination Although we have treated fiscal and monetary policy separately, they are in fact interrelated and should be coordinated. To illustrate: The quantitative significance of, say, a given tax cut will depend upon whether it is accompanied by a "congenial" change in the money supply and the interest rates. Suppose fiscal authorities calculate that a $5 billion cut in personal and business taxes will move the economy to full employment, other things being equal. But in fact, other things—in particular, the interest rate—cannot be expected to remain unchanged as the economy begins to expand under the impetus of the tax cuts. As production and the volume of transactions expand, the demand for money will increase and, given the supply of money, interest rates will rise. The higher interest rates will tend to "crowd out" some investment and thereby partially offset the expansionary impact of the tax reductions. The calculated expansionary effect of the $5 billion tax cut will be partially thwarted unless the monetary authorities counter the greater demand for money with an increase in the money supply in order to keep the interest rate unchanged. The point is that fiscal and monetary policies do not operate in isolation; effective stabilization policy presumes their careful coordination.

Summary

1 Like fiscal policy, the goal of monetary policy is to stabilize the economy. The route, or cause-effect chain, through which monetary policy functions is complex: *a.* Policy decisions affect commercial bank reserves; *b.* changes in reserves affect the supply of money; *c.* changes in the supply of money influence the interest rate and the availability of bank credit; and *d.* changes in the interest rate and availability of credit affect investment, the equilibrium NNP, and the price level.

2 For a consideration of monetary policy, the most important assets of the Federal Reserve Banks are gold certificates, securities, and loans to commercial banks. The basic liabilities are the reserves of member banks, Treasury deposits, and Federal Reserve Notes.

3 Table 16-3 draws together all the basic notions relevant to the application of tight and easy money policies.

4 Monetary policy is subject to a number of limitations. *a.* The excess reserves which an easy money policy provides may not be used by banks to expand the supply of money. *b.* Policy-instigated changes in the supply of money may be partially offset by changes in the velocity of money. *c.* The Treasury's desire for low interest rates conflicts with the higher rate of interest which tight money entails. *d.* A tight money policy is of questionable relevance in correcting cost-push inflation. *e.* The weight of the many noninterest determinants of investment, the ability of monopolistic firms to pass increases in interest costs on to consumers through price increases, and internal financing may all weaken the ability of tight money to curtail investment spending.

Table 16-3 A SUMMARY OF MONETARY POLICY

I. Problem: unemployment and deflation	I. Problem: inflation
II. Remedy: to induce an expansion in the supply of money, and therefore spending, by reducing the cost and increasing the availability of bank credit.	II. Remedy: to induce a contraction in the supply of money, and therefore spending, by increasing the cost and reducing the availability of bank credit
III. Techniques:	III. Techniques:
A. Major, quantitative controls: easy money policy	*A.* Major, quantitative controls: tight money policy
1. Lower reserve ratio.	1. Raise reserve ratio.
2. Buy bonds in the open market.	2. Sell bonds in the open market.
3. Lower discount rate.	3. Raise discount rate.
B. Minor, qualitative controls	*B.* Minor, qualitative controls
1. Lower margin requirements.	1. Raise margin requirements.
2. Ease credit regulations on consumer durables and real estate.	2. Tighten credit regulations on consumer durables and real estate.
3. Use moral suasion to induce banks to lend.	3. Use moral suasion to encourage banks to be more selective in lending.

5   The advantages of monetary policy include its flexibility and political acceptability. Further, the monetarists feel that the supply of money is the single most important determinant of the level of national output.

6   Figure 16-2, which provides a summary statement of Keynesian employment theory and policy, merits careful study by the reader.

Questions and Study Suggestions

1   Key terms and concepts to remember: monetary policy; Reserve Bank credit; quantitative controls; reserve ratio; open-market operations; discount rate; easy and tight money policies; qualitative (selective) controls; margin requirement; moral suasion; velocity of money.

2   What is the basic objective of monetary policy? Describe the cause-effect chain through which monetary policy is made effective. Critics of monetary policy assert that this cause-effect chain contains too many "loose links." What do they mean?

3   Suppose you are a member of the Board of Governors of the Federal Reserve System. The economy is experiencing a sharp and prolonged inflationary trend. What changes in *a.* the reserve ratio, *b.* the discount rate, and *c.* open-market operations would you recommend? Explain in each case how the change you advocate would affect commercial bank reserves and influence the money supply.

4   Use commercial bank and Federal Reserve Bank balance sheets in each case to demonstrate the impact of each of the following transactions upon commercial bank reserves:

   a.   The Federal Reserve Banks purchase securities from private businesses and consumers.

   b.   Commercial banks borrow from the Federal Reserve Banks.

   c.   The Board of Governors reduces the reserve ratio.

5   Evaluate the overall effectiveness of monetary policy. Why have open-market operations evolved as the primary means of controlling commercial bank reserves? Discuss the specific limitations of monetary policy.

6   In the table on page 354 you will find simplified consolidated balance sheets for the commercial banking system and the twelve Federal Reserve Banks. In columns 1 through 3, indicate how the balance sheets would read after each of the three ensuing transactions is completed. Do not cumulate your answers; that is, analyze each transaction separately, starting in each case from the given figures. All accounts are in billions of dollars.

   a.   Suppose a decline in the discount rate prompts commercial banks to borrow an additional $1 billion from the Federal Reserve Banks. Show the new balance-sheet figures in column 1.

   b.   The Federal Reserve Banks sell $3 billion in securities to the public, who pay for the bonds with checks. Show the new balance-sheet figures in column 2.

   c.   The Federal Reserve Banks buy $2 billion of securities from commercial banks. Show the new balance-sheet figures in column 3.

   d.   Now review each of the above three transactions, asking yourself these three questions: (1) What change, if any, took place in the money supply as a direct and immediate result of each transaction? (2) What increase or decrease in commercial banks' reserves took place in each transaction? (3) Assuming a reserve ratio of 20 percent, what change in the money-creating potential of the commercial banking *system* occurred as a result of each transaction?

CONSOLIDATED BALANCE SHEET:
ALL COMMERCIAL BANKS

	(1)	(2)	(3)
Assets:			
Reserves $ 33			
Securities 60			
Loans 60			
Liabilities and net worth:			
Demand deposits $150			
Loans from the Federal Reserve Banks 3			

CONSOLIDATED BALANCE SHEET:
TWELVE FEDERAL RESERVE BANKS

	(1)	(2)	(3)
Assets:			
Gold certificates $20			
Securities 40			
Loans to commercial banks 3			
Liabilities and net worth:			
Reserves of commercial banks $33			
Treasury deposits 3			
Federal Reserve Notes 27			

7   Summarize the theory of employment, using the aggregate demand–aggregate supply approach. Show in detail how monetary and fiscal policies might affect the various components of aggregate demand.

8   Why is it unrealistic to expect fiscal and monetary policies to result in complete economic stability? What might be done to improve monetary and fiscal policies?

9   Design an antirecession stabilization policy, involving both fiscal and monetary policies, which is consistent with *a.* a relative decline in the public sector, *b.* greater income equality, and *c.* a high rate of economic growth. Explain: "Truly effective stabilization policy presumes the coordination of fiscal and monetary policy."

Selected References

Board of Governors of the Federal Reserve System: *The Federal Reserve System: Purposes and Functions,* 6th ed. (1974), particularly chaps. 1, 4, 5.

Chandler, Lester V., and Stephen M. Goldfeld: *The Economics of Money and Banking,* 7th ed. (New York: Harper & Row, Publishers, Incorporated, 1977), chaps. 21–26.

Maisel, Sherman J.: *Managing the Dollar* (New York: W. W. Norton & Company, Inc., 1973).

Ritter, Lawrence S., and William L. Silber: *Money,* 3d ed. (New York: Basic Books, Inc., 1977).

Thorn, Richard S.: *Introduction to Money and Banking* (New York: Harper & Row, Publishers, Incorporated, 1976), chaps. 18–25.

Last Word
Problems in Controlling the Money Supply

Arthur F. Burns, Chairman of the Board of Governors, outlines some of the problems which the Federal Reserve System encounters in trying to control the money supply and interest rates.

Factors which limit the System's ability to control the money supply in the short run include the indirect relationship between Federal Reserve actions and the money supply, [and] the sizable and growing proportion of deposits not subject to Federal Reserve reserve requirements. . . . Some of these factors can also affect the precision with which longer-run control can be attained.

Actions taken by the Federal Reserve System affect the money supply indirectly. Through open market operations, the Federal Reserve can control with certainty only its holdings of U.S. Government securities. Purchases or sales of securities by the Federal Reserve add to or subtract from the level of bank reserves and hence the base supporting member bank deposits, which constitute the major portion of the money supply. . . .

. . . However, the System cannot exert direct control over the use of reserves by banks and the public. Banks may wish to hold excess reserves. While banks in the past two decades have normally maintained minimal excess reserves on average, the amounts are quite volatile in the short-run and often absorb more or less of the reserve supply than expected. These unused reserves would not, of course, support deposits.

The System also cannot directly control the public's preferences for various types of deposits. These preferences are influenced by the interest rate structure, by transaction needs, and by a wide variety of transitory and random factors. Depending on changes in public preferences, reserves supplied may be used to support more time deposits rather than demand deposits, or vice-versa. . . .

. . . monetary control problems are made more difficult over both the short and long run because reserve requirements on certain money supply-type deposits held by nonmember banks and savings institutions are not subject to Federal Reserve requirements.

Nonmember commerical banks hold one-fifth of total demand deposits, and this percentage has been gradually increasing. State-dominated reserve requirements on nonmember banks are variable from one jurisdiction to another, and can be held in the form of cash, deposits with other banks, and (in some cases) interest-bearing securities. Holdings in the last two of these forms do not contribute to the monetary policy function of reserves, since the funds so used finance additional credit and deposit expansion. Hence, the state system of reserve requirements complicates the task and reduces the precision of monetary control.

The potential development at thrift institutions of savings accounts with transfer features similar to checking accounts poses a new threat to controllability of the money supply, defined on functional grounds to include such accounts along with demand deposits. As with nonmember commerical banks, nonbank savings institutions are not subject to Federal Reserve reserve requirements. To the extent they develop deposits of a money-supply type, the linkage between monetary reserves and deposits will be further loosened. . . .

From *How Well Are Fluctuating Exchange Rates Working?*, Hearings before the Subcommittee on International Economics of the Joint Economic Committee, 93d Congress, 1st Session, Washington, 1973, pp. 190–192, abridged.

Monetarism: An Alternative View

The Keynesian conception of employment theory and stabilization policy, summarized in the discussion regarding Figure 16-2, presents the prevailing or majority view of macroeconomics. In the past decade or so, however, this theory has been challenged by an alternative conception of macroeconomics in the form of *monetarism*. Both schools of thought are led by distinguished scholars. MIT's Paul Samuelson, Yale's James Tobin, and Minnesota's Walter Heller are among the distinguished spokesmen for the Keynesian position. The University of Chicago's Milton Friedman is the intellectual leader of the monetarist school. Winner of the 1976 Nobel prize in economics, his pioneering empirical and theoretical research asserts that the role of money in determining the level of economic activity and the price level is much greater than suggested by Keynesian thought.

The overall purpose of this chapter is to outline the monetarist view and to contrast it philosophically, analytically, and in terms of policy implications with the Keynesian view.

PHILOSOPHICAL-IDEOLOGICAL DIFFERENCES

Explicit recognition of important philosophical and ideological differences between Keynesians and monetarists is most helpful in appreciating their disagreements in the areas of theory and policy.

☐ Keynesians: Political Liberalism

Keynesians feel that capitalism and, more particularly, the free-market system suffer from inherent shortcomings. The market system does not provide public goods; it seriously misallocates resources where externalities and monopolies exist; and it yields a highly unequal distribution of income (Chapter 6). More important for the present debate is the contention that capitalism contains no mechanism to guarantee macroeconomic stability. Imbalances of planned investment and saving *do* occur and the result is business fluctuations—periodic episodes of inflation or unemployment. Government, therefore, can and should play a positive, activist role in stabilizing the economy; discretionary fiscal and monetary policies are needed to alleviate the severe economic ups and downs which would otherwise characterize capitalism's course.

For two reasons Keynesians are especially enamored of fiscal policy. First, for reasons to be specified later, they believe it is a much more powerful stabilizing tool than is monetary policy. Second, fiscal policy—the manipulation of taxes and government spending—can also be used to achieve microeconomic goals in the areas of resource allocation and income distribution which Keynesians think are desirable and meritorious in their own right. For example, a tax cut or an increase in government spending can be used, not only to pull the economy out of a current recession, but also to increase the share of the national income going to the poor or to expand currently underproduced social goods and services.

☐ Monetarists: Laissez Faire and Conservativism

In contrast, monetarists have a strong *laissez faire* or free-market orientation. They emphasize the capacity of the competitive market system automatically to allocate resources efficiently. Conversely, governmental decision making is held to be bureaucratic, inefficient, harmful to individual incentives, and frequently characterized by policy mistakes. Furthermore, centralized decision making by government inevitably erodes individual freedoms.[1]

Perhaps more important for present purposes is the monetarist view that the market system can potentially be the source of a high degree of macroeconomic stability. That is, the market system would tend to provide substantial stability in output, employment, and the price level *were it not for ill-advised governmental interference with the functioning of the economy.* Most monetarists would be sympathetic to the classical theory's contention that downward wage-price flexibility would greatly cushion, if not eliminate, the adverse effects of a decline in aggregate demand upon the levels of real output and employment (Chapter 11). The problem, as the monetarists see it, is that government has fostered and promoted downward wage-price inflexibility through the minimum-wage law, pro-union legislation, farm price supports, pro-business monopoly legislation, and so forth. The free-market system could provide substantial macroeconomic stability, but, despite good intentions, government interference has undermined this capability. Furthermore, as we shall detail momentarily, the monetarists argue that government has contributed to the instability of the system—to the business cycle—through its clumsy and mistaken attempts to achieve greater stability through discretionary fiscal and monetary policies.

Note that Keynesians and monetarists are almost diametrically opposed in their conceptions of the private and public sectors. To the Keynesian, the instability of private invest-

[1] Friedman's conservative philosophy is effectively expounded in two of his books: *Capitalism and Freedom* (Chicago: The University of Chicago Press, 1962), and *An Economist's Protest* (Glen Ridge, N.J.: Thomas Horton and Company, 1972).

ment causes the economy to be unstable. Government plays the "good guy" role by applying appropriate stabilization medicine. To the monetarist, government is the "bad guy." Government creates rigidities which weaken the capacity of the market system to provide substantial stability and it embarks upon monetary and fiscal measures which, although well intentioned, aggravate the very instability they are designed to cure.

THE BASIC EQUATIONS

Keynesian economics focuses upon aggregate demand and its components. The basic equation of the Keynesian model is:

$$C + I_n + G = \text{NNP} \qquad (1)$$

This theory says in essence that the aggregate amount spent by buyers is equal to the total value of the goods and services sold. In equilibrium, $C + I_n + G$ (aggregate demand) is equal to NNP (aggregate supply).

Monetarism, as the label suggests, focuses upon money. The basic equation of monetarism is the *equation of exchange:*

$$MV = PQ \qquad (2)$$

where M is the supply of money; V is the income or circuit velocity of money, that is, the number of times per year the average dollar is spent on final goods and services; P is the price level or, more specifically, the average price at which each unit of physical output is sold; and Q is the physical volume of goods and services produced.

It should be emphasized at the outset that both approaches are useful and insightful to the understanding of macroeconomics.

The difference between the two approaches can be compared with two ways of looking at the flow of water through a sewer pipe—say, at the rate of 6000 gallons per hour. A neo-Keynesian investigator might say that the flow of 6000 gallons an hour consisted of 3000 gallons an hour from a paper mill, 2000 gallons

an hour from an auto plant, and 1000 gallons an hour from a shopping center. A monetarist investigator might say that the sewer flow of 6000 gallons a day consisted of an average of 200 gallons in the sewer at any one time with a complete turnover of the water 30 times every hour.[2]

In fact, the Keynesian equation can be quite readily "translated" into monetarist terms. According to the monetarist approach, total spending or aggregate demand is simply the supply of money multiplied by its velocity. In short, MV is the monetarist counterpart of $C + I_n + G$. Because MV is the total amount spent on final goods in one year, it is obviously equal to NNP. Furthermore, we know from Chapter 9 that NNP is the sum of the physical outputs of various goods and services (Q) multiplied by their respective prices (P). That is, $\text{NNP} = PQ$. Thus, we can restate the Keynesian $C + I_n + G = \text{NNP}$ equation as the monetarist equation of exchange, $MV = PQ$. In a very real sense, the two approaches are two ways of looking at the same thing. But the critical question remains: Which theory is the more accurate portrayal of macroeconomics and therefore the better basis for economic policy?

□   **Spotlight on Money**

The Keynesian equation clearly puts money in a secondary role. Indeed, you will recall (Chapter 16) that the Keynesian conception of monetary policy entails a rather lengthy transmission mechanism:

Change in monetary policy	→	Change in commercial bank reserves	→

Change in money supply	→	Change in the interest rate	→	Change in investment

[2]Werner Sichel and Peter Eckstein, *Basic Economic Concepts* (Chicago: Rand McNally College Publishing Company, 1974), p. 344.

Keynesians feel there are many loose links in this cause-effect chain with the result that monetary policy is an uncertain, unreliable, and weak stabilization tool when compared with fiscal policy. Remember some of the weaknesses of monetary policy cited in the previous chapter: for example, an easy money policy may be ineffective if banks are not anxious to lend or the public eager to borrow; the investment-demand curve may be steep or may shift adversely so the impact of a change in the interest rate upon investment spending is muted or offset.

The monetarists believe that money and monetary policy are much more important in determining the level of economic activity than do the Keynesians. In fact, the monetarists hold that changes in the money supply are the single most important factor in determining the levels of output, employment, and prices. They believe that the cause-effect chain between the supply of money and the level of economic activity is short, direct, and tight. Specifically, *if V, the velocity of money, is stable or nearly so, the equation of exchange suggests that changes in the money supply will have a direct and predictable effect upon the level of NNP (= PQ).* That is, if V is constant, an increase in M will obviously increase P or Q or *both P and Q.* The precise effects on P and Q will depend upon whether the economy is experiencing recession or full employment at the time M is increased. If the economy is in a severe recession, an increase in M will raise Q more or less proportionately, with virtually no change in P. But if the economy is at full employment, Q becomes constant because the economy is producing its capacity or maximum output; hence, increases in M will be purely inflationary and will cause P to increase proportionately. Or, as range 2 of Figure 10-1 reminds us, P and Q may both rise in response to an increase in M as the economy approaches full employment.

Monetarism implies a simpler and much more direct transmission mechanism than does the Keynesian model. In the monetarist view:

$$\text{Change in money supply} \longrightarrow \text{Change in NNP}$$

Monetarists feel that the weight of empirical evidence clearly supports their position. In Figure 17-1 the money supply and the money national output (PQ) are both plotted. Monetarists note the remarkably close positive correlation and conclude that the money supply is obviously the critical causal factor in determining the NNP.

Keynesians respond that *correlation* and *causation* are quite different things. Is it not possible that the changes in money GNP portrayed in Figure 17-1 were in fact caused by changes in aggregate demand, that is, in $C + I_n + G$, as suggested by the Keynesian model? And is it not also possible that the indicated growth in the national output prompted—indeed, necessitated—that businesses and consumers borrow more money over time from commercial banks in order to finance this rising volume of economic activity? In other words, Keynesians claim that causation may in fact run from aggregate demand *to* national output *to* the money supply, rather than from the money supply *to* national output as the monetarists contend. The important point, argue the Keynesians, is that the data of Figure 17-1 are as consistent with the Keynesian view as they are with the monetarist position.

We shall return momentarily to the question of the stability of V and the analytical aspects of the monetarists' transmission mechanism.

□ **The Fiscal Policy Debate**

The differences in the Keynesian and monetarist theories spill over into the area of stabilization policy.

Keynesians favor fiscal measures as the cornerstone of stabilization policy. There are two reasons for this. First and foremost, they contend that fiscal policy is a much more pow-

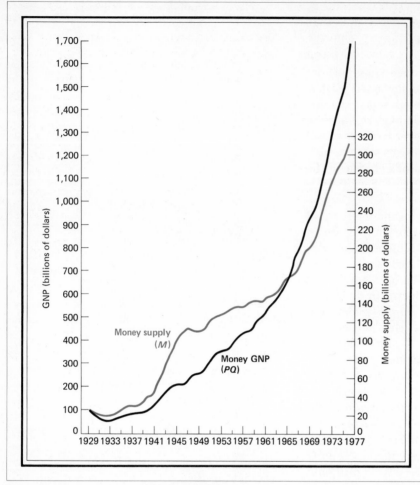

FIGURE 17-1 THE MONEY SUPPLY AND THE GNP, 1929-1976

Monetarists cite the close positive correlation between the money supply and money GNP as evidence in support of their position that money is the critical determinant of economic activity and the price level. They assume that the money supply is the "cause" and the GNP is the "effect," an assumption which Keynesians question. (*Economic Report of the President.*)

erful stabilization device than is monetary policy. This is implied by the basic equation of Keynesianism. Government spending, after all, is a direct component of aggregate demand. And taxes are only one short step removed in that tax changes allegedly affect consumption and investment in dependable and predictable ways. Second, fiscal policy can be used to remedy the microeconomic deficiencies which Keynesians perceive in the economy, but monetary policy cannot. Thus, as previously noted, an increase in government spending can simultaneously stimulate the economy *and* provide currently underproduced public goods and services. Similarly, a

tax increase imposed on the very rich can simultaneously restrain demand-pull inflation and ameliorate the degree of income inequality.

Monetarists seriously downgrade or, in the extreme, reject fiscal policy as both a reallocative and a stabilization device. First, as suggested earlier, they contend that the use of fiscal policy to do "good deeds" is usually ill-advised. For example, tax changes to promote greater income equality tend to affect adversely incentives to work, invest, and bear risks, so that the total national income "pie" is decreased to the detriment of all. Similarly, increased government spending typically results in the production of public goods and services of dubious need *or* in the public sector's usurping production which could be achieved more efficiently through the private sector's price system. Second and more important for present purposes, monetarists feel that fiscal policy is weak and ineffectual because of the *crowding-out effect* (Chapter 13). Monetarists' reasoning goes like this: Suppose government runs a budgetary deficit by selling bonds, that is, by borrowing from the public. By borrowing, they argue, government is obviously competing with private businesses for funds; that is, government borrowing will increase the demand for money, raise the interest rate, and thereby crowd out a substantial amount of private investment which otherwise would have been profitable. Hence, the net effect of a budget deficit upon aggregate demand is unpredictable and, at best, modest. So sayeth Friedman: ". . . in my opinion, the state of the budget by itself has no significant effect on the course of nominal [money] income, on inflation, on deflation, or on cyclical fluctuations."[3] Admittedly, if a deficit was financed by the issuing of new money,[4] the crowding-out effect could be avoided and the deficit would be followed by economic expansion. *But,* the monetarists point out, the expansion would be due, *not* to the fiscal deficit per se, but rather, to the creation of additional money!

Keynesians respond that investment spending is *not* particularly sensitive to changes in the interest rate—that is, the investment-demand curve has a steep slope—so that the amount of investment crowded out by the higher interest rate will be small. Hence, the net effect of a deficit will be substantial. It *is* acknowledged by Keynesians that a deficit financed by creating new money will have a greater stimulus than one financed by borrowing.

It will come as no surprise that recent stabilization efforts are accorded vastly different interpretations by Keynesians and monetarists. Consider the 1964 tax cut and the 1968 tax increase.

> The Keynesians claim that the power of fiscal policy was demonstrated by the success of the 1964 tax cut in bringing the economy up to a high level of employment. The monetarists contend . . . that it was the rapid expansion of the money supply during the months preceding the tax cut that did the job. They also point to the failure of the 1968 tax surcharge to stop inflation. The Keynesians respond by asserting that acceleration of the war in Vietnam undid the impact of the 1968 tax increase.[5]

□ **The Monetary Rule**

Although monetarists feel that the money supply is the critical determinant of the level of economic activity, most of them do *not* advise the use of easy and tight money policies to modify the "downs" and "ups" of the business cycle. Professor Friedman contends that, historically, the *discretionary* changes in the money supply made by the monetary authorities have in fact been a *destabilizing* influence in the economy. Examining the monetary history of the United States from the Civil War up to the establishment of the Federal Reserve System in 1914 and comparing this with the post-1914 record, Friedman concludes that, even if the war and immediate postwar periods are ignored, the latter period was clearly more unstable. Much of this decline in economic stability after the Federal Reserve System became effective is attributed to faulty decisions on the part of the monetary authorities; *economic instability is more a product of monetary mismanagement than of any inherent destabilizers in the economy.*

According to the monetarists, there are

---

[3]Statement by Friedman in Milton Friedman and Walter Heller, *Monetary vs. Fiscal Policy* (New York: W. W. Norton & Company, Inc., 1969), p. 51.
[4]See Chapter 13, footnote 11.

[5]Lawrence S. Ritter and William L. Silber, *Money,* 2d ed. (New York: Basic Books, Inc., Publishers, 1973), p. 150.

two important sources of monetary misman-agement. First, there is the matter of *time lags*. Although the monetary transmission mechanism is direct and straightforward, changes in the money supply have their impact upon NNP only after a rather long and varia-ble time period. Friedman's empirical work suggests that a change in the money supply may significantly change NNP in as short a period as 4 to 6 months or in as long a period as two or two and a half years! Because it is virtually impossible to predict the time lag involved in a given policy action, there is little chance of determining accurately when specific policies should be invoked or, in fact, which policy measure—easy or tight money—is ap-propriate. Indeed, given the uncertain dura-tion of this time lag, the use of discretionary monetary policy to "fine-tune" the economy for cyclical "ups" and "downs" may backfire and intensify these cyclical changes. For ex-ample, suppose an easy money policy is in-voked because the various economic indicators suggest a mild recession. But assume now that within the ensuing six months the economy, for reasons quite unrelated to public policy actions, reverses itself and moves into the prosperity-inflationary phase of the cycle. At this point in time the easy money policy be-comes effective and reinforces the inflation.

Second, monetarists argue that the mone-tary authorities have fallen into a trap by using the current level of interest rates as a guide to policy decisions. More specifically, it is argued that the Board of Governors has often tried to stabilize interest rates and in so doing they have actually made decisions of a *destabilizing* nature. Consider an example. Suppose the economy is coming out of a reces-sion and is currently approaching full employ-ment; that is, the economy is in range 2 of Figure 10-1 with aggregate demand, output, employment, and the price level all increasing. This expanding volume of economic activity will cause the demand for money to increase and therefore cause the interest rate to rise. Now, if the monetary authorities reason that

their task is to stabilize interest rates, they will embark upon an easy money policy. But this expansionary monetary policy will add to ag-gregate demand at a time when the economy is already on the verge of an inflationary boom. That is, the attempt to stabilize interest rates will fan existing inflationary fires and tend to make the economy less stable. A similar sce-nario is applicable to an economy moving into a recession.

Monetarist moral: The monetary authori-ties should stabilize, not the interest rate, but the rate of growth of the money supply. Spe-cifically, Friedman advocates legislating the *monetary rule* that the money supply be ex-panded each year at the same annual rate as the potential growth of our real GNP; that is, the supply of money should be increased steadily at 3 to 5 percent per year.[6]

> Such a rule, it is claimed, would eliminate . . . the major cause of instability in the econ-omy—the capricious and unpredictable impact of countercyclical monetary policy. As long as the money supply grows at a constant rate each year, be it 3, 4, or 5 percent, any decline into recession will only be temporary. The liquidity provided by a constantly growing money supply will cause aggregate demand to expand. Similarly, if the supply of money does not rise at a more than average rate, any inflationary increase in spending will burn itself out for lack of fuel.

Keynesian response: Despite a somewhat spotty record, it would be foolish to replace discretionary monetary policy with a mone-tary rule. Arguing that *V* is variable both cyclically and secularly, Keynesians contend that a constant annual rate of increase in the money supply could contribute to substantial fluctuations in aggregate demand and promote economic instability. As one Keynesian has quipped, the trouble with the monetary rule is that it tells the policy maker: "Don't do some-thing, just stand there."

[6]Ibid., pp. 134–135.

VELOCITY: STABLE OR UNSTABLE?

The critical theoretical issue involved in the Keynesian-monetarist debate centers on the question of whether the velocity of money, V, is stable. If it is, the equation of exchange tells us that the monetarists are indeed correct in claiming that a direct and dependable relationship exists between the money supply and the money NNP ($= PQ$). In the extreme case of an absolutely constant V, a 10 percent increase (decrease) in the money supply will result in a proportionate 10 percent increase (decrease) in PQ or money NNP. But if V is *not* stable, the Keynesian contention that money plays a secondary role in macroeconomics is valid. That is, if V is quite variable, the link between M and PQ will be loose and uncertain. (This chapter's Last Word section is a minidebate on this very issue.)

□ Empirical Evidence

The stability of V is obviously an empirical question and an appeal to "the facts" would seem sufficient to settle the issue. But, unfortunately, the facts are not easy either to discern or to interpret. For example, monetarists point to data such as those shown earlier in Figure 17-1 in support of their contention that V is stable. Given that $MV = PQ$, the close positive correlation between the money supply and PQ (money output) clearly suggests that the velocity of money is stable.

But Keynesians are unimpressed with such data. They point out that by simple manipulation of $MV = PQ$, we find that $V = PQ/M = \text{NNP}/M$. That is, we can empirically calculate the value of V by dividing each year's money output (NNP) by the money supply. Keynesians contend that the resulting data, shown in Figure 17-2, repudiate

FIGURE 17-2 THE VELOCITY OF MONEY AND THE INTEREST RATE, 1929-1976

Keynesians argue that the velocity of money varies both cyclically and secularly. Hence, they conclude that any link between a change in the money supply and the subsequent change in NNP is tenuous and uncertain. More specifically, Keynesians argue that the speculative demand for money causes the size of money balances to vary inversely with – and therefore velocity to vary directly with – the rate of interest. (*Economic Report of the President.*)

the monetarist contention that V is stable.[7] Velocity, in the Keynesian view, is variable both cyclically and secularly and these variations seriously downgrade the role of money as a determinant of output, employment, and the price level. Keynesians add this reminder: Given the large size of the money supply, a small variation in velocity can have a very substantial impact on NNP. For example, assume M is $300 billion and V is 5. A modest 10 percent increase in V will cause a $150 billion increase in money NNP! That is, MV—and therefore PQ—are initially $1500 billion ($= \$300 \cdot 5$). Now, if V increases by 10 percent to 5.5, PQ will be $1650 billion ($= MV = 5.5 \cdot 300$). Stated in terms of the issue at hand, a very small variation in V can offset a large change in M.

□   **Velocity and the Demand for Money**

Given that an appeal to the facts is inconclusive, let us consider the question of the stability of V at the level of theory.

What determines V? Most generally stated, the answer is the demand for money, that is, the amount of money which households and businesses want to hold in comparison with their incomes. If a family receives and spends, say, $10,000 per year and holds or "demands" on the average a $2500 money balance of currency and demand deposits, this means that the family is "turning over" its money 4 times a year. Velocity for this family is obviously 4. Given its $10,000 income, if it demanded and held a $4000 average money balance, V would only be $2\frac{1}{2}$. If it demanded and held only a $1000 average money balance, V would be 10. It is obvious that, given income, *velocity varies inversely with the size of the money balances held*. More specifically, the following formula is useful in determining velocity for a household:

$$\text{Velocity} = \frac{\text{annual income}}{\text{average money balance}} \quad (3)$$

[7] Ignore the interest rate data for the moment.

Hence, for our first example:

$$4 = \frac{\$10,000}{\$2500}$$

This concept of velocity is applicable to the economy as a whole. As noted earlier, simple manipulation of the equation of exchange, $MV = PQ$, tells us that $V = PQ/M$ or NNP$/M$. That is, velocity for the economy is the national output divided by the amount of money supplied and being held by households and businesses. Hence, if the economy's NNP is, say, $400 billion and households and businesses are holding an aggregate money balance (that is, money supply) of $100 billion, then velocity will be 4.

$$V = \frac{\text{NNP}}{M} = \frac{\$400}{\$100} = 4$$

□   **Monetarists: *V* Is Stable**

Monetarists are of the opinion that velocity is quite stable. They reason that money is primarily a *medium of exchange* or, stated differently, that the demand for money is basically a *transactions demand*. This implies that the absolute amount of money the public wants to hold is directly and closely linked to the aggregate volume of transactions or, in other words, to the level of NNP. Hence, the NNP$/M$ relationship—that is, V—is constant.

Monetarists stress that the size of the money balances which the public wants to hold relative to incomes is quite fixed or invariable in the short run because the relationship is determined by spending habits and such institutional factors as the length of pay periods, the availability of credit cards and other forms of short-term credit, and so forth.[8]

[8] The longer the pay period, the larger will be the average money balance held. For example, assume a family earns and spends $500 per week. If it is paid $500 weekly, its average money balance will be $250. But if it is paid $1000 biweekly, its average money balance will be $500. Short-term credit allows a person to better synchronize income and expenditures, thereby permitting a buyer to hold smaller money balances. The increasing availability of credit cards and other forms of consumer credit since

These factors change only slowly and predictably through time. For example, short-term consumer credit and credit cards have been introduced in a relatively slow, evolutionary way so as to increase *V gradually* over an extended period of time (Figure 17-2). But, all things considered, *V* is quite stable in the short run.

☐ Keynesians: *V* Is Unstable

Keynesians reason much differently. They stress that, in addition to the transactions demand for money, there is also a *speculative demand for money.* That is, beyond demanding money for the making of day-to-day purchases, households and businesses may also want to hold some of their financial wealth as money rather than securities (stocks, bonds, and so forth). Keynesians, in other words, say that money is not merely a medium of exchange, but also a *store of value;* money is one form in which financial wealth may be stored. The Keynesian position is that the size of the money balances held to satisfy the speculative demand is *not* related in any systematic way to the NNP and therefore the NNP/*M* relationship—the value of *V*—can and does vary. More precisely, *the speculative demand for money—the amount of money held as a store of value—varies inversely and significantly with the rate of interest, causing V to be unstable.*

Let us explore the Keynesian rationale in some detail. Given that securities yield interest income and idle money balances do not, it may seem foolish to hold money balances beyond the amount needed for transactions. But this is not the case when we envision the choice between securities (let us simplify and limit our discussion to bonds) and money within a context of uncertainty and speculation over future changes in the rate of interest. Thus, it makes a great deal of sense to hold money now rather than bonds *if* interest rates are expected

to be higher in the future than they are currently. Conversely, it is rational to hold bonds as wealth rather than money *if* interest rates are believed to be higher now than they are expected to be in the future.

Further explanation: Assume that at any point in time there is some interest rate which the public considers to be "normal." If the actual interest rate is currently low or "below normal," the public will choose to hold large speculative balances as opposed to bonds. Why? Because the public is speculating that the interest rate will be higher in the future— closer to "normal"—and therefore bonds will be a better buy later on than they are now. The critical point is that the larger speculative demand for money will increase the denominator of Equation (3) and thereby *decrease V.* Conversely, if the current interest rate is high, that is, "above normal," the public will choose to buy bonds and therefore hold smaller speculative balances. People will shift their financial assets from money to bonds to take advantage of the currently high interest rate. The resulting decline in the size of speculative money balances will reduce the denominator of Equation (3) and thereby *increase V.* Note that the Keynesian analysis suggests that a change in the money supply will cause a change in velocity *in the opposite direction* (Chapter 16). An increase in *M* will reduce the interest rate, the public will hold larger speculative balances, and *V* will fall. Conversely, a decrease in *M* will increase the interest rate, inducing the public to hold smaller speculative balances, and *V* will therefore rise. Therefore, a change in the money supply may or may not change aggregate demand (*MV*). Or, more realistically, the size of the change in aggregate demand and, hence, in NNP, which follows from a given change in the supply of money is unpredictable.

To summarize the Keynesian position: The amount of money which the public will want to hold for speculative purposes (as a store of value) is inversely related to the rate of interest. The velocity of money varies in-

---

World War II has been an important factor in reducing money balances in comparison with income and thereby increasing the velocity of money (Figure 17-2).

versely with the size of speculative money balances and, therefore, directly with the rate of interest. An *increase* in the interest rate will *reduce* the size of speculative money balances and therefore V will *rise*. Conversely, a *decrease* in the interest rate will *increase* the size of speculative money balances and V will therefore *fall*. Keynesians contend that empirical data support their view. Referring again to Figure 17-2, note that the velocity of money and the interest rate[9] correlate quite closely as the Keynesian analysis predicts.

□ **Monetary Policy Revisited**

It is informative to relate these two contrasting views of the demand for money and velocity to monetary policy. First, consider, say, an easy money policy in terms of the monetarist position. Assume initially that M is $100 billion and PQ or NNP is $400 billion, so that V is 4. Suppose, too, that this is an equilibrium situation in that households and businesses desire or want to hold an amount of money exactly equal to the available supply of money. Equilibrium exists because the *desired* and *actual* money supplies are equal. In the monetarist scenario, an increase of, say, $10 billion in the money supply will upset this equilibrium in that the public will now be holding more money or liquidity than it wants; the actual amount of money being held exceeds the desired amount. What happens? According to the monetarists, the excess money balances will be spent on *real assets*— that is, on consumer and investment goods. This obviously means that NNP will rise. By how much? By $40 billion. The rationale is that when NNP reaches $440 billion, the *actual* money supply will again be the amount which the public *desires* to hold and, by definition, equilibrium will be reestablished. That is, NNP will rise to $440 billion, at which the

desired level of V is restored ($V = \text{NNP}/M = \$440/\$110 = 4$). Note the alleged theoretical verification of the direct and dependable link between a change in the money supply and the subsequent change in NNP asserted earlier in the monetarist transmission mechanism.

What say the Keynesians? In terms of their conception of the transmission mechanism, they argue that an increase in the money supply will lower the interest rate. And this lower interest rate will prompt the public to hold larger speculative balances in anticipation of a higher interest rate in the future. That is, the lower interest rate will cause some significant portion of the increase in the money supply to be added to the total money balances which the public wants to hold. Hence, velocity declines, making decidedly uncertain the possible impact of the change in the money supply upon NNP. In brief, as the money supply increases, velocity changes perversely so there is no direct and dependable link between the increase in the money supply and the subsequent change in NNP.

In fact, the Keynesians go further. Although the monetarists' basic equation seems to preclude the use of fiscal policy as an effective stabilization device, Keynesians argue that this is not the case. They contend that in a monetarist framework fiscal policy is made effective through changes in V. Here is the purported scenario: Assume government embarks on an expansionary fiscal policy by increasing government spending. The resulting budget deficit is financed by government borrowing. Given the money supply, this increase in the demand for money will raise the interest rate, causing the public to hold smaller speculative money balances. This means, of course, that V will rise. In brief, in the Keynesian view, deficit spending will be "financed" by an increase in V. Therefore, even though the money supply is constant, fiscal policy *can* be effective. In terms of the monetarists' equation, given M, an expansionary fiscal policy will increase V and therefore increase the NNP.

[9]Technical note: The short-term interest rate used here is the rate on three-month Treasury bills.

☐ A Continuing Debate

Our discussion of the theoretical and policy issues raised by the Keynesian-monetarist debate only skims the surface; vigorous pursuit of these analytical and policy questions soon takes one to the mirky frontiers of economic knowledge. For several reasons we can be quite certain that this "great debate" will persist for some time to come. First, both positions are inherently plausible. "Each theory . . . provides a sensible framework for the orderly investigation of economic developments."[10] Second, the late 1960s and the 1970s have proven to be an extraordinarily turbulent "laboratory" for the testing of the two views. For example, the simultaneous inflation and unemployment of the 1970s and the external shocks caused by the OPEC oil cartel have generated an unusually complex "real world"

[10]Paul Wonnacott, *Macroeconomics* (Homewood, Ill.: Richard D. Irwin, Inc., 1974), p. 36.

in which to trace and verify or reject the policy prescriptions of either school of thought. Finally, recall that the two views are imbedded in fundamentally different ideological stances; that is, differences relate not only to facts and theories, but also to subjective value judgments.

The controversy has been healthy in the sense that it has forced economists of all persuasions to rethink some of the very fundamental aspects of macroeconomics. For example, economists and policy makers have reexamined in depth the stabilization policy-mix issue and have recognized more fully the importance of coordinating monetary and fiscal policies. While the debate goes on, it is correct to say that at the present time the Keynesian view is most widely accepted. The majority of economists seem to share the position of one prominent Keynesian who summarized his stance by asserting: "Money, yes; monetarism, no."

Summary

The following statements attempt to contrast the Keynesian and monetarist positions on a number of critical points.

1 *Ideological orientation.* The *Keynesian* view is that the price system is conducive to macroeconomic instability, the misallocation of resources, and income inequality. An activist public policy, centered upon fiscal policy, is required to remedy these shortcomings. The *monetarist* view is that public sector activities have tended to undermine the stabilizing potential of the price system and to result in wasteful, counterproductive programs for the purpose of remedying largely imagined socioeconomic ills.

2 *Analytical framework.* To *Keynesians* the basic determinant of real output, employment, and the price level is the level of aggregate demand. Hence, their basic equation is $C + I_n + G = \text{NNP}$. The components of aggregate demand are determined by a wide variety of factors which, for the most part, are unrelated to the supply of money. The basic equation of *monetarism* is the equation of exchange: $MV = PQ$. Because velocity V is basically stable, the critical determinant of real output and employment (Q) and the price level (P) is the supply of money M.

3 *Monetary policy.* *Keynesians* argue that monetary policy entails a lengthy transmission mechanism, involving monetary policy decisions, bank reserves, the interest rate, investment, and finally the NNP. Uncertainties at each step in the mechanism limit the effectiveness and dependability of monetary policy. Money matters, but its manipulation through monetary policy is not a powerful stabilization device. In terms of the monetarist framework, the presence of the speculative demand for money makes *V* unstable so that the relationship between, and the change in, the money supply and a subsequent change in NNP is uncertain and unpredictable. *Monetarists* believe that the relative stability of *V* indicates a rather tight and dependable link between the money supply and the money NNP. However, monetarists feel that because of **a.** variable time lags in becoming effective and **b.** the incorrect use of the interest rate as a guide to policy, the application of discretionary monetary policy to "fine-tune" the economy is likely to fail. In practice, monetary policy has tended to destabilize the economy. Monetarists therefore recommend a monetary rule whereby the money supply is increased in accordance with the long-term growth of real NNP.

4 *Fiscal policy.* The *Keynesian* position is that because **a.** government spending is a component of aggregate demand and **b.** tax changes have direct and dependable effects upon consumption and investment, fiscal policy is a powerful stabilization tool. *Monetarists* argue that fiscal policy is weak and uncertain in its effects. In particular, unless financed by an increase in the money supply, deficit spending will raise the interest rate and thereby crowd out private investment spending.

Questions and Study Suggestions

1   Key terms and concepts to remember: Keynesianism; monetarism; equation of exchange; crowding-out effect; monetary rule; velocity of money; medium of exchange; store of value; transactions demand for money; speculative demand for money.

2   Explain: "The debate between Keynesians and monetarists is an important facet of the larger controversy over the role of government in our lives."

3   State and explain the basic equations of Keynesianism and monetarism. Can you "translate" the Keynesian equation into the monetarist equation?

4   What is the transmission mechanism for monetary policy according to **a.** Keynesians and **b.** monetarists? What significance do the two schools of thought apply to money and monetary policy as a determinant of economic activity? According to monetarism, what happens when the actual supply of money exceeds the amount of money which the public wants to hold?

5   Why do monetarists recommend that a "monetary rule" be substituted for discretionary monetary policy? Explain: "One cannot assess what monetary policy is doing by just looking at interest rates." Indicate how an attempt to stabilize interest rates can be destabilizing.

6   Explain why monetarists feel fiscal policy is weak and ineffective. Explain through the equation of exchange how Keynesians reach the conclusion that fiscal policy is strong and effective.

7   Indicate the precise relationship between the demand for money and the velocity of money. Discuss in detail: "The crucial issue separating Keynesians from monetarists is whether or not the demand for money is sensitive to changes in the rate of interest." Explain the Keynesian contention that a change in *M* is likely to be accompanied by a change in *V* in the opposite direction.

8   Explain and evaluate these statements in terms of the Keynesian-monetarist controversy:

a. "If the national goal is to raise income, it can be achieved only by raising the money supply."

b. "The size of a Federal budget deficit is not important. What is important is how the deficit is financed."

c. "There is no reason in the world why, in an equation like $MV = PQ$, the V should be thought to be independent of the rate of interest. There is every plausible reason for the velocity of circulation to be a systematic and increasing function of the rate of interest."

Selected References

Friedman, Milton, and Walter W. Heller: *Monetary vs. Fiscal Policy* (New York: W. W. Norton & Company, Inc., 1969).

Heller, Walter W.: *The Economy: Old Myths and New Realities* (New York: W. W. Norton & Company, Inc., 1976).

Humphrey, Thomas M.: "The Quantity Theory of Money: Its Historical Evolution and Role in Policy Debates," *Economic Review* (Federal Reserve Bank of Richmond), May–June 1974, pp. 2–19.

Hutchinson, Harry D.: *Money, Banking, and the United States Economy,* 3d ed. (Englewood Cliffs, N.J.: Prentice-Hall, Inc., 1975), chap. 16.

Lindert, Peter H.: *Prices, Jobs, and Growth: An Introduction to Macroeconomics* (Boston: Little, Brown and Company, 1976), chap. 10.

Ritter, Lawrence S., and William L. Silber: *Money,* 2d ed. (New York: Basic Books, Inc., Publishers, 1973), chaps. 2, 4.

Wonnacott, Paul: *Macroeconomics* (Homewood, Ill.: Richard D. Irwin, Inc., 1974), chap. 10.

Last Word
Inflation: A Monetary Phenomenon?

How "tight" is the relationship between the money supply and the price level? The monetarist view, expressed here by Milton Friedman, is that the relationship is tight and dependable. The second and more eclectic view, stated by Lawrence S. Ritter and William L. Silber, is that the relationship is loose and undependable.

Monetarist view:. . . the central fact is that inflation is always and everywhere a monetary phenomenon. Historically, substantial changes in prices have always occurred together with substantial changes in the quantity of money relative to output. I know of no exception to this generalization, no occasion in the United States or elsewhere when prices have risen substantially without a substantial rise in the quantity of money relative to output or when the quantity of money has risen substantially relative to output without a substantial rise in prices. And there are numerous confirming examples. Indeed, I doubt that there is any other empirical generalization in economics for which there is as much organized evidence covering so wide a range of space and time.

Some confirming examples are extremely dramatic and illustrate vividly how important the quantity of money is by comparison with everything else. After the Russian Revolution of 1917, there was a hyperinflation in Russia when a new currency was introduced and printed in large quantities. Ultimately, it became almost valueless. All the time, some currency was circulating which had been issued by the prerevolutionary Czarist government. The Czarist government was out of power. Nobody expected it to return to power. Yet, the value of the Czarist currency remained roughly constant in terms of goods and rose sharply in terms of the Bolshevik currency. Why? Because there was nobody to print any more of it. It was fixed in quantity and therefore it retained its value. Another story has to do with the United States Civil War. Toward the end of the war, the Union troops overran the place where the Confederates had been printing paper money to finance the war. In the course of moving to a new location, there was a temporary cessation of the printing of money. As a result, there was also a temporary interruption in the price rise that had been proceeding merrily.

Eclectic view:. . . money is not so clearly and uniquely the culprit when it comes to the real problem of our times, creeping inflation. The "fit" between the money supply and the cost of living exists, but it is rather loose and a bit baggy.

Take, for example, the last four decades:

1 From the end of 1930 to the end of 1940, the money supply increased by 70 percent, but prices, instead of rising, fell 15 percent.

2 From 1940 to 1950, the money supply increased by 175 percent, but prices rose by only 80 percent, less than half as much.

3 From the end of 1950 to the end of 1960 provides the best fit; the money supply grew by about 25 percent and the consumer price index rose by about 20 percent.

4 However, from 1960 through 1970 the relationship sags again; the money supply increased by 40 percent, but prices by just 20 percent.

Even the close relationship during the 1950s turns out to be less impressive upon further examination. During the first half of the decade the money supply increased twice as fast as prices, while during the second half prices increased twice as rapidly as the money supply. At the end of the 1960s, the money supply was about $4\frac{1}{2}$ times larger than it had been in 1940, but prices were "only" about $2\frac{1}{2}$ times higher. . . .

Over the long run, an increase in the money supply is a *necessary* condition for the continuation of inflation, creeping or otherwise.

But it is not a *sufficient* condition. Increases in the money supply do not always result in inflation.

Milton Friedman, "What Price Guideposts?" in George P. Shultz and Robert Z. Aliber, eds., *Guidelines, Informal Controls, and the Market Place* (Chicago: The University of Chicago Press, 1966), pp. 25–26, © 1966 by The University of Chicago; Lawrence S. Ritter and William L. Silber, *Money,* 2d ed. (New York: Basic Books, Inc., Publishers, 1973), pp. 67–68, abridged.

18

Unemployment and Inflation: New Problems and New Policies

In the mid-1960s the American economy was healthy and expanding. Furthermore, political leaders and the public had great confidence in the knowledge and policy prescriptions of economists. The great tax cut of 1964 had increased output and employment and accelerated the growth of real GNP as Keynesian economists had predicted. In 1965 inflation was virtually absent; the price level increased that year by only 1.9 percent. Furthermore, the economy was practically at full employment. But the past ten or twelve years have been turbulent for the economy. In the 1970s we have been faced with the worst of all possible macroeconomic worlds. Specifically, *stagflation*—the stagnation of output and employment coupled with inflation—has been the paramount problem of the 1970s. The inability of economists to satisfactorily explain this problem—much less resolve it through policy recommendations—has shaken the public's confidence in economists and their policy recommendations.

The present chapter attempts to explain this turnabout. Specific goals are as follows:

1 The so-called Phillips Curve is introduced to explain stagflation, that is, the possible coexistence of unemployment and inflation.

2 We next consider policies other than traditional fiscal and policy measures which might be used to alleviate the problem of stagflation.

3 The economic developments of the 1960s and 1970s are surveyed to indicate the challenges which these events have posed for

371

macroeconomic theory in general and the Phillips Curve concept in particular.

4 Finally, we briefly ponder some lessons and controversial issues which have evolved from the turbulent economic events of the past decade.

Warning: This chapter deals with important, unsettled questions in modern economics; therefore, although opinions and judgments are plentiful, unassailable evidence and clear-cut policy prescriptions are scarce.

■ DEMAND-PULL INFLATION

Inflation has been regarded traditionally as the consequence of excess total demand. Recall our aggregate demand–aggregate supply approach to income determination in terms of Figure 12-5. We reasoned that if aggregate demand is initially deficient at $(C + I_n)_2$, the economy will experience unemployment. But the use of expansionary fiscal and monetary policies can be used to shift the aggregate demand schedule upward to $(C + I_n)_0$, closing the recessionary gap and establishing full employment. Our *assumption* has been that the expansion of aggregate demand up to the full-employment level would increase employment and real output, *but leave the price level unchanged*. Hence, the "right" level of aggregate demand—$(C + I_n)_0$ in Figure 12-5—would give us the best of all possible macroeconomic worlds wherein society enjoyed full employment *and* price level stability simultaneously.

Demand-pull inflation occurs when the economy attempts to spend beyond its capacity to produce. In popular jargon, demand-pull inflation occurs when "too much money is chasing too few goods." If aggregate demand is in excess of the economy's full-employment output (as valued at current or existing prices), an *inflationary gap* will exist; $(C + I_n)_1$ entails such a gap in Figure 12-5. Because the economy already is at full employment and operating at a point on its production possibilities curve, real output is fixed and cannot be ex-

panded in response to this excess demand; hence, the excess of total demand will have the effect of pulling up the price level.[1]

These comments can be succinctly restated in terms of the monetarists' equation of exchange $(MV = PQ)$. Assuming unemployment initially, an expanding aggregate demand (MV) will cause real output (Q) to rise but leave the price level (P) unchanged. But once full employment is reached, Q becomes constant or fixed and any further expansion of MV will simply pull up P.

The assumed compatibility of full employment and price level stability can be demonstrated graphically in Figure 18-1. Here we show the annual rate of inflation on the left

---

[1] Recall from Chapter 12 the dynamic character of the inflationary process. In particular, a rising price level *may* have feedback effects on both consumption and investment spending and thereby accelerate through time. This means that a new equilibrium with price level stability may *not* be realized at $510 billion, as Figure 12-5 implies.

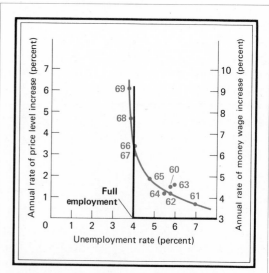

FIGURE 18-1 PRICE LEVEL-UNEMPLOYMENT RELATIONSHIPS

The blue curve is drawn on the assumption that full employment and price level stability are compatible goals. The brown Phillips Curve, which is fitted to data for the 1960s, suggests there is a trade-off between unemployment and inflation.

vertical axis[2] and the unemployment rate on the horizontal axis. We assume, for reasons given in Chapter 10, that "full employment" exists when no more than 4 percent of the labor force is unemployed. The blue L-shaped line with the right-angle kink at full employment reflects the assumption that full employment and price level stability are compatible.[3] Hence, starting with a severe recession where unemployment is 8 or 9 percent, increases in aggregate demand would have the sole effect of *reducing* the unemployment rate and thereby *increasing* real output (Q) until full employment is achieved; the price level (P) would remain constant up to the 4 percent full-employment point. As aggregate demand rises beyond that required for full employment and thereby becomes excess demand, the sole consequence would be increases in the price level (P); real output (Q) would remain constant at the full-employment level.

The demand-pull theory of inflation is widely accepted by economists, and over the years it has provided a useful and reasonably accurate explanation of many of our inflationary experiences. For example, the inflationary pressures of World War II, although partially suppressed by wage and price controls, were explainable in terms of demand-pull. So was most of the postwar inflation of the late 1940s, the inflation associated with the Korean war, and the inflation of 1966–1968.

THE PHILLIPS CURVE: PREMATURE INFLATION

Unfortunately, the experience of the United States and other advanced capitalistic nations suggests that this simplistic demand-pull scenario is an incomplete explanation of inflation. At times the economy has encountered signif-

icant increases in the price level *before* full employment has been achieved; that is, inflation has occurred *before* aggregate demand became excessive.

These events prompted economists to reexamine the problem of inflation in an effort to determine whether such episodes were "special cases" or whether "premature inflation" was a fact of economic life. The resulting pioneering empirical work of the late 1950s and 1960s on the relationship between the rate of unemployment and the rate of inflation yielded the so-called Phillips Curve,[4] which seems to confirm that the price level typically does rise *before* full employment is achieved.

Consider again Figure 18-1 wherein the rate of increase in the price index and the corresponding unemployment rate in the United States have been plotted for the 1960s. The brown Phillips Curve fitted to these data points suggests an unfortunate relationship: Low rates of unemployment seem to be associated with high rates of inflation and, conversely, price stability or low rates of inflation apparently are associated with high rates of unemployment. In short, there seems to be a trade-off between employment and the price level.[5] Specifically, these data suggest that to achieve full employment—defined as 4 percent of the labor force unemployed (Chapter 10)—society must endure an accompanying inflation on the order of a 3 or $3\frac{1}{2}$ percent annual increase in the price level. Conversely, the achievement of near price level stability requires the existence of an unemployment rate of about 6 or 7 percent. Most importantly, note that the Phillips Curve provides an explanation of the simultaneous existence of inflation and unemployment.

---

[2] Ignore the right vertical axis for the moment.
[3] This assumption has been implicit throughout all our earlier analysis with the exception of the brief discussion surrounding Figure 10-1 and the concluding section of Chapter 12.

[4] Named after the British economist A. W. Phillips, who developed this concept. See his "The Relationship between Unemployment and the Rate of Change in Money Wage Rates in the United Kingdom, 1862–1957," *Economica*, November 1958, pp. 283–299.
[5] You may remember the notion of premature inflation as presented earlier in Figure 10-1, which is simply the Phillips Curve trade-off "flopped over" graphically.

☐ Logic of the Phillips Curve

How can the Phillips Curve be explained? What causes the unfortunate trade-off between full employment and price level stability? Basically, there are two sets of complementary considerations which explain premature inflation.

1   Labor Market Imbalances   A partial explanation lies in certain imbalances—"bottlenecks" and structural problems—which arise in labor markets as the economy expands toward full employment. The basic point here is that "the" labor market in the United States in fact comprises an extremely large number of individual labor markets which are stratified and distinct both occupationally and geographically. This labor market diversity suggests that, as the economy expands, full employment will *not* be realized simultaneously in each individual labor market. While full employment and labor shortages may exist for some occupations and some areas, unemployment will persist for other occupations and regions. To illustrate: In 1971 the overall unemployment rate was 5.9 percent. But the unemployment rate for professional and technical workers was only 2.9 percent, while the rate for all blue-collar workers was 7.4 percent. Furthermore, within the blue-collar classification, common laborers experienced an unemployment rate of almost 11 percent, while the rate for craftsmen and foremen was only 4.7 percent. Similarly, unemployment was unusually high in California (7.0 percent), Michigan (8.2 percent), and Washington (10.9 percent), partially because of reductions in military-space expenditures. This disparity means that in an expanding economy, even though the overall unemployment rate may be 5 or 6 percent, scarcities will develop for specific kinds of labor and for labor in certain geographic areas, and the wage rates of such workers will rise. Rising wage rates mean higher costs and necessitate higher prices. The net result is rising prices even though overall unemployment persists.

It is fair to ask why labor market adjustments do not eliminate these bottleneck problems. Why, for example, do not unemployed laborers become craftworkers? The answer, of course, is that such shifts cannot be made with sufficient speed to eliminate labor market bottlenecks. The training for a new occupation is costly in terms of both time and money. Furthermore, even if he has the ability, time, and money to acquire the needed skills and to relocate, an unemployed laborer in Kalamazoo may just not be aware of the shortage of skilled craftworkers in Kenosha. Then, too, artificial restrictions upon the shiftability of workers sustain structural imbalances. For example, discrimination on the basis of race, ethnic background, or sex can keep qualified workers from acquiring available positions. Similarly, licensing requirements and union restrictions upon the number of available apprenticeships inhibit the leveling out of imbalances between specific labor markets. An unemployed real estate salesman or beautician in Kankakee may be unable to take an available job a relatively short distance away in Keokuk, if licensing requirements in Illinois and Iowa are significantly different. In brief, labor market adjustments are neither sufficiently rapid nor complete enough to prevent production costs and product prices from rising *before* overall full employment is achieved.

2   Market Power: Cost-Push Inflation   A complementary explanation of the Phillips Curve is based upon the assumption that labor unions and big businesses both possess significant amounts of monopoly or market power with which to raise wages and prices and that this power becomes easier to exert as the economy approaches full employment. Hence, the "wage-push" or "cost-push" inflationary scenario goes something like this: As the economy moves toward full employment, labor markets tighten and unions become more aggressive in their wage demands. Furthermore, increasing prosperity will tend to enhance the willingness of businesses to grant union wage demands. On the one hand, firms will hesitate to resist union demands and risk a costly strike at the very time when business activity is becoming increasingly profitable. On the other hand, economic expansion provides a favorable environment in which monopoly power can be used to pass wage increases on to consumers in the form of higher product prices.

Alternatively, market-power inflation may be "profit-push"; that is, inflation may be initiated by businesses as they seek higher profit margins. Large corporations which have the ability to manipulate or administer their prices may decide to increase prices to expand profits. Whether wage-push, profit-push, or some combination of the two is responsible, the result is a rising price level in the absence of excess aggregate demand.

☐   The Wage Rate–Productivity Nexus

It is important to recognize at this point that not all increases in money wage rates are destined to be inflationary. *Only money wage increases which are greater than average productivity increases will cause labor costs per unit of output to rise.* This becomes clear once it is recognized that labor cost per unit of output, L, is equal to the money wage rate, W, divided by the average productivity of labor, P_L. That is, L, equals W/P_L. Consider a simple example. Suppose that the productivity (output) of labor per hour is 10 units. If the wage rate is $5.00 per hour, the labor cost *per unit of output* is obviously $0.50 (= $5.00/10). If both W and P_L now increase at the same percentage rate, L will be constant. If productivity and wage rates both rise, say, by 10 percent, labor cost per unit of output will remain at $0.50 (= $5.50/11). However, if the wage rate increases by, say, 20 percent while productivity rises by only 10 percent, then labor cost per unit of output will rise to approximately

$0.55 (= $6.00/11). The important point for immediate purposes is that increases in wage rates must exceed productivity increases in order to increase labor costs per unit of output and be inflationary.

Look back at Figure 18-1 once again and consider the right-hand vertical axis which measures the annual percentage increase in wage rates. Observe that the difference in the left-hand (price) scale and the right-hand (wage rate) scale is the assumed 3 percent annual average increase in labor productivity. Hence, as our example indicates, a 3 percent increase in wage rates (right axis) translates into a constant, or "0 percent change," in the price level (left axis). Why? Because the assumed 3 percent average increase in labor productivity "absorbs" the 3 percent increase in wage rates; therefore, unit labor costs and product prices remain unchanged. Similarly, a 5 percent average increase in wage rates is only partially offset by the 3 percent labor productivity increase, so unit labor costs and prices will rise by 2 percent, and so on. All this assumes that firms do *not* attempt to expand their profit margins but merely allow higher unit labor costs to "pass through" to the consumer.

☐   Stabilization Policy Dilemma

The Phillips Curve embodies a serious policy dilemma because traditional fiscal and monetary policies merely alter aggregate demand and therefore do nothing to correct the labor market imbalances and the market power which bring forth premature inflation. More specifically, the manipulation of aggregate demand through fiscal and monetary measures simply has the effect of moving the economy *along* the given Phillips Curve. Hence, the expansionary fiscal policy and the easy money policy which combine to boost aggregate demand and bring full employment will simultaneously entail inflation. Point A on the Phillips Curve of Figure 18-2 is illustrative. Conversely, a restrictive fiscal policy and a tight money policy can be used to achieve price level stability, but only at the cost of excessive unemployment and forgone production. Point *B* in Figure 18-2 is relevant. *Traditional macroeconomic policies can be used to manipulate aggregate demand and thereby to choose a point on the Phillips Curve, but such policies do not improve upon the "unemployment rate–rate of inflation" menu embodied in the Phillips Curve.* What has eluded recent United States fiscal and monetary policies is the outcome suggested by point *C* in Figure 18-2 where full employment and price stability are simultaneously attained.

NEW POLICY OPTIONS

These circumstances have led most of the advanced capitalist nations, including the United States, to supplement traditional macroeconomic policy with additional policies designed to shift the Phillips Curve leftward to a more desirable position, that is, to a position wherein full employment and price level stability are more compatible. The broken Phillips Curve in Figure 18-2 is illustrative. Generally speaking, two categories of policies have been proposed: *market policies* and *wage-price policies*.

☐ **Market Policies**

Market policies are designed to eliminate the underlying causes of the Phillips Curve. Two kinds of market policies can be distinguished. *Manpower policy* is intended to reduce or eliminate imbalances and bottlenecks in labor markets. A *procompetition policy* attempts to reduce the market power of unions and large corporations.

Manpower Policy The goal of manpower policy is to improve the efficiency of labor markets so that any given level of aggregate demand will be associated with a lower level of unemployment. In other words, the purpose of manpower policy is to achieve a better match-

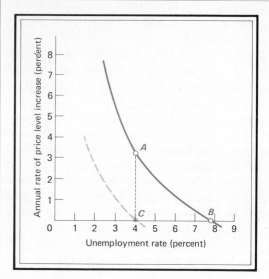

FIGURE 18-2 THE PHILLIPS CURVE AND PUBLIC POLICY

The Phillips Curve poses a cruel dilemma in that fiscal and monetary policies force society to accept inflation in order to achieve full employment (point *A*) or to accept unemployment to achieve price level stability (point *B*). As a result, many societies have experimented with market policies and wage-price policies designed to shift the Phillips Curve leftward, as indicated by the broken curve, so as to make full employment and price level stability compatible goals (point *C*).

ing of workers to jobs, thereby reducing labor market imbalances. Successful manpower policies will shift the Phillips Curve to the left. Several different kinds of programs will provide a better matching of workers to jobs.

1 Programs of vocationally oriented education and training will permit marginal and displaced workers to be more quickly reemployed. The Manpower Development and Training Act (MDTA) of 1962 is the landmark piece of legislation in this area in that it provides for both institutional and on-the-job training for the unemployed, for disadvantaged youth, and for older workers whose skills are meager or obsolete.[6]

[6]The Act also requires the publication of an annual *Manpower Report of the President* which discusses labor-force developments and problems and contains descriptions of major manpower programs.

2 A second type of manpower policy is concerned with improving the flow of job information between unemployed workers and potential employers and with enhancing the geographic mobility of workers. For example, a number of proposals have been made in recent years to modernize the United States Employment Service in order to increase its effectiveness in bringing job seekers and employers together. Similarly, various pieces of Federal legislation have experimented with subsidies to help defray the relocation costs of workers who are willing to move from high-unemployment areas to more prosperous regions. Programs have also been legislated to help revitalize economically depressed areas, such as the Appalachia region which has suffered from shrinking employment opportunities in both mining and agriculture.

3 Another facet of manpower policy is concerned with the reduction or elimination of artificial obstacles to employment. Prejudice and discrimination have been an important roadblock in the matching of workers and jobs; discrimination is a basic factor in explaining why unemployment rates for blacks are roughly twice as high as for whites. The Civil Rights Act of 1964 attempts to improve manpower utilization by removing discrimination because of race, religion, sex, or ethnic background as an obstacle to employment or union membership.

By their very nature, these programs are not easily evaluated. Because they generally involve disadvantaged individuals with little education who have been discouraged by past job market experiences, the expectation of sudden and spectacular success is perhaps unwarranted. On the other hand, there is small doubt that these manpower programs reflect a realistic appraisal of what must be done if America's employment and price stability records are to be improved.

Procompetition Policy A second avenue for improving the unemployment rate–rate of inflation trade-off is to reduce the monopoly or market power of unions and businesses. The contention here is that the monopoly power of unions must be reduced so that they will be less able to push up wage rates ahead of average productivity increases. Similarly, more competition in the product market will reduce the discretionary power of large corporations to raise prices.

How can the economy be made more competitive? A basic recommendation is to apply our existing antitrust (antimonopoly) laws much more vigorously to big businesses and to remove existing legal restrictions upon entry to certain regulated industries (Chapter 34). Similarly, the elimination of tariffs and other restrictions upon foreign imports will tend to increase the competitiveness of American markets. On the labor front, it is periodically argued that the antimonopoly laws should be applied to unions. Another proposal is that unions should be prohibited from bargaining on a centralized, nationwide level, forcing each local union to bargain with its immediate employer. This decentralization of union power and authority, it is hoped, would ameliorate cost-push inflationary pressures.

But serious questions can be raised about such proposals. In the first place, political realities are such that any administration is unlikely to undertake a vigorous antimonopoly or antiunion crusade. Antitrust legislation has been a fact of life in the United States for almost a century, yet there is no clear answer on whether it has significantly retarded the growth of monopoly, much less increased competition. Indeed, some economists feel that large monopolistic corporations are necessary if the economy is to enjoy the economies of mass production and a high rate of technological progress. Hence, although an effective antimonopoly policy might be helpful in containing cost-push inflation, it might also entail diminished productive efficiency now and in the future. Nor is it at all clear that antitrust policies can be applied to labor without virtually destroying unions and the institution of collective bargaining. Unions and collective bargaining perform a number of desirable functions for workers which would be largely sacrificed by a campaign that reduces the bargaining power of unions. Finally, there is little compelling evidence to suggest that localized wage setting results in more socially acceptable wage rates than does centralized bargaining. Indeed, interlocal union rivalries, petty grievances, and limited ability to envision social consequences may all tend to make local bargaining more aggressive and potentially more inflationary than centralized bargaining.

□ **Wage-Price Policies**

A second general approach to the Phillips Curve dilemma accepts the existence of monopoly power and labor market imbalances as more-or-less inevitable facts of economic life, and seeks to alter the behavior of labor and product-market monopolists so as to make their wage and price decisions more compatible with the twin goals of full employment and price level stability. Although they differ primarily in degree, it is meaningful to distinguish between wage-price *guideposts* and wage-price *controls*. In essence, guideposts and controls differ in that the former rely upon the voluntary cooperation of labor and business, whereas the latter have the force of law.

Wage-price guideposts and wage-price controls are sometimes called *incomes policies*. The reason for this label is that a person's real income—the amount of goods and services one can obtain with one's money income—obviously depends upon the size of that money income and the prices of the goods and services he or she buys. Guideposts and controls are designed to constrain both money incomes and prices paid, thereby affecting real incomes.

Wage-Price Guideposts: Voluntary Restraints In the period from 1962 to 1966, the Kennedy and Johnson administrations attempted to shift the Phillips Curve to the left by setting forth "guideposts for noninflation-

ary wage and price behavior."[7] The guideposts were essentially a set of wage and price rules which, if followed by labor and management, would prevent the occurrence of premature inflation.

1 Wage guidepost The basic wage guidepost was that wage rates *in all industries* should rise in accordance with the rate of increase in labor productivity for the nation as a whole. The rationale of this guidepost is that if the average hourly output of workers increases by, say, 3 percent, then employers can raise money wage rates by 3 percent without experiencing any overall increase in labor costs per unit of output. Of course, the productivity increases of some industries will exceed, while those of others will fall short of, the overall or average increase in national productivity. Hence, for an industry whose productivity rises by less than national productivity, unit labor costs will rise. For example, if national productivity rose by 3 percent while productivity rose by only 1 percent in industry X, then, with money wage rates increasing by 3 percent, that industry would experience approximately a 2 percent *increase* in its unit labor costs. Conversely, if productivity rose by 5 percent in industry Y, then the 3 percent increase in money wages would *decrease* unit labor costs by about 2 percent.

2 Price guidepost The basic price guidepost was that prices should change to compensate for changes in unit labor costs. This meant that in industries whose rate of productivity was equal to the national average, prices would be constant because unit labor costs would be unchanged. For industries where productivity rose by less than the national average, prices could be increased by enough to cover the resulting increase in unit labor costs. Industry X, cited earlier, could increase its prices by 2 percent. For industries wherein productivity increases exceeded the

---

[7] *Economic Report of the President, 1962* (Washington), pp. 185–190.

national average, prices would be expected to fall in accordance with the resulting decline in unit labor costs. Industry Y should lower its prices by 2 percent. These price increases and decreases would cancel out and leave the overall price level unchanged.

The guidepost approach was implemented through the use of moral suasion, or what skeptics have labeled an "open mouth" or "jawbone" policy. The President, the Secretary of Labor, and other high administration officials addressed appeals and admonitions to labor and business leaders, urging them to be "socially responsible" by exercising self-restraint in reaching wage-price decisions. In practice, moral suasion was sometimes supplemented by ad hoc measures: for example, threats of antitrust investigation or the abolition of protective tariffs for potential offenders.

Wage-Price Controls: Mandatory Restraints

Wage-price controls have typically been a wartime phenomenon in the United States. Thus, during World War II, controls were widely used to repress inflationary pressures. In 1971, however, peacetime controls were introduced as a part of President Nixon's New Economic Policy. Faced with stagflation—an unfortunate combination of unemployment and rising prices—taxes were cut by some $7 to $8 billion to stimulate aggregate demand and, it was hoped, output and employment. The problem, however, was to prevent this expansionary fiscal policy from being translated into additional inflation rather than into increases in employment and real output. The Nixon response was to invoke authority, given him under the Economic Stabilization Act of 1970, in ordering a 90-day freeze on wages, prices, and rents. More precisely, the President's Executive order made it illegal to (1) increase wages or salaries, (2) charge more for a product than the highest price charged in the 30-day period prior to the freeze, and (3) raise the rents landlords charged tenants.

The Wage-Price Policy Debate

There has been heated and prolonged debate in the United States as to the desirability and efficacy of incomes policies. The debate centers on three points.

1   Workability and compliance   Critics argue that the voluntary *guideposts* approach is doomed to failure because it asks business and labor leaders to abandon their primary functions and to forgo the goals of maximum profits and higher wages. A union leader will not gain favor with the rank and file by not insisting on attainable wage increases; nor does a corporate official become endeared to stockholders by bypassing potentially profitable price increases. For these reasons little voluntary cooperation can be expected from labor and management.

Wage and price *controls* have the force of law and, therefore, labor and management can be forced to obey. Nevertheless, problems of enforcement and compliance can be severe, particularly if wage and price controls are quite comprehensive and if they are maintained for an extended time. The basic problem is that, over time, strong economic incentives develop to evade controls. For example, it can be highly profitable to violate controls upon products and resources which are particularly scarce. The reason is that to be effective, the maximum legal price will be less than the free-market price; therefore, it will be profitable to violate the controls. Hence, it is not surprising that, despite strong patriotic motivation for compliance and the sizable enforcement bureaucracy which accompanied the World War II controls, illegal *black markets*—wherein prices were above legal limits—flourished for many products.

Furthermore, firms can effectively circumvent price controls by lowering the quality or size of their product. If the price of a candy bar is frozen at 15 cents, its price can be effectively doubled by reducing its size by one half!

Proponents of incomes policies respond that available evidence suggests such policies have been workable. Admittedly, the problem of measuring empirically the effectiveness of guidelines or controls is complex. Nevertheless, some important statistical studies suggest that the guideposts did make at least a modest contribution to wage-price stability in the middle 1960s.[8] Furthermore, the rate of inflation did decline perceptibly after the imposition of the wage-price freeze in 1971. And most economists would agree that the use of direct wage-price controls during World War II did contain—or at least defer—the serious inflation which would otherwise have occurred. In general, although wage-price policies may encounter problems of compliance and workability when applied over an extended period, proponents contend there is reason to believe that such policies can be helpful in controlling short-term episodes of premature inflation.

2   Allocative efficiency Opponents of incomes policies contend that effective guideposts or controls interfere with the allocative function of the price system. The crucial point is that product and resource prices must be allowed to fluctuate freely and fully in response to changing market conditions—that is, to changes in demand, changes in resource supplies, and changes in technology—in order for allocative efficiency to be sustained through time (Chapter 5). Effective price controls would prohibit the market system from making these adjustments. For example, if an increase in the demand for some product should occur, its price could *not* rise to signal society's wish for more output and therefore more resources in this area of production. In fact, controls strip the market mechanism of its rationing function, that is, of its ability to equate quantity demanded and quantity supplied, and product shortages will result. Question: Which buyers are to obtain the product and which are to do without? One possibility is that the product can be rationed on a first-come–first-serve basis or by favoritism. But

this is likely to be highly arbitrary and inequitable; those who are first in line or those able to cultivate a friendship with the seller get as much of the product as they want while others get none at all. In the interest of equity, government may have to undertake the task of rationing the product to consumers. This was done for a wide variety of products during World War II by issuing ration coupons to buyers on an equitable basis. Note, however, that governmental rationing contributes to the compliance-bureaucracy problem noted earlier.

Defenders of incomes policies respond as follows: If effective guideposts or controls are imposed upon a competitive economy, then in time the resulting rigidities will undoubtedly impair allocative efficiency. But is it correct to assume that resource allocation will be efficient in the absence of a wage-price policy? After all, cost-push inflation arises *because* big labor and big businesses possess monopoly power and consequently have the capacity to distort the allocation of resources. In short, it is not at all clear that a wage-price policy would further distort resource allocation in an economy already characterized by monopoly and allocative inefficiency. In fact, if guideposts or controls are specifically applied to those industries characterized by monopoly, it can be plausibly argued that allocative efficiency may be improved.[9]

3   The freedom issue Libertarians are quick to point out that guideposts and controls seriously conflict with freedom of action. Restraints upon wage and price decisions are obviously coercive and therefore at odds with the capitalistic ideology's insistence upon free markets and prices. Guideposts and controls move society "in an authoritarian direction" and in effect create a new and more crucial trade-off problem between the goal of full employment with price stability, on the one hand, and freedom of choice, on the other.

Proponents of incomes policies respond

---

[8]John Sheahan, *The Wage-Price Guideposts* (Washington: The Brookings Institution, 1967), chap. 7.

[9]This assertion will be explained in Chapter 27 in the section on "Regulated Monopoly."

that free economic decision making is not an unmitigated good. Certainly, free choices which promote socially desirable ends are to be protected. Hence, freedom of choice is virtuous within the context of a competitive price system because the "invisible hand" is effectively at work to translate free choices based upon self-interest into socially desirable outcomes (Chapter 5). But the discretionary decisions of unions and business monopolists which are the target of wage-price policies are clearly not of this type. When the market system is characterized by monopoly, the "invisible hand" fumbles the ball so that decisions made on the basis of self-interest are at odds with the social interest. More specifically, free decisions by monopolists in the pursuit of private gain may come at the expense of price level stability and allocative efficiency. Incomes policy proponents contend that social control of such antisocial decision making makes sense both economically and philosophically.[10]

A final point: The validity of the criticisms of wage-price policy depends upon the rigidity, comprehensiveness, and duration of such a policy. A "loose," informal, flexible policy applied to a few key sectors of the economy for a relatively short period should wreak little havoc on resource allocation and economic freedom. But an inflexible, "no exceptions" system applied comprehensively to the entire economy for an extended time would clearly raise serious problems. The dilemma, of course, is that the informal and flexible system may be inadequate to the task of effectively improving upon the unemployment rate–rate of inflation options available to society.

Penalties and Rewards Some economists have argued the effectiveness of a wage-price guidepost program would be enhanced if it embraced a clear-cut system of penalties for noncompliance or rewards for compliance.

For example, a special *excess wage settlement tax* might be imposed upon firms which grant inflationary wage increases in excess of, say, the 3 percent indicated by the guidepost. The more the wage increase exceeds 3 percent, the larger would be the special surtax on the firm's profits. The purpose of the tax would be to stiffen management's resistance to union wage demands and thus to result in collective bargaining agreements more conducive to price stability. Proponents of the plan argue that it could be made effective without the need for a new and costly administrative bureaucracy; that it does not call for radical institutional surgery on either unions or businesses; that it is quite compatible with the market system; and, even more important, that it would work.[11]

Another suggestion, the *real wage insurance plan,* calls for government to exempt workers and employers from a portion of their social security (payroll) taxes if they voluntarily obey stated wage and price guideposts. That is, government would reward them for compliance by paying a part of their payroll tax out of general tax revenues. Government would also guarantee participants that, if the consumer price index were to increase in excess of some specified amount, those who obeyed the guideposts would be reimbursed through a tax credit. The intent of this program is that, if the fear that their real incomes will be eroded by inflation is alleviated or removed, workers and businesses will be willing to constrain their wage demands and price policies.

■ ─────────────────────────────

STAGFLATION: THE AWKWARD SEVENTIES

The Phillips Curve and its implications were the focal point of macroeconomics in the 1960s. The unemployment-inflation trade-off

─────────────────────────────

[10]Jerry E. Pohlman, *Inflation Under Control?* (Reston, Va.: Reston Publishing Company, Inc., 1976), pp. 154–156.

[11]For details, see Sidney Weintraub, "An Incomes Policy to Stop Inflation," *Lloyds Bank Review,* January 1971, pp. 1–12; and Henry C. Wallich and Sidney Weintraub, "A Tax-based Incomes Policy," *Journal of Economic Issues,* June 1971, pp. 1–19.

seemed to be a logical extension of Keynesian economics in that it apparently explained the periodic coexistence of unemployment and inflation. Much discussion was devoted to the use of both market and incomes policies as potential supplements to fiscal and monetary measures. Furthermore, economists and policy makers debated the "optimum" position on the curve. Was it better to choose point B (price stability accompanied by unemployment) in Figure 18-2 or point A (full employment with inflation) through the management of aggregate demand?

But then, in the late 1960s and early 1970s, the whole concept of the Phillips Curve—the notion of a stable, dependable trade-off between inflation and unemployment—came into question. Both analytical and real-world considerations played a role in this reevaluation. At the analytical level, some economists expressed concern that the data for certain post-World War II periods did not fit tightly the usual conception of the Phillips Curve. Although the data for the 1960s (Figure 18-1) seemed to confirm the notion of a Phillips Curve, a glance at Figure 18-3 reveals a wide dispersion of points around the curve. This "looseness of fit" implies that factors other than the unemployment rate—perhaps price expectations or the level of business profits—may also be important in determining the actual rate of inflation. But the primary source of doubt about the Phillips Curve was the real-world course of events. Data for the 1950s and 1960s, as the heavy fitted curve in Figure 18-3 suggests, were generally consistent with the Phillips Curve concept in that high unemployment rates were accompanied by modest inflation, whereas low unemployment rates coincided with high rates of inflation. But the points for the 1970s seem clearly to lie further to the right. How might this be interpreted? There are a number of options. One option is that the Phillips Curve has, for some reason, shifted to the right—to a less desirable position—as suggested by the thin curve in Figure 18-3. Another possibility is that the

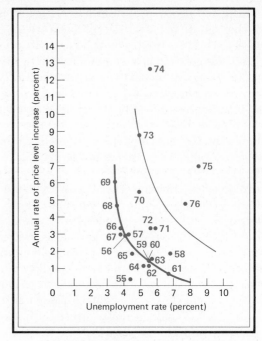

FIGURE 18-3 STABILITY OF THE PHILLIPS CURVE

While data for the 1955–1969 period generally conform to the concept of the Phillips Curve, data for the 1970s lie to the right of this curve. Economists debate whether the 1970 data represent (a) a temporary departure from the curve caused by "random shocks"; (b) a rightward shift of the curve caused by inflationary expectations and changes in the composition of the labor force; or (c) evidence that a traditional Phillips Curve does not exist.

points for, say, 1973–1976 are "special cases." That is, certain unlikely, random events or "shocks" have temporarily generated more inflation and more unemployment than is usual, but as these shocks are absorbed, the economy's future performance will again be consistent with the heavy Phillips Curve. In other words, the curve has *not* shifted, but certain special forces have caused the economy to stray temporarily from the Phillips Curve path. Finally, one might legitimately examine *all* the points plotted in Figure 18-3 and proclaim that the Phillips Curve trade-off simply does not exist! For example, considering the entire 1955–1976 period, one can argue that a vertical line located at the 5 or 5½ percent rate of unemployment summarizes the unemployment-inflation "relationship" as well, or perhaps better, than the heavy Phillips Curve.

It is not a matter of indifference as to which of these various interpretations is the more accurate. *If* the traditional Phillips Curve trade-off does not exist, then macro policy based upon its assumed existence is misguided and, in fact, may do more harm than good. Furthermore, *if* plausible reasons can be offered for a rightward shift of the curve in the 1970s, we then have an understanding of stagflation. That is, a stable Phillips Curve explains the simultaneous *existence* of unemployment and inflation; but it cannot be easily reconciled with simultaneous *increases* in both the rate of inflation and the rate of unemployment.

Aided by Figure 18-4, let us now briefly trace our recent macroeconomic history in an attempt to shed some light on economic developments in the 1970s and their implications for the Phillips Curve in particular and Keynesian economics in general.

□ **The 1960s:**
Stimulus and Demand-Pull

The early 1960s were characterized by a sluggish economy in terms of employment and growth. At the same time, the price level was relatively constant; in the first half of the 1960s, the average annual increase in the price level was only about 1½ percent per year. In 1964, as you may recall from Chapter 13, the Johnson Administration accomplished an $11 billion tax cut. Accompanied by a congenial

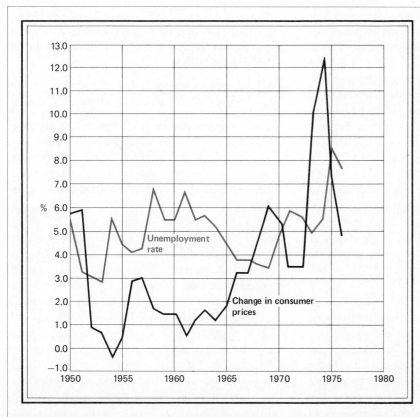

FIGURE 18-4 RATES OF INFLATION AND UNEMPLOYMENT, 1950–1976

The 1950s and much of the 1960s were generally consistent with the notion of a stable Phillips Curve in that relatively high rates of unemployment were accompanied by relatively low rates of inflation and vice versa. But in the 1970s unemployment and inflation rates both rose to their highest levels in the postwar period, implying that the Phillips Curve had shifted to a less desirable position. [*Committee for Economic Development, Fighting Inflation and Promoting Growth (New York: CED, 1976), p. 13. Updated by author. Unemployment rates are annual averages; changes in consumer prices are measured December-to-December.*]

monetary expansion, full employment was virtually achieved by 1965. The rate of inflation in that year was a modest 1.9 percent.

But this enviable economic situation was interrupted by the economic aspects of the war in Vietnam. Specifically, President Johnson made the decision to accelerate the war effort and government spending for the military rose significantly in the 1965–1968 period. These added government expenditures were imposed on a fully employed economy without concurrent increases in taxes. Bluntly stated, the President did not want to bear the political burden of asking the public to finance an unpopular war through higher taxes. The obvious result, reflected in Figure 18-4, was a quite strong demand-pull inflation in the 1966–1969 period.

□ **The Nixon "Game Plan"**

Thus, when Richard Nixon assumed the Presidency in 1969, he used a combination of fiscal and monetary policies to restrict aggregate demand and thereby control inflation which in 1969 was running at a 6 percent annual rate. Nixon, consistent with the accepted Phillips Curve analysis, intended to move the economy southeast along the curve; he had chosen—he thought—to trade an increase in unemployment for a lower rate of inflation. But the Nixon "game plan" failed. Comparing the 1970 and 1969 dots in Figure 18-3, we find that, as expected, the unemployment rate rose. But inflation persisted! Had the economy moved off the Phillips Curve which seemed relevant for the 1960s? If so, why? Or had the Phillips Curve shifted to the right? Again, if so, why?

One point was becoming increasingly clear. The persistence of inflation in 1970 and 1971, despite the government's policy of constraining aggregate demand, suggested the roots of the inflationary problem did *not* lie in demand-pull pressures but rather in cost-push or supply considerations. Some observers noted that the Nixon Administration had

strongly rejected the use of wage-price policies in 1968, and perhaps this action was taken by big business and big labor as a signal to boost wages and prices aggressively without fear of governmental intervention or reprisals. Others pointed out that the prolonged inflation of 1966–1969 had inflamed inflationary expectations and therefore inflation had developed a momentum which made it immune to a simple restriction of aggregate demand. A closely related point was that the 1966–1969 inflation had created income inequities; income receivers who had fallen behind—or felt they had fallen behind—in the past four or five years of accelerating inflation moved aggressively to restore their relative income positions.

The Nixon Administration responded to the persisting inflation by reversing its earlier commitment *not* to employ wage-price controls. We noted earlier that, in August 1971, the President declared a 90-day freeze on wages, prices, and rents. These controls persisted in various forms until early 1973, and during their tenure the rate of inflation moderated (Figure 18-4).

□ **Severe Cost-Push Shocks**

The economy in 1972 was not in the best of health. The rate of inflation was 3.4 percent; the unemployment rate stood at 5.6 percent. But then matters took a sharp turn for the worse as the result of a series of inflation-causing shocks.

1 A severe worldwide agricultural shortfall occurred, reflecting poor harvests, particularly in Asia and the Soviet Union. American agricultural exports expanded sharply, thereby reducing domestic supplies of foodstuffs. Result? Domestic food prices rose by a dramatic 35 percent during 1973–1974.

2 Worldwide shortages of certain strategic raw materials developed, causing substantial increases in material prices.

3 In the 1971–1973 period, the dollar was devalued to help ease the United States' chronic balance of payments deficits (Chapter 44). Devaluation means that it now takes more dollars to buy units of foreign monies; this in turn causes the prices of all American imports to rise. In brief, devaluation sharply boosted American import prices.

4 The effective formation of the Organization of Petroleum Exporting Countries (OPEC) in late 1973 resulted in the dramatic quadrupling of the world price of oil. There ensued price increases for a whole range of petroleum products and energy in general which quickly permeated the entire economy.

Other less evident inflationary forces were also at work. Ironically, the Nixon wage-price controls which were terminated in January 1973 may have left an inflationary legacy. The price controls had caused shortages of many products and resources which could only be eliminated by substantial price increases now that controls were abolished. Furthermore, businesses and workers who felt their real incomes had been unduly constrained during the period of controls sought to restore their real incomes through substantial wage and price increases.

As a consequence of this convergence of forces, inflation accelerated very sharply to almost 9 percent in 1973 and to over 12 percent in 1974! These inflation rates were the highest encountered by the United States during the entire post-World War II period. But, as Figure 18-4 reveals, the rate of unemployment also rose in the 1973–1975 period, reaching a postwar peak of 8.5 percent in 1975. The economy clearly had a very serious case of stagflation.

□ **Why Stagflation?**

The puzzling question was this: Why— contrary to Keynesian economics and the Phillips Curve—did unemployment *rise* during this period of sharp inflation? Many explanations have been offered, but perhaps the most convincing one is that the rapid inflation of this period reduced the real spendable incomes of consumers and investors. That is, unem-ployment was not merely a coincidental accompaniment of inflation, but rather unemployment occurred *because of* the rapid acceleration of the price level. The dramatic oil price increase was tantamount to a gigantic excise tax paid by American consumers and businesses to the OPEC nations. Like any other "tax" increase, the effect was contractionary with respect to output and employment. And, ironically, the built-in stability feature of our tax system worked perversely during this period. As the *money* incomes of households and businesses inflated rapidly, so did personal and corporate income tax payments. In short, the OPEC "tax" and higher domestic tax bills left consumers and businesses with less to spend on domestic consumer and investment goods. Results? Falling real output and rising unemployment. Some economists stress that the unemployment problem was seriously exacerbated by misguided public policy. Specifically, they maintain that government mistakenly perceived of the 1973–1974 inflation as being caused by demand-pull forces. Hence, in late 1973 and 1974, monetary and fiscal policies were used to constrain aggregate demand. But, because the causes of inflation were largely on the cost or supply side, the restricting of aggregate demand did *not* exert any direct control over the rate of inflation. What it did achieve was an intensification of the declines in output and employment!

The equation of exchange, $MV = PQ$, serves us well in elaborating this explanation of stagflation. Assume that cost-push forces (rising oil prices, material shortages, agricultural shortfalls) cause the price level P to rise. Now, if MV (aggregate demand) is constant, Q (real output and, implicitly, employment) must fall. A given level of aggregate demand will take a smaller real output off the market when cost-push pressures increase the price level. Furthermore, if government mistakenly judges the inflation to be demand-pull and therefore invokes policies to reduce MV, the decline in Q will be intensified.

THE PHILLIPS CURVE REVISITED

What are the implications of all this for the Phillips Curve? A few economists believe that the events of the 1970s reflect "random shocks" and that, in time, our unemployment-inflation trade-offs will once again approximate the stable Phillips Curve of the 1960s (Figure 18-1). But most economists are debating other options: Has the curve shifted to the right? Or is the traditional Phillips Curve nonexistent?

☐ The Accelerationist View

At this point our monetarist-Keynesian debate of Chapter 17 resurfaces. The Phillips Curve is an extension of, or amendment to, Keynesian economics. Therefore, it is not surprising to find monetarists like Milton Friedman taking the position that the Phillips Curve does *not* exist as a stable, "long-run" phenomenon. This stance is labeled the *accelerationist view* because, as we shall discover momentarily, it concludes that Keynesian full-employment policies, based on the incorrect assumption that the Phillips Curve *does* exist, will result in an accelerating rate of inflation.

Analysis A simplified explanation of the accelerationist theory is as follows. Assume that the "normal" or full-employment rate of unemployment is higher than believed. Suppose it is, say, 6 percent (as shown by point A_1 in Figure 18-5) rather than 4 percent.[12] But government decides that a 6 percent rate of unemployment is economically and politically intolerable and therefore invokes expansionary

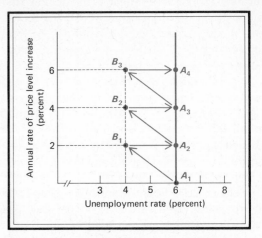

FIGURE 18-5 THE ACCELERATIONIST VIEW

The accelerationists note that an expansion of aggregate demand may temporarily increase profits and therefore output and employment (A_1 to B_1). But money wages will soon rise, reducing profits and thereby negating the short-run stimulus to production and employment (B_1 to A_2). Consequently, in the long run there is no trade-off between the rates of inflation and unemployment; the long-run Phillips Curve is vertical. This suggests that Keynesian expansionary policies will generate accelerating inflation rather than a lower rate of unemployment.

fiscal and monetary policies. The resulting increase in aggregate demand pulls up the price level and, *given the level of money wages,* business profits increase. Firms respond to expanded profits by increasing output and therefore hiring additional workers. The economy thus moves to point B_1, which, in contrast with A_1, obviously entails a higher level of employment along with a higher rate of inflation. This A_1 to B_1 shift, you will note, is consistent with our earlier conception of the Phillips Curve. The economy has simply accepted some inflation as the "cost" of achieving a reduced level of unemployment.

But according to the accelerationist view, point B_1 is *not* a stable equilibrium position. And the reason, according to Friedman, is that workers will recognize that their *real* wages and incomes have fallen; that is, their *money* wages have been constant at a time when the

[12]There may be a number of reasons why the full-employment rate of unemployment has increased in recent years. For example, the composition of the labor force has changed so that women and youths—demographic groups characterized by above-normal unemployment rates—now constitute larger proportions of the labor force. Furthermore, there is evidence that our unemployment compensation system allows unemployed workers to seek reemployment at a more leisurely pace.

level of product prices has increased. Workers will therefore demand and receive money wage increases to restore the purchasing power they have lost. But, as money wages rise to restore the previous level of real wages which existed at A_1, business profits will be reduced to their earlier level. This profit reduction means that the original motivation of businesses to increase output and employ more workers will disappear. Consequence? Unemployment returns to its original 6 percent level at point A_2. Note, however, that the economy is now faced with a higher rate of inflation—2 percent rather than zero percent. That is, the higher level of aggregate demand which originally moved the economy from A_1 to B_1 still exists and, hence, the inflation which it created persists. In brief, as Friedman sees it, an along-the-Phillips-Curve kind of shift from A_1 to B_1 is merely a "short-run" or transient phenomenon. In the "long run"—that is, after money wages catch up with price level increases—unemployment will return to the normal rate at A_2.

The process may now be repeated. Government may reason that certain extraneous, chance events have frustrated its expansionist policies. Hence, government tries again. Policy measures are used to increase aggregate demand and the scenario repeats itself. Prices rise momentarily ahead of money wages, profits expand, and output and employment increase (A_2 to B_2). But, in time, workers now press for, and are granted, higher money wages to restore their level of real wages. Profits, therefore, fall to their original level, causing employment to gravitate back to the normal rate at A_3. Government's "reward" for trying to force the actual rate of unemployment below the natural rate is the perverse one of a still higher (4 percent) rate of inflation!

If we conceive of A_1B_1, A_2B_2, A_3B_3, and so forth as indicating a series of "short-run" Phillips Curves, the accelerationist view can be interpreted as saying that, ironically, governmental attempts through policy to move along the short-run Phillips Curve (A_1B_1) *cause* the curve to shift to a *less* favorable position (A_2B_2, then A_3B_3, and so on). In other words, a stable Phillips Curve with the dependable series of unemployment rate–inflation rate trade-offs which it implies simply does not exist. There is, in fact, no *constant* rate of inflation (such as 2 percent at B_1) which can be accepted as the "cost" of reduced unemployment (6 percent to 4 percent) in the *long run*. To keep unemployment at the desired 4 percent level, government must continuously expand the level of aggregate demand. The "cost" of a 4 percent unemployment rate is *not* a constant 2 percent annual rate of inflation at B_1, but rather an accelerating rate of inflation, that is, an annual rate of inflation that increases from 2 percent (B_1) to 4 percent (B_2) to 6 percent (B_3), and so forth. Stated differently, the *long-run relationship* between unemployment and inflation is shown by the vertical line through A_1, A_2, A_3, and A_4. The Phillips Curve as portrayed earlier in Figure 18-1 does not exist.

This explanation assumes that increases in money wages lag behind increases in the price level. This lag gives rise to temporary increases in profits which in turn temporarily stimulate employment. But is it not more reasonable to suppose that labor will not be content to play "catch up"? Won't workers soon come to anticipate inflation and build this expectation into their wage demands? If we make the alternative assumption that workers correctly and fully anticipate the amount of price inflation and adjust their current money wage demands accordingly so as to maintain their real wages, then the temporary increases in profits, output, and employment will *not* occur. In this case, instead of the temporary increase in employment shown by the movement from A_1 to B_1 in Figure 18-5, the movement will be directly from A_1 to A_2. Fully anticipated inflation by labor means there will be no short-run decline in unemployment. Price inflation which is fully anticipated in the money wage demands of workers will generate a vertical line through A_1, A_2, A_3, and A_4 in Figure 18-5. Policy implication: Keynesian measures to achieve a (misspecified) full-employment rate of unemployment will generate an accelerating rate of inflation, not a lower rate of unemployment. Note, incidentally, that Friedman's accelerationist theory is consistent with his philosophy that government's attempts to do good deeds typically fail and at considerable cost to society. In this instance the "cost" is in the form of accelerating inflation.

Evidence   What about empirical evidence? Are the data of Figure 18-1 to be shrugged off as incorrect or meaningless? Proponents of the accelerationist view make two points. First, it must be recognized that the price level–unemployment rate observations of Figure 18-1 merely trace the historical path of the economy and therefore do *not* necessarily describe or trace out a point-in-time conceptual relationship. For example, recall from Chapter 4 that, if one were to plot the historical data for price and quantity demanded (sold) for, say, automobiles in recent years, they would reveal a *direct* relationship. Yet, the conceptual relationship we call a demand curve embodies an *inverse* relationship between price and quantity demanded. Similarly, according to the accelerationists, the inverse relationship shown by historical inflation–unemployment rate data for, say, the 1961–1969 period (Figure 18-1) does not conflict with the use of a vertical line to describe the conceptual relationship between inflation and the unemployment rate. Second, if one insists upon generalizing from plotted historical data, one should reconsider the data for the entire period since, say, the mid-1950s as shown in Figure 18-3. Clearly, there is no obvious relationships which leaps out at the beholder. In fact, a vertical line through these data located at about the 5 or $5\frac{1}{2}$ percent unemployment rate describes the "relationship" as well, or better than, a traditional Phillips Curve.

□   **Keynesian Position**

Needless to say, Keynesians have not been anxious to accept the accelerationist theory which concludes that aggregate demand management is a futile and costly exercise. Their response generally has been that the events of the late 1960s and 1970s reflect, not the non-existence of the Phillips Curve, but rather, the impact of certain forces which have shifted the curve to the right. What are these special forces?

Changing   Labor-Force   Composition
One contention is that the Phillips Curve has been shifting to the right in the 1960s and 1970s because of important changes which have occurred in the composition of the labor force. In particular, in the past decade or so teenagers and women have come to constitute larger and larger proportions of the total labor force. This is significant because the unemployment rates associated with teenage and women workers are substantially above that for the labor force as a whole. Hence, with these high-unemployment groups more dominant in the labor force, the level of aggregate demand which would previously yield, say, 4 percent inflation and $3\frac{1}{2}$ percent unemployment, now results in 4 percent inflation and $5\frac{1}{2}$ percent unemployment. This obviously implies a worse inflation–unemployment rate trade-off, that is, a rightward shift of the Phillips Curve.

Inflationary Expectations   The Phillips Curve may also have shifted to the right in the 1970s because of changes in inflationary expectations. If the public—workers and businesses—expect substantial inflation in the future, these expectations will be included in their wage demands and price policies. And, if so, the position of the Phillips Curve may worsen. *Scenario 1:* Assume a 5 percent unemployment rate and a recent history of price level stability. Given this past price stability, there are no expectations of future inflation. Unions therefore bargain for, say, a 3 percent increase in money wages. If productivity also increases by this amount, we know that unit labor costs will be constant and there will be no wage-push pressure for the price level to rise. Assuming businesses exert no effort to increase their profit margins, prices will remain constant. In this case a 5 percent unemployment rate is associated with a zero rate of inflation. *Scenario 2:* Suppose a 5 percent unemployment rate once again, but a recent history of rather substantial inflation. Unions, anticipating continuing inflation, demand and obtain, say, a 6 percent increase in money wages. Given a 3 percent increase in productivity, this wage increase translates into a 3 percent increase in unit labor costs. Businesses anticipate that continuing inflation will erode their real profits and therefore boost their prices by 4 percent, that is, by 3 percent to cover their higher labor costs and by 1 percent to help preserve their real profits. Result: A 5 percent unemployment rate is now associated with a 4 percent rate of inflation. Scenario 2 obviously implies a point on a Phillips Curve which is higher, or to the right of, the curve suggested by Scenario 1. Conclusion: Other things being equal, the development or strengthening of inflationary expectations can shift the Phillips Curve to a less desirable position. Recalling that the mild inflation of the early 1960s gave way to increasingly strong demand-pull inflation in the late 1960s, it is reasonable to argue that inflationary expectations were aroused and the Phillips Curve for the 1970s therefore shifted to the right (Figure 18-3).

□ **Policy Implications**

Where do these interpretations leave Keynesian policy? Admittedly, the possibility of a shifting Phillips Curve complicates Keynesian policy and perhaps calls for its modification. More precisely, a Keynesian economist might respond in this way. If the economy is faced with a serious recession, Keynesian demand management policies can clearly be effective in moving the economy *toward* full employment. But, as full employment is approached, increasingly rapid inflation will occur (note the steepness of the Phillips Curve in Figure 18-1 for the 1966–1969 period) *and,* worse yet, inflationary expectations may evolve. These expectations may shift the Phillips Curve to the right. If so, further increases in aggregate demand may generate accelerating inflation rather than more jobs. Therefore, the appropriate policy-mix may be to bring the economy to, say, a $5\frac{1}{2}$ or 5 percent rate of unemployment through Keynesian demand management, but then put greater emphasis upon manpower or wage-price policies in an attempt to realize further reductions in unemployment. Caution: These comments are controversial; there exists a wide spectrum of views as to the implications of the events of the 1970s for Keynesian theory and policy.

■────────────────────

LESSONS AND ISSUES

What observations or lessons, if any, have emerged from our economic experiences of the past ten or fifteen years? And what salient issues remain to be decided? Let us consider these questions in the order stated.

□ **Lessons of the 1970s**

At least four important observations have evolved from the economic turbulence of recent years.

1 Interdependence The United States has become increasingly linked to the world economy, and this growing international interdependence can be an added source of macroeconomic instability. Recall that rising foreign oil prices, worldwide shortages of strategic raw materials, and the devaluation of the dollar were all key forces in the 1973–1974 inflation. Increasing economic interdependence means that our domestic economy may be subject to more and more destabilizing "shocks" which we cannot directly control.

2   Supply versus Demand   The distinction between inflation resulting from excessive demand and that caused by cost or supply-side phenomena is critical for policy. In particular, the application of the aggregate demand management tools of Keynesian economics to an inflation problem derived from cost or supply considerations may not only be ineffective, but blatantly harmful.

3   Policy   A point closely related to the previous two is that the mere management of aggregate demand along Keynesian lines may not be enough to achieve stability. Given a stable Phillips Curve, the standard fiscal and monetary remedies suggest we can temper sharp inflation *or* alleviate excessive unemployment. But, if the Phillips Curve is in fact unstable and periodically shifts to the right, the consequent stagflation cannot be cured by the mere manipulation of aggregate demand. That is, aggregate demand management cannot alleviate unemployment and inflation *at the same time*. It is at this point that policy makers—often with reluctance and trepidation —turn to incomes and procompetition policies.

4   Institutional-Structural Factors   Economists have become increasingly interested in structural-institutional changes and their possible impacts upon the economy and upon public policies. That is, considerations which economists have typically ignored or regarded as "given" in their theories are now being scrutinized to determine whether the overall economic environment has changed sufficiently so that accepted theories and policies must be revised. Consider some far-ranging examples.

First, has the market power of giant corporations and huge labor unions evolved to the stage wherein cost-push inflation—and perhaps stagflation—will become increasingly common and severe problems?

Second, have changes occurred in the economy which call for an upward revision of the "full-employment rate of unemployment" from 4 percent to, say, 5 or $5\frac{1}{2}$ percent? Note, on the one hand, the composition of the labor force has changed so that certain demographic groups which are characterized by high unemployment rates—youths and women, in particular—now bulk larger proportionately in the labor force. Observe, furthermore, that there is mounting evidence that our unemployment insurance system prompts workers to seek new jobs at a more leisurely pace, thus increasing the unemployment rate. This is an important matter because full-employment policies based on a full-employment rate of unemployment which is "too low" will inject an inflationary bias into the economy as implied by the accelerationist view.[13]

Third, should expectations be accorded a more integral role in macroeconomic theory and policy? Some economists feel that the stubborness of inflation in the 1970s is related to the intensification of inflationary expectations. After five or six years of continuous inflation, expectations of continuing inflation came to be widely held and built into labor contracts, consumption and investment decisions, interest rates, and so on. These actions generated continued inflationary pressures, even in the face of constraints on aggregate demand. More recently, increasing attention is being paid to the disturbing possibility that policy decisions may be negated by the expectations which those policies generate. Recall the accelerationist model of Figure 18-5: If workers do *not* anticipate that inflation will accompany an increase in aggregate demand, then an expansionary policy will yield a short-run payoff in terms of less unemployment and a larger real output (A_1 to B_1). But if government announces a program of economic stimulus and labor responds by revising its expectations of inflation—and therefore its

[13]This upward revision is suggested in the *Economic Report of the President, 1977* (Washington), pp. 48–51.

money wage demands—upward, then the short-run beneficial effects upon output and employment will not occur (A_1 to A_2)! This obviously suggests that, by acting rationally upon their expectations, private decision makers—workers, consumers, and businesses—can greatly complicate the task of public policy.

☐ Keynesianism and Planning

Perhaps the fundamental question evolving from the awkward decade of the 1970s is whether Keynesian economics (Figure 16-2) is losing its relevance as an analytical model and as a basis for policy. Does the stagflation of the 1970s reflect the fortuitous convergence of a series of "random shocks" which, although temporarily disruptive to the economy, do *not* invalidate Keynesian economics and its policy prescriptions? Having absorbed these shocks, are we once again returning to a "Keynesian world" wherein the traditional fiscal and monetary policies are applicable and effective? Or are the 1970s an indication that certain fundamental changes have occurred in the institutional and structural framework of the economy which undermine the validity of Keynesian economics? Are we now operating in a new environment wherein the old generalizations no longer apply? Economists are now deeply involved in various aspects of this great debate, and it will undoubtedly be some time before a clear consensus emerges.

Regardless of how this debate is resolved, it is evident that the apparent intractability of simultaneous inflation and unemployment in the 1970s has rekindled interest in the adoption of some form of *central economic planning* as a means of improving economic performance. The intent here is not to provide a Soviet-style economic blueprint which sets production targets for every factory or office (Chapter 45), but rather, the creation of a new and sophisticated planning apparatus at the Federal level to (1) generate better information for economic forecasting; (2) establish specific economic targets for the rates of unemploy-

ment, inflation, and growth; and (3) coordinate a variety of critical policy decisions—including fiscal and monetary policies—to achieve those targets. Proponents argue that the Federal government is *now* deeply involved in decisions which have a profound impact upon the performance of the economy. But these decisions are made on a haphazard, uncoordinated basis in response to existing problems. These uncoordinated decisions are often at cross purposes; for example, fiscal policy may be expansionary while the independent Federal Reserve Board is following a contractionary course with respect to monetary policy. As a result, public policy is as likely to reinforce economic instability as it is to relieve it. Furthermore, there is an obvious need to *anticipate* potentially critical problems as they appear on the horizon (for example, the energy crisis) so that appropriate policies may be invoked to avoid or ameliorate the harmful effects. Proper planning, it is argued, would have revealed our growing dependence upon foreign oil at an early date and allowed us to enact policies to reduce that dependence prior to the OPEC embargo and price increases. The Humphrey-Hawkins bill (officially the Full Employment and Balanced Growth Act of 1976) now in Congress embodies this philosophy of planning. It advocates establishment of a long-range planning process designed to achieve a 3 percent rate of adult unemployment within four years of the bill's enactment. Furthermore, government is designated as "the employer of last resort"; that is, government work projects will guarantee jobs for those who cannot find employment in the private sector.

But there are those who view the prospect of planning with both skepticism and fear. Their concerns are many. First, government is now deeply involved in the decision-making processes which determine our macroeconomic performance, and there is no compelling evidence that these public decisions have made a significant contribution to stability. Indeed, one can make a strong case that the application of monetary and fiscal policies have on balance been *de*stabilizers. Given this dubious record, should we not be reluctant to assign government the more comprehensive task of national economic planning? Second, planning is now done on a decentralized basis by individual economic units. Government planning will necessarily subordinate or supplant this private planning; in other words, central planning is necessarily coercive and at odds with freedom of choice. Stated more generally, central planning represents a long stride on the road to socialism and this step should not be taken precipitously. Third, private firms have a direct monetary interest in the effectiveness and correctness of their plans; government bureaucrats do not have a similar interest in central plans (Chapter 6). This suggests that decentralized planning through the market is likely to be superior to centralized decision making. Finally, studies of French planning suggest that government planners may come

to be dominated by the major corporations of the economy, much as government regulatory agencies now tend to be "captured" by the industries they are supposed to regulate (Chapter 34). The result could be, not planning in the social interest, but an unfortunate government–big business collaboration at the expense of consumers and taxpayers.

One point is unassailable: The recent revival of the central planning question is precipitating a lively and prolonged controversy.[14]

[14]To pursue the issue, you might consult the following: John Kenneth Galbraith, Henry Wallich, Melville J. Ulmer, and Murray L. Weidenbaum, "The Case for and against National Economic Planning," *Challenge,* March–April 1976, pp. 30–38; Hubert H. Humphrey, "The New Humphrey-Hawkins Bill," *Challenge,* May–June 1976, pp. 21–29 (this issue also contains the text of the bill); Henry Hazlitt, "Planning Disaster," *Challenge,* July–August 1975, pp. 44–46; and Wassily Leontief and Herbert Stein, *The Economic System in an Age of Discontinuity: Long-Range Planning or Market Reliance?* (New York: New York University Press, 1976).

Summary

1   The simple theory of demand-pull inflation is based upon the implicit assumption that full employment and price level stability are compatible goals. However, recent inflationary episodes suggest that premature inflation occurs as the economy approaches full employment.

2   Empirical studies of premature inflation have yielded the Phillips Curve, which suggests that society must accept inflation to realize full employment or accept unemployment to achieve price level stability. Although labor market imbalances and monopoly power underlie the Phillips Curve, it is significant that only wage rate increases in excess of average labor productivity increases are inflationary.

3   Traditional macro policy—fiscal and monetary policies—allows society to select a position on the Phillips Curve, but does not improve upon the unemployment-versus-inflation trade-offs implicit in the curve itself. Hence, other policies designed to provide a more desirable Phillips Curve have been developed. These consist of *a.* market policies—manpower policies designed to reduce labor market imbalances and procompetition policies which reduce the market power of unions and corporations—and *b.* wage-price policies in the form of voluntary guideposts or mandatory controls.

4   Economists have evaluated wage-price policies in terms of their workability and compliance, impact upon resource allocation, and compatibility with freedom of choice.

5   In the 1970s the economy has been plagued by stagflation. The rapid inflation stemmed from agricultural shortfalls, raw-material shortages, devaluation of the dollar, and dramatic increases in the price of imported oil. The level of money demand did not keep pace with the resulting supply or cost-push inflation, and consequently, real output and employment declined.

6 Monetarists argue through their accelerationist view that the stagflation of the 1970s undermines the Phillips Curve concept. Keynesians feel the curve has shifted to the right because of *a.* changes in the composition of the labor force and *b.* the more prominent role of inflationary expectations in decision making.

7 The fundamental questions raised by the turbulent 1970s are these: *a.* Are Keynesian economics and its policy prescriptions becoming obsolete? *b.* Is central economic planning a logical and desirable means of dealing with stagflation and related problems?

Questions and Study Suggestions

1 Key terms and concepts to remember: demand-pull inflation; Phillips Curve; stagflation; cost- (wage-, profit-) push inflation; stabilization policy dilemma; incomes policy; wage-price guideposts; wage-price controls; excess wage settlement tax; real wage insurance plan; inflationary expectations; accelerationist view; central economic planning; Humphrey-Hawkins bill.

2 Compare the causes and implications of *a.* demand-pull inflation and *b.* premature inflation. Draw a Phillips Curve and explain its shape. Illustrate and explain the dilemma which the Phillips Curve poses for traditional stabilization policy.

3 Assume the following information is relevant for an industrially advanced economy in the 1978–1980 period:

Year	Price level index	Rate of increase in labor productivity	Index of industrial production	Unemployment rate	Average hourly wage rates
1978	167	4 %	212	4.5%	$3.00
1979	174	3	208	5.2	3.25
1980	181	2.5	205	5.8	3.55

Describe in detail the macroeconomic situation faced by this society. Is cost-push inflation in evidence? What policy proposals would you recommend?

4 "There is no way to make full employment, price stability, and free markets compatible." Do you agree? Explain.

5 Distinguish between market policies and wage-price policies as means of shifting the Phillips Curve to a more desirable position.

6 Explain the wage-price guideposts, indicating in detail the relationship between money wages, productivity, and unit labor costs. What specific problems are associated with the use of wage-price guideposts and controls? Evaluate these problems and note the arguments in favor of guideposts and controls. Would you favor a special tax on firms which grant wage increases in excess of productivity increases?

7 "Controlling prices to halt inflation is like breaking a thermometer to control the heat. In both instances you are treating symptoms rather than causes." Do you agree? Does the correctness of the statement vary when applied to demand-pull and to cost-push inflation? Explain.

8   Contrast the causes of inflation in **a.** the late 1960s and **b.** the 1970s. Why was the inflation of the 1970s accompanied by rising unemployment?

9   Why is the issue of the stability or the existence of the Phillips Curve important for public policy? Explain and evaluate: "Monetary and fiscal policy are more likely to guarantee inflation without full employment than they are to provide full employment without inflation."

10   Use an appropriate diagram to explain the accelerationist's rationale for concluding that the Phillips Curve is a vertical line. Explain how private expectations might frustrate public policy.

11   Evaluate: "The viability of an economy characterized by the concentration of market power, a high degree of international interdependence, and deeply ingrained inflationary expectations, can only be assured through central economic planning." Is planning consistent with political democracy? With a system of free markets?

Selected References

Chase, Richard X.: "The Failure of American Keynesianism," *Challenge,* March–April 1976, pp. 43–51.

Committee for Economic Development: *Fighting Inflation and Promoting Growth* (New York: CED, 1976).

Economic Report of the President, 1977 (Washington), chaps. 1, 2, 4.

Humphrey, Thomas M.: "Changing Views of the Phillips Curve," *Monthly Review* (Federal Reserve Bank of Richmond, July 1973), pp. 2–13.

Pohlman, Jerry E.: *Inflation Under Control?* (Reston, Va.: Reston Publishing Company, Inc., 1976).

Snellings, Aubrey N.: "Stabilization Policy: Time for a Reappraisal?" *Monthly Review,* Federal Reserve Bank of Richmond, March–April 1976, pp. 3–9.

Last Word
The Slow Road to Full Employment

Okun's Law embodies the unhappy message that the real GNP must grow much faster than it has historically to reduce our current high unemployment rate.

One fundamental limitation on what economic managers can accomplish is the ornery fact that it takes a lot of economic growth to produce even a small reduction in the unemployment rate. The relationship between growth and unemployment is summed up in what has come to be called Okun's Law, worked out by economist Arthur M. Okun.

Okun's Law begins with the proposition that the economy has to grow in line with the long-term trend rate, about 4 percent a year, just to keep the unemployment rate from going higher. In other words, with normal improvement in productivity it takes normal growth of output to create enough additional jobs to offset the normal yearly growth in the labor force. This much is obvious enough, but now comes the surprising part. Okun's Law holds that for each percentage point by which real GNP growth falls below the 4 percent trend, the unemployment rate increases by only one-third of a point. And for each percentage point of growth above the trend, the unemployment rate declines by only one-third of a point. In brief, the unemployment rate is "sticky" both on the downside and on the upside.

Obviously intended as a rough rule of thumb rather than as a rigorous formula, Okun's Law has worked out remarkably well over the years. It works because of the varying sensitivity of the underlying factors to turns in the business cycle. In a recession, employers do not lay off workers as rapidly as they scale down output. (As a result, productivity worsens.) The increased difficulty of finding a job induces some workers to leave the labor force or discourages others from entering it; these effects help to hold down the official unemployment rate.

The bleak outlook for jobs is indicated by these three lines showing what various rates of growth in real GNP would do to the unemployment rate over the next five years. Growth at the long-term trend rate of 4 percent would leave unemployment unchanged from its expected average of 9 percent this year [1975]. A long stretch of 6 percent growth—exceeding the fastest pace the U.S. has sustained for more than two years in a row since World War II—would still leave unemployment above 5.5 percent in 1980. Even if output grew at 8 percent, a rate that the U.S. has achieved only in brief spurts, it would take until 1979 to bring unemployment down to the 4 percent rate that used to be considered "full employment." All three lines are plotted in accord with "Okun's Law." (*Fortune Art Department/Vahe Kirishjian*)

During upturns, of course, the reverse happens: output increases faster than employment, with the result that productivity rises rapidly. And people are pulled into the labor force as prospects for employment improve.

As the chart makes plain, Okun's Law spells bad news about unemployment in years ahead. According to his formula, a year of 6 percent real growth would reduce the unemployment rate by only two-thirds of 1 percent. So it would take six years of 6 percent growth to reduce unemployment by four points—from, say, 9.5 to 5.5. And by the standards of the past, six years of 6 percent growth would be an extraordinary economic performance.

Only once in the past twenty years has the U.S. economy come close to the growth record that would be necessary, according to Okun's Law, to bring the unemployment rate below 6 percent by 1980. That was during the period 1962–66, when, in sharp contrast to the current period, the economy had the benefit of a mild rate of inflation, moderate budget deficits, and a labor movement willing to abide by wage guideposts.

Whether the economy can stage a rerun of that boom, even from its present depressed level, is at best problematical. Yet some economists insist that we should try to do better than that. Arthur Okun himself wants to push the economy along at something like an 8 percent growth rate.

Aside from wars and brief rebounds from deep recessions, the American economy has never been able to maintain rates of growth even approaching 8 percent. And many economists believe that under present circumstances such a rate would soon bring supply bottlenecks and spiraling inflation.

Lewis Beman, "The Slow Road Back to Full Employment," *Fortune,* June 1975. Reprinted by permission from *Fortune* magazine.

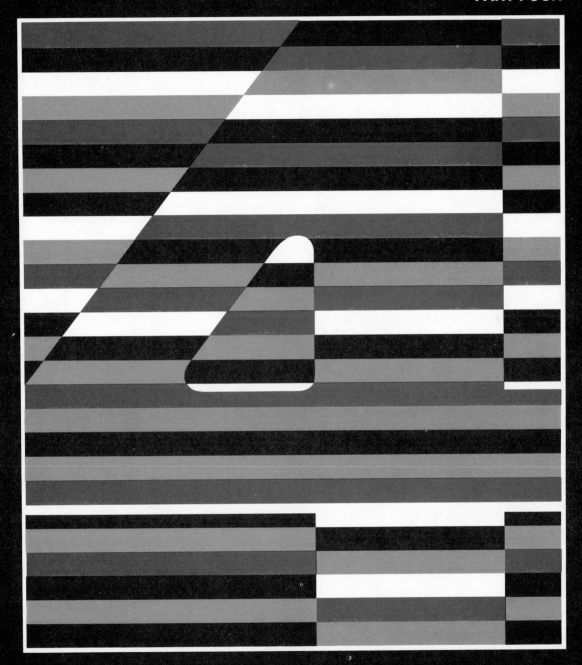

PART FOUR

ECONOMIC GROWTH:
ANALYSIS AND POLICY

The Simple Analytics of Economic Growth

In the past 200 years our economy has grown from an industrial infant to a vigorous, productive giant. This long-run growth has not occurred at a steady pace. On the contrary, it has been punctuated by periods of instability—unemployment and inflation. Parts 2 and 3 of this book have dealt with the causes and potential cures of short-run economic instability. The business cycle, the theory of employment, and fiscal and monetary policy have been the focal points of our analysis.

The task of Part 4 is to take a searching look at economic growth. In Chapter 19 we are concerned primarily with the basic theory of economic growth. Chapter 20 summarizes the growth record of the United States and analyzes recent debate over the desirability of economic growth. In Chapter 21 we shall look at the problem of economic growth from the viewpoint of the developing countries.

GROWTH ECONOMICS

Modern employment theory—detailed along with stabilization policy in Parts 2 and 3—is of a static or short-run character. That is, it assumes the economy has fixed amounts of resources or inputs available and therefore is capable of producing some capacity or full-employment level of national output. The central question of modern employment theory is: How can output be increased by more fully utilizing *existing* productive capacity? The essence of Keynes's answer, of course, is that aggregate demand should be adjusted through fiscal and monetary measures to the full-employment level of output at which actual NNP will equal capacity or potential NNP. In terms of Figure 16-2, modern employment theory *assumes* that at full employment the economy can produce some fixed aggregate output and therefore concentrates on the forces which determine whether $C + I_n + G$ will be sufficient to induce the production of that capacity output.

We now turn to the economics of growth, which is concerned with this question: After full employment is reached and actual NNP equals capacity or full-employment NNP, how can the economy's output be further increased? Thus, whereas employment theory is couched in terms of a fixed-capacity or full-employment output (Figure 12-5), the economics of growth takes a long-run perspective and seeks to uncover the forces that alter the economy's capacity to produce over time. Employment theory is concerned primarily with the adjustment of aggregate demand, while the emphasis in growth theory is upon changes in aggregate real output or supply.

□ Two Definitions

"Economic growth" is a much-used and much-abused term. Indeed, it is a slippery concept. What is economic growth? Two related definitions are commonly offered.

Definition One Economic growth may be defined as an increase in the economy's *real* gross national product, or *real* national income. An expanding real output means that the economy is growing. A stable or declining output means that the economy is static or declining. Note that this definition hinges upon *real* and not *money* output. The production of a larger amount of goods and services signifies growth; paying a larger number of dollars for a fixed or declining quantity does not.

Definition Two A second and somewhat more refined definition links economic growth to increases in real *per capita* output. This definition correctly recognizes that the standard of living of any economy is best measured in terms of real output per person. The actual standard of living could decline in an economy if the population increased at a faster rate than the volume of real output.

Which of these definitions is best? It depends upon the specific problem with which one is dealing. If we are concerned with the question of military potential, for example, total real output is the more appropriate measure of growth. On the other hand, per capita real income is obviously superior for comparisons of living standards among regions or nations. Both definitions suffer from important limitations. The measures do not directly reflect, for example, changes in leisure and environmental quality. We know, too, that the good life involves political, spiritual, and cultural, as well as material, objectives. Nevertheless, our definitions of economic growth will be useful because (1) our immediate concern as students of economics is with material well-being, and (2) as a matter of fact, a nation which is wealthy in material things is in a strategic position to realize, if it chooses, the environmental and nonmaterial aspects of the good life.

□ Importance of Growth

Why be concerned with economic growth? Why should an economy grow? The answer to these questions is almost self-evident: The growth of total output relative to population means a higher standard of living. An expanding real output means greater material abundance and implies a more satisfactory answer to the economizing problem. Our questions can be answered from a slightly different perspective. *A growing economy is in a superior position to meet new needs and resolve socioeconomic problems both domestically and in-*

ternationally. A growing economy, by definition, enjoys an increment in its annual real output which it can use to satisfy existing needs more effectively or to undertake new projects. An expanding real wage or salary income makes new opportunities available to an individual and his family—a trip to Europe, a new stereo, a college education for each child, and so forth—without the sacrifice of other opportunities and enjoyments. Similarly, a growing economy can, for example, undertake new programs to alleviate poverty and clean up the environment *without* impairing existing levels of consumption, investment, and social goods production. *Growth lessens the burden of scarcity.* To a degree, a growing economy, unlike a static one, can have its cake and eat it too. By easing the burden of scarcity—by relaxing society's production constraints—economic growth allows a nation to realize existing economic goals more fully and to undertake new output-absorbing endeavors.

□ **Arithmetic of Growth**

Laymen sometimes wonder why economists get so excited about seemingly minuscule changes in the rate of growth. Does it really matter very much whether our economy grows at 4 percent or 3 percent? It matters a great deal! For the United States, which has a current real GNP of about $1265 billion, the difference between a 3 and a 4 percent growth rate is about $12 billion worth of output per year. For a very poor country, a .5 percent change in the growth rate may well mean the difference between starvation and mere hunger.

Furthermore, when envisioned over a period of years, an apparently small difference in the rate of growth becomes exceedingly important because of the "miracle" of compound interest. Example: Suppose Alphania and Betania have identical GNPs. But Alphania begins to grow at a 4 percent annual rate, while Betania grows at only 2 percent. Recalling our "rule of 70" of Chapter 10, Alphania would find

that its GNP would double in only about eighteen years ($= 70 \div 4$); Betania would take thirty-five years ($= 70 \div 2$) to accomplish the same feat. Example: For the United States with its $1265 billion real GNP, the difference between a 3 and a 4 percent annual rate of growth over a ten-year period amounts to some $170 billion of total output! The importance of the growth rate is undeniable.

■

INGREDIENTS OF GROWTH: A FIRST LOOK

What are the sources of economic growth? Basically, there are six strategic ingredients in the growth of any economy. Four of these factors relate to the physical ability of an economy to grow. They are (1) the quantity and quality of its natural resources, (2) the quantity and quality of its human resources, (3) the supply or stock of capital goods, and (4) technology. These four items may be termed the *supply factors* in economic growth. These are the physical agents of greater production. It is the availability of more and better resources, including the stock of technological knowledge, which permits an economy to produce a greater real output.

But the ability to grow and the actual realization of growth may be quite different things. Specifically, two additional considerations contribute to growth. First, there is a *demand factor* in growth. To realize its growing productive potential, a nation must obviously provide for the full employment of its expanding supplies of resources. This requires a growing level of aggregate demand. Second, there is the *allocative factor* in growth. To achieve its productive potential, a nation must provide not only for the full employment of its resources, but also for full production from them. The ability to expand production is not a sufficient condition for the expansion of total output; the actual utilization of available resources *and* the allocation of those resources in such a way as to get the maximum amount of useful goods produced are also required.

These factors can be placed in proper perspective by recalling the production possibilities curve, reproduced in Figure 19-1. This is a best-performance curve in that it indicates the various *maximum* combinations of products the economy can produce, given the quantity and quality of its natural, human, and capital resources, and its stock of technological know-how. Obviously, an improvement in any of the supply factors will push the production possibilities curve to the right, as indicated by the shift from *AB* to *CD* in Figure 19-1. Increases in the quantity or quality of resources and technological advances push the curve to the right. But the demand and allocative factors remind us that the economy need not realize its maximum productive potential; the curve may shift to the right and leave the economy behind at some level of operation *inside* the curve. In particular, an increase in

the productive *potential* of the economy will not be realized if the economy fails to generate a level of aggregate demand sufficient to provide full employment, and fails to maintain the flexibility to adjust to those changes in the allocation of resources demanded by changes in the relative supplies of resources or technological knowledge. In other words, to stay on the rightward-shifting production possibilities curve, the economy must avoid *un*employment (apparent unemployment) and *under*employment (disguised unemployment).

Example: The net increase in the labor force of the United States is roughly 2 million workers per year. As such, this increment raises the productive capacity, or potential, of the economy. But the realization of the extra output these additional workers are capable of producing presumes an appropriate increase in aggregate money demand. Furthermore, achieving the maximum additional output from this increase in the labor force presumes that these new workers will be efficiently allocated within the economy; that is, additions to the labor force should be apportioned to those industries and firms wherein the value of their contribution to total output will be greatest.

It is notable that the supply and demand factors in growth are related. For example, unemployment tends to retard the rate of capital accumulation and may slow expenditures for research. And, conversely, a low rate of innovation and investment can be a basic cause of unemployment.

FIGURE 19-1 ECONOMIC GROWTH AND THE PRODUCTION POSSIBILITIES CURVE

Economic growth is indicated by an outward shift of the production possibilities curve, as from *AB* to *CD*. Increases in the quantity and quality of resources and technological advance permit this shift; full employment and allocative efficiency are essential to its realization.

GROWTH: A MORE SOPHISTICATED VIEW

Recognizing that growth can be represented by a rightward shift of the production possibilities curve, we now come to a more sophisticated conception of growth economics. *The degree to which total output can be expanded depends upon the proportion in which resource inputs are expanded.* Curve C_1R_1 in Figure 19-2a shows the production possibilities curve for an economy which has available certain given quantities of human and property resources. Now assume that each of the resources of this economy is suddenly doubled. What will happen to total output? Common sense correctly deduces that a doubling of resource inputs will double output, as suggested by the shift of C_1R_1 to C_2R_2.[1] Note that $OC_1 = C_1C_2$ and $OR_1 = R_1R_2$. Furthermore, with the doubling of both the number of labor inputs and total output, it is clear that output per worker will be the same for both production possibilities curves. Increasing resource inputs by the same absolute amounts once again would shift the production possibilities curve to C_3R_3, where $R_2R_3 = R_1R_2 = OR_1$ and $C_2C_3 = C_1C_2 = OC_1$.

□ Law of Diminishing Returns

But an economy may find it extremely difficult to increase *all* its resources in a balanced or proportionate manner. Land, in particular, is a relatively fixed resource. Typically, the mineral deposits and amount of arable land available to a nation can be increased only within narrow limits. What will happen

to total output when inputs are increased *dis*proportionately, that is, when property resources (land) are held constant and more labor is applied to them? The answer to this question has its roots in the famous *law of diminishing returns*,[2] which has applications both to the economy as a whole and to individual firms and industries (Chapters 25 and 30).

The concept of diminishing returns can best be understood by performing an easy mental experiment. Imagine an economy whose property resources (land and real capital) are absolutely fixed. In particular, visualize a primitive, underdeveloped economy whose stock of capital goods is negligible and whose supply of arable land is fixed. Assume, too, that technology—the stock of technological knowledge—is fixed; this means that the *quality* of both capital and labor is given. Assuming its population is growing, this simple agrarian society is concerned primarily with adding labor to a fixed amount of land and a few rudimentary farm tools to produce the food and fiber needed by its population. What happens to total output as equal increments—equal doses—of labor are added to a

---

[1]We shall find later, in Chapter 25, that, because of *economies of scale,* this may not be precisely true. But we can regard this statement as substantially correct.

[2]This law goes by other names: for example, the principle of diminishing marginal productivity and the law of variable proportions.

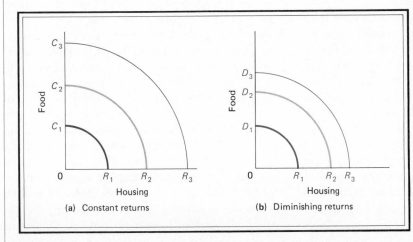

FIGURE 19-2 (a) CONSTANT AND (b) DIMINISHING RETURNS

If all inputs are increased proportionately, total output should increase proportionately. That is, if all inputs are doubled, then total output should double, as indicated by the shift of the production possibilities curve from C_1R_1 to C_2R_2 in **(a)**. But if one or more resources are fixed, as is assumed in **(b)**, then equal increases in another resource (say, labor) will result in smaller and smaller increases in total output. That is, diminishing returns will result because labor is now being combined with smaller amounts of other resources per worker.

(a) Constant returns

(b) Diminishing returns

fixed amount of property (primarily land) resources? The law of diminishing returns indicates that *as successive equal increments of one resource (labor, in this case) are added to a fixed resource (land and property), beyond some point the resulting increases in total output will diminish in size.* The *increase* in total product resulting from each successive dose of labor is called the *marginal physical product* or simply *marginal product.* Our law, then, says that as successive inputs of labor are added to a fixed amount of some other resource(s), the resulting *marginal* product will diminish beyond some point.

Qualification: Note we say "beyond some point." The initial increments or doses of labor may be subject to *increasing returns*—marginal product may rise for a time. The reason for this is that initially, with a very small labor force, property resources will be grossly underutilized. The fixed supplies of land and capital will be seriously undermanned. A very small amount of labor combined with a very large amount of land will result in relatively inefficient production. As equal increments or doses of labor are added to the fixed amount of land, the problem of underutilization is overcome and the resulting marginal product will increase for a time.

But this stage of increasing returns will inevitably reverse itself. As more and more labor is added to the fixed amount of property resources, a point will be reached where land and capital come to be overmanned or overutilized. That is, *each* worker will be equipped with smaller and smaller amounts of land and capital. In our simple agrarian society, more and more workers will be farming each acre of arable land and *each* worker will have fewer tools with which to work. Hence, successive equal doses of labor will result in smaller and smaller increases in total output. Diminishing returns have been encountered; the marginal product of successive doses of labor diminishes and may eventually become negative in the extreme!

□ **The Production Possibilities Curve and Diminishing Returns**

Let us now interpret the law of diminishing returns within the framework of the production possibilities curve. Whereas a proportionate increase in *all* inputs will cause total output to increase proportionately, as suggested by Figure 19-2a, a disproportionate increase in inputs—increasing the labor force while holding property resources constant—will cause total output to increase less than proportionately to the increase in labor. As Figure 19-2b indicates, if the labor force is doubled and the inputs of property resources are held constant, total output will less than double. The production possibilities curve will move from D_1R_1 to only D_2R_2. Why? Because property resources will tend to be overmanned. Double the labor force again and the overutilization of property resources will become more severe. This means that total output will rise by a still smaller amount—from D_2R_2 to, say, D_3R_3. Note that $OR_1 > R_1R_2 > R_2R_3$ and $OD_1 > D_1D_2 > D_2D_3$.

□ **Diminishing Returns: Arithmetic Example**

Table 19-1 presents a more conventional and somewhat more sophisticated illustration of the law of diminishing returns. It provides us with a reference point from which we can further explore the causes of, and the constraints upon, economic growth. Here we are adding equal increments or doses of labor to fixed amounts of land and capital. To simplify our exposition, total output (real GNP) consists of only one product—say, corn (food). Column 2 indicates the total output which will result from each level of labor input in column 1. Column 3, marginal physical product, shows us the *change* in total output associated with each additional unit of labor. Note that with no labor inputs, total output is zero; empty, untilled land will yield no output. The first

Table 19-1   A MACROECONOMIC ILLUSTRATION OF DIMINISHING RETURNS
(*hypothetical data*)

(1) Inputs of labor (millions of man-years)	(2) Total product, TP (millions of bushels of food)	(3) Marginal physical product, MP (millions of bushels of food)	(4) Average physical product, AP (bushels of food per man-year)
0	0		—
		100	
1	100		100
		150	
2	250		125
		125	
3	375		125
		101	
4	476		119
		74	
5	550		110
		50	
6	600		100
		30	
7	630		90
		−6	
8	624		78

two doses of labor reflect increasing returns, their MPs being 100 and 150 tons of food, respectively. But then, beginning with the third increment of labor, marginal physical product—the increase in total output—diminishes continuously and actually becomes negative with the eighth dose of labor.

Figure 19-3a and b show the law of diminishing returns in terms of total product and marginal product respectively. The MP curve reflects the increases in total product associated with each successive dose of labor. Geometrically, marginal physical product is the slope of the total product curve. Note that so long as MP is positive, TP is increasing. And when MP is zero, TP is at its peak. Finally, when MP becomes negative, TP is necessarily declining. Increasing returns are reflected in a rising marginal physical product curve; diminishing returns, in a falling marginal physical product.

In our discussion we will find it particularly useful to note what the law of diminishing returns means for *average product* or output per input of labor. AP is calculated in column 4 of Table 19-1 simply by dividing TP by the number of inputs of labor, that is, by dividing column 2 by column 1. Note in both the table and Figure 19-3b that AP reflects the

same general "rising-maximum-declining" relationship between variable inputs of labor and output with which the law of diminishing returns has already familiarized us.

Also note this technical point concerning the relationship between MP and AP: Where MP exceeds AP, the latter must rise. And wherever MP is less than AP, then AP must be declining. It follows that MP intersects AP where the latter is at a maximum. This relationship is a matter of mathematical necessity. You raise your average grade in a course only when your score on an additional (marginal) examination is greater than the average of all your past scores. If your grade on an additional exam is below your current average, your average will be pulled down.

☐   **Optimum Population**

Average physical product is a convenient and important indicator of growth because output per worker (AP) and real income per worker are essentially the same thing. That is, average physical product or output per worker is our second definition of economic growth. In Table 19-1 and Figure 19-3a and b we find that growth in terms of definition 1 continues through the seventh input of labor. But in

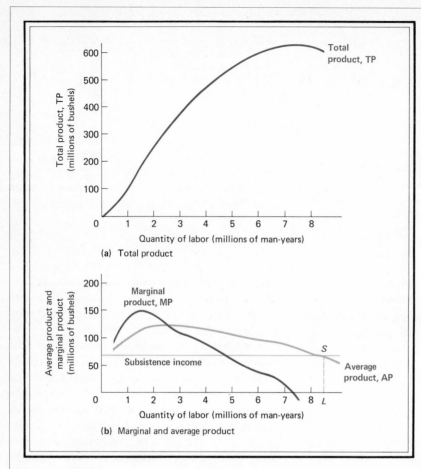

FIGURE 19-3 THE LAW OF DIMINISHING RETURNS

As a variable resource (labor) is added to fixed amounts of other resources (land and capital), the resulting total product will eventually increase by diminishing amounts, reach a maximum, and then decline as in **(a)**. Marginal product in **(b)** reflects the changes in total product associated with each input of labor. Average product is simply output per worker. Note that marginal product intersects average product at the maximum average product.

terms of definition 2—output per worker—growth reaches a maximum at some point between the second and third units of labor.

That particular population size at which real output or income per person is at a maximum is called the *optimum population* for society. The optimum population is that population which, given the economy's property resources and technology, will yield the greatest income per person. This concept reinforces an earlier point: Population growth may be a mixed blessing insofar as growth is concerned. An expansion of the population and labor force typically (but not always) increases real GNP, that is, contributes to growth in the sense

of definition 1. But in terms of definition 2, population may be either too large or too small.

□ Malthus and Misery

Diminishing returns correctly suggest that the relationship between the size of a country's population (labor force) and its property resources is highly relevant in determining both its total output and its output per person or standard of living. Indeed, this fact was perceived by the English economist Thomas R. Malthus at the close of the eighteenth century and enunciated in his famous *Essay on the*

Principle of Population (1798). Malthus's explicit purpose was "to account for much of that poverty and misery observable among the lower classes of every nation," and his explanation of this misery was rooted firmly in the law of diminishing returns.

The essence of Malthus's thesis is quite simple: *The population of a nation tends to outrun its capacity to produce the food and fiber needed to sustain itself.* Population tends to increase at a constant geometric rate (2, 4, 8, 16, 32, 64, 128, 256, and so on). But the output of food, on the other hand, increases *at best* only at a constant arithmetic rate (1, 2, 3, 4, 5, 6, and so forth). Given these different rates of increase, population will in time inevitably press upon the food supply and the results will be subsistence living levels, misery, and, in the extreme, starvation. But why won't the food supply increase at a more rapid rate? Because of diminishing returns. As the growing population puts more and more laborers to work on a fixed amount of arable land, both marginal and then average product (Figure 19-3*b*) will diminish. Each worker is combined with less and less land, so his productivity declines.

We have just seen that a society's output per worker is its income per worker. A diminishing average product therefore means a falling standard of living. In short, the pressure of an expanding population and labor force upon fixed land resources invokes the law of diminishing returns. Total output increases less than proportionately to population, so the standard of living necessarily declines. In the eighteenth century, the result was the widespread misery and poverty which Malthus readily observed. We might draw a subsistence level-of-living line in Figure 19-3*b* and summarize Malthus's position by saying that, given the reality of diminishing returns, persistent and substantial population growth (a rightward movement along the horizontal axis) will keep the level of living (vertical axis) perilously close to the bare subsistence level (point *S*). Only the gloomy team of disease, malnutrition,

and famine will bring population growth to a halt at *OL*.

We are all well aware that mankind has been undergoing an extraordinary expansion of numbers. The magnitude of this unparalleled population explosion is portrayed vividly in Figure 19-4. World population growth in just the last two centuries has been 3 times larger than the cumulated expansion of mankind during all the previous millennia of man's existence! Given this incredible growth of population and its projected continuance, *and* given the hard fact that only a finite amount of land exists on our planet, it is highly relevant to inquire as to the extent to which Malthus's gloomy forecast has come to pass. Is the Malthusian prediction being realized in any of today's nations?

Clearly the specter of Malthus stalks many of the so-called underdeveloped nations of the world. In India, for example, rapid population growth has been a basic factor in making malnutrition, famine, and disease a way of life—and of death. Indeed, many of the nations of Africa, South America, and Asia are finding it extremely difficult to raise their living standards, because rapid population growth means that year after year there are more mouths to feed and more bodies to clothe and shelter. While Egypt's Aswan Dam makes a substantial contribution to that nation's output of food, the growth in population which occurred during the period of construction has had the effect of leaving per capita food production substantially unchanged!

□ **Rising Productivity and Growth**

In contrast, the "advanced" nations of the world—the United States, Canada, the countries of Western Europe, Australia, New Zealand, and Japan—enjoy high and rising standards of living despite considerable population growth. The question is: Why the differences? Why poverty in India and plenty in Indiana? The answer can be found by pursuing our dis-

FIGURE 19-4 THE LONG-RUN TREND OF WORLD POPULATION GROWTH

A dramatic acceleration of world population growth has been experienced in modern times. (*John D. Durand, "A Long-range View of World Population Growth," The Annals, January 1967 p. 3.*)

cussion of diminishing returns. While Figure 19-3*a* and *b* imply the possibility of Malthusian misery, these same curves, and more specifically, *the assumptions upon which they are based,* suggest the possibility of growth and a rising standard of living.

Let us perform a second mental experiment similar to that underlying Figure 19-3*a* and *b*. Again we add a growing labor force to a constant conglomerate of property resources and technical knowledge, as before. But now let us assume that these property resources are fixed at a higher level both quantitatively and qualitatively.[3] Specifically, suppose each worker, instead of being equipped with a negligible amount of capital, is aided in his productive efforts with, say, $100 worth of machinery and equipment. Suppose, too, that technology is better than in our first experiment; for example, farmers now have discovered the contribution which contour plowing and crop rotation can make to output. And let us assume the labor force itself is qualitatively superior—physically and mentally—to that of our first experiment.

Would these changes—more capital, an improved technology, and a better labor force—revoke the law of diminishing returns? Although "revoke" is perhaps too strong a word, these factors can offset or forestall diminishing returns. We can envision what happens by looking at the curves in Figure 19-5. The average-product curve designated as AP_1 is taken from Figure 19-3*b* and merely repeats the results of our original experiment. AP_2 portrays the results of our second experiment. Note that this new curve still reflects the law of diminishing returns but is at a higher level, and the point at which average product begins to fall corresponds with a larger population or labor force. Why? Because each level of labor input is now equipped with more capital and better technological know-how, and the labor force itself is superior. For all these reasons, any given number of workers will produce a larger total output, and hence a larger output per worker, than under the inferior conditions of our first experiment. A third experiment involving still more capital, a further advanced

[3]In Chapter 21 we shall find that less tangible "resources"—for example, attitudes and institutional arrangements—must often be changed if growth is to occur.

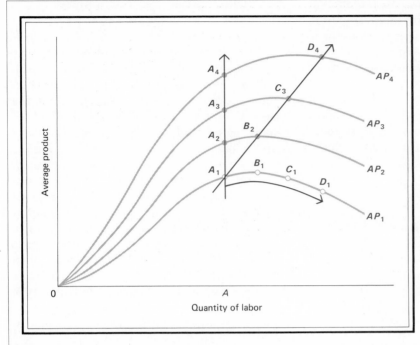

FIGURE 19-5 RISING
PRODUCTIVITY AND
ECONOMIC GROWTH

The "forces of growth"—increases in the stock of capital, technological progress, and improvements in the quality of labor—may offset diminishing returns by shifting the average-product curve upward. A growing economy with a constant population will follow the $A_1 A_2 A_3 A_4$ path. A growing economy with an expanding population will achieve a higher output per worker along the $A_1 B_2 C_3 D_4$ path. A nongrowing economy whose population is expanding will follow the $A_1 B_1 C_1 D_1$ path on an unchanging average-product curve and will be subject to a declining output per worker.

technology, and a labor force of even higher quality will again raise the average-product curve and locate its maximum point further to the right, as indicated by AP_3. Still further improvements in the quantity of capital, technology, and labor force would yield AP_4.

A bit of reflection reveals that, for any nation with a growing population and labor force, we can think of the course of its standard of living as the net result of two opposed forces. On the one hand, diminishing returns cause the application of successive inputs of labor to result eventually in smaller and smaller increases in total product, a declining average product, and a falling standard of living. On the other hand, we have the "forces of growth"—increases in the stock of capital, technological progress, and a qualitatively improved labor force—tending to offset diminishing returns by violating the very assumptions or conditions upon which the functioning of the law depends.

Now, and at the hazard of oversimplifica-

tion, what has happened in the less developed countries is that the forces of growth have been absent or, at best, present in only modest degrees, so that diminishing returns have prevailed. And, as Malthus envisioned, population has indeed tended to press upon the food supply, to the end that living standards have remained pitifully low (Table 21-1). In Figure 19-5 this case can be envisioned as the movement down a stable average-product curve, as from A_1 to B_1 to C_1 and so forth, on curve AP_1. As our diagram suggests, such an economy is literally going "over the hill."

At the other extreme, suppose population and the labor force are constant at, say, OA in Figure 19-5 and the forces of growth are strongly evident. These improvements in technology and the labor force and increases in the stock of capital would shift the average-productivity curve upward and trace the path suggested by A_1, A_2, A_3, and A_4. In general, the developed countries of the world have been experiencing growth in their populations and labor forces. But at the same time, the forces of growth have been pushing their *AP* curves upward. Hence, the advanced nations have been following the kind of path suggested by A_1, B_2, C_3, and D_4. Diminishing returns have *tended* to be at work, but these nations, by adding to their stocks of capital and of knowledge and by improving the quality of their labor forces, have been able to more than offset diminishing returns and to achieve a higher and higher standard of living over time.

AGGREGATE DEMAND AND GROWTH

Up to this point our discussion has centered upon the supply side of economic growth, that is, upon those factors which determine the productive capacity of the economy. We now want to consider the demand side of economic growth.

□ Keeping Pace with Capacity

The essence of the problem is that in an economy whose productive capacity is expanding, the full-employment noninflationary NNP will obviously be increasing over time. Therefore, the realization or achievement of that desired output clearly depends upon an expanding level of aggregate demand. Figure 19-6 is based upon the simple income-determination model of Figure 12-5 wherein we assume the full-employment NNP in year 1 is $490 billion and that, fortunately, aggregate demand is at $(C + I_n + G)_1$, so that full employment is being realized. But now, in a growth context, we must acknowledge that the economy's productive capacity—its full-employment NNP—will be increasing through time. That is, increases in the quantity and quality of resources and technological advances will make it possible for the economy to produce a larger full-employment NNP in year 2. Sup-

FIGURE 19-6 AGGREGATE DEMAND AND FULL EMPLOYMENT IN A GROWING ECONOMY

As the result of increases in the quantity and quality of resources and technological progress, the full-employment NNP will increase over time, for example, from $490 in year 1 to $510 in year 2. To utilize this expanded productive capacity, aggregate demand must increase from $(C + I_n + G)_1$ to $(C + I_n + G)_2$.

pose these supply factors in growth permit a 4 percent increase in real output so that the full-employment NNP is approximately $510 billion in year 2. The obvious point is that, in order for this enhanced productive potential to be realized, aggregate demand must expand at a rate sufficient to maintain full employment. In this instance, aggregate demand must shift upward to $(C + I_n + G)_2$. If aggregate demand grows less or not at all, the consequence will be underutilized productive capacity, unemployed resources, and a retarded growth rate. On the other hand, if aggregate demand shifts above $(C + I_n + G)_2$, the economy will realize its increased capacity to produce but it will also incur inflation. Note that fiscal and monetary policies must now be manipulated to hit a moving target!

□ **Full-Employment Growth Model**

More sophisticated growth models focus attention upon the investment component of aggregate demand. Figure 19-6 stresses the *income-creating* aspect of net investment; that is, investment is regarded solely as a generator of output, income, and employment. But we must now recognize that net investment also has a *capacity-creating* aspect. Net investment represents an addition to the nation's stock of capital goods and this enhances the productive capacity of the economy. An economy which engages in net investment in year 1 is expanding its "national factory" and will thereby have the capacity to produce a larger full-employment NNP in year 2.

Assumptions Table 19-2 embodies a simple macroeconomic growth model which highlights the capacity-creating role of net investment and allows us to isolate certain crucial factors which determine an economy's full-employment growth rate. We begin by making several simplifying assumptions which are reflected in the first row of the table. Assume, first, a private economy wherein aggregate demand is composed of only consumption and investment. Suppose, too, the economy is currently (year 1) in equilibrium at the full-employment NNP of $100 billion. Third, assume that the average propensity to save (APS) is .20.[4] Now, noting that saving is $20 billion (.20 × $100 billion), we know that the level of investment required to achieve full employment is also $20 billion $(S = I_n)$. In short, the year 1 figures of Table 19-2 represent a very simple income-determination model a la Chapter 12.

Capital-Output Ratio But now we must introduce the capacity-creating aspect of net investment and observe that this economy will be able to produce a larger full-employment NNP in year 2. The question is: How much larger? This depends upon the *capital-output ratio,* that is, the ratio or relationship between net investment and the resulting increase in productive or output capacity of the economy. Let us suppose this ratio is 4:1 or, more simply, 4. This means that every $4 of net investment

[4]To avoid complications, we assume the APS is constant at various levels of NNP.

Table 19-2 FULL-EMPLOYMENT GROWTH RATES (*hypothetical data, in billions*)

(1) Year	(2) Full-employment NNP	(3) Full-employment level of saving	(4) Full-employment level of investment	(5) Increase in full-employment NNP
1	$100	$20	$20	
2	105	21	21	$5 $(= 20 \div 4)$
3	110.25	22.05	22.05	5.25 $(= 21 \div 4)$
4	115.76	23.15	23.15	5.51 $(= 22.05 \div 4)$
5	——	——	——	

in year 1 makes the economy capable of producing $1 of additional output in year 2 and succeeding years. Knowing that it takes $4 worth of net investment to increase productive capacity by $1, we can simply divide year 1's $20 billion of net investment by the capital-output ratio of 4 to find the increase in the economy's full-employment NNP as the result of year 1's investment. In column 5 of Table 19-2 we find that the answer is $5 billion; full-employment output in year 2 is $105 billion, compared with year 1's $100 billion.

Succeeding rows in Table 19-2 merely repeat this procedure. We find that in year 2 the full-employment level of saving will be $21 billion (= $105 billion × .20). It is assumed in column 3 that net investment is just sufficient to offset this saving leakage so that full employment is again realized. Same question: By how much will year 2's net investment increase productive capacity in year 3? Again, in column 5 we get the answer by dividing net investment by the capital-output ratio. Year 2's net investment will permit the economy to produce an extra $5.25 billion (= $21 billion ÷ 4) in year 3. The reader is urged to follow through on this procedure for years 3 and 4 and to calculate the omitted figures for year 5.

The Growth Rate It is important to stress that Table 19-2 traces through the growth scenario of an economy wherein aggregate demand grows by just that amount necessary to sustain full employment through time. The figures of the table therefore reflect the *full-employment* growth rate for this economy. Inspection of column 2 indicates that the full-employment NNP is growing by 5 percent per year. Similarly, by inspection we find that the growth in net investment which is required to sustain full employment is also 5 percent. Furthermore, although the growth *rates* of NNP and net investment are constant, this obviously means that the *absolute* increases in NNP and net investment are larger and larger each year.

Let us now generalize: Column 5 of Table 19-2 tells us that each year NNP increases by the proportion of the NNP which is saved and invested (determined by the APS) *divided by* the capital-output ratio. Hence, we can say that:

The full-employment growth rate

$$\bullet \quad = \frac{\text{average propensity to save}}{\text{capital-output ratio}}$$

For the illustrative data of Table 19-2:

$$5\% \text{ or } .05 = \frac{.20}{4}$$

Obviously, any alteration in the basic data of our model—any change in the APS or the capital-output ratio—will change the full-employment growth rate. Specifically, from our formula it is clear that, *given the APS, a decline in the capital-output ratio will increase the growth rate.* For example, with an APS of .20, a decline in the capital-output ratio from 4 to 2 will increase the growth rate from 5 to 10 percent. On reflection this is not at all surprising: A lower capital-output ratio implies that the productivity of capital or investment goods has increased. That is, when the capital-output ratio declines from 4 to 2, it means that now, because of, say, technological progress, only one-half as much additional capital goods are required to increase NNP by $1 as were necessary before. Similarly, *given the capital-output ratio, an increase in the APS will increase the full-employment growth rate.* Given our capital-output ratio of 4, an increase in the APS to, say, .40 would increase the economy's full-employment growth rate from 5 to 10 percent. The rationale for this generalization is rooted in Figure 2-4; other things being equal, an economy which saves and invests a larger proportion of its national output will grow more rapidly. Question 6 at the end of the chapter provides an opportunity for further confirmation of these generalizations.

ALLOCATIVE EFFICIENCY AND GROWTH

The forces of growth—both the supply factors and an appropriately expanding level of aggregate demand—will call for changes in the allocation of the economy's resources over time. If these changes in resource use do not occur with reasonable speed and completeness, the economy will fail to realize fully its capacity for growth.

On the supply side, if we were to disaggregate the economy's overall growth, we would find that the productive capacities of some industries and firms are expanding rapidly while those of others are growing slowly or perhaps even contracting. Such changes obviously imply appropriate adjustments in the allocation of resources. Where, for example, do expanding industries obtain the resources which their growth requires? In part, they may be obtained from current increases in our total supplies of resources. Thus, an expanding industry may get a part of the additional labor it needs from new labor force entrants. It may obtain the remainder of its added labor from other, declining industries. In either event some mechanism is needed to guide new resources into their most productive uses or, as the case may be, to direct currently employed resources from low-productivity to high-productivity employments. In short, changes in technology (as reflected in either new productive techniques or new goods) and changes in the relative scarcities, and therefore prices, of resources which are germane to growth call for constant reallocations of human and property resources among alternative uses. As noted earlier, if these resource realignments do not occur with reasonable rapidity and completeness, the economy's capacity for growth may be underfulfilled.

The need for sustained allocative efficiency also has roots on the demand side. We already know that aggregate demand must expand appropriately if the full-capacity output of an expanding economy is to be realized. This generalization, however, conceals the fact that as total demand grows, its composition or structure will change. The demands for some goods will be highly sensitive to increases in income. For other goods, demand might be quite insensitive to income growth. For example, the demands for potatoes, soap, and wheat grow very modestly as income expands, but the demands for steak, education, jewelry, and automobiles tend to increase sharply as income rises. In any event, extensive shifts in the allocation of resources will again be necessary.

Summary

1 Economic growth may be defined either in terms of **a.** an expanding real national output (income) or **b.** an expanding per capita real output (income). Growth lessens the burden of scarcity and provides increases in the national output which can be used in the resolution of domestic and international socioeconomic problems.

2 The supply factors in economic growth are **a.** the quantity and quality of a nation's natural resources, **b.** the quantity and quality of its human resources, **c.** its stock of capital facilities, and **d.** its technology. Two other factors—a sufficient level of aggregate demand and allocative efficiency—are essential if the economy is to realize its growth potential.

3 The principle of diminishing returns exercises a constraint upon growth where one or more resources are fixed in supply. This law tells us that with a given technology, the addition of successive units of one resource (labor) to fixed amounts of other resources (land and capital) will ultimately result in smaller and smaller

increases in total output. That is, the increases in output will be less than proportionate to the increases in the inputs of the variable resource. This means that the
average output or productivity per worker will ultimately diminish as more and more
labor is added (Figure 19-3).

4   Thomas Malthus used the law of diminishing returns over a century and a
half ago to explain the widespread poverty which then existed. In particular, he
argued that rapid population growth, coupled with diminishing returns in agricultural
production, was tending to keep real income per capita at the subsistence level.

5   Technological progress, increases in the stock of capital, and improvements in
the quality of labor have the effect of offsetting diminishing returns by increasing the
productivity of labor (Figure 19-5).

6   An expanding productive potential will not be achieved unless aggregate
demand expands at an appropriate rate. Growth models emphasize the capacity-
creating aspect of net investment and demonstrate that the economy's full-employment growth rate can be calculated by dividing the APS by the capital-output ratio.
The APS and the growth rate are directly related; the capital-output ratio and the
growth rate are inversely related.

7   The realization of the growth potential of an economy presumes that appropriate reallocations of resources are achieved.

Questions and Study Suggestions

1   Key terms and concepts to remember: economic growth; supply, demand, and
allocative factors in growth; law of diminishing returns; total, marginal, and average
product; optimum population; income-creating and capacity-creating aspects of
investment; capital-output ratio; full-employment growth rate.

2   What difficulties are involved in measuring economic growth? Why is economic growth important? Explain why the difference between a 3.5 percent and a 3.0
percent annual growth rate might be of great importance.

3   What are the major causes of economic growth? "There are both a demand
and a supply side to economic growth." Explain. Illustrate the operation of both sets
of factors in terms of the production possibilities curve.

4   State fully and precisely the law of diminishing returns. Use production
possibilities curves to illustrate economic growth under conditions of constant and
diminishing returns. Why are diminishing returns significant for a nation's economic
growth?

5   Explain: "Rapid population growth may both contribute to, and detract
from, a nation's economic progress." What is meant by an "optimum population"?

6   What is the full-employment growth rate? How can it be calculated? If the
capital-output ratio is 3, what will the full-employment growth rate be when the APS
is .10, .20, and .30? If the APS is .30, what will the full-employment growth rate be
when the capital-output ratio is 5, 4, and 3? What two generalizations can you derive
from these examples?

7   How did Malthus explain the extremely low levels of income which were so
common in the eighteenth century? To what extent, if any, is Malthus's explanation
of poverty relevant today? How can an economy with a rapidly growing population
and labor force effectively offset diminishing returns?

8   Use the following data to calculate marginal physical product and average
physical product. Plot total, marginal, and average physical product and explain in

detail the relationship between each pair of curves. What is the optimum population or labor force for this economy?

Inputs of labor	Total physical product	Marginal physical product	Average physical product
1	15	_____	_____
2	34	_____	_____
3	51	_____	_____
4	65	_____	_____
5	74	_____	_____
6	80	_____	_____
7	83	_____	_____
8	82	_____	_____

Selected References

Brown, Lester R.: *In the Human Interest: A Strategy to Stabilize World Population* (New York: W. W. Norton & Company, Inc., 1974).

Fabricant, Solomon: *A Primer on Productivity* (New York: Random House, 1969).

Gill, Richard T.: *Economic Development: Past and Present,* 3d ed. (Englewood Cliffs, N.J.: Prentice-Hall, Inc., 1972), particularly chaps. 1–4.

Rostow, W. W.: *The Stages of Economic Growth,* 2d ed. (New York: Cambridge University Press, 1971).

Last Word
Population and the Growth Mystique

The national Commission on Population Growth argues that there is no convincing economic argument for continued population growth in the United States.

. . . we find no convincing economic argument for continued national population growth. On the contrary, most of the plusses are on the side of slower growth. This finding is at variance with much opinion, especially in the business community and among many civic leaders. We have sought to find the reason for this seeming contradiction.

Periods of rapid population growth in this country have generally been periods of rapid economic expansion as well. It is not surprising, therefore, that we associate population growth with economic progress. However, the historical association of population growth with economic expansion would be an erroneous guide to the formulation of population policy for the future.

This connection reflects in large part the fact that periods of rapid expansion attracted immigrants to our shores and thus quickened population growth as a result. Additions to population through immigration are far more stimulating to economic growth than are additions by natural increase. This is because, while babies remain dependent for many years before beginning to contribute to output, many immigrants are of working age and thus become immediately productive. . . .

This answer may not satisfy the gas station owner, local food retailer, or banker, to whom it seems obvious that "more people" means more customers or more savings accounts. Once again, however, we need to examine the *kind* of growth that means more business, and its relationship to local economic expansion. The rapid local population growth that means more business results chiefly from other people moving in, not more people being born and raised. Adults moving in make ready customers and ready employees. They have grown up elsewhere, their education has been paid for elsewhere, and being young, they impose few of the demands of the dependent aged. Since mobile people are, on the average, better qualified than those who do not move, it is no surprise that they provide an extra boost to local establishments.

We have studied the effects of lower national population growth rates on the economic well-being of urban and rural areas within the nation. Is there reason to fear that the ills typical of areas of population decline today would become more serious or widespread if national population growth rates declined? We conclude that there is not; such fears are based on a mistaken belief that population decline causes economic decline. In reality, the chain of causation in distressed areas runs from (1) the decline of regional competitive capability to (2) unemployment to (3) net outmigration to (4) population loss. Accordingly, there is little reason to suppose that local problems of unemployment or obsolescence of physical facilities would be more serious in a situation of zero or negative national population growth than they would be at any positive level of national population growth. In the future, as in the past, areas of relatively high unemployment will tend to be areas of relative population loss; but the relative population loss will be the consequence and not the cause of local unemployment.

The diminished burden of providing for dependents, and for the multiplication of facilities to keep up with expanding population, should make more of our national output available for many desirable purposes: new kinds of capital formation, including human resources investment; public expenditure involving qualitative improvement and modernization; and greater attention to environmental and amenity objectives. Thus, whatever the future problems of urban areas and regions may be, we should have more ample per capita resources to attack them in a situation with a lower rate of population growth than we would have with a higher rate.

Report of the Commission on Population Growth and the American Future, *Population and the American Future* (Washington, 1972), pp. 51–53, abridged.

20

Economic Growth: Fact and Controversy

This chapter has three main objectives. The first is to state and explain the growth record of the United States. Secondly, we will outline the current debate over the *desirability* of growth as an economic goal. Thirdly, we will examine the question: Is continued economic growth *feasible?* In dealing with this question we will present and critically discuss the so-called Doomsday models of economic growth.

GROWTH RECORD OF THE UNITED STATES

Table 20-1 gives us a rough idea of economic growth in the United States over the past seven decades as viewed through our two definitions of growth. Column 2 summarizes the economy's growth as measured by increases in real GNP. Although not steady, the growth of real GNP has been quite remarkable. The *real GNP has increased almost elevenfold in this century.* It is remarkable that the growth in the real GNP since 1965 is roughly equal to its total growth in the entire period between 1776 and 1940!

But our population has also grown significantly. Hence, using our second definition of growth, we find in column 3 that *real per capita GNP has more than doubled since 1940.* The growth portrayed in Table 20-1 is expected to continue.[1]

[1] Donald E. Kutscher, "Revised BLS Projections to 1980 and 1985: An Overview," *Monthly Labor Review,* March 1976, pp. 3–8, and author's calculations.

Table 20-1 REAL GNP AND PER CAPITA GNP, 1900–1976

(1) Year	(2) GNP, billions of 1958 dollars	(3) Per capita GNP, 1958 dollars
1900	$ 77	$1011
1910	120	1299
1920	140	1315
1925	179	1549
1930	183	1490
1935	169	1331
1940	227	1720
1945	355	2538
1950	355	2342
1955	438	2650
1960	488	2699
1965	618	3180
1970	723	3555
1976	835	3882

Source: U.S. Department of Commerce, *Historical Statistics of the United States: Colonial Times to 1970* (Washington, 1975), p. 224, and Department of Commerce data.

What about our *rate* of growth? Statistical data (Table 20-2) suggest that the long-term growth rate of the United States' real GNP has been on the order of 3½ percent per year, while real GNP per capita has grown at about 2 percent per year.

For at least two reasons these quantitative conclusions understate the economic growth which the American economy has actually experienced.

1 The figures of Tables 20-1 and 20-2 do *not* fully take into account improvements in product quality. Purely quantitative data do not provide an accurate comparison between an era of crystal sets and one of stereophonic phonographs.

2 The increases in real GNP and per capita GNP shown in Table 20-1 were accomplished despite very sizable increases in leisure. The seventy-hour workweek is a thing of the distant past. The standard workweek is now less than forty hours.

On the other hand, in our discussion of the growth controversy we shall find that these measures of growth do *not* take into account adverse effects upon the physical environment or upon the quality of life itself.

While impressive, the United States' growth record has been somewhat less dramatic than those achieved by some other developed countries. As Table 20-2 indicates, in recent years Japan and a number of countries of Western Europe—not to mention the Soviet Union (Chapter 45)—have reached comparable or superior rates of growth.

Table 20-2 GROWTH OF REAL GNP AND REAL GNP PER CAPITA IN SELECTED COUNTRIES

	Growth rates of real GNP		Growth rates of real GNP per capita	
	1870–1969	1950–1974	1870–1969	1950–1974
United States	3.7%	3.6%	2.0%	2.2%
Japan	4.2	8.9	—	7.7
Germany	3.0	6.0	1.9	4.9
United Kingdom	1.9	2.8	1.3	2.3
France	2.0	5.3	1.7	4.3
Italy	2.2	5.2	1.5	4.5
Canada	3.6	5.0	1.8	2.9

Source: U.S. Department of Commerce, *Historical Statistics of the United States: Colonial Times to 1970* (Washington, 1975), p. 225; and *Statistical Abstract of the United States, 1976*, p. 394.

SOURCES OF UNITED STATES GROWTH

This growth record can be explained largely in terms of the growth ingredients outlined in Chapter 19. Our comments here are brief and largely unqualified.

□ Natural Resources

Climate, soil, rainfall, mineral deposits, and sources of power are all important facets of any nation's natural resource base. These natural resource endowments constitute an obvious but fundamental factor in its capacity to expand, because, in contrast to the quantity and quality of labor and capital resources, the quantity and quality of a nation's natural resources are relatively fixed. Note that we say "relatively" fixed: Within limits, *available* natural resources can be increased in supply. True, given a nation's territorial limits, its mineral deposits of, for example, lead, copper, and zinc are present only in fixed amounts. The same holds true for petroleum and natural gas deposits. Yet the discovery and appropriation of existing deposits can add significantly to available, or usable, supplies of these resources. The discovery in 1969 of vast new oil reserves in Alaska's Prudhoe Bay is a relevant illustration. Similarly, arable land, pasture land, and timberland which have been exploited can frequently be renewed by modern conservation practices. Irrigation and drainage can add significantly to the supply of arable land, and have already done so. Finally, technological advance can augment available resource supplies through the development of new equipment for the detection and recovery of natural resources, on the one hand, and the discovery of new substitute materials for particularly scarce resources, on the other. For example, the perfection of offshore drilling techniques is adding significantly to our known petroleum reserves.

The United States has been most generously endowed in both the quantity and the quality of its natural resources. It is generally agreed that, with the possible exception of the Soviet Union, the United States has a larger variety and greater quantities of resources than any other nation. This is not to deny, however, that a growing population and rising affluence may put enormous demands upon our resources to the end that natural resource bottlenecks—absolute scarcities of specific materials—may become more common and more severe in the future than they have been heretofore.

□ Human Resources

The expansion of real GNP depends upon not only the quantity but also the quality of the labor force. Figure 20-1 provides us with the overall quantitative picture. A quite high birthrate, a declining death rate, and—for a

FIGURE 20-1 POPULATION AND LABOR FORCE GROWTH, 1928–1976

The United States labor force has been a stable proportion—about 40 percent—of the total population during this century. Since 1900 both the population and the labor force have roughly tripled. (*Bureau of Census data.*)

time—heavy immigration have teamed to provide the United States with substantial population growth through most of its history. The population quadrupled during the first half of the nineteenth century. It more than trebled during the last half, and has increased over two and a half times since 1900. There are almost ten times as many Americans today as there were in 1850. In 1976 the population exceeded the 215 million level, and it continues to grow. However, recent evidence suggests a decline in the birthrate, a transition from a three-child to a two-child average family. Whether this trend is permanent remains to be seen. In any event, "low fertility" projections suggest a population of 245 million by the year 2000, and "high fertility" projections envision a population of 287 million. In either case, there is little prospect that the nation's future economic growth will be retarded by a labor shortage!

More labor means more output, but it also means more people as consumers. The trick to increasing real GNP *per capita*—to raising the standard of living—depends upon improving the productivity of labor. And this depends in part upon the quality of labor itself. Worker for worker, the United States labor force is among the best in the world. Its overall health, education, and training all contribute to its high quality.

Figure 20-2 indicates that impressive gains have been made in educational attainment in recent years. Between 1952 and 1974 the percentage of workers aged eighteen or over who have finished high school rose from about 43 percent to about 69 percent. The percentage of labor-force members who have completed four or more years of college increased from 8 to 15 percent over the same period. In fact, some responsible scholars are suggesting that Americans may now be "overeducating" themselves relative to anticipated job openings. In particular, we may be building up an expanding surplus of workers with bachelor and advanced degrees (33,000 Ph.D. degrees were awarded in

FIGURE 20-2 RECENT CHANGES IN THE EDUCATIONAL ATTAINMENT OF THE LABOR FORCE

The percentage of the labor force completing high school and college has been rising steadily in recent years, while the percentage who did not go to high school or complete elementary school has been falling. (*Manpower Report of the President 1975.*)

1974, compared with 10,000 in 1960) who will encounter difficulty in finding jobs which utilize fully their training and skills.[2]

□ **Technological Advance**

Generally speaking, technological progress involves the more efficient use of resources, that is, combining or employing given resources in new ways so as to result in a larger output. In practice, technological advance and capital formation (investment) are closely related processes; technological advance typically entails investment in new machinery and equipment. The idea that there is a more efficient way to catch a rabbit than running it down led to investment in the bow and arrow. Yet in some instances technological advance and capital accumulation are distinct. Example: Modern crop-rotation practices and con-

[2]See Richard B. Freeman, *The Overeducated American* (New York: Academic Press, Inc., 1976), for an excellent discussion of the downturn in the labor market for college-trained manpower.

tour plowing are ideas which contribute greatly to output, although they do not necessarily entail the use of more capital equipment. In any event, we shall find it rewarding to discuss technological advance and capital formation separately, recognizing that the two are usually birds of a feather.

What has been the rate of technological advance in the United States? Casual observation suggests that, historically, it has been both rapid and profound. Gas and diesel engines, conveyer belts, and assembly lines come to mind as obviously significant developments of the past. More recently, the lamp of technology has freed the automation jinni and with it the potential wonders of the electronic brain and the push-button factory. Television, supersonic jets, the transistor and integrated circuitry, computers, microwave ovens, Xerox copiers, Polaroid cameras, containerized shipping, and nuclear power—not to mention space travel—are technological achievements which were in the realm of fantasy a mere generation ago.

Although it is difficult to measure unambiguously a nation's scientific output, total expenditures on research and development (R & D) constitute a rather widely accepted indicator of a nation's effort to advance technologically. The overall picture for the United States since World War II has been one of dramatic expansion of private and public R & D spending. From less than $3 billion in 1950, R & D expenditures are currently approaching $35 billion per year. Nevertheless, there is concern that R & D spending is now tending to retard the rate of growth of real GNP! Why so? The primary reason is that since the mid-sixties, R & D spending has been *declining as a percentage of GNP*. In 1975, R & D amounted to 2.3 percent of GNP, down substantially from the 3 percent of the 1964–1967 period. National Science Foundation projections suggest that this ratio may stabilize at about 2.2 percent for the next decade. The United States seems to be ploughing back a declining fraction of its output into the development of new technological knowledge, and this cutback suggests a lower future growth rate.

□ **Capital Formation: Investment**

To a very considerable degree workers, regardless of their skills and training, are no better than the capital goods with which they are equipped. The indirect or roundabout production which capital goods afford is a basic means of enhancing productive efficiency.

It is important to remember a message made explicit in the previous chapter's full-employment growth model (Table 19-2): The decision to save—to refrain from current consumption—is the prerequisite of investment or capital accumulation. In the 1970s *gross* investment in the United States averaged about 15 percent of GNP. However, much of this investment went into the replacement of depreciated capital goods; hence, *net* investment in this decade has averaged only about 5 percent of GNP.

Over time, this saving-and-investment process has yielded an extremely large stock of capital. A mid-1960s study estimated the value of our national capital at $2 *trillion,* a figure which means that the *average* American worker uses almost $30,000 worth of capital goods! This is an average figure and in many industries the amount of capital per worker is much higher; for example, in petroleum refining each worker is combined with about $180,000 of real capital. From an historical point of view, the long-term trend has been toward the use of more real capital per worker. For example, since 1889 the stock of capital goods has increased sixfold and, over this same period, labor-hours have doubled. Hence, the quantity of capital goods per labor-hour is roughly three times what it was near the end of the nineteenth century.[3]

[3] Figures and illustrations in this paragraph are from Solomon Fabricant, *A Primer on Productivity* (New York: Random House, Inc., 1969), chap. 5.

☐ Instability and Growth

An expanding productive capacity as such does not guarantee growth in the real GNP. We know from Chapter 19 that aggregate demand must expand by an appropriate amount in order for an expanded productive capacity to be utilized.

Figure 10-2 reminds us vividly of the extent to which the actual performance of our economy has fallen short of its potential output in recent years. The result? A wasteful GNP gap and a rate of growth substantially less than that which higher levels of aggregate demand would have brought about. For example, over the 1955–1958 period the annual growth rate was about 0.5 percent—a far cry from our long-run rate of $3\frac{1}{2}$ percent—due to a deficient level of total spending. Looking back further into history, we find that the Great Depression of the 1930s was a serious blow to the United States' long-run growth record. Between 1929 and 1933 our real GNP (measured in 1972 prices) actually *declined* from $315 to $222 billion! In 1939 the real GNP was approximately at the same level as in 1929 (see line 17 of the table on the inside front cover).

But this is only a part of the picture. Cyclical *un*employment can have certain harmful "carry-over" effects upon the growth rate in subsequent years of full employment through the adverse effects it may have upon the supply factors in growth. For example, unemployment depresses investment and capital accumulation. The case is similar for investment in human capital: Families simply do not have sufficient financial resources to spend on additional education and training. Furthermore, why spend time and money on college training for teaching or engineering when these job markets are slack? Recession may also cause a shorter workweek, which is frequently demanded by organized labor as a technique to more equitably apportion the burden of unemployment; the expansion of research budgets may be slowed by recession; union resistance to technological change may

stiffen, and so forth. Though it is impossible to quantify the impact of these considerations upon the growth rate, they undoubtedly can be of considerable importance.

☐ Allocative Efficiency

The social environment of an economy can be every bit as significant as its physical environment in influencing economic growth. The social environment of any society must meet two requirements to facilitate economic growth. First, it must encourage those changes in products, productive techniques, and capital facilities which are vital to economic growth. Second, it must provide a suitable mechanism for negotiating with reasonable efficiency the reallocations of resources which are appropriate to the development of new products, new productive techniques, and changes in resource supplies and the structure of demand.

The overall social-cultural-political environment of the United States generally has been conducive to economic growth. Several interrelated factors contribute to this favorable environment. First, as opposed to many other nations, there are virtually no social or moral taboos upon production and material progress. Indeed, American social philosophy has embraced the notion that material advance is an attainable and highly desirable economic goal. The inventor, the innovator, and the business executive are accorded high degrees of prestige and respect in American society. Second, Americans have traditionally possessed healthy attitudes toward work and risk taking; our society has benefited from a willing labor force and an ample supply of entrepreneurs. Third, our economy has been characterized by a stable political system wherein internal order, the right of property ownership, the legal status of enterprise, and the enforcement of contracts have been fostered. Though not subject to quantification, this bundle of characteristics has undoubtedly provided an excellent foundation for American economic growth.

New methods, new products, and changes in resource supplies and consumer demand all call for realignments of resources. And the price system, we have seen, provides the carrot of profits and the stick of losses to induce the expansion of innovating industries and to force the contraction of those industries whose products have been rendered obsolete or less desirable by these changes. How effectively have these realignments been negotiated? This is not an easily answered question. However, some evidence of the reallocative capacity of the economy is shown in Figure 20-3. Over the years, rather massive shifts have occurred in the industrial-occupational allocation of the labor force. In particular, there has been a dramatic exodus of labor from agricultural into service industries and the public sector. The implication is that the United States economy has been characterized by considerable resource mobility.

This is not to deny that there have been important impediments to the resource re-

alignments necessitated by growth and change. Specific businesses and resource suppliers caught in declining industries have often sought—sometimes with government's help—to impede the reallocations of resources essential to economic growth. Monopolies in both product and resource markets have retarded the reallocations of resources required for economic growth. Business monopolies may find it more profitable to suppress a newly discovered product or productive technique than to have their present capital facilities rendered obsolete before they have been fully depreciated. Furthermore, remember that the expansion of prosperous industries is a self-limiting process; as new firms enter growing industries, economic profits are competed away. Therefore, firms now established in these prosperous industries may contrive monopolistic restrictions upon the entry of new firms in an effort to preserve economic profits for themselves. Some labor unions have followed similar policies, resisting new work methods which

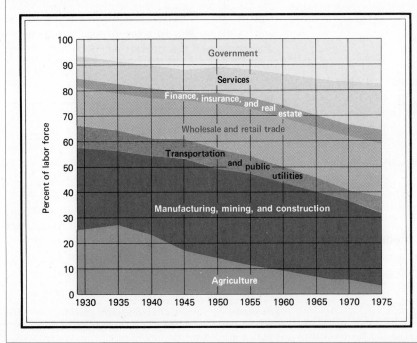

FIGURE 20-3 THE CHANGING OCCUPATIONAL STRUCTURE OF THE LABOR FORCE, 1929-1975

Long-term occupational shifts suggest that the price system has worked quite effectively in reallocating labor among alternative uses.

threaten to cause unemployment by making workers more productive. To illustrate: Unions in the building trades have frequently resisted the use of spray guns, fearing that workers will paint themselves out of jobs. And some unions, following restrictive membership policies, such as those of limiting the number of apprentices or charging high initiation fees, have created an artificial obstacle to labor mobility and have therefore limited the reallocation of human resources demanded by economic growth.

These artificial impediments to growth are enforced by certain inherent resource immobilities. Apart from union and business monopolies, resources are far from perfectly mobile. The obstacles to labor mobility, for example, are many and varied. Geographic immobility stems from the reluctance of workers to break existing social ties, move to a new community, meet new people, and take roots. Moreover, insofar as occupational mobility is concerned, it is no easy chore to abandon one's life work at, say, middle age and assume the responsibility, costs, and inconvenience of learning a new trade.

☐ **Relative Importance**

Is it possible to assess the relative importance of the various ingredients in the economic growth of the United States? Table 20-3 summarizes the findings of one pioneering study which provides such estimates. Although these sources of growth do not perfectly dovetail with our discussion—in particular, natural resources are assumed to be completely fixed and the role of aggregate demand is not explicit—the resulting estimates are highly informative.

Note that there are two fundamental ways by which any society can increase its real income: (1) by increasing its inputs of resources and (2) by increasing the productivity of those inputs. We find that slightly less than half (45 percent) of our recent growth has been due to the use of more inputs and slightly more than

Table 20-3 THE SOURCES OF GROWTH IN U.S. REAL NATIONAL INCOME, 1948–1969

Source of growth	Percent of total growth
Increase in inputs	
Increase in quantity of labor	24%
Increase in quantity of capital	21
Increase in productivity	
Improved technology	34
Improved education and training	12
Improved resource allocation	9
Total	100%

Source: Edward F. Denison, *Accounting for United States Economic Growth, 1929–1969* (Washington: The Brookings Institution, 1974), p. 130.

half (55 percent) is the consequence of rising productivity, that is, more output per unit of labor and capital input. Also observe that the productivity of labor and capital has been increased by three means. Technological advance—more specifically, improvements in the quality of capital and in managerial and organizational knowledge—has been the major factor. Secondly, improvements in the quality of labor through education and training are also significant. Finally, the reallocation of resources from less to more productive uses has also increased the overall productivity of each unit of labor and capital.[4]

IS GROWTH DESIRABLE?

So much for the facts and causes of American economic growth. We now turn to the task of evaluation. Two related questions arise. First, is economic growth *desirable?* Is the United States' growth record to be envied or avoided? Second, is future growth *possible?* Are there unavoidable limits upon the process of economic growth? Let us treat these two questions in the order stated.

[4]There has been concern in recent years over the perceived slowdown in the rate of productivity growth. The interested reader should look ahead to the "Recent Slowdown" section of Chapter 31.

☐ The Case against Growth

In recent years serious questions have been raised as to the desirability of continued economic growth for already affluent nations. A number of interrelated arguments comprise this antigrowth sentiment.

1   Pollution   Current concern with environmental deterioration is an important component of the antigrowth position. The basic point here is that industrialization and growth result in serious problems of air, water, and land pollution. Furthermore, economic growth means industrial noise and stench, ugly cities, traffic jams, and many other of the disamenities of modern life. These adverse social or spillover costs are held to be the consequence of the obvious fact that the production of the GNP changes the form of resources, but does not destroy them. Virtually all inputs in the productive process are eventually returned to the environment in some form of waste. For example, in the United States each person accounts for an estimated 2000 pounds of solid wastes per year. The more rapid our growth and the higher our standard of living, the more waste there is for the environment to absorb—or attempt to absorb. An economic policy designed to maximize the GNP is allegedly a policy which maximizes resource depletion and environmental pollution.

Growth critics argue that society must come to grips with the fact that the production of more goods and services simultaneously creates "bads" and "disservices." Indeed, in an already wealthy society, further growth may mean only the satisfaction of increasingly trivial wants at the cost of mounting threats to our ecological system.

Antigrowth economists feel that a more rational policy should be based upon the proposition that future growth should be purposely constrained. A few economists would recommend a policy of zero growth—both *zero economic growth* (ZEG) and *zero population growth* (ZPG). Others merely argue that the GNP should be constrained by some socially acceptable standard of living which is significantly below the maximum attainable.

2   Problem Resolution?   There is little compelling evidence that economic growth has been a solvent for socioeconomic problems, as its proponents claim. Antigrowth economists assert, for example, that the domestic problem of poverty—income inequality—is essentially a problem of distribution, not production. The United States, it is argued, has possessed for many years the productive capacity to provide all its citizens with a decent standard of living, but it has not been sufficiently charitable to do so. The requisites for solving the poverty problem are commitment and political courage, not further increases in output. In general, there is no compelling evidence that growth has been, or will be, a palliative for domestic problems.

3   Human Obsolescence and Insecurity   Antigrowth economists contend that rapid growth—and in particular the changing technology which is the core of growth—poses new anxieties and new sources of insecurity for man. Both high-level and low-level workers face the prospect of having their hard-earned skills and experience rendered obsolete by an onrushing technology.[5]

> Since change today is faster and more thorough than it was, say, a generation ago, and the generation hence will be faster yet, every one of us, manager, workman or scientist, lives closer to the brink of obsolescence. Each one of us that is adult and qualified feels menaced in some degree by the push of new developments which establish themselves only by discarding the methods and techniques and theories that he has learned to master.

4   Growth and Human Values   Critics of growth also offer a group of related arguments which say, in effect, that while growth may

---

[5] E. J. Mishan, *Technology and Growth* (New York: Frederick A. Praeger, Inc., 1970), p. 115.

permit us to "make a living," it does not provide us with "the good life." We may, in fact, be producing more, but enjoying it less. Indeed, the requisites of growth may preclude attainment of the good life. For example, growth focuses upon the quantitative relationship between inputs and outputs. Output satisfies wants. Therefore, any increase in output from a given quantity of inputs means growth and presumably an improvement in human welfare. Antigrowth economists retort that one must also recognize that human welfare depends upon the character of the inputs. Must not the "loss of aesthetic and instinctual gratification suffered by ordinary working men over two centuries of technological innovation that changed them from artisans and craftsmen into machine-minders and dial-readers" be entered on the liability side of the balance sheet of economic growth? More specifically, it is charged that growth means industrialization, uncreative and unsatisfying mass-production jobs, and workers who are alienated in that they have little or no control over the decisions which affect their lives.

At a more philosophical level it is argued that a growth-oriented society confers a "sweat-and-strain, look-to-the-future" conception of life upon its members.[6]

> Thus, the pure taste of the present eludes us. For in this world that we are intent on changing as rapidly as we can, the material advantages are to be reaped by those who look farthest ahead—those who treat the receding present as a jumping-off ground for the future. But this "futurism," this greed for the rewards of the future, this impatience to realize the shape of things to come, which inspires and fuels the present technological revolution, is just the phenomenon that hastens us through our brief lives and effectively cheats us of all sense of the spaciousness of time.

Or, as another critic has put it:[7]

Less than fifty years ago a person could reach the economic goals of his life when he married, bought and furnished a house, educated his children, and accumulated some savings for his old age. Today he is lured further and further away from rest and satisfaction by more and more new goods and gadgets; they keep him tied to the leash of work and acquisition until he is buried without ever having reached a moment of peace where he could look back to his work and say: It is good.

Now, admittedly, a part of our increasing affluence has been taken in the form of a declining workweek, and individuals therefore have more *nonwork time* available to them. But this does not mean they have more *leisure*. Some workers have responded to a shortened workweek by "moonlighting"—by taking a second job. Some male workers undertake more work around the home because their wives have entered the labor force. Still others find their shortened workweek offset by increased commuting time. As a matter of fact, one can argue that with rising productivity, leisure has become more costly. Rising productivity means that output and real income per hour of work have risen. This in turn means that leisure is more costly. Because leisure is more expensive in terms of goods, fewer leisure activities are "worth the time." A growth-oriented society thus tends to become goods-rich and time-poor. People attempt to adjust to this imbalance by crowding more and more activities into a limited amount of nonwork time. The unfortunate result is a "harried leisure class."[8]

□ **In Defense of Growth**

But many economists defend growth as a high-priority goal, making such arguments as follow.

---

[6] Ibid., p. 122.
[7] Walter A. Weisskopf, "Economic Growth and Human Well-being," *Quarterly Review of Economics and Business,* Summer 1964, p. 20.

[8] For an intriguing and readable discussion of this theme, see Staffan Linder, *The Harried Leisure Class* (New York: Columbia University Press, 1970). Also see Chap. 24.

1 Costs and Benefits The process of economic growth necessarily involves the structural transformation of society, along with concomitant changes in institutions, interrelationships, and values. The essence of economic growth is the shift away from agricultural to industrial production and, ultimately, from industry to services. Advancing technology means an increase in the scale of productive units—a shift from small-scale personal enterprise and the individual craftsman to large, impersonal corporations and mass-production jobs. Furthermore, growth entails the transformation of a rural society into an urban society, with the attendant costs involved in the uprooting of individuals and their adjustment to the greater anonymity of urban life. And growth inevitably means disruption of the natural environment.

The basic point made by growth proponents is that, as with any economic goal, the realization of the benefits from growth necessarily entails certain costs. The trade-offs are such that a society cannot be relatively wealthy in terms of material goods and services without accepting the costs and disamenities which that wealth inevitably entails. The defender of growth says, in effect, "Show me a pastoral society with an untouched environment, an abundance of leisure, and nonsecular values, and I will show you an underdeveloped, poverty-ridden country." More positively, growth entails both benefits and costs and there is no compelling evidence that the benefits from additional growth do not outweigh the costs. In evaluating growth we must not overlook the obvious fact that *economic growth is the primary path to material abundance. Growth makes the unlimited wants–scarce resources dilemma less acute.* It is ultimately through economic growth that any society achieves a higher standard of living.

2 Growth and the Environment Growth proponents feel that the connection between growth, on the one hand, and the environment, on the other, is overdrawn. To a considerable degree these are separable issues. If society should flatly abandon the goal of growth and produce a constant real output every year, it would still have to make choices about the composition of output which would affect the environment and the quality of life. Society would still have to weigh the relative merits of enjoying the natural beauty of a forest or cutting the timber for productive uses. And, if the timber were cut, society would have to decide whether it would be used for housing or billboards. And, as one defender of growth has quipped, even in a zero-growth society "some people would still bring transistor radios to the beach."

More importantly, it is basically incorrect to envision pollution as the inevitable by-product of economic growth. Pollution arises primarily because of a shortcoming of the price system; specifically, much of the environment—streams, lakes, oceans, and the air—are treated as "common property" and no charge is made for their use.

> Factories, power plants, municipal sewers, drivers of cars, strip-miners of coal and deep-miners of coal, and all sorts of generators of waste are allowed to dump that waste into the environment, into the atmosphere and into running water and the oceans, without paying the full cost of what they do.[9]

Hence, our environmental resources are overused and debased. Recalling Chapter 6's terminology, environmental pollution is a case of spillover or external costs, and the correction of this problem entails regulatory legislation or the imposition of special taxes ("effluent charges") to remedy the price system's flaw and eliminate the misuse of the environment. There are, to be sure, serious pollution problems. But limiting growth is the wrong re-

[9] Robert M. Solow, "Is the End of the World at Hand?" *Challenge,* March–April 1973, p. 49.

sponse. "The way to control pollution is to control pollution, not growth."[10]

Finally, one need not be a growth fanatic to point out that programs to clean up the environment are going to make substantial demands upon the national output. If we decide on a zero-growth policy, the required output must come at the expense of our current standard of living. But with growth—with an expanding income pie—we can simultaneously sustain or even increase per capita income *and* devote a larger slice of the national output to antipollution endeavors.

3 Income Inequality Growth is the only practical way of achieving a more equitable distribution of income in our society. "It is inevitably less likely that a middle-class electorate will vote to redistribute part of its own income to the poor than it will be willing to allocate a slightly larger share of a growing total."[11] In fact, the distribution of income in the United States has been basically stable since World War II (Chapter 37); it follows that the basic means for improving the economic position of the poor is to move the entire distribution of income upward through economic growth. This argument is even more compelling for the underdeveloped countries of the world. The basic means by which the people of Asia, Africa, and Latin America can achieve a decent standard of living is through a rising real GNP. A no-growth policy would substantially eliminate the prospect for the world's poor to improve their economic positions.

4 Nonmaterial Considerations Defenders of growth argue that its retardation or cessation will not automatically foster humanistic goals nor promote "the good life." Indeed, we should expect the contrary. For

example, the ending of growth will not mean the elimination of production-line work; historically, growth has been accompanied by a *decline* in the fraction of the labor force so employed. Nor has growth uniformly made labor more unpleasant or hazardous. New machinery is usually less taxing and less hazardous than the machinery it replaces. Furthermore, why would the retardation or prohibition of growth reduce materialism or alienation? Would we not expect the results to be quite the opposite? The loudest protests against materialism are heard in those nations and from those groups who now enjoy the highest levels of material security! More positively, it is the high standards of living which growth provides that make it possible for more people "to take the time for education, reflection, and self-fulfillment."[12]

THE DOOMSDAY MODELS

Out of the debate over the *desirability* of growth a more sobering controversy has evolved as to whether or not continued growth is *possible*. The cornerstone of this controversy is the notion that resources are ultimately finite on "spaceship earth." Pessimists worry about both the availability of resources or *inputs* and the effects of *outputs*. Modern productive technology is heavily dependent upon exhaustible natural resources; it also employs the environment—the absorptive capacity of which is limited—for waste disposal. Hence, on the one hand, there is concern that we must ultimately run out of certain kinds of natural resources—oil, coal, copper, manganese, arable land—which are obviously critical to the productive process. On the other hand, there is fear that the increased waste which inevitably results from economic growth will overwhelm the absorptive capacity of the ecological system.

Using elaborate computer models devel-

[10] Marc J. Roberts, "On Reforming Economic Growth," in Mancur Olson and Hans H. Landsberg (eds.), *The No-Growth Society* (New York: W. W. Norton & Company, Inc., 1973), p. 125.

[11] Solow, op. cit., p. 41.

[12] Roberts, op. cit., p. 133.

oped at MIT, the Club of Rome—a group of some one hundred scientists, businessmen, and academicians—recently triggered a worldwide controversy with its conclusion that continued economic growth is impossible. According to their scenario, the current growth paths of population, output, and pollution are on a catastrophic collision course with production limits imposed by natural resources and the pollution-absorbing capacity of the environment.

> If the present growth trends in world population, industrialization, pollution, food production, and resource depletion continue unchanged, the limits to growth on this planet will be reached sometime within the next one hundred years. The most probable result will be a rather sudden and uncontrollable decline in both population and industrial capacity.[13]

[13]Dennis L. Meadows and others, *The Limits to Growth* (Washington: Potomac Associates, 1972), p. 29. The inter-

Figure 20-4 shows the "standard run" Doomsday model. Data for 1900 through 1970 are actual historical trends; the data for 1971 through 2100 are computerized forecasts of these trends based upon the assumption that "there will be in the future no great changes in human values nor in the functioning of the global population-capital system as it has operated for the last one hundred years." The Club of Rome concludes that:[14]

> The behavior mode of the system . . . is clearly that of overshoot and collapse . . . the collapse occurs because of nonrenewable resource depletion. The industrial capital stock grows to

ested reader should also consult E. F. Schumacher, *Small Is Beautiful* (New York: Harper & Row, Publishers, Incorporated, 1973), and Paul R. Ehrlich and Anne H. Ehrlich, *The End of Affluence* (New York: Ballantine Books, Inc., 1974).

[14]Meadows, op. cit., pp. 131–132.

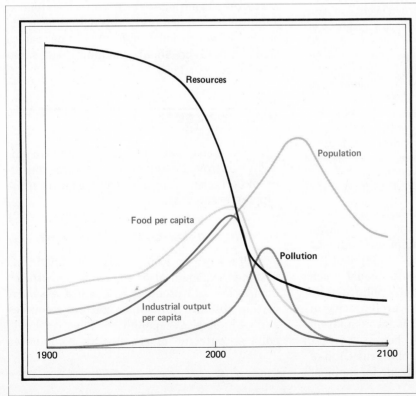

FIGURE 20-4 GROWTH AND COLLAPSE: A DOOMSDAY MODEL

This computer model "assumes no major change in the physical, economic, or social relationships that have historically governed the development of the world system. . . . Food, industrial output, and population grow exponentially until the rapidly diminishing resource base forces a slowdown in industrial growth. Because of natural delays in the system, both population and pollution continue to increase for some time after the peak of industrialization. Population growth is finally halted by a rise in the death rate due to decreased food and medical services." [Dennis L. Meadows and others, *The Limits to Growth* (*Washington: Potomac Associates, 1972*), *p. 129.*]

a level that requires an enormous input of resources. In the very process of that growth it depletes a large fraction of the resource reserves available. As resource prices rise and mines are depleted, more and more capital must be used for obtaining resources, leaving less to be invested for future growth. Finally investment cannot keep up with depreciation, and the industrial base collapses, taking with it the service and agricultural systems, which have become dependent on industrial inputs (such as fertilizers, pesticides, hospital laboratories, computers, and especially energy for mechanization). For a short time the situation is especially serious because population, with the delays inherent in the age structure and the process of social adjustment, keeps rising. Population finally decreases when the death rate is driven upward by lack of food and health services.

The exact timing of these events is not meaningful, given the great aggregation and many uncertainties in the model. It is significant, however, that growth is stopped well before the year 2100. We have tried in every doubtful case to make the most optimistic estimate of unknown quantities, and we have also ignored discontinuous events such as wars or epidemics, which might act to bring an end to growth even sooner than our model would indicate. In other words, the model is biased to allow growth to continue longer than it probably can continue in the real world. *We can thus say with some confidence that, under the assumption of no major change in the present system, population and industrial growth will certainly stop within the next century, at the latest.*

Other Club of Rome computer runs entail much more optimistic assumptions, but the end result is always a dramatic collapse of the system. For example, a computer model which doubles usable resources, cuts pollution by three-fourths, quadruples the productivity of land and raw materials, and halts population growth still leads to collapse before the year 2100. The dismal conclusion of all the Club of Rome models is: "The basic behavior mode of

the world system is exponential growth of population and capital, followed by collapse."[15] If natural resource limits do not precipitate collapse, then famine or pollution will.

If the Doomsday models are at all meaningful, what policies can be recommended to avoid their "overshoot-and-collapse" prophecies? The road to survival calls for a stop to both economic and population growth. That is, top-priority policies entail zero economic growth (ZEG) and zero population growth (ZPG). For example, the Club of Rome concludes that a no-growth "stationary state" can be achieved in the next century *if* (1) population growth is zero; (2) there is no net investment in real capital; and (3) technology reduces resource consumption per unit of industrial output to one-fourth of its 1970 level; (4) pollution is reduced to one-fourth of its 1970 level; and (5) real capital is shifted from industrial production to food and services. The result is a no-growth equilibrium—a state of stagnation—which can be extended more or less indefinitely through time. The projected worldwide average income per capita figure would be about one-half the United States' current level.

NEW HORIZONS?

The Doomsday models have sparked an ongoing controversy and, in the process, considerable criticism. Consider the following overlapping arguments.

☐ Fun and Games with Numbers?

The Club of Rome, it is contended, has *assumed* exponential or geometric growth for population and production and has *assumed* certain absolute limits upon natural resources and technological capabilities. The overshoot-collapse outcome of the resulting computer

---

[15] Ibid., p. 149.

runs is merely the inevitable consequence of these assumptions. The fundamental question is: Are these assumptions—and therefore the predictions drawn from them—realistic? To paraphrase an old joke, one can project the reproduction rate of alligators and conclude that in X years we will be up to our eyeballs, or thereabouts, in alligators. Indeed, several years ago a demographer, with tongue in cheek, projected a slight decline in the Japanese birthrate and forecast the absolute depopulation of that nation! The point is that a different—and equally or even more plausible—set of assumptions would yield a much happier portrayal of mankind's future. Recall that Malthus's model (Chapter 19) is not unlike the Doomsday models in that it forecasts subsistence living levels as the result of geometric expansion of the population and arithmetic expansion of the food supply. And, while the simple projection of these assumptions does inevitably lead to the indicated conclusion, the assumptions of the model have really not been accurate for the United States, Canada, Western Europe, Japan, the Soviet Union, and a number of other advanced and semiadvanced nations.

☐ **Role of Technology**

The Doomsday pessimists may have grossly underestimated the capabilities of technological progress. Specifically, technological progress—which has been highly instrumental in botching Malthus's dismal predictions—may offset the predictions of the Doomsday models in a variety of ways.

1 Applying Existing Knowledge There are potentially great benefits to be realized by the wider application of *existing* technology. For example, British economist-journalist Norman Macrae has recently argued that "if all the land now cultivated were brought up to Dutch standards of efficiency, then the world could feed 60 billion people, 15 times today's

population."[16] This great potential increase in food production is alleged to be an understatement because it does not take into account that, currently, only 3 percent of the earth's surface is farmed or the fact that much of the agricultural output of poor countries is now eaten by easily destroyable pests. Macrae predicts that we shall "find ourselves swimming in food gluts" within the next three decades.

2 New Resource Discoveries The Doomsday models fail to recognize adequately that the supply of natural resources should not be regarded as fixed, but rather as resources the supplies of which increase as the result of technological advance. Specifically, technological progress can "create new uses for formerly worthless substances, make available heretofore inaccessible stocks, and make feasible the extraction of formerly high-cost, low-quality materials."[17] The impact of technological advance over time is thus to continually raise resource ceilings and forestall the production-resource collision embodied in the Doomsday models. Is this reality or wishful thinking? According to one expert, "in the United States, technology has kept ahead of increased use, and the relative costs of resource inputs have declined."[18]

Consider, more specifically, the much-discussed case of petroleum:[19]

Oil was discovered in the United States in 1859 . . . in a well that was some 35 feet deep. . . . We are now drilling wells 30,000 feet deep and the result is that we are now drilling oil at the rate of billions of barrels per year instead of 2 or 3 million barrels in the earlier period. Who knows that in a decade or two we will not be

[16] Norman Macrae, *America's Third Century* (New York: Harcourt Brace Jovanovich, Inc., 1976), p. 49.
[17] Thomas M. Humphrey, "The Dismal Science Revisited," *Monthly Review of the Federal Reserve Bank of Richmond,* March 1973, p. 11.
[18] Roberts, op. cit., p. 121.
[19] W. N. Peach, *The Energy Outlook for the 1980's,* A Study Prepared for the Joint Economic Committee (Washington, 1973), p. 6.

able to drill wells 60,000 feet and we may find 10 or 20 times as much oil as we now know about?

Interestingly, world oil reserves are larger today than they were in 1935, despite high and accelerating rates of consumption! And, contrary to the Doomsday conception of things, recent testimony by geologists, engineers, and economists before congressional committees leads to the conclusion that there is no global physical shortage of energy resources.

3 New Resources and Resource Productivity It must also be recognized that technological progress entails a history of substituting newly discovered or newly developed resources for old ones. Many of the industrial materials used today—for example, plastics—were not even conceptually recognized a short time ago. Similarly, in our early history wood was the basic source of energy. But, aided by technological advances, society has shifted to coal, petroleum, and natural gas, thereby greatly expanding our supplies of energy resources. Optimists now envision solar, geothermal, and nuclear power on the horizon. Thus one recent authoritative estimate indicates that known reserves of fossil fuels are sufficient to last over 500 years at current consumption rates. But by adding *known* nuclear technology, energy resources become sufficient to last for over 8000 years. "With breeder reactors, and more dramatically with a fusion technology, there is virtually unlimited energy available."[20]

Equally significant is the possibility of using technology to increase the productivity of natural resources. Because, historically, labor has been the largest component of production costs, technological advances have been designed to increase the productivity of labor. But if future growth increases the relative scarcity and therefore the relative cost of natural resources, we can expect technological advances to become increasingly oriented toward achieving greater output per input of natural resources. And, in fact, one can point to some remarkable resource-saving innovations.

> . . . microminiaturisation with integrated circuits means that it is going to be increasingly economic to put on a chip the size of a postage stamp properly connected electrical circuits which would previously have required assemblies of machinery that fill a room.[21]

The obvious point is that technological progress holds the potential for greatly expanding the output obtainable from a given amount of natural resource inputs.

4 Increasing Returns to Technology Most important and with obviously crucial implications for the previous three points, technological knowledge—the ability to solve the problems associated with the geometric expansion of population and industrial production—may also expand at a geometric rate. Indeed, the "knowledge explosion" of the post-World War II era suggests that this has been the case. If technology does, or can be made to, expand at a geometric rate, output could continue to grow as new technology is substituted for labor, capital, and nonaugmentable natural resources.

Barnett and Morse have argued that technological progress is self-generating and is therefore subject to increasing, rather than diminishing, returns:

> . . . a strong case can be made for the view that the cumulation of knowledge and technological progress is automatic and self-reproductive in modern economies, and obeys a law of increasing returns. Every cost-reducing innovation opens up possibilities of application in so many new directions that the stock of knowledge, far from being depleted by new

[20]William D. Nordhaus, "Resources as a Constraint on Growth," *American Economic Review,* May 1974, p. 25.

[21]Macrae, op. cit., p. 52.

developments, may even expand geometrically.[22]

If this observation is reasonably realistic, it makes sense—despite the indisputable finiteness of the earth—to think in terms of unrestrained economic progress.

□ Feedback Mechanisms

Critics also contend that the Doomsday models make inadequate allowance for various feedback mechanisms which can function so as to prevent the occurrence of the predicted overshoot-collapse scenario.

The Price System The price system is, of course, the basic mechanism by which market economies signal and react to changes in relative scarcity. As reserves of, say, copper or aluminum become increasingly scarce, their prices will rise. Two responses automatically occur. On the one hand, resource users become more strongly motivated to conserve such resources either by employing substitutes (for example, plastic for copper pipes in new housing) or by developing new resource-saving production techniques. On the other hand, higher resource prices provide an incentive for resource producers to expand output by mining lower-grade ores or by recycling, both of which may have been economically unfeasible at lower prices. The point is that the price mechanism automatically induces responses which tend to alleviate resource shortages. "The economy is not a mindless glutton that will devour the last morsel before it notices that the plate is empty."[23]

Behavioral Patterns Critics of the Doomsday position argue that in the long run alterations in human behavior may be more important than the finiteness of the world's resources in determining man's materialistic future.

There is evidence, for example, that mankind can and will adjust behavioral patterns with respect to procreation so that we will not breed ourselves into economic oblivion. In the United States the "baby boom" of the late 1940s has more recently become a "birth dearth." This change is attributable to improved birth control techniques, wider acceptance of family planning to achieve an "ideal" family size, and changed attitudes toward abortion. Birthrates in the United States are currently at, or slightly below, zero population growth levels! It is highly relevant for the present discussion to note that economic growth *may* be a prerequisite for the control of population growth. That is, the opportunity cost of children rises as growth increases average incomes. In wealthy nations high wage rates mean that more income is forgone when parents spend time rearing children. It is therefore economically rational to have fewer children. Conversely, in poor nations the opportunity cost of children is low and, indeed, a large family is hopefully regarded as a substitute for the inability of parents to accumulate savings for retirement.

Consider how the so-called world food problem might be remedied by changes in human behavior designed to correct existing inefficiencies. According to Macrae, the world's pig population consumes seven times more primary protein than do North Americans. The world's horses, used primarily for recreation, consume more than the Chinese people. Cows, a third of which are located in Africa and Asia and serve no nutritive purpose, consume more grain than the entire world population. The point is that the potential exists through the altering of human decisions to discontinue highly inefficient practices in converting grain into meat and thereby greatly to alleviate the "food problem."[24]

Finally, there is growing evidence of be-

---

[22]Harold Barnett and Chandler Morse, *Scarcity and Growth* (Baltimore: The Johns Hopkins University Press, 1963), p. 236.
[23]Roberts, op. cit., p. 121.

[24]See Macrae, op. cit., p. 50.

havioral changes which have dealt effectively with the problem of pollution. The reclamation of Germany's once-polluted Ruhr valley is a classic example of pollution problems getting better, not worse. Furthermore, "the pollution level in London has been reduced by 85 percent in the last 15 years, doubling the hours of winter sunshine and adding 55 species of fish to the once-moribund Thames."[25]

Whether one comes down on the side of the Doomsday pessimists or the technology-to-the-rescue optimists, certain important messages and questions do emerge from the growth debate. We are reminded, for example, that the fundamental question of scarcity has

[25]Roger Leroy Miller, *The Economics of Macro Issues* (San Francisco: Canfield Press, 1976), p. 169.

a time dimension. Absolutely exhaustible resources which are used today will obviously not be available tomorrow. What is the optimum way to allocate such resources through time? Can this optimum allocation be more effectively achieved via the market mechanism or government decision making, for example, by some sort of national or international planning? The debate also emphasizes that growth is not an unmitigated good. The impact of an ever-expanding output upon the environment and, more elusively, upon "life-styles" must be taken into account in any comprehensive evaluation of future growth. Finally, the debate points out that factors which fall essentially outside the pale of economics—in particular, population growth—have a critical bearing upon economic well-being.

Summary

1 The long-term growth rate of real GNP for the United States has been about $3\frac{1}{2}$ percent; real GNP per capita has grown at about 2 percent.

2 The real GNP of the United States has grown, not only because of increased inputs of labor and capital, but also because of increases in the productivity of labor and capital.

3 Critics of economic growth *a.* cite adverse environmental effects; *b.* argue that domestic and international problems are essentially matters of distribution, not production; *c.* contend that growth is a major source of human obsolescence and insecurity; and *d.* argue that growth is frequently in conflict with certain human values.

4 Proponents of growth stress that *a.* growth means a better solution to the wants-means dilemma; *b.* environmental problems are only loosely linked to growth; *c.* growth is the only feasible means by which greater income equality can be realized; and *d.* growth is more consistent with "the good life" than is stagnation.

5 Recent Club of Rome computer models portray an "overshoot-collapse" scenario as the result of the collision between current growth paths of population, production, and pollution and output limits imposed by natural resources and nature's pollution-absorbing capacity. Zero economic and population growth—ZEG and ZPG—are recommended policies for avoiding overshoot and collapse.

6 Critics argue that the Doomsday models *a.* are based upon unrealistic assumptions, *b.* fail to emphasize sufficiently the scarcity-offsetting capacity of technological progress, and *c.* neglect the role of such feedback mechanisms as the price system and changes in human behavior.

Questions and Study Suggestions

1   Key terms and concepts to remember: R & D; Club of Rome; Doomsday models; zero economic growth; zero population growth; feedback mechanisms.

2   Briefly describe the growth record of the United States in this century. Compare the rates of growth in real GNP and real GNP per capita, explaining any differences. To what extent might these figures understate or overstate economic well-being?

3   To what extent have increases in our real GNP been the result of more capital and labor inputs? Of increasing productivity? Are the United States data of Table 20-2 generally consistent with the data of Table 20-3? Explain.

4   Describe the Doomsday models. "Our prime national goal . . . should be to reach a zero growth rate as soon as possible. Zero growth in people, in GNP, and in our consumption of everything. That is the only hope of attaining a stable economy: that is, of halting deterioration of the environment on which our lives depend." Do you agree? What programs and policies might be used if we sought to accelerate our rate of growth?

5   "If we want economic growth in a free society, we may have to accept a measure of instability." Evaluate. The noted philosopher Alfred North Whitehead once remarked that "the art of progress is to preserve order amid change and to preserve change amid order." What did he mean? Is this contention relevant for economic growth? What implications might this have for public policy? Explain.

6   Comment on the following statements:

a. "The price mechanism is the greatest conserver of scarce natural resources."

b. "Technological advance is destined to play a more important role in economic growth in the future than it has in the past."

c. "Income inequality is a matter of redistribution, not of further growth."

d. "The issues of economic growth and environmental pollution are separable and distinct."

e. "Nature imposes particular scarcities, not an inescapable general scarcity."

Selected References

Beckerman, Wilfred: *Two Cheers for the Affluent Society* (New York: St. Martin's Press, 1974).

Heilbroner, Robert L.: *The Economic Transformation of America* (New York: Harcourt Brace Jovanovich, Inc., 1977).

Macrae, Norman: *America's Third Century* (New York: Harcourt Brace Jovanovich, Inc., 1976).

Meadows, Dennis, and others: *The Limits to Growth* (Washington: Potomac Associates, 1972).

Olson, Mancur, and Hans H. Landsberg (eds.): *The No-Growth Society* (New York: W. W. Norton & Company, Inc., 1973).

Schumacher, E. F.: *Small is Beautiful* (New York: Harper & Row, Publishers, Incorporated, 1973).

Scientific American, *The Human Population* (San Francisco: W. H. Freeman and Company, 1974), particularly chaps. 1, 2, 6–11.

Thurow, Lester, "The Implications of Zero Economic Growth," *Challenge,* March–April 1977, pp. 36–43.

Weintraub, Andrew, Eli Schwartz, and J. Richard Aronson (eds.): *The Economic Growth Controversy* (White Plains, N.Y.: International Arts and Sciences Press, Inc., 1973).

Last Word
Summer of '73

Humorist Art Buchwald reflects on the long-term implications of the gasoline shortage.

"Daddy, tell me again what it was like in 1973 when anyone who wanted to could drive a car."

"I know you're not going to believe this son, but all you had to do was drive up to a gas station and say to the attendant, 'Fill 'er up.' And you know what? He had to wipe your windshield, too, or you wouldn't buy any gas from him."

"Aw, come on Daddy, you're putting me on."

"I'm telling the truth, son. And not only that but we used to have these big cars—three times the size of the ones you see now—with four doors and air conditioning and everything. Some of them got 9, 10 miles to a gallon. I think there are some pictures of them in the encyclopedia here."

"Gosh, those were some cars."

"In those days you could drive your car to work or to the city all alone without violating the law. You'd see people in eight-passenger station wagons all by themselves."

"Is it true you could drive to the beach or to the mountains or a football game 100 miles away without getting a special pass from the Automobile Authority?"

"Yup. One time your mother and I drove all the way to Florida, and we didn't have to ask permission from a soul. We just went."

"What happened, Daddy?"

"Nobody really knows. People just kept using up gasoline and oil until there was none left. I remember in '73 Detroit announced it had had its greatest year. Sold more big cars than any time in its history.

"But nobody bothered to tell Detroit there would be nothing to put in the big gas tanks. They said it wasn't their problem.

"It was really funny because in Washington they were arguing about automobile pollution and the emission standards for 1976 when, in fact, the problem solved itself. There was no fuel left to pollute anything."

"Why didn't Detroit build smaller cars that wouldn't use so much gasoline?"

"Because they said Americans wouldn't go for it. They said Americans had always had big cars, and they deserved big cars because big cars were what made America great. Of course now they have no choice but to manufacture two-cylinder automobiles because that's the only kind of car Americans can afford. I mean when gas is selling for $9.50 a gallon and you've got rationing coupons, nobody in his right mind is going to make a *four*-cylinder car."

"Is that why we moved back to the city, because you couldn't drive to work any more?"

"Yup. We lived in the suburbs when you were very little, but when the country ran out of gasoline we had to move back here. Oh, I tried bicycling to work, but it was 40 miles each way and I was pretty pooped by the time I got home. So we came back. And it was curious because up until that time the blacks lived in the cities and the whites lived in the suburbs.

"Now, of course, all the whites live in the cities and the blacks live in the suburbs because that's the only housing the blacks can afford. The blacks didn't want to go to the suburbs, but the whites kept buying up the ghettos and the blacks had no choice. They're probably happier out there, anyway, living among their own kind."

"Who was to blame for our running out of gasoline?"

"Detroit blamed it on Ralph Nader, the President blamed it on Congress, the Arabs blamed it on Israel and the oil companies blamed it on the caribou in Alaska."

"It must have been fun living in 1973."

"It was. Do you know one time we drove 30 miles just to have a sirloin steak?"
What's a steak?"

"Oh, the hell with it. It hurts too much to talk about it."

Art Buchwald, *Los Angeles Times*, April 17, 1973. Reprinted by permission.

Growth and the Underdeveloped Nations

It is exceedingly difficult for the typical American family, whose 1976 average income was $16,500, to grasp the hard fact that some two-thirds of the world's population persistently lives at, or perilously close to, the subsistence level. Ironically, most Americans are too preoccupied with problems associated with affluence—pollution, rapid urban growth, the monotony and alienation which often accompany employment in large-scale enterprises—to acknowledge the abject poverty which characterizes much of our planet. But, in fact, hunger, squalor, and disease prevail in most nations of the world.

UNDERSTANDING UNDERDEVELOPMENT

The purposes of this chapter are to identify the underdeveloped nations; to understand why they are underdeveloped; and to discuss policies and strategies by which they might achieve more rapid growth.

□ Low per Capita Income

The underdeveloped nations of the world bear a common brand: poverty—low per capita incomes as compared with such industrially advanced countries as the United States, Great Britain, and Canada. Table 21-1 identifies most of the underdeveloped nations. Of course, where one draws the line between "developed," "semideveloped," and "underdeveloped" is an arbitrary matter. Nevertheless, in Table 21-1 we can roughly envision these three classifications. Looking at the 1973 data, we might tag those nations with per capita incomes of $2000 or more as developed, or advanced, nations. Included here, primarily, are the United States, Canada, Australia, New Zealand, most countries of Western Europe, Japan, Israel, and the Soviet Union. Next is the semideveloped group, whose per capita incomes vary from, say, $1000 to $1999 per year. This heterogeneous group is largely composed of several Central and South American countries plus several more European nations. The rest of the world—including most of Asia, Africa, and Latin America—bear the designation "underdeveloped," or "less developed."

□ Dimensions of Inequality

The vast income disparities between the advanced and the underdeveloped countries are further dramatized in Figure 21-1. Here the world is divided into three groups of nations: (1) the industrially advanced market economies, dominated by the United States, the European Economic Community (the "Common Market"), and Japan; (2) the centrally planned economies, comprising mainly the Soviet Union, her satellites, and the People's Republic of China; and (3) the so-called *Third World* countries—the semideveloped and underdeveloped countries. Note that in 1973 the industrialized market economies, with less than 18 percent of the world population, generated about 65 percent of world output! Indeed, although the United States embodies less than 6 percent of the world's population, it enjoyed over 27 percent of world output. The Third World, encompassing slightly over half the world's population, generated only about 12 percent of world output. The Indian subcontinent, with over one-fifth of the world's population, produced less than 2 percent of the world's output.

Furthermore, a closer examination of Table 21-1 reveals very significant differences in the progress of the Third World nations. Some have achieved substantial growth of per capita GNP while many others—sometimes labeled Fourth World nations—have made minuscule progress or no progress at all. Whether or not a Third World nation achieves some degree of development depends upon a variety of factors including the presence of strategic raw materials, rates of population growth, foreign aid, and the degree of internal political stability. It is important to note that aggregated figures suggest that the income gap between rich and poor nations has been widening; in terms of per capita GNP the advanced nations as a group are growing at about 2.5 percent annually, while Third World nations are growing at 1.5 percent per year.

□ Implications

But statistics both reveal and conceal. The human implications of the poverty which characterizes so much of our planet merits emphasis:[1]

> The poverty of underdeveloped countries means that their people, on a broad average, have a life expectancy only about half that of the people of the highly developed countries. They suffer much of the time from malaria, dysentery, tuberculosis, trachoma, or other ills. . . . Their food supply is about one-third less, measured in calories, than that of the developed countries, and when account is taken of the needs of the human body for the relatively expensive "protective" foods, such as milk and meat, the extent of malnutrition is found to be very great indeed. The opportunity to attend school is limited to a small minority. . . . Only one person in four or five, again on a broad average of underdeveloped countries, knows how to read or write. The supply of cloth for clothing, home furnishing, and other purposes is about one-fourth as great per person in underdeveloped as in highly developed countries. Nonhuman en-

[1] Eugene Staley, *The Future of Underdeveloped Countries* (New York: Harper & Row, Publishers, Incorporated, for the Council on Foreign Relations, 1954), pp. 15–18.

Table 21-1 PER CAPITA GNP, 1973, AND AVERAGE ANNUAL GROWTH RATE, 1965–1973, FOR COUNTRIES WITH
POPULATIONS OF 1 MILLION OR MORE

Country	GNP per capita		Country	GNP per capita		Country	GNP per capita	
	Amount (US$)	Growth rate(%) 1965–73		Amount (US$)	Growth rate (%) 1965–73		Amount (US$)	Growth rate (%) 1965–73
United States	6200	2.5	Iran	870	7.4	Cameroon	250	4.9
Switzerland	6100	3.0	Iraq	850	2.9	Bolivia	230	2.2
Sweden	5910	2.4	Brazil	760	6.0	Nigeria	210	8.3
Canada	5450	3.5	Chile	720	1.4	Mauritania	200	1.2
Germany, Fed.			Costa Rica	710	3.5	Togo	180	2.5
Rep. of	5320	4.0	China, Rep. of	660	7.3	Kenya	170	3.3
Denmark	5210	3.8	Peru	620	1.8	Sierra Leone	160	1.5
Norway	4660	3.8	Turkey	600	4.4	Central African		
Belgium	4560	4.6	Malaysia	570	3.7	Rep.	160	1.0
France	4540	5.0	Algeria	570	4.3	South Vietnam	160	−0.7
Australia	4350	3.0	Mongolia	550	1.6	Malagasy Rep.	150	0.9
Netherlands	4330	4.3	Cuba	540	−0.7	Uganda	150	1.2
New Zealand	3680	2.0	Nicaragua	540	1.6	Zaire	140	2.9
Japan	3630	9.6	Dominican Rep.	520	5.1	Sudan	130	−0.6
Finland	3600	5.2	Guatemala	500	3.8	Tanzania	130	2.6
Libyan Arab			Angola	490	3.2	Indonesia	130	4.5
Rep.	3530	5.7	Albania	460	5.1	Haiti	130	0.7
Austria	3510	5.1	Tunisia	460	4.9	India	120	1.5
United Kingdom	3060	2.3	Colombia	440	3.1	Sri Lanka	120	2.0
Israel	3010	6.7	Zambia	430	−0.2	Pakistan	120	2.5
German Dem.			Rhodesia	430	3.5	Benin, People's		
Rep.	3000	2.9	Paraguay	410	2.2	Rep. of	110	1.5
Czechoslovakia	2870	2.6	Papua New			Malawi	110	3.7
Italy	2450	4.2	Guinea	410	5.0	Yemen, People's		
Puerto Rico	2180	5.2	Syrian Arab			Dem. Rep. of	110	n.a.
Ireland	2150	3.9	Rep.	400	3.6	Vietnam, Dem.		
Poland	2090	4.2	Korea, Rep. of	400	8.7	Rep. of	110	−0.5
U.S.S.R.	2030	3.5	Ivory Coast	380	3.0	Guinea	110	0.1
Greece	1870	7.6	Ecuador	380	2.8	Niger	100	−4.6
Hungary	1850	2.7	Mozambique	380	4.1	Yemen Arab		
Singapore	1830	9.4	El Salvador	350	0.8	Rep.	100	n.a.
Spain	1710	5.3	Jordan	340	−2.6	Lesotho	100	2.6
Argentina	1640	2.9	Korea, Dem.			Nepal	90	−0.1
Venezuela	1630	1.3	Rep. of	340	2.7	Ethiopia	90	1.6
Saudi Arabia	1610	10.1	Congo, People's			Afghanistan	90	0.9
Bulgaria	1590	3.6	Rep. of	340	1.9	Somalia	80	1.6
Hong Kong	1430	5.8	Morocco	320	2.5	Chad	80	−3.3
Portugal	1410	8.0	Honduras	320	1.1	Bangladesh	80	−1.6
Trinidad and			Liberia	310	4.7	Burma	80	0.7
Tobago	1310	2.2	Ghana	300	0.8	Burundi	80	1.4
South Africa	1050	2.0	Senegal	280	−2.8	Cambodia	70	−5.2
Yugoslavia	1010	4.5	Philippines	280	2.6	Rwanda	70	3.2
Jamaica	990	4.8	China, People's			Upper Volta	70	−1.1
Uruguay	950	0.0	Rep. of	270	4.6	Mali	70	0.5
Lebanon	940	3.5	Thailand	270	4.5	Bhutan	60	−0.2
Panama	920	4.3	Egypt, Arab			Laos	60	2.5
Mexico	890	2.8	Rep. of	250	0.8			

Source: World Bank, *World Bank Atlas,* 1975. Countries with populations of one million or more. GNP per capita rounded to nearest US $10.

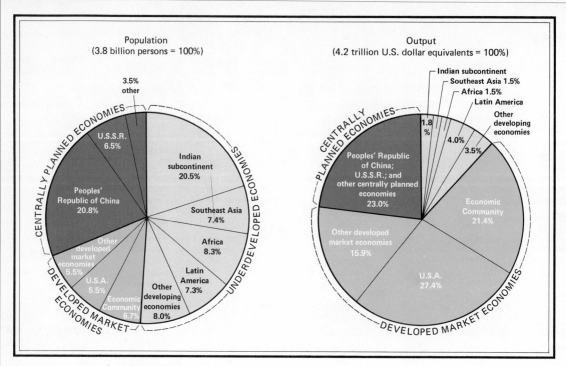

FIGURE 21-1 GLOBAL POPULATION AND OUTPUT

The industrially advanced nations produce about two-thirds of world output, although their population is only 18 percent of the total. In contrast the underdeveloped nations, with over half the world's population, generate only about one-eigth of global output. (*The Conference Board. Population data are for 1973; output data are for 1972.*)

ergy to supplement the labor of human beings in industry, agriculture, transport, and household tasks is less than one-twentieth as plentiful, measured in horsepower-hours per person. Incomes, on the average, are less than one-tenth as high.

In Table 21-2 various socioeconomic indicators for selected Third World nations are contrasted with those for the United States and Japan. These data clearly verify the major points stressed in the above quotation.

☐ **Viewpoint of Underdeveloped Nations**

The bulk of the people in the underdeveloped nations are not resigned to their fate. Far from it. Most seek, and feel they have a right

to, a better life. As they see it, poverty is not inescapable.

Two recent developments—one economic and the other political—have fanned the desire of the underdeveloped nations for material and social betterment:

1 As noted, the per capita income gap between the economically advanced nations and the underdeveloped nations has not merely persisted, but has widened. Among nations, the rich have been getting richer and the poor have been getting relatively poorer.[2]

[2]The grim jokes of the day mirror the widening economic gap between the United States and the less developed nations:

Polish Communist party secretary: "Hear you've got a

Table 21-2   SELECTED SOCIOECONOMIC INDICATORS OF DEVELOPMENT

Country	(1) Per capita GNP, 1973	(2) Life expectancy at birth, 1970–1975 average	(3) Infant mortality per 1000 live births	(4) Literacy	(5) Per capita public education expenditures, 1972	(6) Per capita energy consumption, 1973*
United States	$6200	71 years	18	98%	$314	11,897
Japan	3630	73	26	94	103	3,103
Brazil	760	61	94	67	16	625
China, People's Republic of	270	62	55	25	7	583
Mauritania	200	38	189	1–5	6	115
India	120	50	139	34	3	192
Ethiopia	90	38	181	5	2	37
Bangladesh	80	36	132	22	1	32
Upper Volta	70	38	182	5–10	2	13

*Kilogram coal equivalent.
Source: Roger D. Hansen, *The U.S. and World Development: Agenda for Action, 1976* (New York: Praeger Publishers, 1976), Table A-7, pp. 132–141.

This widening has intensified the discontent of the peoples of the underdeveloped countries. The equation for social unrest is no secret:

Aspirations − standard of living
= social unrest

As the living standards of the advanced nations have improved, the economic goals and aspirations of the underdeveloped nations have increased accordingly. But their actual standard of living in most instances has shown meager growth. The differential—social unrest—has clearly been on the increase. Witness the political instability in many of the underdeveloped nations.

2 It has been only since World War II that many of the underdeveloped lands have achieved political independence. Accompanying this freedom from colonial status has been a tremendous upsurge of nationalistic spirit. The less developed countries seek the eco-nomic independence, respect, and social status which they feel are due them as independent nations.

☐   **Dubious Lessons of History**

It is disarmingly tempting for the advanced nations to offer less fortunate nations a simple formula for economic development: "Do what we did." Such a formula is glib, inaccurate, and, to the informed citizens of poor nations, downright insulting. The truth is that the now advanced nations initiated their development in an environment vastly different from that currently faced by the underdeveloped countries. Witness the favorable setting for American economic development: abundant and diverse mineral resources, opulent sources of power, navigable rivers, fertile and free farmland, a temperate climate, a small but energetic and (for that time) intelligent labor force, and finally, the virtual absence of social and moral taboos on business and commerce. This is an environment ripe for economic growth. Throw these characteristics into reverse and you have the typical underdeveloped nation: a niggardly resource base, a

brother out of work in Detroit. Why don't you write him and tell him to come home?"

Warsaw automobile worker: "Sure, but who'd send us the food parcels?"

lack of power, low-quality land, a teeming and untrained population, a tropical climate, and a host of fetishes narrowly circumscribing any existing spirit of enterprise. The spontaneous growth arising from the favorable environs of the North American continent is not likely to blossom in such a brier patch.

BREAKING THE POVERTY BARRIER

The avenues of economic growth are essentially the same for both advanced and underdeveloped nations:

1 Existing supplies of resources must be used more efficiently. This entails not only the elimination of unemployment but also the achievement of greater efficiency in the allocation of resources.

2 The supplies of productive resources must be altered—typically, increased. By expanding the supplies of raw materials, capital equipment, effective manpower, and technological knowledge, a nation can push its production possibilities curve to the right (Chapter 19).

Why have some nations been so successful in pursuing these avenues of growth while other countries have lagged far behind? The answer, as noted above, lies in differences in the physical and sociocultural environments of the various nations. Our plan of attack is to examine the obstacles in the underdeveloped countries to altering the quantities and improving efficiency in the use of (1) natural resources, (2) human resources, (3) capital goods, and (4) technological knowledge. Emphasis here will be upon the private sector of the economy. In addition, social and institutional impediments to growth will be illustrated. And finally, the roles of government and foreign aid in the development process will be analyzed.

☐ **Natural Resources**

There is no simple generalization with respect to the role of natural resources in the economic development of Third World nations. This is true mainly because the distribution of natural resources among these nations is very uneven. Some underdeveloped nations encompass valuable deposits of bauxite, tin, copper, tungsten, nitrates, petroleum, and so forth. In a few instances the underdeveloped countries have been able to use their natural resource endowments to achieve rapid growth and a significant redistribution of income from the rich to the poor nations. The Organization of Oil Producing Countries, (OPEC), of course, is the outstanding example. On the other hand, we must recognize that in many cases natural resources are owned or controlled by the huge multinational corporations of the industrially advanced countries to the end that the economic benefits from these resources are largely diverted abroad. Other Third World nations simply lack mineral deposits, face a paucity of arable land, and have few sources of power. It is important to note that the vast majority of the less developed countries are located in Central and South America, Africa, the Indian subcontinent, and Southeast Asia where tropical climates prevail. The hot, humid climate is not conducive to productive labor; crop and livestock diseases are widespread; and weed and insect infestations plague agriculture.

In a very real sense a weak resource base can pose a particularly serious obstacle to growth. Real capital can be accumulated and the quality of the labor force can be improved through education and training. But the natural resource base is largely unaugmentable. Hence, it is unrealistic for many of the underdeveloped nations to envision an economic destiny comparable with that of the United States, Canada, or the Soviet Union. Automated steel, automobile, and aluminum plants are not a part of their foreseeable economic futures. But, again, we must be careful in generalizing: Switzerland, Israel, and Japan, for example, have achieved relatively high levels of living *despite* restrictive natural resource bases.

□ Employment of Human Resources

Three statements describe the typical underdeveloped nation's circumstances with respect to human resources:

1 It is overpopulated.

2 Underemployment is widespread.

3 The quality of the labor force is exceedingly low.

Overpopulation Figure 21-1 suggests that many of the nations with the most meager natural and capital resources have the largest populations to support. Table 21-3 compares population densities and population growth rates of a few selected nations with those of the United States and the world as a whole. Most important for the long run is the vivid contrast of population growth rates: In the last twenty years the underdeveloped nations have experienced about a 2.5 percent annual increase in population as compared with a 0.8 percent

Table 21-3 POPULATION STATISTICS FOR SELECTED COUNTRIES, 1975

Country	Population per square kilometer	Annual rate of population increase, 1970–1975
United States	23	0.8%
Hong Kong	4179	2.0
Bengladesh	533	2.4
Puerto Rico	347	2.6
Sri Lanka	213	2.2
India	182	2.1
Haiti	165	1.6
Rwanda	157	2.7
Philippines	142	2.9
World	**29**	**1.9**

Source: United Nations, *Demographic Yearbook, 1975.*

annual rate for the advanced countries. Recalling the "rule of 70," the current rate suggests that the Third World's total population will double in about 28 years! These simple statistics are a significant reason why the per capita income gap between underdeveloped and advanced nations has tended to widen. In some of the underdeveloped countries, the Malthusian population doctrine, rooted in the law of diminishing returns, is all too apparent. Population actually presses upon the food supply to the extent that per capita food consumption is pulled down perilously close to the subsistence level. In the worst instances, it is only the despicable team of malnutrition and disease and the high death rate they engender which keeps incomes near subsistence.

It would seem at first glance that, since

Per capita standard of living

$$= \frac{\text{consumer goods (food) production}}{\text{population}}$$

the standard of living could be raised merely by boosting consumer goods—particularly food—production. But in reality the problem is much more complex than this, because any increase in consumer goods production which initially raises the standard of living is likely to induce a population increase. This increase, if sufficient in size, will dissipate the improvement in living standards, and subsistence living levels will again prevail.

But why does population growth tend to accompany increases in output? First, the nation's *death* or *mortality rate* will decline with initial increases in production. This decline is the result of (1) a higher level of per capita food consumption, and (2) the basic medical and sanitation programs which almost invariably accompany the initial phases of economic development. Second, the *birthrate* will remain high or may even increase, particularly so as the medical and sanitation programs cut the rate of infant mortality. The cliché that "the rich get richer and the poor get children" is uncomfortably accurate for many of the underdeveloped nations of the world. In short, an increase in the per capita standard of living may give rise to a population upsurge which will cease only when the standard of living has again been reduced to the level of bare subsistence. This chapter's Last Word segment on Mexico's population problem is relevant.

In addition to the fact that rapid population growth can translate an expanding GNP into a stagnant or slow-growing GNP per capita, there are less obvious reasons why population expansion is an obstacle to development. On the one hand, large families reduce the capacity of households to save, and this inability restricts the economy's capacity to accumulate capital. On the other hand, high birthrates result in a larger proportion of children in the population or, in other words, a smaller productive work force relative to total population.

Most authorities advocate birth control as the obvious and most effective means for breaking out of this dilemma. And breakthroughs in contraceptive technology in the last two decades have made this solution increasingly relevant. But the obstacles to population control are great. Low literacy rates make it difficult to disseminate information on the use of contraceptive devices. In peasant agriculture, large families are a major source of labor. Furthermore, adults may look upon having many children as a kind of informal social security system; the more children one has, the greater the probability of having a relative to care for one during old age. Finally, many nations which stand to gain the most through birth control are often the least willing, for religious and sociocultural reasons, to embrace contraception programs. Population growth in Latin America, for example, is among the most rapid in the world.

Caution: Not all underdeveloped nations suffer from overpopulation, nor may one conclude that a large population necessarily means underdevelopment. The points to note are: (1) A large and rapidly growing population may pose a special obstacle to economic development; and (2) many of the underdeveloped and semideveloped nations are so burdened.[3]

Unemployment Aside from the drag of overpopulation, the underdeveloped countries are faced with serious unemployment problems. In contrast to the unemployment in advanced nations, the problem is not so much cyclical fluctuations—most underdeveloped nations are too poor to afford a business cycle!—but rather, a chronic and large-scale overallocation of labor to agriculture.

How has this problem of disguised unemployment come about? The predominance of agriculture is common to virtually all the underdeveloped nations. It is very likely that two-thirds, four-fifths, or more of an underdeveloped nation's labor force are engaged in agricultural pursuits. Much—possibly 25 to 30 percent—of this farm labor is underemployed, or surplus, labor,[4] that is, labor which contributes little or nothing to total agricultural output. In Chapter 19's discussion of the principle of diminishing returns, the agricultural "plant" (the fixed supply of arable land) of most underdeveloped nations is grossly overmanned, to the extent that the marginal product of one-fourth or one-third of the nation's agricultural labor force may be zero or even negative! This means that a large fraction of an underdeveloped nation's labor force might be reallocated from agricultural to industrial pursuits with little or no decline, and possibly an increase, in food production.

But the opportunity for such productivity-increasing reallocation of labor has not been realized in most countries. It is true that rural population pressures have often caused

[3] The interested reader should consult Clifford M. Hardin (ed.), *Overcoming World Hunger* (Englewood Cliffs, N.J.: Prentice-Hall, Inc., 1969), and The Editors of Scientific American, *The Human Population* (San Francisco: W. H. Freeman and Company, 1974), particularly chaps. 1, 2, 9, and 10.
[4] See Ragnar Nurkse, *Problem of Capital Formation in Underdeveloped Countries* (Fair Lawn, N.J.: Oxford University Press, 1967), p. 35.

substantial migrations to the cities. However, the lack of industrial growth means that relatively few jobs are available in urban areas. And, even when jobs are available, the transplanted workers frequently do not possess the minimum levels of training and education to qualify for the jobs. Hence, unemployment is often extremely high in the seemingly endless slums which surround the cities of the underdeveloped countries.

Quality of the Labor Force Though long on numbers, the populations of the underdeveloped nations are pitifully short on quality. Poor countries have simply not been able to invest sufficiently in their human capital (Table 21-2, columns 4 and 5); that is, expenditures on health and education have been meager. Low levels of literacy, malnutrition, the absence of proper medical care, and insufficient educational facilities all contribute to populations ill equipped for economic development and industrialization. Particularly vital is the absence of a vigorous entrepreneurial class willing to bear risks, accumulate capital, and provide the organizational requisites essential to economic growth. Closely related is the dearth of labor that is prepared to handle the routine supervisory functions basic to any program of development.

□ **Capital Accumulation**

Most economists feel that an important focal point of economic development is the accumulation of capital goods. There are several reasons for this emphasis upon capital formation:

1 All underdeveloped countries do suffer from a critical shortage of capital goods—factories, machinery and equipment, public utilities, and so forth. There can be no doubt that better-equipped labor forces would greatly enhance the productivity of the underdeveloped nations and help to boost the per capita standard of living.

2 Increasing the stock of capital goods is crucial because of the very limited possibility of increasing the supply of arable land. If there is little likelihood of offsetting the law of diminishing returns in agriculture by increasing the supply of land, the obvious alternative is to counter its operation by better equipping the available agricultural manpower or by providing industrial capital to which this labor can be reallocated. In terms of Figure 19-5, the accumulation of capital may permit a nation to achieve the $A_1B_2C_3D_4$ path to development as opposed to the $A_1B_1C_1D_1$ route to stagnation.

3 Once initiated, the process of capital accumulation can be cumulative. If capital accumulation can increase output ahead of population growth, a margin of saving may arise which permits further capital formation. In a sense, capital accumulation can feed upon itself.

Let us first consider the prospects for underdeveloped nations to accumulate capital domestically. Then we shall examine the possibility of foreign capital flowing into them. In each case we are concerned with private capital; public investment will be considered later.

Domestic Capital Formation How does an underdeveloped nation—or any nation for that matter—accumulate capital? The answer: through the processes of saving and investing. A nation must save, that is, refrain from consumption, to release resources from consumer goods production. Investment spending must then occur to absorb these released resources in the production of capital goods. But the impediments to saving and investing are much greater in a low-income nation than in an advanced economy.

The savings potential Consider first the savings side of the picture. The savings potential of the underdeveloped countries is low. Statistics indicate that they manage to save at best some 5 percent of their national incomes, whereas the advanced nations save 10 percent or more. In explaining this point, it is important to distinguish between (1) the masses of people, who are unable or unwilling to save, and (2) the very wealthy, who can save, but who do not make their savings available for the accumulation of productive capital goods.

1 Saving is a luxury far beyond the reach of the masses of people in the underdeveloped nations; most consume their entire incomes to keep body and soul intact. Incomes are just too low to permit the masses to save. But this is only half the picture. There is serious doubt as to whether significant increases in per capita incomes will generate much saving. Most experts agree that the propensities of underdeveloped nations to consume—that is, their willingness to spend—depend not only upon their own levels of income but also upon the relationship of their income levels to those of the advanced nations. Better communications, increased literacy, expanding hordes of affluent tourists, and, in some instances, the presence of foreign troops have made the peoples of the underdeveloped nations increasingly aware of the superior consumption levels of the advanced nations. This whets the appetites of the poverty-ridden and intensifies their dissatisfaction with their own standard of living. New wants and higher aspirations lead to a high propensity to consume.[5] The underdeveloped nations, in short, are most eager to consume, not save, any forthcoming increases in their national incomes.

2 This is not to say that no one saves in an underdeveloped nation. We have noted that saving might be as high as 5 percent of the national income. This saving stems from the highly unequal distribution of income which characterizes most of the underdeveloped nations. Ironically, both the poorest and the richest families of the world reside in the least developed countries. Those fortunate few with astronomical incomes—the tribal chieftains, the kings, the large landowners, the oil-rich shieks, and the political leaders—do have ample capacity to save. Unfortunately, these high-income receivers frequently dispense their wealth on luxury goods, trivialities, foreign

[5] Ibid., p. 58.

travel, the hoarding of precious metals, or the purchase of existing properties in the form of land or urban real estate. The monetary saving which does occur often flows abroad for safekeeping or to take advantage of the more convenient saving outlets provided by the securities markets of the advanced nations. The important point is that those few who have the ability to save are often unwilling to do so or, if they are willing, do not make their savings available for investment in productive facilities.

Investment obstacles The investment side of the capital formation process abounds with equally serious obstacles. These obstacles undermine the rate of capital formation even when a sufficient volume of savings is available to finance the needed investment. *The major obstacles to investment fall into two categories: the lack of investors and the lack of incentives to invest.*

Oddly enough, in some underdeveloped countries—Turkey and Pakistan, for example—the major obstacle to investment is basically the lack of businessmen who are willing to assume the risks associated with investment. This, of course, is a special case of qualitative deficiencies of the labor force previously discussed.

But even if substantial savings and a vigorous entrepreneurial class are present, an essential ingredient in capital formation—the incentive to invest—may be weak. And clearly a host of factors may combine in an underdeveloped nation to cripple investment incentives. Political and social instability—in particular, the fear of nationalization of industry—may dampen the incentive to invest. Similarly, very low incomes mean a limited domestic market—a lack of demand—for most nonagricultural goods. This factor is especially crucial when one recognizes that the chances of successfully competing with the mature industries of the advanced nations in international markets are typically nil. Then, too, the previously cited lack of trained administrative and operating personnel may be a vital factor in retarding investment. Finally, many of the underdeveloped countries simply do not have a sufficient accumulation of the *basic social capital,* that is, the public utilities, which is prerequisite to private investment of a productive nature. Poor roads, inadequate railways, little gas and electricity production, antiquated communications, unsatisfactory housing, and meager educational and public health facilities scarcely provide an inviting environment for investment spending.

The absence of basic social capital presents more of a problem than one might first surmise. The dearth of social capital means that a great deal of investment spending which does not *directly* result in the production of goods and which may not be capable of bearing profits must take place prior to, and simultaneously with, productive investment in manufacturing machinery and equipment. Statistics for the advanced nations indicate that about 60 percent of gross investment goes for housing, public works, and public utilities, leaving about 40 percent for directly productive investment in manufacturing, agriculture, and commerce.[6] These figures probably understate the percentage of total investment which must be devoted to social capital in the emerging nations. The volume of investment required to initiate economic development may be much greater than it first appears.

There is one potential bright spot in this otherwise dismal picture: the possibility of accumulating capital through *nonfinancial investment,* or investment in kind. Given the prerequisite leadership and willingness to cooperate, capital can be accumulated by transferring surplus agricultural labor to the improvement of agricultural facilities or to the construction of basic social capital. If each agricultural village would allocate its surplus manpower to the construction of irrigation canals, wells, schools, sanitary facilities, and roads, significant amounts of capital might be

accumulated at no sacrifice of consumer goods production. Nonfinancial investment simply bypasses the problems embodied within the financial aspects of the capital accumulation process. Such investment does not require consumers to save portions of their money income, nor does it presume the presence of an entrepreneurial class anxious to invest. In short, provided the leadership and cooperative spirit are present, nonfinancial investment is a promising avenue for the accumulation of basic capital goods.

□ Technological Advance

Technological advance and capital formation are frequently part of the same process. Yet, there are advantages in treating technological advance, or the accumulation and application of new ideas concerning methods of producing, and capital formation, or the accumulating of capital goods, as separate processes.

This is particularly so in discussing the underdeveloped countries. We view technological advance in the industrially advanced nations as an essentially evolutionary process wherein researchers first inch forward the boundaries of technological knowledge. Then follow the financing and construction of the ever larger amounts of complex capital equipment which the technological advance demands. But this picture is not accurate for the less developed countries. The rudimentary state of their current technology puts these nations far from the frontiers of technological advance. There already exists an enormous body of technological knowledge accumulated by the advanced nations which the underdeveloped countries might adopt and apply without undertaking the expensive tasks of research. For example, the adoption of modern crop-rotation practices and the introduction of contour plowing require no additional capital equipment, and they may contribute very significantly to productivity. By raising grain storage bins a few inches above the ground, a

---

[6]W. Arthur Lewis, *The Theory of Economic Growth* (Homewood, Ill.: Richard D. Irwin, Inc., 1955), p. 210.

large amount of grain spoilage can be avoided. Such changes may sound minor to people of advanced nations. However, the resulting gains in productivity can mean the difference between subsistence and starvation in some poverty-ridden nations.

In most instances the application of either existing or new technological knowledge entails the use of new and different capital goods. But, within limits, this capital can be obtained without an increase in the rate of capital formation. That is, if the annual flow of replacement investment is rechanneled from technologically inferior to technologically superior capital equipment, productivity can be increased out of a constant level of investment spending. Actually, some technological advances may be *capital-saving* rather than *capital-using*. A new fertilizer, better adapted to a nation's topography and climate, might be cheaper than that currently employed. A seemingly high-priced metal plow which will last ten years may be cheaper in the long run than an inexpensive but technologically inferior wooden plow which requires annual replacement.

All this is not to deny that, before a nation's development program is far along, further technological process will call for an expanding flow of investment in capital goods. However, even here we must keep in mind that the productivity increases which the most fundamental technological advances permit may provide an increase in the standard of living sufficient to generate a part of the saving prerequisite to meeting the nation's expanding capital goods requirements. By boosting incomes, basic technological advances may provide for the capital accumulation upon which still further technological progress depends. To a degree, technological advance and capital formation may feed upon one another. But we must guard against overoptimism even when this mutual reinforcement of technological and capital accumulation occurs. Remember that the lack of entrepreneurs, of qualified indus-

trial labor, or of essential natural resources can block technological progress as effectively as can a dearth of capital equipment.

□ Sociocultural and Institutional Factors

Purely economic considerations are not sufficient to explain the occurrence or the absence of economic growth. Massive social and institutional readjustments are usually an integral part of the growth process. Economic development entails not only changes in a nation's physical environment (that is, new transportation and communications facilities, new schools, new housing, new plants and equipment), but also drastic changes in the ways in which people think, behave, and associate with one another. Emancipation from custom and tradition is frequently the fundamental prerequisite of economic development. Possibly the most crucial but least tangible ingredient in economic development is "the will to develop." Economic growth may hinge upon "what individuals and social groups *want,* and *whether they want it badly enough to change their old ways of doing things* and to work hard at installing the new."[7]

Sociocultural impediments to growth are numerous and varied. Consider a few examples.

1 Some of the least developed countries have failed to achieve the preconditions for a national economic unit. Tribal allegiances take precedence over national identity. Warring tribes confine all economic activity within the tribe, eliminating any possibility for production-increasing specialization and trade.

2 Religious beliefs and observances may seriously restrict the length of the work day and divert resources which might otherwise have been used for investment to ceremonial uses. In rural India, for example, total ceremonial expenditures are estimated at about 7

[7] Staley, op. cit., p. 218.

percent of per capita income.[8] More generally, religious and philosophical beliefs may be dominated by the "capricious universe view," that is, the notion that there is little or no correlation between an individual's activities and endeavors, on the one hand, and the outcomes or experiences he encounters, on the other.

> If the universe is deemed capricious, the individual will learn to expect little or no correlation between actions and results. This will result in a fatalistic attitude. . . .
>
> These attitudes impinge on all activities including saving, investment, long-range perspective, supply of effort, and family planning. If a higher standard of living and amassing of wealth is treated as the result of providence rather than springing from hard work and saving, there is little rationale for saving, hard work, innovations, and enterprise.[9]

3 The existence of a caste system—formal or informal—causes labor to be allocated to occupations on the basis of caste or tradition rather than on the basis of skill or merit.

Consider now some growth obstacles of an institutional character. Political corruption and bribery are commonplace in many Third World nations. School systems and public service agencies are often ineptly administered and their functioning impaired by petty politics. Tax systems are frequently arbitrary, unjust, cumbersome, and detrimental to incentives to work and invest. Political decisions are often motivated by the desire to enhance the nation's international prestige, rather than to foster development. For example, India's explosion of a nuclear bomb in 1974 (Last Word section of Chapter 2) created a substantial controversy over societal priorities.

[8] Inder P. Nijhawan, "Socio-Political Institutions, Cultural Values, and Attitudes: Their Impact on Indian Economic Development," in J. S. Uppal (ed.), *India's Economic Problems* (New Delhi: Tata McGraw-Hill Publishing Company, Ltd., 1975), p. 31.
[9] Ibid., p. 33.

Because of the predominance of farming in the underdeveloped nations, the problem of achieving that institutional environment in agriculture which is most conducive to increasing production must be a vital consideration in any growth program. More specifically, the institutional problem of *land reform* demands attention in virtually all underdeveloped nations. But the needed reform may vary tremendously between specific nations. In some underdeveloped countries the problem assumes the form of excessive concentration of land ownership in the hands of a few wealthy families. This situation is demoralizing for the tenants, weakening their incentive to produce, and is typically not conducive to capital improvements. At the other extreme is the absurd arrangement whereby each and every family owns and farms a minute fragment of land far too small for the application of modern agricultural technology. An important complication to the problem of land reform lies in the fact that political considerations often push reform in that direction which is least defensible on economic grounds. For many nations, land reform may well be the most acute institutional problem to be resolved in initiating the process of economic development.

THE VICIOUS CIRCLE: A SUMMING UP

It is important to recognize that many of the characteristics of the underdeveloped countries just described are simultaneously causes and consequences of their poverty. These countries are caught in a vicious circle: they are poor because they are poor! Consider Figure 21-2. The fundamental feature of an underdeveloped nation is low per capita income. Being poor, a family has little ability or incentive to save. Furthermore, low incomes mean low levels of demand. As a result, there are few available resources, on the one hand, and no strong in-

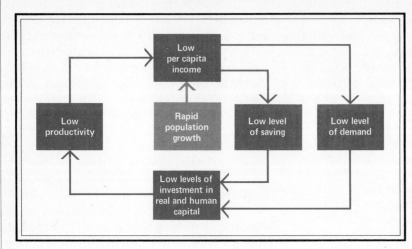

FIGURE 21-2 THE VICIOUS CIRCLE OF UNDERDEVELOPMENT

Low per capita incomes make it extremely difficult for poor nations to save and invest, a condition that perpetuates low productivity and low incomes. Furthermore, rapid population growth may quickly absorb increases in per capita real income and thereby may negate the possibility of breaking out of the underdevelopment circle.

centives, on the other, for investment in real or human capital. This means that labor productivity is low. And, since output per person is real income per person, it follows that per capita income is low.

Many experts feel that the key to breaking out of this vicious circle is to increase the rate of capital accumulation, that is, to achieve a level of investment of, say, 12 percent of the national income. But Figure 21-2 reminds us that the real villain for many underdeveloped nations—rapid population growth—may be waiting in the wings to undo the potentially beneficial effects of this higher rate of capital accumulation. Recall our macro growth model based upon Table 19-2. Suppose an underdeveloped country manages to increase its average propensity to save to 12 percent, and that all this saving is absorbed as investment in real capital. Now, if we assume, not unrealistically, that the capital-output ratio is, say, 4, then real output will rise by 3 percent per year.[10] Given a stable population, real income per person will also rise by 3 percent per year. If

[10] Recall from Chapter 19 that:

$$\text{Growth rate} = \frac{\text{average propensity to save}}{\text{capital-output ratio}}$$

Hence, in this case, .12/4 = .03, or 3 percent.

this per capita growth rate persists, the standard of living will *double* in about twenty-three years. But what if population grows at, say, the Latin American rate of about 3 percent per year? Then real income per person is unchanged and the vicious circle persists!

More optimistically, *if* population can be kept constant or constrained to some growth rate significantly below 3 percent, then real income per person will rise. And this implies the possibility of still further enlargement in the flows of saving and investment, continued advances in productivity, and the continued growth of per capita real income. In short, if a process of self-sustaining expansion of income, saving, investment, and productivity can be achieved, the self-perpetuating vicious circle of poverty can be transformed into a self-regenerating, beneficent circle of economic progress. The trick, obviously, is to make effective those policies and strategies which will accomplish this transition.

CRUCIAL ROLE FOR GOVERNMENT

Economists agree that, at least during the initial stages of growth, government can be expected to play a major role. The reasons for this stem from the character of the obstacles facing these nations.

1 Some of the poorest countries are plagued by widespread banditry and intertribal warfare which divert both attention and resources from the task of development. A strong and stable national government is needed to establish domestic law and order and to achieve peace and unity.

2 The absence of a sizable and vigorous entrepreneurial class, ready and willing to accumulate capital and initiate production, indicates that in many cases private enterprise is intrinsically not capable of spearheading the growth process.

3 Many of the basic obstacles to economic growth center upon deficiencies of social goods and services. Sanitation and basic medical programs, education, irrigation and soil conservation projects, and the construction of highways and transportation-communication facilities are all essentially indivisible goods and services yielding widespread spillover benefits. These characteristics largely preclude their production by private enterprise and distribution to consumers through the price system. Government is the sole institution in a position to provide these goods and services in required quantities.

4 Government action may also be required to break through the saving-investment dilemma which impedes capital formation in the underdeveloped nations. We have noted that when the ability to save does exist, the desire to emulate the consumption standards of the advanced nations may make an underdeveloped nation's citizenry unwilling to save. And, when an entrepreneurial class exists, the deficiency of domestic markets and the temptation to invest in the advanced nations may similarly slow capital formation.

It may well be that only governmental fiscal action can provide a solution by forcing the economy to accumulate capital. The alternatives here are essentially twofold. One is to force the economy to save by increasing taxes. These tax revenues can then be chan-

neled into top-priority investment projects. The problems of honestly and efficiently administering the tax system and achieving a relatively high degree of compliance with tax laws are frequently very great.

The other alternative is to force the economy to save through inflation; that is, the government can finance capital accumulation by printing and spending new money or by selling bonds to banks and spending the proceeds. The resulting inflation, you will recall, is the equivalent of an arbitrary tax upon the economy. There are serious arguments against the advisability of saving through inflation. In the first place, inflation tends to distort the composition of investment away from productive facilities to such items as luxury housing, precious metals and jewels, or foreign securities, which provide a better hedge against rising prices. Furthermore, significant inflation may reduce voluntary saving as potential savers become less willing to accumulate depreciating money or securities payable in money of declining value. Internationally, inflation may boost the nation's imports and retard its flow of exports, creating balance of payments difficulties.

5 Government is obviously in the key position to deal effectively with the social-institutional obstacles to growth. Population growth is a basic problem which calls for the broad approach that only government can provide. The same can be said for the particularly crucial problem of land reform and the difficulties entailed in inducing the migration of labor from agriculture to industrial pursuits. And government is in an advantageous position to stimulate the will to develop, to change a philosophy of "Heaven and faith will determine the course of events" to one of "God helps those who help themselves."

6 The underdeveloped nations seek *rapid* economic growth. The surging spirit of nationalism and the widening gap between the aspirations and the economic positions of the peoples of the poorer nations constantly fan this passion to catch up with the advanced nations. The price system, you will remember, operates slowly, without certainty, and often with little regard for considerations of equity. It may be that government is the only mechanism through which the development process can be accelerated with certainty and with a reasonably equitable distribution of costs.

But all this must not blind us to certain potential problems and disadvantages which a governmentally directed development program may entail. If entrepreneurial talent is lacking in the private sector, can we expect men of quality to be present in the ranks of government? Is there not a real danger that government bureaucracy, not to mention outright maladministration and corruption, will prove an impediment, not a stimulus, to much-needed social and economic change? And, too, what of the tendency of centralized economic planning to favor the spectacular "showpiece" projects at the expense of less showy but more productive programs? Might not political objectives take precedence over the economic goals of a governmentally directed development program?

It must also be emphasized strongly that we are not here advocating socialism or communism as the most likely path to opulence. The point is that government might well be obligated by the environmental characteristics of an underdeveloped country to provide the incentive and the means of *initially* breaking the poverty barrier. With economic growth there may evolve a price system, an entrepreneurial class, and all the institutions and attitudes prerequisite to a strong private economy. Government may then relinquish its key role, assured that the private sector of the economy is capable of sustaining the growth process.

ROLE OF THE ADVANCED NATIONS

What are the ways by which the advanced nations can help the less developed countries in their quest for growth? To what degree have these avenues of assistance been pursued?

Generally speaking, underdeveloped nations can benefit from (1) an expanding volume of trade with advanced nations; (2) flows of private capital from the more affluent nations; and (3) foreign aid, that is, grants and loans from the governments of advanced nations. Let us consider these possibilities in the order stated.

□ Expanding Trade

Some authorities maintain that the simplest and most effective means by which the United States and other advanced nations can aid the underdeveloped nations is by lowering international trade barriers, thereby enabling Third World nations to expand their national incomes through an increased volume of trade.

Though there is undoubtedly some truth in this view, lowered trade barriers are not a panacea. It is true that some Third World nations need only large foreign markets for their raw materials to achieve some measure of growth. But the problem for most of the developing nations is not that of obtaining markets for the utilization of existing productive capacity or the sale of relatively abundant raw materials, but rather, the more fundamental one of getting the capital and technical assistance needed to produce something for export!

Furthermore, it must be recognized that close trade ties with advanced nations are not without disadvantages. The old quip, "When Uncle Sam gets his feet wet, the rest of the world gets pneumonia," contains considerable truth for many less developed nations. In particular, a recession in the First World can have disastrous consequences for the prices of raw materials and the export earnings of Third World nations. For example, in mid–1974 the price of copper was $1.52 per pound; by the end of 1975 it had fallen to $.53 per pound! Stability and growth in the industrially advanced nations are clearly important to progress in the underdeveloped countries.

Private Capital Flows

Our vicious circle of underdevelopment emphasizes the importance of capital accumulation in achieving economic growth. Foreign capital—both private and public—can obviously supplement an emerging country's saving and investment efforts and play a crucial role in breaking the circle of underdevelopment.

The underdeveloped countries have in fact received substantial flows of private capital from the advanced nations. In the 1960s these flows amounted to $3 or $4 billion per year. Inspired undoubtedly by an intensified search for oil, private flows grew dramatically in the 1970s. The figure for 1975 exceeded $21 billion.

The advanced nations and their huge multinational corporations contend that the flow of private capital would be much larger if conditions in the Third World nations were more receptive. That is, in addition to all the previously mentioned deterrents to domestic capital accumulation in the poor nations, there are special obstacles to foreign investment. For example, foreign capital is often subject to (1) discriminatory taxation, (2) limitations or prohibitions upon the withdrawal of profits, (3) cumbersome governmental regulations and red tape, and (4) the ever-present danger of nationalization without adequate compensation.

Foreign Aid: Public Loans and Grants

Many obstacles to economic development cannot be overcome by private capital alone. In particular, most of the underdeveloped nations are sadly lacking in the basic social capital—irrigation and public health programs and educational, transportation, and communications systems—prerequisite to the attraction of either domestic or foreign private capital. Foreign public aid is needed to tear down this major roadblock to the flow of private capital to the underdeveloped countries.

Direct Aid The United States has assisted the underdeveloped nations directly through a variety of programs and through participation in international institutions designed to stimulate economic development. Over the past decade, American economic aid—including both loans and grants—has averaged $3 to $4 billion per year. The bulk of this aid is administered by our Agency for International Development (AID). A significant amount, however, takes the form of grants of surplus food under the Food for Peace program. Other advanced nations have also embarked upon substantial foreign aid programs. In 1975 foreign aid from all noncommunist nations was about $14 billion.

The World Bank Group The United States is a major participant in the World Bank, the major objective of which is to assist underdeveloped nations in achieving growth. The 127 member nations have subscribed to the Bank's $26 billion worth of stock roughly in proportion to their economic strength. The Bank not only lends out of its capital funds, but also (1) sells bonds and lends the proceeds, and (2) guarantees and insures private loans.

Several characteristics of the World Bank merit comment.

1 The World Bank is in a sense a "last resort" lending agency; that is, its loans are limited to productive projects for which private funds are not readily available.

2 Because many World Bank loans have been for basic development projects—multipurpose dams, irrigation projects, health and sanitation programs, communications and transportation facilities—it has been hoped that the Bank's activities will provide the basic social capital prerequisite to substantial flows of private capital.

3 The Bank has played a significant role in providing technical assistance to underdeveloped nations by helping them discover what avenues of growth seem most appropriate for their economic development.

In recent years two World Bank affiliates

have come into existence, functioning in areas where the World Bank has been weak. The International Finance Corporation (IFC) has the primary function of investing in *private* enterprises in underdeveloped nations. The International Development Association (IDA) makes "soft loans"—that is, loans which may not be self-liquidating—to the very poorest of the underdeveloped countries on much more liberal terms than does the World Bank.

NEOCOLONIALISM?

Despite growing flows of private investment and foreign aid, the Third World nations are far from content with their relationships vis-à-vis the industrially advanced nations. The feeling is widespread among Third World nations that their economies are being dominated by the business interests of the United States and Europe. The advanced nations, it is argued, are not genuinely interested in the economic progress of the Third World, but rather in exploiting the natural resources, the raw materials, the cheap labor, and the markets which exist there. Many of the underdeveloped nations have emerged from colonial status only since World War II. Despite political independence, they feel that an economically based *neocolonialism* persists. Both private investment and public aid, it is contended, have tended to exploit the Third World economies and keep them dependent upon, and subservient to, the rich nations.

Consider private capital flows. Underdeveloped countries seek to make their economies more diversified. They want to develop home markets on the one hand, and to reduce their dependence upon world markets and the economic well-being of the advanced nations on the other. Foreign private capital, however, seeks out those industries which are currently the most profitable, that is, the ones which are now producing for the export market. In brief, while the underdeveloped nations strive for less dependence on world markets, flows of foreign private capital often tend to enhance that dependence. Exxon, Alcoa, United Fruit, British Shell, and the rest are after profits and they allegedly have no particular interest in the overall progress of the less developed countries. Indeed, progress in the form of industrialization might in time mean unwanted competition in world markets.

Consider foreign aid. First, the Third World countries argue that the flow of foreign aid has been grossly inadequate. True, on the surface the United States' $4 billion of aid in 1975 seems like an impressive amount. But in fact it is only one-fourth of 1 percent of its GNP! In comparative terms, at least, one cannot say that American economic aid to the underdeveloped nations has been extravagant. As one authority has put it,[11]

> There is practically no danger that the United States government will spend more than our national interest requires on economic aid to underdeveloped countries. The danger is all the other way. Underdeveloped countries are not represented in Congress where the appropriation logs are rolled, and the compelling American interest in the advancement of the underdeveloped parts of the free world is less easy for statesmen to explain than for narrow-mindedness and shortsightedness to obscure.

Other considerations have tended to diminish the effectiveness of foreign aid. (1) Much aid is "tied" to the granting or lending country; for example, "tied" American loans and grants must be spent by the recipient nation upon American goods and services. This means that underdeveloped nations are denied the opportunity to "shop around" in world markets for potentially better buys on capital goods and technological assistance.

[11]Staley, op cit., p. 372. For a highly critical view of foreign aid see C. R. Hensman, *Rich Against Poor: The Reality of Aid* (Baltimore, Md.: Penguin Books, Inc., 1971).

(2) Inflation in the United States and other aid-giving countries has acted to erode the real value of aid dollars to recipient nations. (3) The current foreign debt of the Third World is on the order of $175 billion. Hence, a large portion of the foreign aid received by many underdeveloped countries must go to pay interest on outstanding debt, rather than to finance development.

A second complaint is that the size and the direction of foreign aid are strongly influenced by the national interests of the donor country, rather than based upon need or the prospects for development. The United States, for example, is continuously redirecting its aid to promote its political, military, and economic interests overseas. At best, aid is viewed as a device for sustaining pro-American and pro-capitalistic governments, even though those governments may be undemocratic, unprogressive, and unpopular. At worst, aid is held to be part of a larger overall imperialistic strategy which encompasses political-military pressure, far-flung military bases, "imperialistic wars," and the clandestine subversion of revolutionary movements which might lead to the establishment of "unfriendly" political regimes.[12]

■ _____

THE FUTURE

What next? What will be the fate of the Third World nations over, say, the remainder of this century and beyond? Will substantial progress be made? Or, with perhaps a few exceptions, will stagnation and poverty prevail? Obviously, the forecasts required to respond to these questions cannot be made with any reasonable degree of certainty. Yet a number of intriguing and plausible scenarios have been offered.

1 The most optimistic view is this: In the

[12]The section entitled "Imperialism" in Chapter 40 expands upon these arguments.

past decade or so the overall growth of the GNPs of the Third World nations has been on the order of 5 or 6 percent, quite comparable to many of the more advanced nations. Given important breakthroughs in birth-control technology and a rapidly expanding awareness of the need to control populations, this growth of GNP will be translated into an improving standard of living. Furthermore, the potentialities of the "Green Revolution," that is, the important technological breakthroughs in agriculture which have created new high-yield strains of rice and wheat, may be realized on an expanded scale to resolve basic food and nutritional problems within the foreseeable future.

2 Another scenario envisions the Third World improving its economic status through the exercise of greater economic muscle in its relationships with the advanced countries. Inspired by the success of the OPEC oil cartel and the apparent vulnerability of the industrialized nations to raw material embargoes, it is envisioned that various groups of less developed nations will form cartels (monopolies) to control the worldwide supply of some particular raw material. Following the OPEC lead, the cartels will increase the prices of their raw materials sharply and thereby significantly redistribute world income and wealth from the rich to the poor countries. Given the substantial contribution of OPEC's higher oil prices to the worldwide stagflation of the 1970s, there is no doubt that this scenario implies the serious disruption of the international economic system which now exists.

3 A final scenario envisions a rich nations–poor nations confrontation of frightening proportions. Assume that the population problem perseveres; that is, that Malthus's grim prognosis is realized in many Third World countries and population expands at unmanageable rates. Suppose, too, that nuclear capability spreads to the underdeveloped nations. The result, it is argued, is the horrendous possibility of "wars of redistribution." That is, as the rich nations get richer and the economic situation of the underdeveloped countries deteriorates under the burden of population pressures, it becomes increasingly possible that radical poor nations will threaten a nuclear holocaust as a means of blackmailing rich nations into sharing their wealth.[13]

[13]See Robert L. Heilbroner, *An Inquiry into the Human Prospect* (New York: W. W. Norton & Company, Inc., 1974), and Heilbroner, "Second Thoughts on *The Human Prospect*," *Challenge*, May–June 1975, pp. 21–28.

Summary

1 Most nations of the world are underdeveloped (low per capita income) nations. Spurred by *a.* the widening gap between their incomes and those of the advanced nations, and *b.* the rising spirit of nationalism, the people of the underdeveloped nations are far from content with their current economic status.

2 Initial scarcities of natural resources and the limited possibility of augmenting existing supplies may impose a rigid limitation upon a nation's capacity to develop.

3 The presence of large populations in the underdeveloped countries contributes to low per capita incomes. In particular, increases in per capita incomes frequently induce rapid population growth, to the end that per capita incomes again deteriorate back to near-subsistence levels.

4 Disguised unemployment in the form of surplus agricultural labor exists in most of the underdeveloped nations. This underemployment stems from the absence of alternative job opportunities on the one hand, and the occupational and geographic immobility of agricultural labor on the other.

5 In the underdeveloped nations both the saving and investment aspects of the capital formation process are impeded by formidable obstacles. The vast majority of households in the underdeveloped nations receive incomes too small to permit them to save. Furthermore, little saving may be forthcoming even out of incomes considerably higher than those currently received by this group. A high propensity to consume accounts for this expectation. The very wealthy have considerable ability to save but prefer to spend lavishly or to invest their savings in socially unproductive ways.

6 The absence of a vigorous entrepreneurial class and the weakness of investment incentives are the major obstacles to capital accumulation when money capital is readily available. Political and social instability, the lack of large domestic markets, shortages of operating and administrative personnel, and deficiencies of basic social capital all contribute to an uninviting environment for private investment. Some degree of capital accumulation can usually be achieved, however, through nonfinancial investment.

7 Appropriate social and institutional changes and, in particular, the presence of "the will to develop" are essential ingredients in economic development.

8 The vicious circle of underdevelopment brings together many of the obstacles to growth and says in effect that "poor countries are poor because of their poverty." Low incomes inhibit saving and the accumulation of real and human capital, making it difficult to increase productivity and incomes. Rapid population growth can offset otherwise promising attempts to break the vicious circle.

9 The role of government in the development of the underdeveloped nations is likely to be considerable. The nature of the obstacles to growth—the absence of an entrepreneurial class, the dearth of social capital, the saving-investment dilemma, and the presence of social-institutional obstacles to growth—and the fact that the underdeveloped nations seek rapid growth suggest the need for government action in intitiating the growth process.

10 The advanced nations can assist in development by reducing trade barriers and by providing both private and public capital. However, many underdeveloped nations feel their trade, investment, and aid relationships with the advanced nations are such that they constitute a new form of economic colonialism.

Questions and Study Suggestions

1 Key terms and concepts to remember: underdeveloped nation; Third World; investment in human capital; nonfinancial investment; basic social capital; capital-saving and capital-using technological advance; the "will to develop"; vicious circle of poverty; World Bank; the "Green Revolution"; neocolonialism.

2 What are the major characteristics of an underdeveloped nation? List the major avenues of economic development available to such a nation. State and explain the obstacles which face the underdeveloped nations in breaking the poverty barrier. Use the "vicious circle of underdevelopment" to outline in detail the steps which an underdeveloped country might take to initiate economic development.

3 Discuss and evaluate:

a. "The path to economic development has been clearly blazed by American capitalism. It is only for the underdeveloped nations to follow this trail."

b. "Economic inequality is conducive to saving, and saving is the prerequisite of investment. Therefore, greater inequality in the income distribution of the underdeveloped countries would be a spur to capital accumulation and growth."

c. "The spirit of nationalism sometimes aids and sometimes impedes the process of economic growth."

d. "The advanced economies fear the complications which stem from oversaving; the underdeveloped countries bear the yoke of undersaving."

e. "The core of the development process involves changing human beings more than it does altering a nation's physical environment."

f. "America's 'foreign aid' program is a sham. In reality it represents neocolonialism—a means by which the underdeveloped nations can be nominally free in a political sense but remain totally subservient in an economic sense."

g. "Poverty and freedom cannot persist side by side; one must triumph over the other."

4 Much of the initial investment in an underdeveloped country must be devoted to basic social capital which does not directly or immediately lead to a greater production of goods and services. What bearing might this have upon the degree of inflation which results as government finances capital accumulation through the printing and spending of new money? Be specific.

5 "The nature of the problems faced by the underdeveloped nations creates a bias in favor of a governmentally directed as opposed to a decentralized development process." Do you agree? Substantiate your position.

6 Assume an underdeveloped country saves and invests 16 percent of its national income each year and that its capital-output ratio is 4. What does this mean for the growth of per capita incomes if population is increasing by 6 percent per year? By 4 percent per year? By 1 percent per year? What, if anything, does this example suggest with respect to growth policies?

Selected References

Blanchfield, William C.: *Economic Development* (Columbus, Ohio: Grid, Inc., 1976).

Hagen, Everett E.: *The Economics of Development,* rev. ed. (Homewood, Ill.: Richard D. Irwin, Inc., 1975).

Meier, Gerald M. (ed.): *Leading Issues in Economic Development,* 3d ed. (New York: Oxford University Press, 1976).

Morgan, Theodore: *Economic Development: Concept and Strategy* (New York: Harper & Row, Publishers, Incorporated, 1975).

Ranis, Gustav (ed.): *The United States and the Developing Economies,* rev. ed. (New York: W. W. Norton & Company, Inc., 1973).

Stanford, Quentin H.: *The World's Population: Problems of Growth* (New York: Oxford University Press, 1972).

Last Word
The Thunder of Tiny Feet

Population growth is the Achilles' heel of economic development; the development efforts of many poor countries are frustrated by rapid population growth. Consider the case of Mexico.

Mexico is known to millions of Americans as the land of the mariachi; of fabulous but still reasonably priced vacations; and of one of the world's best economic growth rates. If you believe, however, in simple statistical projections, Mexico is in deep trouble.

The enemy is the stork. Mexico's population of 50 million is growing at 3.7% a year, a full 1% higher than India's disastrous birthrate. Even allowing for a slowdown in the birthrate, there will be 100 million Mexicans within 20 years, and nowhere in sight are the food and jobs to sustain them. Not even zero population growth would save the situation, because past growth has created too many potential mothers who are about to reach childbearing age. More than half the population is under 20 years old.

The economy is not at fault. It has been growing at an average annual rate of 7% or so for 20 years; only Japan beats that for fast, sustained growth. Even though agriculture, the traditional occupation, is bogged down in low productivity, this vital, vibrant economy is providing something like 250,000 new jobs every year in commerce and industry. But something like 700,000 young Mexicans come into the job market every year, maybe more.

In a country where there is no such thing as a dole and where social security covers only an elite of 3 million workers and their families, life is merciless: No job, no food. You see this not only in the beggars, but in the thousands of people trying to eke out a few pesos selling lottery tickets or chewing gum in the streets of every large city. The desperation shows all along the U.S.-Mexican border, where the illegal migrants—wetbacks—increase year by year. . . .

Mexico is one of the great contradictions of the modern world. Here is a once poor country that has done everything right. It has achieved stability, established the rule of law, encouraged free enterprise and greatly raised the level of education. Yet all this prosperity and stability has only made the population problem worse. Mexico is smothering in people. Mexico City, the El Dorado for the rural poor, now has 8.5 million inhabitants and gains 700,000 every year. What has been called the "terrible patter of tiny feet" has become thunder to all thoughtful Mexicans.

A major consequence of the population problem is that the prosperity has been uneven. About half of the population, the people with jobs and businesses, is sharing in it—with shoes, with bicycles, even with cars, refrigerators and TVs. The other half, the masses of peasants, are living roughly as they lived 30 years ago: Twenty-eight percent of the population is still illiterate, 20% is shoeless. . . .

The healthy part of Mexico's economy has never been healthier. . . . Industrial production is growing at a rate of 10% a year; basic industries like cement and chemicals and steel are growing 12% to 15%.

Foreign businessmen with plants in the country have nothing but praise for the Mexican worker: dexterous, intelligent, unafraid of hard work. At least one American businessman is convinced that Mexican plants could eventually turn out consumer goods for the U.S. market if U.S. tariffs would permit it; already Volkswagen recreation vehicles, called "Things," manufactured in Mexico are being sold in the U.S. In the so-called border industries, U.S. companies use Mexican workers on Mexican soil to make parts and to assemble U.S. products for export overseas.

Morever, Mexico is investing heavily and intelligently in its most promising industry: tourism. European tourism is being hurt by devaluation of the dollar; Caribbean tourism is being hurt by high prices and by black power hostility to white skins. But Mexico has everything going for it: proximity to the U.S., good weather and reasonable prices. . . .

But meanwhile, the stork keeps right on coming. Mexico gained about 35,000 people last week and will gain 35,025 next week and 35,050 the week after, and on and on as far as the mind can stretch.

"The Stork vs. the Steel Mill." Reprinted by permission of *Forbes Magazine* from the August 15, 1973, issue.

PART FIVE

THE ECONOMICS OF THE FIRM
AND RESOURCE ALLOCATION

22

The Market Structures of American Capitalism

Scarce resources and unlimited wants, you will recall, are the foundation of economic science. The efficient management of scarce resources is a major goal of our economic system. Furthermore, there are two major facets to the problem of achieving efficient resource use. The first, which we have examined in Parts 2 and 3 and, to some degree, in Part 4 of this book, centers upon the full employment of available resources. The second aspect of the economizing problem—the one to which we now turn—has to do with allocating employed resources among alternative uses in the most efficient manner. Stated differently, Parts 2, 3, and 4 focused upon the last of the Five Fundamental Questions posed in Chapter 2: "Can the economy achieve the full employment of its available resources?" Part 5 deals with the first four questions: "Can the economy produce that output most desired by society?" "Will the production of that output be organized in the most efficient manner?" "Can the economy successfully distribute that output?" "Is the economy capable of maintaining efficiency in the use of its resources in the face of changes in the relative supplies of resources, changes in consumer tastes, and changes in technology?" All four of these questions obviously have an important bearing on the problem of achieving and maintaining an efficient allocation of available resources.

We are well aware that one of the major characteristics of capitalistic economies is their heavy reliance upon a price system as a means for allocating resources (Chapter 5). Our major topics of discussion, then, are prices and the price system. Specifically, our basic goal in the ensuing chapters is to acquire a comprehensive understanding of the operation and relative efficiency of the *price system* in allocating resources within the framework of American capitalism. As a means to achieving this primary goal, we also seek a thorough analysis of *individual prices* under a variety of contrasting market arrangements.

Using the product market as a point of reference, the present chapter defines and describes the various market arrangements we propose to examine. In the subsequent chapters in Part 5, we shall review and apply our previous analysis of demand and supply, enhance our understanding of the demand side of the market, explore the production (supply) side of the market through a discussion of production costs—the major determinant of a firm's willingness to supply a given product—and examine in some detail the interaction of supply and demand under the various market arrangements described in the present chapter. Our attention will then shift to the functioning of prices in the resource market. Finally, the overall operation of the price system in American capitalism is examined.

FOUR BASIC MARKET MODELS

There is no such thing as an "average" or "typical" industry. Detailed examination of the business sector of American capitalism reveals an almost infinite number of different market situations; no two industries are alike. At one extreme we may find a single producer completely dominating a particular market. At the other we discover thousands upon thousands of firms, each of which supplies a minute fraction of market output. Between these extremes lies an almost unlimited variety of market arrangements, most of which shade into one another.

Obviously, any attempt to examine each specific industry would be an endless and impossible task. There are simply too many of them. Hence, we seek a more realistic objective—to define and discuss several basic market structures, or models. In so doing, we shall acquaint ourselves with the *general* way in which price and output are determined in most of the market types which characterize American capitalism.

But the use of a few market models as typifying most of American industries calls for a word or two of caution.

1 The market models to be considered are necessarily abstractions. They are merely first approximations and, as such, do not purport to present a complete picture of reality (see Chapter 1). In no case will the market models we are about to define provide a *detailed* explanation of the functioning of any specific firm. Yet they will do a reasonably good job of outlining the operation of many firms.

2 Some firms and industries will not fall neatly within any of the market models we are about to outline; rather, they will bear characteristics of two or more of these models. This means that the classification of a given firm or industry might entail an element of arbitrariness. This is the same type of problem which other scientists encounter. The botanist, for example, classifies all plants under three family groups—algae and fungi (thallophytes), moss plants (bryophytes), and vascular plants (tracheophytes). Yet many forms of plant life do not neatly fit into any one of these families, but rather, are borderline cases. So it is with the economist in classifying industries.

3 Finally, it is important to recognize at the outset that the economist's definitions of the basic market models do not coincide with those typically employed by businessmen and laymen. The definitions which follow are not of commonsense vintage. "Competition," for example, has a much more precise meaning to the economist than it does to the average businessman.

Economists envision four relatively distinct market situations. These are (1) pure competition, (2) pure monopoly, (3) monopolistic competition, and (4) oligopoly. The immediate task is to describe the major characteristics of each of these four market models. In doing so, we shall use the seller's side of the product market as a point of reference. We shall see later that the same general models also are relevant for the buying side of the market.

□ Pure Competition

A purely competitive market has several distinct characteristics which set it off from other market structures.

1 A main feature of a purely competitive market is the presence of a large number of independently acting sellers, usually offering their products in a highly organized market.

2 Competitive firms are producing a standardized or virtually standardized product. Given price, the consumer is indifferent as to the seller from which he purchases. In a competitive market the products of firms B, C, D, E, and so forth are looked upon by the buyer as perfect substitutes for that of firm A.

3 In a purely competitive market *individual firms* exert no significant control over product price. This characteristic follows from the preceding two. Under pure competition each firm produces such a small fraction of total output that increasing or decreasing its output will have no perceptible influence upon total supply or, therefore, product price. To illustrate, assume there are 10,000 competing firms, each of which is currently producing 100 units of output. Total supply is obviously 1,000,000. Now suppose one of these 10,000 firms cuts its output to 50 units. Will this affect price? No. And the reason is clear: This restriction of output by a single firm has an almost imperceptible impact on total supply—specifically, the total quantity supplied declines from 1,000,000 to 999,950. This is obviously not enough of a change in total supply to affect product price noticeably. In short, the individual competitive producer is a *price*

taker; he cannot adjust market price, but can only adjust to it.

Stated differently, the individual competitive producer is at the mercy of the market; to him product price is a given datum over which he exerts no influence. He can get the same price per unit for a large output as he can for a small output. To ask a price higher than the going market price would be futile. Consumers will not buy anything from firm A at a price of $2.10 when its 9999 competitors are selling an identical, and therefore a perfect substitute product at $2 per unit. Conversely, because firm A can sell as much as it chooses at $2 per unit, there is no reason for it to charge some lower price, say, $1.95. Indeed, to do so would shrink its profits.

Finally, a subtle but highly important point: Although the *individual* firm cannot influence product price by varying its output, all firms in a competitive industry acting *as a group* can cause market price to vary. Should all 10,000 firms cut their outputs from 100 to 50 units, the total quantity supplied will decline from 1,000,000 to 500,000 units. This is most certainly a very significant change and can be expected to boost product price considerably. In brief, the individual firm cannot significantly influence price, but all firms as a group can. Although product price to an individual competitive seller is fixed, that price is free to move up or down in accordance with changes in either *total* demand or *total* supply.

4 New firms are free to enter and existing firms are free to leave purely competitive industries. In particular, no significant obstacles—legal, technical, financial, or other—exist to prohibit new firms from coming into being and selling their outputs in competitive markets.

5 Because purely competitive firms are producing a standardized product, there is virtually no room for *nonprice competition,* that is, competition on the basis of differences in product quality, advertising, or sales promotion. By definition each firm in a competitive market is producing an identical product.

Hence, no firm has a quality edge over its rivals. Advertising by individual firms will be to no avail, because each firm's product has no distinguishing features to be advertised or promoted. Buyers will know that the products of all firms in the industry have the same features. Advertising has virtually no chance of convincing them otherwise.

What about examples? Really precise examples of pure competition are few and far between. If we neglect the government's farm program, agriculture provides us with most of the good illustrations. Thus, we find, for example, that there are hundreds of thousands of farmers producing class I corn—a product which is obviously standardized or uniform. Class I corn is class I corn! Each firm supplies such a small fraction of the total that no single farmer has any control over the market price for class I corn. He accepts the market price which exists in the highly organized market as a datum over which he has no influence; the individual farmer can sell as much or as little as he wants without affecting that price. He does not squander his financial resources on advertising or sales promotion. Farmer Jones knows that thousands upon thousands of other farmers are producing an identical product and that buyers are well aware of this. Hence, advertising would be futile, a sheer waste of time, effort, and money. The markets for wheat, cotton, barley, oats, the various types of livestock, and a good many other farm staples also fit rather well into the competitive mold we have outlined. Although only a few industries approximate pure competition, the purely competitive market model provides a norm against which less competitive markets can be evaluated.

□   **Pure Monopoly**

Now we turn to the other extreme of the spectrum. Pure monopoly provides us with the sharpest contrast to pure competition.

1 A pure, or absolute, monopolist is a one-firm industry. A single firm is the only producer of a given product or the sole supplier of a service; hence, the firm and the industry are synonymous.

2 It follows from this first characteristic that the monopolist's product is unique in the sense that there are no good, or close, substitutes available. From the buyer's point of view, this means that he has no reasonable alternatives to which he can turn. He must buy the product from the monopolist or do without.

A question arises at this point: When are products "good" substitutes? There is no clear answer to this query. In a very broad sense, all goods and services which compete for the consumer's dollar are substitutes. A down payment on a house may be a substitute for a new automobile. A two-week vacation may be a substitute for a television set. A pair of shoes may be a substitute for a new pair of slacks. A symphony concert may be a substitute for a fraternity dance. Yet, in a more restricted sense of the term, it is clear that some products and services simply do not have reasonably good substitutes. Candles and kerosene lamps are not good substitutes for electric lights. Spices are poor substitutes for salt. Bus or train transportation may be a poor substitute for owning one's own automobile. To some, a symphony concert is no substitute at all for the Signa Phi Nothing formal.

In our discussion we shall employ the idea of substitution in the narrower sense of the term. Hence, we can agree that, as most consumers see it, there are no good substitutes for the water piped into our homes by the municipal waterworks or the electric power provided by the local power company. Digging a well or importing water from a neighboring community is not a realistic substitute for running water in one's home. And few would regard kerosene lighting as an acceptable substitute for electric lights. In any event your television set will not run on kerosene. Up to World War II, manufacturers whose products entailed the need for a strong but lightweight metal had little choice but to purchase aluminum from

Alcoa; no competing aluminum producers were in existence prior to the war.

3 We have emphasized that the individual firm operating under pure competition exercises no influence over product price. This is so because it contributes only a negligible portion of total supply. In vivid contrast, the pure monopolist is a *price maker;* he exercises considerable control over price. And the reason is obvious: He is responsible for, and therefore controls, the total quantity supplied. Given a downsloping demand curve for his product, the monopolist can cause product price to change by manipulating the quantity of the product supplied. If it is to his advantage, we can expect him to use his power in this way.

4 If, by definition, a pure monopolist has no immediate competitors, there must be a reason for this lack of competition. And there is: The existence of monopoly depends upon the existence of barriers to entry. Be they economic, technological, legal, or other, certain obstacles must exist to keep new competitors from coming into the industry if monopoly is to persist. Entry is not easy under conditions of pure monopoly; on the contrary, it is blocked. More of this in Chapter 27.

5 Depending upon the type of product or service involved, monopolists may or may not engage in extensive advertising and sales promotion activity. Local public utilities see no point in large expenditures for advertising; any local citizen who wants water, gas, and electric power and telephone service already knows from whom he must buy.

If pure monopolists do advertise, such advertising is likely to be of a public relations, or goodwill, character rather than highly competitive, as is the advertising associated with, say, cigarettes, detergents, and beer. Because they have no immediate rivals, monopolists, in trying to induce more people to buy their products, need not invoke the ours-is-better-than-theirs type of advertising which plagues radio, television, and otherwise scenic highways. Rather, the monopolist's pitch is likely to be, "We're really nice fellows and certainly wouldn't do anything to exploit other firms, our beloved employees, or, heaven forbid, consumers." Or the monopolist may be anxious for the public to recognize that at least 90 percent of the firm's stock is held by destitute widows and orphans. Or, finally, the monopolist may be content merely to point out the technological progress for which the firm has been responsible.

Because pure monopoly is admittedly an extreme market model, we once again find relatively few precise illustrations. Most local public utilities are pure monopolists for the municipalities which they serve. Thus, consumers either purchase their water, electricity, gas, and telephone service from the local utility or do without. Much the same may hold true of railway service in rural areas. On a nationwide basis, American Telephone and Telegraph approximates a pure monopoly. As we have said, Alcoa was a virtual monopolist in the production of most basic aluminum products until World War II; now it faces some competition from Reynolds and Kaiser. The United Shoe Machinery Company is the only manufacturer of certain equipment used in the production of shoes. IBM is the only source of certain calculating machines.

This is not to say that the pure monopolist will charge the highest price he can get for his product or service. Consumers may find it impossible to do without some amount of water and highly inconvenient to do without some quantity of electricity. But the amounts they purchase will vary inversely with price. If the prices of electricity and water were extremely high, the poor (but cheap) substitutes of kerosene lamps and drawing water from a well would become relevant. And an extremely high price on office machines might induce firms to substitute bookkeepers for the machines.

□ **Monopolistic Competition**

As its name indicates, monopolistic competition stands between the extremes of pure competition and pure monopoly. It embraces characteristics of both, but it stands closer to pure competition.

1 As is the case with pure competition, monopolistic competition entails a large number of sellers acting independently. This does not mean that there need be 1,000, 10,000, or 1,000,000 firms in the industry; 30, 40, or 100 firms of more or less equal size may prevail. The important point is that each firm produces a fairly small share of the total output.

2 In contrast to pure competition, wherein the product is standardized, *product differentiation* is a major characteristic of monopolistically competitive industries. Product differentiation entails not only physical differences in the products of various producers or sellers in the industry, but also differences in such factors as the location and "snob appeal" of the seller's store, the packaging of the product, the cordiality of the firm's salespeople, the effectiveness of its advertising, the availability of credit, the company's reputation for servicing or "making good" on defective products, and so forth. The net result is that, although all firms in such an industry are producing the same general type or class of product, the particular product of each firm will have certain distinguishing features which set it off to some extent from those of other firms in the industry. In other words, the products of monopolistically competitive firms are close, but not perfect, substitutes. Just as the presence of a relatively large number of firms makes for competition, product differentiation gives rise to a measure of monopoly power. Indeed, monopolistic competition is sometimes called "the case of differentiation and large numbers."

3 Monopolistically competitive producers have a limited amount of control over product price. The control that exists depends essentially upon the degree of product differentiation and the number and proximity of competitors. The monopolistically competitive producer can raise his price modestly without having his sales fall to zero. Why? Because buyers recognize some differences between the products of various sellers. In the presence of product differentiation, consumers are likely to have definite preferences for the products of specific sellers, and relatively small price increases by one firm will not cause all buyers to seek out the close substitute products of rival firms in that industry. Generally, when the rivals of a monopolistically competitive firm are many in number and in close proximity, each firm's control over price will be less than would otherwise be the case.

4 Entry into monopolistically competitive industries is typically easy. Nevertheless, entry may be a bit more difficult under monopolistically competitive conditions than when pure competition prevails. This is so because of product differentiation. A new firm must not only obtain the capital necessary to go into business but must also win clients away from existing firms. Securing a share of the market may entail considerable research and product development costs by the new firm to ensure that its product will have features which distinguish it from products already on the market. Similarly, considerable advertising outlays may be necessary to inform consumers of the existence of a new brand and to convince a number of them that it will be to their advantage to switch to the new product. In short, greater financial obstacles may face the potential newcomer under monopolistic competition than under pure competition.

5 Because products are differentiated, monopolistically competitive industries are ordinarily characterized by vigorous competition in areas other than price. Economic rivalry, as we have seen, may be based not only on price, but also on product quality, advertising, and conditions or services associated with the sale of a product. Great emphasis is placed upon trademarks and brand names as means for convincing the consumer that the products of one's rivals are not as good substitutes for brand X as they might first seem. Indeed, quality and advertising competition go hand in hand. Advertising proclaims and, if possible, magnifies real differences in product quality. While quality competition manipulates the firm's product, advertising and sales promotion attempt to manipulate the consumer.

A considerable number of industries approximate the conditions of monopolistic competition (see Table 28-1). At the manufacturing level the women's dress industry provides a good example; New York City and a few other large metropolitan areas are the locations of the many small manufacturers which constitute this industry. The shoe industry also has features which make it reasonably close to being monopolistically competitive. A good many types of retail trade, particularly in cities of any size, occur under conditions which approximate monopolistic competition. Most cities contain a fairly large number of grocery stores, cleaning establishments, clothing shops, gasoline stations, restaurants, hairdressers, and so forth, all of which are providing differentiated products and services.

□   Oligopoly

The remaining market model—oligopoly—is less precisely defined by economists than are the three market structures just discussed. Two reasons go far to explain this lack of preciseness. On the one hand, oligopoly includes a wider range of market structures than do the other three market models; in effect it embraces all the remaining market situations which do not fit the rather clearly defined market models of pure competition, monopolistic competition, and pure monopoly. On the other hand, as we shall discover in a moment, oligopoly has certain characteristics which make it difficult to come up with hard and fast predictions about the behavior of oligopolistic industries.

1 The basic characteristic of oligopoly is "fewness." Oligopoly exists whenever a few firms dominate the market for a product. When we hear of the "Big Three," "Big Four," or "Big Six," we can be relatively certain that the industry is oligopolistic. This does not mean, of course, that the Big Three or Four necessarily share the total market. The domi-

nant few may control, say, 70 or 80 percent of a market, with a competitive fringe—a group of smaller firms—sharing the remainder.

When a few firms dominate a market, each of these firms will have a share of the market sufficiently large so that its actions and policies will have repercussions on the other firms. Because each firm supplies a large portion of the total industry output, actions taken by any one firm to improve its share of the market will directly and immediately affect its rivals. Hence, each firm must carefully weigh the expected reactions of its rivals when considering changes in product price, advertising outlays, product quality, and so forth. Such clear-cut *mutual interdependence* is peculiar to oligopoly. It is not present in pure competition or monopolistic competition because of the large numbers of firms involved. The pure monopolist has no need to worry about the reactions of rivals, because he has none. Indeed, it can be said that oligopoly exists whenever the number of sellers is so few that the actions of one will have obvious and significant repercussions on the others. The firms of an oligopolistic industry are all in the same boat. If one rocks the boat, the others will be affected and in all probability will know the identity of the responsible firm and can retaliate.

2 Oligopolists may be producing virtually standardized products or differentiated products. Speaking very generally, those oligopolistic industries which are producing raw materials or semifinished goods are typically offering virtually uniform products to buyers. For example, most metal products—steel, copper, zinc, lead, and aluminum—along with cement, rayon, explosives, industrial alcohol, and some building materials, are virtually uniform goods produced in markets in which a few large firms are dominant. On the other hand, oligopolistic industries producing finished consumer goods are typically offering differentiated products to buyers. Automobiles, tires, petroleum products, soap, cigarettes, ballpoint pens, breakfast foods, aircraft, farm implements, plus a host of electrical appliances—refrigerators, radios, electric razors, and so forth—are produced by oligopolistic industries wherein product differentiation is considerable.[1]

3 An individual oligopolistic firm's control over price tends to be closely circumscribed by the mutual interdependence which characterizes such markets. Specifically, if a given firm lowers price, it will initially gain sales at the expense of its several rivals. However, these adversely affected rivals will have little choice but to retaliate to recover their shrinking shares of the market; they will match or even undercut the given firm to preserve their market share. The result may be a price war and possibly losses for all firms. Conversely, if a given oligopolist increases his price, rival firms stand to gain sales and profits by adhering to their present prices. That is, a price-boosting oligopolist runs the risk of "pricing himself out of the market" to the benefit of his rivals. For both these reasons, there is a strong tendency for firms in oligopolist markets not to alter their prices very frequently.

The potentially adverse effects of price warring or pricing oneself out of the market can be largely avoided by a group of oligopolistic firms through the establishment of some sort of collusive agreement by which all firms either increase or decrease their prices as a group. Under such an arrangement the firms as a group can exert control over price in much the same way as can a pure monopolist.

4 Obstacles to entry are typically formidable in oligopolistic industries. The ownership of strategic patents or essential raw materials by existing firms may virtually prohibit the entry of new firms. Furthermore, the technology of heavy industry may demand that a new competitor be a large-scale producer from the outset, thus ruling out the possibility of a new firm starting on a small-scale basis and

in time expanding into a significant rival of existing firms. In addition, certain advantages of being established—that is, the mere fact that existing firms are producing well-known, highly advertised products and selling them through long-established marketing outlets—may work against the successful entrance of new firms into the industry. Yet, in contrast to pure monopoly, entry is not usually blocked completely in oligopolistic industries. For example, the entry of Sylvania Electric into the electrical equipment industry after World War II presented a formidable rival for General Electric and Westinghouse. Entry into oligopolistic industries is very difficult, but by no means impossible.

5 Oligopolistic industries frequently channel considerable amounts of resources into advertising and other promotional activities. But the type and amount of advertising will depend upon whether the firms are producing standardized or differentiated products.

Advertising competition is likely to be strong among oligopolists who are producing differentiated products. For example, each major automobile producer or cigarette manufacturer will have a large budget for convincing the consumer that his particular product is significantly superior to those of his rivals. Such advertising is likely to be of a highly competitive ours-is-better-than-theirs nature. On the other hand, public relations advertising is the bill of fare for oligopolists who are producing virtually standardized products. United States Steel does not try to convince the public that its sheet steel is superior to that produced by Republic, Bethlehem, or any of its other rivals. Skilled buyers who purchase the raw or fabricated steel products from these firms know that any differences are negligible. Hence, advertising in such industries is to keep the company in the public's eye, to convince the public that big business is an essential cog in the American economy, and so forth. It must be added that the producers of both standardized and differentiated products may engage in "social responsibility" advertising,

[1] Illustrations are from Joe S. Bain, *Pricing, Distribution, and Employment,* rev. ed. (New York: Holt, Rinehart and Winston, Inc., 1953), pp. 273–274, 333.

for example, advertising which proclaims that the corporation is doing good deeds with respect to pollution, the hiring of minorities, and so forth.

Quality competition may be intense under oligopoly, particularly when product differentiation prevails. The research and design departments of many oligopolistic industries have become increasingly important over the years. Indeed, it is through research and rapid product development that the entry of potential rivals into the industry may be thwarted.

A good many American industries fall under the heading of oligopoly. As a matter of fact, most of those industries which come to mind when we think of "big business" are some form or another of oligopoly. In addition to the specific examples previously mentioned, Table 29-1 contains a list of industries which are oligopolistic.

□ **Imperfect Competition**

We shall find it convenient from time to time to distinguish between the characteristics of a purely competitive market and those of all other basic market arrangements—pure monopoly, monopolistic competition, and oligopoly. To facilitate such comparisons we shall employ "imperfect competition" as a generic term to designate all those market structures which deviate from the purely competitive market model.

THE BUYER'S SIDE OF THE MARKET

The preceding definitions of the four basic market models are couched in terms of the seller's side of the market. The same variety of market arrangements can and does exist on the buying or demand side. Here, however, the classification is almost exclusively based on the number of buyers. For example, a very large number of purchasers obviously means pure competition on the buying side of the market. *Monopsony* describes the situation in which there is only one buyer. When a few buyers dominate a market, *oligopsony* exists. *Monopsonistic competition* designates the presence of a fairly large number of buyers.

With the selling and buying sides of the market placed together as in Figure 22-1, it is easy to recognize that an almost infinite number of seller-buyer relationships can exist. A few representative examples will help underscore this point. The public utilities field is usually characterized by pure monopoly on the selling side and pure competition on the buying side. The market for raw tobacco links a great many purely competitive tobacco farmers on the selling side with a few large buyers—American, Liggett and Myers, Lorillard, and Reynolds—dominating the demand side. Where a strong union exists, specific labor markets often approximate *bilateral monopoly*—pure monopoly on one side and pure monopsony on the other. The local union is the

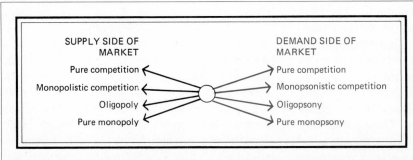

SUPPLY SIDE OF MARKET
- Pure competition
- Monopolistic competition
- Oligopoly
- Pure monopoly

DEMAND SIDE OF MARKET
- Pure competition
- Monopsonistic competition
- Oligopsony
- Pure monopsony

FIGURE 22-1 SOME BASIC MARKET RELATIONSHIPS

The four basic market models are pertinent to both the selling and buying sides of markets; this suggests the existence of a very large number of selling-buying relationships.

"seller" of labor services, and the company is the single buyer. In the "original equipment" segment of the automobile tire market, we have oligopsonistic buyers—General Motors, Ford, and Chrysler—linked with oligopolistic sellers—Goodyear, Firestone, U.S. Rubber, and B. F. Goodrich. A similar arrangement exists in the market for tin plate—a few large steel companies are the sole producers, and two large tin-can manufacturers are the major buyers. And so it goes. When all the hybrid cases falling between the four basic market models are taken into account, it is clear that the number of possible market arrangements can be and actually is extremely large.

OTHER COMPETITIVE DIMENSIONS

It is important that we qualify and amend the foregoing definitions and explanations of the various market models in several ways.

□　Geographic Factor

In practice the competitiveness of an industry or a firm is a geographic phenomenon. That is, the degree of competition in a particular industry depends upon the size of the market. Although a given city may have seventy or eighty grocery stores, a particular supermarket in a suburban area may, for all practical purposes, be competing only with three other chain stores and one or two independent corner groceries. Similarly, commercial banking appears to be highly competitive at first glance—after all, there are some 14,600 banks in our economy providing essentially identical services. But to the farmer in What Cheer, Iowa, borrowing from the Chase Manhattan Bank in New York or the Bank of America in California is out of the question. In negotiating a loan, Farmer Jones will look to the What Cheer State Bank or possibly one or two of the larger banks in a nearby city. These comments correctly imply that improved transportation and communication tend to strengthen com-

petition; more efficient, lower-cost transportation and communication bring geographically remote producers into competition with one another.

In short, before hastily labeling an industry as "competitive" or "monopolistic," we must be very sure that we have properly delineated the geographic boundaries of the market. The number of firms alone is not a sufficient criterion by which to gauge the competitiveness of an industry; proximity is important, too.

□　Interindustry Competition

It is important to recognize the significance of interindustry or interproduct competition. Although a few firms may be the only ones producing a specific product, they may face rather severe rivalry from other somewhat distinct products. Illustrations of such interproduct competition are numerous. The aluminum industry is a strong oligopoly with three firms—Alcoa, Reynolds, and Kaiser—dominating the market. Buyers who must use aluminum have no choice but to do business with one of these industrial giants. However, in many cases other materials—steel, copper, and even wood or plastics—are suitable substitutes for aluminum. Hence, steel competes with aluminum in the manufacturing of many automobile parts. Aluminum and copper contest the market for transmission lines. Aluminum battles both steel and wood in the construction field. These comments add up to the fact that the control over price which the Big Three of the aluminum industry possess is subject to limitations dictated by the prices of distinct but nevertheless competing products. Another example: The Big Two of the tin-can industry—American Can and Continental Can—dominate over 80 percent of their market. From within the industry they face little serious competition. But from without, they face the competition of glass, plastic, and paper containers.

□ Nonprice Competition

This is a convenient juncture at which to restate a point emphasized earlier: Competition is something more than the willingness and ability to cut prices. Competition in other areas than price may be vigorous and important in an industry. Variations in product quality, advertising and promotional activities, and so forth are important elements of competition which may supplement or, in some cases, supplant price competition.

□ Technological Advance

The previous explanations of the four basic market models tend to classify the various markets at some particular *point* in time. Hence, they neglect an important competitive force which functions only over a *period* of time. That competitive force is technological advance. The development of new products and new techniques of production can result in new competition for producers who previously enjoyed a considerable degree of monopoly power. Thus the leading proponent of the role of technological advance as a competitive force has argued that[2]

> In capitalist reality . . . it is . . . competition from the new commodity, the new technology, the new source of supply, the new type of organization (the largest-scale unit of control for instance)—competition which commands a decisive cost or quality advantage and which strikes not at the margins of the profits and the outputs of the existing firms but at their foundations and their very lives. This kind of competition is . . . so . . . important that it becomes a matter of comparative indifference whether competition in the ordinary sense functions more or less promptly; the powerful lever that in the long run expands output and brings down prices is in any case made of other stuff.

. . . that competition of the kind we now have in mind acts not only when in being but also when it is merely an ever-present threat. It disciplines before it attacks. The businessman feels himself to be in a competitive situation even if he is alone in his field. . . . In many cases, though not in all, this will in the long run enforce behavior very similar to the perfectly competitive pattern.

Some examples may help to underscore this point. For over a decade a single firm enjoyed the position of a pure monopolist in the production of rayon. Its profits, enormous by any standard, were the result of the successful competition this innovation provided for other textiles. But more recently the development of acetates, nylon, acrylic, and other "miracle fibers" has in turn provided considerable competition for rayon.[3] In a similar manner, the rapid development of the dehydrated and quick-frozen food industries during World War II has permitted an intensification of the competition which paper, fiber, and plastic containers provide for the Big Two of the tin-can industry. Consider, finally, the widespread repercussions of the transistor. Its development spawned new firms—Texas Instruments, Fairchild, and Intel, among others—which have made serious inroads on the electronics components businesses once dominated by such giants as General Electric, Sylvania, and Westinghouse. Similarly, innovative Japanese firms used the transistor to undermine the leadership of such American firms as GE and RCA in the radio market. And in the past few years the semiconductor technology which created the transistor has been applied to watchmaking, and, as a result, Switzerland's watchmaking industry has faced severe competition from the digital watches of American electronics firms.

[2]Joseph A. Schumpeter, *Capitalism, Socialism, and Democracy,* 3d ed. (New York: Harper & Row, Publishers, Incorporated, 1950), pp. 84–85.

[3]A. D. H. Kaplan, *Big Enterprise in a Competitive System,* rev. ed. (Washington: The Brookings Institution, 1964), p. 185.

DETERMINANTS OF MARKET STRUCTURE

Agriculture is an almost purely competitive industry. The clothing industry fits roughly into the mold of monopolistic competition. The steel and automobile industries are obviously oligopolistic. American Telephone and Telegraph nationally, and public utilities locally, approximate pure monopolies. What forces explain the emergence of these different market structures? What factors have caused agriculture to remain highly competitive and the automobile industry, spiced in its infancy with seventy-odd producers, now to be a tight oligopoly dominated by the Big Three? Although there exists no short, easy answer to these questions, we can put our fingers on some of the more important forces which historically have played significant roles in determining the competitive structures of the various American industries. Generally speaking, such factors as (1) legislation and government policy, (2) the policies and practices of business firms, (3) technological considerations, and (4) institutions and characteristics inherent in the capitalistic ideology, go far to explain the variety of market structures which characterizes American capitalism.

□   Legislation and Government Policy

Government has promoted both monopoly and competition. By issuing *exclusive franchises* to so-called natural monopolies (for example, public utilities), government has purposely created many pure monopolies in industries which might otherwise have attained some degree of competition. Federal government commissions—the Interstate Commerce Commission, Civil Aeronautics Board, and Federal Communications Commission—play the major role in determining the degree of competition in the land and air transportation, radio, and television industries. Similarly, *patent laws* often have pro-

moted monopoly by giving innovating firms the exclusive right to manufacture a product for extended periods of time. *Tariffs* and other artificial barriers to international trade have promoted and preserved monopoly power in many domestic industries. On the other hand, there is but little doubt that the liberal Homestead Act of 1862 provided a competitive base for American agriculture. *Antitrust legislation*—the Sherman and Clayton Acts—is explicitly designed to curb the abuses of monopoly power.

We find here seemingly inconsistent government policies; but this inconsistency can be at least partially explained. Although government has pursued a generally antimonopolistic social policy, it simultaneously seeks other social objectives. One of these goals is the promotion of technological advance—an aim which patent legislation tends to foster. And in the case of public utilities, competition has simply not functioned effectively; here government has condoned and promoted monopoly, but has then provided regulatory commissions designed to prevent the abuse of this government-sponsored monopoly power.

□   Business Policies and Practices

The practices and policies pursued by various firms and industries can also be critical in determining the structure of industry. In some industries, mergers, consolidations, and the development of holding companies have pushed in the direction of oligopoly or monopoly. The evolution of the corporate form of business enterprise and collusive practices between legally independent firms have played a similar role. In other industries, cutthroat competition has resulted in some firms driving others from existence, thereby lowering the number of competitors in the industry. In still other instances, firms have acquired ownership or control over vital raw materials so as to eliminate present rivals and destroy the possibility of new firms coming into being. These practices and developments, however, have occurred unevenly among various industries, causing some to move in the direction of monopoly and others to remain quite highly competitive.

□   **Technology**

Technology has undoubtedly been an important determinant of industrial structure. In a good many industries, technology has developed to the point where the existence of large industrial giants is necessary if efficient low-cost production is to be achieved. Technology has given rise to economies of mass production which only large producers can realize. This means that, given consumer demand, efficient production necessitates the existence of a few large producers rather than many small producers. It is thus that technological advance has "forced" the market structure of many "heavy" industries—for example, the automobile, steel, and aluminum industries—in the direction of oligopoly. Economists differ in evaluating the extent to which technological factors require bigness; we shall examine the conflicting views in greater detail in Chapter 34.

In some industries, technological advance has worked toward the same end but in a somewhat different manner. Superior research on product development has permitted some firms to outgrow and often eliminate less progressive rivals. Furthermore, this tendency is frequently cumulative; by gaining a larger share of the market through its superior research, a firm realizes the financial rewards that facilitate a widening of the technological advantages which it possesses over its rivals.

□   **Capitalistic Institutions**

We must be reminded that the institutions of American capitalism are permissive of the concentration of economic power and the development of oligopoly and monopoly. The relatively free, individualistic economic environment of the economy is a fertile ground for the most efficient, the most courageous, the most fortunate, or the most crafty producer to conquer his rivals in an effort to free himself from the regulatory powers of competition. Freedom of contract, private property, and inheritance rights have also contributed to the concentration of economic power. And, too, the business cycle has probably abetted the tendency toward monopoly. As one scholar puts it:[4]

> Weaklings may still fail, and disappear, especially in more difficult times. Good times make it easy to finance consolidations, and tempting for the strong company to expand and the weak to sell out. Thus, both adversity and prosperity work alike to reduce the number of firms in an industry.

[4]John K. Galbraith, *American Capitalism,* rev. ed. (Boston: Houghton Mifflin Company, 1956), p. 35.

Summary

1   American industry is characterized by differing degrees of competition. The market models of *a.* pure competition, *b.* pure monopoly, *c.* monopolistic competition, and *d.* oligopoly are classifications into which most industries can be fitted with reasonable accuracy. These market models, however, are merely first approximations of reality.

2   Table 22-1 provides a convenient summary of the major characteristics of these four market models.

3   Similar market classifications, based essentially upon numbers, are applied to the buying, or demand, side of the market.

Table 22-1   CHARACTERISTICS OF THE FOUR BASIC MARKET MODELS

Characteristic	Market model			
	Pure competition	Monopolistic competition	Oligopoly	Pure monopoly
Number of firms	A very large number	Many	Few	One
Type of product	Standardized	Differentiated	Standardized or differentiated	Unique; no close substitutes
Control over price	None	Some, but within rather narrow limits	Circumscribed by mutual interdependence; considerable with collusion	Considerable
Conditions of entry	Very easy, no obstacles	Relatively easy	Significant obstacles present	Blocked
Nonprice competition	None	Considerable emphasis on advertising, brand names, trademarks, etc.	Typically a great deal, particularly with product differentiation	Mostly public relations advertising
Example	Agriculture	Retail trade, dresses, shoes	Steel, automobiles, farm implements, many household appliances	AT&T, local utilities

4   The economist's definitions of the four market models focus attention upon *a.* the number of firms, *b.* the degree of product differentiation, and *c.* the ease or difficulty encountered by new firms in entering the industry. However, certain other important factors which have a bearing upon the competitive nature of an industry must also be considered: *a.* In practice, any meaningful description of the market structure of an industry requires a proper definition of the geographic limits of the market. *b.* Interindustry or interproduct competition is a significant force in many markets which might otherwise appear to be lacking in competition. *c.* Nonprice competition may be an important supplement to price competition. *d.* Technological advance, working as a competitive force through time, often undermines existing industries characterized by strong monopolistic elements.

5   Legislation, government policies, research and technological development, industry practices, and a variety of other factors have all played significant roles in determining the present structure of American industry.

Questions and Study Suggestions

1   Key terms and concepts to remember: pure competition; pure monopoly; monopolistic competition; oligopoly; imperfect competition; standardized product; product differentiation; nonprice competition; monopsony; monopsonistic competition; oligopsony; bilateral monopoly; interindustry competition.

2   Elaborate and illustrate: "The structure of the American economy displays a highly diverse terrain from almost complete monopoly to nearly perfect competition."

3   Under which of the four market classifications discussed in the chapter does each of the following most accurately fit: *a.* a supermarket located in your home town; *b.* the steel industry; *c.* a Kansas wheat farm; *d.* the commercial bank in which you or your family has an account; *e.* the automobile industry. In each case justify your classification. In making your classifications, specify assumptions you have made about the geographic limits of the various markets.

4   "Purely competitive producers have no price policy, but monopolistically competitive, oligopolistic, and purely monopolistic firms do." Explain. Why doesn't a purely competitive producer advertise his product?

5   The president of E. I. du Pont de Nemours & Company once made the following statements:

> The difference between three and one [firms] is very substantial. It is the difference between monopoly and no monopoly. Oligopoly . . . to me is meaningless, because there is either competition or there is not. If there is competition, the public interest is being served.

What differences, if any, can you detect between this definition of "competition" and the economist's definition of "pure competition"? Do you feel that all industries can be meaningfully categorized as competitive or not competitive? Explain your answers.

6   A single farmer is "at the mercy of the market" in that he must regard the market price for his products as being fixed. Yet, agricultural prices are very flexible. Reconcile these two statements.

7   What is interindustry competition? How important is it in each of the following industries? In each case specify the competing products or industries: *a.* automobile; *b.* railway; *c.* cement; *d.* steel; *e.* coal; and *f.* glass container.

8   What is nonprice competition? How prevalent do you think nonprice competition to be in the industries mentioned in questions 3 and 7?

9   "Competition should be judged solely on the basis of the number of firms in the industry; the larger the number, the greater the competition." Critically evaluate.

10   What are some of the major forces which determine the market structure of industries? Drawing on your knowledge of American history, evaluate the relative significance of these forces in explaining the market structures of the following industries: *a.* automobile; *b.* television; *c.* tobacco; *d.* steel; *e.* petroleum; and *f.* agriculture. Be as specific as you can in your answers.

11   "Technological advance has both encouraged and limited the development of monopoly." Do you agree? Explain.

Selected References

Averitt, Robert T.: *The Dual Economy: The Dynamics of American Industry Structure* (New York: W. W. Norton & Company, Inc., 1968).

Baird, Charles W.: *Prices and Markets: Microeconomics* (St. Paul: West Publishing Company, 1975), chap. 6.

Galbraith, John Kenneth: *Economics and the Public Purpose* (Boston: Houghton Mifflin Company, 1973).

Stern, Louis W., and John R. Grabner, Jr.: *Competition in the Marketplace* (Glenview, Ill.: Scott, Foresman and Company, 1970), chaps, 1–3.

Weiss, Leonard W.: *Economics and American Industry* (New York: John Wiley & Sons, Inc., 1961), chap. 1.

Last Word
Galbraithian Economics

In a series of influential books—including *The New Industrial State* (1967) and *Economics and the Public Purpose* (1973)—John Kenneth Galbraith has challenged the orthodox conception of American industry. Galbraith envisions a business sector divided into the dominant "planning system" of the large corporation and the "market system" of small, more competitive firms. The following summary of Galbraith's position is authored by Melville J. Ulmer of the University of Maryland.

In place of the traditional, "impersonal" competitive forces of the market, the prime mover in Galbraith's portrait of modern capitalism is the managerial elite of the great corporations. Less than 400 industrial corporations currently own three-fourths of *all* assets employed in manufacturing in the United States. Concentration nearly as high prevails in most branches of finance, transportation, electric power, merchandising and mining. Guiding the nation's top 1000 firms or so is what Galbraith calls the "technostructure," consisting of the "complex of scientists, engineers and technicians; of sales, advertising and marketing men; of public relations experts, lobbyists, lawyers and men with a specialized knowledge of the Washington bureaucracy and its manipulations; and of coordinators, managers and executives." It is their interests and objectives that comprise the most powerful single force shaping the country's economic decisions—its allocation of resources, the composition of its output, its technology, consumption habits, the form and manner of its governmental policies and, in some significant degree, its culture.

In orthodox economic literature, which includes virtually all university textbooks, reference is customarily made to the term "entrepreneur," the classic owner-manager of the business firm. The entrepreneur is buffeted by the forces of supply and demand over which he has no influence. Steadfastly, he strives to minimize costs and maximize profits. Even when textbooks recognize the existence of big corporate business, in the form of oligopoly or monopoly, the classic image of the lonely entrepreneur is revised only slightly. In its place is set the corporation's top management (or often just its president), which also strives to maximize profits within the constraints of the costs that it faces and the capricious demands of consumers, neither of which can it control. The great corporation, too, is subject to the discipline of competition, the trials and tests of the market. So goes the popular legend. . . .

Galbraith presents an opposite view that discloses an aspect of business behavior that classical models overlook: the technostructure preoccupied with its own welfare. Stockholders by and large have no effective control over the firms they "own" and ordinarily no knowledge at all concerning their operations. In this era of complicated techniques even boards of directors are commonly at sea when specific, substantive business problems are raised. . . . The technostructure—the firm's bureaucracy of engineering, scientific, marketing, managerial and financial experts—represents the corporate brains, and its interest is primarily in growth and security: growth so that the corporate bureaucracy can prosper with a constantly expanding scope of activity, rising salaries, prompt promotions and always ascending prestige, responsibilities and personnel; security because growth is faster and more predictable when the strategic determining variables are safely under the corporation's bureaucratic control.

So through advertising and other forms of promotion the technostructure takes care of demand. Consumers are riveted so firmly to the need for deodorants, flashy cars, crackly breakfast cereals, electric dishwashers, color TV's and other symbols of affluence or conspicuous waste that some poorer families would rather go without food and medicine than resist the blandishments of Madison Avenue—and as the Census Bureau reports they sometimes do. As Galbraith sees it the giant corporations do not passively produce what consumers want (in accord with orthodox theory), but instead get consumers to want what they produce.

Further the corporations, for security and growth, must control costs, which they do by buying out or dominating smaller suppliers and by cultivating industry-wide and reasonably predictable contracts with labor unions. They must control prices, partly by shaping demand through massive advertising and partly by developing a peaceful modus vivendi to their mutual advantage with firms in the same or related industries. They must control government policies through close "symbiosis" with the Senate or House committees or the bureaucracies of the government departments or regulating agencies, that might affect them. They must control foreign trade, which they do by direct investments abroad, in the familiar multinational pattern and by surreptitious cooperation in cartels. In short the business of the giant corporations is not left to the whimsical trends of the market, of capricious consumer tastes or of political ideologies; all is painstakingly and effectively planned. Profits are required as a means to an end. A predictable and satisfactory flow of net income is essential for the technostructure so that growth can flourish and stockholders can be placated for the use of their money with adequate dividends and/or capital gains.

So successful is this "planning system" and so gluttonous are its appetites for the nation's resources that according to Galbraith, it effectively starves the rest of the economy of output and income and cuts the nation's households off from some of their vital satisfactions. Within the planning system incomes are high, production efficient and abundant. Outside the realm of big business is what Galbraith calls the "market system"—some 12 million small firms, farms, and many millions of service workers from repairmen to housecleaners. Here without the benefits of mass production techniques and often exploited in one way or another by the bargaining power of big business, efficiency and incomes stagnate; as in medical care, mass transportation, the arts and housing, output is also typically inadequate. In recognition of this disparity, he says, are the numerous and usually ineffective measures of government to redress the imbalance in aids to agriculture, cheap credit and technical assistance for small business, housing subsidies, price maintenance protection for retailers, medicare, medicaid and so on. And of course outside the planning system, too, is government, deliberately downgraded and systematically used and abused by big business. Neither the environment nor the population's health can be preserved while such domination of government by business is allowed to prevail. Such observations lead the author to say that "in its mature form the (giant) corporation can be thought of as an instrument principally for perpetuating inequality."

In summary Galbraith faults the American economy for gross inequities, costly irrationalities, ridiculous extravagance in some sectors coupled with dangerous deprivation in others, all attributable to the arrogant, undemocratic, public-be-damned dominance of big business. His prescription for correction is many-sided and deals with a variety of specific issues such as environmental protection, inflation and poor relief. But his central and most significant proposal follows directly from his belief that the competitive market system of the United States has so grievously deteriorated that it is now beyond repair. He concludes that in a substantial part of the economy, the private, profit-seeking market must be replaced by a comprehensive system of governmental economic planning; that planning would entail public ownership and operation of the means of production—a "new socialism," Galbraith calls it, born of necessity rather than ideology.

Melville Ulmer, "The Managerial Elite," *The New Republic,* Oct. 13, 1973, pp. 24–26, abridged. Reprinted by permission.

23

Demand, Supply, and Elasticity: Some Applications

In Chapter 4 we familiarized ourselves with the rudiments of demand and supply analysis. In the present chapter we seek a more sophisticated understanding of demand and supply. Specifically, the tasks of this chapter are threefold. First, a brief summary of the elements of demand and supply analysis is presented. Second, we shall consider the concept of elasticity as applied to both demand and supply. Third, some specific applications of demand and supply analysis are discussed.

■ DEMAND, SUPPLY, AND MARKET PRICE[1]

Demand and supply both refer to schedules. The demand schedule shows the relationship between various possible prices of a product and the quantities which consumers will purchase at each of these prices (Table 23-1, columns 1 and 2). The price–quantity-demand relationship thus portrayed is an inverse one. Consumers typically buy less at a high price than at a low price. This commonsense relationship is called the *law of demand*. Graphically the demand curve is downsloping (*DD* in Figure 23-1).

The supply schedule embodies the relationship between possible product prices and the quantities which producers will supply at each of those prices (Table 23-1, columns 2 and

[1]This review is not a substitute for Chapter 4. The student is strongly urged to reread Chapter 4 at this point.

Table 23-1 THE DEMAND FOR, AND SUPPLY OF, CORN (*hypothetical data*)

(1) Total quantity demanded per week	(2) Price per bushel	(3) Total quantity supplied per week	(4) Surplus (+) or shortage (−) (arrow indicates effect on price)
2,000	$5	12,000	+10,000↓
4,000	4	10,000	+ 6,000↓
7,000	3	7,000	0
11,000	2	4,000	− 7,000↑
16,000	1	1,000	−15,000↑

3). The relationship between price and quantity supplied is a direct one. The *law of supply* states that producers will find it profitable to devote more resources to the production of a good when its price is high than they will when it is low. When graphed, this direct relationship results in an upsloping supply curve (*SS* in Figure 23-1).

The intersection of demand and supply determines the market, or equilibrium, price and quantity. Both Table 23-1 and Figure 23-1 clearly show that the demand and supply data

here assumed result in an equilibrium price of $3 and an equilibrium quantity of 7000 units. Competition guarantees that any other price will be unstable. The shortages which accompany *below*-equilibrium prices will prompt competing buyers to bid up the price, as consumers want to avoid doing without the product. A rising price will (1) induce firms to allocate more resources to the production of this good, and (2) ration some consumers out of the market. These adjustments are illustrated in Figure 23-1 by the arrows moving up the supply curve and up the demand curve respectively. The surpluses which result at any *above*-equilibrium price will induce competing sellers to shade their prices to work off these excess stocks. The falling price will (1) prompt firms to allocate fewer resources to this line of production, and (2) ration some additional buyers into the market. These adjustments are shown by the arrows moving down the supply and demand curves respectively in Figure 23-1.

Changes in the determinants of either demand or supply can cause the demand and

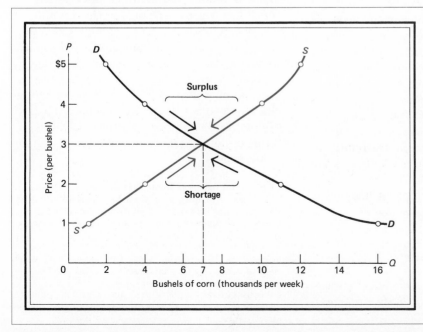

FIGURE 23-1 THE EQUILIBRIUM PRICE FOR CORN AS DETERMINED BY MARKET DEMAND AND MARKET SUPPLY

Equilibrium price and equilibrium quantity are determined by the intersection of demand *DD* and supply *SS*.

supply schedules (curves) to shift. Variations in consumer tastes, incomes, the prices of related goods, consumer expectations, and the number of buyers in the market all will account for shifts in demand. Changes in any of those factors which affect production costs—for example, technology or resource prices—will cause supply to shift. The relationship between a change in demand and the resulting changes in equilibrium price and quantity is a direct one. An inverse relationship exists between a change in supply and the ensuing change in price. However, the relationship between a change in supply and the ensuing change in quantity is direct.

ELASTICITY OF DEMAND

The law of demand tells us that consumers will respond to a price decline by buying more of a product. But the degree of responsiveness of consumers to a price change may vary considerably from product to product. Furthermore, we will find that consumer responsiveness typically varies substantially between different price ranges for the same product.

Economists measure how responsive, or sensitive, consumers are to a change in the price of a product by the concept of *elasticity*. The demand for some products is such that consumers are relatively responsive to price changes; price changes give rise to very considerable changes in the quantity purchased. The demand for such products is said to be *elastic*. For other products, consumers are relatively unresponsive to price changes; that is, price changes result in modest changes in the amount purchased. In such cases demand is *inelastic*.

□   **The Elasticity Formula**

Economists measure the degree of elasticity or inelasticity by the *elasticity coefficient,* or E_d, in this formula:

$$E_d = \frac{\text{percentage change in quantity demanded}}{\text{percentage change in price}}$$

One calculates these *percentage* changes, of course, by dividing the change in price by the original price and the consequent change in quantity demanded by the original quantity demanded. Thus, we can restate our formula as

$$E_d = \frac{\text{change in quantity demanded}}{\text{original quantity demanded}} \div \frac{\text{change in price}}{\text{original price}}$$

Use of Percentages   But why use percentages rather than absolute amounts in measuring consumer responsiveness? The answer is that if we use absolute changes, our impression of buyer responsiveness will be arbitrarily affected by the choice of units. To illustrate: If the price of product X falls from $3 to $2 and consumers, as a result, increase their purchases from 60 to 100 pounds, we get the impression that consumers are quite sensitive to price changes and therefore that demand is elastic. After all, a price change of "one" has caused a change in the amount demanded of "forty." But by changing the monetary unit from dollars to pennies (why not?), we find a price change of "one hundred" causes a quantity change of "forty," giving the impression of inelasticity. The use of percentage changes avoids this problem. The given price decline is 33 percent whether measured in terms of dollars ($1/$3) or in terms of pennies (100¢/300¢).[2]

[2]The careful reader will note that the elasticity coefficient of demand will always be negative. This is so for the obvious reason that the demand curve is downsloping; that is, price and quantity are inversely related. Economists are generally inclined to ignore the minus sign (as we do here) in order to avoid an ambiguity which might otherwise arise. It can be confusing to say that an elasticity coefficient of −4 is greater than one of −2; this possible confusion can be avoided if we simply say a coefficient of 4 indicates greater elasticity than one of 2. This difficulty does not arise with supply because price and quantity are directly related.

Interpretations   Now let us interpret our formula. Demand is *elastic* if a given percentage change in price results in a larger percentage change in quantity demanded. Example: If a 2 percent decline in price results in a 4 percent increase in quantity demanded, demand is elastic. In all such cases, where demand is elastic, the elasticity coefficient will obviously be greater than 1. If a given percentage change in price is accompanied by a relatively smaller change in the quantity demanded, demand is *inelastic*. Illustration: If a 3 percent decline in price gives rise to a 1 percent increase in the amount demanded, demand is inelastic. It is apparent that the elasticity coefficient will always be less than 1 when demand is inelastic. The borderline case which separates elastic and inelastic demands occurs where a percentage change in price and the accompanying percentage change in quantity demanded chance to be equal. For example, a 1 percent drop in price causes a 1 percent increase in the amount sold. This special case is termed *unit elasticity,* because the elasticity coefficient is exactly 1, or unity.

It must be emphasized that when economists say demand is "inelastic," they do not mean consumers are completely unresponsive to a price change. The term *perfectly inelastic* demand designates the extreme situation wherein a change in price results in no change whatsoever in the quantity demanded. Approximate example: an acute diabetic's demand for insulin. A demand curve parallel to the vertical axis—such as D_1 in Figure 23-2— shows this situation graphically. Conversely, when economists say demand is "elastic," they do not mean that consumers are completely responsive to a price change. In the extreme situation, wherein there is some small price reduction which would cause buyers to increase their purchases from zero to all they could obtain, we say that demand is *perfectly elastic*. A perfectly elastic demand curve is a line parallel to the horizontal axis; D_2 in Figure 23-2 is illustrative. We shall find later in

FIGURE 23-2 PERFECTLY INELASTIC AND ELASTIC DEMAND

A perfectly inelastic demand curve, D_1, graphs as a line parallel to the vertical axis; a perfectly elastic demand curve, D_2, is drawn parallel to the horizontal axis.

this chapter that such a demand curve applies to a firm which is selling in a perfectly competitive market.

□ **Refinement: Midpoints Formula**

An annoying problem arises in applying the elasticity formula. To illustrate: In calculating the elasticity coefficient for corn for the $5–$4 price range in Table 23-2, should we use the $5–2000-bushel price-quantity combination or the $4–4000-bushel combination as a point of reference in calculating the percentage changes in price and quantity which the elasticity formula requires? Our choice will influence the outcome. Using the $5–2000-bushel reference point, we find that the percentage decrease in price is 20 percent and the percentage increase in quantity is 100 percent. Substituting in the formula, the elasticity coefficient is 100/20, or 5. But, using the $4–4000-bushel reference point, we find that the percentage increase in price is 25 percent and the percentage decline in quantity is 50 percent. The elasticity coefficient is therefore 50/25, or

2, in this case. Although the formula indicates that demand is elastic in both cases, the two solutions involve a considerable difference in the degree of elasticity. In other instances— experiment, for example, with the $3–$2 price range—the formula may indicate a slightly elastic demand for one price-quantity combination and slight inelasticity of demand for the other.

Economists have reached a workable compromise to this problem by using the averages of the two prices and the two quantities under consideration for reference points. In the $5–$4 price-range case, the price reference is $4.50 and the quantity reference 3000 bushels. The percentage change in price is now about 22 percent and the percentage change in quantity about 67 percent, giving us an elasticity coefficient of 3. Instead of gauging elasticity at either one of the extremes of this price-quantity range, this solution estimates elasticity at the midpoint of the $5–$4 price range. More positively stated, we can refine our earlier statement of the elasticity formula to read

$$E_d = \frac{\text{change in quantity}}{\text{sum of quantities}/2} \div \frac{\text{change in price}}{\text{sum of prices}/2}$$

Substituting data for the $5–$4 price range, we get

$$E_d = \frac{2000}{6000/2} \div \frac{1}{9/2} = 3.00$$

In column 5 of Table 23-2 we have calculated the elasticity coefficients for the demand data of Table 23-1, using the midpoints formula. The reader should verify each of these calculations.

□ **The Total-Revenue Test**

Perhaps the easiest way to gauge whether demand is elastic or inelastic is to note what happens to total revenue or receipts—total expenditures from the buyer's viewpoint— when product price changes.

1 If demand is *elastic,* a decline in price will result in an increase in total revenue. Why? Because even though a lesser price is being received per unit, enough additional units are now being sold to more than make up for the lower price. This is illustrated in Figure 23-3 for the $5–$4 price range of our demand curve from Table 23-1. Total revenue, of course, is price times quantity. Hence, the area shown by the rectangle OP_1AQ_1 is total revenue ($10,000) when price is P_1 ($5) and quantity demanded is Q_1 (2000 bushels). Now when price declines to P_2 ($4), causing the quantity demanded to increase to Q_2 (4000 bushels), total revenue changes to OP_2BQ_2 ($16,000), which is obviously larger than OP_1AQ_1. It is larger because the *loss* in revenue due to the lower price per unit (area P_2P_1AC) is *less* than the *gain* in revenue due to the larger sales (area Q_1CBQ_2) which accompanies the lower price. This reasoning is reversible: If demand is elastic, a price increase will reduce total revenue. Why? Because the *gain* in total revenue caused by the higher unit price (area P_2P_1AC) is less than the *loss* in revenue associated with the accompanying fall in sales (Q_1CBQ_2).

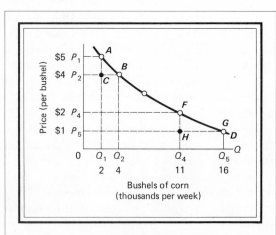

FIGURE 23-3 ELASTICITY AND TOTAL REVENUE

If demand is elastic, as in the $5–$4 price range, a change in price will cause total revenue to change in the opposite direction. Conversely, if demand is inelastic, as in the $2–$1 price range, price and total revenue will move in the same direction.

Generalization: *If demand is elastic, a change in price will cause total revenue to change in the opposite direction.*

2 If demand is *inelastic,* a price decline will cause total revenue to fall. The modest increase in sales which occurs will be insufficient to offset the decline in revenue per unit, and the net result is that total revenue declines. This situation exists for the $2–$1 price range of our demand curve, as shown in Figure 23-3. Initially, total revenue is OP_4FQ_4 ($22,000) when price is P_4 ($2) and quantity demanded is Q_4 (11,000 bushels). If we reduce price to P_5 ($1), quantity demanded will increase to Q_5 (16,000 bushels). Total revenue will change to OP_5GQ_5 ($16,000), which is obviously less than OP_4FQ_4. It is smaller because the loss in revenue due to the lower unit price (area P_5P_4FH) is larger than the *gain* in revenue due to the accompanying increase in sales (area Q_4HGQ_5). Again our analysis is reversible: If demand is inelastic, a price increase will increase total revenue. Generalization: *If demand is inelastic, a change in price will cause total revenue to change in the same direction.*

3 In the special case of *unit elasticity*, an increase or decrease in price will leave total revenue unchanged. The loss in revenue due to a lower unit price will be exactly offset by the gain in revenue brought about by the accompanying increase in sales. Conversely, the gain in revenue due to a higher unit price will be exactly offset by the loss in revenue associated with the accompanying decline in the amount demanded.

Columns 3 and 4 of Table 23-2 apply the total-revenue test to the entire demand curve for corn.

□ **Characteristics**

The alert reader may have detected two subtle but notable characteristics of elasticity from our applications of the elasticity formula and the total-revenue tests.

Elasticity and Price Range First, elasticity typically varies over the different price ranges of the same demand schedule or curve. For most demand curves—including our illustrative demand for corn in Table 23-2—demand tends to be more elastic in the upper-left portion than in the lower-right portion. This is essentially a consequence of the arithmetic properties of the elasticity measure. Specifically, in the upper-left portion the percentage change in quantity tends to be large because the original quantity from which the percentage quantity change is derived is small.

Table 23-2 ELASTICITY OF DEMAND AS MEASURED BY THE TOTAL-RECEIPTS TEST AND THE ELASTICITY COEFFICIENT (*hypothetical data*)

(1) Total quantity demanded per week	(2) Price per bushel	(3) Total revenue (expenditures)	(4) Total-revenue test	(5) Elasticity coefficient E_d (approximate)
2,000	$5	$10,000		
			Elastic	$\dfrac{2,000}{6,000/2} \div \dfrac{1}{9/2} = 3.00$
4,000	4	16,000		
			Elastic	$\dfrac{3,000}{11,000/2} \div \dfrac{1}{7/2} = 1.91$
7,000	3	21,000		
			Elastic	$\dfrac{4,000}{18,000/2} \div \dfrac{1}{5/2} = 1.11$
11,000	2	22,000		
			Inelastic	$\dfrac{5,000}{27,000/2} \div \dfrac{1}{3/2} = 0.56$
16,000	1	16,000		

Similarly, in this portion the percentage change in price tends to be small because the original price from which the percentage price change is calculated is large. The relatively large percentage change in quantity divided by the relatively small change in price yields an elastic demand. The reverse holds true for the lower-right portion of the demand curve. Here the percentage change in quantity tends to be small because the original quantity from which the percentage change is determined is large. Similarly, the percentage change in price tends to be large because the original price from which the relative price change is calculated is small. The relatively small percentage change in quantity divided by the relatively large change in price results in an inelastic demand.

Elasticity versus Slope In the second place, the graphic appearance, that is, the slope, of a demand curve is *not* a sound basis upon which to judge its elasticity. For example, in Figure 23-3 we find that because the demand curve has a steeper slope at relatively higher prices and a flatter slope at relatively lower prices, one is tempted to associate an inelastic demand with high prices and an elastic demand with low prices. But this is dangerous reasoning. Have we not just discovered that the elasticity formula and the total-revenue test indicate that the reverse is true? The catch lies in the fact that the slope—the flatness or steepness—of a demand curve is based upon *absolute* changes in price and quantity, while elasticity has to do with *relative* changes in price and quantity. The difference between slope and elasticity can also be made quite clear by calculating elasticity for various price-quantity combinations on a straight-line demand curve. You will find that, although the slope is obviously constant throughout, demand tends to be elastic in the high-price range and inelastic in the low-price range. Question 18 at the end of this chapter is relevant.

□ **Determinants of Elasticity of Demand**

There are no iron-clad, exceptionless generalizations concerning the determinants of the elasticity of demand. The following points, however, are usually accepted as valid and helpful.

1 Substitutability Generally speaking, the larger the number of good substitute products available, the greater the elasticity of demand. We shall find later in this chapter that in a purely competitive market, where by definition there is an extremely large number of perfect substitutes for the product of any given seller, the demand curve to that single seller will be perfectly elastic (Figure 23-9a). If one competitive seller of wheat or corn raises his price, buyers will turn to the readily available perfect substitutes of his many rivals. At the other extreme, the diabetic's demand for insulin is undoubtedly highly inelastic. It is worth noting that the elasticity of demand for a product depends upon how narrowly the product is defined. The demand for Texaco motor oil is more elastic than is the overall demand for motor oil. A number of other brands are readily substitutable for Texaco's oil, but there is no good substitute for motor oil per se.

2 Proportion of Income Other things being equal, the larger a good bulks in one's budget the greater will tend to be the elasticity of demand for it. A 10 percent increase in the price of pencils or chewing gum will amount to only a few pennies and elicit little response in terms of amount demanded. A 10 percent increase in the price of automobiles or housing means price increases of, say, $450 and $3500 respectively. These latter increases are significant fractions of the annual incomes of many families, and quantities purchased could be expected to diminish significantly.

3 Luxuries versus Necessities The demand for "necessities" tends to be inelastic; the demand for "luxuries" tends to be elastic. Bread and electricity are generally regarded as necessities; we "can't get along" without them. A price increase will not reduce significantly the amount of bread consumed or the amounts of lighting and power used in a household. A more extreme case: One does not decline an operation for acute appendicitis because the physician's fee has just gone up! On the other hand, French cognac and emeralds are luxuries which, by definition, can be forgone without undue inconvenience. If the price of cognac or emeralds rises, one need not purchase and, in so deciding, one will encounter no great hardship. The demand for salt tends to be highly inelastic on several counts. It is a "necessity"; unsalted cooking leaves much to be desired. There are no good substitutes available. Finally, salt is a negligible item in the family budget.

4 Time Generally speaking, the demand for a product tends to be more elastic the longer the time period under consideration. One aspect of this generalization has to do with the fact that many consumers are creatures of habit. When the price of a product rises, it takes time to seek out and experiment with other products to see if they are acceptable to us. The social drinker may not immediately reduce his purchases to any significant degree when the price of bourbon rises by, say, 10 percent. But, given time, he may shift his affections to Scotch or vodka for which he has now "developed a taste." Another facet of this generalization has to do with product durability. Studies show that the "short-run" demand for gasoline is more inelastic at .2 than is the "long-run" demand at .7. Why so? Because in the long run, large, gas-guzzling automobiles wear out and, in a context of rising gasoline prices, are replaced by smaller, higher-mileage cars.

In Chapter 30 we shall discover that a somewhat different group of factors determines the elasticity of demand for resources.

☐ **Some Practical Applications**

The concept of elasticity of demand is something more than a theoretical notion designed to confuse unwary students. It is a notion of great practical significance. Some examples will make this evident.

1 The United Automobile Workers once contended that automobile manufacturers should raise wages and simultaneously cut automobile prices. Arguing that the elasticity of demand for automobiles was about 4, the UAW concluded that a price cut would help check inflation, boost the total receipts of manufacturers, and preserve or even increase the profits of producers. A spokesman for the Ford Motor Company, however, claimed that available studies suggest an elasticity of demand for automobiles in the 0.5–1.5 range. He held that price cuts would therefore shrink profits or result in losses for manufacturers. In this case, the elasticity of demand for automobiles was a strategic factor in labor-management relations and wage bargaining.[3]

2 Another example: Studies indicate that the demand for most farm products is highly inelastic. As a result, increases in the output of farm products due to a good growing season or to productivity increases depress both the prices of farm products and the total receipts (incomes) of farmers. For farmers as a group, the inelastic nature of the demand for their products means that a bumper crop may be a mixed blessing. For policy makers it means that higher farm incomes depend upon the restriction of farm output.

3 Finally, the impact of automation, that is, of rapid technological advance, upon the

[3]See the statement by Theodore Yntema, vice president of finance, Ford Motor Company, before the Subcommittee on Antitrust and Monopoly of the Committee on the Judiciary, United States Senate, Feb. 4–5, 1958.

level of employment depends in part upon the elasticity of demand for the product being manufactured. Suppose a firm installs new laborsaving machinery, resulting in the technological unemployment of, say, 500 workers. Suppose too that a part of the cost reduction resulting from this technological advance is passed on to consumers in the form of reduced product prices. Now, the effect of this price reduction upon the firm's sales and therefore the quantity of labor it needs will obviously depend upon the elasticity of product demand. An elastic demand might increase sales to the extent that some of, all, or even more than, the 500 displaced workers are reabsorbed by the firm. An inelastic demand will mean that few, if any, of the displaced workers will be reemployed, because the increase in the volume of the firm's business will be small.

These examples could be multiplied; we will examine the important question of tax incidence through use of the elasticity concept in a moment. But the main point is clear. Elasticity of demand is vitally important to businessmen, farmers, labor, and government policy makers.

□ **Elasticity of Supply**

The concept of price elasticity can also be applied to supply. If producers are responsive to price changes, supply is elastic. If they are relatively insensitive to price changes, supply is inelastic.

The elasticity formula is pertinent in determining the degree of elasticity or inelasticity of supply. The only obvious alteration is the substitution of "percentage change in quantity *supplied*" for "percentage change in quantity *demanded*."

The main determinant of the elasticity of supply is the amount of *time* which a producer has to respond to a given change in product price. Generally speaking, we can expect a greater output response—and therefore greater elasticity of supply—the longer the amount of time a producer has to adjust to a given price

change. Why? Because a producer's response to an increase in the price of product X depends upon his ability to shift resources from the production of other products[4] to the production of X. And the shifting of resources takes time: the greater the time, the greater the resource "shiftability." Hence, the greater will be the output response and the elasticity of supply.

In analyzing the impact of time upon the elasticity of supply, economists find it useful to distinguish between the immediate market period, the short run, and the long run.

1 The Market Period The immediate market period is so short a time that producers cannot respond to a change in demand and price. Example: Suppose a small truck farmer brings his entire season's output of tomatoes—one truckload—to market. His supply curve will be perfectly inelastic; he will sell the truckload whether the price is high or low. Why? Because he cannot offer more tomatoes than his one truckload if the price of tomatoes should be higher than he had anticipated. Even though he might like to offer more, tomatoes cannot be produced overnight. It will take him another full growing season to respond to a higher-than-expected price by producing more than one truckload. Similarly, because his product is perishable, he cannot withhold it from the market. If the price is lower than he had anticipated, he will still sell the entire truckload. Costs of production, incidentally, will not be important in making this decision. Even though the price of tomatoes may fall far short of his production costs, he will nevertheless sell out to avoid a total loss through spoilage. In a very short time, then, our farmer's supply of tomatoes is fixed; he can offer one truckload no matter how high the price. The perishability of his product forces him to sell all, no matter how low the price.

Figure 23-4*a* illustrates the truck farmer's perfectly inelastic supply curve in the market

---

[4]The prices of which we assume to remain constant.

period. Note that he and other truck farmers are unable to respond to an assumed increase in demand; they do not have time to increase the amount supplied. The price increase from P_o to P_m simply rations a fixed supply to buyers, but elicits no increase in output.[5]

2 The Short Run   In the short run, the plant capacity of individual producers and of the industry is presumed to be fixed. But firms do have time to use their plants more or less intensively. Thus in the short run, our truck farmer's plant, which we shall consider as his land and farm machinery, is presumed fixed. But he does have time in the short run to cultivate tomatoes more intensively by applying more labor and more fertilizer and pesticides to his crop. The result is a greater output response to the presumed increase in demand; this greater output response is reflected in a

[5] The supply curve need not be perfectly inelastic (vertical) in the market period. If the product is not perishable, producers may choose, at low current prices, to store some of their product for future sale. This will cause the market supply curve to have some positive slope.

more elastic supply of tomatoes, as shown by S_s in Figure 23-4b. Note that the increase in demand is met by a larger quantity adjustment (Q_o to Q_s) and a smaller price adjustment (P_o to P_s) than in the market period; price is therefore lower than in the market period.

3 The Long Run   The long run is a time period sufficiently long so that firms can make all desired resource adjustments; individual firms can expand (or contract) their plant capacities, and new firms can enter (or existing firms can leave) the industry. In the "tomato industry" our individual truck farmer is able to acquire additional land and buy more machinery and equipment. Furthermore, more farmers may be attracted to tomato production by the increased demand and higher price. These adjustments mean an even greater supply response, that is, an even more elastic supply curve S_L. The result, shown in Figure 23-4c, is a small price effect (P_o to P_l) and a large output effect (Q_o to Q_l) in response to the assumed increase in demand.

The solid supply curve in Figure 23-4c

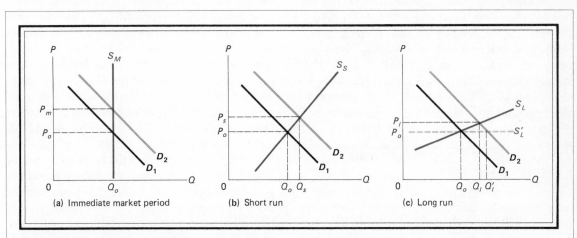

FIGURE 23-4 TIME AND THE ELASTICITY OF SUPPLY

The greater the amount of time producers have to adjust to a change in demand, the greater will be their output response. In the immediate market period **(a)** there is insufficient time to change output, and so supply is perfectly inelastic. In the short run **(b)** plant capacity is fixed, but output can be altered by changing the intensity of its use; supply is therefore more elastic. In the long run **(c)** all desired adjustments—including changes in plant capacity—can be made, and supply becomes still more elastic.

entails a new long-run equilibrium price P_l which is somewhat higher than the original price, P_o, in Figure 23-4a. Why higher? The presumption is that tomato farming is an "increasing cost" industry, meaning simply that the industry's expansion causes the prices of relevant resources to rise. The increased demand for fertilizer and farm equipment has pushed their prices up somewhat; the expanded demand for land has increased its value. In short, it is common and realistic to expect the expansion of an industry to result in "increasing costs." Hence, while P_o was sufficient for profitable production in Figure 23-4a, a higher price, P_l, is required for profitable production in the enlarged industry. If the tomato industry hired very small or negligible portions of relevant resources, then its increased demand for these inputs would leave their prices unchanged. In this "constant-cost" industry case the long-run supply curve would be perfectly elastic, as shown by the dashed curve in Figure 23-4c. The new price would be equal to the original price, P_o, in Figure 23-4a. We shall discuss these cases more fully in Chapter 26.

A final point: You may have noted that no mention has been made of a total-revenue test for elasticity of supply. Indeed, there is none. Supply shows a direct relationship between price and the amount supplied; that is, the supply curve is upsloping. Thus, regardless of the degree of elasticity or inelasticity, price and total receipts will always move together.

APPLICATIONS OF SUPPLY AND DEMAND ANALYSIS

Supply and demand analysis and the elasticity concept will be applied repeatedly in the remainder of this book. Let us strengthen our understanding of these analytical tools and their significance by examining three important applications: (1) legal prices, (2) the incidence of sales taxes, and (3) demand from the viewpoint of the individual firm.

□   Legal Prices

For the most part, the price system functions effectively in rationing goods and services and in allocating resources. Yet, under certain circumstances and in certain sectors of the economy, government has established by law prices which are above or below the equilibrium level. Let us briefly examine what happens to the functioning of the market when legal price fixing occurs.

Price Ceilings and Shortages   Price ceilings—maximum prices fixed by government which are *below* equilibrium prices—were used extensively during World War II and to a lesser extent during the Korean conflict as anti-inflationary devices. More recently, wage-price policies have been applied to alleviate the problem of premature inflation embodied in the Phillips Curve (Chapter 18).

Let us turn back the clock to World War II and analyze the effects of a ceiling price upon, say, butter. The booming wartime prosperity of the early 1940s was shifting the demand for butter to the right so that, as in Figure 23-5, the equilibrium or market price P was, say, $1.20 per pound. On the one hand, the rapidly rising price of butter was contributing to inflation and, on the other, rationing out of the butter market those families whose money incomes were not keeping pace with the soaring cost of living. Hence, to help stop inflation and to keep butter on the poor man's table, government imposed a ceiling price P_c of, say, $.90 per pound.

What will be the effects of this ceiling price? The rationing ability of the free market will be rendered ineffective. At the ceiling price there will be a persistent shortage of butter. That is, the quantity of butter demanded at P_c is Q_d and the quantity supplied is only Q_s; hence, a persistent shortage in the amount $Q_s Q_d$ occurs. Stated differently, the legal price P_c prevents the usual market adjustment wherein competition among buyers would bid up price, thereby simultaneously inducing

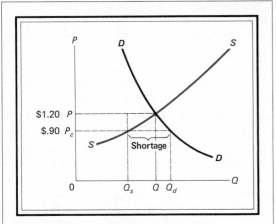

FIGURE 23-5   CEILING PRICES RESULT IN PERSISTENT SHORTAGES

Because the imposition of a price ceiling such as P_c results in a persistent product shortage, as indicated by the distance Q_sQ_d, government must undertake the job of rationing the product in order to achieve an equitable distribution.

more production and rationing some buyers out of the market until the shortage disappears at the equilibrium price and quantity, P and Q.

Now, by preventing this free-market adjustment process from occurring, the ceiling price poses problems born of the market disequilibrium. First, how is the available supply Q_s to be apportioned among buyers who want the amount Q_d? Should the supply be distributed on a first-come–first-served basis, that is, to those who are willing and able to stand in line the longest? Should the grocer distribute his butter on the basis of favoritism? The point is that an unregulated shortage is hardly conducive to the equitable distribution of butter. Hence, to avoid catch-as-catch-can distribution, government must establish some formal system of rationing the product to consumers. This was accomplished during World War II by issuing ration coupons to individuals on an equitable basis. An effective rationing system entails the printing of ration coupons equal to Q_s pounds of butter and the equitable distribution of these coupons among consumers so that, for example, the rich family

of four and the poor family of four will both get the same number of coupons.

But the use of rationing coupons does not prevent a second problem from arising. Specifically, the demand curve in Figure 23-5 tells us there are many buyers who are willing to pay more than the ceiling price. And, of course, it is more profitable for grocers to sell above the ceiling price. Hence, despite the sizable enforcement bureaucracy which accompanied World War II price controls, illegal *black markets*—markets wherein products were bought and sold at prices above the legal limits—flourished for many goods.

Finally, recall from Chapter 18 that ceiling prices entail the larger problem of prohibiting the price movements which are essential to preserve allocative efficiency through time. Example: Rent controls in New York City have contributed to a persistent housing shortage. Although the short-term effect of such controls may be to keep housing within reach of some of the poor, their longer-term impact is to inhibit alleviation of the housing shortage. Given low rents, investors are reluctant to construct new housing and investing in repairs tends to be unprofitable. The point is that rent controls prevent the rent increases needed to signal the profitable allocation of more resources to the construction of new housing and the renovation of old housing in New York City. The Last Word segment of this chapter is relevant.

Price Supports and Surpluses   Price supports—minimum prices fixed by government which are *above* equilibrium prices—have generally been invoked when society has felt that the free functioning of the market system has failed to provide an equitable distribution of income. Minimum-wage legislation and the support of agricultural prices are the two most widely discussed examples of government price supports. Let us examine price supports as applied to a specific farm commodity.

Suppose the going market price for corn is $3 per bushel, and as a result of this price, farmers realize extremely low incomes. Government decides to lend a helping hand by establishing a legal support price of, say, $4 per bushel.

What will be the effects? At any price above the equilibrium price, quantity supplied will obviously exceed quantity demanded; there will be a persistent surplus of the product. Farmers will be willing to produce and offer for sale more than private buyers are willing to purchase at the supported price. The size of this surplus will vary directly with the elasticity of demand and supply. The greater the elasticity of demand and supply, the greater the resulting surplus. As is the case with a ceiling price, the rationing ability of the free market obviously has been disrupted by the imposition of a legal price.

Figure 23-6 provides us with a graphic illustration of the effect of a supported price. Let SS and DD be the supply and demand curves for corn. Equilibrium price and quantity are obviously P and Q, respectively. If

government imposes a supported price of P_s, farmers will be willing to produce Q_s, but private buyers will only take Q_d off the market at that price. The surplus entailed is measured by the excess of Q_s over Q_d.

Government inherits the task of coping with the surplus which a supported price entails. There are two general approaches open to government. First, it might invoke certain programs to restrict supply (for example, acreage allotments) or to increase demand (for example, research on new uses for agricultural products) in order to reduce the difference between the equilibrium price and the supported price and thereby the size of the resulting surplus. If these efforts are not wholly successful, then, secondly, government must purchase the surplus output (thereby subsidizing farmers) and store or otherwise dispose of it. We shall have more to say about agricultural surpluses in Chapter 35.

The same reasoning as used in our agricultural price support example will lead us to conclude in Chapter 31 that, although the minimum wage is intended to improve the economic position of low-income workers, its actual effect may be to increase unemployment among such workers. The reader is urged to work through the implications of an above-equilibrium minimum wage in terms of Figure 23-6.

Recapitulation: Ceiling and supported prices rob the free-market forces of supply and demand of their ability to bring the supply decisions of producers and the demand decisions of buyers into accord with one another. Freely determined prices automatically ration products to buyers; legal prices do not. Therefore, government must accept the administrative problem of rationing which stems from price ceilings and the problem of buying or eliminating surpluses which price supports entail. Legal prices tend to break down unless accompanied by programs to control consumption or production. But remember this: Although legal prices involve knotty problems for government by upsetting the rationing and allocation functions of the market mechanism,

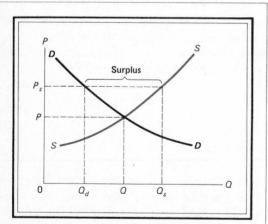

FIGURE 23-6 SUPPORTED PRICES RESULT IN PERSISTENT SURPLUSES

A price support such as P_s gives rise to a persistent product surplus as indicated by the distance Q_dQ_s. Government must either purchase these surpluses or take measures to eliminate them by restricting product supply or increasing product demand.

one must be careful not to prejudge ceilings or supports as undesirable. Legal prices are designed to correct alleged inequities which free-market prices entail.

□   **Tax Incidence**

The concepts of supply and demand *and* the notion of elasticity are useful in determining who pays a sales or excise tax. Suppose that Figure 23-7 shows the market for a certain domestic wine and that the no-tax equilibrium price and quantity are $4 and 15 million bottles. Now assume that government levies a specific sales or excise tax of $1 per bottle on this wine. Who actually pays this tax—producers or consumers? In technical terms (Chapter 8), what is the *incidence* of this tax?

Division of Burden   Assuming that government imposes the tax upon sellers (suppliers), it can be viewed as an addition to the supply price of the product. Therefore, the tax has the effect of shifting the supply curve upward by the amount of the tax. Thus, while sellers were willing to offer 5 million bottles of untaxed wine at $2 per bottle, they must now receive $3 per bottle—$2 plus the $1 tax—to offer the same 5 million bottles. Sellers must now get $1 more for each quantity supplied in order to receive the same per unit price as they were getting before the tax. The tax-caused upshift in the supply curve is shown in Figure 23-7, where S is the "no-tax" supply curve and S_t is the "after-tax" supply curve.

Careful comparison of after-tax supply and demand with the pretax equilibrium reveals that the new equilibrium price is $4.50, compared with the before-tax price of $4.00. In this particular case, one-half of the tax is paid by consumers and the other half by producers. Consumers obviously pay 50 cents more per bottle and, after remitting the $1 tax per unit to government, producers receive $3.50, or 50 cents less per bottle. In this instance, consumers and producers share the burden of the tax equally; producers shift half the tax for-

FIGURE 23-7   THE INCIDENCE OF A SALES TAX

The imposition of a sales tax of a specified amount, say $1 per unit, shifts the supply curve upward by the amount of the tax. This results in a higher price ($4.50) to the consumer and a lower after-tax price ($3.50) to the producer. In this particular case the burden of the tax is shared equally by consumers and producers.

ward to consumers in the form of a higher price and bear the other half themselves.

Note, incidentally, that the equilibrium quantity has fallen from 15 to 12½ million bottles. This reduction in output may well have been an intended outcome of the imposition of the tax. That is, government may have reasoned that certain spillover or social costs result from the consumption of alcoholic beverages and therefore imposed an excise tax to adjust the market supply curve for these costs and reduce the amount of resources allocated to wine production (Chapter 6).

Elasticities   If the elasticities of demand and supply were different from those shown in Figure 23-7, the incidence of the tax would also be different. Two generalizations are relevant.

1 *Given supply, the more inelastic the demand for the product, the larger the portion of the tax shifted forward to consumers.* The easiest way to verify this is to sketch graphically the extreme cases where demand is perfectly inelastic and perfectly elastic. In the first case the tax is shifted entirely to consumers; in the second instance the incidence of the tax is entirely upon sellers. Figure 23-8a contrasts the more likely cases where demand might be relatively elastic (D_e) or relatively inelastic (D_i) in the relevant price range. In the elastic demand case, a small portion of the tax (P_oP_e) is shifted forward to consumers, and most of the tax is borne by producers. In the inelastic demand case, most of the tax (P_oP_i) is shifted to consumers, and only a small amount is paid by producers. Note, too, that the reduction in equilibrium quantity is greater the more elastic the demand. This suggests that, if government's primary purpose in levying an excise tax is to raise revenue rather than reallocate resources, then, other things being equal, the tax should be levied on products having relatively inelastic demand. This reasoning may help explain the heavy excise taxes levied upon liquor, cigarettes, and tires.

2 *Given demand, the more inelastic the supply the larger the portion of the tax borne by producers.* Figure 23-8b explains this generalization. S_e is a relatively elastic, and S_i is a relatively inelastic, supply curve. S_{et} and S_{it} show these two curves after the imposition of an identical sales or excise tax. With the inelastic supply, we find that price rises by only P_oP_i; so a large portion of the tax must be borne by producers or sellers. But if supply is elastic, price will rise by the larger amount P_oP_e, so most of the tax is shifted to buyers and sellers bear only a small part of it. Quantity also declines less with an inelastic supply than it does with an elastic supply.

Implications   There are many additional implications which can be derived from this kind of analysis. For example, recall that subsidies are negative taxes. Therefore, a specific subsidy paid to a producer shifts the supply curve *downward* by the amount of the subsidy. What generalizations can you derive which relate the incidence of the benefits from a subsidy of some fixed amount per unit of output to the elasticity of demand? The elasticity of supply? Also, you might demonstrate graphically how excise taxes and subsidies can be used to adjust output and therefore improve

FIGURE 23-8 ELASTICITY AND THE INCIDENCE OF A SALES TAX

In **(a)** we find that if demand is elastic (D_e) in the relevant price range, price will rise modestly (P_o to P_e) when a sales or excise tax is imposed; hence the producer bears most of the tax burden. But if demand is inelastic (D_i) in the relevant price range, price will increase substantially (P_o to P_i) and most of the tax will be shifted to consumers. Part **(b)** demonstrates that a sales or excise tax of a given amount will fall primarily upon producers when supply is inelastic (S_i), but largely upon buyers when supply is elastic (S_e).

(a) Taxes and demand elasticity

(b) Taxes and supply elasticity

the allocation of resources when substantial spillover costs and benefits are present in the production or consumption of certain goods (Chapter 6). Finally, you might compare the amount of tax revenue a given sales or excise tax will yield when demand is elastic with its yield when demand is inelastic. The point to be stressed is that the tools of supply and demand and elasticity are of great significance in analyzing the full implications of taxes and subsidies.

☐ Demand from the Individual Firm's Viewpoint

The concepts of demand and supply are also of vital importance from the seller's point of view. Whereas demand indicates price and amount purchased from the consumer's standpoint, it simultaneously reflects revenue per unit and sales from the seller's standpoint. We first seek to examine the demand or average-revenue curve of an individual competitive producer.

Demand to a Purely Competitive Seller
You will recall (Chapter 22) that a purely competitive market entails a very large number of producers selling a standardized prod-

uct. Because he offers a negligible fraction of total supply, the individual competitive seller exerts no perceptible influence on market price. Price is set by the market, and the individual firm can sell as much or as little as it chooses at that price. Stated differently, the demand schedule is perfectly elastic to the individual competitive firm.

But a word of caution is in order. We are *not* saying that the *market* demand curve is perfectly elastic in a competitive market. Indeed, it is not, but rather, it is typically a downsloping curve as shown in Figure 23-9*b*. As a matter of fact, the total-demand curves for most agricultural products are quite *in*elastic, even though agriculture is the most competitive industry in our economy. We are saying that the demand schedule faced by the *individual firm* in a purely competitive industry is perfectly elastic. The distinction comes about in this way. For the industry—that is, for all firms producing a particular product—a larger volume of sales can be realized only by accepting a lower product price. All firms, acting independently but simultaneously, can and do affect total supply and therefore market price. But not so for the individual firm. If a single producer increases or decreases his output, the outputs of all other competing

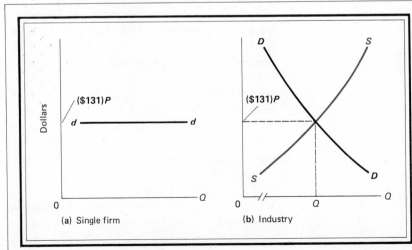

FIGURE 23-9 THE INDIVIDUAL COMPETITIVE FIRM'S DEMAND CURVE (a) AND DEMAND TO A COMPETITIVE INDUSTRY (b)

Industry demand is downsloping, such as *DD* in (b); that is, firms as a group must accept a lower price in order to sell a greater output. However, the product price which is determined by market demand and supply is given to the individual firm, making his demand curve *dd* perfectly elastic at that price, as shown in (a).

(a) Single firm

(b) Industry

firms being constant, the effect on total supply and market price is negligible. The single firm's sales schedule is therefore perfectly elastic, as shown in Figure 23-9a. This is an instance in which the fallacy of composition is worth remembering. What is true for the group of firms (a downsloping, less than perfectly elastic, demand curve) is *not* true for the individual firm (a perfectly elastic demand curve).

Columns 1 and 2 of Table 23-3 show a perfectly elastic demand curve where market price is assumed to be $131. Note that the firm cannot obtain a higher price by restricting output; nor need it lower price in order to increase its volume of sales.

Average, Total, and Marginal Revenue to a Purely Competitive Seller

A moment's reflection reveals that this demand schedule is simultaneously a revenue schedule. What appears in column 1 as price per unit to the purchaser is obviously revenue per unit, or *average revenue,* to the seller. To say that a buyer must pay a price of $131 per unit is to say that the revenue per unit, or average revenue, received by the seller is $131. Price and average revenue are the same thing looked at from different points of view.

Total revenue for each level of sales can obviously be determined by multiplying price by the corresponding quantity which the firm can sell. Multiply column 1 by column 2, and the result is column 3. In this case, total receipts increase by a constant amount, $131, for each additional unit of sales. Each unit sold adds exactly its price to total revenue.

Whenever a firm is pondering a change in its output, it will be concerned with how its revenue will change as a result of that shift in output. What will be the additional revenue from selling another unit of output? *Marginal revenue* is the addition to total revenue, that is, the extra revenue, which results from the sale of one more unit of output. In other words, in Table 23-3, marginal revenue is simply the rate of change in total revenue. In column 3 we note that total revenue is obviously zero when zero units are being sold. The first unit of output sold increases total revenue from zero to $131. Marginal revenue—the increase in total revenue resulting from the sale of the first unit of output—is therefore $131. The second unit sold increases total revenue from $131 to $262, so marginal revenue is again $131. Indeed, you will note in column 4 that marginal revenue is a constant figure of $131. Why? Because total revenue increases at a constant rate with every extra unit sold. Under purely competitive conditions, product price is constant to the individual firm; added units therefore can be sold without lowering product price. This means that each additional unit of sales adds exactly its price—$131 in this case—to total revenue. And marginal revenue is this rate of increase in total revenue. Marginal revenue is constant under pure competition because additional units can be sold at a constant price.

The competitive firm's demand curve and total- and marginal-revenue curves are shown graphically in Figure 23-10. The demand or average-revenue curve is perfectly elastic. The

Table 23-3 THE DEMAND AND REVENUE SCHEDULES FOR AN INDIVIDUAL PURELY COMPETITIVE FIRM (*hypothetical data*)

Firm's demand or average-revenue schedule		Revenue data	
(1) Product price (average revenue)	(2) Quantity demanded (sold)	(3) Total revenue	(4) Marginal revenue
$131	0	$ 0	
131	1	131	$131
131	2	262	131
131	3	393	131
131	4	524	131
131	5	655	131
131	6	786	131
131	7	917	131
131	8	1048	131
131	9	1179	131
131	10	1310	131

FIGURE 23-10 DEMAND, MARGINAL REVENUE, AND TOTAL REVENUE OF A PURELY COMPETITIVE FIRM

Because it can sell additional units of output at a constant price, the marginal-revenue curve (MR) of a purely competitive firm coincides with its perfectly elastic demand curve (*D*). The firm's total-revenue curve (TR) is a straight upsloping line.

marginal-revenue curve coincides with the demand curve because the market is a purely competitive one, and as a result, product price is constant to the single firm. Each extra unit of sales increases total revenue by $131. Total revenue is a straight line up to the right. Its slope is constant—that is, it is a straight line—because marginal revenue is constant.

In order to test your grasp of these new concepts, you should pause at this point and explain both tabularly and graphically what happens to average, total, and marginal revenue if price is, say, increased to $151 or lowered to $81.

Demand to an Imperfectly Competitive Seller

Let us now consider the nature of the demand and revenue schedules faced by imperfectly competitive producers, that is, firms which are pure monopolies, monopolistically competitive, or oligopolistic. Though they differ in details, the demand schedules facing imperfectly competitive firms have one basic point in common: They are downsloping. The demand curve of a pure monopolist, a monopolistically competitive producer, and an oli-

gopolist may differ considerably in elasticity; yet all are less than perfectly elastic and therefore downsloping.

Why? An imperfectly competitive producer sells a significant percentage of the industry's total output. Therefore any decision one firm makes to increase or reduce its output will have a noticeable effect on total supply and consequently on market price. This is most obvious in the case of the pure monopolist, where the firm and the industry are synonymous. Here the firm's output and market output are identical.

Specifically, when an imperfectly competitive producer attempts to sell more, market supply increases in relation to market demand, and price falls. As a result, the demand schedule faced by the individual firm is downsloping, that is, less than perfectly elastic. The firm must accept a lower price to achieve a larger volume of sales. Columns 1 and 2 of Table 23-4 portray this situation. We assume in this particular instance that the firm must accept a $10 price cut in order for it to sell each succeeding unit of output.

Table 23-4 THE DEMAND AND REVENUE SCHEDULES FOR AN INDIVIDUAL IMPERFECTLY COMPETITIVE FIRM (*hypothetical data*)

Firm's demand or average-revenue schedule		Revenue data	
(1) Product price (average revenue)	(2) Quantity demanded (sold)	(3) Total revenue	(4) Marginal revenue
$172	0	$ 0	
162	1	162	$162
152	2	304	142 (= 152 − 10)
142	3	426	122 (= 142 − 20)
132	4	528	102 (= 132 − 30)
122	5	610	82 (= 122 − 40)
112	6	672	62 etc.
102	7	714	42
92	8	736	22
82	9	738	2
72	10	720	−18

Average, Total, and Marginal Revenue to an Imperfectly Competitive Seller   As with the purely competitive firm, price and average revenue are identical to the imperfectly competitive producer. Total revenue is again the product of price and the corresponding volume of sales. Note, however, that the rate of increase in total revenue is *not* constant, as it was under purely competitive conditions. As a matter of fact, total revenue reaches a maximum of $738 with the ninth unit sold and declines thereafter. Why so?

Under pure competition, each successive unit sold adds the same amount—its price—to total revenue. Marginal revenue is constant under competition because price is constant to the individual firm. But with imperfect competition, price declines as sales increase. Hence, we should expect marginal revenue to decline. It does, and as a glance at columns 1 and 4 in Table 23-4 reveals, it falls *faster* than does price. Why? The catch is this: *When an imperfectly competitive firm cuts price to increase its volume of sales, this lower price will apply not only to the extra unit sold but also to all other units of sales.* For example, when our imperfectly competitive firm is selling 1 unit at $162, total revenue is obviously $162. To increase its sales to 2 units, price must be cut by $10 to $152. This new price applies not only to the extra (second) unit of sales but also to the first unit, which could have been sold at $162. In short, the second unit adds $152 (its price) less $10 (the price cut which the firm must take on the first unit), or $142, to total revenue. Similarly, to sell 3 units the firm must lower price from $152 to $142. The resulting marginal revenue will be just $122—the $142 addition to total revenue which the third unit of sales provides less $10 price cuts on the first 2 units of output. These calculations are

FIGURE 23-11   DEMAND, MARGINAL REVENUE, AND TOTAL REVENUE OF AN IMPERFECTLY COMPETITIVE FIRM

Because it must lower price to increase its sales, the marginal-revenue curve (MR) of an imperfectly competitive firm lies below its downsloping demand curve (D). Total revenue (TR) increases at a decreasing rate, reaches a maximum, and then declines.

shown in the marginal-revenue column in Table 23-4. Note that with the tenth unit of sales, marginal revenue becomes negative. Why?

Graphically, the data of Table 23-4 appear as in Figure 23-11. The points of contrast with Figure 23-10 are clear. The demand or average-revenue curve is, of course, downsloping. Total revenue increases, but at an ever-declining rate. In time, total revenue reaches a maximum and then actually declines. Aside from the first unit of sales, marginal revenue lies below the demand curve. The reason? Marginal revenue is derived from total revenue and therefore reflects price declines not only on the extra unit sold but also on all prior units of output which otherwise could have been sold at a higher price.

Summary

1   The present chapter extends the rudiments of demand and supply analysis developed in Chapter 4. The summarizing statements pertinent to that chapter should be reviewed at this point.

2   Elasticity of demand measures the responsiveness of consumers to price changes. If consumers are sensitive to price changes, demand is elastic. If consumers are unresponsive to price changes, demand is inelastic.

3   The price elasticity formula measures the degree of elasticity or inelasticity of demand. The formula is

$$E_d = \frac{\text{percentage change in quantity demanded}}{\text{percentage change in price}}$$

The averages of the prices and quantities under consideration are used as reference points in determining the percentage changes in price and quantity. If E_d is greater than 1, demand is elastic. If E_d is less than 1, demand is inelastic. Unit elasticity is the special case in which E_d equals 1.

4   Price elasticity of demand can be determined by observing the effect of a price change upon total receipts from the sale of the product. If price and total receipts move in opposite directions, demand is elastic. If price and total receipts move in the same direction, demand is inelastic.

5   The number of available substitutes, the size of an item in one's budget, whether the product is a luxury or necessity, and the time period involved are all considerations which influence elasticity of demand.

6   Elasticity varies at different price ranges on a demand curve. Furthermore, it is not safe to judge elasticity by the steepness or flatness of a demand curve on a graph.

7   The elasticity concept is also applicable to supply. Elasticity of supply depends upon the shiftability of resources between alternative employments. This shiftability in turn varies with the amount of time producers have to adjust to a given price change.

8   Legally fixed prices upset the rationing function of free-market prices. Effective price ceilings result in persistent product shortages, and if an equitable distribution of the product is sought, government will have to ration the product to consumers. Price supports give rise to product surpluses; government must purchase these surplus products *or* eliminate them by imposing restrictions on production or by increasing private demand.

9   Sales and excise taxes affect supply and therefore equilibrium price and quantity. The more inelastic the demand for a product, the greater is the portion of the tax which is shifted to consumers. The greater the inelasticity of supply, the larger the portion of the tax borne by sellers.

10   The demand or average-revenue curve faced by a purely competitive seller is perfectly elastic. In contrast, the demand curve facing an imperfectly competitive seller is downsloping, that is, less than perfectly elastic.

11   Under pure competition, product price is constant to the individual seller; therefore each extra unit of output adds exactly the same amount (its price) to total revenue. In other words, marginal revenue is constant and equal to price. Graphically, the marginal-revenue curve coincides with the firm's perfectly elastic demand curve. Total revenue is a straight upsloping line.

12   The imperfectly competitive seller must lower price to sell more, and this lower price will apply to all prior units of sales. As a result, marginal revenue is less than price. Graphically, the firm's marginal-revenue curve lies below its demand curve. Total revenue increases at a declining rate, reaches a maximum, and finally declines.

Questions and Study Suggestions

1   Key terms and concepts to remember: elasticity formula; elastic versus inelastic demand; perfectly inelastic demand; perfectly elastic demand; total-revenue test; elasticity of supply; market period; the short run and long run; price ceiling; price support; tax incidence; average revenue; total revenue; marginal revenue.

2   Answer questions 2, 4, and 11 at the end of Chapter 4.

3   In many oligopolistic industries, for example, the petroleum industry, producers justify their reluctance to lower prices by arguing that the demand for their products is inelastic. Explain.

4   How will the following changes in price affect total receipts (expenditures)—that is, will total receipts *increase, decline,* or *remain unchanged?*

   a.   Price falls and demand is inelastic.

   b.   Price rises and demand is elastic.

   c.   Price rises and supply is elastic.

   d.   Price rises and supply is inelastic.

   e.   Price rises and demand is inelastic.

   f.   Price falls and demand is elastic.

   g.   Price falls and demand is of unit elasticity.

5   Determine the elasticity of demand and supply for the following demand and supply schedules. Use the total-revenue test to check the answers given by the E_d formula.

E_s	Quantity supplied	Product price	Quantity demanded	Total revenue	E_d
____	28,000	$10	10,000	$____	____
____	22,500	9	13,000	____	____
____	17,000	8	17,000	____	____
____	15,500	7	22,000	____	____
	11,000	6	25,000	____	____

6   What are the major determinants of elasticity of demand? Use these determinants in judging whether the demand for the following products is elastic or inelastic: *a.* oranges; *b.* cigarettes; *c.* Winston cigarettes; *d.* gasoline; *e.* butter; *f.* salt; *g.* automobiles; *h.* football games; *i.* diamond bracelets; and *j.* this textbook.

7   Why is it difficult to judge elasticity of demand or supply by merely observing the appearance of a demand or supply curve on a graph?

8   Empirical estimates suggest the following demand elasticities: .6 for physicians' services; 4.0 for foreign travel; .1 for newspapers; and 1.2 for radio and television receivers. Use the generalizations for the determinants of elasticity developed in this chapter to explain each of these figures.

9   Empirical estimates indicate that the elasticity of supply for cabbage is .36 in the short run and 1.20 in the long run. Can you explain the different figures?

10 Why is it desirable for ceiling prices to be accompanied by government rationing? And for price supports to be accompanied by surplus-purchasing or output-restricting or demand-increasing programs? Show graphically why price ceilings entail shortages and price supports result in surpluses. What effect, if any, does the elasticity of demand and supply have upon the size of these shortages and surpluses? Explain.

11 New York City has had rent controls since 1941. What effect do you think they have had upon the demand for housing? Upon the construction of new housing?

12 How would you expect the elasticity of supply of product X to differ in a situation of full employment in industry X, on the one hand, and of considerable unemployment in the industry, on the other? Explain.

13 "If the demand for farm products is highly inelastic, a bumper crop may reduce farm incomes." Evaluate and illustrate graphically.

14 What is the incidence of *a.* a sales tax and *b.* a subsidy, when demand is highly inelastic? Elastic? What effect does the elasticity of supply have upon the incidence of a sales tax? A subsidy?

15 Suppose you are chairman of a state commission that is responsible for establishing a program to raise new revenue through the use of excise taxes. Would elasticity of demand be important to you in determining those products upon which excises should be levied? Explain.

16 Use the following demand schedule to determine total and marginal revenues for each possible level of sales.

Product price	Quantity demanded	Total revenue	Marginal revenue
$2	0	$————	
2	1	————	$————
2	2	————	————
2	3	————	————
2	4	————	————
2	5	————	————
2	6	————	————

    a. What can you conclude about the structure of the industry in which this firm is operating? Explain.

    b. Graph the demand, total-revenue, and marginal-revenue curves for this firm.

    c. Why do the demand and marginal-revenue curves coincide?

    d. "Marginal revenue is the rate of change in total revenue." Do you agree? Explain verbally and graphically, using the above data.

17 Now determine total and marginal revenues for each level of sales for this set of data:

Product price	Quantity demanded	Total revenue	Marginal revenue
$7	0	$————	
6	1	————	$————
5	2	————	————
4	3	————	————
3	4	————	————
2	5	————	————
1	6	————	

   a.   What can you conclude about the structure of the industry in which this firm is operating? Explain.

   b.   Graph the demand, total-revenue, and marginal-revenue curves for this firm.

   c.   Why does the marginal-revenue curve lie below the demand curve?

   18   *Advanced analysis.* The price-quantity data of question 17 constitute a straight-line demand curve. Use either the elasticity coefficient or the total-revenue test to determine the elasticity of demand for each possible price change. What can you conclude about the relationship between the slope of a curve and its elasticity? Use your answer to 17*b* to derive a generalization concerning the relationship between marginal revenue and the elasticity of demand.

   19   *Advanced analysis.* Explain the error in the following argument: "For the past four years the prices of automobiles have been rising and each year people have purchased more autos. Price and quantity are directly related and the economists' law of demand is obviously incorrect."

Selected References

Allen, Clark Lee: *The Framework of Price Theory* (Belmont, Calif.: Wadsworth Publishing Company, Inc., 1967), chaps. 2–4.

Boulding, Kenneth E.: *Economic Analysis: Microeconomics,* 4th ed. (New York: Harper & Row, Publishers, Incorporated, 1966), chaps. 7–12.

Brennan, Michael J.: *Theory of Economic Statics,* 2d ed. (Englewood Cliffs, N.J.: Prentice-Hall, Inc., 1970), chaps. 4–8.

Kaish, Stanley: *Microeconomics: Logic, Tools, and Analysis* (New York: Harper & Row, Publishers, Incorporated, 1976), chap. 3.

Rogers, Augustus J., III: *Choice: An Introduction to Economics* (Englewood Cliffs, N.J.: Prentice-Hall, Inc., 1971), chaps. 2–3.

Last Word
Rent Controls: A Self-Fulfilling Prophecy

Rent controls may aggravate the very problem they are designed to rectify.

To the Editor:

Your recent news article on rent control prompts some comments.

Rent control (or stabilization) may not be forever but it is likely to be for a very long time. Once installed, controls have an immediate and passionate constituency which virtually guarantees their continuance regardless of need. For example, in my own county of Westchester, some 80,000 units are now subject to either rent control or rent stabilization. This represents a bloc of over 100,000 voters out of a total population of somewhat under 900,000. No conceivable coalition of builders, apartment owners and other "interests" is going to be able to match that political muscle. New York City's controls were enacted in the midst of a world war and have now lasted one third of a century with no end in sight.

Rent controls will depress the construction of new rental housing. Since controls limit profit opportunities but not loss possibilities, this conclusion seems inevitable. Capital will be shifted from areas with controls to areas without controls. Controls are thus a self-fulfilling prophecy. Brought into being by a housing shortage, they depress construction, helping to perpetuate the shortage which justifies their existence. Controls will lead to lower housing quality. If a unit must be rented at below market rates (otherwise controls have no meaning) the motivation to improve it disappears. The rational course for the owner is to improve his short-term cash flow by disinvesting.

Controls will shift the property tax burden. Since property taxes on rental properties are paid out of rents, controlled rents mean less capacity to pay taxes. Thus the burden will be shifted from controlled properties to owner-occupied residences and commercial structures. As in other areas of life, "there is no free lunch."

As an instrument of income redistribution—from wealthy landlords to poor tenants—controls leave a lot to be desired because not all landlords are rich and not all tenants are poor. It would make more sense to subsidize poor tenants directly than to control the entire market to help those who cannot survive in it unassisted.

Rent control (or stabilization) is politically attractive because tenants far outnumber landlords and because it appears to protect the weak against the powerful. But like some other quick fixes, its short-term effects are much more pleasant than its long-term effects.

John M. Levy
Dobbs Ferry, N.Y.

24

Further Topics in the Theory of Consumer Demand[1]

In Chapter 23 we extended our understanding of demand and supply by introducing the concept of price elasticity and by discussing some specific applications of demand and supply analysis. The present chapter is devoted to further consideration of the demand side of the market. In Chapter 25 we shall discuss production costs, which, we shall discover, are the major determinant of supply. The goal of Chapters 26 to 29 is to use our understanding of demand and supply in analyzing pricing and output decisions under the various market structures which were outlined in Chapter 22.

Now for a more detailed look at the two main objectives of the present chapter. First, we seek a more sophisticated explanation of the law of demand. Second, we want to understand how consumers allocate their money incomes among various goods and services. Why does a consumer buy some specific bundle of goods rather than any one of a number of other collections of goods which are available to him?

TWO EXPLANATIONS OF THE LAW OF DEMAND

Thus far, we have accepted the law of demand as a commonsense notion. We have simply appealed to observation in claiming an inverse

[1]To the instructor: This is an optional chapter which may be omitted without impairing the continuity and meaning of ensuing chapters.

relationship between price and quantity demanded. A high price usually does discourage consumers from buying; a low price typically does encourage them to buy. Now let us explore two complementary explanations of the downsloping nature of the demand curve which will back up our everyday observations.[2]

□ Income and Substitution Effects

One explanation of the law of demand says in essence that as the price of a product declines, consumers will be both *able* and *willing* to buy more of it.

Income Effect As the price of steak declines, you are obviously able to buy more of it with your money income. With a constant money income of, say, $20 per week you can purchase 10 pounds of steak at a price of $2 per pound. But if the price of steak falls to $1 per pound and you buy 10 pounds of steak, $10 per week is freed for buying more of this and other commodities. A decline in the price of steak increases the real income of the consumer. This is called the *income effect*.

Substitution Effect But being able to buy more steak at a lower price is not a complete explanation of why you actually do buy more. As the price of steak falls—the prices of other products being unchanged—steak will become more attractive to the buyer. At $1 per pound it is a "better buy" than at $2 per pound. Consequently, the lower price will induce the consumer to substitute steak for some of the now less attractive items in his budget. Steak may well be substituted for pork, chicken, veal, and a variety of other foods. A lower price increases the relative attractiveness of a product

and makes the consumer willing to buy more of it. This is known as the *substitution effect*.

The income and substitution effects combine to make a consumer able and willing to buy more of a specific good at a a low price than at a high price.

□ Law of Diminishing Marginal Utility

A second explanation centers upon the notion that, although consumer wants in general may be insatiable, wants for specific commodities can be fulfilled. In a given span of time, wherein the tastes of buyers are unchanged, consumers can get as much of specific goods and services as they want. The more of a specific product a consumer obtains, the less anxious he is to get more units of the same product. This can be most readily seen for durable goods. A consumer's want for an automobile, when he has none, may be very strong; his desire for a second car is much less intense; for a third or fourth, very weak. Even the wealthiest of families rarely have more than a half-dozen cars, despite the fact that their incomes would allow them to purchase and maintain a whole fleet of them.

Economists put forth the idea that specific consumer wants can be fulfilled with succeeding units of a commodity in the *law of diminishing marginal utility*. Let us dissect this law to see exactly what it means. A product has utility if it has the power to satisfy a want. *Utility* is want-satisfying power. Two characteristics of this concept must be emphasized: First, "utility" and "usefulness" are by no means synonymous. Paintings by Picasso may be useless in the functional sense of the term yet be of tremendous utility to art connoisseurs. Second—and implied in the first point—utility is a subjective notion. The utility of a specific product will vary widely from person to person. A nip of Old Tennisshoes will yield tremendous utility to the Skid Row alcoholic, but zero or negative utility to the local WCTU president.

By *marginal* utility we simply mean the

---

[2] A third explanation, based upon *indifference curves,* is in some respects more precise and more sophisticated than the two we now discuss. The interested reader should refer to Richard H. Leftwich, *The Price System and Resource Allocation,* 6th ed. (Hinsdale, Ill.: The Dryden Press, Inc., 1976), chap. 5; or Edwin Mansfield, *Microeconomics: Theory and Applications,* 2d ed., (New York: W. W. Norton & Company, Inc., 1975), chaps. 2, 3.

extra utility, or satisfaction, which a consumer gets from one additional unit of a specific product. In any relatively short time wherein the consumer's tastes can be assumed not to change, the marginal utility derived from successive units of a given product will decline.[3] Why? Because a consumer will eventually become saturated, or "filled up," with that particular product. The fact that marginal utility will decline as the consumer acquires additional units of a specific product is known as the *law of diminishing marginal utility*.

We have noted that utility is a subjective concept. As a result, it is not susceptible to precise quantitative measurement. But for purposes of illustration, let us assume that we can measure satisfaction with units we shall call "utils." This mythical unit of satisfaction is merely a convenient pedagogical device which will allow us to quantify our thinking about consumer behavior. Thus, in Table 24-1, we can illustrate the relationship between the quantity obtained of a product—say, product A—and the accompanying extra utility derived from each successive unit. Here we assume that the law of diminishing marginal utility sets in with the first unit of A obtained. Each successive unit yields less and less extra utility than the previous one as the consumer's want for A comes closer and closer to fulfillment. Total utility can obviously be found for any number of units of A by cumulating the marginal-utility figures as indicated in Table 24-1. The third unit of A has a marginal utility of 7 utils; 3 units of A yields a total utility of 25 utils ($= 10 + 8 + 7$).

Now, how does the law of diminishing marginal utility explain why the demand curve for a specific product is downsloping? If successive units of a good yield smaller and smaller amounts of marginal, or extra, utility, the consumer will buy additional units of a

Table 24-1 THE LAW OF DIMINISHING MARGINAL UTILITY AS APPLIED TO PRODUCT A (*hypothetical data*)

Unit of product A	Marginal utility, utils	Total utility, utils
First	10	10
Second	8	18
Third	7	25
Fourth	6	31
Fifth	5	36
Sixth	4	40
Seventh	3	43

product only if its price falls. The consumer for whom these utility data are relevant may buy, say, 2 units of A at a price of $1. But, owing to diminishing marginal utility from additional units of A, he will choose *not* to buy more at this price, because giving up money really means giving up other goods, that is, alternative ways of getting utility. Therefore, additional units of A are "not worth it" unless the price (sacrifice of other goods) declines. From the seller's viewpoint, diminishing marginal utility forces the producer to lower the price in order to induce buyers to take a larger quantity of the product.

■
THEORY OF CONSUMER BEHAVIOR

In addition to providing a basis for explaining the law of demand, the idea of diminishing marginal utility also plays a key role in explaining how a consumer should allocate his money income among the many goods and services which are available for him to buy.

□ **Consumer Choice and Budget Restraint**

We can picture the situation of the typical consumer as being something like this:

1 Rational Behavior The average consumer is a fairly rational fellow. He attempts to dispose of his money income in such a way

[3]For a time the marginal utility of successive units of a product may increase. A third cigarette may yield a larger amount of extra satisfaction than the first or second. But beyond some point, we can expect the marginal utility of added units to decline.

as to derive the greatest amount of satisfaction, or utility, from it. This is not to say he is always able to achieve the maximum amount of utility from his money income; for example, inadequate knowledge of the goods available to him and the force of habit work against achieving the utility-maximizing pattern of expenditures. But we may safely assume that the typical consumer wants to get the most for his money.

2 Preferences We may suppose, too, that the average consumer has rather clear-cut preferences for various goods and services available in the market. We assume that buyers have a pretty good idea of how much marginal utility they will get from successive units of the various products which they might choose to purchase.

3 Budget Restraint The consumer's money income is limited in amount. Because he supplies limited amounts of human and property resources to businesses, the money income he receives will be limited. Whether the consumer finds himself at the top or bottom of the income pyramid, his income will be a finite amount. With a few exceptions—Nelson Rockefeller, oilman H. L. Hunt, and Saudi Arabia's King Khalid—all consumers are subject to a *budget restraint.*

4 Prices The goods and services available to consumers have price tags on them. Why? Because they are scarce in relation to the demand for them, or, stated differently, their production entails the use of scarce and therefore valuable resources. In the ensuing examples we shall suppose that product prices are not affected by the amounts of specific goods which the individual consumer buys; pure competition exists on the buying or demand side of the market.

Obviously, if a consumer has a limited number of dollars in his pocket and the products he wants have price tags on them, he will be able to purchase only a limited amount of goods. The consumer cannot buy everything he might want when each purchase exhausts a portion of his limited money income. It is precisely this obvious point which brings the economic fact of scarcity home to the individual consumer.[4]

> In making his choices, our typical consumer is in the same position as the Western prospector . . . who is restocking for his next trip into the back country and who is forced by the nature of the terrain to restrict his luggage to whatever he can carry on the back of one burro. If he takes a great deal of one item, say baked beans, he must necessarily take much less of something else, say bacon. His job is to find that collection of products which, in view of the limitations imposed on the total, will best suit his needs and tastes.

In short, the consumer must make compromises; he must do some picking and choosing among alternative goods to obtain with his limited money resources the collection of goods and services most satisfying to him.

▢ **Utility-maximizing Rule**

The question then boils down to this: Of all the collections of goods and services which a consumer can obtain within the limit of his budget, which specific collection will yield him the greatest utility or satisfaction? Bluntly put, the rule to be followed in maximizing his satisfactions is that *the consumer should allocate his money income so that the last dollar spent on each product purchased yields the same amount of extra (marginal) utility.* We shall call this the *utility-maximizing rule.* When the consumer is "balancing his margins" in accordance with this rule, there will be no incentive for him to alter his expenditure pattern. He will be in equilibrium, and, barring a change in his tastes, his income, or the prices of the various goods, he will be worse off—his

[4] E. T. Weiler, *The Economic System* (New York: The Macmillan Company, 1952), p. 89.

total utility will decline—by any alteration in the collection of goods he is purchasing.

Now a detailed illustration will help explain the validity of the rule. For simplicity's sake we limit our discussion to just two products. Keep in mind that the analysis can readily be extended to any number of goods. Suppose that consumer Brooks is trying to decide which combination of two products—A and B—he should purchase with his limited daily income of $10. Obviously, Brooks's preferences for these two products and their prices will be basic data determining the combination of A and B which will maximize his satisfactions. Table 24-2 summarizes Brooks's preferences for products A and B. Column 2a shows the amount of extra or marginal utility Brooks will derive from each successive unit of A. Column 3a reflects Brooks's preferences for product B. In each case the relationship between the number of units of the product obtained and the corresponding marginal utility reflects the law of diminishing marginal utility. Diminishing marginal utility is assumed to set in with the first unit of each product purchased.

But before we can apply the utility-maximizing rule to these data, we must put the marginal-utility information of columns 2a and 3a on a per-dollar-spent basis. Why? Because a consumer's choices will be influenced not only by the extra utility which successive units of, say, product A will yield, but also by how many dollars (and therefore how many units of alternative good B) he must give up to obtain those added units of A. Example: Brooks may clearly prefer to own a Cadillac rather than a Ford; he may be twice as happy with a Cadillac than with a Ford. Yet he may buy a Ford because a Cadillac costs three or four times as much as a Ford. Brooks may feel that *per dollar spent,* a Ford is a better buy. The point is this: To make the amounts of extra utility derived from differently priced goods comparable, marginal utility must be put on a per-dollar-spent basis. This is done in columns 2b and 3b. These figures are obtained by dividing the marginal-utility data of columns 2a and 3a by the assumed prices of A and B—$1 and $2, respectively.

Now we have Brooks's preferences—on unit and per dollar bases—and the price tags of A and B before us. Brooks stands patiently with $10 to spend on A and B. In what order should he allocate his dollars on units of A and

Table 24-2   THE UTILITY-MAXIMIZING COMBINATION OF PRODUCTS A AND B OBTAINABLE WITH AN INCOME OF $10* (*hypothetical data*)

(1)	(2) Product A: price = $1		(3) Product B: price = $2	
Unit of product	(a) Marginal utility, utils	(b) Marginal utility per dollar (MU/price)	(a) Marginal utility, utils	(b) Marginal utility per dollar (MU/price)
First	10	10	24	12
Second	8	8	20	10
Third	7	7	18	9
Fourth	6	6	16	8
Fifth	5	5	12	6
Sixth	4	4	6	3
Seventh	3	3	4	2

* It is assumed in this table that the amount of marginal utility received from additional units of each of the two products is independent of the quantity of the other product. For example, the marginal-utility schedule for product A is independent of the amount of B obtained by the consumer.

B to achieve the highest degree of utility within the limits imposed by his money income? And what specific combination of A and B will he have obtained at the time that he exhausts his $10?

Concentrating on columns 2b and 3b of Table 24-2, we find that Brooks should first spend $2 on the first unit of B. Why? Because its marginal utility per dollar of 12 utils is higher than A's. But now Brooks finds himself indifferent about whether he should buy a second unit of B or the first unit of A. Suppose he buys both of them: Brooks now has 1 unit of A and 2 of B. Note that with this combination of goods the last dollar spent on each yields the same amount of extra utility. Does this combination of A and B therefore represent the maximum amount of utility which Brooks can obtain? The answer is "No." This collection of goods only costs $5 $[=(1 \times \$1) + (2 \times \$2)]$; Brooks has $5 of income remaining, which he can spend to achieve a still higher level of total utility.

Examining columns 2b and 3b again, we find that Brooks should spend the next $2 on a third unit of B. But, now with 1 unit of A and 3 of B, we find he is again indifferent to a second unit of A and a fourth unit of B. Let us again assume Brooks purchases one more unit of each. Marginal utility per dollar is now the same for the last dollar spent on each product, *and* Brooks's money income of $10 is exhausted $[(2 \times \$1) + (4 \times \$2)]$. *The utility-maximizing combination of goods attainable by Brooks is 2 units of A and 4 of B.*[5]

It is to be emphasized that there are other combinations of A and B which are obtainable with $10. But none of these will yield a level of total utility as high as do 2 units of A and 4 of B. For example, 4 units of A and 3 of B can be obtained for $10. However, this combination violates the utility-maximizing rule; total util-

ity here is only 93 utils, clearly inferior to the 96 utils yielded by 2 of A and 4 of B. Furthermore, there are other combinations of A and B (such as 4 of A and 5 of B *or* 1 of A and 2 of B) wherein the marginal utility of the last dollar spent is the same for both A and B. But such combinations are either unobtainable with Brooks's limited money income (as 4 of A and 5 of B) or fail to exhaust his money income (as 1 of A and 2 of B) and therefore do not yield him the maximum utility attainable.

□ **An Algebraic Restatement**

We are now in a position to restate the utility-maximizing rule in simple algebraic terms. Our rule simply says that a consumer will maximize his satisfaction when he allocates his money income in such a way that the last dollar spent on product A, the last on product B, and so forth, yield equal amounts of additional, or marginal, utility. Now the marginal utility per dollar spent on A is indicated by MU of product A/price of A (column 2b of Table 24-2) and the marginal utility per dollar spent on B by MU of product B/price of B (column 3b of Table 24-2). Our utility-maximizing rule merely requires that these ratios be equal. That is,

$$\frac{\text{MU of product A}}{\text{price of A}} = \frac{\text{MU of product B}}{\text{price of B}}$$

and, of course, the consumer must exhaust his available income. Our tabular illustration has shown us that the combination of 2 units of A and 4 of B fulfills these conditions in that

$$\frac{8}{1} = \frac{16}{2}$$

and the consumer's $10 income is spent.

If the equation is not fulfilled, there will be some reallocation of the consumer's expenditures between A and B, from the low to the high marginal-utility-per-dollar product, which will increase the consumer's total utility. For example, the consumer may spend his $10 on 4 of A and 3 of B. But here we find that

---

[5]To simplify, we assume in this example that Brooks spends his entire income; he neither borrows nor saves. Saving can be regarded as a utility-yielding commodity and incorporated in our analysis. It is treated thus in question 5 at the end of the chapter.

$$\frac{\text{MU of A: 6 utils}}{\text{price of A: \$1}} < \frac{\text{MU of B: 18 utils}}{\text{price of B: \$2}}$$

The last dollar spent on A provides only 6 utils of satisfaction, and the last dollar spent on B provides 9. On a per dollar basis, units of B provide more extra satisfaction than units of A. The consumer will obviously increase his total satisfaction by purchasing more of B and less of A. As dollars are reallocated from A to B, the marginal utility from additional units of B will decline as the result of moving *down* the diminishing marginal-utility schedule for B, and the marginal utility of A will rise as the consumer moves *up* the diminishing marginal-utility schedule for A. At some new combination of A and B—specifically, 2 of A and 4 of B—the equality of the two ratios and therefore consumer equilibrium will be achieved. As we already know, the net gain in utility is 3 utils ($= 96 - 93$).

MARGINAL UTILITY AND THE DEMAND CURVE

It is a quite simple step from the utility-maximizing rule to the construction of an individual's downsloping demand curve. Recall from Chapters 4 and 23 that the basic determinants of an individual's demand curve for a specific product are (1) his preferences or tastes, (2) his money income, and (3) the prices of other goods. Now the utility data of Table 24-2 reflect our consumer's preferences. Let us continue to suppose that his money income is given at $10. And, concentrating upon the construction of a simple demand curve for product B, let us assume that the price of A—representing "other goods"—is given at $1. We should now be able to derive a simple demand schedule for B by considering alternative prices at which B might be sold and determining the corresponding quantity our consumer will choose to purchase. Of course, we have already determined one such price-quantity combination in explaining the utility-maxi-

mizing rule: Given tastes, income, and the prices of other goods, the rational consumer will purchase 4 units of B at a price of $2. Now assume the price of B falls to $1. This means that the marginal-utility-per-dollar data of column 3b will double, because the price of B has been halved; the new data for column 3b are in fact identical to those shown in column 3a. The purchase of 2 units of A and 4 of B is no longer an equilibrium combination. By applying the same reasoning used to develop the utility-maximizing rule, we now find Brooks's utility-maximizing position entails 4 units of A and 6 of B. That is, we can sketch Brooks's demand curve for B as in Table 24-3. This, of course, confirms the downsloping demand curve discussed in earlier chapters.

CRITICISMS: THE TIME DIMENSION

The marginal-utility theory of consumer behavior is a meaningful explanation of how consumers seek to maximize their satisfaction. Though the process may be crude, consumers do make marginal comparisons in allocating their limited incomes. A family must choose between, say, buying a food freezer or a color television. And the college student must weigh the relative satisfaction to be derived from spending $15 on a Saturday-night date as opposed to a new pair of jeans.

Nevertheless, the theory of consumer behavior is not without criticism. Most obviously, we have no "utilometer" by which the consumer's preferences can be set down precisely, as in Table 24-2. Nor is it easy to incorporate large, indivisible products, such as houses, automobiles, pianos, and a college education, in our analysis. In fact, owing largely to the

Table 24-3 THE DEMAND SCHEDULE FOR PRODUCT B

Price per unit of B	Quantity demanded
$2	4
1	6

pioneering work of Gary Becker,[6] economists recently have been rethinking and generalizing the theory of consumer choice. Becker begins by noting that both consumption and production activities have a common characteristic—they take time. And time is obviously a valuable economic resource; by working—by using an hour in productive activity—one may earn $6, $10, or $50, depending upon one's education, skills, and so forth. By using that hour for leisure or in consumption activities, one obviously incurs the opportunity cost of forgone income; you sacrifice the $6, $10, or $50 you could have earned by working.

□ The Value of Time

Becker points out that the traditional marginal-utility theory of consumer behavior is inadequate because it lacks a time dimension; the theory unrealistically assumes that consumption is an instantaneous act. Specifically, Becker contends that the "prices" of consumer goods should include, not merely the market price, but also the value of the time required in the consumption of the good. In other words, the denominators of our earlier marginal-utility/price ratios are inadequate because they do not reflect the "full price"—market price *plus* the value of the consumption time—of the product.

Imagine a consumer who is considering the purchase of a round of golf, on the one hand, and a concert, on the other. The market price of the golf game is $5 and the concert is $8. But wait, says Becker, the golf game is more time-intensive than the concert. Suppose you will spend four hours on the golf course, but only two hours at the concert. If your time is worth, say $4 per hour—as evidenced by the $4 wage rate you can obtain by working—then we must recognize that the "full price" of the golf game is $21 (the $5 market price *plus* $16

worth of time). Similarly, the "full price" of the concert is $16 (the $8 market price *plus* $8 worth of time). We find that, contrary to what market prices alone would indicate, the "full price" of the concert is really *less* than the "full price" of the golf game. If we now invoke the simplifying assumption that the marginal utility derived from successive golf games and concerts are identical, traditional theory would indicate that one should consume more golf games than concerts because the market price of the former is lower ($5) than the latter ($8). But Becker would say that, when time is taken into account, the situation is reversed and golf games are more expensive ($21) than are concerts ($16). Hence, it is rational to consume more concerts than golf games!

□ Some Implications

Becker contends that his approach explains certain observable phenomena which the traditional theory does not. It may be rational for the unskilled worker or retiree whose time has little or no market value to ride a bus from New York to Chicago. But the corporate executive, whose time is very valuable, will find it cheaper to fly, even though bus fare is only a fraction of plane fare. It is sensible for the retiree, living on a modest social security check and having ample time, to spend many hours shopping for bargains. It is equally intelligent for the highly paid physician, working 55 hours per week, to patronize fast-food restaurants and to buy a new television set over the phone. Affluent Americans are observed by foreigners to be "wasteful" of food and other material goods, but "overly economical" in the use of time. Americans who visit less developed countries find that time is used casually or "squandered," while material goods are very highly prized and carefully used. According to Becker, these differences are not a paradox or a case of radically different temperaments. The differences are primarily a quite rational reflection of the fact that the high labor productivity which is characteristic

---

[6] Becker's classic article, "A Theory of the Allocation of Time," *Economic Journal,* September 1965, pp. 493–517, is not easily digested by the beginning student.

of an advanced society gives time a high market value, whereas precisely the opposite is true in a less developed country.

A final point: As labor productivity has increased historically with the growth of our economy, time has become more valuable in the labor market. Or, stated differently, time used on pure leisure and various consumer activities has become more expensive. As a result, we make a great effort to use nonwork time more "productively." Where possible, we try to increase the pleasure or utility yield per hour by consuming more per unit of time. In some cases this means making consumption more goods-intensive; for example, by buying or renting a motorized golf cart, the time required for a round of golf can be reduced. One watches the news on television because it takes less time than reading the newspaper. In other instances, we consume two or more items simultaneously. After dinner, the consumer "may find himself drinking Brazilian coffee,

smoking a Dutch cigar, sipping a French cognac, reading *The New York Times,* listening to a Brandenburg Concerto and entertaining his Swedish wife—all at the same time, with varying degrees of success."[7] But the yield from certain uses of time—pure idleness, cultural pursuits, and the "cultivation of mind and spirit"—cannot be readily increased. Hence, time tends to be shifted from these uses to areas where the yield is greater. This helps explain why, although economic development may bring affluence in the form of goods, it also increases the relative scarcity of time and creates a more hectic life-style. Economic growth, it is argued, cannot produce abundance in all respects; total affluence—an abundance of *both* goods and time—is a logical fallacy.

[7] Staffan B. Linder, *The Harried Leisure Class* (New York: Columbia University Press, 1970), p. 79. This book is required reading for the person who wants to pursue the many implications of the increasing value of time.

Summary

1   The law of demand can be explained on the basis of the income and substitution effects or the law of diminishing marginal utility.

2   The income effect says that a decline in the price of a product will enable the consumer to buy more of it with his fixed money income. The substitution effect points out that a lower price will make a product relatively more attractive and therefore increase the consumer's willingness to substitute it for other products.

3   The law of diminishing marginal utility states that beyond some point, additional units of a specific commodity will yield ever-declining amounts of extra satisfaction to a consumer. It follows that a lower price will be needed to induce the consumer to increase his purchases of such a product.

4   We may assume that the typical consumer is rational and acts on the basis of rather well-defined preferences; consumers act sensibly and know roughly the satisfaction they will derive from successive units of various products available to them. Because his income is limited and goods have prices on them, the consumer cannot purchase all the goods and services he might like to have. He should therefore select that attainable combination of goods which will maximize his utility or satisfaction.

5   The consumer's utility will be maximized when he is allocating his income so that the last dollar spent on each product purchased yields the same amount of extra satisfaction. Algebraically, the utility-maximizing rule is fulfilled when

$$\frac{\text{MU of product A}}{\text{price of A}} = \frac{\text{MU of product B}}{\text{price of B}}$$

and the consumer's income is spent. Though subject to limitations, this rule is a meaningful guide in explaining consumer behavior.

6   The utility-maximizing rule and the downsloping demand curve are logically consistent.

7   Recently economists have been concerned with modifying and generalizing the theory of consumer choice by taking into account the time required in the consumption of various goods and services.

Questions and Study Suggestions

1   Key terms and concepts to remember: income effect; substitution effect; utility; law of diminishing marginal utility; utility-maximizing rule.

2   Explain the law of demand through the income and substitution effects, using a price increase as a point of departure for your discussion. Explain the law of demand in terms of diminishing marginal utility.

3   Mrs. Peterson buys loaves of bread and quarts of milk each week at prices of 50 cents and 40 cents, respectively. At present she is buying these two products in amounts such that the marginal utilities from the last units purchased of the two products are 80 and 70 utils, respectively. Is Mrs. Peterson currently buying the best, that is, the utility-maximizing, combination of bread and milk? If not, in what manner should she reallocate her expenditures between the two goods?

4   "Nothing is more useful than water: but it will purchase scarce any thing; scarce any thing can be had in exchange for it. A diamond, on the contrary, has scarce any value in use; but a very great quantity of other goods may frequently be had in exchange for it."[8] Explain.

5   Columns 1 through 4 of the following table show the marginal utility, measured in terms of utils, which Mr. Black would get by purchasing various amounts of products A, B, C, and D. Column 5 shows the marginal utility Black gets from saving. Assume that the prices of A, B, C, and D are $24, $4, $6, and $18, respectively, and that Black has a money income of $106.

Column 1		Column 2		Column 3		Column 4		Column 5	
Units of A	MU	Units of B	MU	Units of C	MU	Units of D	MU	No. of dollars saved	MU
1	36	1	15	1	24	1	72	1	5
2	30	2	12	2	15	2	54	2	4
3	24	3	8	3	12	3	45	3	3
4	18	4	7	4	9	4	36	4	2
5	13	5	5	5	7	5	27	5	1
6	7	6	4	6	5	6	18	6	$\frac{1}{2}$
7	4	7	$3\frac{1}{2}$	7	2	7	15	7	$\frac{1}{4}$
8	2	8	3	8	1	8	12	8	$\frac{1}{8}$

   a.   What quantities of A, B, C, and D will Black purchase in maximizing his satisfactions?

[8] Adam Smith, *The Wealth of Nations* (New York: Modern Library, Inc., originally published in 1776), p. 28.

b.   How many dollars will Black choose to save?

c.   Check your answers by substituting in the algebraic statement of the utility-maximizing rule.

6   "In the long run it may be irrational to purchase goods on the basis of habit; but in the short run habitual buying may prove to be a very sensible means of allocating income." Do you agree? Explain.

7   Summarize Becker's revision of the theory of consumer choice. Discuss the implications of the following statement: "Although time must be considered as a scarce resource to be allocated among different uses, time differs from other resources in that its supply cannot be augmented."

8   Explain:

a.   "Before economic growth, there were too few goods; after growth, there is too little time."

b.   "It is irrational for an individual to take the time to be completely rational in his economic decision making."

9   *Advanced analysis.* Let $MU_a = z = 10 - x$ and $MU_b = z = 21 - 2y$, where z is marginal utility measured in utils, x is the amount spent on product A, and y is the amount spent on product B. Assume the consumer has \$10 to spend on A and B; that is, $x + y = 10$. How is this \$10 best allocated between A and B? How much utility will the marginal dollar yield?

Selected References

Bennett, Peter D., and Harold H. Kassarjian: *Consumer Behavior* (Englewood Cliffs, N.J.: Prentice-Hall, Inc., 1972).

Cole, Charles L.: *Microeconomics: A Contemporary Approach* (New York: Harcourt Brace Jovanovich, Inc., 1973), chaps. 2–4.

Ferguson, C. E., and S. Charles Maurice: *Economic Analysis,* rev. ed. (Homewood, Ill.: Richard D. Irwin, Inc., 1974), chaps. 3, 4.

Leftwich, Richard H.: *The Price System and Resource Allocation,* 6th ed. (Hinsdale, Ill.: The Dryden Press, Inc., 1976), chaps. 5–7.

Linder, Staffan B.: *The Harried Leisure Class* (New York: Columbia University Press, 1970).

Mansfield, Edwin: *Microeconomics: Theory and Applications,* 2d ed. (New York: W. W. Norton & Company, Inc., 1975), chaps. 2, 3.

Last Word

Does Money Buy Happiness?

The theory of consumer behavior tells us that more money expenditures mean more of the material benefits of life. But do these material benefits result in greater happiness?

The question simply is: Do the facts actually indicate that people who get more money typically feel happier?

The conclusions to which the evidence points, in brief, are these. *In all societies, more money for the individual typically means more individual happiness. However, raising the incomes of all does not increase the happiness of all.* The happiness-income relation provides a classic example of the logical fallacy of composition—*what is true for the individual is not true for society as a whole.*

The resolution of this paradox lies in the relative nature of welfare judgments. Individuals assess their material well-being, not in terms of the absolute amount of goods they have, but relative to a social norm of what goods they ought to have. At any given time, those above the norm typically feel happier than those below. Over time, however, the process of economic advance leads, not only to a general increase in incomes, but also to a corresponding rise in the social norm by which material well-being is judged. This increase in material aspirations in a society, itself produced by material progress, thus negates the positive impact of income growth on happiness that one might have expected from the happiness-income relation among individuals prevailing at any point of time. . . .

What do the data show on the comparative happiness of income groups within a country at a given time? Does greater happiness go with higher income? The answer is, quite clearly, yes. This does not mean that there are no unhappy people among the rich and no happy people among the poor. On the average, however, higher-income people are happier than the poor. For example, in a December 1970 survey of the American population, not much more than a fourth of those in the lowest income group (under $3000 annual income) reported that they were "very happy." In the highest income group identified in the survey (over $15,000) the proportion that was "very happy" was almost twice as great. In successive income groups from low to high, the proportion "very happy" rose steadily. For the typical individual, it would seem, more money brings with it more happiness.

This positive relation between happiness and income appears in every single one of the 30 national population surveys studied. Eleven of these surveys relate to the United States between 1946 and 1970, and 19 other countries, including three communist nations (Poland, Yugoslavia, and Cuba) and 11 countries in Asia, Africa, and Latin America. Note that the association between greater individual happiness and more money appears without exception in widely different countries and social systems—in non-Western as well as Western societies, poor as well as rich countries, Communist as well as non-Communist nations. . . .

In simple comparisons within countries, there is a repeated positive association between income and happiness; but when one compares rich and poor countries, or higher and lower income situations in a given country at two different times, the happiness differences by income levels do not appear.

How can one explain this paradoxical result? If for the individual more money typically means more happiness, why not for society as a whole? The answer lies in the way that people form their welfare judgments. The satisfaction one gets from his material situation depends not on the absolute amount of goods he has, but on how this amount compares with what he thinks he needs. A lot of goods relative to perceived needs makes for a lot of material satisfaction and thus greater happiness; if goods are low compared with needs, the result is relatively less happiness.

A crucial question, then, is how are needs determined. If perceived needs were essentially the same for all people in all times and places, being determined, say, primarily by physiological considerations, then more money would mean more happiness, not only among individuals at a given time, but also in those societies which grow richer over time.

In fact, however, what people perceive as their needs is socially determined, and those who live in richer times and places perceive their needs in more ambitious terms than those in poorer societies. Needs, or material aspirations, are formed as the result of prior and on-going experience in a society—in the language of sociology, through the socialization experience of the individual. Thus what one "needs" as he reaches adulthood typically depends on the impressions he has formed of "how to live" from observing life around him and in his society while growing up.

25

The Costs of Production

Product prices are determined by the interaction of the forces of demand and supply. Preceding chapters have focused our attention upon the factors underlying demand. The basic factor underlying the ability and willingness of firms to supply a product in the market is the cost of production. The production of any good requires the use of economic resources which, because of their relative scarcity, bear price tags. The amount of any product which a firm is willing to supply in the market depends upon the prices (costs) and the productivity of the resources essential to its production, on the one hand, and the price which the product will bring in the market, on the other. The present chapter is concerned with the general nature of production costs. Product prices are introduced in the following several chapters, and the supply decisions of producers are then explained.

ECONOMIC COSTS

The economist's notion of costs goes back to the basic fact that resources are scarce and have alternative uses. Thus, to use a bundle of resources in the production of some particular good means that certain alternative products have been forgone. *Costs in economics have to do with missed opportunities or forgone alternatives.* This conception of costs is clearly embodied in the production possibilities curve of Chapter 2. Note, for example, that at point C in Table 2-1 the cost of producing 100,000 *more* units of bread is the 3000 units of drill presses which must be forgone. This notion of cost is called the *opportunity* or *alternative cost doctrine.* The steel that is used for armaments is not available for the manufacture of automobiles or apartment buildings. And if an assembly-line worker is capable of producing automobiles or washing machines, then the cost to society in employing this worker in an automobile plant is the contribution he would otherwise have made in producing washing machines. The cost to you in reading this chapter is the alternative uses of your time which you must forgo.

□   Explicit and Implicit Costs

Let us now consider costs from the viewpoint of an individual firm. Given the notion of opportunity or alternative costs, we can say that *economic costs are those payments a firm must make, or incomes it must provide, to resource suppliers in order to attract these resources away from alternative lines of production.* These payments or incomes may be either *explicit* or *implicit.* The monetary payments—that is, cash outlays which a firm makes to those "outsiders" who supply labor services, materials, fuel, transportation services, power, and so forth—are called *explicit costs.* But, in addition, a firm may use certain resources which the firm itself owns. Our notion of opportunity costs tells us that, regardless of whether a resource is owned or hired by an enterprise, there is a cost involved in using that resource in a specific employment. The costs of such self-owned, self-employed resources are nonexpenditure or *implicit costs.* To the firm, those implicit costs are the money payments which the self-employed resources could have earned in their best alternative employments. For example, suppose Brooks operates a corner grocery as a sole proprietor. He owns his store building and supplies all his own labor and money capital. Though his enterprise has no explicit rental or wage costs, implicit rents and wages are incurred. By

using his own building for a grocery, Brooks sacrifices the $400 monthly rental income which he could otherwise have earned by renting it to someone else. Similarly, by using his money capital and labor in his own enterprise, Brooks sacrifices the interest and wage incomes which he otherwise could have earned by supplying these resources in their best alternative employments. And, finally, by running his own enterprise, Brooks forgoes the earnings he could realize by supplying his managerial efforts in someone else's firm.

□   Normal Profits as a Cost

The minimum payment required to keep Brooks's entrepreneurial talents engaged in this enterprise is sometimes called a *normal profit.* As is true of implicit rent or implicit wages, his normal return for the performing of entrepreneurial functions is an implicit cost. If this minimum, or normal, return is not realized, the entrepreneur will withdraw his efforts from this line of production and reallocate them to some alternative line of production. Or the individual may cease being an entrepreneur in favor of becoming a wage or salary earner.

In short, the economist includes as costs all payments—explicit and implicit, the latter including a normal profit—required to retain resources in a given line of production.

□   Economic, or Pure, Profits

Our discussion of economic costs correctly suggests that economists and accountants use the term "profits" differently. By "profits" the accountant generally means total receipts less explicit costs. But to the economist, "profits" means total receipts less *all* costs (explicit and implicit, the latter including a normal return to the entrepreneur). Therefore, when an economist says that a firm is just covering its costs, he means that all explicit and implicit costs are being met and that the entrepreneur is therefore receiving a return just large enough to retain his talents in his present line of production. If a firm's total receipts exceed all its economic costs, any residual accrues to the entrepreneur. This residual is called an *economic,* or *pure, profit.* It is not a cost, because by definition it is a return in excess of the normal profit required to retain the entrepreneur in this particular line of production. In Chapter 32 we shall find that economic profits are associated with risk bearing and monopoly power.

□   **Short Run and Long Run**

The costs which a firm or an industry incurs in producing any given output will depend upon the types of adjustment it is able to make in the amounts of the various resources it employs. The quantities employed of many resources—labor, raw materials, fuel, power, and so forth—can be varied easily and quickly. But the amounts of other resources demand more time for adjustment. For example, the capacity of a manufacturing plant, that is, the size of the factory building and the amount of machinery and equipment therein, can only be varied over a considerable period of time. In some heavy industries it may take several years to alter plant capacity.

These differences in the time necessary to vary the quantities of the various resources used in the productive process make it essential to distinguish between the short run and the long run. The *short run* refers to a period of time too brief to permit an enterprise to alter its plant capacity, yet long enough to permit a change in the level at which the fixed plant is utilized. The firm's plant capacity is fixed in the short run, but output can be varied by applying larger or smaller amounts of manpower, materials, and other resources to that plant. Existing plant capacity can be used more or less intensively in the short run.

From the viewpoint of existing firms, the *long run* refers to a period of time extensive enough to allow these firms to change the quantities of *all* resources employed, including plant capacity. From the viewpoint of an in-

dustry, the long run also encompasses enough time for existing firms to dissolve and leave the industry and for new firms to be created and to enter the industry. *While the short run is a "fixed-plant" time period, the long run is a "variable-plant" time period.*

Some examples will make clear the distinction between the short run and the long run. If a General Motors plant were to hire an extra 100 workers or to add an entire shift of workers, this would be a short-run adjustment. If the same GM plant were to add a new wing to its building and install more equipment, this would be a long-run adjustment.

It is important to note that the short run and the long run are conceptual rather than specific calendar time periods. In light manufacturing industries, changes in plant capacity may be negotiated almost overnight. A small firm making men's clothing can increase its plant capacity in a few days or less by ordering and installing a couple of new cutting tables and several extra sewing machines. But heavy industry is a different story. It may take Ford or General Motors several years to construct a new assembly plant and to install elaborate assembly-line equipment.

We turn now to the task of analyzing production costs in the short-run, or fixed-plant, period. Following this we consider costs in the long-run, or variable-plant, period.

■

**PRODUCTION COSTS IN THE
SHORT RUN**

A firm's costs of producing any output will depend not only upon the prices of needed resources, but also upon technology—the quantity of resources it takes to produce that output. It is the latter, technological aspect of costs with which we are concerned for the moment. In the short run a firm can change its output by adding variable resources to a fixed plant. Question: How does output change as more and more variable resources are added to the firm's fixed resources?

□   Law of Diminishing Returns

The answer is provided in general terms by the *law of diminishing returns.* (You will recall that we applied this famous law in aggregative terms in Chapter 19). This engineering law states that *as successive units of a variable resource (say, labor) are added to a fixed resource (capital), beyond some point the extra, or marginal, product attributable to each additional unit of the variable resource will decline.* Stated somewhat differently, if additional workers are applied to a given amount of capital equipment, as is the case in the short run, eventually output will rise less than in proportion to the increase in the number of workers employed. A couple of examples will illustrate this law.

Suppose a farmer has a fixed amount of land—say, 80 acres—in which he has planted corn. Assuming the farmer does not cultivate his cornfields at all, his yield will be, say, 40 bushels per acre. If he cultivates the land once, output may rise to 50 bushels per acre. A second cultivation may increase output to 57 bushels per acre, a third to 61, and a fourth to, say, 63. But further cultivations will add little or nothing to total output. Successive cultivations add less and less to the land's yield. If this were not the case, the world's needs for corn could be fulfilled by extremely intense cultivation of this single 80-acre plot of land. Indeed, if diminishing returns did not occur, the world could be fed out of a flowerpot.

The law of diminishing returns also holds true in nonagricultural industries. Assume a small planing mill is manufacturing wood furniture frames. The mill has a given amount of equipment in the form of lathes, planers, saws, sanders, and so forth. If this firm hired just one or two workers, total output and production per man would be very low. These workers would have a number of different jobs to perform, and the advantages of specialization would be lost. Time would also be lost in switching from one job operation to another, and the machines would stand idle much of the time. In short, the plant would be undermanned, and production therefore would be inefficient. These difficulties would disappear as more workers were added. Equipment would be more fully utilized, and workers could now specialize on a single job. Thus, as more workers are added to the initially undermanned plant, the extra or marginal product of each will tend to rise as a result of more efficient production. But this cannot go on indefinitely. As still more workers are added, problems of overcrowding will arise. Workers must wait in line to use the machinery, so now *workers* are underutilized. The extra, or marginal, product of additional workers declines because the plant is overmanned. There is too much labor in proportion to the fixed amount of capital goods. In the extreme case, the continuous addition of labor to the plant would use up all standing room, and production would be brought to a standstill.

Table 25-1 illustrates the law of diminishing returns numerically. In this instance, diminishing marginal product is incurred with the hire of the third worker. Total product is found by simply accumulating the extra, or marginal, product attributable to each successive worker. Total product will increase so long as marginal product is positive.

Table 25-1   THE LAW OF DIMINISHING RETURNS (*hypothetical data*)

(1) Inputs of the variable resource (labor)	(2) Total product	(3) Extra, or marginal, product
0	0	
		5
1	5	
		8
2	13	
		5
3	18	
		4
4	22	
		3
5	25	
		2
6	27	

□ Fixed, Variable, and Total Costs

The production data described by the law of diminishing returns must be coupled with resource prices to determine the total and per unit costs of producing various outputs. We have already emphasized that in the short run some resources—those associated with the firm's plant—are fixed. Others are variable. This correctly suggests that in the short run, costs can be classified as either fixed or variable.

Fixed Costs *Fixed costs are those costs which in total do not vary with changes in output.* Fixed costs are associated with the very existence of a firm's plant and therefore must be paid even if the firm's rate of output is zero. Such costs as interest on a firm's bonded indebtedness, rental payments, a portion of depreciation on equipment and buildings, insurance premiums, and the salaries of top management and key personnel are generally fixed costs. In column 2 of Table 25-2 we have

assumed that the firm's fixed costs are $100. Note that this fixed-cost figure prevails at all levels of output, including zero.

Variable Costs *Variable costs are those costs which increase with the level of output.* They include payments for materials, fuel, power, transportation services, most labor, and similar variable resources. In column 3 of Table 25-2 we find that the total of variable costs changes with output; but note that the increases in variable costs associated with each one-unit increase in output are not constant. As production begins, variable costs will for a time increase by a decreasing amount; this is true through the fourth unit of output. Beyond the fourth unit, however, variable costs rise by increasing amounts for each successive unit of output. The explanation of this behavior of variable costs lies in the law of diminishing returns. Because of increasing marginal product, smaller and smaller increases in the amounts of variable resources will be needed

Table 25-2 TOTAL- AND AVERAGE-COST SCHEDULES FOR AN INDIVIDUAL FIRM IN THE SHORT RUN (*hypothetical data*)

Total-cost data, per week				Average-cost data, per week			
(1) Total product	(2) Total fixed cost	(3) Total variable cost	(4) Total cost	(5) Average fixed cost	(6) Average variable cost	(7) Average total cost	(8) Marginal cost
(Q)	(TFC)	(TVC)	(TC) $TC = TFC + TVC$	(AFC) $AFC = \dfrac{TFC}{Q}$	(AVC) $AVC = \dfrac{TVC}{Q}$	(ATC) $ATC = \dfrac{TC}{Q}$	(MC) $MC = \dfrac{\text{change in TC}}{\text{change in Q}}$
0	$100	$ 0	$ 100				
1	100	90	190	$100.00	$90.00	$190.00	$ 90
2	100	170	270	50.00	85.00	135.00	80
3	100	240	340	33.33	80.00	113.33	70
4	100	300	400	25.00	75.00	100.00	60
5	100	370	470	20.00	74.00	94.00	70
6	100	450	550	16.67	75.00	91.67	80
7	100	540	640	14.29	77.14	91.43	90
8	100	650	750	12.50	81.23	93.73	110
9	100	780	880	11.11	86.67	97.78	130
10	100	930	1030	10.00	93.00	103.00	150

for a time to get successive units of output produced. This means that total variable costs will increase by decreasing amounts. But when marginal product begins to decline as diminishing returns are encountered, it will be necessary to use larger and larger additional amounts of variable resources to produce each successive unit of output. Total variable costs will therefore increase by increasing amounts.

Total Cost *Total cost* is self-defining: it is the *sum of fixed and variable costs at each level of output.* It is shown in column 4 of Table 25-2. At zero units of output, total cost is equal to the firm's fixed costs. Then for each unit of production—1 through 10—total cost varies at the same rate as does variable cost.

Figure 25-1 shows graphically the fixed-, variable-, and total-cost data of Table 25-2. Note that total variable cost is measured from the horizontal axis and total fixed cost is added vertically to total variable cost in locating the total-cost curve.

FIGURE 25-1 TOTAL COST IS THE SUM OF FIXED AND VARIABLE COSTS

Variable costs (VC) vary with output. Fixed costs are independent of the level of output. The total cost (TC) of any output is the vertical sum of the fixed and variable costs of that output.

The distinction between fixed and variable costs is of no little significance to the businessman. Variable costs are those costs which the businessman can control or alter in the short run by changing his level of production. On the other hand, fixed costs are clearly beyond the businessman's control; such costs are incurred and must be paid regardless of output level.

□ **Per Unit, or Average, Costs**

Producers are certainly interested in their total costs, but they are equally concerned with their per unit, or average, costs. In particular, average-cost data are more usable for making comparisons with product price, which is always stated on a per unit basis. Average fixed cost, average variable cost, and average total cost are shown in columns 5 to 7 of Table 25-2. It is important that we know how these unit-cost figures are derived and how they vary as output changes.

Average fixed cost (AFC) is found by dividing total fixed cost (TFC) by the corresponding output (Q). That is,

$$\text{AFC} = \frac{\text{TFC}}{Q}$$

AFC declines as output increases. Whereas total fixed costs are, by definition, independent of output, AFC will decline as output increases. As output increases, a given total fixed cost of $100 is obviously being spread over a larger and larger output. When output is just 1 unit, total fixed costs and AFC are equal— $100. But at 2 units of output, total fixed costs of $100 become $50 worth of fixed costs per unit; then $33.33, as $100 is spread over 3 units; $25, when spread over 4 units; and so forth. This is what businessmen commonly refer to as "spreading the overhead." We find in Figure 25-2 that AFC graphs as a continually declining figure as total output is increased.

Average variable cost (AVC) is calculated

by dividing total variable cost (TVC) by the corresponding output (Q):

$$AVC = \frac{TVC}{Q}$$

AVC declines initially, reaches a minimum, and then increases again. Graphically, this provides us with a U-shaped or saucer-shaped AVC curve, as is shown in Figure 25-2.

Because total variable cost reflects the law of diminishing returns, so must the AVC figures, which are derived from total variable cost. Because of increasing returns it takes fewer and fewer additional variable resources to produce each of the first 4 units of output. As a result, variable cost per unit will decline. AVC hits a minimum with the fifth unit of output, and beyond this point AVC rises as diminishing returns necessitate the use of more and more variable resources to produce each additional unit of output. In more direct terms, at low levels of output production will be relatively inefficient and costly, because the

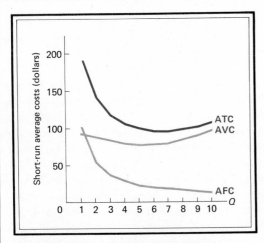

FIGURE 25-2 THE AVERAGE-COST CURVES

Average total cost (ATC) is the vertical sum of average variable cost (AVC) and average fixed cost (AFC). AFC necessarily falls as a given amount of fixed costs is apportioned over a larger and larger output. AVC initially falls because of increasing physical returns but then rises because of diminishing physical returns.

firm's fixed plant is undermanned. Not enough variable resources are being combined with the firm's plant; production is inefficient, and per unit variable costs are therefore relatively high. As output expands, however, greater specialization and a more complete utilization of the firm's capital equipment will make for more efficient production. As a result, variable cost per unit of output will decline. As more and more variable resources are added, some point will eventually be reached where diminishing returns are incurred. The firm's capital equipment will now be overmanned, and the resulting overcrowding and overutilization of machinery impair efficiency. This means that AVC will increase.

Average total cost (ATC) can be found by dividing total cost (TC) by total output (Q) or, more simply, by adding AFC and AVC for each of the ten levels of output. That is,

$$ATC = \frac{TC}{Q} = AFC + AVC$$

These data are shown in column 7 of Table 25-2. Graphically, ATC is found by adding vertically the AFC and AVC curves, as in Figure 25-2. Thus the vertical distance between the ATC and AVC curves reflects AFC at any level of output.

□ **Marginal Cost**

There remains one final and very crucial cost concept—marginal cost. *Marginal cost (MC) is the extra, or additional, cost of producing one more unit of output.* MC can be determined for each additional unit of output simply by noting the change in total cost which that unit's production entails.

$$MC = \frac{change\ in\ TC}{change\ in\ Q}$$

In Table 25-2 we find that production of the first unit of output increases total cost from \$100 to \$190. Therefore, the additional, or marginal, cost of that first unit is \$90. The marginal cost of the second unit is \$80

(= \$270 − \$190); the MC of the third is \$70 (= \$340 − \$270); and so forth. MC for each of the ten units of output is shown in column 8 of Table 25-2. MC can also be calculated from the total-variable-cost column. Why? Because the only difference between total cost and total variable cost is the constant amount of fixed costs. Hence, the change in total cost and change in total variable cost associated with each additional unit of output is the same.

Marginal cost is a strategic concept because it designates those costs over which the firm has the most direct control. More specifically, MC indicates those costs which are incurred in the production of the last unit of output and, simultaneously, the cost which can be "saved" by reducing total output by the last unit. Average-cost figures do *not* provide this information. For example, suppose the firm is undecided as to whether it should produce 3 or 4 units of output. At 4 units of output Table 25-2 indicates that ATC is \$100. But the firm does not increase its total costs by \$100 by producing, nor does it "save" \$100 by not producing, the fourth unit. Rather, the change in costs involved here is only \$60, as the MC column of Table 25-2 clearly reveals. A firm's decisions as to what output to produce are marginal decisions, that is, decisions to produce a few more or a few less units. Marginal cost reveals the change in costs which one more unit or one less unit of output entails. When coupled with marginal revenue, which we found in Chapter 23 indicates the change in revenue from one more or one less unit of output, marginal cost allows a firm to determine whether it is profitable to expand or contract its level of production. The analysis in the next four chapters centers upon these marginal calculations.

Marginal cost is shown graphically in Figure 25-3. Note that marginal cost declines sharply, reaches a minimum, and then rises rather sharply. This mirrors the fact that variable cost, and therefore total cost, increases

FIGURE 25-3   THE RELATIONSHIP OF MARGINAL COST TO AVERAGE TOTAL COST AND AVERAGE VARIABLE COST

Marginal cost (MC) cuts both ATC and AVC at their minimum points. This is so because whenever the extra or marginal amount added to total cost (or variable cost) is less than the average of that cost, the average will necessarily fall. Conversely, whenever the marginal amount added to total (or variable) cost is greater than the average of total cost, the average must rise.

first by decreasing amounts and then by increasing amounts (see Figure 25-1 and columns 3 and 4 of Table 25-2).

MC and Marginal Product   The shape of the marginal-cost curve is a reflection of, and the consequence of, the law of diminishing returns. The relationship between marginal product and marginal cost can be readily grasped by looking back to Table 25-1. If each successive unit of a variable resource (labor) is hired at a constant price, the marginal cost of each extra unit of output will *fall* so long as the marginal product of each additional worker is *rising*. This is so because marginal cost is simply the price or cost of an extra worker divided by his marginal product. Hence, in Table 25-1 suppose each worker can be hired at a cost of \$10. Because the first worker's marginal product is 5 and the hire of this worker increases the firm's costs by $10, the marginal cost of each of these 5 extra units of output will be $2 (= $10 ÷ 5). The second worker also increases costs by $10, but his marginal product is 8, so that the marginal cost of each of these 8 extra units of output is $1.25 (= $10 ÷ 8). In general, so long as marginal product is rising, marginal cost will be falling. But as diminishing returns set in—in this case, with the third worker—marginal cost will begin to rise. Thus, for the third worker, marginal cost is again $2 (= $10 ÷ 5); $2.50 for the fourth worker; $3.33 for the fifth; and $5 for the sixth. The relationship between marginal product and marginal cost is evident: *Given the price* (*cost*) *of the variable resource, increasing returns* (*that is, a rising marginal product*) *will be reflected in a declining marginal cost and diminishing returns* (*that is, a falling marginal product*) *in a rising marginal cost.*

Relation to AVC and ATC It is also notable that marginal cost cuts both AVC and ATC at their minimum points. This marginal-average relationship is a matter of mathematical necessity, which a commonsense illustration can make readily apparent. Suppose a baseball pitcher has allowed his opponents an average of 3 runs per game in the first three games he has pitched. Now, whether his average falls or rises as a result of pitching a fourth (marginal) game will depend upon whether the additional runs he allows in that extra game are fewer or more than his current 3-run average. If he allows fewer than 3 runs—for example, 1—in the fourth game, his total runs will rise from 9 to 10, and his average will fall from 3 to $2\frac{1}{2}$ (= 10 ÷ 4). Conversely, if he allows more than 3 runs—say, 7—in the fourth game, his total will rise from 9 to 16 and his average from 3 to 4 (= 16 ÷ 4). So it is with costs. When the amount added to total cost (marginal cost) is less than the average of total cost, ATC will fall. Conversely, when marginal cost exceeds ATC, ATC will rise. This means in Figure 25-3

that so long as MC lies below ATC, the latter will fall, and where MC is above ATC, ATC will rise. Therefore at the point of intersection where MC equals ATC, ATC has just ceased to fall but has not yet begun to rise. This, by definition, is the minimum point on the ATC curve. Because MC can be defined as the addition either to total cost or to total variable cost resulting from one more unit of output, this same rationale explains why MC also cuts AVC at the latter's minimum point. No such relationship exists for MC and average fixed cost, because the two are not related; marginal cost embodies only those costs which change with output, and fixed costs by definition are independent of output.

Let us now turn to the relationship between output and unit costs when all inputs are variable.

PRODUCTION COSTS IN THE LONG RUN

In the long run all desired resource adjustments can be negotiated by an industry and the individual firms which it comprises. The firm can alter its plant capacity; it can build a larger plant or revert to a smaller plant than that assumed in Table 25-2. The industry can also change its plant size; the long run is an amount of time sufficient for new firms to enter or old firms to leave an industry. The impact of the entry and exodus of firms from an industry will be discussed in the next chapter; here we are concerned only with changes in plant capacity made by a single firm. And in considering these adjustments, we couch our analysis in terms of ATC, making no distinction between fixed and variable costs for the obvious reason that all resources and therefore all costs are variable in the long run.

Suppose a single-plant manufacturing enterprise starts out on a small scale and then, as the result of successful operations, expands to successively larger plant sizes. What will happen to average total costs as this growth occurs? The answer is this: For a time successively larger plants will bring lower average total costs. However, eventually the building of a still larger plant will cause ATC to rise.

Figure 25-4 illustrates this situation for five possible plant sizes. ATC-1 is the average-total-cost curve for the smallest of the five plants, and ATC-5 for the largest. The relationship of the five plant sizes to one another is clearly that stated above. Constructing a larger plant will entail lower per unit costs through plant size 3. But beyond this point a larger plant will mean a higher level of average total costs.

The dotted lines perpendicular to the output axis are crucial. They indicate those points at which the firm should change plant size in order to realize the lowest attainable per unit costs of production. To illustrate in terms of Figure 25-4: For all outputs up to 20 units, the lowest per unit costs are attainable with plant size 1. However, if the firm's volume of sales expands to some level greater than 20 but less than 30 units, it can achieve lower per unit costs by constructing a larger plant—plant size 2. For any output between 30 and 50 units, plant size 3 will yield the lowest per unit costs.

For the 50- to 60-unit range of output, plant size 4 must be built to achieve the lowest unit costs. Lowest per unit costs for any output in excess of 60 units demand the construction of the still larger plant of size 5.

Tracing these adjustments, we can conclude that the long-run ATC curve for the enterprise will comprise segments of the short-run ATC curves for the various plant sizes which can be constructed. *The long-run ATC curve shows the least per unit cost at which any output can be produced after the firm has had time to make all appropriate adjustments in its plant size.* In Figure 25-4 the heavy, bumpy curve is the firm's long-run ATC curve or, as it is often called, the firm's planning curve. In most lines of production the choice of plant sizes is much wider than that assumed in our illustration. In fact, in many industries the number of possible plant sizes is virtually unlimited. This means that in time, very small changes in the volume of output (sales) will prompt appropriate changes in the size of the plant. Graphically, this suggests there is an unlimited number of short-run ATC curves, as suggested by Figure 25-5. The minimum ATC of producing each possible level of output is shown by the long-run ATC curve.

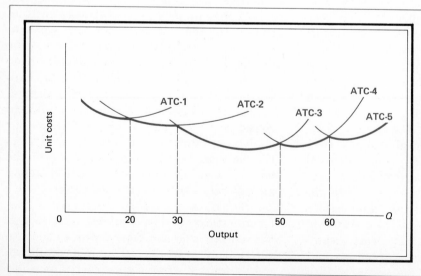

FIGURE 25-4   THE LONG-RUN AVERAGE-COST CURVE: FIVE POSSIBLE PLANT SIZES

The long-run average-cost curve is made up of segments of the short-run cost curves (ATC-1, ATC-2, etc.) of the various-sized plants from which the firm might choose. Each point on the bumpy planning curve shows the least unit cost attainable for any output when the firm has had time to make all desired changes in its plant size.

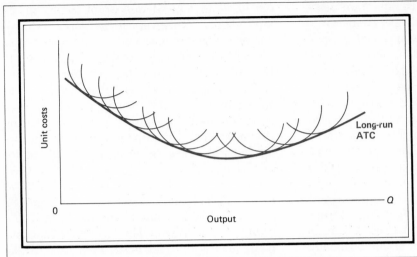

FIGURE 25-5 THE LONG-RUN AVERAGE-COST CURVE: UNLIMITED NUMBER OF PLANT SIZES

If the number of possible plant sizes is very large, the long-run average-cost curve approximates a smooth curve. Economies and diseconomies of scale cause the curve to be U-shaped.

Rather than being comprised of *segments* of short-run ATC curves as in Figure 25-4, the long-run ATC curve is made up of all the *points of tangency* of the unlimited number of short-run ATC curves from which the long-run ATC curve is derived. Hence, the planning curve is smooth rather than bumpy. Note that, with the exception of the minimum point on the long-run ATC curve, the long-run ATC curve is *not* tangent to the short-run ATC curves at the minimum points of the latter. Where the long-run ATC curve is diminishing, the points of tangency are to the left of the minimum points on the short-run ATC curves. Conversely, where long-run ATC is rising, the tangency points are to the right of the minimum points on the short-run ATC curves.

□ **Economies and Diseconomies of Scale**

We have patiently accepted the contention that for a time a larger and larger plant size will entail lower unit costs but that beyond some point successively larger plants will mean higher average total costs. Now we must explain this point. Exactly why is the long-run ATC curve U-shaped? It must be emphasized, first of all, that the law of diminishing returns is *not* applicable here, because it presumes that one resource is fixed in supply and, as we have seen, the long run assumes that all resources are variable. Furthermore, our discussion assumes that resource prices are constant. What, then, is our explanation? The U-shaped long-run average-cost curve is explainable in terms of what economists call "economies and diseconomies" of large-scale production.

Economies of Large Scale Economies of scale or, more commonly, economies of mass production, explain the downsloping part of the long-run ATC curve. As the size of a plant increases, a number of considerations will for a time give rise to lower average costs of production.

1 Labor Specialization Increased specialization in the use of labor is feasible as a plant increases in size. The hire of more workers means that jobs can be divided and subdivided. Instead of performing five or six distinct operations in the productive process, each worker may now have just one task to perform. Workers can be used full time on those particular operations at which they have special skills. In a small plant a skilled machinist may spend half his time performing unskilled tasks. This makes for high production costs. Further, the dividing of work operations which large scale allows will give workers the opportunity to become very proficient at the specific tasks assigned them. The jack-of-all-trades who is burdened with five or six jobs will not be likely to become very efficient in any of them. When allowed to concentrate on one task, the same worker may become highly efficient. Finally, greater specialization tends to eliminate the loss of time which accompanies the shifting of workers from one job to another.

2 Managerial Specialization Large-scale production also permits better utilization of, and greater specialization in, management. A foreman capable of handling fifteen or twenty men will be underutilized in a small plant hiring only eight or ten men. The production staff can be doubled with no increase in administrative costs. In addition, small firms will not be able to use management specialists to best advantage. In a small plant a sales specialist may be forced to divide his time between several executive functions—for example, marketing, personnel, and finance. A larger scale of operations will mean that the marketing expert can devote full time to supervising sales and product distribution while appropriate specialists are added to perform other managerial functions. Greater efficiency and lower unit costs are the net result.

3 Efficient Capital Small firms are often not able to utilize the most efficient productive equipment. In many lines of production the most efficient machinery is available only in very large and extremely expensive units. Furthermore, effective utilization of this equipment demands a high volume of production. This means only large-scale producers are able to afford and operate efficiently the best available equipment.

To illustrate: In the automobile industry the most efficient fabrication method entails the use of extremely elaborate assembly-line equipment. The efficient use of this equipment

demands an annual output of thousands of automobiles. Only very large-scale producers can afford to purchase and use this equipment efficiently. The small-scale producer is between the devil and the deep blue sea. To fabricate automobiles with the use of other equipment is inefficient and therefore more costly per unit. The alternative of purchasing the most efficient equipment and underutilizing it with a small level of output is equally inefficient and costly.

4 By-products The large-scale producer is in a better position to utilize by-products than is a small firm. The large meat-packing plant makes glue, fertilizer, pharmaceuticals, and a host of other products from animal remnants which would be discarded by smaller producers.

All these technological considerations—greater specialization in the use of labor and management, the ability to use the most efficient equipment, and the effective utilization of by-products—will contribute to lower unit costs for the producer who is able to expand his scale of operations.

Diseconomies of Large Scale But in time the expansion of a firm *may* give rise to diseconomies and therefore higher per unit costs.

The main factor causing diseconomies of scale has to do with certain managerial problems involved in efficiently controlling and coordinating a firm's operations as it becomes a large-scale producer. In a small plant a single key executive may render all the basic decisions relative to his plant's operation. Because of the firm's smallness, he is close to the production line. He can, therefore, readily comprehend the various aspects of the firm's operations, easily digest the information fed to him by his subordinates, and render clear and efficient decisions.

This neat picture changes, however, as a firm grows. The management echelons between the executive suite and the assembly line become many; top management is far removed from the actual production operations of the plant. It becomes impossible for one man to assemble, understand, and digest all the information essential to rational decision making in a large-scale enterprise. Authority must be delegated to innumerable vice-presidents, second vice-presidents, and so forth. This expansion in the depth and width of management entails problems of coordination and bureaucratic red tape and the possibility that the decisions of various subordinates will fail to mesh. The result is impaired efficiency and rising average costs.

The relevance of diseconomies of scale is not universally accepted by economists. Indeed, the existence and continued growth of such gigantic corporations as General Motors, AT&T, Exxon, and Prudential Life Insurance seem to cast doubt on the concept. In practice, computer-assisted communication systems have often been developed and applied for the purpose of overcoming or forestalling the decision-making problems embodied in the notion of diseconomies of scale. In cases where these efforts are successful, the long-run average-cost curve would fall and then become more or less constant as economies of scale are exhausted.

☐ **Significance**

Economies and diseconomies of scale are something more than a plausible pipe dream of economic theorists. Indeed, in most American manufacturing industries economies of scale have been of great significance. Firms which have been able to expand their scale of operations to realize the economies of mass production have survived and flourished. Those unable to achieve this expansion have found themselves in the unenviable position of high-cost producers, doomed to a marginal existence or ultimate insolvency.

Diseconomies of scale, when encountered, can be equally significant. The organizational structure of General Motors, for example, is

designed to avoid managerial diseconomies which its gigantic size would otherwise entail. This industrial colossus has subdivided itself into some thirty-seven operating subdivisions, each of which is basically autonomous and in some cases—for example, its five automobile-producing divisions (Chevrolet, Buick, Oldsmobile, Pontiac, and Cadillac)—competing. A degree of decentralization has been sought

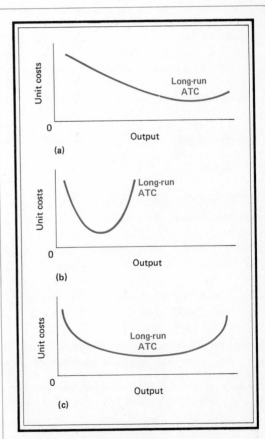

FIGURE 25-6 VARIOUS POSSIBLE LONG-RUN AVERAGE-COST CURVES

(a) When economies of scale are many and diseconomies remote, the ATC will fall over a wide range of production. (b) If economies of scale are few and diseconomies are quickly incurred, minimum unit costs will be encountered at a relatively low output. (c) Where economies of scale are rather rapidly exhausted and diseconomies not encountered until a considerably large scale of output has been achieved, long-run average costs will be relatively constant over a wide range of output.

which will allow full realization of the economies of mass production yet help to avoid diseconomies of scale.[1] Another example: Some economists feel that over the years U.S. Steel has declined in relative importance in the steel industry because of diseconomies of scale. One authority has described U.S. Steel as[2]

> . . . a big sprawling inert giant, whose production operations were improperly coordinated; suffering from a lack of a long-run planning agency; relying on an antiquated system of cost accounting; with an inadequate knowledge of the costs or of the relative profitability of the many thousands of items it sold; with production and cost standards generally below those considered everyday practice in other industries; with inadequate knowledge of its domestic markets and no clear appreciation of its opportunities in foreign markets; with less efficient production facilities than its rivals had; slow in introducing new processes and new products.

These comments correctly imply that economies and diseconomies of scale are a fundamental determinant of the structure of any industry. Where economies of scale are many and diseconomies are remote, the long-run ATC curve will decline over a long range of output, as in Figure 25-6a. Such is the case in the automobile, aluminum, steel, and a host of other heavy industries. This means that, given consumer demand, efficient production will be achieved only with a small number of large producers. On the other hand, where economies of scale are few and diseconomies quickly encountered, minimum unit costs will be achieved at a modest level of production. The long-run ATC curve for such a situation is shown in Figure 25-6b. In such industries a given level of consumer demand will support a large number of relatively small producers. Many of the retail trades and some types of farming fall into this category. So do certain types of light manufacturing, for example, the baking, clothing, and shoe industries. Fairly small firms are as efficient as, or more efficient than, large-scale producers in such industries.

In some industries we find a mixture of large and small producers operating with roughly the same degree of efficiency—the meat-packing, furniture, and some aspects of the household-appliance industries are representative. In such industries the long-run ATC curve may be such that there exists a wide range of output between the point at which available economies of scale are exhausted and the point at which diseconomies of scale are encountered. Or, alternatively, economies and diseconomies of scale may be largely self-canceling over an extended range of output. Figure 25-6c illustrates the situation in which average costs are relatively constant over a wide range of output.

Caution: We are not implying here that long-run unit costs are the only determinant of the structure of industry. Indeed, it was stressed in Chapter 22 that the major determinants of the competitiveness of industry are several and varied. We are saying that there is considerable evidence that cost considerations are one important force in determining the number and size of firms in a particular industry.

---

[1] See Leonard W. Weiss, *Economics and American Industry* (New York: John Wiley & Sons, Inc., 1961), pp. 347–350.
[2] Statement by George Stocking, cited in Walter Adams (ed.), *The Structure of American Industry*, 4th ed. (New York: The Macmillan Company, 1971), pp. 112–113.

Summary

1 Economic costs include all payments which must be received by resource owners in order to assure their continued supply in a particular line of production. This definition includes explicit costs which flow to resource suppliers who are separate from a given enterprise and also implicit costs which are the remuneration of self-owned and self-employed resources. One of the implicit cost payments is a normal profit to the entrepreneur for the functions he performs.

2 In the short run a firm's plant capacity is fixed. The firm can use its plant more or less intensively by adding or subtracting units of variable resources, but the firm does not have sufficient time to alter its plant size.

3 The law of diminishing returns describes what happens to output as a fixed plant is used more intensively. The law states that as successive units of a variable resource such as labor are added to a fixed plant, beyond some point the resulting marginal product associated with each additional worker will decline.

4 Because some resources are variable and others fixed, costs can be classified as variable or fixed in the short run. Fixed costs are those which are independent of the level of output. Variable costs are those which vary with output. The total cost of any output is the sum of fixed and variable costs at that output.

5 Average fixed, average variable, and average total costs are simply fixed, variable, and total costs per unit of output. Average fixed costs decline continuously as output increases, because a fixed sum is being apportioned over a larger and larger number of units of production. Average variable costs are U-shaped, reflecting the law of diminishing returns. Average total cost is the sum of average fixed and average variable costs; it too is U-shaped.

6 Marginal cost is the extra, or additional, cost of producing one more unit of output. Graphically, marginal cost cuts ATC and AVC at their minimum points.

7 The long run is a period of time sufficiently long for a firm to vary the amounts of all resources used, including plant size. Hence, in the long run all costs are variable. The long-run ATC, or planning, curve is composed of segments of the short-run ATC curves, which represent the various plant sizes a firm is able to construct in the long run.

8 The long-run ATC curve is generally U-shaped. Economies of scale are first encountered as a small firm expands. A number of considerations—greater specialization in the use of labor and management, the ability to use the most efficient equipment, and the more complete utilization of by-products—contribute to these economies of scale. Diseconomies of scale stem from the managerial complexities which accompany large-scale production. The relative importance of economies and diseconomies of scale in an industry is often a major determinant of the structure of that industry.

Questions and Study Suggestions

1 Key terms and concepts to remember: economic (opportunity) cost; explicit and implicit costs; normal and economic profits; short run and long run; law of diminishing returns; fixed costs; variable costs; total cost; average fixed cost; average variable cost; average total cost; marginal cost; economies and diseconomies of scale.

2 Distinguish between explicit and implicit costs, giving examples of each. What are the explicit and implicit costs of going to college? Why does the economist classify normal profits as a cost? Are economic profits a cost of production?

3 Which of the following are short-run and which are long-run adjustments? *a.* General Motors builds a new assembly plant; *b.* Acme Steel Corporation hires 200 more workers; *c.* a farmer increases the amount of fertilizer used on his corn crop; and *d.* an Alcoa plant adds a third shift of workers.

4 Explain the law of diminishing returns. What bearing does this law have upon short-run costs? Be specific. "When marginal product is rising, marginal cost is falling. And when marginal product is diminishing, marginal cost is rising." Illustrate and explain graphically and through a numerical example.

5   Why can the distinction between fixed and variable costs be made in the short run? Classify the following as fixed or variable costs: advertising expenditures, fuel, interest on company-issued bonds, shipping charges, payments for raw materials, real estate taxes, executive salaries, insurance premiums, wage payments, depreciation and obsolescence charges, sales taxes, and rental payments on leased office machinery. "There are no fixed costs in the long run; all costs are variable." Explain.

6   Assume a firm has fixed costs of $60 and variable costs as indicated in the following table. Complete the table. When finished, check your calculations by referring to question 5 at the end of Chapter 26.

Total product	Total fixed cost	Total variable cost	Total cost	Average fixed cost	Average variable cost	Average total cost	Marginal cost
0	$____	$ 0	$____	$____	$____	$____	
1	____	45	____	____	____	____	$____
2	____	85	____	____	____	____	____
3	____	120	____	____	____	____	____
4	____	150	____	____	____	____	____
5	____	185	____	____	____	____	____
6	____	225	____	____	____	____	____
7	____	270	____	____	____	____	____
8	____	325	____	____	____	____	____
9	____	390	____	____	____	____	____
10	____	465	____	____	____	____	____

a. Graph fixed cost, variable cost, and total cost. Explain how the law of diminishing returns influences the shapes of the variable-cost and total-cost curves.

b. Graph AFC, AVC, ATC, and MC. Explain the derivation and shape of each of these four curves and the relationships which they bear to one another. Specifically, explain in nontechnical terms why MC cuts both AVC and ATC at their minimum points.

7   Use the concepts of economies and diseconomies of scale to explain the shape of a firm's long-run ATC curve. What bearing may the exact shape of this curve have upon the structure of an industry?

Selected References

Bain, Joe S.: *Industrial Organization,* 2d ed. (New York: John Wiley & Sons, Inc., 1968), pp. 166–180.

Kaish, Stanley: *Microeconomics: Logic, Tools, and Analysis* (New York: Harper & Row, Publishers, Incorporated, 1976), chap. 6.

Robinson, E. A. G.: *The Structure of Competitive Industry* (Chicago: The University of Chicago Press, 1958).

Stigler, George J.: *The Theory of Price,* 3d ed. (New York: The Macmillan Company, 1966), chaps. 6–8.

Watson, Donald S. (ed.): *Price Theory in Action,* 2d ed. (Boston: Houghton Mifflin Company, 1969), part 3.

Last Word
Economies of Scale at American Motors

The Chairman of the Board discusses economies of scale as they relate to American Motors.

A few years ago the Small Business Administration declared American Motors to be a small business. At the time, AMC had 40,000 employees, ranked as the 100th largest American corporation, and turned out 300,000 cars a year. *Small?* By the standards of its competition—General Motors with $36 billion in sales, Ford with $23 billion—AMC is small. But small on this scale doesn't have to mean inefficient.

"We all build cars the same way," says American Motors' Chairman Roy Chapin, "and we know that in the basic assembly structure of our vehicle—between the time the body starts and the time it comes off as a finished vehicle—our hours per car are *less* than some of our competitors'. Our return on equity is about the same as GM's. We think we've done a more efficient job of organizing our manpower, our tooling, the speeds at which we run our lines."

AMC's present prosperity is so impressive as to lend grist to the claims of Senator Philip Hart (Dem., Mich.) and others that medium-sized companies are just as efficient as huge ones and that GM, as a consequence, ought to be split up into as many as 12 independent companies.

"The one area where Senator Hart has validity," Chapin says, "is that when you get beyond a certain size, the economies of scale do not just continue *ad infinitum*. You can build a very profitable, viable automobile company on a volume of between 300,000 and 500,000 units a year. At American Motors we really have only two major product categories: the Matador/Ambassador and the Hornet/Gremlin. Both have basically the same tooling and use the same parts, but the vehicles look different and serve somewhat different purposes. If your volume, like ours, runs between 150,000 and 350,000 units in each of those categories, your cost per unit will be just a few dollars more than somebody making twice as many."

Which is why AMC now looks like a winner again. With the demand for AMC's small cars booming, the production economies that worked against it when it was producing 300,000 cars a year have now—at 420,000—begun working for it.

"Here's a quick lesson in automotive economics. You have a big block like this," Chapin says, shaping an invisible square with his hands. "That's your fixed costs. That's me, the building, utilities, amortization of your tooling—all the things that are constant whether you make a car or you don't. What you then have to do is make enough vehicles with enough marginal profit to cover that block. Let's say that marginal profit is $1,000 a vehicle. Once you get above that so-called break-even point, every extra $1,000 goes into your pocket. Since you don't have any additional fixed costs, those extra $1,000s are, in effect, free up to a certain point.

"At that point you have to build another assembly plant, fill another assembly line, buy another set of tools, put in another set of supervisors, hire more typists to fill out schedules. You have to duplicate almost all of your fixed costs. The trick is to get maximum productivity out of a given set of fixed costs, without having to add another set."

How soon those additional costs start paying for themselves depends on volume. "Say we want to build another 200,000 units to keep pace with demand," says Chapin. "Once you pass the 500,000 mark, the first 50,000 are going to cost you money; the next 100,000 will probably not leave you much better off, if any. Until you get to 650,000 you haven't really got your bait back for building all those new facilities. These are not our numbers, by the way, but the principle is correct."

Chapin is not simply musing in a vacuum. AMC is already near the half-million-car maximum capability of its existing organization. "We'll make $50 million, let's say, this year on our 400,000 units, but if we went to 700,000 and had to duplicate all this all over again, that $50 million might turn out to be $75 million or something like that." Except that Chapin can't double AMC's sales or production overnight. So in the meantime any increase in size would probably be less efficient.

"The Economies of Scale Do Not Just Continue." Reprinted by permission of *Forbes Magazine* from the May 15, 1974, issue.

26

Price and Output Determination: Pure Competition

We now have at our disposal the basic tools of analysis needed to understand how product price and output are determined. These analytical tools are applicable to all four basic market models—pure competition, pure monopoly, monopolistic competition, and oligopoly. In this chapter we focus attention upon price and output determination in a purely competitive industry.

PURE COMPETITION: CONCEPT AND OCCURRENCE

Pure competition, you will recall, presupposes that certain specific conditions are fulfilled.

1 By definition, a purely competitive industry is composed of a large number of independent sellers.

2 The firms offer a standardized product. This feature rules out nonprice competition, that is, advertising, sales promotion, and so forth.

3 No individual firm supplies enough of the product to influence its market price noticeably.

4 In a competitive industry no artificial obstacles prevent new firms from entering, or existing firms from leaving, the industry. Firms and the resources they employ are shiftable, or mobile.

The third characteristic is particularly important. The individual competitive firm has nothing to say about determining market price. Because it supplies a negligible portion of total output, the competitive firm cannot significantly influence the market price which the forces of total demand and supply have established. The competitive firm does not have a price policy, that is, the ability to adjust price. Rather, the firm can merely *adjust to* the market price, which it must regard as a given datum determined by the market. The competitive seller is said to be a price *taker,* rather than a price *maker.*

Pure competition is rare in practice. This does not mean, however, that an analysis of how competitive markets work is a useless and irrelevant exercise in logic.

1 In the first place, there are a few industries which more closely approximate the competitive model than they do any other market structure. For example, much can be learned about American agriculture by understanding the functioning of competitive markets.

2 Moreover, pure competition provides the simplest context in which to apply the revenue and cost concepts developed in previous chapters. Pure competition is a clear and meaningful starting point for any discussion of price and output determination.

3 Finally, in the concluding section of this chapter we shall discover that the operation of a purely competitive economy provides us with a standard, or norm, against which the efficiency of the real-world economy can be compared and evaluated.

Though pure competition is a relatively rare market structure in our economy, it is one of considerable analytical and some practical importance.

Our analysis of pure competition centers upon three major objectives. First, we seek an understanding of how a competitive producer adjusts to market price in the short run. Next, the nature of long-run adjustments in a competitive industry is explored. Finally, we seek to evaluate the efficiency of competitive industries from the standpoint of society as a whole.

PROFIT MAXIMIZATION IN THE SHORT RUN

In the short run the competitive firm has a fixed plant and is attempting to maximize its profits or, as the case may be, minimize its losses by adjusting its output through changes in the amounts of variable resources (materials, labor, and so forth) it employs. The economic profits it seeks are obviously the difference between total revenue and total costs. Indeed, this points out the direction of our analysis. The revenue data of Chapter 23 and the cost data of Chapter 25 must be brought together in order that the profit-maximizing output for the firm can be determined.

There are two complementary approaches to determining the level of output at which a competitive firm will realize maximum profits or minimum losses. The first involves a comparison of total revenue and total costs; the second, a comparison of marginal revenue and marginal cost. Both approaches, incidentally, can be applied not only to a purely competitive firm but also to firms operating in any of the other three basic market structures. To ensure an understanding of output determination under pure competition, we shall invoke both approaches, emphasizing the marginal approach. Furthermore, hypothetical data in both tabular and graphic form will be employed to bolster our understanding of the two approaches.

□ Total-Receipts–Total-Cost Approach

Given the market price of its product, the competitive producer is faced with three related questions: (1) Should we produce? (2) If so, what amount? (3) What profit (or loss) will be realized?

At first glance, the answer to question 1 seems obvious: "You should produce if it is profitable to do so." But the situation is a bit more complex than this. In the short run a part of the firm's total costs is variable costs, and the remainder is fixed costs. The latter will have to be paid "out of pocket" even when the firm is closed down. In the short run a firm takes a loss equal to its fixed costs when it is producing zero units of output. This means that, although there may be no level of output at which the firm can realize a profit, the firm might still produce, provided that in so doing, it can realize a loss less than the fixed-cost loss it will face in closing down. In other words, the correct answer to the "Should we produce?" question is this: *The firm should produce in the short run if it can realize either an economic profit or a loss which is less than its fixed costs.*

Assuming the firm *will* produce, the second question becomes relevant: "How much should be produced?" The answer here is fairly obvious: *In the short run the firm should produce that output at which it maximizes profits or minimizes losses.*

Now let us examine three cases which will demonstrate the validity of these two generalizations and answer our third query by indicating how profits and losses can be readily calculated. In the first case the firm will maximize its profits by producing. In the second case it will minimize its losses by producing. In the third case the firm will minimize its losses by closing down. Our plan of attack is to as-

sume given short-run cost data for all three cases and to explore the firm's production decisions when faced with three different product prices.

Profit-maximizing Case In all three cases we employ cost data with which we are already familiar. Columns 3 through 5 of Table 26-1 merely repeat the fixed-, variable-, and total-cost data which were developed in Table 23-2. Assuming that market price is $131, we can derive total revenue for each level of output by simply multiplying output times price, as we did in Table 23-3. These data are presented in column 2. Then in column 6 the profit or loss which will be encountered at each output is found by subtracting total cost from total revenue. Now we have all the data needed to answer the three questions.

Should the firm produce? Yes, because it can realize a profit by doing so. How much? Nine units, because column 6 tells us that this is the output at which profits will be at a maximum. The size of that profit? $299.

Figure 26-1a compares total revenue and total cost graphically. Total revenue is a straight line, because under pure competition each additional unit adds the same amount— its price—to total revenue (Chapter 23). Total

Table 26-1 THE PROFIT-MAXIMIZING OUTPUT FOR A PURELY COMPETITIVE FIRM: TOTAL-REVENUE–TOTAL-COST APPROACH (PRICE = $131) (*hypothetical data*)

(1) Total product	(2) Total revenue	(3) Total fixed cost	(4) Total variable cost	(5) Total cost	(6) Profit (+) or loss (−), = (2) − (5)
0	$ 0	$100	$ 0	$ 100	$−100
1	131	100	90	190	− 59
2	262	100	170	270	− 8
3	393	100	240	340	+ 53
4	524	100	300	400	+124
5	655	100	370	470	+185
6	786	100	450	550	+236
7	917	100	540	640	+277
8	1048	100	650	750	+298
9	1179	100	780	880	+299
10	1310	100	930	1030	+280

(a) Profit-maximizing case

(b) Loss-minimizing and close-down cases

FIGURE 26-1 THE PROFIT-MAXIMIZING (a), LOSS-MINIMIZING, AND CLOSE-DOWN CASES (b), AS SHOWN BY THE TOTAL-REVENUE-TOTAL-COST APPROACH

A firm's profits are maximized in (a) at that output at which total revenue exceeds total cost by the maximum amount. A firm will minimize its losses in (b) by producing at that output at which total cost exceeds total revenue by the smallest amount. However, if there is no output at which total revenue exceeds variable costs, the firm will minimize losses in the short run by closing down.

costs increase with output; more production requires more resources. But the rate of increase in total costs varies with the relative efficiency of the firm. Specifically, the cost data reflect Chapter 25's law of diminishing returns. That is, for a time the rate of increase in total cost is less and less as the firm utilizes its fixed resources more efficiently. Then, after a time, total cost begins to rise by ever-increasing amounts because of the inefficiencies which accompany overutilization of the firm's plant. Comparing total cost with total revenue in Figure 26-1*a*, we note that a *break-even point* occurs at about 2 units of output. And, if our data were extended beyond 10 units of output, another such point would be incurred where total cost would catch up with total revenue, as is shown in Figure 26-1*a*. Any output outside of these points will entail losses. Any output within these break-even points will entail an economic profit. The maximum profit is obviously achieved where the vertical difference between total revenue and total cost is greatest. For our data this is at 9 units of output and the resulting maximum profit is $299.

Loss-minimizing Case Assuming no change in costs, the firm may not be able to realize economic profits if the market yields a price considerably below $131. To illustrate: Suppose the market price is $81. As column 6 of Table 26-2 indicates, at this price all levels of output will entail losses. But the firm will not close down. Why? Because, by producing, the firm can realize a loss considerably less than the fixed-cost loss it would incur by closing down. Specifically, the firm will minimize its losses by producing 6 units of output. The resulting $64 loss is clearly preferable to the $100 loss which closing down would involve. Stated differently, by producing 6 units the firm earns a total revenue of $486, sufficient to pay all the firm's variable cost ($450) and also a substantial portion—$36 worth—of the firm's $100 of fixed costs. There are, you will note, several other outputs which entail a loss less than the firm's $100 fixed costs; but at 6 units of output the loss is minimized.

Close-down Case Assume finally that the market price is a mere $71. Given short-run costs, column 9 of Table 26-2 clearly indi-

Table 26-2 THE LOSS-MINIMIZING OUTPUTS FOR A PURELY COMPETITIVE FIRM: TOTAL-REVENUE–TOTAL-COST APPROACH (PRICES = $81 and $71) (*hypothetical data*)

	Product price = $81					Product price = $71		
(1) Total product	(2) Total revenue	(3) Total fixed cost	(4) Total variable cost	(5) Total cost	(6) Profit (+) or loss (−), = (2) − (5)	(7) Total revenue	(8) Total cost	(9) Profit (+) or loss (−), = (7) − (8)
0	$ 0	$100	$ 0	$ 100	$−100	$ 0	$ 100	$−100
1	81	100	90	190	−109	71	190	−119
2	162	100	170	270	−108	142	270	−128
3	243	100	240	340	− 97	213	340	−127
4	324	100	300	400	− 76	284	400	−116
5	405	100	370	470	− 65	355	470	−115
6	**486**	**100**	**450**	**550**	**− 64**	426	550	−124
7	567	100	540	640	− 73	497	640	−143
8	648	100	650	750	−102	568	750	−182
9	729	100	780	880	−151	639	880	−241
10	810	100	930	1030	−220	710	1030	−320

cates that at all levels of output, losses will exceed the $100 fixed-cost loss the firm will incur by closing down. Obviously, then, the firm will minimize its losses by closing down, that is, by producing zero units of output.

Figure 26-1*b* demonstrates the loss-minimizing and close-down cases graphically. In the loss-minimizing case, the total-revenue line TR ($P = \$81$) exceeds total variable cost by the maximum amount at 6 units of output. Here total revenue is $486, and the firm recovers all of its $450 of variable costs and also $36 worth of its fixed costs. The firm's minimum loss is $64, clearly superior to the $100 fixed-cost loss involved in closing down. In the close-down case, the total-revenue line TR ($P = \$71$) lies below the total-variable-cost curve at all points; there is no output at which variable costs can be recovered. Therefore, the firm, by producing, would incur losses in excess of its fixed costs. The firm's best choice is to close down and pay its $100 fixed-cost loss out of pocket.

□ **Marginal-Revenue–Marginal-Cost Approach**

An alternative means for determining the amounts which a competitive firm will be willing to offer in the market at each possible price is for the firm to determine and compare the amounts that each *additional* unit of output will add to total revenue, on the one hand, and to total cost, on the other. That is, the firm should compare the *marginal revenue* (MR) and the *marginal cost* (MC) of each successive unit of output. Any unit whose marginal revenue exceeds its marginal cost should obviously be produced. Why? Because on each such unit, the firm is gaining more in revenue from its sale than it adds to costs in getting that unit produced. Hence, the unit of output is adding to profits or, as the case may be, subtracting from losses. Similarly, if the marginal cost of a unit of output exceeds its marginal

revenue, the firm should avoid producing that unit. It will add more to costs than to revenue; such a unit will not "pay its way."

MR = MC Rule In the initial stages of production, where output is relatively low, marginal revenue will usually (but not always) exceed marginal cost. It is therefore profitable to produce through this range of output. But at later stages of production, where output is relatively high, rising marginal costs will cause the reverse to be true. Marginal cost will exceed marginal revenue. Production of units of output falling in this range is obviously to be avoided in the interest of maximizing profits. Separating these two production ranges will be a unique point at which marginal revenue equals marginal cost. This point is the key to the output-determining rule: *The firm will maximize profits or minimize losses by producing at that point where marginal revenue equals marginal cost.* For convenience we shall call this profit-maximizing guide the MR = MC rule. For most sets of MR and MC data, there will be no nonfractional level of output at which MR and MC are precisely equal. In such instances the firm should produce the last complete unit of output whose MR exceeds its MC.

Three Characteristics Three features of this MR = MC rule merit comment. First, a qualification: The rule assumes that the firm will choose to produce rather than close down. Shortly, we shall note that marginal revenue must be equal to, or must exceed, average variable cost, or the firm will find it preferable to close down rather than produce the MR = MC output.

Second, it is to be emphasized that the MR = MC rule is an accurate guide to profit maximization for all firms, be they purely competitive, monopolistic, monopolistically competitive, or oligopolistic. The rule's application is *not* limited to the special case of pure competition.

A third and related point is that the MR = MC rule can be conveniently restated in a slightly different form when being applied to a purely competitive firm. You will recall that product price is determined by the broad market forces of supply and demand, and although the competitive firm can sell as much or as little as it chooses at that price, the firm cannot manipulate the price itself. In technical terms the demand, or sales, schedule faced by a competitive seller is perfectly elastic at the going market price. The result is that product price and marginal revenue are equal; that is, each extra unit sold adds precisely its price to total revenue (see Figure 23-10). Thus under pure competition—and *only* under pure competition—we may substitute price for marginal revenue in the rule, so that it reads as follows: *To maximize profits or minimize losses the competitive firm should produce at that point where price equals marginal cost* ($P = MC$). This $P = MC$ rule is simply a special case of the MR = MC rule.

Now let us apply the MR = MC or, because we are considering pure competition, the MR $(P) = MC$ rule, using the same three prices employed in our total-revenue–total-cost approach to profit maximization.

Profit-maximizing Case Table 26-3 reproduces the unit- and marginal-cost data derived in Table 25-2. It is, of course, the marginal-cost data of column 5 in Table 26-3 which we wish to compare with price (equal to marginal revenue) for each unit of output. Suppose first that market price, and therefore marginal revenue, is $131, as shown in column 6. What is the profit-maximizing output? It is readily seen that each and every unit of output up to and including the ninth adds more to total revenue than to total cost. That is, price, or marginal revenue, exceeds marginal cost on all of the first 9 units of output. Each of these units therefore adds to the firm's profits and should obviously be produced. The tenth unit, however, will not be produced, because it would add more to costs ($150) than to revenue ($131).

The level of economic profits realized by the firm can be readily calculated from the unit-cost data. Multiplying price ($131) times

Table 26-3 THE PROFIT-MAXIMIZING OUTPUT FOR A PURELY COMPETITIVE FIRM: MARGINAL-REVENUE-EQUALS-MARGINAL-COST APPROACH (PRICE = $131) (*hypothetical data*)

(1) Total product	(2) Average fixed cost	(3) Average variable cost	(4) Average total cost	(5) Marginal cost	(6) Price = marginal revenue
0				$ 90	$131
1	$100.00	$90.00	$190.00	80	131
2	50.00	85.00	135.00	70	131
3	33.33	80.00	113.33	60	131
4	25.00	75.00	100.00	70	131
5	20.00	74.00	94.00	80	131
6	16.67	75.00	91.67	90	131
7	14.29	77.14	91.43	110	131
8	12.50	81.23	93.73	130	131
9	11.11	86.67	97.78	150	131
10	10.00	93.00	103.00		

output (9), we find total revenue to be $1179. Total cost of about[1] $880 is found by multiplying average total cost ($97.78) by output (9). The difference of $299 is economic profits. An alternative means of calculating economic profits is to determine profit *per unit* by subtracting average total cost ($97.78) from product price ($131) and multiplying the difference (per unit profits of $33.22) by the level of output (9). The skeptical reader should calculate profits at outputs other than those indicated to be most profitable by the MR (*P*) = MC rule to verify that they entail either losses or profits less than $299.

Figure 26-2 makes the comparison of price and marginal cost graphically. Here per unit economic profit is indicated by the distance *AP*. When multiplied by the profit-maximizing output, the resulting total economic profit is shown by the brown rectangular area.

---

[1] In most instances the unit-cost data are rounded figures. Therefore, economic profits calculated from them will typically vary by a few cents from the profits determined in the total-revenue–total-cost approach. We here ignore the few-cents differentials and make our answers consistent with the results of the total-revenue–total-cost approach.

It should be noted that the firm is seeking to maximize its *total* profits, not its *per unit* profits. Per unit profits are largest at 7 units of output, where price exceeds average total cost by $39.57 ($131 minus $91.43). But by producing only 7 units, the firm would be forgoing the production of additional units of output which would clearly contribute to total profits. The firm is happy to accept lower per unit profits if the resulting extra units of sales more than compensate for the lower per unit profits.

Loss-minimizing Case   Now let us apply the same reasoning on the assumption that market price is $81 rather than $131. Should the firm produce? If so, how much? And what will the resulting profits or losses be? The answers, respectively, are "Yes," "Six units," and "A loss of $64."

Column 6 of Table 26-4 shows the new price (equal to marginal revenue) alongside the same unit- and marginal-cost data presented in Table 26-3. Comparing columns 5 and 6, we find that the first unit of output adds $90 to total cost but only $81 to total revenue. One might be inclined to conclude: "Don't pro-

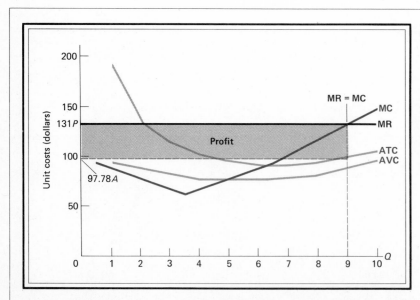

FIGURE 26-2 THE SHORT-RUN PROFIT-MAXIMIZING POSITION OF A PURELY COMPETITIVE FIRM

The *P* = MC output allows the competitive producer to maximize profits or minimize losses. In this case price exceeds average total cost at the *P* = MC output of 9 units. Economic profits per unit of *AP* are realized; total economic profits are indicated by the brown rectangle.

Table 26-4 THE LOSS-MINIMIZING OUTPUTS FOR A PURELY COMPETITIVE FIRM: MARGINAL-REVENUE-EQUALS-MARGINAL-COST APPROACH (PRICES = $81 AND $71) (*hypothetical data*)

(1) Total product	(2) Average fixed cost	(3) Average variable cost	(4) Average total cost	(5) Marginal cost	(6) $81 price = marginal revenue	(7) $71 price = marginal revenue
0						
				$ 90	$81	$71
1	$100.00	$90.00	$190.00	80	81	71
2	50.00	85.00	135.00	70	81	71
3	33.33	80.00	113.33	60	81	71
4	25.00	75.00	100.00	70	81	71
5	20.00	74.00	94.00	80	81	71
6	**16.67**	**75.00**	**91.67**	90	81	71
7	14.29	77.14	91.43	110	81	71
8	12.50	81.23	93.73	130	81	71
9	11.11	86.67	97.78	150	81	71
10	10.00	93.00	103.00			

duce—close down!" But this would be hasty. Remember that in the very early stages of production, marginal physical product is low, making marginal cost unusually high. The price–marginal-cost relationship might improve with increased production. And it does. On the next 5 units—2 through 6—price exceeds marginal cost. Each of these 5 units adds more to revenue than to cost, more than compensating for the "loss" taken on the first unit. Beyond 6 units, however, MC exceeds MR (*P*). The firm should therefore produce at 6 units. In general, the profit-seeking producer should always compare marginal revenue (or price under pure competition) with the *rising* portion of his marginal-cost schedule or curve.

Will production be profitable? No, it will not. At 6 units of output, average total costs of $91.67 exceed price of $81 by $10.67 per unit. Multiply by the 6 units of output, and the firm's total loss is about $64. Then why produce? Because this loss is less than the firm's $100 worth of fixed costs—the $100 loss the firm would incur in the short run by closing down. Looked at differently, the firm receives enough revenue per unit ($81) to cover its variable costs of $75 and also provide $6 per unit, or a total of $36, to apply against the payment

of fixed costs. Therefore, the firm's loss is only $64 (= $100 − $36), rather than $100.

This case is shown graphically in Figure 26-3. Whenever price exceeds the minimum average variable cost but falls short of average total cost, the firm can pay a part of, but not all, its fixed costs by producing. In this instance total variable costs are shown by the area *OVGF*. Total revenue, however, is *OPEF*, greater than total variable costs by *VPEG*. This excess of revenue over variable costs can be applied against total fixed costs, represented by area *VACG*. Stated differently, by producing 6 units the firm's loss is only area *PACE*; by closing down, its loss would be its fixed costs shown by the larger area *VACG*.

Close-down Case Suppose now that the market yields a price of only $71. In this case it will pay the firm to close down, to produce nothing. Why? Because there is no output at which the firm can cover its average variable costs, much less its average total cost. In other words, the smallest loss it can realize by producing is greater than the $100 worth of fixed costs it will lose by closing down. The smart thing is obviously to close down. This can be verified by comparing columns 3 and 7 of Table

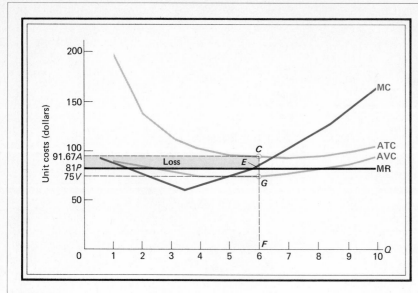

FIGURE 26-3 THE SHORT-RUN LOSS-MINIMIZING POSITION OF A PURELY COMPETITIVE FIRM

If price exceeds the minimum AVC but is less than ATC, the $P = MC$ output of 6 units will permit the firm to minimize its losses. In this instance losses are AP per unit; total losses are shown by the area $APEC$.

26-4 and can be readily visualized in Figure 26-4. Price comes closest to covering average variable costs at the MR $(P) = MC$ output of 5 units. But even here, price or revenue per unit would fall short of average variable cost by \$3 ($= \$74 - \$71$). By producing at the MR (P) $= MC$ output, the firm would lose its \$100 worth of fixed costs *plus* \$15 (\$3 on each of the five units) worth of variable costs, for a total loss of \$115. This clearly compares unfavorably with the \$100 fixed-cost loss the firm would incur by choosing to close down. In short, it

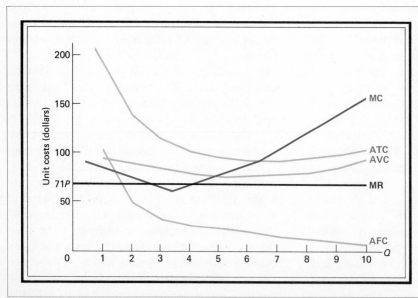

FIGURE 26-4 THE SHORT-RUN CLOSE-DOWN POSITION OF A PURELY COMPETITIVE FIRM

If price falls short of minimum AVC, the competitive firm will minimize its losses in the short run by closing down. There is no level of output at which the firm can produce and realize a loss smaller than its fixed costs.

will obviously pay the firm to close down rather than operate at a $71 price or, for that matter, at any price less than $74.

The close-down case obligates us to modify our MR (P) = MC rule for profit maximization or loss minimization. *A competitive firm will maximize profits or minimize losses in the short run by producing at that output at which MR (P) = MC, provided that price exceeds the minimum average-variable-cost figure.*

Marginal Cost and the Short-run Supply Curve   Now the astute reader will recognize that we have simply selected three different prices and asked how much the profit-seeking competitive firm, faced with certain costs, would choose to offer or supply in the market at each of these prices. This information— price and corresponding quantity supplied— obviously constitutes the supply schedule for the competitive firm. Table 26-5 summarizes the supply-schedule data for the three prices we have chosen—$131, $81, and $71. The reader is urged to apply the MR (P) = MC rule (as modified by the close-down case) to verify the quantity-supplied data for the $151, $111, $91, and $61 prices and calculate the corresponding profits or losses. The supply schedule is obviously upsloping. In this instance, price must be $74 (equal to minimum average variable cost) or greater before any output is supplied. The profit-seeking firm is induced to offer more of the product as higher and higher prices are equated with the mar-

Table 26-5   THE SUPPLY SCHEDULE OF A COMPETITIVE FIRM CONFRONTED WITH THE COST DATA OF TABLE 26-3 (*hypothetical data*)

Price	Quantity supplied	Maximum profit $(+)$ or minimum loss $(-)$
$151	10	$_____
131	9	$+299$
111	8	_____
91	7	_____
81	6	-64
71	0	-100
61	0	_____

ginal cost of larger and larger outputs in the cost table.

Figure 26-5 generalizes upon our application of the MR (P) = MC rule. Here we have drawn the appropriate cost curves. Then from the vertical axis we have extended a series of marginal-revenue lines from some of the various possible prices which the market might set for the firm. The crucial prices are P_2 and P_4. Our close-down case reminds us that at any price *below* P_2—that price equal to the minimum average variable cost—the firm should close down and supply nothing. Actually, by producing Q_2 units of output at a price of P_2, the firm will just cover its variable costs, and its losses will be equal to its fixed costs. The firm therefore would be indifferent as between closing down *or* producing Q_2 units of output. But at any price below P_2, such as P_1, the firm will close down and supply zero units of output. P_4 is strategic because it is the price at which the firm will just break even by producing Q_4 units of output, as indicated by the MR (P) = MC rule. Here total revenue will just cover total costs (including a normal profit). At P_3 the firm supplies Q_3 units of output and, in so doing, minimizes its losses. At any other price between P_2 and P_4, the firm will minimize its losses by producing to the point where MR (P) = MC. At any price above P_4, the firm will maximize its economic profits by producing to the point where MR (P) = MC. Thus at P_5 and P_6 the firm will realize the greatest profits by supplying Q_5 and Q_6 units of output.

The basic point is this: Each of the various MR (P) = MC intersection points shown in Figure 26-5 indicates a possible product price and the corresponding quantity which the profit-seeking firm would supply at that price. These points, by definition, constitute the supply curve of the competitive firm. Because nothing would be produced at any price below the minimum average variable cost, we can conclude that *the portion of the firm's marginal-cost curve which lies above its average-variable-cost curve is its short-run supply curve.* The heavy segment of the marginal-cost

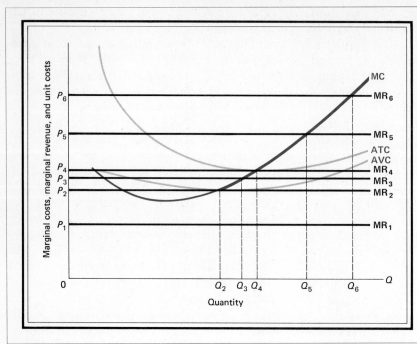

FIGURE 26-5 MARGINAL COST AND THE COMPETITIVE FIRM'S SHORT-RUN SUPPLY

Application of the $P = MC$ rule, as modified by the close-down case, reveals that the segment of the firm's MC curve which lies above AVC is its short-run supply curve. At any price between P_2 and P_4, such as P_3, losses will be minimized by producing the $P = MC$ output. At any price above P_4, such as P_5 or P_6, profits will be maximized at the $P = MC$ output.

curve is the short-run supply curve in Figure 26-5. This is the link between production costs and supply in the short run.

☐ Short-run Competitive Pricing

Let us now pause to summarize the main points we have made concerning short-run competitive pricing. Table 26-6 provides a con-venient check sheet on the total-revenue–total-cost and MR = MC approaches to deter-mining the competitive firm's profit-maximiz-ing output. This table warrants careful study by the reader. In the MR = MC approach it is noteworthy that in deciding whether or not to produce, it is the comparison of price with minimum average *variable* cost which is all-important. Then, in determining the profit-

Table 26-6   SUMMARY OF COMPETITIVE OUTPUT DETERMINATION IN THE SHORT RUN

	Total-revenue–total-cost approach	Marginal-revenue–marginal-cost approach
Should the firm produce?	Yes, if TR exceeds TC or if TC exceeds TR by some amount less than total fixed costs.	Yes, if price is equal to, or greater than, minimum average variable cost.
What quantity should be produced to maximize profits?	Produce where the excess of TR over TC is a maximum or where the excess of TC over TR is a minimum (and less than total fixed costs).	Produce where MR or price equals MC.
Will production result in an economic profit?	Yes, if TR exceeds TC. No, if TC exceeds TR.	Yes, if price exceeds average total cost. No, if average total cost exceeds price.

maximizing or loss-minimizing amount to produce, it is the comparison—or better yet, the equality—of MR (*P*) and MC which is crucial. Finally, in determining the actual profit or loss associated with the MR (*P*) = MC output, price and average *total* cost must be contrasted. A final basic conclusion implied in Table 26-6 is that the segment of the short-run marginal-cost curve which lies above the average-variable-cost curve is the competitive firm's short-run supply curve. This conclusion stems from the application of the MR (*P*) = MC rule and the necessary modification suggested by the close-down case.

□   **Firm and Industry: Equilibrium Price**

Now one final wrap-up step remains. Having developed the competitive firm's short-run supply curve through the application of the MR (*P*) = MC rule, we must determine which of the various price possibilities will actually be the equilibrium price. Recalling Chapter 4, we know that in a purely competitive market, equilibrium price is determined by *total,* or market, supply and total demand. To derive total supply, we know that the sales schedules or curves of the individual competitive sellers must be summed. Thus in Table 26-7, columns 1 and 3 repeat the individual competitive firm's supply schedule just

derived in Table 26-5. Let us now conveniently assume that there are a total of 1000 competitive firms in this industry, each having the same total and unit costs as the single firm we have been discussing. This allows us to calculate the total- or market-supply schedule (columns 2 and 3) by multiplying the quantity-supplied figures of the single firm (column 1) by 1000.

Now, in order to determine equilibrium price and output, this total-supply data must be compared with total-demand data. For purposes of illustration, let us assume total-demand data are as shown in columns 3 and 4 of Table 26-7. Comparing the total quantity supplied and total quantity demanded at the seven possible prices, we readily determine that the equilibrium price is $111 and that equilibrium quantity is 8000 units for the industry and 8 units for each of the 1000 identical firms.

Will these conditions of market supply and demand make this a prosperous or an unprosperous industry? Multiplying product price ($111) by output (8), we find the total revenue of each firm to be $888. Total cost is $750, found by multiplying average total cost of $93.73 by 8, or simply by looking at column 5 of Table 26-1. The $138 difference is the economic profit of each firm. Another way of calculating economic profits is to determine *per unit* profit by subtracting average total cost ($93.73) from product price ($111) and multiplying the difference (per unit profits of $17.27) by the firm's equilibrium level of output (8). For the industry, total economic profit is obviously $138,000. This, then, is a prosperous industry.

Figure 26-6*a* and *b* shows this analysis graphically. The individual supply curves of each of the 1000 identical firms—one of which is shown as *ss* in Figure 26-6*a* are summed horizontally to get the total-supply curve *SS* of Figure 26-6*b*. Given total demand *DD,* equilibrium price is found to be $111, and equilibrium quantity for the industry is 8000 units. This equilibrium price is given and unalterable to the individual firm; that is, the typical firm's

Table 26-7   FIRM AND MARKET SUPPLY AND MARKET DEMAND (*hypothetical data*)

(1) Quantity supplied, single firm	(2) Total quantity supplied, 1000 firms	(3) Product price	(4) Total quantity demanded
10	10,000	$151	4,000
9	9,000	131	6,000
8	**8,000**	**111**	**8,000**
7	7,000	91	9,000
6	6,000	81	11,000
0	0	71	13,000
0	0	61	16,000

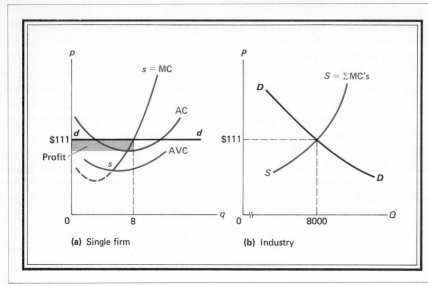

FIGURE 26-6 SHORT-RUN
COMPETITIVE EQUILIBRIUM
FOR A REPRESENTATIVE
FIRM (a) AND THE
INDUSTRY (b)

The horizontal sum of the
1000 firms' supply curves
(*ss*) determines the industry
supply curve (*SS*). Given
industry demand (*DD*), the
short-run equilibrium price
and output for the industry
are $111 and 8000 units.
Taking the equilibrium
price as given datum, the
representative firm es-
tablishes its profit-maximizing output at 8 units and,
in this case, realizes the
economic profit shown
by the brown area.

demand curve is perfectly elastic at the equilibrium price, as indicated by *dd*. Because
price is given and constant to the individual
firm, the marginal-revenue curve coincides
with the demand curve. Price obviously exceeds average total cost at the firm's equilibrium MR (*P*) = MC output, resulting in a situation of economic profits similar to that
already portrayed in Figure 26-2.

Assuming that no changes in costs or
market demand occur, these diagrams reveal a
genuine short-run equilibrium situation.
There are no shortages or surpluses in the
market to cause price or total quantity to
change. Nor can any of the firms making up
the industry improve their profits by altering
their output. Note, too, that higher unit and
marginal costs, on the one hand, or a weaker
market demand situation, on the other, could
have posed a loss situation similar to Figure
26-3. The student is urged to sketch, in Figure
26-6*a* and *b,* how higher costs and a less favorable demand could cause a short-run equilibrium situation entailing losses.

Figure 26-6*a* and *b* brings out a final notable point. We have emphasized that product
price is a given datum to the *individual* com-

petitive firm. But at the same time, the supply
plans of all competitive producers *as a group*
are a basic determinant of product price. If we
recall the fallacy of composition, we find there
is no inconsistency here. Though each firm,
supplying a negligible fraction of total supply,
cannot affect price, the sum of the supply
curves of all the many firms in the industry
constitutes the industry supply curve, and this
curve does have an important bearing upon
price. In short, under competition, equilibrium
price is a given datum to the individual firm
and simultaneously is the result of the production (supply) decisions of all firms taken as a
group.

PROFIT MAXIMIZATION IN THE LONG RUN

The long run permits firms to make certain
adjustments which time does not allow in the
short run. In the short run there are a given
number of firms in an industry, each of which
has a fixed, unalterable plant. True, firms may
close down in the sense that they produce zero
units of output in the short run; but they do

not have sufficient time to liquidate their assets and go out of business. By contrast, in the long run firms already in an industry have sufficient time either to expand or to contract their plant capacities, and, more important, the number of firms in the industry may either increase or decrease as new firms enter or old firms leave. We want to discover how these long-run adjustments modify our conclusions concerning short-run output and price determination.

It will facilitate our analysis greatly to make certain simplifying assumptions, none of which will impair the general validity of our conclusions.

1 We shall suppose that the only long-run adjustment is the entry and exodus of firms. Furthermore, for simplicity's sake we shall ignore the short-run adjustments already analyzed, in order to grasp more clearly the nature of long-run competitive adjustments.

2 It will also be assumed that all firms in the industry have identical cost curves. This allows us to talk in terms of an "average," or "representative," firm with the knowledge that all other firms in the industry are similarly affected by any long-run adjustments which occur.

3 We assume for the moment that the industry under discussion is a constant-cost industry. This means simply that the entry and exodus of firms will *not* affect resource prices or, therefore, the locations of the unit-cost schedules of the individual firms.

Now our goal is to describe long-run competitive adjustments both verbally and through simple graphic analysis. It will be well to state in advance the basic conclusion we seek to explain: *After all long-run adjustments are completed, that is, when long-run equilibrium is achieved, product price will be exactly equal to, and production will occur at, each firm's point of minimum average total cost.* This conclusion follows from two basic facts: (1) Firms seek profits and shun losses, and (2) under competition, firms are free to enter and leave industries. If price initially exceeds aver-

age total costs, the resulting economic profits will attract new firms to the industry. But this expansion of the industry will increase product supply until price is brought back down into equality with average total cost. Conversely, if price is initially less than average total cost, the resulting losses will cause firms to leave the industry. As they leave, total product supply will decline, bringing price back up into equality with average total cost.

Our conclusion can best be demonstrated and its significance evaluated by assuming that the average or representative firm in a purely competitive industry is initially in long-run equilibrium. This is shown in Figure 26-7a, where price and minimum average total cost are equal at $50. Economic profits here are zero; hence, the industry is in equilibrium or "at rest," because there is no tendency for firms to enter or leave the industry. As we know, the going market price is determined by total, or industry, demand and supply, as shown by D_1D_1 and S_1S_1 in Figure 26-7b. (The market supply schedule, incidentally, is a *short-run* schedule; the industry's long-run supply schedule will be developed in our discussion.) By examining the quantity axes of the two graphs, we note that if all firms are identical, there must be 1000 firms in the industry, each producing 100 units, to achieve the industry's equilibrium output of 100,000 units.

□ **Entry of Firms Eliminates Profits**

Now our model is set up. Let us upset the serenity of this long-run equilibrium situation and trace the subsequent adjustments. Suppose that a change in consumer tastes increases product demand from D_1D_1 to D_2D_2. This favorable shift in demand obviously makes production profitable; the new price of $60 exceeds average total cost. *These economic profits will lure new firms into the industry.* Some of the entrants will be newly created firms; others will shift from less prosperous industries. But as the firms enter, the market

FIGURE 26-7 TEMPORARY PROFITS AND THE REESTABLISHMENT OF LONG-RUN EQUILIBRIUM IN A REPRESENTATIVE FIRM (a) AND THE INDUSTRY (b)

A favorable shift in demand (D_1D_1 to D_2D_2) will upset the original equilibrium and cause economic profits. But profits will cause new firms to enter the industry, increasing supply (S_1S_1 to S_2S_2) and lowering product price until economic profits are once again zero.

supply of the product will increase, causing product price to gravitate downward from $60 toward the original $50 level. Assuming, as we are, that the entry of new firms has no effect upon costs, economic profits will persist, and entry will therefore continue until short-run market supply has increased to S_2S_2. At this point, price is again equal to minimum average total cost at $50. The economic profits caused by the boost in demand have been competed away to zero, and as a result, the previous incentive for more firms to enter the industry has disappeared. Long-run equilibrium has been restored at this point.

Figure 26-7 tells us that upon the reestablishment of long-run equilibrium, industry output is 110,000 units and that each firm in the now expanded industry is producing 100 units. We can therefore conclude that the industry is now composed of 1100 firms; that is, 100 new firms have entered the industry.

□ Exodus of Firms Eliminates Losses

To strengthen our understanding of long-run competitive equilibrium, let us throw our analysis into reverse. In Figure 26-8a and b, the heavy lines show once again the initial

long-run equilibrium situation used as a point of departure in our previous analysis of how the entry of firms eliminates profits.

Now let us suppose that consumer demand falls from D_1D_1 to D_3D_3. This forces price down to $40, making production unprofitable. *In time these losses will force firms to leave the industry.* As capital equipment wears out and contractual obligations expire, some firms will simply toss in the sponge. As this exodus of firms proceeds, however, industry supply will decrease, moving from S_1S_1 toward S_3S_3. And as this occurs, price will begin to rise from $40 back toward $50. Assuming costs are unchanged by the exodus of firms, losses will force firms to leave the industry until supply has declined to S_3S_3, at which point price is again exactly $50, barely consistent with minimum average total cost. The exodus of firms continues until losses are eliminated and long-run equilibrium is again restored.

The reader will note from Figure 26-8a and b that total quantity supplied is now 90,000 units and each firm is producing 100 units. This obviously means that the industry is now populated by only 900 firms rather than the original 1000. Losses have forced 100 firms out of business.

FIGURE 26-8 TEMPORARY LOSSES AND THE REESTABLISHMENT OF LONG-RUN EQUILIBRIUM IN A REPRESENTATIVE FIRM (a) AND THE INDUSTRY (b)

An unfavorable shift in demand (D_1D_1 to D_3D_3) will upset the original equilibrium and cause losses. But losses will cause firms to leave the industry, decreasing supply (S_1S_1 to S_3S_3) and increasing product price until all losses have disappeared.

Our prestated conclusion has now been verified. Competition, as reflected in the entry and exodus of firms, forces price into equality with the minimum long-run average total cost of production, and each firm produces at the point of minimum long-run average total cost. Observe, too, that these expanding- and declining-industry cases comprise an explanation of the functioning of consumer sovereignty, a concept which we encountered at a less sophisticated level in Chapter 5.

□ **Long-run Supply for a Constant-Cost Industry**

We now ask: What is the nature of the long-run supply curve which evolves from this analysis of the expansion or contraction of a competitive industry? Even though our discussion is concerned with the long run, we have noted that the market supply curves of Figures 26-7b and 26-8b are short-run industry supply curves. However, the analysis itself permits us to sketch the nature of the long-run supply curve for this competitive industry. The crucial factor in determining the shape of the industry's long-run supply curve is the effect, if any, which changes in the number of firms in the industry will have upon the costs of the individual firms in the industry.

In the foregoing analysis of long-run competitive equilibrium we assumed the industry under discussion was a *constant-cost industry*. By definition, this means that the expansion of the industry through the entry of new firms will have no effect upon resource prices or, therefore, upon production costs. Graphically, the entry of new firms does *not* change the position of the long-run average-cost curves of the individual firms in the industry. When will this be the case? For the most part, when the industry's demand for resources is small in relation to the total demand for those resources. And this is most likely to be the situation when the industry is employing unspecialized resources which are being demanded by many other industries. In short, when the particular industry's demand for resources is a negligible component of the total demand, the industry can expand without significantly affecting resource prices and costs.

What will be the nature of the long-run supply curve for a constant-cost industry? The answer is contained in our previous discussion of the long-run adjustments toward equilibrium which profits or losses will initiate. Here we assumed that entrance or departure of firms would not affect costs. The result was that the entry or exodus of firms would alter industry output but always bring product price back to the original $50 level, where it is just consistent with the unchanging minimum average total cost of production. Specifically, we discovered that the industry would supply 90,000, 100,000, or 110,000 units of output, all at a price of $50 per unit. In technical terms, *the long-run supply curve of a constant-cost industry is perfectly elastic.*

This is demonstrated graphically in Figure 26-9, where the illustrative data from Figures 26-7 and 26-8 are retained. Suppose that industry demand is originally D_1D_1, industry output is Q_1 (100,000), and product price is Q_1P_1 ($50). This situation, referring to Figure 26-7, is one of long-run equilibrium. Now assume that demand increases to D_2D_2, upsetting this equilibrium. The resulting economic

profits will attract new firms. Because this is a constant-cost industry, entry will continue and industry output will expand until price is driven back down to the unchanged minimum average-total-cost level. This will be at price Q_2P_2 ($50) and output Q_2 (110,000).

This analysis, now using Figure 26-8 as a reference point, is reversible. A decline in short-run industry demand from D_1D_1 to D_3D_3 will cause an exodus of firms and ultimately a restoration of equilibrium at price Q_3P_3 ($50) and output Q_3 (90,000). A line which connects all points, such as these three, shows the various price–quantity supplied combinations which would be most profitable for the industry when it has had sufficient time to make *all* desired adjustments to assumed changes in industry demand. By definition, this line is the industry's long-run supply curve. In the case of a constant-cost industry we note that this line, S_1S_1 in Figure 26-9, is perfectly elastic.

□ Long-run Supply for an Increasing-Cost Industry

But constant-cost industries are a special case. In most instances the entry of new firms will affect resource prices and therefore unit costs for the individual firms in the industry. When an industry is using a significant portion of some resource whose total supply is not readily increased, the entry of new firms will increase resource demand in relation to supply and boost resource prices. This is particularly so in industries which are using highly specialized resources whose initial supply is not readily augmented. The result of higher resource prices will be higher long-run average costs for firms in the industry. These higher costs, it should be noted, take the form of an upward shift in the long-run average-cost curve for the representative firm.

The net result is that when an increase in product demand causes economic profits and attracts new firms to the industry, a two-way squeeze on profits will occur to eliminate those profits. On the one hand, the entry of new

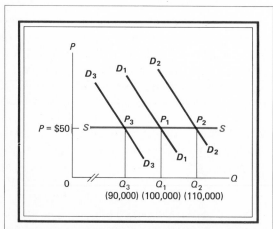

FIGURE 26-9 THE LONG-RUN SUPPLY CURVE FOR A CONSTANT-COST INDUSTRY IS PERFECTLY ELASTIC

Because the entry or exodus of firms does not affect resource prices or, therefore, unit costs, an increase in demand (D_1D_1 to D_2D_2) will cause an expansion in industry output (Q_1 to Q_2) but no alteration in price ($Q_1P_1 = Q_2P_2$). Similarly, a decrease in demand (D_1D_1 to D_3D_3) will cause a contraction of output (Q_1 to Q_3) but no change in price ($Q_1P_1 = Q_3P_3$). This means that the long-run industry supply curve (*SS*) will be perfectly elastic.

firms will increase market supply and lower product price, and, on the other, the entire average-total-cost curve of the representative firm will shift upward. This means that the equilibrium price will now be higher than it was originally. The industry will only produce a larger output at a higher price. Why? Because expansion of the industry has increased average total costs, and in the long run product price must cover these costs. A greater industry output will be forthcoming at a higher price, or, more technically, the industry supply curve for an increasing-cost industry will be upsloping. Instead of getting either 90,000, 100,000, or 110,000 units at the same price of $50, in an increasing-cost industry 90,000 units might be forthcoming at $45; 100,000 at $50; and 110,000 at $55. The higher price is required to induce more production because costs per unit of output increase as the industry expands.

This can be seen graphically in Figure 26-10. Original market demand, industry output, and price are D_1D_1, Q_1 (100,000) and Q_1P_1 ($50) respectively. An increase in demand to D_2D_2 will upset this equilibrium and give rise to economic profits. As new firms enter, (1) industry supply will increase, tending to drive price down, and (2) resource prices will rise, causing the average total costs of production to rise. Because of these average-total-cost increases, the new long-run equilibrium price will be established at some level above the original price, such as Q_2P_2 ($55). Conversely, a decline in demand from D_1D_1 to D_3D_3 will make production unprofitable and cause an exodus of firms from the industry. The resulting decline in the demand for resources relative to their supply will lower resource prices and cause average total costs of production to decline. Hence, the new equilibrium price will be established at some level below the original price, such as Q_3P_3 ($45).

Which situation—constant- or increasing-cost—is characteristic of American industry? Economists generally agree that increasing-cost industries are most common. Ag-

FIGURE 26-10 THE LONG-RUN SUPPLY CURVE FOR AN INCREASING-COST INDUSTRY IS UPSLOPING

In an increasing-cost industry the entry of new firms in response to increases in demand (D_3D_3 to D_1D_1 to D_2D_2) will bid up resource prices and thereby increase unit costs. As a result, an increased industry output (Q_3 to Q_1 to Q_2) will be forthcoming only at higher prices ($Q_2P_2 > Q_1P_1 > Q_3P_3$). The long-run industry supply curve (SS) is therefore upsloping.

riculture and extractive industries such as mining and lumbering are increasing-cost industries because each utilizes a very large portion of some basic resource—farmland, mineral deposits, and timberland. Expansion will significantly affect the demand for these resources and result in higher costs. It is less easy to generalize with respect to manufacturing industries. In their early stages of development, such industries may well be relatively constant-cost industries.[2] But as continued

[2]Under certain, very special circumstances, an industry may be for a time a *decreasing-cost industry*. For example, as more mines are established in a given locality, each firm's costs in pumping out water seepage may decline. With more mines pumping, the seepage into each is less, and pumping costs are therefore reduced. Furthermore, with only a few mines in an area, industry output might be so small that only relatively primitive and therefore costly transportation facilities are available. But as the number of firms and industry output expand, a railroad might build a spur into the area and thereby significantly reduce transportation costs. Under such special conditions, a firm's long-run supply curve may shift *downward*. We will have more to say about this kind of cost economy in Chapter 36.

expansion increases the importance of these industries in resource markets, they may in time become increasing-cost industries.

AN EVALUATION OF COMPETITIVE PRICING

Whether a purely competitive industry is one of constant or increasing costs, the final long-run equilibrium position for each firm will have the same basic characteristics. As shown in Figure 26-11, price (and marginal revenue) will settle at the level where they are equal to minimum average cost. However, we discovered in Chapter 25 that the marginal-cost curve intersects, and is therefore equal to, average cost at the point of minimum average cost. In the long-run equilibrium position, "everything is equal." MR (P) = AC = MC. This triple equality is of more than geometric interest. It tells us that, although a competitive firm may realize economic profits or losses in the short run, it will barely break even by producing in accordance with the MR (P)

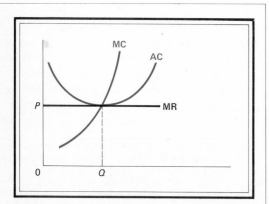

FIGURE 26-11 FOR THE COMPETITIVE FIRM IN LONG-RUN EQUILIBRIUM, P = AC = MC

The equality of price and minimum average cost indicates that the firm is using the most efficient known technology and is charging the lowest price P and producing the greatest output Q consistent with its costs. The equality of price and marginal cost indicates that resources are being allocated in accordance with consumer preferences.

= MC rule in the long run. Furthermore, this triple equality suggests certain conclusions concerning the efficiency of a purely competitive economy which are of great social significance. It is to an evaluation of competitive pricing from society's point of view that we now turn.

You will recall that the overview of the price system in Chapter 5 yielded some general conclusions with respect to the efficiency of any economy characterized by a competitive price system. Equipped now with a better understanding of costs and price-output determination under competition, we are in a position to sharpen our understanding of the efficiency of a competitive price economy. Specifically, we want to see how our analysis of long-run competitive equilibrium implies certain highly desirable features of a competitive price system.

☐   **Efficient Allocation of Resources**

Most economists argue that, subject to certain limitations and exceptions, a purely competitive economy will lead to the most efficient, or "ideal," allocation of resources. That is, *a competitive price economy will tend to allocate the fixed supplies of resources available to society in such a way as to maximize the satisfactions of consumers.* Actually, there are two related points which underlie this conclusion. First, it is argued that under pure competition firms will be forced to produce those goods which consumers want the most. Second, competition forces firms to use the most efficient, or least-cost, methods in the production of these goods. To facilitate our discussion, we shall examine the second point first.

1 P = AC   We have just noted that in the long run, competition forces firms to produce at the point of minimum average total cost of production and to charge that price which is just consistent with these costs. This is obviously a most desirable situation from the consumer's point of view. It means that firms must use the best available (least-cost) technology or they will not survive. And, too, it means that consumers benefit from the highest volume of production and the lowest product price which are possible under the cost conditions which currently prevail. Furthermore, the costs involved in each instance are only those costs essential in producing a product. Because products are standardized in competitive industries, there will be no selling or promotional costs which must be added to production costs in determining product price.

2 $P = MC$ But the competitive production of *any* collection of goods does not necessarily make for an efficient allocation of resources. Production must not only be technologically efficient, but it must also entail the "right goods," that is, the goods that consumers want the most. The competitive price system will see to it that resources are allocated so as to result in a total output whose composition best fits the preferences of consumers.

Let us see precisely how this comes about. We must first grasp the social meaning of competitive product and resource prices. The money price of any product—product X—is society's measure, or index, of the relative worth of that product at the margin. Similarly, recalling the notion of opportunity costs, we see that the marginal cost of producing X measures the value, or relative worth, of the other goods that the resources used in the production of an extra unit of X could otherwise have produced. In short, product price measures the benefit, or satisfaction, which society gets from additional units of X, and the marginal cost of an additional unit of X measures the sacrifice, or cost to society, of other goods in using resources to produce more of X. Now, under competition, the production of each product will occur up to that precise point at which price is equal to marginal cost (Figure 26-11). The profit-seeking competitor will realize the maximum possible profit only by equating price and marginal cost. To pro-

duce short of the MR $(P) = MC$ point will mean less than maximum profits to the individual firm and an *under*allocation of resources to this product from society's standpoint. The fact that price exceeds marginal cost indicates that society values additional units of X more highly than the alternative products which the appropriate resources could otherwise produce.

For similar reasons, the production of X should not go beyond the output at which price equals marginal cost. To do so would entail less than maximum profits for producers and an *over*allocation of resources to X from the standpoint of society. To produce X at some point at which marginal cost exceeds price means that resources are being used in the production of X at the sacrifice of alternative goods which society values more highly than the added units of X. In brief, *under pure competition, profit-motivated producers will produce each commodity up to that precise point at which price and marginal cost are equated. This means that resources are efficiently allocated under competition.* Each good is produced to the point at which the value of the last unit is equal to the value of the alternative goods sacrificed by its production. To alter the production of X would necessarily reduce consumer satisfactions. To produce X beyond the $P = MC$ point would result in the sacrifice of alternative goods whose value to society exceeds that of the extra units of X. To produce X short of the $P = MC$ point would involve the sacrifice of units of X which society values more than the alternative goods resources can produce.

A further attribute of the competitive price system is its ability to negotiate appropriate adjustments in resource use as changes occur in basic data of the economy. In a competitive economy, any changes in consumer tastes, resource supplies, or technology will automatically set in motion appropriate realignments of resources. As we have already explained, an increase in consumer demand for product X will increase its price. Disequilibrium will occur in that, at its present output, the price of X will now exceed its marginal cost. This will create economic profits in industry X and stimulate its expansion. Its profitability will permit the industry to bid resources away from less pressing uses. Expansion in this industry will end only when the price of X is again equal to its marginal cost, that is, when the value of the last unit produced is once again equal to the value of the alternative goods society forgoes in getting that last unit of X produced. Similarly, changes in the supplies of particular resources or in the techniques pertinent to various industries will upset existing price–marginal-cost equalities by either raising or lowering marginal cost. These inequalities will cause business executives, in either pursuing profits or shunning losses, to reallocate resources until price once again equals marginal cost in each line of production. In so doing, they correct any inefficiencies in the allocation of resources which changing economic data may temporarily impose upon the economy.

A final appealing feature of a purely competitive economy is that the highly efficient allocation of resources which it fosters comes about because businesses and resource suppliers freely seek to further their own self-interests. That is, the "invisible hand" (Chapter 5) is at work in a competitive market system. In a competitive economy, businesses employ resources until the extra, or marginal, costs of production equal the price of the product. This not only maximizes the profits of the individual producers but simultaneously results in a pattern of resource allocation which maximizes the satisfactions of consumers. The competitive price system organizes the private interests of producers along lines which are fully in accord with the interests of society as a whole.

☐ **Shortcomings of the Competitive Price System**

Despite these several virtues, economists acknowledge certain limitations of the price system which may impair its ability to allocate resources efficiently. Some of these criticisms have been previously noted in a less sophisticated way in Chapter 5.

The Income Distribution Problem The contention that the competitive price system will allocate resources efficiently—that is, will produce the collection of goods and services which maximizes the satisfaction of consumer wants—is predicated upon some given distribution of money income. In other words, money income is distributed among households in some specific way, and this distribution results in a certain structure of demand. The price system then brings about an efficient allocation of resources or, stated differently, an output of goods and services whose composition maximizes the fulfillment of these particular consumer demands. But what if the distribution of money income is altered so that the structure of demand changes? Would the competitive price system negotiate a new allocation of resources? The answer, of course, is "Yes"; the price system would reallocate resources and therefore change the composition of output to maximize the fulfillment of this new pattern of consumer wants. The problem, then, is, Which of these two "efficient" allocations of resources is the "most efficient"? Which allocation of resources yields the greatest level of satisfaction to society? There is no *scientific* answer to this question because we do not know how to measure and compare the satisfaction derived by various individuals from goods and services. If all people were precisely alike in their capacities to obtain satisfaction from income, economists could recommend that income be distributed equally and that the allocation of resources which would be appropriate to *that* distribution would be the "best" or "most efficient" of all. But, in fact, people are different by virtue of their education, experiences, and environment, not to mention their inherited mental and physical characteristics. Such differences can be used to argue for an unequal distribution of income.

The basic point for present purposes is that the distribution of income associated with the workings of the competitive price system is quite unequal and therefore may lead to the production of trifles for the rich while denying the basic needs of the poor. Hence, many economists believe that the distribution of income which pure competition provides should be modified by public action. They maintain that allocative efficiency is hardly a virtue if it comes in response to an income distribution which offends prevailing standards of equity. The question of income inequality will be accorded detailed treatment in Chapter 37.

Market Failure: Spillovers and External Goods The competitive price system does not accurately measure costs and benefits where spillover costs and benefits are significant. Under competition each producer will assume only those costs which he *must* pay. This correctly implies that in some lines of production there are significant costs which producers can and do avoid. Recall from Chapter 6 that these avoided costs accrue to society and are aptly called *spillover* or *external costs.* Firms may avoid the cost of properly disposing of waste materials or of buying smoke- and dust-abatement equipment. The result is significant spillover costs in the form of polluted rivers, smog, and a generally debased community. Similarly, unbridled competition may cause profit-seeking firms to brutally exploit farmland, timberland, and mineral deposits through the use of the cheapest production methods. The cost to society is the permanent loss of irreproducible natural resources. On the other hand, the consumption of certain goods and services, such as chest x-rays and polio shots, yields widespread satisfactions, or benefits, to society as a whole. These satisfactions are called *external* or *spillover benefits.*

Now the significance of spillover costs and benefits for present purposes is this: The profit-seeking activities of producers will bring about an allocation of resources which is efficient from society's point of view only if marginal cost embodies *all* the costs which production entails and product price accurately reflects *all* the benefits which society gets from a good's production (see Figure 6-1). Only in this case will competitive production at the MR $(P) =$ MC point balance the *total* sacrifices and satisfactions of society and result in an efficient allocation of resources. To the extent that price and marginal cost are not accurate indexes of sacrifices and satisfactions—in other words, to the extent that spillover costs and benefits exist—production at the MR $(P) =$ MC point will *not* signify an efficient allocation of resources.

Remember, too, the point of the lighthouse example in Chapter 6: The market system does not provide for social or public goods, that is, for goods to which the exclusion principle does not apply. Despite its other virtues, the competitive price system ignores an important class of goods and services—national defense, flood-control programs, and so forth—which can and do yield satisfaction to consumers but which cannot be priced and sold through the market system.

Productive Techniques The competitive price system may not always entail the use of the most efficient productive techniques or the development of improved techniques. There are both a static or "right now" aspect and a dynamic or "over time" aspect of this general criticism. The static aspect argues that in certain lines of production, existing technology may be such that a firm must be a large-scale producer in order to realize the lowest unit costs of production. Given consumer demand, this suggests that a relatively small number of efficient, large-scale producers is needed if production is to be carried on efficiently. In other words, existing mass-production economies might be lost if such an industry were populated by the large number of small-scale producers which pure competition requires. This point was discussed in some detail in Chapter 25.

The dynamic aspect of this criticism concerns the willingness and ability of purely competitive firms to undertake technological advance. The progressiveness of pure competition is debated by economists. For present purposes we merely call attention to the belief of some authorities that a purely competitive economy would *not* foster a very rapid rate of technological progress. They argue, first, that the incentive for technological advance may be weak under pure competition because the profit rewards accruing to an innovating firm as the result of a cost-reducing technological improvement will be quickly competed away by rival firms who readily adopt the new technique. Second, the small size of the typical competitive firm and the fact that it tends to "break even" in the long run raise serious questions as to whether such producers could finance substantial programs of organized research. We will return to this controversy in Chapter 29.

Range of Consumer Choice The competitive price system may not provide for a sufficient range of consumer choice or for the development of new products. This criticism, like the previous one, has both a static and a dynamic aspect. Pure competition, it is contended, entails product standardization, whereas other market structures—for example, monopolistic competition and, frequently, oligopoly—entail a wide range of types, styles, and quality gradations of any product. This product differentiation widens the consumer's range of free choice and simultaneously allows his preferences to be more completely fulfilled. Similarly, critics of pure competition point out that, just as pure competition is not likely to be progressive with respect to the development of new productive techniques, neither is this market structure conducive to the improvement of existing products or the creation of completely new ones.

The question of the progressiveness of the various market structures in terms of both productive techniques and product development will be a recurring one in the following three chapters.

Summary

1 A purely competitive industry comprises a large number of independent firms producing a standardized product. Pure competition assumes that firms and resources are mobile among different industries. No single firm can influence market price in a competitive industry; price therefore equals marginal revenue.

2 Short-run profit maximization by a competitive firm can be analyzed by a comparison of total revenue and total cost or through marginal analysis. A firm will maximize profits by producing that output at which total revenue exceeds total cost by the greatest amount. Losses will be minimized by producing where the excess of total cost over total revenue is at a minimum and less than total fixed costs.

3 Provided price exceeds minimum average variable cost, a competitive firm will maximize profits or minimize losses by producing at that output at which price or marginal revenue is equal to marginal cost. If price is less than average variable cost, the firm will minimize its losses by closing down. If price is greater than average variable cost but less than average total cost, the firm will minimize its losses by producing the $P = $ MC output. If price exceeds average total cost, the $P = $ MC output will provide maximum economic profits for the firm.

4 Applying the MR $(P) = $ MC rule at various possible market prices leads to the conclusion that the segment of the firm's short-run marginal-cost curve which lies above average variable cost is its short-run supply curve.

5   In the long run, competitive price will tend to equal the minimum average cost of production. This is so because economic profits will cause firms to enter a competitive industry until those profits have been competed away. Conversely, losses will force the exodus of firms from the industry until product price once again barely covers unit costs.

6   The long-run supply curve is perfectly elastic for a constant-cost industry, but upsloping for an increasing-cost industry.

7   In a purely competitive economy the profit-seeking activities of producers will result in an allocation of resources which maximizes the satisfactions of consumers. The long-run equality of price and minimum average cost indicates that competitive firms will use the most efficient known technology and charge the lowest price consistent with their production costs. The equality of price and marginal cost indicates that resources will be allocated in accordance with consumer tastes. The competitive price system will reallocate resources in response to a change in consumer tastes, technology, or resource supplies so as to maintain allocative efficiency over time.

8   Economists recognize four possible deterrents to allocative efficiency in a competitive economy. *a.* There is no reason why the competitive price system will result in an optimum distribution of income. *b.* In allocating resources, the price system does not allow for spillover costs and benefits or of the production of social goods. *c.* A purely competitive industry may preclude the use of the best-known productive techniques and foster a slow rate of technological advance. *d.* A competitive system provides neither a wide range of product choice nor an environment conducive to the development of new products.

Questions and Study Suggestions

1   Key terms and concepts to remember: profit-maximizing case; break-even point; loss-minimizing case; close-down case; MR (P) = MC rule; short-run supply curve; long-run supply curve; constant-cost industry; increasing-cost industry.

2   Strictly speaking, pure competition never has existed and probably never will. Then why study it?

3   Why is the equality of marginal revenue and marginal cost essential for profit maximization in all market structures? Explain why price can be substituted for marginal revenue in the MR = MC rule when an industry is purely competitive.

4   Explain: "A competitive producer must look to average variable cost in determining whether or not to produce in the short run, to marginal cost in deciding upon the best volume of production, and to average total cost to calculate his profits or losses." Why might a firm produce at a loss in the short run rather than close down?

5   Assume the unit-cost data shown on page 556 is for a purely competitive producer:

   a.   At a product price of $32, will this firm produce in the short run? Why, or why not? If it does produce, what will be the profit-maximizing or loss-minimizing output? Explain. Specify the amount of economic profit or loss per unit of output.

   b.   Answer the questions of 5a on the assumption that product price is $41.

   c.   Answer the questions of 5a on the assumption that product price is $56.

   d.   Complete the short-run supply schedule given on page 556 for the same firm, and indicate the profit or loss incurred at each output (columns 1 to 3).

Total product	Average fixed cost	Average variable cost	Average total cost	Marginal cost
0				
1	$60.00	$45.00	$105.00	$45
2	30.00	42.50	72.50	40
3	20.00	40.00	60.00	35
4	15.00	37.50	52.50	30
5	12.00	37.00	49.00	35
6	10.00	37.50	47.50	40
7	8.57	38.57	47.14	45
8	7.50	40.63	48.13	55
9	6.67	43.33	50.00	65
10	6.00	46.50	52.50	75

e. Explain: "That segment of a competitive firm's marginal-cost curve which lies above its average-variable-cost curve constitutes the short-run supply curve for the firm." Illustrate graphically.

(1) Price	(2) Quantity supplied, single firm	(3) Profit (+) or loss (−)	(4) Quantity supplied, 1500 firms
$26	——	$——	——
32	——	——	——
38	——	——	——
41	——	——	——
46	——	——	——
56	——	——	——
66	——	——	——

f. Now assume there are 1500 identical firms in this competitive industry; that is, there are 1500 firms, each of which has the same cost data as shown here. Calculate the industry supply schedule (column 4).

g. Suppose the market demand data for the product are as follows:

Price	Total quantity demanded
$26	17,000
32	15,000
38	13,500
41	12,000
46	10,500
56	9,500
66	8,000

What will equilibrium price be? What will equilibrium output be for the industry? For each firm? What will profit or loss be per unit? Per firm?

6 Using diagrams for both the industry and a representative firm, illustrate competitive long-run equilibrium. Employing these diagrams, show how **a.** an increase, and **b.** a decrease, in market demand will upset this long-run equilibrium. Trace graphically and describe verbally the adjustment processes by which long-run equilibrium is restored. Assume the industry is one of constant costs.

7 Distinguish carefully between a constant-cost and an increasing-cost industry. Answer question 6 on the assumption that the industry is one of increasing costs. Compare the long-run supply curves of a constant-cost and an increasing-cost industry.

8 Suppose a decrease in demand occurs in a competitive increasing-cost industry. Contrast the product price and industry output which exist after all long-run adjustments are completed with those which originally prevailed.

9 In long-run equilibrium, $P = AC = MC$. Of what significance for the allocation of resources is the equality of P and AC? The equality of P and MC?

10 Explain why some economists believe that an unequal distribution of income might impair the efficiency with which a competitive price system allocates resources. What other criticisms can be made of a purely competitive economy?

Selected References

Leftwich, Richard H.: *The Price System and Resource Allocation,* 6th ed. (Hinsdale, Ill.: The Dryden Press, Inc., 1976), chap. 10.

Mansfield, Edwin: *Microeconomics: Theory and Applications,* 2d ed. (New York: W. W. Norton & Company, Inc., 1975), chap. 8.

Stigler, George J.: *The Theory of Price,* rev. ed. (New York: The Macmillan Company, 1952), chap. 10.

Stonier, Alfred W., and Douglas C. Hague: *A Textbook of Economic Theory,* 3d ed. (New York: Longmans, Green & Co., Inc., 1964), chaps. 6, 7.

Thompson, Arthur A., Jr.: *Economics of the Firm: Theory and Practice,* 2d ed. (Englewood Cliffs, N.J.: Prentice-Hall, Inc., 1977), chap. 10.

Last Word
Technology and Competition

Competitive pressures are often rooted in technological progress.

New electronic technology coupled with good, solid marketing should be the secret to successful business performance. But instead, this combination of functions has turned out to be disastrous for several industries.

Two prime examples are pocket calculators and digital watches.

The technology came first. Innovators were able to develop a calculator that you could hold in the palm of your hand, and a watch that flashed the time at the touch of a button.

The watches came out at $200 or more and the calculators at $100 or more. And they started to sell, even at these prices.

So the manufacturers pushed more money into marketing. And competitors saw the potential and rushed into the market place with new products.

But competition and rapid improvement in technology started pushing prices down dramatically. Retailers weren't about to stock up on $99.95 watches when they knew virtually the same watches would hit the market a month later at $79.95.

So the guy who made the $99.95 watch was stuck with it. Or he had to peddle it at a loss to keep up with the lower prices. And that forced several companies out of business and into bankruptcy.

During the holiday season, wristwatches bearing a nationally advertised name and containing the very same technology that sold for $200 a couple of years ago are available at about $16. Calculators are selling for less than $10.

And now, we can see the same thing happening all over again to some new industries: citizens band radios and electronic video games.

A year ago, these items generally were priced at $100 and up. Last week, stores were selling nationally advertised brands of CB radios and video games for as little as $39.95. And by next year, who knows?

One thing is sure, the technology-marketing combination has fractured several companies, but consumers are enjoying every minute of it.

"Watches That Sold for $200 Now Cost $16," *Lincoln Evening Journal,* Dec. 28, 1976. Reprinted by permission of the Chicago Daily News.

27

Price and Output Determination: Pure Monopoly

Let us now jump to the opposite end of the industry spectrum and examine the characteristics, the bases, the price-output behavior, and the social desirability of pure monopoly.

PURE MONOPOLY: CONCEPT AND OCCURRENCE

Pure or absolute monopoly exists when a single firm is the sole producer of a product for which there are no close substitutes. By the absence of close substitutes we mean that there are no other firms producing the same product or products varying only in very minor ways from that of the monopolist. For example, there is no close substitute for the electricity or water supplied by local utilities. Nor is there a good substitute for telephone service. On the international scene the De Beers diamond syndicate controls the noncommunist world's supply of diamonds. In small and geographically isolated towns the single local bookstore or movie theater may approximate pure monopoly. Of course, there is almost always *some* competition. Candles or kerosene lights are very imperfect substitutes for electricity; letters and carrier pigeons can be substituted for the telephone. Rubies, emeralds, and other precious stones are substitutable for diamonds. The important point arising out of all these cases is that the pure monopolist is the only supplier of a product or service for which there are no *close* substitutes available. Defined in this way, pure monopoly is admittedly a rare phenomenon.

Yet, a brief analysis of pure monopoly is important for two related reasons. First, some industries are reasonable approximations of pure monopoly. The behavior of firms with 80, 70, or even 60 percent of a market can often be explained with considerable accuracy through the pure monopoly market model. For all practical purposes the dominant firm *is* the industry in such instances. Second, a study of pure monopoly provides us with valuable insights concerning the more realistic market structures of monopolistic competition and oligopoly, which will be discussed in Chapters 28 and 29. These two market situations combine in differing degrees the characteristics of pure competition and pure monopoly.

■ BARRIERS TO ENTRY

It was noted in Chapter 22 that the absence of competitors which characterizes pure monopoly is largely explainable in terms of barriers to entry, that is, considerations which prohibit additional firms from entering an industry. These barriers are also pertinent in explaining the existence of oligopoly and monopolistic competition between the market extremes of pure competition and pure monopoly. In the case of pure monopoly, entry barriers are sufficiently great to block completely all potential competition. Somewhat less formidable barriers permit the existence of oligopoly, that is, a market dominated by a few firms. Still weaker barriers permit the fairly large number of firms which characterizes monopolistic competition. The virtual absence of entry barriers helps explain the very large number of competing firms which is the basis of pure competition. The important point is this: Barriers to entry are pertinent not only to the extreme case of pure monopoly but also to the "partial monopolies" which are so characteristic of American capitalism.

What forms do these entry barriers assume?

□ Economies of Scale

Modern technology in many industries is such that efficient, low-cost production can be achieved only if producers are extremely large both absolutely and in relation to the market. Where economies of scale are very significant, a firm's average-cost schedule will decline over a wide range of output (Figure 25-6a). Given market demand, the achieving of low unit costs and therefore low unit prices for consumers depends upon the existence of a small number of firms or, in the extreme case, only one firm. The automobile, aluminum, and steel industries are a few of many heavy industries which reflect such conditions. If three firms currently enjoy all available economies of scale and each has roughly one-third of a market, it is easy to see why new competitors may find it extremely difficult to enter this industry. On the one hand, new firms entering the market as small-scale producers will have little or no chance to survive and expand. Why? Because as small-scale entrants they will be unable to realize the cost economies enjoyed by the existing "Big Three" and therefore will be unable to realize the profits necessary for survival and growth. New competitors in the steel and automobile industries will not come about as the result of the successful operation and expansion of small "backyard" producers. They simply will not be efficient enough to survive. The other option is to start out big, that is, to enter the industry as a large-scale producer. In practice, this is virtually impossible. It is extremely unlikely that a new and untried enterprise will be able to secure the money capital needed to obtain capital facilities comparable to those accumulated by any of the Big Three in the automobile industry. The financial obstacles in the way of starting big are so great in many cases as to be prohibitive.

□ Public Utilities: Natural Monopolies

In a few industries, economies of scale are particularly pronounced, and at the same time competition is impractical, inconvenient, or simply unworkable. Such industries are called *natural monopolies,* and most of the so-called public utilities—the electric and gas companies, bus and railway firms, and water and communication facilities—can be so classified. These industries are generally given exclusive franchises by government. But in return for this sole right to supply electricity, water, or bus service in a given geographic area, government reserves the right to regulate the operations of such monopolies to prevent abuses of the monopoly power it has granted.

Let us examine some illustrations. It would be exceedingly wasteful for a community to have a number of firms supplying water or electricity. Technology is such in these industries that heavy fixed costs on generators, pumping and purification equipment, water mains, and transmission lines are required. This problem is aggravated by the fact that capital equipment must be sufficient to meet the peak demands which occur on hot summer days when lawns are being watered and air conditioners turned on. These heavy fixed costs mean that unit costs of production decline with the number of cubic feet of water or kilowatt hours of electricity supplied by each firm. The presence of several water and electricity suppliers would divide the total market and reduce the sales of each competitor. Each firm would be pushed back up its declining average-cost curve. Firms would underutilize their fixed plants, with the result that unit cost and therefore electricity and water rates would be unnecessarily high. In addition, competition might prove to be extremely inconvenient. For example, the presence of a half-dozen telephone companies in a municipality would entail the inconvenience of having six telephones and six telephone books—not to mention six telephone bills—to ensure communications with all other residents in the same town.

Because firms are eager to spread their fixed costs and thereby achieve lower unit costs, cutthroat price competition tends to break out when a number of firms exist in these public utilities industries. The result may be losses, the bankruptcy of weaker rivals, and the eventual merger of the survivors. The evolving pure monopoly may be anxious to recoup past losses and to profit fully from its new position of market dominance by charging exorbitant prices for its goods or services.

To spare society from such disadvantageous results, government will usually grant an exclusive franchise to a single firm to supply water, natural gas, electricity, telephone service, or train or bus transportation. In return, government reserves the right to designate the monopolist's geographic area of operation, to regulate the quality of its services, and to control the prices which it may charge. The result is a regulated or government-sponsored monopoly—monopoly designed to achieve low unit costs but regulated to guarantee that consumers will benefit from these cost economies. We shall examine some of the problems associated with regulation later in this chapter.

□ **Ownership of Essential Raw Materials**

The institution of private property can be used by a monopoly as a means of achieving an effective obstacle to potential rivals. A firm owning or controlling a raw material which is essential in production can obviously prohibit the creation of rival firms. There are several classic examples. The Aluminum Company of America retained its monopoly position in the aluminum industry for many years by virtue of its control of all basic sources of bauxite, the major ore used in aluminum fabrication. The International Nickel Company of Canada controls approximately 90 percent of the world's known nickel reserves. As noted earlier, most of the world's known diamond mines are owned by the De Beers Company of South Africa.

□ Patents and Research

By granting an inventor the exclusive right to control a product for some seventeen years, American patent laws are aimed at protecting him from having his product or process usurped by rival enterprises which have not shared in the time, effort, and money outlays which have gone into its development. By the same token, of course, patents may provide the inventor with a monopoly position for the life of the patent. Patent control figures prominently in the growth of many modern-day industrial giants—National Cash Register, General Motors, General Electric, du Pont, to name a few. The United Shoe Machinery Company provides a notable example of how patent control can be abused to achieve monopoly power. In this case United Shoe became the exclusive supplier of certain essential shoemaking machines through patent control. It extended its monopoly power to other types of shoemaking machinery by requiring all lessees of its patented machines to sign a "tying agreement" in which shoe manufacturers agreed also to lease all other shoemaking machinery from United Shoe. This allowed United Shoe to monopolize the market until partially effective antitrust action was taken by the government in 1955.

Research, of course, underlies the development of patentable products. Firms which gain a measure of monopoly power by their own research or by purchasing the patents of others are in a strategic position to consolidate and strengthen their market position. The profits provided by one important patent can be used to finance the research required to develop new patentable products. Monopoly power achieved through patents may well be cumulative.

□ Unfair Competition

A firm's rivals may be eliminated and the entry of new competitors blocked by aggressive, cutthroat tactics. Familiar techniques entail product disparagement, pressure on resource suppliers and banks to withhold materials and credit, the hiring away of strategic personnel, and aggressive price cutting designed to bankrupt competitors. Though many of these facets of unfair competition are now illegal or fringe upon illegality, they are of more than historical interest. For example, although Federal legislation prohibits price cutting intended to reduce competition, how is one to distinguish in practice between legitimate price competition based upon cost advantages and price competition designed to bankrupt rivals?

□ Economies of Being Established

A bit of reflection will reveal that for a variety of reasons an established, going concern has numerous advantages over new, embryonic rivals. There are good reasons why existing firms should survive and prosper, whereas new firms have every reason to founder and fail. Established firms which have proved themselves by their continued existence and prosperity will have relatively easy access to the capital market, on favorable terms. This advantage is not unrelated to the fact that an established concern will tend to have a relatively efficient administrative framework staffed by competent and experienced personnel. The firm's longevity will have allowed it to eliminate inappropriate policies and to have screened the dolts from its administrative ranks. It must be added that going concerns will also be in a position to expand their size and market share by internal financing.

The new concern may have great difficulties in securing needed money capital. Its personnel and policies are untried and untested; it is an industrial question mark. If funds are available to newcomers, the added risks of investing in a new concern are likely to make the terms unattractive to the firm.

In addition, an established firm will be likely to have a widely known and highly advertised product, which it sells through well-established marketing channels to long-standing customers. A new firm faces serious financial obstacles in developing and advertising a product, in establishing marketing outlets, and in building up a clientele.

□ Two Implications

Our discussion of barriers to entry suggests two noteworthy points. First, barriers to entry are rarely complete; indeed, this is merely another way of stating our earlier point that pure monopoly is rare. Although, as we have seen, research and technological advance may strengthen the market position of a firm, technology may also undermine existing monopoly power. Existing patent advantages may be circumvented by the development of new and distinct, yet substitutable, products. New sources of strategic raw materials may be found. It is probably not an overstatement to say that monopoly in the sense of a one-firm industry persists over time only with the sanction or aid of government.

Second, it is implied in our discussion that monopolies may be desirable or undesirable from the standpoint of economic efficiency. The public utilities and economies-of-scale arguments suggest that market demand and technology may be such that efficient low-cost production presupposes the existence of monopoly. On the other hand, our comments upon materials ownership, patents, and unfair competition as sources of monopoly imply more undesirable connotations of business monopoly.

With these points in mind, let us analyze the price-output behavior of a pure monopolist. Important insights with respect to the social desirability of monopoly will be revealed.

PRICE AND OUTPUT DETERMINATION

Let us assume a pure monopolist who, through, say, patent and materials control, is able to block the entry of new firms to the market. Suppose, too, that the monopolist is unhampered by the existence or the prospect of a regulatory commission. In short, we have a monopolist who is ideally situated to exploit his market fully. The pure monopolist will determine his profit-maximizing output on the basis of his cost and demand data.

□ Monopoly Demand

The crucial difference between a pure monopolist and a purely competitive seller lies on the demand side of the market. We recall from Chapter 26 that the purely competitive seller faces a perfectly elastic demand schedule at the market price determined by industry supply and demand. The competitive firm can sell as much or as little as it wants at the going market price. It follows that each additional unit sold will add a constant amount—its price—to the firm's total revenue. In other words, for the competitive seller marginal revenue is constant and equal to product price. But the competitive seller can do nothing about market price; he has no price policy. For better or worse, he is a "price taker" and therefore must accept the market-determined price.

The monopolist's demand curve is much different. Because the pure monopolist *is* the industry, his demand, or sales, curve is the industry demand curve. And the industry demand curve is not perfectly elastic, but rather, is downsloping.[1] This is illustrated by columns 1 and 2 of Table 27-1. There are two implications of a downsloping demand curve which must be understood.

---

[1] Beware of this pitfall: Because the individual competitive firm's demand curve is perfectly elastic, it does not follow that the monopolist's demand curve will be perfectly *inelastic*. Remember: Even though the individual competitor regards his demand as perfectly elastic, the demand curve for a competitive *industry* is downsloping. The pure monopolist's demand curve is downsloping, but not perfectly inelastic, because here the firm *is* the industry. As with competitive-industry demand, the degree of elasticity or inelasticity which characterizes the pure monopolist's demand curve depends upon those elasticity-determining factors discussed in Chapter 23.

Table 27-1   REVENUE AND COST DATA OF A PURE MONOPOLIST (*hypothetical data*)

Revenue data				Cost data			
(1) Quantity of output	(2) Price (average revenue)	(3) Total revenue	(4) Marginal revenue	(5) Average total cost	(6) Total cost	(7) Marginal cost	(8) Profit (+) or loss (−)
0	$172	$ 0			$ 100		$ −100
			$162			$ 90	
1	162	162		$190.00	190		− 28
			142			80	
2	152	304		135.00	270		+ 34
			122			70	
3	142	426		113.33	340		+ 86
			102			60	
4	132	528		100.00	400		+128
			82			70	
5	**122**	**610**		**94.00**	**470**		**+140**
			62			80	
6	112	672		91.67	550		+122
			42			90	
7	102	714		91.43	640		+ 74
			22			110	
8	92	736		93.73	750		− 14
			2			130	
9	82	738		97.78	880		−142
			−18			150	
10	72	720		103.00	1030		−310

Price Exceeds Marginal Revenue   In the first place, a downsloping demand curve means that a pure monopoly can increase its sales only by charging a lower unit price for its product. *Furthermore, the fact that the monopolist must lower price to boost sales causes marginal revenue to be less than price (average revenue) for every level of output except the first.* The reason? Price cuts will apply not only to the extra output sold but also to all other units of output which otherwise could have been sold at a higher price. Each additional unit sold will add to total revenue its price *less* the sum of the price cuts which must be taken on all prior units of output.[2] The marginal revenue of the second unit of output in Table 27-1 is $142 rather than its $152 price, because a $10 price cut must be taken on the first unit to increase sales from 1 to 2 units. It is this rationale which explains why the marginal-revenue data of column 4 of Table 27-1 fall short of product price in column 2 for all levels of output save the first.

Price Maker   The second implication of a downsloping demand curve is this: In all imperfectly competitive markets in which such

demand curves are relevant—that is, purely monopolistic, oligopolistic, and monopolistically competitive markets—firms have a price policy. By virtue of their ability to influence total supply, the output decisions of such firms necessarily affect product price. This is most evident, of course, in the present case of pure monopoly, where one firm controls total output. Faced with a downsloping demand curve, wherein each output is associated with some unique price, the monopolist unavoidably determines price in deciding what volume of output to produce. The monopolist simultaneously chooses both price and output. In columns 1 and 2 of Table 27-1 we find that the monopolist can sell only an output of 1 unit at a price of $162, only an output of 2 units at a price of $152 per unit, and so forth.[3]

But all this is not to imply that the monopolist is "free" of market forces in establishing price and output or that the consumer

[2] At this point it may be helpful to reread the discussion of the mechanics of this process in Chapter 23.

[3] The notion of a supply curve does not apply in a purely monopolistic (or any other imperfectly competitive) market because of the ability of the seller to control product price. A supply curve shows the amounts producers will offer at various *given* prices which may confront them in the market. But prices are not "given" to the pure monopolist; he does not respond to a fixed price, but rather, sets the price himself.

is somehow completely at the monopolist's mercy. In particular, the monopolist's downsloping demand curve means that high prices are associated with low volumes of sales and, conversely, low prices with larger outputs. The monopolist cannot raise price without losing sales or gain sales without charging a lower price. The question which now arises is this: What specific price-quantity combination on his demand curve will the pure monopolist choose? This depends not only upon demand and marginal-revenue data but also upon costs.

□ **Cost Data**

On the cost side of the picture we shall assume that, although the firm is a monopolist in the product market, it hires resources competitively and employs the same technology as our competitive firm in the preceding chapter. This permits us to use the cost data developed in Chapter 25 and applied in Chapter 26, thereby facilitating a comparison of the price-output decisions of a pure monopoly with those of a pure competitor. Columns 5 through 7 of Table 27-1 merely restate the pertinent cost concepts of Table 25-2.

□ **Equating Marginal Revenue and Marginal Cost**

A profit-seeking monopolist will employ the same rationale as a profit-seeking firm in a competitive industry. He will produce each successive unit of output so long as it adds more to his total revenue than it does to his total costs. In technical language, the firm will produce up to that output at which marginal revenue equals marginal cost.

A comparison of columns 4 and 7 in Table 27-1 indicates that the profit-maximizing output is 5 units; the fifth unit is the last unit of output whose marginal revenue exceeds its marginal cost. What price will the monopolist charge? His downsloping demand curve of col-

umns 1 and 2 in Table 27-1 shows him that there is only one price at which 5 units can be sold: $122.

This same analysis is presented graphically in Figure 27-1, where the demand, marginal-revenue, average-total-cost, and marginal-cost data of Table 27-1 have been drawn. A comparison of marginal revenue and marginal cost again indicates that the profit-maximizing output is 5 units or, more generally, Q_m. The unique price at which Q_m can be sold is found by extending a perpendicular up from the profit-maximizing point on the output axis and then at right angles from the point at which it hits the demand curve to the vertical axis. The indicated price is P_m. By charging a price higher than P_m, the monopolist must move up his demand curve, and this means that his sales will fall short of the profit-maximizing level Q_m. Specifically, the firm will be failing to produce units of output whose marginal revenue exceeds their marginal cost. If the monopolist charges less, it would involve a volume of sales in excess of the profit-maximizing output.

Columns 2 and 5 of Table 27-1 indicate that, at 5 units of output, product price of $122 exceeds average total cost of $94. Economic profits are therefore $28 per unit; total economic profits are then $140 ($= 5 \times$28$). In Figure 27-1, per unit profit is indicated by the distance AP_m, and total economic profits —the brown area—are found by multiplying this unit profit by the profit-maximizing output Q_m.

The same profit-maximizing combination of output and price can also be determined by comparing the total revenue and total costs incurred at each possible level of production. The reader should employ columns 3 and 6 of Table 27-1 to verify all the conclusions we have reached through the use of marginal-revenue–marginal-cost analysis. Similarly, an accurate graphing of total revenue and total cost against output will also show the greatest differential (the maximum profit) at 5 units of output.

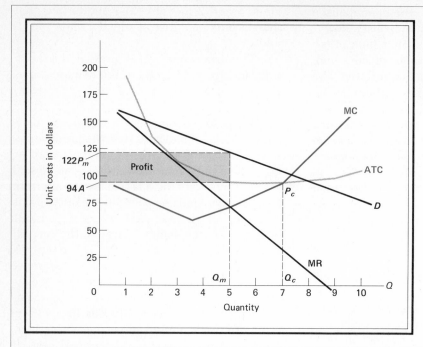

FIGURE 27-1 THE PROFIT-MAXIMIZING POSITION OF A PURE MONOPOLIST

The pure monopolist maximizes profits by producing the MR = MC output. In this instance profit is AP_m per unit, total profits are measured by the brown rectangle.

□ Misconceptions Concerning Monopoly Pricing

Our analysis explodes some popular fallacies concerning the behavior of monopolies.

1   Not Highest Price   Because a monopolist can manipulate output and price, it is often alleged that a monopolist "will charge the highest price he can get." This is clearly a misguided assertion. There are many prices above P_m in Figure 27-1, but the monopolist shuns them solely because they entail a smaller than maximum profit. Total profits are the difference between total revenue and total costs, and each of these two determinants of profits depends upon the quantity sold as much as upon the price and unit cost.

2   Total, not Unit, Profits   The monopolist seeks maximum *total* profits, not maximum *unit* profits. In Figure 27-1 a careful comparison of the vertical distance between average cost and price at various possible outputs indi-

cates that per unit profits are greater at a point slightly to the left of the profit-maximizing output Q_m. This is more readily seen in Table 27-1, where unit profits are $32 at 4 units of output as compared with $28 at the profit-maximizing output of 5 units. In this instance the monopolist is accepting a lower-than-maximum per unit profit for the simple reason that the additional sales more than compensate for the lower unit profits. A profit-seeking monopolist would obviously rather sell 5 units at a profit of $28 per unit than 4 units at a profit of $32 per unit.

3   Losses   It must also be emphasized that pure monopoly does not guarantee economic profits. True, the likelihood of economic profits is greater for a pure monopolist than for a purely competitive producer. In the long run the latter is doomed by the free and easy entry of new firms to a normal profit; barriers to entry permit the monopolist to perpetuate economic profits in the long run. Of course, like the pure competitor, the monopolist cannot

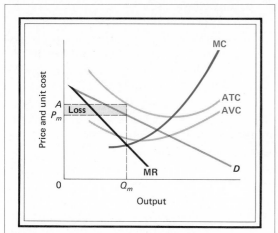

FIGURE 27-2 THE LOSS-MINIMIZING POSITION OF A PURE MONOPOLIST

If demand D is weak and costs are high, the pure monopolist may be unable to make a profit. He will minimize his losses in the short run by producing at that output where MR = MC. Loss per unit is AP_m, and total losses are indicated by the blue rectangle.

Public Scrutiny In the first place, the monopolist does not have anonymity; the identity of monopolistic sellers is typically well known. It follows that the monopolist who fully exploits his market position may find himself the target of public criticism or the object of moral suasion designed to enforce a "voluntary" wage-price policy (Chapter 18). After all, in Figure 27-1 there are many prices less than P_m which will entail outputs greater than Q_m and still yield substantial economic profits to the monopolist. If criticism is widespread and persistent, it can lead to a loss of goodwill or, worse yet from the firm's viewpoint, some form of governmental intervention—antitrust action, rate regulation, government stimulation of new competitors, or, at the extreme, nationalization of the firm. Thus, from a very long-run standpoint it may be sensible for the monopolist to avoid unfavorable comment with respect to his market behavior, even at the sacrifice of some profits.

The "Long View" Secondly, the monopoly may deliberately limit its profits so as not to attract new competitors. A highly profitable monopoly may cause potential rivals to double their efforts to overcome the monopolist's barriers. And remember: Barriers to entry are rarely insurmountable over time. Full exploitation of a monopolist's position in the short run may destroy that monopolistic position in the long pull.

The importance of these "voluntary" restraints is subject to heated debate. It would be a mistake to say that they undermine our profit-maximizing analysis; at best they probably cause minor deviations from the most profitable price-output combination.

PRICE DISCRIMINATION

The aforementioned restraints on monopoly *may* tend to make its price-output policies somewhat more socially acceptable. We must

persistently operate at a loss. He must realize a normal profit or better in the long run or he will not survive. However, if the demand and cost situation faced by the monopolist is less favorable than that shown in Figure 27-1, he may realize short-run losses. Despite his dominance in the market, the monopolist shown in Figure 27-2 realizes a loss in the short run by virtue of a weak demand and high costs.

☐ **Possible Restraints upon Profit Maximization**

The foregoing comments indicate that certain restraints are imposed upon the monopolist by the market. Cost and demand considerations set restrictions upon the monopolist's price-output behavior. Actually, certain other forces may cause the monopolist to exercise restraint; these forces may cause him purposely to charge a lower price and produce a greater output than are consistent with maximum profits. Two of these restraints merit further comment.

now recognize that through *price discrimination* a monopolist might exploit and profit from his market position to an even greater extent than Figure 27-1 indicates. *Price discrimination takes place when a given product is sold at more than one price and these price differences are not justified by cost differences.* The monopolist's downsloping demand curve suggests that price discrimination can be a highly profitable policy. After all, the segment of the demand curve lying above the profit area in Figure 27-1 tells us that there are buyers of the product who would be willing to pay *more than P_m* ($122) rather than forgo the product. If the monopolist can somehow identify and segregate each of these buyers and thereby charge the maximum price each would pay, his profits would be expanded considerably. In columns 1 and 2 of Table 27-1 we note that the buyers of the first 4 units of output would be willing to pay more than the equilibrium price of $122. If the seller could somehow extract the maximum price each would pay, total revenue would increase from $610 (= $122 × 5) to $710 (= $122 + $132 + $142 + $152 + $162) and profits would increase from $140 (= $610 − $470) to $240 (= $710 − $470).

Price discrimination is not an isolated occurrence; it is much more common in our economy than we recognize. A surgeon may charge a well-to-do patient $500 for an operation, while a less affluent patient is billed for only $200. Lawyers frequently set their fees for a given service on the basis of ability to pay; a rich man may pay a substantially larger legal fee for a divorce than a poor man. A car sales representative may sell identical cars at different prices to two different buyers. A manufacturer sells the same whiskey at a high price under a prestige label, but at a lower price under a different label. An appliance or tire manufacturer sells its product directly to the public at one price and through Sears or Ward's at a lower price. Other common examples will follow.

□ **Conditions**

The opportunity to engage in price discrimination is not readily available to all sellers. In general, price discrimination is workable when three conditions are realized.

1 Most obviously, the seller must be a monopolist or, at least, possess some degree of monopoly power. Under competition the buyer who is confronted with a higher, discriminatory price would quickly shift his patronage to another seller.

2 The seller must be able to segment the market; that is, he must be able to sort out those buyers whose demand is inelastic (relatively insensitive to price) from those whose demand is elastic. These differences in elasticity of demand may be related to differences in buyer incomes or ability to pay, consumer tastes, or availability of substitute goods or services. As we shall discover, the buyer whose demand is inelastic will be charged a higher price than the buyer whose demand is elastic.

3 The original purchaser cannot resell the product or service. If those who buy in the low-price segment of the market can easily resell in the high-price segment, the resulting decline in supply would increase price in the low-price segment and the increase in supply would lower price in the high-price segment. The price discrimination policy would thereby be undermined.

Some further examples of price discrimination reflect the significance of these conditions. The sales representative who must communicate important information to corporate headquarters has a highly inelastic demand for long-distance telephone service and pays the high daytime rate. The college student making a periodic "reporting in" call to the folks at home has an elastic demand and defers the call to take advantage of lower evening or weekend rates. Electric utilities frequently segment their markets by end uses, such as lighting and heating. The absence of reasonable substitutes means that the demand for electricity for illumination is inelastic and the price per kilowatt hour for this use is high. But the availability of natural gas and petroleum as alternatives to electrical heating makes the demand for electricity elastic for this purpose and the price charged is therefore lower. Similarly, industrial users of electricity are typically charged lower rates than residential users because the former may have the alternative of constructing their own generating equipment while the individual household does not. Movie theaters and golf courses vary their charges on the basis of time (higher rates in the evening and on weekends when demand is strong) and age (ability to pay). Railroads vary the rate charged per ton mile of freight according to the market value of the product being shipped. The shipper of 10 tons of television sets or costume jewelry will be charged more than the shipper of 10 tons of gravel or coal. Note that these illustrations not only demonstrate the various bases for market segmentation (condition 2), but most of them involve services which the buyer cannot resell (condition 3).

□ Desirability

Is the practice of price discrimination socially desirable? The term itself carries an unfavorable connotation and, indeed, there is no doubt that price discrimination allows many monopolistic sellers to expand their profits beyond those which a single-price monopolist would realize.

On the other hand, price discrimination is not without defenses. While the general public may look upon the charging of discriminatory fees by doctors as a rip-off, the physicians themselves argue that, by charging high fees to the wealthy, they can treat low-income patients at token fees. Price discrimination, they contend, redistributes income from rich to poor, not from the general public to the medical profession. Furthermore, it is claimed that the survival of certain vital industries may depend upon the practice of price discrimina-

tion. Look back at Figure 27-2. Suppose this diagram shows the equilibrium position for, say, an electric utility. At the uniform monopoly price of P_m, the firm fails to cover its average total cost and in the long run the utility would be forced out of business. But such natural monopolies are providing an essential service to a municipality or region and the cessation of service is unthinkable. What can be done? One option, of course, might be a public subsidy of some sort. Another is to allow the utility to engage in price discrimination for the purpose of enlarging its revenues so as to cover total costs and ensure the survival of the firm.

■ ECONOMIC EFFECTS

Let us now evaluate pure monopoly from the standpoint of society as a whole. Our emphasis will be upon (1) price, output, and resource allocation; (2) the distribution of income; and (3) economic progress, that is, technological advance. To sharpen our analysis we ignore any possible restraints upon the monopolist's policies and presume that it seeks the maximum profit that its cost-revenue situation permits. We also assume that no price discrimination occurs.

□ Price, Output, and Resource Allocation

In Chapter 26 we concluded that pure competition would result in a highly efficient, or "ideal," allocation of resources. In the long run the free entry and exodus of firms would force firms to operate at the optimum rate of output where unit costs of production would be at a minimum. Product price would be at the lowest level consistent with average total costs. To illustrate: In Figure 27-1 the competitive firm would sell Q_c units of output at a price of Q_cP_c. Furthermore, long-run competitive equilibrium would also entail an efficient allocation of resources, in that production would occur up to that point at which price (the measure of a product's value to society) would equal marginal cost (the measure of the alternative products forgone by society in the production of any given commodity).

Figure 27-1 indicates that, given the same costs, a purely monopolistic firm will produce much less desirable results. As we have already discovered, the pure monopolist will maximize his profits by producing an output of Q_m and charging a price of P_m. It can be readily seen that *the monopolist will find it profitable to sell a smaller output and to charge a higher price than would a competitive producer.*[4] Furthermore, it is clear that, at Q_m

[4] In Figure 27-1 the price-quantity comparison of monopoly and pure competition is from the vantage point of the single purely competitive *firm* of Figure 26-6a. An equally illuminating approach is to start with the purely competitive *industry* of Figure 26-6b, which is reproduced below. Recall that the competitive industry's supply curve S is the horizontal sum of the marginal-cost curves of all the firms in the industry. Comparing this with industry demand D, we get the purely competitive price and output of P_c and Q_c. Now suppose that this industry becomes a pure monopoly as a result of a wholesale merger or one firm's somehow buying out all its competitors. Assume, too, that no changes in costs or market demand result from this dramatic change in the industry's structure. What were formerly, say, 100 competing firms are now a pure monopolist consisting of 100 branch plants.

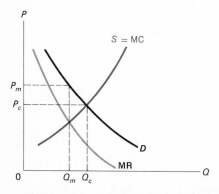

The industry supply curve is now simply the marginal-cost curve of the monopolist, the summation of the MC curves of its many branch plants. The important change, however, is on the market-demand side. From the viewpoint of each individual competitive firm, demand was perfectly elastic, and marginal revenue was therefore equal to price. Each firm equated MC to MR (and therefore to

units of output, product price is considerably greater than marginal cost. This means that society values additional units of this monopolized product more highly than it does the alternative products which resources could otherwise produce. In other words, the monopolist's profit-maximizing output results in an underallocation of resources; the monopolist finds it profitable to restrict output and therefore employ fewer resources than are justified from society's standpoint.

To summarize: Given identical costs, a purely monopolistic firm will find it profitable to charge a higher price, produce a smaller output, and foster an allocation of economic resources inferior to that of a purely competitive firm. These contrasting consequences are rooted in the barriers to entry which characterize monopoly.

There is one basic exception to these conclusions: The assumption that the unit costs available to the purely competitive and the purely monopolistic firm are the same may not hold in practice. Given production techniques and therefore production costs, consumer demand may not be sufficient to support a large number of competing firms producing at an output which permits each of them to realize all known economies of scale. In such instances a firm must be large in relation to the market—that is, it must be monopolistic—to produce efficiently (at low unit cost). Our previous discussion of economies of scale as a barrier to entry and the desirability of establishing public utilities in certain fields is based primarily upon such cost considerations (see Chapter 25).

How important is this exception? Most

P) in maximizing profits (Chapter 26). But industry demand and individual demand are the same to the pure monopolist; the firm *is* the industry, and thus the monopolist correctly envisions a downsloping demand curve D. This means that marginal revenue MR will be less than price; graphically the MR curve lies below the demand curve. In choosing the profit-maximizing MC = MR position, the monopolist selects an output Q_m which is smaller, and a price P_m which is greater, than would be the case if the industry were organized competitively.

economists feel that it applies for the most part only to public utilities and is therefore not significant enough to undermine our general conclusions concerning the restrictive nature of monopoly. The best available evidence (see footnote 7 in Chapter 7) suggests that the giant corporations which populate many manufacturing industries now have more monopoly power than can be justified on the grounds that these firms are merely availing themselves of existing economies of scale.

☐ **Income Distribution**

Business monopoly probably contributes to inequality in the distribution of income. By virtue of their market power, monopolists charge a higher price than would a purely competitive firm with the same costs; monopolists are in effect able to levy a "private tax" upon consumers and thereby to realize substantial economic profits. These monopolistic profits, it should be noted, are not widely distributed because corporate stock ownership is largely concentrated in the hands of upper income groups. The owners of monopolistic enterprises thereby tend to be enriched at the expense of the rest of society.

Assuming monopoly does contribute to income inequality, is this necessarily undesirable? There is no agreement here, and no scientifically correct answer will ever be found because any view entails a value judgment on what one feels the distribution of income ought to be. Nevertheless, there is a rather widespread feeling in our society that the extreme degrees of income inequality to which pure monopoly frequently contributes are undesirable (see Chapter 37).

☐ **Technological Advance**

We have already qualified our condemnation of pure monopoly by noting that in a few instances *existing* mass-production economies may be lost if an industry comprises a large number of small, competing firms. There is

also a dynamic aspect to this line of reasoning. To be specific, will competition or monopoly foster the more rapid improvement of products and productive techniques over time? This is fertile ground for honest differences of opinion.

The Competitive Model Competitive firms certainly have the incentive—indeed, a market mandate—to employ the most efficient *known* productive techniques. We have seen that their very survival depends upon being efficient. But at the same time, competition tends to deprive firms of economic profit—an important means and a major incentive to develop *new* products and *new* improved productive techniques. The profits of technological advance will be short-lived to the innovating competitor. An innovating firm in a competitive industry will find that its many rivals will soon duplicate or imitate any technological advance it may achieve; rivals will share the rewards but not the costs of successful technological research.

The Monopoly Model In contrast, we have seen that—thanks to entry barriers—a monopolist may persistently realize substantial economic profits. Hence, the pure monopolist will have greater financial resources for technological advance than will competitive firms. But what about the monopolist's incentives for technological advance? Here the picture is clouded.

There is one imposing argument which suggests that the monopolist's incentives to develop new products and new techniques will be weak: The absence of competitors means that there is no automatic stimulus to technological advance in a monopolized market. Because of its sheltered market position, the pure monopolist can afford to be inefficient and lethargic. The keen rivalry of a competitive market penalizes the inefficient; an inefficient monopolist does not face this penalty simply because it has no rivals. The monopolist has every reason to become satisfied with the status quo, to become complacent. It might well pay the monopolist to withhold or "file" technological improvements in both product and productive techniques in order to exploit existing capital equipment fully. New and improved products and techniques, it is argued, may be suppressed by monopolists to avoid any losses caused by the sudden obsolescence of existing machinery and equipment. And, even when improved techniques are belatedly introduced by monopolists, the accompanying cost reductions will accrue to the monopolist as increases in profits and only partially, if at all, to consumers in the form of lower prices and an increased output. Proponents of this view point out that in a number of industries which approximate pure monopoly—for example, steel and aluminum—the interest in research has been minimal. Such advances as have been realized have come largely from outside the industry or from the smaller firms which make up the "competitive fringe" of the industry.

Basically, there are at least two counterarguments:

1 Technological advance is a means of lowering unit costs and thereby expanding profits. As our analysis of Figure 27-1 implies, lower costs will give rise to a profit-maximizing position which involves a larger output and a lower price than previously. Furthermore, any expansion of profits will not be of a transitory nature; barriers to entry protect the monopolist from profit encroachment by rivals. In short, technological progress is profitable to the monopolist.

2 Research and technological advance may be one of the monopolist's barriers to entry; hence, the monopolist must persist and succeed in the area of technological advance or eventually fall prey to new competitors. Technological progress, it is argued, is essential to the maintenance of monopoly.

A Mixed Picture Which view is more accurate? Frankly, economists are not sure. Most economists do not envision pure monopoly as a particularly progressive market structure. At the same time, they acknowledge that agriculture, the industry which most nearly fits the competitive model, has only on rare occasions provided itself with innovations in product and method. Government research and the oligopolistic firms which produce farm equipment have provided this competitive industry with most of its improvements in products and techniques. As we shall see in Chapter 29, some respected economists seem to feel that oligopolistic industries, wherein firms are large enough to have the ability to finance research and at the same time are compelled to engage in such research because of the presence of a moderate number of rivals, may be more conducive to technological advance than any other market structure.

Now what can be offered by way of a summarizing generalization on the economic efficiency of pure monopoly? Simply this: In a static economy, wherein economies of scale are equally accessible to purely competitive and monopolist firms, pure competition will be superior to pure monopoly in that pure competition forces use of the best-known technology and allocates resources in accordance with the wants of society. On the other hand, when economies of scale available to the monopolist are not attainable by small competitive producers, or in a dynamic context in which changes in the rate of technological advance must be considered, the inefficiencies of pure monopoly are not so evident.

REGULATED MONOPOLY

Most purely monopolistic industries are "natural monopolies" and therefore subject to social regulation. In particular, the prices or rates which public utilities—railroads, telephone companies, natural gas and electricity suppliers—can charge are determined by a Federal, state, or local regulatory commission or board. Can such regulation improve the social acceptability of monopoly?

Figure 27-3 is informative. We know that

FIGURE 27-3   REGULATED MONOPOLY

Price regulation can improve the social consequences of a
natural monopoly. The socially optimum price P_r will result
in an efficient allocation of resources but is likely to entail
losses and therefore call for permanent public subsidies. The
"fair-return" price P_f will allow the monopolist to break
even, but will not fully correct the underallocation of
resources.

P_m and Q_m are the profit-maximizing price and
output which the unregulated monopolist
would choose. Because price exceeds average
total cost, the monopolist enjoys a substantial
economic profit which is likely to contribute to
income inequality. Furthermore, price exceeds
marginal cost, which indicates an underallocation of resources to this product or service.

□   **Socially Optimum Price**

If the objective of our regulatory commission is to achieve an efficient allocation of resources, it should obviously establish a legal
(ceiling) price for the monopolist that is equal
to marginal cost. Remembering that each
point on the market demand curve designates
a price-quantity combination, and noting that
marginal cost cuts the demand curve only at
point R, it is quite obvious that P_r is the only
price which is equal to marginal cost. The
imposition of this maximum or ceiling price
causes the monopolist's effective demand curve
to become $P_rRD;$ the demand curve becomes

perfectly elastic, and therefore $P_r = $ MR out to
point R, where the regulated price ceases to be
effective. The important point is that, given
the legal price P_r, the monopolist will maximize profits by producing Q_r units of output,
because it is at this output that MR (P_r) = MC.
By making it illegal to charge more than P_r per
unit, the regulatory agency has eliminated the
monopolist's incentive to restrict output in
order to benefit from a higher price. In short,
by imposing the legal price P_r and letting the
monopolist choose his profit-maximizing output, the allocative results of pure competition
can be simulated. Production takes place
where $P_r = $ MC, and this equality indicates an
efficient allocation of resources to this product
or service. This reasoning, incidentally, is the
basis for the argument made in Chapter 18
that mandatory price controls imposed in an
imperfectly competitive economy might improve resource allocation.

□   **"Fair-return" Price**

But the socially optimum price P_r is likely
to pose a problem of losses for the regulated
firm. The price which equals marginal cost is
likely to be so low that average total costs are
not covered. The inevitable result is losses.
The reason for this lies in the basic character of
public utilities. Because they are required to
meet "peak" demands (both daily and seasonally) for their product or service, they tend to
have substantial excess productive capacity
when demand is relatively "normal." This
high level of investment in capital facilities
means that unit costs of production are likely
to decline over a wide range of output. In
technical terms, the market demand curve in
Figure 27-3 cuts marginal cost at a point to
the left of the marginal-cost-average-total-
cost intersection, so the socially optimum
price is necessarily below AC. Therefore, to
enforce a socially optimum price upon the
regulated monopolist would mean short-run
losses, and in the long run, bankruptcy for
the utility.

What to do? One option would be a public subsidy sufficient to cover the loss which the socially optimum price would entail. Another possibility is to condone price discrimination in the hope that the additional revenue gained thereby will permit the firm to cover costs. In practice, regulatory commissions have pursued a third option; they have tended to back away somewhat from the objective of allocative efficiency and marginal-cost pricing. Most regulatory agencies in the United States are concerned with establishing a "fair-return" price. This is so in no small measure because, as the courts have envisioned it, an unembellished socially optimum price would lead to losses and eventual bankruptcy and thereby deprive the monopoly's owners of their private property without "due process of law." Indeed, the Supreme Court has held that the regulatory agencies must permit a "fair return" to owners.

Remembering that total costs include a normal or "fair" profit, we see that the "fair" or "fair-return" price in Figure 27-3 would obviously be P_f, where price equals *average* cost. Because the demand curve cuts average cost only at point F, it is clear that P_f is the only price which permits a fair return. The corresponding output at regulated price P_f will be Q_f.

□   **Dilemma of Regulation**

A comparison of the results of the socially optimum price and the fair-return price suggests a policy dilemma. When price is set to achieve the most efficient allocation of resources $(P = MC)$, the regulated utility is likely to suffer losses. Survival of the firm would presumably depend upon permanent public subsidies out of tax revenues. On the other hand, although a fair-return price $(P = AC)$ allows the monopolist to cover costs, it only partially resolves the underallocation of resources which the unregulated monopoly would foster. That is, the fair-return price would only increase output from Q_m to Q_f, whereas the socially optimum output is Q_r. Despite this knotty problem, the basic point is that regulation can improve upon the results of monopoly from the social point of view. Price regulation can simultaneously reduce price, increase output, and reduce the economic profits of monopolies.

Summary

1   A pure monopolist is the sole producer of a commodity for which there are no close substitutes.

2   Barriers to entry, in the form of *a.* economies of scale, *b.* natural monopolies, *c.* the ownership or control of essential raw materials, *d.* patent ownership and research, *e.* unfair competition, and *f.* economies of being established, help explain the existence of pure monopoly and other imperfectly competitive market structures. Barriers to entry which are very formidable in the short run may prove to be surmountable in the long run.

3   The pure monopolist's market situation differs from that of a competitive firm in that the monopolist's demand curve is downsloping, causing the marginal-revenue curve to lie below the demand curve. Like the competitive seller, the pure monopolist will maximize profits by equating marginal revenue and marginal cost. Barriers to entry may permit a monopolist to acquire economic profits even in the long run. It is noteworthy, however, that *a.* the monopolist does not charge "the highest price he can get"; *b.* the maximum total profit sought by the monopolist rarely coincides with maximum unit profits; and *c.* high costs and a weak demand may prevent the monopolist from realizing any profit at all.

4   A monopolist can increase his profits by practicing price discrimination, provided he can segregate buyers on the basis of different elasticities of demand and the product or service cannot be readily transferred between the segmented markets.

5   Given the same costs, the pure monopolist will find it more profitable to restrict output and charge a higher price than would a competitive seller. This restriction of output causes resources to be misallocated, as is evidenced by the fact that price exceeds marginal cost in monopolized markets.

6   Monopoly tends to increase income inequality.

7   Economists disagree as to how conducive pure monopoly is to technological advance. Some feel that pure monopoly is more progressive than pure competition because its ability to realize economic profits provides for the financing of technological research. Others, however, argue that the absence of rival firms and the monopolits's desire to exploit fully his existing capital facilities weaken the monopolist's incentive to innovate.

8   Price regulation can be invoked to eliminate wholly or partially the tendency of monopolists to underallocate resources and to earn economic profits.

Questions and Study Suggestions

1   Key terms and concepts to remember: pure monopoly; barriers to entry; natural monopoly; unfair competition; economies of being established; price discrimination; socially optimum price; fair-return price; the dilemma of regulation.

2   "No firm is completely sheltered from rivals; all firms compete for the dollars of consumers. Pure monopoly, therefore, does not exist." Do you agree? Explain.

3   Discuss the major barriers to entry. Explain how each barrier can foster monopoly or oligopoly. Which barriers, if any, do you feel give rise to monopoly that is socially justifiable?

4   Critically evaluate and explain:

a.   "Because they can control product price, monopolists are always assured of profitable production by simply charging the highest price consumers will pay."

b.   "The pure monopolist seeks that output which will yield the greatest per unit profit."

c.   "An excess of price over marginal cost is the market's way of signaling the need for more production of a product."

d.   "The more profitable a firm, the greater its monopoly power."

e.   "The monopolist has a price policy; the competitive producer does not."

f.   "With respect to resource allocation, the interests of the seller and of society coincide in a purely competitive market but conflict in a monopolized market."

g.   "In a sense the monopolist makes a profit for not producing; the monopolist produces profits more than he does goods."

5   Carefully evaluate the following widely held viewpoint. Can you offer any arguments to the contrary?[5]

Competition is congenial to material progress. It keeps the door open to new blood and new ideas. It communicates to all producers the improvements made by any one of them. Monopoly, as such, is not conducive to progress. The large

---

[5]Clair Wilcox, *Public Policies toward Business* (Homewood, Ill.: Richard D. Irwin, Inc., 1955), p. 12.

firm may engage in research and invent new products, materials, methods and machines. But when it possesses a monopoly, it will be reluctant to make use of these inventions if they would compel it to scrap existing equipment or if it believes that their ultimate profitability is in doubt. The monopolist may introduce innovations and cut costs, but instead of moving goods by reducing prices he is prone to spend large sums on alternative methods of promoting sales. His refusal to cut prices deprives the community of any gain.

6   Suppose a pure monopolist is faced with the demand schedule shown below and the same cost data as the competitive producer discussed in question 5 at the end

Price	Quantity demanded	Marginal revenue
$100	1	$_____
83	2	
71	3	_____
63	4	_____
55	5	_____
48	6	_____
42	7	_____
37	8	_____
33	9	_____
29	10	_____

of Chapter 26. Calculate marginal revenue and determine the profit-maximizing price and output for this monopolist. What is the level of profits? Verify your answer graphically. If this firm could engage in perfect price discrimination, that is, if it could charge each buyer the maximum acceptable price, what would be the level of profits?

7   Explain verbally and graphically how price (rate) regulation may improve the performance of monopolies. What is the "dilemma of regulation"?

8   How does the demand curve faced by a purely monopolistic seller differ from that confronting a purely competitive firm? Why does it differ? Of what significance is the difference? Why is the pure monopolist's demand curve not perfectly inelastic?

9   Assume a pure monopolist and a purely competitive firm have the same unit costs. Contrast the two with respect to **a.** price, **b.** output, **c.** profits, **d.** allocation of resources, and **e.** impact upon the distribution of income. Since both monopolists and competitive firms follow the MC = MR rule in maximizing profits, how do you account for the different results?

Selected References

Adams, Walter (ed.): *The Structure of American Industry,* 5th ed. (New York: The Macmillan Company, 1977), chaps. 9, 11.

Cox, Eli P.: "A Case for Price Discrimination," *Business Topics* (Michigan State University), Summer 1975, pp. 39–46.

Koch, James V.: *Microeconomic Theory and Applications* (Boston: Little, Brown and Company, 1976), chap. 9.

Robinson, E. A. G.: *Monopoly* (London: Nesbit and Company, 1941).

Schumpeter, Joseph A.: *Capitalism, Socialism, and Democracy,* 3d ed. (New York: Harper & Row, Publishers, Incorporated, 1950), chaps. 7, 8.

Last Word
Monopoly in Professional Basketball

Dr. Roger G. Noll analyzes monopoly pricing by professional basketball teams.

Basketball teams are organized into leagues which grant each club a franchise to provide its services in a designated geographic area. The franchise is a valuable economic asset because it not only gives the club the right to operate in an area, but grants it the privilege of being the sole provider of the service there. Thus, if anybody in the city wishes to see a live basketball game, he must buy it from the franchisee, or not at all. . . .

In the area of providing professional sports contests, we have in fact turned such monopoly power over to private interest to handle as they wish. . . .

One consequence of uncontrolled monopoly rights is monopoly pricing. In a competitive industry, prices tend to converge to the point where they equal the incremental [marginal] costs of providing one more consumer with output from the industry. If prices are above incremental costs, some firms will expand output or enter the industry in response to the potential for profit. This expansion will lower prices until costs and price fall into rough equality. If prices are below incremental costs, some firms will cut back on output or leave the industry to avoid losses on sales. In a noncompetitive market, the expansion of output to equate prices and incremental costs does not occur, for the monopolist can earn higher profits if prices are above—and output level below—the competitive level.

In basketball, the incremental cost of serving an additional spectator is almost solely the cost of improving team quality. [Data show that] improving the record of the team 10-percent increases attendance by 47,000 persons. And the teams who have done relatively better in winning games over the past few years, winning around 60 to 70 percent of their games, normally pay $10,000 to $20,000 more per player than average. This translates roughly to a cost of about $125,000 to increase attendance by 50,000. Since other costs—ushers, extra publicity, maintenance—are likely to be relatively small, the incremental cost of providing a live basketball game to an additional fan is certainly under $3, and probably not much above $2.50. However, [average ticket price is $4.50 and] many arenas have no seats at all priced as low as $2.50, the true incremental cost.

The preceding analysis indicates the following characterization of basketball operations. First, the handful of lucrative franchises exercise their full monopoly powers by charging very high prices. Then because the monopoly revenues in these cities are not significantly shared with other teams, the remaining borderline and losing franchises are also forced to charge monopoly prices to minimize losses. The result is a pricing structure that excludes many fans who are willing to pay the true incremental cost of letting them view a game. Yet, such pricing still does not prevent widespread financial losses within the sport because the monopoly profits are retained by a small group of rich franchises.

Basketball has gone to the extreme of creating monopoly franchises and charging monopoly prices, but without equalization of the monopoly revenues to make the leagues economically viable. From the point of view of the fans, this is the worst possible arrangement. His own ticket prices are higher than the costs of providing him with the service, but the extra revenues he pays are not used to improve the financial position of weak teams and thereby make competition more even. Consequently, fans in the cities with poorer teams are, and will continue to be, faced with the unattractive alternatives of having no team at all or having a very highly priced poor team. Fans in large cities also face high prices, and they can watch good teams—but they must watch their good teams play a large number of games against unnecessarily weak opposition because the very high profits of their own team are not shared.

From *Professional Basketball,* Hearings before the Subcommittee on Antitrust and Monopoly of the Committee on the Judiciary, U.S. Senate, 92d Congress, 1st Session, Washington, 1971, pp. 389–390, abridged.

28

Price and Output Determination: Monopolistic Competition

Pure competition and pure monopoly are the exception, not the rule, in American capitalism. Most market structures fall somewhere between these two extremes. In Chapter 29 we shall discuss oligopoly, a market structure which stands close to pure monopoly. In the present chapter we are concerned with monopolistic competition. Monopolistic competition correctly suggests a blending of monopoly and competition; more specifically, monopolistic competition involves a very considerable amount of competition with a small dose of monopoly power intermixed.

Our basic objectives in this chapter are:

1 To define and discuss the nature and prevalence of monopolistic competition.

2 To analyze and evaluate the price-output behavior of monopolistically competitive firms.

3 To explain and assess the role of nonprice competition, that is, competition based upon product quality and advertising, in monopolistically competitive industries.

MONOPOLISTIC COMPETITION: CONCEPT AND OCCURRENCE

First of all, let us recall, and also expand upon, the definition of monopolistic competition.

□ **Relatively Large Numbers**

Monopolistic competition refers to that market situation in which a relatively large number of small producers or suppliers are offering similar but not identical products. The contrasts between this and pure competition are important. Monopolistic competition does not require the presence of hundreds or thousands of firms but only a fairly large number—say 25, 35, 60, or 70.

Several important characteristics of monopolistic competition follow from the presence of relatively large numbers. In the first place, each firm has a comparatively small percentage of the total market, so each has a very limited amount of control over market price. Then too, the presence of a relatively large number of firms also ensures that collusion—concerted action by the firms to restrict output and rig price—is all but impossible. Finally, with numerous firms in the industry, there is no feeling of mutual interdependence among them; that is, each firm determines its policies without considering the possible reactions of rival firms. And this is a very reasonable way to act in a market in which one's rivals are very numerous. After all, the 10 or 15 percent increase in sales which firm X may realize by cutting price will be spread so thinly over its 20, 40, or 60 rivals that, for all practical purposes, the impact upon their sales will be imperceptible. Rivals' reactions can be ignored because the impact of one firm's actions upon each of its many rivals is so small that these rivals will have no reason to react.

◻ **Product Differentiation**

Also in contrast to pure competition, monopolistic competition has the fundamental feature of *product differentiation.* Purely competitive firms produce a standardized product; monopolistically competitive producers turn out variations of a given product. A number of firms produce cosmetics, but the product of each differs from its rivals in one or more respects. Indeed, it must be emphasized that product differentiation has more dimensions than are immediately apparent. "Real," or physical, differences involving functional features, materials, design, and workmanship

are obviously important aspects of product differentiation. But "imaginary" differences created through advertising, packaging, and the use of trademarks and brand names can be equally significant. Finally, the conditions of sale make for differentiation; the location of a store, the courteousness of its clerks, the firm's reputation for servicing its products, and the availability of credit are all facets of product differentiation.

The significance of product differentiation is basically twofold. On the one hand, despite the presence of a relatively large number of firms, monopolistically competitive producers do have limited amounts of control over the prices of their products because of differentiation. Consumers have preferences for the products of specific sellers and *within limits* will pay a higher price to satisfy those preferences. Sellers and buyers are no longer linked at random, as in a purely competitive market. On the other hand, product differentiation adds a new and complicating factor to our analysis: *nonprice competition.* Because products are differentiated, it can be supposed that they can be varied over time and that the differentiating features of each firm's product will be susceptible to advertising and other forms of sales promotion. In a monopolistically competitive market, economic rivalry centers not only upon price but also upon product variation and product promotion.

◻ **Entry Conditions**

Entry into monopolistically competitive industries tends to be relatively easy. The fact that monopolistically competitive producers are typically small-sized firms, both absolutely and relatively, suggests that economies of scale and capital requirements are few. On the other hand, as compared with pure competition, there may be some added financial barriers posed by the need for deriving a product different from one's rivals and the obligation to advertise that product. Existing firms may hold patents on their products and copyrights on their brand names and trademarks, enhancing the difficulty and cost of successfully imitating them.

In short, monopolistic competition refers to industries that comprise a relatively large number of firms, operating noncollusively, in the production of differentiated products. Nonprice competition accompanies price competition. Ease of entry makes for competition by new firms in the long run.

□   Illustrations

It is difficult to find clear-cut illustrations of monopolistically competitive industries. Many industries which approximate monopolistic competitions also embody one or more characteristics of oligopoly. Table 28-1 lists a group of manufacturing industries which approximate monopolistic competition. Retail stores in metropolitan areas are generally monopolistically competitive; grocery stores, gasoline stations, barber shops, dry cleaners, clothing stores, and so forth, operate under conditions similar to those we have described.

PRICE AND OUTPUT DETERMINATION

Let us now analyze the price-output behavior of a monopolistically competitive firm. To facilitate this task we assume initially that the firms in the industry are producing *given* products and are engaging in a *given* amount of promotional activity. Later we shall note how product variation and advertising modify our discussion.

□   The Firm's Demand Curve

Our explanation is couched in terms of Figure 28-1a. The basic feature of this diagram, which sets it off from our analyses of pure competition and pure monopoly, is the elasticity of the firm's individual demand, or sales, curve. The demand curve faced by a monopolistically competitive seller is highly, but not perfectly, elastic. It is much more elastic than the demand curve of the pure monopolist, because the monopolistically competitive seller is faced with a relatively large

Table 28-1   PERCENTAGE OF OUTPUT* PRODUCED BY FIRMS IN SELECTED LOW-CONCENTRATION MANUFACTURING INDUSTRIES

Industry	Four largest firms	Eight largest firms	Twenty largest firms
Plywood	34%	43%	61%
Book publishing	19	31	56
Men's and boys' suits and coats	19	31	48
Costume jewelry	17	27	41
Upholstered furniture	14	23	36
Wood furniture	14	22	40
Metal house furniture	13	24	44
Women's and misses' suits and coats	13	18	26
Paperboard boxes	11	17	31
Fur goods	7	12	23
Concrete block and brick	5	18	14

* As measured by value of shipments. Data are for 1972.
Source: Bureau of the Census, *1972 Census of Manufacturers.*

FIGURE 28-1 MONOPOLISTICALLY COMPETITIVE FIRMS TEND TO REALIZE A NORMAL PROFIT IN THE LONG RUN

The economic profits shown in (a) will induce new firms to enter, causing the profits to be competed away. The losses indicated in (b) will cause an exodus of firms until normal profits are restored. Thus in (c), where price just covers unit costs at the MR = MC output, the firm's long-run equilibrium position is portrayed.

perfectly elastic as is the purely competitive producer's:

1 The monopolistically competitive firm has fewer rivals.

2 The products of these rivals are close but not perfect substitutes.

Generally speaking, the precise degree of elasticity embodied in the monopolistically competitive firm's demand curve will depend upon the exact number of rivals and the degree of product differentiation. The larger the number of rivals and the weaker the product differentiation, the greater will be the elasticity of each seller's demand curve, that is, the closer the situation will be to pure competition.

□ The Short Run: Profits or Losses

The firm will maximize its profits or minimize its losses in the short run by producing that output designated by the intersection of marginal cost and marginal revenue, for reasons with which we are now familiar. The representative firm of Figure 28-1a produces an output Q, charges a price P, and is fortunate enough to realize a total profit of the size indicated in brown. But a less favorable cost and demand situation may exist, putting the monopolistically competitive firm in the position of realizing losses in the short run. This is illustrated by the light blue area in Figure 28-1b. In the short run the monopolistically competitive firm may either realize an economic profit or be faced with losses.

□ The Long Run: Break-even

In the long run, however, the tendency is for monopolistically competitive firms to earn a normal profit, that is, to break even. In the short-run profits case, Figure 28-1a, we can expect the economic profits to attract new rivals, because entry is relatively easy. As new firms enter, the demand curve faced by the typical firm will fall (shift to the left) and become more elastic. Why? Because each firm

number of rivals producing close-substitute goods. The pure monopolist, of course, has no rivals at all. Yet, for two reasons, the monopolistically competitive seller's sales curve is not has a smaller share of the total demand and now faces a larger number of close-substitute products. This in turn tends to cause the disappearance of economic profits. When the demand curve is tangent to the average-cost curve at the profit-maximizing output, as shown in Figure 28-1c, the firm is just breaking even. Output Q is the equilibrium output for the firm; as Figure 28-1c clearly indicates, any deviation from that output will entail average costs which exceed product price and, therefore, losses for the firm. Furthermore, economic profits have been competed away, and there is no incentive for additional firms to enter. In the short-run losses case, Figure 28-1b, we can expect an exodus of firms to occur in the long run. Faced with fewer substitute products and blessed with an expanded share of total demand, surviving firms will find that their losses disappear and gradually give way to approximately normal profits.[1]

Note that we have been very careful to say that the representative firm in a monopolistically competitive market *tends* to break even in the long run. There are certain complicating factors which prevent us from being more dogmatic. First, some firms may achieve a measure of product differentiation which cannot be duplicated by rivals even over a long span of time. A given gasoline station may have the only available location at the busiest intersection in town. Or a firm may hold a patent which gives it a slight and more-or-less permanent advantage over imitators. Such firms may realize a sliver of economic profits even in the long run. Second, remember that entry is not completely unrestricted. Because of product differentiation, there are likely to be greater financial barriers to entry than otherwise would be the case. This again suggests that some economic profits may persist even in the long run. A third consideration may work in the opposite direction, causing losses—

below-normal profits—to persist in the long run. The proprietor of a corner delicatessen persistently accepts a return less than he could earn elsewhere, because his business is a way of life to him. The suburban barber ekes out a meager existence, because cutting hair is "all he wants to do." With all things considered, however, the long-run profitless equilibrium of Figure 28-1c is probably a reasonable portrayal of reality.

WASTES OF MONOPOLISTIC COMPETITION

Recalling our evaluation of competitive pricing in Chapter 26, we know that economic efficiency requires the triple equality of price, marginal cost, and average cost. The equality of price and marginal cost is necessary for a correct allocation of resources to the product. The equality of price with minimum average total cost suggests the use of the most efficient (least-cost) technology; this equality means that consumers will enjoy the largest volume of product and the lowest price which prevailing cost conditions will allow.

An examination of Figure 28-1c suggests that the monopolistic element in monopolistic competition causes a modest underallocation of resources to goods produced under this market structure. Price exceeds marginal cost in long-run equilibrium, thereby indicating that society values additional units of this commodity more than the alternative products which the needed resources can otherwise produce.

Furthermore, in contrast to purely competitive firms, as suggested in Figure 28-1c, monopolistically competitive firms produce somewhat short of the most efficient (least unit cost) output. Production entails higher unit costs than the minimum attainable. This in turn means a somewhat higher price than would result under pure competition. Consumers do *not* benefit from the largest output and lowest price which cost conditions permit.

---

[1] For simplicity's sake we assume constant costs; shifts in the cost curves as firms enter or leave would complicate our discussion slightly, but would not alter the conclusions.

Indeed, monopolistically competitive firms must charge a higher than competitive price in the long run in order to manage a normal profit. Looked at differently, if each firm were able to produce at the most efficient output, a smaller number of firms could produce the same total output, and the product could be sold to consumers at a lower price. Monopolistically competitive industries tend to be overcrowded with firms, each of which is underutilized, that is, operating short of optimum capacity. This is typified by many kinds of retail establishments, for example, the thirty or forty gleaming gasoline stations, all operating short of capacity, that populate a medium-sized city. Underutilized plants, consumers penalized through higher than competitive prices for this underutilization, and producers just making a normal return in the long run—these are the so-called "wastes" of monopolistic competition.

But we must not be hypercritical of monopolistic competition. Some economists argue that in many monopolistically competitive industries the price and output results are not drastically different from those of pure competition. The highly elastic nature of each firm's demand curve guarantees that the results are nearly competitive. Furthermore, it must be kept in mind that any deviations from the purely competitive output and price may be offset by the fact that with monopolistic competition the consumer now can choose from among a number of variations of the product; he is not faced with a homogeneous commodity.

NONPRICE COMPETITION

For reasons cited above, we can conclude that the situation portrayed in Figure 28-1c may not be the most beneficial to society. It can also be surmised that it is not very satisfying to the monopolistically competitive producer who barely captures a normal profit for his efforts. We can therefore expect monopolistically competitive producers to take steps to improve upon the long-run equilibrium position. But how can this be accomplished? The answer lies in product differentiation. Each firm has a product which is currently distinguishable in some more-or-less tangible way from those of his rivals. The product is presumably subject to further variation, that is, to product development. Then, too, the emphasis upon real product differences and the creation of imaginary differences may be achieved through advertising and related sales promotion. In short, the profit-realizing producer of Figure 28-1a is loath to stand by and watch new competitors encroach upon his profits by duplicating or imitating his product, copying his advertising, and matching his services to consumers. Rather, he will attempt to sustain these profits and stay ahead of competitors through further product development and by enhancing the quantity and quality of advertising. In this way he might prevent the long-run tendency of Figure 28-1c from becoming a reality. True, product development and advertising will add to the firm's costs. But they can also be expected to increase the demand for his product. If demand increases by more than enough to compensate for development and promotional costs, the firm will have improved its profit position. As Figure 28-1c suggests, the firm may have little or no prospect of increasing profits by price cutting. So why not practice nonprice competition?

☐ **Product Differentiation and Product Development**

The likelihood that easy entry will promote product variety and product improvement is possibly a redeeming feature of monopolistic competition which may offset, wholly or in part, the "wastes" associated with this market structure. There are really two somewhat distinct considerations here: (1) product differentiation at a point in time, and (2) product improvement over a period of time.

1 Differentiation Product differentiation means that at any point in time the consumer will be offered a wide range of types, styles, brands, and quality gradations of any given product. Compared with the situation under pure competition, this correctly suggests possible advantages to the consumer. His range of free choice is widened, and variations and shadings of consumer tastes are more fully met by producers. But skeptics warn that product differentiation is not an unmixed blessing. Product proliferation may reach the point where the consumer becomes confused and rational choice is rendered time-consuming and difficult. Variety may add spice to the consumer's life, but only up to a point. Worse yet, some observers fear that the consumer, faced with a myriad of similar products, may rely upon such a dubious expedient as judging product quality by price; that is, the consumer may irrationally assume that price is necessarily an index of product quality.

2 Development Product competition is an important avenue of technological innovation and product betterment over a period of time. Such product development may be cumulative in two different senses. (*a*) A successful product improvement by one firm obligates rivals to imitate or, if they can, improve upon this firm's temporary market advantage or suffer the penalty of losses. (*b*) Profits realized from a successful product improvement can be used to finance further improvements. Again, however, there are notable criticisms of the product development which may occur under monopolistic competition. Critics point out that many product alterations are more apparent than real, consisting of frivolous and superficial changes in the product which do not improve its durability, efficiency, or usefulness. A more exotic container, bright packaging, or "shuffling the chrome" is frequently the focal point for product development. It is argued, too, that particularly in the cases of durable and semidurable consumer goods, development seems to follow a pattern of "planned obsolescence," wherein firms improve their product only by that amount necessary to make the average consumer dissatisfied with last year's model.

Do the advantages of product differentiation, properly discounted, outweigh the "wastes" of monopolistic competition? It is difficult to say, short of examining specific cases; and even then, concrete conclusions are difficult to come by. For example, a pioneering study of the (oligopolistic) automobile industry attempted to measure the cost of model changes.[2] Specifically, this question was posed: What has been the aggregate annual cost of the increases in automobile size, increases in horsepower, increased gasoline consumption caused by the "horsepower race," "power" accessories, and the cost of factory retooling required by such model changes? The investigators concluded that "the estimated costs of model changes since 1949 . . . run about 5 billion dollars per year over the 1956–60 period." Thus, although there is no question that the automobile today is a better product than it was in 1949, it is nevertheless quite legitimate to inquire: Is it *that much* better?

□ **Advertising**

A monopolistically competitive producer may gain at least a temporary edge on his rivals by manipulating his product. He may achieve the same result by manipulating the consumer through advertising and sales promotion. While product differentiation adapts the product to consumer demand, advertising adapts consumer demand to the product. In practice these two aspects of nonprice competition may be difficult to disentangle. Does a new and colorful method of packaging a product constitute a change in the product, or is it a means of advertising and promotion?

[2] F. M. Fisher, Z. Griliches, and C. Kaysen, "The Costs of Automobile Model Changes since 1949," *Journal of Political Economy,* October 1962, pp. 433–451.

Though we might tentatively agree that product development is a desirable feature of monopolistic competition, the advertising which accompanies it is more difficult to evaluate. The social desirability of extensive advertising expenditures is a very controversial and clouded topic. A basic reason for this is that some advertising is *informative,* that is, accurately descriptive of the qualities and prices of products, while other advertising is *competitive,* consisting of unsubstantiated ours-is-better-than-theirs exhortation. Local newspaper advertising is usually informative, for example, a grocery store's listing of prices and special buys. The beer, soap, and pain-reliever advertisements that the television industry funnels into American living rooms are generally competitive.

This controversy is not an unimportant one. Currently, advertising and promotional expenditures in American capitalism were estimated to be $33 billion in 1976. This exceeded the amount all state and local governments spent on public welfare. Hence, if advertising is generally wasteful, any potential virtues of monopolistically competitive markets are thereby dimmed, and the need for corrective public policies is indicated.

Extreme arguments are prevalent. Some economists are prone to write off all advertising as sheer economic waste. Others—the admen themselves—manage to associate all that is just and good in American society with advertising. An accurate picture lies in the middle ground. Let us survey the basic claims for and the charges against advertising.

The Case for Advertising   Some of the arguments in favor of advertising follow:

1 Advertising allegedly provides the information which assists consumers in making rational choices. In a dynamic, complex economy there is an acute need for the consumer to be closely acquainted with new firms, new products, and improvements in existing products. Advertising is the medium which disperses such information.

2 Advertising supports national communications. Radio, television, magazines, and newspapers are financed wholly or in part through advertising.

3 Advertising is said to be a stimulant to product development. Successful advertising is frequently based upon unique and advantageous features of a firm's product. Hence, a firm is obligated to improve its product to provide "sales points" for competing successfully in the advertising sphere.

4 Through successful advertising a firm can expand its production and thereby realize greater economies of scale. As shown in Figure 28-2, by shifting the firm's demand curve to the right through advertising, production will expand from, say, Q_1 to Q_2. Despite the fact that advertising outlays will shift the firm's average-cost curve upward, unit costs will nevertheless decline from, say, AC_1 to AC_2. Greater productive efficiency resulting from economies of scale more than offsets the increase in unit costs due to advertising. Consumers will

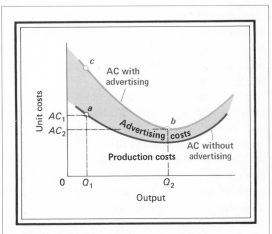

FIGURE 28-2   THE POSSIBLE EFFECTS OF ADVERTISING UPON A FIRM'S OUTPUT AND AVERAGE COSTS

Proponents of advertising contend that resulting economies of scale will expand the firm's production from, say, *a* to *b* and lower unit costs as economies of scale are realized. Some critics argue that advertising is more likely to increase costs and leave output largely unchanged, as is suggested by the movement from *a* to *c*.

therefore get the product at a lower price with advertising than they would in its absence.

5 It is held that advertising is a force which promotes competition. By providing information about a wide variety of substitute products, advertising tends to diminish monopoly power. In fact, intensive advertising is frequently associated with the introduction of new products designed to compete with existing brands.

6 Advertising allegedly promotes full employment by inducing high levels of consumer spending. This is particularly crucial, it is argued, in a wealthy society such as that of American capitalism, where much of total production takes the form of luxury or semiluxury goods which fulfill no basic wants. One need not advertise to sell food to a hungry man, but advertising and sales promotion are essential in persuading families that they need a second car, color television, or an automatic dishwasher. Stability in an opulent society calls for want-creating activities—in particular, advertising—or high levels of production and employment will not be sustainable.

The Case against Advertising   Some of the arguments on the other side of the picture allegedly "debunk" the claims for advertising; others raise new points.

1 Critics of advertising point out that the basic objective of advertising is to persuade, not to inform. Competitive advertising is based upon misleading and extravagant claims which confuse and frequently insult the intelligence of the consumer, not enlighten him. Little of real value in the rendering of rational choices can be garnered from the shampoo and shaving cream advertising which crowds our television screens and adds bulk to our magazines. Indeed, advertising may well persuade consumers in some cases to pay high prices for much-acclaimed but inferior products, forgoing better but unadvertised products selling at lower prices. The Pure Food and Drug and Federal Trade Commission Acts, which are aimed at protecting consumers from product

misrepresentation and misleading advertising, testify to past and present abuses by modern-day hucksters.

2 Advertising expenditures as such are relatively unproductive; they add little or nothing to the well-being of society. Advertising diverts human and property resources from other more pressing areas. For example, lumber which is sorely needed in the production of housing is squandered on the construction of unsightly billboards. In short, advertising contributes to the misallocation of resources. A more specific aspect of this point is the allegation that advertising contributes to the overproduction of private goods relative to public or social goods. It is argued that advertising is peculiar to, and an integral part of, the production and sale of private goods. Gigantic advertising campaigns extol the merits of electric can openers, self-propelled lawnmowers, and quadraphonic phonographs. But no similar force proclaims the virtues of social goods and services; similar persuasion does not exist to whet the consumer's appetite for better schools, improved streets and highways, increased expenditures for medical research, and so forth. The net result, it is contended, is a misallocation of resources; they are overallocated to private goods and underallocated to public goods.

3 Significant external costs are entailed by advertising. Billboards blot out roadside scenery and generally debase the countryside. Sound trucks disrupt suburban serenity. Of potentially greater importance are the effects which advertising's support of national communications may have upon the accuracy and quality of those communications. Will a newspaper present an unprejudiced report of the labor dispute in which its major advertiser is involved? Will a television newscast conveniently ignore the fact that antitrust action has been initiated against its sponsor? Will a firm which distributes its product nationally permit the television playhouse it sponsors to present an honest and frank portrayal of America's racial problems? In more general terms, it is charged that competitive advertising offends the common sense and tries the patience of society. The fact that water consumption rises enormously during television commercials adds some credibility to this latter contention.

Critics of advertising are very dubious of the argument that advertising permits firms to expand, to achieve lower unit costs, and to offer their products at lower prices to consumers. There are several reasons for this doubt. First, it is contended that much advertising tends to be self-canceling. The million-dollar advertising campaign of one cigarette manufacturer is largely offset by equally expensive campaigns waged by its rivals. Few additional people smoke cigarettes. Each firm has about the same portion of the market as it had originally. And the cost, and therefore the price, of cigarettes is higher. In Figure 28-2 self-canceling advertising may move the firm from point *a* to point *c,* not from *a* to *b.* Second, are there not more desirable and less costly alternative means by which a firm might expand output and achieve economies of scale? Would not product development or research on production methods permit a firm to achieve economies of scale and at the same time avoid the upshift in its average-cost schedule which advertising entails? Finally, even if a firm achieves lower unit costs through advertising, will the consumer benefit through proportionate price reductions? This point is particularly pertinent in view of the fact that the expansion of those firms whose advertising is most successful implies that less successful advertisers will fall by the wayside, causing the industry to move away from monopolistic competition and in the direction of oligopoly, wherein firms have greater control over product price.

5 It is claimed that advertising promotes the growth of monopoly. On the one hand, extensive advertising creates financial barriers to entry and thereby intensifies the market power which firms already possess. Furthermore, by creating brand loyalties, consumers become less responsive to price cutting by competitors, thereby enhancing the monopoly power possessed by the firm which is advertising its product.

6 Most economists are reluctant to accept advertising as an important determinant of the levels of output and employment. There has been little evidence of economic stagnation in the post-World War II years that would seem remediable by advertising and promotional outlays. Furthermore, the most volatile aspect of aggregate demand is not so much highly advertised consumer goods as it is little-advertised investment goods. The consensus seems to be that advertising probably affects the composition more than it does the volume of spending. The argument has also been made that advertising expenditures are procyclical, that is, they fluctuate *with* total spending, intensifying unemployment during bad times and adding to inflationary pressures during prosperous times.

7 There is evidence that in some industries advertising has become such a large part of the cost of doing business that it constitutes an important financial barrier to entry. This is generally recognized to be the case in the tobacco industry, where producers as a group may spend considerably in excess of $400 million per year on advertising and related promotional activities. The three major auto manufacturers—GM, Ford, and Chrysler—currently spend over $550 million for advertising per year.

Empirical Evidence The economic implications of advertising have been probed through a number of recent empirical studies. Unfortunately, such studies are subject to serious problems with respect to both the acquisition and analysis of relevant data; hence, conclusions are necessarily tentative. Nevertheless, empirical research suggests that perhaps the microeconomic effects of advertising are *not* as adverse as economists have traditionally assumed. In particular, a substantial portion of total advertising is of an informative type and therefore is a basic means by which consumers are informed of prices and terms of sale. Furthermore, advertising does not seem to be a mechanism by which competition is necessarily reduced; on the contrary, it is frequently a means by which new firms gain entrance to an industry.[3]

☐   **Monopolistic Competition and Economic Analysis**

Our discussion of nonprice competition correctly implies that the equilibrium situation of a monopolistically competitive firm is actually much more complex than the previous graphic analysis indicates. Figure 28-1*a, b,* and *c assume* a given product and a given level of advertising expenditures. But, alas, these we

[3]The pioneering work of Richard G. Telser is recommended to the ambitious student. See his "Advertising and Competition," *Journal of Political Economy,* December 1964, pp. 537–562. Jules Backman's *Advertising and Competition* (New York University Press, 1967) is an interesting and useful summary of empirical studies of advertising.

now know are not given in practice. The monopolistically competitive firm must actually juggle three variable considerations—price, product, and promotion—in seeking maximum profits. What specific variety of product, selling at what price, and supplemented by what level of promotional activity, will result in the greatest level of profits attainable? This complex situation is not readily expressed in a simple, meaningful economic model. At best we can note that each possible combination of price, product, and promotion poses a different demand and cost (production plus promotion) situation for the firm, some one of which will allow it maximum profits. In practice, this optimum combination cannot be readily forecast but must be sought by the process of trial and error. And even here, certain limitations may be imposed by the actions of rivals. A firm may not risk the elimination of advertising expenditures for fear its share of the market will decline sharply, to the benefit of its rivals who do advertise. Similarly, patents held by rivals will rule out certain desirable product variations.

Summary

   1   The distinguishing features of monopolistic competition are: *a.* There is a large enough number of firms so that each has little control over price, mutual interdependence is absent, and collusion is virtually impossible; *b.* products are characterized by real and imaginary differences and by varying conditions surrounding their sale; and *c.* entry to the industry is relatively easy. Many aspects of retailing, and some industries wherein economies of scale are few, approximate monopolistic competition.
   2   Monopolistically competitive firms may earn economic profits or incur losses in the short run. The easy entry and exodus of firms give rise to a long-run tendency for them to earn a normal profit.
   3   The long-run equilibrium position of the monopolistically competitive producer is less socially desirable than that of a purely competitive firm. Under monopolistic competition, price exceeds marginal cost, suggesting an underallocation of resources to the product, and price exceeds minimum average total cost, indicating that consumers do not get the product at the lowest price which cost conditions would allow. However, because the firm's demand curve is highly elastic, these "wastes" of monopolistic competition should not be overemphasized.
   4   Product differentiation provides a means by which monopolistically competitive firms can offset the long-run tendency for economic profits to approximate zero.

Through product development and advertising outlays, a firm may strive to increase the demand for its product more than nonprice competition increases its costs.

5 Although subject to certain dangers and problems, product differentiation affords the consumer a greater variety of products at any point in time and improved products over time. Whether these features fully compensate for the "wastes" of monopolistic competition is a moot question.

6 There is sharp disagreement as to the economic benefits of advertising. Proponents justify advertising on the grounds that it *a.* aids consumers in exercising rational choices, *b.* supports national communications, *c.* speeds product development, *d.* permits firms to realize economies of scale, *e.* promotes competition, and *f.* encourages spending and a high level of employment. Critics assert that advertising *a.* confuses rather than informs, *b.* misallocates resources away from more urgent employments (particularly from the production of social goods), *c.* involves a variety of external costs, *d.* results in higher, not lower, costs and prices, *e.* promotes monopoly, *f.* is not a strategic determinant of spending and employment, and *g.* often constitutes a significant financial barrier to entry.

7 In practice the monopolistic competitor seeks that specific combination of price, product, and promotion which will maximize his profits.

Questions and Study Suggestions

1 Key terms and concepts to remember: monopolistic competition; product differentiation; wastes of monopolistic competition; nonprice competition; informative advertising; competitive advertising.

2 How does monopolistic competition differ from pure competition? From pure monopoly? Explain fully what product differentiation entails.

3 Compare the elasticity of the monopolistically competitive producer's demand curve with that of *a.* a pure competitor, and *b.* a pure monopolist. Assuming identical long-run costs, compare graphically the prices and output which would result under pure competition and monopolistic competition. Explain: "Monopolistically competitive industries are characterized by too many firms, each of which produces too little."

4 "Monopolistic competition is monopoly up to the point at which consumers become willing to buy close substitute products and competitive beyond that point." Explain.

5 What is nonprice competition? "Competition in quality and in service may be quite as effective in giving the buyer more for his money as is price competition." Do you agree? Explain why monopolistically competitive firms frequently prefer nonprice to price competition.

6 Critically evaluate and explain:

a. "In monopolistically competitive industries economic profits are competed away in the long run; hence, there is no valid reason to criticize the performance and efficiency of such industries."

b. "Monopolistic competition is merely a way station on the road to oligopoly."

c. "In the long run monopolistic competition leads to a monopolistic price but not to monopolistic profits."

7 Do you agree or disagree with the following statements? Why?

a. "The amount of advertising which a firm does is likely to vary inversely with the real differences in its product."

   b.   "If each firm's advertising expenditures merely tend to cancel the effects of its rivals' advertising, it is clearly irrational for these firms to maintain large advertising budgets."

   8   Carefully evaluate the two views expressed in the following statements:

   a.   "It happens every day. Advertising builds mass demand. Production goes up—costs come down. More people can buy—more jobs are created. These are the ingredients of economic growth. Each stimulates the next in a cycle of productivity and plenty which constantly creates a better life for you."

   b.   "Advertising constitutes 'inverted education'—a costly effort to induce people to buy without sufficient thought and deliberation and therefore to buy things they don't need. Furthermore, advertising intensifies economic instability because advertising outlays vary directly with the level of consumer spending. Indeed, by contributing to inflation during prosperous periods, advertising may foster political pressures for the curtailment of government spending on much-needed social goods and services, thereby promoting a misallocation of resources."

   Which view do you feel is the more accurate? Justify your position.

Selected References

Adams, Walter (ed.): *The Structure of American Industry,* 5th ed. (New York: The Macmillan Company, 1977), chap. 2.

Bain, Joe S.: *Industrial Organization,* 2d ed. (New York: John Wiley & Sons, Inc., 1968), chaps. 7, 8.

Leftwich, Richard H.: *The Price System and Resource Allocation,* 6th ed. (Hinsdale, Ill.: The Dryden Press, Inc., 1976), chap. 13.

Meyer, Robert A.: *Microeconomic Decisions* (Boston: Houghton Mifflin Company, 1976), chap. 12.

Simon, Julian A.: *Issues in the Economics of Advertising* (Urbana: University of Illinois Press, 1970).

Weiss, Leonard W.: *Case Studies in American Industry,* rev. ed. (New York: John Wiley & Sons, Inc., 1971), chap. 5.

Last Word
Beer: Trouble Brewing

Some economists feel there is a tendency for monopolistically competitive industries to evolve into oligopoly. The following is a brief case study in accord with this view.

When the United States officially went wet again in 1933, 750 breweries across the country—most of them small, family-owned businesses—eagerly reopened their taps. But although beer consumption has grown from 40 million to 133 million barrels in the intervening 40 years, control of the industry has gradually consolidated into the hands of a few giant companies and the number of U.S. breweries has been drastically reduced to a mere 64. The local brewer seems on a path to extinction.

In Chicago, for instance, there is now only one brewery compared with 32 on the day of repeal. In the East, P. Ballantine & Sons was forced to shut down last year and sell its brand name to Falstaff; Piel Bros. plans to close one of its two breweries this fall and has the other up for sale. By 1980, says William M. O'Shea, head of the Brewers Association of America, "there won't be a dozen breweries left in the country."

Many of the locals, of course, fail simply because of poor management. "Many breweries did not keep up with manufacturing techniques and automation," says an official of Adolph Coors Co., the fourth-largest U.S. brewer and a dominant factor in Western markets. "They weren't fast-thinking enough." But the small brewers say their condition wouldn't be so precarious if it weren't for predatory price-cutting by the majors. The little companies have consistently pushed legal action against the three national giants, Anheuser-Busch, Schlitz and Pabst, which account for 44 per cent of all the beer sold in the U.S.

Whether their price-cutting is legal or not, the big brewers have other overpowering advantages. Their huge advertising expenditures create demand for their beer all over the country, a demand they meet from their strategically placed regional breweries. The only way the locals can compete is with low prices.

If the small beer companies could keep their prices a little below those of the majors, they could coexist. But they are often saddled with old, inefficient plants, and their costs keep rising while the majors keep automating and reducing theirs. "Schlitz in Winston-Salem can make beer and ship it into New York 33 cents a case cheaper than we can make it in Brooklyn," says Richard Fisher, Piel's controller.

All the locals aren't quite ready to surrender. G. Heileman of La Crosse, Wis., for instance, has grown right along with the majors, partly by acquiring other brands such as Blatz, and it is now felt something of a regional power. In the past year, two new beer companies have started up in Florida.

The small brewers also are starting to get some help from state legislatures. A New York law that is going into effect this month is designed to curtail the majors' price-cutting ploys. "But when you solve one problem, others always arise," Howard Jones, president of the New York State Brewers Association, says mournfully. "The big brewers could pour in advertising or hold tremendous sales contests, and put us right back where we were."

Indeed, short of a complete dismemberment of the Big Three, there seems little that can be done to protect most of the locals. John C. Maxwell Jr., a leading beer-industry analyst, concludes: "Today, there is no way for a local brewer to survive unless he gets a grant from the Ford Foundation."

Price and Output Determination: Oligopoly

In many of the manufacturing, mining, wholesaling, and retailing industries of American capitalism, a few firms are dominant. Such industries are called *oligopolies*. It is with these industries that the present chapter is concerned. Specifically, we have four objectives. We seek first to define oligopoly, assess its occurrence, and note the reasons for its existence. The second and major goal is to survey the possible courses of price-output behavior which oligopolistic industries might follow. Third, the role of nonprice competition, that is, competition on the basis of product development and advertising, in oligopolistic industries is discussed. Finally, some comments with respect to the economic efficiency and social desirability of oligopoly are offered.

OLIGOPOLY: CONCEPT AND OCCURRENCE

What are the basic characteristics of oligopoly? How frequently is it encountered in American capitalism? Why has this industry structure developed?

□ Fewness

The outstanding feature of oligopoly is "fewness." When a relatively small number of firms dominates the market for a good or service, the industry is oligopolistic. But what specifically is meant by "a few" firms? This is necessarily vague, because the market model of oligopoly covers a great deal of ground, ranging from pure monopoly, on the one hand, to monopolistic competition, on the other. Thus oligopoly encompasses the tin-can industry, in which two firms tend to dominate an entire national market, and the situation in which, say, ten or fifteen gasoline stations may enjoy roughly equal shares of the petroleum products market in a medium-sized town. Table 29-1 lists a number of major industries in which fewness is present in varying degrees. This table correctly suggests that the market structure of oligopoly is very common and very important in American capitalism. At the local level, some aspects of the retail trades—particularly in small- and medium-sized towns—are characterized by oligopoly.

Oligopolies may be *homogeneous* or *differentiated;* that is, the firms in an oligopolistic industry may produce standardized or differentiated products. Many industrial products—steel, zinc, copper, aluminum, lead, cement, industrial alcohol, and so forth—are virtually standardized products in the physical sense and are produced under oligopolistic conditions. Of course, even here slight physical differences may exist, and the service, credit, and speed of delivery may differ between sellers, making for a measure of differentiation. But for most practical purposes these are standardized products. On the other hand, many consumer goods industries—automobiles, tires, typewriters, petroleum products, soap, cigarettes, and a host of electrical appliances—are differentiated oligopolies.

Table 29-1 PERCENTAGE OF OUTPUT* PRODUCED BY FIRMS IN SELECTED HIGH-CONCENTRATION MANUFACTURING INDUSTRIES

Industry	Percentage of industry output produced by first four firms
Locomotives and parts	97
Cellulose fibers	96
Telephone and telegraph equipment	94
Primary lead	93
Motor vehicles	93
Flat glass	92
Electric lamps (bulbs)	90
Turbines and generators	90
Chewing gum	87
Cigarettes	84
Sewing machines	84
Household laundry equipment	83
Typewriters	81
Gypsum products	80
Primary aluminum	79
Tires and inner tubes	73
Metal cans	66
Soap and detergents	62

*As measured by value of shipments. Data are for 1972.
Source: Bureau of the Census, *Concentration Ratios in Manufacturing.*

□ **Underlying Causes**

Why are certain industries composed of only a few firms? Specific reasons are manifold, but two related factors—economies of scale and the advantages of merger—are perhaps of greatest importance.

Economies of Scale We discovered in Chapter 25 that, where economies of scale are substantial (see Figure 25-6a), reasonably efficient production will be possible only with a small number of producers; in other words, efficiency requires that the productive capacity of each firm be large relative to the total market. Indeed, it is an unstable situation for an industry to have a large number of high-cost firms each of which is failing to realize existing economies of scale. In Figure 25-4, for example, a firm currently operating with the small and inefficient plant size indicated by ATC-1 will recognize that this short-run position is unsatisfactory; it can realize substantially lower unit costs and a larger profit by expanding its plant to ATC-2. The same can be said for the move to ATC-3. However, given a reasonably stable market demand, all the many firms with small (ATC-1) plant sizes cannot now survive. The profitable expansion to larger plant sizes by some will necessarily come at the expense of rival producers. In short, the realization of economies of scale by some firms implies that the number of rival producers is simultaneously being reduced through failure or merger.

Historically, what has happened in many industries is that technological progress has made more and more economies of scale attainable over time. Thus many industries started out with a primitive technology, few economies of scale, and a relatively large number of competitors. But then, as technology improved and economies of scale became increasingly pronounced, the less alert or less aggressive firms fell by the wayside and a few producers emerged. For example, estimates suggest that as many as seventy to eighty firms populated the automobile industry in its infancy. Over the years, the development of mass-production techniques reduced the field through failure and combination. Now the Big Three—General Motors, Ford, and Chrysler—have over 80 percent of the automobile market.

But why, you may ask, aren't new firms created to enter the automobile industry? The answer, of course, is that to achieve the low unit costs essential to survival, any new entrants must necessarily start out as large producers. This may require hundreds of millions of dollars worth of investment in machinery and equipment alone. Economies of scale can prove a formidable barrier to entry. Hence, they explain not only the evolution of oligopoly in many industries, but also why such industries are not likely to become more competitive.

We must note that the development or persistence of some oligopolies can be traced at least in part to other entry barriers. In the electronics, chemical, and aluminum industries, the ownership of patents and the control of strategic raw materials have been important. And perhaps prodigious advertising outlays may provide an added financial barrier to entry, as some economists argue has been the case in the cigarette industry. But in general, economies of scale are the dominant barrier in most oligopolies.

The Urge to Merge The second factor in explaining oligopoly or fewness is merger. The motivation for merger has diverse roots. Of immediate relevance is the fact that the combining of two or more formerly competing firms by merger may increase their market share substantially and enable the new and larger production unit to achieve greater economies of scale. Another significant motive underlying the "urge to merge" is the market power which may accompany merger. A firm that is larger both absolutely and relative to the market may have greater ability to control the market for, and the price of, its product than does a smaller, more competitive producer. Furthermore, the large size which merger entails may give the firm the advantage of being a "big buyer" and permit it to demand and obtain lower prices (costs) from input suppliers than previously.

□ **Mutual Interdependence**

Regardless of the means by which oligopoly evolves, it is clear that rivalry among a small number of firms interjects a new and complicating factor into our discussion: *mutual interdependence.* Imagine three firms, A, B, and C, each of which has about one-third of the market for a particular product. If A cuts price, its share of the market will increase. But B and C will be directly, immediately, and adversely affected by A's price cutting. Hence, we can expect some *reaction* on the part of B and C to A's behavior: B and C may match A's price cut or even undercut A, thereby precipitating a price war. This response correctly suggests that no firm in an oligopolistic industry will dare to alter its price policies without attempting to calculate the most likely reactions of its rivals. To be sure, cost and demand data are important to the oligopolist in establishing price, but to these we must add the reaction of rivals—a highly uncertain factor. The situation faced by oligopolistic producers resembles that of participants in games of strategy, such as poker, bridge, or chess. There is no means of knowing beforehand the best way to play your cards, because this depends upon the way other participants play theirs. Each player must pattern his actions according to the actions and expected reactions of his rivals.

It is to be emphasized that the mutual interdependence resulting from fewness, and the consequent need for a firm to weigh the possible reactions of rivals in altering its price policy, are unique features of oligopoly. The large number of rivals, which characterizes pure competition and monopolistic competition, and the absence of rivals, which is the earmark of pure monopoly, rule out mutual interdependence in these market structures. Indeed, a good, workable definition of oligopoly is this: Oligopoly exists when the number of firms in an industry is so small that each must consider the reactions of rivals in formulating its price policy.

ANALYTICAL COMPLEXITIES

The theories of competitive, monopolistic, and monopolistically competitive markets as presented in prior chapters are quite standard and widely accepted segments of microeconomics. But economic analysis offers no standard portrait of oligopoly. In general, there are two major reasons why it is difficult to use formal economic analysis in explaining the price behavior of oligopolies.

1 The previously noted fact that oligopoly encompasses many specific market situations works against the development of a single, generalized explanation or model of how an oligopoly determines price and output. Pure competition, monopolistic competition, and pure monopoly all refer to rather clear-cut market arrangements; oligopoly does not. It includes the situation in which two or three firms dominate an entire market as well as the situation in which twelve or fifteen firms compete. It includes both product differentiation and standardization. It encompasses the cases in which firms are acting in collusion and those in which they are not. It embodies the situations in which barriers to entry are very strong and those in which they are not quite so strong. In short, the many breeds, or strains, of oligopoly preclude the development of any simple market model which provides a general explanation of oligopolistic behavior.

2 The element of mutual interdependence which fewness adds to the analysis is a most significant complication. To be specific, the inability of a firm to predict with certainty the reactions of its rivals makes it virtually impossible to estimate the demand and marginal-revenue data faced by an oligopolist. And without such data, firms cannot determine their profit-maximizing price and output even in theory, as we shall presently make clear.

Despite these analytical difficulties, two interrelated characteristics of oligopolistic pricing stand out. On the one hand, oligopolistic prices tend to be inflexible, or "sticky." Prices change less frequently in oligopoly than they do under pure competition, monopolistic competition, and in some instances, pure monopoly. Figure 10-5 provides some interesting data on this point. On the other hand, when oligopolistic prices do change, firms are likely to change their prices together; that is, oligopolistic price behavior suggests the presence of incentives to act in concert or collusively in setting and changing prices.

PRICE–OUTPUT BEHAVIOR

Let us now examine two oligopolistic market models—noncollusive oligopoly and collusive oligopoly—in an effort to shed some light upon these two pricing characteristics.

☐ **Noncollusive Oligopoly
and Price Rigidity**

Again imagine an oligopolistic industry
comprised of just three firms, A, B, and C, each
having about one-third of the total market for
a differentiated product. Assume the firms are
"independent" in the sense that they do not
engage in collusive practices in setting prices.
Suppose, too, that the going price for firm A's
product is QP and its current sales are Q, as
shown in Figure 29-1. Now the question is,
"What does the firm's demand, or sales, curve
look like?" We have just noted that mutual
interdependence, and the uncertainty of rivals'
reactions which interdependence entails, make
this question difficult to answer. The location
and shape of an oligopolist's demand curve
depend upon how the firm's rivals will react to
a price change introduced by A. There are two
plausible assumptions about the reactions of
A's rivals with which we might experiment.

Match or Ignore?   One possibility is that
firms B and C will exactly match any price
change initiated by A. In this case, A's demand
and marginal-revenue curves will look something like D_1D_1 and MR_1MR_1 in Figure 29-1.
If A cuts price, its sales will increase very modestly, because its two rivals will follow suit and
thereby prevent A from gaining any price advantage over them. The small increase in sales
which A (and its two rivals) will realize is at
the expense of other industries; A will gain no
sales from B and C. If A raises the going price,
its sales will fall only modestly. Why? Because B and C match its price increase, so A
does not price itself out of the market. The
industry now loses some sales to other industries, but A loses no customers to B and C.

The other obvious possibility is that firms
B and C will simply ignore any price change
invoked by A. In this case, the demand and
marginal-revenue curves faced by A will re-
semble D_2D_2 and MR_2MR_2 in Figure 29-1. The
demand curve in this case is considerably more
elastic than under the assumption that B and

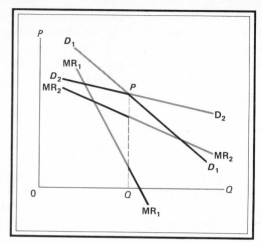

FIGURE 29-1 THE KINKED DEMAND CURVE

The nature of a noncollusive oligopolist's demand and
marginal-revenue curves will depend upon whether his
rivals will match (D_1D_1 and MR_1MR_1) or ignore (D_2D_2
and MR_2MR_2) any price changes which he may initiate
from the current price QP. In all likelihood an oligopolist's
rivals will ignore a price increase but follow a price cut.
This causes the oligopolist's demand curve to be kinked
(dark blue D_2PD_1) and his marginal-revenue curve to have
a vertical break, or gap (dark blue MR_2MR_1).

C will match A's price changes. The reasons
are clear. If A lowers its price and its rivals do
not, A will gain sales sharply at the expense of
its two rivals because it will obviously be
underselling them. Conversely, if A raises price
and its rivals do not, A will be pricing itself out
of the market and will lose many customers to
B and C, which are now underselling it. Because of product differentiation, however, A's
sales do not fall to zero when it raises price;
some of A's customers will pay the higher price
because they have strong preferences for A's
product.

Now, which is the most logical assumption
for A to make as to how its rivals will react to
any price change it might initiate? The answer
is "some of each"! Common sense and observation of oligopolistic industries suggest that
price declines will be matched as a firm's competitors act to prevent the price cutter from
taking their customers, but that price increases

will be ignored, because rivals of the price-increasing firm stand to gain the business lost by the price booster. In other words, the dark blue D_2P segment of the "rivals ignore" demand curve seems relevant for price increases, and the dark blue PD_1 segment of the "rivals follow" demand curve is more realistic for price cuts. It is logical, or at least a good guess, that an oligopolist's demand curve is "kinked" on the order of the dark blue D_2PD_1. The curve is highly elastic above the going price, but much less elastic or even inelastic below the current price. Note also that if it is correct to suppose that rivals will follow a price cut but ignore an increase, the marginal-revenue curve of the oligopolist will also have an odd shape. It, too, will be made up of two segments—the dark blue part of the marginal-revenue curve appropriate to D_1D_1 and the dark blue chunk of the marginal-revenue curve appropriate to D_2D_2. Because of the sharp differences in elasticity of demand above and below the going price, there occurs a gap, or what we can treat as a vertical segment, in the marginal-revenue curve. In Figure 29-1 the marginal-revenue curve is shown by the two dark blue lines connected by the dotted vertical segment, or gap.

Price Inflexibility This analysis is important in that it goes far to explain why price changes are infrequent in noncollusive oligopolistic industries. On the one hand, the kinked-demand schedule gives each oligopolist good reason to believe that any change in price will be for the worse. A firm's customers will desert it in quantity if it raises price. If it lowers price, its sales at best will increase very modestly. Even if a price cut increases its total revenue somewhat, the oligopolist's costs may well increase by a more-than-offsetting amount. Should the dark blue PD_1 segment of its sales schedule be inelastic in that E_d is less than 1, the firm's profits will surely fall. A price decrease will lower the firm's total receipts, and the production of a somewhat larger output will increase total costs. Worse yet, a price cut by A may be *more* than met by

B and C. That is, A's initial price cut may precipitate a price war; so the amount sold by A may actually decline as its rival firms charge still lower prices. These are all good reasons on the demand side of the picture why noncollusive oligopolies might seek "the quiet life" and follow live-and-let-live, or don't-upset-the-applecart, price policies. More specifically, if the resulting profits are satisfactory to the several firms at the existing price, it may seem prudent to them not to alter that price.

A second reason for price inflexibility under noncollusive oligopoly works from the cost side of the picture. The broken marginal-revenue curve which accompanies the kinked demand curve suggests that within limits, substantial cost changes will have no effect upon output and price. To be specific, any shift in marginal cost between MC_1 and MC_2 as shown in Figure 29-2 will result in no change in price or output, because the oligopolist fears a price

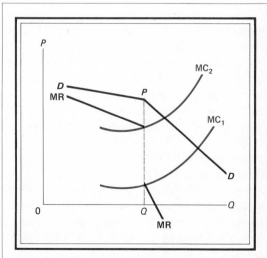

FIGURE 29-2 COST CHANGES AND PRICE STABILITY UNDER OLIGOPOLY

The kinked demand curve *DPD* and the accompanying broken marginal-revenue curve MRMR help explain the price inflexibility which characterizes oligopoly. Because any shift in marginal costs between MC_1 and MC_2 will cut the vertical (dashed) segment of the marginal-revenue curve, no change in either price QP or output Q will occur.

war, on the one hand, and that he may price himself out of the market, on the other.

But the notion of price inflexibility should not be overstated. Rather, it is important to stress that the prices of noncollusive oligopolists *do* change, particularly when significant and mutually applicable cost changes occur, for example, wage or tax increases which collective bargaining or government imposes more-or-less uniformly on the firms. Knowing its rivals are also afflicted with these cost increases, each firm boosts price with considerable certainty that each and every rival will follow suit. The practice of linking price increases to wage or tax hikes has the further advantage of shielding oligopolies from public criticism. To many the price increase—even if in excess of cost increases—will clearly seem the fault of irresponsible unions and the insatiable appetite of government for tax revenues.

□ **Collusion: Joint-Profit Maximization**

The kinked-demand situation just described may be decidedly unappealing to oligopolists. It is surrounded by an air of uncertainty. Although there may be a strong disposition toward price stability, the possibility always does exist that a firm may shade its price to expand its share of the market and thereby precipitate disastrous rounds of price cutting. This is particularly likely if firms have excess capacity because of, say, a general business recession; under these circumstances a firm can lower unit costs by increasing its market share. Then, too, the possibility is always present that new firms may surmount barriers to entry and initiate aggressive price cutting to gain a foothold in the market. In addition, the tendency toward rigid prices may adversely affect profits if general inflationary pressures increase costs.

The kinked-demand analysis is also a source of uneasiness to economists because it contains a crucial shortcoming. The analysis *does not explain how the going price gets to be at PQ* (Figure 29-1) in the first place. Rather,

it merely helps to explain why oligopolists may be reluctant to deviate from an existing price which yields them a "satisfactory" or "reasonable" profit. The kinked demand curve explains price inflexibility but not price itself.

In short, oligopolistic firms frequently behave collusively to avoid the uncertainties of noncollusive oligopoly. Economists are interested in collusive oligopoly in that it provides a more satisfactory explanation of price and output.

Where will price and output be established under collusive oligopoly? To answer this question we must construct a highly simplified situation. Assume once again there are three firms—A, B, and C—producing homogeneous products. Each firm has identical cost curves. Each firm's demand curve is indeterminate unless we know how its rivals will react to any price change. Therefore, let us suppose each firm assumes that its two rivals will match either a price cut or a price increase. In other words, each firm's demand curve is of the D_1D_1 type in Figure 29-1. Assume further that the demand curve for each firm is identical. Given identical cost and identical demand and marginal-revenue data, we can say that Figure 29-3 represents the position of each of our three oligopolistic firms.

What price-output combination should each firm choose? If firm A were a pure monopolist, the answer would be clear enough: Establish output at Q, where marginal revenue equals marginal cost, charge the corresponding price PQ, and enjoy the maximum profit attainable. However, firm A *does* have two rivals selling identical products, and if A's assumption that his rivals will match his price[1] proves to be incorrect, the consequences could be disastrous for A. Specifically, if B and C actually charge prices below PQ, then firm A's demand curve will shift quite sharply to the left as its potential customers turn to its rivals, which are now selling the same product at a lower

[1] Recall that this is the assumption upon which A's demand curve in Figure 29-3 is based.

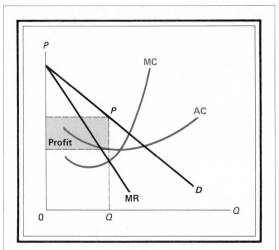

FIGURE 29-3   COLLUSION AND THE TENDENCY TOWARD JOINT-PROFIT MAXIMIZATION

If oligopolistic firms are faced with identical or highly similar demand and cost conditions, they will tend to behave collusively and maximize joint profits. The price and output results are essentially the same as those of pure (unregulated) monopoly; each oligopolist charges price QP and produces output Q.

talk it over"—and agree to charge the same price PQ. As a result, each firm will realize the maximum profit. And for society, the result is likely to be about the same as if the industry were a pure monopoly composed of three identical plants (Chapter 27).

□   Obstacles to Collusion

But we must keep in mind that this discussion of collusive oligopoly and the resulting maximization of joint profits is based upon a number of simplifying assumptions. Release of these assumptions and the introduction of certain legal realities create obstacles to collusion and make the outcome of collusive oligopoly no more than a *tendency* to maximize joint profits. In practice, price collusion may be difficult to achieve and to maintain over time.

Legal Obstacles: Antitrust   Blatant price fixing as described in our collusive-oligopoly model is at odds with existing antitrust legislation (Chapter 34). For example, *cartels*—formal arrangements embodying written or explicit verbal agreements among producers to regulate price or output or to divide markets geographically—are illegal in the United States. This, however, does not mean that collusion is absent, but rather that it takes more informal, more subtle forms. To illustrate, *gentlemen's agreements* are undoubtedly widespread in our economy. Such agreements arise when competing oligopolists reach a verbal agreement on product price, market shares almost invariably being left to the ingenuity of each seller as reflected in nonprice competition. Gentlemen's agreements arise at trade conventions, on the golf course, or at cocktail parties, not in a lawyer's office. Although they too collide with the antitrust laws, their sub rosa and intangible character makes them more difficult to detect and prosecute successfully.

Price leadership is a still less formal means by which oligopolists can coordinate their price behavior and avoid the uncertain-

price. Of course, A can retaliate by cutting its price too; but this will have the effect of moving all three firms down their demand curves, lowering their profits, and perhaps even driving them to some point where average cost exceeds price. So the question becomes, "Will B and C want to charge a price below PQ?" Under the assumptions we have made, and recognizing that A will have little choice except to match any price they may set below PQ, the answer is "No." Faced with the same demand and cost circumstances, B and C will find it in their interest to produce Q and charge PQ. This is a curious situation; each firm finds it most profitable to charge the same price PQ, but only if its rivals will actually do so! How can the three firms realize the PQ-price and Q-quantity solution in which each is keenly interested? How can this be made a reality so that all three can avoid the less profitable outcomes associated with either higher or lower prices? The answer is obvious: The firms will all be motivated to collude—to "get together and ties of noncollusive action. In this case, one firm—usually the largest in the industry—initiates price changes, and all other firms more-or-less automatically follow that price change. In some cases—for example, the oil and cigarette industries—the identity of the price leader may vary over time, whereas in other industries—the steel industry—a single firm may rather persistently enjoy the position of price leader. The importance of price leadership is evidenced in the fact that such industries as farm machinery, anthracite coal, cement, copper, gasoline, newsprint, tin cans, lead, sulfur, rayon, fertilizer, glass containers, and nonferrous metals are practicing, or have in the recent past practiced price leadership. Because price leadership is an informal, tacit agreement involving no written or spoken commitments, it is generally accepted as a legal technique by the courts in interpreting the antitrust laws.

Despite the existence of these less formal techniques of collusion, antitrust legislation is still a formidable obstacle and persistent threat to collusive oligopoly.

Number of Firms   Other things being equal, the smaller the number of firms, the easier it is to achieve price collusion. Agreement on price by three or four producers that control an entire market is much more readily accomplished than it is in the situation where ten firms each have roughly 10 percent of the market, or where the Big Three have, say, 70 percent of the market, while a "competitive fringe" of eight or ten smaller firms do battle for the remainder. Furthermore, some of the smaller firms may aspire to become one of the Big Four and may feel that aggressive pricing below the profit-maximizing level is a means of achieving this goal. The resulting price competition may force the dominant firms to charge prices below that which would maximize joint profits. Or smaller firms may feel that they must compensate for the absence of nationwide advertising by charging a price below that of the Big Three.

Differentiation   Our model of collusive oligopoly assumed identical cost and demand curves for each firm. This is unrealistic. Where products are differentiated, we would certainly expect considerable differences in cost and demand data. Indeed, even with highly standardized products, we would expect that firms might have somewhat different market shares and would operate with differing degrees of productive efficiency. Thus it is likely that even homogeneous oligopolists would have somewhat different demand and cost curves. In either event, differences in costs and demand will mean that the profit-maximizing price for each firm will differ; there will be no single price which is readily acceptable to all. Price collusion therefore depends upon the ability to achieve compromises and concessions—to arrive at a degree of "understanding" which in practice is often difficult to achieve. For example, the MR = MC positions of firms A, B, and C may call for them to charge $12, $11, and $10 respectively, but this price cluster or range may be unsatisfactory to one or more of the firms. Firm A may feel that differences in product quality justify only a $1.50, rather than a $2, price differential between its product and that of firm C. In short, cost and demand differences make it difficult for oligopolists to agree on a single price or a "proper" cluster of prices; these differentials are therefore an obstacle to collusion.

Price Breaks   Legal obstacles, fairly large numbers of firms, and product differentiation are obstacles to collusive pricing. In addition, even when an oligopolistic industry has achieved a deeply entrenched practice of price collusion—for example, through price leadership—this collusion may break down periodically. Two related reasons for such price breaks are the occurrence of a business recession and the temptation of firms to engage in secret price cutting.

1   Slumps   Recession is an enemy of collusion because slumping markets cause average costs to rise. In technical terms, as the oligopolists' demand and marginal-revenue curves shift to the left (Figure 29-4), each firm moves back to a higher point on its average-cost curve. The firms find they have substantial excess productive capacity, sales are down, unit costs are up, and profits are being squeezed. Under such conditions, businesses may feel they are in a better position to avoid serious profit reductions by price cutting in the hope of gaining sales at the expense of rivals.

2 Cheating There is also a more-or-less persistent temptation for collusive oligopolists to engage in clandestine price cutting, that is, to make secret price concessions in order to get a little additional business. This temptation to cheat upon one's price-fixing partners stems from the fact that such action can be profitable *provided* the firm can keep such price concessions secret from (1) rival firms and (2) other customers who are paying a higher price.

Figure 29-4 is instructive. Here our collusive oligopolist is maximizing profits by selling an output of Q_1 at a quoted or list price of P_1. Now, the firm's downsloping demand curve indicates there are other customers who would buy additional output at a price below $P_1 (= Q_1 V)$. For example, buyers would take an additional $Q_1 Q_2$ units at price $P_2 Q_2$. Are these extra sales profitable to the firm? Yes, they are, because they add $Q_1 S P_2 Q_2$ to the firm's total revenue while the firm incurs additional costs of only $Q_1 T U Q_2$ (the area under the marginal-cost curve between Q_1 and Q_2) in producing them. The resulting addition to the firm's profits is the area $T S P_2 U$. In general, so long as the secret price exceeds the firm's marginal cost, the additional secret-price sales will be profitable.[2]

But the profitability and very possibility

[2]Technical note: Contrary to first-glance impressions, this discussion does not violate the MR = MC profit-maximizing rule. This is an instance of price discrimination where, through secrecy, the buyers of Q_1 and $Q_1 Q_2$ are in effect divided into two separate markets. Sales of output to the first group occur up to the profit-maximizing point; added sales to the second group (in the "second market") occur because marginal revenue ($P_2 Q_2$) exceeds the marginal cost of each of these units.

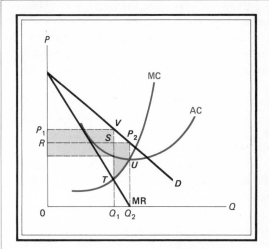

FIGURE 29-4 SECRET PRICE CONCESSIONS UNDER OLIGOPOLY

Secret price concessions can add to an oligopolist's profits. In this case the sale of $Q_1 Q_2$ extra units of output at a price of $Q_2 P_2$ can add the amount $T S P_2 U$ to the profits earned by selling to other customers at the higher price P_1. If other customers or rival firms learn of the price concessions, however, the existing price collusion may break down and profits may decline.

of secret price concessions disappear if either of the aforementioned provisions is violated. If price concessions become an "open secret," other customers will balk at paying P_1 and insist upon paying only $Q_2 P_2$. That is, the firm will be forced to take a price cut on all prior (Q_1) sales. This will trim off a substantial portion ($R P_1 V S$) of the profits derived from sales to these customers. Such a loss in profits, as Figure 29-4 indicates, can more than offset the possible profits from secret price concessions. Stated differently, if all buyers become aware of price concessions by a firm, the firm's ability to practice price discrimination among its customers will vanish. As a result, the firm may end simply by producing beyond the profit-maximizing output and charging a price ($Q_2 P_2$) *to all customers* which is below the profit-maximizing level.

Similarly, buyers receiving price concessions from one oligopolist may use this concession as a wedge to getting even larger price concessions from the firm's rivals. The attempt of buyers to play sellers against one another may precipitate price warring among these firms. In short, although it is potentially profitable, the use of secret price concessions is a threat to the maintenance of collusive oligopoly over time.[3]

◼ OLIGOPOLY AND GAMES[4]

We have already noted that the mutual interdependence which characterizes oligopoly makes it necessary that each firm consider the possible reactions (countermoves) of rivals to any action (move) it initiates. This means that oligopolists face a situation similar to that of participants in such games of strategy as poker or chess. Economists have developed a *theory of games*[5] which is very useful in analyzing possible game strategies. In particular, many of the salient behavioral characteristics of oligopoly can be grasped through a simple game-theory illustration.

☐   The Profits-Payoff Table

Table 29-2 is a *price-profits* or *profits-payoff* table. Let us examine the assumptions upon which it has been constructed and the nature of the data in it. The table assumes that a two-firm oligopoly or *duopoly* exists. We assume that products are differentiated and that the amount of sales and promotional activity is fixed. The figures along the top of the table show three possible prices that oligopolistic firm B might charge for its product; the

[3] For a fascinating case study of collusive pricing, read Clarence C. Walton and Frederick W. Cleveland, Jr., *Corporations on Trial: The Electric Cases* (Belmont, Calif.: Wadsworth Publishing Company, Inc., 1964).

[4] This is an optional section which instructors may choose to omit without impairing the continuity of the discussion.

[5] The interested reader should consult two informative and delightful introductory books on the subject: John D. Williams, *The Compleat Strategyst*, rev. ed. (New York: McGraw-Hill Book Company, 1965), and John McDonald, *Strategy in Poker, Business and War* (New York: W. W. Norton & Company, Inc., 1950).

TABLE 29-2 A PROFITS-PAYOFF TABLE FOR A TWO-FIRM OLIGOPOLY
(*hypothetical data; profit data in thousands of dollars*) .

figures down the left side indicate various prices rival firm A might charge. The entries in the body of the table show the resulting profit payoffs to A and B for each possible combination of prices they might charge. Firm A's profit payoff is shown in the lower left (darker) portion and B's profit is in the upper right (lighter) portion of each box or cell. For example, if B charges $8 and A charges $9, we find in cell VI that B will receive a profit of $23 (thousand) and A a profit of $19 (thousand). Note that even if the firms selected the same price, their profits would differ. This is so because we are assuming differentiated oligopoly, and therefore A and B have different cost and demand data.

Reading across any row, we can see the profits for the two firms as a *given* price for A is compared with all the possible prices B might charge. Thus in row (1) we find that if firm A charges $10, its profits will be $24, $19, or $15 respectively, depending upon whether B reacts with a price of $10, $9, or $8. Similarly, by reading down any column, we can determine the profit payoffs for the two firms as we compare a *given* price for B against the various prices A might charge. For example, reading down column (3), we see that if B charges $8, its profits will be $28, $23, or $18, depending upon whether A charges $10, $9, or $8.

Although the data in Table 29-2 are hypothetical, the profit figures are by no means arbitrarily chosen. We would expect that if one firm (say, A) committed itself to a given price—for example, $10—and did not vary from it, the rival firm (B) generally could increase profits by lowering the price of its product. That is, if A sticks to $10, B can make a profit of $21 by also charging $10, but can increase this profit to $26 and $28 by cutting price to $9 and $8 respectively.[6]

□ Interdependence of Behavior

In examining Table 29-2, we have seen once again that fewness means mutual interdependence. The best (profit-maximizing) price for firm B to charge depends upon firm A's reaction or response to B's price—that is, upon the price A charges. Example: If B initially chooses $10 as its price, A will maximize profit at $26 if its "price strategy" is $9 (cell IV). But with A charging $9, it will pay B to drop price to $8 (cell VI). However, with B now charging $8, A finds that it will maximize profits by dropping price from $9 to $8 (cell IX). Another example: If A sets its price at $10, B will maximize profits at $28 with a price strategy of $8 (cell III). But if B is charging $8,

A will no longer want to keep price at $10; with B charging $8, A will find it most profitable to charge $8 also (cell IX). It is clear that the profit-maximizing price for each firm depends upon the price reaction or price strategy of its rival.

□ Price Rigidity

Our kinked-demand analysis was useful in explaining the price rigidity which is characteristic of oligopoly. The profits-payoff table provides a complementary explanation of this phenomenon.

Price rigidity stems from the expectation of each firm that it will generally be profitable for its rival to ignore a price increase but to follow a price cut. To illustrate: Suppose A and B are both charging $9 and each is realizing profits of $22 (cell V). On the assumption that A will ignore (not follow) a price increase, B will foresee its own profits falling from $22 to $17 if it raises price to $10 (cell V to cell IV). And indeed, our table makes it quite clear why A should want to ignore B's price increase. When B goes to $10 and A stays at $9, A's profits rise from $22 to $26; if A were to follow B and raise price to $10, its profits would rise only from $22 to $24 (cell I). In any event, a price increase by B which A does not follow will cause B's profits to fall. Hence, B will not be eager to raise price.

What about a price cut by B? Again suppose both firms are initially charging $9. Now, if A continues to charge $9, B could increase profits from $22 to $23 (cell V to cell VI) by lowering its price to $8. But A will not want to charge $9 when B has cut price to $8. Why? Because moving from cell V to cell VI cuts A's profits from $22 to $19. Firm A can reduce this profit decline to $21 by also cutting price to $8, thereby moving the two firms to cell IX. When we compare the $9–$9 situation (cell V) with the $8–$8 situation (cell IX), it is obvious that both firms have experienced reduced profits by cutting prices. Hence, neither firm will be eager to cut prices.

---

[6]This need not always be the case. If, for example, B sticks to $10, A can increase its profit from $24 to $26 by lowering its own price from $10 to $9. But a further price cut to $8 lowers A's profit to $25. Why might this happen? The answer is that lower prices mean a larger output, and this expanding output in time will lead to rising unit costs. Also, recall from Chapter 23 that demand tends to become less elastic at lower prices, which means that further price cuts cause total revenue to expand by smaller and smaller amounts. These two factors—rising costs and increasingly modest growth of total revenue—may make it disadvantageous to sell at a price too far below one's rival. Stated differently, price cutting by one firm may bring it to some cost-revenue position beyond which marginal cost exceeds marginal revenue.

The important point is that B's profits will fall if (1) B raises price and A does not follow, *or* (2) B cuts price and A cuts price too. Furthermore, we have seen that there are profit incentives for A to ignore B's price increase and to follow B's price cut! We may conclude that if the two oligopolists are currently charging a mutually satisfactory ("reasonably profitable") price, both may be fearful of altering that price. Hence, the price rigidity which characterizes many oligopolistic industries over time.

□ **Collusion and Merger**

As our previous analysis has demonstrated, another characteristic of oligopoly is that collusive pricing may be mutually profitable. Adam Smith perceptively remarked more than 200 years ago, "People of the same trade seldom meet together, even for merriment and diversion, but the conversation ends in a conspiracy against the public, or in some contrivance to raise prices." The profits-payoff table yields some insights as to why collusive action is tempting under oligopoly.

Assume that through noncollusive action, firms A and B have both settled upon a price of $8. This price may well have been reached as a result of earlier competitive price cutting. Both firms realize that higher prices would be mutually beneficial. That is, A could increase its profits from $21 to $22 and B its profits from $18 to $22 *if* both would raise their prices to $9 (cell IX to cell V). But note that if A raises price to $9 and B stays at $8, B's profits will rise to $23 while A's profits fall to $19 (cell IX to cell VI). Firm A, therefore, may be understandably reluctant to raise price from $8 to $9 without assurance that B will also raise price from $8 to $9. Firm B is confronted with the same situation: If B goes to $9 and A stays at $8, A's profit will jump from $21 to $24 (cell IX to cell VIII). This new $24 profit is obviously superior to the $22 A would realize by also raising price to $9 (cell IX to cell V). So there is a dilemma: Both firms will realize a

greater profit if both charge $9 instead of $8. Yet each is afraid to initiate such a price increase independently of its rival, because each knows there is a profit incentive for the rival *not* to match a price increase. How can A and B both make certain that if either raises price to $9, the other will do the same? The answer, of course, is for them not to act independently, but to engage in collusion by which both firms commit themselves to raise price from $8 to $9. To act noncollusively is to remain at $8–$8 (cell IX) and realize profits inferior to those associated with the $9–$9 situation (cell V) attainable through some form of collusive price fixing.

Now you may ask: Having agreed collusively to increase price from $8 to $9, why don't both firms take the next step and raise their prices to $10? The problem here is that it does not pay firm B to move from the $9–$9 position (cell V) to the $10–$10 position (cell I). Specifically, this move would reduce B's profits from $22 to $21, although it would increase A's from $22 to $24. This conflict of interest could be resolved by forming a trust to coordinate formally the price decisions of the two firms or, alternatively, by negotiating a merger of the two firms. The trust or single firm that evolved from the merger would find it most profitable to have both plants (formerly independent firms) charge $10 (cell I), because the total or joint profits here would be greater at $45 (= $24 + $21) than at a price of $9 (cell V), where profits are $44 (= $22 + $22).

■ ─────────────────────────────

ROLE OF NONPRICE COMPETITION

We have noted that, for several reasons, oligopolists have an aversion to price competition. This aversion may lead to some more-or-less informal type of collusion on price. In the United States, however, price collusion is usually accompanied by nonprice competition. It is typically through nonprice competition that each firm's share of the total market is determined. This emphasis upon nonprice competition has its roots in two basic facts.

1 Price cuts can be quickly and easily met by a firm's rivals. Because of this the possibility of significantly increasing one's share of the market through price competition is small; rivals will promptly cancel any potential gain in sales by matching price cuts. And, of course, the risk is always present that price competition will precipitate disastrous price warring. More positively stated, oligopolists seem to feel that more permanent advantages can be gained over rivals through nonprice competition because product variations, improvements in productive techniques, and successful advertising gimmicks cannot be duplicated so quickly and so completely as can price reductions. And there is less likelihood of nonprice competition's forcing all firms to the wall regarding profits in the manner of unbridled price competition. Nonprice competition is less likely to get out of hand. It might be added that some oligopolistic producers of consumer goods apparently believe that consumers are more product- and advertising-conscious than they are price-conscious.

2 There is a more obvious reason for the tremendous emphasis which oligopolists put upon nonprice competition: Manufacturing oligopolists are typically blessed with substantial financial resources with which to support advertising and product development. Hence, although nonprice competition is a basic characteristic of both monopolistically competitive and oligopolistic industries, the latter are in a financial position to indulge more fully.

We need not restate the pros and cons of advertising. The arguments stated in Chapter 28 with respect to advertising under monopolistic competition are pertinent when applied to oligopoly. However, the implications of the rather prodigious outlays which manufacturing oligopolies sometimes make for technological research on both product quality and productive techniques are a matter of major concern to which we now turn.

OLIGOPOLY AND ECONOMIC EFFICIENCY

The troublesomeness of evaluating the economic efficiency of oligopoly is matched only by the importance of such an evaluation. The root difficulty is that of deciding whether it is more realistic to look at the probable effects of oligopoly in a short-run (static) or in a long-run (dynamic) environment.

□ Restrictive Oligopoly

The more-or-less traditional view holds that because oligopoly is close to pure monopoly in structure, we should expect it to operate in a similar way. Being characterized by barriers to entry, oligopoly can be expected, according to this view, to result in a restriction of output short of the point of lowest unit costs and a corresponding market price which yields substantial, if not maximum, economic profits. These points usually rest upon an analysis similar to that shown in Figure 29-5a. Facing a *given* demand and a *given* cost situation, the oligopolist will find that it pays to be restrictive. As indicated, higher unit costs will soon arise if output is expanded far beyond Q_1, and the lowering of price which such an expansion requires courts the disaster of a price war. Other things being equal, the price and output results under such an oligopoly would be clearly inferior to those of pure competition. Furthermore, we saw earlier that the results of collusive oligopoly may approximate those of pure monopoly. Indeed, one may even argue that oligopoly is actually less desirable than pure monopoly for the simple reason that pure monopoly in the United States is almost invariably subject to government regulation to mitigate abuses of such market power. Informal collusion among oligopolists may yield price and output results similar to pure monopoly, yet at the same time maintain the

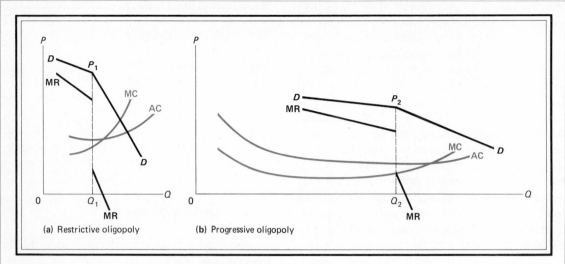

FIGURE 29-5   RESTRICTIVE OLIGOPOLY AND PROGRESSIVE OLIGOPOLY

Restrictive oligopoly (a): Faced with given demand and marginal revenue data (such as DP_1D and MRMR) and given cost data (such as AC and MC), the oligopolist will maximize profits by restricting output to Q_1 and charging price Q_1P_1. In expanding output beyond Q_1, the oligopolist must accept considerable price reductions and run the risk of starting a price war. Furthermore, by expanding the output, the producer may soon encounter rising average costs AC.
Progressive oligopoly (b): In fact some oligopolists have been progressive, achieving lower average costs AC and marginal costs MC through technological advance. Similarly, demand DP_2D and marginal revenue MRMR have been pushed far to the right as a result of product development and want-creating activities. As compared to the restrictive oligopoly of (a), the net result of progressive oligopoly has frequently been a larger output (Q_2 as compared with Q_1) and a lower price (Q_2P_2 as compared with Q_1P_1).

outward appearance of several independent and "competing" firms.

At the level of macroeconomics, we have previously noted that cost-push inflation is based upon the existence of market power. Therefore, oligopoly may also be criticized as a potential source of inflationary pressure.

☐ **Progressive Oligopoly**

The above view of oligopoly seems at odds with the historical facts surrounding the operation of many oligopolistic manufacturing industries, such as the automobile, farm equipment, electronics, home appliance, and steel industries. These industries have been characterized by falling product prices, improvements in product quality, and expanding levels of output and employment over a period of years. But caution is required here. The basic issue is whether this progress would have been even greater had these industries been organized on

a purely competitive basis. And, lacking the ability to conduct controlled laboratory experiments, the economist cannot offer a clear-cut answer. It is evident, however, that there has been significant progress in some oligopolistic industries, and the possibility does exist that in the long run some oligopolistic industries may well have fostered product improvement, lower unit costs, lower prices, and a greater output than the same industry would have provided if organized competitively. Graphically, the restrictive situation portrayed in Figure 29-5a may give way over time to the progressive situation reflected in Figure 29-5b, wherein demand and output have been substantially increased and unit cost and price reduced as compared with Figure 29-5a.[7]

[7]This comparison of restrictive and progressive oligopoly and the graphic presentation of Figure 29-5 are based upon Henry Grayson, *Price Theory in a Changing Economy* (New York: The Macmillan Company, 1965).

Technological Progress: The Argument

Generally speaking, the reasons for this possible progressiveness lie in the fact that many oligopolistic industries focus their competitive energies upon technological competition as reflected in both the development of productive techniques and improvement of product quality. The betterment of productive techniques will have the effect of expanding the range of constant or, better yet, declining unit costs. Advances in product quality, accompanied by advertising and related want-creating activities, will shift the firm's demand curve to the right. As indicated in Figure 29-5b, product price is very likely to decline with declines in unit costs.

There is a rather widely held assumption that modern oligopolies have both greater means and a stronger inclination for technological advance than does any other market structure. Let us summarize the arguments underlying this assumption and then test them against such statistical data as are available.

First, oligopolies typically possess the *means*—substantial profits—with which to undertake the incredibly expensive task of modern research. Technological progress, it is contended, is no longer in the domain of the backyard Edison or the basement Whitney. Rather, it is the result of highly organized and cooperative efforts of a variety of scientists and engineers housed in the elaborate research departments of such giant oligopolies as du Pont and General Electric. Purely and monopolistically competitive firms, being smaller and less prosperous, are decidedly less progressive.

Second, oligopolistic producers have a host of good *incentives* for accelerating technological advance:

1 Given their disposition to avoid price competition, technological, or cost, competition provides an obvious alternative means for enlarging total profits through an expanded product demand and lower unit costs. Like advertising and product development, the discovery of more efficient productive techniques is less certainly and less quickly matched by one's rivals than is a price cut.

2 Technological superiority is a basic means by which an oligopolist can ensure survival in the event that a price war should somehow plague the quiet life of the industry.

3 In contrast to an unrivaled pure monopolist, the presence of several strong rivals puts the oligopolist under considerable pressure to seek maximum productive efficiency. Failure to do so may mean that his several competitors will in time drive him out of business. The pure monopolist, being devoid of rivals, is under no competitive spur to technical progress. But the oligopolist, having a few rivals, clearly is in an environment of technological competition.

4 The existence of barriers to entry gives the progressive oligopolist some assurance that he will actually realize the profit rewards to which his research expenditures may give rise. This is in contrast to a monopolistically competitive market, wherein the rewards of a new productive technique will be shared by many competitors who will quickly copy or imitate a progressive firm without bearing any of the research and development costs. And the presence of a large number of rivals will hasten price reductions to consumers, based upon the cost reductions stemming from the advance. The presence of fewer rivals and the proclivity of oligopolists not to cut price enhance the possibility of the innovating oligopolist's realizing greater profit rewards from his technical progress. This is an important point in an economy such as American capitalism, wherein the basic drive wheel is profits.

Technological Progress: The Evidence[8]

Such data as are available do considerable damage to the image of the oligopolistic indus-

[8]This section draws heavily upon Daniel Hamberg, "Size of Firm, Monopoly, and Economic Growth," in *Employment, Growth, and Price Levels, Hearings of the Joint Economic Committee, Part 7* (Washington, 1959), pp. 2337–2352, and "Invention in the Industrial Research Laboratory," *Journal of Political Economy,* April 1963, pp. 95–115.

try as a mainspring of research and development activity. Available statistics suggest that the research laboratories of giant corporate oligopolies are *not* the fountainhead of technological advance. For example, a study[9] of sixty-one important inventions made since 1900 indicates that over half were the work of independent inventors, quite disassociated from the industrial research laboratories of corporate enterprise. Such substantial advances as air conditioning, power steering, cellophane, the jet engine, insulin, the helicopter, and the catalytic cracking of petroleum have this individualistic heritage. Other equally important advances have been provided by small- and medium-sized firms. According to this study, about two-thirds—forty out of sixty-one—of the basic inventions of this century have been fathered by independent inventors or the research activities of relatively small firms. Other studies—for example, analyses of patent statistics—reinforce the conclusion that a large proportion of basic technological advances originates outside the laboratories of giant oligopolies.

This, of course, is the overall picture and does not in any way repudiate the fact that in a number of oligopolistic industries—for example, the aircraft, chemical, petroleum, and electronics industries—research activity has been pursued vigorously, fruitfully, and on an expanding scale. But even here we must append at least two important qualifications. In the first place, there are other oligopolistic industries wherein it is generally agreed that the interest in research and development activity has been modest at best; the steel, cigarette, and aluminum industries are cases in point. Secondly, a very substantial portion of the research carried on by oligopolistic industries is actually financed with public funds. For example, about 80 percent of the research performed in the aircraft-missile industry is government-sponsored, almost 50 percent in

the electronics and communication industries, and so forth. Despite the increased interest of businesses, the Federal government remains the most important source of funds for research and development activity.

☐   **Countervailing Power**

There is a second consideration which brightens somewhat the traditional dim view of oligopoly. John Kenneth Galbraith has developed the notion that many oligopolies (and monopolies) tend to induce the development of oligopolies (and monopolies) on the opposite side of the market.[10] That is, the existence of a monopolistic (or oligopolistic) seller tends to stimulate the growth of a monopsonistic (or oligopsonistic) buyer, and vice versa. More specifically, there is a tendency for "countervailing power" to evolve on the opposite side of those markets in which strong positions of "original power" have already developed. The development of countervailing power is not a matter of chance. It stems, on the one hand, from the desire of resource suppliers or customers to protect themselves from any abuses of the original-power position and, on the other hand, from the desire to share in the profits of the original-power position. Stated differently, for both defensive and offensive reasons, countervailing power is self-generating. Oligopoly begets oligopoly on the opposite side of the market. Oligopoly, in effect, generates its own antidote.

Significance   The significance of countervailing power is implicit in the concept itself. Countervailing power, or "across-the-market" competition, can be an important competitive force in those very markets in which "same-side-of-the-market" rivalry is weak. Oligopolistic sellers may be restrained by a few large buyers. The Big Four of the tire industry face the Big Three of the automobile

[9]John Jewkes, David Sawers, and Richard Stillerman, *The Sources of Invention* (New York: St. Martin's Press, Inc., 1958).

[10]John Kenneth Galbraith, *American Capitalism,* rev. ed. (Boston: Houghton Mifflin Company, 1956), particularly chap. 9.

industry; chain grocery stores and mail-order houses buy in quantity from oligopolistic food processors and manufacturers. Oligopsonistic buyers may be faced with a small number of sellers. Labor unions face gigantic employers; agricultural marketing cooperatives sell to large food processors. Now, to the degree that these opposed positions of market power are successful in checking or restraining the power of one another, the socially desirable operation of a market system characterized by oligopoly will be furthered. Buyer and seller may cancel the power and negate the potential market abuses of one another. The monopolistic seller who seeks a high monopolistic price is faced with a monopsonistic buyer who obviously is interested in a low monopsonistic price. That is, each seeks to use his market power to raise or depress price to his own advantage. The market power of each may be largely self-canceling, and the resulting compromise price close to the competitive level. Furthermore, given the compromise price, the monopolist will have no incentive to restrict his output and sales as he would be obligated to do in establishing a monopolistic price. Thus the net result of monopoly on both sides of the market may be a price and an output closer to those of pure competition than if monopoly existed on only one side of the market. This is true of oligopoly as well. Countervailing power is an important regulatory force in American capitalism and makes the economy more competitive than any discussion limited to same-side-of-the-market competition would lead one to conclude.[11]

Limitations   Countervailing power, however, is not devoid of shortcomings and criticisms. One shortcoming is that it is not universally present. In the automobile industry, for example, dealers are highly dependent upon manufacturers and thus in a poor position to bargain for lower automobile prices which may

[11]The reader should consult the "bilateral monopoly model" of Chapter 31 for the theoretical details of countervailing power as it might apply to the labor market.

benefit both themselves and consumers. In other cases—for example, the petroleum industry—manufacturers are increasingly integrated vertically down to the consumer, thus excluding the possibility of countervailing power. Because the residential construction industry is composed of thousands of small and unorganized contractors, no countervailing power is exerted against oligopolistic suppliers of building materials.

Even where countervailing power is firmly established, it does not function with equal effectiveness under all economic conditions. In particular, during periods of inflation countervailing power does not operate effectively as a competitive force, because with excess demand buyers are no longer able to restrain sellers. When a resource buyer enjoys a seller's market for his product, he is not apt to offer stiff resistance to the demands of resource suppliers. This is best exemplified in the labor market, where unions as "sellers" of labor are in a most strategic position in bargaining with employers during inflation. Management does not want to risk a work stoppage when consumer demand is burgeoning. Why resist? Increases in wage costs can be readily passed on to the consumer through price increases with no loss of sales, and profits thereby can be maintained or even expanded. The results of this situation are anything but socially desirable (Chapter 18).

Finally, it has been pointed out that the two power positions may both benefit at the expense of the rest of the economy by combining their forces rather than by offsetting one another. Across-the-market rivals may find mutual advantages in collusive action or outright merger rather than in expanding their energies in negating the market power of one another.

□   **Oligopoly: Tentative Appraisal**

Having surveyed the restrictive and progressive oligopoly models, what, if anything, can we conclude about the economic efficiency of oligopolistic industries? Not much more than this: Assuming *given* long-run costs of production, an oligopolistic industry will produce less, provide fewer jobs, and charge a higher product price than would the same industry organized competitively. But to the extent that oligopoly results in lower unit costs and improvements in product quality, this conclusion must be altered in a manner less condemnatory of oligopoly. That is, *if* large oligopolistic producers are in a better position than competitive firms to realize existing (known) economies of scale, or *if* they are more able and willing to develop improved productive techniques and better products, then oligopoly *may* be more desirable socially than competition. However, despite plausible arguments as to why oligopoly may be progressive, such empirical evidence as is available suggests that giant oligopolistic corporations are not the basic source of technological advance in our society. Furthermore, there are many known instances in which oligopolists, unbridled by countervailing power, have sorely abused their market power, to the detriment of society as a whole.[12]

Indeed, the picture is a mixed one. The examination of specific cases will reveal both restrictive and progressive oligopolies. This tentative conclusion is worth venturing: Oligopolistic industries may be much more palatable over time, that is, in the long run, than they seem to be at a particular point in time.

[12]See Walton and Cleveland, *Corporations on Trial*, op. cit.

Summary

1   Oligopolistic industries are characterized by the presence of few firms, each of which has a significant fraction of the market. Firms thus situated are mutually interdependent; the behavior of any one firm directly affects, and is affected by, the actions of rivals. Products may be virtually uniform or significantly differentiated. Underlying reasons for the evolution of oligopoly are economies of scale and the advantages of merger.

2   The wide variety of oligopolistic markets and the uncertainty which stems from mutual interdependence limit the applicability of formal economic analysis to oligopolistic markets. The factual record indicates, however, that **a.** oligopolistic prices tend to be inflexible or "sticky," and **b.** the price changes which do occur are "orderly" and thereby imply some form of collusion.

Noncollusive oligopolists in effect face a kinked demand curve. This curve and the accompanying marginal-revenue curve help explain the price rigidity which characterizes such markets; they do not, however, explain the level of price.

4   The uncertainties inherent in noncollusive pricing are conducive to collusion. There is a tendency for collusive oligopolists to maximize joint profits—that is, to behave somewhat like pure monopolists. However, antitrust legislation, the presence of a "large" number of firms, and differences in cost and demand curves serve as impediments to collusion. Furthermore, collusive price arrangements are difficult to maintain during recessions. Though potentially profitable, secret price concessions can lead to the breakdown of price collusion.

5   Insights into the character and behavior of oligopolistic industries—mutual interdependence, price rigidity, the tendency toward collusion—can be gained through the examination of a profits-payoff table.

6   Market shares in oligopolistic industries are usually determined on the basis of nonprice competition. Oligopolists emphasize nonprice competition because *a.* advertising and product variations are less easy for rivals to match, and *b.* oligopolists frequently have ample financial resources to finance nonprice competition.

7 There is no clear-cut conclusion as to the social desirability of oligopoly; oligopoly may be either restrictive or progressive. Where oligopoly is restrictive, abuses of its market power may sometimes be curbed by countervailing power.

Questions and Study Suggestions

1 Key terms and concepts to remember: oligopoly; mutual interdependence; noncollusive versus collusive oligopoly; kinked demand curve; price rigidity; joint-profit maximization; cartel; gentlemen's agreement; price leadership; price break; theory of games; profit-payoff table; restrictive versus progressive oligopoly; countervailing power.

2 What features distinguish oligopoly from monopolistic competition?

3 "Fewness of rivals means mutual interdependence, and mutual interdependence means uncertainty as to how those few rivals will react to a price change by any one firm." Explain. Of what significance is this for determining demand and marginal revenue? Other things being equal, would you expect mutual interdependence to vary directly or inversely with the degree of product differentiation? Explain.

4 What are the basic characteristics of oligopolistic prices? How are these characteristics best explained?

5 What assumptions concerning a rival's responses to price changes underlie the kinked demand curve? Why is there a gap in the marginal-revenue curve? How does the kinked demand curve help explain oligopolistic price rigidity?

6 Why is there a tendency for price collusion to occur in oligopolistic industries? Assess the economic desirability of collusive pricing. Explain: "If each firm knows that the price of each of its few rivals depends on its own price, how can the prices be determined?"

7 Explain how price leadership might evolve and function in an oligopolistic industry.

8 Explain the general character of the data in the following profits-payoff table for oligopolists C and D. All profit figures are in thousands.

D's price ↓ \ C's price →	$40	$35	$30
$40	$60 / $54	$55 / $59	$49 / $57
$35	$69 / $50	$58 / $55	$50 / $56
$30	$70 / $40	$60 / $49	$52 / $51

a. Use the table to explain the mutual interdependence which characterizes oligopolistic industries.

b. Assuming both firms are initially charging $35 and there is no collusion, explain why each firm may be hesitant to alter its price.

c.   Assuming both firms are charging $30 initially, explain why the firms might find collusive pricing to be mutually advantageous. Why might the firms find it difficult to raise their prices up to $40?

9   "Oligopolistic industries have both the means and the inclination for technological progress." Do you agree? Explain.

10   Under what conditions will oligopoly be economically efficient? Economically inefficient? Which set of conditions do you feel best describes oligopoly in American capitalism? Justify your answer.

11   How does countervailing power differ from ordinary competition? Why is it self-generating? What are its limitations?

Selected References

Adams, Walter (ed.): *The Structure of American Industry,* 5th ed. (New York: The Macmillan Company, 1977), chaps. 3, 5, 13.

Bain, Joe S.: *Industrial Organization,* 2d ed. (New York: John Wiley & Sons, Inc., 1968), chap. 9.

Colberg, Marshall R., Dascomb R. Forbush, and Gilbert R. Whitaker, Jr.: *Business Economics: Principles and Cases,* 4th ed. (Homewood, Ill.: Richard D. Irwin, Inc., 1970), chap. 12.

Galbraith, John K.: *American Capitalism,* rev. ed. (Boston: Houghton Mifflin Company, 1956), chaps. 7, 9.

Koch, James V.: *Industrial Organization and Prices* (Englewood Cliffs, N.J.: Prentice-Hall, Inc., 1974), chaps. 9, 12, 13.

Scherer, F. M.: *Industrial Pricing: Theory and Evidence* (Chicago: Rand McNally & Company, 1970).

Weiss, Leonard W.: *Economics and American Industry* (New York: John Wiley & Sons, Inc., 1961), chaps. 7, 8.

Last Word
Auto Rentals: Trying Too Hard?

Collusive behavior by oligopolists is typically to the detriment of smaller competitors.

Travelers renting cars at most U.S. airports can choose to drive away the Fords of Hertz, the Plymouths of Avis or the Chevies of National Car Rental. Last week the Federal Trade Commission charged that the Big Three of the auto-rental business had combined to make sure that consumers got no other choice. Hertz, Avis and National, said the FTC, have been conspiring since 1968 to freeze competitors out of airport trade, which constitutes 70% of the $700 million-a-year business, and to keep car-rental prices artificially high.

The FTC alleged that Hertz, Avis and National conspired to submit identical bids for concession rights at airports, and persuaded airport managers to set requirements for concessions that disqualified competitors. One rule they are alleged to have promoted requires that "concessionaires have a nationwide reservations network." The FTC also accused the three companies of fixing rental prices and stated that smaller competitors kept out of the airports charged 10% to 40% less.

The commission further charged the rental companies with "entering into anticompetitive arrangements" with automakers—Hertz with Ford, Avis with Chrysler and National with General Motors. According to the complaints, the arrangements provide the rental companies with advertising subsidies from the automakers that average $5 million a year to each, and "have the effect of increasing barriers to entry" to smaller companies, which do not get such large subsidies.

The three rental concerns denied the charges. The FTC chose not to accuse the automakers of any violation, but a spokesman for Ford denied that the advertising agreements were anticompetitive and said the company had similar agreements with some of Hertz's smaller competitors.

A trial of the case before an FTC administrative-law judge may be a year off and the companies could appeal any unfavorable ruling through the federal courts. If the FTC eventually prevails, the three companies could be forced to pay triple damages to any competitors or consumers who win lawsuits. The FTC might also seek to have one or more of the three big rental companies booted out of some airports and replaced by smaller competitors.

"Auto Rentals: Trying Too Hard?" *Time,* June 23, 1975, p. 58. Reprinted by permission from TIME, The Weekly Newsmagazine; Copyright Time Inc. 1975.

Production and the Demand for Economic Resources

The preceding four chapters have been concerned with the pricing and output of goods and services under a variety of product market structures. In producing any commodity, a firm must hire productive resources which, directly or indirectly, are owned and supplied by households. It is appropriate that we now turn from the pricing and production of goods to the pricing and employment of resources needed in accomplishing production. In terms of our circular flow diagram of the economy (Chapter 3), we now shift our attention from the bottom loop of the diagram, where firms supply and households demand products, to the top loop, where households supply and businesses demand resources. It is in part this reversal of roles which makes necessary a separate discussion of resource pricing.

SIGNIFICANCE OF RESOURCE PRICING

There are a number of intertwined reasons for studying resource pricing.

1 The most basic fact about resource prices is that they constitute a major determinant of money incomes. The expenditures which businesses make in acquiring economic resources flow as wage, rent, interest, and profit incomes to those households which in turn supply the human and property resources at their disposal. Here we are concerned with explaining the resource prices which play such a crucial role in determining the distribution of income.

2 Another important aspect of resource pricing is that, just as product prices ration finished goods and services to consumers, so resource prices allocate scarce resources among various industries and firms. An understanding of the manner in which resource prices negotiate the allocation of resources is particularly significant in view of the fact that in a dynamic economy such as American capitalism, the efficient allocation of resources over time calls for continuing shifts in resources among alternative uses.

3 A very special aspect of the resource allocation problem faces the individual firm. To the firm, resource prices are costs, and to realize maximum profits a firm must produce the profit-maximizing output with the most efficient (least costly) combination of resources. Given technology, it is resource prices which play the major role in determining the quantities of land, labor, capital, and entrepreneurial ability that are to be combined in the productive process.

4 Finally, aside from these objective facets of resource pricing, there are a myriad of ethical questions and public policy issues surrounding the resource market. In particular, the amoral nature of resource prices results in considerable inequality in the personal distribution of income. Too, the age-old question of the sizes of the income shares going to specific groups is still very much alive. What is the proper distribution of the national income between profits and wages? What shares should go to farmers, factory workers, white-collar employees? Indeed, the pursuit of these questions leads into a consideration of the alternative economic ideologies. Much of Part 6 of this book is concerned with endeavors—both public and private—to alter the distribution of income. Chapter 37 is concerned specifically with the ethics of income distribution; here the arguments for and against greater income equality are examined.

COMPLEXITIES OF RESOURCE PRICING

Economists are in substantial agreement as to the basic principles of resource pricing. Yet there exists considerable disagreement and sometimes an element of confusion as to the variations in these general principles which must be made as they are applied to specific resources and particular markets. While economists are in general agreement that the pricing and employment of economic resources, or factors of production, are a supply and demand phenomenon, they also recognize that in particular markets, resource supply and demand may assume strange and often complex dimensions. This is further complicated by the fact that the operation of supply and demand forces may be muted or even largely supplanted by the policies and practices of government, business firms, or labor unions, not to mention a host of other institutional considerations.

Our major objective in this chapter is a limited one: to explain the basic factors which underlie the demand for economic resources. We shall couch our discussion in terms of labor, recognizing that the principles we outline are also generally applicable to land, capital, and entrepreneurial ability. In Chapter 31 we shall combine our understanding of resource demand with a discussion of labor supply in analyzing wage rates. Then in Chapter 32 we shall emphasize the supply side of the market for property resources.

MARGINAL PRODUCTIVITY THEORY OF RESOURCE DEMAND

The least complicated approach to resource demand is that which assumes a firm is hiring some specific resource in a competitive market and in turn is selling its product in a competitive market. The simplicity of this situation lies in the fact that under competition the firm can dispose of as little or as much output as it chooses at the going market price. The firm is selling such a negligible fraction of total output that it exerts no influence whatever on product price. Similarly, in the resource market, competition means that the firm is hiring such a small fraction of the total supply of the resource that its price is unaffected by the quantity the firm purchases.

□ Resource Demand as a Derived Demand

Having specified these simplified conditions, we can note the most crucial point: the demand for resources is a *derived* demand, that is, derived from the finished goods and services which resources help produce. Resources do not directly satisfy consumer wants, but do so indirectly by producing goods and services. No one wants to consume an acre of land, an International Harvester tractor, or the labor services of a farmer, but households do want to consume the various food and fiber products which these resources help produce.

□ Marginal Revenue Product (MRP)

The derived nature of resource demand correctly implies that the strength of the demand for any resource will depend upon (1) the capability of the resource in producing a good, and (2) the market value of the good it is producing. In other words, a resource which is highly productive in turning out a commodity highly valued by society will be in great demand. On the other hand, demand will be very weak for a relatively unproductive resource which is only capable of producing some good not in great demand by households. There will be no demand for a resource which is phenomenally efficient in the production of something which no one will want to purchase!

The roles of productivity and product value in determining resource demand can be brought into sharper focus through Table 30-1. Here it is assumed that a firm is adding one variable resource—labor—to its fixed plant. Columns 1 through 3 remind us that the law of diminishing returns will be applicable in this situation, causing the marginal physical product (MPP) of labor to fall beyond some point.[1] For simplicity's sake, it is here assumed that diminishing marginal physical product sets in with the first worker hired.

But we have already emphasized that the derived demand for a resource depends not only upon the productivity of that resource but also upon the price of the commodity it

[1] It might be helpful to review the section "Growth: A More Sophisticated View" in Chapter 19, where the law of diminishing returns is discussed in more detail.

Table 30-1   THE DEMAND FOR A RESOURCE: PURE COMPETITION IN THE SALE OF THE PRODUCT (*hypothetical data*)

(1) Units of resource	(2) Total product	(3) Marginal physical product (MPP), or Δ(2)	(4) Product price	(5) Total revenue, or (2) × (4)	(6) Marginal revenue product (MRP), or Δ(5)
1	15	15	$1	$15	$15
2	27	12	1	27	12
3	36	9	1	36	9
4	42	6	1	42	6
5	45	3	1	45	3
6	46	1	1	46	1

produces. Column 4 adds this price information. Note that product price is constant, in this case at $1, because we are supposing a competitive product market. Multiplying column 2 by column 4, we get the total-revenue data of column 5. From these total-revenue data we can readily compute *marginal revenue product (MRP)—the increase in total revenue resulting from the use of each additional variable input (labor, in this case).* This is indicated in column 6.

□   Rule for Employing Resources: MRP = MRC

The MRP schedule—columns 1 and 6—constitutes the firm's demand schedule for labor. To explain why this is so, we must first discuss the rule which guides a profit-seeking firm in hiring any resource. *To maximize profits, a firm should hire additional units of any given resource so long as each successive unit adds more to the firm's total revenue than it does to its total costs.* Economists have special terms which designate what each additional unit of a resource adds to total cost and what it adds to total revenue. We have just noted that MRP measures how much each successive worker adds to total revenue. The amount which each additional unit of a resource adds to the firm's total (resource) cost is called *marginal resource cost* (MRC). Thus we can restate our rule for hiring resources as follows: *It will be profitable for a firm to hire additional units of a resource up to the point at which that resource's MRP is equal to its MRC.* If the number of workers a firm is currently hiring is such that the MRP of the last worker exceeds his MRC, the firm can clearly profit by hiring more workers. But if the number being hired is such that the MRC of the last worker exceeds his MRP, the firm is hiring workers who are not "paying their way," and it can thereby increase its profits by laying off some workers. The reader will recognize that this MRP = MRC rule is very similar to the MR = MC rule employed throughout our discussion of product pricing. The rationale of the two rules is the same, but the point of reference is now *inputs* of resources, not *outputs* of product.

□   MRP is a Demand Schedule

Just as product price and marginal revenue are equal in a purely competitive product market, so resource price and marginal resource cost are equal when a firm is hiring a resource competitively. In a purely competitive labor market the wage rate is set by the total, or market, supply of, and the market demand for, labor. Because it hires such a small fraction of the total supply of labor, a single firm cannot influence this wage rate. This means that total resource cost increases by exactly the amount of the going wage rate for each additional worker hired; the wage rate and MRC are equal. It follows that so long as it is hiring labor competitively, *the firm will hire workers to the point at which their wage rate (or MRC) is equal to their MRP.*

Accordingly, employing the data in column 6 of Table 30-1, we find that if the wage rate is $14.95, the firm will hire only one worker. This is so because the first worker adds $15 to total revenue and slightly less—$14.95—to total costs. For each successive worker, however, we find that his MRC exceeds his MRP, indicating that it will not be profitable to hire him. If the wage rate is $11.95, we apply the same reasoning and discover that it will pay the firm to hire both the first and second workers. Similarly, if the wage rate is $8.95, three will be hired. If $5.95, four. If $2.95, then five. And so forth. It is evident that *the MRP schedule constitutes the firm's demand for labor, because each point on this schedule (curve) indicates the number of workers which the firm would hire at each possible wage rate which might exist.* This is shown graphically in Figure 30-1.[2]

---

[2]The rationale employed here is familiar to us. Recall in Chapter 26 that we applied the price-equals-marginal cost or $P = MC$ rule for the profit-maximizing *output* to dis-

FIGURE 30-1   THE PURELY COMPETITIVE SELLER'S DEMAND FOR A RESOURCE

The MRP curve is the resource demand curve. The location of the curve depends upon the marginal productivity of the resource and the price of the product. Under pure competition product price is constant; therefore, it is solely because of diminishing marginal productivity that the resource demand curve is downsloping.

□   **Resource Demand Under Imperfect Competition**

Our analysis of labor demand becomes slightly more complex when we assume that the firm is selling its product in an imperfectly competitive market. Pure monopoly, oligopoly, and monopolistic competition in the product market all mean that the firm's product demand curve is downsloping; that is, the firm must accept a lower price in order to increase its sales. Table 30-2 takes this into account. The productivity data of Table 30-1 are retained, but it is now assumed in column 4 that product price must be lowered in order to sell the marginal product of each successive worker. The MRP of the purely competitive seller falls for one reason: marginal physical

product diminishes. But the MRP of the imperfectly competitive seller falls for two reasons: marginal product diminishes, *and* product price falls as output increases.

It must be emphasized that the lower price which accompanies every increase in output applies in each case not only to the marginal product of each successive worker but also to all prior units which otherwise could have been sold at a higher price. To illustrate: The second worker's marginal product is 12 units. These 12 units can be sold for $1.20 each or, as a group, for $14.40. But this is not the MRP of the second worker. Why? Because in order to sell these 12 units, the firm must take a 10-cent price cut on the 15 units produced by the first worker—units which could have been sold for $1.30 each. Thus the MRP of the second worker is only $12.90 [= $14.40 − (15 × 10 cents)]. Similarly, the third worker's MRP is $7.20. Although the 9 units he produces are worth $1.10 each in the market, the third worker does not add $9.90 to the firm's total revenue when account is taken of the 10-cent price cut which must be taken on the 27 units produced by the first two workers. In this case the third worker's MRP is only $7.20 [= $9.90 − (27 × 10 cents)]. And so it is for the other figures in column 6.

The net result is obvious: The MRP curve—the resource demand curve—of the imperfectly competitive producer tends to be less elastic than that of a purely competitive producer. At a wage rate or MRC of $11.95, both the purely competitive and the imperfectly competitive seller will hire two workers. But at $8.95, the competitive firm will hire three and the imperfectly competitive firm only two. And at $5.95, the purely competitive firm will take on four employees and the imperfect competitor only three. This difference in elasticity can be readily visualized by graphing the MRP data of Table 30-2 as in Figure 30-2 and comparing them with Figure 30-1.

It is not surprising that the imperfectly competitive producer is less responsive to wage cuts in terms of workers employed than is the

cover that the portion of the competitive firm's short-run marginal-cost curve lying above average variable cost is the short-run *product* supply curve (Figure 26-5). Presently we are applying the MRP = MRC rule for the profit-maximizing *input* to the firm's MRP curve and determining that this curve is the input or *resource* demand curve.

Table 30-2 THE DEMAND FOR A RESOURCE: IMPERFECT COMPETITION IN THE SALE OF THE PRODUCT (*hypothetical data*)

(1) Units of resource	(2) Total product	(3) Marginal physical product (MPP), or Δ(2)	(4) Product price	(5) Total revenue, or (2) × (4)	(6) Marginal revenue product (MRP), or Δ(5)
1	15		$1.30	$19.50	
		15			$19.50
2	27		1.20	32.40	
		12			12.90
3	36		1.10	39.60	
		9			7.20
4	42		1.05	44.10	
		6			4.50
5	45		1.00	45.00	
		3			0.90
6	46		0.95	43.70	
		1			−1.30

purely competitive producer. The relative reluctance of the imperfect competitor to employ more resources and thereby produce more output when resource prices fall is merely the resource market reflection of the imperfect competitor's tendency to restrict output in the product market. Other things being equal, the imperfectly competitive seller will produce less of a product than would a purely competitive seller. In producing this smaller output, he will demand fewer resources.

But one qualification is pertinent. We noted in Chapters 27 and 29 that in some instances the market structures of oligopoly and pure monopoly might be progressive rather than restrictive. That is, they might give rise to a higher level of production, more employment, and lower prices in the long run than would a purely competitive market arrangement. This seems more likely in the case of oligopoly. The resource demand curve for progressive oligopoly and monopoly would not be so restricted.

FIGURE 30-2 THE IMPERFECTLY COMPETITIVE SELLER'S DEMAND FOR A RESOURCE

An imperfectly competitive seller's resource demand curve slopes downward because marginal product diminishes and product price falls as output increases.

□ **Market Demand for a Resource**

Can we now derive a market demand curve for a resource? Yes, we can. You will recall that the total, or market, demand curve for a product is developed by summing the demand curves of all individual buyers in the market. Similarly, the market demand curve for a particular resource can be derived in essentially the same fashion, that is, by summing the individual demand or MRP curves for all firms hiring that resource.[3]

[3]The matter is actually not quite this simple. The resource demand, or MRP, curve *for each firm* is drawn on the assumption that product price is constant. However, if a lowering of resource price causes *all firms* in the industry to hire more of the resource and thereby expand total output, we can expect product price to decline. The result is that the resource market demand curve will not be quite identical with the sum of the individual firms' demand

CHANGES IN RESOURCE DEMAND

What will alter the demand for a resource, that is, shift the demand curve? The very derivation of resource demand immediately suggests two related factors—the resource's productivity and the market price of the product it is producing. And our previous analysis of changes in product demand (Chapter 4) suggests another factor—changes in the prices of other resources.

☐ Changes in Product Demand

Because resource demand is a derived demand, it is obvious that any change in the demand for the product will affect product price and therefore the MRP of the resource. In Table 30-1, assume an increase in product demand which boosts product price to $2. If you calculate the new labor demand curve and plot it in Figure 30-1, you will find that it lies to the right of the old curve. Similarly, a drop in product demand and price will shift the labor demand curve to the left. Real-world example: In late 1973 the gasoline shortage and rapidly rising gasoline prices twisted the demand for automobiles away from larger models—Cadillacs and Oldsmobiles—and toward compacts—Vegas and Pintos. As a result, workers in the large-car plants were being furloughed and small-car workers were working overtime!

---

curves for that resource. Recall that the resource demand curve of Figure 30-2 is steeper or less elastic than the curve of Figure 30-1 *because* the former is based on a constant product price and the latter upon the assumption that product price falls as output or product supply increases. So it is for the case at hand. A simple horizontal summing of the resource demand curves of the individual firms is unrealistically based upon an unchanging product price. The true market demand curve takes cognizance of the fact that product price will fall as *industry* output expands, and, hence, this curve will be steeper or less elastic than that based upon a constant product price. For details consult Richard B. Freeman, *Labor Economics* (Englewood Cliffs, N.J.: Prentice-Hall, Inc., 1972), pp. 60–62.

☐ Productivity Changes

Changes in productivity will also cause resource demand to shift. The productivity of any resource can be altered in several ways. (1) The marginal productivity data for, say, labor will depend upon the quantities of other resources with which it is combined. The greater the amount of capital and land resources with which labor is combined, the greater will be the marginal productivity and the demand for labor. (2) Technological improvements will have the same effect. The better the quality of the capital, the greater the productivity of labor. Steelworkers employed with a given amount of real capital in the form of modern oxygen furnaces are much more productive than when employed with the same amount of real capital embodied in the old open-hearth furnaces. (3) Improvements in the quality of the variable resource itself—labor—will increase the marginal productivity and therefore the demand for labor. In effect, we have a new demand curve for a different, more skilled kind of labor.

All these considerations, incidentally, are important in explaining why the average level of (real) wages is higher in the United States than in most foreign nations. American workers are generally healthier and better trained than those of foreign nations, and in most industries they work with a larger and more efficient stock of capital goods and more abundant natural resources than do the workers of most other countries. This spells a strong demand for labor. On the supply side of the market, labor is *relatively* scarce as compared with most foreign nations. A strong demand and a relatively scarce supply result in high wage rates. This will be discussed further in Chapter 31.

☐ Prices of Other Resources

Just as changes in the prices of other products will change the demand for a specific commodity, so changes in the prices of other resources can be expected to alter the demand for a particular resource. And just as the effect of a change in the price of product X upon the demand for product Y depends upon whether X and Y are substitute or complementary goods, so the effect of a change in the price of resource A upon the demand for resource B will depend upon their substitutability or their complementariness.

Within limits, resources are typically substitutes for one another. A drop in the price of machinery may prompt a firm to substitute machinery for labor; this is the obvious adjustment to make if the firm seeks to produce any given output in the least costly fashion. At given wage rates, less labor will now be employed. The demand for labor will have fallen. But this *substitution effect* may be offset wholly or in part by an accompanying *output effect*. Because the price of machinery has fallen, the cost of producing various outputs will also have declined. And with lower costs, the firm will find it profitable to produce and sell a larger output. This greater output will tend to increase the demand for all resources, including labor. The net effect of a decline in the price of machinery upon the demand for labor will depend upon the sizes of these two opposed effects. If the substitution effect outweighs the output effect, the demand for labor will decline. If the reverse holds true, the demand for labor will increase.

When resources are complementary or jointly demanded, the situation is a bit more clear-cut. In some situations the nature of the productive process allows little or no room for substituting resources; resources are combined in fixed proportions. Suppose, for example, that a small manufacturer of metal products uses punch presses as its basic piece of capital equipment. Each press is designed to be operated by one worker; the machine is not automated—it won't run itself—and a second worker would be wholly redundant. Now assume that a significant technological advance in the production of these presses substantially

reduces their cost. Other things being unchanged, this reduction in the price of capital goods will induce our manufacturer to use more presses. However, because labor and capital are required in fixed proportions—one man for one machine—there will be no substitution of capital for labor. On the contrary, the purchase of more machines will increase the firm's demand for punch-press operators. The output effect will bolster this increase in labor demand. To the extent that the firm's metal products are reduced in price because of the drop in the cost of the presses, its volume of sales and therefore its demand for labor will increase.

ELASTICITY OF RESOURCE DEMAND

The considerations just discussed are responsible for shifts in the location of resource demand curves. Such changes in demand are to be carefully distinguished from a change in the quantity of a resource demanded. The latter, you will recall, does not entail a shift in the resource demand curve but rather a movement from one point to another on a stable resource demand curve, because of a change in the price of the specific resource under consideration. To illustrate: An increase in the wage rate from $5.95 to $8.95 will reduce the quantity of labor demanded from four to three workers, as can be readily seen in Table 30-1 and Figure 30-1.

This raises a question: What determines the sensitivity of producers to changes in resource prices? Or, more technically, what determines the elasticity of resource demand? Several long-standing generalizations provide some important insights in answering this question.

1 Rate of MRP Decline A purely technical consideration—the rate at which the marginal physical product of the variable resource declines—is important. *If the marginal* *product of labor declines slowly as it is added to a fixed amount of capital, the MRP, or demand curve for labor, will decline slowly and tend to be highly elastic.* A small decline in the price of such a resource will give rise to a relatively large increase in the amount demanded. Conversely, if the marginal productivity of labor declines sharply, the MRP, or labor demand curve, will decline rapidly. This means that a relatively large decline in the wage rate will be accompanied by a very modest increase in the amount of labor hired; resource demand will be inelastic.

2 Ease of Resource Substitutability
The degree to which resources are substitutable for one another is a highly important determinant of elasticity. *The larger the number of good substitute resources available, the greater will be the elasticity of demand for a particular resource.* If a furniture manufacturer finds that some five or six different types of wood are equally satisfactory in making coffee tables, a rise in the price of any one type of wood may cause a very sharp drop in the amount demanded as the producer readily substitutes other woods. At the other extreme, it may be impossible to substitute; bauxite is absolutely essential in the production of aluminum ingots. This means that the demand for it tends to be very inelastic.

3 Elasticity of Product Demand The elasticity of demand for any resource will depend upon the elasticity of demand for the product which it helps produce. *The greater the elasticity of product demand, the greater the elasticity of resource demand.* The derived nature of resource demand would lead us to expect this relationship. A small rise in the price of a product with great elasticity of demand will give rise to a sharp drop in output and therefore a relatively large decline in the amounts of the various resources demanded. Indeed, our comparisons of resource demand when output is being sold competitively (Table 30-1 and Figure 30-1) on the one hand, and

under imperfectly competitive conditions (Table 30-2 and Figure 30-2) on the other, have already suggested that, other things being the same, the greater the elasticity of product demand, the greater the elasticity of resource demand.

4 Labor Cost–Total Cost Ratio *Finally, the larger the portion of total production costs accounted for by a resource, the greater will be the elasticity of demand for that resource.* The rationale here is rather evident. If labor costs account for, say, three-fourths of the total cost of a product, a given increase in wage rates will alter total cost by a relatively large amount, resulting in a significant increase in product price. Given the elasticity of product demand, this substantial price increase will cause a relatively large decline in sales and a sharp decline in the amount of labor demanded. But if labor cost is only 5 or 10 percent of total cost, the same given increase in wage rates will have little effect upon total cost and product price. Given the same elasticity of product demand, a small decline in sales and therefore in the amount of labor demanded will result.

■ _____

A FIRM'S DEMAND FOR SEVERAL RESOURCES

We know that the production of any commodity will involve the use of several inputs. It is therefore important to generalize our discussion of the demand for a single resource to the demand for a number of resources. While our analysis will proceed on the basis of two resources, it can readily be extended to any number one chooses to consider.

□ The Profit-maximizing Combination of Resources

The generalization of our discussion of resource demand to several resources is quite easily accomplished. Assume a firm is hiring two resources, capital and labor, in purely competitive markets. This means that the price of capital and the price of labor (the wage rate) are given to the firm and will not change with the amount purchased. It follows that the prices of labor (P_L) and capital (P_C) and their respective marginal resource costs are equal.

We have seen that in determining the profit-maximizing amount of any single resource—say, labor—to hire, the firm must ask itself: How much will an extra worker add to total costs? And how does this compare with what he will add to total revenue? Or, more formally, what is the marginal resource cost (wage rate) of an extra worker as compared to his marginal revenue product? We know that so long as an extra worker's MRP exceeds his wage rate, it remains profitable to add more workers. But if the firm is employing some quantity of labor such that the wage rate exceeds the MRP, it has hired too large a labor force and can increase profits by terminating the employment of all workers who add more to costs than they do to revenue. In short, the profit-maximizing quantity of labor to employ is that quantity at which the wage rate, or price of labor (P_L), equals the marginal revenue product of labor (MRP_L) or, more simply, $P_L = \text{MRP}_L$.

The same rationale applies to any other resource—for example, capital. Capital will also be employed in the profit-maximizing amount when its price equals its marginal revenue product, or $P_C = \text{MRP}_C$. Thus, in general, we can say that when hiring resources in competitive markets, a firm will realize the profit-maximizing combination of resources when each input is employed up to the point at which its price equals its marginal revenue product:

$$P_L = \text{MRP}_L$$
$$P_C = \text{MRP}_C$$

This rule is sometimes alternatively expressed as

$$\frac{\text{MRP}_L}{P_L} = \frac{\text{MRP}_C}{P_C} = 1 \qquad (1)$$

Note two things. First, in equation (1) it is not sufficient that the MRPs of the two resources be *proportionate to* their prices; the MRPs must be *equal to* their prices and the ratios therefore equal to 1. For example, if $\text{MRP}_L = \$15$, $P_L = \$5$, $\text{MRP}_C = \$9$, and $P_C = \$3$, the firm would be underemploying both capital and labor even though the ratios of MRP to resource price were identical for both resources. That is, the firm could expand its profits by hiring additional amounts of both capital and labor until it had moved down their downsloping MRP curves to the points at which MRP_L was equal to \$5 and MRP_C was \$3. The ratios will now be 5/5 and 3/3 and obviously equal to 1.

Second, the problem faced by the producer is much like that confronting the consumer. You will recall from Chapter 24 that the consumer seeks the particular combination of goods which will yield the maximum utility for his money income. In achieving the utility-maximizing collection of goods, the consumer considers both his preferences as reflected in diminishing marginal-utility data *and* the prices of the various products. The producer is in a similar boat. He obviously wants to maximize his profits, just as the consumer seeks to maximize his utility. In pursuing this combination of resources, the producer must consider both the productivity of the resource as reflected in diminishing marginal-physical-productivity data *and* the prices (costs) of the various resources. A firm may well find it profitable to employ very small amounts of an extremely productive resource if its price is particularly high. Conversely, it may be sensible to hire large amounts of a relatively unproductive resource if its price is sufficiently low.

□ **The Least-Cost Combination of Resources**

Determination of the profit-maximizing combination of several inputs obviously implies repeated comparisons of total revenue and total costs to ascertain that output at which the difference between the two is maximized. Given product price, the maximization of this difference—the maximization of profits—will pinpoint some unique output (Figure 26-1a). But, of course, product price might change and thereby cause some alternative output to become the profit-maximizing level of production (Figure 26-5). In short, depending upon the level of product price, any one of a large number of possible outputs may be the profit-maximizing or loss-minimizing output. However, these various possible outputs can only be a profit-maximizing level of production if each is produced in the least costly way. In other words, a necessary condition for profit maximization is the production of any relevant output with the minimum attainable cost outlay for resources. *Indeed, all the cost curves developed in Chapter 25 and applied in the ensuing product market chapters implicitly assume that each possible level of output is being produced with the least costly combination of inputs.* If this were not the case, then presumably there would exist lower attainable positions for the cost curves (Figure 26-2, for example), and consequently there would be some other (larger) output than that designated at which greater profits could be realized.

When is a firm producing any given output with the least costly combination of resources? The answer is: When the last dollar spent on each resource entails the same marginal physical product. That is, *the cost of any output is minimized when the marginal physical product per dollar's worth of each resource used is the same.* If we are thinking in terms of just two resources, labor and capital, the cost-minimizing position occurs where

$$\frac{\text{MPP of labor}}{\text{price of labor}} = \frac{\text{MPP of capital}}{\text{price of capital}} \quad (2)$$

It is not difficult to see why the fulfillment of this condition means least-cost production. Suppose, for example, that the prices of capital and labor are both $1 per unit, but that capital and labor are currently being employed in such amounts that the marginal physical product of labor is 9 and the marginal physical product of capital is 5. Our equation immediately tells us that this is clearly *not* the least costly combination of resources: MPP_L/P_L is 9/1 and MPP_C/P_C is 5/1. If the firm spends a dollar less on capital and shifts that dollar to labor, it will lose the 5 units of output produced by the marginal dollar's worth of capital, but will gain the 9 units of output from the employment of an extra dollar's worth of labor. *Net* output will increase by 4 (= 9 − 5) units for the same total cost. Note that this shifting of dollars from capital to labor will push the firm down its MPP curve for labor and back up its MPP curve for capital, moving the firm toward a position of equilibrium wherein equation (2) is fulfilled. At this point the MPP of both labor and capital might be, for example, 7.

Whenever the same total cost results in a greater total output, it means that cost per unit—and therefore the total cost of any given level of output—is being reduced. Stated somewhat differently, to be able to produce a *larger* output with a *given* total-cost outlay is the same thing as being able to produce a *given* output with a *smaller* total cost outlay. And as we have seen, the cost of producing any given output can be reduced so long as $\text{MPP}_C/P_C \neq \text{MPP}_L/P_L$. But when dollars have been shifted among capital and labor to the point at which equation (2) holds, then there are no further changes in the amounts of capital and labor employed which will reduce costs more. The least-cost combination of capital and labor is being realized for that output. Question 7 at the end of this chapter stresses the distinction between the profit-maximizing and the least-cost combination of resources.

A subtle, but significant, point: Although we have separated the two for discussion purposes, the profit-maximizing position of equation (1) subsumes the least-cost position of equation (2).[4] That is, a firm which is maxi-

---

[4] Note that if we divide the MRP numerators in equation (1) by product price we obtain equation (2).

mizing its profits *must* be producing the profit-maximizing output with the least costly combination of resources. If it is *not* using the least costly combination of labor and capital, then it could obviously produce the same output at a smaller total cost and realize a larger profit! Thus, a necessary condition for profit maximization is the fulfillment of equation (2). But equation (2) is not a sufficient condition for profit maximization. It is quite possible for a firm to produce the "wrong" output, that is, an output which does not maximize profits, but to produce that output with the least costly combination of resources.

☐ Modifications for Imperfect Competition

Our development of the profit-maximizing and least-cost rules assumes purely competitive markets and therefore constant input prices. We shall find in Chapter 31 that, when a firm is hiring resources under imperfectly competitive conditions, its decision to hire more inputs will affect resource prices. Specifically, if a firm is large relative to a resource market, it will have to increase the current resource price to attract more inputs. And this higher price must be paid not only to the extra inputs employed, but also to all units of the resource already in the employment of the firm. This means that marginal resource cost (MRC)—the cost of an extra input—is actually greater than resource price. The fact that MRC exceeds resource price when resources are hired or purchased under imperfectly competitive conditions calls for appropriate adjustments in equations (1) and (2). Specifically, in making marginal decisions to determine the profit-maximizing and least-cost combination of resources, the firm must substitute MRC for resource price in the denominators of our two equations. That is, with imperfect competition in the hiring of both labor and capital, equation (1) becomes

$$\frac{MRP_L}{MRC_L} = \frac{MRP_C}{MRC_C} = 1 \qquad (1')$$

and equation (2) is restated as

$$\frac{MPP_L}{MRC_L} = \frac{MPP_C}{MRC_C} \qquad (2')$$

As a matter of fact, equations (1) and (2) can be regarded as special cases of (1') and (2') wherein firms happen to be hiring under purely competitive conditions and resource price is therefore equal to, and can be substituted for, marginal resource cost.

Summary

1 Resource prices are a major determinant of money incomes, and simultaneously perform the function of rationing resources to various industries and firms.

2 Though economists agree that resource pricing is a supply and demand phenomenon, they frequently disagree as to the exact characteristics of, and the operation of, supply and demand in particular resource markets.

3 The fact that the demand for any resource is derived from the product it helps produce correctly suggests that the demand for a resource will depend upon its productivity and the market value (price) of the good it is producing.

4 The marginal-revenue-product schedule of any resource is the demand schedule for that resource. This follows from an application of the rule that a firm operating under competitive conditions will find it most profitable to hire a resource up to the point at which the price of the resource equals its marginal revenue product.

5 The demand curve for a resource is downsloping, because the marginal physical product of additional inputs of any resource declines in accordance with the law of diminishing returns. When a firm is selling in an imperfectly competitive market, the resource demand curve will fall, too, because product price must be reduced in order to permit the firm to sell a larger output. The market demand for a resource can be derived by summing the demand curves of all firms hiring that resource.

6 The demand for a resource will change, that is, a resource demand curve will shift, as the result of *a.* a change in the demand for, and therefore the price of, the product the resource is producing; *b.* changes in the productivity of the resource due either to increases in the quantity or improvements in the quality of the resources with which a given resource is being combined, or improvements in the quality of the given resource itself; and *c.* changes in the prices of other resources.

7 A decline in the price of resource A will typically give rise to a substitution effect; that is, resource A will tend to be substituted for resources B and C. But these declines in the demand for resources B and C may be partially, wholly, or more than offset by an output effect; that is, the decrease in cost which the decline in the price of resource A entails will increase output and tend to increase the demand for resources B and C. When resources are not substitutes but are complementary, a decline in the price of resource A will increase the demand for complementary resource B.

8 The elasticity of resource demand depends upon *a.* the rate at which the marginal physical product of the resource declines, *b.* the number of good substitute resources available, *c.* the elasticity of demand for the product, and *d.* the portion of total production costs attributable to the resource.

9 A firm will employ the profit-maximizing combination of resources when the price of each resource is equal to its marginal *revenue* product or, algebraically, when

$$\frac{\text{MRP of labor}}{\text{price of labor}} = \frac{\text{MRP of capital}}{\text{price of capital}} = 1$$

10 Any level of output will be produced with the least costly combination of resources when the marginal *physical* product per dollar's worth of each input is the same, that is, when

$$\frac{\text{MPP of labor}}{\text{price of labor}} = \frac{\text{MPP of capital}}{\text{price of capital}}$$

11 Imperfect competition in hiring labor and capital is accounted for by substituting the marginal resource costs of labor and capital for their prices in the profit-maximizing and least-cost equations.

Questions and Study Suggestions

1 Key terms and concepts to remember: derived demand; marginal physical product; marginal revenue product; marginal resource cost; MRP = MRC rule; substitution and output effects; profit-maximizing combination of resources; least-cost combination of resources.

2 What is the significance of resource pricing? Explain in detail how the factors determining resource demand differ from those underlying product demand. Explain the meaning and significance of the notion that the demand for a resource is a *derived* demand. Why do resource demand curves slope downward?

3 Complete the following labor demand table for a firm which is hiring labor competitively and selling its product in a competitive market.

Units of labor	Total product	Marginal physical product	Product price	Total revenue	Marginal revenue product
1	17	_____	$2	$ _____	$ _____
2	31	_____	2	_____	_____
3	43	_____	2	_____	_____
4	53	_____	2	_____	_____
5	60	_____	2	_____	_____
6	65	_____	2	_____	

a. How many workers will the firm hire if the going wage rate is $27.95? $19.95? Explain why the firm will not hire a larger or smaller number of workers at each of these wage rates.

b. Show in schedule form and graphically the labor demand curve of this firm.

c. Now redetermine the firm's demand curve for labor on the assumption that it is selling in an imperfectly competitive market and that, although it can sell 17 units at $2.20 per unit, it must lower product price by 5 cents in order to sell the marginal physical product of each successive worker. Compare this demand curve with that derived in question 3b. Explain any differences.

4 Distinguish between a change in resource demand and a change in the quantity of a resource demanded. What specific factors might give rise to a change in resource demand? A change in the quantity of a resource demanded?

5 Using the substitution and output effects, explain how a decline in the price of resource A *might* cause an increase in the demand for substitute resource B.

6 What factors determine the elasticity of resource demand? What effect will each of the following have upon the elasticity *or* the location of the demand for resource C, which is being used in the production of commodity X? Where there is any uncertainty as to the outcome, specify the causes of that uncertainty.

a. An increase in the demand for product X.

b. An increase in the price of substitute factor D.

c. An increase in the number of resources which are substitutable for C in producing X.

d. A technological improvement in the capital equipment with which resource C is combined.

e. A decline in the price of complementary resource E.

f. A decline in the elasticity of demand for product X due to a decline in the competitiveness of the product market.

7 Suppose the productivity of labor and capital are as shown below. The output of these resources sells in a purely competitive market for $1 per unit. Both labor and capital are hired under purely competitive conditions at $1 and $3 respectively.

Units of capital	MPP of capital	Units of labor	MPP of labor
1	24	1	11
2	21	2	9
3	18	3	8
4	15	4	7
5	9	5	6
6	6	6	4
7	3	7	1
8	1	8	$\frac{1}{2}$

a.   What is the least-cost combination of labor and capital to employ in producing 80 units of output? Explain.

b.   What is the profit-maximizing combination of labor and capital for the firm to employ? Explain. What is the resulting level of output?

c.   When the firm is employing the profit-maximizing combination of labor and capital as determined in 7*b*, is this combination also the least costly way of producing the profit-maximizing output? Explain.

8   If each input is paid in accordance with its marginal revenue product, will the resulting distribution of income be ethically just?

Selected References

Hyde, Francis E., et al.: *A New Prospect of Economics* (Liverpool: Liverpool University Press, 1958), chap. 7.

Kreps, Juanita M., Gerald G. Somers, and Richard Perlman: *Contemporary Labor Economics* (Belmont, Calif.: Wadsworth Publishing Company, Inc., 1974), chap. 11.

Leftwich, Richard H.: *The Price System and Resource Allocation,* 6th ed. (Hinsdale, Ill.: The Dryden Press, Inc., 1976), chaps. 14, 15.

Mansfield, Edwin: *Microeconomics: Theory and Applications,* 2d ed. (New York: W. W. Norton & Company, Inc., 1975), chaps. 12, 13.

Marshall, F. Ray, Allen M. Cartter, and Allan G. King: *Labor Economics: Wages, Employment, and Trade Unionism,* 3d ed. (Homewood, Ill.: Richard D. Irwin, Inc., 1976), chap. 9.

Last Word
Push-Button Warfare

Increases in the price of labor tend to cause a substitution of capital for labor. In the following case highly paid New York typographical workers face the loss of jobs to new automated equipment.

It was the sort of steamy protest demonstration that The New York Daily News takes special relish in covering. As a cordon of helmeted riot police looked on, some 300 pickets hurled bottles, eggs and epithets at a handful of white-faced truck drivers. "You scab rats," bellowed one sign-toter. "I hope you have an accident." Another picket shook a beefy fist and shouted: "Commit suicide, ya bum." As it happened, however, the Daily News itself was the story. Enmeshed in a complex labor dispute over automation, America's largest newspaper (weekday circulation: 2.1 million) made a bit of hometown history last week when it began producing entire issues without the help of its printers.

The brouhaha is hardly exclusive to the News. Throughout the U.S., cost-conscious newspaper publishers are gradually automating a technology that hasn't seen a major innovation since the invention of the Linotype machine almost a century ago. But automation is being bitterly resisted by printers and other craftsmen who view the new electronic gear as a clear threat to their jobs. The issue is roiling composing rooms in a dozen major cities, but many of the participants believe that the outcome in New York will serve as a national guidepost.

The fireworks began in New York after several weeks of deadlocked contract negotiations between the powerful, 2,500-member Typographical Union No. 6 and the city's three remaining papers—the morning News and Times and the afternoon Post. The union, led by its tough-talking president Bertram A. Powers, wants lifetime job security for all printers—both full-time and substitutes. Big Six, as it is known in the city, focused on the News and staged a prolonged work slowdown that cost the paper more than $2 million in lost advertising. The News countered by moving automated typesetting equipment into its 42nd Street plant—and it pushed the first buttons on Monday night last week. The first issue was only 60 pages (considerably smaller than most editions at this time of the year), and only 687,000 copies were printed.

The initial machine-set editions looked sloppy and crude. Thursday's News had "Tuesday, May 7" printed on its front page."You can't even read it if you have good eyesight," snorted one printer as he scanned the unfamiliar type. But as the week wore on, the glitches disappeared and the paper took on a relatively clean look that clearly deflated the mood on the picket line.

The News's new process—known as "cold type"—is the simplest of several automated systems currently in use at some 800 U.S. dailies. Under the traditional "hot metal" system, a reporter's edited story is sent to the composing room, where a printer punches it out on a Linotype machine—producing lines of type cast from molten lead. Under the new's cold-type system, a typist taps out the story on a keypuncher that transforms it into a strip of perforated tape. The tape is fed into a photo-composing machine, which spits out neat columns of type imprinted on paper. In this system, "justification" (producing even margins by hyphenating words and adjusting the spaces between them) is done by a computer rather than an operator. The system can turn out as many as 150 lines a minute (compared with three lines a minute on a Linotype machine), reducing the number of personnel required for production.

Far more sophisticated gadgetry has recently been installed at papers like The Miami Herald, Los Angeles Times and Detroit News. In Detroit, reporters type on electric keyboards that reproduce their stories on small video screens. The story is then stored in a computer's memory bank until an editor "calls up" the copy by pushing a button on his own video-equipped keyboard, which he uses to make any necessary changes. With another flick of a button, the final version is transmitted to a computer-run composing room. The system is not without bugs; occasionally, whole paragraphs of copy vanish inside the computers. "But when it works," sighs one News executive, "it's just plain beautiful."

Most newspaper craftsmen are resigned to the new technology, but they want their jobs guaranteed. In Washington, the Post and the Star-News have been gearing up for automation, and last year the Post used its new equipment to publish during a wildcat strike. Now both papers have been hit by production delays; as a result, the Star-News decided last week to suspend its Saturday edition for the time being. The papers also terminated their contracts with the printers, although neogtiations continued. The publishers have offered life-time jobs to regular printers, but they balk at prolonging such practices as the setting of "bogus" type—ad copy that is needlessly duplicated to make work for printers. The printers have set a strike vote for this week, and a quick settlement seems unlikely. The Post, vowed publisher Katharine Graham, will no longer seek "peace at any price" from the union.

The battlelines seem equally fixed in New York, where the publishers have never forgiven themselves for caving in to the craftsmen during previous showdowns. "We were burned on the last settlement," says a Times spokesman. "There was a 46 per cent wage increase and we got absolutely nothing in return." Expecting a long labor war, Times publisher Arthur O. Sulzberger has diversified by acquiring other properties, including ten automated papers in Florida. The parent Times company is said to be financially healthy enough to shut down the paper for the rest of the year and still break even on the year.

To a city that has witnessed the demise of five dailies during the past decade, the current confrontation has an ominously familiar tinge. But this time the publishers seem to be holding most of the high cards. As talks with the printers entered a crucial phase last weekend, the Time's Sanger summed up the publisher's tough new mood. "The time has come," he said flatly, "for us to finally enter the twentieth century."

"Push-Button Warfare," *Newsweek,* May 20, 1974, pp. 96–98. Copyright Newsweek, Inc. 1974. Reprinted by permission.

31

The Pricing and Employment of Resources: Wage Determination

Armed with some understanding of the strategic factors underlying resource demand, we must now introduce supply as it characterizes the markets for labor, land, capital, and entrepreneurial ability to see how wages, rents, interest, and profits are determined. For two reasons, we discuss wage rates prior to other resource prices.

1 The marginal productivity theory of resource demand is probably more applicable to an explanation of wage rates than to the pricing of other resources.

2 To the vast majority of households the wage rate is the most important price in the economy; it is the sole or basic source of income. About three-fourths of the national income is in the form of wages and salaries.

Our basic objectives in discussing wage determination are as follows:

1 To understand the forces underlying the general level of wage rates in the United States.

2 To see how wage rates are determined in particular labor markets by presenting several representative labor market models.

3 To discuss the economic effects of the minimum wage.

4 To analyze the impact of unions upon the structure and level of wages.

5 To explain wage differentials.

6 To introduce and briefly discuss the concept of investment in human capital.

Throughout this chapter we shall rely upon the marginal productivity theory of Chapter 30 as an explanation of labor demand.

MEANING OF WAGES

Wages, or wage rates, are the price paid for the use of labor. Economists often employ the term "labor" broadly to apply to the payments received by (1) workers in the narrow sense of the term, that is, blue- and white-collar workers of infinite variety; (2) professional people—physicians, lawyers, dentists, teachers, and so forth; and (3) small businessmen—barbers, plumbers, television repairmen, and a host of retailers—for the labor services they provide in operating their own businesses. This broad definition of labor, incidentally, encompasses individuals who would be considered as profit receivers in national income accounting. Hence, under this definition, wages would clearly amount to more than three-fourths of the national income.

Though in practice wages may take the form of bonuses, royalties, commissions, and monthly salaries, we shall use the term "wages" to mean wage rates per unit of time—per hour, per day, and so forth. This designation has the advantage of reminding us that the wage rate is a price paid for the use of units of labor service. It also permits us to distinguish clearly between "wages" and "earnings," the latter depending upon wage rates *and* the number of hours or weeks of labor service supplied in the market.

It is important, too, to make a distinction between money wages and real wages. *Money wages* are the amount of money received per hour, per day, per week, and so on. *Real wages,* on the other hand, are the quantity of goods and services which one can obtain with his money wages; real wages are the "purchasing power" of money wages. Obviously one's real wages depend upon his money wages and the prices of the goods and services he buys. Note that money wages and real wages need not move together. For example, money wages may rise and real wages simultaneously decline *if* product prices rise more rapidly than do money wages. Unless otherwise indicated, our discussion will be couched in terms of real wage rates by assuming that the level of product prices is constant.

GENERAL LEVEL OF WAGES

Wages tend to differ among nations, among regions, among various occupations, and among individuals. Wage rates are vastly higher in the United States than in China or India; they are generally higher in the North and East of the United States than in the South; plumbers are paid more than cotton pickers; physician Abrams may earn twice as much as physician Bennett for the same number of hours of work. Wage rates also differ by sex and race.

Our approach will involve moving from the general to the specific. In this section we are concerned with explaining why the general level of wages is higher in the United States than in foreign nations. This explanation will be largely applicable to regional wage differences within nations. In the following section we shall seek to explain wages in terms of markets for specific types of labor. In both these discussions a supply and demand approach will offer the most fruitful results.

The general level of wages, like the general level of prices, is a composite concept encompassing a wide range of different specific wage rates. This admittedly vague concept is a useful point of departure in making and explaining international and interregional wage comparisons. Statistical data indicate that the general level of real wages in the United States is among the highest in the world. The simplest explanation of this fact is that in the United States the demand for labor has been great in relation to the supply.

□   Role of Productivity

Let us look behind these forces of demand and supply. We know that the demand for labor—or any other resource—depends upon its productivity. The greater the productivity of labor, the greater the demand for it. And, given the total supply of labor, the stronger the demand, the greater the level of real wages. The demand for American labor has been high because American labor is highly productive. But why the high productivity? The reasons are several:

1 Capital American workers are used in conjunction with large amounts of capital equipment. For example, the average American worker is assisted by some $27,000 worth of machinery and equipment.

2 Natural Resources Natural resources are very abundant in relation to the size of the labor force. The United States is richly endowed with arable land, basic mineral resources, and ample sources of industrial power. The fact that American workers have large amounts of high-quality natural resources to work with is perhaps most evident in agriculture where, historically, the growth of productivity has been dramatic (Chapter 35).

3 Technology The level of technological advance is generally higher in the United States than in foreign nations. American workers in most industries use not only more capital equipment but better (that is, technologically superior) equipment than do foreign workers. Similarly, work methods are steadily being improved through detailed scientific study and research.

4 Labor Quality The health, vigor, education and training, work attitudes, and adaptability of American workers to the discipline of factory production are generally superior to those of the labor of other nations. This means that, even with the same quantity and quality of natural and capital resources, American workers typically would be somewhat more efficient than their foreign counterparts.

5 Other Factors Less tangible, yet important, items underlying the high productivity of American labor are (a) the efficiency and flexibility of American management; (b) a business, social, and political environment which puts great emphasis upon production and productivity; and (c) the vast size of the domestic market, which provides the opportunity for firms to realize mass-production economies.

The reader will recognize that the aforementioned factors are merely a restatement of the cornerstones of economic growth (Chapter 19). It is also notable that the productivity of labor depends to a very great degree upon considerations other than the quality of labor itself, that is, upon the quantity and quality of the property resources at the worker's disposal.

□ **Real Wages and Productivity**

The dependence of real hourly wages upon the level of productivity is indicated in Figure 31-1. Note the relatively close relationship in the long run between real hourly wages and output per labor-hour in nonfarm private industries. When one recalls that real income and real output are two ways of viewing the same thing, it is no surprise that *income per worker can increase only at about the same rate as output per worker.*

□ **Secular Growth**

But simple supply and demand analysis suggests that, even if the demand for labor is strong in the United States, increases in the supply of labor will cause the general level of wages to decline over time. It is certainly true that the American population and the labor force have grown significantly over the decades. However, these increases in the supply of labor have been more than offset by increases in the demand for labor stemming from the productivity-increasing factors discussed above. The result has been a long-run, or secular, increase in wage rates, as suggested by

FIGURE 31-1 OUTPUT PER HOUR AND REAL AVERAGE HOURLY EARNINGS

Over a long period of years there has been a close relationship between real hourly wages and output per man-hour. (Department of Labor, *Employment and Earnings,* September 1976, p.94).

Figure 31-2. One authoritative study indicates that, for the 1889–1969 period, labor productivity, as measured by output per labor-hour, grew at an annual rate of 2.4 percent. This rate of growth translates into a doubling of real output and real wage rates in about thirty years (recall the "rule of 70"), and for the entire eighty-year period under consideration, something in excess of a sixfold increase in real wages per labor-hour.[1]

□   Recent Slowdown?

There has been concern that since the mid-sixties the rate of productivity growth in the United States has been slowing down. The reasons usually cited are complex and manifold, but they include the following: (1) Values and attitudes have changed in recent years so as to impede productivity growth. For example, environmental and quality-of-life concerns have made society skeptical of "materialism" and economic growth. Workers—particularly

[1]Solomon Fabricant, *A Primer on Productivity* (New York: Random House, Inc., 1969), p. 14.

unionized workers—are increasingly resistant to productivity-increasing technological advances because they threaten job security. (2) Intensified efforts by government to foster

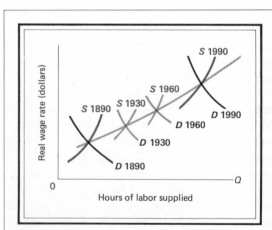

FIGURE 31-2 THE SECULAR TREND OF REAL WAGES IN THE UNITED STATES

The productivity of American labor has increased substantially in the long run, causing the demand for labor to increase in relation to the supply. The result has been increases in real wages.

greater income equality—that is, to redistribute income through the tax-transfer payments system—may be undermining incentives to work, take risks, and invest. (3) Research and development spending has declined as a percentage of GNP since the mid-sixties, partially as a result of declining government support and partially as a consequence of private business's reaction to the high unemployment and rapid inflation of the early 1970s. (4) Increasing governmental intervention in the functioning of the price system has allegedly lowered productivity growth. For example, wage-price controls have presumably (*a*) worsened the efficiency with which resources are allocated, *and* (*b*) restricted profits and, therefore, the level of investment. Similarly, in meeting the requirements of the controversial Occupational Safety and Health Act (OSHA) of 1970, firms have had to use more inputs which do not add perceptibly to real output; hence, productivity tends to decline.[2]

A second and more controversial explanation of the apparent slowdown of productivity growth relates the problem to the existence of our large military establishment. Seymour Melman has argued that, although they may have "political utility," military goods are "devoid of economic use value." That is, war goods do *not* satisfy current economic wants as do consumer goods, nor do they serve, as do capital goods, as inputs for future production. What military spending *does* accomplish, in Melman's view, is a massive shift of real capital, high-level technological manpower, and research and development effort from the civilian to the military sector of the economy. Furthermore, according to Melman, the characteristics of military contracts are such that cost minimization and efficient resource use are subverted. In short, military spending is a drag on the economy as a whole, and the inevitable consequence is that productivity growth languishes.[3]

■
WAGES IN PARTICULAR LABOR MARKETS

We now turn from the general level of wages to the wage structure, that is, to the system of specific wage rates which the general level of wages comprises. The question now is this: What determines the wage rate received by some specific type of worker? Demand and supply analysis again provides the most revealing approach. Our analysis covers some half-dozen basic market models.

□ **Competitive Model**

Let us suppose that there are many—say, 200—firms demanding a particular type of semiskilled or skilled labor.[4] The total, or market, demand for this labor can be determined by summing the labor demand curves (the MRP curves) of the individual firms, as suggested in Figure 31-3a and b. On the supply side of the picture, we assume there is no union; workers compete freely for available jobs. The supply curve for a particular type of labor will be upsloping, reflecting the fact that, in the absence of unemployment, hiring firms as a group will be forced to pay higher wage rates to obtain more workers. Why? Because the firms must bid these workers away from other industries and other localities. Within limits, workers have alternative job opportuni-

---

[2]For a more complete discussion of these and other points, see John W. Kendrick, "Productivity and Business," in Jules Backman and Harold S. Geneen (eds.), *Labor, Technology, and Productivity* (New York: New York University Press, 1974), pp. 125–144.

[3]See Seymour Melman, "Twelve Propositions on Productivity and the War Economy," *Challenge,* March–April, 1975, pp. 7–11, and Melman, *The Permanent War Economy* (New York: Simon & Schuster, Inc., 1974), particularly chap. 4.

[4]These firms need not be in the same industry; industries are defined in terms of the products they produce and not of the resources they employ. Thus firms producing wood-frame furniture, window and door frames, and cabinets will all demand carpenters.

FIGURE 31-3 THE SUPPLY OF, AND THE DEMAND FOR, LABOR IN A SINGLE COMPETITIVE FIRM (a) AND IN A COMPETITIVE MARKET (b)

In a competitive labor market the equilibrium wage rate W_c and number of workers employed Q_c are determined by supply SS and demand DD, as shown in (b). Because this wage rate is given to the individual firm hiring in the market, its labor supply curve, $S = MRC$, is perfectly elastic, as in (a). The firm finds it most profitable to hire workers up to the MRP = MRC point.

ties; that is, they may work in other industries in the same locality, or they may work in their present occupations in different cities or states. In a full-employment economy the group of firms in this particular labor market must pay higher and higher wage rates to attract this type of labor away from these alternative job opportunities.

The equilibrium wage rate and the equilibrium level of employment for this type of labor are obviously determined by the intersection of the labor demand and labor supply curves. In Figure 31-3b the equilibrium wage rate is W_c ($6), and the number of workers hired is Q_c (800). To the individual firm the wage rate W_c is given. Each of the many hiring firms employs such a small fraction of the total available supply of this type of labor that none can influence the wage rate. Technically, the supply of labor is perfectly elastic to the individual firm, as shown by S in Figure 31-3a. Each individual firm will find it profitable to hire workers up to the point at which the going wage rate is equal to labor's MRP. This is merely an application of the MRP = MRC rule developed in Chapter 30. (Indeed, the demand curve in Figure 31-3a is based upon Table 30-1.) As Table 31-1 indicates, *because resource price is given to the individual com-*

petitive firm, the marginal cost of that resource (MRC) will be constant and equal to resource price. In this case the wage rate and hence the marginal cost of labor are constant to the individual firm. Each additional worker hired adds precisely his wage rate to the firm's total resource cost. The firm then will maximize its profits by hiring workers to the point at which their wage rate, and therefore marginal resource cost, equals their marginal revenue product. In Figure 31-3a the "typical" firm will hire q_c (four) workers.

☐ **Monopsony Model**

But in many labor markets workers are not hired competitively. Rather, employers are *monopsonists;* that is, they have some monopolistic buying power. In some instances the monopsonistic power of employers is virtually complete in the sense that there is only one major employer in a labor market. For example, the economies of some towns and cities depend almost entirely upon one major firm. A silver-mining concern may be the basic source of employment in a remote Colorado town. A New England textile mill, a Wisconsin paper mill, or a farm-belt food processor may provide a large proportion of the employ-

Table 31-1   THE SUPPLY OF LABOR: PURE COMPETITION IN THE HIRE OF LABOR (*hypothetical data*)

(1) Units of labor	(2) Wage rate	(3) Total labor cost (wage bill)	(4) Marginal resource (labor) cost
1	$6	$ 6	$6
2	6	12	6
3	6	18	6
4	6	24	6
5	6	30	6
6	6	36	

ment in its locality. Anaconda Mining is the dominant employer in Butte, Montana. The market for professional athletes is characterized by ingenious collusive devices by which employers have attempted with considerable success to limit competition in the hire of labor. The National Football League, the National Basketball Association, and the American and National Baseball Leagues have established systems of rules which tend to tie a player to one team and prevent him from selling his talents to the highest bidder on the open (competitive) market. In particular, through the new player draft, the team which selects or "drafts" a player has the exclusive right to bargain a contract with that player. Furthermore, the so-called reserve clause in each player's contract gives his team the exclusive right to purchase his services for the next season. Though recent court cases have tended to make the labor markets for professional athletes slightly more competitive, collusive monopsony persists.[5] In other cases *oligopsony* may prevail; three or four firms may each hire a large portion of the supply of labor in a particular market. Our study of oligopoly correctly suggests that there is a strong tendency for oligopsonists to act in concert—much like a monopsonist—in hiring labor.

[5]The interested reader should consult Janice M. Westerfield, "Restrictive Labor Practices in Baseball: Time for a Change?" *Business Review,* Federal Reserve Bank of Philadelphia, June 1975, pp. 17–26.

The important point is this: When a firm hires a considerable portion of the total available supply of a particular type of labor, its decision to employ more or fewer workers will affect the wage rate paid to that labor. Specifically, *if a firm is large in relation to the labor market, it will have to pay a higher wage rate in order to obtain more labor.* For simplicity's sake let us suppose there is only one employer of a particular type of labor in a specified geographic area. Obviously, the labor supply curve to that firm and the total supply curve for the labor market are identical. This supply curve, for reasons already made clear, is upsloping, indicating that the firm must pay a higher wage rate to attract more workers. This is shown by *SS* in Figure 31-4. The supply curve is in effect the average-cost-of-labor curve from the firm's perspective; each point on it indicates the wage rate (cost) per worker which must be paid to attract the corresponding number of workers.

But the higher wages involved in attracting additional workers will also have to be paid to all workers currently employed at lower wage rates. If not, labor morale will surely deteriorate, and the employer will be plagued with serious problems of labor unrest because of the wage-rate differentials existing for the same job. As for cost, the payment of a uniform wage to all workers will mean that the cost of an extra worker—the marginal resource (labor) cost (MRC)—will exceed the wage rate by the amount necessary to bring the wage rate of all workers currently employed up to the new wage level. Table 31-2 illustrates this point. One worker can be hired at a wage rate of $6. But the hire of a second worker forces the firm to pay a higher wage rate of $7. Marginal resource (labor) cost is $8—the $7 paid the second worker plus a $1 raise for the first worker. Similarly, the marginal labor cost of the third worker is $10—the $8 which must be paid to attract him from alternative employments plus $1 raises for the first two workers. The important point is that *to the monopsonist, marginal resource (labor) cost will exceed*

FIGURE 31-4 THE WAGE RATE AND LEVEL OF EMPLOYMENT IN A MONOPSONISTIC LABOR MARKET

In a monopsonistic labor market the employer's marginal resource (labor) cost curve (MRC) lies above the labor supply curve (S). Equating MRC with labor demand MRP at point b, the monopsonist will hire Q_m workers (as compared with Q_c under competition) and pay the wage rate W_m (as compared with the competitive wage W_c).

the wage rate. Graphically, the MRC curve (columns 1 and 4 in Table 31-2) will lie above the average cost, or supply, curve of labor (columns 1 and 2 in Table 31-2). This is shown graphically in Figure 31-4.

How much labor will the firm hire, and what wage rate will it pay? To maximize profits the firm will equate marginal resource (labor) cost with the MRP. The number of workers hired by the monopsonist is indicated

Table 31-2 THE SUPPLY OF LABOR: MONOPSONY IN THE HIRE OF LABOR *(hypothetical data)*

(1) Units of labor	(2) Wage rate	(3) Total labor cost (wage bill)	(4) Marginal resource (labor) cost
1	$ 6	$ 6	$ 6
2	7	14	8
3	8	24	10
4	9	36	12
5	10	50	14
6	11	66	16

by Q_m, and the wage rate paid, W_m, is indicated by the corresponding point on the resource supply, or average-cost-of-labor, curve. It is particularly important to contrast these results with those which a competitive labor market would have yielded. With competition in the hire of labor, the level of employment would have been greater (Q_c), and the wage rate would have been higher (W_c). It simply does not pay the monopsonist to hire workers up to the point at which the wage rate and labor's MRP are equal. Other things being equal, he maximizes his profits by hiring a smaller number of workers and thereby paying a less-than-competitive wage rate. In the process, society gets a smaller output,[6] and workers get a wage rate less by bc than their marginal revenue product. Just as a monopolistic seller finds it profitable to restrict product output to realize an above-competitive price for his goods, so the monopsonistic employer of resources finds it profitable to restrict employment so as to depress wage rates and therefore costs, that is, to realize below-competitive wage rates.

Will a monopsonistic employer also be a monopolistic seller in the product market? Not necessarily. The New England textile mill may be a monopsonistic employer, yet face severe domestic and foreign competition in selling its product. In other cases—for example, the automobile and steel industries—firms have both monopsonistic and monopolistic (oligopolistic) power. How does the presence of monopoly or oligopoly power affect our analysis of a monopsonistic labor market? The answer is: through the labor demand curve. If the monopsonistic employer is also a restrictive monopoly or oligopoly, we can expect the resource demand curve of Figure 31-4 to be depressed. (Recall the contrasting labor demand curves of the purely and imperfectly competi-

---

[6]This is analogous to the monopolist's restricting output as he sets product price and output on the basis of marginal revenue, not product demand. In this instance, resource price is set on the basis of marginal labor (resource) cost, not resource supply.

tive sellers as portrayed in Figures 30-1 and 30-2.) The result will be a wage rate even lower than W_m and a volume of employment less than Q_m. On the other hand, a progressive monopoly or oligopoly may entail a resource demand curve to the right of that shown in Figure 31-4, with the result that the wage rate and level of employment will exceed W_m and Q_m. In short, monopoly (oligopoly) power will depress or increase labor demand, depending upon whether the monopoly is restrictive or progressive.

☐ Some Union Models

Thus far, we have been content to assume that workers are actively competing in the sale of their labor services. In a good many markets, workers "sell" their labor services collectively through unions. To envision the economic impact of unions in the simplest context, let us suppose a union is formed in an otherwise competitive labor market. That is, a union is now bargaining with a relatively large number of employers. Later we shall consider the case where the union faces a large single employer, that is, a monopsonist.

Unions seek many goals. The basic objective, however, is to raise wage rates. The union can pursue this objective in several different ways.

Increasing the Demand for Labor   From the union's point of view, the most desirable technique for raising wage rates is to increase the demand for labor. As shown in Figure 31-5, an increase in the demand for labor will result in *both* higher wage rates and more jobs. The relative sizes of these increases will depend upon the elasticity of labor supply. Classic examples are the International Ladies' Garment Workers Union and the Amalgamated Clothing Workers Union, both of which have assisted clothing firms to increase their productivity. The New York locals of the ILGWU have even helped employers in financing advertising campaigns to bolster the demand for

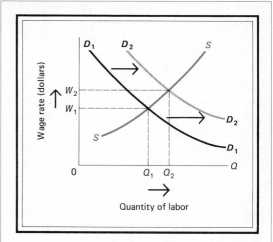

FIGURE 31-5 UNIONS AND THE DEMAND FOR LABOR

When unions can increase the demand for labor (D_1D_1 to D_2D_2), higher wage rates (W_1 to W_2) and a larger number of jobs (Q_1 to Q_2) can be realized.

their products. And it is no accident that some unions have vigorously supported their employers in seeking to maintain protective tariffs designed to exclude competing foreign products. The American Watch Workers Union is a case in point. Some unions have sought to expand the demand for labor by forcing make-work, or "featherbedding," rules upon employers. Prior to fairly recent court rulings, the Railway Brotherhoods forced railroads to hire train crews of a certain minimum size; diesel engines had to have a fireman even though there was no fire.

But the opportunity for unions to increase the demand for labor is limited. The main reason is obvious: As noted in our earlier discussion of the general level of wages, the basic forces underlying the productivity of, and therefore the demand for, labor are largely outside the control of labor unions. The quantity and quality of the capital equipment with which labor is combined are the basic determinants of labor productivity in most firms, and this is a matter over which unions typically have little or no control. It should be noted, too, that in many of the instances in which unions have pleaded for tariff protection and have practiced featherbedding, the situation has been that of a union's attempting to offset or forestall declines in the demand for labor rather than actually to increase the existing demand for a particular type of labor. This comment seems pertinent to the garment-makers, the watchmakers, and the Railway Brotherhoods, all of which find themselves in the unfortunate position of being employed in declining industries or faced with job-destroying technological advances. In view of these considerations, it is not surprising that union efforts to increase wage rates have concentrated upon the supply side of the market.

Exclusive or Craft Unionism   Unions may boost wage rates by reducing the supply of labor, that is, by shifting the supply curve of a particular type of labor to the left. Historically, the labor movement has favored policies designed to restrict the supply of labor to the economy as a whole in order to bolster the general level of wages. Labor unions have supported legislation which has (1) restricted immigration, (2) reduced child labor, (3) encouraged compulsory retirement, and (4) enforced a shorter workweek.

More relevant for present purposes is the fact that specific types of workers have adopted through unions a host of techniques designed to restrict their numbers. This has been especially true of *craft unions*—that is, unions which comprise workers of a given skill, such as carpenters, bricklayers, plumbers, and printers. These unions have in many instances forced employers to agree to hire only union workers, thereby giving the union virtually complete control of the supply of labor. Then, by following restrictive membership policies—long apprenticeships, exorbitant initiation fees, the limitation or flat prohibition of new members—the union causes an artificial restriction of the labor supply. As indicated in Figure 31-6, this results in higher wage rates. For obvious reasons, this approach to achieving wage increases might be called "exclusive"

FIGURE 31-6 EXCLUSIVE OR CRAFT UNIONISM

By reducing the supply of labor ($S_1 S_1$ to $S_2 S_2$) through the use of restrictive membership policies, exclusive unions achieve higher wage rates (W_1 to W_2). However, the restriction of labor supply also reduces the number of workers employed (Q_1 to Q_2).

unionism. Higher wages are the result of excluding workers from the union and therefore from the supply of labor.

Inclusive or Industrial Unionism   Most unions, however, do not attempt to limit their membership. On the contrary, they seek to organize all available or potential workers. This is characteristic of the so-called *industrial unions*—unions, such as the automobile workers and steelworkers, which include all unskilled, semiskilled, and even skilled workers in a given industry. A union can afford to be exclusive when its members are skilled craftsmen for whom substitute workers are not readily available in quantity. But a union that comprises largely unskilled and semiskilled workers will undermine its own existence by limiting its membership and thereby causing numerous highly substitutable nonunion workers to be readily available for employment.

If an industrial union is successful in including virtually all workers in its membership, firms will be under great pressure to come to terms at the wage rate demanded by the union. Why? Because the union can obviously deprive the firm of its entire labor supply.

Inclusive unionism is illustrated graphically in Figure 31-7. Initially, the competitive equilibrium wage rate is W_c, and the level of employment is Q_c. Now suppose an industrial union is formed, and it imposes a higher, above-equilibrium wage rate of, say, W_u. The imposition of this wage rate changes the supply curve of labor to the firm from the preunion SS curve to the postunion $W_u aS$ curve shown by the heavy brown line.[7] No workers will be forthcoming at a wage rate less than that demanded by the union. If the employers decide it is better to pay this higher wage rate than to suffer a strike, they will cut back on employment from Q_c to Q_u. In other words, the above-equilibrium wage rate will cause some unemployment of union workers in this particular labor market.

Needless to say, this unemployment effect constitutes an important restraining influence upon the union in formulating its wage demands. A union cannot expect to maintain solidarity within its ranks if it seeks a wage rate so high that the result will be joblessness for 20, 30, or 40 percent of its members. The elasticity of labor demand is the basic consideration in determining the amount of unemployment which will accompany a wage hike: the more inelastic the demand for labor, the smaller will be the resulting unemployment. You will recall from Chapter 30 that the determinants of the elasticity of labor demand include the elasticity of demand for the product, the portion of total costs for which wages account, and the substitutability of other re-

FIGURE 31-7 INCLUSIVE OR INDUSTRIAL UNIONISM

By organizing virtually all available workers and thereby controlling the supply of labor, inclusive industrial unions may impose a wage rate, such as W_u, which is above the competitive wage rate W_c. The effect is to change the labor supply curve from SS to $W_u aS$. At the W_u wage rate, employers will cut employment from Q_c to Q_u.

sources for labor. It is notable that substitutability and hence elasticity vary directly with time. That is, over a short period—say a few weeks or months—a firm may hire about the same number of workers after a pay hike as it did before. But then, as the months pass, employers have sufficient time to substitute labor-saving capital equipment for workers. The practical significance of this is that, as substitution occurs, workers will be *gradually* unemployed and typically will drift into other jobs and other geographic areas. And with the absence of job opportunities, new workers entering the labor force will be discouraged from entering this line of work. For these reasons the unemployment restraint upon union wage demands may be less pressing than it first appears to be.[8]

[7]Technically, the imposition of the wage rate W_u makes the labor supply curve perfectly elastic over the $W_u a$ range in Figure 31-7. If employers hire any number of workers within this range, the union-imposed wage rate is effective and must be paid, or the union will supply no labor at all—the employers will be faced with a strike. If the employers want a number of workers in excess of $W_u a$ (which they never will when the union sets an above-equilibrium wage rate), they will have to bid up wages above the union's minimum.

[8]In fact, in a growing economy the demand curves for most kinds of labor will be gradually shifting to the right through time, tending to offset unemployment effects. Instead of an absolute decline in the number of jobs in this market, the result may be a decline in the rate of growth of job opportunities.

Even though industrial unions encourage rather than restrict membership, there is clearly a restrictive aspect to this analysis. But, in contrast to the practices of exclusive unionism, the restriction of employment here is made not by directly influencing labor supply, but by enforcing an above-equilibrium wage rate and allowing the market to restrict the number of jobs available.

The United Mine Workers provide an excellent illustration of how an industrial union can achieve substantial wage increases, but only at the cost of a reduction in the number of jobs the industry has to offer. The UMW has clearly done an outstanding job of raising wage rates for miners. In January 1977, the average weekly earnings of bituminous coal workers were $317.77, as compared with $213.64 for all manufacturing industries. However, employment in January 1977 stood at only 188,000 in bituminous coal as compared with a peak figure of almost 705,000 in 1923 and 400,000 in 1945. There is little doubt that UMW wage pressure has been a major cause of this decline in the number of jobs. Labor costs constitute about 70 percent of total costs in bituminous coal production. Hence, union-imposed wage increases have increased the total cost of coal sharply, causing a drop in coal output and in the number of jobs the industry can offer. Simultaneously, the increased cost of labor has accelerated the substitution of machinery for labor, causing further diminutions in the number of miners employed. The UMW has explicitly taken the position that the fattening of pay envelopes which it has brought about more than compensate for the sacrifice of jobs that these high wages have entailed.[9]

☐ **Bilateral Monopoly Model**

Now let us suppose that a strong industrial union is formed in a labor market which is not competitive but monopsonistic. In other

words, let us combine the monopsony model with the inclusive unionism model. The result is a case of *bilateral monopoly*. The union is a monopolistic "seller" of labor in that it can exert an influence over wage rates; it faces a monopsonistic employer (or combination of oligopsonistic employers) of labor who can also affect wages. Is this an extreme or special case? Not at all. In such important industries as steel, automobiles, meatpacking, and farm machinery, "big labor"—one huge industrial union—bargains with "big business"—a few huge industrial giants.

This situation can be shown graphically as in Figure 31-8, which merely superimposes Figure 31-7 upon 31-4. The monopsonistic employer will seek the wage rate W_m and the union presumably will press for some above-equilibrium wage rate such as W_u. Which of these two possibilities will result? We cannot say with any certainty. The outcome is logically indeterminate in the sense that economic theory does not explain what the resulting wage rate will be. We should expect the resulting wage to lie somewhere between W_m and W_u. Beyond that, about all we can say is that

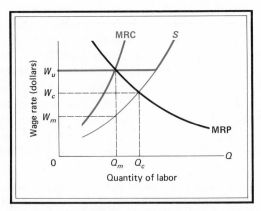

FIGURE 31-8 BILATERAL MONOPOLY IN THE LABOR MARKET

When a monopsonistic employer seeks the wage rate W_m and the inclusive union he faces seeks an above-equilibrium wage rate such as W_u, the actual outcome is logically indeterminate.

[9]See Gordon F. Bloom and Herbert R. Northrup, *Economics of Labor Relations*, 5th ed. (Homewood, Ill.: Richard D. Irwin, Inc., 1965), pp. 469–472.

the party with the most bargaining power and the most effective bargaining strategy will be able to get his opponent to agree to a wage close to the one he seeks.[10]

These comments suggest another important feature of the bilateral monopoly model. The kind of labor market we are here describing may be an important manifestation of countervailing power. If either the union or management prevailed in this market—that is, if the actual wage rate were determined at W_u or W_m—employment would be restricted to Q_m, which is obviously below the competitive level. But now let us suppose the countervailing power of the union roughly offsets the original monopsony power of management and a bargained wage rate of about W_c, which is the competitive wage, is agreed upon. Once management agrees to this wage rate, its incentive to restrict employment disappears; no longer can the employer depress wage rates by restricting employment. Thus management equates the bargained wage rate W_c (= MRC) with MRP and finds it most profitable to hire Q_c workers. In short, with monopoly on both sides of the labor market, it may be possible that the resulting wage rate and level of employment will be closer to competitive levels than if monopoly existed on only one side of the market.

□ **The Minimum-Wage Controversy**

Since the passage of the Fair Labor Standards Act in 1938, the United States has had a Federal minimum wage. The analysis of the effects of union wage-fixing raises the much-debated question of the efficacy of this minimum-wage legislation as an antipoverty device.

[10]Economists have developed a number of bargaining theories. The ambitious reader should consult Carl M. Stevens, *Strategy and Collective Bargaining Negotiation* (New York: McGraw-Hill Book Company, 1963), and Albert Rees, *The Economics of Work and Pay* (New York: Harper & Row, Publishers, Incorporated, 1973), chaps. 8 and 9.

Case against the Minimum Wage Critics, reasoning in terms of Figure 31-7, contend that the imposition of effective (above-equilibrium) minimum wages will simply push employers back up their MRP or labor demand curves because it is now profitable to hire fewer workers. The higher wage costs may even force some firms out of business. The result is that many of the poor, low-wage workers whom the minimum wage was designed to help will now find themselves out of work. Is it not obvious, critics query, that a worker who is unemployed at a minimum wage of $2.30 per hour is clearly worse off than if he were employed at the market wage rate of, say, $1.75 per hour? Some discharged workers may drift off into other labor markets and find employment, but in so doing they increase the supply of labor in these markets and tend to depress wage rates therein.

Case for the Minimum Wage Advocates allege that critics have analyzed the impact of the minimum wage in an unrealistic context. Figure 31-7, advocates claim, assumes a competitive and static market. The imposition of a minimum wage in a monopsonistic labor market (Figure 31-8) suggests that the minimum wage can increase wage rates without causing unemployment; indeed, higher minimum wages may even result in more jobs by eliminating the monopsonistic employer's motive to restrict employment. Furthermore, the imposition of an effective minimum wage may increase labor productivity, shifting the labor demand curve to the right and offsetting any unemployment effects which the minimum wage might otherwise induce. But how might a minimum wage increase productivity? First, a minimum wage may have a *shock effect* upon employers. That is, firms using low-wage workers may tend to be inefficient in the use of labor; the higher wage rates imposed by the minimum wage will presumably force these firms to use labor more efficiently, and so the productivity of labor rises. Second, it is argued that higher wages will tend to increase the incomes and therefore the health, vigor, and motivation of workers, making them more productive.

Evidence   Which view is correct? It is hard to say, because empirical studies of the effects of increases in the minimum wage run into the problems of distinguishing the effects of the minimum wage per se from the effects of other developments—growth, inflation, recession—occurring in the economy. On balance, however, the evidence seems to suggest that periodic increases in the minimum wage are followed by employment declines in affected industries. Empirical studies suggest that the unemployment effect is particularly pronounced among teenage workers. The other side of the coin, of course, is that those who remain employed receive higher incomes and tend to escape poverty. The overall antipoverty effect of the minimum wage may thus be a mixed, ambivalent one. Those who lose their jobs are plunged deeper into poverty; those who remain employed tend to escape poverty.[11]

☐   **Do Unions Raise Wages?**

Our union models (Figures 31-5, 31-6, and 31-7) all imply that unions have the capacity to raise wage rates. Has unionization in fact caused wage rates to be higher than otherwise? On the face of it, this might seem to be a naïve question, the answer to which must be an unqualified "Yes." Don't we persistently read of specific unions successfully bargaining for substantial wage gains? And is it not also true that the average wage for organized workers is 10 to 15 percent higher than for unorganized workers?

Complications   Yet, one may have second thoughts. For example, we know that the long-run trend of real wages in the United

States has been upward (Figure 31-2). So the real question is not solely whether unions successfully bargain for wage increases, but rather, whether these increases are larger than, smaller than, or about the same as those which the subtle, undramatic workings of the market would have brought about. Although the UAW now negotiates wage increases in the automobile industry, we must keep in mind that wages rose in the industry long before it was organized in 1938–1941 and undoubtedly would have risen substantially in the past several decades had the industry remained unorganized. Furthermore, there is the historical fact that unions have been most successful in organizing the more prosperous industries. Many of the now-unionized high-wage industries were also high-wage industries *before* they were organized. Again the automobile industry is a good illustration. Thus one may legitimately ask if the fact that unionized industries pay higher wages than unorganized industries is the result of unionization or, alternatively, if unions are getting credit for wage increases attributable to favorable market forces.

As with the minimum wage, empirical studies which attempt to compare union and nonunion wages encounter severe conceptual obstacles, and their conclusions are invariably questionable. For example, if it is found that unionized carpenters get $8.00 per hour in city X while unorganized carpenters earn only $6.00 per hour in city Y, can we say with certainty that the differential is attributable to unionization or to some other variable? Perhaps city X is a dynamic, growing economic area, while city Y is in a depressed area where wage rates are generally low.

Two Generalizations   Given such difficulties, it is not too surprising that labor economists offer a tentative two-part response to the question "Do unions raise wages?" The first portion of the response compares union with nonunion wages; the second is concerned with the impact of unions upon the wage level of all workers.

[11]See Lloyd G. Reynolds, *Labor Economics and Labor Relations,* 6th ed. (Englewood Cliffs, N.J.: Prentice-Hall, Inc., 1974), pp. 106–110, for an excellent summary of recent empirical work on the minimum wage.

1 *Unions have raised wages modestly in organized industries. Specifically, through unions organized workers have probably achieved wage rates 10 to 15 percent higher than would otherwise be the case.*[12] Although this is not an insignificant accomplishment, the advantage is not so large as to imply that the formation of unions and the determination of wages through collective bargaining somehow permit labor to break free of market restraints and to establish wage rates largely at their discretion. In particular, higher wages tend to mean fewer jobs, and this inverse relationship between wages and employment acts as an important constraint upon the wage-raising activities of labor unions.

2 *On the other hand, unions have probably had little or no perceptible impact upon the average level of real wages received by labor—both organized and unorganized— taken as a whole.*

At first glance these two conclusions may seem inconsistent. But they need not be if the wage gains of organized workers are at the expense of unorganized workers. Imagine an economy divided into two sectors which are identical except that one is unionized and the other is not. Now, consistent with generalization 1 above, suppose the organized sector realizes a 10 percent money-wage increase. Assuming constant productivity, unit production costs and the price level will rise by 10 percent in the organized sector and, given constant prices in the unorganized sector, the overall price level will rise by 5 percent. This will obviously mean that real wages have risen by 5 percent in the organized sector, because money wages have gone up 10 percent, and the price level by only 5 percent. But it also means a *fall* in real wages in the unorganized sector, where money-wage rates have assumedly remained constant while the price level has gone up by 5 percent. This tendency for higher union wages to result in lower nonunion wages

may be reinforced by shifts in labor supply. Higher wages in the organized sector will tend to reduce employment therein; these unemployed workers may then seek jobs in the unorganized sector. This increase in the supply of labor will tend to depress the money and real wages of workers in the unorganized sector. In short, higher real wage rates for organized workers may well be at the expense of unorganized workers with the result that the average level of real wages for labor as a whole is unaltered. Stated differently, the tight relationship between productivity and the average level of real wages shown in Figure 31-1 correctly suggests that unions have little power to raise real wage rates for labor as a whole. But Figure 31-1 is an average relationship and is therefore compatible with certain groups of (union) workers getting higher relative wages if other (nonunion) workers are simultaneously getting lower real wages.

■ ────────────────────────────
WAGE DIFFERENTIALS

We have discussed the general level of wages and the role of supply and demand in a series of specific labor market situations. Yet, the wage differences which persist between different occupations and different individuals in the same occupations still have not been explained. Why does a corporate executive or a movie star receive $300,000 per year while laundry workers and retail clerks get a paltry $5000 per year? Table 31-3 indicates the substantial wage differentials which exist among certain common occupational groups. Our problem is to explain these kinds of differences.

Once again the forces of supply and demand provide a general answer. If the supply of a particular type of labor is very great in relation to the demand for it, the resulting wage rate will be low. But if demand is great and the supply very small, wages will be very high. Though it is a good starting point, this supply and demand explanation is not particularly revealing. We want to know *why* supply

[12] Albert Rees, *The Economics of Trade Unions* (Chicago: The University of Chicago Press, 1962), p. 79.

Table 31-3   AVERAGE HOURLY AND WEEKLY EARNINGS IN SELECTED
INDUSTRIES, JANUARY 1977

Industry	Average hourly gross earnings	Average weekly gross earnings
Bituminous coal	$8.19	$317.77
Motor vehicles	8.01	339.62
Contract construction	7.97	268.59
Chemicals	6.18	255.82
Printing and publishing	5.91	218.67
Fabricated metals	5.63	222.95
Food products	5.21	204.75
Retail trade	3.72	116.81
Apparel and finished textiles	3.55	118.93
Laundries and dry cleaning	3.41	116.96
Hotels and motels	3.20	97.92

Source: U.S. Department of Labor, *Earnings and Employment,* March 1977.

and demand conditions differ in various labor markets. To do this we must probe those factors which lie behind the supply and demand of particular types of labor.

If (1) all workers were homogeneous, (2) all jobs were equally attractive to workers, and (3) labor markets were perfectly competitive, all workers would receive precisely the same wage rate. As such, this is not a particularly startling statement. It merely suggests that in an economy having one type of labor and in effect one type of job, competition will result in a single wage rate for all workers. The statement is important in that it suggests the reasons why wage rates do differ in practice. (1) Workers are not homogeneous. They differ in capacities and in training and, as a result, fall into noncompeting occupational groups. (2) Jobs vary in attractiveness; the nonmonetary aspects of various jobs are not the same. (3) Labor markets are typically characterized by imperfections.

◻ **Noncompeting Groups**

Workers are not homogeneous; they differ tremendously in their mental and physical capacities and in their education and training. Hence, at any point in time the labor force can be thought of as falling into a number of *non-competing groups,* each of which may be composed of several occupations, or possibly just one, for which the members of this group qualify. For example, a relatively small number of workers have the inherent capacity to be brain surgeons, concert violinists, and research chemists, and even fewer have the financial means of acquiring the necessary training. The result is obviously that the supplies of these particular types of labor are very small in relation to the demand for them and that the consequent wages and salaries are high. These and similar groups do not compete with one another or with other skilled or semiskilled workers. The violinist does not compete with the surgeon, nor does the garbage collector or retail clerk compete with either the violinist or the surgeon.

This is not to say that each of the thousands of specific occupations in the United States constitutes a noncompeting group of workers or that workers fall into isolated occupational compartments. A number of unskilled or semiskilled occupations may well fall into one noncompeting group. For example, gasoline station attendants, farmhands, and unskilled construction workers may all be classified in the same group, because each is capable of doing the others' jobs. Yet none of the workers in this group currently offers effective competition for printers or electricians, who find themselves in other, more exclusive groups.

It should be noted, too, that the lack of competition among noncompeting groups of workers is actually a matter of degree. *Within limits* unskilled construction workers can be substituted for printers and electricians. Furthermore, this substitutability will be greater over a period of time than it is in the short run; over time, workers may move from one non-competing group to another as they are able to develop their native capacities through education and training. The assembly-line worker who has an IQ of 130 may become an account-ant or a lawyer by going to night school. But here another obstacle arises: higher education is a costly business. Our ambitious but low-income laborer does not have the same oppor-tunity of entering the higher-paid occupational groups as do the offspring of the lawyers and accountants who are already in those groups. And, needless to say, differences in inherent capacities provide an even more permanent obstacle to occupational mobility. In short, both native capacity and the opportunity to train oneself are unequally distributed, causing the wage differentials of noncompeting groups to persist.

The concept of noncompeting groups is a flexible one; it can be applied to various sub-groups and even to specific individuals in a given group. Some especially skilled surgeons are able to command fees considerably in ex-cess of their run-of-the-mill colleagues who perform the same operations. Dave Cowens, Kareem Abdul-Jabbar, and a few others de-mand and get salaries many times that of the average professional basketball player. Why? Because in each instance their colleagues are only imperfect substitutes.

□ Equalizing Differences

Now, if a group of workers in a particular noncompeting group is equally capable of per-forming several different jobs, one might ex-pect that the wage rate would be identical for each of these jobs. But this is not the case. A group of high school graduates may be equally capable of becoming bank clerks or unskilled construction workers. But these jobs pay dif-ferent wages. In virtually all localities, con-struction laborers receive better wages than do beginning bank clerks.

These differences can be explained on the basis of the *nonmonetary aspects* of the two jobs. The construction job involves dirty hands, a sore back, the hazard of accidents, and irregular employment, both seasonally and cy-clically. The banking job entails a white shirt, pleasant air-conditioned surroundings, and lit-tle fear of injury or layoff. Other things being equal, it is easy to see why workers will prefer picking up a deposit slip rather than a shovel. The result is that construction contractors must pay higher wages than banks pay to compensate for the unattractive nonmonetary aspects of construction jobs. These wage dif-ferentials are sometimes called *equalizing dif-ferences* because they must be paid to compen-sate for the nonmonetary differences in various jobs.

□ Market Imperfections

The notion of noncompeting groups helps explain wage differentials between various jobs for which limited numbers of workers are qual-ified. Equalizing differences aid in under-standing wage differentials on certain jobs for which workers in the same noncompeting group are equally qualified. Market imperfec-tions in the form of various immobilities help explain wage differences paid on identical jobs.

1 Geographic Immobilities Workers take root geographically. They are reluctant to leave friends, relatives, and associates, to force their children to change schools, to sell their houses, and to incur the costs and incon-veniences of adjusting to a new job and a new community. Geographic mobility is likely to be particularly low for older workers who have seniority rights and substantial claims to pension payments upon retirement. Then, too, workers who may be willing to move may simply be ignorant of job opportunities and wage rates in other geographic areas. As Adam Smith noted two centuries ago, "A man is of all sorts of luggage the most difficult to be transported." The reluctance or inability of workers to move obviously causes geographic wage differentials for the same occupation to persist.

2 Institutional Immobilities Geographic immobilities may be reinforced by artificial restrictions on mobility which are imposed by institutions. In particular, we have already noted that craft unions find it to their advantage to restrict their membership. After all, if carpenters and bricklayers become plentiful, the wages they can command will decline. Thus the low-paid nonunion carpenter of Brush, Colorado, may be willing to move to Chicago in the pursuit of higher wages. But his chances of successfully doing so are slim. He will probably be unable to get a union card; and no card, no job. The professions impose similar artificial restraints. For example, at most universities individuals lacking advanced degrees are automatically not considered for employment as teachers. Quite apart from one's competence as a teacher and one's command of the subject matter, a "union card"— an M.A. or a Ph.D.—is the first requisite for employment.

3 Sociological Immobilities Finally, we must acknowledge sociological immobilities. Despite recent regulatory legislation to the contrary, women workers frequently receive less pay than men working at the same job. The consequence of racial and ethnic discrimination is that Negroes, Mexicans, Jews, and other minority groups are often forced to accept lower wages on given jobs than fellow workers receive. We shall have more to say on

the matter of discrimination in Chapters 37 and 38.

A final point: It is more than likely that all three of these considerations—noncompeting groups, equalizing differences, and market imperfections—will play a role in the explanation of actual wage differentials. For example, the differential between the wages of a physician and a construction worker is largely explainable on the basis of noncompeting groups. Physicians fall into a noncompeting group where, because of mental and financial requisites to entry, the supply of labor is small in relation to demand, and wages are therefore high. In construction work, where mental and financial prerequisites are much less significant, the supply of labor is great in relation to demand and wages are low when compared with those of physicians. However, were it not for the unpleasantness of the construction worker's job and the fact that his craft union pursues restrictive membership policies, the differential would probably be even greater than it is.

■

INVESTMENT IN HUMAN CAPITAL

We have just seen that the concept of noncompeting groups is a very important part of the explanation of wage differentials. Let us probe more carefully the question of why these noncompeting groups exist.

□ **The Concept**

According to human capital theory, noncompeting groups—and therefore wage differentials—exist to a large extent because of differing amounts of investment in human capital. Generally speaking, investments in human capital are of three kinds. Each of them is for the purpose of increasing the productivity of workers and thereby of expanding their wages and incomes.

First, expenditures on *education*— including general and specific education, formal and informal education, on-the-job training, and so forth—are the most obvious and perhaps most important kind of investment in human capital. Education contributes to a labor force which is more skilled and more productive. Second, expenditures on *health* are also significant. Better health—the consequence of expenditures on preventive medicine and medical care, improved diet, and better housing—gives rise to greater vigor, longevity, and higher productivity among workers. Finally, expenditures on *mobility* which shifts workers from relatively low to relatively high productivity uses are a less obvious form of investment in human capital. Like education, the geographic movement of workers may raise the value of their labor services. In short, each employable person has embodied within himself a future flow of labor services. According to human capital theory, the productivity and therefore the market value of his labor services (his wages) are determined to a great degree by the amount which the individual, his family, and society have chosen to invest in his education and training, his health, and his location.

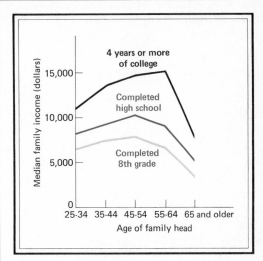

FIGURE 31-9 EDUCATION LEVELS AND FAMILY INCOME

Investment in education yields a return in the form of an income differential enjoyed both initially and throughout one's worklife. (*U.S. Bureau of the Census.*)

□ The Investment Decision

It may seem odd or even repugnant to analyze investment in manpower in the same way one would explore the decision to buy a machine. But, in fact, the two decisions are very similar. The purchase of a machine (real capital) will give rise to a flow of additional net revenues over the estimated years of life of the machine. Potential investors can discount this lifetime flow of earnings, compare their present value with the cost of the machine, and determine a rate of return on the investment. By contrasting this rate of return with the expected rates on alternative investments, a firm can rationally decide whether the purchase of this machine is profitable and, if so, whether it

is the most profitable purchase of real capital it can make. Similarly, one might subject the decision to invest in, say, a four-year college education to the same analysis. Figure 31-9 suggests that the families of those with larger investments in education achieve higher incomes initially and throughout their work careers than do those who have made smaller educational investments. The economic return from investment in a college education can therefore be regarded as the additional lifetime earnings which the college graduate will earn as compared with the earnings of a high school graduate. The present value of this difference in lifetime earnings can be determined and compared with the cost of the education, and the rate of return on the investment in the college education can be calculated. This rate will be useful to the individual in determining whether investment in additional education is economically justifiable. It will be helpful to

society in determining the proper balance between investment in men and investment in
machinery.[13]

□ Explanatory Value

Proponents contend that the theory of
human capital explains a number of phenomena which would otherwise be minor mysteri-
ies. Why do we educate younger, rather than
older, people? Why are younger people more
mobile than older people? Answer to both
questions: Younger people have a longer expected working life over which to realize returns on their investments in education or
mobility. The fact that wages in the South
have been persistently lower than in the rest of
the country is partly the result of different
levels of spending on education. The concept
of human capital is also a part of the explanation of the rising level of real wages which the
United States has enjoyed historically (Figure
31-2). If our economy had the same natural
resources and real capital we now possess, but
a completely uneducated and untrained labor
force or even a labor force with the educational
and skill levels of, say, 1929, our GNP and real
wage levels would obviously be much lower
than they now are. Recall (Table 20-3) that
improved education and training are of great
importance in explaining the economic growth
which our economy has enjoyed.

□ Recent Criticism

We must recognize, however, that in recent years enthusiasm for human capital theory has abated somewhat. The primary reason
for this tarnished image has to do with the
apparent failure of various human capital programs of the 1960s to lessen income inequality.

---

[13] For a discussion of the many problems in estimating the
returns from investment in human capital, see the articles
by Theodore W. Schultz, Harry G. Shaffer, and William G.
Bowen in M. Blaug (ed.), *Economics of Education 1* (Baltimore: Penguin Books, 1968).

Human capital theory assumes the existence of a direct and significant relationship
between investment in human capital and
productivity. Specifically, the hypothesized
cause-effect chain is:

> Investment in human capital
> (expenditures on education)
> *causes*
> Increases in worker productivity
> *which cause*
> Higher wage rates and higher earnings

Now, if these relationships are valid, it follows
that the incomes of poor people can be increased by providing them with more human
capital, that is, more education and training.
This thinking was consistent with, and an en-
dorsement of, a host of manpower programs
(for example, the Job Corps) which were introduced in the 1960s as a part of the "war on
poverty." Although economists still debate the
efficacy of manpower programs, there is empirical evidence which questions the success of
these programs and, more importantly, the
cause-effect chain assumed by human capital
theory. For example, government statistics
indicate that, in fact, the degree of income
inequality has *not* changed in recent years
(Chapter 37). And studies of ghetto labor
markets, at which many of the manpower programs were specifically directed, revealed
that—contrary to what human capital theory
would suggest—the better educated workers
did *not* receive higher wages or experience less
unemployment. Furthermore, much-discussed
studies of a more global character have tended
to downgrade and question the existence of a
positive and significant relationship between
public expenditures on education and an individual's ability to perform in school and in the
labor market. For example, James S. Coleman
and his associates found that the socioeconomic status of one's family—not the quantity
of education—is the critical influence upon an
individual's academic and labor market

achievements.[14] Similarly, Christopher Jencks found only a modest relationship between schooling, on the one hand, and income, on the other.

> Economic success seems to depend on varieties of luck and on-the-job competence that are only moderately related to family background, schooling, or scores on standardized tests. The definition of competence varies greatly from one job to another, but it seems in most cases to depend more on personality than on technical skills.[15]

If we accept this empirical evidence and thereby reject the cause-effect chain of human capital theory, how can we explain the fact (Figure 31-9) that people with "more" education *do* receive higher earnings than people with "less" education? One explanation is the argument that human capital theory has reversed the true relationship; perhaps high incomes cause families to spend more on education, just as they cause people to spend more on clothing, automobiles, and housing. A more complex explanation holds that

[14]James S. Coleman, *Equality of Educational Opportunity* (Washington: U.S. Department of Health, Education, and Welfare, 1966).
[15]Christopher Jencks et al., *Inequality: A Reassessment of the Effect of Family and Schooling in America* (New York: Basic Books, Inc., Publishers, 1972), p. 8.

. . . the only reason that education is correlated with income is that the combination of ability, motivation, and personal habits that it takes to succeed in education happen to be the same combination that it takes to be a productive worker.[16]

According to this view, the high-income "4 years or more of college" group of Figure 31-9 would have received high incomes even if they had chosen not to invest in a college education. The reason? They possess the ability and motivation to succeed in the labor market; the fact that they attended college is incidental to this success. Stated differently, if it is in fact a combination of inherent ability, motivation, and personal habits that is rewarded in the labor market, then the subsidization of individuals who do not possess these characteristics to enable them to stay in school longer or to enroll in manpower training programs will not affect their ultimate earnings.

The essence of our argument is not that human capital theory should be flatly rejected. Indeed, it is the basis for many valuable insights into the workings of the labor market, the causes of economic growth, and so forth. Rather, the point is that the concept should be used judiciously and, more specifically, it has apparent limitations for making policy decisions.

[16]Alice M. Rivlin, "Income Distribution—Can Economists Help?" *American Economic Review,* May 1975, p. 10.

Summary

1   Wages are the price paid per unit of time for the services of labor.

2   The general level of wages in the United States is higher than in foreign nations because the demand for labor is great in relation to the supply. The strong demand for American labor is based upon its high productivity, which in turn depends upon the quantity and quality of the capital equipment and natural resources used by labor, the quality of the labor force itself, the efficiency of management, a favorable sociopolitical environment, and the vast size of the domestic market. Over time these factors have caused the demand for labor to increase in relation to the supply, accounting for the long-run rise of real wages in the United States.

3   The determination of specific wage rates depends upon the structure of the particular labor market. In a competitive market the equilibrium wage rate and level of employment will be determined by the intersection of labor supply and demand.

4 Under monopsony, however, the marginal-resource-cost curve will lie above the resource supply curve, because the monopsonist must bid up wage rates in hiring extra workers and pay that higher wage to *all* workers. The monopsonist will hire fewer workers than he will under competitive conditions in order to achieve less-than-competitive wage rates (costs) and thereby greater profits.

5 A union may raise competitive wage rates by *a.* increasing the derived demand for labor, *b.* restricting the supply of labor through exclusive unionism, and *c.* directly enforcing an above-equilibrium wage rate through inclusive unionism.

6 In many important industries, the labor market takes the form of bilateral monopoly; that is, a strong union "sells" labor to a monopsonistic employer. Although the outcome of this labor market model is logically indeterminate, it might entail an important manifestation of the concept of countervailing power.

7 Economists disagree about the desirability of the minimum wage as an antipoverty mechanism. While it causes unemployment for some low-income workers, it raises the incomes of others who retain their jobs.

8 Unionized workers have probably realized wage rates 10 to 15 percent higher than would otherwise have been the case; but there is little evidence to suggest that unions have been able to raise the average level of real wages for labor as a whole.

9 Wage differentials are largely explainable in terms of *a.* noncompeting groups, that is, differences in the capacities and training of different groups of workers; *b.* equalizing differences, that is, wage differences which must be paid to offset nonmonetary differences in jobs; and *c.* market imperfections in the form of geographic, artificial, and sociological immobilities.

10 Investment in human capital takes the form of expenditures on education and training, health, and location. Despite limitations, the concept of human capital is useful in explaining, for example, the long-run rise in the average level of real wages and geographic wage differentials.

Questions and Study Suggestions

1 Key terms and concepts to remember: money and real wage rates; monopsony; marginal resource cost; exclusive and inclusive unionism; bilateral monopoly; the minimum wage; wage differentials; noncompeting groups; equalizing differences; investment in human capital.

2 Explain why the general level of wages is higher in the United States than in foreign nations. What is the most important single factor underlying the long-run increase in the average real wage rates in the United States? What, if anything, does this suggest concerning the ability of unions to raise real wages?

3 *a.* Describe wage determination in a labor market in which workers are unorganized and many firms are actively competing for the services of labor. Show this situation graphically, using W_1 to indicate the equilibrium wage rate and Q_1 to show the number of workers hired by the firms as a group.

b. Suppose now that the formerly competing firms form an employers' association which hires labor as a monopsonist would. Describe verbally the impact upon wage rates and employment. Adjust the graph drawn for question 3*a*, showing the monopsonistic wage rate and employment level as W_2 and Q_2, respectively.

4 Describe the techniques which unions might employ to raise wages. Evaluate the desirability of each from the viewpoint of **a.** the union, and **b.** society as a whole. Explain: "Craft unionism directly restricts the supply of labor; industrial unionism relies upon the market to restrict the number of jobs."

5   Assume a monopsonistic employer is paying a wage rate of W_m and hiring Q_m workers, as is indicated in Figure 31-8. Now suppose that an industrial union is formed and that it forces the employer to accept a wage rate of W_c. Explain verbally and graphically why in this instance the higher wage rate will be accompanied by an *increase* in the number of workers hired.

6   Complete the following labor supply table for a firm hiring labor competitively.

Units of labor	Wage rate	Total labor cost (wage bill)	Marginal resource (labor) cost
1	$14	$_____	$_____
2	14	_____	_____
3	14	_____	_____
4	14	_____	_____
5	14	_____	_____
6	14	_____	_____

a.   Show graphically the labor supply and marginal resource (labor) cost curves for this firm. Explain the relationships of these curves to one another.

b.   Compare these data with the labor demand data of question 3 in Chapter 30. What will the equilibrium wage rate and level of employment be? Explain.

c.   Now redetermine this firm's supply schedule for labor on the assumption that it is a monopsonist and that, although it can hire the first worker for $14, it must increase the wage rate by $1 to attract each successive worker. Show the new labor supply and marginal labor cost curves graphically and explain their relationships to one another. Compare these new data with those of question 3 for Chapter 30. What will be the equilibrium wage rate and the level of employment? Why does this differ from your answer to question 6*b*?

7   A critic of the minimum wage has contended, "The effects of minimum wage legislation are precisely the opposite of those predicted by those who support them. Government can legislate a minimum wage, but cannot force employers to hire unprofitable workers. In fact, minimum wages cause unemployment among low-wage workers who can least afford to give up their small incomes." Do you agree? What bearing does the elasticity of labor demand have upon this assessment? What factors might possibly offset the unemployment effects of a minimum wage?

8   Explain: "Although unions have altered the wage structure, they have not been successful in raising the average real wage of the American labor force."

9   What are the basic considerations which help explain the wage differentials between particular labor markets?

10   Evaluate and explain these two statements:

a.   "Wage differentials can be explained in terms of two factors: first, vertical immobilities, that is, obstacles to the movement of workers from one occupational level to another; and, second, horizontal immobilities, that is, factors which prevent workers from being perfectly mobile geographically."

b.   "If all workers were of equal capacity and training, all jobs were equally attractive to workers, and labor markets were free of imperfections, all workers would receive the same wage rate."

11   What is meant by investment in human capital? Use this concept to explain **a.** wage differentials, and **b.** the long-run rise in real wage rates in the United States. What criticisms are made of human capital theory?

Selected References

Bloom, Gordon F., and Herbert R. Northrup: *Economics of Labor Relations,* 8th ed. (Homewood, Ill.: Richard D. Irwin, Inc., 1977), chaps. 8–12.

Freeman, Richard B.: *Labor Economics* (Englewood Cliffs, N.J.: Prentice-Hall, Inc., 1972), chaps. 1–5.

Freeman, Richard B.: *The Over-Educated American* (New York: Academic Press, Inc., 1976).

Marshall, F. Ray, Allan M. Cartter, and Allan G. King: *Labor Economics: Wages, Employment, and Trade Unionism,* 3d ed. (Homewood, Ill.: Richard D. Irwin, Inc., 1976), chaps. 7, 8, 10, 11, 13.

McConnell, Campbell R. (ed.): *Perspectives on Wage Determination* (New York: McGraw-Hill Book Company, 1970), parts 2, 4, 5.

Reynolds, Lloyd G.: *Labor Economics and Labor Relations,* 6th ed. (Englewood Cliffs, N.J.: Prentice-Hall, Inc., 1974), chaps. 1–8, 12, 22.

Last Word
Why Doctors Earn So Much

The average earnings of physicians are 70 to 80 percent greater than those of lawyers and Ph.D. scientists.

The medical profession attained the incomparable income levels of the post-World War II period through its trade union powers. The AMA is perhaps the strongest trade union in the United States. It has virtually complete control over the supply of doctors, and actively uses this control to restrict supply and raise doctors' incomes. The source of AMA power lies in the fact that practicing physicians must be licensed and that licenses are given only to graduates from schools in the United States that are approved by the AMA's Council on Medical Education and Hospitals. When doctors' incomes fell during the Depression, the AMA sought to reduce admissions.

Restrictionist policies cut the number of medical school acceptances from 7578 in 1933 to 6211 in 1939 and kept the number below the 1933 "peak" for some 20 years. In 1926, 64% of applicants to medical school were accepted; in 1952, 52%; in 1973 just 35%. While there was a moderate increase in the number of M.D.s conferred (and in approved medical schools) through 1960, and a more rapid increase thereafter, medical schools are the only major segment of higher education that did not expand rapidly in the post-World War II years. In 1950, 5.2% of postbaccalaureate degrees were awarded in medicine; in 1972, 2.9%. In 1950 doctors, dentists, and related practitioneers constituted 3.9% of the professional work force; in 1974, 2.8%. Medical incomes were raised and maintained by the AMA's control over supply.

The economic position of doctors was enhanced even further in the 1960s and 1970s by federal subsidization of medical services under Medicare and Medicaid. Because the increased demand brought about by federal spending had relatively little impact on the output of doctors from American medical schools, the price of doctors' services and their incomes increased greatly. From 1959 to 1969, physicians fees grew at twice the rate of the consumer price index. Median net earnings of physicians rose by 80%. By contrast, the average hourly earnings of production workers grew by just 50%.

Richard B. Freeman, *The Over-Educated American* (New York: Academic Press, 1976), pp. 118–120, abridged. Reprinted by permission.

32

The Pricing and Employment of Resources: Rent, Interest, and Profits

The discussion of wages in Chapter 31 is rather lengthy. In contrast, the discussions of the income shares—rent, interest, and profits—found in the present chapter are relatively brief. There are two reasons for this difference in emphasis.

1 Wage incomes are clearly the major component of the national income. As we will find in the concluding section of this chapter, 70 to 80 percent of the national income is in the form of wage and salary incomes, the remainder accruing as rent, interest, and profit incomes.

2 The economic theories of rent, interest, and profit are very unsettled; there are honest differences among authorities as to definitions, explanations, and implications where nonwage incomes are concerned. For these two reasons we shall concentrate upon the basic features of rent, interest, and profit determination and forgo the many controversial points and the often ambiguous details which are encountered in more advanced discussions of these income shares.

ECONOMIC RENT

To most people the term "rent" means the seemingly exorbitant sum one must pay for a two-bedroom apartment or a dormitory room. To the businessman, "rent" is a payment made for the use of a factory building, machinery, or warehouse facilities. Closer examination finds these commonsense definitions of rent to be confusing and ambiguous. Dormitory room rent, for example, includes interest on the money capital the university has borrowed from the government or private individuals in financing the dormitory's construction, wages for custodial and maid service, utility payments, and so forth. Economists therefore use the term "rent" in a narrower but less ambiguous sense: *Economic rent is the price paid for the use of land and other natural resources which are completely fixed in total supply.* It is the unique supply conditions of land and other natural resources—their fixed supply—which make rental payments distinguishable from wage, interest, and profit payments.

Let us examine this feature and some of its implications through simple supply and demand analysis. To avoid complications, assume, first, that all land is of the same grade or quality—in other words, that each available acre of land is equally productive. Suppose, too, that all land has just one use, being capable of producing just one product—say, corn. And assume that land is being rented in a competitive market—that many corn farmers are demanding and many landowners offering land in the market.

In Figure 32-1, SS indicates the supply of arable farmland available in the economy as a whole and D_2 the demand of farmers for the use of that land. As with all economic resources, demand is a derived demand. It is downsloping because of the law of diminishing returns and the fact that, for farmers as a group, product price must be diminished to sell additional units of output.

The unique feature of our analysis is on the supply side: for all practical purposes the supply of land is perfectly inelastic, as reflected in SS. Land has no production cost; it is a "free and nonreproducible gift of nature." The economy has so much land, and that's that. It is true, of course, that within limits existing land can be made more usable by clearing, drainage, and irrigation. But these programs constitute capital improvements and not changes in the amount of land as such. Fur-

thermore, such variations in the usability of land are a very small fraction of the total amount of land in existence and therefore do not undermine the basic argument that land and other resources are in virtually fixed supply.

The fixed nature of the supply of land means that demand is the only active determinant of land rent; supply is passive. And what determines the demand for land? Those factors discussed in Chapter 30—the price of the product grown on the land, the productivity of land (which depends in part upon the quantity and quality of the resources with which land is combined), and the prices of those other resources which are combined with land. If, in Figure 32-1, the demand for land should increase from D_2 to D_1 or decline from D_2 to D_3, land rent would change from R_2 to R_1 or R_3, but the amount of land supplied would remain unchanged at OS. In technical terms, there is a large price effect and no quantity effect when

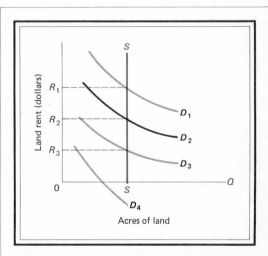

FIGURE 32-1 THE DETERMINATION OF LAND RENT

Because the supply of land and other natural resources is perfectly inelastic (SS), demand is the sole active determinant of land rent. An increase (D_2 to D_1) or decrease (D_2 to D_3) in demand will cause considerable changes in rent (R_2 to R_1 and R_2 to R_3). If demand is very small (D_4) relative to supply, land will be a "free good."

the demand for land changes. If the demand for land is only D_4, land rent will be zero; that is, land will be a "free good" because it is not scarce enough in relation to the demand for it to command a price. This situation was approximated in the free-land era of American history. Changes in economic rent will have no impact upon the amount of land available; the supply of land is simply not augmentable.

☐   **Land Rent is a Surplus**

The perfect inelasticity of the supply of land must be contrasted with the relative elasticity of such property resources as apartment buildings, machinery, and warehouses. These resources are not fixed in total supply. A higher price will give entrepreneurs the incentive to construct and offer larger quantities of these property resources. Conversely, a decline in their prices will induce suppliers to allow existing facilities to depreciate and not be replaced. The same general reasoning applies to the total supply of labor. Within limits, a higher average level of wages will induce more workers to enter the labor force, and lower wages will cause them to drop out of the labor force. In other words, the supplies of nonland resources are upsloping, or, stated differently, the prices paid to such resources perform an *incentive function.* A high price provides an incentive to offer more; a low price, to offer less.

Not so with land. Rent serves no incentive function, because the total supply of land is fixed. If rent is $10,000, $500, $1, or $0 per acre, the same amount of land will be available to society to make a contribution to production. Rent, in other words, could be eliminated without affecting the productive potential of the economy. For this reason economists consider rent to be a *surplus,* that is, a payment which is not necessary to ensure that land will be available to the economy as a whole.[1]

[1]The alert reader will have observed that a portion—in some instances a major portion—of wage and salary incomes may be a surplus in that these incomes exceed the

☐   **A Single Tax on Land?**

If land is a free gift of nature, costs nothing to produce, and would be available even in the absence of rental payments, why should rent be paid to those who by historical accident or inheritance happen to be landowners? Socialists have long argued that all land rents are unearned incomes. Therefore, they argue, land should be nationalized—owned by the state—so that any payments for its use can be utilized by the state in furthering the well-being of the entire population rather than by a landowning minority. The Last Word section of this chapter pokes fun at private ownership and land rent.

In the United States, criticism of rental payments has taken the form of a *single-tax movement* which gained considerable support in the late 1800s. Spearheaded by Henry George's provocative book *Progress and Poverty* (1879), this reform movement centered upon the notion that economic rent might be taxed away completely without impairing the available supply of land or, therefore, the productive potential of the economy as a whole.

George observed that as population grew and the geographic frontier closed, landowners came to enjoy larger and larger rents from their landholdings. These increments in rent were simply the result of a growing demand for a resource whose supply was perfectly inelastic; some landlords were receiving fabulously high incomes, not through rendering any productive effort, but solely as the result of holding advantageously located land. Henry George took the position that these increases in land rent belonged to the economy as a whole; he held that land rents should be taxed away and spent for public uses.

minimum amount necessary to keep an individual in his current line of work. For example, a professional basketball superstar may receive $100,000 or more per year, whereas his next best occupational option, as, say, a high school coach, would earn him only $12,000 or $15,000 per year. Most of his income is therefore a surplus. Observe that in the twilight of their careers, professional athletes sometimes accept sizable salary reductions rather than seek employment in alternative occupations.

To illustrate: If the relevant supply and demand conditions for land are as shown by SS and D_2 in Figure 32-1, land rent will be OR_2 per acre. Suppose government imposes a tax equal to, say, half the rent per acre. That is, a tax of R_2R_3 per acre is levied where $R_2R_3 = \frac{1}{2}OR_2$. Now, you will recall from Chapter 23 the generalization that the more inelastic the supply of a product (or resource), the larger will be the portion of a tax borne by the producer (or resource owner). In the case of land, the supply is completely inelastic, so all the tax must be borne by the landowner; it is impossible to shift any part of the tax to renters. Of course, the landowner could withdraw his land from production, but this would simply mean no rental income for him at all!

As George saw it, the fact that the tax burden remained on the landowner was perfectly justifiable; land rent, after all, was unearned income. Population growth and the closing of the geographic frontier were conferring windfall rental income upon landowners, and government was fully justified in taxing away such rental income. Indeed, George held that there was no reason to tax away only 50 percent of the landowner's unearned rental income. Why not take 70 or 90 or 99 percent? In seeking popular support for his ideas on land taxation, Henry George proposed that taxes on rental income be the only tax levied by government.

Criticisms   Critics of the single tax on land make these points: First, current levels of government spending are such that a land tax alone would clearly not bring in enough revenue; it cannot be considered realistically as a *single* tax. Second, as noted earlier, in practice most income payments combine elements of interest, rent, wages, and profits. Land is typically improved in some manner by productive effort, and economic rent cannot be readily disentangled from payments for capital improvements. As a practical matter, it would be very difficult to determine how much of any given income payment is actually rent. Third,

the question of unearned income goes beyond land and land ownership. One can readily argue that many individuals and groups other than landowners benefit from the receipt of "unearned" income associated with the overall advance of the economy. For example, consider the capital gains income received by an individual who, some fifteen or twenty years ago, chanced to purchase (or inherit) stock in a firm which has experienced rapid growth (say, IBM or Xerox). How is this income different from the rental income of the landowner?

Renewed Concern   On the other hand, there is a renewed interest in land taxation on the part of urban economists, city planners, and public officials. Many of them contend that a strong case can be made on grounds of both equity and efficiency for a heavy tax on land values.

1   Equity   With respect to *equity,* they argue, like Henry George, that much of the value of urban land results from population growth, community development, and, very significantly, public decisions to invest in roads, schools, and water, gas, and sewer utilities. Furthermore, zoning changes made by public bodies can sharply increase the value of affected land overnight. As a result, landowners, who are typically high-income people initially, realize large "unearned increments" of income with little or no expenditure of effort or money. Because the value of urban land is largely determined by public decision and public investment, it is held that the community should recapture the resulting increases in land value through taxation and use these revenues for public purposes.

2   Efficiency   The *efficiency* argument is that a tax on land value has a neutral effect upon the allocation or use of land; unlike most other taxes, a tax on land value does not contribute to the malallocation of resources. For example, glancing back at Figures 23-7 and 23-8, we find that sales and excise taxes have the effect of increasing prices and reducing output. Assuming allocative efficiency initially, the allocation of resources to affected products would obviously be less efficient as a result of the tax. Assume now that Figure 23-7 shows the demand for and supply of labor in a competitive market. The imposition of an income tax of a certain amount per worker per day would have the effect of reducing the supply of labor, distorting the workers' preferred balance between work and leisure away from the optimum. The tax would cause workers to offer less productive effort and to take more leisure. In comparison, the complete inelasticity of the supply of land means that a tax on land rent has no effect on price or output and therefore does not alter resource allocation. "The most profitable use of the [land] site before the tax is imposed continues to be the most profitable use."[2] This outcome is in contrast to property taxes on buildings—the major alternative revenue source for cities—wherein there is an adverse incentive effect; that is, taxes on buildings lower their return to investors and discourage their construction. We will find in Chapter 36 that high property taxes on buildings have been an important factor in the physical deterioration of the central city of many major metropolitan areas. Hence, more and more urban economists favor greater use of taxes on land and less use of property taxes on buildings.

□ **Productivity Differences and Alternative Uses**

Our analysis thus far has proceeded upon the assumption that all units of land are of the same grade. In practice, this is plainly not so. Different acres vary greatly in productivity. These productivity differences stem primarily from differences in soil fertility and such climatic factors as rainfall and temperature. It is these factors which explain why Iowa soil is excellently suited to corn production, the plains of eastern Colorado are much less so,

and desert wasteland of New Mexico is incapable of corn production. These differences in productivity will be reflected in resource demand. Competitive bidding by farmers will establish a high rent for the very productive Iowa land. The less productive Colorado land will command a much lower rent, and the New Mexico land no rent at all. Location may be equally important in explaining differences in land rent. Other things being equal, renters will pay more for a unit of land which is strategically located with respect to materials, labor, and customers than for a unit of land whose location is remote from these markets. Witness the extremely high land rents in large metropolitan areas.

The rent differentials to which quality differences in land would give rise can be easily seen by looking at Figure 32-1 from a slightly different point of view. Suppose, as before, that only one agricultural product, say corn, can be produced on four grades of land, *each* of which is available in the fixed amount OS. When combined with identical amounts of capital, labor, and other cooperating resources, the productivity—or, more specifically, the marginal revenue productivity—of each grade of land is reflected in demand curves D_1, D_2, D_3, and D_4. Grade 1 land is the most productive, as reflected in D_1, whereas grade 4 is the least productive, as is shown by D_4. The resulting rents for grades 1, 2, and 3 land will obviously be R_1, R_2, and R_3 respectively, the rent differentials mirroring the differences in the productivity of the three grades of land. Grade 4 land is so poor in quality that it would not pay farmers to bring it fully into production; it would be a "free" and only partially used resource.

We have also supposed, thus far, that land has only one use. Actually, we know that land usually has a number of alternative uses. An acre of Iowa farmland may be useful in raising not only corn, but also wheat, oats, milo, and cattle, or it may be useful as a site for a house or factory. What is the importance of this obvious point? It indicates that, although land

[2]Dick Netzer, *Economics and Urban Problems,* 2d ed. (New York: Basic Books, Inc., Publishers, 1974), p. 257.

is a free gift of nature and has no production cost from the viewpoint of society as a whole, the rental payments of individual producers are *costs*. The total supply of land will be available to society even if no rent at all is paid for its use, but, from the standpoint of individual firms and industries, land has alternative uses, and therefore payments must be made by specific firms and industries to attract that land from those other uses. Such payments by definition are costs. Once again the fallacy of composition has entered our discussion. From the standpoint of society, there is no alternative but for land to be used by society. Therefore to society, rents are a surplus, not a cost. But because land has alternative uses, the rental payments of corn farmers or any other individual user are a cost; such payments are required to attract land from alternative uses.

INTEREST

The interest rate is the price paid for the use of money. Or, since money is obviously the most liquid of all assets, we can say that the interest rate is the price of liquidity. Two aspects of this income payment are immediately notable.

1 Because it is paid in kind, interest is typically stated as a percentage of the amount of money being borrowed rather than as an absolute amount. It is less clumsy to say that one is paying 5 percent interest than to proclaim that interest is "$50 per year per $1000." Furthermore, stating interest as a percentage facilitates the comparison of interest paid on loans of much different absolute amounts. By expressing interest as a percentage, we can immediately compare an interest payment of, say, $144 per year per $2880 and one of $600 per year per $12,000. In this case both interest payments are 5 percent—a fact not at all obvious from the absolute figures. Remember (Chapter 7) that the Truth in Lending Act calls for the uniform statement of interest costs so that borrowers will understand the interest rate they are paying.

2 Money is not an economic resource. As such, money is not productive; it is incapable of producing goods and services. However, businessmen "buy" the use of money, because money can be used to acquire capital goods—factory buildings, machinery, warehouses, and so forth. And these facilities clearly do make a contribution to production. Thus, in hiring the use of money capital, businessmen are ultimately buying the use of real capital goods. In fact, it is the expected marginal revenue productivity of capital goods which sets an upper limit upon the rate of interest businessmen will pay to obtain the funds needed for the purchase of those capital goods.

□ Range of Rates

Although we often refer to "the" interest rate, in fact there exists a whole range or continuum of rates. The Federal government currently borrows at $7\frac{1}{2}$ percent on its long-term securities. Corporate bonds may pay 8 to 9 percent. Mortgage loans may entail interest rates of $8\frac{1}{2}$ to $9\frac{1}{2}$ percent. Bank loans to consumers for automobile or refrigerator purchases may run from 10 to 18 percent. Those whose credit standing forces them to borrow from consumer finance companies may pay extremely high rates—24 or 36 percent is not uncommon. Why the differences?

1 The varying degrees of *risk* on loans are important. The greater the chance the borrower will not repay the loan, the more interest the lender will charge to compensate for this risk.

2 The *length* of a loan also affects the interest rate. Other things being equal, long-term loans usually command higher rates of interest than do short-term loans, because the long-term lender suffers the inconvenience and possible financial sacrifice of forgoing alternative uses for his money for a greater period of time.

3 Given two loans of equal length and risk, the interest rate will be higher on the smaller of the two loans. This is so because the *administrative costs* of a large and a small loan are about the same absolutely.

4 *Market imperfections* are also important in explaining some interest rate differentials. The small-town bank which monopolizes the local money market may charge high interest rates on loans to consumers because households find it inconvenient to "shop around" at banks in somewhat distant cities. The large corporation, on the other hand, is able to survey a number of rival investment houses in disposing of a new bond issue and thereby to secure the lowest obtainable rate.

To circumvent the difficulties involved in discussing the whole structure of interest rates, economists talk of "the" interest rate or the "pure" rate of interest. This pure rate is best approximated by the interest paid on long-term, virtually riskless bonds such as the long-term bonds of the United States government or of American Telephone and Telegraph. This interest payment can be thought of as being made solely for the use of money over an extended time period, because the risk factor and administrative costs are negligible and the interest on such securities is not distorted by market imperfections. The pure interest rate is currently (mid-1977) about $7\frac{1}{2}$ or 8 percent.

□ **The Money Market: Liquidity Preference Theory**

Given these preliminaries, our task now is to look more systematically at the *money market* or, more specifically, at the *liquidity preference theory* of the interest rate. A brief overview is appropriate before we explore details. The theory involves demand and supply, but both have unique characteristics. On the demand side of the money market, there are three components of the demand for money or liquidity: the transactions, the precautionary, and the speculative demands. The transactions and precautionary demands depend, not upon the interest rate (price of money), but rather, upon the level of national income. In

contrast, the speculative demand is inversely related to the interest rate. On the supply side of the money market, we assume that the amount of money available in the economy is determined by the policy decisions of the monetary authorities. Putting demand and supply together, an equilibrium interest rate is determined. Given this synopsis, let us now examine the theory more systematically.

□ **The Demand for Money**

Consider the components of the demand for money.

1 The *transactions demand* has to do with the use of money—currency and demand deposits—in the usual day-to-day and week-to-week operations of households and businesses. The expenditures of households and businesses are not perfectly timed or synchronized to their income or revenue. Therefore, there is a demand for a certain amount of money to bridge the gap between the receipt of income and expenditures. For example, a household may receive a paycheck every two weeks, but its expenditures occur more or less evenly through time. The household therefore demands a money balance of some average size to bridge the time gap between paydays; this is the transactions demand.

2 The *precautionary demand* for money suggests that households and businesses may want to hold money balances to meet any unforeseen, rainy-day contingencies which might arise. That is, for many households and businesses, the receipt of income and the making of expenditures are not completely predictable. Hence, they may hold money balances to compensate for unpredicted changes in income or expenses. Particularly relevant are those risks which one cannot fully protect oneself against by purchasing insurance—prolonged illness, unemployment, unfavorable shifts in consumer demand, and so forth.

The transactions and precautionary motives for holding money depend primarily upon the level of national income, rather than upon the rate of interest. A high level of national income implies a large volume of economic transactions which, in turn, suggests that households and businesses will need to hold a large amount of money balances to finance these transactions. Similarly, households and businesses can afford to hold larger amounts of money for precautionary purposes when their incomes are high. In short, the amount of money which will be held for transactions and precautionary purposes will vary *directly* with the level of national income.

Look now at Figure 32-2. Here we are concerned with the relationship between the amount of money demanded *and the interest rate.* Because the transactions and precautionary demands for money depend upon the level of national income and are independent of the rate of interest, we show these two demands graphically by the dashed vertical line arbitrarily located at $150 billion. In technical terms the transactions and precautionary demands for money are perfectly inelastic with respect to the interest rate. Interpretation: The amount of money or liquidity demanded

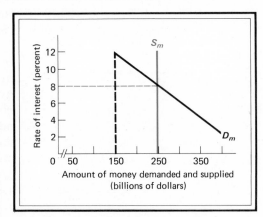

FIGURE 32-2 THE MONEY MARKET: LIQUIDITY PREFERENCE THEORY OF INTEREST

The demand for money, D_m, is comprised of the transactions, precautionary, and speculative demands. The fixed supply, S_m, is determined by the monetary authorities. In this instance the equilibrium rate of interest is 8 percent.

for transaction and precautionary purposes is unrelated to the interest rate.

3 Finally, the *speculative demand* for money indicates that, rather than hold their financial wealth in the form of securities (stocks, bonds, and so forth), households and businesses may choose to hold money. Given the fact that securities yield interest income and idle money balances do not, it may seem irrational to hold money beyond that needed for transactions and precautionary purposes. However, this is not the case when we envision the choice between securities—let us simplify and limit our discussion to *bonds*—and money within a framework of uncertainty and speculation over future changes in interest rates. That is, it makes a great deal of sense to hold money now rather than bonds *if* interest rates are expected to be higher in the future than they are currently. Conversely, it is rational to hold bonds rather than money as wealth *if* interest rates are believed to be higher now than they will be in the future.

Explanation: At any point in time there is some interest rate which the public considers to be about "normal." If the current interest rate is high, that is, above normal, the public will choose to buy bonds and therefore hold small amounts of money for speculative purposes. In other words, people will shift their financial assets from money to bonds to take advantage of the currently high interest rates. Buy bonds now rather than hold money because the future interest rate is likely to be lower—closer to "normal"—than it is currently. Conversely, if the interest rate is currently below normal, the public will choose to hold large speculative money balances as opposed to bonds. The reason is that the public is speculating that the interest rate will be higher in the future—closer to "normal"—and therefore bonds will be a better buy later on than they are now. This explanation suggests that *the amount of money which the public will want to hold for speculative purposes is inversely related to the rate of the interest.* Consider the matter from a slightly different perspective. The advantage or benefit of being liquid—of holding money as an asset—is that it puts one in a position to take advantage of favorable opportunities (a higher interest rate) which may occur in the money market. On the other hand, the cost of hold money is an opportunity cost—the interest income one forgoes by *not* holding bonds. We are simply saying that the lower the interest rate—the lower the cost of holding money—the larger the amount of money the public will want to hold. Conversely, the higher the interest rate—in other words, the higher the forgone interest-income cost of holding money—the smaller the amount of speculative balances the public will want to hold.

In Figure 32-2 this inverse relationship between the amount of money demanded for speculative purposes and the interest rate is reflected in the downsloping solid line. Note that we have added this speculative demand horizontally to the vertical dashed line representing the transactions and precautionary demands for money. Hence, the solid line, labeled D_m, represents the total demand for money. This line tells us the amount of money or liquidity the economy prefers at each possible interest rate. Hence, the designation "liquidity preference" theory of interest.

□ **Supply of Money and Equilibrium**

Determination of the equilibrium rate of interest obviously depends not only upon the demand for money, but also upon the supply. The supply of money is portrayed in Figure 32-2 by the vertical line S_m. Our assumption here is that the money supply is some fixed amount, determined by the policy decisions of the monetary authorities. If we suppose the money supply is $250 billion, we find in Figure 32-2 that the equilibrium interest rate is 8 percent, the only rate at which the amount of money which economic units want to hold is equal to the stock of money supplied.

Economists sometimes refer to the interest rate as an "administered price." By this they mean, of course, that the monetary authorities purposely manipulate the supply of money so as to influence the interest rate and thereby the overall performance of the economy. More specifically, the interest rate affects both the *level* and the *composition* of investment goods production.

Interest, Investment, and National Output Recall from Part 3 that the interest rate can be adjusted to affect the level of investment and thereby the levels of output and

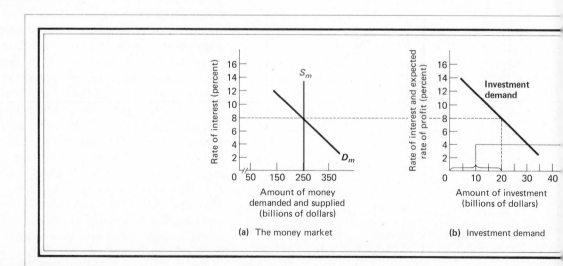

(a) The money market

(b) Investment demand

employment. With the aid of Figure 32-3, let us examine the relevant relationships in a more sophisticated fashion. Figure 32-3a merely restates our money market diagram of Figure 32-2. In Figure 32-3b the equilibrium interest rate of 8 percent is projected off the investment-demand curve developed in Chapter 11; the investment-demand curve used here is identical to Figure 11-5. We find that at the 8 percent interest rate, it will be profitable for businesses in the aggregate to invest $20 billion. In moving to Figure 32-3c, we simply plug this $20 billion of investment into the simple leakages-injections model for the private sector to determine the equilibrium net national product (NNP). Figure 32-3c is the same as Figure 12-2 and therefore yields the same $470 billion NNP as derived in Chapter 12. In Chapter 12, however, we essentially *assumed* $20 billion of investment; in the present discussion, we have used the money market or interest rate along with the investment-demand curve to *explain* why investment is at the $20 billion level.

It is a simple matter to use Figure 32-3 to reveal the theoretical underpinnings of monetary policy. If the $470 billion level of NNP entails unemployment, an easy money policy will shift S_m to the right, lower the equilibrium interest rate, increase the volume of profitable

investment opportunities, shift the I_n curve upward, and increase the equilibrium NNP. Conversely, if demand-pull inflation is the problem, a tight money policy will shift S_m to the left, increase the interest rate, and choke off some investment to close the inflationary gap.

Several additional points are essential to the complete understanding of Figure 32-3.

1 Note that in Figure 32-3a we are concerned with *financial investment* (exchanging money for securities) by *lenders,* while Figure 32-3b involves *real investment* (the purchase of capital goods) by *borrowers.* These differences make it easy to reconcile the fact that financial investment by lenders is *encouraged* by high interest rates (Figure 32-3a) with the fact that high interest rates *discourage* real investment by borrowers (Figure 32-3b).

2 The functioning of monetary policy as portrayed in Figure 32-3 may be complicated by unfavorable shifts in the investment-demand curve. Recall that the interest rate is only one of many forces which have a bearing upon the investment plans of businesses. The rate of technological advance, population growth, the acquisition and operating costs of capital goods, government tax and expenditure policies, the stocks of capital goods on hand,

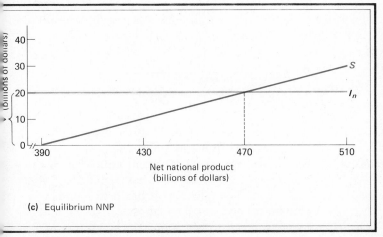

(c) Equilibrium NNP

FIGURE 32-3 THE MONEY MARKET AND EQUILIBRIUM NNP

By projecting the equilibrium interest rate from the money market in (a) to the investment-demand curve in (b) we determine the amount of investment which the business sector finds it profitable to undertake. Comparing this aggregate level of investment with the saving schedule in (c), the equilibrium NNP is determined. The reader should use this series of graphs to trace through the effects of tight and easy money policies.

anticipated market conditions, and business confidence are all important determinants of investment (Figure 16-2). Changes in any or all of these factors may easily offset any alterations in the interest rate which government may initiate in seeking to influence investment spending and employment. To illustrate: We know that the purpose of an easy money policy is to lower the interest rate, move businessmen down the investment-demand curve, thereby stimulating real investment and the equilibrium NNP. *But* the very recession which the easy money policy is designed to cure may very well be accompanied by a deterioration of business confidence and expectations which has the effect of shifting the investment-demand curve to the left. If substantial, this leftward shift *may* mean *less* investment spending, despite the fact that the interest rate is lower. Hence, monetary policy is frustrated. Similar reasoning can be applied to a tight money policy.[3]

3 The alert reader may have sensed that Figure 32-3 embodies a "circularity" or "feedback" problem which complicates monetary policy. Recall that the transactions and precautionary components of the money demand curve D_m depend directly upon the the level of NNP. This means that the increase in the NNP which an easy money policy brings about will in turn *increase* the demand for money, tending to offset or blunt the interest-reducing effect of the easy money policy. Conversely, a tight money policy will tend to reduce the NNP. But this in turn will *decrease* the demand for money and tend to dampen the initial interest-increasing effect of the tight money policy.

Interest and the Allocation of Capital
Prices, you will recall, are rationing devices. The interest rate is no exception; it performs

[3]The effectiveness of monetary policy is also dependent upon (1) the interest elasticities of the money demand and investment-demand curves and (2) the slope (MPS) of the saving schedule. The reader should tackle question 5 at the end of this chapter.

the function of allocating money capital and therefore real capital to various firms and investment projects. It rations the available supply of money or liquidity to those investment projects whose rate of return or expected profitability is sufficiently high to warrant payment of the going interest rate. If the expected rate of net profits of additional real capital in industry X is 12 percent and the required funds can be secured at an interest rate of 8 percent, industry X will be in a position, in terms of profit, to borrow and expand its capital facilities. On the other hand, if the expected rate of net profits of additional capital in industry Y is expected to be only 4 percent, it will be unprofitable for this industry to accumulate more capital goods. In short, the interest rate allocates money, and ultimately real capital, to those industries in which it will be most productive and therefore most profitable. Such an allocation of capital goods is obviously in the interest of society as a whole.

But the interest rate does not perform perfectly the task of rationing capital to its most productive uses. Large oligopolistic borrowers are in a better position than competitive borrowers to pass interest costs on to consumers by virtue of their ability to manipulate their prices. And, too, the sheer size and prestige of large industrial concerns might allow them to obtain money capital on favorable terms, whereas the market for loanable funds screens out less well known firms whose profit expectations might actually be superior.

BUSINESS PROFITS AND ECONOMIC PROFITS

As is the case with rent, economists find it advantageous to define profits more narrowly than do businessmen or accountants. To most businessmen, "profit" is what remains of a firm's total revenue after it has paid individuals and other firms for materials, capital, and labor supplied to the firm. To the economist, this conception is too broad and therefore ambiguous. The difficulty, as the economist sees it, is that this view of profits takes into account only *explicit* costs, that is, payments made by the firm to outsiders. It therefore ignores *implicit* costs, that is, payments to similar resources which are owned and self-employed by a firm. In other words, the businessman's concept of profits fails to allow for implicit wage, rent, and interest costs. *Economic,* or *pure, profits* are what remain after *all* opportunity costs—both explicit and implicit wage, rent, and interest costs and a normal profit—have been subtracted from a firm's total revenue (Chapter 25). Economic profits may be either positive or negative (losses).

An example may sharpen these comments. As the economist sees it, a farmer who owns his land and equipment and provides all his own labor is grossly overstating his economic profits if he merely subtracts his payments to outsiders for seed, insecticides, fertilizer, gasoline, and so forth, from his total receipts. Actually, much or possibly all of what remain are the implicit rent, interest, and wage costs which the farmer forgoes in deciding to self-employ the resources he owns rather than make them available in alternative employments. Interest on the capital or wages for the labor contributed by the farmer himself are no more profits than are the payments which would be made if outsiders had supplied these resources. In short, the businessman's definition and the economist's definition of profits are compatible only if the businessman includes both explicit and implicit costs in determining total costs. Economic profits are a residual—the total revenue remaining after *all* costs are taken into account.

☐ **Economic Profits and the Entrepreneur**

Speaking very generally, the economist views profits as the return to a very special type of human resource—entrepreneurial ability. A part of this return, you will recall, is called a *normal profit*. This is the minimum return or payment necessary to retain the entrepreneur in some specific line of production. By definition, this normal profit payment is a cost (Chapter 25). However, we know that a firm's total revenue may exceed its total costs (explicit, implicit, and inclusive of a normal profit). This extra or excess revenue above all costs is an *economic,* or *pure, profit*. This residual—which is *not* a cost because it is in excess of the normal profit required to retain the entrepreneur in the industry—accrues to the entrepreneur. The entrepreneur, in other words, is the residual claimant.

Economists offer several theories to explain why this residual of economic profit might occur. As we will see in a moment, these explanations relate to:

1 The risks which the entrepreneur necessarily bears as he functions in a dynamic and therefore uncertain environment or as he undertakes innovational activity.

2 The possibility of attaining monopoly power.

☐ **Sources of Economic Profit**

Our understanding of economic profits and the entrepreneur's functions can be both deepened and widened by describing an artificial economic environment within which pure profits would be zero. Then, by noting real-world deviations from this environment, we can lay bare the sources of economic profit.

In a purely competitive, static economy, pure profits would be zero. By a static economy we mean one in which all the basic data—resource supplies, technological knowledge, and consumer tastes—are constant and unchanging. A static economy is a changeless one in which all the determinants of cost and supply data, on the one hand, and demand and revenue data, on the other, are constant. Given the static nature of these data, the economic future is perfectly foreseeable; economic uncertainty is nonexistent. The outcome of price and production policies is accurately predictable. Furthermore, the static nature of such a society precludes any type of innovational change. Under pure competition any pure profits (positive or negative) which might have existed initially in various industries will disappear with the entry or exodus of firms in the long run. All costs—both explicit and implicit—will therefore be precisely covered in the long run, leaving no residual in the form of pure profits.

The notion of zero economic profits in a static, competitive economy enhances our understanding of profits by suggesting that the presence of profits is linked to the dynamic nature of real-world capitalism and the accompanying uncertainty. Furthermore, it indicates that economic profits may arise from a source apart from the directing, innovating, risk-bearing functions of the entrepreneur. And that source is the presence of some degree of monopoly power.

Uncertainty, Risk, and Profits In a dynamic economy the future is always uncertain. This means that the businessman necessarily assumes risks. Profits can be thought of in part as a reward for assuming these risks.

In linking pure profits with uncertainty and risk bearing, it is important to distinguish between risks which are insurable and those which are not. Some types of risks—for example, fires, floods, theft, and accidents to employees—are measurable in the sense that actuaries can estimate their average occurrence with considerable accuracy. As a result, these risks are typically insurable. Firms can avoid, or at least provide for, them by incurring a small known cost in the form of an insurance premium. It is the bearing of uninsurable risks, then, which is a potential source of economic profits.

What are such uninsurable risks? Basically, they are uncontrollable and unpredictable changes in demand (revenue) and supply (cost) conditions facing the firm. Some of these uninsurable risks stem from unpredictable changes in the general economic environment or, more specifically, from the business

cycle. Prosperity brings substantial windfall profits to most firms, whereas depression means widespread losses. But in addition, changes are constantly taking place in the structure of the economy. Even in a full-employment, noninflationary economy, changes are always occurring in consumer tastes, resource supplies, and so forth. These changes continually alter the revenue and cost data faced by individual firms and industries, leading to changes in the structure of the business population as favorably affected industries expand and adversely affected industries contract. Changes in government policies are pertinent at both levels. Appropriate fiscal and monetary policies of government may reverse a recession, whereas a tariff may significantly alter the demand and revenue data of the protected industry.

The point is this: Profits and losses can be associated with the assumption of uninsurable risks stemming from both cyclical and structural changes in the economy.

Uncertainty, Innovations, and Profits The uncertainties just discussed are external to the firm; they are beyond the control of the individual firm or industry. One other extremely important dynamic feature of capitalism—innovation—occurs at the initiative of the entrepreneur. Business firms deliberately introduce new methods of production and distribution to affect their costs favorably and new products to influence their revenue favorably. The entrepreneur purposely undertakes to upset his existing cost and revenue data in a way he hopes will be profitable to him.

But once again, uncertainty enters the picture. Despite exhaustive market surveys by well-established firms, new products or modifications of existing products may prove to be economic failures. Three-dimensional movies, not to mention Edsel and Corvair automobiles, come readily to mind as product failures. Nor is it known with certainty whether a new machine will actually provide the cost economies predicted for it while it is still in the blueprint stage. Innovations purposely undertaken by entrepreneurs entail uncertainty, just as do those changes in the economic environment over which an individual enterprise has no control. In a sense, then, innovation as a source of profits is merely a special case of risk bearing.

Under competition and in the absence of patent laws, innovational profits will be temporary. Rival firms will imitate successful (profitable) innovations, thereby competing away all economic profits. Nevertheless, innovational profits may always exist in a progressive economy as new, successful innovations replace those older innovations whose associated profits have been eroded or competed away.

Monopoly Profits Thus far, we have emphasized that profits are related to the uncertainties and uninsurable risks surrounding dynamic events which enterprises are exposed to or initiate themselves. The existence of monopoly in some form or another is a final source of economic profits. As explained previously, because of his ability to restrict entry, a monopolist may persistently enjoy economic profits, provided demand is strong relative to cost (Figure 27-1). This profit stems from the monopolist's ability to restrict output and influence product price to his own advantage.

There are both a causal relationship and a notable distinction between uncertainty, on the one hand, and monopoly, on the other, as sources of profits. The causal relationship involves the fact that an entrepreneur can reduce uncertainty, or at least manipulate its effects, by achieving monopoly power.[4] The competitive firm is unalterably exposed to the vagaries of the market; the monopolist, however, can control the market to a degree and thereby offset or minimize potentially adverse effects of uncertainty. Furthermore, innovation is an important source of monopoly power; the short-run uncertainty associated with the introduction of new techniques or new products may be borne for the purpose of achieving a measure of monopoly power.

The notable distinction between profits stemming from uncertainty and from monopoly has to do with the social desirability of the two sources of profits. Bearing the risks inherent in a dynamic and uncertain economic environment and the undertaking of innovations are socially desirable functions. The social desirability of monopoly profits, on the other hand, is very doubtful. Monopoly profits typically are founded upon output restriction, above-competitive prices, and a contrived misallocation of resources.

□   **Functions of Profits**

Profit is the prime mover, or energizer, of the capitalistic economy. As such, profits influence both the level of resource utilization and the allocation of resources among alternative uses. It is profits—or better, the *expectation* of profits—which induce firms to innovate. And innovation stimulates investment, total output, and employment. Innovation is a fundamental aspect of the process of economic growth, and it is the pursuit of profit which underlies most innovation. We know from our previous analysis of the determination of national income that profit expectations are

---

[4]The extensive efforts of large corporations to avoid risk and uncertainty constitute a major theme running through John Kenneth Galbraith's recent writings. He argues as follows: In resource markets, corporations vertically integrate their structure so as to guarantee themselves reliable sources of materials. Similarly, they finance their capital investment internally to insulate themselves from the vagaries of capital markets. The modern corporation reduces product market uncertainty by supplanting consumer sovereignty with producer sovereignty (recall the Last Word section of Chapter 5), using advertising and other forms of salesmanship to "manage" consumers so they will buy those goods corporations want to sell at the prices they want to charge. Finally, uncertainties of a larger sort— economic fluctuations—are mitigated indirectly by inducing government to undertake appropriate countercyclical policies. Galbraith's *Economics and the Public Purpose* (Boston: Houghton Mifflin Company, 1973) and *The New Industrial State* (Boston: Houghton Mifflin Company, 1967) are relevant.

highly volatile, with the result that investment, employment, and the rate of growth
have been unstable. Profits have functioned
imperfectly as a spur to innovation and investment.

Profits perform more effectively the task
of allocating resources among alternative lines
of production. Recall the message of Chapter
5: Businessmen seek profits and shun losses.
The occurrence of economic profits is a signal
that society wants that particular industry to
expand. Indeed, profit rewards are more than
an inducement for an industry to expand; they
also are the financial means by which firms in
such industries can add to their productive
capacities. Losses, on the other hand, signal
society's desire for the afflicted industries to
contract; losses penalize businesses which fail
to adjust their productive efforts to those
goods and services most preferred by consumers. This is not to say that profits and
losses result in an allocation of resources which
is now and forever attuned to consumer preferences. In particular, the presence of monopoly in both product and resource markets impedes the shiftability of firms and resources, as
also do the various geographic, artificial, and
sociological immobilities discussed in Chapter
31.

INCOME SHARES

The discussions of Chapters 31 and 32 would
be incomplete without a brief empirical summary as to the importance of wages, rent, interest, and profits as proportions or relative
shares of the national income. Table 32-1 provides an historical look at income shares in
terms of the income categories used in our
national income accounts. Unfortunately,
these accounting conceptions of income do not
nearly fit the economist's definitions of wages,
rent, interest, and profits. In particular, the
national income-accounting conceptions are
often mixtures of these four types of income.
Notable example: Much of "proprietors' in-

come" is wages and salaries, but most unincorporated businesses provide their own capital
and entrepreneurial talent and, in the case of
farming, their own land. Hence, a portion of
proprietors' income is interest, profits, and
rent. Recognizing this kind of limitation, what
do our national income data tell us about the
relative size and trends of income shares?

□   **Current Shares**

Looking at the most recent 1971–1976 figures in the table, we note immediately the
dominant role of labor income. Defining labor
income narrowly as "wages and salaries," labor
currently receives about 75 percent of the national income. But some economists argue
that since proprietors' income is largely comprised of wages and salaries, it should be added
to the official "wages and salaries" category to
determine labor income. When we use this
broad definition, labor's share rises to 84 percent of national income. Interestingly, although we label our system a "capitalist economy," the capitalist share of national
income—which we will define as the sum of
"corporate profits," "interest," and "rent"—is
substantially less than 20 percent of the national income.

□   **Historical Trends**

What can be deduced from Table 32-1 with
respect to historical trends? Let us concentrate on the dominant wage share. Using the
narrow definition of labor's share as simply
"wages and salaries," we note an increase from
about 55 to 76 percent in this century. Although there are several tentative explanations of this growth, one prominent theory
stresses the structural changes which have occurred in our economy. Two specific points are
made. First, noting the relative constancy of
the capitalist share (the sum of columns 4, 5,
and 6)—which was roughly 20 percent in both
the 1900–1909 and the 1971–1976 periods—we
find that the expansion of labor's share has

Table 32-1   RELATIVE SHARES OF NATIONAL INCOME, 1900–1976 *(decade or period averages of shares for individual years)*

(1) Decade	(2) Wages and salaries	(3) Proprietors' income	(4) Corporate profits	(5) Interest	(6) Rent	(7) Total
1900–1909	55.0%	23.7%	6.8%	5.5%	9.0%	100%
1910–1919	53.6	23.8	9.1	5.4	8.1	100
1920–1929	60.0	17.5	7.8	6.2	7.7	100
1930–1939	67.5	14.8	4.0	8.7	5.0	100
1939–1948	64.6	17.2	11.9	3.1	3.3	100
1949–1958	67.3	13.9	12.5	2.9	3.4	100
1954–1963	69.9	11.9	11.2	4.0	3.0	100
1963–1970	71.7	9.6	12.1	3.5	3.2	100
1971–1976	76.1	7.8	8.6	5.6	2.0	100

Source: Irving Kravis, "Income Distribution: Functional Share," *International Encyclopedia of Social Sciences.* vol. 7 (New York: The Macmillan Company and Free Press, 1968), p. 134, updated.

come primarily at the expense of the share going to proprietors. This suggests that the evolution of the corporation as the dominant form of business enterprise (Chapter 7) is an important explanatory factor. Put bluntly, the individual who would have operated his own corner grocery in the 1920s is the hired manager of a corporate supermarket in the 1960s or 1970s. Second, the changing output-mix and therefore the industry-mix which have occurred historically have tended to increase labor's share. Overall, there has been a long-term change in the composition of output and industry which has been away from land- and capital-intensive production and toward labor-intensive production. Again, crudely stated, there has been an historical realloca-tion of labor from agriculture (where labor's share is quite low) to manufacturing (where labor's share is rather high) and, finally, to private and public services (where labor's share is very high). These shifts account for much of the growth of labor's share reflected in column 2 of Table 32-1.

One is tempted to explain an expanding wage share in terms of the growth of labor unions. But there are difficulties with this approach. First, the growth of the labor move-ment in the United States does not fit very well chronologically with the growth of labor's share of the national income. Most of the growth of "wages and salaries" occurred be-tween 1900 and 1939; much of the growth in the labor movement came in the last few years of the 1930s and the war years of the early 1940s. Second, recall from Chapter 31 the pos-sibility that wage increases for union members may come at the expense of the wages of unor-ganized workers. That is, in obtaining higher wages, unions restrict employment opportuni-ties (Figures 31-6 and 31-7) in organized indus-tries. Unemployed workers and new labor force entrants therefore seek jobs in the non-union sectors. The resulting increases in labor supply tend to depress wage rates in nonunion jobs. If this scenario is correct, then higher wages for union workers may be achieved, not at the expense of the capitalist share, but rather, at the expense of the nonunion wage share. Overall, the total labor share—union plus nonunion—could be unaffected by unions. Finally, if the national income is dis-aggregated into industry sectors (as in Table 7-5) and the historical trend of the wage share in each sector is examined, we reach a curious conclusion. Generally speaking, labor's share has grown more rapidly in those sectors where unions are weak than in sectors which are highly unionized!

Other economists perceive substantial stability in the shares of national income that go to labor and capital. That is, if we recognize that most of "proprietors' income" is wages and therefore define labor's share broadly as the sum of "wages and salaries" and "proprietors' income," we note a high degree of stability in labor's share historically. Labor's share, defined as the sum of columns 2 and 3, and the capitalist share, composed of columns 4, 5, and 6, have divided the national income roughly on an 80–20 percent basis throughout the entire period. Economists who have treated the statistics in this way have attempted to explain the stability of labor's share. The "pursuit and escape" theory, for example, is an intriguing explanation with considerable intuitive ap-

peal. It draws upon a number of ideas developed in Chapter 18. Labor and business are envisioned in effect as being engaged in a contest of pursuit and escape. Labor attempts to encroach upon the capitalist share—profits, in particular—by increasing money wages. But businesses can escape this encroachment in either of two ways: (1) through increasing productivity, which has the effect of absorbing increases in money wages and preserving profits; and (2) by increasing product prices as a means of passing increases in wage costs on to consumers. According to the theory, it has been the effective use of these two escape techniques which explains the perceived historical stability of labor's share.[5]

[5]See Clark Kerr, "Labor's Income Share and the Labor Movement," in George W. Taylor and Frank C. Pierson (eds.), *New Concepts in Wage Determination* (New York: McGraw-Hill Book Company, 1957), pp. 260–298.

Summary

1 Economic rent is the price paid for the use of land and other natural resources whose total supplies are fixed.

2 Rent is a surplus in the sense that land would be available to the economy as a whole even in the absence of all rental payments. The notion of land rent as a surplus gave rise to the single-tax movement of the late 1800s. Currently, many urban economists and planners advocate a tax on land value on both equity and efficiency grounds.

3 Differences in land rent are explainable in terms of differences in productivity due to the fertility and climatic features of land and in its location.

4 Land rent is a surplus rather than a cost to the economy as a whole; however, because land has alternative uses from the standpoint of individual firms and industries, rental payments of firms and industries are correctly regarded as costs.

5 Interest is the price paid for the use of money or liquidity. The liquidity preference theory of interest envisions a total demand for money comprised of transactions, precautionary, and speculative demands. The supply of money is primarily the consequence of monetary policy.

6 The equilibrium interest rate influences the level of investment and helps ration capital goods to specific firms and industries.

7 Economic, or pure, profits are the difference between a firm's total revenue and its total costs, the latter defined to include implicit costs and a normal profit. Profits accrue to entrepreneurs for assuming the uninsurable risks associated with the organizing and directing of economic resources and innovating. Profits also result from monopoly power.

8 Profit expectations influence innovating and investment activities and therefore the level of employment. The basic function of profits and losses, however, is to induce that allocation of resources which is in general accord with the tastes of consumers.

9 The largest share of the national income goes to labor. Narrowly defined as "wages and salaries," labor's relative share has increased through time. When more broadly defined to include "proprietors' income," labor's share has been about 80 percent and the capitalist share about 20 percent of national income since 1900.

Questions and Study Suggestions

1 Key terms and concepts to remember: economic rent; incentive function; single-tax movement; the pure rate of interest; liquidity preference theory of interest; transactions, precautionary, and speculative demands for money; economic or pure profit; static economy; insurable and uninsurable risks; pursuit and escape theory.

2 How does the economist's usage of the term "rent" differ from everyday usage? "Though rent need not be paid by society to make land available, rental payments are very useful in guiding land into the most productive uses." Explain.

3 Explain why economic rent is a surplus to the economy as a whole but a cost of production from the standpoint of individual firms and industries. Explain: "Rent performs no 'incentive function' in the economy." What arguments can be made for and against a heavy tax on land?

4 If money capital, as such, is not an economic resource, why is interest paid and received for its use? What considerations account for the fact that interest rates differ greatly on various types of loans? Use these considerations to explain the relative size of the interest rates charged on the following: *a.* a long-term $1000 government bond; *b.* a $20 pawnshop loan; *c.* an FHA mortgage loan on a $37,000 house; *d.* a $4500 commercial bank loan to finance the purchase of an automobile; and *e.* a $100 loan from a personal finance company.

5 Use a set of diagrams similar to Figure 32-3 to verify the following statement: Other things being equal, monetary policy will be more effective (*a*) the less elastic the demand-for-money curve; (*b*) the more elastic the investment-demand curve; and (*c*) the flatter the saving schedule. Indicate how monetary policy might be complicated or frustrated by (*a*) unfavorable shifts in the investment-demand curve and (*b*) a feedback problem.

6 What are the major economic functions of the interest rate? Of economic profits? How might the fact that more and more businesses are financing their investment activities internally affect the efficiency with which the interest rate performs its functions?

7 How do the concepts of business profits and economic profits differ? Why are economic profits smaller than business profits? What are the three basic sources of economic profits? Classify each of the following in accordance with these sources: *a.* the profits acquired by a firm from developing and patenting a ball-point pen containing a permanent ink cartridge; *b.* the profit of a restaurant which results from construction of the interstate highway past its door; *c.* the profit received by a firm benefiting from an unanticipated change in consumer tastes.

8 Why is the distinction between insurable and uninsurable risks significant for the theory of profits? Carefully evaluate: "All economic profits can be traced to either uncertainty or the desire to avoid it."

9 Explain the absence of economic profit in a purely competitive, static economy. Realizing that the major function of profits is to allocate resources in accordance with consumer preferences, evaluate the allocation of resources in such an economy.

10   What has happened to the wage, profit, interest, and rent shares of national income over time? Explain the alleged growth of labor's share in terms of structural changes in the economy. Explain the alleged stability of labor's share in terms of the "pursuit and escape" theory.

Selected References

Clower, Robert W., and John F. Due: *Microeconomics* (Homewood, Ill.: Richard D. Irwin, Inc., 1972), chaps. 13–16.

Hansen, Alvin: *A Guide to Keynes* (New York: McGraw-Hill Book Company, 1953), chaps. 6, 7.

Humphrey, Thomas M.: "Income Distribution and Its Measurement: Distribution among the Factors of Production," *Monthly Review* (Federal Reserve Bank of Richmond, August 1971).

Stonier, Alfred W., and Douglas C. Hague: *A Textbook of Economic Theory,* 3d ed. (New York: Longmans, Green & Co., Inc., 1964), chaps. 13–15.

Last Word
Land Rent Goes Ape

An American poet, Edmund Vance Cooke (1866–1932), satirizes the private-property, land-rent issue.

UNCIVILIZED

An ancient ape, once on a time,
Disliked exceedingly to climb,
And so he picked him out a tree
And said, "Now this belongs to me.
I have a hunch that monks are mutts
And I can make them gather nuts
And bring the bulk of them to me,
By claiming title to this tree."

He took a green leaf and a reed
And wrote himself a title deed,
Proclaiming pompously and slow:
"All monkeys by these presents know."
Next morning when the monkeys came
To gather nuts, he made his claim:
"All monkeys climbing on this tree
Must bring their gathered nuts to me,
Cracking the same on equal shares;
The meats are mine, the shells are theirs."

"But by what right?" they cried, amazed,
Thinking the ape was surely crazed.
"By this," he answered; "if you'll read
You'll find it is a title deed,
Made in precise and formal shape
And sworn before a fellow ape,
Exactly on the legal plan
Used by that wondrous creature, man,
In London, Tokyo, New York,
Glengarry, Kalamazoo and Cork.

Unless my deed is recognized,
It proves you quite uncivilized."

"But," said one monkey, "you'll agree
It was not you who made this tree."
"Nor," said the ape, serene and bland,
"Does any owner make his land,
Yet all of its hereditaments
Are his and figure in the rents."

The puzzled monkeys sat about;
They could not make the question out.
Plainly, by precedent and law,
The ape's procedure showed no flaw;
And yet, no matter what he said,
The stomach still denied the head.

Up spoke one sprightly monkey then:
"Monkeys are monkeys, men are men;
The ape should try his legal capers
On men who may respect his papers.
We don't know deeds; we do know nuts,
And spite of 'ifs' and 'ands' and 'buts,'
We know who gathers and unmeats 'em,
By monkey practice also eats 'em.
So tell the ape and all his flunkies
No man tricks can be played on monkeys."
Thus, apes still climb to get their food,
Since monkeys' minds are crass and crude,
And monkeys, all so ill-advised,
Still eat their nuts, uncivilized.

From *The Public,* May 24, 1919, p. 546.

33

General Equilibrium: The Price System and Its Operation[1]

It is the basic purpose of this chapter to draw together the discussion of product and resource markets which has been the dominant theme of Part 5. We have analyzed the various categories of individual product and resource markets in some detail. Our present goal is to reemphasize that the many diverse markets of our economy are interwoven into a highly complex *price system*. This price system is responsible for the production of about four-fifths or more of our national product and therefore for the allocation of a comparable proportion of available resources. It is imperative that we grasp how this price system works.

PARTIAL AND GENERAL EQUILIBRIUM

Thus far, our discussion of prices has been compartmentalized; we have examined representative product and resource prices one at a time, in isolation, and apart from any detailed interrelationships each may bear to the other. In the jargon of the economist, we have been concerned with *partial equilibrium analysis*—a study of equilibrium prices and outputs in the many specific markets which are the component *parts* of the price system.

But the economy is not merely a myriad of isolated and unrelated markets. On the con-

[1]As a prologue to the present chapter, it might be helpful for the reader to scan Chapter 5 and the concluding section of Chapter 26, which evaluates competitive pricing.

trary, it is an interlocking network of prices wherein changes in one market are likely to elicit numerous and significant changes in other markets. Hence, our vantage point now shifts from individual markets and prices in isolation to an analysis of the price system as a whole. In technical language, our discussion now shifts to *general equilibrium analysis*—an overall big-picture view of the interrelationships among all the various prices (parts) which make up the price *system.*

We shall attempt to grasp the interrelatedness of various industries and markets through a series of three general equilibrium illustrations. We begin with a verbal model of the automobile industry wherein the many possible repercussions of a change in demand are traced. Next we turn to a hypothetical model of two industries which makes explicit use of the formal analytical tools of microeconomics. At this point we will digress to summarize the implications of the functioning of a purely competitive price system for allocative efficiency and to recall some real-world complications. A third and final model views the interdependence of the various sectors of the economy through what is called input-output analysis. The chapter closes with a discussion of the relevance of general equilibrium analysis for economic understanding.

MARKET INTERRELATIONSHIPS: AUTOMOBILES[2]

Suppose initially that general equilibrium exists—in other words, that all product and resource markets are "at rest." Now assume there occurs an increase in the demand for automobiles. What will be the effects?

The immediate impact is obviously an increase in automobile prices. As automobile manufacturers react by increasing production, an increase will occur in the derived demands

for, and therefore the prices of, all those resources used in the production of automobiles. These interrelationships between product and resource prices are not new to us; they were a key point in our analysis of resource demand (Chapter 30). In any event, the prospect of higher earnings in the automobile industry will attract resources to it. Industries losing labor to the automobile industry may find it necessary to pay higher wages to counteract this loss, and these higher wage costs imply declining profits for the affected industries. Furthermore, if the shift of labor to the automobile industry involves a geographic relocation of workers and their families, we can expect repercussions upon a number of other industries. For example, the residential construction industry—and therefore cement, lumber, and glass suppliers in the area—will experience an increase in the demand for their products. Too, the demand for the services of various skilled and semiskilled construction workers will increase, imposing additional changes on the other labor markets. A similar analysis would apply to nonlabor resources. An increase in the demand for automobiles will increase the demand for steel, and we know that the list of firms and industries using substantial amounts of steel reads like a *Who's Who* of American industry. In brief, innumerable other industries using the same types of land, labor, and capital as the automobile industry will find that their costs have increased. This will give rise to increases in the prices and declines in the sales of the products produced by these industries.

But we must not conclude that the effects of an increase in the demand for automobiles emanate solely from the resource market. An increase in the price of automobiles will affect the demand for, and prices of, other goods. The demand for, and prices of, such products as gasoline, motor oil, and tires will increase in response to the initial increase in the demand for automobiles. The demand for, and prices of, the services provided by bus lines, interurban railways, and taxis will tend to decline.

[2]This illustration follows the excellent example discussed in Francis E. Hyde et al., *A New Prospect of Economics* (Liverpool: Liverpool University Press, 1958), chap. 9.

And these changes in the prices of goods and services will be communicated back into the resource markets relevant to all these industries.

This is still not all: An equally subtle series of price alterations will emanate in the resource market from the initial price increases of resources used by the automobile industry. To illustrate: If the increase in the automobile industry's derived demand for steel significantly increases the price of steel, automobile manufacturers may substitute aluminum where possible for engine and body parts. Many other industries using steel may make similar substitutions. As the prices of resources change, all industries and firms employing these resources will tend to shuffle the quantities of the various resources used to reachieve the least costly combination of resources (Chapter 30). This will affect the demand for, and prices of, these resources.

Noteworthy, too, is the fact that all the changes in resource prices which we have sketched will affect the personal distribution of income. In our example, automobile workers will find themselves moving into higher income brackets as the result of the initial increase in the demand for automobiles. They may well react by demanding more superior, or normal, goods such as butter and steak and less of such inferior goods as oleomargarine and potatoes. Indeed, they may even decide to buy still more automobiles, prompting a whole new series of price interactions such as we have already outlined.

The reader will readily note many loose ends in our discussion. If one had the patience and inclination, these price interrelationships could be pursued almost indefinitely. But our discussion is sufficiently detailed to emphasize our major point. Individual prices are interrelated in a number of both evident and subtle ways. Any initial disturbance such as a change in demand, a change in technology, or a change in resource supply will set off a highly complex economic chain reaction.

GENERAL EQUILIBRIUM: A TWO-INDUSTRY MODEL

Let us now consider a hypothetical illustration which explicitly embodies the formal tools of economic analysis. In Figure 33-1, which is merely a somewhat sophisticated version of Figure 3-4, the discussion focuses upon two product markets, X and Y. And although each industry would actually employ a number of different inputs, it will facilitate our analysis to concentrate only upon the labor market relevant to each industry. It is assumed that industry X uses type A labor and Y uses type B labor.

☐   Behind the Curves

A word or two is in order to remind us of the concepts which underlie the demand and supply curves of both product and resource markets. The product demand curves are downsloping because of *diminishing marginal utility* (Chapter 24). Successive units of a given product yield less and less additional satisfaction or utility to buyers, so that consumers will purchase more of that product only if its price falls. The upsloping product supply curves are based upon the concept of *increasing marginal costs* (Chapter 25). Because extra units of output are more costly, firms must receive a higher price before it will be profitable for them to produce this extra output. The downsloping labor demand curves are based upon the law of diminishing returns or *diminishing marginal physical productivity* (Chapter 30). Beyond some point, the addition of labor or any other variable resource to fixed resources will result in smaller and smaller increases in total output. And as we recall these concepts from earlier chapters, do not overlook the obvious link between the upsloping product supply curve and the downsloping resource demand curve. It is the diminishing marginal productivity of the resource which *causes*

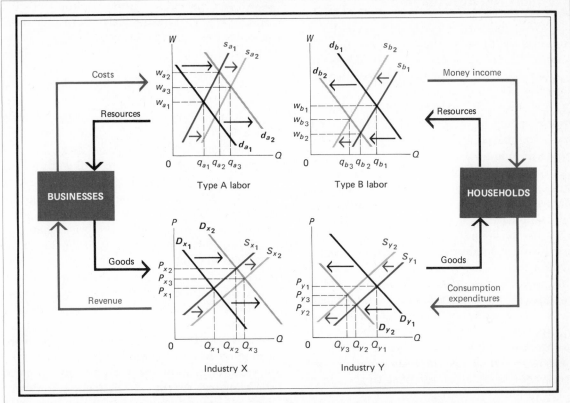

FIGURE 33-1 GENERAL EQUILIBRIUM AND THE INTERACTION OF PRODUCT AND RESOURCE MARKETS

These diagrams show the short-run and long-run adjustments resulting from an assumed increase in the demand for product X and assumed decline in the demand for product Y. Emphasis here is upon product and resource market interactions, and the diagrams therefore conceal many of the less obvious repercussions. For example, the given changes in demand for X and Y will affect the demands for substitute and complementary goods and alter the distribution of income.

marginal costs to increase as output is increased. If each successive unit of labor (hired at a constant wage cost) adds less and less to output, then the cost of *each* successive unit of output must be more and more. Finally, the upsloping labor supply curves reflect the *work-leisure preferences* of individuals. A firm or an industry must pay higher and higher wage rates to obtain larger amounts of labor service.

We assume long-run equilibrium initially, so that P_{x1} and w_{a1} are the equilibrium product price and wage rate for industry X, and P_{y1} and w_{b1} represent the equilibrium price and wage

for industry Y. Firms are making normal profits, and there is no reason for either industry to expand or contract. The two labor markets are similarly "at rest"; there is no incentive for workers to move out of or into either market.

Suppose now that something happens to upset this equilibrium. What will be the character of the resulting adjustments? Specifically, let us say that a change occurs in consumer preferences or tastes so that consumer demand for X increases and consumer demand for Y simultaneously decreases.

□ **Short-run Adjustments**

What short-run adjustments will occur in response to these changes in consumer demand? First of all, production, which was normally profitable in industry X before demand rose from D_{x1} to D_{x2}, now results in economic profits. Firms in industry X, faced with the new higher price of P_{x2}, find it profitable to move to some point further up and to the right on their marginal-cost curves (Figure 26-5). Collectively, these marginal-cost curves are the supply curve S_{x1} for the industry. Thus, in Figure 33-1 existing firms find it profitable to expand output as a group from Q_{x1} to Q_{x2}.

But to expand output, the firms in industry X must acquire more resources, such as type A labor. Remembering that the demand for resources is a *derived demand,* it is no surprise that the expansion of output by firms in X will increase the demand for labor from d_{a1} to, say, d_{a2}. Workers in this labor market are willing to offer more of their services, perhaps by working longer hours or more days per week, moving up s_{a1} in response to the higher wage rate w_{a2}.

An opposite set of short-run adjustments will be experienced in industry Y. Product demand falls to, say, D_{y2}, causing price to fall from P_{y1} to P_{y2}. At this lower price, individual firms incur losses. These firms will react by moving down and to the left on their marginal-cost curves as they seek their loss-minimizing positions. The decline in demand for product Y is reflected back in the resource market. In particular, the demand for type B labor falls from d_{b1} to d_{b2}, causing the equilibrium wage rate to decline to w_{b2}.

□ **Long-run Adjustments**

But we have only traced the first round of market adjustments. At the conclusion of these short-run adjustments, the production of X still yields an economic profit, while losses persist in industry Y. This means that, given sufficient time, new firms will enter industry X, while firms will fall into bankruptcy and fail in industry Y. That is, the presumed changes in consumer demand have made X a prosperous, expanding industry and Y an unprosperous, declining industry.

As new firms enter X, the industry supply curve will shift to the right from S_{x1} to, say, S_{x2}. This increase in supply tends to bring price back down to, say, P_{x3}. Equilibrium output of X has further increased to Q_{x3}. If P_{x3} and Q_{x3} represent a new long-run equilibrium, as we assume is the case, we can note in passing that industry X must be an increasing-cost industry. Why? Because the new long-run equilibrium entails a higher price than the initial equilibrium price P_{x1} (Figure 26-10). If this was a constant-cost industry, the new price would be the same as the old price. It is to be emphasized that, in the new equilibrium position, consumers are getting a larger output of X—which is, of course, precisely what they wanted. In other words, these adjustments are a manifestation of *consumer sovereignty*.

Losses in industry Y force firms to leave the industry. As they do, industry supply will decline from S_{y1} to, say, S_{y2}. This raises price somewhat from P_{y2} to P_{y3}. If we assume industry Y is also an increasing-cost industry, contraction of the industry will lower unit costs. Thus, in the new long-run equilibrium position at P_{y3}, price will be lower than originally, production will be normally profitable once again, and industry size will be stabilized.

These long-run adjustments have counterparts in the resource markets. The supply curve for type B labor, s_{b1}, is drawn on the assumption that other wage rates—for example, the wage rate received by type A labor—are given. The same holds true for the type A labor supply curve, s_{a1}. But our short-run changes in the demand for labor have increased the wage rate for type A labor and reduced the wage rate for type B labor. The stage is set for type B labor to shift from industry Y, where job opportunities and wage rates have been declining, to industry X, where employment has been expanding and wage rates have been increasing. Thus we would expect the supply of type A labor to increase from s_{a1} to, say, s_{a2} and the supply of type B labor to fall from s_{b1} to, say, s_{b2}. As a result, wage rates for type A labor fall somewhat from w_{a2} to w_{a3}. And for type B labor, wage rates tend to go back up from w_{b2} to, say, w_{b3}.

But note several related points about these labor market adjustments. First, we are assuming that type B labor can become qualified as type A labor without too much difficulty and retraining. We know from Chapter 18 that occupational shifts may actually be complicated and costly to achieve. A second and closely related point is that supply shifts might take a substantial period of time. As suggested, type B workers may in fact require additional education, job retraining, and geographic relocation before becoming type A workers. Finally, because of various immobilities (Chapter 31), we would not expect the supply curve shifts to be sufficiently great to restore the wage rates of the original equilibrium. The new equilibrium wage rate will be w_{a3} (higher than w_{a1}) for type A labor and w_{b3} (lower than w_{b1}) for type B labor. Indeed, these long-run wage adjustments are consistent with, and a factor in, the assumed increasing-cost character of industries X and Y.

□ **Further Adjustments**

But this is only the beginning of the repercussions which stem from our original change in the structure of consumer demand. There are innumerable, more subtle adjustments which we might take into account.

Other Industries Consider now a third industry—call it industry Z. Will the initial increase in the price of X have any impact upon industry Z? It might! Recall that one of the determinants of the demand for Z are the prices of related goods, and X just might be "related" to Z. But any shift in the demand for Z which stems from the increase in the price of X depends on precisely how products X and Z are related. Recall (Chapter 4) that any two products might be *substitutes* (butter and oleo), *complements* (gas and oil), or substantially *independent* (raisins and wristwatches). If X and Z are independent, then a rise in the price of X will have no significant effect on the demand for Z. But if X and Z are substitutes, the rise in the price of X will increase the demand for Z. Therefore, a series of adjustments will be precipitated in the product and resource markets for Z similar to those just sketched for X. And if X and Z are complements, the higher price for X will lower the demand for Z. This would precipitate adjustments in Z like those already traced for industry Y.

Other Resources The initial changes in the demands for type A and type B labor may have an impact upon other resource markets. Suppose that technology in industry X is such that labor and capital must be used in virtually fixed proportions, for example, one machine is needed for every two workers. This means that the expansion in the employment of type A labor will stimulate the demand for relevant kinds of capital goods.

Income Distribution It is also quite evident that our short-run and long-run adjustments will alter the distribution of income. Workers and entrepreneurs associated with industry X will receive higher incomes; those in industry Y, lower incomes. It is realistic to assume some differences in tastes which will be transformed into further changes in the structure of consumer demand. These new changes in demand will trigger new rounds of short-run and long-run adjustments.

We could go on, but the basic point is clear. The adjustments stemming from our initial changes in demand are much more complex and go far beyond the simple supply and demand shifts portrayed in Figure 33-1.

ECONOMIC WELFARE AND THE PRICE SYSTEM

Now that we have some appreciation of the mechanics of the price system and the many complex market interrelationships it implies, we must inquire once again as to the efficiency of the system. How effectively does the price system function?

Although there is no unequivocal answer to this question, we can certainly say some things on behalf of a competitive price system. The fundamental argument for it is that *its operation is conducive to an efficient allocation of resources.* More precisely, *given the distribution of income among consumers, purely competitive product and resource markets tend to give rise to the production of that collection of goods and services which maximizes the satisfactions of consumers.* Earlier discussion, particularly in Chapters 5 and 26, provided the analytical grounding for this claim of allocative efficiency. The following three technical points simply suggest that the price system provides economically desirable answers to the questions: What should the economy produce? How should that output be produced? And for whom should it be produced?

1 Self-interest drives purely competitive firms to produce that output at which price equals marginal cost. Remember that the price of a product reflects its value or worth to society, while marginal cost measures the value of the resources needed in its production. This means that additional units of any product are produced as long as they are valued by society more highly than are the alternative products which the needed resources could otherwise have produced. In other words, the "right" or most desirable output of each commodity—and therefore the best mixture of goods and services—gets produced.

2 Pure competition also results in the production of each good at minimum average cost (Figure 26-11). In terms of the resource market, competition forces producers to use the least costly combination of resources or, more specifically, that combination wherein the last dollar spent on each resource entails the same marginal physical product (Chapter 30).[3]

3 Not only does competition cause the right collection of goods and services to be produced and production to be at least cost, but free choice by consumers in competitive markets will result in the distribution of this output so as to maximize consumer satisfactions. *Given his income and his tastes,* each consumer will purchase that collection of goods and services which is most satisfying to him. Technically speaking, he will buy various products in such amounts that the last dollar spent on each item yields equal amounts of extra satisfaction or marginal utility.[4]

And finally, remember that these desirable consequences follow from the free decisions of participants made in their own self-interest. Businessmen are motivated in their decision making to maximize profits; resource suppliers, to increase their incomes; consumers, to maximize their satisfactions. Quite miraculously, the overall outcome of these freely rendered decisions, once coordinated and synchronized by the price system, is in the public interest. Scarce resources are apparently used with maximum efficiency.

THE REAL WORLD AND IMPERFECT COMPETITION

Having discussed the adjustments of a purely competitive price system in moving toward long-run equilibrium and the consequences of

---

[3] If any two resources—labor and capital—are being employed, then costs will be minimized when they are used in such amounts that

$$\frac{\text{MPP of labor}}{\text{price of labor}} = \frac{\text{MPP of capital}}{\text{price of capital}}$$

[4] If the consumer is buying just two products, X and Y, he will maximize his utility by purchasing them in such quantities that

$$\frac{\text{MU of product X}}{\text{price of X}} = \frac{\text{MU of product Y}}{\text{price of Y}}$$

these adjustments for allocative efficiency, we must now understand that the competitive price system is clearly a rough approximation of reality. The competitive model is essentially a simplified way of envisioning the operation of a market economy; it does not purport to be a description of reality.

One basic way in which the real world differs from our model is that, in actuality, most product and resource markets are imperfectly competitive; they deviate in varying degrees from the purely competitive model. As a result, resources may well be allocated less efficiently than under pure competition. Imperfectly competitive producers find it in their private interest as profit seekers to produce short of the price-equals-marginal-cost output, and an underallocation of resources to the production of such goods will occur. The private interest of the imperfectly competitive firm is at odds with society's interest in allocative efficiency. Similarly, monopsony (Figure 31-4) or monopoly (Figure 31-7) can cause prices in the resource market to vary from the competitive level and impair allocative efficiency.

Imperfect competition also means that adjustments of the type described in our general equilibrium models will be more sluggish and less complete. This is not to say the price system won't make generally appropriate adjustments. It will. But under imperfect competition, these adjustments will be only rough approximations of those described, for example, in our two-industry model. In general, most economists are willing to conclude that with imperfect competition, resource allocation is less efficient and the price system less responsive to changes in tastes, technology, or resource availability than if pure competition prevailed. On the other hand, the possibility of more rapid technological progress and the alleged advantages stemming from greater product variety under imperfectly competitive conditions must be regarded as potential offsets to diminished allocative efficiency (Chapter 28).

OUTPUT, INCOME, AND ETHICS

Even if the purely competitive model of the price system were an accurate portrayal of the real world, we would nevertheless be justified in questioning its capacity to allocate resources efficiently. This is so for at least two reasons.

□   Allocative Activities of Government

In the first place, we know that the production of certain products may entail benefits and costs which are external to the demand and supply curves of the market. If substantial *spillover benefits* are involved in the production or consumption of some good or service (for example, education), the market will understate the demand for such goods, and resources will be underallocated to their production. Conversely, if the production or consumption of some good entails significant *spillover costs* (for example, air pollution), the market supply curve will understate costs, and resources will be overallocated to that commodity's production. The imposition of special excise taxes (Chapters 6 and 23) is one of several ways of correcting for this overallocation of resources which accompanies spillover costs. Recall that special public subsidies can be useful in correcting the underallocation of resources which characterizes the production of goods whose spillover benefits are substantial. Furthermore, the price system would ignore or grossly neglect the production of such *social goods* as national defense, streets and highways, flood control, courthouses, and so forth.

□   Government and Distributive Justice

A most perplexing question—to which economists as social scientists do not know the answer—now looms before us. The question is this: What is the "best" or optimal distribution of income?

Let us back up a moment and reexamine

our claim that, aside from social goods and instances of substantial spillover benefits and costs, a competitive price system will negotiate that allocation of resources which maximizes consumer satisfaction. This claim is predicated upon a "given" or "assumed" distribution of income. Money income is presumably distributed among consumers in a certain way, and on the basis of their incomes, each consumer makes his wants effective in the various markets by his expenditures for different goods. This is what we rather quaintly termed "dollar voting" in Chapter 5. In any event, these consumer decisions, based upon money income, are reflected in the product demand curves of our general equilibrium models. Given the structure of demand which results from this distribution of income, we have seen that it is a primary virtue of the price system that it brings about the allocation of resources and resulting product-mix which best fulfills the wants of consumers.

This is all well and good. But now an awkward question arises. *If* we were now to suppose, or bring about, a *different* distribution of money income so as to get a *different* structure of consumer demand, would not the competitive price system negotiate a new allocation of resources and a new product-mix which would result in the maximum satisfaction of this new pattern of consumer demand? The answer is: Yes, this is exactly what the price system would do! This answer leads inevitably to a further question: Which of these two allocations of resources—the one which is "most efficient" for the first income distribution or the one which is "most efficient" for the second income distribution—is truly optimal or best?

Economists have been unable to provide a satisfactory answer because they cannot measure and compare the ability of various individuals to derive satisfaction or utility from money income. If every individual were precisely identical in his capacity to enjoy income, economists would say that income should be distributed equally and that the allocation of resources which is most efficient in response to

that distribution of income would result in the greatest possible level of consumer satisfaction. But people differ by virtue of their inherited physical and mental characteristics, not to mention their education, training, environment, experiences, and so forth. And we cannot meaningfully gauge the extent to which they are different; the capacity to derive satisfaction or utility is a highly subjective, psychological thing, elusive of measurement. So how can we determine whether some distribution of income, other than the existing one, is superior or inferior? In short, the whole question of what is the optimum distribution of income remains an ethical one. We will return to this question of distributive justice in Chapter 37 and discuss in some detail the ways in which government has altered the distribution of income from that which the unmodified price system would have provided. Indeed, all the chapters of Part 6 bear upon the question of income distribution.

■

GENERAL EQUILIBRIUM: INPUT-OUTPUT ANALYSIS

The relatively simple general equilibrium models thus far explored contain important insights into the operation and social implications of the price system. They also serve the major purpose of emphasizing the interrelatedness of the many decision makers who comprise the economy. Further appreciation of the intricate interrelationships between the various sectors or industries of the economy can be gained through an input-output table.

☐ Input-Output Table

Table 33-1 is a very much simplified hypothetical input-output table for an economy.[5] Listed down the left side of the table are the

[5] Wassily W. Leontieff is largely responsible for input-output analysis. See his simplified discussion of "Input-Output Economics," *Scientific American*, October 1951, pp. 15–21. Table 33-1 and portions of the accompanying

Table 33-1 A SIMPLIFIED INPUT-OUTPUT TABLE (*hypothetical data*)

Producing sectors	Consuming or using sectors					
	(1) Metal	(2) Machinery	(3) Fuel	(4) Agriculture	(5) Households (labor)	(6) Total output
(1) Metal	10	65	10	5	10	100
(2) Machinery	40	25	35	75	25	200
(3) Fuel	15	5	5	5	20	50
(4) Agriculture	15	10	50	50	525	650
(5) Labor (households)	100	200	100	550	50	1000

five producing sectors (industries) of the economy. Column 6 shows the total output associated with each of the five sectors; the metal sector produces 100 units, the machine sector 200 units, and so on. These same five sectors are also the consuming sectors of the economy and are shown in this capacity across the top of the table. Looking across each of the horizontal rows of figures, we can see how the total output of each sector is disposed of, or consumed, among the five sectors. For example, of the 200 units of output of the machinery sector, 40 units go to the metal sector, 25 to the machinery sector itself (because it takes machines to produce machines!), and 35, 75, and 25 units go to the fuel, agriculture, and household sectors, respectively, thereby exhausting the units produced.

Following through on this disposition-of-output procedure for all five sectors, we find that each vertical column must and does show the units of output of each producing sector which are consumed as inputs by the five sectors. For example, we find in column 2 that to produce 200 units of machinery, inputs of 65 units of metal, 25 of machinery, 5 of fuel, 10 of agricultural products, and 200 of labor are required. In this way, the table vividly reveals the highly interdependent character of the

various sectors or industries. Any given industry or sector employs the outputs of other sectors—and indeed, some of its own output—as its inputs! And the outputs of that given sector are similarly the inputs of the other sectors. To cite a real-world example: While outputs of steel are inputs in the production of railroad cars, these railroad cars are, in turn, used to transport both finished steel and the various inputs—coke, pig iron, and so forth—which are necessary to the production of steel.

□ **Interdependencies**

The interdependence of the economy's sectors or industries can be further demonstrated by tracing the repercussions of an assumed change in the output of some commodity.

Consider, for example, the repercussions of a 20-unit (10 percent) increase in machinery production. This means that a 10 percent increase in the production of all the outputs which are used as inputs in the production of machinery is required.[6] These inputs, as we know, are listed in column 2 of the table. Applying the 10 percent figure, we find that 6.5 additional units (outputs) of metal, 0.5 unit of fuel, 1 unit of agricultural products, 20 units of

---

discussion are from Francis M. Boddy, "Soviet Economic Growth," in Robert T. Holt and John E. Turner (eds.), *Soviet Union: Paradox and Change* (New York: Holt, Rinehart and Winston, Inc., 1962), pp. 77–79, with permission of the publisher.

[6]We invoke here one of the simplifying assumptions underlying the input-output table, namely, that production occurs under conditions of constant returns to scale (see Chapter 25).

labor, and 2.5 units of machinery will be needed to produce another 20 units of machinery.

But this is just the beginning: obviously, a myriad of further adjustments are also required. Because each sector which supplies inputs to the machinery sector must expand its output, these supplying sectors in turn will require more inputs from other sectors. Example: The additional 6.5 units of metal needed as inputs to produce the extra 20 units of machinery will in turn call for an appropriate—6.5 percent, in this case—increase in the production of all the inputs shown in column 1 to be needed in producing metal. The same reasoning, of course, is applicable to the fuel, agriculture, and labor sectors. That is, the 0.5-unit increase in fuel production required in producing the extra 20 units of machinery will call for an appropriate (1 percent) increase in the production of all the inputs listed in column 3, and similarly for the agricultural and labor sectors. Example: We noted earlier that the production of 20 more units of machinery output requires as inputs the production of 2.5 units of machinery. This 2.5-unit increase will require "second-round" increases (of 1.25 percent in this case) in the inputs of all the resources shown in column 2 in the same general fashion as did the initial 20-unit increase in machinery output.

The reader will clearly recognize that the chain reaction is by no means at an end. All the repercussions cited in these examples call for still further adjustments similar to those already described. The crucial point, of course, is that, because of the high degree of interrelatedness among the sectors of the economy, a change in the figure in any one "cell" or "box" of the input-output table will precipitate an almost endless series of adjustments in other figures. In our illustration, the expansion of production in one sector has nearly innumerable repercussions which reach into virtually every nook and cranny of the economy.

GENERAL EQUILIBRIUM AND ECONOMIC UNDERSTANDING

In what respects, if any, is a knowledge of general equilibrium analysis important? Is an understanding of the interrelationships of prices or sectors useful? Up to a point, at least, an understanding of these interrelationships is an indispensable tool in evaluating the overall operation of the economy, in understanding specific economic problems, and in formulating policies. A failure to recognize price and sector interrelationships is an important source of misunderstanding and faulty reasoning about major economic problems. Furthermore, input-output analysis lends itself to an abundance of practical applications.

☐   Some Illustrations

Some examples will clarify these points. One might expect that the effect of a general or widespread wage cut is to reduce the costs of specific firms. And, other things being equal, lower costs will cause a firm to lower prices, increase production, and hire more workers. But general equilibrium analysis suggests that this seemingly obvious conclusion is of doubtful validity. Lower wages mean lower incomes, which are communicated into the product market as general declines in the demand for, and prices of, products. These price declines are then projected back into the resource market once again as declines in resource demand. And these declines in resource demand will mean unemployment. The immediate impact of wage cuts (more employment) which partial equilibrium analysis suggests may be swallowed up by the secondary effects (less employment), which are discernible only by an understanding of general equilibrium analysis.

Another example: Many people favor protective tariffs levied on, say, Japanese or German toys, because the immediate and obvious effect is to increase the price of foreign toys and therefore increase the demand for American-made toys. The result is that output and employment rise in the American toy industry. But this ignores the fact that incomes in Japan and Germany will decline as a result of their inability to sell toys in the United States. And with smaller incomes they will be less able to buy from American industries exporting machine tools, chemicals, grains, and so forth. The obvious increase in employment in the protected industry may well be offset, wholly or in part, by the indirect, subtle declines in employment in American export industries. As a matter of fact, apart from any decline in domestic employment stemming from tariff-induced declines in exports, general equilibrium analysis reminds us that the extra resources which are shifted into the expanding toy industry must come from other industries. That is, in a full-employment economy the tariff-inspired expansion of the toy industry will entail a contraction in the production of other goods.

A final illustration: It would not be legitimate to consider the impact of a general sales tax upon the production of one industry in isolation, thereby ignoring its simultaneous effects upon related products. In analyzing the effects of the imposition of a sales tax upon the butter industry, one must not ignore the fact that oleomargarine will also be subject to the same tax.

□ **Forecasting and Planning**

Although our interest in input-output analysis has centered upon the pedagogical goal of emphasizing that "everything depends upon everything else" in the economy, it should be noted that input-output analysis has resulted in empirical measurement of the various interactions between sectors of the economy, and these measurements have proved of considerable value as an instrument of economic forecasting and planning. Assume for the moment a much more detailed input-output table containing 50 or even 500 individual sectors with each box filled with accurate em-

pirical data. Now, for example, if the government should decide to undertake the production of fifty new supersonic bombers, the impact of this decision upon affected sectors could be quite accurately predicted; we can forecast quantitatively "what it will take" in terms of the outputs of all the many affected industries to fulfill this goal. Input-output analysis also has great relevance for the less developed nations, virtually all of which seek growth through some form of planning (Chapter 21) and for more advanced centrally planned systems, such as the Soviet Union (Chapter 45). By revealing the quantitative interrelationships among various sectors of the economy, input-output analysis allows the planners to determine how realistic—how feasible—planned production targets actually are. By tracing the repercussions of, say, a planned increase in steel production of 10 percent, the Central Planning Board of the U.S.S.R. can determine what outputs of coal, iron ore, transportation, manpower, relevant capital equipment, and all other inputs used in the production of steel will be needed to fulfill this target. In this way, potential bottlenecks to the realization of this goal (or others) may be uncovered; for example, transportation problems may be revealed, or it may be found that the additional plant capacity required conflicts severely with the planned production of housing or the planned expansion of the chemicals industry. Appropriate adjustments may therefore be made in the production targets for steel or other products to make the plan more realistic and more consistent with the constraints imposed by technology and overall scarcities of economic resources.

General equilibrium analysis provides a broader perspective for analyzing the effects of given economic disturbances or policies than does partial equilibrium analysis. Partial equilibrium analysis shows merely "the big splash" of an initial disturbance; general equilibrium analysis traces the waves and ripples emanating from the big splash. In some instances the waves and ripples are relatively unimportant; in others they may prove to be a tidal wave which completely changes conclusions one would draw from the big splash viewed in isolation. As we noted in Chapter 1, a basic task of the economist is that of ascer- taining which waves and ripples are important to the analysis of a given question and which can be safely ignored. In any event, a grasp of the general equilibrium point of view is essential in understanding and evaluating our economy.

Summary

1 General equilibrium analysis is concerned with the operation of the entire price system and the interrelationships among different markets and prices. These interrelationships are important in that they might modify or negate the immediate effects of economic disturbances or policies which partial equilibrium analysis reveals.

2 A purely competitive price system would tend to allocate resources so as to provide the maximum satisfaction of consumer wants.

3 The fact that imperfect competition generally exists in both product and resource markets detracts from the price system's capacity to allocate resources efficiently.

4 Efficient resource allocation would depend on an active role for government even if the price system were purely competitive. The price system would under- produce goods which entail substantial spillover benefits and overproduce those which embody substantial spillover costs. Also, the price system would tend to ignore the production of social goods.

5 Because of the inability to measure and compare the capacity of various individuals to derive satisfaction from income, economists are unable to define the optimum distribution of income.

6 The input-output table provides a kind of general equilibrium analysis which reveals the overall fabric of the economy by focusing upon the interdependencies that exist among the various sectors or industries which it comprises. Input-output analysis has practical applications to economic forecasting and planning.

Questions and Study Suggestions

1 Key terms and concepts to remember: partial equilibrium analysis; general equilibrium analysis; input-output analysis.

2 Compare partial and general equilibrium analysis. In what respect is each useful?

3 Trace through the price system the economic effect of: *a.* the development of a man-made fiber which never wears out, fades, or stains; *b.* a permanent increase in the demand for leather; *c.* a sharp decline in the size of the labor force; *d.* the development of a new production technique which cuts the cost of color television by 50 percent; *e.* the imposition of a 20 percent excise tax on shoes; *f.* the discovery of an effective vaccine for the common cold.

4 Explain the following statements:

a. "Allocative efficiency does not mean distributive justice."

b. "There is an 'efficient' or 'optimal' allocation of resources for every conceivable distribution of money income."

5 What is an input-output table? Using Table 33-1, trace some of the repercussions of a 5-unit (10 percent) increase in fuel production. What insights might input-output analysis provide as to the operation of a capitalistic system? How might input-output analysis be used as a "mechanism of coordination" in a centrally planned system?

Selected References

Brennan, Michael J.: *Theory of Economic Statics,* 2d ed. (Englewood Cliffs, N.J.: Prentice-Hall, Inc., 1970), chap. 25.

Köhler, Heinz: *Welfare and Planning* (New York: John Wiley & Sons, Inc., 1966), particularly chaps. 1–5.

Miernyk, William H.: *The Elements of Input-Output Analysis* (New York: Random House, Inc., 1965).

Phelps-Brown, E. H.: *The Framework of the Pricing System* (London: Chapman & Hall, Ltd., 1936).

Ryan, W. J. L.: *Price Theory* (New York: St. Martin's Press, Inc., 1958), chap. 8.

Stigler, George J.: *The Theory of Price,* rev. ed. (New York: The Macmillan Company, 1952), chap. 16.

Last Word
The English Cotton Famine

The relevance of general equilibrium analysis is illustrated by the myriad effects of the marked decline of American cotton exports to England during the Civil War.

The Civil War led to a near suspension of English imports of American cotton, which in 1860 had accounted to about four-fifths of the English supply. The price of cotton at Liverpool rose from 8 pence per pound in June of 1860 to a peak of 31½ pence in July of 1864. The effects of this cotton famine provide some notion of the interrelationships of prices: the famine was severe (imports of cotton fell by three-fifths from 1861 to 1862) and the cotton industry was very large (employing about 500,000 people in a total labor force of 9 million), so wide effects are noticeable.

The famine led to a great decrease in the demand for cotton fabrication, and hence in the demand for the services of cotton mills and their laborers. The margin between the prices of raw cotton and cloth (taking 39-inch shirtings as an example) declined from 7 pence a pound in 1860, almost equal to the cost of the raw cotton, to 1 or 2 pence in 1862 and 1863. Wage (piece) rates fell an unknown amount, and workers' earnings fell much more when they were forced to work with the inferior Surat cotton.

Of course a large expansion took place in rival fabrics. The production of flax quadrupled between 1861 and 1864 in Ireland, and yarn imports rose greatly; even so, prices of linen goods rose about 60 per cent between 1862 and 1864. Similarly, the wool industry experienced a great boom: imports of wool rose by a third during the period, and raw wool prices rose more than 40 per cent, but the Yorkshire industry was overtaxed and processing margins increased by half. Some migration of cotton workers and entrepreneurs to Yorkshire, and of weaving of woolens to Lancashire, helped the latter area.

The unemployment in Lancashire caused great distress. The big decrease in consumer expenditures in the area hit shopkeepers hard, and landlords even harder: families doubled up, marriages fell by more than a third, and poor rates increased. By 1863 about one-fourth of the families requiring public assistance were not directly connected with the textile industry.

Of course the effects reached to industries for which cotton textiles was an important customer. The textile machinery industry had a bad slump until 1864, and the warehouses of the region suffered also. The Lancashire and Yorkshire Railway, unlike other English roads, had a decline in both freight and passenger traffic in 1862 and 1863.

We could cast our net farther to uncover more relationships of substitution and complementarity and buyer and seller, and subject only to the limitations of imagination and energy, we shall continue to find them. In Birmingham, to give only one example, the button and needle industries had to discharge many workers, but the edged-tool industry expanded greatly to provide tools for new cotton plantings in India and Egypt.

Perhaps this brief and highly incomplete sketch is sufficient to illustrate the basis for the economist's faith, for such it is, in the general interdependence of economic phenomena. It does not seem bold to conjecture that everyone in England was somehow affected by the cotton famine: as a consumer, in the price of clothing; as a laborer, in the altered directions of consumer spending; in the effects on transport, banking, and commerce; as a capitalist, in the return on investments in textiles and other industries.

PART SIX

CURRENT ECONOMIC PROBLEMS

The Monopoly Problem: The Social Control of Industry

Previous chapters have made these two contrasting points:

1 Many important American industries are characterized by considerable monopoly power. Some of these industries were shown in Table 29-1.

2 One of the basic economic functions of government is to preserve competition as a key mechanism of control in the economy (Chapter 6).

It is the overall goal of the present chapter to describe and evaluate governmental policies toward business monopolies. More specifically, the objectives of this chapter are threefold:

1 To examine the case for, and then the case against, business monopolies

2 To understand and appraise government policies toward business monopolies

3 To explore several possible future public policy alternatives

BIG BUSINESS AND MONOPOLY

Before considering the pros and cons of business monopoly, we must pause to define our terminology. In Chapters 22 and 27 we developed and applied a very strict definition of monopoly. A *pure,* or *absolute,* monopoly, we said, is a one-firm industry—a situation in which a unique product is produced entirely by one firm, entry to the industry being blocked by certain insurmountable barriers. When a single firm controls an entire market, pure monopoly exists.

In the present chapter we shall find it convenient to use the term "monopoly" in a broader, generic sense. *Monopoly exists whenever a small number of firms controls all, or a large portion of, the output of a major industry.* This definition, which comes closer to the way the man in the street understands monopoly, includes a large number of industries which we have heretofore designated under the category of oligopoly.

What is the difference between monopoly (as we have just defined it) and big business? The term "big business" may be defined in terms either of a firm's share of the total market for its product or of some absolute measure, such as the volume of its assets, sales, or profits, the number of workers employed, or the number of stockholders. A firm can obviously be large *in relation to* the size of the total market but small in an *absolute* sense. The Weeping Water General Store may almost completely dominate the local market for a good many products, yet be exceedingly small by any meaningful absolute standard. Conversely, a firm might be very large in the absolute sense but small in relation to the total market. For example, American Motors is large by most absolute standards one can employ. In 1976 its net sales revenue was $2,315,470,000, and some 31,000 employees were on its payroll. Yet American Motors sells only about 3 percent of all automobiles in the United States. Insofar as the automobile industry is concerned, American Motors is a small producer. However, *in a good many instances, absolute and relative bigness go hand in hand.* A firm which is large in absolute terms very frequently controls a significant portion of the market for its product. Thus, although "big business" and "monopoly" are not necessarily synonymous, they frequently do go together.

The present chapter is concerned with the type of situation in which absolute and relative bigness are both present. In using the term "business monopoly" in this chapter, we refer to those industries in which firms are large in absolute terms *and* in relation to the total market. Examples are the electrical equipment industry, where General Electric and Westinghouse, large by any absolute standard, dominate the market; the automobile industry, where General Motors, Ford, and Chrysler are similarly situated; the chemical industry, dominated by du Pont, Union Carbide, and Allied Chemical; the aluminum industry, where three industrial giants—Alcoa, Reynolds, and Kaiser—reign supreme; and the cigarette industry, where the four giant firms of Reynolds, Liggett and Myers, American Tobacco, and Lorillard currently command the lion's share of this large market.[1]

■───────────────────────────

MONOPOLY: GOOD OR EVIL?

It is not at all clear whether business monopolies are, on balance, advantageous or disadvantageous to the functioning of American capitalism. Note the following two statements—one bitterly opposed to monopoly in any form or context, and the other viewing business monopoly as an integral part of modern American capitalism. The first view:[2]

> Monopoly power must be abused. It has no use save abuse. . . . There must be an outright dismantling of our gigantic corporations and persistent prosecution of producers who organize, by whatever methods, for price maintenance or output limitation.

> . . . Legislation must prohibit, and administration effectively prevent, the acquisition by any private firm, or group of firms, of substantial monopoly power.

The second view:[3]

---

[1]See George J. Stigler, "The Case against Bigness in Business," *Fortune,* May 1952, p. 123.

[2]Henry C. Simons, *Economic Policy for a Free Society* (Chicago: The University of Chicago Press, 1948), pp. 129, 158.

[3]A. D. H. Kaplan, *Big Enterprise in a Competitive System* (Washington: The Brookings Institution, 1954), p. 248.

In our economy big business undertakes the major role of coordinating individual efforts and resources into collective achievement. This is a function that must be undertaken under modern technology, whether by private enterprise or by the state. In the United States it has been possible so to mix dispersion with centralization that the major job can be left to private competition, under government regulation. Big business has not merely been kept effectively subject to a competitive system; on the whole it has also made an essential contribution to its scope, vitality, and effectiveness.

These are not propaganda blasts sponsored by antimonopoly and promonopoly pressure groups. Rather, they are the well-considered arguments of respected scholars. These two assertions accurately show that there is ample room for serious disagreement as to the desirability of business monopolies in American capitalism. Extensive debate on this issue has precipitated a series of rather well-defined arguments on both sides. Our immediate goal is to outline these divergent and contradictory views.

■───────────────────

THE CASE FOR MONOPOLY

Business monopoly is not without substantial defenses. A series of plausible arguments with which we are only partially familiar has been evolved to explain and justify the existence of the giant business enterprises which currently dominate various markets.

□ "Workable Competition"

It is alleged, first of all, that, although the stringent conditions of pure competition as set forth in Chapter 26 are rarely if ever met, the presence of *workable competition* effectively regulates the operations of big businesses. It is argued that there exist certain types of competition, more subtle than the mere presence of a large number of rival producers, which in fact make so-called monopolistic industries "workably competitive." This contention suggests that any judgment of the competitiveness of an industry which rests solely on the number of existing producers is incomplete and misleading because it overlooks other important dimensions of competition.

What are some of these more subtle dimensions of competition?

1 Pervasive Competition All products are in competition for the dollars of consumers. A down payment on a house is often a good substitute for a new automobile. Two or three LP records, on the one hand, compete with a new pair of blue jeans, on the other. Refrigerators compete with washing machines, television sets, and air conditioners.

2 Interproduct Competition The contention that competition is pervasive shades into the notion of interproduct competition. Although only a small number of firms may produce certain specific products, these apparent monopolists may in fact face severe competition from firms producing distinct but highly substitutable products. The fact that a handful of firms are responsible for the nation's output of aluminum belies the competition which aluminum faces in specific markets from steel, copper, wood, plastics, and other products. These first two aspects of workable competition both suggest that the demand for the products of a monopolistic industry may be considerably more elastic than the small number of firms in that specific industry would seem to imply.

3 Innovative Competition Technological advance operates over time so as to circumscribe and undermine existing monopoly positions. Innovation, in particular the development of new products, is a force which persistently destroys the market power of individual firms, making monopoly power a precarious and transitory phenomenon. Witness the devastating competition which hand calculators have provided the manufacturers of slide rules in recent years. Similarly, digital watches pose a serious threat to the markets held by conventional watchmakers.

4 Countervailing Power Competition in the form of countervailing power must not be ignored (Chapter 29). If an original position of monopoly power induces the growth of monopoly power on the opposite side of the market, the consequent across-the-market competition can provide effective checks, or restraints, on both the original and the countervailing power position. Countervailing power can effectively prevent abuses of monopoly power in those very markets in which traditional same-side-of-the-market competition is weak.

5 Potential Competition It is argued that *potential* competition and the fear of censure can regulate the behavior of monopolists almost as effectively as does the actual presence of numerous rivals. The possibility that new rival firms will be formed or that other industrial giants will branch out works against the monopolist's exploiting his market power. The fear of public censure, the embarrassment of an antitrust suit, or the possibility of government regulation may also contribute to the monopolist's disinclination to exert his monopoly power.

Economists who emphasize the importance of workable competition feel that firms and industries should be judged not on the basis of their market structure but rather in terms of their performance. Such characteristics as the number of firms in the industry and the importance of barriers to entry should be supplanted by criteria of performance—price, efficiency of production, and rate of technological advance—in gauging the social desirability of an industry or a specific firm. Defenders of business monopoly contend that many industries which fall short of the large-numbers no-

barriers criteria nevertheless perform very well, efficiently producing a quality product at a low price.

☐ **Technological Determinism: A New Industrial State?**

The second major defense of monopoly centers upon technology as an aspect of efficient industry performance. Two related arguments are made.

Mass-production Economies Existing mass-production economies can be realized only by big businesses. Where existing technology is highly advanced, only large producers—firms which are large both absolutely and in relation to the market—can realize low unit costs and therefore sell to consumers at relatively low prices. In short, the traditional antimonopoly contention that monopoly means less output, higher prices, and an inefficient allocation of resource assumes that cost economies would be equally available to firms whether the industry's structure was highly competitive or quite monopolistic. In fact, this may not be the case; economies of scale may be accessible only if competition is absent.

Technological Advance: Galbraith's Thesis It is also contended that monopolistic industries—in particular, three- and four-firm oligopolies—are conducive to a high rate of technological progress. John Kenneth Galbraith, for example, has argued that oligopolistic firms have both the financial resources and the incentives to undertake technological research.[4]

The modern industry of a few large firms [is] an excellent instrument for inducing technical change. It is admirably equipped for financing technical development. Its organization provides strong incentives for undertaking devel-

[4]John Kenneth Galbraith, *American Capitalism,* rev. ed. (Boston: Houghton Mifflin Company, 1956), pp. 86–88.

opment and for putting it into use. . . . In the modern industry shared by a few large firms, size and the rewards accruing to market power combine to insure that resources for research and technical development will be available. The power that enables the firm to have some influence on prices insures that the resulting gains will not be passed on to the public by imitators (who have stood none of the costs of development) before the outlay for development can be recouped. In this way market power protects the incentive to technical development.

Galbraith has extended this theme in his well-known book *The New Industrial State*.[5] He argues that "technological imperatives" have brought the corporate giant to a dominant role in the American economy. Production requires not only huge quantities of capital, but also a highly sophisticated technology, and this means that firms must be large to be efficient. Furthermore, the successful functioning of giant enterprises presumes detailed planning, not only of innovations and new productive processes, but also of the manipulation of consumer demand. According to Galbraith, the "technostructure"—the technicians and professional managers of the corporation—carry out these planning and decision-making functions.

A primary goal of the modern "mature" corporation is security and stability—the avoidance of risk. In seeking security the giant corporation attempts to insulate itself from the vagaries of free markets. Thus the corporation integrates vertically; that is, it creates, controls, or merges with materials suppliers. It engages in the internal financing of capital expansion to eliminate its dependence upon the capital market. On the demand side, the corporation controls its customers through ad-

vertising and techniques of salesmanship, thereby supplanting "consumer sovereignty" with "producer sovereignty." In these ways the corporation dominates both suppliers and consumers, thereby signaling the demise of the free-market system as traditionally conceived. Furthermore, the corporate giant, by virtue of its size and crucial role in production, has achieved autonomy from government control. In fact, Galbraith feels that big business and government are in the process of establishing a tacit alliance to manage the economy. On the one hand, government plans and undertakes various functions—the stabilization of aggregate demand, the financing of research and development, the provision of highly educated manpower—which the technostructure and the corporate giants require for security and growth. On the other hand, the industrial giants assume responsibility for the planning of much of society's production. Galbraith feels that these trends are a "part of the broad sweep of economic development"; technological advance makes these developments necessary and immutable if productive efficiency is to be realized.

□   **Other Defenses: Stability and Responsibility**

Although the primary defenses of monopoly cluster around the arguments of workable competition and technological determinism, two other points merit brief mention.

Macro Stability   Business monopolies are alleged to exert a stabilizing influence upon the economy because of both their investment and their pricing policies. Concerning investment policies, it is argued that the absolute and the relative size of business monopolies permit them to gear their investment spending to long-run business prospects rather than to the short-term cyclical upswings and downswings which are so influential in determining the investment outlays of smaller, competitive

---

[5]John Kenneth Galbraith, *The New Industrial State* (Boston: Houghton Mifflin Company, 1967). This book is highly recommended reading; the terse summary presented here does not do justice to Professor Galbraith's arguments.

firms. Thus it has been argued that a part of the stability achieved in the post-World War II era arose from the fact that the long-term investment programs of large monopolies were continued despite short-term changes in inventory investment and consumer spending. It is also asserted that the ability of business monopolies to resist price reductions during recession (coupled with the propensity of unions to resist wage cuts) helps thwart the development of a cumulative wage-price deflationary spiral and the accompanying declines in output and employment.

Social Responsibility A few economists and most business groups suggest that business leaders are blessed with a strong sense of social responsibility which will mitigate, if not eliminate entirely, abuses of monopoly power. Although industry leaders command tremendous economic power, we are assured that they have the social maturity not to wield this power in a manner detrimental to the public interest. The public-be-damned attitude of business monopolies in earlier decades is allegedly a thing of the past.[6]

THE CASE AGAINST MONOPOLY

The essence of the case against monopoly was stated in Chapter 27. Let us summarize and extend those arguments.

□ Inefficiency and Inequality

Monopolists find it possible and profitable to restrict output and charge higher prices than would competitive producers. Furthermore, the monopolist's profit-maximizing output entails a misallocation of economic resources. It is through his ability to block or retard the entry of new firms and resources into an industry that the monopolist can real-

ize economic profits in the long run. These profits are an indication that consumers want more resources allocated to the production of the monopolized commodity. Finally, the persistent economic profits which monopolists can realize contribute to inequality in the distribution of income.

□ Obstacle to Progress?

Antimonopoly economists have attacked (1) the notion that only giant corporations can realize the economies of large-scale production, and (2) Galbraith's argument that monopoly is essential to technological progress. In so doing, they make a variety of interrelated arguments.

1 Empirical studies suggest that in the vast majority of manufacturing industries, fewness is not essential to the realization of economies of scale. In most industries, firms need only realize a small percentage of the total market to achieve low-cost production; monopoly is *not* a prerequisite of productive efficiency.[7]

2 The basic unit for technological efficiency is not the firm, but the individual plant. Thus one can correctly argue that productive efficiency calls for, say, a large-scale, integrated steel-manufacturing plant. But it is perfectly consistent to argue that there is no technological justification for the existence of U.S. Steel, which is essentially a giant business corporation composed of a number of geographically distinct plants. Similarly, it is contended, for example, that the Chevrolet, Pontiac, Oldsmobile, Buick, and Cadillac divisions of General Motors are, for operating purposes, independent producers. How, then, can their legal unification be justified on the basis of mass-production economies? As one observer has put it:[8]

---

[6] The interested student will find Paul T. Heyne, *Private Keepers of the Public Interest* (New York: McGraw-Hill Book Company, 1968), to be challenging reading.

[7] The classic study is Joe S. Bain, *Barriers to New Competition* (Cambridge, Mass.: Harvard University Press, 1956).
[8] Assar Lindbeck, *The Political Economy of the New Left* (New York: Harper & Row, Publishers, Incorporated, 1971), p. 94.

I do not think that the loss in economic efficiency connected with returns to scale would be dramatic if big American companies were subdivided, for instance, five or even ten times. The average cost curve seems to be rather flat over long intervals, and the experience of relatively small firms (internationally speaking), like manufacturing firms in Sweden, for instance, do not indicate that firms have to be nearly as large as those in the United States to be efficient, particularly as an increase in competition by itself is likely to increase efficiency.

Furthermore, there are no efficiency grounds for the existence of huge conglomerate corporations engaged in the production of such widely divergent products as frozen foods, shoes, cosmetics, and office equipment. In short, many existing monopolies have attained a size and structure far larger than necessary for the realization of existing economies of scale.

3 Nor does technological progress depend upon the existence of huge corporations with substantial monopoly power. It is held that the evidence—one might review the closing pages of Chapter 29—does not support the view that large size and market power correlate closely with technological progress. Indeed, the sheltered position of the monopolist is conducive to inefficiency and lethargy; there is no competitive spur to productive efficiency. Furthermore, monopolists are inclined to resist or suppress technological advances which may cause the sudden obsolescence of their existing machinery and equipment.

Critics of Galbraith's technological determinism offer contrary case studies. For example, the American steel industry, dominated by a few industrial giants, should neatly fit Galbraith's portrayal of large firms as efficient planners for technological progress. But, critics contend, the steel industry is in fact sorely at odds with Galbraith's model.[9]

[9]Testimony of Walter Adams at *Hearing before a Subcommittee of the Select Committee on Small Business* (Washington, June 29, 1967).

The U.S. Steel industry, which ranks among the largest, most basic, and most concentrated of American industries, certainly part of the industrial state that Professor Galbraith speaks of, affords a dramatic case in point. It spends only 0.7 percent of its revenues on research and, in technological progressiveness, the giants which dominate this industry lag behind their smaller domestic rivals as well as their smaller foreign competitors. Thus, the basic oxygen furnace—considered the "only major breakthrough at the ingot level since before the turn of the century" was invented in 1950 by a miniscule Austrian *firm* which was less than one-third the size of a single *plant* of the United States Steel Corp. The innovation was introduced in the United States in 1954 by McLouth Steel which at the time had about 1 percent of domestic steel capacity—to be followed some 10 years later by the steel giants: United States Steel in December 1963, Bethlehem in 1964, and Republic in 1965. . . .

Only after they were subjected to actual and threatened competition from domestic and foreign steelmakers in the 1960's did the steel giants decide to accommodate themselves to the oxygen revolution. Thus, it was the cold wind of competition, and not the catatonia induced by industrial concentration, which proved conducive to innovation and technological progress.

□ **Instability**

Monopoly is held by its critics to be an obstacle to the achievement of economic stability, that is, full employment with reasonable price stability. Two somewhat distinct assertions underlie this point. On the one hand, it was noted in Chapter 16 that business monopolies are in a position of relative immunity insofar as an anti-inflationary (tight) money policy is concerned. Indeed, the ability of monopolists to manipulate prices may cause a tight money policy to contribute indirectly to inflation as monopolists pass interest rate increases on to consumers through product price increases. On the other hand, we saw in Chapter 18 that business monopolies, in conjunction with labor monopolies, can cause cost-push inflation in the absence of full employment through the exertion of their market power.[10] Conversely, during recession monopolists resist price reductions to the end that output and employment fall dramatically (Figure 10-5).

☐ Political Dangers

The conventional conception of government is that of an institution whose activities and policies promote "the public interest" (Chapter 6). Some observers contend that this conventional portrayal of government as a doer of good deeds is wishful thinking because the power of giant monopolies has been extended to the political state. Big business actively finances the campaigns of probusiness politicians who, upon election, behave so as to further the interests of big business. Similarly, the nonelected public bureaucracy is recruited heavily from the ranks of big business; a substantial flow of executive personnel persists between government and the corporate giants. Thus there evolves a symbiotic relationship—a relationship of mutual dependence—between government and big business. And this implies the functioning of the political state for the furtherance of the private ends of the corporate giants at the expense of the general welfare. In short, huge corporations exert effective control over government, and this control is reflected in legislation and government policies which are congenial, not to the public interest, but rather, to the preservation and growth of these industrial giants. Big businesses allegedly have exerted political power to become the primary beneficiaries of defense contracts, tax loopholes, patent policy, tariff and quota protection, and a variety of other subsidies and privileges. Witness, for example, the curious character of public policy toward the heavily concentrated and politically active petroleum industry:[11]

> Under the antitrust laws, it is a per se offense for private firms to fix prices or allocate markets, yet in the name of conservation the government does for the oil companies what they could not legally do for themselves. The process is familiar. The Bureau of Mines in the Department of Interior publishes monthly estimates of the market demand for petroleum (at current prices, of course). Under the Interstate Oil Compact, approved by Congress, these estimates are broken down into quotas for each of the oil producing states which, in turn, through various prorationing devices, allocate "allowable production" to individual wells. Oil produced in violation of these prorationing regulations is branded as "hot oil," and the federal government prohibits its shipment in interstate commerce. Also, to buttress this government sanctioned cartel against potential competition, oil imports by sea are limited to slightly more than one million barrels a day. Finally, to top off these indirect subsidies with more visible favors and to provide the proper incentives for an industry crucial to the national defense, the government authorizes oil companies to charge off a $27\frac{1}{2}$ percent depletion allowance against their gross income. In all, the industry has been estimated to receive special favors of $3.5 billion . . . [to] $4.0 billion . . . in addition to having a government sanctioned cartel provide the underpinning for its control of markets and prices.

It is recognized that the 1973–1974 energy crisis significantly altered government policies with respect to the oil industry. In particular, limitations upon domestic production and import quotas were both abandoned, as was the tax subsidy provided by the depletion allowance. On the other hand, critics point out that production limitations and depletion allowances may have exacerbated the energy crisis by allowing American petroleum firms to make

---

[10]See, for example, Gardiner C. Means, "Simultaneous Inflation and Unemployment: A Challenge to Theory and Policy," *Challenge,* September–October 1975, pp. 6–20.

[11]Walter Adams, "The Military-Industrial Complex and the New Industrial State," *American Economic Review,* May 1968, p. 654.

substantial profits from existing wells and facilities, thereby blunting their incentives to explore for new oil fields and to construct new refining facilities.

This controversial question of the political aspects of economic power will be encountered again when we discuss the military-industrial complex (Chapter 39), and the radical economists' interpretation of capitalism (Chapter 40).

□ **Character of Society**

Finally, there is the more elusive contention that giant corporate monopolies have become *the* dominant force in our society and, in that role, have fostered dehumanizing institutional arrangements and questionable values. For example, the emphasis of big business upon organizational structures which are presumably conducive to productive efficiency have allegedly resulted in bureaucracies and occupational hierarchies wherein most workers and many managers are confined to uninspiring, noncreative, stultifying jobs. Similarly, corporate advertising has had a great impact upon life-styles, stressing the virtues of materialism and tacitly downgrading other goals and values. The criticism, in brief, is that many of the less admirable characteristics of the "American way of life" are a reflection of the dominant role which the giant corporation plays in our society.

□ **Empirical Evidence**

A number of pioneering empirical studies have attempted to measure the quantitative impact of monopoly (imperfect competition) upon the economy. In general, these studies reach two basic conclusions. First, the distinction which economists make between "competitive" and "monopolistic" industries is a valid one. In particular, evidence suggests that monopolistic industries do realize larger profits than competitive ones and do cause a misallocation of resources. Second, monopoly profits are not so much greater than those under competition as economic theory might lead us to believe; nor is the malallocation of resources caused by monopoly nearly so severe as some economists maintain.

One of the recent estimates suggests that the dollar-value loss of output due to monopoly is on the order of 6 percent of the GNP, leading the investigator to conclude that the "inefficiency burden of monopoly does not appear to be overwhelming. But it is also not so slight that it can be ignored."[12] Postscript: Empirical research on the economic effects of monopoly is plagued by severe limitations, and conclusions must be regarded as rough estimates or best guesses.

■──────────────────

PUBLIC POLICY TOWARD MONOPOLY

In view of the sharp conflict of opinion over the relative merits of business monopoly, it is not surprising to find that government policy toward business monopolies has been something less than clear-cut and consistent. As reflected in major pieces of legislation, the Federal government's stated policy objective is the maintenance of competition. Yet the government has passed legislation and at times pursued policies which have furthered the development of monopoly power. As one scholar has aptly phrased it,[13]

> Governments, apparently, have never been able to make up their minds as to which they dislike more, competition or monopoly. . . . Whether government activities, on the basis of the presently existing body of law, are on balance more favorable to monopoly or competition is controversial.

Government, in short, has both restrained business monopoly and promoted it.

[12] F. M. Scherer, *Industrial Market Structure and Economic Performance* (Chicago: Rand McNally & Company, 1970), p. 408.
[13] Fritz Machlup, *The Political Economy of Monopoly* (Baltimore: Johns Hopkins Press, 1952), p. 182.

☐ **Legislation and Policies Restricting Monopoly**

Historically, American capitalism, steeped in the philosophy of free, competitive markets, has been a fertile ground for the development of a suspicious and fearful public attitude toward business monopolies. Though relatively dormant in the nation's early years, this fundamental distrust of monopoly came into full bloom in the decades following the Civil War. The widening of local markets into national markets as transportation facilities improved, the ever-increasing mechanization of production, and the increasingly widespread adoption of the corporate form of business enterprise were important forces giving rise to the development of "trusts"—that is, business monopolies—in the 1870s and 1880s. Trusts developed in the petroleum, meat-packing, sugar, lead, coal, whiskey, and tobacco industries, among others, during this era. Not only were questionable tactics employed in monopolizing the various industries, but the resulting market power was almost invariably exerted to the detriment of all who did business with these monopolies. Farmers and small businessmen, being particularly vulnerable to the growth and tactics of the giant corporate monopolies, were among the first to censure their development. Consumers and labor unions were not far behind in voicing their disapproval of monopoly power.

Given the development of certain industries wherein market forces no longer provided adequate control to ensure socially tolerable behavior, two man-made techniques of control have been adopted as substitutes for, or supplements to, the market. First, in those few markets where economic realities are such as to preclude the effective functioning of the market—that is, where there tends to be a "natural monopoly"—we have established public *regulatory agencies* to control economic behavior. Second, in most other markets wherein economic and technological conditions have not made monopoly essential, social con-

trol has taken the form of antimonopoly or *antitrust legislation* designed to inhibit or prevent the growth of monopoly. Let us examine these two forms of social control in the order stated.

☐ **The Regulation of Natural Monopolies**

In certain industries, economies of scale are so great that a single firm can supply an entire market at lower per unit cost than could a number of competing firms (see Figure 25-6a). Competition, in short, is uneconomic. Two alternatives present themselves as means of ensuring socially acceptable behavior on the part of a "natural monopoly" or "public utility." One is public ownership, and the other, widely preferred in the United States, is to provide for public regulation. We now have public regulatory commissions in such fields as transportation, communications, electric power, and radio and television.

Background To illustrate: The first of our several regulatory laws, the Interstate Commerce Act of 1887, was based on the supposition that competition was unworkable in the railroad industry. Certain industry characteristics ruled out the possibility of effective competition:

1 Relatively large fixed costs—for roadbed, track, engines, rolling stock, and so on—entailed the necessity of large-scale operations by each firm in order to achieve efficient, low-cost service.

2 The existence of several firms in this industry would entail the wasteful duplication of very costly capital facilities.

3 The service being supplied—transportation—was essential to many firms and individuals.

And, as a matter of fact, "competition" had not worked well in this industry. Price competition aimed at the fuller realization of economies of scale often degenerated into cutthroat competition and losses for all participants. The results would be either the elimination of the weaker competitors and the evolution of monopoly or the establishment of a collusive price agreement of some sort by which the competitors sought to improve their lot. If monopoly resulted, the exploitation of that power through discriminatory pricing—that is, charging what the traffic would bear—was likely. If a collusive price resulted, the industry would then operate in much the same manner as a pure monopoly, at least until another round of price warring was precipitated.

In view of such circumstances, the Interstate Commerce Act was passed by Congress to make railroads regulated monopolies. Although their management and actual operation remained in private hands, the Interstate Commerce Commission was established to regulate the rates and monitor the services of the railroads.

The intent of this "natural monopoly" legislation is to regulate such industries effectively and for the benefit of the public, to the end that consumers may be assured quality service at reasonable rates. The rationale is this: If competition is inappropriate, *regulated* monopolies should be established to avoid possible abuses of uncontrolled monopoly power (Chapter 27). In particular, regulation should guarantee that consumers benefit from the economies of scale—that is, the lower per unit costs—which their natural-monopoly position allows public utilities to achieve. Few would quarrel with this reasoning.

Problems But there is considerable disagreement about the effectiveness of the regulatory commissions in controlling the various natural monopolies. Two major criticisms are common:

1 The regulatory commissions function inadequately because they are frequently "captured" or controlled by the very industries they are supposed to regulate. Hence, regulation is not in the public interest, but rather, it protects and nurtures the comfortable position of the natural monopolist. It is alleged that regulation typically becomes a means of guaranteeing profits and protecting the regulated industry from potential new competition which technological change might create.[14]

> Regulation has too often resulted in protection of the *status quo*. Entry is often blocked, prices are kept from falling, and the industry becomes inflexible and insensitive to new techniques and opportunities for progress. Competition can sometimes develop outside the jurisdiction of a regulatory agency and make inroads on the regulated companies, threatening their profitability or even survival. In such cases, pressure is usually exerted to extend the regulatory umbrella to guard against this outside competition, so that the problems of regulation multiply and detract from the original purpose of preventing overpricing and unwanted side effects.

2 A more complex, long-run problem also exists. If a regulatory agency operates in the public interest and thereby effectively limits profits to a competitive level, the natural monopoly may encounter serious difficulties in attracting the money capital needed to sustain, modernize, and expand its facilities. Why the problem? Because the natural monopoly is competing for money capital with unregulated oligopolies which are more attractive to financial investors because of their higher, above-competitive profits. Hence, a dilemma: The regulatory commission must either allow the natural monopoly to realize above-competitive rates of return by charging above-competitive prices to consumers *or* face the prospect of a gradual deterioration of capital facilities and therefore of service to consumers.

What are the alternatives to regulation? Some recommend government ownership as an alternative. But nationalization entails prob-

---

[14] *Economic Report of the President, 1970* (Washington), p. 107. The reader who is interested in the problems of regulation will do well to consult Paul W. MacAvoy (ed.), *The Crisis of the Regulatory Commissions* (New York: W. W. Norton & Company, Inc., 1970).

lems of its own; for example, critics envision strong political pressures dominating economic considerations in determining rates and services. Others feel that regulation is now obsolete and should be abandoned. For example, the monopoly position which the railroads enjoyed some ninety or a hundred years ago has been undermined by the evolution of barge, air, and motor transportation. Hence, economically satisfactory results can be achieved by letting the various segments of the transportation industry openly and freely compete.

□   **Antitrust Legislation**

A number of antitrust laws have been passed to foster or enhance competition in those industries wherein technological and economic conditions do not make monopoly inevitable. The rationale underlying these laws contrasts sharply with that underlying the regulatory commissions. The basis of antitrust is[15]

> the assumption that by controlling or modifying certain aspects of industrial structure and competitive conduct, the public can avoid government intervention in the economically and politically hazardous thicket of specifying industrial performance. . . . [Antitrust] does not tell businessmen what and how much to produce or at what price to sell their products. Rather, the antitrust approach is directed at maintaining sufficient competition in the market place so that market forces will "compel" desirable economic performance.

Three pieces of legislation, the Sherman Act, the Clayton Act, and the Federal Trade Commission Act, as refined and extended by various amendments, constitute the basic law of the land with respect to corporate size and concentration.

The Sherman Act of 1890   Acute public resentment of the trusts which developed in the 1870s and 1880s culminated in the passage

of the Sherman Antitrust Act in 1890. This cornerstone of antitrust legislation is surprisingly brief and, at first glance, directly to the point. The core of the act is embodied in two major provisions:

In Section 1:

> Every contract, combination in the form of a trust or otherwise, or conspiracy, in restraint of trade or commerce among the several states, or with foreign nations is hereby declared to be illegal. . . .

In Section 2:

> Every person who shall monopolize, or attempt to monopolize, or combine or conspire with any person or persons, to monopolize any part of the trade or commerce among the several states, or with foreign nations, shall be deemed guilty of a misdemeanor. . . .

The act had the effect of making monopoly and "restraints of trade" criminal offenses against the Federal government. Either the government or parties injured by business monopolies could file suits under the Sherman Act. Firms found in violation of the act could be ordered dissolved by the courts, or injunctions could be issued to prohibit practices deemed unlawful under the act. Fines and imprisonment were also possible results of successful prosecution. Further, parties injured by illegal combinations and conspiracies could sue for triple the amount of damages done them. The Sherman Act seemed to provide a sound foundation for positive government action against business monopolies.

A study of key antitrust cases indicates that at times the Sherman Act has been applied with great verve and effectiveness, whereas at other times it has lain dormant. Two considerations go far to explain this inconsistency:

1 The Federal government has varied considerably in its willingness to apply the act. Administrations "friendly" toward big business

---

[15] Willard F. Mueller, *A Primer on Monopoly and Competition* (New York: Random House, Inc., 1970), p. 132.

have sometimes emasculated the act by the simple process of ignoring it or by cutting the budget appropriations of enforcement agencies.

2 The courts have run hot and cold in interpreting the Sherman Act and its various amendments. At times, the courts have applied the Sherman Act with vigor, adhering closely to the spirit and objectives of the law. In other cases, the courts have interpreted the act in such ways as to render it all but completely innocuous.

These varying interpretations of the act by the courts undoubtedly arose in good measure from its loose and general wording. Not too many years after the passage of the Sherman Act, it was quite evident that a more explicit statement of the government's antitrust sentiments was in order.

The Clayton Act of 1914   This needed elaboration of the Sherman Act took the form of the 1914 Clayton Antitrust Act. The following sections of the Clayton Act were designed to strengthen and make explicit the intent of the Sherman Act:

Section 2 *outlaws price discrimination* between purchasers when such discrimination is not justified on the basis of cost differences.

Section 3 *forbids exclusive, or "tying," contracts* whereby a producer would sell a product only on the condition that the buyer acquire other products from the same seller and not from competitors.

Section 7 *prohibits the acquisition of stocks* of competing corporations when the effect is to lessen competition.

Section 8 *prohibits the formation of interlocking directorates*—the situation where a director of one firm is also a board member of another firm—in large corporations where the effect would be to reduce competition.

Actually, there was little in the Clayton Act which had not already been stated by implication in the Sherman Act. The Clayton Act merely attempted to sharpen and make clear the general provisions of the Sherman Act. Furthermore, the Clayton Act attempted

to outlaw the techniques by which monopoly might develop and, in this sense, was a preventive measure. The Sherman Act, by contrast, was aimed more at the punishment of existing monopolies.

The Federal Trade Commission Act of 1914   The Federal Trade Commission Act was based on the belief that preventive rather than more punitive measures were needed to sustain competition. Specifically, the act was designed to prevent competition from assuming certain aggressive forms which would tend to undermine competition and bring about the development of monopoly power. The act created the Federal Trade Commission, a permanent five-man board, and charged it with the power to investigate unfair competitive practices on its own initiative or at the request of injured firms. The Commission could hold public hearings on such complaints and, if necessary, issue cease-and-desist orders where "unfair methods of competition in commerce" were discovered.

The antitrust potential of the FTC has been limited by subsequent court rulings which have restricted the investigatory powers of the Commission and made it clear that the courts, not the FTC, have the final authority in interpreting the meaning of the antitrust laws. Then, in 1938, the Wheeler-Lea Act amended the Federal Trade Commission Act by prohibiting "unfair or deceptive acts or practices in commerce." As a result, a primary task of the FTC now is the prohibition of false and misleading advertising and the misrepresentation of products.

More Recent Antitrust Legislation   More recent antitrust legislation has taken the form of amendments designed to plug loopholes in—and thereby strengthen—the Clayton Act.

The Robinson-Patman Act of 1936 amended Section 2—the price discrimination section—of the Clayton Act. This section, you will recall, attempted to eliminate the practice by which producers charged different prices to different buyers, where the objective was to drive competing producers from business. The various trusts frequently employed such cut-throat tactics—charging extremely low prices in markets in which small competitors persisted and higher prices in markets where competition had already been eliminated—as a method of improving and strengthening their monopoly positions. The Robinson-Patman Act, or "Chain Store Law," had a different background. It was aimed at the growing number of chain stores which, so argued independent retailers, were obtaining large and unjustified price discounts from wholesalers because of their strong bargaining positions as large buyers. By passing some of these cost savings on to consumers in the form of price reductions, the chains allegedly were driving their independent competitors into bankruptcy. The Robinson-Patman Act outlaws quantity discounts to large buyers when such discounts are not justified on the basis of actual cost economies arising from mass buying. And, in turn, the act prohibits retailers from selling "at unreasonably low prices" when the purpose is to eliminate competitors. Many economists feel that the effect of the act has been not so much to deter the growth of monopoly as to stifle price competition, particularly at the retail level, and therefore to sustain inefficient retailers who would otherwise succumb to more vigorous competition.

Finally, the Celler-Kefauver Antimerger Act of 1950 amended Section 7 of the Clayton Act, the section which prohibits one firm from acquiring the *stock* of competitors when the acquisition would reduce competition. This provision had been weakened by court decisions and had been dodged by firms who merged with competitors by acquiring their *assets* rather than their stock. The Celler-Kefauver Act attempted to tighten the stock acquisition ban and also prohibits the acquisition of the assets of competitors when the effect would be to lessen competition.

Effectiveness of Antitrust Reasonable men can, and do, disagree about the relevance and effectiveness of antitrust. At one extreme, Galbraith's view is that the antitrust laws are a charade. These laws have not been used to attack the *existence* of monopoly power, but rather are applied only when *anticompetitive behavior* is evidenced. Galbraith therefore contends that, in fact, the giant corporation which already has vast market power is substantially immune from antitrust prosecution. But if substantially smaller firms in the same industry attempt to merge so as to compete more effectively with the dominant giant, they will run afoul of antitrust. Furthermore, by giving the public the illusion that the market remains a viable form of social control, the antitrust laws protect the largest corporations from the alternative of public regulation. The Last Word for this chapter elaborates Galbraith's view.

On the other hand, many economists are of the opinion that the antitrust laws have worked reasonably well and that stronger antitrust laws, coupled with more vigorous and more discriminating enforcement, would do much to make our economy even more competitive. It is felt in some quarters that faulty judicial interpretations, legal loopholes, and indifferent Federal administrations have at times undermined and considerably weakened antitrust policy. Most importantly, there is rather widespread agreement that many of the government's most notable legal victories in applying the antitrust laws have proved to be economic defeats. That is, the guilty firms have agreed to cease-and-desist orders or have been subject to minor penalties rather than forced to dissolve. Indeed, even when dissolution has occurred, the economic benefits have been dubious: When it comes to price and output policies, a tight three- or four-firm oligopoly is likely to behave much as the absolute monopoly which once comprised it.

On the positive side, it must be recognized that there currently exists widespread interest in antitrust. Examples: The Senate Subcommittee on Antitrust and Monopoly has conducted detailed investigations of administered prices in the automobile, steel, and drug industries; the Department of Justice indicted the nation's principal electrical equipment producers in late 1960 for conspiracy in violation of the Sherman Act; and, finally, economists have reasserted their long-standing interest in the monopoly problem as the cost-push theory of inflation has emphasized market power as a cause of rising prices.

The Conglomerates: A Special Problem

Existing antitrust laws, properly enforced, are quite adequate to cope with horizontal and vertical mergers (Chapter 8). But the vast majority of the mergers of the last decade were conglomerate mergers; that is, a company in one industry took over companies in unrelated industries. To illustrate:[16]

> The International Telegraph & Telephone Company (ITT) is a huge international conglomerate operating over 150 affiliated companies in fifty-seven countries; it is the fourth largest private industrial employer in the world. Most of its present size can be traced to the hundreds of mergers it has made during the years. During 1961–1968 it acquired at least 120 businesses with combined assets of nearly $2 billion. Perhaps more than any other corporation, ITT has acquired companies that are themselves large and leaders in their fields. For example, it has acquired Avis, the second largest car rental corporation; Sheraton Corporation, the largest hotel chain; Continental Baking Company, the country's largest bakery products manufacturer; and Educational Services, one of the leading suppliers of educational exhibit materials. During the first nine months of 1969, ITT's board of directors approved the consummation of thirty-three more acquisitions. Three of these were industry leaders with combined assets of about $2.2 billion: Grinnel Corporation, the

nation's leading maker of automatic fire protection equipment, Canteen Corporation, one of the largest vending machine companies, and Hartford Fire Insurance Company, a leader in several lines of insurance.

On the surface, conglomerate mergers would seem less detrimental to the public interest than would, for example, a horizontal merger of firms which directly compete in the same market. But conglomerates do pose serious problems. First, as the ITT illustration indicates, conglomerates are obviously a means for achieving great concentrations of wealth and economic power. As emphasized in the arguments against monopoly, such vast concentrations of economic power can have adverse political effects. This is particularly so if the conglomerate is a multinational, that is, a corporation with investments and subsidiaries located abroad. Multinationals may become an unofficial, disruptive, and highly controversial aspect of American "foreign policy." Recall the 1972 scandal surrounding ITT's efforts to prevent the election of socialist Salvador Allende as President of Chile. These efforts were prompted, of course, by ITT's fears that Allende would nationalize its assets in Chile. Second, this amassed wealth can be used to weaken or destroy competitors in the conglomerates' various product markets. That is, the profits derived from markets wherein a conglomerate's monopoly power is currently great can be used to subsidize and promote its power in other markets which are currently quite competitive. Third, by their very nature conglomerates are in a position to use *reciprocal selling* as an anticompetitive device. Since its operations span many different markets, the conglomerate may be in the unique position to say to potential customers, "I'll buy from you if you'll buy from me," which puts it at an obvious advantage over competing nonconglomerate firms which can only plead to customers, "Please buy from me." Finally, it is notable that the growth of the conglomerates

---

[16]Ibid., pp. 80–81.

is not based upon technological imperatives; indeed, there is "persuasive evidence that many jerry-built conglomerates are less efficient than were the individual companies they absorbed."[17]

Although the Justice Department has challenged a few conglomerate mergers in the courts, it is not clear that existing antitrust legislation can be used effectively against the conglomerates. In any event, the conglomerate merger movement peaked in the 1960s and, spurred by two or three widely publicized failures, has subsided in the 1970s.

□   **Legislation and Policies
Promoting Monopoly**

Let us now consider briefly the other side of the picture. Government has directly and indirectly promoted the growth of monopoly in several different ways. Consider some important examples.

Exemptions to Antitrust   Over the years government has enacted certain laws which have either exempted certain specific industries or, alternatively, have excluded certain trade practices from antitrust prosecution. In doing so, the government has tended indirectly to foster the growth of monopoly power.

In 1918 the Webb-Pomerene Act exempted American exporters from the antitrust laws by permitting them to form export trade associations. Although the act was intended to put American exporters in a stronger competitive position with international cartels, the effect has probably been to reduce competition in both international and domestic markets. Similarly, we have already noted that the Robinson-Patman Act of 1936 had the effect of dampening price competition at the retail level.

It should be noted, too, that labor unions and agricultural cooperatives have been exempt, subject to limitations, from the antitrust

[17]Ibid., p. 155.

laws. We shall see in the next chapter that Federal legislation and policy have attempted to provide some measure of monopolistic power for agriculture, feeling that this would help alleviate the farm problem. Similarly, in a subsequent chapter we shall discover that since 1930, Federal legislation on balance has generally promoted the growth of strong labor unions. This federally sponsored growth has resulted, according to some authorities, in the development of union monopolies.

Patent Laws   Technological research is a costly and risky procedure. American patent laws—the first of which was passed in 1790—are aimed at providing sufficient monetary incentive for innovators by granting them exclusive rights to produce and sell a new product or machine for a period of seventeen years. Patent grants have the effect of protecting the innovator from competitors who would otherwise quickly imitate his product and share in the profits, though not the cost and effort, of his research. Few contest the desirability of this particular aspect of our patent laws, particularly when it is recalled that innovation can weaken and undermine existing positions of monopoly power.

However, patents are a mixed blessing. The granting of a patent frequently amounts to the granting of monopoly power in the production of the patented item. Many economists feel that the length of patent protection—seventeen years—is much too long. Such an extended period of protection from competitors is likely to allow the innovator to entrench himself firmly in a monopoly position to the extent that he is able to block successfully any potential competition after his patent expires. This is particularly true if the innovating firm extends its patent rights longer than seventeen years by patenting improved models of the original innovation. By this and similar procedures, innovating firms have often been able to extend their exclusive jurisdiction over a product for three or four decades!

When patents are licensed to competitors, the innovating firm has the right to specify the prices which these competitors may charge for the product, the markets in which they may sell, and even the amounts which they may produce. The result is that the innovator faces no genuine competition. The worst abuses of patent rights occur when one firm accumulates by research or purchase a large number of related patents or, alternatively, several firms in an industry "pool" the patents which they own and exclude potential rivals from their use. In such situations, patents can constitute a very formidable barrier to entry and thereby create and perpetuate monopoly power.

And finally, a patent monopoly is an excellent basis for a tying agreement and the subsequent extension of monopoly power. The classic case is that of the United Shoe Machinery Corporation, which leased the machinery over which it has exclusive patents only on the condition that shoe manufacturers would purchase all their other machinery from United. This practice stripped its competitors of their customers and firmly entrenched United as the dominant firm in the industry.

The importance of patent laws in the growth of business monopoly must not be underestimated. Such well-known firms as du Pont, General Electric, American Telephone and Telegraph, Eastman Kodak, Alcoa, and innumerable other industrial giants have attained various measures of monopoly power in part through their ownership of certain patent rights.[18]

Protective Tariffs   Although we must postpone any detailed discussion of tariffs until a later chapter, it is relevant at this point to recognize that tariffs and similar trade barriers have the effect of shielding American producers from foreign competition. Protective tariffs are in effect discriminatory taxes against the goods of foreign firms. These taxes make it difficult and often impossible for foreign producers to compete in domestic markets with American firms. The result? A less competitive domestic market and an environment frequently conducive to the growth of domestic business monopolies.

■ ───────────────────────────────

FUTURE POLICY ALTERNATIVES

Now let us look ahead. What is the most desirable path for public policy to follow in the future? There are three general positions and a host of hybrid views on this important question. There are those who are satisfied with the structure and performance of American industry and therefore generally content with the status quo or even in favor of some relaxation of antitrust enforcement. There are those who feel that American capitalism has no choice but to move in the direction of increased governmental regulation and/or ownership of monopolized industries. There are those who believe that it is both desirable and possible to make American industry more competitive.[19] The serious consequences of any choice between these sharply contrasting policy alternatives demand that we weigh each rather carefully.

☐   **Maintaining the Status Quo**

Those who advocate maintaining the status quo are convinced that the presence of business monopolies and the degree of concentration of economic power which now exists are not only essential but also desirable. Supporting arguments are generally those made earlier in this chapter on the side of business monopoly.

Competition of all products for the dollars of consumers, interproduct competition, nonprice competition, countervailing power, po-

---

[18]For a sophisticated and detailed discussion of this topic, see Scherer, op. cit., chap. 16.

[19]The present discussion follows the general pattern outlined in Walter Adams (ed.), *The Structure of American Industry,* 5th ed. (New York: The Macmillan Company, 1977), chap. 14.

tential competition and the fear of government regulation, and technological advance all render "workably competitive" industries which appear at first glance to be monopolistic. Then, too, it is contended that business leaders have attained levels of maturity and social responsibility far beyond those attained by their predecessors. Business leaders are trustees of economic power and can be expected not to abuse that trust.

But the most significant and the most frequently heard tenet for preservation of the status quo is the doctrine of *technological determinism*. The current advanced stage of technological development, it is argued, makes it imperative that big businesses prevail. Business monopolies are necessary if the economy is to realize the productive efficiencies which modern technology now makes available. Furthermore, bigness is essential to continued large-scale expenditures on research and development and, therefore, to a future high rate of technological progress. A return to competition, in the sense of a large number of small producers, would be to forgo economies of scale and a rapid rate of technological advance. Any restoration of large-numbers competition is a step in the direction of economic *in*efficiency and the misuse of scarce resources.

□ **Toward Public Regulation and Ownership**

There are many observers who are less satisfied with the current structure of American industry. Public regulation or even public ownership and operation are envisioned as inevitable consequences of the need to control private monopoly power.

This position rests on three points:

1 Modern technology, it is assumed, is such that business monopoly is here to stay if we are to achieve and maintain productive efficiency.

2 The arguments underlying the status quo position are discounted by those who view public regulation as the only course for future policy. It is naïve to assume that monopolists will exercise self-restraint in using the economic power at their disposal. Workable competition is more a myth than a reality; it does not function as an effective regulatory device. Further, countervailing power is subject to many exceptions, and where relevant, it functions in a very imperfect manner.

3 Present antitrust laws are deemed too weak to curb abuses of monopoly power, and if strengthened and vigorously enforced, antitrust laws would entail the loss of the productive efficiencies which modern technology now provides.

It is concluded that the only real alternative is the social control of business monopolies through government regulation. Only in this way can business monopoly be operated in the public interest.

□ **Restoring Vigorous Competition**

A final alternative seeks the restoration of "effective" competition in what now are monopolistic industries. The objective sought is not the establishment of *pure* competition; this is recognized as unrealistic and in some instances economically undesirable. Rather, the goal is the establishment of markets wherein (1) the number of producers is sufficiently large so that no individual firms possess considerable market power, (2) collusion is absent, and (3) the entry to markets is relatively unrestricted.

Proponents of this policy alternative contend that the goal of effective competition is realistic, attainable, and highly desirable. They argue that the status quo is intolerable. Monopoly power exists, workable competition and countervailing power to the contrary, and it is being sorely abused. No effective market or moral forces exist to protect consumers from business monopolies. Hence, the restoration of competition to such industries is highly desirable.

In the second place, it is felt that in most industries the growth of big business monopolies has far exceeded that necessary for the attainment of all the economies of scale which modern technology allows. A considerable degree of competition *can* be reestablished in most now-monopolized markets with little or no impairment of productive efficiency or the rate of technological progress.

And, it is argued, past experience indicates that public regulation of monopoly has generally failed to function in the public interest. Public monopolies can abuse their power in the same way as can private monopolies.

Through what techniques is competition to be restored? On the one hand, antitrust laws should be strengthened and vigorously applied. A rearguard defensive application of antitrust legislation to retard the rate of monopoly growth is wholly inadequate. It is imperative that all exceptions to antitrust be eliminated and that monopoly-promoting patent laws and protective tariffs be abandoned. Furthermore, the restoration of effective competition calls for positive action designed to *increase* the degree of competition in industries in which monopoly power is considerable.

A recent legislative proposal, offered by Senator Philip Hart, chairman of the Senate Subcommittee on Antitrust and Monopoly, is consistent with this "restore competition" position. According to the provisions of his proposed Industrial Reorganization Act, evidence of monopoly would no longer depend upon a firm's undertaking certain conspiratorial acts to reduce competition, but would hinge simply upon the fulfillment of certain criteria. Specifically, the proposed legislation assumes that monopoly exists if any one of these three criteria is fulfilled: (1) the concentration ratio, that is, the percentage of industry sales made by the four largest firms, exceeds 50 percent; (2) the firms in the industry have not engaged in price competition for three years; and (3) a firm's rate of profits has exceeded 15 percent for five consecutive years. A firm which fulfills one or more of these criteria would be an illegal monopoly unless it is able to demonstrate that its existence is economically justifiable, for example, that economies of scale would be sacrificed if the firm should be dissolved. Needless to say, legislative proposals which redefine monopoly as a "state of being" rather than in terms of anticompetitive acts are bound to be highly controversial.

Summary

1 The role of business monopolies in American capitalism is a highly controversial one. The defense of business monopoly is built around the following points: *a.* "Workable competition" prevails in many industries in which large-numbers competition is absent; *b.* the realization of mass-production economies often necessitates the presence of business monopolies; *c.* monopoly provides both the means and incentives for rapid technological advance; *d.* the investment and price policies of monopolies tend to stabilize the economy; and *e.* business monopolies are socially responsible.

2 The case against business monopoly centers upon the contentions that business monopoly *a.* results in high prices and output restriction; *b.* contributes to the misallocation of resources; *c.* promotes income inequality; *d.* retards the rate of technological advance; *e.* is an obstacle to the achievement of economic stability; *f.* poses a threat to political democracy; and *g.* dominates our culture and life-style.

3 Government has attempted to exert social control over monopoly by *a.* establishing regulatory commissions in markets where technological and economic considerations are conducive to natural monopoly, and *b.* applying antitrust laws to markets wherein monopoly is not a prerequisite of economic efficiency.

4 The cornerstone of antitrust policy consists of the Sherman Act of 1890 and the Clayton Act of 1914. The Sherman Act specifies that "Every contract, combination . . . or conspiracy in the restraint of interstate trade . . . is . . . illegal," and that any person who monopolizes or attempts to monopolize interstate trade is guilty of a misdemeanor. The general wording of the act, however, has resulted in a variety of court interpretations, many of which have limited the effectiveness of the act.

5 The Clayton Act was designed to bolster and make more explicit the provisions of the Sherman Act. To this end the Clayton Act declared that price discrimination, tying contracts, intercorporate stockholdings, and interlocking directorates are illegal when the effect of their use is the lessening of competition.

6 The Federal Trade Commission Act of 1914 created the Federal Trade Commission to investigate antitrust violations and to prevent the use of "unfair methods of competition." Empowered to issue cease-and-desist orders, the Commission now serves as a watchdog agency for the false and deceptive representation of products.

7 Though designed to sustain competition between retail distributors, the Robinson-Patman Act of 1936 has stifled retail price competition by prohibiting chain stores from *a.* acquiring "unjustified" discounts in buying from wholesalers, and *b.* selling to consumers at "unreasonably" low prices.

8 The Celler-Kefauver Antimerger Act of 1950 prohibits one firm from acquiring the assets of another firm where the result is a lessening of competition.

9 Government, however, has also done much to promote both directly and indirectly the concentration of economic power and the growth of monopoly. Industrial exceptions to antitrust laws include *a.* the exclusion of exporters by the Webb-Pomerene Act of 1918; *b.* partial exclusion of retailers by the Robinson-Patman Act of 1936; and *c.* the exemption of unions and agricultural cooperatives. Patent laws and protective tariffs also constitute bases for the development of business monopoly.

10 Possible future policies for dealing with business monopolies include *a.* maintenance of the status quo; *b.* increasing public regulation and ownership of industry; and *c.* the restoration of effective competition.

Questions and Study Suggestions

1 Key terms and concepts to remember: monopoly; big business; workable competition; countervailing power; technological determinism; regulatory agencies; Interstate Commerce Act; Sherman Act; Clayton Act; Federal Trade Commission Act; interlocking directorate; tying agreement; cease-and-desist order; Wheeler-Lea Act; Robinson-Patman Act; Celler-Kefauver Act; conglomerate mergers; reciprocal selling; Webb-Pomerene Act; patent laws.

2 "All big firms are monopolistic, but not all monopolistic firms are big." Appraise critically.

3 Suppose you are president of one of the Big Three automobile producers. Discuss critically the case against business monopoly. Now suppose you are a spokesman for a farm organization and are attempting to convince a congressional committee that the presence of business monopolies is a significant factor contributing to the farm problem. Critically evaluate the case for business monopoly.

4 Discuss the evolution and the social desirability of the giant corporation as envisioned in Galbraith's *The New Industrial State.*

5 What stake do you, as a consumer, have in the application of antitrust legislation? Do you feel that antitrust legislation should be applied to labor unions? Explain. Which of the three policies outlined just before the chapter summary do you feel is the most desirable? What criticisms can be made of each of the three positions? Be as specific as you can.

6 How does countervailing power differ from competition as we defined it in Chapter 26? What implication, if any, does countervailing power have for the application of antitrust policy?

7 What proposals can you make to strengthen the antitrust laws in their application to business monopolies? Be specific. Explain how conglomerates might tend to diminish competition.

8 "The social desirability of any given business enterprise should be judged not on the basis of the structure of the industry in which it finds itself, but rather, on the basis of the market performance of that firm." Analyze critically.

9 Would you favor legislation, such as the proposed Industrial Reorganization Act, which identifies illegal monopolies on the basis of a high degree of industry concentration, high profit rates, and the absence of price competition? Critics contend that such legislation would merely penalize efficiently managed firms. Do you agree?

Selected References

Caves, Richard: *American Industry: Structure, Conduct, Performance,* 4th ed. (Englewood Cliffs, N.J.: Prentice-Hall, Inc., 1977).

Goldschmid, Harvey J., H. Michael Mann, and J. Fred Weston (eds.): *Industrial Concentration: The New Learning* (Boston: Little, Brown and Company, 1974).

Koch, James V.: *Industrial Organization and Prices* (Englewood Cliffs, N.J.: Prentice-Hall, Inc., 1974).

Mansfield, Edwin (ed.): *Monopoly Power and Economic Performance,* 3d ed. (New York: W. W. Norton & Company, Inc., 1974).

Reid, Samuel Richardson: *The New Industrial Order* (New York: McGraw-Hill Book Company, 1976).

Thompson, George C., and Gerald P. Brady: *Antitrust Fundamentals* (St. Paul, Minn.: West Publishing Company, 1974).

Warren, Russell G.: *Antitrust in Theory and Practice* (Columbus, Ohio: Grid, Inc., 1975).

Weiss, Leonard, and Allyn D. Strickland: *Regulation: A Case Approach* (New York: McGraw-Hill Book Company, 1976).

Last Word
The Antitrust Charade

John Kenneth Galbraith takes the controversial position that the antitrust laws are a charade. More specifically, the laws are discriminatory in their effect; firms which are already large are virtually immune, while smaller firms are fully exposed to antitrust prosecution.

The most effective manifestation of economic power, all must agree, is simply the big firm. To be big in general and big in an industry is by far the best way of influencing prices and costs, commanding capital, having access to advertising and selling resources, and possessing the other requisites of market power. And . . . by common agreement the heartland of the industrial economy is now dominated by large firms. The great bulk of American business is transacted by very large corporations.

And here enters the element of charade in the antitrust laws. If a firm is already large it is substantially immune under the antitrust laws. If you already have the basic requisite of market power, you are safe . . .

Meanwhile, the antitrust laws are effective in two instances where the firms do not have market power but are seeking to achieve it. Where firms are few and large they can, without overt collusion, establish and maintain a price that is generally satisfactory to all participants. Nor is this an especially difficult calculation, this exercise of power. This is what we economists with our genius for the neat phrase have come to call oligopolistic rationality. And this market power is legally immune or very nearly so. It is everyday practice in autos, steel, rubber, and virtually every other industry shared or dominated by, relatively, a few large firms. But if there are 20 or 30 or more significant firms in the industry, this kind of tacit price-making—this calculation as to what is mutually advantageous but without overt communication—becomes more difficult, may be very difficult. The same result can only be achieved by having a meeting or by exchanging information on prices and costs and price intentions. But this is illegal. It is also legally vulnerable. And it is, in fact, an everyday object of prosecution as the Department of Justice will confirm. What the big firm in the concentrated industry can accomplish legally and effortlessly because of its size, the small firm in the unconcentrated industry does at the pain of civil and even criminal prosecution. . . .

The second manifestation of the charade has to do with mergers. If a firm is already large, it has as a practical matter nothing to fear under antimerger provisions of the Clayton Act. It will not be demerged. It can continue to grow from its own earnings; if discreet, it can even, from time to time, pick up a small and impecunious competitor, for it can reasonably claim that this does little to alter the pattern of competition in the industry. But if two medium-sized firms unite in order to deal more effectively with this giant, the law will be on them like a tiger. Again if large, you are exempt. If you seek to become as large, or even if you seek to become somewhat larger, although still much smaller, you are in trouble.

Here we have the nature of modern antitrust activity. It conducts a fairly effective war on small firms which seek the same market power that the big firms already, by their nature, possess. Behind this impressive facade the big participants who have the most power bask in nearly total immunity. And since the competitive market, like God and a sound family life, is something that no sound businessman can actively oppose, even the smaller entrepreneurs who are the natural victims of this arrangement do not actively protest. It is possible that they do not know how they are being used. . . . The antitrust laws give the impression of protecting the market and competition by attacking those who exercise it most effectively.

From *Planning, Regulation, and Competition,* Hearing before Subcommittees of the Select Committee on Small Business, U.S. Senate, 90th Congress, 1st Session, Washington, 1967, pp. 7–9, abridged.

35

Rural Economics: The Farm Problem

Traditionally, American agriculture has been something of a paradox. Characterized by a rate of productivity growth substantially in excess of any other major sector of the economy, our agricultural abundance has been the envy of the world. But, ironically, farmers have typically received below-average incomes for their remarkable production feats. This irony is perhaps underscored by the fact that agriculture is the only major industry which approximates the purely competitive model of Chapter 26. We must try to discover why the functioning of competitive forces in farming have not yielded incomes comparable to those realized in nonfarm sectors of the economy.

The major objectives of this chapter are:

1 To describe "the farm problem" and outline its causes

2 To discuss public policy toward agriculture and comment upon its effectiveness

3 To inquire as to whether, in the 1970s, American agriculture has entered a new, more prosperous era

HISTORY OF THE FARM PROBLEM

The two decades prior to World War I were exceedingly prosperous ones for agriculture; indeed, this period has been dubbed "the golden age of American agriculture." The demand for farm products, farm prices, and farm incomes all rose. World War I intensified these good times. Foreign demand for the output of American farmers skyrocketed during, and immediately following, the war. Foreign countries, diverting resources from agriculture to war goods production, turned to American agriculture for food and fiber. High prices and an almost insatiable demand were the happy lot of American farmers.

These highly favorable conditions were not to last. A sharp postwar depression in 1920 was a sudden and severe shock to agriculture. In particular, the large volume of mortgage indebtedness incurred during the previous years of prosperity proved a heavy burden. The economy as a whole quickly recovered from this downturn, however, and by 1921 the booming twenties were upon us. But agriculture failed to share in this prosperity to the extent that other segments of the economy did.

The reasons for this were several. European agriculture not only recovered from the war but also began to expand rapidly under the impetus of new technological advances. Hence, foreign demand for American farm goods began to level off and then to decline. American foreign trade policies also contributed to this deterioration in foreign demand. High tariffs on goods imported to the United States helped undermine foreign demand for American farm products. To the extent that foreigners could not sell to us because of trade restrictions, they were unable to earn the funds they needed to buy from American producers. Furthermore, the domestic demand for farm products did not rise very much in the twenties. American stomachs were full, and as a result, income increases were used to buy automobiles, refrigerators, and a host of new products of industry. Finally, on the supply side of the picture, technological advances boosted farm output markedly. The net result of a lagging, inelastic demand and a sharply increasing supply of farm products was low farm prices and incomes.

The Great Depression of the 1930s was a particularly acute blow to American agriculture. The highly competitive nature of agriculture makes it especially vulnerable to bad

times. Unlike sellers who possess a modicum of monopoly power, farmers are unable to influence their prices. They are "price takers" at the mercy of the market. Therefore, when market demand declines as it did during the Depression, farm prices and farm incomes fall sharply. Ironically, farmers buy in markets which are basically noncompetitive. Hence, while their incomes fell by very large amounts, the prices of farmers' purchases declined very modestly. Farmers in the 1920s and 1930s found themselves in a harsh price-cost squeeze.

World War II provided welcome but temporary relief for the farmer. Both domestic and foreign demand for agricultural products boomed during the war, and prosperity returned to agriculture. Except for the 1948–1949 slump, the middle and the late forties were peak years for American farmers. Then in the 1950s a slow but certain relapse became evident, and agriculture was once again encountering difficulty.

■───────────────────────────

FARM INCOMES

The relative deterioration of the economic position of the farmer can be readily seen through income statistics. Indeed, low incomes are the most obvious symptom of the farm problem. Table 35-1 provides us with a comparison of per capita farm and nonfarm incomes since the mid-thirties. Generally speaking, farm incomes have been substantially less than nonfarm incomes. (As we will find later in this chapter, the data for 1973, wherein the reverse was true, reflects an unusual convergence of forces highly favorable to agriculture.) In 1975 per capita farm income was about 90 percent of per capita nonfarm income. Historically, the relationship has been more unfavorable to farmers; for example, in 1965 and 1970 per capita farm incomes were only 68 and 74 percent respectively of nonfarm incomes.

Given the farm-nonfarm income disparity, it is not surprising to find that rural people

Table 35-1 PER CAPITA DISPOSABLE INCOME OF FARM AND NONFARM PEOPLE, SELECTED YEARS, 1934–1975

Year	Farm people	Nonfarm people
1934	$ 163	$ 500
1937	283	638
1940	245	671
1944	630	1151
1948	913	1351
1952	949	1596
1956	877	1838
1960	1086	2014
1965	1692	2480
1970	2510	3390
1973	4665	4267
1975	4553	5081

Source: U.S. Department of Agriculture, *Farm Income Statistics.*

bear a disproportionate share of poverty. Although only about a third of all families live outside metropolitan areas, these families constitute about 40 percent of all families who live in poverty. On the other hand, it would be a gross error to conclude that *all* farmers are poor. Table 35-2 indicates there is great income disparity *within* agriculture. These figures show that in 1975, 4 percent of the farms in the United States accounted for 47 percent of total farm output. At the other extreme, cumulating the figures for the bottom two economic classes makes it clear that 43 percent of all farms sold less than $5000 worth of farm products in 1975 and that the output of these farms was a mere 3 percent of the total amount of farm products sold in that year. Note further that the 48 percent of our farms which market $10,000 or more each year produce 95 percent of all marketed farm products. The remaining 52 percent account for only 5 percent of marketed output. It is in this latter group that extremely low incomes—the main symptom of the difficulties which plague American agriculture—are predominant.

The data of Table 35-2 suggest a second point about which more will be said later: A substantial amount of human and property resources could leave agriculture without causing a very significant decline in total farm output.

CAUSES OF THE FARM PROBLEM

It is a bit misleading to talk of "the" farm problem. Actually, the changes which have occurred in farm incomes suggest the presence of both a long-run problem and a short-run problem. The long-run problem concerns those forces which have tended to cause farm prices and incomes to lag behind the trends of prices and incomes for the economy as a whole. The short-run problem has to do with the extreme year-to-year instability of farm incomes.

☐ The Long-run Problem

Complex problems can rarely be stated accurately in brief terms. This is certainly true of the long-run problem which plagues American agriculture. Nevertheless, a workable picture of the problem can be portrayed through the economic tools of demand and supply. In these terms, we may say that the causes of the long-run farm problem are embodied in

1 The *price inelasticity* of the demand for agricultural products

Table 35-2 DISTRIBUTION OF COMMERCIAL FARMS BY ECONOMIC CLASS, 1975

Value of farm products sold	Percent of total farms	Percent of total output
$100,000 or more	4	47
$40,000–$99,999	12	24
$20,000–$39,999	20	19
$10,000–$19,999	12	5
$5,000–$9,999	9	2
$2,500–$4,999	17	2
Less than $2,500	26	1
Total	100	100

Source: U.S. Department of Agriculture, *Farm Income Statistics.*

2 The *shifts* which have occurred over time in the demand and supply curves for farm products

3 The relative *immobility* of agricultural resources

The Inelastic Demand for Agricultural Products

In most developed societies, the price elasticity of demand for agricultural products is low. For farm products in the aggregate, the elasticity coefficient is estimated to be from .20 to .25.[1] These figures suggest that the prices of agricultural products would have to fall by 40 to 50 percent in order for consumers to increase their purchases by a mere 10 percent. Consumers apparently put a low value on additional agricultural output as compared with alternative goods. Why is this so? You will recall that the basic determinant of elasticity of demand is substitutability. That is, when the price of a product falls, the consumer will tend to substitute *that* product for other products whose prices presumably have not fallen. But in wealthy societies this "substitution effect" (Chapter 24) is very modest. People simply do not switch from three to six or eight meals each day in response to declines in the relative prices of agricultural products. An individual's capacity to substitute food for other products is subject to very real biological constraints. The inelasticity of agricultural demand can also be explained in terms of diminishing marginal utility. In a wealthy society, the population by and large is well fed and well clothed, that is, relatively saturated with the food and fiber of agriculture. Therefore, additional agricultural output entails rapidly diminishing marginal utility. Thus it takes very large price cuts to induce small increases in consumption. Curve *D* in Figure 35-2 on page 719 portrays an inelastic demand.

Technological Advance and Rapid Increases in Agricultural Supply

An inelastic demand for farm products is, in and of itself, innocent enough. It is the accompanying fact that the supply of agricultural products has increased in relation to the demand for them that has spelled declining farm incomes.

On the supply side of the picture, a rapid rate of technological advance, particularly since World War I, has caused significant increases in the supply of agricultural products. This technological progress has many roots: the virtually complete electrification and mechanization of farms; improved techniques of land management and soil conservation; irrigation; the development of hybrid crops; the availability of improved fertilizers and insecticides; improvements in the breeding and care of livestock; and so forth.

How meaningful have these technological advances actually been? Very! The simplest index is the increasing number of people which a single farmer's output will support. In 1820 each farm worker produced enough food and fiber to support four persons. By 1976 each farmer produced enough to support about sixty! There can be no question but that productivity in agriculture has risen significantly. Since World War II, productivity in agriculture has advanced at a rate which is *twice* as fast as that of the nonfarm economy.

Two additional important points must amend this discussion of the increasing productivity in American farming:

1 Most recent technological advances have not been initiated by farmers but are, rather, the result of government-sponsored programs of research and education and the work of farm machinery producers. Land-grant colleges, experiment stations, county agents of the Agricultural Extension Service, the inexhaustible supply of educational pamphlets issuing from the U.S. Department of Agriculture, and the research staffs of John Deere and International Harvester are the sources of technological advance in American agriculture.

---

[1] Dale E. Hathaway, *Problems of Progress in the Agricultural Economy* (Chicago: Scott, Foresman and Company, 1964), p. 10. This short book is an incisive and highly readable survey of the farm problem.

2 Technological advance has not occurred evenly throughout agriculture. Many farmers—particularly those resting on the bottom rung of the income ladder—are undermechanized, uninformed, and inefficient.

Lagging Demand for Agricultural Products

Increases in the demand for agricultural commodities have failed to keep pace with technologically inspired increases in their supply. Why? The answer lies in the two major determinants of agricultural demand—incomes and population.

In less developed countries, consumers must devote the bulk of their meager incomes to the products of agriculture—food and clothing—to sustain themselves. But as income expands beyond the subsistence level and the problem of hunger eventually gives way to one of obesity, consumers will increase their outlays on food and clothing at ever-declining rates. Once a consumer's stomach is filled, his or her thoughts turn to the amenities of life which industry, not agriculture, provides. Economic growth in the United States has boosted average per capita income far beyond the level of bare subsistence. As a result, *increases in the incomes of American consumers lead to less than proportionate increases in expenditures on farm products.* In technical terms, the demand for farm products is *income-inelastic;* that is, the demand for most agricultural products is quite insensitive to increases in income. Estimates indicate that a 10 percent increase in real per capita disposable income entails at the most an increase in the consumption of farm products of only 2 percent.[2]

Population is a somewhat different proposition. Despite the fact that, after a minimum income level is reached, each individual consumer's intake of food and fiber will become relatively fixed, more consumers obviously will mean an increase in the demand for farm prod-

[2]Joint Economic Committee, *Staff Report on Employment, Growth, and Price Levels* (Washington, 1960), p. 190.

ucts. And this increase has occurred. But population increases, added to the relatively small increase in the purchase of farm products which occurs as incomes rise, have simply not been great enough to match the concomitant increases in farm output.

Graphic Portrayal   When coupled with the inelastic demand for agricultural products, these shifts in supply and demand have resulted in declining farm incomes. This is illustrated in Figure 35-1, where a large increase in supply is shown against a very modest increase in demand. Because of the inelastic demand for farm products, these shifts have resulted in a sharp decline in farm prices accompanied by relatively small increases in sales. Farm incomes therefore decline. Diagrammatically, income before the increase in supply occurs (measured by rectangle $OPAQ$) will exceed farm income after supply increases (OP_1BQ_1). The income "loss" of P_1PAC is not fully offset by the income "gain" of $QCBQ_1$. In summary,

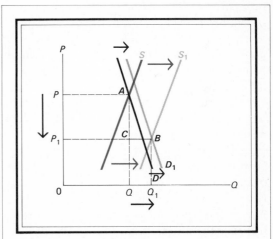

FIGURE 35-1   A GRAPHIC SUMMARY OF THE LONG-RUN FARM PROBLEM

In the long run, increases in the demand for agricultural products (D to D_1) have not kept pace with the increases in supply (S to S_1) which technological advances have permitted. Coupled with the fact that agricultural demand is inelastic, these shifts have tended to depress farm prices (as from P to P_1) and incomes (as from $OPAQ$ to OP_1BQ_1).

given an inelastic demand for farm products, an increase in the supply of farm products relative to the demand for them has created persistent tendencies for farm incomes to fall. This is not to say that farm incomes have fallen absolutely, but rather, that farm incomes have clearly lagged behind the nonfarm sector of the economy (Table 35-1).

Immobility of Resources Our previous discussion of the workings of the price system (Chapter 33) would certainly suggest an obvious and automatic solution to the long-run problem faced by agriculture. As noted earlier, agriculture is a highly competitive industry, characterized by large numbers of independent firms each of which produces a minute fraction of the overall output of quite highly standardized products. One would expect declining farm prices and incomes to signal an exodus of resources from agriculture. Prices and incomes which are low in relation to the rest of the economy would seemingly prompt farmers to leave their farms in favor of more lucrative occupations. The adjustments of a competitive industry, as outlined in Chapters 5 and 26, indicate that this exodus of farmers would reduce industry supply in relation to demand, thereby boosting farm prices and incomes. This reallocation of resources away from agriculture and toward industry, one can assume, would bring farm incomes into rough accord with those of the rest of the economy.

Human resources *have* shifted out of agriculture in large numbers as the competitive market model would predict. But, except for the minute portion of total farmland which borders on metropolitan areas, most farmland has no real alternative uses. Farmers leave, but the land they leave stays in production. Hence, the mass outmigration of labor from agriculture, shown in Table 35-3, has failed to close the farm-nonfarm income gap embodied in Table 35-1. Furthermore, we must recognize that the farm-nonfarm disequilibrium is not the result of a single, one-shot imbalance. Hence, even as labor leaves agriculture in the

Table 35-3 THE DECLINING FARM POPULATION, SELECTED YEARS, 1910–1976

Year	Farm population, millions	Percentage of the total population
1910	32.1	35
1920	31.9	30
1930	30.5	25
1935	32.2	25
1940	30.5	23
1945	24.4	18
1950	23.0	15
1955	19.1	12
1960	15.6	9
1965	12.4	6
1970	9.7	5
1973	9.5	5
1976	8.3	4

Source: Statistical Abstract of the United States, 1962, p. 613, and Economic Report of the President, 1977, p. 292.

pursuit of higher incomes in nonfarm sectors of the economy, the components of the long-run farm problem *continue* to depress farm incomes and to set the stage for a further exodus. Despite the remarkable secular decline in the farm population displayed in Table 35-3, agricultural economists still talk of surplus labor in the agricultural sector. It must be appended that evidence for the 1970s suggests that the human resource exodus from farming *may* be coming to an end. The reasons for this are several. First, there is the simple fact that the farm population is now at an historical low, and therefore the possibility of further outmigration is diminished. Second, the rate of growth in agricultural productivity seems to be declining in recent years. Finally, as we shall discover shortly, agricultural demand, and thus the demand for farm labor, has risen in the 1970s.

It is correct to say that, historically, the relative slowness of the reallocation of farmers from agriculture to industry is the crux of the farm problem. Ironically enough, in an industry long associated with the word "surplus," we find that the biggest and most fundamental farm surplus of all is the number of farmers.

Indeed, the farm problem can be correctly envisioned as a problem of resource misallocation. It is the fact that too many farmers are sharing agriculture's shrinking slice of the national income pie that makes income per farmer small.

□   **The Short-run Problem**

The lag of farm incomes behind the rest of the economy is evidence of the long-run agricultural problem. Substantial year-to-year fluctuations in farm prices and therefore in incomes reflect a short-run problem. This short-run instability can be traced back to the inelastic demand for agricultural products which contributes to the instability of farm prices and incomes in two different ways.

Fluctuations in Output   On the production side of the picture, the inelastic demand for farm products causes small changes in agricultural production to be magnified into relatively larger changes in farm prices and incomes. To understand this point, we must first note that farmers possess only limited control over their production. In the first place, floods, droughts, an unexpected frost, insect damage, and similar disasters can mean short crops. Conversely, an excellent growing season may mean bumper crops. Weather factors are beyond the control of farmers, yet they exert an important influence upon production. Second, the highly competitive nature of agriculture makes it virtually impossible for farmers to form a huge combination to control their production. If all the millions of widely scattered and independent producers should by chance plant an unusually large or abnormally small portion of their land, extra large or small outputs would result even if the growing season were normal.

Now, putting the instability of farm production together with an inelastic demand for farm products, we can readily discover why farm prices and incomes are highly unstable. Figure 35-2 is pertinent. Even if we assume

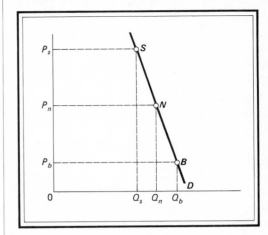

FIGURE 35-2   THE EFFECT OF OUTPUT CHANGES ON FARM PRICES AND INCOMES

Because of the inelasticity of demand for farm products, a relatively small change in output (Q_n to Q_s or Q_b) will cause relatively large changes in farm prices (P_n to P_s or P_b) and incomes (OP_nNQ_n to OP_sSQ_s or OP_bBQ_b).

that the market demand for agriculture products is stable at D, the inelastic nature of demand will magnify small changes in output into relatively large changes in farm prices and income. For example, assume that a "normal" crop of Q_n results in a "normal" price of P_n and a "normal" farm income of OP_nNQ_n. But a bumper crop or a short crop will cause large deviations from these normal prices and incomes; these results stem from the inelasticity of demand for farm products.

If an unusually good growing season occurs, the resulting bumper crop of Q_b will cause farm incomes to *fall* from OP_nNQ_n to OP_bBQ_b. Why? Because when demand is inelastic, an increase in the quantity sold will be accompanied by a *more than* proportionate decline in price. The net result is that total receipts, that is, total farm income, will decline. Similarly, for farmers as a group, a short crop caused by, say, drought may boost farm incomes. A short crop of Q_s will raise total farm income from OP_nNQ_n to OP_sSQ_s. Why? Because a decline in output will cause a *more than* proportionate increase in price when demand is inelastic. Ironically, for farmers as a group, a short crop may be a blessing and a bumper crop a hardship. Our conclusion is this: Given a stable market demand for farm products, the inelasticity of that demand will turn relatively small changes in output into relatively larger changes in farm prices and incomes.

Fluctuations in Demand   The other aspect of the short-run instability of farm incomes has to do with shifts in the demand curve for agricultural products. Let us suppose that somehow agricultural output is stabilized at the "normal" level of Q_n in Figure 35-3. Now, because of the inelasticity of the demand for farm products, short-run fluctuations in the demand for these products will cause markedly different prices and incomes to be

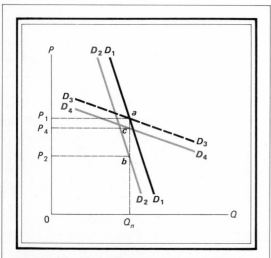

FIGURE 35-3 THE EFFECT OF DEMAND CHANGES ON FARM PRICES AND INCOMES

Because of the highly inelastic demand for agricultural products, a small shift in demand (D_1D_1 to D_2D_2) will cause drastically different levels of farm prices (P_1 to P_2) and farm incomes (OP_1aQ_n to OP_2bQ_n) to be associated with a given level of production Q_n. Note that equal changes in a more elastic demand curve (D_3D_3 to D_4D_4) will be accompanied by much smaller price (P_1 to P_4) and income (OP_1aQ_n to OP_4cQ_n) alterations.

associated with this level of production that we assume to be constant. That is, a slight drop in demand from D_1D_1 to D_2D_2 will cause farm incomes to fall from OP_1aQ_n to OP_2bQ_n. A relatively small decline in demand gives farmers a drastically reduced money reward for the same amount of production. Conversely, a slight increase in demand will bring an equally sharp increase in farm incomes for the same volume of output. These large price-income changes are linked to the fact that demand is inelastic. This relationship can be grasped by observing the much smaller price-income changes which accompany an equal shift in demand from the more elastic demand curve D_3D_3.[3] If demand drops from D_3D_3 to D_4D_4, price will fall very modestly from P_1 to P_4 and income will fall only from OP_1aQ_n to OP_4cQ_n.

It is tempting to argue that the sharp declines in farm prices which accompany a decrease in demand will cause many farmers to close down in the short run, thereby reducing total output and alleviating these price-income declines. But farm production is relatively insensitive to price changes, because the farmer's fixed costs are high compared with his variable costs. Interest, rental, tax, and mortgage payments on buildings and equipment are the major costs faced by the farmer. These are clearly fixed charges. Furthermore, the labor supply of the farmer and his family can also be regarded as a fixed cost. So long as he stays on his farm, the farmer cannot reduce his costs by firing himself! This means that his variable costs are for the small amounts of hired help he may employ, plus expenditures for seed, fertilizer, and fuel. As a result of this high volume of fixed costs, the farmer is almost invariably better off when working his land than when sitting idle and attempting to pay his fixed costs out of pocket. The other factors, noted previously, which contribute to the rela-

[3]Though they may not appear so graphically, these two shifts in demand are equal in the sense that in each instance buyers want to purchase the same amount less at each possible price.

tive immobility of farmers are also pertinent. In particular, if a decline in the demand for farm output is part of an overall recession, there will be no real incentive for farmers to stop production in order to seek nonexistent jobs in industry. In fact, a migration in the opposite direction—from the city to the farm—often accompanies a full-scale depression. Note in Table 35-3 the absolute *increase* in the farm population which occurred between 1930 and 1935. Note, too, in Figure 10-5 that between 1929 and 1933, farm prices fell by 63 percent and farm output by a mere 6 percent.

□ **A Restatement**

Let us pause at this point to bring our knowledge of the causes of the long- and short-run farm problems into sharper focus. The long-run problem is the result of the unhappy combination of four factors.

1 The demand for agricultural commodities is inelastic.

2 Rapid technological advance has given rise to significant increases in the supply of farm products.

3 The demand for agricultural commodities has increased very modestly. This consideration, combined with factors 1 and 2, has resulted in a tendency for farm prices and incomes to fall or to grow only modestly.

4 The relatively fixed nature of agricultural resources—land, capital, and farmers themselves—has caused low prices and incomes to persist; resources have not been reallocated from agriculture rapidly enough to offset the tendency for agricultural prices and incomes to decline.

In the short run, the extreme sensitiveness of farm prices and incomes is based upon the inelastic demand for agricultural products which transforms small changes in farm output and demand into much larger changes in farm prices and incomes.

□ **Agriculture and Growth**

An alternative explanation correctly puts emphasis upon resource misallocation as the core of the long-run farm problem and couches the problem in terms of a growing economy. Of necessity, primitive or underdeveloped countries have essentially agrarian economies. The total population of such a nation must devote its efforts to agricultural endeavors to provide enough food and fiber to sustain itself. But, as technological advance increases productivity per farmer, the economy can maintain or even increase its consumption of food and clothing and simultaneously transfer a portion of its population into nonagricultural pursuits. This is the path which any expanding, progressive economy follows. Indeed, the shift of resources from agricultural to industrial pursuits is the earmark of a growing economy. The experience of the United States is illustrative. About 90 percent of our population was devoted to agriculture in the eighteenth century. At present about 4 percent of the population is in farming, the remaining 96 percent being free to produce refrigerators, furniture, automobiles, and the thousands of other goods and services which make up a high standard of living. But, in American capitalism, the actual shift of resources to nonagricultural employments has not kept pace with the rate of reallocation which rapid technological advance permits. The result has been persistent downward pressure on farm prices and incomes.

RATIONALE FOR PUBLIC POLICY

Historically, many arguments have been used in seeking and rationalizing public aid to agriculture. It has been contended, for example, that farming, and particularly the family farm, is a fundamental American institution and should be nurtured as "a way of life." Furthermore, farmers are subject to certain extraordinary hazards—floods, droughts, and invasion by hordes of insects—to which other industries are not exposed. It has been held, too, that agriculture is a major cog in the American economy, and therefore prosperity for farmers is a prerequisite for prosperity in the economy as a whole.

Two additional arguments for special aid to agriculture are of greater substance and merit more detailed consideration.

□ Costs-of-Progress Argument

While agriculture has made great contributions to the nation's economic growth, it has had to bear a disproportionately large share of the costs associated with this progress. The high degree of progressiveness of American agriculture has resulted in substantial and widespread benefits to the economy as a whole. The population has been able to get more and better food and fiber from agriculture in exchange for a smaller portion of its money income. Furthermore, over the years agriculture has been a major source of labor for industry (Table 35-3).[4]

> Farm families have for years produced children well in excess of the numbers needed to replace retiring members of the farm labor force. This, together with the absolute decline in the number of people on farms, means that a very substantial portion of our present productive nonfarm labor force was raised on a farm, educated in schools heavily dependent upon farm taxes, and migrated to the cities after finishing school.

On the other hand, the peculiar combination of economic circumstances already discussed—an inelastic demand for farm products, rapid technological progress, the slow growth of demand, and the relatively fixed nature of agricultural resources—has caused farm people to bear a large share of the costs of agricultural progress in the form of incomes substantially below those of nonfarm income receivers.

[4]Hathaway, op cit., p. 5.

□ Market-power Argument

A second argument focuses upon the question of market power. Agriculture is a highly competitive industry, comprising hundreds of thousands of small, geographically dispersed producers. As a result, farmers have no control over the prices at which they must sell their products. Nonagricultural industries, on the other hand, have varying degrees of market power and, within limits, the capacity to adjust their prices. In particular, most of the firms from which farmers buy machinery, fertilizer, gasoline, and so forth, have some capacity to control their prices. Given the farmer's unenviable market position in comparison with the nonfarm sectors, it is not surprising that he gets a disproportionately small share of the national income. It is argued on the basis of this rationale that a special farm program to help agriculture is justified as a means of compensating for the weak market position of farmers. Stated differently, agriculture is the last stronghold of pure competition in an otherwise imperfectly competitive economy; it warrants public aid to offset disadvantageous terms of trade which result.

FARM POLICY: OLD AND NEW

On the basis of these arguments and the disproportionately large voice which farmers have historically had in Congress, a detailed "farm program" concerning (1) farm prices, incomes, and output; (2) soil conservation; (3) agricultural research; (4) farm credit; (5) crop insurance; and other factors has come into being and persisted since the 1930s.

But the thrust of our farm policy has shifted through time. At the risk of oversimplification, our *traditional policies*—policies which prevailed during the 1930s, 1940s, and 1950s—were characterized by government market intervention. Specifically, traditional policy was largely designed to restrict farm production for the purpose of raising farm prices and incomes. These "price-centered" policies were a reflection of the excess productive capacity which characterized agriculture during most of this period. But, in the 1960s and particularly in the 1970s, the problems of excess productive capacity and chronically depressed farm incomes have diminished in importance, thanks largely to substantial increases in the overseas demand for American farm products. Hence, public policy in the 1960s and 1970s has shifted away from market intervention and output restriction. The focus of *new policies* in the 1970s is toward freer farm markets and the realization of low-cost increases in agricultural production. We shall consider first the traditional policies, beginning with the concept of parity.

◼ TRADITIONAL POLICY: PARITY

The Agricultural Adjustment Act of 1933 established the concept of *parity* as a cornerstone of agricultural policy. The simple rationale of the parity concept can be readily envisioned in both real and money terms. In real terms, parity says that year after year for a given output of farm products, a farmer should be able to acquire a given total amount of goods and services. A given real output should always result in the same real income. "If a man could take a bushel of corn to town in 1912 and sell it and buy himself a shirt, he should be able to take a bushel of corn to town today and buy a shirt." In money terms, the parity concept suggests that the relationship between the prices received by farmers for their output and the prices they must pay for goods and services should remain constant. Hence, if the prices of the items farmers purchase increase, then the prices which farmers receive for their products *should* rise accordingly.

☐ Price Supports

The practical importance of the notion of parity prices is that it provides the rationale for government price supports on farm prod-

ucts. The fact that, in the long run, the market prices received by farmers have not generally kept abreast of prices paid by them means that to achieve parity or some percentage thereof, the government is likely to be required to establish above-equilibrium, or "support," prices on farm products.

Support prices have a number of significant effects. Suppose, in Figure 35-4, that the support price is P_s as compared with the equilibrium price P_e.

1 Surplus Output The most obvious effect is that product surpluses will result. Private consumers will be willing to purchase only OQ units at the supported price, while farmers will supply OQ_s units. The amount QQ_s is a surplus. What happens to this surplus? The government must buy it in order to

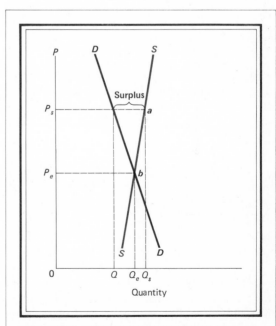

FIGURE 35-4 EFFECTIVE PRICE SUPPORTS RESULT IN FARM SURPLUSES

Application of the parity concept obligates government to support farm prices at above-equilibrium levels. These supported prices result in persistent surpluses of farm products.

make the above-equilibrium support price effective. Because of such purchases, huge surpluses accumulated during most of the 1950s and persisted until the late 1960s. These large accumulated surpluses were economically undesirable on two counts. First, their very existence indicates a misallocation of the economy's resources. Government-held surpluses reflect the fact that the economy is devoting large amounts of resources to the production of commodities which, *at existing supported prices,* are simply not wanted by consumers. Second, the storing of surplus products is an expensive undertaking which has added to the cost of the farm program and ultimately to the consumer's tax bill. Storage costs on surpluses have run as high as $1 billion per year when accumulated stocks were particularly large.

2 Consumers' Loss Consumers "lose" in two ways. First, they will be paying a higher price (P_s rather than P_e) and consuming less (Q rather than Q_e) of the product. Second, they will be paying higher taxes to finance the government's purchase of the surplus. In Figure 35-4, this added tax burden will amount to the surplus output QQ_s, multiplied by its price P_s. Storage costs, of course, add to this tax burden.

3 Farmers' Gain Farmers, of course, gain from price supports. In Figure 35-4, gross receipts rise from the free-market level of OP_ebQ_e to the supported level of OP_saQ_s.

□ **Surplus Controls**

By what means might government cope with the surplus farm output which accompanies effective price supports? An elementary knowledge of the tools of supply and demand suggests that programs designed to reduce market supply or increase market demand would help bring the market price up to the desired supported price, thereby reducing or eliminating farm surpluses (Figure 35-4).

Restricting Supply On the supply side, public policy has long been aimed at restricting farm output. In particular, *acreage allotment programs* have accompanied the application of price supports. In return for the privilege of getting price supports on their crops, farmers must agree to limit the number of acres planted. Attempting to bring quantity supplied and quantity demanded into balance, the Department of Agriculture estimates the amount of each product which private buyers will take at the supported price. This amount is then translated into the number of acres of planting which will produce this amount. The total acreage figure is apportioned among states, counties, and ultimately individual farmers. Similarly, various *acreage reserve programs* have been employed whereby the Department of Agriculture makes direct payments to farmers for removing land entirely from crop production. For example, under the "soil bank" program, the government in effect rented land from farmers. Such idle land was to be planted in cover crops or timber, not in cash crops.

Have these supply-restricting programs been successful? It is difficult to give an unqualified answer. Certainly they have not eliminated surplus farm production. The basic reason is that acreage reduction invariably results in less than proportionate declines in production. Why? Farmers retire their worst land and keep their best in production. Those acres which are tilled are cultivated more intensively. The use of better seed, more and better fertilizer and insecticides, and more manpower will enhance output per acre. However, without these output controls, there is no doubt that accumulated farm surpluses and their associated costs would have been much greater than has actually been the case.

Bolstering Demand Government has followed a number of paths in seeking to augment the demand for agricultural products.
1 Both government and private industry have spent considerable sums for research to

uncover new uses for agricultural commodities. Overall, the results have been modest.

2 A variety of programs has been invoked to augment the domestic consumption of farm products. For example, the *food stamp program* is designed to distribute surplus farm products to low-income families. *School lunch programs* and the distribution of surpluses to welfare and charitable institutions have also had the effect of enhancing the domestic demand for farm output.

3 A number of measures have been undertaken to increase foreign demand for American farm products. For example, our Food for Peace program under Public Law 480 has permitted the less developed countries to buy our surplus farm products with their own currencies, rather than with dollars. Furthermore, in international trade bargaining, our negotiators have pressed hard to persuade foreign nations to reduce protective tariffs and other barriers against our farm products.

□   **Evaluation**

How successful has public policy been in resolving the long-run farm problem? Although it is difficult to offer an unequivocal answer, economists are generally critical of American farm policy. Let us note two major criticisms.

Symptoms and Causes   First and foremost, the farm program has failed to get at the causes of the farm problem. Public policy toward agriculture is designed to treat symptoms and not causes. The root *cause* of the farm problem has been a misallocation of resources between agriculture and the rest of the economy. Historically, the problem has been one of too many farmers. The effect or symptom of this misallocation of resources is low farm incomes. *For the most part, public policy in agriculture has been oriented toward supporting farm prices and incomes rather than toward alleviating the resource allocation problem, which is the fundamental cause of these sagging farm incomes.*

Some critics go further and argue that price-income supports have encouraged people to stay in agriculture when they otherwise would have migrated to some nonfarm occupation. That is, the price-income orientation of the farm program has deterred the very reallocation of resources which is necessary to resolve the long-run farm problem. On the other hand, one can argue that the extra income provided by price supports may have enabled farmers to provide more education for their children, thereby preparing them for better and higher-paying nonfarm jobs.

Misguided Subsidies   A second criticism is that price-income support programs have most benefited those farmers who least need government assistance. Assuming the goal of our farm program is the bolstering of low farm incomes, it follows that any program of government aid should be aimed at farmers at the bottom of the farm income distribution. But the poor, small-output farmer simply does not produce and sell enough in the market to get much aid from price supports. It is the large corporate farm which reaps the benefits by virtue of its large output. Individual subsidy checks running into hundreds of thousands of dollars are not easy to justify. If public policy must be designed to supplement farm incomes, a strong case can certainly be made for making those benefits vary inversely with one's position in the income distribution. An income-support program should be geared to *people,* not *commodities.* Many economists contend that, on equity grounds, direct income subsidies to poor farmers are highly preferable to indirect price support subsidies which go primarily to large and prosperous farmers.

The other side of the picture here is that our price support programs are also output-restricting programs. Remember that to receive price supports, a farmer must agree to restrict his supply. If only small (low-income) farmers were eligible for price supports, little or no restricting of farm output would have occurred and our farm surplus problems would have been much more acute.

THE SEVENTIES: WINDFALL OR WATERSHED?

In the 1970s, conditions in American agriculture changed quite dramatically. Against this backdrop of change, important alterations occurred in farm policy. What were these changes in agricultural conditions and policy?

□   A New Era?

Recall that since World War II the basic problem in agriculture has been one of excess productive capacity. Consequently, farm policy has been essentially restrictive, that is, public policy has focused upon the restriction of farm output for the purpose of increasing farm prices and income. Thus, for example, since the early 1960s, about one-sixth of the nation's cropland has been held out of production.

But in 1972 and 1973 the agricultural picture was dramatically altered. Specifically, a number of interrelated factors accounted for a sharply increasing foreign demand for American agricultural products. As Figure 35-5 indicates, our agricultural exports spurted dramatically from about $6 billion in 1969 to almost $22 billion in 1975. Why did this happen?

1 On a worldwide basis—and especially in Western Europe and Japan—incomes have been expanding rapidly. But most countries have little or no excess capacity in agriculture; indeed, many countries were already large importers of food. Hence, much of their increased food and fiber demand has been for American output.

2 Dietary habits in Europe and Japan have been shifting toward the consumption of more red meat and poultry. Since it takes about 6 pounds of grain to produce 1 pound of meat, the increased demand for grains has been especially strong.

3 Poor harvests in many countries also accelerated the demand for American foodstuffs.

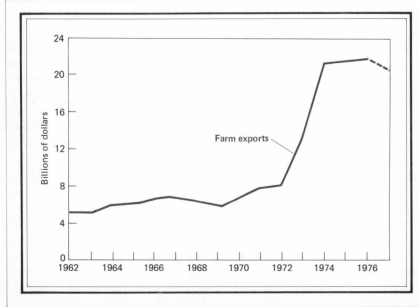

FIGURE 35-5 U.S. AGRICULTURAL EXPORTS

Our exports of farm products expanded sharply in the early 1970s and have remained at high levels. Causes of this export growth include bad harvests, rising incomes, and changing dietary habits abroad, in addition to the devaluation of the dollar. (*Department of Agriculture.*)

4 A further stimulus occurred in 1971 and another in 1973 as a result of the devaluation of the dollar in international trade. That is, dollars became less expensive in terms of other currencies, making American products—including farm products—cheaper for foreigners to buy (Chapter 44).

5 Finally, the opening of communist markets to American farm products bolstered demand. The controversial sale of over $1 billion of grain to the Soviet Union in 1972–1973 was particularly significant.

In short, all these factors, coupled with a rather strong expansion of incomes domestically, sharply boosted agricultural demand, farm prices, and receipts.

□   **A New Farm Program**

Many critics of past agricultural policy take the position that an ultimate solution to the farm problem must entail, in general, less government involvement in agriculture and, in particular, a return to freer markets. Seizing upon the very favorable agricultural situation of the 1970s, Congress passed new farm legislation which tends to move in these directions. Specifically, the Agriculture and Consumer Protection Act of 1973 embodies a four-year program with the following basic features.

1 **Target Prices** The price supports previously legislated have been replaced with a system of *target prices* which are established by law. The target price is essentially a floor, or guaranteed minimum, price on basic agricultural products. The target prices were established substantially below the very high price levels of 1973, but generally above the support prices of prior legislation. These price floors operate so that "when market prices are above the targets, no Government 'deficiency payments' are made to farmers and the Government has little involvement in agriculture. In years when market prices fall below the target prices, Government payments to farmers make up the difference between target and market prices. . . ."[5] Subsidies to farmers under this target price program could be small or nonexistent *if* farm prices remain high; but a return to agricultural "hard times" could make the program extremely costly to taxpayers.

2 **All-out Production** Although the new legislation extends the previously legislated authority to take land out of production, the implementation of this authority is now at the discretion of the Secretary of Agriculture. And, in fact, in the mid-1970s, the Secretary has given farmers the green light to produce as much as they choose. Temporarily, at least, American agricultural policy has shifted from restriction to the encouragement of all-out production.

3 **Subsidy Ceilings** The new program also deals more effectively than prior legislation with the problem of paying huge subsidies to large, prosperous farmers. The 1973 law limits total payments to $20,000 per individual farmer for all commodity programs combined.

In short, under the current farm legislation we are moving from price supports toward a more market-oriented policy, on the one hand, and from output restriction toward expanded production in response to market incentives, on the other.

□   **Consequences and Implications**

The agricultural "boom" of the 1970s, along with the new agricultural policies, has a number of salient implications.

1 **Alleviated Income Problem** There is no doubt that the expanded demand for agricultural products has generally been of considerable benefit to farmers. But there have been offsetting considerations. While the cash receipts of farmers from the sale of their products have increased sharply, so have produc-

[5] *Economic Report of the President, 1974* (Washington), p. 133.

tion costs. For example, livestock producers are major buyers of grains for feed; hence, rapidly rising grain prices mean higher costs for cattle production. Furthermore, historically American farmers have obtained a substantial fraction of their incomes from government subsidies. But most of these subsidies vary inversely with the incomes farmers receive from the market. Thus, when market prices and incomes go up, farm income from public subsidy tends to fall. The point is that net farm incomes do *not* rise in proportion to gross farm receipts.

2 End of Excess Capacity? Excess productivity capacity in American agriculture *may* be disappearing. For example, under the new farm policy, some 60 million acres of land were released from acreage controls in the 1972–1974 period, but only 37 million acres were added to the nation's cultivated area in those years. This suggests that substantial investments are required to bring more land into production, and current farm prices are insufficient to justify that investment. Furthermore, much of the increase in export demand has been met by sales of grain from reserve stockpiles. As a result, these reserves have been substantially depleted. In 1973, total grain stocks reached their lowest levels since 1953. The depletion of these reserves means that the United States and the rest of the world are more vulnerable to poor harvests and consequent food shortages.

3 Domestic-Foreign Trade-off In the past, excess productive capacity and large grain reserves made it possible for the United States to increase food exports without significantly affecting domestic food prices. But in the current situation, as more foodstuffs are shipped abroad, available domestic supplies are reduced and prices rise. Rising food prices were a major factor in the domestic inflation of the early 1970s. In 1973, retail food prices rose at the most rapid rate in over a quarter of a century; in August 1973, food prices were 23 percent higher than they had been ten months earlier! It is no wonder that the issue of export embargoes on farm products was accorded considerable attention in the 1976 Presidential campaign.

4 Greater Price Instability? Some experts feel that the problem of farm price instability may be aggravated in the present situation. Why so? Historically, price instability was cushioned by manipulating farm product reserves or changing the amount of land in production. Potential price increases could be softened by drawing on reserves and bringing more land into production. Conversely, a price fall could be offset by adding to reserves and withdrawing land from production. But fallow land reserves and surplus stocks are no longer available, at least to the degree they were under traditional farm policies. Furthermore, agricultural prices are obviously more exposed to the vagaries of international markets.

> The domestic agricultural policies of the European Community and Japan inhibit the adjustments that can take place in their agricultural markets. Consequently, the burden of adjustment to changing conditions of demand and supply is pushed onto the United States and other exporting countries. In addition, the growing involvement of the U.S.S.R. in world trade in recent years has transmitted to world markets the shocks stemming from fluctuations in the relatively unstable agricultural sector of that country. Some 80 percent of the year-to-year fluctuations in the world wheat trade since 1960 have been accounted for by swings in Soviet wheat trade.[6]

5 International Aspects Two implications of the growing role of export markets for American farm products merit comment at this point. First, the recent upsurge of our

---

[6]*Economic Report of the President, 1975* (Washington), p. 173.

agricultural exports has been very helpful in dealing with our balance of payments problem (Chapters 43 and 44). Crudely put, the earnings from our growing farm exports have been helpful in financing our rapidly expanding imports of petroleum. Second, it is estimated that about two-thirds of our agricultural exports are subject to some form of restrictive trade barriers in foreign markets. The United States is now engaged in multilateral negotiations to reduce or eliminate barriers to international trade. It is obviously of great importance to the prosperity of American farmers that protected foreign markets be opened to our agricultural exports.

The current agricultural situation is clouded with uncertainties. How well will the new, market-oriented farm policy work? Will the foreign demand for American farm products remain strong? Has agriculture moved permanently from a situation of chronic excess capacity and abundance to an environment of full capacity and scarcity? Or will the forces underlying our traditional long-run farm problem eventually reassert themselves?

Summary

1 Rapid technological advance, coupled with a highly inelastic and relatively constant demand for agricultural output, has caused low farm incomes. Because of the relatively fixed nature of both property and human resources, the price system has failed to correct the farm problem by reallocating sufficient amounts of resources out of agriculture. In the short run, the highly inelastic nature of agricultural demand translates small changes in output and small shifts in demand into large fluctuations in prices and incomes.

2 The two basic arguments for public assistance to agriculture are *a.* farmers have borne a disproportionately large share of the costs of economic progress, and *b.* farmers have little market power, compared with other sectors of the economy.

3 Historically, agricultural policy has been price-centered and based upon the parity concept. The application of price supports, based upon the parity concept, gives rise to surplus agricultural output. The government has pursued a variety of programs to reduce the supply of, and increase the demand for, agricultural products in order to limit the size of these surpluses.

4 Farm policy has been criticized for treating symptoms (low incomes) rather than causes (resource misallocation) and for maintaining the inverse relationship between the size of farm subsidies and economic need.

5 Owing largely to substantial increases in export demand, agriculture enjoyed considerable prosperity in the early 1970s. Consequences of this prosperity include rapidly rising domestic food prices and the reduction of excess productive capacity.

6 The Agriculture and Consumer Protection Act of 1973 shifts agricultural policy in the direction of freer markets, encourages all-out food production, and imposes a maximum $20,000 limit on commodity subsidies per farmer.

Questions and Study Suggestions

1 Key terms and concepts to remember: long-run farm problem; short-run farm problem; Agricultural Adjustment Act; parity concept; price supports; Public Law 480: Food for Peace program; acreage allotment program; soil bank; Agriculture and Consumer Protection Act; target price.

2   Explain how each of the following contributes to the farm problem: *a.* the inelasticity of the demand for farm products, *b.* rapid technological progress in farming, *c.* the modest long-run growth in the demand for farm commodities, *d.* the competitiveness of agriculture, and *e.* the relative fixity or immobility of agricultural resources.

3   What relationship, if any, can you detect between the fact that the farmer's fixed costs of production are large and the fact that the supply of most agricultural products is generally inelastic? Be specific in your answer.

4   "The supply and demand for agricultural products are such that small changes in agricultural supply will result in drastic changes in prices. However, large changes in farm prices have modest effects on agricultural output." Carefully evaluate. *Hint:* A brief review of the distinction between *supply* and *quantity supplied* may be of assistance.

5   "The whole process of economic growth is one of making agriculture less fundamental in the economic system. The fewer people the nation needs to employ in the production of food and fiber, the better off it is—and the better off farm people are."[7] Evaluate this statement.

6   The key to efficient resource allocation is the shifting of resources from low-productivity to high-productivity uses. Given the high and expanding physical productivity of agricultural resources, explain why many economists want to get more resources out of farming in the interest of greater allocative efficiency.

7   "Industry complains of the higher taxes it must pay to finance subsidies to agriculture. Yet the fact that the trend of agricultural prices has been downward while industrial prices have been moving upward suggests that on balance agriculture is actually subsidizing industry." Explain and evaluate.

8   "Because consumers as a whole must ultimately pay the total incomes received by farmers, it makes no real difference whether this income is paid through free farm markets or through supported prices supplemented by subsidies financed out of tax revenues." Analyze this statement very carefully.

9   Suppose you are the president of a local chapter of one of the major farm organizations. You are directed by the chapter's membership to formulate policy statements for the chapter which cover the following topics: *a.* antitrust policy, *b.* monetary policy, *c.* fiscal policy, and *d.* tariff policy. Briefly outline the policy statements which will best serve the interests of farmers. What is the rationale underlying each statement? Do you see any conflicts or inconsistencies in your policy statements?

10   Explain and evaluate the following statements:

a.   "Price supports intensify rather than resolve the farm problem."

b.   "The best farm program is the Employment Act of 1946."

c.   "The trouble with parity prices in agriculture is that they strip the price mechanism of its ability to allocate resources."

11   Reconcile these two statements: "The farm problem is one of overproduction." "Despite the tremendous productive capacity of American agriculture, plenty of Americans are going hungry." What assumptions about the price system are implied in your answer?

12   Briefly describe the Agriculture and Consumer Protection Act of 1973. Is it a significant departure from prior farm legislation? Justify your answer.

13   What factors account for the great increase in American farm exports in the 1970s? Do you feel these factors are sustainable?

[7]Lauren Soth, *Farm Trouble* (Princeton, N.J.: Princeton University Press, 1957), p. 40.

Selected References

Duncan, Marvin R., Blaine W. Bickel, and Glenn H. Miller, Jr.: *International Trade and American Agriculture* (Federal Reserve Bank of Kansas City, 1976).

Economic Report of the President, 1975 (Washington), pp. 160–186.

Harshbarger, C. Edward, and Richard D. Rees: "The New Farm Program—What Does It Mean?" *Monthly Review,* Federal Reserve Bank of Kansas City, January 1974.

Heady, Earl O.: *A Primer on Food, Agriculture, and Public Policy* (New York: Random House, Inc., 1967).

U.S. and World Food Situation, Hearings before the Senate Committee on Agriculture and Forestry (Washington, 1974).

Last Word
Farming: The Good Life?

In early 1977 the Senate Committee on Agriculture, Nutrition, and Forestry held hearings to obtain reactions to pending farm legislation and to gain insight into farm problems. This last Word is comprised of two short excerpts from statements made by farmers at these hearings.

(*First excerpt: A Kansas wheat farmer explains his economic plight.*) . . . our total result from our 1976 crops was a loss of $347.71. Our deductible expenses were in excess of $60,000.00. A continuation of the present prices for our grain leaves us nothing to live on; nothing for food, clothing, housing, health insurance, life insurance or recreation, etc. No compensation for the endless hours of labor, nothing as return on our land, nothing with which to make other capital investment, no put-back for depreciating equipment . . . it kills incentive. What America does not need is farmers who don't care, who suddenly cannot care. We cannot, being in sound mind, continue to plant knowing we will have further loss.

We were forced this year to mortgage a quarter of ground in order to have the money to plant 1977 crops. Two more years like this and we'll be not just $200,000.00 in debt, we'll be bankrupt. Loans only add to our burden, we must have more for the products we raise.

(*Second excerpt: A midwestern farm wife decries the effects of government policies.*) The farming industry is in serious trouble. Through a combination of circumstances over which we, as producers, have very little control, the future looks extremely grim.

One of these circumstances was the world-wide grain shortage of 1973. In fear of another back to back shortage, we were asked, by our country, to plant fence row to fence row to replenish our grain stocks. We complied. Now we are faced with a world-wide surplus, and cannot even meet our cost of production due to a declining market.

In 1974 we faced a sugar shortage. In 1975 we were encouraged to "all out" production. Again we responded, and provided a significant increase. This increase, coupled with an increase of imports of about 20% over 1975, has created [low prices and] an impossible situation.

We, as farmers, try to live with the weather, insects, crop diseases and other natural disasters. It is extremely difficult, however, to fight these man-made disasters. It is time for people to realize farmers are consumers too. We are, in fact, one of the few, if not the only, industry that must purchase inputs at retail prices, and sell outputs at wholesale prices. In 1973 we were forced to accept higher prices and in some cases "black market" prices for fertilizer. Where were the protesters then? Why were these exports [of fertilizer] not controlled? We must have help controlling our production costs. We will not be satisfied with another pat on the head and a big thank you for our part of the balance of trade.

. . . farmers are outraged at the way they have been treated. Other industries set their own price for a margin of profit. We must take what is offered. Other industries "pass along" cost increases they receive. We must "swallow" these increases, and just try harder. This discrimination must be stopped. Why is an industry so necessary to all people handled as it has been in the past? Every day more farmers are quitting. These people will soon be showing up on unemployment lists. If this mass migration is allowed to continue, farming, as we know it today, is finished. Farming of the future may well be done by large corporations who will be able to command and receive a profitable price.

From *General Farm and Food Legislation,* Hearings before the Committee on Agriculture, Nutrition, and Forestry, U.S. Senate, 95th Congress, 1st Session, Washington, 1977, pp. 206, 193–194, respectively.

36

Urban Economics: The Problems of the Cities

America's cities are a curious paradox. They are the depositories of great wealth and the source of abundant incomes; they are the nucleus of economic activity and opportunity. Yet these same cities simultaneously embody blighted neighborhoods, faltering school systems, an acutely deteriorating physical environment, and a growing sense of social unrest and alienation.[1]

> Fly over Manhattan or Nob Hill or the Chicago Loop and the breathtaking skyline will excite your pride with the very grandeur of the American achievement. These towering symbols give dramatic character to the core of our giant cities. But their shadows cannot hide the disgrace at their feet.
>
> There we find the decayed and decaying center cities, traffic-clogged, smoke-polluted, crime-ridden, recreationally barren. It is there we find the segregated slum with its crumbling tenement house, waiting to crush the hope of the Negro and displaced farmer who has pursued his dream into the city. There too we find the suburbs ringing the cities in their rapid, undisciplined growth with ugly, congested webs of ticky-tacky houses and macadam-burst shopping centers. . . .
>
> How have we built, or let build, this somewhat lacking, somehow defective, maculate home for man?

[1]Terry Sanford, "The States and the Cities: The Unfinished Agenda," in Brian J. L. Berry and Jack Meltzer (eds.), *Goals for Urban America* (Englewood Cliffs, N.J.: Prentice-Hall, Inc., 1967), pp. 52–53.

This chapter will explore a number of the paradoxes and problems posed by the dominant role of the city in American life. First, what is the rationale for the evolution of cities? Why have cities developed and grown? A second and closely related objective is to explain the more recent phenomenon of suburban growth. What economic considerations underlie urban sprawl? Next, we will consider some problems which have been spawned by the dynamics of urban growth. These include transportation problems, environmental pollution, and central-city poverty. Finally, we will consider some possible solutions to the problems of the cities.

As a prelude to these questions and issues, we must first determine the extent to which the United States is urbanized. Today the United States is clearly an urban nation. But, as Table 36-1 indicates, this has not always been so. Musty records reveal that in 1790 some 95 percent of our population lived in rural areas, mostly on farms. But by 1920 a majority of the population had become urban. Currently, almost three-fourths of our population is located in urban areas. While future

Table 36-1   URBAN POPULATION GROWTH IN THE UNITED STATES (*in millions*)

Year	Urban population	Rural population	Urban as a percent of total population
1790	.2	3.7	5
1810	.5	6.7	7
1830	1.1	11.7	9
1850	3.5	19.6	15
1870	9.9	28.7	25
1890	22.1	40.8	35
1910	42.0	50.0	46
1930	69.0	53.8	56
1950	96.5	54.2	64
1970	149.8	53.9	73
1974	155.0	56.4	73
1980*	197.0	53.0	79

* Projected.
Source: U.S. Bureau of the Census. "Urban areas" are defined by the Census Bureau as cities and other incorporated places which have 2500 or more inhabitants.

demographic changes are difficult to forecast, there is no question that the United States is—and will continue to be—a nation of city dwellers.

WHY CITIES DEVELOP

There are substantial economic reasons why modern cities have evolved and grown. Let us look at these reasons—the economic rationale for cities—in both general and specific terms. Consider first the production or supply aspect of this rationale.

□   In General: Where to Produce?

The decision about where certain kinds of businesses should locate is as important as the decision to produce, say, more television sets and fewer radios. The very important question of business location was hidden in Chapter 5's discussion of the Five Fundamental Questions. In fact, the question of organizing production—*how* to produce?—implies the problem of location, or *where* to produce. Our analysis of the firm (particularly in Chapter 25) implicitly assumed that all production took place at some fixed geographic point. In effect, we supposed that the market for inputs was located at the firm's back door, and the market for outputs at its front door. This is obviously unrealistic; transportation or transfer costs are involved both in getting raw materials and other inputs to the plant and in delivering the finished product to buyers. Production decisions have a spatial or locational aspect.

Stated differently, one of the important costs in organizing resources for production is the cost of overcoming geographic space, that is, the amounts of time and resources necessary for transportation and communication. If producers locate close to those from whom they purchase inputs and to those to whom they sell their outputs, transportation and communication costs will obviously be reduced. Crudely put, there are economic advantages accruing to firms which agglomerate, that is, locate in proximity to one another and to their markets. These spatial advantages are fundamental to the economic rationale of urban growth.

□ **In Particular: Economies of Agglomeration**

But let us back up and explain the economic reasons for the evolution of cities in more detail. In the first place, the necessary condition for the development of cities is the capacity of a nation's agriculture to produce surplus food and fiber. The rapidly expanding productivity of American agriculture, detailed in Chapter 35, has freed the vast majority of our population from farming so that this labor might turn to the production of nonagricultural goods and services. Because man is a social animal and because specialized industrial production demands large numbers of workers, it was only natural that labor, when released from an increasingly efficient agriculture, would cluster in villages, towns, and cities.

Although an increasingly efficient agricultural sector has "pushed" labor out of farming, it has been *economies of agglomeration* which have "pulled" population and industry to the villages, towns, and cities. What specifically are agglomeration economies? Generally speaking, agglomeration economies refer to the "cheapening" of production or marketing which results from the fact that firms locate relatively close to one another. The economies which result from such agglomeration are of several interrelated and admittedly overlapping types.

Internal Economies of Scale Perhaps the simplest basis for spatial concentration is the economies of large-scale production. Recall that where economies of scale are substantial, reasonably efficient production will be possible only with a few producers relative to the total market. This suggests that one large producer can serve a number of market areas

more cheaply than can many small, decentralized producers. Cities have large populations and therefore large potential markets which give producers the opportunity to move down their long-run average-cost curves and achieve low unit costs (Figure 25-6*a*).

Locational (Transport) Economies The location of business enterprise is strongly influenced by the availability of transportation facilities. Transport costs will obviously be higher for a firm if required inputs and markets for outputs are not readily accessible. Hence, at any given time the locational choice of a firm will be strongly influenced by the existing transportation network. It is no accident that our major cities historically have grown around low-cost natural or man-made transportation nodes, that is, along seaboards (New York, San Francisco), on major rivers (St. Louis), or around railroad terminals (Chicago).

Perhaps less obvious as an incentive to agglomeration is the matter of "industrial linkages." Technological progress has caused the chain of goods production and assembly to become longer and more complex. The outputs of a growing number of firms and industries constitute the inputs of still other firms and industries. This growing specialization in production means that industrially linked firms can realize substantial economies in transportation and communication by locating in proximity. It is not difficult to see why the attraction of industry and therefore of population to the cities tends to be a self-perpetuating process. For obvious reasons, the location of an automobile assembly plant in a given city may induce tire and glass producers, for example, to locate plants in the same area. In turn, the existence of the glass and tire plants may induce still another automobile manufacturer to establish an assembly plant in the area. And so it goes.

Urban Economies: Specialization and Infrastructure The foregoing discussion of internal economies of scale and locational economies is not sufficient to explain fully the phenomenon of urban growth. Nor does it explain why the larger cities have grown at the expense of the smaller cities. A more complete explanation involves *external economies of specialization* and the *infrastructure* of urban areas.

The economies of scale discussed earlier were labeled "internal economies of scale" because their realization depends solely upon the decisions and fortunes of individual firms. In other words, technology confronts the firm with a *given* average-cost curve which declines over a very substantial range, such as in Figure 25-6a, and it is entirely up to the firm to achieve the high levels of production prerequisite to low unit costs. Now we must consider scale economies of a different type. Specifically, there may exist certain economies which cause the average-cost curves of firms to *shift* downward. These downward shifts of the average-cost curves of individual firms depend upon the expansion of the entire *industry* or group of firms, not of the single *firm*. Therefore, such economies are *external economies of scale,* for their realization lies beyond, or is external to, the actions and decisions of any single firm.

Specifically, as a number of firms agglomerate, they may *as a group* be able to realize lower input prices and therefore lower cost curves than if they were geographically dispersed. That is, as firms agglomerate, it tends to become profitable for specialized firms to perform certain functions for the industry on a larger scale—and therefore more cheaply—than can each firm internally. For example, prior to agglomeration a manufacturer may be forced to repair its own machinery or conduct its own technological or marketing research. But, as the number of firms in an industry, or even in different industries, concentrate in an area, the volume of repair or research business of the firms as a group becomes sufficient to support a firm specializing in these functions. The agglomerated firms can realize lower input

prices—and lower unit costs—by "farming out" these functions to specialists rather than undertaking the tasks themselves.

This growing specialization obviously leads to an increased interdependence among various types of manufacturing and service establishments. Thus, the location of the individual establishments which are highly interdependent is, in a sense, determined simultaneously. Broadly speaking, producers of final goods must have easy access both to the intermediate goods and services needed as inputs and to the markets for their final product. Similarly, the suppliers of intermediate goods and services must have easy access to markets sufficient in scale to realize internal economies of large-scale production. It follows that the solution for both groups is the same—to cluster in cities that alone can provide both inputs and markets in sufficient scale and variety to meet their total needs. Thus, it is not difficult to see why the attraction of industry and therefore of population to the cities tends to be a self-perpetuating process.

Another illustration: The geographic concentration of many firms requiring, say, unskilled and semiskilled labor may attract large pools of these kinds of labor to the area. The result? Lower wage rates for labor inputs and therefore lower average costs for the firms.

The *infrastructure* of an urban area is a source of economies or cost advantages not entirely unlike external economies of scale. Specifically, a city provides its firms with important services and facilities upon which producers rely and which would be costly for each firm to provide in the small amounts it alone needs. This infrastructure comprises such obvious things as ample water, electrical power, waste treatment facilities, transportation facilities, educational research and engineering facilities, financial and banking institutions, management and public relations consultants, and so forth.

A rich and varied infrastructure may be the strongest agglomerative force explaining the continuing and persistent growth of our largest urban areas. For example, one of the conclusions of a 1960 study of the New York metropolitan area pertained to the importance of the area's infrastructure in attracting new enterprises. The study noted that even though the New York metropolitan area has lost nearly every industry it has ever had—flour mills, foundries, meat-packing plants, textile mills, and tanneries—the area continues to grow and earn above-average income. The report stated that New York's propensity for growth and above-average income can be attributed to its rich infrastructure which attracts new enterprises that require highly specialized and sophisticated services.

□ **Demand Considerations**

Aside from the importance of market demand as a requisite for firms and industries to realize both internal and external economies of scale, market demand plays another role in explaining urban growth. The large populations of the cities mean that a wider variety of products and services are available. Put bluntly, while the populations of Chicago and Philadelphia will generate a market demand sufficient to support Chinese restaurants and shops specializing in exotic imports, the demand for such products in Grand Mound, Iowa, or Eureka, Montana, is insufficient to make such enterprises profitable. Similarly, the live theater, symphony orchestras, highly specialized medical and professional facilities, and professional athletics are commercially feasible only in larger cities. In general, many of the refinements and amenities of modern life are urban-based because of adequate demand. This means that cities are places not only where goods and services can be produced more cheaply, but also where consumers can attain a higher level of satisfaction from a given expenditure because of a finer matching of their wants with the wider variety of available goods and services.

□ **Deglomerative Forces**

The advantages of agglomeration cannot be reaped indefinitely. Beyond some critical and difficult-to-specify point—a point which many of our larger cities may have passed—continued city growth and geographic concentration of industry will tend to create counterforces which give rise to higher production costs. That is, continued efforts to realize the economies of agglomeration may create certain offsetting diseconomies, or what might be termed *deglomerative forces*. Certain costs associated with geographic concentration are internal to, and therefore must be borne by, the producers themselves. For example, a growing concentration of industry in a given geographic area will mean higher land values and rents. (Figure 32-1 reminds us that a rising demand for a perfectly inelastic supply of centrally located sites will have a large price effect.) In turn, rising land values will make it increasingly costly for new firms to locate in an area or for existing firms to expand facilities. Furthermore, the intensified demand for labor which accompanies industrial agglomeration may be reflected in increased bargaining power for workers and rising wage costs.

Other costs which accompany industrial agglomeration may be shifted by individual producers to society as a whole, that is, to other firms and to the population at large. These spillover costs in the form of air and water pollution or traffic congestion and noise contribute to the general debasement of the area and make it a less attractive place for firms and people to locate. The pollution problem merits separate discussion later in this chapter.

Have deglomerative forces become sufficiently important in recent years so that they offset some of the advantages of agglomeration? Recent changes in urbanization patterns seem to indicate that this is the case. The growth of suburbia, the decentralization of central business districts, and the recent resurgence in the growth of smaller cities and towns are consistent with the notion that deglomerative forces are at work. Note, however, that the simple fact of urban growth will result in urban spread—the fanning out of people and businesses from the central city.

THE FLIGHT TO THE SUBURBS: URBAN SPRAWL

This brief introduction to the economies and diseconomies of agglomeration helps explain the paradox stated at the outset of this chapter. The cities are centers of great wealth and income. They are centers of economic activity and for many people a magnet of economic opportunity. But the very growth and maturation of the modern city spawn spillover costs, not to mention the inevitable social tensions which characterize areas of high population density. These latter features of the cities obviously tend to make urban life less attractive. Hence, actual or potential urban residents—both businesses and households—ask themselves this question: How can the advantages and opportunities of the metropolitan area be realized without also incurring the disadvantages? How can one tap the economic activity of the city and realize a higher income *and* at the same time enjoy fresh air, space, privacy, and tranquillity?

Millions of more affluent Americans have answered: Move to the suburbs! It is significant that the percentage of our population living in the central city has actually been declining since the turn of the century; virtually all our metropolitan population growth has been in the suburbs. Many factors have contributed to this rapid growth. Rising postwar incomes, abetted by governmentally guaranteed mortgage credit, have made suburban living accessible to more and more families. Automobile ownership, as a convenient means of commuting, has been an important permissive factor.

Suburban growth has resulted not merely in the relocation of people, but also in the movement of businesses. The reasons for this are complex and diverse.[2] In the first place, it is easy to see why many of the retail and personal service industries—groceries, hardware and furniture stores, laundries and cleaners, barber and beauty shops—have moved to the suburbs. Such establishments must be close to people; in particular, to people who have money! But many manufacturing firms have also fled the central city. We have already hit upon a couple of reasons for such shifts. Rising land costs make plant expansion very costly in the central city. And spillover costs make downtown locations less attractive. Firms which are large enough to have their own truck transportation encounter costly problems of traffic congestion, loading and parking, and so forth. In addition, technological changes have encouraged many manufacturers to migrate to the suburbs. The rapid development of truck transportation has freed many firms from the need to locate near downtown railroad terminals and harbor facilities. Perhaps more important is the great emphasis that modern production technology has put upon highly integrated, continuous processes which assume an extensive one-story plant layout. Space for the utilization of this technology is not available—or only available at prohibitive cost—in the central city.

Now this reasoning is not to suggest that *all* major businesses have fled to the suburbs. Certain kinds of businesses have remained—and prospered—in the central cities:[3]

These are the highly specialized areas of finance, business services, and central office administration, whose inputs are skill or knowledge or information, whose outputs are not goods but service or advice or decisions. It is these establishments—banks and law offices,

[2]The following discussion is based upon Benjamin Chinitz (ed.), *City and Suburb* (Englewood Cliffs, N.J.: Prentice-Hall, Inc., 1964), pp. 23–27.
[3]Ibid., p. 26.

advertising agencies and central administrative offices, consulting firms and government agencies—which are filling more and more of the central cities of most urban areas, and are becoming the primary function of . . . the city's central business district.

Overall, however, the trend has been to the suburbs.

☐ Political Fragmentation

This dramatic flight to the suburbs has been accompanied by the political balkanization of our large cities. That is, the central cities have become encircled with a large number of new suburbs, each of which is a separate political entity. Figure 36-1 shows the case of St. Louis. The St. Louis urban area is served by 474 local governments which are almost equally divided between Illinois and Missouri. These 474 governmental units include over 100 separate municipalities. St. Louis is hardly an exceptional case. There are over 1400 separate units of government in the New York City metropolitan area and almost 1000 in the San Francisco Bay area.

☐ Economic Imbalance

Political fragmentation is the source of many urban problems. But it is particularly troublesome because the process of urban decentralization or suburban growth has brought about a highly unequal distribution of wealth and incomes geographically. The more prosperous people and many of the newer and more profitable industries have fled the central city in favor of the suburbs. By and large, the poor people and many of the less profitable industries have been left behind in the central city.

This dramatic process of change in the structure of metropolitan areas has been self-reinforcing and cumulative. The migration of both the wealthier people and businesses to new political entities in the suburbs seriously erodes the property tax base of the central cities.[4] New plants and new housing are built in the suburban ring, not in the central cities. To maintain public services, property tax *rates* must be increased in the central city. But these rising rates provide further incentive for both households and businesses to flee to the suburbs.

Furthermore, the poor, predominantly black families who by virtue of their poverty and discrimination are left behind in the central cities, are "high cost" citizens. An unusually high percentage are on welfare. Children are numerous, and education costs are high. High population densities—New York's Harlem has 67,000 people per square mile—mean that the costs of governing, of collecting garbage, of maintaining law and order are high.

All this is complicated and given further impetus by the fact that central-city decay, or urban blight, tends to be a cumulative process.[5]

The older structures concentrated near the city center lose their economic usefulness as the functions of the downtown areas change. Extensive conversion, rehabilitation, and reconstruction are needed. If a few buildings need to be replaced or renovated in an otherwise prosperous area, the market provides private developers and builders with sufficient incentives to undertake the work. However, when a pattern of decay permeates a large area, the dilapidation of neighboring buildings reduces the profitability of improving a particular property. A large area must then be improved as a single unit, and the cost and difficulties of acquiring and redeveloping a large tract of central city land are likely to deter private investors from the undertaking.

To summarize: The basic consequence of the dynamics of urban growth and the accompanying political fragmentation has been "to

---

[4] Recall from Table 8-4 that property taxes are the main source of revenue for local units of government.
[5] *Economic Report of the President, 1965,* pp. 149–150.

FIGURE 36-1 POLITICAL FRAGMENTATION: THE CASE OF ST. LOUIS

The dynamics of urban expansion has given rise to the growth of numerous politically distinct subdivisions around the central city. The 474 units of local government which comprise the St. Louis metropolitan area are quite typical of this political balkanization.(*Advisory Commission on Intergovernmental Relations, Urban America and the Federal System, Washington, 1969, p. 85.*)

forge a white, middle- and high-income noose around the increasingly black and poor inner city. . . ." The losers in the flight to politically splintered suburbs have been the central cities, saddled with an inadequate and shrinking tax base and the burgeoning expenditure demands "incident to the governing, educating, and 'welfaring' of an increasing proportion of rela-tively poor [and usually] black families."[6] The winners, on the other hand, have been the more wealthy white suburban localities wherein income and wealth have been suffi-

[6] Advisory Commission on Intergovernmental Relations, *Urban America and the Federal System* (Washington, 1969), pp. 2, 8.

cient to underwrite viable public services with relatively modest tax efforts.

The dynamics of urban growth and the crazy quilt of political entities which has accompanied this growth have spawned a host of acute and interrelated problems. Let us now briefly survey some of these problems and sketch possible avenues for their resolution. Although the problems of the cities are manifold and not subject to simple classification, we will concentrate on three main problem areas: urban transportation, the ghettos and central-city poverty, and pollution.

THE URBAN TRANSPORTATION PROBLEM

We have seen that one fundamental characteristic of urban growth is the direct relationship one finds between distance from the central city and income and wealth. Generally speaking, those living furthest from "downtown" are the professional, technical, and white-collar workers. A large proportion of these higher-income people work downtown; that is, they are employed in the banking and financial firms, the legal and consulting firms, and the advertising agencies which have remained in the central city. On the other hand, we have seen that many kinds of manufacturing, wholesale, retail, and personal service industries—industries which require blue-collar and less skilled workers—have moved to suburbia. The result is a significant locational mismatch of jobs and labor force between suburbs and central city. This mismatch creates the need for an effective transportation system to negotiate the required cross-hauling of the population.

But the need for efficient transportation is even more pervasive. Accessibility is the *sine qua non* of effective participation in urban life. Most of the cultural and social advantages of city life can only be efficiently realized through a viable transportation system. Museums, art galleries, and concert halls are indivisible, or "lumpy," social goods; since they cannot be divided and taken home by consumers, the consumer must go to them. Similarly, comparative shopping in the city assumes adequate transportation.

Given the convenience of private automobile travel, most suburbanites have chosen this form of transportation. Furthermore, large Federal subsidies to highway construction have created a substantial financial bias in favor of the automobile. But, ironically, dramatic increases in metropolitan automobile use and highway construction—Los Angeles is the classic case—have not solved the transportation problem. Indeed, the expanded use of auto transportation has given rise to increasingly acute problems of traffic congestion, not to mention the automobile's substantial contribution to air pollution. The response to traffic congestion, of course, has been to construct more highways. But the additional highways permit the growth of still more distant suburbs and elicit more traffic. Alas, more highways beget more autos. So mammoth highway construction programs have been accompanied by more—not less—traffic congestion and parking problems. We have witnessed a vicious cycle of more autos, more highways which induce more autos, and the construction of still more highways.

The other side of the coin has been the general deterioration of the mass-transit systems of the cities. The vast geographic dispersion of population throughout the suburbs has made it difficult for mass-transit systems to realize the heavy trunk-line operations requisite to their prosperity or survival. Again, we encounter a cumulative process. As patronage declines, unit costs rise and commuter fares must be increased, on the one hand, and the quality of both equipment and service deteriorates, on the other. So more people choose to drive their cars to work, and the process repeats itself.

Unfortunately, not all people can afford the automobile–mass-transit choice. The poor and less skilled of the central city must rely upon mass transit. Shrinkage and service deterioration of the transit system, accompanied by the shift of blue-collar jobs to the suburbs, unfortunately leave many of the central-city residents isolated from the economic opportunities of the metropolitan area.

◼ IMPROVING URBAN TRANSPORTATION

In considering possible solutions, it is both convenient and meaningful to consider the urban transport problem in two parts: the short-run problem and the long-run problem.

☐ The Short Run: User Charges and Peak Pricing

First, there is a short-run problem: Given existing transportation facilities and technology, how can this transportation "plant" be used most efficiently? What is the best way of utilizing *existing* freeway–street-parking and mass-transit facilities? We have already noted that, historically, governmental subsidies have been heavily biased in favor of automobile transportation. Specifically, urban freeway and street construction has been heavily subsidized by Federal grants; financing also comes from state gasoline-tax revenues. A number of urban economists feel that a system of *user charges* on drivers would be very useful in achieving a better balance in the use of mass transit and auto transportation and, in particular, in alleviating the problem of traffic congestion. They contend that the city's streets and highways are overused and congested because drivers do not bear the full cost of driving; they are in fact subsidized by society (taxpayers) at large. More specifically, it is argued that automobile drivers should be confronted "as near as possible in time and place to the act of making the decision to drive" with a price—a user charge—which covers the full cost of driving. By "full cost" is meant not only the cost of highway construction and repair but also the cost of traffic control devices

and traffic police and even automobile pollution costs. Price, after all, is a rationing device or disciplining mechanism, and traffic congestion is a symptom of quantity demanded in excess of quantity supplied at the going price. "Surely, we would have traffic jams in the aisles of food stores and 'shortages' of food if we tried to administer free food stores supported by general taxation. The food shortages would be analogous to the shortages of street space per automobile (traffic jams) and the shortages of parking places that characterize our underpriced and tax-supported urban transportation industry."[7]

What specifically will be the effects of a system of user charges on drivers? First, some will be rationed out of the "driving market"; that is, they will use the public transportation system or, if they have the option, will make fewer trips downtown. This response, of course, has the desired effect of relieving traffic congestion. Second, those who continue to drive will contribute more funds for the expansion and improvement of highway and parking facilities.

Recognizing that the morning and evening rush hours are the focal points of the urban transportation problem, many advocates of user charges also contend that the pricing of both auto and mass-transit facilities should vary according to the time of day. That is, *peak pricing* should be used; charges should be higher during the peak or rush hours and lower during off-peak hours. The purpose, of course, is to "ration out" travelers whose need to travel during rush hours is less pressing or less necessary. For example, shoppers might be induced by a system of peak prices to alter the timing of their trips to and from downtown so that they do not coincide with the travel times of commuting workers.

Those who favor user charges admit that significant problems of application exist. For example, how does one calculate the costs of

[7] Wilbur R. Thompson, *A Preface to Urban Economics* (Baltimore: The Johns Hopkins Press, 1965), pp. 340–341.

air pollution, noise, and delay, and the opportunity cost of the land used in freeway and street construction in determining the full cost of an automobile trip to the downtown area? Then, too, there is the difficult problem of assessing and collecting user charges from drivers; can tolls be collected without creating toll station bottlenecks? Or is it possible to "include highly sophisticated electronic sensing devices mounted on cars and in the streets, which could result in computer-written monthly bills to motorists . . . , charging them more for the use of congested routes in crowded hours"?[8]

□ **The Long Run: Mass Transit**

This brings us to the long-run aspect of the urban transportation problem: What should be the character of future public investments in urban transportation facilities? For a variety of reasons, there has been a revival of interest in the revitalization and development of public mass-transit systems—commuter railroads, subways, buses, monorails, and so forth. First, given projections of suburban population growth and the consequent possibility that the volume of urban automobile traffic may double in the next twenty years, many city planners and public officials feel that effective alternatives to auto transportation are imperative. This is particularly so in view of the previously noted point that increased investment in streets and freeways often seems to induce a higher volume of traffic, rather than relieve congestion. Second, interest in public mass transit has been stimulated by the recognition that past transportation subsidies have favored the automobile and that there is now a need to achieve a better balance between auto and mass transit. Finally, it is felt that an expanded and improved mass-transit system can yield substantial social benefits in terms of (1) a viable and revitalized central city with an expanding property tax base, (2) greater accessibility to suburban jobs for the central-city poor, and (3) avoidance of an increasingly acute pollution problem which an expansion of automobile transportation is likely to entail.

The Urban Mass Transit Acts of 1964 and 1970 have been passed in response to this interest in mass transit, providing Federal funds for the revitalization and technological improvement of public transportation systems. It should be emphasized, however, that the solution—if there is one—to the urban transportation problem will not entail an either-or choice; some workable combination of automobile and public mass transit will be essential to a viable transportation system.

■
**THE POLLUTION PROBLEM:
THE EFFLUENT SOCIETY?**

Cities do not have a monopoly on the pollution problem. Yet, the high population densities and high levels of industrial concentration which are the earmarks of urban life make pollution problems most acute in the cities.

□ **Dimensions of the Problem**

The seriousness of water, air, and solid-waste pollution has been well documented in the popular press and needs only brief review here. We know that rivers and lakes have been turned into municipal and industrial sewers. Not only has Lake Erie deteriorated into a national cesspool, but the Cuyahoga River which feeds into it has become so permeated with sludge and oil that it has been labeled a fire hazard! Leaks from offshore wells have plagued the Southern California and Gulf coasts. The drainage of DDT into streams and lakes has imperiled our fish and bird populations. Almost half our population drinks water of dubious quality. A growing body of evidence links air pollution to lung cancer, emphysema, pneumonia, and other respiratory diseases.

[8]Dick Netzer, *Economics and Urban Problems* (New York: Basic Books, Inc., Publishers, 1970), p. 211.

The toxics in New York City's air make a day's walking and breathing the equivalent of smoking two packages of cigarettes.[9] Cynics tell us that one wakes up in Los Angeles to the sound of birds coughing. Each American accounts for some 2000 pounds of solid wastes—including, for example, 250 tin cans per person—each year.

Possible longer-run consequences of environmental pollution are even more disturbing. Competent scientists suggest that if current trends in automobile use continue, large, densely populated areas of our country may become uninhabitable, the source of certain suffocation. Some scientists contend that the concentrations of industry, people, structures, and cement which constitute cities might create air and heat pollution sufficient to cause irreversible and potentially disastrous changes in the earth's climate and weather patterns.

□   **Causes: Materials Balance Approach**

The roots of the pollution problem can best be envisioned through the *materials balance approach,* which is the notion that the weight of the inputs (fuels, raw materials, water, and so forth) used in the economy's production processes will ultimately result in a roughly equivalent residual of wastes. For example, each year:[10]

> The economy . . . takes in about . . . [a] billion tons of minerals and food and forest products.

[9]In a penetrating satire on New York City ("fume city"), Dick Schaap made this observation in *New York* magazine (April 15, 1968):

> Beyond its natural loveliness, pollution serves the city of New York in so many ways. It helps keep the City from becoming over-populated; it insures that only the fittest survive and the rest move to the suburbs. It helps keep the City from becoming overgrown with foliage; it kills roses and tulips and other harmful weeds. It provides employment for window washers and car-washers and eager little shoe-shine boys. And it saves money: it provides all the joys of cigarette smoking without any of the expenses.

[10]U.S. Department of Health, Education and Welfare, *Toward a Social Report* (Washington, 1969), p. 28.

Consumers use these goods in the form they receive them, or further transform them (e.g., by eating), but must sooner or later dispose of the end product, whether it be empty tin cans, "throw away" bottles, worn-out refrigerators, plastic toys or human excreta.

Fortunately, the ecological system—Nature, if you are over thirty—has the self-regenerating capacity which allows it, within limits, to absorb or recycle such wastes. But the problem is that the volume of such residuals has outrun this absorptive capacity; Nature is no longer a free good.

Why has this happened? Why do we have a pollution problem? Causes are manifold, but perhaps four are paramount.

1 There is the simple matter of population growth. An ecological system which may accommodate 50 or 100 million people may begin to break down under the pressures of 200 or 300 million. As noted, the absorptive capacity of our natural environment, an increasingly scarce resource, is most evident in urban areas where the concentration of population and economic activity is so great.

2 Per capita incomes have been rising. Industrial production, for example, has been growing at $4\frac{1}{2}$ percent per year, which means that industrial output will increase sevenfold by the year 2020.[11] The materials balance approach reminds us that, barring significant changes in technology or the composition of output, the total weight of wastes generated will also increase tenfold. Paradoxically, the affluent society helps to spawn the effluent society. A rising GNP (gross national product) means a rising GNG (gross national garbage). Thus a high standard of living permits Americans to own some 100 million automobiles. But autos are a primary source of air pollution and, concomitantly, give rise to the hard problem of disposing of some 7 or 8 million junked autos each year. Furthermore, the fact that more leisure has been a component of our rising standard of living has increased public

[11]Ibid., p. 28.

awareness of the pollution problem. When you have time to spend on a beach or at a lake, you become concerned that the water may be unfit for swimming or that the fish may have been killed by thermal or chemical pollution.

3 Technological change is another contributor to pollution. For example, the expanded use of pesticides, herbicides, and insecticides has proved to be a deadly enemy of our fish and bird populations. The addition of lead to gasolines poses a serious threat to human health. The development and widespread use of "throw-away" containers made of virtually indestructible aluminum or plastic add substantially to the solid-waste crisis. Detergent soap products have been highly resistant to sanitary treatment and recycling.

4 A final and crucial factor concerns economic incentives. Specifically, businesses find their private production costs will be lowered by polluting. In technical terms, pollution is a problem in spillover costs (Chapters 6 and 26). Profit-seeking manufacturers choose the least-cost combination of inputs and will find it advantageous to bear only unavoidable costs. If they can dump waste chemicals into rivers and lakes rather than pay for expensive treatment and proper disposal, businesses will be inclined to do so. If manufacturers can discharge smoke and the hot water used to cool machinery rather than purchase expensive abatement and cooling facilities, they will tend to do so. The result is air and water pollution—both chemical and thermal—and, in the economist's jargon, the shifting of certain costs to the community at large as spillover costs. Enjoying lower "internal" costs than if he had not polluted the environment, the producer can sell his product more cheaply, expand his production, and realize larger profits. The supply curve of a polluting firm or industry lies too far to the right because it omits the cost which society bears in the form of a debased environment. The result is an overallocation of resources to the polluter's commodity.

But it is neither just nor accurate to lay the entire blame for pollution at the door of industry. Given the fact that an important function of government is to correct the misallocation of resources which accompany spillover costs (Chapter 6), it is ironic that most major cities are heavy contributors to the pollution problem. Municipal power plants are frequently major contributors to air pollution; many cities discharge untreated or inadequately treated sewage into rivers or lakes because it is cheap and convenient to do so. Similarly, individuals seek to avoid the costs of proper refuse pickup and disposal by burning their garbage. We also find it convenient to use throw-away containers rather than recycle "return" containers. And note in particular that a well-intentioned firm which wants to operate in a socially responsible way with respect to pollution finds itself in an awkward position. If an individual firm "internalizes" all its external or spillover costs by installing, say, water-treatment and smoke-abatement equipment, the firm will find itself at a cost disadvantage in comparison to its polluting competitors. The socially responsible firm will have higher costs and will be forced to raise its product price. The "reward" for the pollution-conscious firm is a declining market for its product, diminished profits, and, in the extreme, the prospect of bankruptcy. This correctly suggests that effective action to combat pollution must be undertaken collectively through government.

□ **Antipollution Policies**

Because environmental pollution is a problem in spillover or external costs,[12] the task of antipollution policy is to devise ways of "internalizing" the external costs of pollution. The objective is to make the polluter pay *all* the costs associated with his activities. In terms of Figure 6-1*b* we want to eliminate the discrepancy between private and total costs by shifting SS to, or at least toward, S_tS_t.

[12] Rereading the section entitled "Spillovers or Externalities" in Chapter 6 may be useful at this point.

1   Direct Controls through Legislated Standards   One obvious approach is for governmental units to pass legislation which prohibits or regulates pollution. Legislation may establish minimum standards for air and water which polluters must observe or face legal sanctions. The legislation of pollution standards will presumably force polluters to install water-treatment and air-filter equipment and thereby to bear costs which would otherwise be shifted to society. A much-publicized illustration of this approach is Federal legislation requiring automobile manufacturers to meet exhaust-emission standards. On a broader front, the Environmental Protection Agency was established by Congress in 1969 to develop quality standards for air and water in cooperation with state and local governments.

2   Special Taxes: Emission Fees   A second approach is to levy special charges or taxes—emission or effluent fees—on polluters. That is, a special tax or fee should be assessed per ton of pollutant discharged into the air or water. Ideally, fees would be set so that spillover costs would be exactly covered and each producer's cost curve would reflect *all* production costs.

For example, suppose a chemical plant is polluting a river. The resulting external costs are manifold: Other manufacturers and municipalities located downstream must pay to purify the water prior to use; businesses based upon fishing or recreational uses of the river will be injured; individuals will suffer the loss of recreational uses; the river may become a health hazard; and so forth. If a special tax or emission fee covering these spillover costs is imposed upon the chemical plant, these external costs will become internalized to the plant. The chemical firm must recalculate its cost alternatives. On the one hand, it can purchase pollution-abatement equipment and thereby reduce or eliminate the payment of emission fees. Or it can continue to pollute and pay the required fees. In the second case, govern-

ment can use the revenue from the emission fees to cleanse the downstream water or to compensate injured parties. A system of water pollution fees has been used effectively in Germany's Ruhr River basin for some time.

3   A Market for Pollution Rights   One of the most novel policy suggestions is to create a market for pollution rights.[13] The rationale for this proposal is that the air, rivers, lakes, oceans, and public lands, such as parks and streets, are all primary objects for pollution because the *rights* to use these resources are either held "in common" by society or are unspecified by law. As a result, no specific private individual or institution has any incentive to restrict the use or maintain the purity or quality of these resources because he does not have the right to realize a monetary return from doing so. One maintains the property he owns—you paint and repair your home periodically—because he will capture the value of these improvements at the time of resale. But, as long as the "rights" to air, water, and certain land resources are commonly held and these resources made freely available, there will be no incentive to maintain them or restrict their use. Hence, these natural resources are "overconsumed" and thereby polluted.

The proposal is therefore made that an appropriate pollution-control agency should determine the amount of pollutants which can be discharged into the water or air of a given region each year and still maintain the quality of the water or air at some acceptable standard. For example, the agency may determine that 500 tons of pollutants may be discharged into Metropolitan Lake and be "recycled" by Nature. Hence, 500 pollution rights, each entitling the owner to dump 1 ton of pollutants into the lake in the given year, are made available for sale each year. The resulting supply of pollution rights is fixed and therefore

[13]J. H. Dales, *Pollution, Property and Prices* (Toronto: University of Toronto Press, 1968).

perfectly inelastic, as shown in Figure 36-2. The demand for pollution rights will take the same downsloping form as will the demand for any other input. At high prices, polluters either will stop polluting or will pollute less by acquiring pollution-abatement equipment. Thus, a market price for pollution rights will be determined at which an environment-preserving quantity of pollution rights will be rationed to polluters. Note that without this market, 750 tons of pollutants would be discharged into the lake and it would be "overconsumed," or polluted, in the amount of 250 tons. And over time, as human and business populations expand, demand will increase, as from D_{1978} to D_{1988}. *Without* a market for pollution rights, pollution would occur in 1988 in the amount of 500 tons beyond that which can be assimilated by Nature. *With* the market for pollution rights, price will now rise from $100 to $200 and the amount of pollutants will

remain at 500 tons—the amount which the lake can recycle.

This proposal has a number of advantages. Potential polluters are confronted with an explicit monetary incentive not to pollute. Conservation groups can fight pollution by buying up and withholding pollution rights, thereby reducing actual pollution below governmentally determined standards. As the demand for pollution rights increases over time, the growing revenue from the sale of the given quantity of pollution rights could be devoted to environment improvement. Similarly, with time the rising price of pollution rights should stimulate the search for improved techniques to control pollution.

Problems The problems involved in establishing and administering these antipollution proposals are both numerous and substantial. First, pollution standards are difficult to establish because of incomplete and disputed technological and biological information. We simply do not know with certainty the effects—the economic and human costs—of certain pollutants. Witness the prolonged dispute over the use of DDT. This lack of information is important because it is not economically rational to prohibit or flatly eliminate pollution, but rather to use benefit-cost analysis (Chapter 6) to determine the optimum extent to which antipollution programs should be pursued. This entails the very difficult problem of calculating the marginal benefits and marginal costs of such programs. Second, the administration and enforcement of legislated controls or standards can be both difficult and costly. Finally, governmental units—the very institutions we would expect to create and enforce antipollution policies—are themselves major polluters![14]

FIGURE 36-2 THE MARKET FOR POLLUTION RIGHTS

Pollution can be controlled by having a public body determine the amount of pollution which the atmosphere or a body of water can safely recycle and sell these limited rights to polluters. The effect is to make the environment a scarce resource with a positive price. Economic and population growth will increase the demand for pollution rights over time, but the consequence will be an increase in the price of pollution rights rather than more pollution.

[14]If you are inclined to pursue the economics of pollution, you will find Thomas D. Crocker and A. J. Rogers, III, *Environmental Economics* (Hinsdale, Ill.: The Dryden Press, Inc., 1971), to be entertaining reading. Maurice F. Strong (ed.), *Who Speaks for Earth?* (New York: W. W. Norton & Company, Inc., 1973), is also recommended.

■

THE GHETTOS:
APARTHEID AMERICAN STYLE[15]

A combination of complex and interrelated forces—many of which are pointedly discussed in the Last Word section of this chapter—have given rise to central-city ghettos, populated disproportionately by Negroes and other minority groups. The poverty and debased conditions of life which are pervasive in the ghettos are well known. The oldest, most deteriorated, and most crowded housing is in the central-city ghetto. In general, schools are grossly inadequate, and, as a result, ghetto students fall further behind nonghetto students with each level of school completed. Mortality rates are high, the result of inadequate nutrition, high incidence of disease, drug use, insufficient medical care, deplorable levels of sanitation, and so forth. Social disintegration is acute, and crime rates are high. And, perhaps most important, ghetto income levels are abysmally low; nearly 40 percent of central-city blacks live in poverty.

What combination of circumstances accounts for the ghettos? Most important, the whole process of urban decentralization is very much involved. Historically, the better-educated, better-trained, more prosperous whites have moved in large numbers from the central city to the suburbs, leaving behind obsolete housing in decaying neighborhoods. Their places have been taken by poorly educated, unskilled, low-income Negroes migrating largely from the rural South, by Puerto Ricans, by Chicanos, and by Indians. Secondly, the dynamics of urban growth have shifted: "The activities which have been the traditional points of labor force entry for the urban unskilled—manufacturing, wholesale and retail trade, construction—are precisely those that

have been suburbanizing most rapidly, making entry for the central-city poor difficult indeed."[16] And this movement of jobs to the suburbs is particularly adverse because of the previously noted deterioration of the public transportation system; it is both difficult and costly for central-city residents—many of whom do not own cars—to get to the suburbs for jobs.

But, from a long-run viewpoint, racial discrimination is perhaps the most important force underlying the black ghettos. The Kerner Commission put the matter quite bluntly in asserting that past and present policies of discrimination have divided the nation into two societies, "one largely Negro and poor, located in the central cities; the other, predominantly white and affluent, located in the suburbs and outlying areas."[17] Discrimination has taken many forms: Blacks have been denied adequate education; they have been denied entry to certain occupations; they have been paid lower wages than whites on given jobs; and they have been the last hired and the first fired (Chapter 37).

Given the complexity of the problems of the ghettos, our discussion of remedies will necessarily be brief and incomplete. To facilitate matters we will treat the human (poverty) and the physical (housing) aspects of the ghetto problem separately; in fact, they are obviously very closely interrelated.

□ The Human Aspect:
Alleviating Ghetto Poverty

How can the poverty which is endemic to the black ghetto be alleviated? The causes and characteristics of the ghettos imply possible solutions.

1 More and Better Jobs Unemployment among central-city blacks is notoriously high and a major cause of poverty. The unem-

---

[15]The organization and content of this section follows Dick Netzer, *Economics and Urban Problems,* 2d ed. (New York: Basic Books, Inc., Publishers, 1974), chaps. 3 and 4. Netzer's book, which is both readable and perceptive, is recommended reading.

[16]Ibid., p. 29.
[17]*Report of the National Advisory Commission on Civil Disorders* (New York: Bantam Books, 1968), p. 22.

ployment rate for nonwhites is generally twice that for whites. Black teenagers face a chronic depression; their unemployment rates are typically 20 to 25 percent! Given the present education and and qualifications of the ghetto labor force, how can the unemployment situation be improved?

Two complementary approaches present themselves: Bring ghetto residents to existing jobs in the suburbs, *and* bring new jobs to the ghettos. Consider the first approach. Mobility in terms of residence is extremely difficult for ghetto dwellers. On the one hand, the incomes of most central-city blacks are so low that they simply cannot afford to move to the suburbs. On the other hand, those who can afford suburban housing are confronted with severe problems of discrimination. Real estate agencies and landlords have used a variety of both crude and subtle techniques for prohibiting or restricting these moves. Many suburban areas have purposely zoned for large minimum lot sizes and have enacted strict building and housing codes which push up housing prices to prohibit any influx of lower-income (black) families from the central city. A recent government report has summarized the situation in this way: "The different income levels of whites and Negroes contribute to the segregated pattern in housing. But race is a far better predictor of where a person will live than is income—or any other attribute."[18]

Another means of making suburban employment opportunities more accessible to the ghetto labor force is to provide improved transportation facilities. We have already discussed the urban transportation problem and noted that the renewed interest in mass transit is partially motivated by the ghetto worker's need for greater accessibility to suburban jobs.

The second approach is to create new job opportunities in the ghettos. *Black capitalism* is a generic term which refers to the creation of new businesses, owned and operated by Negroes, in ghetto areas. A variety of proposals—a few of which have become operational—have been made in support of black capitalism. These proposals advocate governmentally sponsored programs to provide liberal credit, tax incentives and subsidies, managerial assistance and training, and so forth, to present or potential black entrepreneurs. Related proposals urge subsidies to major corporations which are willing to build plants in the ghettos and to train black workers to staff them. The fundamental criticisms of black capitalism are twofold. First, the concept is flatly at odds with the strong economic forces which underlie the decentralization of economic activity in urban areas. Second, the types of industries which will be attracted to the ghetto are likely to be low-wage operations which provide largely "dead-end" jobs.

2 Income Maintenance But a large fraction—perhaps as much as one-half—of the ghetto poor will not be helped by improved employment opportunities. The aged, the disabled, and the mothers of dependent children can be assisted effectively only by some sort of income-maintenance program. The deficiencies of our present welfare programs and new proposals for a comprehensive income-maintenance program will be discussed in Chapter 37.

3 Improved Education and Training Many of the ghetto blacks who are fully employed nevertheless live in poverty. The reason? They have not had access to sufficient education and training to qualify for jobs which pay higher wages.

But education and training should not be viewed as a panacea for ghetto dwellers. In fact, recent empirical work suggests that, although ghetto blacks have been obtaining more education, they have *not* been able to translate their efforts into an improved eco-

[18]U.S. Department of Health, Education, and Welfare, op. cit., p. 37.

nomic status because of a deficiency of suitable job opportunities.[19]

> . . . as a short-run antipoverty policy instrument, education without a supply of jobs which utilize and reward the capabilities of ghetto workers is unlikely to have much impact. The prevalence of ghetto unemployment, involuntary parttime employment, and substandard wages, . . . strongly suggests that existing urban labor markets under-utilize ghetto workers and do not permit these individuals to realize their potential productivities. If this interpretation is correct, then the remedy must be sought in opening up *new* urban job markets to the ghetto poor, markets whose jobs are physically accessible to ghetto residents, whose availability is made known to them, and whose entry level wages and promotional possibilities will in fact lead to a significant improvement in their levels of living.

☐ **The Physical Aspect: Housing and Urban Renewal**

The urban ghetto is not only a visible and potentially explosive concentration of poverty. It is also characterized by extensive deterioration of the physical environment; much of the housing and many commercial buildings are substandard and dilapidated. Given the fact that all levels of government have long and varied histories of involvement in the housing industry, the persistence of urban blight may come as something of a surprise. Consider some of the better-known public efforts to stimulate construction.

1 For many years government—working through such agencies as the Federal Housing Administration (FHA) and the Veterans Administration (VA)—has attempted in a variety of ways to reduce the cost and increase the availability of mortgage funds to finance housing purchases.

[19] Bennett Harrison, "Education and Underemployment in the Urban Ghetto," *American Economic Review,* December 1972, p. 811.

2 Since the late 1930s the Federal government has heavily subsidized the efforts of state and local governments to provide low-rent public housing for the poor.

3 Urban renewal programs—again, subsidized with Federal funds—have attempted to reverse the spread of urban blight by rebuilding central-city areas.

4 The National Housing Act of 1949 set forth the goal of "a decent home and a suitable living environment for every American family." The Housing Act of 1968 translated this goal into a projection of 26 million new and rehabilitated housing units in the 1968–1978 decade.

Despite these programs and well-intentioned goals, there is general agreement that efforts to provide adequate housing for all America's population have been inadequate and unsuccessful. The housing problem remains particularly acute for low-income families. Why have we failed? Why do we seem to be losing the battle against urban blight? The reasons are varied.

1 Program Inadequacies In many instances our housing programs have been inappropriate or inadequate to the task. Mortgage subsidies, for example, have been most helpful to middle- and high-income groups in obtaining good housing. But low-income people have generally not been able to enjoy the low FHA and VA interest rates (nor the tax deductibility of mortgage interest payments) because they simply have not been able to qualify for such loans. Lofty statements of goals to the contrary, some housing programs have foundered for the lack of adequate financing. Public housing and rent subsidy programs have undoubtedly helped some low-income families, but the poorest families cannot afford even the subsidized rental payments.

Ironically, on balance, urban renewal programs have *reduced* the supply of housing available to low-income families. Some urban renewal efforts have not been primarily concerned with housing, but rather, the strategy has been to shore up the vitality of the central city by replacing slum neighborhoods with new office buildings to house both public services and private enterprises. This tendency helps explain the paradox that many ghetto dwellers are opposed to urban renewal. Witness the slogan: "Urban renewal is Negro removal." Furthermore, some families have been uprooted several times by public housing projects which have in fact increased the supply of housing available to middle-income families, but reduced it for low-income families.

But the relative ineffectiveness of government involvement in the physical restoration of the cities goes beyond the inadequacies of particular programs. Two other important considerations merit comment.

2   Problems of the Construction Industry   The residential construction industry has been technologically unprogressive and hampered by the inability of thousands of small contractors to realize economies of scale. Furthermore, construction is cyclically vulnerable, being highly sensitive to changes in interest rates and the availability of mortgage funds. Building codes frequently perpetuate the use of traditional materials and archaic working methods; the very abundance and diversity of these codes impede standardization in construction methods. Strong craft unions which control the supply of labor, coupled with material scarcities, have contributed significantly to high and rapidly rising construction costs. The high cost of urban housing has been aggravated by soaring land values and zoning regulations which specify large-sized lots.

3   Discrimination   Discrimination in housing has been a basic consideration in restricting Negroes and other minorities to the decaying ghettos of the central cities. It is true that the incomes of many central-city blacks are so low that they cannot afford to move to the suburbs. But some could and would if housing were available to them.

One need merely recall the simple tools of

supply and demand to grasp the impact of discrimination upon housing prices and rents. The immediate effect is to make available a disproportionately small supply of housing to blacks. This restricted supply means higher housing prices and rents. One result is that blacks are forced to use a very high proportion of their income for housing. But even so, the housing is likely to be of inferior quality. High rents induce ghetto families to "double up" on available housing. Landlords respond on the supply side by subdividing apartments. And, needless to say, a captive market provides little incentive for owners to repair or improve their property. The overall consequence is typically high rents for crowded and dilapidated housing.

SOLVING URBAN PROBLEMS: THE PREREQUISITES

We have outlined the general character of certain problems of the cities and have indicated specific remedies. We must now recognize that there exist certain institutional and financial prerequisites to these solutions. An obvious prerequisite to all proposed solutions is sufficient financial resources. This is not to say that urban problems will automatically disappear if we simply "throw money at them." Our knowledge of appropriate techniques and strategies for dealing effectively with the problems of the cities is embryonic and deficient. Nevertheless, adequately financed programs are essential. Furthermore, certain institutional changes may be required, not only to obtain adequate financing, but also to provide an effective and efficient decision-making environment.

□   Political Consolidation

Most urbanologists agree that one of the basic prerequisites to resolving urban problems is political consolidation. In particular, the design of efficient and equitable solutions to the problems of the cities depends in good measure on overcoming the political fragmentation which now exists in most cities.

Urban areas are in fact highly integrated and highly interdependent economic units. Most urban problems—transportation; discrimination in housing, employment, and education; pollution; land use—are clearly areawide in character. The individual, fragmented political units of the cities do not have effective jurisdiction over these problems; in our large cities, the local units of government have been losing the capacity to govern effectively. The realization of efficient and equitable—as opposed to politically feasible—solutions to urban problems depends upon coordinated, areawide action, that is, upon political consolidation.

Efficiency   Looked at from the economist's point of view, political consolidation can stimulate more efficient decision making in dealing with urban problems for several reasons.

1 Small political subdivisions will frequently be unable to realize economies of scale in providing certain public facilities, such as water and sewage systems. Levels of output will be low and these facilities will operate at points high on their unit-cost curves (Figure 25-6a).

2 A closely related point is that in such endeavors as police and fire protection, street construction, and public transit, political fragmentation results in the loss of certain qualitative advantages which would stem from the planning and coordination of these public services at the metropolitan level. "The case for bigness in public services probably rests more on quality than on cost; an area-wide police force is better coordinated for traffic control and hot pursuit, and big enough to afford scientific crime detection facilities and specialists in juvenile and race problems."[20] Similarly, although the actual unit cost (per

mile) of producing streets may be roughly the same whether provided by many small, independent municipalities or by a large metropolitan government, there are obvious advantages in having an overall plan to coordinate a given volume of street construction in the interest of maximum effectiveness.

3 Still another reason why most urban economists favor political consolidation is that, because of the small geographic size of existing urban political units, many of the benefits associated with the provision of needed public facilities in such areas as, say, education, recreation, and environmental improvement will accrue to individuals and businesses residing in other political units. For example, a small urban political unit which builds an excellent school system, provides for the treatment of sewage and industrial wastes, and constructs ample recreational facilities will be providing benefits which in part spill over its political boundaries, that is, are external to it in that they are realized by the residents of other political units. Many of the graduates of its school system will take jobs in other areas. And those living in other political subdivisions will use its parks and playgrounds and benefit from its antipollution activities. The crucial point is that, when spillover benefits are large, a good or service will tend to be underproduced (Figure 6-1c). More specifically, the voters in each small political entity will not be anxious to tax themselves heavily to provide services and facilities whose benefits accrue in significant amounts to others.

Equity   The case for political consolidation also rests on grounds of equity. Political fragmentation has created serious fiscal disparities within the urban areas. Resources and needs have become separated in the political jungle of the cities:[21]

> Most of America's wealth and most of America's domestic problems reside in the metropol-

[20] Thompson, op. cit., pp. 267–268.

[21] Advisory Commission on Intergovernmental Relations, op. cit., p. 1.

itan areas. Why, then, cannot this vast wealth be applied through vigorous social measures to meet the growing problems? Because the resources exist in one set of jurisdictions within the metropolitan areas and the problems in another. . . . This disparity between needs and resources is the disparity between the central city and its suburbs.

Political consolidation would obviously have the desirable effect of putting resources and needs within the same political jurisdiction.

Avenues of Consolidation   Political consolidation can be achieved in a variety of ways: the annexation of surrounding suburban areas by the city; the consolidation of city and county governments; the establishment of special regional authorities to deal with such particular problems as transportation or pollution.

But it would be unrealistic to expect that consolidation will be easily and quickly achieved. The "haves" of the wealthier suburbs have shown little inclination to assume the moral and financial responsibility for the glaring problems of the "have nots" in the central city. Nor can we expect the officials of local governmental units to be eager to give up their power and functions. More positively, one can make counterarguments in favor of the present fragmented system. First, small local government is likely to be more conducive to personal political participation and more responsive to the needs and aspirations of its constituents than is a metropolitanwide government. A specific example: Some blacks feel that with fragmentation, they can gain political control of those geographic areas wherein they are numerically dominant, whereas, with consolidation, they are destined to be a largely ignored minority. Second, "bureaucracy"—diseconomies of scale in public administration—may tend to offset assumed cost economies in the provision and coordination of public goods and services by a consolidated urban

government (Chapter 6). Finally, some would argue that small local governments contribute to the heterogeneity of urban living areas in that they provide residents with a variety of choices as to levels of local taxes and amounts and quality of public services. Thus, although most urbanologists endorse political consolidation, the case is not as clear-cut as one might at first suppose.

☐   **The Larger Fiscal Problem**

The recent and much-publicized financial crisis in New York City differs in magnitude more than in kind from the problems faced by many large cities. The causes of the fiscal difficulties faced by large cities are manifold. The equity argument for political consolidation focuses upon the problem of residential segregation by income and the urban fiscal dilemma it creates: Public service needs are divorced from the tax base. Although political consolidation will put resources and needs within the same political jurisdiction, a larger fiscal question remains. Even with political consolidation, it is questionable that the tax resources of the urban areas will be sufficient to meet the rising costs of urban governments. Consider some specific factors which have made urban government very costly. Most big cities are old and, as a result, their physical plant—public buildings, sewer and electrical systems, streets, and so forth—is costly to maintain. Given the central city's dense concentrations of low-income and minority populations, it is no surprise that crime rates—and hence law-enforcement costs—are high. Welfare costs are very high and the public provision of many basic services (for example, medical care) is extensive. Financially troubled mass-transit systems require public subsidies. More recently, strong government employee unions have evolved and have aggressively pushed up wages and fringe benefits, including ofttimes-generous pension systems. Civil service or collective bargaining contracts restrict or impair the altering of job descriptions or reallocations of public workers in the interest of greater efficiency. Finally, the sheer size of big city bureaucracies may lead to diseconomies of scale which would not arise in smaller cities and towns. Empirical data show that the number of municipal workers per 1000 of population grows steadily as city size increases. Finally, the combination of high rates of inflation and unemployment which has plagued much of the 1970s has intensified the budget difficulties of municipal governments.

There are a number of proposed solutions to the revenue crisis faced by local governments: (1) Federal revenue sharing, (2) the shifting of certain fiscal burdens to the Federal government, and (3) the restructuring of the property tax.[22]

Federal Revenue Sharing   We are already familiar with the first proposal (Chapters 8) and its underlying rationale. The Federal government has great tax-raising ability but limited responsibilities for public spending on civilian goods and services. Local governments, on the other hand, are largely responsible for spending on civilian public needs, but are obstructed by the severe revenue-raising limitations associated with their heavy dependence upon property taxation. The enactment of Federal revenue sharing in 1972 and its 1976 extension have helped to ease the fiscal crunch faced by many cities.

Shifting Financial Responsibility   Another recommendation is to have the Federal or state governments assume the financial responsibility for meeting certain urban problems and obligations. In Chapter 37 we will discuss the suggestion that the Federal government establish and finance an income-maintenance program to relieve poverty, thereby reducing the heavy welfare costs now borne by city governments. Similarly, the shifting of all local costs of elementary and

secondary education to the Federal government would not only relieve the fiscal crisis of the cities, but might also help to ensure greater equality of educational opportunity.

Overhauling the Property Tax   Like sin, everyone deplores the property tax. It is regressive because low-income people spend a larger proportion of their incomes for rental housing than do high-income people. It is difficult and costly to administer. Equitable assessment of property is difficult. Furthermore, we have seen that rising property-tax rates have been a part of the self-reinforcing process by which wealthy people and prosperous businesses have fled to the suburbs. Yet the property tax is clearly the main source of revenue for local governments (Table 8-4) and is likely to remain so. It is therefore relevant to ask: Is it possible to restructure and revitalize the property tax so as to provide more revenue, on the one hand, and to reduce its harmful economic effects, on the other?

The basic proposal here is to shift the property-tax emphasis from buildings to land. We noted in Chapter 32 the reasons for a renewed interest in land-value taxation. The equity argument is that much of the value of urban land reflects public decisions with respect to zoning and the provision of roads, schools, and utilities. Most of the dramatic increases in urban land values are windfall gains in the sense that they are not the consequence of the efforts or expenditures of landowners. It would seem fair for society to tax away much of the increase in land value which society's decisions and expenditures have provided. The efficiency argument is that a tax on land has a neutral effect upon the use or allocation of land; a land-value tax does not contribute to a malallocation of land.

In the cities the present arrangement of relatively high property taxes on buildings and relatively low taxes on land tends to have perverse effects upon incentives. Specifically, heavy taxes on buildings harm the incentives of builders and property owners to construct

[22]This discussion generally follows the recommendations of the Advisory Commission on Intergovernmental Relations, ibid.

new buildings and improve existing ones. This fact helps to explain central-city decay and blight. The relatively light taxes on land mean that landowners find the tax costs involved in holding vacant land to be comparatively small, and so they are encouraged to withhold land from productive uses in order to speculate on increases in its value. Such action—or inaction—prevents growth of the property-tax base and contributes to the fiscal problems of the cities. But higher taxes on land values are advocated for reasons that go beyond the raising of additional revenue for city government:[23]

> There is poetic justice in heavy land value taxation: at present land is typically taxed at rates, relative to market value, that are less than half those applied to buildings. We now, perversely, favor the speculator who impedes development and discourage the investor in new and better buildings.

Postscript: The greater application of user charges which was recommended in connection with both the urban traffic and pollution problems would also be helpful in providing additional local revenue.

☐ New Cities

Some observers—dismayed at our apparent inability to cope with specific urban problems, dubious about the prospects for political consolidation and fiscal relief for the cities, and alarmed at the prospect of 100 million new city dwellers within the next thirty years—argue for the development of entirely new cities. These new cities might be satellites within the socioeconomic orbit of existing metropolitan areas, or they might be new, independent cities which are self-contained and distant from existing urban areas. In either event the prospect of "starting from scratch," and thereby avoiding the costly task of reversing the historical trends of urban dynamics and the associated problems, is appealing. High central-city land values would be circumvented, as would the burden of prevailing building-code and zoning regulations. And there would be a number of more positive advantages.[24]

> Designing and building a new community from the ground up provides a unique opportunity to plan for orderly growth with the most desirable location, timing, and sequence. It is possible to relate the new community development to areawide, regional, and national urban development plans and objectives. The continuous planning process required permits adjustments between the actual rate of growth of a new community and job opportunities within or near the community and the need for public facilities, transportation, public services, and commercial and retail establishments. Public investments can be related both to a projected and an actual rate of growth and anticipated need and capacity can be incorporated into current construction, thereby avoiding the necessity for later costly replacement or upgrading.

> Planning and design in a new community can be on a large enough scale to incorporate features which are difficult to obtain on a piecemeal design basis. For example, an improved relationship between work and residential locations can be established through balanced development and distribution of economic activity. Greater ease of internal movement can be planned by separating types of motor vehicle traffic and in turn isolating them from pedestrians. Moreover, the size and location of commercial and public buildings and other facilities can be more easily related to traffic patterns in order to minimize congestion.

> The large-scale planning required for a new community can also produce an improved esthetic environment and provide amenities not otherwise available.

---

[23] Netzer, op. cit., p. 258.

[24] Advisory Commission on Intergovernmental Relations, *Urban and Rural America: Policies for Future Growth,* (Washington, 1968), pp. 99–100.

Despite the potential attractiveness of the "new cities" approach, it has been subjected to thoughtful criticism. Is the new cities concept merely a copout, a means of running away from the problems which our cities now face? The vast bulk of our population will continue to live in existing cities. Is it realistic to expect that model cities can make significant contributions to the problems confronting these people? Furthermore, existing cities have evolved and grown for compelling economic reasons. Can we expect contrived model cities—constructed to get away from the problems of existing cities—to have a viable economic base?[25]

[25]See, for example, William Alonso, "The Mirage of New Towns," *The Public Interest*, Spring 1970, pp. 3–17.

Summary

1 The economies of agglomeration are significant in explaining the growth of cities. Similarly, deglomerative forces account for the shift of population and economic activity from the central city to the suburbs. Political fragmentation and pronounced economic imbalances have accompanied urban sprawl.

2 The short-run urban transportation problem is concerned with the most efficient use of existing transportation facilities. Although administrative problems are substantial, user charges and peak pricing are advocated by many economists. The long-run problem is concerned with the character of future investment in transportation facilities. For a variety of reasons, city planners and public officials tend to favor expanded and improved mass-transit systems.

3 Pollution is a problem of spillover or external costs. Most proposed solutions—legislated controls and standards, emission fees, and markets for pollution rights—seek to internalize these spillover costs to offending firms.

4 The central-city ghettos are heavily populated by blacks and other minorities who, because of low incomes and discrimination, cannot escape to suburban areas. Enlarged job opportunities, income-maintenance programs, and improved education and training are obvious ways of reducing ghetto poverty. Urban renewal and public housing programs have met with limited success in revitalizing the central-city areas and generally have done little to increase the supply of low-income housing.

5 Because of the areawide character of urban problems and the unequal distribution of income and wealth between central city and suburbs, political consolidation would be very helpful in resolving many of the problems of the cities.

6 Even if political consolidation is realized, fiscal assistance in such forms as Federal revenue sharing and the shifting of fiscal responsibility for certain specific urban problems and obligations to the Federal government may be necessary. The cities may reduce the harmful effects of property taxation and simultaneously obtain more revenue by shifting the relative burden of the property tax away from buildings and toward land.

7 Some observers argue that many advantages may be realized by planning and building entirely new cities to accommodate future population growth.

Questions and Study Suggestions

1 Key terms and concepts to remember: economies of agglomeration; internal and external economies of scale; infrastructure; deglomerative forces; urban sprawl; political fragmentation; user charges; peak pricing; materials balance approach; emission fees; market for pollution rights; black capitalism.

2 Explain: "To agglomerate is to economize." What, specifically, are the economies of agglomeration? Distinguish between internal and external economies of scale. What is the urban infrastructure? Discuss the demand aspects of urban growth.

3 What socioeconomic forces underlie urban sprawl? Explain in detail why the process of urban sprawl has been to the economic and fiscal disadvantage of the central city. Of what significance is the fact that suburbs are typically separate political entities? What arguments can be made for and against political consolidation?

4 "If cities are too large to be efficient or are poorly organized, the problem can be traced in large part to a failure to charge people for all the costs they impose or to reward them fully for the benefits of their action." Explain. Do you agree?

5 What is the nature of the urban transportation problem? Explain: "Although improved transportation has been a necessary condition for decentralization and urban sprawl, this decentralization has also created acute transportation problems."

6 What are the main causes of environmental pollution? Explain: "Clean air and water have become increasingly scarce and valuable resources precisely because they have been treated in the past as if they were free and unlimited in supply." What methods might be used to internalize spillover costs?

7 What is the role of racial discrimination in explaining the poverty of central cities? Analyze the economics of the ghetto housing market. Explain: "Urban blight—the cumulative deterioration of entire neighborhoods or areas—occurs because individual owners have no economic incentive to improve their property."

8 "We can go far to solve the central-city housing crisis by simply changing tax policy. First, tax unused land at higher rates than land with buildings on it. Second, tax new and improved housing at low rates and dilapidated and old housing at high rates." Do you think these policies would have the indicated results? Explain.

9 "Increases in the value of land in cities are the consequence of public decisions about zoning and investment in public utilities and facilities, not the result of individual efforts by owners. Therefore, the city should recapture the unearned incomes from rising land values by taxation and use these revenues for public purposes." Do you agree?

10 Analyze the fiscal problems of the cities. What solutions do you recommend? "The purpose of user charges is to confront decision-makers with the spillover costs of their decisions and in so doing cause them to alter their decisions." Explain this statement in terms of the urban transportation and pollution problems.

Selected References

Bish, Robert L., and Hugh O. Nourse: *Urban Economics and Policy Analysis* (New York: McGraw-Hill Book Company, 1975).

Downs, Anthony: *Urban Problems and Prospects,* 2d ed. (Chicago: Rand McNally & Company, 1976)

Emerson, M. Jarvin, and F. Charles Lamphear: *Urban and Regional Economics: Structure and Change* (Boston: Allyn and Bacon, Inc., 1975).

Hochman, Harold M. (ed.): *The Urban Economy* (New York: W. W. Norton & Company, Inc., 1976).

Netzer, Dick: *Economics and Urban Problems,* 2d ed. (New York: Basic Books, Inc., Publishers, 1974).

Ward, Barbara: *The Home of Man* (New York: W. W. Norton & Company, Inc., 1976).

Last Word
The Ghetto as an Economic Subsystem

Professor Daniel R. Fusfeld of the University of Michigan explains why the urban ghettos persist as underdeveloped areas within a generally prosperous national economy.

The ghetto economy differs markedly from the rest of the economic system. It is the home of the bulk of our urban poverty. It is permanently depressed, with unemployment rates normally at the high levels that are characteristic of depressions when they occur in the national economy. It is backward and underdeveloped, lacking the dynamic, progressive changes that bring advancement to the rest of the economy. Its manpower is employed in the low wage sector of the economy, primarily, and provides a pool of low skilled labor for an economy in which this resource is needed less and less. Within the ghetto an irregular economy functions, partly legal and partly illegal, which provides many of the services needed by the low income ghetto residents which they cannot afford to pay for in the normal channels of commerce or which the regular economy does not provide at all.

When we look at the relationships between the ghetto and the progressive sector of the economy, two phenomena quickly become evident. First, there is a continuous drain of income and other resources out of the ghetto. Second, there is a continuing accretion of people into it, cast off as unuseable by the progressive sector, which wholly or partially counterbalances those who are able to climb up and out.

The drain of resources includes savings, income, physical capital and human resources. The savings of ghetto residents, small though they may be, are deposited in financial institutions whose loans are made to business firms or mortgage borrowers outside the ghetto, with a much smaller flow of capital into the ghetto for these purposes, leaving a net outflow. The size of the net outflow is unknown, but its presence is acknowledged by those who are familiar with the financial institutions that serve the ghetto.

Income is drained out in more easily observed ways. Products sold in the ghetto and to ghetto residents are produced outside the ghetto. The owners of the retail stores that sell these products and gain the profits live largely outside the ghetto. The same is true of the wholesale and shipping firms, advertising media and other elements of the economy that service retail establishments. A large portion of the employees of ghetto retail firms live outside the ghetto, although this has been less true after the 1967–68 riots than before.

Physical capital flows out of the ghetto largely through failure to replace depreciation of housing and public facilities. The ghetto landlord takes a large portion of his gains in the form of capital withdrawals that come from failure to maintain his property. This drain is large. Typically, 70 to 80 percent of ghetto residents rent their housing (as compared with 22% in the nation as a whole) and rent takes some 35 to 60 percent of family income (as compared with 25 to 30 percent in the economy as a whole). A large portion of those rental payments represent a drain of capital out of housing. Public facilities are subject to the same outward flow, through failure to maintain schools, streets, sidewalks, parks and other public facilities in ghetto areas.

Manpower also leaves, when it can. Many persons move up and out of the urban ghetto through education, skill, initiative and luck. They move out primarily through education and jobs in the high wage sector of the economy, and take with them a large part of the entrepreneurship and skill that any substantial population group generates.

The net result of the drain of income and resources from the urban ghetto is the poor, backward, undeveloped slum that continues to exist in the midst of a growing and progressive society. It is drained of all those resources which might form the base for economic development. When this is added to a weak community structure, inadequate public services, and relatively few professional skills, it is not hard to understand why the urban ghetto has been such an intractable problem.

From Daniel R. Fusfeld, "Transfer Payments and the Ghetto Economy," in Kenneth E. Boulding, Martin Pfaff, and Anita B. Pfaff (eds.), *Transfers in an Urbanized Economy: Theories and Effects of the Grants Economy* (Belmont, Calif.: Wadsworth Publishing Company, 1973), pp. 85–87. Reprinted by permission.

37

The Economics of Income Distribution: Inequality and Poverty

The question of how income should be distributed has a long and controversial history in both economics and philosophy. In the past decade this interest has been fanned by a rather heated debate over the issue of egalitarianism. Should our national income and wealth be more or less equally distributed than is now the case? Or, in terms of Chapter 5, is society making the proper response to the "For whom" question? The egalitarian debate has produced a wide spectrum of responses and positions. At one extreme we are urged to believe that greater equality is the basic prerequisite of capitalism's survival. At the other, we are warned that the "rush toward equality" will undermine the system and lead to its demise.

In this chapter we begin by surveying some basic facts and trends concerning the distribution of income. Next, some basic arguments for and against income inequality are summarized. Then we specifically look at the poverty problem and the way in which poverty is related to racial discrimination. Finally, we consider public policy; existing income-security programs are outlined and the possibility of introducing a negative income tax to alleviate poverty is discussed.

INCOME INEQUALITY

First we must examine rather carefully available factual data on the distribution of income. Average income in the United States is among the highest in the world. The median income for all families was $11,800 in 1975. But now we must envision how income is distributed around the average. Table 37-1 is instructive. At the low end of the scale we find that 20 percent of all families receive about 4 percent of total personal income. Only 16 percent of the total income went to the 42 percent of the families receiving under $10,000 per year in 1975. At the top of the income pyramid we find that 12 percent of the families received incomes of $25,000 or more per year; this group received about 30 percent of total personal income. These figures suggest *there is considerable income inequality in the United States.*

□   **Causes of Income Inequality**

The price system is an impersonal mechanism. It has no conscience, and it does not cater to any set of ethical standards concerning what is an "equitable," or "just," distribution of income. In fact, the basically individualistic environment of the capitalist economy is more than permissive of a high degree of income inequality. Some of the more specific factors contributing to income inequality include:

1   Native Abilities   Nature has been very arbitrary in apportioning mental, physical, and aesthetic talents. Some individuals have had the good fortune to inherit the exceptional mental qualities essential to entering the relatively high-paying fields of medicine, dentistry, and law. Others, rated as "dull normals" or "mentally retarded," are assigned to the most menial and low-paying occupations or are incapable of earning income at all. Some are blessed with the physical capacity and coordination to become highly paid professional athletes. The clumsy and frail must settle for much less. Some have the aesthetic qualities prerequisite to becoming great artists or musicians. Others are not blessed with such talents. In brief, native talents put some individuals in a position to make contributions to total output which command very high incomes. Others are in much less fortunate circumstances.

2   Training, Education, and Opportunities to Advance   Opportunities to develop latent talents and to acquire new abilities are not equally available to all. Discrimination on the basis of race, religion, ethnic background, and sex blocks many paths of self-betterment.

Table 37-1   THE DISTRIBUTION OF PERSONAL INCOME BY FAMILIES, 1975

(1) Personal income class	(2) Percentage of all families in this class	(3) Percentage of total personal income received by families in this class	(4) Percentage of all families in this class and all lower classes	(5) Percentage of income received by this class and all lower classes
Under $5,000	20	4	20	4
$5,000–$9,999	22	12	42	16
$10,000–$14,999	20	19	62	35
$15,000–$19,999	16	20	78	55
$20,000–$24,999	10	15	88	70
$25,000–$49,999	11	24	99	94
$50,000 and over	1	6	100	100
	100	100		

Source: Bureau of the Census, *Household Money Income in 1975 and Selected Social and Economic Characteristics of Households,* Current Population Reports, Series P-60, No. 104, March 1977.

The virtual closing of certain occupational doors by unions or professional associations are equally effective obstacles. Furthermore, the acquisition of the training and skills one needs to enter highly paid occupations can be extremely costly. Most poorer families are unable to afford such investments in human capital, implying that income inequality may tend to be self-perpetuating. In short, even if everyone were blessed with identical physical and mental talents, income inequality would still result because opportunities to develop and employ those talents are not equally available.

3   Property Ownership   The ownership of property resources, and hence the receipt of property incomes, is very unequal. The vast majority of households own little or no property resources, while the remaining few supply very great quantities of machinery, real estate, farmland, and so forth. For example, a study of the ownership of private assets indicates that, in 1962, the poorest 25 percent of all families had no net worth, that is, their debts equaled their assets, while the wealthiest 20 percent of the population owned over 75 percent of all private assets. Furthermore, the richest 8 percent of the population owned 60 percent, and the wealthiest 1 percent owned over 26 percent, of all private assets.[1] Basically, property incomes account for the position of those households at the very pinnacle of the income pyramid. The right of inheritance and the fact that "wealth begets wealth" reinforce the role played by unequal ownership of property resources in determining income inequality.

4   Ability to Exert Market Power   Ability to "rig the market" on one's own behalf is undoubtedly a major factor in accounting for income inequality. Certain unions and profes-

sional groups have adopted policies which limit the supplies of their productive services, thereby boosting the incomes of those "on the inside." Exorbitant initiation fees, prolonged apprenticeship periods, flat refusal to accept new members, and the setting of unrealistic standards of performance are well-known and frequently employed tactics for manipulating the market on the behalf of a particular group. Legislation which provides for occupational licensure for barbers, beauticians, accountants, taxi drivers, and so forth can also be a basis for exerting market power in favor of the licensed group. The same holds true in the product market: profit receivers in particular stand to benefit when their firm develops some degree of monopoly power.

5   Unequal Distribution of Misfortune   Many households are at the base of the income pyramid as a result of economic misfortune. A host of economic hazards in such forms as prolonged illness, serious accident, death of the family breadwinner, and unemployment may plunge a family into relative poverty. The burden of such misfortunes is borne very unevenly by the population and hence contributes to the degree of income inequality.

6   Miscellaneous Factors   There are obviously other important forces which play a part in explaining income inequality. Luck, chance, and "being in the right place at the right time" have all caused individuals to stumble into fortunes. Discovering oil on a run-down farm, meeting the right press agent, and making a favorable impression on the boss's daughter have accounted for many high incomes. Nor can personal contacts and political influence be discounted as means of attaining the higher income brackets.

☐   **Trends in Income Inequality**

We know from Chapter 20 that economic growth has brought increases in incomes: *Absolutely,* the entire distribution of income has

---

[1] Dorothy S. Projector, "Survey of Financial Characteristics of Consumers," *Federal Reserve Bulletin,* March 1964, pp. 285–293.

been moving upward over time. Changes in the *relative* distribution of income are quite another thing. Incomes can move up absolutely, and the degree of inequality may or may not be affected. Table 37-2 is instructive on the relative distribution of income. Here we divide the total number of income receivers into five numerically equal groups, or *quintiles,* and show the percentage of total personal income received by each.

These data suggest that a significant reduction in income inequality occurred between 1929 and 1947. Note in Table 37-2 the declining percentage of personal income going to the top quintile and the increasing percentage received by the other four quintiles during this period. Many of the forces at work during World War II undoubtedly contributed to this decline in inequality. War-born prosperity eliminated the many low incomes caused by the severe unemployment of the 1930s, brought a reduction of wage and salary differentials, boosted depressed farm incomes through sharp increases in farm prices, temporarily diminished discrimination in employment, was accompanied by a decline in property incomes as a share of the national income, and so forth.

But the data since 1947 tell a different story. *The relative distribution of income has been basically stable since World War II.* Apparently, the forces making for greater equality during the war ceased to be of great import after the war.

A subtle point: Over time, all families—poor and rich—have been sharing in the fruits of economic progress in that incomes seem to be growing at roughly the same rate in all income classes. However, the application of the same growth rate to high and low incomes results in widening absolute dollar gaps between, for example, the richest fifth and the poorest fifth of all families. Hence, while the data of Table 37-2 suggest relative stability in the distribution of income, the absolute dollar differentials between the various quintiles have been growing.

□ **Of Taxes, Time, and Transfers**

The perceptive reader may raise several objections about our data.

Taxes Do taxes affect the distribution of income? Tables 37-1 and 37-2 are both in terms of before-tax incomes. Isn't the tax system an income-leveling mechanism? Is not after-tax income more equally distributed? The answer is no. *In the United States the before-tax and after-tax distributions of income are not noticeably different.* Recalling Table 8-6, we see that the overall tax system is proportional. Hence, taxes reduce everyone's income by about the same percentage, and as a result, relative incomes are unchanged. *Both the before-tax and the after-tax*

Table 37-2 PERCENTAGE OF TOTAL BEFORE-TAX INCOME RECEIVED BY EACH ONE-FIFTH, AND BY THE TOP 5 PERCENT, OF FAMILIES, SELECTED YEARS

Quintile	1929	1935–1936	1947	1955	1962	1972	1975
Lowest ⎫ Second ⎬	12.5	4.1 9.2	5.0 11.8	4.8 12.2	5.0 12.1	5.4 11.9	4.3 10.4
Third	13.8	14.1	17.0	17.7	17.6	17.5	17.1
Fourth	19.3	20.9	23.1	23.7	24.0	23.9	24.7
Highest	54.4	51.7	43.0	41.6	41.3	41.4	43.4
Total	100.0	100.0	100.0	100.0	100.0	100.0	100.0
Top 5 percent	30.0	26.5	17.2	16.8	15.7	15.9	16.3

Source: U.S. Bureau of the Census data. Details may not add up to totals because of rounding.

average incomes of the richest quintile are about eight times as much as those of the poorest quintile.[2]

Time A second possible objection to our discussion of inequality is that our data might well conceal the shifting of families up and down the income ladder, so when a time dimension is added to our analysis, the distribution of income is more nearly equal. For example, is the lifetime distribution of income more nearly equal than the annual distribution because of economic mobility? What are the chances, in Table 37-1, that a family falling in, say, the "under $5,000" class will progress to the "$10,000–$14,999" class next year or five years from now?

Although data are sketchy, the evidence suggests that, in the short run, economic mobility is not great. For example, one study[3] indicates that 70 percent of the families who are living in poverty in any given year will also be in poverty the next year. Of the remaining 30 percent, 11 percent will have been dissolved as the result of death or other reasons. Of the 19 percent who escape poverty, most will hover close to the poverty line. Similar observations apply to high-income receivers. In fact, experts have concluded that "distributions of income would probably not be noticeably different if they were collected on a lifetime rather than on an annual basis."[4]

But what about the long run? Does the income status of families change from one generation to the next? Intergenerational income mobility is important because it provides some indication as to the distribution of economic opportunity. If the sons and daughters of the rich all end up being rich, and, similarly, the children of the poor remain poor, then the

implication is that our society is falling far short of the goal of equal economic opportunity. Data are limited, but one recent study concludes that:

> . . . there does not seem to be *any* mechanism available to most upper-middle class parents for maintaining their children's privileged economic position. Insofar as incomes are relative rather than absolute, most upper-middle class children simply end up worse off than their parents. Among men born into the most affluent fifth of the population, for example, we estimate that less than half will be part of this same elite when they grow up. Of course, it is also true that very few will be in the bottom fifth. Rich parents can at least guarantee their children that much. Yet if we follow families over several generations, even this will not hold true. Affluent families often have at least one relatively indigent grandparent in the background, and poor families, unless they are black or relatively recent immigrants, have often had at least one prosperous grandparent.[5]

Furthermore, one-third of the children of top-quintile parents received below-average incomes and, conversely, one-third of the children of bottom-quintile parents achieve above-average incomes. In short, one's income status is not generally inherited; a reasonable degree of economic opportunity seems to exist.

Transfers Edgar K. Browning has criticized the official Census Bureau data of Table 37-2 for its treatment of transfer payments. While including cash or money transfers (such as social security payments and unemployment compensation), the data exclude nonmonetary or *in-kind transfers,* that is, transfers of goods and services which take place under such programs as Medicare, medicaid, housing assistance, food stamps, and job-training programs. Browning points out that in-

[2] Lester C. Thurow and Robert E. B. Lucas, *The American Distribution of Income: A Structural Problem,* Joint Economic Committee (Washington: Government Printing Office, 1972), pp. 4–5.

[3] *Economic Report of the President, 1965* (Washington), pp. 164–165.

[4] Thurow and Lucas, op. cit., p. 13.

[5] Christopher Jencks et al., *Inequality: A Reassessment of the Effect of Family and Schooling in America* (New York: Basic Books, Inc., Publishers, 1972), p. 216.

Table 37-3 RELATIVE INCOME DISTRIBUTION ADJUSTED FOR IN-KIND TRANSFERS* (*in percentage*)

Quintile	1962	1972
Lowest	8.8	11.7
Second	14.4	15.0
Third	18.2	18.2
Fourth	23.1	22.3
Highest	35.4	32.8
Total	100.0	100.0

* Data are also adjusted for personal taxes and differences in average family size.
Source: Edgar K. Browning, "How Much More Equality Can We Afford?" *The Public Interest,* Spring, 1976, p. 93.

kind transfers have increased dramatically in the past fifteen years and that, when these are taken into account, three observations emerge. First, we find a much more equal distribution of income in each year. Second, we observe "a marked trend toward equality" over the last twenty years. Compare Browning's adjusted data for 1962 and 1972 in Table 37-3 with the Census Bureau's data of Table 37-2 for the same years. Finally, Browning also contends that when in-kind transfers are taken into account, poverty, as officially defined, has virtually been eliminated.[6]

□ **The Case against Income Inequality**

The desirability of income inequality is anything but a new subject for debate. Indeed, the long-standing nature of the controversy has resulted in the development of a more-or-less standardized set of arguments that condemn, and an equally traditional group of contentions that defend, income inequality.

Three points constitute the case against inequality in the distribution of income:

1 Maximizing Satisfactions It is alleged that income inequality is a large obstacle in maximizing consumer satisfaction. The underlying reasoning is this: Money income is

[6] Edgar K. Browning, "How Much More Equality Can We Afford?" *The Public Interest,* Spring 1976, pp. 90–110.

subject to the principle of diminishing marginal utility. In any time period, income receivers spend the first dollars received on those products which they value most, that is, on products whose marginal utility is high. As their most pressing wants become satisfied, consumers will spend additional dollars of income on increasingly frivolous, lower-marginal-utility items. Suppose, for example, that $40,000 worth of annual income is unequally distributed between Brooks and Anderson— the former getting $32,000 and the latter $8000. As a result, the last, or marginal, dollars spent by Brooks will yield him relatively small increments of satisfaction or utility. Why? Because these dollars will be spent in satisfying less urgent needs; that is, they will be spent on frivolous products or on extra units of items already possessed in abundance. In either event the marginal utility of these dollars will be relatively low.

But, alas, $8000-a-year Anderson is in a much different situation. His annual pittance is such that his marginal dollars are spent on very basic, high-marginal-utility products. He is able to buy such small quantities of most products that the marginal utility of added units is still relatively high. It is concluded that any transfer of money income from high-income Brooks to low-income Anderson will increase the satisfactions or utility of the latter by more than it will decrease those of the former. The result is a *net* increase in *total* consumer satisfaction. Greater income equality has moved the economy closer to the goal of maximizing aggregate satisfaction.

In a slightly altered form, this argument contends that income inequality causes economic resources to be misallocated. As Chapter 33's discussion of distributive justice noted, the market economy allocates resources efficiently only if it starts with an optimum distribution of income. Hence, if we begin with the "wrong" distribution of dollar votes, resources will be drawn into the production of frivolous products for the rich at the expense of necessities for the poor. Critics assert there is ample evidence that our distribution of income is far from optimal. Witness the face-to-face ads in *The New Yorker* magazine: One ad pictures a pathetic little girl over the caption "Hunger is all she has ever known" as it asks for charitable contributions; the other displays a dog's sterling silver feeding dish as offered by Saks Fifth Avenue. The point, critics argue, is that there is nothing in the functioning of the market system to generate an optimal distribution of income and that the result is a malallocation of resources.[7]

Harvard philosopher John Rawls has recently developed the case for income equality along somewhat different lines. Suppose, he argues, we are starting a society "from scratch" and no one has any idea what his future income position may be. What principle of income distribution will this society choose? According to Rawls, they will opt for an equal distribution. The reason, he contends, is that people are basically "risk averters" and, in this case, they want to avoid the risk of receiving a low income. And how does society avoid the risk of low incomes? By choosing a distribution of income which involves the maximum or highest "low income" that one might receive. And that distribution, obviously, is an equal distribution of income.[8]

[7]Many economists have been reluctant to take a strong position for greater income equality because of a technical loophole in the above argument: The argument against inequality assumes that Brooks and Anderson have equal capacities to enjoy income. In fact, however, *interpersonal comparisons* of the subjective concept of utility cannot be scientifically made. It is unlikely that Brooks and Anderson are equally capable of enjoying income. The chances are at least 50-50 that Brooks has a greater capacity to derive satisfaction from spending money income than does Anderson. Were this actually the case, an *unequal* distribution of income would be required to achieve maximum consumer satisfaction. So, although this argument for greater income equality cannot be disproved, it also cannot be proved valid. The ability to derive satisfaction from the expenditure of money income eludes quantitative measurement (Chapter 33). As for the malallocation criticism, the rebuttal is that there is in fact no way to specify or define an optimum distribution of income.

[8]John Rawls, *A Theory of Justice* (Cambridge: Harvard University Press, 1971).

2 Productivity It is also argued that excessive income inequality impairs productivity. In the first instance, laborers who find themselves at the base of the income pyramid may not be able to obtain that minimum of food and shelter needed to maintain their physical and mental vigor, not to mention the effects which poverty may have upon their morale. And, ironically enough, inequality may impair the productivity of those at the pinnacle of the pyramid. Leveling off the income peak might induce the "idle rich" and the "I retired at thirty-five" segment of the economy's human resources back into harness. That is, less income inequality might stimulate incentives to produce and invest.

3 Political Inequality Another pillar in the case against inequality joins income inequality to political and social inequality. In the era of the ITT and Watergate scandals, one need hardly be reminded that "in politics, money talks!" By supporting lobbyists and financing the campaigns of "right-minded" politicians, the wealthy can exert a disproportionate influence over legislation and political policy. Furthermore, recall the inequities of military conscription which arose in part from income inequality: Youth from higher-income families could afford college and thereby obtain deferments, while the youth from lower-income families could not.

☐ **The Case for Income Inequality**

Three long-standing arguments anchor the defense of income inequality.

1 Capital Formation Income inequality gives rise to sizable amounts of private savings which, when invested, provide the capital goods that are the core of economic growth. Indeed, it is primarily as a result of this expanding stock of capital which the savings of high-income recipients finance that the productivity and standard of living of the entire economy are bettered. The savings of the very wealthy, it is argued, provide the means for improving, over time, the lot of the very poor.

2 Incentive Effects   Income inequality is also defended on the ground that it furnishes the incentives to work, produce, and innovate which are the driving forces of any economy. Monetary gain—the opportunity to better oneself financially—is alleged necessary to induce workers and entrepreneurs to rise above mediocrity. Income inequality is essential if risky ventures are to be undertaken and workers are to perform effectively and faithfully over time. In short, financial rewards are the basic motivator in the capitalistic system. If these rewards are lessened in the interest of greater income equality, the operating efficiency of the economy will be impaired.

Recent empirical work by Edgar K. Browning has led him to conclude that our present tax-transfer payments system has resulted in marginal tax rates which are so high that any further redistribution of income toward greater equality may have serious adverse effects upon incentives. He estimates that most upper-income families face marginal tax rates of at least 40 to 50 percent. Furthermore, transfer income—which Browning argues constitutes more than two-thirds of the income of the poor (defined as the lowest quintile)—is typically embodied in programs wherein the amount of money or in-kind transfer received is inversely related to income. For example, a poor family participating in the Aid to Families with Dependent Children (AFDC) program will lose $.67 in program benefits for every $1 of income earned. This means that, in effect, the marginal tax rate on this family's earnings is 67 percent. Noting that (1) some families participate in several transfer programs and (2) poor families pay sales and excise taxes on their expenditures of earnings or money transfers, Browning concludes that the marginal tax rate on poor families "can exceed 70 or even 80 percent." His calculations lead him to assert that "redistrib-

uting even one percent more [of national income] will probably require marginal tax rates to rise by at least 10 percentage points for most, if not all, families." Browning concludes that "rates this high pose a danger of seriously undermining incentives that is too great to be acceptable." In short, he feels the American economy cannot afford more income equality.[9]

3 The "Good Life"   Defenders of inequality also claim that high-income consumers have played a crucial role in the development of new products. The rich, it is said, support new industries in their high-cost, high-price infancies. This support allows low-cost mass production to evolve, bringing the products within the financial means of the masses of consumers. Stated differently, in the face of a drastic leveling of incomes, "The production of all first-quality goods would cease. The skill they demand would be lost and the taste they shape would be coarsened." A closely related and more general point is that the sociocultural fiber and viability of any society are directly related to, and dependent upon, income inequality. In short, it is alleged that the highly egalitarian society promises to be intellectually uncreative, culturally unappealing, technologically unprogressive, and socially unrewarding.[10]

■
THE DISMAL ECONOMICS OF POVERTY

Many people are less concerned with the larger question of income distribution than they are with the more specific issue of income inadequacy. Therefore, armed with some background information on income inequality, let us now turn to the poverty problem. How extensive is poverty in the

[9]Browning, op. cit., pp. 94–102.
[10]Bertrand de Jouvenel, *The Ethics of Redistribution* (New York: Cambridge University Press, 1952), pp. 41, 46, 54.

United States? What are the characteristics of the poor? And what is the best strategy in a war on poverty?

□ Who Are the Poor?

Poverty does not lend itself to precise definition. But, as a broad generalization, we might say that a family lives in poverty when its basic needs exceed its available means of satisfying them. A family's needs have many determinants: its size, its health, the ages of its members, and so forth. Its means include currently earned income, transfer payments, past savings, property owned, and so on. The definitions of poverty accepted by concerned government agencies are based on family size. Hence, in 1974 an unattached individual receiving less than $2658 per year was living in poverty. For a family of four the poverty line was $5040. For a family of six, about $6700. Applying these definitions to income data for the United States, it is found that *slightly less than 12 percent of the nation lives in poverty.*

Who are these 24 million or so souls who live in poverty? Unfortunately for purposes of public policy, the poor are heterogeneous; they can be found in all geographic regions, they are whites and nonwhites, they include large numbers of both rural and urban people, they are both old and young. Yet, despite this pervasiveness, poverty is far from randomly distributed:[11]

> ... the poverty population has a greater proportion of the elderly, female-headed families, blacks, the poorly educated, and unrelated individuals (especially elderly unrelated individuals) than the general population. For example, 46 percent of poor families are headed by a female, and children in female-headed families are about 6 times as likely to be poor as children in male-headed families (52 percent

vs. 9 percent). Blacks are more than 3 times as likely as whites to be poor; blacks comprise almost one-third of the poor population, compared to only 11 percent of the total population. About 16 percent of the elderly are poor, compared to a poverty rate of 12 percent for the general population, and the elderly constitute 14 percent of the poverty population. Only one-third of poor persons over 14 years have a high-school diploma. Although about two-thirds of poor families receive some earnings, employment tends to be unstable; only 19 percent of poor families have full-time, year round employment.

□ The "Invisible" Poor

These facts and figures on the extent and character of poverty may be a bit difficult to accept. After all, ours is presumably the affluent society. How does one square the depressing statistics on poverty which permeate both government and private reports with everyday observations of abundance? The answer lies in good measure in the fact that much American poverty is hidden; it is largely invisible. First of all, poverty is increasingly isolated in the hearts of large cities, because the middle and upper classes have migrated away from them to suburbia. Poverty persists in the slums and ghettos not readily visible from the freeway or subway. Secondly, much poverty embraces the aged and infirm, who rarely venture from their meager rented rooms. Thirdly, rural poverty and the chronically depressed areas of Appalachia are also off the beaten path. Finally, and perhaps most important,[12]

> The poor are politically invisible. ... [They] do not, by far and large, belong to unions, to fraternal organizations, or to political parties. They are without lobbies of their own; they put forward no legislative program. As a group

[11]U.S. Department of Health, Education, and Welfare, *The Measure of Poverty* (Washington, 1976), pp. 111-112.

[12]Michael Harrington, *The Other America* (Baltimore: Penguin Books, Inc., 1962), p. 14. This admirable and disturbing little book is required reading for anyone seriously interested in the poverty problem.

they are atomized. They have no face; they have no voice.

Indeed, the American poor have been labeled "the world's least revolutionary proletariat."

DISCRIMINATION AND POVERTY

Noting that blacks bear a disproportionately large burden of poverty, it is important that we consider the economic aspects of discrimination. Assuming genetic similarity among all races and ethnic groups, the degree of discrimination can be measured by comparing the incomes of those who are favored and those who are injured by discrimination. The comparison of median income figures of whites and nonwhites gives us a rough index of the degree of discrimination. As Table 37-4 indicates, the median income of nonwhite families is only 64 percent that of white families.

□   **Dimensions of Discrimination**

There is compelling evidence that this large income differential is firmly rooted in a number of different types of discrimination, some of which are reflected in Table 37-4.

1 *Wage discrimination* occurs when black and other minority workers are paid less than whites for doing the same work. This kind of discrimination is of declining importance because of its unsubtle character and the fact that it clearly violates Federal law.

2 *Employment discrimination* means that unemployment is concentrated among minorities. Blacks are frequently the last hired and the first fired. Hence, for the past fifteen or

Table 37-4   SELECTED MEASURES OF DISCRIMINATION AND INEQUALITY OF OPPORTUNITY, 1975

Selected measure	Whites	Negroes and other nonwhite races
*Income**		
Median income of families	$12,340	$7,935
Percent of households in poverty	10	29
Percent of families with incomes of $7,000 or more	73	55
Education		
Percent of labor force 16 years and over completing 4 years of high school or more		
Males	71	54
Females	75	62
Percent of labor force 16 years and over completing 4 years of college or more	16	11
Employment (percent of total civilian employment)		
White-collar occupations	52	34
Craftsmen-foremen occupations	13	9
Unemployment rate (percent of civilian labor force)		
Adult males	7.2	13.7
Adult females	8.6	14.0
Teenagers†	19.7	39.4

*Income data are for 1976.
†Males, 16 and 17 years old.
Sources: Statistical Abstract of the United States and *Manpower Report of the President, 1976* (Washington).

twenty years the unemployment rate for blacks has been roughly double that for whites (Table 37-4).

3 *Occupational discrimination* means that minority workers have been arbitrarily restricted or prohibited from entering the more desirable, higher-paying occupations. Negro executives and salesmen, not to mention electricians, bricklayers, and plumbers, are few and far between. Many craft unions have effectively barred Negroes from membership and hence from employment. Simple supply and demand analysis suggests how occupational discrimination contributes to income disparity between whites and blacks. Imagine two occupations—say, carpenters and dockworkers—for which blacks and whites are equally well qualified. Now assume that carpentry becomes a "white man's job" and blacks are effectively barred by either the union or construction firms. This means that the supply of carpenters will decline and the wages of carpenters—all of whom are white—will rise. Conversely, blacks, who can no longer obtain employment as carpenters, will shift into the dockworkers' labor market, increasing labor supply and causing wages to decline. A more revealing model of occupational discrimination and its consequences can be found in the "Women in the Labor Market" section of Chapter 38.

4 *Human-capital discrimination* occurs when investments in education and training are lower for blacks than for whites. The smaller amount (Table 37-4) and inferior quality of the education received by Negroes have had the obvious effect of denying them the opportunity to increase their productivity and qualify for better jobs. Unfortunately, a vicious circle seems to exist here. Many blacks are poor because they have acquired little human capital. Being poor, blacks have less financial ability to invest in education and training. They also have less economic motivation to invest in human capital: Facing the very real possibility of wage, employment, and occupational discrimination, blacks tend to receive a lower rate of return on their investments in education and training.

5 *Other forms of discrimination* may make the nonwhite's economic status even worse than Table 37-4 suggests. A number of recent studies have demonstrated that the nonwhite generally gets less for his dollar than does the white consumer. In particular, the supply of housing available to Negroes is sharply restricted, forcing them to pay higher rents for poorer housing than do whites. Ironically, urban renewal has typically resulted in a net reduction in the supply of housing for low-income Negroes. In addition to housing, the limited consumer, banking and credit, insurance, and legal facilities found in urban ghettos have the effect of limiting supply, causing Negroes to pay higher prices for these goods and services than do whites.

□ **Costs of Discrimination**

Given the diverse types of discrimination, naturally the economic costs of discrimination are difficult to estimate. However, the Council of Economic Advisers[13] has estimated that if economic and social policies were successful in lowering the Negro unemployment rate to the level of the white rate, and if education and training opportunities were made available to the Negro labor force so that the average productivity of Negro labor became equal to that of white workers, the total output of the economy would rise by about 4 percent. For 1976 the economic cost of racial discrimination would be on the order of $65 to $70 billion!

TWO PHILOSOPHIES

Given the existence and characteristics of poverty, the question arises as to whether it is an appropriate area for public policy. A fundamental philosophical disagreement focuses on this point.

[13] *Economic Report of the President, 1966* (Washington), p. 110.

□   Personal Shortcomings?

One view holds that most of the poor are ultimately responsible for their circumstances. They have forfeited or frittered away their educational opportunities. They lack salable skills and won't enroll in retraining programs. They live in now-depressed areas and, instilled with a "homing instinct," refuse to move. They have large families and are too short-sighted to use contraceptives. They have been spendthrifts in the days of youth and high earning power and now, in their old age, are unable to supplement their social security benefits or welfare payments. Some are poor because they are slothful or lazy. The bohemians, the hippies, and the skid-row alcoholics have willfully, and perhaps even joyously, chosen poverty as a way of life. In short, poverty is largely a matter of personal inadequacies, "attitudes of shiftlessness," shortsightedness, and, in some instances, preference. Poverty is therefore deserved and should be dealt with, if at all, through private charity and philanthropy.

□   Social Victims?

The virtually diametrically opposed position is that poverty is essentially the result of self-perpetuating cultural and social deficiencies which are beyond the capacities of individuals to remedy through self-help. The very characteristics of poverty suggest that poor families are by and large the victims of society and their environment. Some are the victims of rapid technological change. Others cannot find employment because of racial discrimination or because society has not provided them with adequate education and training. And certainly the millions of children who live in poverty can hardly be held responsible for their plight. Can those suffering from physical or mental infirmities be held responsible for these tragedies? In brief, for the most part poverty is the social by-product of a complex, highly interdependent, dynamic economy; therefore, responsibility for alleviating this poverty rests primarily upon society rather than on the individuals so afflicted.

□   The Evidence

The evidence resulting from this debate is not conclusive, and, of course, one can cite anecdotal support for both views. But a detailed analysis of the welfare rolls suggests that the vast majority of those receiving assistance are not self-supporting for legitimate cause.[14]

It is evident that as prosperity has opened up new job opportunities, enabling people who are employable to cross the subsistence threshold, those left behind are the less-fortunate who are unable to fend for themselves because of circumstance, whether it be age, sickness or other incapacitation, lack of training, responsibility for young children, or whatever disability stands in the way of earning a decent living. . . .

The outstanding fact emerging from [Bureau of Labor Statistics] studies is that most of the poor in the working age brackets, who might reasonably be expected to be in the labor force, in fact were in the labor force and a large proportion were employed.

SOCIAL SECURITY SYSTEM

The existence of a wide variety of income-security programs is ample evidence that the alleviation of poverty has been accepted as a legitimate objective of public policy. Indeed, transfer payments under the various programs which constitute our "social security" or "welfare" system have been the most rapidly expanding component of the Federal budget. In 1965, just prior to the Johnson Administration's "war on poverty," Federal outlays on "health and income security" totaled $27.5

[14]Committee for Economic Development, *Improving the Public Welfare System* (New York: CED, 1970), pp. 35–36, 43.

billion. In 1976 these outlays were $163 billion or about 43 percent of the Federal budget. Table 37-5 lists many of the major programs in our income-maintenance system and serves as a focal point for a brief commentary on each program.

□ **OASDI**

OASDI—old age, survivors, and disability insurance—is essentially a gigantic social insurance program financed by compulsory payroll taxes levied upon both employers and em-

ployees. As its name implies, the program is designed to replace earnings lost because of a worker's retirement, disability, or death. A payroll tax of 5.85 percent is levied on both worker and employer and applies to the first $16,500 of wage income. Workers may retire at 65 with full benefits or at 62 with reduced benefits. When the worker dies, benefits accrue to his survivors. Special provisions provide benefits for disabled workers. Currently, social insurance covers over 90 percent of all employed persons in the United States. In 1975 some 31 million people were receiving

Table 37-5 CHARACTERISTICS OF MAJOR INCOME-MAINTENANCE PROGRAMS

Program	Basis of eligibility	Source of funds	Form of aid	Fiscal 1975 Expenditures* (billions of dollars)	Fiscal 1975 Beneficiaries (monthly average; millions)
OASDI	Age, disability, or death of parent or spouse Individual earnings	Federal payroll taxes on employers and employees	Cash	$62.6	30.9
Unemployment compensation	Unemployment	State and Federal payroll tax on employers	Cash	13.0	16.0
Supplemental security income (SSI)	Age or disability Income	Federal revenues	Cash	5.5	4.0
AFDC	Certain families with children Income	Federal-state-local revenues	Cash and services	8.6	11.1
Food stamp	Income	Federal revenues	Vouchers	4.4	17.1
Medicare	Age or disability	Federal payroll tax on employers and employees	Subsidized health insurance	14.1	24.7
Medicaid	Persons eligible for AFDC, or SSI and medically indigent	Federal-state-local revenues	Subsidized health services	13.0	8.3

*Expenditures by Federal, state, and local governments; excludes administrative expenses.
Source: Economic Report of the President, 1976 (Washington), p. 94.

OASDI checks averaging about $170 per month.

There has been considerable controversy recently concerning both the short-term and long-term problems of financing OASDI. The program is financed essentially on a pay-as-you-go basis whereby benefits paid this year are derived primarily from this year's contributions. The short-term problem stems from the unseemly combination of inflation and unemployment which we have experienced in the 1970s. On the one hand, legislation has tied benefits to the cost of living; hence, rapid inflation has increased disbursements to beneficiaries. On the other hand, unemployment has eroded payroll tax payments into the program. The long-term problem is largely a reflection of demographic trends. Declining birth rates suggest that in the future there will be fewer workers contributing to the program at a time when the number of retirees will have increased substantially. For example, one projection suggests that the number of beneficiaries per 100 workers will increase from 30 to 45 between now and the year 2030.[15]

☐ **Unemployment Compensation**

All fifty states sponsor unemployment insurance programs. These programs are financed by taxes on employers which average about $1\frac{1}{2}$ percent of covered payrolls. Any insured worker who finds himself unemployed can, after a short waiting period (usually a week), become eligible for benefit payments. Currently over 80 percent of all workers are covered by the program. Size of payments and the number of weeks they may be received vary considerably from state to state. Generally speaking, benefits approximate one-half a worker's wage up to a certain maximum payment, which in many states is about $90. Ob-

---

[15]The interested reader should consult Warren Shore, *Social Security: The Fraud in Your Future* (New York: The Macmillan Company, 1975).

viously, the number of beneficiaries and the level of total disbursements vary greatly over the business cycle. It is to be recalled that unemployment compensation benefits are one of our important built-in stabilizers.

☐ **SSI and AFDC**

Many needy persons who do not qualify for OASDI or unemployment compensation are assisted through other programs. Beginning in 1974 Federal grants to states for public assistance to the aged, the blind, and the disabled were terminated and a new Federally financed and administered Supplemental Security Income (SSI) program was created. The purpose of SSI is to establish a uniform, nationwide minimum income for these three categories of workers who are unable to work. Over half the states provide additional income supplements to the aged, blind, and disabled.

The Aid to Families with Dependent Children (AFDC) program is state-administered, but is partly financed with Federal grants. The purpose is to provide aid to families in which dependent children do not have the financial support of a parent, usually the father, because of death, disability, or desertion.

☐ **Food Stamp Program**

The food stamp program, which has grown very rapidly in recent years, is designed to provide all low-income Americans with a "nutritionally adequate diet." Under the program eligible households receive monthly allotments of coupons which are redeemable for food. The value of the coupon or stamp allotment varies directly with household size and inversely with income. Thus, eligible households with little or no income receive free stamps, whereas households at the upper end of the eligibility range may pay 75 or 85 percent of the value of the stamps. The difference between the retail value of the stamps and the amount paid for them is obviously a government food subsidy.

☐ Medicare and Medicaid

Medicare is a Federal program designed to provide medical benefits to the aged. Compared with the rest of the population, older people tend to be ill more frequently and for longer periods of time. Because many old people have very modest incomes and the costs of hospitalization and medical care have been rising rapidly, it has become increasingly difficult for the aged to afford adequate medical treatment. Against this background Congress passed the Medicare program in 1965. This program provides, first, for compulsory hospitalization insurance covering up to sixty days for each "spell of illness." The beneficiary pays only the first $104 for each period of hospitalization. The cost of the program is financed by a 1.8 percent addition to the OASDI payroll tax. Secondly, Medicare provides a low-cost ($6.70 per month to the beneficiary) voluntary insurance program which helps pay doctor fees. *Medicaid* helps finance medical expenses of individuals participating in the SSI and AFDC programs.

It is anticipated that government's role in the financing of medical care will expand in the future. Congress is now considering several proposals to establish a national health insurance program. Spiraling medical costs, the catastrophic economic implications of prolonged illness, and the simple fact that millions of Americans—aside from the aged and indigent—do not have medical insurance, are all factors which have generated interest in such a program.

☐ "The Welfare Mess"

Now there can be no doubt that the social security system—not to mention local relief, public housing, minimum-wage legislation, agricultural subsidies, and private transfers through charities, pensions, supplementary unemployment benefits, and so forth—provides important means of alleviating poverty. Indeed, as Figure 37-1 indicates, the growth of

FIGURE 37-1 THE DECLINE OF POVERTY

Since the mid-1960s there has been a substantial decline in the number of people living in poverty. Note, however, that recently high unemployment rates have reversed the trend. (*U.S. Bureau of the Census*)

the social security or welfare system, along with overall economic progress, has substantially reduced the number of people living in poverty.

On the other hand, the welfare system, broadly defined, has been subject to a wide variety of criticisms in recent years.

1 Incentives It is argued that many programs impair incentives to work. For example, efforts to encourage AFDC mothers to work and become self-supporting have been largely unsuccessful. Since $.67 of benefits will be lost for every $1 earned, there is little incentive to become a productive member of society. Similarly, unemployment compensation benefits allow unemployed workers to seek new jobs at a more leisurely pace, contributing to both the volume and duration of unemployment. At the other end of the income scale, it is held that growing welfare benefits are financed by higher and higher taxes on the more productive, higher-income members of society, thereby weakening their incentives to work, take risks, and invest.

2 Abuses and Inequities The regulations of many income-maintenance programs are such that those who are *not* needy can benefit. To illustrate: The food stamp program has been criticized because stamps have been made available to striking workers and college students from middle-income families. Public housing projects have allegedly assisted middle-income groups more than the poor. On the other hand, it is pointed out that our income-maintenance system is a patchwork of programs and, depending upon the state or area in which one lives, benefits are subject to considerable disparities. Furthermore,

> Many of those who might be eligible for existing assistance programs—the aged, blind, disabled, dependent children and spouses—do not qualify for benefits because of the variety of Federal, State, and local nonfinancial eligibility requirements. Program features and regulations often seem designed to restrict benefits through the imposition of residence requirements, tests of "moral worthiness," mandatory acceptance of social services, overly stringent asset tests, income limits set below the poverty line, and the like. . . .
>
> Some persons decline to participate in welfare and food programs because of demeaning administrative techniques. Many people never are eligible for some programs because the States, counties, or cities in which they live have not elected to participate in the programs. . . .[16]

3 Administrative Costs and Problems
Critics charge that the willy–nilly growth of our welfare programs has created a clumsy and inefficient system, characterized by red tape and dependent upon a huge bureaucracy for its administration.

[16]President's Commission on Income Maintenance Programs, *Poverty Amid Plenty: The American Paradox* (Washington, 1969), p. 6.

4 Inflation It has been contended that the rapid growth of our welfare system has contributed to inflation in two ways. In the first place, dramatic increases in government spending for income-maintenance programs have outstripped the growth of tax revenues and thereby contributed very significantly to government deficits. These deficits have been a major source of demand-pull inflation. Secondly, middle-income workers—trade unionists in particular—have attempted to maintain the historical income differentials they have enjoyed over the bottom-bracket income receivers. As the welfare system has pulled bottom-bracket incomes upward, middle-income workers, through their unions, have pressed vigorously for larger wage increases to maintain their income differential. The result? Added pressure for cost-push inflation.

There are other criticisms: AFDC regulations encourage family breakup. Various programs foster social divisiveness between welfare recipients and low-income workers. In-kind transfers interfere with freedom of consumer choice. And so forth.

NEGATIVE INCOME TAX (NIT)

There has emerged from this array of criticism growing support for a new approach to income maintenance. This approach entails the establishment of a *guaranteed minimum income* which, proponents argue, can be integrated with, and effectively administered through, the existing Federal income tax system by making provisions for a *negative income tax*. That is, the present tax system takes funds from families whose incomes exceed some minimum amount. The modified system would also provide income transfers ("negative tax" payments) to families whose incomes fall below some minimum level.

Proponents argue that the massive administrative apparatus now required to administer our hodgepodge of welfare programs will no longer be needed. The Internal Revenue Service can quickly and cheaply handle the new program, mailing out negative tax payments to the poor as it now mails out tax refunds. In short, the NIT can yield more income maintenance bang for a buck. There is no doubt that NIT is an attractive option. Yet, as the following analysis will reveal, it is difficult to devise such a program which will simultaneously eliminate poverty, maintain incentives, and entail reasonable costs.

□ **Illustration**

Table 37-6 presents a hypothetical illustration of how a negative income tax might be employed to implement an income maintenance program. Assume we are considering a family of four and that society agrees that a minimum income of $4000 is desirable for a family of this size. Now families with earned incomes of less than $4000 can be assisted by applying a negative income tax. That is, the Federal income tax might be structured so that, while a family pays taxes to the government for income earned in excess of $4000, the government will make negative tax (subsidy) payments to the family on the amount by which its earned income falls short of $4000. In Table 37-6 the negative tax rate is assumed to be 50 percent. This means, for example, that if the family's earned income is zero and its "income deficit" is therefore $4000, the family will be entitled to a subsidy or negative tax payment equal to 50 percent of its income deficit, or $2000. Similarly, a family which

Table 37-6 NEGATIVE INCOME TAX: PLAN ONE (*hypothetical data*)

(1) Minimum income	(2) Earned income	(3) Income deficit	(4) Income subsidy	(5) = (2) + (4) Total income
$4000	$ 0	$4000	$2000	$2000
4000	1000	3000	1500	2500
4000	2000	2000	1000	3000
4000	3000	1000	500	3500
4000	4000	0	0	4000

earns $1000 will get a subsidy equal to 50 percent of its $3000 income deficit, or $1500. Adding this subsidy to the family's $1000 earned income will provide a total income of $2500. When the family's earned income reaches the $4000 minimum level—that is, when its income deficit is zero—it ceases to receive subsidies.

□ **Goals and Conflicts**

Ideally, an income maintenance program of this general type should accomplish three objectives. First, it obviously should guarantee some minimum income for all poor people. Second, it should preserve incentives to work; that is, the program should not encourage people to drop out of the labor force in order to "go on welfare." Finally, the program should be efficient in that it should eliminate or ameliorate poverty to some stipulated extent at a minimum cost. In particular, the program should not subsidize people who are not poor. Unfortunately, as Table 37-6 implies, these three objectives conflict with one another, and compromises or trade-offs are necessary.

The negative tax program of Table 37-6 is specifically designed to sustain incentives to work. That is, the negative tax rate is 50 percent so that the family's subsidy falls by only one-half of any increase in its earned income. Thus when earned income rises by $1000, the family's subsidy falls by only $500. A family always gets a larger total income by earning more income.

But the catch is that this particular negative tax program does *not* bring the poor family up to the $4000 minimum income level. Any family whose earned income falls below $4000 will get an income subsidy insufficient to bring total income to $4000. What to do? One obvious alternative is to alter the income subsidies so as to bring every family's total income to the $4000 level, that is, to make the income subsidies in column 4 equal to the income deficits shown in column 3 of Table 37-6. Specifically, change the subsidies of column 4 to read: $4000, $3000, $2000, $1000, and $0. This, of course, would raise the cost of the program substantially. And, more importantly, it would tend to undermine work incentives. In effect, the tax rate *on earned income* now becomes 100 percent because the family will lose $1 of subsidy for every additional $1 it earns. Why work harder and longer to increase your income by $500 when the government will respond by reducing your negative income tax subsidy by the same amount? Indeed, any family earning less than $4000 would be tempted to withdraw its breadwinners from the labor force and simply enjoy a $4000 subsidy. Why work for $4000 a year, receive no subsidy, and realize a total income of $4000 when you can decide not to work and realize the same total income?

The question, then, is this: How do we adjust our program to get all incomes up to the $4000 minimum level and still maintain work incentives? The answer: Apply the negative income tax to higher income levels. For example, substitute $8000 for $4000 in column 1 of Table 37-6, and apply the 50 percent negative tax rate to the resulting higher deficits. Table 37-7 demonstrates how this would work. We find that all total incomes are now at the $4000 minimum or above, remedying the basic shortcoming of Table 37-6. Furthermore, work incentives are provided for as in Table 37-6: for every $1000 increase in earned income the income subsidy falls by only $500. The rub, of course, is that many people—in fact, every family with some earned income—will be subsidized to the extent that their total incomes

will exceed the minimum level of $4000. By extending Table 37-7, you will find that families whose earned incomes are $4000 to $8000—people who are *not* poor—will receive substantial income subsidies. Hence, this particular program will be costly and inefficient in the sense that people above the $4000 poverty level will be subsidized.

To summarize: Negative income tax proposals which are structured to maintain work incentives either fail to bring incomes to desired minimum levels or provide subsidies for families that are not poor. Proposals which bring incomes to the poverty level without subsidizing families whose incomes are above the poverty level tend to impair work incentives.

■────────────────────────────

THE BIG TRADE-OFF[17]

One of the most profound changes in our society in the past half-century has been the emergence of a strong egalitarian movement. The roots of this movement are imbedded in a fundamental divergence between our political and social institutions, on the one hand, and our economic system, on the other. In principle, at least, our political and social institutions are based upon notions of equality; but our economic institutions, centered on the market system, generate substantial disparities in income and wealth. This inherent conflict has undoubtedly been a critical factor in providing societal support for egalitarianism. More specifically, efforts to redistribute income and alleviate poverty are a public response to the tensions created by the conflict between the political principles of democracy and the economic principles of capitalism.

But egalitarianism poses a fundamental trade-off between economic efficiency and economic equality.

Table 37-7 NEGATIVE INCOME TAX: PLAN TWO (*hypothetical data*)

(1) Minimum income	(2) Earned income	(3) Income deficit	(4) Income subsidy	(5) = (2) + (4) Total income
$8000	$ 0	$8000	$4000	$4000
8000	1000	7000	3500	4500
8000	2000	6000	3000	5000
8000	3000	5000	2500	5500
8000	4000	4000	2000	6000

[17]This section is based directly upon Arthur M. Okun, *Equality and Efficiency: The Big Tradeoff* (Washington, D.C.: The Brookings Institution, 1975).

The contrasts among American families in living standards and in material wealth reflect a system of rewards and penalties that is intended to encourage effort and channel it into socially productive activity. To the extent that the system succeeds, it generates an efficient economy. But that pursuit of efficiency necessarily creates inequalities. And hence society faces a trade-off between equality and efficiency.[18]

Thus the problem for a society inclined toward egalitarianism is how to achieve a given redistribution of income in such a way as to minimize the adverse effects upon economic

[18] Ibid., p. 1.

efficiency. Consider this parable. Assume society agrees to shift income from the rich to the poor. But the money must be transferred from affluent to indigent in a leaky bucket. How much leakage will society accept and continue to endorse the redistribution? In other words, if cutting the income pie in more equal slices tends to shrink the pie, what amount of shrinkage will society tolerate? The more technical problem is how to minimize the leak. What specific combination of tax and transfer programs will have the minimum adverse effect upon economic efficiency?

We can be assured that "the big trade-off" will be the basic issue lurking behind future debates over specific modifications and extensions of our income-maintenance system.

Summary

1 The distribution of personal income in American capitalism reflects considerable inequality. Though income inequality lessened quite significantly between 1929 and the end of World War II, little change has occurred in the postwar period.

2 Three arguments constitute the case against income inequality. Income inequality **a.** impedes the maximization of consumer satisfaction; **b.** impairs productivity; and **c.** fosters noneconomic inequalities.

3 Income inequality is defended as follows: **a.** Income inequality is conducive to a high rate of saving, a rapid rate of capital accumulation, and therefore rapid economic growth; **b.** income inequality is essential as an incentive to work and invest; and **c.** income inequality is essential to a viable, progressive society.

4 Current statistics suggest that about 12 percent of the nation lives in poverty. Although the poor are a heterogeneous group, poverty is concentrated among the poorly educated, the aged, and families headed by women. The incomes of blacks and other minorities are very substantially below those of whites, primarily because of wage, employment, occupational and human-capital discrimination.

5 Our current income-maintenance system has been an important factor in reducing poverty. However, critics of the system urge that it be replaced by a negative income tax.

Questions and Study Suggestions

1 Key terms and concepts to remember: income inequality; money versus in-kind transfers; discrimination; OASDI; food stamp program; unemployment compensation; Medicare; Medicaid; AFDC; SSI; negative income tax.

2 What are the major causes of income inequality? Outline and critically evaluate the arguments for and against income inequality. Which position do you favor? Why? Should a nation's income be distributed to its members according to their contributions to the production of that total income or to the members' needs? Should society attempt to equalize income *or* economic opportunities?

3 Are the issues of "equity" and "equality" in the distribution of income synonymous? To what degree, if any, is income inequality equitable?

4 Comment upon or explain:

a. "To endow everyone with equal income will certainly make for very unequal enjoyment and satisfaction."

b. "Poverty [in America] is not an economic malady so much as it is a social disgrace."

c. "The social and economic optimum is the same. The best economic solution will be the best social solution."

d. "Equality is a 'superior good'; the richer we become, the more of it we can afford."

e. "The mob goes in search of bread, and the means it employs is generally to wreck the bakeries."

f. "Under our welfare system we have foolishly clung to the notion that employment and receipt of assistance must be mutually exclusive."

g. "Some freedoms may be more important in the long run than freedom from want on the part of every individual."

h. "Capitalism and democracy are really a most improbable mixture. Maybe that is why they need each other—to put some rationality into equality and some humanity into efficiency."

5 Compare and account for differences in the economic status of whites and nonwhites. Distinguish between the various kinds of economic discrimination.

6 A prominent economist has argued:[19]

It is a striking historical fact that the development of capitalism has been accompanied by a major reduction in the extent to which particular religious, racial, or social groups have operated under special handicaps in respect of their economic activities; have, as the saying goes, been discriminated against. . . . there is an economic incentive in a free market to separate economic efficiency from other characteristics of the individual.

Do you agree with this view? Justify your position.

7 Comment on the following statement.[20]

Education is the principal route to a high status occupation, but it is not obvious whether, on balance, it promotes social mobility. . . . In part . . . education is a "transmission belt," whereby initial advantages stemming from the family are maintained for the fortunate, whereas initial disadvantages are perpetuated for the unfortunate. On the other hand, education allows some able people to rise to a higher relative position in the society.

Do you believe on balance that the distribution of education and training in our society alleviates, or contributes to, income inequality? Explain.

[19] Milton Friedman, *Capitalism and Freedom* (Chicago: University of Chicago Press, 1962), pp. 108–109.
[20] U.S. Department of Health, Education, and Welfare, *Toward a Social Report* (Washington, 1969), p. 19.

8   What is the negative income tax proposal? Discuss the case for and against NIT as a means of eliminating poverty. "The dilemma of the negative income tax is that you cannot bring families up to the poverty level on the one hand, and simultaneously preserve work incentives and minimize program costs on the other." Explain in detail.

Selected References

Gans, Herbert J.: *More Equality* (New York: Pantheon Books, Inc., 1973).

Harrington, Michael: *The Other America: Poverty in the United States,* rev. ed. (New York: The Macmillan Company, 1970).

Okun, Arthur M.: *Equality and Efficiency: The Big Tradeoff* (Washington, D.C.: The Brookings Institution, 1975).

Rejda, George E.: *Social Insurance and Economic Security* (Englewood Cliffs, N.J.: Prentice-Hall, Inc., 1976).

Rivlin, Alice M.: "Income Distribution—Can Economists Help?" *American Economic Review,* May 1975, pp. 1–15.

Thurow, Lester C.: *Generating Inequality* (New York: Basic Books, Inc., Publishers, 1975).

Tuckman, Howard P.: *The Economics of the Rich* (New York: Random House, Inc., 1973).

Last Word
Dangers of the Welfare State

In his farewell address as Secretary of Health, Education, and Welfare, Casper W. Weinberger offered some sobering thoughts on America's welfare state.

Federal spending has shifted away from traditional Federal functions such as defense and toward programs that reduce the remaining freedom of individuals and lessen the power of other levels of government.

This shift in Federal spending has transformed the task of aiding life's victims from a private concern to a public obligation. There are benefits and burdens in this:

One benefit is that the care of the less fortunate is guaranteed under law. The sweep of our social program commitments has brought secure incomes for the elderly, the ill, those who are alone, and those who are disabled. We have provided health care for millions and opened the doors of college to young people whose families could not otherwise have given their sons and daughters this opportunity.

But in the process of pouring out all of these compassionate and humanitarian blessings and institutionalizing our social obligations, we have built an edifice of law and regulation that is clumsy, inefficient and inequitable. Worst of all, the unplanned, uncoordinated and spasmodic nature of our responses to these needs—some very real, some only perceived—is quite literally threatening to bring us to national insolvency.

We are also creating a massive welfare state that has intruded into the lives and personal affairs of our citizens. This intrusion affects both those it seeks to help and those who do the helping. The entire human resources field is under the lash of Federal law—doctor, hospital, teacher, college president, student, voluntary agency, city hall and State capital.

There is another overriding danger inherent in the growth of an American welfare state. The danger simply is that we may undermine our whole economy. If social programs continue growing for the next two decades at the same pace they have in the last two, we will spend more than half of our whole Gross National Product for domestic social programs alone by the year 2000.

Should that day ever come, half of the American people will be working to support the other half. At that point, government would be like a gigantic sponge, sopping up all the Nation's surplus capital needed for industrial growth and modernization. Lacking funds for these vital purposes, we would no longer have enough surplus capital left to invest in job producing activities in the private sector—and it is that kind of investment which has always pulled us out of recessions and depressions in the past. In all likelihood, we could not maintain our free enterprise, incentive capitalistic economy, if 50 percent of the whole GNP had to be used to pay for domestic social programs alone. And if we lose our free enterprise, incentive system, we will have destroyed, by inaction, the system that has brought more benefits to more people at home and throughout the world than any other system since recorded history began.

Those who urge still more social programs view the problem upside down. It is not more social programs that will solve our Nation's ills, but more economic growth. Growth alone provides the jobs that reduce social ills. Growth alone provides the revenues that finance our social program commitments, yet one of the most iniquitous of the new philosophies we hear today is the smug assertion that "less is better and more is worse."

What we do have to limit is the growth of the welfare state in America. We must summon up a common determination as a people to change drastically our present approach because it is not only not working—it can ruin all of us. Only a wave of public sentiment in this direction can give Congress the nerve to say "no" to more social programs. As it is, Congress quite evidently believes that the road to popularity and re-election is to say "yes" to every demand for every increase in all existing programs and to agree to most demands for new ones.

Above all, we must recognize that personal freedoms diminish as the welfare state grows. The price of more and more public programs is less and less private freedom.

It is also the propensity of welfare states to spend beyond their means, leaving the day of fiscal reckoning to another generation. The news today is that we *are* that other generation.

Caspar W. Weinberger, "A View of the Federal Government," speech before the Commonwealth Club of San Francisco, July 21, 1975, excerpts.

Unionism, Collective Bargaining, and Women at Work

Over 20 million workers—almost 25 percent of the nonagricultural labor force—now belong to labor unions. Bare statistics, however, understate the importance of unions. The wage rates, hours, and working conditions of nonunionized firms and industries are influenced by those determined in organized industries. Unions are clearly permanent and powerful institutions of American capitalism.

In this chapter we seek, first, an understanding of the historical background and the present status of labor unions. Attainment of this objective necessarily involves a discussion of government policy toward organized labor, because labor legislation and union growth are intimately related. A friendly government and prolabor legislation cause unions to flourish and grow; an indifferent government and unfavorable legislation can result in stagnation and decay of the labor movement. Second, we want to analyze labor-management relations. Here our discussion will center upon the process of collective bargaining. Finally, we will discuss the increasingly important role of women in the labor market and the discrimination which they have encountered.

BRIEF HISTORY OF AMERICAN UNIONISM

The history of the labor movement in America is long, colorful, and flavored with violence.

In terms of national labor policy the American labor movement has gone through three phases: repression (1790 to 1930), encouragement (1930 to 1947), and intervention (1947 to date). Though the dates are somewhat arbitrary, these three phases serve as an excellent guide for our discussion.[1]

☐ Repression Phase: 1790 to 1930

Labor unions have existed in the United States for over 180 years. The shoemakers, carpenters, printers, and other skilled craftsmen formed unions of some permanence in the early 1790s. As Figure 38-1 indicates, despite this early start, union growth was relatively slow and sporadic until the 1930s. Two considerations go far to account for this meager progress: (1) the hostility of the courts toward labor unions, and (2) the extreme reluctance of American businessmen to recognize and bargain with unions.

Unions and the Courts It was not until the 1930s that legislation spelled out the Federal government's policy toward labor unions. In the absence of a national labor policy, it was up to the courts to decide upon specific union-management conflicts. And, much to the dismay of organized labor, the courts were generally hostile toward unions. Their hostility had two sources.

1 Most judges had propertied-class backgrounds.

2 The courts are inherently conservative institutions charged with the responsibility of protecting *established* property rights. Unions, throughout the 1800s and the early decades of the 1900s, were in the unenviable position of seeking rights for labor at the expense of the *existing* rights of management.

The hostility of the courts was first given

[1] The following are highly recommended: U.S. Department of Labor, *Brief History of the American Labor Movement* (1970); Richard B. Morris (ed.), *The American Worker* (Washington: Government Printing Office, 1976); Foster Rhea Dulles, *Labor in America,* 3d ed. (New York: Thomas Y. Crowell Company, 1960); and Joseph G. Rayback, *A History of American Labor* (New York: The Free Press, 1966).

vent in the *criminal conspiracy doctrine.* This doctrine, "imported" by the American courts from English common law at the turn of the nineteenth century, was unbelievably narrow by modern standards. The doctrine flatly concluded that combinations of workmen to raise wages were criminal conspiracies and hence illegal. Though weakened by subsequent court rulings in the 1840s, the shadow of the conspiracy doctrine hung heavy over organized labor throughout most of the 1800s. Although unions, as such, were later recognized by the courts as legal organizations, the techniques employed by unions to press their demands—strikes, picketing, and boycotting—were generally held to be illegal. And, in the latter part of the 1800s, the courts employed both antitrust laws and injunctions in such a way as to impede the labor movement significantly.

Although Congress passed the Sherman Act of 1890 for the express purpose of thwarting the growth of business monopolies, the courts interpreted the loose wording of the act to include labor unions as conspiracies in restraint of trade and frequently so applied the act.

A simpler and equally effective antiunion device was the *injunction*. An injunction, or restraining order, is a court order directing that some act not be carried out, on the ground that irreparable damage will be done to those affected by the action. The attitude of the courts toward unions was such that it was extremely easy for employers to obtain injunctions from the courts, prohibiting unions from enforcing their demands by striking, picketing, and boycotting. Stripped of these weapons, unions were relatively powerless to obtain the status and rights they sought.

To summarize: The courts employed the criminal conspiracy doctrine, the Sherman Act, and injunctions, to the end that union growth was greatly retarded during the 1790–1930 period.

Antiunion Techniques of Management
American businessmen did not rely entirely

upon the courts in their attempt to impede the growth of unions. The business community, hostile to unions from their inception, developed a group of techniques to undermine unions. A startlingly simple antiunion technique was that of ferreting out and firing prounion workers. Too, the average employer felt it his duty to inform fellow employers that the discharged workers were "troublemakers" and "labor agitators" and not fit to be hired. This combination of *discriminatory discharge* and *blacklisting* made it extremely risky for workers even to think in terms of organizing a union. One's present and future employment opportunities were at stake.

Another potent weapon in management's struggle to keep unions down was the *lockout,* management's counterpart of the strike. By closing up shop for a few weeks, employers were frequently able to bring their employees to terms and to destroy any notions they might have about organizing a union. In some cases this might prove a bit costly to the employer in the short run. In other cases, when business was slack, the lockout was a good means of killing two birds with one stone— working off excess inventories and undermining worker attempts to organize. Remember: Workers of the late 1800s and early 1900s were not blessed with savings accounts or multi-million-dollar strike funds to draw upon in such emergencies.

Where workers were determined to organize, pitched battles often ensued. Rocks, clubs, shotguns, and an occasional stick of dynamite were the shadowy ancestors of collective bargaining. Some of the darkest pages of American labor history concern the violent clashes between workers and company-hired *strikebreakers.* The Homestead strike of 1892, the Pullman strike of 1894, and the Ludlow Massacre of 1914 are cases in point. Less dramatic skirmishes erupt down to the present time.

But management tactics were often more subtle than a cracked skull. The *yellow-dog contract* was one of the more ingenious antiunion devices fostered by management. In such contracts workers agreed to remain nonunion as a condition of employment. They often had little choice but to sign such contracts—no contract, no job. Violation of a yellow-dog contract exposed a worker to a lawsuit by his employer, the result of which might be a court-imposed fine or even imprisonment.

As a last resort, an employer might shower his work force with such amenities as group insurance and pension programs and stock ownership and profit-sharing schemes to convince them that employers would look after the interests of the workers as effectively as would unions established by "outsiders." The next step beyond such *paternalism* was employee-representation schemes or *company unions,* that is, employer-dominated "dummy" unions which, it was hoped, would discourage the establishment of genuine unions. Paternalism and company unions were decidedly effective in retarding union growth as late as the 1920s.[2]

Evolution of Business Unionism The growth which occurred in the labor movement during the 1800s not only was modest, but it also embodied a variety of union philosophies. The mid-1800s were in effect a laboratory wherein American labor experimented with alternative forms of unionism—Marxism, utopianism, reformism, and a host of other isms. But such unions usually foundered in the span of a few short years because of the internal conflict between the workers' interest in short-run practical goals (higher wages and shorter hours) and the long-run utopian goals (producer cooperatives, creation of a labor party, and so forth) of the union leaders.

Then, in 1886, a new labor organization—

---

[2] During a prolonged strike in the bituminous coal industry in 1902, a spokesman for the mine operators, George F. Baer, issued the classic statement of business paternalism: "The rights and interests of the laboring man will be protected and cared for—not by the labor agitators, but by the Christian men to whom God in His infinite wisdom has given the control of the property interests of this country."

the American Federation of Labor—which was to dominate the labor movement for the next fifty years was formed. Under the leadership of Samuel Gompers, labor charted a conservative course which has been very influential down to the present date.[3] Appropriately honored as "the father of the American labor movement," Gompers preached three fundamental ideas: (1) practical business unionism, (2) political neutrality for labor, and (3) the autonomy of each trade or craft.

1 Business unionism Gompers was firmly convinced that "safe and sane" business unionism was the only course for American labor to follow. In 1903 he declared:[4]

> I want to tell you, Socialists, that I have studied your philosophy; read your works on economics . . . studied your standard works. . . . I have heard your orators and watched the work of your movement the world over. I have kept close watch upon your doctrines for thirty years; have been closely associated with many of you, and know how you think and what you propose. I know, too, what you have up your sleeve. And I want to say that I am entirely at variance with your philosophy. I declare it to you, I am not only at variance with your doctrines, but with your philosophy. Economically, you are unsound; socially, you are wrong; industrially, you are an impossibility.

Gompers flatly rejected long-run idealistic schemes entailing the overthrow of the capitalistic system. He spurned intellectuals and theorizers and emphasized that unions should be concerned with practical short-run economic objectives—higher pay, shorter hours, and improved working conditions. In the words of one scholar, Gompers felt that "you must offer the American working man bread and butter in the here and now instead of pie in the sky in the sweet by and by."[5]

2 Political neutrality In addition to espousing "bread and butter" unionism, Gompers had strong opinions on labor's role in politics and the basis upon which workers should be organized. Insofar as politics was concerned, Gompers was convinced that government should keep its nose out of labor-management relations and collective bargaining. Although he recognized that governmental interference on behalf of labor might be a boon to union growth, Gompers was equally certain that antiunion government policies could stifle the progress of the entire labor movement. In pursuing the idea of political neutrality, Gompers cautioned organized labor not to align itself with any political party. Preoccupation with long-run political goals, he argued, merely causes labor to lose sight of the short-run economic objectives it ought to seek. Gompers admonished organized labor to follow one simple principle in the political arena: Reward labor's friends and punish its enemies at the polls without regard to political affiliation.

3 Trade autonomy Finally, Gompers was firmly convinced that "autonomy of the trade," that is, unions organized on the basis of specific crafts, was the only permanent foundation for the labor movement. Unions composed of many different crafts lack the cohesiveness, he argued, that is essential to strong, hard-hitting, business unionism. These craft unions should then be affiliated in a national federation. "One union to each trade, affiliated for one labor movement."

This philosophy—conservative business unionism, political "neutrality," and the craft

---

[3] This is not to say that all unions have followed conservative paths since Gompers first espoused the virtues of business unionism. The Industrial Workers of the World, founded in 1905, advocated a decidedly revolutionary brand of left-wing unionism. And in the late thirties and early forties, Communists infiltrated a number of CIO unions. In 1949 and 1950, the CIO expelled eleven affiliated unions whose leadership had come to be dominated by Communists.

[4] From the *Proceedings* of the 1903 AFL convention, reprinted in George P. Shultz and John R. Coleman, *Labor Problems: Cases and Readings,* 2d ed. (New York: McGraw-Hill Book Company, 1959), pp. 16–17.

[5] Charles C. Killingsworth, "Organized Labor in a Free Enterprise Economy," in Walter Adams (ed.), *The Structure of American Industry,* 3d ed. (New York: The Macmillan Company, 1961), p. 570.

principle of union organization—was destined to dominate the AFL and the entire labor movement for the next half-century. Indeed, the AFL, operating under Gompers's leadership, met with considerable success—at least for a time. AFL membership hit a high-water mark of about 4 million members by the end of World War I. Then a combination of circumstances arose in the 1920s which forced the AFL into an eclipse (see Figure 38-1). One factor was a strong antiunion drive by employers. Spearheaded by the National Association of Manufacturers, businesses waged a last-ditch effort to stem the rising tide of organized labor. Then, too, many firms introduced employee representation plans, company unions, and a host of paternalistic schemes to convince workers that employers were better prepared to look out for their employees' interests than were labor leaders. Finally, the AFL clung tenaciously to the craft principle of union organization, thereby ignoring the ever-increasing number of unskilled workers employed by the rapidly expanding mass-production industries—the automobile and steel industries in particular.

☐ Encouragement Phase: 1930 to 1947

Two significant events occurred in the 1930s which revived the labor movement and inaugurated a period of rapid growth. Most important, the attitude of the Federal government toward unions changed from one of indifference, not to say hostility, to one of encouragement. Also, a major structural change in the labor movement accompanied the founding of the Committee (later the Congress) of Industrial Organizations in 1936. Both events, coupled with the wartime prosperity of the 1940s, greatly swelled the ranks of organized labor.

Prolabor Legislation of the 1930s Against the background of the depressed thirties, the Federal government enacted two decidedly prolabor acts. In part, the passage of these acts reflects the strong opposition of organized labor to the previously described weapons employed by the courts and by management to suppress unions. In part, they reflect a Democratic administration replacing a

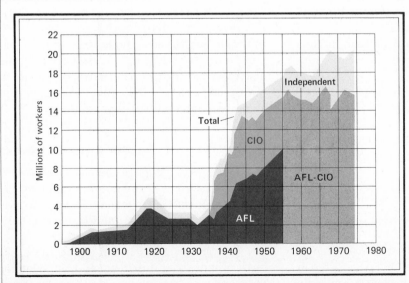

FIGURE 38-1 THE GROWTH OF UNION MEMBERSHIP

Most of the growth in organized labor has occurred since 1935. (*U.S. Bureau of the Census and Bureau of Labor Statistics.*)

Republican administration. In part, they echo the widely held opinion that strong unions, by achieving higher wages through collective bargaining, would increase total spending—or at least prevent it from falling—and help alleviate the Great Depression.

The Norris–La Guardia Act of 1932 did much to clear the path for union growth by outlawing two of the more effective antiunion weapons. Specifically, the act

1 Made it decidedly more difficult for employers to obtain injunctions against unions

2 Declared that yellow-dog contracts were unenforceable

Three years later, in 1935, the Federal government took more positive steps to encourage union growth. The Wagner Act (officially the National Labor Relations Act) guaranteed the "twin rights" of labor: the right of self-organization and the right to bargain collectively with employers. The act listed a number of "unfair labor practices" on the part of management. Specifically it

1 Forbade employers from interfering with the right of workers to form unions

2 Outlawed company unions

3 Prohibited antiunion discrimination by employers in hiring, firing, and promoting

4 Outlawed discrimination against any worker who files charges or gives testimony under the act

5 Obligated employers to bargain in good faith with a union duly established by their employees

The Wagner Act was clearly "labor's Magna Charta."

A National Labor Relations Board was established by the act and charged with the authority to investigate unfair labor practices occurring under the act, to issue cease-and-desist orders in the event of violations, and to conduct worker elections in deciding which specific union the workers wanted to represent them.

The Wagner Act was tailored to accelerate union growth. It was extremely successful in achieving this goal. The protective umbrella provided to unions by this act in conjunction with the Norris–La Guardia Act played a major role in causing the ranks of organized labor to mushroom from about 4 million in 1935 to 15 million in 1947.

Industrial Unionism We have already noted that one of the causes of stagnation in the AFL during the 1920s was its unwillingness to organize the growing masses of unskilled assembly-line workers. Though the majority of AFL leaders chose to ignore the unskilled workers, a vocal minority under the leadership of John L. Lewis contended that craft unionism would be completely ineffective as a means of organizing the hundreds of thousands of workers in the growing mass-production industries. According to Lewis and his followers, the basis for organization should be shifted from *craft unionism* to *industrial unionism,* that is, away from unions which only encompass a specific type of skilled workers to unions which include all workers—both skilled and unskilled—in a given industry or group of related industries. This conflict came to a head, and in 1936 Lewis and his sympathizers withdrew their unions (and were simultaneously expelled) from the AFL.

The withdrawing unions established themselves as the Congress of Industrial Organizations. The CIO met with startling success in organizing the automobile and steel industries. So great was this success that the AFL also moved in the direction of organizing on an industrial basis. By 1940, total union membership approximated 9 million workers.

□ **Intervention Phase: 1947 to Date**

Since World War II there has been a decided increase in government regulation of, and intervention in, labor-management relations. It is important to understand the background of this governmental interference.

The prolabor legislation of the 1930s, the birth of industrial unionism, and the booming prosperity of the war years brought rapid union growth (see Figure 38-1). As unions gathered strength—both numerical and financial—it became increasingly evident that labor unions could no longer be regarded as the weak sister or underdog in their negotiations with management. Just as the growing power of business monopolies brought a clamor for public control in the 1870s and 1880s, the upsurge of union power in the 1930s and 1940s brought a similar outcry for regulation. This pressure for union control came to a head in the years immediately following World War II.

Many people felt that the wartime strike record of American labor left much to be desired. Despite no-strike pledges, work stoppages reached a new high at the height of the war effort in 1944. Equally harmful to the favorable climate of public opinion which labor enjoyed in the 1930s was the series of nationwide strikes which broke out during the reconversion period in such basic industries as steel, coal, meat-packing, and railway transportation. The man in the street felt that these strikes not only slowed the reconversion process but also inaugurated the severe wage-price inflationary spiral which was to plague the immediate postwar years (see Chapter 10). Many businessmen, needless to say, were happy to fan the flames of public resentment. By the mid-forties the prolabor climate of the prior decade had done a virtual turnabout.

Taft-Hartley Act of 1947   This growing public hostility toward unions was crystallized in the Taft-Hartley Act (officially the Labor–Management Relations Act) in 1947. A very detailed piece of legislation, this act mirrors the increasing complexity of labor-management relations. Generally its specific provisions fall under four headings: (1) provisions which designate and outlaw certain "unfair union practices"; (2) provisions which regulate the internal administration of unions; (3) provisions which specify collective bargaining procedures and regulate the actual contents of bargaining agreements; and (4) provisions for

the handling of strikes imperiling the health and safety of the nation.

1   Unfair union practices   You will recall that the Wagner Act outlined a number of "unfair labor practices" on the part of management. A new and crucial feature of the Taft-Hartley Act was that it listed a number of "unfair labor practices" on the part of unions. These unfair practices, which constitute some of the most controversial sections of the act, are as follows: (*a*) Unions are prohibited from coercing employees to become union members. (*b*) *Jurisdictional strikes* (disputes between unions over the question of which has the authority to perform a specific job) are forbidden, as are *secondary boycotts* (refusing to buy or handle products produced by another union or group of workers) and certain *sympathy strikes* (strikes designed to assist some other union in gaining employer recognition or some other objective). (*c*) Unions are prohibited from charging excessive or discriminatory initiation fees or dues. (*d*) *Featherbedding,* a mild form of extortion wherein the union or its members receive payment for work not actually performed, is specifically outlawed. (*e*) Unions cannot refuse to bargain in good faith with management.

2   Union administration   Taft-Hartley also imposes significant controls on the internal processes of labor unions: (*a*) Unions are obligated to make detailed financial reports to the National Labor Relations Board and to make such information available to its members. (*b*) Unions are prohibited from making political contributions in elections, primaries, or conventions which involve Federal offices. (*c*) Originally, union officials were required to sign non-Communist affidavits.

3   Contract contents   Other Taft-Hartley provisions are designed to control the actual collective bargaining process and the contents of the work agreement resulting therefrom: (*a*) The *closed shop* (which requires that a firm hire only workers who are already union members) is specifically outlawed for workers engaged in interstate commerce; that is, a closed-shop arrangement cannot be written into a collective bargaining agreement. (*b*) The *checkoff* (whereby union dues are deducted from the workers' pay checks by the employer and turned over to the union in a lump sum) cannot be written into a bargaining agreement unless authorized in writing by individual workers. (*c*) Collective bargaining agreements must provide that, where they exist, welfare and pension funds are kept separate from other union funds and jointly administered by the union and management. (*d*) Bargaining agreements must contain termination or *reopening clauses* whereby both labor and management must give the other party 60 days' notice of the intent to modify or terminate the existing work agreement.

4 "Health and safety" strikes Finally, the Taft-Hartley Act outlines a procedure for avoiding major strikes which might disrupt the entire economy and thereby imperil the health or safety of the nation. According to this procedure, the President may obtain an injunction to delay such strikes for an 80-day "cooling off" period. Within this period the involved workers are polled by the NLRB as to the acceptability of the last offer of the employer. If the last offer is rejected, the union can then strike. The government's only recourse—one of questionable legality—is seizure of the industry.

The Taft-Hartley Act is difficult to evaluate.[6] It has been a subject of heated debate since its enactment. Unions have condemned Taft-Hartley as a "slave labor act," claiming that it has undermined the status of unions and imperiled many of organized labor's basic weapons. Most employers feel that the act is merely a step in the right direction—a long-overdue attempt to restore a better balance of power between labor and management.

This much is agreed upon: The Taft-Hartley Act represented a marked shift in public policy. This shift is essentially one from "government-sponsored" collective bargaining to "government-regulated" collective bargaining. The underlying philosophy of the Wagner Act was that a balance of bargaining power between labor and management should be established. This balance would be conducive to effective collective bargaining free of government intervention. The Taft-Hartley Act, however, envisioned a need for detailed and continuous government control of collective bargaining to assure labor-management relations which are not unduly injurious to the welfare of the general public. Most objective observers feel that this shift in public policy was a necessary one. Disagreement persists, however, with respect to the form these controls should take and the manner in which they should be applied.

Landrum-Griffin Act of 1959 Government regulation of the internal processes of unions was extended by passage of the Landrum-Griffin Act (officially the Labor-Management Reporting and Disclosure Act) in the fall of 1959. This act places regulations upon union elections and union finances and guarantees certain rights of union members. Specifically, the act regulates union elections by requiring regularly scheduled elections of officers and the use of secret ballots; restrictions are placed upon ex-convicts and Communists in holding union offices. Furthermore, union officials are now held strictly accountable for union funds and property. Officers handling union funds must be bonded; the embezzlement of union funds is made a Federal offense; and close restrictions are placed upon a union's loans to its officers and members. The act is also aimed at preventing autocratic union leaders from infringing upon certain rights of their constituents. The individual worker's rights to attend and participate in union meetings, to vote in union proceedings, and to nominate officers are guaranteed. The act permits a worker to sue his union if it denies him these rights. Under the act the Secretary of Labor is given broad powers in investigating violations of the act.

[6]See "The Taft-Hartley Act after Ten Years: A Symposium," *Industrial and Labor Relations Review,* April 1958.

☐ Labor Unity

In 1955 unity was formally reestablished in the American labor movement with the merger of the AFL and the CIO. Many forces were significant in closing the breach which had existed between the two for almost two decades:

1 The AFL's increased willingness to accept and practice industrial unionism lessened the original structural differences between the AFL and the CIO.

2 The political and legislative setbacks which labor has encountered since the prolabor era of the 1930s convinced labor leaders that unity in the labor movement was a necessary first step toward bolstering the political influence of organized labor.

3 Failure to achieve the desired rate of growth in the ranks of organized labor in the post-World War II years made evident to organized labor that a concerted, unified effort was needed to organize currently nonunion firms and industries.

4 Then, too, considerable turnover in top leadership in both the AFL and the CIO pushed into the background certain personality conflicts which had proved to be a significant obstacle to reunification of the labor movement at an earlier date.

☐ The Postmerger Era: Stagnation?

The achievement of labor unity seemed to set the stage for vigorous growth of the labor movement. In fact, the period since the AFL-CIO merger has *not* been characterized by a resurgence of organized labor. Union membership was virtually static between 1955 and 1965. Labor economists talk of an "organizational plateau" and "stagnation" in the labor movement. A number of factors, both within the movement and external to it, have made union growth difficult.

Internal Obstacles   In the first place, the AFL-CIO merger did not really resolve the issue of craft versus industrial unionism. Given the fact that the number of blue-collar jobs has been shrinking, both industrial and craft unions have been anxious to establish their rights to jobs. The persistent internal squabbles which have resulted over job jurisdiction have diverted energies from expansion of the labor movement.

A second and more subtle consideration is apathy within the labor movement itself. Whereas union members of the 1930s fought to establish their unions, workers currently accept membership as a convenient, businesslike arrangement. The member pays his dues and receives certain kinds of security and representation in return. Except in times of crisis there is little activism and ideological zeal among union members.

Finally, leadership rivalries continue to exist. For example, persistent differences between George Meany and Walter Reuther caused the latter to disaffiliate his 1.5-million-member United Auto Workers in May of 1968, creating a significant new threat to a unified labor movement.

External Obstacles   Nor have external forces been conducive to rapid union growth.

First, the traditional organizational base of unions has not expanded significantly. In fact, the historical shift in the composition of the labor force from blue- to white-collar employment has probably reduced the potential membership base of organized labor. Despite some inroads, organized labor has not as yet found an effective formula for bringing large numbers of white-collar workers into the fold. Remaining unorganized blue-collar workers are in smaller plants, in agriculture, in service industries, and in the South—all of which are "hard-to-organize" areas. Furthermore, women—who comprise an increasing percentage of the total work force (Table 38-1)—are perhaps less susceptible to unionization because many of them are less permanently attached to the labor force.

Second, legislative reversals—namely, the shift of public policy from encouragement to intervention—pose a more hostile legal environment for organized labor.

Lastly, organized labor seems to have suffered from a deteriorating public image. Some liberal observers contend that labor's traditional progressive stance has given way to conservativism, complacency, and bureaucracy. Many unions—the craft unions in particular—have followed membership policies which foster racial discrimination. Furthermore, the growing number of public sector strikes, involving schoolteachers, garbage collectors, and municipal transit workers, has entailed more direct adverse effects upon the public than is usually the case with private sector strikes. Hence, such strikes have contributed to public impatience and dissatisfaction with unions.

At present the AFL-CIO boasts some 16 million members. Independent unions, of which the Teamsters, the United Auto Workers, and the United Mine Workers are the major ones, add another 4 million members. Hence, the ranks of organized labor now embody about 20 million workers, or slightly more than one-fourth of the nonfarm labor force.

Public Sector Bargaining   Although unionism has been relatively stagnant in the private sector, since 1965 a rapid and dramatic unionization of government employees has occurred at Federal, state, and especially local levels. The number of unionized public employees increased from a little over a million in 1960 to 5.3 million in 1974. For example, the American Federation of State, County, and Municipal Employees raised its membership from 185,000 in 1960 to 700,000 in 1975, while the American Federation of Government Employees grew from 70,000 to 325,000 in the same period. The fact that the public sector has been providing an expanding proportion of total employment has undoubtedly been conducive to this surge of union growth. Moreover, many public employees have sought to offset the adverse effects of the inflation of the late 1960s and the 1970s upon their real incomes by joining unions.

The rapid development of public sector bargaining has a number of interesting and important implications. First, in general, strikes by public employees are legally prohibited. Should public employee strikes—strikes by transit workers, schoolteachers, garbage collectors, and police and firemen—be legalized? Second, the unionization of public employees has been accompanied by traumatic redistributions of power and sovereignty. Decisions which were once made unilaterally by agency chiefs or school boards are now subject to worker protest and bilateral review. Third, public sector bargaining has probably contributed substantially to cost-push inflationary pressures. Partially because of unionization, wage rates have been increasing rapidly in the public sector. However, it is generally agreed that productivity advances in the public sector have been modest. As we recall from Chapter 18, the combination of substantial wage increases and small productivity increases means significant cost-push pressures.[7]

COLLECTIVE BARGAINING

As a result of the rapid growth of unions in recent decades, collective bargaining has become a way of life in labor-management relations. It is estimated that over 165,000 collective bargaining agreements are now in force in the United States.

☐   The Bargaining Process

To the outsider, collective bargaining is a dramatic clash every two or three years between labor and management. Chief participants are a John L. Lewis–type character with

[7] The interested reader should consult Sam Zagoria (ed.), *Public Workers and Public Unions* (Englewood Cliffs, N.J.: Prentice-Hall, Inc., 1972).

baggy suit, bushy eyebrows, and calloused hands, and, on the other side of the table, a Daddy Warbucks with diamond stickpin and formal attire. Furthermore, one gets the impression from the newspapers that labor and management settle their differences only with strikes, picketing, and not infrequent acts of violence.

These impressions are largely inaccurate. Collective bargaining is a somewhat less colorful process than most people believe. In negotiating important contracts, the union is represented by top local and national officials, duly supplemented with lawyers and research economists. Management representatives include top policy-making executives, plant managers, personnel and labor relations specialists, lawyers, and staff economists. The union usually assumes the initiative, outlining its demands. These take the form of specific adjustments in the current work agreement. The merits and demerits of these demands are then debated. Typically, a compromise solution is reached and written into a new work agreement. Strikes, picketing, and violence are clearly the exception and not the rule. In recent years it has generally held true that less than one-fifth of 1 percent of all working time has been lost each year as a result of work stoppages resulting from labor-management disputes! *Labor and management display a marked capacity for compromise and agreement.* We must keep in mind that strikes and labor-management violence are newsworthy, whereas the peaceful renewal of a work agreement hardly rates a page-5 column.

□ **The Work Agreement**

Collective bargaining agreements assume a variety of forms. Some agreements are amazingly brief, covering two or three typewritten pages; others are highly detailed, involving 200 or 300 pages of fine print. Some agreements involve only a local union and a single plant; others set wages, hours, and working conditions for entire industries. There is no such thing as an "average" or "typical" collective bargaining agreement. Nevertheless, the following skeleton agreement, based on an actual contract, provides a fairly accurate notion of the scope and content of collective bargaining.

CONTRACT AND AGREEMENT

□ **Sample Agreement**

Article I. Intent, union status, management prerogatives *Section 1* This agreement entered into June 30, 1978, between the Deep South Manufacturing Company, hereinafter referred to as the "Employer," and the International Brotherhood of Boilermakers, Iron Shipbuilders, and Helpers of America, Local No. 167, hereinafter referred to as the "Union." It is the intent and purpose of the parties hereto that this Agreement will promote and improve industrial relations between the Employer and the Union.

Section 2 The Employer recognizes the Union as the sole and exclusive bargaining agency for the purpose of determining rates of pay, hours of employment, and all other conditions of employment for all the Employer's production and maintenance employees. It is understood and agreed that the Union shall designate a representative who is duly authorized and will be consulted in all matters pertaining to the application of this work agreement.

Section 3 There shall be in each unit no less than one (1), nor more than two (2), Shop Stewards, these Stewards to be appointed by the Union. A unit shall be defined as any part of the Company Organization that provides for a foreman. Shop Stewards may leave their work during their regular working hours, without loss of pay, for the purpose of adjusting grievances.

Section 4 The Employer shall have the sole right of determining plant layout, the means of manufacturing and distributing products, the scheduling of production operations, and the setting of work shifts.

Section 5 Upon receipt of a written authorization by an employee the Employer shall deduct from the first pay each month and remit to the local Union such sum as the employee shall specify in said authorization.

Article II. Wages, hours of work, holidays **Section 1** The minimum wage rates per hour shall be as follows:

Layout men	$5.50
Welders	5.20
Tackers	4.60
Painters	4.25
Riveting machine operators	4.10
Truck drivers	4.00
Helpers	3.60

When employees are transferred to a new job, their rate of pay shall not be changed for a period of fifteen (15) working days. If they are retained on the new job after this probationary period, the job rate called for by this agreement shall then be paid to them. If such job change involves a pay raise, the new rate shall be retroactive to the date the job was assigned.

Section 2 Wage rates shall be adjusted every three (3) months in accordance with changes in the U.S. Department of Labor's Index of Consumer Prices. For each one (1) point change upward in the Index, there shall be a two (2) cent per hour raise in wages. For each one (1) point downward change in the Index, there shall be a two (2) cent per hour decrease in wages. Wages in no case shall fall by more than six (6) cents per hour in any three-month period.

Section 3 All employees shall receive a two (2) percent longevity increase in hourly wages for each year of service. This two (2) percent shall be based on the previous year's hourly base rates.

Section 4 Forty (40) hours shall constitute the workweek, from Monday to Friday, inclusive. The established schedule of hours shall be from 8 A.M. to 12 noon and from 12:30 noon to 4:30 P.M.

Section 5 Time and one-half shall be paid for work performed in excess of eight (8) hours in one day and for hours worked on Saturday. Double time shall be paid for hours worked on Sunday.

Section 6 When the following legal holidays—New Year's Day, Memorial Day, Fourth of July, Labor Day, Veteran's Day, Thanksgiving Day, and Christmas Day—occur or are celebrated during the employee's workweek, he/she shall receive said holidays off duty with his/her regular straight-time pay, provided that he/she shall have been in the employ of the Employer at least thirty (30) calendar days. If said holiday falls on Saturday, it shall be celebrated on Friday, and if it falls on Sunday, celebration shall be on Monday. In the event an employee is required to work on one of the above-named holidays, he/she shall receive double time for such time worked in addition to his regular holiday pay. However, if any employee shall refuse to work on a holiday if he/she is requested by the Employer, he/she shall forfeit his holiday pay, but only if he/she refuses for other than a legitimate reason.

Section 7 All overtime work shall be divided among the workers according to seniority.

Section 8 All employees within the bargaining unit of the Union who shall have been in the service of the company one (1) year and less than three (3) years shall receive a paid vacation of five (5) days; those who have been in the service of the company three (3) years or more shall receive a paid vacation of ten (10) days.

Article III. Seniority and job opportunities **Section 1** Seniority is defined as the principle that if, because of lack of work, the employer deems it advisable to reduce his work force, the last person hired shall be the first person laid off, and, in rehiring, the last person laid off shall be the first person rehired, until the list of former employees is exhausted.

Section 2 Seniority shall be the determining factor regarding layoff and reemployment, transfers, demotions, promotions, or other job changes where the necessary skill and ability are present to perform the work required.

Section 3 Seniority shall be lost for the following reasons: (*a*) voluntary quitting; (*b*) discharge for cause; (*c*) layoff for twelve (12) months; (*d*) if laid-off employee is notified by the Employer by registered mail sent to his/her last known address to return and fails to do so within five (5) days of mailing the letter, unless a reasonable excuse shall be established.

Section 4 A seniority list shall be maintained and kept up to date by the Employer and shall be available to the Union at all times.

Article IV. Grievance procedure Section 1 In the event a grievance arises between an employee or group of employees and the Employer, such grievance shall be handled as follows:

Section 2 The employee or employees having a grievance shall report the same in a signed statement to the Shop Steward, who will in turn take up the grievance with the Foreman verbally. The Foreman will attempt to make a satisfactory settlement and will advise the Steward of his/her decision.

Section 3 If the Steward and employee are not satisfied with the decision of the Foreman, the Steward shall then submit the grievance to the Plant Superintendent verbally. The Superintendent shall make his/her decision within ten (10) days of the time the grievance is submitted to him/her. If the Steward or employee is not satisfied with the decision of the Superintendent, the Steward shall report the grievance to the Union's President, who shall submit the grievance to the management within ten (10) days and endeavor to reach an agreement.

Section 4 If no agreement is reached

within ten (10) days, the grievance shall be submitted to an impartial arbitrator. The arbitrator shall be jointly selected by the Employer and the Union. The arbitrator shall be required to hand down a decision within thirty (30) days. This decision shall be binding, so long as it does not change the terms of this Agreement in any way.

Article V. Termination Section 1 This Agreement shall remain in full force and effect until June 30, 1979, and thereafter from year to year unless, within the ten (10) day period immediately preceding the sixty (60) days prior to the day of expiration, notice is given in writing to the other party indicating a desire to change the agreement.

Section 2 Anything in this Agreement found to be contrary to any state or national law shall be automatically voided.

. . . .

International Brotherhood of Boilermakers, Iron Shipbuilders, and Helpers of America, Local 167
Deep South Manufacturing Company

□ **Basic Contract Areas**

This contract is representative in that it covers four basic areas: (1) the degree of recognition and status accorded the union and the prerogatives of management (Article I); (2) wages and hours (Article II); (3) seniority and job opportunities (Article III); and (4) a procedure for settling grievances (Article IV).

Union Status and Managerial Prerogatives Unions enjoy differing degrees of recognition from management. Listed in order of the union's preference are (1) the closed shop, (2) the union shop, and (3) the open shop.

Prior to being outlawed by the Taft-Hartley Act, the *closed shop* afforded the greatest security to a union. Under a closed shop a worker must be a union member before the employer can hire him. A *union shop,* on the other hand, permits the employer to hire nonunion workers but provides that these workers must join the union in a specified period—say, thirty days—or relinquish their jobs. Since it is not specified to the contrary, we may assume, in our sample contract, that an *open shop* exists (Article I, section 2). Management may apparently hire union or nonunion workers. Those who are nonunion are not obligated to join the union; they may continue on their jobs indefinitely as nonunion workers. In this contract, the union is the bargaining agent for *all* the firm's production and maintenance workers. In other cases the union may bargain only for union members. In some instances union or open-shop status will be supplemented with *preferential hiring.* Management agrees to hire union members so long as they are available; then it can hire nonunion workers. Finally, we must also mention the *nonunion shop.* Here no union exists, and the employer makes a conscious effort to hire those workers who are least inclined to form or join a union.

One of the most controversial aspects of union status has grown out of the (in)famous section 14(b) of the Taft-Hartley Act. Section 14(b) makes the union shop a legal form of union status *unless* prohibited by state legislation. Some twenty states now have so-called *right-to-work laws* which make compulsory union membership, and therefore the union shop, illegal.

Proponents of these laws (mainly employers) hold that an individual should be free to refrain from joining any organization without being denied access to a job. No worker, as a condition of employment, should be forced to join and support financially an organization whose principles he may hold to be unacceptable or which he feels is corrupt. Opponents (mainly organized labor) counter that employer support of right-to-work laws is motivated more by the desire to undermine unions than by an urge to protect the freedom of workers. Furthermore, the union shop is held to be a desirable means of eliminating "free riders"—nonunion workers who benefit from, but do not, financially or otherwise, support, the union. Finally, opponents of the right-to-work laws argue that an open-shop union, which must constantly strive to secure its position and gain wider worker support, is frequently forced to make unreasonable demands as a means of obtaining this support; a union whose existence is secure through a union shop can approach collective bargaining more reasonably and responsibly.

No easy resolution of the right-to-work controversy is apparent. Chances are that it will remain a prominent bone of contention in labor-management relations for some time to come.

The other side of the union-status coin is the issue of managerial prerogatives. Many businessmen fear that in time the expansion of the scope of collective bargaining may reach the point where certain fundamental management decisions will become matters to be decided jointly by management and labor. It is felt by businessmen that such an eventuality will "tie the hands" of management to the extent that efficient business operation may be jeopardized. For this reason, at the insistence of management an increasing number of work agreements contain clauses outlining certain decisions which are to be made solely by management. These *managerial prerogatives* usually cover such matters as the size and location of plants, products to be manufactured, types of equipment and materials used in production, and the scheduling of production (Article I, section 4). Frequently the hiring, transfer, discipline, discharge, and promotion of workers are decisions made solely by management but are subject to the general principle of seniority and to challenge by the union through the grievance procedure.

Wages and Hours   The focal point of any bargaining agreement is wages and hours. Our skeleton agreement is representative of most contracts in that basic hourly pay rates, length of workweek, overtime rates, holidays, and vacations are all specified (Article II).

Both labor and management tend to be highly pragmatic in wage bargaining. The standards, or "talking points," most frequently invoked by labor in demanding (and by management in resisting) wage boosts are (1) "what others are getting," (2) productivity, (3) ability to pay, and (4) cost of living. If a given firm has basic rates below those of comparable firms, the union is likely to stress that wages should be increased to bring them into line with what workers employed by other firms are getting. Similarly, if the firm has had a banner year, the union is likely to demand high wages on the ground that the company has ample ability to grant such increments. In recent years unions have achieved considerable success in tying wages to the cost of living. It is estimated that work agreements covering about 7.7 million workers embody some kind of "escalator clause." This is true of our sample agreement (Article II, section 2). And some contracts link wage rates to productivity; wages automatically increase in terms of an estimated "improvement factor."

Three points should be mentioned in connection with these wage criteria. In the first place, they are clearly two-edged propositions. For example, the cost-of-living criterion is invoked by the union only when prices are hurrying upward; unions conveniently ignore this criterion when prices are stable or declining. Similarly, the union considers the ability-to-pay argument to be of importance only when profits are large. Management is equally inconsistent in the evaluation it places on the various wage-bargaining standards.

Secondly, these wage criteria are considerably less objective than might first appear. Most people might agree that it is only fair that wage rates be adjusted for increases in productivity and the cost of living. But then arises the difficult question, "By how much?" What wage boost should accompany, say, a 2-point increase in the Consumer Price Index? Furthermore, productivity increases—particularly in the area of services—can be very difficult to measure.

A third noteworthy point: Wage changes —either increases or declines—based on these criteria are not necessarily desirable on either economic or equity grounds. Many economists fear, for example, that the widespread use of the cost-of-living criterion will cause a wage-price inflationary bias to be built into our economy. In like manner, indiscriminate application of the what-others-are-getting standard may push a relatively inefficient firm out of business, causing considerable hardship for its workers.

Seniority and the Control of Job Opportunities   The uncertainty of employment in a capitalistic economy, coupled with the fear of antiunion discrimination on the part of employers, has made workers and their unions decidedly "job-conscious." The explicit and detailed provisions covering job opportunities which most work agreements contain reflect this concern. The importance of seniority as the guiding principle in controlling job opportunities is apparent from Article III of our work agreement. It should be noted, however, that in many cases seniority is not rigidly applied. Strategic workers, or "key" personnel, will often be exempt from seniority regulations. And unions are typically willing to recognize that, particularly where promotion is concerned, ability must take precedence over seniority (Article III, section 2).

Grievance Procedure   It has been quipped that a collective bargaining agreement is to labor relations what the wedding ceremony is to domestic relations—only the beginning. Despite formal agreements, it is the "living together" that counts. It is unthinkable that even the most detailed and comprehensive work agreement can anticipate all the issues and problems which might occur during its life. What if Local 167 members show up for work on a Monday morning to find that for some reason—say, a mechanical failure—the plant is closed down? Should they be given "show-up" pay amounting to, say, two or four hours' pay? This event is not covered in the contract and would therefore be a problem which might be ironed out through the grievance machinery. Then, too, there may be some disagreement in interpreting points covered in the work agreement. For example, the abbreviated work agreement upon which our discussion is centered poses some possible questions of interpretation which may necessitate invoking the grievance procedure. What is a "legitimate reason" for refusing to work on a holiday (Article II, section 6)? Exactly how are "necessary skill and ability" to be defined in specific cases (Article III, section 2)? What is meant by "discharge for cause" (Article III, section 3)?

As a result, virtually all agreements contain a more-or-less explicit procedure for the handling of disputes which arise during the life of an agreement. In our sample agreement, a very complete four-step procedure is clearly outlined. In this instance the grievance machinery culminates in arbitration, that is, a neutral third party is designated to render a decision by which both labor and management must abide.

□ **Three Implications**

Three points implicit in our discussion of collective bargaining merit emphasis:

1 Collective bargaining is concerned not only with wage rates but also with the security and status of workers and of the union itself. Man does not live by bread alone. Workers seek protection from arbitrary actions by management; they seek a voice in determining the conditions under which they must work; they seek a means of voicing their grievances; they seek the status and dignity which accompany membership in economically powerful institutions. These objectives are fulfilled wholly or in part by membership in unions.

2 Also worthy of emphasis is the fact that collective bargaining is a continuous process.

True, the *negotiation* of an agreement is an important and often dramatic point of departure. But this is followed by the equally important and continuing tasks of *administering* and *interpreting* (through the grievance procedure) the agreement. Collective bargaining involves much more than a periodic clash of labor and management.

3 Finally, labor-management relations occur in a dynamic climate. Technological advance, business fluctuations, population changes, changes in the legislative framework, and changes in the character of business and of unions themselves constitute some of the obvious dynamic aspects of the environment in which bargaining occurs. Changes such as these virtually preclude the reaching of final, once-and-for-all solutions to labor-management problems. At best, collective bargaining provides short-run, temporary adjustments to labor-management conflicts—adjustments which the changing economic milieu is likely to render obsolete in a relatively short span of time. In view of this observation, the previously cited paucity of work stoppages due to labor-management disputes is all the more remarkable.

WOMEN IN THE LABOR MARKET[8]

Perhaps the most profound labor market development since World War II has been the increasingly important role of women in the labor force.

As Table 38-1 clearly indicates, not only has a growing percentage of all working-age women entered the labor market, but women have become a rising proportion of the total labor force. In fact, in the 1950–1975 period 16.2 million women entered the labor force as compared to only 9.6 million men!

---

[8] This section draws heavily upon chap. 4 of the *Economic Report of the President, 1973* (Washington).

Table 38-1   WOMEN IN THE LABOR FORCE, 1900–1976

Year	Women in labor force (thousands)	Women in labor force as percent of	
		Total labor force	All women of working age
1900	5,114	18.1	20.4
1920	8,180	20.4	23.3
1940	12,845	24.3	25.4
1945	19,270	29.6	35.7
1955	20,634	30.2	35.7
1965	26,232	34.0	39.3
1970	31,560	36.7	43.4
1973	34,510	38.9	45.7
1976	39,117	40.9	48.0

Source: U.S. Bureau of Labor Statistics.

□   Increased Participation Rate

What influences have caused this increase in the rate at which women participate in the labor force? An incomplete list of factors includes the following.

1   Opportunities   The rising wage rates and expanding job opportunities which have accompanied economic growth have provided obvious economic incentives for women to seek paid employment. In particular, the service sector of the economy, which contains a disproportionately large number of "women's jobs," has expanded rapidly since World War II. Interestingly, one might think that the substantial increases in husbands' earnings that have occurred since World War II would induce married women—who, incidentally, compose the lioness's share of female labor-force entrants—to stay out of the job market. But once it is recognized that a woman's entry into the labor force means, not a substitution of work for leisure, but rather, the substitution of paid work in the market for unpaid work at home, the wholesale entry of women into paying jobs is easily understood. Furthermore, although the pursuit of greater economic independence is an important reason that some women enter the labor force, for many women

work is a matter of sheer economic necessity. About two-fifths of all working women are either single, divorced, separated, or widowed; they must in large measure support themselves.

2   Education   Like men, women have been acquiring more education, thereby increasing their productivity and earning capacity in the labor market. Statistics make it clear that the more education a woman has, the more likely she is to work.

3   Family Size   The improvement of birth control technology, coupled with changing attitudes toward family size, has tended to increase the labor-force participation rate for women. Not only has the average number of children per family diminished historically, but the timing of births has been altered to expedite a mother's labor-force career.

4   Increased Working Life   A related point is that the expected working life of women has been rising because of longer life expectancy and the tendency of today's women to complete their childbearing at an earlier age. "This lengthening of a woman's expected working life is significant because it increases her return on her investment in training and education; the greater the number of years in which to collect the return, the greater is the return."[9]

5   Substituting Capital for Labor at Home   It has become increasingly economic to substitute capital for labor in the home, thereby freeing women from housework and permitting them to enter the labor market. The development of relatively low-cost, time-saving household appliances, for example, dishwashers, vacuum cleaners, and microwave ovens, is illustrative. As the opportunity cost to housewives, that is, the earnings women forgo by not

[9]Ibid., p. 93.

entering the labor force, has risen, it has become more and more rational in economic terms to purchase and substitute this household capital for women's work at home in order that they may enter the labor force.

☐ Economic Status of Women

Are women in the labor force accorded a status equal to that of men? There is convincing evidence of substantial economic bias against women workers. For example, in 1974 median earnings for full-time male workers were $11,835; the comparable figure for females was only $6,772. Stated differently, the average female earned only 57 percent as much as the average male worker. In 1975 the median income for households headed by males was $15,873 as compared to $7,201 for households headed by females. Furthermore, this earnings gap, measured both absolutely and relatively, has been widening. Figure 38-2 is also instruc-

tive in that it reveals substantial income differentials when men and women of the same age and education are compared. In addition, these differentials widen through much of the working lives of men and women. Note that men with a *high school* education earn more, over much of their working lives, than do women with a *college* education!

The various forms of discrimination encountered by women are essentially the same as those confronting blacks (Chapter 37), but studies of discrimination against women single out the importance of job segregation, that is, male-female occupational differences which reflect deeply ingrained attitudes about the labor market characteristics and capabilities of women.

> The division of labor on the basis of sex appears to be a universal characteristic of every society. . . . Moreover, occupational segregation by sex within the labor market mirrors the traditional relations of women and men

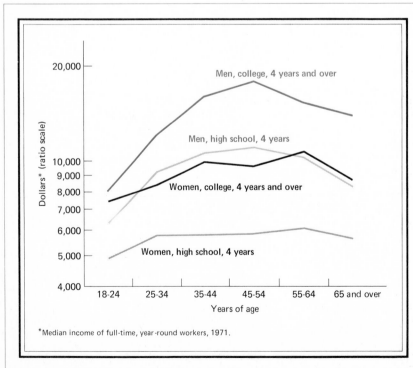

FIGURE 38-2 ANNUAL INCOME BY AGE FOR MALE AND FEMALE HIGH SCHOOL AND COLLEGE GRADUATES

Men receive a substantial income advantage over women with the same amount of education; this differential tends to widen over much of the working lives of men and women. During almost all their working years, men with a high school education are paid more than are women with a college education. (*U.S. Department of Commerce.*)

*Median income of full-time, year-round workers, 1971.

within the family unit. Within the family, the work of women and men is generally viewed as complementary rather than competitive. Sexual segregation of the labor market and the resultant division of female and male workers into two noncompeting groups preserves this basic characteristic that governs the relations of women and men in the family. . . .

The force of these institutional factors operates on both the supply and demand side to restrict the employment opportunities of women.

On the supply side, girls are socialized to aspire to and train for what are considered to be appropriate female occupations. The educational system frequently further intensifies this problem by channeling women into traditionally feminine pursuits and maintaining quotas on women students in graduate and professional schools in male dominated fields.

On the demand side, there is no reason to assume that employers as a group should be free from socially prevalent attitudes as to what constitutes appropriate female tasks. . . .[10]

[10]Francine Blau Weisskoff, "'Women's Place' in the Labor Market," *American Economic Review,* May 1972, pp. 163–164.

Thus we find women disproportionately represented in elementary teaching, retail sales, clerical jobs, and nursing. Men dominate medicine, dentistry, law, engineering, blue-collar craft jobs, and virtually all business positions which entail significant decision-making and supervisory authority.

□   **Occupational Discrimination:
A Simple Model**

The character and consequences of occupational discrimination can be revealed through a very simple supply and demand model.[11] We make the following simplifying assumptions.

1 The labor force is equally divided between males and females (or white and black) workers. Let us say there are 6 million male and 6 million female workers.

2 The economy is comprised of three industries, each having identical labor demand curves as shown in Figure 38-3.

[11]This portrayal is a slight modification of the analysis of sex discrimination presented in Paul A. Samuelson, *Economics,* 10th ed. (New York: McGraw-Hill Book Company, 1976), pp. 791–793.

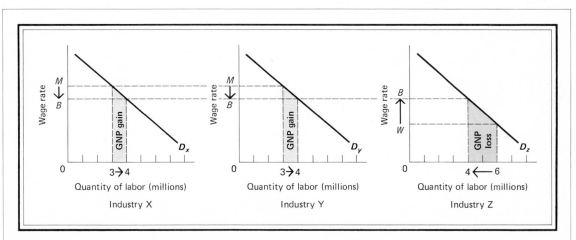

FIGURE 38-3 THE SIMPLE ECONOMICS OF SEX DISCRIMINATION

By crowding women into one industry, men enjoy high wage rates of *OM* in industries *X* and *Y* while women receive low wages of *OW* in industry *Z*. The abandonment of discrimination will equalize wage rates at *OB and* result in a net increase in national output.

3 Men and women (whites and blacks) are homogeneous with respect to their labor force characteristics; each of the three industries' labor-force needs could be filled equally well by men or women.

Suppose now that, as a consequence of irrational discrimination, the 6 million women are excluded from industries X and Y and confined to industry Z. Men distribute themselves equally among industries X and Y so there are 3 million male workers in each industry and the resulting common wage rate is *OM*. (Assuming no barriers to mobility, any initially different distribution of males between X and Y would result in a wage differential which would prompt labor shifts from low- to high-wage industry until wage equality was realized.) Note that women, on the other hand, are crowded into industry Z and, as a consequence of this occupational segregation, receive a much lower wage rate *OW*. Given the reality of discrimination, this is an equilibrium situation. Women *cannot,* because of bigotry, reallocate themselves to industries X and Y in the pursuit of higher wage rates.

Assume at this point that through legislation or sweeping changes in social attitudes, discrimination disappears. What are the results? Women, attracted by higher wage rates, will shift from Z to X and Y. Specifically, 1 million women will shift into X and another 1 million into Y, leaving 4 million workers in Z. At this point 4 million workers will be in each industry and wage rates will be equal to *OB* in all three industries. This new, nondiscriminatory equilibrium is to the obvious advantage of women, who now receive higher wages, and to the disadvantage of men, who now get lower wages. Women were initially exploited through discrimination to the benefit of men; the termination of discrimination corrects that situation.

But that's not all: There is a net gain to society. Recall that the labor demand curve reflects labor's marginal revenue product (Chapter 30) or, in other words, labor's contribution to the national output.[12] Hence, the shaded areas for industries X and Y show the *increases* in national output—the market value of the marginal or extra output—realized by adding 1 million women workers in each of those two industries. Similarly, the shaded area for industry Z shows the *decline* in national output caused by the shifting of the 2 million women workers from industry Z. By inspection we note that the sum of the two additions to national output exceed the subtraction from national output when discrimination is ended. This is to be expected: after all, women workers are reallocating themselves from industry Z, where their contribution to national output (their MRP) is relatively low, to alternate employments in X and Y, where their contributions to national output (their MRPs) are relatively high. Conclusion: *Society gains from a more efficient allocation of resources when discrimination is abandoned.*

☐   **Conflicting Explanations**

How can the inferior economic position of women—for example, the fact that their earnings are roughly 40 percent below those of men—be explained? Is this disparity simply a reflection of discrimination? Or are other factors at work? Some researchers have argued that nondiscriminatory factors explain a part of the earnings differential. First, part-time work is more common for women than for men. Second, the typical work-life cycle of married women who have children involves a continuous period of work until birth of the first child, then a five- to ten-year period of nonparticipation or partial participation in the labor force related to childbearing and child care, followed by a more continuous period of work experience when the mother is in her late thirties or early forties. The net result is that, on the average, married women have accumu-

[12]Technical note: This assumes pure competition in product and resource market.

lated only about half the labor-force experience as men in the same age group.[13] Furthermore, family ties provide women with less geographic mobility in job choice than is the case with males. In fact, married women may give up good positions to move with husbands who decide to accept jobs located elsewhere. And some married women may put convenience of job location and flexibility of working hours ahead of occupational choice.[14]

But even after adjustments are made for factors such as these, that is, when full-time male and female workers with equal amounts of education and work experience are compared, large earnings differentials remain. These differences must be attributable to discrimination. Furthermore, cause and effect are difficult to unravel as one tries to analyze labor market behavior. A self-fulfilling prophecy may occur which works to the disadvantage of women. Employers, believing married women are more likely to quit their jobs in order to follow their husbands to a new job

location or to have children, deny them access to on-the-job training and assign them to dead-end jobs at low rates of pay. However, these are the very kinds of jobs where quit rates for *all* workers tend to be high. Thus women do leave these kinds of jobs in relatively large numbers, reaffirming the initial beliefs of employers.

It is difficult to forecast whether the relative economic position of women will improve significantly in the foreseeable future. The large number of female labor-force entrants in recent years has undoubtedly tended to sustain, if not widen, the income differential between men and women. But counter influences are at work. The Women's Liberation Movement has played a positive role in publicizing the discriminatory treatment of women in the labor force. On the legal front the Civil Rights Act of 1964 prohibits discrimination on the basis of sex, as well as of race, religion, and ethnic background. Finally, proponents of the controversial Equal Rights Amendment, which provides that "equality of rights under the law shall not be denied or abridged by the United States or by any State on account of sex," contend that it would go far to eliminate the differential treatment of women.

[13]U.S. Department of Labor, *Manpower Report of the President, 1974* (Washington), p. 119.
[14]Sar A. Levitan, Garth Mangum, and Ray Marshall, *Human Resources and Labor Markets,* 2d ed. (New York: Harper & Row, Publishers, Incorporated, 1976), pp. 85, 88.

Summary

1   The growth of labor unions was slow and irregular until the 1930s. The repression of unions by the courts and by management was an important factor in accounting for this retarded growth. The courts employed the conspiracy doctrine, injunctions, and the antitrust laws against unions. Management invoked such varied antiunion techniques as discriminatory discharge, blacklisting, lockouts, strikebreakers, yellow-dog contracts, paternalism, and company unions in slowing the development of unions.

2   The AFL dominated the American labor movement from 1886 until the CIO was formed in 1936. Its philosophy was essentially that of Samuel Gompers—business unionism, political neutrality, and craft unionism.

3   Union growth was rapid in the 1930s and 1940s. The shift toward industrial unionism, triggered by the formation of the CIO in 1936, was a significant factor in this growth. Equally important were the prolabor legislation passed by the Federal government in the 1930s and the wartime prosperity of the 1940s.

4 The Norris–La Guardia Act of 1932 rendered yellow-dog contracts unenforceable and sharply limited the use of injunctions in labor disputes. The Wagner Act of 1935—"labor's Magna Charta"—guaranteed labor the rights to organize and to bargain collectively with management. The act prohibited certain "unfair labor practices" on the part of management, thereby paving the way for unions to organize, unimpeded by management.

5 The Taft-Hartley Act of 1947 brought about a shift from government-sponsored to government-regulated collective bargaining. The act *a.* specifically outlaws certain "unfair practices" of unions; *b.* regulates certain internal operations of unions; *c.* controls the content of collective bargaining agreements; and *d.* outlines a procedure for handling "national health and welfare" strikes.

6 The Landrum-Griffin Act of 1959 was designed to regulate the internal processes of unions—in particular the handling of union finances and the union's relationships with its members.

7 At the present time over 20 million workers are union members; this constitutes about one-fourth of the nonfarm labor force. Although the labor movement has been relatively stagnant in the private sector, rapid unionization of public employees has occurred in the past decade.

8 Labor and management "live together" under the terms of collective bargaining agreements. These work agreements cover four major topics: *a.* union status and managerial prerogatives; *b.* wages and hours; *c.* seniority and job control; and *d.* a grievance procedure. Experience indicates that both labor and management are very willing to compromise and reach agreement short of work stoppages.

9 Historically, an increasing percentage of all working-age women have entered the labor market, and women constitute a rising percentage of the total labor force.

10 The median income of full-time female workers is about 57 percent that of males. This differential is partially the result of discrimination and, in particular, job segregation; but it also reflects differences in labor market behavior.

Questions and Study Suggestions

1 Key terms and concepts to remember: criminal conspiracy doctrine; injunction; discriminatory discharge; blacklisting; lockout; yellow-dog contract; company union; business unionism; Norris–LaGuardia Act of 1932; Wagner Act of 1935; National Labor Relations Board; Taft-Hartley Act of 1947; jurisdictional strike; sympathy strike; secondary boycott; featherbedding; closed shop; union shop; open shop; nonunion shop; right-to-work law; checkoff; Landrum-Griffin Act of 1959; preferential hiring; seniority; arbitration; American Federation of Labor (AFL); Congress of Industrial Organizations (CIO); craft and industrial unions; female participation rate; occupational discrimination.

2 Briefly describe the repression, encouragement, and intervention phases of the American labor movement. "In the 1930s public opinion was prolabor, but by the mid-1940s the public was of an antilabor disposition." Account for this turnabout.

3 What are the major provisions of the Taft-Hartley Act? If you had the power to revise this act, what changes would you make? In what ways has the Taft-Hartley Act directly affected the sample work agreement studied in this chapter? Be specific.

4 It has been said that the Taft-Harley Act was passed to achieve three major goals: *a.* to reestablish an equality of bargaining power between labor and management to maintain industrial peace; *b.* to protect "neutrals," that is, third parties who are not directly concerned with a given labor-management dispute; *c.* to protect the rights of individual workers in their relations with unions. Review the Taft-Hartley provisions as outlined in this chapter, and relate each to these three major goals.

5 Summarize the controversy surrounding the so-called right-to-work laws.

6 Suppose you are the president of a newly established local union which is about to bargain with an employer for the first time. Make a list of those points which you would want to be covered explicitly in the work agreement. Assuming the economic climate which exists at this moment, what criteria would you use in backing your wage demands? Explain.

7 "There are legislative, executive, and judicial aspects to collective bargaining." Explain.

8 Explain the increasing participation rate for women in the labor force. Use demand and supply to explain the economic impact of job segregation by sex upon the relative earnings of men and women.

9 Evaluate and comment:

a. "In general, women are simply less productive workers than men. And, in particular, there are certain kinds of jobs in which women are not physically or temperamentally equipped to perform."

b. "Equal pay legislation may not be very helpful to women because such laws tend to further reduce on-the-job training opportunities for women and thereby reinforce job segregation."

Selected References

Levitan, Sar A., Garth L. Mangum, and Ray Marshall: *Human Resources and Labor Markets,* 2d ed. (New York: Harper & Row, Publishers, Incorporated, 1976), chaps. 5, 23.

Marshall, F. Ray, Allan M. Cartter, and Allan G. King: *Labor Economics,* 3d ed. (Homewood, Ill.: Richard D. Irwin, Inc., 1976), chaps. 1–5, 16–18, 23.

Rowan, Richard L. (ed.): *Readings in Labor Economics and Labor Relations* (Homewood, Ill.,: Richard D. Irwin, Inc., 1976), parts 1–4, 7.

U.S. Department of Labor, *Monthly Labor Review Reader* (Washington: Government Printing Office, 1975), chaps. 8, 9.

U.S. Department of Labor, *Monthly Labor Review.* Contains statistics and articles of current interest on collective bargaining and industrial relations.

Last Word
Work and Alienation

A controversial report of an HEW Task Force argues that both "blue-collar blues" and "white-collar woes" are endemic to our labor force.

. . . significant numbers of American workers are dissatisfied with the quality of their working lives. Dull, repetitive, seemingly meaningless tasks, offering little challenge or autonomy, are causing discontent among workers at all occupational levels. This is not so much because work itself has greatly changed; indeed, one of the main problems is that work has not changed fast enough to keep up with the rapid and wide-scale changes in worker attitudes, aspirations and values. A general increase in their educational and economic status has placed many American workers in a position where having an interesting job is now as important as having a job that pays well. Pay is still important: it must support an "adequate" standard of living, and be perceived as equitable—but high pay alone will not lead to job (or life) satisfaction.

There have been some responses to the changes in the workforce, but they have been small and slow. As a result, the productivity of the worker is low—as measured by absenteeism, turnover rates, wildcat strikes, sabotage, poor quality products, and a reluctance by workers to commit themselves to their work tasks. Moreover, a growing body of research indicates that, as work problems increase, there may be a consequent decline in physical and mental health, family stability, community participation and cohesiveness, and "balanced" sociopolitical attitudes, while there is an increase in drug and alcohol addiction, aggression, and delinquency. . . .

Our economic, political, and cultural system has fostered the notion of independence and autonomy, a part of which is the belief that a hardworking person, even if he has little capital, can always make a go of it in business for himself. Or, to put it another way, if things get too bad in a dependent work situation, it has been felt that the individual could always strike out on his own.

This element of the American Dream is rapidly becoming myth, and disappearing with it is the possibility of realizing the character traits of independence and autonomy of going into business for oneself. The trend of the past seventy years or more, and particularly in recent years, has been a decrease in small independent enterprises and self-employment, and an increase in the domination of large corporations and government in the work force.

Yet, the more democratic and self-affirmative an individual is, the less he will stand for boring, dehumanized, and authoritarian work. Under such conditions, the workers either protest or give in, at some cost to their psychological well-being. Anger that does not erupt may be frozen into schizoid depressed characters who escape into general alienation, drugs, and fantasies. More typically, dissatisfying working environments result in the condition known as alienation.

Alienation exists when workers are unable to control their immediate work processes, to develop a sense of purpose and function which connects their jobs to the over-all organization of production, to belong to integrated industrial communities, and when they fail to become involved in the activity of work as a mode of personal self-expression.

Social scientists identify four ingredients of alienation: (1) powerlessness (regarding ownership of the enterprise, general management policies, employment conditions and the immediate work processes), (2) meaninglessness (with respect to the character of the product worked on as well as the scope of the product or the production process), (3) isolation (the social aspect of work), and (4) self-estrangement ("depersonalized detachment," including boredom, which can lead to "absence of personal growth"). As thus broken down, alienation is inherent in pyramidal, bureaucratic management patterns and in advanced, Taylorized technology, which divides and subdivides work into minute, monotonous elements. The result of alienation is often the withdrawal of the worker from community or political activity or the displacement of his frustrations through participation in radical social or political movements.

It seems fair to conclude that the combination of the changing social character of American workers, declining opportunities to establish independence through self-employment, and an anachronistic organization of work can create an explosive and pathogenic mix.

From *Work in America:* Report of a special Task Force to the Secretary of Health, Education, and Welfare, 93d Congress, 1st Session, Washington, 1973, pp. x–xi, 18–19, abridged.

39

The Economics of War and Defense

Perhaps no issue has generated more debate—both rational and impassioned—than that of the appropriate size of the military establishment. This debate reached fever pitch during the Vietnam war. Unfortunately, the "solution" to that war has not resolved the various problems associated with the military-industrial complex. Indeed, periodic warfare in the Middle East makes it clear that we live in a highly uncertain world in which the economics of war and defense will demand continuing attention. This chapter is a brief outline of the economic implications of the war industry.

But a caveat is immediately in order: There are many questions of a political-ideological, technological, and moral character—not to mention issues of integrity and honor—associated with our military posture. The economist has no particular expertise in these areas. That is, the size and character of our military posture cannot be prescribed on economic grounds alone. Nevertheless, economists can shed light upon some basic questions. Are we making too many or not enough resources available to the military? Are these resources being used efficiently in the acquisition of weapons systems and other military goods? What is the most efficient means of acquiring military manpower? Does the existence of the defense sector pose any special problems for the achievement of economic stability? Perhaps the most difficult problem for the economist in examining the war industry is that in applying benefit-cost analysis (Chapter

6), great difficulties arise in measuring accurately the spillover benefits of defense. Economists speak with some certainty about the cost or burden of our defense posture; they speak with considerably less certainty about the necessity or desirability of that cost.

SIZE OF THE WAR INDUSTRY

It is essential at the outset to grasp an overall understanding of the aggregate size of America's military spending. At the height of the Vietnam war in 1970, our military expenditures—primarily purchases by the Department of Defense (DOD)—were over $80 billion. This figure was about 41 percent of the total Federal budget for that year and slightly less than 10 percent of the GNP (Figure 39-1). Measured in terms of manpower, defense spending provided jobs for about 10 percent of the labor force.

The cessation of hostilities brought about a temporary decline in military spending. But by the mid-seventies public and political sentiment toward national defense seemed to be becoming more favorable. As the memories of Vietnam have faded, so have the antimilitarist sentiments generated by that war. Furthermore, the lack of progress in achieving mutual arms reduction with the Soviet Union has reminded us that, even for a superpower, the world can be a dangerous place. Hence, military spending was on the order of $93 billion in 1976, with projected Pentagon outlays expected to rise above $100 billion in 1977. Note in Figure 39-1b that, in relative terms, military spending in the 1970s has persisted at about 5½ percent of the GNP.

Except for World War I, defense spending in the half-century prior to World War II was less than 1 percent of national output. Two important factors contributed to this low level of spending. First, before the development of nuclear weapons and technologically advanced delivery systems, the United States was sheltered by geographic distance. Second, past wars were "GNP wars" in the sense that time was available to shift resources from civilian to war goods production. These interrelated considerations are now substantially changed. The existence of ICBMs and nuclear-armed submarines has virtually eliminated the protection afforded by distance. Furthermore, the amount and technological superiority of our immediately available military hardware will likely determine the "winner" of a third world war, if indeed such a designation is meaningful.

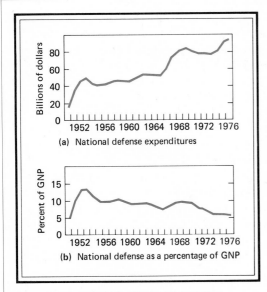

FIGURE 39-1   FEDERAL EXPENDITURES FOR NATIONAL DEFENSE

Expenditures by the Department of Defense were approximately $93 billion in 1976; this amounted to about 5½ percent of the GNP. (*U.S. Department of Commerce and Council of Economic Advisers. Data are in current dollars.*)

☐   **Measurement Problems**

One can argue that Figure 39-1 understates the size and importance of the war industry. In the first place, at least portions of the budgets of certain other governmental agencies, for example, NASA and the Atomic Energy Commission, have important military aspects, and therefore these amounts should be added to our total military-defense budget. Moreover, DOD purchases exclude such war-related expenditures as various veterans' benefits and interest on the public debt. The latter, you will recall (Chapter 13), is largely the consequence of financing World War II. These two items are of considerable magnitude—$19 and $35 billion respectively in 1976—and would add substantially to our measure of the war industry's aggregate size. It should be emphasized, however, that interest on the public debt and veterans' pensions are non-exhaustive transfer payments as opposed to exhaustive government purchases (Chapter 8). However, the higher taxes necessary to finance these transfers presumably have adverse effects in terms of incentives to work and invest and, in this sense, they involve a cost.[1]

□ **Other Implications**

Aggregate data on the level of military spending conceal other important ramifications of the war industry. First, it is significant that purchases of military goods and facilities entail the expansion of government's direct role as a consumer of output. In contrast to transfer payments, which shift income among various groups within the private sector, rising military spending means that government is directly absorbing a portion of GNP which could otherwise have been available for private uses. Much of the increase in military spending seems to have come at the expense of consumption; since 1929, military spending has risen from 1 to almost 6 percent of GNP, and

during the same period consumption has fallen from 73 to 64 percent. Military spending accounts for almost four-fifths of all Federal expenditures for goods and services.

Second, it is of considerable significance that a relatively small number of quite large corporations are the recipients of the majority of defense contracts; military outlays contribute to the concentration of economic power in industry. But a word of caution is in order here: Although DOD contract recipients are large, they are *not* typically such corporate giants as General Motors, U.S. Steel, or AT&T.

Third, military spending is also subject to very considerable geographic concentration. Some ten states receive about two-thirds of all military contracts; three of these—California, New York, and Texas—receive about one-third. This obviously implies that disarmament might necessitate serious economic readjustments for particular industries and particular areas of the country.

Finally, a sizable portion—about 40 percent—of the nation's research and development activities is oriented toward defense and space. We will momentarily confront the argument that this emphasis upon military R & D has stifled productivity and growth in the civilian economy.

ECONOMIC COSTS

Waiving the possibility of understatement, do the military expenditure data of Figure 39-1 accurately represent the burden of our military posture? Does our national security cost us about 6 percent of our national output?

□ **Alternative to Unemployment?**

The answer depends upon one's assumption concerning opportunity costs, that is, the alternative outputs society forgoes by allocating 6 percent of its resources to the military. It can be argued that it is a gross overstatement

---

[1]It has been estimated that the ultimate cost of a war, including such nonexhaustive outlays as veterans' benefits and interest on war debt, may exceed the immediate costs of a war by a factor of three! For example, the total immediate costs of military operations in Vietnam were estimated at $110 billion by the end of 1970; the addition of long-term costs in the form of veterans' benefits and interest on war loans results in an estimated total cost of $352 billion. Statement of James L. Clayton in Subcommittee on Economy in Government, *The Military Budget and National Economic Priorities, Part 1* (Washington, 1969), pp. 143–150.

to say that the military costs us almost 6 percent of the GNP; it can be argued in the extreme that the cost of our military preparation is zero! The rationale for this view is that massive defense spending is the prerequisite of a high level of aggregate demand and therefore of full employment. After all, large military outlays have gone hand in hand with a generally prosperous economy for some thirty years. Indeed, was it not the upsurge in military spending occasioned by World War II which pulled our society out of the Great Depression of the 1930s? In brief, one can assume that resources devoted to defense would otherwise be idle and unemployed. Hence, our military posture in effect is "free" in the sense that society is not forgoing alternative civilian goods.

□ Prosperity without Arms

The difficulty with this line of reasoning is that it is based upon a highly pessimistic view of the economy's vitality and the efficacy of monetary and fiscal policy. In fact, the economy adjusted remarkably well to the massive decline in military outlays at the conclusion of World War II (Chapter 10). The appropriate use of monetary and fiscal policy—for example, easy money and tax cuts—provides an obvious means of compensating for any decline in defense spending. Many would argue that a reduction in government spending on military goods can and should be replaced by increased government spending on the civilian economy—education, welfare, health, urban renewal, antipollution programs, and so forth (see footnote 16). In short, most economists would argue that defense spending is not the *sine qua non* of a prosperous economy and that our military posture clearly does come primarily at the cost of forgone civilian output.

Foreign experience bolsters the view that military spending is not a prerequisite of full employment and therefore that military outlays *are* a burden. The capitalist nations of Western Europe have enjoyed full employment

for the past twenty-five years with defense budgets much smaller—both absolutely and relatively—than those of the United States. Indeed, casual observation suggests a negative correlation between military expenditures as a percentage of GNP and an economy's growth rate. West Germany, France, and the Scandinavian countries immediately come to mind (Table 20-2). But Japan is perhaps the outstanding example; it has had virtually no military establishment since World War II and has been the world's outstanding performer in terms of economic growth. One can readily argue that Japan's remarkable technological progress in such fields as electronics, shipbuilding, and watchmaking is a reflection of the fact that virtually all of Japan's scientific and technical personnel have been available for civilian production. In fact, in the post–World War II period the United States has been partially defending Western European allies and Japan. That is, a portion of America's military resources has been transferred to these nations, permitting them to devote more of their domestic resources than they otherwise could to the development of their economies.

□ The Issue Restated

These two views can be readily restated in terms of the production possibilities curve shown in Figure 39-2. The view that our military posture imposes no real cost on the civilian economy presumes that without defense spending, the economy would be at a position of unemployment such as A. Defense outlays move the economy from A to B, and the economy has gained AB in guns with no sacrifice of butter. The second view holds that the economy can enjoy full employment and be on the production possibilities curve at, say, C without a high level of military spending. Therefore, more military goods necessarily means a shift from C to B, and the cost is obviously less butter. Turning the issue around, if the economy is at full employment at B and "peace

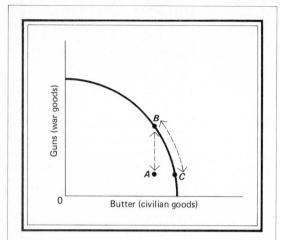

FIGURE 39-2   THE WAR INDUSTRY AND THE PRODUCTION POSSIBILITIES CURVE

The cost of an increase in military spending will be the sacrifice of civilian output in a full-employment economy (C to B). But in an economy characterized by unemployment and excess productive capacity, more war goods can be produced at no cost in terms of civilian goods and services (A to B).

breaks out," we want to move from *B* to *C* if the civilian economy is to benefit from the release of resources by the military. But if stabilization policies fail to compensate for the decline in military spending, the economy will lapse from *B* to *A*, and society will have squandered a potential "peace dividend" on unemployment and idle resources.

But Figure 39-2 assumes that the issue of military versus civilian spending is a simple either-or proposition. Is there really a strict dichotomy between spending for military and for civilian goods? If certain kinds of military outlay entail significant and beneficial spillover effects for the civilian economy, then it is an overstatement to contend that, say, $93 billion of military spending imposes a burden of $93 billion upon a fully employed civilian economy. There is, in fact, some spillover or fallout from military outlays which benefits the civilian economy: rockets designed for military uses can be used to launch civilian weather and communication satellites; many

civilian airline pilots and electronics personnel received their early training in the military; military-space research gives rise to new materials, new products, and new production techniques which are relevant to the civilian economy; and so forth. But careful estimates suggest that, in the aggregate, these beneficial spillover effects are quite modest, amounting to perhaps no more than 10 or 15 percent of total military spending.

■ _____

ALLOCATIVE ASPECTS

Let us shift our attention now from the aggregate size and cost of the military to its organizational and institutional characteristics. This is a necessary prelude to a discussion of the military establishment's microeconomic efficiency.

☐   The Military Establishment and the Firm

It is informative to contrast the military establishment—in particular, the Department of Defense—with a private firm.[2]

1   A most obvious difference is that the military establishment derives its revenue from the Federal government's budget, not from the sale of products in the market. But it must be noted that, like the private firm, the military establishment has a sales problem; that is, it is selling a "psychological product" called national security:[3]

> The salesmen consist of the officers who work with the legislators and legislative committees which command the appropriations. There are also public relations officers who work with the general public who pay the taxes. The almost unfailing appearance of some kind of external

[2]This discussion is based upon Kenneth E. Boulding, "The World War Industry as an Economic Problem," in Emile Benoit and Kenneth E. Boulding (eds.), *Disarmament and the Economy* (New York: Harper & Row, Publishers, Incorporated, 1963).

[3]Ibid., p. 8.

threat in the news stories before the appropriations . . . are to be passed is a phenomenon strongly related to some things which go on in Madison Avenue.

2 Another difference is that the military establishment is a nonprofit public bureaucracy. Recalling our discussion of public sector failure in Chapter 6, this may contribute to chronic complaints of waste and the misuse of resources by the military establishment. One can argue that the military establishment is a kind of monopolist—the sole supplier of national security—and, much like a private, profit-seeking monopolist, it can obtain a total revenue larger than is essential to provide a given output or level of national security. This will be the focal point for our discussion of military procurement.

3 A third point of contrast between a private firm and the military establishment is that the demand for the latter's product is based upon the existence of another, potentially hostile military establishment in some other country. Looked at on a worldwide basis, the war industry produces its own demand. The existence of a military establishment in the United States can only be justified by the existence of large military establishments in the Soviet Union, the People's Republic of China, and certain other countries.

☐ **War Goods Procurement**

With these distinctions in mind, let us now explore the operation of the military establishment in the product market. The Department of Defense does not itself produce military hardware, but it contracts with private firms to design and produce armaments systems. Has this process of arms procurement by the military been efficient? There is considerable evidence to suggest that it has not.

Ideally, taxpayers might hope for a bilateral monopoly confrontation (Figure 31-8) between the military and such giant corporate suppliers as General Dynamics, Lockheed,

McDonnell Douglas, and General Electric, wherein the military acts as a monopsonist and seeks below-competitive prices, and the corporations act as monopolists by seeking above-competitive prices. And one might hope that the outcome would approximate the ideal countervailing power solution wherein actual price and output roughly approximate competitive results. But the relationships are more involved than the countervailing power model suggests, and the outcome is likely to be less socially desirable.

First, some observers charge that a tacit "understanding" exists between the military and its weapons suppliers. Galbraith and others have argued that the two have common interests—an expanding defense budget—and that in fact the suppliers come perilously close to being a part of the military bureaucracy.[4]

> There is the fiction that the specialized arms contractor is separate from the [military] services. The one is in the public sector. The other is private enterprise. . . . [But] the dividing line between the services and their specialized suppliers exists increasingly in the imagination. Where a corporation does all or nearly all of its business with the Department of Defense; uses much plant owned by the Government; gets its working capital in the form of progress payments from the Government; does not need to worry about competitors for it is the sole source of supply; accepts extensive guidance from the Pentagon on its management; is subject to detailed rules as to its accounting; and is extensively staffed by former service personnel, only the remarkable flexibility of the English language allows us to call it private enterprise. Yet this is not an exceptional case, but a common one. General Dynamics, Lockheed, North American-Rockwell and such are public extensions of the bureaucracy. Yet the myth that they are private allows a good deal of freedom in pressing the case for weapons, encouraging unions and

---

[4]Statement by John Kenneth Galbraith before the Subcommittee on Economy in Government, *The Military Budget and National Economic Priorities,* op. cit., pp. 5–6.

politicians to do so, supporting organizations such as the Air Force Association which do so, allowing executives to press the case and otherwise protecting the military power. We have an amiable arrangement by which the defense firms, though part of the public bureaucracy, are largely exempt from its political and other constraints.

□   **"Pentagon Capitalism"**

An even harsher critic of the military establishment contends that we have moved significantly and ominously beyond the military-industrial complex about which President Eisenhower warned us in his now famous farewell address in 1961. General Eisenhower had in mind a rather loose and informal group of high military officers, defense-oriented firms, and certain members of the Congress and executive branch of government who were bound together by a common "ideology" favorable to the maintenance and expansion of American military power. Seymour Melman has contended that during the Kennedy administration the military-industrial complex was in effect reorganized on the basis of the principles of corporate management into a "state-management" system. Under the new state-management the Pentagon is the central management office, and producers of military goods in effect have become subsidiary enterprises of the Pentagon. That is, the buyer-seller market relationship which formerly existed between the Pentagon and military contractors and provided at least a measure of independence between the two was altered into state-management of the war industry because of the great dependence of the firms upon military contracts and the fact that elaborate military procurement procedures and practices resulted in deep penetration of the managerial decision making of military suppliers by the Pentagon. In Melman's words:[5]

An industrial management has been installed in the federal government, under the Secretary of Defense, to control the nation's largest network of industrial enterprises. With the characteristic managerial propensity for extending its power . . . the new state-management combines peak economic, political, and military decision-making. Hitherto, this combination of powers in the same hands has been a feature of statist societies—communist, fascist, and others—where individual rights cannot constrain central rule.

According to Melman, the primary motivation of this new state-management is the maintenance and extension of its decision-making power; that is, like other large industrial managements, it is inclined to measure its own success by the volume of goods produced, the number of employees under its control, the volume of its investments, and so forth. Melman contends that this new military state-management system, which dwarfs such corporate giants as General Motors and AT&T, and its motivation to expand have resulted in decisions which are irrational on both military and economic grounds. Examples: The United States has developed an incredible overkill capacity whereby "we can now deliver more than six tons of TNT for each person on our planet";[6] the prolongation and expansion of an extremely costly war in Vietnam without discernible political-ideological or economic benefits; the Pentagon's position that the United States' balance of payments deficit should be alleviated, not by cutting military expenditures abroad, but by expanding international arms sales; the preference for universal military training or, at least, the military draft as a method of military procurement. All these decisions and positions, according to Melman, can be deemed "rational" only when viewed against the state-management's objective of maintaining and extending its control and size. We will evaluate the Galbraith-Melman views later in our discussion.

[5]Seymour Melman, *Pentagon Capitalism* (New York: McGraw-Hill Book Company, 1970), p. 1.

[6]Ibid., p. 17.

□ **The Costs of Military Procurement**

Congressional and other studies claim that literally billions of dollars have been wasted each year in the process of military procurement. For example, major weapons systems have frequently resulted in final costs two or three times as great as initial cost estimates. Consider two much-publicized illustrations. The original cost estimate of the F-111 airplane order was $4.9 billion in 1963. By 1968 a cost overrun of $9.7 billion had spiraled the cost of the original order to $14.6 billion, or $8.6 million per plane! Air Force cost estimates of $3.4 billion for 120 C-5A jet transports in 1965 had grown to $5.3 billion in 1968—a cost overrun of almost $2 billion.[7] In general, the final cost of military goods in the 1960s averaged about twice their estimated costs. More recently, estimated costs of the controversial B-1 bomber have nearly tripled, from $30 million per plane in 1970 to $84 million in 1975.

Why has this happened? The basic answer seems to be that the practices and procedures of armaments procurement are faulty and wasteful and therefore have resulted in "a vast subsidy to the defense industry, particularly the larger contractors."[8] Or, as we will note later, cost overruns may be a more-or-less inevitable consequence of the technological complexity and experimental character of most new weapons systems.

It does seem clear that a basic problem in military procurement is the inability of the military to enforce effective cost controls upon suppliers. For example, most contracts are not awarded on the basis of competitive bidding, but rather, by direct negotiation with a single supplier. Some experts believe that the absence of competitive bidding by rival suppliers causes procurement costs to be 25 to 50 percent higher than they would otherwise be.

More importantly, defense procurement is based upon what amounts to *cost-plus contracts;* hence, the higher the total cost of a weapons system, the greater the profit to the firm.

> If a private sector firm devises a lower cost method of production, it is rewarded with bigger profits. Defense contractors are not rewarded for cutting costs and may in fact be penalized. The defense firm's negotiated profits are a direct function of the estimated cost of the contract. Lower costs mean smaller profits. After winning a contract the defense producer may decide not to lower costs. Although cost reduction will yield higher profits on the current project, future profits may be cut. Future estimated program costs depend heavily on the projection of present actual expenses. A reduction in the costs of a current project will yield less profits in future years. A labor-saving capital investment can have particularly harmful effects on profitability. The cost-reducing plant and equipment investment will lower the expense base for determining profits.[9]

Furthermore, suppliers employ the "buy in, get well later" method for obtaining defense contracts; that is, a contractor bids "a lower price, higher performance, and earlier delivery than his rivals, knowing Pentagon officials will accept increased costs, less than promised performance, and late delivery."[10] It is also a common occurrence that the development of complex military equipment will necessitate changes in design and production after a contract is awarded. For example, the Minuteman missile program embodied the issuance of thousands of "change orders." Contractors can use change orders as a means for disproportionately inflating costs, contract prices, and their profits. Moreover, the Pentagon makes "progress payments" which reimburse contractors for as much as 90 percent of their

---

[7] Ibid., pp. 21, 64, and Subcommittee on Economy in Government, *The Economics of Military Procurement* (Washington, 1969), p. 19.

[8] *The Economics of Military Procurement,* op. cit., p. 4.

[9] James M. Saurez, "Profits and Performance of Aerospace Defense Contractors," *Journal of Economic Issues,* June 1976, pp. 399–400.

[10] *The Economics of Military Procurement,* op. cit., p. 5.

incurred costs; these payments mean that the government is extending interest-free credit to suppliers in advance of product delivery. The government also follows an extremely liberal patent policy in dealing with contractors. Contractors are allowed to obtain exclusive patent rights without charge on inventions developed in carrying out government contracts. "The contractor, in other words, obtains a monopoly which he can exploit for his own private gain in the commercial market for inventions paid for by public moneys."[11] Given the fact that most government contracts are awarded to large corporations, this "fringe benefit" undoubtedly tends to increase the concentration of economic power.

The Military in the Labor Market[12]

Historically, the military and private firms have differed dramatically in obtaining labor resources. The traditional use of conscription, or the "draft," as a means of acquiring much of its manpower puts the military at extreme odds with the traditional capitalist concept of free or voluntary occupational choice. Prior to the elimination of conscription in 1973, young men reaching eighteen years of age were required to register with the Selective Service System and were liable for military conscription for one year. The manpower needs of the military, however, were substantially less than the number of potentially eligible young people available. Thus a kind of rationing problem existed: From the relatively large number potentially eligible for military service, who would actually serve? This rationing problem was "resolved" through an elaborate system of exemptions, deferments, and rejections which functioned with dubious equity.

[11]Ibid., p. 7.
[12]The present discussion draws heavily upon James C. Miller, III (ed.), *Why the Draft?* (Baltimore: Penguin Books, 1968), and *Report of the President's Commission on an All Volunteer Armed Force* (Washington, 1970).

Case for a Volunteer Army

Most economists felt that in the absence of a major war, a volunteer army would be a much superior alternative to the draft. Their arguments involved the following points.

1 Equitable Distribution of Manpower Costs Under post-World War II conscription a small minority of Americans—those eligible young people who were draftees or "reluctant volunteers"—bore a large and discriminatory implicit tax. That is, they shouldered a disproportionately large and inequitable share of the cost of national defense. The discriminatory tax borne by the draftee was composed of two parts. First, there was the difference between a draftee's pay (say $2500 per year) and the income (say $4500 per year) he might have earned in his best available civilian employment. But this $2000 differential was based upon the assumption that the draftee would have felt the same toward military and civilian employment if the pay rates had been the same. In fact, we can assume that draftees and reluctant volunteers had some occupational preference for civilian employments; that is, the military might not have had to pay just $4500—an amount equal to that obtainable in civilian employment—but perhaps an additional $500 as an "equalizing difference" (Chapter 31). Thus the total implicit tax was roughly equal to the difference between what the draftee was paid and the wage needed to induce him to volunteer for military service. In our example, that tax is $2500 (= $5000 − $2500). Actual estimates suggest that under conscription, this tax was high, for example, 40 to 50 percent of civilian income. Stated more positively, with the volunteer army, manpower is acquired by paying a market price (income) substantially higher than that paid to draftees. Taxpayers pay higher taxes to finance the higher price for military labor, but this distribution of military manpower costs is much more equitable than a high and discriminatory implicit tax on the very small percentage of our total population who might be draftees and reluctant volunteers.

But one may raise this question: Even if the voluntary army results in greater equity in sharing the cost burden of national defense, won't the total cost of military manpower be substantially increased?

2 A Volunteer Army Is Less Costly

There is no question but that a volunteer army entails higher budgetary or *money* costs than would a conscripted army of the same size; the higher pay associated with our shift to the volunteer army added over $3 billion to the military budget in 1974. This is the case because the hidden implicit tax on draftees is shifted to taxpayers and therefore made explicit. But there are good reasons why a volunteer army entails a smaller *real* cost than conscription. That is, a volunteer army of a given size can provide greater defensive capability or effectiveness than a conscripted army of the same size.[13] What real cost savings or increases in efficiency might be achieved through a volunteer army?

First, it is argued that the very high turnover rate for draftees (over 90 percent) is reduced by substituting a volunteer army. This reduces training costs, on the one hand, and results in a more experienced, more professional, and therefore more effective military force, on the other. Similarly, the morale and "productivity" of military personnel who are serving as the result of free choice are higher than those of men who are coerced to serve. It is also hoped that a higher monetary price for military manpower—one which more accurately reflects real costs—causes more efficient decision making in the use of that manpower. Under a conscripted army, the low budgetary cost of manpower is conducive to the use of too much labor and not enough capital in both combat and noncombat undertakings (Chapter

30). Furthermore, it is argued that at a higher level the increased budgetary costs of military manpower will cause voters and the Congress to examine military budgets more critically and to force the elimination of wasteful uses of military labor. Finally, it is held that a volunteer army has beneficial allocative effects in the civilian economy. Employers can hire the best qualified workers rather than those least likely to be drafted. Young people are less inclined to make irrational decisions with respect to occupational choice, education, and marriage as means of acquiring a draft deferment or exemption.

Consistent with Freedom of Choice A fundamental tenet of the capitalistic system is that laborers should have freedom of occupational choice. Conscription is a system of "involuntary servitude" and is fundamentally inconsistent with free occupational choice. In a more positive sense, a volunteer army would necessarily entail higher wages and better working conditions than the draft in order to attract an armed force of a given size. Therefore, a volunteer army would provide a new and improved occupational alternative to young people, thereby extending their range of free occupational choices.

☐ Objections

There are objections to the volunteer army, two of which merit comment.[14]

1 It is argued that a volunteer army "will cost too much." We know the answer to this point: The monetary or budgetary costs do indeed rise as the result of removing the heavy implicit tax on draftees and making this cost explicit. But, as we have seen, the real cost— the sacrifice of real output by the civilian economy for a given level of military manpower effectiveness—falls.

2 The volunteer army means a powerful,

---

[13]Or, alternatively stated, a given level of military manpower effectiveness could be attained with a smaller volunteer army.

[14]For a more extended discussion, the reader should consult Miller, op. cit.

professional military elite—an army of mercenaries—which, in accordance with Melman's
fears, may constitute a growing threat to democratic processes and political freedom. The
answer to this criticism is that the military's
officers, and particularly the senior officers, are
professionals, or "mercenaries," under the alternative of conscription. It must be admitted,
however, that the problem implied here might
be aggravated by a volunteer army. The possible development of a professional army whose
corps of junior officers, noncommissioned officers, and enlisted men feel a primary allegiance
to their senior officers and not to the nation is
a disquieting prospect.

□ **Other Manpower Problems**

The shift from conscription to the volunteer army has not relieved the military of all
criticism of its manpower policies. On the one
hand, the military has been criticized for poor
manpower utilization. Only 15 percent of all
personnel are in combat forces; the remainder
are in combat-support positions. Furthermore,
the National Guard and the Reserves were
virtually unused in Vietnam. If these trained
personnel are not to be utilized, why retain
them on military payrolls? On the other hand,
the military has been subject to "grade creep."
That is, there is evidence to suggest the military has become topheavy with officers:[15]

> There are more field grade and flag officers to
> command 2.2 million men today than there
> were to command 12.1 million men in 1945;
> also, there are more sergeants than there are
> recruits today, compared with a 1945 ratio of
> seven recruits per sergeant. . . . [I]f the grade
> structure existing at the end of World War II
> were in effect today, payroll costs at today's
> pay scales would be $2.7 billion less than they
> actually are.

[15] William Burke, "Pentagon Problems," *Business &
Financial Letter,* Federal Reserve Bank of San Francisco,
Nov. 2, 1973, p. 3.

■ AGGREGATIVE ASPECTS

We have examined the size of the war industry,
the costs associated with its existence, and
some of the microeconomic aspects of the military establishment's operations in both the
product and labor markets. Let us now turn to
the implications of the war industry for aggregate economic stability.

□ **Defense Spending and Stability**

Perhaps the main characteristic of military spending by government is the fact that
its underlying motivation and rationale are
noneconomic. Government military outlays
alter in response to international political and
military events, rather than in terms of the
goal of domestic economic stability. It is not
surprising, then, that changes in military
spending have been an important source of
economic instability in the post-World War II
period. Since World War II, defense spending
has tended to fluctuate more than consumption, investment, or the expenditures of state
and local governments.

From a long-term, historical standpoint,
war has been closely linked with inflation.
Figure 39-3 is instructive. Consumer prices
rose on the order of 15 and 13 percent per year
respectively during the Civil War and World
War I. Inflation was less dramatic—about 5 or
6 percent per year—during World War II. But
this more modest price rise was the result of
our entering the war with substantial unemployment and excess productive capacity and
of the fact that inflationary pressures were
suppressed with direct wage and price controls
during the war. These controls largely shifted
inflationary pressures into the immediate
postwar period (Figure 39-3). The Korean war
was much less resource-demanding, but nevertheless gave rise to a sharp, but short, upsurge
in prices. Finally, the inflation of the late
1960s and early 1970s is traceable to the esca-

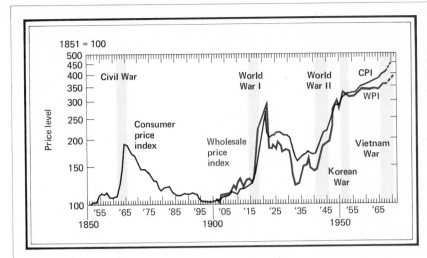

FIGURE 39-3 WAR AND INFLATION

Historically war—and, more specifically, high levels of spending on armaments—has been a cause of inflation in the United States. (*First National City Bank of New York*, Monthly Economic Letter, *December 1969, p. 140.*)

lation of the Vietnam war in the mid-sixties (Chapter 18).

Why does this close tie exist between war and inflation? A partial answer is to the effect that "War always fills the purse faster than the pantry." That is, during war, civilian output is curtailed, or at least its growth is retarded, as resources are reallocated to the production of military goods. But the prosperity to which military spending contributes pumps a rising flow of money income into the civilian economy. The result is a classic case of demand-pull inflation in the civilian sector. However, this explanation is incomplete; we must add the supposition that government is unwilling or regards it inadvisable to levy sufficiently high taxes to match the flows of civilian demand and civilian goods output to the end that the prices of civilian goods and services remain stable. That is, sharp tax increases and a restrictive monetary policy could restrain consumption and investment in the civilian sector and prevent inflation. But government may simply lack the political will to take these steps, as was the case during the Vietnam War. Or, as occurred during World War II, government might take the position that taxes would have to be so high to prevent inflation that

work and investment incentives would be undermined. As a result, government may choose to finance a part of its military outlays by borrowing. If it borrows extensively from the central and commercial banks, debt financing will expand the supply of money and tend to be particularly inflationary (Chapter 13). In any event, war does tend to spawn inflation.

☐   **Détente and Disarmament**

What if peace "breaks out"? What if East-West détente is achieved and the world secures a genuine and lasting peace? The answer, quite obviously, is that the resulting demobilization will permit each nation to realize a potential "peace dividend" in the form of expanded civilian output. But the achievement of a peace dividend requires appropriate management of the national economy and careful advanced planning to cope with demobilization.

Fiscal-Monetary Policies   We know in general the kinds of macroeconomic policies which would be appropriate in offsetting a significant cutback in government military spending: (1) reduce net taxes—that is, reduce taxes and increase transfer payments; (2) increase government nondefense expenditures; and (3) move toward an easier money policy. The obvious purpose of all these measures is to bolster the nondefense components of aggregate demand so as to compensate for the cuts in military outlays.

Our experience with disarmament at the conclusion of World War II suggests that reconversion to civilian production can be achieved quite smoothly and without encountering significant unemployment (see table inside covers for 1945–1947, lines 1–5 and 26). Although military outlays fell from about $74 billion in 1945 to just $15 billion in 1946 and $9 billion in 1947, unemployment did not rise above 4 percent in the 1946–1948 period. On the other hand, disarmament took place under conditions which favored a smooth transition to peacetime production. A large portion of the war was financed by government borrowing rather than taxation; hence, consumers and businesses emerged from the war with large stocks of liquid assets or near-monies. Furthermore, the private sector had experienced an extended period of product shortages, the result of the war itself and the preceding Great Depression. Households and businesses converted near-monies into money at the war's end and indulged in a spending spree. Thus consumption and investment rose sharply at the conclusion of hostilities, compensating for most of the decline in military spending. Similarly, spending on civilian social goods and services by state and local governments increased quite spectacularly. Export demand also rose sharply as the devastated countries of Europe looked to America to provide the goods needed for economic recovery. National economic policy was also favorable: tax rates were reduced, and monetary policy made ample credit available at low interest rates. On the other hand, although unemployment was avoided after the war, we have noted that inflation was significant in the immediate postwar period.

Two other points are relevant. First, the task of maintaining full employment so as to realize a substantial peace dividend through disarmament depends upon the size and rapidity of the declines in military spending. Large and sudden cuts in military outlays will obviously be the most difficult to cope with. Second, it is clear that the policy-mix chosen will determine the general form in which a peace dividend is taken. For example, cutting taxes is a decision to take the peace dividend in the form of additional private consumption and investment goods. Increased transfer payments imply the bolstering of social insurance and welfare payments or the inauguration of a negative income tax program (Chapter 37). Increased nonmilitary spending by government suggests new or expanded programs in such areas as urban development, pollution abatement, health and education, and crime prevention. The various forms which a peace dividend might take imply a final point: Advanced planning and general agreement on priorities for a peace dividend are crucial "so that wrangling will not paralyze action when the need arises."[16]

Structural Problems The efficient adjustment to demobilization entails not only the maintenance of aggregate demand, but also the minimization of structural or allocational problems. In particular, disarmament means substantial changes in the structure of aggregate demand. While the market system tends automatically to negotiate the shift of resources from defense to civilian uses, we know that the market system works slowly and imperfectly. We also know that certain industries and regions are very heavily dependent upon military contracts. For example, firms and regions which are very largely committed to the production of aircraft, missiles, munitions, and electronics equipment for the military might well be hard hit by disarmament. Areas such as Seattle, Boston, Wichita, Los Angeles,

---

[16]Roger E. Bolton, *Defense and Disarmament* (Englewood Cliffs, N.J.: Prentice-Hall, Inc., 1966), p. 38.

and San Diego, wherein military-aerospace work has been the dominant source of employment, are obviously vulnerable to serious economic repercussions. Government might want to alleviate the pains of reconversion to peacetime production in very adversely affected industries by granting temporary tax relief or other subsidies during the period of transition.

□ **The Current Malaise**

Seymour Melman, whose concept of "Pentagon capitalism" was introduced earlier in this chapter, attributes the American stagflation of the 1970s to the presence of a large military sector. Briefly stated, his reasoning follows along these lines: Although military goods yield "political utility," they do not have economic use value. War goods do not satisfy current wants as do consumer goods, nor do they contribute to future production as do capital goods. Military goods are an economic waste. But the production of large quantities of these goods has a series of unintended and uniformly undesirable effects on the economy. Most crucially, the rate of growth of the nation's productivity is reduced. Why so? On the one hand, military spending entails a massive shift of real capital, high-level technical manpower, and research and development activity from the civilian to the military sector. On the other hand, the realities of military procurement are such that there are no significant pressures upon suppliers to minimize cost; as noted earlier, in effect military-goods producers enjoy cost-plus contracts. Hence, there is no reason to use resources efficiently. The resulting overall decline in the nation's productive efficiency contributes to rising costs and higher prices. Foreign firms thereby become more successful in selling in American markets; conversely, American firms become less competitive in world markets. For both reasons, American workers lose jobs. The problem is compounded as private American investment capital flows abroad where unit labor costs are less. As a consequence, not only are more jobs lost, but our domestic stock of productive facilities tends to become antiquated and productivity falls further. According to Melman,

> . . . there is solid evidence to support the thesis that [the military] has preempted capital and technology resources on so vast a scale as to induce deterioration in the production facilities of the civilian economy. The military economy, as the core of a new cost maximizing system, has infected the rest with its trained incapacities for offsetting rising costs. This, in turn, has led to a sharply lowered rate of productivity growth. The consequent inability of American-based firms to meet competition encouraged the flow of capital abroad and implanted durable unemployment in the U.S. economy.[17]

IN DEFENSE OF DEFENSE

What can be said in defense of the war industry? Let us first consider rebuttals to some of the specific criticisms of it; then we will consider a more basic, positive point.

□ **Guns and Butter?**

Has the war industry drained the economic cupboard of resources to the extent claimed by critics? One can argue to the contrary, starting with the basic point that in a growing economy we can simultaneously have more guns and more butter. In fact, despite high levels of military spending, many important domestic programs have been initiated and accelerated during past decades. Furthermore, it may be a gross overstatement to contend that the employment of large amounts of high-level scientific manpower by the military-industrial complex has been a primary

[17]Seymour Melman, "Decision Making and Productivity as Economic Variables: The Present Depression as a Failure of Productivity," *Journal of Economic Issues,* June 1976, pp. 230–231. See also Melman's *The Permanent War Economy* (New York: Simon and Schuster, 1974), particularly chap. 4.

cause of technological deficiencies in the private economy. We must recognize that our weapons expenditures affect not only the demand side of the labor market, but also the supply side. By providing fellowships, research grants, and training programs, the defense effort has *directly* increased the supplies of scientists, engineers, and technicians. And, by providing a very favorable labor market, the war industry has *indirectly* increased the supply of high-level scientific and technical manpower by inducing young people to enter these occupations. One can argue that the military-industrial complex has been a vital force in upgrading the quality of our labor force—an accomplishment which may yield substantial long-run social benefits. Finally, although certain industries have remained in the "technological backwaters," this may be more the result of the lethargy and indifference of those industries than of scarcities of scientific talent.

□ Technological-Organizational Spillovers

There is no question that the war industry has absorbed large amounts of scientific and technical resources which otherwise might have been available for civilian uses. But it must also be recognized that expenditures on defense and space have resulted in important technological "spillovers" for the civilian economy. The existence or commercial feasibility of nuclear power, transport aircraft, and high-speed computers is related to military R & D. Similarly, military research was highly instrumental in the development of silicon transistors, improved anti–motion-sickness drugs, and new flameproofing for fabrics.[18] The space effort has resulted in significant developments in the fields of communication, weather control, and navigation which can have important economic repercussions for the civilian economy in both the short and long run. More

generally, profound advances in the sciences and technology have been a consequence of generous military budgets.

Finally, complex weaponry and space programs have demonstrated both the ability and methods for organizing massive amounts of human and property resources in the resolution of complex, large-scale problems. These abilities and techniques may prove to be highly relevant in resolving domestic socioeconomic problems.

□ Is War Inherently Inflationary?

While there seems to be a positive correlation between wartime spending and rising prices (Figure 39-3), is it entirely accurate to say flatly that "military spending is inflationary"? Or is it perhaps fairer to say that "inflation has accompanied wartime spending because government has failed to invoke counterbalancing monetary and fiscal policies"? For example, inflation during and following World War II was quite severe; but during the Korean war, inflation was modest. Although much of the differential undoubtedly resulted from differences in the magnitudes of the conflicts, one can argue that the methods of finance were also of significance. During World War II, heavy reliance was placed on deficit financing in contrast to the emphasis upon tax financing during the Korean war. These choices contributed to the differing severity of inflation. Similarly, while it is correct to say that rising military expenditures in Vietnam were an important factor in the inflation of the 1960s (Chapter 18), it is generally agreed that more restrictive fiscal and monetary measures could have thwarted this price level instability.

□ Cost Overruns: Are They Inevitable?

Perhaps the much-publicized question of cost overruns in military procurement deserves more dispassionate treatment than it has received in public hearings and in the press.

[18] Charles J. Hitch and Roland N. McKean, *The Economics of Defense in the Nuclear Age* (New York: Atheneum, Publishers, 1967), p. 83.

At the outset, it is important to note that cost overruns are neither new nor peculiar to the military. Two examples: Construction of the interstate highway system and the Rayburn addition to the House Office Building both entailed very substantial cost overruns.[19]

> An office building is not a very complicated structure in comparison with modern military aircraft and guided missiles. . . . Yet we all know of office building after office building for commercial account in which substantial cost overruns were experienced. The same is true in the history of innumerable people who contracted for a house. They wind up paying substantially more than they originally bargained for in the building of their home . . . let us not be carried away by the current list of horrible [cost overrun] examples in the military and assume that this is the product of some evil conspiracy between the government and manufacturers of military goods.

Government committees and journalists who are critical of apparent waste in the military have equally unkind comments to make concerning public programs in such civilian areas as urban renewal, highway construction, Medicare, aid to education, and so forth.

Secondly, the alleged wastes and inefficiencies associated with military procurement may in fact be inevitable consequences of the transactions and products involved. A genuine market system does not and cannot exist for modern weapons, and it is therefore misleading to judge efficiency by conventional market standards or measures. The military, after all, is not purchasing mules and muskets, but highly complex and technologically advanced weapons systems, many of which are often only in the "idea stage" when contracts are let. Furthermore, the financial costs for requisite R & D and investment in productive capacity far exceed the resources of even the largest corporations. And the uncertainty over whether technical specifications desired by the

military can in fact be realized may be highly doubtful. Private firms simply cannot undertake such financial risks and uncertainties on their own initiative. Hence, it should not be too surprising that the close interrelationship between buyer and seller and all that goes with it—contracts by negotiation, cost-plus-fixed-fee contracts, progress payments, government provision of real capital—are characteristic of modern weapons production. Also, certain kinds of desired military hardware will inevitably prove not to be technologically feasible or, alternatively, the equipment will be rendered technologically obsolete before it is fully developed. Stated differently, when working at the frontiers of technology, we should not be too surprised when a project such as the F-111 fighter turns sour.

It is also important to recognize that technical performance is a much more compelling criterion in weapons acquisition than it is in most civilian goods. In a field noted for rapid technological progress and high rates of obsolescence, it makes little sense to stress cost minimization at the risk of technically inferior weaponry. Although rivalry on price may be relatively weak in the weapons acquisition process, DOD can argue with some plausibility that supplier rivalry on the basis of scientific-technical capability is both strong and fundamental.

□   **Survival in a Nuclear Age**

But a more positive case can be made for the military: The basic prerequisite of economic development is peace. If we are to survive and to realize the socioeconomic fruits of our scientific and technological progress, major military conflict must be avoided. Ironically, "the very fearsomeness of the threat [of thermonuclear] war is an invitation to a calculating, ruthless power to remove it by force if any happy circumstance presents itself—as, for example, the temporary impotence or vulnerability of the opposing strategic air force; or his own temporary invulnerability resulting from,

---

[19] David Novick, "A Balanced View of Cost Overruns," *Business Horizons,* April 1970, p. 72.

say, a break-through in air defense technology."[20] In short, given Communist ideological objectives and agreement by Western experts that the Soviet Union "would not hesitate to use force or the threat of force to gain advantage over the West,"[21] the United States has little choice but to make a substantial resource commitment to war goods in order to achieve a position of "mutual deterrence," or what Winston Churchill more pointedly termed a "balance of terror." Former Secretary of Defense Robert McNamara carried the point further, arguing that national security is "inherently priceless" and cannot be measured in terms of dollars: "Our children will hardly admire us for our frugality [in defense spending] if it is achieved at a price they will have to pay in blood and suffering."

■
THE NATIONAL PRIORITIES DEBATE

The substantial role of the military, on the one hand, and the growing acuteness and increasing awareness of domestic socioeconomic problems, on the other, have set the stage for profound national debate concerning the character and objectives of our society.

> Two major schools of political thought have become locked in a contest for the mind and soul of America. One school draws much of its strength from the revolution of military technology, the other from the revolution of rising expectations. One school tends to regard communism as a centrally directed conspiracy that threatens our survival as a free people. The other school believes that communism is

breaking up into independent national movements, and sees the main threat to free institutions in the deterioration of our cities and the sickness of our society. One school seeks overwhelming military power to deter fresh Communist adventures, and is willing to risk war in order to prevent the geographic expansion of communism. The other school seeks wider social justice and better economic conditions for Negroes and others who have not participated fully in the advance of prosperity, and holds that the force of moral example can contribute more to our national security than additional bombs or missiles.[22]

The focal point of this debate has been the Federal budget and, in particular, its division between military and civilian uses. In a very real sense the debate is concerned with the establishing of national priorities. Charles L. Schultze, former Director of the Bureau of the Budget, has put the matter this way: "The benefits and costs of proposed military programs cannot be viewed in isolation. They must be related to and measured against those other national priorities which, in the context of limited resources, their adoption must necessarily sacrifice." To this end, Schultze proposed the establishment of an "appropriate committee," staffed in part with senators and representatives chiefly concerned with domestic issues, to achieve a more careful assessment of national priorities as the result of rational and responsible debate which evaluates military and domestic needs directly against one another.[23]

[20]Hitch and McKean, op. cit., p. 12.
[21]Subcommittee on Economy in Government, *The Military Budget and National Economic Priorities,* op. cit., p. 8.

[22]Arthur F. Burns, in Jacob K. Javits, Charles J. Hitch, and Arthur F. Burns, *The Defense Sector and the American Economy* (New York: New York University Press, 1968), pp. 85–86.
[23]Subcommittee on Economy in Government, *The Military Budget and National Economic Priorities,* op. cit., pp. 45, 56–57.

Summary

1 Department of Defense expenditures indicate that the military currently absorbs almost 6 percent of the GNP. For a variety of reasons these figures may understate the economic significance of the war industry. On the assumption that full employment can be realized without a large defense establishment, military outlays are a rough measure of the economic burden or real cost of our military posture.

2 The military establishment has encountered severe criticism in recent years as the result of allegedly wasteful practices in the acquisition of weapons systems; in addition, some critics express serious alarm concerning the institutional and political overtones associated with the evolution of the "military-industrial complex" or "Pentagon capitalism." Critics also contend that the drain of high-level manpower, capital goods, and R & D activity to the military has undermined the economy's rate of productivity growth and contributed to the stagflation of the 1970s.

3 The conscription of military manpower has been replaced by the volunteer army. The latter has several important advantages: **a.** It results in a more equitable distribution of military manpower costs; **b.** it lowers the real cost of achieving a given level of military manpower effectiveness; and **c.** it is consistent with free occupational choice.

4 Defenses of the war industry include the following: **a.** Given international uncertainties, a high level of United States military preparedness is essential to peace and, hence, to continued economic development; **b.** military expenditures have resulted in technological advances of great importance to the civilian economy; and **c.** given the size and technological complexities of modern weapons systems, market tests of efficiency in weapons procurement are not relevant.

5 Disarmament implies a potential "peace dividend" as resources are reallocated from military to civilian uses. Full realization of this dividend assumes that demobilization will be unimpeded by unemployment or serious allocative bottlenecks.

Questions and Study Suggestions

1 Key terms and concepts to remember: war industry; military-industrial complex; "Pentagon capitalism"; cost-plus contract; cost overrun; peace dividend; volunteer army.

2 What is the aggregate size of Department of Defense spending in the United States? How might this figure **a.** understate, or **b.** overstate, the cost of our military posture?

3 Explain and evaluate:

a. "The United States is an affluent society and therefore does not have to choose between guns and butter."

b. "The largest money costs of a war come after the fighting stops."

c. "Federal spending will continue to be a major source of instability so long as it consists predominantly of military outlays."

4 Compare the objectives and characteristics of the military establishment with those of a private firm. Why are any differences important? Explain why the procurement of weapons systems by the Department of Defense frequently entails large cost overruns.

5 How does the concept of "Pentagon capitalism" differ from the notion of a "military-industrial complex"?

6 What are the economic advantages of an all-volunteer army as compared with conscription? Explain: "A volunteer army will result in higher budgetary costs, but lower real costs, for a given level of military manpower effectiveness."

7 Comment upon, or critically evaluate, each of the following statements:

a. "A great virtue of the volunteer army is that the difficult problems of determining deferments, exemptions, and in particular conscientious objector status under the draft are all automatically resolved."

b. "The trouble with a volunteer army is that it results in a professional army of mercenaries and the likelihood of a military *coup* or civilian control *by* the military is greatly enhanced."

c. "Decisions concerning who might die in defense of our country are too fundamental to be decided by the market."

8 Explain: "If taken literally, the questions, 'What can we afford for defense?' and 'What are our needs?' are the wrong ones to ask in deciding upon the size of the defense effort. The right question is, 'How much is needed for defense more than it is needed for other purposes?'"

Selected References

Benoit, Emile, and Kenneth E. Boulding (eds.): *Disarmament and the Economy* (New York: Harper & Row, Publishers, Incorporated, 1963).

Clayton, James L. (ed.): *The Economic Impact of the Cold War* (New York: Harcourt, Brace & World, Inc., 1970).

Hitch, Charles J., and Roland N. McKean: *The Economics of Defense in the Nuclear Age* (New York: Atheneum, 1967).

Ilchman, Warren F., and Joe S. Bain (eds.): *The Political Economy of the Military-Industrial Complex* (Berkeley, Calif.: University of California Institute of Business and Economic Research, 1973).

Melman, Seymour (ed.): *The War Economy of the United States* (New York: St. Martin's Press, 1971).

Melman, Seymour: *The Permanent War Economy* (New York: Simon and Schuster, 1974).

Weidenbaum, Murray L.: *The Economics of Peacetime Defense* (New York: Praeger Publishers, 1974).

Last Word

Apollo: A Technological Superstunt

Sociologist Amitai Etzioni contends that the Apollo Project drained resources and diverted attention from domestic socioeconomic problems and yielded few economic, scientific, or military benefits.

The most hopeful epitaph for Project Apollo might be: This was the last gasp of a technologically addicted, public-relations-minded society, the last escapade engineered by an industrial-military coalition seeking conquests in outer space, while avoiding swelling needs on earth.

And what a gasp it was! Never before had so many taxpayers spent so many billions, and so many thousands of talented technologists and scientists labored so hard on a civilian project that yielded so little. Apollo's irrationality stands second only to one—our inclination to get involved in far-off wars, at even greater cost and distraction from our domestic problems.

Both tendencies are part of our difficulty in turning toward self-reform as the ages of exploiting nature and dealing in other people's lands come to an inevitable end.

The astronauts set out to investigate the moon, but their journeys told us more about ourselves than about that arid pile of orbiting rocks. They told us that in the decade in which poverty, social injustice, pollution, mental illness, subquality housing, inadequate education and crime went untreated, we invested more new public resources and scarce research-and-development manpower, staggering amounts of our muscle and mind, in a combination of a technological superstunt and a geological excavation.

Project Apollo reveals both the how and why of decisions which set the course of the nation. The commitment to put Americans on the moon was made by President John F. Kennedy during a few days in late April and mid-May of 1961 following brief staff reviews of the social, economic and international implications of the project.

And a good part of the review available was opposed to the emphasis on expensive, probably unnecessary, manned flights. Among those questioning such a venture was a task force headed by Jerome B. Wiesner and the outgoing President's scientific advisory committee. We do not reflect long before we jump, often disregarding our experts' advice.

Soon, a presidential speech to a joint session of Congress, a quick approval by the legislature, and we were on our way. In the years that followed, with a rapidly growing space industry promoting the lunar visits, and scientists, many working on the project, testifying in its behalf, an impartial evaluation of the decision was practically impossible.

Once the executive starts a multi-billion public work rolling, don't count on Congress' annual review to stop it.

The underlying motives for the go-ahead included the public relations notion that the prospect of a moon voyage would provide a new topic for a nation despondent over the failure of the Cuban invasion; that Apollo would demonstrate to the world that we could match recent Soviet technological feats (the Russians had just put Yuri Gagarin in space); and that the giant project would help revitalize a recessed economy.

Arguments in favor of other domestic projects were pushed aside, then and since, on the ground they would not "sell" as well as lunar flights. Mundane, unphotogenic dispersed activities, such as the collection of garbage in thousands of streets, arrests of muggers on myriad corners, and the reading and writing habits of kids all over America, it was said, do not compare to the Apollo spectaculars on TV.

And, unlike any earthly project, going to the moon was a project the federal government could control without violating states' rights, building highways through minority communities, or having to gain the cooperation of the natives.

Once the space coalition was formed, every value dear to man was emblazoned on its banners. Only now we begin to see how absurd most of that razzle-dazzle was. Generals argued the moon was essential to national security as a "high ground," for observation and fire purposes, disregarding those who pointed out that our reconnaissance satellites would soon be able to gather more detailed information about "the enemy" than we know what to do with, and that it would be rather silly for the Russians to shoot missles at us from the moon, when they could fire them from much nearer bases.

There is no question the space race did help to develop our military technology. However, we entered the Age of Apollo with an existing and guaranteed capacity to kill twice over every man, woman and child alive. How much more did we need?

Nor did the military yet acknowledge that, in the war fought in the last decade, its Buck Rogers space gadgets and supermissiles did us very little good, to put it mildly.

The promise of economic "spin-offs" from the lunar gear into other areas was touted by NASA, and indeed there were some. If you burn 27-odd billion dollars, you generate some heat, but pitiful little it was. It turned out that most outer-space products, fuels and alloids, geared to extreme temperatures, vacuums, acceleration and weightlessness, have no use in our earthly schools, hospitals and bedrooms.

Scientists promised to look on the moon for the origin of life, which many Americans understood to mean other civilizations, one-legged beings with two antenna sticking out of their pear-shaped heads. Actually, at issue was if there were any organic molecules, and if something could be gleaned about the rise and fall of the solar system. So far, Apollo has delivered no major scientific breakthroughs and, many experts agree, not even middle-sized ones.

Finally, we were informed Apollo would provide a peaceful outlet for the world's superpower contest, unite the nation, and enrich the human spirit. But at the cost of keeping one of NASA's missiles from catching a cold, Nixon achieved more peace through his ping-pong diplomacy with China and in SALT talks, than a decade of space jumps.

The nation surely was divided more over these years than in the preceding decade, among other things over the objectives of the space race, which polls show about half of America never came to accept.

The space coalition is still drawing more per year for its space antics than many domestic missions (recently, it got us committed to buying Skylabs). The space budget should be be cut below the half-billion mark, focused on near space and economical nonmanned efforts (weather control, communication satellites). Every school child, citizen and inchoate politician should be required to study what Apollo taught us.

Then we can cease chasing moons in the quest for a new America.

40

The Radical Critique: The Economics of Dissent

The overriding goal of this book is to present the orthodox—the "traditional" or "mainstream"—view of how capitalism operates, the sources of its problems, and the various policies which might be appropriate in alleviating those problems. The general tenor of this presentation is acceptable to the vast majority of economists; they agree that it is a rough approximation of reality.

But in the 1960s and early 1970s there emerged a relatively small group of economists—variously labeled "New Left," neo-Marxist, or radical economists. Although radical economics encompasses an important intellectual tradition which traces back to Karl Marx, its recent growth is rooted in (1) the radicalization of university campuses in the late 1960s which occurred primarily in response to the Vietnam war and racial injustice, and (2) the apparent inability of capitalistic society to resolve a number of deeply rooted problems such as the unequal distribution of income, wealth, and power both domestically and internationally; the wasteful use of resources; deterioration of the environment; discrimination; the urban malaise; and the Phillips Curve dilemma. More specifically, radical economists flatly reject the portrayal of capitalism presented in this textbook; they regard it essentially as an apology for, or a legitimization of, the existing system. Furthermore, the radicals are pessimistic about the prospects for reform of the existing society from within for the simple reason that those who benefit most from the status quo dominate and control the political system.

The basic objective of the present chapter is to present—in as systematic and objective a fashion as possible—those basic ideas and contentions which constitute radical economics. This is not an easy task. On the one hand, just as there are many different postures or schools of thought within orthodox economics, so there are many divergent views within the radical position. On the other hand, the literature of radical economics is vast and far-ranging; hence, the summary statement offered here is necessarily abrupt and incomplete.[1]

The agenda is as follows. First, a thumbnail sketch of Marxian economics—the historical predecessor of radical economics—is presented. Next, we shall examine certain fundamental differences between orthodox and radical economics in the areas of methodology and problem perception. Third, our main task will be to outline in some detail a radical model of modern capitalism. Finally, we shall consider the orthodox rebuttal to the economics of dissent.

THE MARXIAN HERITAGE: THE "OLD LEFT"

The roots of the radical critique of capitalism go back to Karl Marx (1818–1883). An intellectual of the first rank, Marx was both a radical journalist and an active revolutionary. Expelled from continental Europe for his activities, Marx spent some thirty-five years in England engaged in scholarly research.

During this period he was eyewitness to the depressing picture presented by the industrial revolution in capitalistic England.[2]

> Workers in the new factories were paid low wages. . . . Hours of work were long, women and children were employed in substantial numbers and often in hard and dangerous jobs, factory discipline was often harsh and rigorous, and in some areas company-owned stores profited from exclusive selling rights among employees. Particularly in the textile and coal industries, competition kept selling prices low, and firms competed with each other by squeezing labor costs whenever possible.

> The realities of industrial life created sharp contrasts between the growing wealth of the new industrialists and bankers and the poverty of those without property who formed the work force in the factories of the slum-ridden cities. . . .

> . . . industrialization promised abundance. For the first time it seemed as though it might be possible to produce everything men could want and that the great struggle for existence could be resolved. Yet the gray slums of Manchester and the black country of the coal mines told a different story. The promise and the reality were vastly different.

Marx grasped the inconsistencies of capitalism and, in particular, the promise of abundance and the reality of widespread poverty. Hence, in his great work *Capital,* Marx's attention was devoted primarily to an explanation of how the dynamic forces and contradictions within capitalism would cause the system to break down. In capsule form, Marx's theory of capitalistic development and collapse runs as follows.

[1] Most radical economists belong to the Union for Radical Political Economics (URPE), which publishes the quarterly *Review of Radical Political Economics.* Formed in 1968, URPE now claims some 2000 members. The *Monthly Review* is also an important outlet of radical thought. The references at the end of this chapter present important summaries and critiques of the radical view. For an excellent summary of "the major tenets and general orientation" of radical thought by two radical economists, consult Raymond S. Franklin and William K. Tabb, "The Challenge of Radical Political Economics," *Journal of Economic Issues,* March 1974, pp. 127–150.

[2] Daniel R. Fusfeld, *The Age of the Economist,* 3d ed. (Glenview, Ill.: Scott, Foresman and Company, 1977), p. 57.

☐ The Class Struggle

To Marx the economist, mankind is engaged in a struggle with nature. Initially, this is a struggle to wrest subsistence from the physical resources which nature provides. But over time the development of factory production and improved machine technology increase man's ability to obtain material wealth from nature and pose the prospect of economic abundance. However, to Marx the social philosopher, there is a simultaneous struggle which pits person against person. Human beings as workers are also a part of nature; they, too, are productive resources. Hence, it is possible for some individuals to improve their material well-being by wresting output from other individuals. Pointing to the slave-based economies of ancient societies and the serfdom of the Middle Ages, Marx argued that this man-versus-man struggle has been a central theme of history. In Marx's time, this class struggle centered upon the wage system of capitalism—a system based upon the private ownership of capital.

☐ Private Property and the Exploitation of Labor

In the man-against-man struggle Marx envisioned two great groups of protagonists— capitalists (the bourgeoisie) and workers (the proletariat). The former, thanks to the capitalistic institution of private property, own the machinery and equipment necessary to production in an industrial society. The propertyless working class is therefore dependent upon the capitalists for employment and for its members' livelihood. Given the worker's inferior bargaining position and the capitalist's pursuit of profits, the capitalist will exploit labor by paying a daily wage which is much less than the value of the worker's daily production. In short, the capitalist can and will pay his workers a subsistence wage and expropriate the remaining fruits of their labor as profits, or what Marx called *surplus value*.

☐ Capital Accumulation and Its Consequences

The dynamics of the capitalistic system put pressures upon the capitalist-entrepreneur. In the early stages of capitalism, there exist severe competitive pressures which force the capitalist to become more efficient, more productive. The capitalist reacts to these pressures by investing the profits he has expropriated from his labor in additional and technologically superior machinery and equipment. The capitalist who fails to accumulate capital faces the prospect of losing out to those rivals who do; the capitalist must accumulate or be accumulated.

This *law of capitalist accumulation* has a number of consequences in the capitalist system. First and expectedly, it is a basic source of the expanding national output which capitalism is potentially able to produce. Marx, it should be noted, expressed great admiration for the productive potential of the capitalistic system. His hostility toward the system was based on the belief that, although labor was the ultimate source of all output, a large portion of this output was denied labor by property-owning capitalists. Second, capital accumulation results in the substitution of capital for labor in the productive process; Marx argued that capital accumulation would cause technological unemployment and give rise to a growing body of unemployed workers, which he termed the *industrial reserve army*. This unemployment would be aggravated by the growing productive capacity of capitalism, coupled with the inadequate purchasing power of the masses of low-wage workers. Finally and paradoxically, Marx held that the capitalist's investment in machinery and equipment, motivated by the desire to preserve his profits, would in fact *lower* his rate of profits. Why so? Because the capitalist's source of surplus value or profits is (the exploitation of) his labor force and not his capital goods. Therefore, as the capitalist substitutes machinery for labor, a growing proportion of his outlays is for non-profitable machinery and a declining proportion for profit-generating labor. Hence, the *rate* of profits must fall.

☐ Increasing Degradation of the Working Class

An inevitable consequence of these developments is the increased immiseration of the working class. Consider the forces bearing upon workers. The institution of private property divorces them from the means of production—machinery and equipment—and allows the capitalist to pay a subsistence wage and expropriate much of their production as profits. The substitution of capital for labor, coupled with the growing divergence between capitalism's capacities to produce and consume, leads to a growing body of unemployed workers. Finally, in an effort to offset falling profit rates, capitalists will increase their exploitation of labor by increasing the intensity of work, lengthening the work day, and bringing more women and children into the labor force.

☐ Monopoly Capitalism and Imperialism

The forces of capitalistic development also impose serious changes upon the capitalist class. In particular, the competition which characterizes the early stages of capitalism will give way to the increased monopolization of industry in its later stages. Bluntly put, the falling rate of profits and the growing gap between production and consumption will force the weaker capitalists out of business. Hence, over time the ownership and control of industry will become increasingly concentrated in the hands of a diminishing number of capitalists. The smaller, financially weaker business owners who have succumbed to the forces of capitalistic development will join the ranks of the working class. The combined impact of increased degradation of the working class and the monopolization of industry yields Marx's famous assertion that under capitalism, the rich get richer (and fewer in number) and the poor get poorer (and increasingly numerous).

These circumstances would give rise to *imperialism,* the final stage of capitalistic development.[3] That is, faced with falling profits, diminishing ability to further exploit the domestic labor force, and increasing difficulty in selling their products domestically because of the inadequate incomes and purchasing power of the masses of workers, monopoly capitalists will inevitably turn their attention to the exploitation of the less developed countries. The underdeveloped areas are typically characterized by abundant and therefore cheap labor and, frequently, cheap raw materials. Furthermore, their primitive state of economic development makes them lucrative targets for capitalist investment or accumulation. These developments allegedly explain the colonization and domination of the world's underdeveloped areas by "imperialistic powers," a process which reached its peak in the period between 1890 and World War II. The important point is that imperialism transforms the class struggle from a domestic to a worldwide conflict.

☐ Revolution and Socialism

But the imperialistic phase merely prolongs capitalism's life span. The ultimate results of the internal contradictions—falling profit rates, difficulties in finding markets for output, and especially the increasing exploitation of labor—inevitably culminate in worker revolution and the overthrow of capitalism. Consider the impassioned prose of Marx's *Capital:*

> Along with the constantly diminishing number of the magnates of capital, who usurp and

[3]Lenin, not Marx, was responsible for the analysis of the imperialistic stage of capitalism.

monopolize all advantages of this process of transformation, grows the mass of misery, oppression, slavery, degradation, exploitation; but with this too grows the revolt of the working-class, a class always increasing in numbers, and disciplined, united, organized by the very mechanism of the process of capitalist production itself. . . . Centralization of the means of production and socialization of labour at last reach a point where they become incompatible with their capitalist integument. This integument bursts asunder. The knell of capitalist private property sounds. The expropriators are expropriated.

Marx envisioned the political state in capitalism as a means through which the capitalist class will sustain its capacity to exploit the working class. The period following the worker revolution would be characterized by a "dictatorship of the proletariat," or working class; its primary task would be to socialize the means of production and thereby to abolish the capitalist class. The specific program for transforming society under proletariat leadership was presented by Marx and his lifelong associate Friedrich Engels (1820–1895) in *The Communist Manifesto*. Specific measures included the nationalization (socialization) of all basic productive resources, including land, factories, the banking system, and the transportation and communication systems. A heavily progressive income tax was advocated and the right of inheritance was to be canceled. Child labor was also to be abolished and free public education provided for all children. But in time the establishment of a classless society would mean the elimination of the primary function of the state—the oppression of one class (labor) by another (capitalist)—and hence the state would "wither away" and some unspecified form of communism would evolve.

Given this terse outline of the economics of the Old Left, let us now consider its modernization by the New Left.

ORTHODOX AND RADICAL ECONOMICS: BASIC DIFFERENCES

In the radical or New Left view, the methodological shortcomings of orthodox economics render it incapable of understanding, and dealing effectively with, the "big problems" of capitalist society. Radicals envision two related methodological deficiencies: First, orthodox economists have a naïve and incorrect conception of the realities—the institutions and operations—of the capitalistic system; second, orthodox economics is too narrow a discipline to permit a clear understanding of real-world problems. Let us consider these two criticisms in the order stated.

☐ Harmony or Conflict?

Consider the comments of a leading Marxist on the first point:[4]

> Orthodox economics takes the existing social system for granted, much as though it were a part of the natural order of things. Within this framework it searches for harmonies of interest among individuals, groups, classes, and nations; it investigates tendencies toward equilibrium; and it assumes that change is gradual and non-disruptive.

But it is contended that capitalist reality is not so placid:

> . . . the world we live in is not one of harmonies of interest, tendencies to equilibrium, and gradual change. . . . Conflicts of interest, disruptive forces, abrupt and often violent change—these are clearly the *dominant* characteristics of capitalism on a world-wide scale today.

[4] Paul M. Sweezy, *Modern Capitalism and Other Essays* (New York: Monthly Review Press, 1972), pp. 53–55. The Last Word segment of Chapter 1 contains a more complete statement of Sweezy's argument.

Orthodox economists, in other words, envision a basic harmony in capitalism which allows the system to realize a satisfactory and workable reconciliation of divergent interests. Where product and resource markets are reasonably competitive, the market system promotes a rough identity of private and social interests through the "invisible hand" (Chapter 5). In other cases, monopoly is countered with monopoly—big business faces big labor—so that market outcomes are usually socially tolerable. Where the market fails—for example, in the cases of unbridled monopoly, spillover costs, and income inequality—a benevolent government will intervene so as to protect and promote the general welfare. Modern capitalism is a pluralistic system wherein power is rather widely dispersed among business, labor, consumers, and government so that consensus decisions are reached which are consistent with the general welfare. Hence, argue mainstream economists, the system's problems and shortcomings can be ameliorated or resolved within its present institutional and ideological framework. Indeed, the system is not only viable, but in most respects works extremely well.

But the radical economists see in modern capitalism the deep class conflicts envisioned by Marx. In particular, in capitalist reality, power lies with the giant, monopolistic corporation—with the capitalist class—which dominates the productive system of industrialized capitalism. Furthermore, rather than functioning as a catalyst in the resolution of conflicts of interest, the public sector is dominated by, and is an instrument of, the large corporations. Rather than promote socioeconomic harmony and further the general welfare, the public sector is essentially a tool by which the capitalists preserve and promote their own selfish interests—both domestically and internationally—to the detriment of the rest of society. Following Marx, the radicals conclude that the system is laden with contradictions and irrationalities and therefore is beyond redemption. The "solution" to capitalism's problems lies in a radical change in the ideology and institutions upon which it is based; in particular, the private ownership of capital goods and reliance upon the market system as a decision-making mechanism must be eliminated in favor of some form of socialism.

□ **Disciplinary Narrowness**

A related criticism centers upon the disciplinary narrowness of economics. The radicals charge that orthodoxy concentrates upon the purely economic aspects of society and turns its back upon the critical interactions among economic, political, sociological, and technological facets of modern society. Orthodox economists, argue the radicals, devote their energies to the technical treatment of highly specialized and esoteric matters which are remote from the real problems of the day. A primary example of this shortcoming is the failure of orthodox economics to recognize the political character of the modern corporation:[5]

> When the modern corporation acquires power over markets, power in the community, power over the state, power over belief, it is a political instrument, different in form and degree but not in kind from the state itself.

The net result is that fundamental questions surrounding the distribution and use of *power* in capitalist society are largely ignored by orthodox economists. This neglect results in a failure to understand the root causes of most of the problems which plague modern capitalism.

THE RADICAL CONCEPTION OF CAPITALISM

Modern radical economists have constructed a model of American capitalism which is essen-

[5]John Kenneth Galbraith, "Power and the Useful Economist," *America Economic Review,* March 1973, p. 6. Galbraith is not considered a radical economist. The Last Word section of Chapter 22 is a capsule statement of his conception of the American economy.

tially an extension and updating of Marxian thought. Let us outline the main features of the radical conception.

□ Corporate or Monopoly Capitalism

The radical view holds that capitalism has reached an advanced stage in the United States wherein huge monopolistic corporations dominate the economy. Small corporations have succumbed through merger or bankruptcy. Proprietorships and partnerships flourish only on the relatively unimportant fringes of the economy. Even agriculture is increasingly dominated by corporate farming. The dynamics of capitalist expansion has resulted in gigantic multiproduct enterprises, frequently of a multinational character. All major industries are now characterized by a high degree of concentration of economic activity among a small number of giant corporations. And, most importantly, the two hundred or so largest industrial, financial, and commercial corporations shape and define the character of our economy and society.[6]

> The reality is we now have an integrated industrial economy dominated by corporate collectives with resources greater than those of most States and many nations. These control technological innovation, administer prices, generate unending consumer wants, while expanding to an international scale. . . . Highly accomplished profit gatherers, they are able to shift risk and social costs to the consumer, the taxpayer and the less powerful.

□ Domination of the State

The evolution of corporate giants might not be such an ominous development if appropriate public surveillance through antitrust or regulation were to yield socially satisfactory (near-competitive) results. The radical view,

however, is that the corporate giants have come to dominate the political state; hence, rather than control corporate power in socially desirable ways, the public sector has become the handmaiden of the corporate giants. Or, at a minimum, a situation of mutual interdependence—a symbiotic relationship—has developed between the corporate giants and government. The success of political parties in realizing and maintaining power depends upon the financial support of wealthy corporations; in turn, government follows policies which are responsive to the needs of the large corporations. The radicals contend that there is substantial evidence of this mutual dependence of big business and government. Consider some of the ways by which government has catered to the corporate giants.

Failure of Social Control   The regulatory commissions which are designed to control natural monopolies are ineffective for the simple reason that they are controlled by the very corporate monopolies they are supposed to regulate! Witness, for example, the assessment of government regulation recently offered by the chairman of the Federal Trade Commission:[7]

> Though most government regulation was enacted under the guise of protecting the consumer from abuse, much of today's regulatory machinery does little more than shelter producers from normal competitive consequences of lassitude and inefficiency. In some cases, the world has changed reducing the original threat of abuse. In other cases, the regulatory machinery has simply become perverted. In still other cases, the machinery was a mistake from the start. In any case, the consumer, for whatever presumed abuse he is being spared, is paying plenty in the form of government-sanctioned price fixing.

> The fact of the matter is that most regulated industries have become federal protectorates,

---

[6]Statement by Robert Engler in *Controls or Competition*, Hearings before the Senate Subcommittee on Antitrust and Monopoly (Washington, 1972), p. 261.

[7]Lewis A. Engman, speech before the 1974 Fall Conference, Financial Analysts Federation, Detroit, Oct. 7, 1974.

living in the cozy world of cost-plus, safely protected from the ugly specters of competition, efficiency and innovation.

Similarly, antitrust legislation is applied half-heartedly, if at all, to large corporations; at best, the flagrant violations of antitrust by giant enterprises result in harmless admonitions or token penalties.

Public Subsidies The radical economists also argue that the public sector uses tax revenues derived from a substantially regressive tax system to subsidize the corporate giants in a variety of ways. For example, the tax-supported educational system provides corporate enterprise with the technical, scientific, and administrative manpower which it needs to operate profitably. Similarly, government finances most of the new scientific and technological developments upon which corporate enterprise depends. Governmentally sponsored construction of streets and highways has amounted to a tremendous subsidy to the automobile industry and all the related industries which feed inputs to it. The radicals emphasize that, in striking contrast, underprivileged minorities are powerless to obtain quality education, decent health care, and, frequently, adequate housing and food from the public treasury.

Provision of Markets Government has also played a primary role, both directly and indirectly, in providing markets for the output of the corporate giants. High levels of military spending—at times in excess of $90 billion per year—have created major markets for many of the large corporations. Similarly, monetary and fiscal policies have tended to eliminate or mitigate recessions, the major source of financial losses for corporate monopolies. Finally, the government has assisted corporations in establishing and expanding their overseas markets through various "imperialistic" measures.

□ **Dynamics of Capitalist Expansion**

Despite the friendly affiliation of monopoly capitalists with the state, capitalist expansion does involve dynamics that pose a serious problem for the corporate capitalists. Competition among capitalists compels each to protect himself against his rivals by producing more goods, accumulating more capital, and realizing more profits. This process, the radicals argue, spawns a variety of evils and irrationalities within the capitalistic system. The problem is this: As Marx foresaw, the accumulation of real capital by the corporate giants increases their productive capacity; therefore, their continued prosperity depends upon ever-expanding markets.[8]

> The pressure created by the necessity to find markets for expanding production constitutes one of the most fundamental characteristics of capitalism. . . . competition induces capitalists to expand sales and production of goods in order to realize profits. Greater output leads to expanded profits and capital accumulation. . . , but in order to realize profits on the newly accumulated capital, even greater sales of output are required.

According to the radicals, the consequences of corporate capitalism and capitalist expansion are manifold and uniformly bad. The domination of society—including the political state—by huge, powerful, profit-seeking corporations creates a variety of "big" problems and inhibits the resolution of others. The problems allegedly spawned or aggravated by corporate capitalism run the gamut from worker exploitation, income inequality, and alienation to militarism and imperialism.

[8] Richard C. Edwards, Michael Reich, and Thomas A. Weisskopf (eds.), *The Capitalist System: A Radical Analysis of American Society* (Englewood Cliffs, N.J.: Prentice-Hall, Inc., 1972), p. 98.

□ Exploitation

Orthodox economics explains the distribution of income largely in terms of marginal productivity. That is, under competitive conditions any resource, say some particular kind of labor, will be employed up to the point at which its wage rate equals its marginal revenue product (Chapters 30 and 31). Putting the matter very simply, this implies that any specific kind of labor is paid in accordance with its contribution to the national output at the margin. The theory can also be applied to land or capital so that all resources are rewarded in accordance with what they have produced or contributed to the national output. Furthermore, it is a situation wherein one class of resources cannot possibly exploit or take advantage of another. Note: Neither radical economists nor most mainstream economists believe the resulting distribution of income is equitable or just. For example, we know from Chapter 37 that, even under pure competition, differences in natural abilities and the random (unequal) distribution of misfortune can result in a highly unequal distribution of wage incomes.

Radical economists stress three basic defects in the marginal productivity theory of income distribution. They point out, first, that this theory rests upon the assumption of competitive markets, while in fact monopoly has replaced competition in both labor and product markets. Corporate capitalists thus have the power to exploit workers in both labor and product markets. In labor markets, the competitive model of Figure 31-3 has given way to the monopsony model of Figure 31-4, and monopsonistic employers—the large corporations—find it profitable to pay workers an amount *less* than their marginal revenue productivity (MRP). Similarly, the markets for most products are dominated by a few large corporations which use their market power to "rig" the market against workers as consumers.

A second point is less obvious. Even if all markets are competitive and labor resources are paid their marginal revenue product, the ability of workers to generate MRP may be constrained arbitrarily by exploitative or discriminatory factors. That is, if the opportunity of individuals to develop their natural abilities through education and training is arbitrarily and unequally distributed *or* if society discriminates among workers on the basis of race or sex, then those workers are exploited in that their "actual" MRP and hence their wage payments will be arbitrarily held below their "potential" MRP.

Third, radical economists challenge the legitimacy of income payments to the owners of real capital. Their reasoning goes thus: To be sure, physical capital is productive; when combined with labor, machinery and equipment obviously enhance total output. *But* the productivity of real capital—created, incidentally, by the past efforts of labor—must be distinguished from the capitalist owner's ability to command profit income from the productive contribution of real capital.[9]

> Radicals admit that a machine may increase production, that workers need them, and that they increase the worker's productivity. . . . But it is the physical capital that is productive (jointly with the worker), *not* the capitalist. The capitalist owns the capital, but he is not himself the machine. The machine does the work (with the worker); the capitalist gets the profit.

Stated somewhat differently, the mere owning of capital is *not* a productive activity and the income derived from capital ownership is unearned and unjustified.

[9]E. K. Hunt and Howard J. Sherman, *Economics: An Introduction to Traditional and Radical Views* (New York: Harper & Row, Publishers, Incorporated, 1972), p. 226.

☐ **Inequality**

The factual characteristics of income inequality in the United States have already been examined (Chapter 37). Recall that the personal distribution of income has *not* changed significantly since 1947 (Table 37-2). The point stressed by radicals is that capitalistic institutions create most of this inequality and cause it to persist. Hence, the following comments on inequality tie in closely with the discussion of exploitation.

Unearned Income and Power First, by providing unearned incomes to capitalist owners, the institution of private property is a basic source of income inequality. Wealth is even more highly concentrated than is income. One authoritative study, for example, concluded that 1.6 percent of the adult population owns 27.6 percent of the nation's total personal wealth, while at the other extreme one-half the adult population owns only 8.3 percent. [10] Radicals hold that weak and easily avoided inheritance taxes allow the economic inequality arising from private property to be perpetuated through time.

In the second place, inequality is created and fostered by the exercise of economic power by one group against other groups. As the comments on exploitation indicate, in corporate capitalism giant firms can use their market power in both labor and product markets to the detriment of noncapitalists as workers and consumers. As a result, monopoly profits accrue and income inequality is reinforced.

Third, political power has sustained economic inequality. Given the domination of the state by the monopoly capitalists, it is no surprise that big business has benefited from a variety of tax loopholes and subsidies, from protection against foreign competition, and from lucrative government contracts. The progressivity of the Federal tax system has

been eroded over time and, when coupled with regressive state and local tax systems, the overall tax structure turns out at best to be proportional. Therefore, the tax system has failed to function as a "great equalizer" of incomes. And the so-called welfare system has been underfinanced and of little benefit to those groups most deeply mired in poverty. Indeed, American capitalism has displayed no propensity to alter significantly the distribution of income which the market provides.

These factors which cause and sustain income inequality, argue the radicals, are cumulative and self-reinforcing. The very high concentration of wealth fattens the bank accounts of those at the top of the income distribution. And it is only these high-income receivers who are able to save in substantial amounts. What do they do with their saving? They invest it in more income-producing assets from which they receive still more income, which they reinvest in still more property resources, and so on. Much the same holds true with respect to economic opportunity. Education—particularly higher education—is traditionally viewed as an income equalizer; college is the ladder by which the children of the poor presumably gain the human capital—the skills and training—to climb out of poverty and into higher income brackets. Not so, say the radicals. The rich have not only more real capital, but also greater access to human capital. Those who go to college are increasingly the youth from higher income groups. The poor and middle-income groups find it increasingly difficult to afford college training, not merely because of the rising out-of-pocket costs associated with higher education, but because the opportunity cost—the income forgone by not entering the labor market—is relatively high. Crudely stated, poor families attach greater relative importance to the income which a son or daughter could earn by *not* attending college. Thus the educational system has become a mechanism for the intergenerational perpetuation of economic inequality. And, finally, the college graduate from the rich family is

[10] Robert J. Lampman, *The Share of Top Wealth-Holders in National Wealth: 1922–1956* (Princeton, N.J.: Princeton University Press, 1962), p. 213.

likely to get a better job than the graduate from the poor family because of his or her "connections." One starts out higher and moves up more rapidly in the business world if Daddy owns the business!

Dual Labor Markets In the past several years the foregoing explanation of capitalist inequality has been supplemented by the concept of *dual* or *segmented labor markets*. In abbreviated form, the radical view is that labor markets are increasingly of two distinct types. The *primary labor market* is characterized by relatively high and rising wage rates, employment stability, good and well-defined opportunities for advancement, and the presence of advanced production techniques and efficient management. The *secondary labor market* embraces the opposite characteristics: Wages are low and stagnant; employment is casual and unstable; available jobs are "dead ends"; relevant technology is archaic; and management is inefficient and exploitative.

The historical reasons for the evolution of these two distinct labor markets are diverse and largely complementary. One view is that dual labor markets are essentially a reflection of the alleged duality found in product markets. That is, the giant corporations which dominate major industries give rise to primary labor markets, whereas the competitive fringes of the economy are conducive to secondary labor markets. Another position is of a more conspiratorial nature: labor-market segmentation is the result of an historical effort by capitalists to retard the evolution of a homogeneous and unified labor force which might threaten and overthrow capitalist dominance of the economy.

A third interpretation is that the characteristics of both primary and secondary labor markets are self-reinforcing and over time cause the two markets to diverge. The features of the primary labor market lead to a benign cycle of progress; those of the secondary labor market spawn a vicious cycle of perpetual stagnation and poverty. That is, the high wages of the primary labor markets put firms under constant pressure to innovate and use technologically advanced capital goods. But such progress calls for more skills, and management invests in the training of its work force. Improved real capital and investment in labor's human capital both increase labor's productivity and lead to further wage increases which cause the cycle to repeat itself. Similarly, the fact that employers have invested in the training of their work force gives them a vested interest in greater employment stability; a firm must keep labor turnover low to realize a return on its investment in human capital. Hence, a self-reinforcing cycle of events occurs which allow those workers fortunate enough to be in the primary labor market to be relatively well off and to share to some extent in the gains of general economic advance. Substantially the opposite occurs in the secondary labor market. At poverty wage rates there is no reason for a firm to be labor-saving or technologically innovative; technology and capitalization languish. Indeed, secondary labor markets are typically highly competitive and, motivation aside, firms are financially unable to invest in real or human capital. Workers therefore tend to be unskilled and relatively unproductive. And high worker turnover is acceptable to the firm; indeed, it may be helpful in discouraging unionization. In fact, a kind of symbiotic relationship evolves wherein worker behavior mirrors the characteristics of the secondary labor market. Employment is unstable, so workers become "unreliable." Because production is technologically backward, workers have no motivation to upgrade their education and skills. The important point is that, while workers in the primary labor market achieve some economic progress, those in the secondary labor market are confined to a vicious cycle of stagnation and poverty. Furthermore, as the two labor markets diverge, it is increasingly difficult for workers to achieve mobility between the markets. The growing skill gap between the two markets, reinforced by discrimination based on race and sex and the geographic segregation of secondary labor markets in urban ghettos, makes upward occupational mobility less and less likely for secondary labor market workers. In the radical view this scenario is meaningful in explaining the persistence of income inequality and poverty through time.

☐ Alienation

Radical economists argue that the institutions and operations of capitalism are a major source of *alienation*. That is, under corporate capitalism, individuals have less and less control over their lives and activities; the masses of people are increasingly remote from the decision-making processes which determine the character and quality of their lives.[11]

> In general, people in capitalist society do not participate in making the basic decisions that affect their lives; instead, these decisions are made through capitalist institutions over which most individuals have little or no control. The actual decisions are likely, if not inevitably, independent of the interests of the persons involved, and the consequences of these decisions will be contrary to their needs.

The causes and forms of alienation are manifold. First, corporate dominance has largely eliminated the possibility of achieving independence and autonomy by going into business for oneself. Second, the sheer size of corporations and their bureaucratic structure put most workers—both blue- and white-collar—in positions where they have little or no decision-making power. Both blue- and white-collar workers have jobs which are segmented and subject to authoritarian direction. Even middle-managers feel that they have no influence upon the organizational decisions which they are obligated to implement. In general, the sheer size of corporations is conducive to jobs which are constrained by inflexible work rules and procedures. Third, radicals

envision a fundamental contradiction between an individual's desire for "self-realization" and creativity, on the one hand, and the progressive division of labor which accompanies technological advance, on the other. Blue-collar workers in particular are confronted with the dehumanization of assembly-line production. In general, in their drive for profits, corporations ride roughshod over the individual's needs and his or her desire for self-fulfillment and meaningful participation. The dynamics of capitalism entails mass-production technology, boring and stultifying jobs, and a highly constraining work environment.

☐ The Irrational Society: Production for Waste

Orthodox economists generally argue that one of the great virtues of capitalism is the capacity of the market system to allocate resources with considerable efficiency. Radical economists, however, cite what they feel is overwhelming evidence that resources are used most irrationally under capitalism. Furthermore, this wasteful production is rooted in the institutions of capitalism and, ironically, in the price system itself.

The radical position is that simple evidence of the eye makes clear that capitalism uses its resources irrationally. The economy produces incredible quantities of automobiles, television sets, cosmetics, and alcoholic beverages while, at the same time, many households are without adequate housing, medical care, or diet. The fact that over $30 billion is squandered each year on advertising is ample evidence that the production of many consumer goods fails to fulfill the true needs of consumers. At a time when the nation spends $90 billion or more per year on military hardware, the maintenance of overseas military bases, and "space circuses," such areas as urban decay, mass transit, and social services are woefully ignored. Furthermore, environmental pollution has been an inevitable by-product of capitalist production.

[11]Edwards, Reich, and Weisskopf, op. cit., p. 255.

Why do these apparent irrationalities—this gross misuse of scarce resources—occur under capitalism? The answer, according to the radical position, lies basically in the dynamics of capitalist expansion abetted by the system's emphasis upon market signals, individual profit incentives, and its highly unequal distribution of income and wealth.

The essence of capitalistic expansion is that the pursuit of profits induces the giant corporations to expand their productive capacities. But this enhanced capacity necessitates ever-expanding markets if this additional productive capacity is to be profitably utilized. "The pursuit of profits and the desire to accumulate lead to more and more production for the sake of production. . . ."[12] The consequences are quite obvious. In the first place, the great emphasis upon industrial growth and materialism in capitalism exacerbates the problem of environmental deterioration. Resources are devoured and waste products are dumped into the environment at an accelerating rate (Chapter 20). The monopoly capitalist's concern is solely with private benefits and costs; spillover or external costs are uniformly ignored. Second, an ever-expanding demand is required if the expanding productive capacity of the monopoly capitalists is to be profitably utilized. Capitalists attempt to assure themselves of an adequate demand for their products both directly and indirectly. Direct efforts center upon want-creating, consumer-manipulating activities. Given the highly unequal distribution of income under capitalism, the poor cannot afford to partake of an expanding output. The rich, in contrast, are already glutted with most goods. Hence, the heavy hand of advertising and the technique of "planned obsolescence" are mustered to induce the consumption of essentially unneeded output. The demand for capitalistic production is supported indirectly by the public sector. Starkly put, government engages in wasteful and unnecessary military spending to absorb the output of the capitalistic system. Furthermore, government engages in imperialistic activities on a global basis to create and sustain overseas markets and to secure cheap sources of inputs. The basic point is that under capitalism, production priorities are determined not on the basis of the real needs of the people, but rather in accordance with what is profitable to the capitalist class. The outcome is the irrational use of resources, on the one hand, and the creation of a "commodity fetish culture" with undue emphasis upon rank materialism, on the other. Capitalism, so to speak, is producing more and enjoying it less.

□ **Imperialism**

Given the dynamics of capitalism, it is inevitable that monopoly capitalism will transcend national boundaries to dominate and exploit the less developed areas of the world. This "internationalization of capitalism" is, of course, imperialism.

Radicals envision orthodox explanations of underdevelopment as hoaxes. In particular, they argue that it is patently incorrect to explain underdevelopment in terms of overpopulation or natural resource deficiencies. High population density and economic growth do *not* correlate significantly and, in fact, the underdeveloped countries are a major source of natural resources. Similarly, the familiar "vicious circle of poverty"—the argument that in poor countries, incomes are so low that there is no economic surplus to invest in capital goods with which to increase productivity and per capita incomes—is rejected by radical economists.[13]

In the radical view . . . the main obstacles to development are *not* natural or biological factors inherent in the underdeveloped countries, and *not* sexual desires and procreation, laziness, low intelligence or lack of natural resources. The obstacles are in the present so-

---

[12] Ibid., p. 363.

[13] Howard Sherman, *Radical Political Economy* (New York: Basic Books, Inc., 1972), pp. 151–152.

cial relationships of man to man: the fact that all the peasants' and workers' surplus over immediate need is extracted from them by the landlords, moneylenders, tax collectors, and foreign corporations.

Furthermore, orthodox theories of underdevelopment provide

> the perfect defense against the suspicion of these peoples that their problems are due to antiquated social systems, rapacious ruling classes and—above all—foreign domination and exploitation.[14]

More specifically, radicals contend that imperialism is the basic obstacle to the development of poor nations. In the first place, capitalist aid supports reactionary ruling classes (landlords, moneylenders, and the government itself) who in turn expropriate the economic surplus of workers and peasant farmers. For what purposes? For luxury consumption, for show-case (nonproductive) construction projects, for investment in advanced nations, and for military goods to repress domestic "liberation" movements.

Secondly, contrary to the Marxian view that imperialism entails a flow of investment from mature capitalist countries to the underdeveloped areas of the world, modern radicals hold that the underdeveloped countries have, in fact, made very substantial contributions to the capital accumulation of the United States and other imperialistic countries. That is, over time the imperialistic countries derive profit incomes from their overseas investments which far exceed the value of these investments, thereby contributing to a growing income gap between the have and have-not nations. Finally, trade between the advanced capitalist nations and the poor countries occurs on terms which are highly favorable to the former; in addition, the pattern of that trade tends to inhibit growth in the underdeveloped countries. That is, the underdeveloped countries are essentially exporters of raw materials and importers of finished goods, a trade pattern which fosters economic dependence rather than industrialization and growth.

It is perhaps in connection with imperialism or neocolonialism that the domination of the state by monopoly capitalists is most apparent.

> On the international front, U.S. trade and especially foreign investments grew enormously throughout the capitalist world during the postwar period and became increasingly important as sources of profits for U.S. corporations. Successive national administrations protected these expanding profitable international activities by the general policy of keeping as much of the world as possible open for trade, investment, and raw materials acquisition by giant corporations. This aim was pursued by economic aid to "friendly" governments (that is, those receptive to U.S. direct investment and trade or those in strategic positions to further the global aims of the U.S.), partly to strengthen them economically, partly to provide supporting overhead capital for U.S. private enterprise, and partly to increase export markets for U.S. corporations. Postwar administrations have also extended military aid to "friendly" governments, for the purposes of fostering the weapons and aircraft output of U.S. corporations and of protecting these client governments from the militant opposition of some of their own people. The U.S. has, moreover, conducted counterinsurgency operations throughout the underdeveloped capitalist world, and when all has failed, it has used military force in pursuit of its basic aim—the maximization of the area of the world that is open for profitable corporate activities.[15]

☐ **Socialist Visions**

What kind of new society do the radicals envision or advocate? The heterogeneity of the radical critique becomes most apparent at this point:

[14] Ibid., p. 152.

[15] John G. Gurley, "The Future of American Capitalism," *Quarterly Review of Economics and Business,* Autumn 1972, pp. 7–8.

. . . every radical in the United States has his own view of exactly what socialism should be like. All agree that there should be no private profit, that it should be decent and human, that it should be based on a genuinely democratic process. But beyond that, there is disagreement on every particular.[16]

A few radical economists are attracted to the Soviet model (Chapter 45), but most are repulsed by its repressive features. Others recommend market socialism, that is, public ownership and the preservation of the price system. A few are content to advocate anarchism; many espouse some new form of economic organization based upon producer cooperatives. Some kind of socioeconomic organization along the lines of China's communes appeals to many radicals. Still others advocate "participatory socialism":[17]

Most fundamentally, socialism means democratic, decentralized and *participatory* control for the individual: it means having a say in the decisions that affect one's life. Such a participatory form of socialism certainly requires equal access for all to material and cultural resources, which in turn requires the abolition of private ownership of capital and the redistribution of wealth. But it also calls for socialist men and women to eliminate alienating, destructive forms of production, consumption, education and social relations. Participatory socialism requires the elimination of bureaucracies and all hierarchical forms and their replacement, not by new state or party bureaucracies, but by a self-governing and self-managing people with directly chosen representatives subject to recall and replacement. Participatory socialism entails a sense of egalitarian cooperation, of solidarity of people with one another; but at the same time it respects individual and group differences and guarantees individual rights. It affords to all individuals the freedom to exercise human rights and civil liberties that are not mere abstractions but have concrete day-to-day meaning.

[16]Hunt and Sherman, op. cit., 564.
[17]Edwards, Reich, and Weisskopf, op. cit., p. 520.

■
THE ORTHODOX REBUTTAL

The radical critique of capitalism is not merely an enumeration of this or that sin, but rather a unified and systematic frontal attack on the whole system. That is, the entire spectrum of socioeconomic problems—exploitation, inequality, alienation, pollution, militarism, imperialism, and so forth—has a common cause. That cause, of course, is the ideology of capitalism; the private ownership of property resources and the functioning of the price system have spawned monopolistic corporations and their ultimate domination of the state and society. Let us briefly consider the response of orthodox economists to the economics of dissent.

□   **Invalid Perceptions**

We have seen that radical economics rejects the orthodox perception of modern capitalism as a pluralistic system characterized by a socially responsive public sector. Similarly, orthodox economists reject the radical model of capitalism as a grossly distorted caricature; the radical view, they argue, is inconsistent with commonsense observation and therefore not realistic and believable.

Consider, for example, the following points. If worker exploitation depends directly upon the degree of monopsony power possessed by a firm, why is it that the large corporations generally pay the highest wages? How can radical economics square the upward drift of labor's share of national income and the virtual constancy of the corporate profit share (Table 32-1) with their contention that monopoly capitalists are exploiting labor? Where do such phenomena as the social security and welfare systems, Medicare, and minimum-wage legislation fit into the conception of government as handmaiden of the monopoly capitalists? Similarly, how does the long-term decline in protective tariffs square with government as a protector and promoter of capitalist profits?

Is the radical notion that militarism is necessary to sustain aggregate demand credible in view of the fact that inflation, not overproduction and unemployment, has been the primary problem of capitalist countries since World War II? How is prosperous, capitalistic Japan, with its minimum military establishment, to be reconciled with the radical notion of militarism as an economic prop? As for imperialism,[18]

> It seems to be a mistake to believe that the business society generally considers foreign-policy confrontations advantageous to the business community. This is certainly suggested by the declines in stock exchange prices that usually accompany international political crisis and the rises that usually follow rumors of peace.

Is the radical notion of imperialism consistent with the fact that

> the great bulk of . . . (our) exports and of our foreign investments involve the developed areas of Europe and Canada, rather than areas where we are fighting wars or supporting dictators and supplying arms.[19]

At a more philosophical level, orthodox economists reject the radicals' deterministic conception of capitalism, that is, the view that the problems and contradictions of modern capitalism are the *inevitable* consequences of the laws of capitalist production. The underlying mode of production, so say the radicals, *necessarily* results in a highly unequal distribution of income, wealth, and power; in worker alienation; in wasteful production; and in imperialism and militarism. Orthodox economists are unwilling to accept this deterministic interpretation of capitalism. Furthermore, even if this deterministic interpretation were

correct, would it not transcend ideological and institutional arrangements and therefore also apply to alternative (socialistic) systems? In fact, it has been argued that there may be more-or-less inevitable consequences of socialistic systems, for example, that the seizure of power by force (socialist revolution) may be conducive to the selection of an "authoritarian and cruel" leadership, and that viable socialistic systems are necessarily highly centralized and bureaucratic.

□ **Nonobjectivity**

Orthodox economists have grave reservations concerning the methodology of radical economics; radicals, they contend, are strongly inclined to substitute rhetoric for reasoning. The claim is that radical economics is doctrinaire, dogmatic, and deficient in scientific objectivity. Put uncharitably, radicals are alleged to employ a "cowboys and Indians mentality" in their interpretation of capitalism. Any and all actions by capitalists or government are envisaged within a conspiratorial framework, for they are the "bad guys." The "good guys"—those who ultimately suffer from the actions of monopoly capitalists and government—are, of course, "the people." The radical method, argue orthodox economists, is to interpret current problems and policies to fit their preconceived conception of capitalist society, rather than to modify or retreat from their conception when the problems and policies in fact do *not* fit. Radicals, it is alleged, display a cavalier disregard for facts—both statistical and anecdotal—and for alternative explanations which are at odds with the neo-Marxist framework.[20] In interpreting problems to dovetail the radical model, great reliance is placed upon simple two-variable analysis to explain issues and situations which are decidedly more complex. For example, to the radical economist the pollution problem is

---

[18] Assar Lindbeck, *The Political Economy of the New Left* (New York: Harper & Row, Publishers, Incorporated, 1971), p. 21.

[19] Charles Perrow (ed.), *The Radical Attack on Business* (New York: Harcourt Brace Jovanovich, Inc., 1972), p. 88.

[20] Radical reply: Transpose "orthodox" and "radical" in the foregoing statements and you have a basic radical criticism of orthodox economics.

clearly the consequence of profit-hungry corporations shifting costs to society, an indirect form of exploitation. Alternative explanations, for example, those centering upon population growth and its geographic concentration, are conveniently ignored. Similarly, we have seen that the radical conceives of the relationships between rich and poor countries entirely within an imperialistic framework, stressing the flow of benefits (capital) from the underdeveloped to the advanced capitalistic nations. The concept of comparative advantage and the consequent possibility that international intercourse could be *mutually* advantageous is carefully excluded from their thinking.

□   Importance of Ideology

Orthodox economists are highly skeptical of the radical assertion that each and every problem present in American capitalism is traceable to the ideological-institutional bases of the system. Other world economies with very different ideological bases seem to suffer from the same kinds of problems. Consider, for example, the question of income inequality. What is there to guarantee that the socialization of any economy will result in greater income equality? Socialization might merely redistribute income from private to public sectors and not from rich to poor. Furthermore, empirical studies show that a substantial portion of income inequality in the United States results from differences in the distribution of *human,* rather than *property* or *real,* capital. Hence, the nationalization of real capital would lessen, but not resolve, the inequality issue. We note, incidentally, that wage income is unequally distributed in the Soviet Union, perhaps as much so as in the United States.

Consider imperialism. Can one seriously argue that imperialism correlates highly with the private ownership of resources and monopoly capitalism?

Preindustrial and precapitalist societies certainly have been characterized by militarism,

aggressive foreign policy, and imperialism— and present day noncapitalist societies are hardly free of a military-industrial complex and an aggressive nationalist foreign policy![21]

Soviet policy toward Estonia, Latvia, and Lithuania, among other countries (and more recently, toward Hungary and Czechoslovakia) make it abundantly clear that monopoly capitalism does not have a monopoly on imperialism.

What about the critical problem of the distribution of *power?* One might concede the existence of casual evidence suggesting that the distribution of power has become increasingly concentrated in the United States. But by what means is the nationalization of property resources going to alleviate the problem?

> We would expect the problem to be accentuated, for then the bulk of economic power over physical assets would be concentrated in the one hand which also happens to exert political and military power: that is, the hand of centrally placed politicians and administrators.[22]

Similarly, there is ample evidence of environmental pollution, alienation, discrimination, not to mention repression, in other systems with widely varying ideological bases and institutions. The point is this: Radical economics offers no convincing evidence that the ideological-institutional changes which it prescribes will provide the will, the resources, and the social technology to remedy the problems and contradictions it envisions in capitalism. Is the ideological-institutional structure of a society really the crucial determinant of its character and the source of its shortcomings? Or are such problems as inequality, imperialism, alienation, pollution, and so on, indigenous to any complex social system?

[21] Lindbeck, op. cit., p. 62.
[22] Ibid., pp. 59–60.

□ **Viable Options**

It is relatively easy to criticize the existing system; it is much more difficult to set forth a viable system which will effectively overcome the fancied and real deficiences of modern capitalism. The essence of rational choice calls for the objective comparison of realistic and attainable alternatives. The radical economists are therefore obliged to state clearly and in detail the nature of the alternative system which they advocate. This they have not done.[23]

> What the New Left lacks . . . is a practical, comprehensive solution. . . . The radicals know what must come down, but not what should be left standing or what should go up. . . . revolutionaries call for destruction first and experimentation afterward. One may be reluctant to sign up for such an uncertain future.

Orthodox economists argue that the radical position is bankrupt insofar as viable alternatives are concerned. Specifically, most radicals reject *both* the market system *and* the bureaucracy of government as means of providing a satisfactory solution to the economic problem. Since the price system and the public bureaucracy are the only two basic alternatives for economic decision making, the rejection of both leaves an operational vacuum. The orthodox economist says, in effect, "reread the earlier statement on the character of participatory socialism and attempt to discern how that system would actually operate." How would the system respond to the everyday questions which are at the core of *any* economy's functioning? How, specifically, would it decide what to produce? How would production be organized? What productive techniques would be selected? How would output be distributed? How would the "What, How, and For Whom" decisions be coordinated? Would resources be fully employed? How

would resources be reallocated over time from uses of declining importance to those of increasing importance? And what incentives would exist for citizens to undertake all the required tasks and decisions? Radical conceptions of idyllic communal societies (wherein the distinction between director and worker is obliterated and "self-fulfillment" is given priority over materialistic objectives) are superficially attractive, but they fail to respond to the hard question: "How do you plan to run the steel industry?"

Radical response: We are not irresponsible, scatterbrained critics. Our movement is relatively new and our energies have been absorbed in uncovering and articulating the shortcomings of the existing system and in developing a critique of orthodox economic analysis. Radicals are just now getting seriously into the formidable task of framing meaningful, workable alternatives which will avoid the evils of both the market system and the bureaucracy. It is not a simple matter to create a viable system based upon equality and egalitarianism, cooperation, and self-realization as opposed to inequality, competition, and alienation. But give us time!

The evidence is quite clear that radical economics has established itself as an alternative, competing explanation of socioeconomic phenomena. And whether one greets the economics of dissent with delight or dismay, there is no doubt that a nodding acquaintance with the radical view contributes a new, skeptical dimension to one's interpretation of the economic, political, and social milieu. Furthermore, whether one finds their answers relevant or reasonable, the radical economists perform a useful service in underscoring some of the perennial problems associated with advanced capitalism. Finally, radical economics is useful in reminding us that economics, narrowly defined, provides only a limited perspective on the real world and that this perspective is not always the most relevant for understanding.

[23]Perrow, op. cit., p. 4.

Summary

1   Radical economics is essentially a modernization and an extension of Marxian economics.

2   Radical economists criticize the method of orthodox economics for accepting the existing ideological-institutional framework, for stressing harmony of interests and conflict resolution, and for maintaining disciplinary narrowness.

3   In the radical view, giant monopolistic corporations dominate capitalistic society, including the political state. The dynamics of capitalist expansion entails the continual pursuit of profits within a context of expanding productive capacity.

4   According to the radical position, capitalist expansion creates or intensifies a variety of problems: for example, the exploitation of labor, income inequality, alienation, irrational or wasteful production, and imperialism.

5   Radical visions of a new society range from anarchy to centralized socialism; "participatory socialism" is a frequently discussed possibility.

6   Orthodox economists criticize the radical position on the grounds that it *a.* embraces an inaccurate interpretation or portrayal of modern capitalism; *b.* lacks scientific objectivity; *c.* overemphasizes ideology and institutions as the source of socioeconomic problems; and *d.* fails to offer viable alternatives to the market system or the public bureaucracy.

Questions and Study Suggestions

1   Key terms and concepts to remember: Marxian economics; radical economics; class struggle; bourgeoisie and proletariat; surplus value; law of capitalist accumulation; industrial reserve army; monopoly capitalism; exploitation; dual labor markets; alienation; imperialism; participatory socialism.

2   Briefly summarize Marxian economics, using the concepts of class struggle, exploitation, and the increasing degradation of the working class in your discussion.

3   How might a radical economist explain or interpret *a.* income inequality, *b.* environmental pollution, *c.* the military budget, *d.* minimum-wage legislation, *e.* the social security system, and *f.* the Employment Act of 1946? How might an orthodox economist interpret the same phenomena?

4   "The activities and policies of the American national state are responsive to the needs and objectives of the capitalist class." Cite both supporting and conflicting evidence.

5   Critically evaluate each statement:

a.   "Human behavior and the ultimate character of any society are determined by its economic ideology and institutions."

b.   "The economic processes in a capitalistic system inevitably generate irreconcilable conflicts between the various groups in society who have contradictory goals and needs."

c.   "Under the banners of free enterprise, democracy, and the protection of underdeveloped countries from communism, the United States has waged imperialistic wars, exploited foreign labor, stripped underdeveloped countries of their material resources, and supported unpopular and undemocratic governments."

d.   "The trouble with the radical position is twofold: First, too many government policies clearly *are* in the public interest, and second, they offer no operationally viable system which will eliminate the alleged evils of capitalism."

6 Explain how radical economists use the concept of dual labor markets to explain income inequality and the persistence of poverty in the United States.

7 In the radical view, what are the specific relationships between exploitation and income inequality? Capitalist expansion and militarism? Capitalist expansion and imperialism? Explain the radical argument that capitalism results in a grossly inefficient allocation of resources.

Selected References

Bronfenbrenner, Martin: "Radical Economics in America: A 1970 Survey," *The Journal of Economic Literature,* September 1970, pp. 747–766.

Edwards, Richard C., Michael Reich, and Thomas E. Weisskopf (eds.): *The Capitalist System: A Radical Analysis of American Society* (Englewood Cliffs, N.J.: Prentice-Hall, Inc., 1972).

Hunt, E. K., and Howard J. Sherman: *Economics: An Introduction to Traditional and Radical Views,* 2d ed. (New York: Harper & Row, Publishers, Incorporated, 1975).

Lindbeck, Assar: *The Political Economy of the New Left* (New York: Harper & Row, Publishers, Incorporated, 1971).

Mermelstein, David (ed.): *Economics: Mainstream Readings and Radical Critiques,* 2d ed. (New York: Random House, Inc., 1973).

Perrow, Charles (ed.): *The Radical Attack on Business* (New York: Harcourt Brace Jovanovich, Inc., 1972).

Sherman, Howard J.: *Radical Political Economy: Capitalism and Socialism from a Marxist-Humanist Perspective* (New York: Basic Books, Inc., 1972).

Sherman, Howard J.: *Stagflation: A Radical Theory of Unemployment and Inflation* (New York: Harper & Row, Publishers, Incorporated, 1976).

Weaver, James H. (ed.): *Modern Political Economy* (Boston: Allyn and Bacon, Inc. 1973).

Last Word

Monopoly Capitalism at Work

This excerpt is an extension of Chapter 7's Last Word. The testimony provides anecdotal evidence to support the radical argument that huge corporations dominate government as a means of exploiting both human and property resources.

[The conditions in West Virginia] result, in large measure, from the domination, economically and politically, of the coal industry which in turn is controlled by a handful of large out-of-State corporations. . . .

West Virginia is comprised of 55 counties containing less than 1,900,000 people. The nine southernmost counties contain approximately 30 percent of the State's total population and produce about 70 percent of the State's coal. Nine corporations own more than 33 percent of these nine counties with real estate holdings worth over $90 million at grossly underassessed values. The top 25 landowners in the nine counties control more than one-half the total land area through their collective ownership of more than 1,600,000 acres of land. Of these nine corporations, only one is a West Virginia corporation doing business principally within the State.

The effects of this corporate giantism have been devastating in many ways. Despite the fact that coal, oil and gas entrepreneurs have prospered almost beyond measure, the land and its inhabitants have not. West Virginia is not a poor State—it is a rich State inhabited by poor people. Employment in the coal industry has dropped from a high of 135,000 to barely 40,000 with automation. Coal production, on the other hand, is soaring. Contrary to the prevailing myth, the company's size is no index of safety. The most recent mine disaster at Farmington, W. Va., took the lives of 78 miners employed by Consolidation Coal Company, the largest producer in the State. Aside from the continuing high rate of injuries, the toll of black lung victims has been dramatically increased by virtue of the continuous miner—a formidable machine developed by the corporate giants.

The magnitude of the wealth of the huge companies which own many areas of West Virginia is matched only by the magnitude of the poverty of the people who live in these same areas. There are counties in West Virginia where one out of every four families is on the welfare program—an inadequate program at that. In the last 20 years, West Virginia has lost 15 percent of its population and the people are still leaving. Our streams are badly polluted from coal wastes and acid mine drainage. Our air is filthy from burning gob piles and slag heaps. Factories and powerplants dump their industrial garbage with little restraint. . . .

Public services such as education, health care, environmental protection and public welfare are in a condition not dissimilar to the land itself—shabby. Through the coal industry's heavy influence in the State legislature, combined with the power of the manufacturers and the utilities, State taxes are kept so regressive and so unproductive that all services which are dependent upon public revenues are doomed to remain inadequate. Until recently the entire coal industry paid less in taxes to the State of West Virginia than the State collected from cigarette smokers. West Virginia coal production at the same time, approximated 150 million tons per year.

Not only is the private government of the giant corporations beyond the reach of the citizenry, but it is beyond the State itself. The total annual budget of the State of West Virginia approximates $500 or $600 million a year. The total annual budget for any one of the giant corporations which compose the private government of West Virginia far exceeds that total. Members of the West Virginia Legislature just last year received a raise from

$1,500 to $3,000 per year. The legislature meets only a few months out of the year. Staff facilities available to them are severely limited; they do not even have an office. On the other hand, lobbyists for the private government of the corporate giants are paid upwards of $25,000 per year and are supported by lawyers, researchers, and experts in abundance.

The West Virginia Public Service Commission which is supposed to control all public utilities and common carriers operating in the State is required by law to be supported financially by the very corporations it is supposed to regulate, and its funding is minimal. Most of the State regulatory agencies are required by law to include corporate representatives on their governing boards, their appeal boards, or their advisory boards.

Until recently, the president of Amherst Coal Company was also chairman of the State air pollution control commission, for example. He is still on the commission. An executive vice president of the Continental Oil-Consolidation Coal setup is a former State tax commissioner. The executive secretary of the West Virginia Coal Association is a former speaker of the West Virginia House of Delegates. His predecessor with the coal association was a former president of the West Virginia Senate. A high official of Continental Oil Company was once director of the West Virginia Department of Natural Resources, our conservation commission. The chairman of the State senate commission on natural resources is in the oil and gas business, as was the immediate past president of the West Virginia Senate. I could go on and on.

In short, however, the State and its people are ill equipped to deal with the corporate giants which have tremendous power over their lives. . . .

From *Controls or Competition,* Hearings before the Subcommittee on Antitrust and Monopoly of the Committee on the Judiciary, U.S. Senate, 92d Congress, 1st Session, Washington, 1972, pp. 143–144. Statement by Paul Kaufman, Director, Appalachian Research and Defense Fund, Inc.

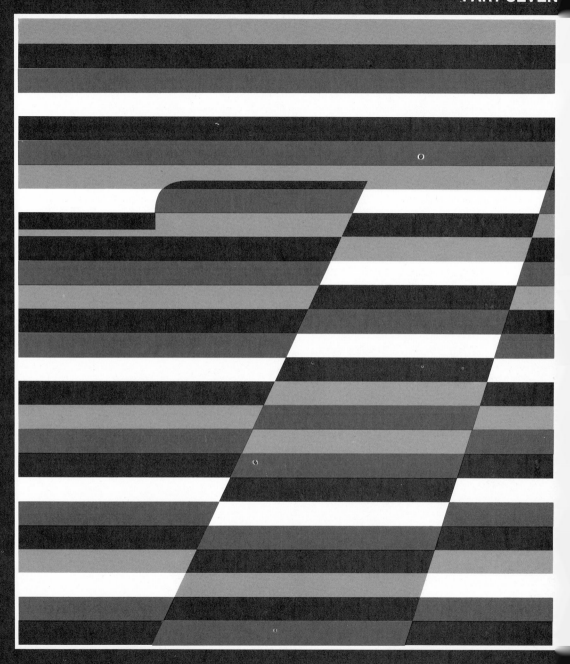

PART SEVEN

INTERNATIONAL ECONOMICS
AND THE WORLD ECONOMY

41

International Trade and Comparative Advantage

Thus far, our analysis of American capitalism has been based upon the assumption that it is an isolated or *closed economy*. This is obviously not true. Ours is an *open economy* in that it is linked to other nations of the world through a complex network of international trade and financial relationships. It is the purpose of this and the following three chapters to describe and analyze these relationships and to assess both the advantages and the problems associated with them.

The goals of the present chapter are modest in number, but of fundamental importance. First, we will look briefly at the volume and unique characteristics of international trade. Next, we want to explain the basis for international trade and to assess its microeconomic impact. Our third objective is to analyze the macroeconomic implications of world trade.

IMPORTANCE OF WORLD TRADE

Is the volume of world trade sufficiently great, or are its characteristics so unique, as to merit special consideration?

□ Quantitative Aspects

Table 41-1 provides us with a rough index of the importance of world trade for a number of representative countries. Many nations which have restricted resource bases and limited domestic markets simply cannot produce

851

Table 41-1 EXPORTS AS A PERCENTAGE OF GROSS NATIONAL PRODUCT, SELECTED COUNTRIES, 1976

Country	Exports	
	Percentage of GNP	Total volume (billions of dollars)
Belgium	46	$ 22.8
The Netherlands	43	34.8
Canada	22	33.5
West Germany	21	90.0
Italy	20	34.8
United Kingdom	19	44.1
France	16	53.0
Japan	12	55.8
United States	7	119.9
Soviet Union	4	33.3

Source: Central Intelligence Agency, *Handbook of Economic Statistics, 1976.*

with reasonable efficiency all the goods they want to consume. For such countries, exports may run from 30 to 35 percent or more of their GNP. Other countries—the United States and the Soviet Union, for example—have rich and highly diversified resource bases and vast internal markets and are therefore less dependent upon world trade.

But even in the case of the United States, where exports and imports are a small proportion of total output, international trade can be extremely important.

1 In this country, 7 percent of the GNP is a very large figure in absolute terms. In 1976, for example, American exports of goods and services totaled about $120 billion, and imports were about $124 billion. Though there are nations which derive a third or more of their national incomes from international trade, *the absolute volume of American imports and exports exceeds that of any other nation.*

2 Despite the versatility of American capitalism, we are almost entirely dependent upon other countries for our supplies of specific commodities. Bananas, cocoa, coffee, spices, tea, raw silk, nickel, tin, natural rubber, and diamonds are cases in point. Casual observation suggests that imported goods compete strongly in many of our domestic markets: Japanese cameras and tape recorders, French and Italian wines, English bicycles, and Japanese motorcycles are a few cases in point. Foreign cars have made persistent gains in American markets and now account for about 20 percent of total sales in the United States. Equally obvious—and potentially ominous—is the growing dependence of the United States upon foreign oil. Ironically, even the great American pastime—baseball—relies heavily upon imported gloves!

But world trade is a two-way street, and a host of American industries are highly dependent upon foreign markets. Almost all segments

Table 41-2 PRINCIPAL COMMODITY EXPORTS AND IMPORTS OF THE UNITED STATES, 1976 (*in millions*)

Exports	Amount	Percentage of total	Imports	Amount	Percentage of total
Machinery	$ 31,289	28	Petroleum and products	$ 31,795	26
Transport equipment	18,221	15	Automobiles and parts	13,104	11
Grains, cereals, etc.	10,911	9	Electrical machinery	7,424	6
Chemicals	9,958	8	Iron and steel products	4,347	4
Soybeans	3,315	3	Coffee	2,632	2
Iron and steel manufactures	1,906	2	Metal ores	2,251	2
			Textiles	1,635	1
All other exports	44,296	37	All other imports	60,728	49
Total	$119,896	100	Total	$123,916	100

Source: U.S. Department of Commerce, *Survey of Current Business,* March 1977, pp. S-22 and 24. Details may not add to totals because of rounding.

of agriculture rely heavily upon foreign markets—rice, wheat, cotton, and tobacco exports vary from one-fourth to more than one-half of total output. The chemical, automobile, machine tool, and computer industries are only a few of many American industries which sell significant portions of their output in international markets. Table 41-2 shows some of the major commodity exports and imports of the United States.

3 Changes in net exports, that is, in the difference between the value of a nation's exports and that of its imports, have multiple effects upon the level of national income in roughly the same fashion as do fluctuations in the various types of domestic spending. A small change in the volume of American imports and exports can have magnified repercussions upon the domestic levels of income, employment, and prices.

With these points in mind, we need not belabor the significance of international trade for such nations as the Netherlands, Japan, Australia, and Great Britain, whose volumes of international trade constitute substantial fractions of their national incomes.

□ **Unique Aspects**

Aside from essentially quantitative considerations, world trade has certain unique characteristics which require us to devote special attention to it.

1 Though the difference is a matter of degree, the mobility of resources is considerably less among nations than it is within nations. American workers, for example, are free to move from Iowa to California or from Maine to Texas. Of course, there are sociological limits on this mobility, but otherwise there are no serious obstacles. If a worker wants to move, he can do so. Crossing international boundaries is a different story. Immigration laws, not to mention language and cultural barriers, put severe restrictions upon the migration of labor between nations. Different tax laws, different governmental regulations, different business practices, and a host of other institutional barriers limit the migration of real capital over international boundaries.

International trade is a substitute for the international mobility of resources. If human and property resources do not move readily among nations, the movement of goods and services can provide an effective substitute.

2 Each nation uses a different currency. This poses complications (Chapter 43). For example, in buying a British automobile you must first buy British pounds sterling (£) and then spend these pounds on the Jaguar or MG of your choice.

3 As we will note shortly, international trade is subject to political interferences and controls which differ markedly in degree and kind from those applying to domestic trade.

THE ECONOMIC BASIS FOR TRADE

But why do nations trade? What is the basis for trade between nations? Stated most generally, international trade is a means by which nations can specialize, increase the productivity of their resources, and thereby realize a larger total output than otherwise. As we saw in Chapter 3, specialization according to comparative advantage results in more output from a given volume of resources than does nonspecialized production. Interpersonal and interregional specialization and trade involve a more efficient use of economic resources. The advantages of specialization transcend international boundaries. Sovereign nations, like individuals and regions of a nation, can gain by specializing in those products which they can produce with greatest relative efficiency and by trading for those goods they cannot produce efficiently.

While the above rationale for world trade is quite correct, it in a sense begs the question. A more sophisticated answer to the question "Why do nations trade?" hinges upon two points. First, the distribution of economic resources—natural, human, and man-made—

among the nations of the world is quite un-even; nations are substantially different in their endowments of economic resources. Second, the efficient production of various goods requires different technologies or combinations of resources.

The character and interaction of these two points can be readily illustrated. Japan, for example, has a large and quite well-educated labor force; skilled labor is abundant and therefore cheap. Hence, Japan can produce efficiently (at low cost) a variety of goods whose production requires much skilled labor: cameras, transistor radios, and tape recorders are some examples of such *labor-intensive* commodities. In contrast, Australia has vast amounts of land in comparison with its human and capital resources and hence can cheaply produce such *land-intensive* commodities as wheat, wool, and meat. Brazil possesses the soil, tropical climate, rainfall, and ample supplies of unskilled labor requisite to the efficient low-cost production of coffee. The United States possesses the iron ore, coal, large amounts of capital equipment, and a labor force of considerable skill and competence requisite to the production of steel. Similarly, the United States and other industrially advanced nations are in a strategic position to produce cheaply a variety of *capital-intensive* goods, for example, automobiles, machinery, and chemicals.

It is important to emphasize that the economic efficiency with which nations can produce various goods can and does change over time. Both the distribution of resources and technology can change so as to alter the relative efficiency with which goods can be produced by various countries. For example, in the last forty to fifty years the Soviet Union has substantially upgraded the quality of its labor force and has greatly expanded its stock of capital. Hence, although Russia was primarily an exporter of agricultural products and raw materials a half-century ago, it now exports large quantities of manufactured goods. Similarly, the new technologies which gave rise to man-made fibers and synthetic rubber drastically altered the resource-mix needed to produce these goods and thereby changed the relative efficiency of nations in manufacturing them. In short, as national economies evolve, the size and quality of their labor forces may change, the volume and composition of their capital stocks may shift, new technologies will develop, and even the quantity and quality of land and natural resources may be altered (Chapter 19). As these changes occur, the relative efficiency with which a nation can produce various goods will also change.

■─────────────────────────

INTERNATIONAL SPECIALIZATION AND COMPARATIVE ADVANTAGE

Let us now recall the concept of comparative advantage from Chapter 3 and employ it in analyzing the basis for international specialization and trade in a more sophisticated manner.[1] We employ a simplified trade model to reveal most clearly the basic principles involved.

□   Two Isolated Nations

Suppose the world economy is composed of just two nations, say, the United States and Brazil. Assume further that each is capable of producing both steel and coffee, but at differing levels of economic efficiency. To be specific, let us suppose that the United States and Brazilian domestic production possibilities curves for coffee and steel are as shown in Figure 41-1*a* and *b*. Two characteristics of these production possibilities curves must be stressed.

1   Constant Costs   We have purposely drawn the "curves" as straight lines, in contrast to the concave-from-the-origin type of production possibilities boundaries introduced

─────────────────────────

[1]The reader might want to review pages 49 to 52 at this point.

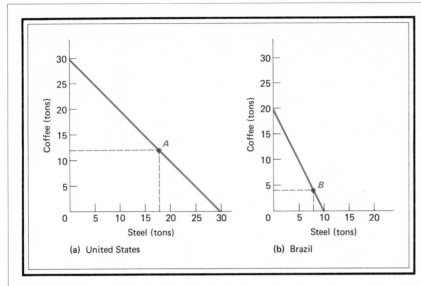

FIGURE 41-1 PRODUCTION POSSIBILITIES FOR THE UNITED STATES AND BRAZIL

The two production possibilities lines show the amounts of coffee and steel the United States **(a)** and Brazil **(b)** can produce domestically. The production possibilities for both countries are straight lines because we are assuming constant costs. The different cost ratios—$1S = 1C$ for the United States and $1S = 2C$ for Brazil—are reflected in the different slopes of the two lines.

(a) United States

(b) Brazil

in Chapter 2. That is, we have in effect replaced the law of increasing costs with the assumption of constant costs. This simplification will greatly facilitate our discussion. With increasing costs, the comparative costs of the two nations in producing coffee and steel would obviously vary with the amounts produced, and comparative advantages might even change. The assumption of constant costs permits us to complete our entire analysis without having to shift to different comparative-cost ratios with every variation in output. The constant-cost assumption will not seriously impair the validity of our analysis and conclusions. We shall note later in our discussion the effect of the more realistic assumption of increasing costs.

2   Different Costs   The production possibilities lines of the United States and Brazil are obviously different, reflecting different resource-mixes and differing levels of technological progress. More specifically, the opportunity costs of producing steel and coffee differ between the two nations. We note in Figure 41-1a that under full-employment condi-

tions, the United States can increase its output of steel 1 ton by forgoing 1 ton of coffee output. That is to say, in the United States the domestic exchange ratio or *cost ratio* for the two products is 1 ton of steel for 1 ton of coffee, or simply $1S = 1C$. The United States, in effect, can "exchange" a ton of steel for a ton of coffee domestically by shifting resources from steel to coffee. Our constant-cost assumption means that this exchange or cost ratio prevails for all possible shifts on the United States' production possibilities curve. Brazil's production possibilities line in Figure 41-1b reveals a different exchange or cost ratio. In Brazil the domestic cost ratio for the two goods is 1 ton of steel for 2 tons of coffee, or $1S = 2C$.

If the United States and Brazil are isolated and therefore self-sufficient, each must choose some output-mix on its production possibilities line. Let us assume that point A in Figure 41-1a is regarded as the optimum output-mix in the United States. The choice of this combination of 18 tons of steel and 12 tons of coffee is presumably rendered through the price system, as described in Chapters 5 and 33. Suppose Brazil's optimum product-mix is 8

Table 41-3 INTERNATIONAL SPECIALIZATION ACCORDING TO COMPARATIVE ADVANTAGE AND THE GAINS FROM TRADE (*hypothetical data; in tons*)

Country	Outputs before special- ization	Outputs after special- ization	Amounts exported ($-$) and imported ($+$)	Outputs available after trade	Gains from special- ization and trade
United States	18 steel	30 steel	-10 steel	20 steel	2 steel
	12 coffee	0 coffee	$+15$ coffee	15 coffee	3 coffee
Brazil	8 steel	0 steel	$+10$ steel	10 steel	2 steel
	4 coffee	20 coffee	-15 coffee	5 coffee	1 coffee

tons of steel and 4 tons of coffee, as indicated by point *B* in Figure 41-1*b*. These choices are also reflected in column 1 of Table 41-3.

□ **Specialization According to Comparative Advantage**

Given these different cost ratios, is there any rule or guideline which will tell us the products in which the United States and Brazil should specialize? Yes, there is: The *principle of comparative advantage* says that total output will be greatest when each good is produced by that nation which has the lower opportunity cost. For our illustration, the United States' opportunity cost is lower for steel, that is, the United States need only forgo 1 ton of coffee to produce 1 ton of steel, whereas Brazil must forgo 2 tons of coffee for 1 ton of steel. *The United States, therefore, has a comparative (cost) advantage in steel, and it should specialize in steel production.* The "world" (the United States and Brazil) obviously is *not* economizing in the use of its resources if a given product (steel) is produced by a high-cost producer (Brazil) when it could have been produced by a low-cost producer (the United States). To have Brazil produce steel would mean that the world economy would have to give up more coffee than is necessary to obtain a ton of steel.

Conversely, Brazil's opportunity cost is lower for coffee, that is, Brazil must sacrifice only $\frac{1}{2}$ ton of steel in producing 1 ton of coffee,

whereas the United States must forgo 1 ton of steel in producing a ton of coffee. *Brazil has a comparative advantage in coffee, and therefore it should specialize in coffee production.* Again, the world would *not* be employing its resources economically if coffee were produced by a high-cost producer (the United States) rather than a low-cost producer (Brazil). If the United States produced coffee, the world would be giving up more steel than would be necessary to obtain each ton of coffee. *Economizing—using given quantities of scarce resources so as to obtain the greatest total output—requires that any particular good be produced by that nation which has the lower opportunity cost, that is, which has the comparative advantage.* In our illustration, the United States should produce steel and Brazil should produce coffee.

By looking at column 2 of Table 41-3, we can quickly verify that specialized production in accordance with the principle of comparative advantage does, indeed, allow the world to get more output from given amounts of resources. By specializing completely in steel, the United States can produce 30 tons of steel and no coffee. Similarly, by specializing completely in coffee, Brazil produces 20 tons of coffee and no steel. We note that the world has more steel—30 tons as compared with 26 ($= 18 + 8$) tons—*and* more coffee—20 tons as compared with 16 ($= 12 + 4$) tons—than in the case of self-sufficiency or unspecialized production.

Terms of Trade

But the consumers of each nation will want *both* steel and coffee. Specialization implies the need to trade or exchange the two products. What will be the *terms of trade?* That is, at what exchange ratio will the United States and Brazil trade steel and coffee? We know that because $1S = 1C$ in the United States, the United States must get *more than* 1 ton of coffee for each ton of steel exported or it will not pay the United States to export steel in exchange for Brazilian coffee. That is, the United States must get a better price (more coffee) for its steel in the world market than it can get domestically, or else trade will not be advantageous. Similarly, because $1S = 2C$ in Brazil, we know that Brazil must be able to get 1 ton of steel by exporting some amount *less than* 2 tons of coffee. Brazil must be able to pay a lower price for steel in the world market than it must pay domestically, or it will not wish to engage in international trade. Thus we can be certain that the international exchange ratio or *terms of trade* must lie somewhere between

$$1S = 1C$$

and

$$1S = 2C$$

But where will the actual world exchange ratio fall between the $1S = 1C$ limit (established by cost conditions in the United States) and the $1S = 2C$ limit (determined by cost conditions in Brazil)? This question is very important, because the exchange ratio determines how the gains from international specialization and trade are divided among the two nations. Obviously, the United States will prefer a rate close to $1S = 2C$, say, $1S = 1\frac{3}{4}C$. Americans want to get a great deal of coffee for each ton of steel they export. Similarly, Brazil desires a rate approximating $1S = 1C$, say, $1S = 1\frac{1}{4}C$. Brazil wants to export as little coffee as possible for each ton of steel it receives in exchange.

The actual exchange ratio that will materialize between the two limits depends upon world supply and demand conditions for the two products. If the overall world demand for coffee is weak relative to its supply and the demand for steel is strong relative to its supply, the price of coffee will be low and that of steel high. The exchange ratio will settle near the $1S = 2C$ figure preferred by the United States. Under the opposite world supply and demand conditions, the ratio will settle near the $1S = 1C$ level most favorable to Brazil.

The Gains from Trade

Let us arbitrarily suppose that the international exchange ratio or terms of trade are actually $1S = 1\frac{1}{2}C$. The possibility of trading on these terms permits each nation to supplement its domestic production possibilities line with a *trading possibilities line*. This can be seen in Figure 41-2a and b. Just as a production possibilities line shows the options that a full-employment economy has in obtaining one product by shifting resources from the production of another, so a trading possibilities line shows the options that a nation has by specializing in one product and trading (exporting) its speciality to obtain the other product. The trading possibilities lines in Figure 41-2 are drawn on the assumption that both nations specialize in accordance with comparative advantage and therefore that the United States specializes completely in steel (point S in Figure 41-2a) and Brazil completely in coffee (point c in Figure 41-2b). Now, instead of being constrained by its domestic production possibilities line and having to give up 1 ton of steel for every ton of coffee it wants as it moves up its domestic production possibilities line from point S, the United States, through trade with Brazil, can get $1\frac{1}{2}$ tons of coffee for every ton of steel it exports to Brazil as it moves up the trading line SC'. Similarly, we can think of Brazil as starting at point c, and instead of having to move down its domestic production

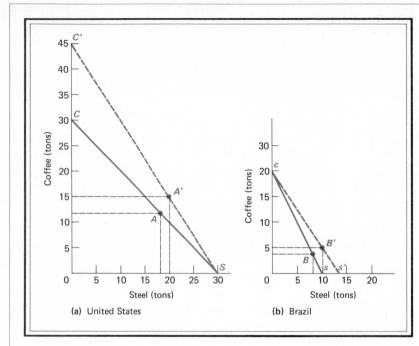

FIGURE 41-2 TRADING POSSIBILITIES LINES AND THE GAINS FROM TRADE

As a result of international specialization and trade, the United States and Brazil can both realize levels of output superior to those attainable on their domestic production possibilities curves. For example, the United States in (a) can move from point A on its domestic production possibilities line to point A' on its trading possibilities line; similarly, Brazil in (b) can move from B to B'.

possibilities line and thereby having to give up 2 tons of coffee for each ton of steel it wants, it can now export just 1½ tons of coffee for each ton of steel it wants by moving down its *cs'* trading possibilities line. Specialization and trade give rise to a new exchange ratio between steel and coffee which is reflected in a nation's trading possibilities line. This new exchange ratio is superior to the self-sufficiency exchange ratio embodied in the nation's production possibilities line. By specializing in steel and trading for Brazil's coffee, the United States can obtain *more than* 1 ton of coffee for 1 ton of steel. Similarly, by specializing in coffee and trading for the United States' steel, Brazil can get 1 ton of steel for *less than* 2 tons of coffee.

The crucial fact to note is that by specializing according to comparative advantage and trading for those goods produced with the least relative efficiency domestically, both the United States and Brazil can realize combinations of steel and coffee which lie beyond their

production possibilities boundaries. *Specialization according to comparative advantage results in a more efficient allocation of world resources, and larger outputs of both steel and coffee are therefore available to the United States and Brazil.* To be more specific, suppose that at the $1S = 1\frac{1}{2}C$ terms of trade, the United States exports 10 tons of steel to Brazil and Brazil in return exports 15 tons of coffee to the United States. How do the new quantities of steel and coffee available to the two nations compare with the optimum product-mixes that existed before specialization and trade? Point A in Figure 41-2a reminds us that the United States chose 18 tons of steel and 12 tons of coffee originally. Now, by producing 30 tons of steel and no coffee, and by trading 10 tons of steel for 15 tons of coffee, the United States can enjoy 20 tons of steel and 15 tons of coffee. This new, superior combination of steel and coffee is shown by point A' in Figure 41-2a. Compared with the nontrading figures of

18 tons of steel and 12 tons of coffee, the United States' gains from trade are 2 tons of steel and 3 tons of coffee. Similarly, we assumed Brazil's optimum product-mix was 4 tons of coffee and 8 tons of steel (point *B*) before specialization and trade. Now, by specializing in coffee and thereby producing 20 tons of coffee and no steel, Brazil can realize a combination of 5 tons of coffee and 10 tons of steel by exporting 15 tons of its coffee in exchange for 10 tons of American steel. This new position is shown by point *B'* in Figure 41-2*b*. Brazil's gains from trade are 1 ton of coffee and 2 tons of steel. *As a result of specialization and trade, both countries have more of both products.* Table 41-3 is a summary statement of all these figures and merits careful study by the reader.

The fact that points *A'* and *B'* are positions superior to *A* and *B* is extremely important. You will recall from Chapters 2 and 19 that the only ways a given nation can penetrate its production possibilities boundary are (1) to expand the quantity and improve the quality of its resources or (2) to realize technological progress. We have now discovered a third means—international trade—by which a nation can circumvent the output constraint imposed by its production possibilities curve. The effects of international specialization and trade are tantamount to having more and better resources or discovering improved production techniques.

□   **Increasing Costs**

In formulating a straightforward statement of the principles underlying international trade, we have invoked a number of simplifying assumptions. Our discussion was purposely limited to two products and two nations in order to minimize verbiage; multination and multiproduct examples yield similar conclusions. The assumption of constant costs, on the other hand, is a more substantive simplification. Let us therefore pause to consider the significance of increasing costs (concave-from-the-origin production possibility curves) for our analysis.

Suppose, as in our previous constant-cost illustration, that the United States and Brazil are at positions on their production possibilities curves where their cost ratios are initially $1S = 1C$ and $1S = 2C$ respectively. As before, comparative advantage indicates that the United States should specialize in steel and Brazil in coffee. But now, as the United States begins to expand its steel production, its $1S = 1C$ cost ratio will *rise;* that is, it will have to sacrifice *more than* 1 ton of coffee to get 1 additional ton of steel. Resources are no longer perfectly shiftable between alternative uses, as the constant-cost assumption implied. Resources less and less suitable to steel production must be allocated to the American steel industry in expanding steel output, and this means increasing costs—that is, the sacrifice of larger and larger amounts of coffee for each additional ton of steel. Similarly, Brazil, starting from its $1S = 2C$ cost ratio position, expands coffee production. But as it does, it will find that its $1S = 2C$ cost ratio begins to *fall.* Sacrificing a ton of steel will free resources which are only capable of producing something less than 2 tons of coffee, because these transferred resources are less suitable to coffee production.

Hence, as the American cost ratio rises from $1S = 1C$ and Brazil's falls from $1S = 2C$, a point may be reached at which the cost ratios are equal in the two nations, for example, at $1S = 1\frac{1}{2}C$. At this point the underlying basis for further specialization and trade—differing cost ratios—has obviously disappeared, and further specialization is uneconomic. And most important, this point of equal cost ratios may be realized where the United States is still producing *some* coffee along with its steel and Brazil is producing *some* steel along with its coffee. *The primary effect of increasing costs is to make specialization less than complete.*

MICROECONOMIC EFFECTS OF WORLD TRADE

What are the major economic effects of international specialization and trade?

☐ Resource Allocation and Output

We are familiar with the impact of specialization and trade upon resource allocation and output. International specialization causes each country to shift resources away from that product in which it has a comparative disadvantage and toward that product in which it has a comparative advantage. In our example, the United States shifts resources from coffee to steel and Brazil reallocates its resources from steel to coffee. Under the assumption of constant costs, specialization—and hence the reallocation of resources—would be complete. But, as we have just seen, under the more realistic assumption of increasing costs, the reallocation of resources is partial and specialization less than complete. These reallocations of resources in accordance with comparative advantage give rise to the production of a larger world output from fixed amounts of resources. Once again, specialization and trade between nations on the basis of comparative advantage entail the more efficient use of world resources.

☐ Product Prices

International specialization and trade bring about the redirection of demand so that product prices in the trading countries move toward equality. Recall that prior to trade, steel was relatively cheap in the United States; it would take only 1 ton of coffee to get a ton of steel in the United States. Conversely, steel was relatively expensive in Brazil; it would take 2 tons of coffee to obtain a ton of steel in Brazil. With specialization and trade, Brazilians redirected their demand for steel

from their domestic steel to American steel. The consequence was that the total demand (domestic plus foreign) for American steel rose, pulling up the price of American steel. Or, looking at the matter from the other vantage point, as American exports of steel augmented domestic supplies in Brazil, the price of steel in Brazil fell. Take your choice: either approach implies an equalization of the price of steel in the two countries as the result of trade. That is, a single world market and therefore a single world price for steel will result.[2] Recall that, in real terms, the price of 1 ton of steel before trade was 1 ton of coffee in the United States and 2 tons of coffee in Brazil. With trade, the price of a ton of steel became $1\frac{1}{2}$ tons of coffee in both countries.

The same rationale applies to coffee. Before trade, coffee was relatively expensive in the United States; 1 ton of steel had to be forgone to obtain a ton of coffee. Conversely, coffee was relatively cheap in Brazil where only $\frac{1}{2}$ ton of steel had to be sacrificed to obtain a ton of coffee. With specialization and trade, the demand for Brazilian coffee was augmented by a redirected American demand, and the price of coffee in Brazil therefore went up. Or we can think of Brazilian coffee flowing into the United States, increasing our domestic supply and therefore lowering the price in America. In either event, the price of coffee will tend to be equal in the two countries as the result of trade. In our example, after specialization and trade the world price of coffee became $\frac{2}{3}$ ton of steel for both countries.

☐ Resource Prices

Specialization and trade will also *tend* to equalize resource prices in the two countries. Capital is presumably relatively abundant and land relatively scarce in the United States. Conversely, in Brazil land is apparently rela-

[2] We are simplifying here in that we ignore transportation costs, tariffs, and market imperfections.

tively abundant and capital relatively scarce. It is these differences in resource endowments which give rise to the different domestic production costs and give the United States a comparative advantage in steel (a capital-intensive good) and Brazil a comparative advantage in coffee (a land-intensive good). These differences in resource availability will be mirrored in resource prices: the price of capital is relatively low in the United States, while the price of land is relatively high. The opposite is true in Brazil: the price of capital is relatively high and that of land relatively low.

International trade obviously permits both the United States and Brazil to specialize in that good whose production demands the relatively abundant resource. That is, trade allows the United States to increase its output of steel, a capital-intensive good. Brazil produces more coffee, a land-intensive good. The stimulus for this redirection of production is a redirection of demand. Through trade, the United States' domestic demand for steel is now supplemented by the foreign (Brazilian) demand for American steel. This increased demand for American steel is reflected in the resource market as an increase in the demand for capital. Hence, the price of capital in the United States rises. Conversely, as a result of opening up trade with Brazil, American demand for coffee is redirected from domestic to Brazilian coffee. In the American resource market, this is reflected in a decline in the demand for land, and the price of land therefore falls.

The opposite tendencies are at work in Brazil. Through trade, Brazil's domestic demand for coffee is now supplemented by foreign (American) demand. In the Brazilian resource market, the demand for land will increase and its price will rise. Trade also causes Brazil's domestic demand for steel to be redirected toward American steel; hence the demand for and price of capital will tend to fall in Brazil.

Note carefully what is happening here: In both countries the prices of abundant, relatively cheap resources (capital in the United States and land in Brazil) tend to rise while the prices of the scarce, relatively expensive resources (land in the United States and capital in Brazil) tend to fall. In short, international trade shifts demand from the scarce toward the abundant resource in both countries, *tending* to equalize resource prices in the two countries.

□   **Other Considerations**

Two final points merit emphasis. First, we noted earlier that international trade is a substitute for the international mobility of resources. The meaning of this assertion should now be evident. If capital resources, for example, could move freely between the United States and Brazil, capital would actually flow from the United States (where its price is initially low) to Brazil (where its price is initially high), and this would obviously increase the price of capital in the United States and lower it in Brazil. This would continue until the price of capital was equal in the two countries. While capital has not moved between the two countries, free trade has brought about similar changes in capital prices. The redirecting of Brazil's steel demand from its domestic producers to the United States has increased the price of capital in the United States and simultaneously reduced the price of capital in Brazil. In this sense, trade is a substitute for resource mobility.

Second, our discussion of the impact of trade upon commodity and resource prices rests on a number of simplifying assumptions. We have assumed (as noted) that there are no transportation costs or barriers to trade—for example, tariffs and quotas. Further, both economies are presumably at full employment, and domestic product and resource markets are highly competitive. To the extent that these conditions are not realized, the weaker will be the tendency for product and resource prices to move toward equality.

MACROECONOMIC EFFECTS OF WORLD TRADE

Not only does world trade affect the allocation of resources and the structure of product and resource prices, but it can also alter aggregate demand and thereby the levels of output, income, and employment. If world trade increases a nation's aggregate demand, then domestic income, output, and employment will rise. If trade diminishes aggregate demand, then income, output, and employment will fall.

□   **Net Exports and Aggregate Demand**

First, consider exports. Recall from Chapter 9 that—like consumption, investment, and government purchases—exports (X) give rise to domestic production, income, and employment. Even though the goods and services produced in response to such spending flow abroad, foreign spending on American goods increases production and creates jobs and incomes in the United States. Exports must therefore be added as a new component of aggregate demand. Conversely, imports of the United States—spending by Americans on foreign goods—will clearly induce production and create jobs and incomes abroad rather than domestically. Hence, in measuring aggregate demand for domestic goods, we must subtract expenditures for imports. Stated differently, imports—like the leakages of saving and taxes—represent a use for income other than spending on domestic goods and services. In short, for a nontrading or closed economy, aggregate demand is $C + I_n + G$. But for a trading or open economy, aggregate demand is $C + I_n + G + (X - M)$. Or, recalling from Chapter 9 that net exports (X_n) equals $(X - M)$, we can say that aggregate demand for an open economy is $C + I_n + G + X_n$.

Now we must ask: What determines the volume of a nation's exports and imports?

What determines whether the net export figure added to aggregate demand is positive or negative? The answers are complex. The basic consideration, we know, is comparative costs and the terms of trade. And we will find in Chapter 42 that trade barriers can be significant. But given these considerations, the volume of American exports will depend primarily and directly upon the levels of incomes in foreign nations. That is, if such major trading partners as Japan, Britain, and West Germany are prosperous, they will purchase much from us and American exports will be relatively large. But if these economies are depressed, their purchases from the United States—American exports—will be relatively small. Note that American exports are independent of the level of *domestic* national income. On the other hand, it is reasonable to assume that any nation's imports will vary directly with domestic income in the same general fashion as does domestic consumption. That is, as our domestic net national product (NNP) rises, we can expect households to buy not only Fords and more Schlitz, but also more Ferraris and more Scotch.

□   **Exports, Imports, and NNP**

Let us now add exports and imports to our discussion of income determination as presented in Part 2. Columns 1 and 2 of Table 41-4 merely repeat columns 2 and 9 from Table 13-1, where the equilibrium NNP for a closed economy was $490 billion. In column 3, we have added exports of $30 billion, which are dependent upon the incomes of foreign countries and therefore independent of domestic NNP. Imports are added in column 4; it is assumed that imports increase by $2 billion for every $20 billion increase in domestic national income. Column 5 combines exports and imports to show net exports. In column 6, we have adjusted the domestic aggregate demand of column 2 for net exports, giving us aggregate demand for an open economy.

Table 41-4 DETERMINATION OF THE EQUILIBRIUM LEVELS OF OUTPUT AND INCOME: PRIVATE, PUBLIC, AND FOREIGN SECTORS (*hypothetical data*)

(1) Possible levels of aggregate supply (NNP = NI = PI), billions	(2) Aggregate demand for closed economy $(C + I_n + G)$, billions	(3) Exports, billions	(4) Imports, billions	(5) Net exports, billions (3) − (4)	(6) Aggregate demand for open economy $(C + I_n + G + X_n)$, billions (2) + (5)
$370	$400	$30	$18	$12	$412
390	415	30	20	10	425
410	430	30	22	8	438
430	445	30	24	6	451
450	460	30	26	4	464
470	475	30	28	2	477
490	490	30	30	0	490
510	505	30	32	−2	503
530	520	30	34	−4	516

The particular export and import figures we have selected are such that foreign trade leaves the equilibrium NNP unchanged. That is, net exports are zero at the closed economy's equilibrium NNP of $490 billion, so aggregate demand for the open economy (column 6) equals aggregate supply (column 1) at $490 billion. Figure 41-3 portrays these results graphically. The $C + I_n + G$ schedule is aggregate demand for the closed economy, plotted from column 2 of Table 41-4. The $(C + I_n + G + X_n)_0$ schedule is aggregate demand for the open economy and reflects the figures of column 6. Observe that aggregate demand for the open economy intersects aggregate supply at the same point as does aggregate demand for the closed economy and therefore the $490 billion equilibrium NNP is unaltered in this case by world trade.

But there is no reason why net exports will have a neutral effect on equilibrium NNP. For example, by *either* reducing exports by $7 billion (from $30 to $23 billion) *or* increasing imports by $7 billion at each level of NNP, we would find that net exports would be *minus* $7 billion at the $490 billion NNP. Recalculating aggregate demand in column 6 of Table 41-4, we see that the resulting new equilibrium NNP

will be $470 billion. Graphically, the new open-economy aggregate demand schedule is shown by $(C + I_n + G + X_n)_1$ in Figure 41-3. This schedule lies $7 billion below $(C + I_n + G + X_n)_0$, reflecting the assumed $7 billion decline in net exports. Hence, at the original $490 billion equilibrium NNP, a contractionary gap of $7 billion exists which causes the equilibrium NNP to decline to $470 billion.

Conversely, by *either* increasing exports by $7 billion (from $30 to $37 billion) *or* decreasing imports by $7 billion at each NNP level, one discovers that net exports are now *plus* $7 billion at the original $490 billion NNP. Again, the recalculation of aggregate demand in column 6 of Table 41-4 reveals that the equilibrium NNP will shift from $490 to $510 billion. In Figure 41-3 the new open economy aggregate demand line is $(C + I_n + G + X_n)_2$, which lies $7 billion above $(C + I_n + G + X_n)_0$ because of the assumed $7 billion increase in net exports. This creates a $7 billion gap at the original $490 equilibrium NNP, and, as a result, the equilibrium NNP increases to $510 billion. As shown in Figure 12-5, this increase may be in terms of money NNP or real NNP, depending upon

FIGURE 41-3 NET EXPORTS AND THE EQUILIBRIUM NNP

An increase in net exports raises the aggregate demand schedule as from $(C + I_n + G + X_n)_0$ to $(C + I_n + G + X_n)_2$ and increases the equilibrium NNP. Conversely, a decrease in net exports shifts the aggregate demand schedule downward as from $(C + I_n + G + X_n)_0$ to $(C + I_n + G + X_n)_1$ and lowers the equilibrium NNP. Note also that net exports reduce the slope of the aggregate demand schedule which implies a smaller multiplier.

whether the economy is currently at full employment.

The generalizations which can be distilled from these examples are quite obvious. A decline in net exports—that is, a decrease in exports or an increase in imports—decreases aggregate demand and has a contractionary effect on domestic NNP. Conversely, an increase in net exports—the result of either an increase in exports or a decrease in imports—increases aggregate demand and has an expansionary effect on domestic NNP.

□ **Open-economy Multiplier**

A final and rather technical point: You undoubtedly noted in Figure 41-3 that the slope of the aggregate demand schedule is reduced by the introduction of international trade. This diminished slope correctly implies a smaller multiplier. Specifically, in the above illustrations we noted that a $7 billion change in net exports would cause a $20 billion change in equilibrium NNP, indicating a multiplier of $2\frac{6}{7}$ ($= \$20/\$7$). Why does this new *open-economy multiplier* differ from the multiplier of 4 associated with the closed economy of Table 13-1 and columns 1 and 2 of Table 41-4?

Recall that for the closed economy the multiplier is 1/MPS or, for our data, 1/.25, or 4. In other words, the multiplier is the reciprocal of the MPS, where we define the MPS as the fraction of any change in national income which "leaks" into saving. Now in moving to an open economy, we add a second leakage in the form of expenditures on imports. That is, saving and imports are similar in that both are ways of disposing of income other than spending it on *domestically* produced goods. Defining the *marginal propensity to import* (MPM) as the fraction of any change in national income which is spent on imports, we can add the

MPM to the MPS in the denominator of the multiplier formula so that the multiplier becomes $\dfrac{1}{\text{MPS} + \text{MPM}}$ for an open economy. For the data of Table 41-4 the MPM is $\frac{2}{20}$, or .10. Hence,

$$\frac{1}{\text{MPS} + \text{MPM}} = \frac{1}{.25 + .10} = 1/.35 = 2\frac{6}{7}$$

To repeat: Because it entails another leakage from the domestic income-expenditures stream, international trade tends to reduce the size of the multiplier.

Summary

1 International trade is important, quantitatively and otherwise, to most nations. World trade is vital to the United States in several respects. *a.* The absolute volumes of American imports and exports exceed those of any other single nation. *b.* The United States is completely dependent upon trade for certain commodities and materials which cannot be obtained domestically. *c.* Changes in the volume of net exports can have magnified effects upon the domestic levels of output and income.

2 International and domestic trade differ in that *a.* resources are less mobile internationally than domestically; *b.* each nation uses a different currency; and *c.* international trade is subject to more political controls.

3 World trade is ultimately based upon two considerations: the uneven distribution of economic resources among nations, and the fact that the efficient production of various goods requires particular techniques or combinations of resources.

4 Mutually advantageous specialization and trade are possible between any two nations so long as the cost ratios for any two products differ. By specializing according to comparative advantage, nations can realize larger real incomes with fixed amounts of resources. The terms of trade determine how this increase in world output is shared by the trading nations. Increasing costs impose limits upon the gains from specialization and trade.

5 In addition to reallocating resources toward those products in which a nation has a comparative advantage, international specialization creates tendencies for both product and resource prices in trading countries to move toward equality.

6 An increase in a country's exports or a decrease in its imports will have an expansionary effect upon its NNP. Conversely, a decline in exports or an increase in imports will have a contractionary impact on NNP.

7 Because imports are a leakage, the multiplier for an open economy is equal to the reciprocal of the sum of the marginal propensities to save and import.

Questions and Study Suggestions

1 Key terms and concepts to remember: open economy, labor- (land-, capital-) intensive commodity; cost ratio; comparative advantage; terms of trade; gains from trade; trading possibilities line; net exports; marginal propensity to import; open-economy multiplier.

2 In what ways are domestic and foreign trade similar? In what ways do they differ?

3 Answer question 8 at the end of Chapter 3.

4 Assume that by using all its resources to produce X, nation A can produce 80 units of X; by devoting all its resources to Y, it can produce 40 Y. Comparable figures for nation B are 60 X and 60 Y. Assuming constant costs, in which product should each nation specialize? Why? Indicate the limits of the terms of trade. Explain the effects of trade upon resource and product prices in the two nations.

5 "The United States can produce product X more efficiently than can Great Britain. Yet we import X from Great Britain." Explain.

6 Analyze the following statement carefully and completely:[3]

In the international division of labor it is not *absolute* advantage that counts; a country's resources may be more productive in all branches of industry than those of another country, and yet trade might be profitable for both countries, provided that they concentrate their efforts on the products in which they have a *comparative* advantage. *It is the productivity [cost] ratios within a country that should differ from the productivity ratios in the partner country.* Commerce is profitable between countries that are unequal, at least in economic structure. *Levels of productivity are tremendously important to the real income of a country, but they do not indicate the possibilities of international trade.*

7 The data in columns 1 and 2 of the following table are for a closed economy.

(1) Aggregate supply (NNP = DI), billions	(2) Aggregate demand, closed economy, billions	(3) Exports, billions	(4) Imports, billions	(5) Net exports, billions	(6) Aggregate demand, open economy, billions
$200	$240	$20	$18	$ _____	$ _____
250	280	20	22	_____	_____
300	320	20	26	_____	_____
350	360	20	30	_____	_____
400	400	20	34	_____	_____
450	440	20	38	_____	_____
500	480	20	42	_____	_____
550	520	20	46	_____	_____

a. Use columns 1 and 2 to determine the equilibrium NNP and the multiplier for the closed economy.

b. Now open this economy for international trade by including the export and import figures of columns 3 and 4. Determine the equilibrium NNP and the multiplier for the open economy. Explain why these figures differ from those for the closed economy.

c. Given the import figures of column 4, what would be the level of equilibrium NNP if exports were $48 billion? $6 billion? What generalization concerning the level of exports and the equilibrium NNP can you derive from these examples?

d. Given the original $20 billion level of exports, what would be the equilibrium NNP if imports were $14 billion larger at each level of NNP? Or $14 billion smaller at each level of NNP? What generalization concerning the level of imports and the equilibrium NNP is illustrated by these examples?

[3]Jan Pen, *A Primer on International Trade* (New York: Random House, Inc., 1967), p. 17.

Selected References

Baldwin, Robert E., and J. David Richardson (eds.): *International Trade and Finance: Readings* (Boston: Little, Brown and Company, 1974), part 1.

Caves, Richard E., and Ronald W. Jones: *World Trade and Payments: An Introduction,* 2d ed. (Boston: Little, Brown and Company, 1977), chaps. 1–4.

Humphrey, Thomas M.: "Changing Views of Comparative Advantage," *Monthly Review* (Federal Reserve Bank of Richmond, July 1972).

Kenen, Peter B., and Raymond Lubitz: *International Economics,* 3d ed. (Englewood Cliffs, N.J.: Prentice-Hall, Inc., 1971), particularly chaps. 1, 2, 4.

Pen, Jan: *A Primer on International Trade* (New York: Random House, Inc., 1967).

Snider, Delbert A.: *Introduction to International Economics,* 6th ed. (Homewood, Ill.: Richard D. Irwin, Inc., 1975), chaps. 1–6.

Last Word
Imperialism and World Trade

Orthodox economics employs the notion of comparative advantage to explain mutually advantageous trade between nations. Radical or Marxist economics explains trade in terms of capitalist nations exploiting less developed areas of the world.

. . . according to Marxists, foreign trade continues to play an important role as capitalism develops. By means of this trade, older capitalistic countries can take advantage of both larger markets for their manufactures and cheaper sources of foodstuffs and raw materials. To regulate the terms of this trade, however, so that they can obtain the major benefits from trade, the mature capitalistic nations tighten and extend their control over poorer areas by building up colonial empires. In other words, Marxists maintain that colonialism is designed to increase the degree of exploitation in the poorer countries for the benefit of the advanced capitalistic nations.

Foreign markets become even more important as capitalism moves into what Marxists term its monopoly stage. This occurs when the concentration and centralization of capital gradually eliminate most areas of free competition in the economy. At this stage imperialism emerges. As Lenin says, "Imperialism is capitalism in that stage of development in which the dominance of monopolies and finance capital has established itself; . . . in which the division of the world among the international trusts has begun; in which the division of all territories of the globe among the great capitalist powers has been completed."

At this point in capitalist development, so argue the Marxists, the forces of stagnation in the form of a low rate of profit and chronic overproduction are conditions that press ever harder upon the economy. The older capitalistic countries turn more and more to the foreign sector in order to postpone their final destruction. The export of capital to backward areas in which the rate of profit is higher becomes a major means of attempting to lessen the tendency towards stagnation. This also becomes a means for encouraging the export of commodities which relieves the pressures of overproduction at home.

According to the Marxist view, further domination of the poorer countries by the advanced capitalist countries accompanies this export of capital. There are resistances to be overcome within these areas, if foreigners are to find profitable outlets and exploit the people. Each capitalist power also desires to exclude competition from other capitalist nations who are in similar difficulties. Consequently, the governments of the great powers step in and forcibly create conditions favorable to the process of exploitation. In all this, the people of the poorer regions benefit little, if any. Traditional habits and customs are destroyed; handicraft industries are wiped out by cheap manufacturing imports; and the masses are stripped of their means of production. In short, "Finance capital and the trusts are increasing instead of diminishing the differences in the rate of development of the various parts of world economy."

Gerald M. Meier and Robert E. Baldwin, *Economic Development: Theory, History, Policy* (New York: John Wiley & Sons, Inc., 1957), pp. 59–60. Copyright © 1957 by John Wiley & Sons, Inc. Reprinted by permission of John Wiley & Sons, Inc.

CHAPTER

The Economics of Free Trade and Protection

The fundamental conclusion of Chapter 41 is that nations can enjoy an expanded world output by specializing in accordance with comparative advantage and by freely engaging in trade. Despite the apparent advantages of uninhibited world trade, nations embrace a variety of policies which restrict such trade. Hence, the goals of this chapter are to (1) restate the case for free trade; (2) discuss trade barriers and their economic consequences; (3) set forth and critically evaluate the arguments for protectionism; and (4) summarize the evolution of international trade policy.

THE CASE FOR FREE TRADE

The compelling logic of the case for free trade is hardly new. Indeed, in 1776 Adam Smith got to the heart of the matter by asserting:[1]

> It is the maxim of every prudent master of a family, never to attempt to make at home what it will cost him more to make than to buy. The taylor does not attempt to make his own shoes, but buys them of the shoemaker. The shoemaker does not attempt to make his own clothes but employs a taylor. The farmer attempts to make neither the one nor the other, but employs those different artificers. All of them find it for their interest to employ their whole industry in a way in which they have some advantage over their neighbors, and

[1] Adam Smith, *The Wealth of Nations* (New York: Modern Library, Inc., 1937), p. 424.

to purchase with a part of its produce, or what is the same thing, with the price of a part of it, whatever else they have occasion for.

In modern jargon, the case for free trade comes down to this one potent argument. *Through free trade based upon the principle of comparative advantage, the world economy can achieve a more efficient allocation of resources and a higher level of material well-being.* The resource mixes and technological knowledge of each country are different. Therefore, each nation can produce particular commodities at different real costs. Each nation should produce goods for which its costs are low relative to those of other nations and exchange these specialties for products for which its costs are high relative to those of other nations. If each nation does this, the world can fully realize the advantages of geographic and human specialization. That is, the world—and each free-trading nation—can realize a larger real income from the given supplies of resources available to it. Protection—barriers to free trade—lessens or eliminates the gains from specialization. If nations cannot freely trade, they must shift resources from efficient (low-cost) to inefficient (high-cost) uses in order to satisfy their diverse wants.

A collateral benefit of free trade also should be noted: Unimpeded international trade deters the establishment of domestic business monopolies. As opposed to free trade, protection from foreign competition creates a domestic economic environment more conducive to the development of monopoly and the host of restrictive practices associated therewith.

It is fair to say that the vast majority of economists embrace the case for free trade as an economically valid position. However, economists do, as we shall note shortly, acknowledge the relevance of short-run and politically motivated exceptions to the case for free trade.

TRADE BARRIERS

No matter how compelling the logic of the case for free trade, in fact a wide variety of barriers to free trade do exist. Our discussion will center upon the two most widely used barriers.

□   Protective Tariffs and Import Quotas

Tariffs are simply excise taxes on imported goods; they may be imposed for purposes of revenue or protection. *Revenue tariffs* are usually applied to products which are not produced domestically, for example, tin, coffee, and bananas in the case of the United States. Rates on revenue tariffs are typically modest. *Protective tariffs,* on the other hand, are designed to shield domestic producers from foreign competition. Although protective tariffs are usually not high enough to prohibit the importation of foreign goods, they obviously put foreign producers at a competitive disadvantage in selling in domestic markets.

Import quotas specify the maximum amounts of specific commodities which may be imported in any period of time. Frequently, import quotas are more effective in retarding international commerce than are tariffs. A given product might be imported in relatively large quantities despite high tariffs; low import quotas, on the other hand, completely prohibit imports once the quotas are filled. We will emphasize protective tariffs in the following discussion of protectionism.

□   Motivations

The imposition of protective tariffs and import quotas is rooted in several motivations.

1   Special Interests   While nations as a whole gain from free international trade, particular industries and groups of resource suppliers can be hurt. In our earlier example, specialization and trade adversely affected the

American coffee industry and the Brazilian steel industry. It is easy to see why such groups may seek to preserve or improve their economic positions by persuading the government to impose tariffs or quotas to protect them from the deleterious effects of free trade. Such groups have sometimes been highly vocal and politically powerful.

2 Domestic Stimulus During depressions or recessions, nations have sometimes attempted to stimulate their domestic economies by controlling or manipulating their world trade. In particular, as we saw in Chapter 41, a decline in imports tends to shift the aggregate demand schedule upward, thereby increasing domestic income and employment.

3 Defense Post-World War II international tensions prompted nations to use tariffs and quotas to protect domestic producers of materials and goods essential to mobilization and war.

4 Industrialization In Chapter 21 we found that underdeveloped nations have sometimes turned to tariffs and quotas in attempting to industrialize and diversify their economies.

☐ **Economic Impact of Tariffs**

Let us now employ simple supply and demand analysis to examine the economic effects of the most widely used trade barrier—protective tariffs. The D_d and S_d curves in Figure 42-1 show domestic demand and supply for a product in which the United States has a comparative *dis*advantage, for example, tape recorders. In the absence of world trade, the domestic price and output would be OP_d and OQ_{d1}. Assume now that the domestic economy is opened to world trade, and that the Japanese, having a comparative advantage in tape recorders, begin to sell their products in the American market. Specifically, suppose

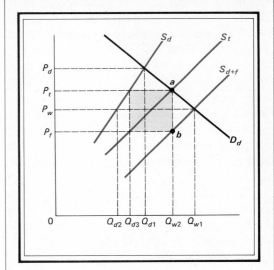

FIGURE 42-1 THE ECONOMIC EFFECTS OF A PROTECTIVE TARIFF

By restricting supply from S_{d+f} to S_t, tariffs increase price from OP_w to OP_t and lower quantity from QQ_{w1} to QQ_{w2} to the domestic consumer. Domestic producers enjoy a higher price—OP_t instead of OP_w—and sell a larger output—QQ_{d3} rather than QQ_{d2}. Foreign exporters, however, are penalized as their prices and sales both fall; price falls from OP_w to OP_f and sales decline from $Q_{d2}Q_{w1}$ to $Q_{d3}Q_{w2}$. The brown area indicates the amount of tariffs paid by American consumers.

imported tape recorders from Japan augment our domestic supply to the extent that total supply—domestic plus foreign—available in the United States is S_{d+f}. At the resulting free-trade or world price of OP_w, total consumption is OQ_{w1}, of which OQ_{d2} is domestic production and $Q_{d2}Q_{w1}$ is imports. We observe here the benefits of specialization and free trade in accordance with comparative advantage; American consumers obtain more tape recorders and at a lower price.

Now suppose a tariff of ab $(= P_tP_f)$ per tape recorder is imposed. Given that a tariff is merely a sales tax on imports, it is no surprise that its economic consequences are similar to those of a sales or excise tax (see Figure 23-7). Specifically, the tariff shifts the supply curve upward by ab or P_tP_f, that is, from S_{d+f} to S_t. The new equilibrium price is higher, OP_t rather than OP_w, and as a result, fewer tape recorders, OQ_{w2} rather than OQ_{w1}, are purchased. Observe that the gains from specialization and trade are partially lost to consumers. If the tariff were higher, so that the S_t curve coincided with the S_d curve, imports would fall to zero and the gains from trade would be entirely lost to consumers as price and quantity would be back at the closed-economy levels of OP_d and OQ_{d1}.

What about foreign and domestic producers? Japanese exporters are clearly hurt. They receive less per tape recorder sold and, in addition, their sales in the United States diminish. Specifically, the after-tariff price to Japanese exporters is OP_f $(= OP_t$ minus the tariff of ab or P_tP_f) rather than OP_w; sales are reduced from $Q_{d2}Q_{w1}$ to only $Q_{d3}Q_{w2}$. Note that total tariff revenue collected by government is P_tP_f, tariff per unit, multiplied by $Q_{d3}Q_{w2}$, the number of tape recorders imported; this is shown by the brown area in Figure 42-1. These tariff revenues are essentially a transfer of income from consumers to government and do not represent any net change in the nation's economic well-being; government gains what consumers lose. On the other hand, domestic producers of tape recorders will now enjoy both higher prices and expanded sales. Specifically, American producers—who, of course, are *not* subject to the tariff—will receive a price of OP_t per unit. And, because OP_t is higher than the pretariff or world price OP_w, the domestic tape recorder industry will move up its supply curve S_d, increasing domestic output from OQ_{d2} to OQ_{d3}. These favorable effects obviously explain the interest of domestic producers in imposing protective tariffs.

There are more subtle effects of tariffs which go beyond our simple supply and demand diagram. Because of diminished sales of tape recorders in the United States, Japan will now earn fewer dollars with which to buy American exports. That is, American export

industries—industries in which the United States has a comparative advantage—will cut production and release resources. These are highly efficient industries, as is evidenced by their comparative advantage and their ability to sell goods in world markets. In short, tariffs directly promote the expansion of relatively inefficient industries which do not have a comparative advantage *and* indirectly cause the contraction of relatively efficient industries which do have a comparative advantage. This obviously means that tariffs cause resources to be shifted in the wrong direction. This is not surprising. The big message of Chapter 41 was that specialization and unfettered world trade based on comparative advantage would lead to the efficient use of world resources and an expansion of the world's real output. The purpose and effect of protective tariffs are to reduce world trade. Therefore, aside from their specific effects upon consumers and foreign and domestic producers, tariffs diminish the world's real output.

THE CASE FOR PROTECTION: A CRITICAL REVIEW

Although free-trade advocates tend to prevail in the classroom, protectionists often dominate the halls of Congress. What arguments do protectionists make to justify trade barriers? Of what validity are these arguments?

☐ Military Self-Sufficiency Argument

The argument here is not economic, but rather, it is of a political-military nature: Protective tariffs are needed to preserve or strengthen industries producing strategic goods and materials essential for defense or war. It very plausibly contends that in an uncertain world, political-military objectives (self-sufficiency) must take precedence over economic goals (efficiency in the allocation of world resources).

Unfortunately, there is no objective criterion for weighing the relative worth of the increase in national security on the one hand, and the decrease in productive efficiency on the other, which accompany the reallocation of resources toward strategic industries when such tariffs are imposed. The economist can only call the politician's attention to the fact that certain economic costs are involved when tariffs are levied to enhance military self-sufficiency.

Although we might all agree that it is probably not a good idea to import our missile guidance systems from the Soviet Union, the self-sufficiency argument is nevertheless open to serious abuse. Virtually every industry can directly or indirectly claim a contribution to national security. Can you name an industry which did *not* contribute in some small way to the execution of World War II? Aside from abuses, are there not means superior to tariffs which will provide for needed strength in strategic industries? When achieved through tariffs, self-sufficiency gives rise to costs in the form of higher domestic prices on the output of the shielded industry. Hence, the cost of enhanced military security is apportioned arbitrarily among those consumers who buy the industry's product. Virtually all economists agree that a direct subsidy to strategic industries, financed out of general tax revenues, would entail a more equitable distribution of these costs.

☐ **Protect Domestic Living Standards**

Proponents of tariff protection frequently argue that tariffs are essential to *protect high wages and the high standard of living* now enjoyed in American capitalism. Cheap foreign labor, it is contended, will cause cheap foreign goods to flow into the United States. As a result, the prices of American goods and ultimately wage rates and the level of living will be driven down by this competition.

This appeal is tempting. But the argument falsely assumes that low foreign wages will automatically mean low prices on foreign goods and that high domestic wages mean high prices on domestic goods. This is not necessarily the case. Indeed, the argument conveniently ignores the fact that wage rates and per unit production costs are related through productivity. Hourly wage rates may be high and unit costs and product price low, if productivity is high. And what determines the productivity of labor? Basically, the quality of labor and the quality and quantity of the capital with which it is equipped. As compared with most other nations, American labor is high in quality and is extremely well equipped. The consequence is that high wages in the United States usually are accompanied by relatively low unit costs and relatively low product prices. As we have already discovered (Chapter 31), wages are high in the United States for the simple reason that productivity is high!

These comments, of course, do not rule out the fact that in the production of certain articles, higher American productivity is more than offset by the low money wages paid foreign workers. This is particularly likely to be true where production of a commodity requires much hand labor and little capital equipment, for example, Swiss watches or Japanese toys. Is protection warranted under these circumstances? Certainly not on economic grounds. These nations will simply have a comparative advantage in these lines of production. Limiting American imports of such goods by imposing tariffs will also curtail American exports; in the long run, other nations must be able to sell to us in order to earn dollars so they can buy from us. The result is that American workers will be released from efficient, high-productivity export industries and absorbed in relatively inefficient, low-productivity industries which can survive only under an umbrella of protective tariffs. This reallocation will lower, not increase, real wages domestically and impair the domestic standard of living.

□ Increase Domestic Employment

This argument for tariffs becomes increasingly fashionable as an economy encounters a recession. It is rooted in the macro analysis of Chapter 41. Aggregate demand in an open economy is comprised of $C + I_n + G + X - M$. By reducing imports, M, aggregate demand will rise, stimulating the domestic economy by boosting income and employment. In the short run this policy may work, but there are important shortcomings.

1 Although the immediate effect of an export surplus is to bolster domestic employment, it is obvious that all nations cannot simultaneously succeed in this endeavor. The exports of one nation must be the imports of another. To the extent that one country is able to stimulate its economy through an excess of exports over imports, some other economy's unemployment problem is worsened by the resulting excess of imports over exports. It is no wonder that tariff boosts and the imposition of import quotas for the purposes of achieving domestic full employment are termed "beggar my neighbor" policies.

2 Nations adversely affected by tariffs and quotas are likely to retaliate, causing a competitive raising of trade barriers which will choke off trade to the end that all nations are worse off. It is not surprising that the Smoot-Hawley Tariff Act of 1930, which imposed the highest tariffs ever enacted in the United States, backfired miserably. Rather than stimulate the American economy, this tariff act only induced a series of retaliatory restrictions by adversely affected nations. This caused a further contraction of international trade and tended to lower the income and employment levels of all nations.

3 Lastly, in the long run an excess of exports over imports is doomed to failure as a device for stimulating domestic employment. Remember: It is through American imports that foreign nations earn dollars with which to purchase American exports. In the long run a nation must import in order to export. Hence, the long-run impact of tariffs is not to increase domestic employment but at best to reallocate workers away from export industries and toward protected domestic industries. This shift implies a less efficient allocation of resources, that is, an increase in disguised unemployment. Tariffs shift resources away from those industries in which production is so efficient as to provide a comparative advantage. There is little doubt that intelligent, well-timed monetary and fiscal policies are far superior to tariff and quota adjustments as anticyclical techniques.

□ Diversification for Stability

Closely related to the increase-domestic-employment argument for tariff protection is the diversification-for-stability argument. The point here is that highly specialized economies—for example, Brazil's coffee economy or Cuba's sugar economy—are dependent upon international markets for their incomes. Wars, cyclical fluctuations, and adverse changes in the structure of industry will force large and frequently painful readjustments upon such economies. It is therefore alleged that tariff and quota protection is needed in such nations to induce greater industrial diversification and consequently less dependence upon world markets for one or two products. This will help insulate the domestic economy from wars and depressions abroad and from random fluctuations in world supply and demand for one or two particular commodities, thereby providing greater domestic stability.

There is undoubtedly some truth in this argument. There are also serious qualifications and shortcomings. (*a*) The argument has little or no relevance to the United States and other advanced economies. (*b*) The economic costs of diversification may be great; one-crop economies may be highly inefficient in manufacturing.

□ **Infant-Industry Argument**

The infant-industry argument contends that protective tariffs are needed for the purpose of allowing new domestic industries to establish themselves. Temporarily shielding young domestic firms from the severe competition afforded by more mature and therefore currently more efficient foreign firms will give the infant industries a chance to develop and become efficient producers. This argument for protection rests upon an alleged exception to the case for free trade. The exception is that all industries have not had, and in the presence of mature foreign competition, will never have, the chance to make long-run adjustments in the direction of larger scale and greater efficiency in production. The provision of tariff protection for infant industries will therefore correct a current misallocation of world resources now perpetuated by historically different levels of economic development between domestic and foreign industries.

Though the infant-industry argument has logical validity, these qualifying points must be noted. (*a*) This argument is not particularly pertinent to industrially advanced nations such as the United States. (*b*) In the underdeveloped nations it is very difficult to determine which industries are the infants capable of achieving economic maturity and therefore deserving of protection. (*c*) Unlike old soldiers, protective tariffs rarely fade away, but rather, tend to persist and increase even after industrial maturity has been realized. (*d*) Most economists feel that if infant industries are to be subsidized, there are better means than tariffs for doing it. Direct subsidies, for example, have the advantage of making explicit which industries are being aided and to what degree.

□ **The Diffusion-of-Technology Argument**

A more sophisticated and complex argument for protection has evolved in recent years. It challenges the traditional view that comparative advantage is rooted in each nation's differing endowments of climate, natural resources, labor, and capital. Simply put, the argument is that the comparative advantage of industrially advanced nations, such as the United States, is based increasingly upon technological superiority. That is, the United States has a comparative advantage in certain commodities because it has achieved a technological lead with respect to their production.

Rapid Diffusion The significance of a shift from a resource-endowment explanation to a technological-superiority interpretation of comparative advantage is that technological superiority is alleged to be a much more temporary or transient source of comparative advantage. While the United States cannot duplicate South Africa's diamond- or gold-producing capacities or cheaply install the climate and land characteristics which underlie Brazil's coffee-producing ability, it is a relatively easy matter for other nations—for example, Japan and West Germany—to emulate American technological advances in the production of manufactured goods. Furthermore, it is argued that the rate at which technological knowledge is being dispersed around the world is rising, making it increasingly difficult for the United States to generate innovations sufficient to sustain its comparative advantages and hence its capacity to export.[2]

Trade in research-intensive new products, international licensing and sale of patents, foreign travel by scientists and professionals, private direct investment, and, of course, faster means of transportation and communication all serve as vehicles for the rapid transmission of technical knowledge. The more rapid spread of technology, of course, shrinks the average lead-time that U.S. producers have to profitably exploit foreign markets. In

[2]Thomas M. Humphrey, "Changing Views of Comparative Advantage," *Monthly Review* (Federal Reserve Bank of Richmond, July 1972), p. 13. The present discussion draws heavily upon this article.

short, acceleration in the rate of transfer of technology may have increased the required rate of innovative activity while simultaneously reducing the potential profitability of any given innovation and thus the incentive of U.S. producers to undertake it.

The recent growth of multinational firms also accelerates the rate of technological diffusion. When American firms establish or acquire overseas subsidiaries, they usually directly transfer production techniques and related worker and managerial skills. Furthermore, "the increased competition provided by United States subsidiaries stimulates local producers to adopt the latest technology and spurs them to undertake innovative activity of their own."[3]

Protectionist View   How does all this relate to the free trade–protectionism debate? Protectionists content that, given this more dynamic conception of comparative advantage, the risks and economic costs of free trade are significantly increased. Because comparative advantage now shifts more rapidly among nations, a greater degree of flexibility and adaptability is required of free-trading nations than can be actually achieved. The industrially advanced trading economy cannot adjust its product-mix or reallocate its resources rapidly enough to keep pace with changing comparative cost conditions; the result is that free trade contributes to structural maladjustment and resource unemployment. Furthermore, protectionists contend that the balance of payments problems which have plagued the United States for over two decades (Chapter 44) are ample evidence of the inability of our economy to adjust to the rapid worldwide diffusion of technological knowledge.

Free-Trade Position   Free traders respond along the following lines. It may very well be true that comparative advantage is

subject to more rapid shifts than in the past. They argue, however, that the domestic economy displays a high degree of flexibility; after all, rapid technological change and substantial shifts in consumer demand are common events *within* the United States, and, curiously, protectionists do *not* recommend *intra*national trade restrictions to protect adversely affected industries and regions. Advocates of free trade contend that, in any event, trade barriers are the wrong remedy for adaptability problems; protectionism will only tend to reduce adaptability. By shielding domestic producers from the rigors of international competition, protectionism will make American industry increasingly lethargic and less adaptable to change. Protectionist policies, by attempting to resist economic change, tend to freeze resources into uses which become more and more uneconomic with the passing of time. It is much better for society to undertake tax-financed programs to hasten the required reallocations of resources than to resort to protectionism. For example, worker retraining programs and relocation subsidies, along with tax relief and low-interest loans for adversely affected businesses, enhance the economy's adaptability by redirecting labor and industry from less to more efficient uses. Finally, although the rapid dissemination of technological knowledge may contribute to American deficits in merchandise trade, it is argued that future earnings from the export of our technological knowledge, managerial skills, and technologically advanced real capital can be expected to compensate for imbalances in our exports and imports of goods.

□   **A Summing Up**

Though the arguments for protection are many and varied, they fail to overshadow the case for free trade: Unimpeded international trade permits greater specialization and a more efficient allocation of world resources. Under proper conditions, the infant-industry argu-

[3] Ibid.

ment stands as a valid exception, justifiable on economic grounds. And on political-military grounds, the self-sufficiency argument can be used to validate protection. Both arguments, however, are susceptible to severe abuses, and both neglect alternative means of fostering industrial development and military self-sufficiency. Most other arguments are semi-emotional appeals in the form of half-truths and outright fallacies. These arguments note only the immediate and direct consequences of protective tariffs. They ignore the plain truth that in the long run a nation must import in order to export.

INTERNATIONAL TRADE POLICIES

As Figure 42-2 makes clear, tariffs in the United States have had their ups and downs.[4] Generally speaking, the United States tended to be a high-tariff nation over much of its history. Note that the Smoot-Hawley Tariff

[4]Technical footnote: Average tariff-rate figures understate the importance of tariffs by not accounting for the fact that some goods are *excluded* from American markets because of existing tariffs. Then, too, average figures conceal the extremely high tariffs on particular items: watches, china, hats, woolens, scissors, wine, jewelry, glassware, and so forth.

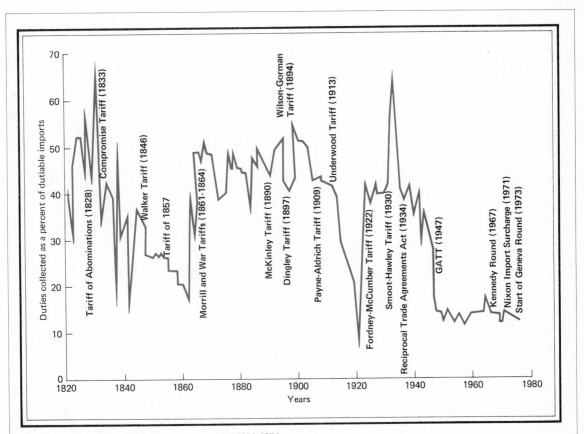

FIGURE 42-2 UNITED STATES TARIFF RATES, 1820-1976

American tariff rates have fluctuated historically. But beginning with the Reciprocal Trade Agreements Act of 1934, the trend has been downward. (*U.S. Department of Commerce data.*)

Act of 1930 embodied some of the highest tariff rates ever imposed by the United States.

Given the case for free trade, this high-tariff heritage may be a bit surprising. If tariffs are economically undesirable, why has Congress been so willing to employ them? The answer lies in the political realities of tariff making. Those interest groups who stand to benefit from protection have done an effective job of lobbying for tariffs. And, in a sense, the pressure for protection is cumulative. With some tariff protection, domestic producers increase their economic strength. This means they have greater financial resources to plead for more protection—and also more to lose if they fail in their efforts to sustain it. Most consumers, unaware of all the economic implications of tariffs, are impressed by not only the vigor but also the plausibility ("Cut imports and prevent domestic unemployment") and the patriotic ring ("Buy American!") of the protectionists. Alleged tariff benefits seem immediate and clear-cut to the public. The adverse effects cited by economists appear ever so obscure and widely dispersed over the economy. Then, too, the public is likely to stumble on the fallacy of composition: "If a protective tariff on Swiss watches will preserve profits and employment in the American watch industry, how can it be detrimental to the economy as a whole?" Those relatively few individuals who do recognize that the benefits gained by protected industries come at the expense of the general welfare are incapable of financing lobbyists to offset the protectionists. When political logrolling is added in—"You back tariffs for industry X in my state and I'll do the same for industry Y in your state"—the sum can be protective tariffs and import quotas.

☐   **Reciprocal Trade Act and GATT**

The downward trend of tariffs since Smoot-Hawley was inaugurated with the Reciprocal Trade Agreements Act of 1934. Specifically aimed at tariff reduction, the act had two main features:

1   Negotiating Authority   It authorized the President to negotiate agreements with foreign nations which would reduce American tariffs up to 50 percent of the existing rates. Tariff reductions were to hinge upon the willingness of other nations to reciprocate by lowering tariffs on American exports.

2   Generalized Reductions   By incorporating *most-favored-nation clauses* in these agreements, the resulting tariff reductions not only would apply to the specific nation negotiating with the United States, but they would be *generalized* so as to apply to all nations.

But the Reciprocal Trade Act gave rise to only bilateral (two-nation) negotiations. This approach was broadened in 1947 when twenty-three nations, including the United States, signed a General Agreement on Tariffs and Trade (GATT). GATT is based on three cardinal principles: (1) equal, nondiscriminatory treatment for all member nations; (2) the reduction of tariffs by *multilateral* negotiations; and (3) the elimination of import quotas. Basically, GATT is a forum for the negotiation of reductions in tariff barriers on a multilateral basis. Over ninety nations now belong to GATT, and there is little doubt but that it has been an important force in the trend toward liberalized trade. Under its sponsorship, six "rounds" of negotiations to reduce trade barriers have been completed in the post-World War II period.

☐   **Economic Integration:
The Common Market**

Another crucial development in trade liberalization has taken the form of economic integration. The most dramatic illustration is the European Economic Community (EEC), or the Common Market, as it is popularly known. The EEC was begun in 1958 with France, West Germany, Italy, Belgium, the Netherlands, and Luxembourg as members. Britain, Denmark, and Ireland joined in 1973.

Goals   The Common Market calls for (1) the gradual abolition of tariffs and import quotas on all products traded among the nine participating nations; (2) the establishment of a common system of tariffs applicable to all goods received from nations outside the Common Market; (3) the eventual free movement of capital and labor within the Market; and (4) the creation of common policies with respect to a number of other economic matters of joint concern, for example, agriculture, transportation, and restrictive business practices. The Common Market, with a population of 258 million and a combined GNP in excess of $1360 billion, has tremendous economic and political implications.

Results   Evidence of the success of the Common Market is reflected in high rates of economic growth (Table 20-2) and a dramatic expansion of both internal and external trade. Although it is impossible to determine how much of the Common Market's economic success has been due to economic integration as such, one can plausibly argue that economic integration has been a major contributing factor in European economic progress. First, integration generally promotes a more rational allocation of Europe's economic resources in accordance with the principle of comparative advantage. Second, integration of the national economies of Western Europe creates a large-scale mass market which is essential for European industries in realizing economies of large-scale production. More efficient production for a large-scale market permits European industries to realize the lower costs which small, localized markets have historically denied them. This enhanced productive efficiency has made European producers more competitive in world markets—often at the expense of American firms. All things considered, there can be little doubt that the Common Market as an institution has been a significant factor in the buoyancy and expansion of the economies of its member nations.

Nonmembers   Although economic integration is an important means of reducing trade barriers among members, serious problems can arise for nonmembers. The reduction of internal tariffs to zero and the simultaneous establishment of a common external tariff can make it more difficult for the United States and other nonmembers to sell their goods in the Common Market. For example, *before* the establishment of the Common Market, American, German, and French automobile manufacturers all faced the same tariff in selling their products to, say, Belgium. However, with the establishment of internal free trade among EEC members, Belgian tariffs on German Volkswagens and French Renaults fell to zero, but an external tariff of, say, 25 or 30 percent still applies to all nonmember nations such as the United States. This obviously puts American firms and those of other nonmember nations at a serious competitive disadvantage. And, of course, to the extent that this disadvantage results in a growing mass market for European producers, they may realize greater economies of scale (lower unit costs) and find themselves increasingly able to compete with American manufacturers in the export market of nations outside the Common Market. Moreover, the Common Market embodies a rapidly growing, but as yet relatively unsaturated, market for our manufactured goods. European incomes and living standards are rising, and the Common Market nations have entered the "high mass-consumption" stage of their economic development. High Common Market external tariffs on imports from the United States will tend to make increasingly inaccessible to U.S. manufacturers a growing mass market for consumer durables and semi-durables—those very products which American firms produce with such great efficiency. We shall see in Chapter 44 that any shrinkage in exports to Europe tends to aggravate the United States' balance of payments problem.

The economic relationship between the United States and the Common Market also has crucial political overtones. Close economic ties are conducive to close political ties. But the persistence of substantial trade barriers between the EEC and the United States can result in a free world which is divided both economically and politically.

□ The Kennedy Round

Against this background, it became increasingly evident in the early 1960s that, if the United States' economic isolation from the Common Market and potential political disunity were to be avoided, the United States should take the initiative to reduce trade barriers against the Common Market. This initiative took the form of the Trade Expansion Act of 1962, which provided the President with broad powers to negotiate reciprocal trade reductions. In particular, the act gave American negotiators the authority to reduce tariffs up to 50 percent on broad classes of industrial products and to eliminate tariffs completely on goods where tariffs have been only 5 percent or less. The reductions were to be made by reciprocal negotiations and to embody "most-favored-nation" clauses, automatically extending the lower tariffs to many other countries.

A unique feature of the act was its explicit acknowledgment that the sweeping tariff reductions required for a closer alignment of the Common Market and the United States economies will entail certain costs. For example, a number of domestic industries, when relieved of tariff protection, will be faced with declining markets, falling profits, and unemployment. The act therefore provided for *trade adjustment assistance* to those who are adversely affected. Specifically, workers who lose their jobs because of increased import competition can get vocational training, relocation allowances, and cash payments. Adversely affected businesses can get tax relief and loans and technical assistance for the modernization and reorganization of plants.

The Trade Expansion Act was the legislative basis for the "Kennedy Round" of tariff negotiations under the auspices of GATT,

which were concluded in 1967.[5] The Kennedy Round was generally successful in that it achieved tariff cuts averaging more than 35 percent on some $40 billion worth of goods. The underdeveloped nations also benefited from the negotiations in that special efforts were made to reduce tariffs on products of particular interest to these nations without requiring full reciprocity. The main disappointment from the United States' viewpoint was the EEC's reluctance to reduce tariffs on agricultural products because American competition in foodstuffs would jeopardize the Common Market's program of agricultural price supports.

□ New Initiative: The Geneva Round

In September of 1973, representatives of some 105 nations, including the United States, met to lay the groundwork for a new round of comprehensive trade negotiations. This new effort to further dismantle trade barriers is particularly timely for several reasons. First, the reductions of trade barriers negotiated in the Kennedy Round have now been implemented; a new initiative is appropriate to sustain the movement toward freer trade. Second, the recent expansion of Common Market membership, along with continuing reductions and eliminations of trade barriers among members, makes the negotiation of further declines in trade barriers important to nonmembers so that they can continue to sell their products in the Common Market. Third, as we shall find in Chapter 44, the international monetary system is undergoing basic reform; this reform requires "mutually supportive" improvements in the world's trade policies. Finally, the historic lowering of tariffs as the result of prior negotiations has increased the visibility and relative importance of a number of nontariff barriers to trade; it is time that the nations of the world critically examined these nontariff impediments to trade.[6]

[5]So called because this sixth "round" of trade negotiations came about largely at the initiative of President Kennedy.
[6]*Economic Report of the President, 1974* (Washington), pp. 212–213.

Trade Reform Act The Trade Reform Act of 1974 enables United States participation in this new seventh round of GATT negotiations now going on in Geneva. Emphasis is upon the reduction of *nontariff barriers* (NTBs) to trade. Under the previous six rounds of negotiations, many tariffs have been reduced substantially or eliminated. But trade is also impeded by a variety of NTBs in the form of import quotas, licensing requirements, unreasonable standards for product quality, unnecessary red tape in customs procedures, and so forth. To illustrate: Japan and the European countries frequently require importers to obtain licenses. By restricting the issuance of licenses, imports can be effectively restricted. Great Britain bars the importation of coal in this way. Similarly, unrealistic health and safety standards may be applied to foreign products to the end that their importation is discouraged. The United States has "Buy American" legislation which puts restrictions on the Federal government's purchasing foreign goods. Unnecessarily complex procedures in the administration of customs can also reduce the flow of trade. The NTBs will undoubtedly pose serious problems for Geneva Round negotiators because many of them are difficult to quantify for purposes of reciprocal reduction. Furthermore, there is the problem of distinguishing between NTBs designed to fulfill some desirable social goal—for example, the protection of consumers from hazardous products—and those which exist for the purpose of economic protection.

Raw-Material Access The Geneva Round also focuses upon a relatively new problem—freedom of access to raw materials and foodstuffs. Until the 1970s the industrially advanced nations had little difficulty in obtaining raw materials and foodstuffs relatively cheaply from one another and from the underdeveloped countries. But the economies of the advanced countries expanded simultaneously in the early 1970s, causing a rapid and substantial increase in the demand for raw materials and foodstuffs. The result was rapidly rising food and raw-material prices (Chapter 35). Many governments responded with measures to restrict exports and encourage imports for the purpose of expanding domestic supplies and alleviating the upward price pressures.

> With the booming worldwide demand for foodstuffs and raw materials, prices of such commodities rose to record heights. This increase in domestic prices as a result of foreign demand pressure caused considerable resentment in many producing countries and led to public demands that domestic supplies be protected. The situation was further aggravated when some governments imposed price controls in an effort to contain the inflationary pressures. Since export prices remained uncontrolled, domestic producers had an increased incentive to export their goods, with the result that the domestic shortages created by the initial imposition of the price controls were aggravated by increased exports. To alleviate the domestic shortages, a number of governments imposed controls on exports.[7]

For example, in 1973 the United States imposed export controls on soybeans and other high-protein grains and scrap steel. Other countries—Canada, Brazil, and Australia, for example—also imposed export controls on foodstuffs. The most dramatic example of export controls, of course, was the politically motivated embargo on oil shipments to the United States and other countries friendly to Israel by most of the Middle East Arab (OPEC) nations (the Organization of Petroleum Exporting Countries). The important point is that a priority item for the Geneva Round negotiations will be the development of a "code of good conduct for exporting countries, and the adoption of more systematic procedures for the resolution of disputes over the access to [raw-material and foodstuff] supplies. . . ."[8]

[7]Ibid., p. 210.
[8]Ibid., p. 212.

Agriculture A special problem exists between the United States and the Common Market nations with respect to agriculture. The United States—whose farmers are highly efficient and enjoy a comparative advantage—seek reductions in European barriers to American farm products. Recall from Chapter 35 that recent expansions in American farm exports have allowed us to move from a policy of price supports and output restriction to a freer market policy at considerable saving to taxpayers. The earnings from these expanded exports have been helpful in financing our growing petroleum imports. The United States obviously has an interest in maintaining or expanding its sales of farm products overseas. Common Market nations, however, fear that the reduction of existing barriers to our agricultural products will have a devastating effect upon their relatively small and inefficient farmers.

Prospects? Bargaining at Geneva will be difficult and substantial reductions in trade barriers cannot be taken for granted. On the one hand, the issues are more complex and diverse than in the past. Reducing NTBs and negotiating accessibility agreements with respect to raw materials and foodstuffs are likely to prove more difficult than achieving tariff reductions. Furthermore, the present world environment—wherein many nations are faced with stagflation and balance of payments problems resulting from oil-price increases—is hardly conducive to concession and agreement. On the contrary, protectionist pressures tend to be reasserted in such an unhealthy environment. For example, organized labor in the United States—traditionally in the free-trade camp—has tended to alter its position in the face of unemployment associated with rising imports. On the other hand, the long-term trend toward freer trade has been mutually beneficial. And the increasing interdependence which has accompanied the expanding volume of trade will make it costly for nations *not* to pave the way for a further liberalization of world commerce.

☐ United States–Communist Trade

Since World War II, American policy has leaned toward greater trade liberalization with respect to noncommunist countries. But over most of this period, our policies toward trade with communist countries—the Soviet Union and its Eastern European satellites, China, and North Korea—have been highly restrictive. In the late 1960s, for example, United States trade with the communist nations accounted for less than 1 percent of both our trade and their trade. In particular, the United States has severely restricted exports to communist nations for the purpose of preventing these nations from acquiring goods and technologies which might enhance their industrial-military capacities.

But, beginning in 1969, United States policy began to change. And for several reasons. First, the political climate between the United States and the communist countries began to ease; the reestablishment of American political contact with the People's Republic of China is particularly notable. Second, the Soviet Union began to display a growing interest in both American capital goods and industrial products. Underlying this interest is a declining Soviet growth rate and the hope that imports embodying advanced Western technology will provide a stimulus to Soviet productivity and growth. Third, rather persistent Soviet agricultural shortfalls have resulted in agreements to buy substantial quantities of American grain. Finally, recognition was growing that the restrictionist American policy was unrealistic and substantially a failure. There was increasing awareness, on the one hand, that the sale of consumer and capital goods to the communist countries would benefit our economy—not to mention our balance of payments—as much as theirs. On the other hand, other nations of Western Europe as well as Japan *were* liberalizing their trade with the communists and supplying the goods and technologies which the United States was withholding. Why should not American firms get a piece of the action?

Opportunities The potential for United States–communist trade is considerable. For example, the Soviet Union is clearly an important new market for American grains and other farm products. And, as just noted, the U.S.S.R. is interested in American capital and technological knowledge which can further its industrial growth and help develop its enormous natural resources in the areas of oil, natural gas, timber, and nonferrous metals. The United States, of course, could alleviate its energy, natural gas, and lumber shortages by sharing in expanded Soviet production. Hence, there is some basis for an expanding complementary trade. In fact, some attention has been given to "coproduction agreements" whereby American firms would provide the capital, technology, and managerial expertise to develop certain fuel and mineral resources in the Soviet Union in return for a share of the resulting production. Similarly, the communist systems of Eastern Europe embody growing markets for many consumer goods in which American manufacturers have a comparative advantage. Finally, China could become an export market for American machinery, computers, chemical fertilizers, and certain food products. Aside from the mutual economic benefits of an expanding East-West trade, important political benefits can also accrue. Trade can lead to mutual interdependence and greater communication, not to mention enhanced scientific-technical and cultural interaction, all of which contribute to mutual understanding and encourage a rational approach to the resolution of areas of disagreement.

Problems But the problems involved in establishing and sustaining a prosperous flow of East-West trade are substantial. First, the market-oriented economies of the West do business in ways which are a far cry from the practices and policies of the centrally planned communist economies. Western nations typically engage in multilateral trade wherein X may send goods to Y in order to get other goods from Z (Figure 3-1); the communist countries find bilateral trade much more compatible with central planning. Second, the communist and the Western nations march to different drummers with respect to copyright and patent protection, the settlement of commercial disputes, and so forth. For example, how can an American firm which has licensed technological knowledge in the Soviet Union be certain it is receiving proper compensation when Soviet production and sales data are held secret? Third, the communist nations do not belong to either GATT or the international monetary institutions to which Western nations subscribe. Can the rules of the international trading and financial game as practiced by the capitalistic nations be modified so as to facilitate East-West trade, or must entirely new institutions and techniques be evolved? Finally, Soviet ideology is steeped in the notion of autarchy—of self-reliance and economic independence from the surrounding capitalistic world. Hence, the rapid growth of East-West trade would be at the cost of some ideological disruption.

Trade Growth What does the record show? While it is too early to offer predictions about the long-term course of United States–Soviet trade, there *has* been substantial trade expansion in the 1970s. For example, Soviet trade with the West—that is, with non-communist, industrially advanced nations—grew more than threefold between 1970 and 1975. In the same period, Soviet trade with the United States grew almost tenfold! Even when adjusted for inflation, these figures reflect extraordinary growth. On the other hand, these data include large Soviet grain purchases which may or may not reoccur, depending upon the vagaries of Soviet harvests. Furthermore, the Soviet Union has had problems financing its trade with the West; its exports to the West have not earned sufficient amounts of Western currencies to finance a larger volume of imports from the West.

The recent expansion of East-West trade indicates that the Soviet Union is allowing itself to become increasingly intertwined in international trade. It may soon reach the point where its dependence upon Western capital goods, technology, and foodstuffs is such that it would be extremely costly for it to return to economic self-isolation. If East-West trade does continue to expand, the increased economic interdependence may foster more harmonious international political relationships. Although there are too many unknowns clouding the picture for firm predictions, present signs are favorable for a continued expansion of trade. But keep in mind that Soviet history makes it clear that its leadership has been willing to pay a high price for economic independence.[9]

[9]Those interested in pursuing this topic should consult Marshall I. Goldman, "Autarchy or Integration: The USSR and the World Economy," and Jack Brougher, "USSR Foreign Trade: A Greater Role for Trade with the West," both of which appear in Joint Economic Committee, *Soviet Economy in a New Perspective* (Washington, 1976), pp. 81–96 and 677–694 respectively.

Summary

1 The basic argument for free trade is that it fosters a more efficient allocation of resources and a higher standard of living for the world as a whole.

2 The most common trade barriers take the form of protective tariffs and quotas. Supply and demand analysis reveals that protective tariffs increase the prices and reduce the quantities demanded of affected goods. Foreign exporters find their sales and prices both diminish. Domestic producers, however, enjoy higher prices and enlarged sales. Tariffs promote a less efficient allocation of domestic and world resources.

3 When applicable, the strongest arguments for protection are the infant-industry and military self-sufficiency arguments. Most of the other arguments for protection are half-truths, emotional appeals, or fallacies which typically emphasize the immediate effects of trade barriers while ignoring long-run consequences.

4 The Reciprocal Trade Agreements Act of 1934 was the beginning of a trend toward lower American tariffs. In 1947 the General Agreement on Tariffs and Trade was formed *a.* to encourage nondiscriminatory treatment for all trading nations, *b.* to achieve tariff reduction, and *c.* to eliminate import quotas.

5 Economic integration is an important means of liberalizing trade. The outstanding illustration is the nine-member European Common Market wherein internal trade barriers are abolished, a common system of tariffs is applied to non-members, and the free internal movement of labor and capital is perceived. The Kennedy Round of reciprocal tariff reductions under GATT was initiated to make the Common Market more accessible to American producers. The Geneva Round, which accords special attention to nontariff barriers, raw-material accessibility, and trade policies toward agricultural products, is now in progress.

6 The United States has begun to relax its highly restrictive trade policies with communist nations and there are signs of a growing mutually advantageous trade with the Soviet Union, the People's Republic of China, and the Eastern European nations.

Questions and Study Suggestions

1 Key terms and concepts to remember: revenue and protective tariffs; import quotas; Reciprocal Trade Agreements Act of 1934; most-favored-nation clause; General Agreement on Tariffs and Trade (GATT); economic integration; European Economic Community (Common Market); Trade Expansion Act of 1962; Kennedy Round; Trade Reform Act of 1974; Geneva Round; nontariff barriers (NTBs).

2   State the economist's case for free trade. Given this case, how do you explain the existence of artificial barriers to international trade?

3   Draw a domestic supply and demand diagram for a product in which the United States does not have a comparative advantage. Indicate the impact of foreign imports upon supply and domestic price and quantity. Now show a protective tariff which eliminates approximately one-half the assumed imports. Indicate the price-quantity effects of this tariff to **a.** domestic consumers, **b.** domestic producers, and **c.** foreign exporters.

4   Carefully evaluate the following statements:

a.   "Protective tariffs limit both the imports and the exports of the nation levying tariffs."

b.   "The extensive application of protective tariffs destroys the ability of the international price system to allocate resources efficiently."

c.   "Apparent unemployment can often be reduced through tariff protection, but by the same token disguised unemployment typically increases."

d.   "American imports and exports since World War II are higher than they have ever been. This indicates that tariffs are not restricting the volume of trade."

e.   "Given the rapidity with which technological advance is dispersed around the world, free trade will inevitably yield structural maladjustments, unemployment, and balance of payments problems for industrially advanced nations."

f.   "Free trade can improve the composition and efficiency of domestic output. Only the Volkswagen forced Detroit to make a compact car, and only foreign success with the oxygen process forced American steel firms to modernize."

5   "The most valid arguments for tariff protection are also the most easily abused." What are these arguments? Why are they susceptible to abuse?

6   Suppose the existing American tariffs on Swiss watches were abolished. What would be the short-run economic effects upon the American and Swiss watch industries? Upon total American exports to and imports from Switzerland? What would be the long-run effects of this abolition upon **a.** the volume of employment, **b.** the allocation of resources, and **c.** the standard of living in the two nations?

7   Carefully evaluate the use of artificial trade barriers, such as tariffs and import quotas, as a means of achieving and maintaining full employment.

8   Use the "economies of scale" analysis of Chapter 25 to explain why the Common Market has enabled many European industries to compete more effectively in international markets. Explain: "Economic integration leads a double life: it can further free trade for members, but pose serious trade obstacles for nonmembers."

9   "The future of United States trade with the communist nations depends primarily upon political, not economic considerations." Do you agree? What are some of the practical problems involved in increasing East-West trade?

Selected References

Baldwin, Robert E., and J. David Richardson (eds.): *International Trade and Finance: Readings* (Boston: Little, Brown and Company, 1974), part 1.

Humphrey, Thomas M.: "Changing Views of Comparative Advantage," *Monthly Review* (Federal Reserve Bank of Richmond, July 1972).

Kenen, Peter B., and Raymond Lubitz: *International Economics,* 3d ed. (Englewood Cliffs, N.J.: Prentice-Hall, Inc., 1971), particularly chaps. 1, 2, 4.

Pen, Jan: *A Primer on International Trade* (New York: Random House, Inc., 1967).

Snider, Delbert A.: *Introduction to International Economics,* 6th ed. (Homewood, Ill.: Richard D. Irwin, Inc., 1975), chaps. 1–6.

Last Word
Petition of the Candlemakers, 1845

The French economist Frédéric Bastiat (1801–1850) devastated the proponents of protectionism by satirically extending their reasoning to its logical and absurd conclusions.

PETITION of the Manufacturers of Candles, Wax-lights, Lamps, Candlesticks, Street Lamps, Snuffers, Extinguishers, and of the Producers of Oil Tallow, Rosin, Alcohol, and, Generally, of Everything Connected with Lighting.

TO MESSIEURS THE MEMBERS OF THE CHAMBER OF DEPUTIES.

Gentlemen,—You are on the right road. You reject abstract theories, and have little consideration for cheapness and plenty. Your chief care is the interest of the producer. You desire to emancipate him from external competition, and reserve the *national market* for *national industry*.

We are about to offer you an admirable opportunity of applying your—what shall we call it? your theory? No; nothing is more deceptive than theory; your doctrine? your system? your principle? but you dislike doctrines, you abhor systems, and as for principles, you deny that there are any in social economy: we shall say, then, your practice, your practice without theory and without principle.

We are suffering from the intolerable competition of a foreign rival, placed, it would seem, in a condition so far superior to ours for the production of light, that he absolutely *inundates* our *national market* with it at a price fabulously reduced. The moment he shows himself, our trade leaves us—all consumers apply to him; and a branch of native industry, having countless ramifications, is all at once rendered completely stagnant. This rival . . . is no other than the Sun.

What we pray for is, that it may please you to pass a law ordering the shutting up of all windows, sky-lights, dormerwindows, outside and inside shutters, curtains, blinds, bull's-eyes; in a word, of all openings, holes, chinks, clefts, and fissures, by or through which the light of the sun has been in use to enter houses, to the prejudice of the meritorious manufactures with which we flatter ourselves we have accommodated our country,—a country which, in gratitude, ought not to abandon us now to a strife so unequal.

If you shut up as much as possible all access to natural light, and create a demand for artificial light, which of our French manufactures will not be encouraged by it?

If more tallow is consumed, then there must be more oxen and sheep; and, consequently, we shall behold the multiplication of artificial meadows, meat, wool, hides, and, above all, manure, which is the basis and foundation of all agricultural wealth.

The same remark applies to navigation. Thousands of vessels will proceed to the whale fishery; and, in a short time, we shall possess a navy capable of maintaining the honour of France, and gratifying the patriotic aspirations of your petitioners, the undersigned candlemakers and others.

Only have the goodness to reflect, Gentlemen, and you will be convinced that there is, perhaps, no Frenchman, from the wealthy coalmaster to the humblest vender of lucifer matches, whose lot will not be ameliorated by the success of this our petition.

Frédéric Bastiat, *Economic Sophisms* (Edinburgh: Oliver and Boyd, Tweeddale Court, 1873), pp. 49–53, abridged.

43

The Balance of Payments and Exchange Rates

Chapter 41 was concerned with comparative advantage as the basis for international trade; Chapter 42 stressed the fact that free trade would tend to maximize the potential gains from international specialization. The present chapter, building upon these notions, has the following specific objectives: (1) to introduce explicitly the monetary or financial aspects of international trade, (2) to define, analyze, and interpret the international balance of payments, and (3) to explain the various mechanisms for correcting a balance of payments disequilibrium.

FINANCING INTERNATIONAL TRADE

Although the particular techniques of financing international transactions are rather detailed, their general nature can be readily grasped. The basic feature which distinguishes international from domestic payments is that two different national currencies are obviously involved. Thus, for instance, when American firms export goods to British firms, the American exporter will want to be paid in dollars. But the British importers have pounds sterling. The problem, then, is to exchange pounds for dollars to permit the American export transaction to occur.

□ American Export Transaction

Suppose our American exporter agrees to sell $30,000 worth of computers to a British firm. Assume that the *rate of exchange*—that is, the rate or price at which pounds can be exchanged for, or converted into, dollars, and vice versa—is $2 for £1. This means that the British importer must pay £15,000 to the American exporter. Let us summarize what occurs in terms of simple bank balance sheets (Figure 43-1) such as those employed in Part 3.

a. To pay for the American computers, the British buyer draws a check on his demand deposit in a London bank for £15,000.

b. The British firm then sends this £15,000 check to the American exporter. But the rub is that the American exporter must pay his employees and materials suppliers, as well as his taxes, in dollars, not pounds. So the exporter sells the £15,000 check or draft on the London bank to some large American bank, probably located in New York City, which is a dealer in foreign exchange. The American firm is given a $30,000 demand deposit in the New York bank in exchange for the £15,000 check.

c. And what does the New York bank do with the £15,000? It in turn deposits it in a correspondent London bank for future sale. To simplify, we assume this correspondent bank is the same bank from which the British firm obtained the £15,000 draft.

Note these salient points. First, American exports create a foreign demand for dollars, and the satisfaction of this demand increases the supply of foreign monies—pounds, in this case—held by American banks and available to American buyers. Second, the financing of an American export (British import) reduces the supply of money (demand deposits) in Britain and increases the supply of money in the United States by the amount of the purchase.

☐ **American Import Transaction**

But a question persists: Why would the New York bank be willing to give up dollars for pounds sterling? As just indicated, the New York bank is a dealer in foreign exchange; it is in the business of buying—for a fee—and, conversely, in selling—also for a fee—pounds for dollars. Having just explained that the New York bank would buy pounds with dollars in connection with an American export transaction, we shall now examine how it would sell pounds for dollars in helping to finance an American import (British export) transaction. Specifically, suppose that an American retail concern wants to import £15,000 worth of woolens from a British mill. Again we rely on simple commercial bank balance sheets to summarize our discussion (Figure 43-2).

a. Because the British exporter must pay his own obligations in pounds rather than dollars, the American importer must somehow exchange dollars for pounds. He can obviously

LONDON BANK		NEW YORK BANK	
Assets	Liabilities and net worth	Assets	Liabilities and net worth
	Demand deposit of British importer $-£15,000(a)$	Deposit in London bank $+£15,000(c)$ ($30,000)	Demand deposit of American exporter $+$30,000(b)$
	Deposit of New York bank $+£15,000(c)$		

FIGURE 43-1 FINANCING A U.S. IMPORT TRANSACTION

American export transactions create a foreign demand for dollars. The satisfaction of this demand increases the supplies of foreign monies held by American banks.

LONDON BANK		NEW YORK BANK	
Assets	Liabilities and net worth	Assets	Liabilities and net worth
	Demand deposit of British exporter +£15,000(*b*)	Deposit in London bank −£15,000(*a*) ($30,000)	Demand deposit of American importer −$30,000(*a*)
	Deposit of New York bank −£15,000(*a*)		

FIGURE 43-2 FINANCING A U.S. EXPORT TRANSACTION

American import transactions create an American demand for foreign monies. The satisfaction of that demand reduces the supplies of foreign monies held by American banks.

do this by going to the New York bank and purchasing £15,000 for $30,000—perhaps he purchases the very same £15,000 which the New York bank acquired in the previous American export transaction. This purchase reduces the American importer's demand deposit in the New York bank by $30,000 and, of course, the New York bank gives up its £15,000 deposit in the London bank.

b. The American importer sends his newly purchased check for £15,000 to the British firm, which deposits it in the London bank.

Note that American imports create a domestic demand for foreign monies (pounds sterling, in this case) and that the fulfillment of this demand reduces the supplies of foreign monies held by American banks. Moreover, an American import transaction increases the supply of money in Britain and reduces the supply of money in the United States.

By putting these two transactions together, a further point comes into focus. American exports (in this case, computers) make available, or "earn," a supply of foreign monies for American banks, and American imports (British woolens, in this instance) create a demand for these monies. That is, in a broad sense, *any nation's exports finance or "pay for" its imports.* Exports provide the foreign currencies needed to pay for imports. From Britain's point of view, we note that its exports of woolens earn a supply of dollars, which are then used to meet the demand for dollars associated with its imports of computers.

THE INTERNATIONAL BALANCE OF PAYMENTS

The generalization that "exports finance imports" is only a first approximation, because the economic relationships among nations involve much more than the exporting and importing of goods and services. The spectrum of international transactions is reflected in a nation's balance of payments. Specifically, nations of the world systematically record and summarize *all* the transactions which take place between their residents (including individuals, businesses, and governmental units) and the residents of all other foreign nations and present them in an annual accounting statement called the *international balance of payments.* Despite its name, this statement is more like a business firm's profit and loss statement than a balance sheet. Like a profit and loss statement a nation's balance of payments records its sales to, and purchases from, all other nations, and it accounts for any differences between its sales (receipts) and its purchases (expenditures). A simplified balance of payments for the United States in 1976 is

Table 43-1   THE UNITED STATES BALANCE OF PAYMENTS, 1976 (*in billions*)

(1) United States exports		$+164.2
(*a*) Goods	$+119.9	
(*b*) Services	+21.7	
(*c*) Income from United States investments abroad · · · · · · · · · ·	+22.7	
(2) United States imports ·		−159.8
(*a*) Goods	$−123.9	
(*b*) Services	−23.8	
(*c*) Income from foreign investments in United States · · · · · · · · · ·	−12.1	
(3) Net balance due United States on exports and imports · · · · · · · · · ·		$ +4.4
(4) Net remittances ·		−1.9
(5) Net government transactions: grants, loans, etc. · · · · · · · · · · · · · ·		−3.1
(6) Net capital movements		−20.5
(*a*) United States capital inflow · · · · · · · · · · · · · · · · · ·	$ −40.5	
(*b*) Foreign capital inflow to United States	+20.0	
(7) Errors and omissions ·		+10.5
(8) Balance due United States (+) or rest of world (−) · · · · · · · · · · · ·		$ −10.6
(9) Financing (balancing) transactions		
(*a*) Decrease in United States holdings of foreign currencies		−2.5
(*b*) Increase in liquid dollar balances held by foreigners		+13.1
		$ 0.0

Source: Survey of Current Business, March 1977. Details may not add to totals because of rounding.

presented in Table 43-1. Let us analyze this accounting statement to see what it reveals about American international trade and finance. Specifically, what does it tell us about our position in world trade and finance?

☐ **Exports and Imports of Goods and Services**

The most obvious and perhaps most basic segment of the balance of payments involves the export and import of goods and services. As items 1 and 2 in Table 43-1 indicate, exports and imports are broadly defined. There is no question about the inclusion of items 1*a* and *b* as a part of American exports. As with domestic trade, international trade involves the exchange of both goods and services. The United States exports not only machinery, automobiles, and farm products, but also sells transportation services, insurance, and brokerage services to residents of foreign nations. Note, however, that one of the very special services

which foreigners get from the United States consists of the services of American money capital which has been invested abroad. As item 1*c* indicates, the dividend and interest income received from the use of American capital which has been invested in foreign nations is a payment for the American "export" of the services of this capital. United States imports, item 2, obviously include three analogous items. Americans import goods and services, including the services of foreign money capital which has been invested in the United States.

In Table 43-1 we have designated American exports with *plus* signs and American imports with *minus* signs. You will recall from our earlier discussion of foreign exchange that American exports entail payments of dollars from foreign buyers to the United States. These transactions, which involve dollar "inpayments" to the United States, have been marked plus (+). Conversely, American imports require that Americans make dollars available to foreigners. Such transactions, which involve dollar "outpayments" from the United States, have been marked minus (−). Thus the fact that the balance-due figure is a *plus* $4.4 billion indicates that net inpayments of that amount are due the United States from the rest of the world (item 3).

□ **Remittances**

A second component of the United States' balance of payments involves remittances— item 4 in Table 43-1. These are private gifts or grants: for example, immigrants' remittances sent to their families in the "old country," contributions to overseas missions, and pensions going to American citizens who are now living abroad. Note that net remittances to the rest of the world amounted to some $1.9 billion during 1976.

□ **Government Transactions**

Item 5 reflects the fact that the United States government makes substantial loans and grants to many nations. These loans and grants are for economic and military aid and in part reflect our ideological competition with the Soviet Union (Chapter 45). In 1976 these government transactions entailed dollar outpayments of $3.1 billion. That is, American government transactions were a source of that much purchasing power to foreign nations. The United States government was, in effect, "importing" claims against foreign nations in the case of loans and goodwill or, as it has been facetiously put, "thank-you notes" in the case of grants.

□ **Net Capital Movements**

Americans—both individuals and businesses—may choose to make investments in, and extend loans to, other nations. For example, many American corporations have become multinational by purchasing or constructing plants or outlets in foreign countries. Or Americans may buy the securities—stocks and

bonds—of foreign firms. Or American individuals or firms may make dollar deposits in foreign banks.

All such transactions involve capital outflows in monetary or real form. That is, just like American imports of goods, these American investing and lending transactions provide foreigners with American dollars. Indeed, it is quite appropriate to think of American investors and lenders as importing securities— claims of ownership to foreign assets, claims against foreign borrowers, and passbook claims against foreign banks. As item 6a indicates, American capital flows going abroad amounted to $40.5 billion in 1976.

Of course, foreigners can and do engage in similar capital transactions. They may purchase real assests in the United States, buy American stocks and bonds, make deposits in United States banks, and so forth. In these instances, the United States is in effect exporting securities and claims and, as with merchandise or service exports, getting inflows or inpayments of dollars in return. In 1976 capital inflows to the United States were $20.0 billion, as shown by item 6b.

It is appropriate to ask: Why did the United States experience a *net* capital outflow of $20.5 billion in 1976? Why don't Americans make all their investments in, and loans to, American firms rather than foreign firms? The answer is that Americans invest and lend abroad when they expect the rates of return from these foreign loans and investments to be greater than they can realize domestically. Given the rapid pace of economic expansion experienced by the countries of Western Europe and by Japan (Table 20-2), Americans have simply found it profitable to channel a large volume of loans and investments overseas.

□ **Errors and Omissions**

The gathering of data for the balance of payments statement is a complex and highly imperfect process. Hence, an "errors and omissions" item will invariably appear. Item 7 is essentially a bookkeeping entry which simply reflects the difference between all known in-payment and outpayment items. In 1976 errors and omissions were unusually large at $10.5 billion. It is generally agreed that most of this item reflects unrecorded capital inflows (note the plus sign) to the United States.

Let us now summarize our discussion to this point. Taking items 1 through 7 into account, we find that in 1976 the United States exported more goods and services than it imported and, as a result, other countries "owed" the United States $4.4 billion. But as the consequence of American remittances abroad, United States government grants and loans, private net capital outflows from this country, and taking the errors and omissions item into account, foreign nations actually obtained $15.0 billion, more than enough to cover this "debt." Stated differently, as the result of trade and financial transactions with the United States in 1976, the net dollar earnings of foreigners was $10.6 billion.

□   **Financing Transactions**

The $10.6 billion shown as item 8 measures the United States' *balance of payments deficit* for 1976. This deficit, which we shall define in more detail shortly, means that the United States provided more dollars to the world as a result of its imports, remittances, grants, and net public and private capital outflows than it earned back through its exports. That is, our exports were not sufficiently large to finance the sum of our imports, public and private grants and remittances, and public and private capital outflows.

What must the United States do to settle up the $10.6 billion difference? Briefly stated, the United States' $10.6 billion payments deficit can be financed in essentially two ways. First, it may expend some of its international monetary reserves, that is, some of the foreign cur-

rencies which it may have on hand.[1] Certain currencies—for example, German marks and Japanese yen—are widely acceptable as an international medium of exchange and therefore can be used to finance deficits. As Table 43-1 indicates, however, we did not use these reserves to finance our payments deficit; on the contrary, we increased our foreign currency holdings by $2.5 billion.

A second way in which the United States payments deficit can be handled is simply for foreign countries to hold a part or all of the surplus dollars which reflect the deficit. That is, the United States can increase its outstanding dollar liabilities. These dollar balances represent claims against the future output of the United States economy. Hence, in holding larger dollar balances, foreign countries are in effect granting us credit; they are saying to us: "We'll settle up later." In 1976 foreign holdings of dollars increased by $13.1 billion.

Items 9*a* and 9*b* in Table 43-1 tell us that the United States settled its 1976 payments deficit by having foreign nations increase their *net* credit to the United States by $10.6 billion (= $13.1 billion − $2.5 billion). That is, the difference between the $13.1 billion of credit foreign nations granted the United States and the $2.5 billion in credit which we granted them covered our $10.6 balance of payments deficit for 1976.

□   **A Peculiar Deficit**

Balance of payments deficits usually occur when a nation's imports exceed its exports of goods and services and it does not receive sufficient inflows of remittances or public and private loans and grants to cover the difference. It must then draw upon its international monetary reserves to finance the deficit.

Our analysis of Table 43-1 makes it clear

---

[1] In Chapter 44 we will find that a nation with a payments deficit can finance it by borrowing, within rather strict limits, from the International Monetary Fund (IMF).

that the balance of payments deficits which the United States has been encountering for a number of years are rather untypical. This country has usually had exports in excess of imports. The problem has been that net outflows of remittances and private capital, plus substantial public foreign aid disbursements, have been greater than that excess. Hence, despite its ability to sell more goods and services in international markets than it buys, the United States has been faced with growing accumulations of foreign-held dollars. We will examine the historical causes of the United States deficit problem, along with a number of potential remedies, in Chapter 44.

INTERNATIONAL DISEQUILIBRIUM

The meaning of international disequilibrium or, in the present instance, the meaning of a payments deficit, merits further discussion. The balance of payments statement must always balance, for the simple reason that every transaction must be settled, or accounted for, in one way or another. But the fact that this accounting statement balances is of little economic significance. The really important aspect of the balance of payments is the means by which that balance is achieved.

☐   An Analogy

Consider a crude analogy comparing two families. Family 1's earnings or income substantially exceeds its expenditures on goods and services. It uses its unconsumed income to buy stocks and bonds (make loans), to buy real assets such as real estate (make investments), perhaps to make some grants, and to add to its monetary reserves. We would agree that all is well with family 1; it is in good financial shape. Moreover, this family is in equilibrium in the sense that it can indefinitely maintain this position.

Family 2 is in a different situation. Its expenditures exceed the sum of its earnings plus any loans or grants it might be fortunate enough to receive. Family 2 is in financial difficulty; it is "living beyond its income" and must draw upon its monetary reserves or must borrow to finance the shortfall of its receipts relative to its expenditures. Note that in an accounting sense, inpayments and outpayments are in balance for both families; each family's "balance of payments" with the rest of the economy is in balance. Yet family 2 is clearly in a nonmaintainable or disequilibrium position. Its monetary reserves are presumably limited, and so is its credit, and it therefore cannot continue indefinitely to spend in excess of its receipts. Family 2 will be obliged to get its financial house in order.

☐   Autonomous and Accommodating Transactions

The same general kind of comparison can be applied to nations. Once again, the important consideration is not the fact that the balance of payments balances, but what kinds of transactions occur in achieving that balance. To pursue this point, we must distinguish between autonomous transactions, on the one hand, and accommodating or compensating transactions, on the other.

Autonomous transactions are independent of the balance of payments in the sense that they arise from, or are caused by, factors lying outside the balance of payments statement itself. Five of the items discussed in Table 43-1 (items 1, 2, 4, 5, and 6) are generally considered to be autonomous: exports, imports, remittances, public transactions, and net capital movements. Thus Americans buy goods and services from, and sell goods and services to, foreign nations because of differences in comparative costs. Remittances and government grants and loans are based upon humanitarian, political, or military considerations. Capital movements occur on the expectation that the income earned abroad on investments and loans will exceed the income which is anticipated domestically.

Accommodating transactions occur in order to account or compensate for differences between the inpayments and outpayments which arise from a nation's autonomous transactions. Accommodating transactions can be thought of as balancing transactions, that is, transactions which take place to accommodate or finance payment imbalances associated with the autonomous transactions. Illustration: Suppose a nation's autonomous transactions are such that its exports are $10 billion and its imports are $15 billion; it receives remittances of $1 billion and public grants and loans of another $1 billion; finally, it receives net capital inflows of $1 billion. The outpayments associated with these autonomous transactions are $15 billion, and the inpayments or receipts are only $13 (= $10 + $1 + $1 + $1) billion. The country has a $2 billion *dis*equilibrium or, more specifically, a $2 billion deficit, in its balance of payments. The nation must undertake $2 billion worth of financing or accommodating transactions to account for the difference between autonomous outpayments and inpayments. These financing transactions will involve reductions in its balances of foreign monies or increases in the balances of its currency held by other nations.

We can therefore say that the occurrence of accommodating or financing transactions is evidence of a balance of payments disequilibrium. In Table 43-1, items 9a and 9b are accommodating transactions and are evidence of the United States payments deficit. They indicate that the United States is not "paying its way" internationally. And although the United States has been realizing deficits for a period of years, these accommodating transactions cannot be maintained indefinitely. In the next chapter we shall discover that in the early 1970s, our persistent deficits precipitated fundamental changes in the international monetary system.

RESTORING INTERNATIONAL EQUILIBRIUM

Because it is a nonmaintainable situation, some adjustments must ultimately occur to correct a balance of payments disequilibrium. The basic problem is to bring autonomous inpayments or receipts into balance or equality with autonomous outpayments. Let us assume for simplicity's sake that a nation's imports exceed its exports and that all other autonomous transactions are zero (in other words, remittances, government transactions, and net capital flows are zero). In this simple framework the disequilibrium can be corrected by reducing imports, increasing exports, or both. There are essentially three means by which the country can adjust imports and exports and thereby return to equilibrium. If exchange rates are *fixed*—that is, if the prices of international currencies in terms of one another are stable—then a nation can correct a payments deficit in two ways: It can permit adjustments in domestic levels of output, employment, and prices to occur; *or* it can invoke governmental controls over international trade and finance. If exchange rates are *flexible* or *floating*, then exchange rates will automatically change in such a way as to tend to correct a balance of payments disequilibrium.

□ Freely Floating Exchange Rates

When foreign currencies can be freely bought and sold, the rate of exchange between any two currencies will be determined by the forces of supply and demand. Let us examine the rate, or price, at which American dollars might be exchanged for, say, British pounds sterling. As indicated in Figure 43-3, the demand for pounds will be downsloping, and the supply of pounds will be upsloping. Why? The downsloping demand for pounds shown by D_0D_0 indicates that, if pounds become less expensive to Americans, British goods will become cheaper to Americans. This fact causes

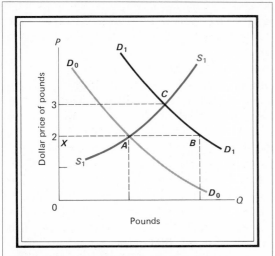

FIGURE 43-3 ADJUSTMENTS UNDER FLEXIBLE EXCHANGE RATES, THE GOLD STANDARD, AND EXCHANGE CONTROLS

Under flexible rates an American trade deficit at the $2-for-£1 rate would be corrected by an increase in the rate to $3 for £1. Under the gold standard the deficit would cause changes in domestic prices and incomes, which would shift the demand for $(D_1 D_1)$ and the supply of $(S_1 S_1)$ pounds into equilibrium at the $2-for-£1 rate. Under exchange controls the government would ration the available supply of pounds XA among persons demanding the quantity XB.

rate of exchange is $2 to £1. At this rate American-British trade is in balance; American imports from Great Britain create a demand for the precise quantity of pounds which American exports to Great Britain make available.

The Adjustment Process Now let us assume that our national tastes change so that Americans begin to import more British goods. They want more Triumph automobiles, more Scotch whisky, and more Harris tweeds. This obviously causes America's imports to exceed its exports, and, if not offset by long-term private loans, investments, and unilateral transfers from Britain, an American balance of payments deficit results. The immediate impact of the increase in American imports from Britain is an increase in the American demand for pounds, as indicated by the shift from $D_0 D_0$ to $D_1 D_1$ in Figure 43-3. Because of this shift, a shortage of pounds equal to AB now appears at the existing $2-for-£1 exchange rate. Since this is a free competitive market, the shortage will change the exchange rate (the dollar price of pounds) from $2 for £1 to, say, $3 for £1. This obviously means that the value of the dollar has *depreciated*—that is, the dollar is worth less—in international trade.

But at this point we must recognize that the exchange rate is a very special price. Why? Because it is the link between *all* domestic (United States) prices and *all* foreign (British) prices. A change in the exchange rate therefore alters the prices of all British goods to Americans and all American goods to potential British buyers. Specifically, this particular change in the exchange rate will alter the relative attractiveness of American imports and exports in such a way as to restore equilibrium in the balance of payments of the United States. From the American point of view, as the dollar price of pounds changes from $2 to $3, the Triumph automobile priced at £1500, which formerly cost an American $3000, now costs $4500. Other British goods will also be more expensive to Americans. Hence, Ameri-

Americans to demand larger quantities of British goods and therefore larger amounts of pounds with which to buy those goods. The supply of pounds is upsloping, as $S_1 S_1$, because, as the dollar price of pounds *rises* (that is, the pound price of dollars *falls*), the British will be inclined to purchase more American goods. The reason, of course, is that at higher and higher dollar prices for pounds, the British can obviously get more American dollars and therefore more American goods per pound. In other words, American goods become cheaper to the British, inducing the British to buy more of these goods. Such purchases, we have seen, will make larger and larger quantities of pounds available to Americans.

The intersection of the supply and demand for pounds will determine the dollar price of pounds. Suppose that the equilibrium can imports of British goods will tend to decline. Graphically, this is shown as a move from point *B* toward point *C* in Figure 43-3.

Conversely, from Britain's standpoint the exchange rate, that is, the pound price of dollars, has fallen (from £.50 to £.33 for $1). The international value of the pound has *appreciated*. The British previously got only $2 for £1; now they get $3 for £1. American goods are therefore cheaper to the British, and as a result American exports to Great Britain tend to rise. In Figure 43-3 this is indicated by the move from point *A* toward point *C*. The two adjustments described—a decrease in American imports from Great Britain and an increase in American exports to Great Britain—are precisely those needed to correct the American balance of payments deficit. (The reader should reason through the operation of freely fluctuating exchange rates in correcting an initial American balance of payments surplus in its trade with Great Britain). In short, the free fluctuation of exchange rates in response to shifts in the supply of, and demand for, foreign monies tends to restore international equilibrium automatically. As a matter of fact, if floating rates worked perfectly, a balance of payments disequilibrium would not occur.

Disadvantages   Though freely fluctuating exchange rates automatically correct a balance of payments disequilibrium, they may entail several significant problems:

1   Risks   The risks associated with flexible exchange rates are likely to discourage the flow of trade. To illustrate: Suppose an American automobile dealer contracts to purchase ten Triumph cars for £15,000. At the current exchange rate of, say, $2 for £1, the American importer expects to pay $30,000 for these automobiles. But if in the two- or three-month shipping period the rate of exchange shifts to $3 for £1, the £15,000 payment contracted by the American importer will now amount to $45,000. Obviously, this unheralded increase in the dollar price of pounds may easily turn the

potential American importer's anticipated profits into substantial losses. Aware at the outset of the possibility of an adverse change in the exchange rate, the American importer may simply not be willing to assume the risks involved. He therefore confines his operations to domestic automobiles, with the result that international trade does not occur in this item.

The same rationale applies to investment. Assume that, when the exchange rate is $3 to £1, an American invests $30,000 (or £10,000) in a British enterprise. He estimates a return of 10 percent, that is, he anticipates earnings of $3000 or £1000. Suppose his expectations prove correct in the sense that the British firm earns £1000 the first year on his £10,000 investment. But suppose that during the year, the value of the dollar depreciates to $2 = £1. His absolute return is now only $2000 (rather than $3000) and his rate of return falls from the anticipated 10 percent to only $6\frac{2}{3}$ percent ($= \$2000/\$30,000$). Investment is inherently risky. The added risk posed by adverse changes in exchange rates may persuade the potential American investor to shy away from overseas ventures.[2]

2   Terms of trade   A nation's terms of trade will tend to be worsened by a decline in the international value of its currency. For example, an increase in the dollar price of pounds will mean that the United States must export a larger volume of goods and services to finance a given level of imports from Britain.

3   Instability   Freely fluctuating exchange rates may also have some destabilizing effects upon the domestic economy as wide fluctuations stimulate and then depress those industries producing internationally traded goods. If the American economy is operating at full employment and the international value of its currency depreciates as in our illustration, the subsequent rise in American exports and de-

---

[2] At modest cost and inconvenience, a *trader* can circumvent the risk of unfavorable exchange rate fluctuations by "hedging" in the "futures market" for foreign exchange. However, there is no long-term investment futures market; hence, the *investor* must bear the risk.

cline in imports will tend to increase net exports and cause domestic price inflation. Conversely, appreciation of the dollar could lower exports and increase imports, tending to cause unemployment. Looked at from the vantage point of policy, acceptance of floating exchange rates may complicate the use of domestic fiscal and monetary policies in seeking full employment and price stability.

4   Effective? Some economists make the related contention that in fact floating exchange rates may *not* effectively correct a payments imbalance. The argument goes something like this: Assume the United States economy is at full employment and has a payments deficit. The deficit causes the dollar to depreciate, stimulating American exports and reducing our imports and thereby tending to eliminate our payments deficit. But now a counterproductive feedback intrudes upon this adjustment process. The increase in our net exports means that aggregate demand has risen (Chapter 41) and, given full employment, inflation will result in the United States. Inflation, however, makes our exports less attractive and imports of foreign goods more attractive. These changes are obviously at odds with the increase in exports and decrease in imports originally triggered by the depreciation of the dollar. The point is that reductions in American exports and increases in American imports caused by inflation work against the achievement of a balance of payments equilibrium.

☐ **Changing Price and Income Levels**

As the preceding paragraphs explained, allowing the international value of the dollar to depreciate—that is, letting the dollar price of pounds rise—is one way to correct a payments deficit. Example: A ton of American steel may sell for $20 domestically. This ton of American steel will obviously cost a British buyer £10 if the exchange rate is $2 for £1, but only £6.67 when $3 exchange for £1. Depreciation of the value of the dollar as reflected in a

shift in the exchange rate from $2 equals £1 to $3 equals £1 will stimulate American exports and help correct a United States payments deficit.

But domestic *deflation* can have an effect equivalent to that of exchange rate depreciation. *Given the $2-for-£1 exchange rate,* a decline in the domestic price of American steel from $20 to $13.33 per ton will have the same stimulating effect on steel exports, for at this exchange rate it will take only £6.67 to buy a ton of American steel! Obviously, *inflation* in Britain would also tend to correct an American payments disequilibrium by making British goods less attractive to American importers.

If domestic price level changes—deflation in the United States and inflation in Britain—are a possible cure for an American payments deficit, how are these price level adjustments to be brought about? In the first place, the payments deficit itself would automatically tend to cause them. Recall from Figure 43-2 that American imports decrease the supply of money in the United States and increase the money supply in Britain. This obviously means that the net effect of a United States payments deficit—an excess of imports over exports, in our simple case—will be to reduce the money supply in the United States. And this reduction, we know from Chapter 16, tends to be deflationary. Conversely, the balance of payments surplus incurred by Britain will increase her supply of money and tend to cause inflation. In the second place, appropriate monetary and fiscal policies might be necessary in the two countries to ensure that the price level changes are sufficiently great to correct the payments disequilibrium. In particular, the United States might need to invoke a tight money policy and a contractionary fiscal policy to bring about the degree of deflation needed to eliminate its payments deficit.

Equilibrium: At What Price?   The main advantage of this means of correcting a balance of payments disequilibrium is that it sidesteps the disadvantages associated with freely fluctuating exchange rates. Because exchange rates are held constant, the risks and uncertainties which accompany fluctuating rates and tend to discourage international trade are avoided, as is the prospect of worsening terms of trade.

But a moment's reflection will reveal formidable objections to stable exchange rates accompanied by domestic price level adjustments.

1 We know (Chapter 10) that changing price levels mean arbitrary changes in the distribution of real income. If these changes are severe, inflation and deflation can seriously disrupt normal economic activity.

2 More important, however, is the fact that the changes in the money supply which international disequilibrium entails will affect not only the price level, but also the levels of national output and employment. Recalling (Chapter 17) the equation of exchange, $MV = PQ$, we see that a decline in M (the money supply) will tend to cause both P (the price level) and Q (real output and, implicitly, the level of employment) to decline. As a matter of fact, we know that prices are quite sticky or inflexible in a downward direction, so the brunt of any decline in aggregate demand (MV) will probably fall on output and employment rather than on the price level. Most economists take the position that such distasteful domestic adjustments are far too high a price to pay for a balance of payments equilibrium. In our example, the "price" of exchange rate stability for the United States is falling price, output, and employment levels—in other words, a recession! Achieving a balance of payments equilibrium and realizing domestic stability are both important national economic objectives; but to sacrifice the latter for the former is to let the tail wag the dog.

The Gold Standard

It is interesting to note that for a half-century prior to World War I, and again for a brief period in the 1920s, most of the major trading nations accepted and participated in an international monetary system whose operation was characterized by exchange rate stability and therefore domestic adjustment of price and output levels as a basic means of achieving balance of payments equilibrium. This system was the international gold standard.

Conditions   A nation is on the gold standard when it fulfills two conditions:

1 It must define its monetary unit in terms of a certain quantity of gold and stand ready to convert gold into paper money and paper money into gold at the rate stipulated in its definition of the monetary unit.

2 It must allow gold to be freely exported and imported.

If each nation defines its monetary unit in terms of gold, the different currencies will have a fixed relationship to one another. For example, suppose the United States defines a dollar as being worth, say, 25 grains of gold and Britain defines its pound sterling as being worth 50 grains of gold. This means that a British pound is worth $^{50}/_{25}$ dollars or, simply, £1 equals $2.

Gold flows   Now, if we momentarily ignore the costs of packing, insuring, and shipping gold between countries, under the gold standard the rate of exchange would not vary from this $2-for-£1 rate. And the reason is clear: No one in the United States would pay more than $2 for £1, because he could always buy 50 grains of gold for $2 in the United States, ship it to Britain, and sell it for £1. Nor would an Englishman pay more than £1 for $2. Why should he, when he could buy 50 grains of gold in England for £1, send it to the United States, and sell it for $2?

Of course, in practice the costs of packing, insuring, and shipping gold must be taken into account. But these costs would only amount to a few cents per 50 grains of gold. For example, if these costs were 3 cents for 50 grains of gold, Americans wanting pounds would pay up to $2.03 for a pound rather than buy and export 50 grains of gold to get that pound. Why? Because it would cost them $2 for the 50 grains of gold plus 3 cents to send it to England to be exchanged for £1. This $2.03 exchange rate, above which gold would begin to flow out of the United States, is called the *gold export point*. Conversely, the exchange rate would fall to $1.97 before gold would flow into the United States. Englishmen wanting dollars would accept as little as $1.97 in exchange for £1, because from the $2 which they could get by buying 50 grains of gold in England and reselling it in the United States, 3 cents must be subtracted to pay shipping and related costs. This $1.97 exchange rate, below which gold would flow into the United States, is called the *gold import point*. Our basic conclusion is that under the gold standard the flow of gold between nations would result in exchange rates which for all practical purposes are fixed.

Domestic adjustments But these gold flows would do more than stabilize exchange rates. They would also cause internal adjustments within the domestic economies which would tend to restore equilibrium in the balance of payments.

Suppose, once again, that the United States incurs a balance of payments deficit by importing more from Great Britain than it exports to her. The immediate result is that the dollar price of pounds will move up to the $2.03 gold export point and, if at this exchange rate the quantity of pounds demanded still exceeds the quantity supplied, gold will flow from the United States to Great Britain to settle the deficit. But as gold leaves the United States, bank reserves and the amount of money in circulation will decline, credit availability will be lessened, and interest rates tend to rise. Other things being unchanged, this is conducive to a decline in aggregate demand and therefore in national income and, perhaps, the price level in the United States. The opposite occurs in Great Britain; the inflow of gold expands bank reserves and the money supply, causing aggregate demand, national income, and the price level to rise, and exerting downward pressure on interest rates. Declining American prices and rising British prices will encourage American exports to, and discourage American imports from, Great Britain, thereby tending to correct the initial American payments deficit. Income changes will work toward the same end. As their incomes fall, Americans import fewer British goods. As their incomes rise, the British buy more American exports.

Graphic portrayal Gold standard adjustments can be envisioned in terms of Figure 43-3. You will recall that under a system of freely fluctuating exchange rates, an American payments deficit would be corrected by a rise in the exchange rate from, say, $2 to $3. In the case of the gold standard, gold flows between the two nations hold the exchange rate approximately at the $2 level. But gold flows result in changes in the price, income, and employment levels of the nations receiving and losing gold. These domestic adjustments shift the demand for and supply of foreign exchange so as to achieve equilibrium at the fixed $2-to-£1 exchange rate. Specifically, given the initial American payments deficit and the resulting American pound shortage of AB at the $2 exchange rate, gold will flow from the United States to Great Britain. The contractionary impact in the United States will tend to lower the American demand for pounds, and the expansionary impact in Great Britain will tend to increase the available supply of pounds. These shifts continue until equilibrium is restored at the $2-for-£1 gold standard rate. Graphically, this means the D_1D_1 curve of Figure 43-3 will shift to the left, and the S_1S_1 curve to the right, providing a new intersection (equilibrium) point somewhere on the broken line between points A and B.

Evaluation The gold standard entails obvious advantages:

1 The stable exchange rates which it fosters reduce the riskiness and thereby stimulate the volume of international trade.

2 The gold standard automatically corrects balance of payments disequilibria. International equilibrium under the gold standard does not require the action of governmental bodies; inevitable gold flows adjust trade deficits or surpluses to the end that a balance of payments disequilibrium will be resolved.

The basic drawback of the gold standard is apparent from our discussion of the adjustment processes it entails. Nations on the gold standard must accept domestic adjustments in such distasteful forms as deflation, unemployment, and falling incomes, on the one hand, or inflation, on the other.

□ Public Controls

By allowing the forces of supply and demand in the foreign exchange market to alter the exchange rate or by permitting internal employment, output, and price level adjustments to occur in response to a balance of payments disequilibrium, the government is assuming an essentially passive role. Government is permitting "market forces" to work themselves out in ameliorating or correcting a balance of payments deficit or surplus. A third option is for government to adopt specific policies—to take positive action—to correct, say, a payments deficit by interfering with the functioning of market forces. In general, there are two variants of this method of adjustment to consider: (1) government control of the foreign exchange market and thereby the rate of exchange, and (2) control of the flow of international trade itself. Both attempt to correct a balance of payments disequilibrium by suppressing or altering the functioning of market forces.

Foreign Exchange Controls To see how exchange controls work, let us suppose the United States government has fixed the legal dollar price of pounds at $2 to £1, as in Figure 43-3. Now assume as before that American imports increase, resulting in an American payments deficit. The main symptom of this deficit is an American foreign exchange shortage of AB in Figure 43-3. Under exchange controls, the government handles this problem by requiring that all foreign exchange obtained by American exporters and other recipients be sold to it. Then, in turn, the government allocates or rations this short supply of pounds (XA) among the various American importers and other users, who demand the quantity XB. In this way government can restrict American imports to the amount of foreign exchange earned by American exports. In effect, *government rationing of foreign exchange "forces" a balance of payments equilibrium by restricting imports to the value of exports.* The rationing process necessarily involves government discrimination between different importers, typically denying foreign exchange for the importation of luxury, or nonessential, goods in order to made the short supply available for necessary, or essential, goods.

But there are many objections to exchange controls.

1 They obviously impinge upon freedom of consumer choice; American buyers may be forced to forgo Scotch and settle for bourbon. American importing firms will obviously be hurt by exchange controls, because imports are restricted to the volume of exports.

2 The government will be faced with an enforcement problem; the market forces of supply and demand indicate that there are American importers who want foreign exchange badly enough to pay *more* than the $2 equals £1 official rate, and this sets the stage for extralegal or "black market" foreign exchange dealings.

3 Exchange controls do not free nations from internal price and income adjustments. Specifically, the restriction of imports in the control nation leads to domestic scarcities of certain goods and materials ordinarily imported. The prices of these products and resources therefore tend to rise. This is reinforced by the fact that the restricting of imports to the value of exports will increase national income in the control economy; expenditures formerly made on imported goods are now reallocated to domestically produced goods. Conversely, countries with which the control country trades will tend to experience contractionary consequences.

Trade Controls   The government of a nation faced with a payments deficit—say, the United States—can also undertake to manipulate imports and exports through the use of tariffs, quotas, subsidies, and the like. In correcting a payments deficit, the problem obviously is to reduce imports and increase exports. On the one hand, imports can be reduced by imposing tariffs or import quotas (Chapter 42). Special taxes on foreign lending and investing by Americans have a similar effect in that such taxes tend to reduce United States capital outflows or, looked at differently, to cut our imports of foreign securities. Similarly, special taxes or outright limits might be imposed upon the expenditures of American tourists. On the other hand, the United States government might subsidize certain American exports to make them more competitive in world markets and thereby to increase the volume of their sales.

The fundamental problem with these trade controls, and also with exchange controls, is that they reduce the volume of world trade and distort its composition or pattern away from that which is economically desirable. That is, exchange and trade controls can be imposed only at the sacrifice of some portion of the economic gains or benefits attainable from a free flow of world trade based upon the principle of comparative advantage. These effects should not be underestimated; remember that the imposition of exchange or trade controls can elicit retaliatory responses from other nations whose balance of payments are adversely affected.

Summary

1   America exports create a foreign demand for dollars and make a supply of foreign exchange available to Americans. Conversely, American imports simultaneously create a demand for foreign exchange and make a supply of dollars available to foreigners. Generally speaking, a nation's exports earn the foreign currencies needed to pay for its imports.

2   The balance of payments is an annual accounting statement of all a nation's international trade and financial transactions. In 1976 the United States' exports exceeded its imports by $4.4 billion. But remittances from the United States, government loans and grants, and net capital movements from the United States totaled $15.0 billion, resulting in a balance of payments deficit of $10.6 billion. Payments deficits have been common to the United States since the early 1950s.

3   In general, a balance of payments disequilibrium occurs when the inpayments and outpayments resulting from a nation's autonomous transactions do not balance. This imbalance necessitates accommodating or financing transactions. In the case of a deficit, financing transactions typically involve reductions in the nation's holdings of foreign monies and increases in the amount of its liquid liabilities to nonresidents—mostly foreign central and commercial banks.

4   A balance of payments disequilibrium can be corrected by means of *a.* freely fluctuating exchange rates, *b.* changes in domestic levels of output and prices, and *c.* government controls over international trade and finance.

5   Freely fluctuating exchange rates restore international equilibrium primarily by affecting the relative attractiveness of internationally traded goods.

6   Given stable exchange rates, a nation can correct a payments deficit by undertaking contractionary policies domestically. Historically, the gold standard provided exchange rate stability. But, under this system, gold flows between nations precipitated sometimes painful changes in price, income, and employment levels in bringing about international equilibrium.

7 Through exchange controls, government can force imports into equality with exports by rationing foreign exchange. Similarly, trade controls—tariffs, import quotas, export subsidies, and so forth—can be used to alleviate or correct a payments disequilibrium.

Questions and Study Suggestions

1 Key terms and concepts to remember: rate of exchange; international balance of payments; remittances; net capital movements; financing transactions; balance of payments deficit and surplus; international monetary reserves; international disequilibrium; autonomous and accommodating transactions; floating exchange rates; exchange rate depreciation and appreciation; international gold standard; gold import and export points; foreign exchange controls; trade controls.

2 Explain how an American automobile importer might finance a shipment of Renaults from France. Explain: "American exports earn supplies of foreign monies which American can use to finance imports."

3 "A rise in the dollar price of pesos necessarily means a fall in the peso price of dollars." Do you agree? Illustrate and elaborate: "The critical thing about exchange rates is that they provide a direct link between the prices of goods and services produced in all trading nations of the world."

4 "Exports pay for imports. Yet in 1976 the rest of the world imported about $4.4 billion more worth of goods and services from the United States than were exported to the United States." Resolve the apparent inconsistency of these two statements.

5 Use the distinction between autonomous and accommodating transactions to explain the notion of international disequilibrium.

6 Explain in detail the adjustments which must occur to resolve a balance of payments surplus under *a.* the gold standard, *b.* flexible exchange rates, and *c.* exchange controls. Now trace the adjustments entailed by a payments deficit. Evaluate the virtues and shortcomings of *a.* the gold standard and *b.* flexible exchange rates.

7 "The operation of the international gold standard undermines domestic full-employment policies, and, conversely, the active pursuit of full employment domestically is inimical to the operation of the gold standard." Explain and evaluate this statement.

Selected References

Grubel, Herbert G.: *The International Monetary System* (Middlesex, England: Penguin Books, Ltd., 1970).

Kreinin, Mordechai E.: *International Economics: A Policy Approach,* 2d ed. (New York: Harcourt Brace Jovanovich, Inc., 1975), chaps. 1–6.

Root, Franklin R.: *International Trade & Investment,* 3d ed. (Cincinnati: South-Western Publishing Company, Incorporated, 1973), chaps. 6–10.

Stevens, Robert Warren: *A Primer on the Dollar in the World Economy* (New York: Random House, Inc., 1972).

Last Word
Are Floating Exchange Rates Desirable?

In early 1973 the international monetary system changed from fixed to flexible or floating exchange rates. Dr. Arthur F. Burns, Chairman of the Board of Governors of the Federal Reserve System, questions the long-term desirability of floating rates.

For the longer run, thinking of a reformed international monetary system, I remain skeptical about the desirability of a general system of floating exchange rates. I hold this view even though I recognize the usefulness of floating rates in particular situations, such as the present. Some reasons for my skepticism are as follows:

First, in my judgment, the floating exchange-rate system that has figured so heavily in academic discussions is a dream that will continue to elude us. Even for a country with as low a ratio of international trade to gross national product as that of the United States, the repercussions of exchange-rate changes on the domestic economy can be substantial. Under a floating exchange-rate system, governments are always apt to be subject to political pressure by business, agricultural, and labor interests for protection against large movements of exchange rates—which may mean new controls or central bank intervention or both. . . .

Second, a system of floating exchange rates may lead to political friction and competitive national economic policies. From time to time suspicions will be generated that this or that country has been manipulating its exchange rate at the expense of the interests of its trading partners. In such an atmosphere, whether for defensive or retaliatory reasons, governments may impose controls on capital flows or on current transactions. It is true, of course, that suspicion and political friction may be present under any type of exchange-rate regime. And we know from experience that governments often imposed controls on international transactions when they were trying to defend fixed exchange rates that were unrealistic. Nonetheless, I fear that such problems would be greater with widespread permanent floating of the major currencies.

Third, the uncertainties associated with floating exchange rates may lead in time to some erosion of international trade, particularly in the case of equipment purchases that require long-term financing and when profit margins are slim. These uncertainties may also weaken private foreign investment—especially in long-term bond issues.

Fourth, exchange-rate fluctuations under a floating regime may add further to the difficulties that some governments already have in carrying out suitable fiscal and monetary policies. There is danger, for example, that a temporary exchange-rate depreciation will get translated into permanent price-level increases through upward revisions of nominal [money] wages. Moreover, floating exchange rates may themselves become a tool of business-cycle policy, and thereby lead at times to neglect of appropriate domestic policies.

From *How Well Are Fluctuating Exchange Rates Working?,* Hearings before the Subcommittee on International Economics of the Joint Economic Committee, 93d Congress, 1st Session, Washington, 1973, p. 173, abridged.

International Trade and Finance: Problems and Policies

With the elements of international trade and finance in mind, we are now in a position to explore current international economic problems and policies. In particular, our discussion will center upon two interrelated problems: chronic United States balance of payments deficits and the recent reform of the international monetary system. We begin with a brief historical synopsis.

A BACKWARD GLANCE

During most of the nineteenth century a harmonious network of international trade and finance linked the nations of the world. Some nations—particularly those of northwestern Europe—quickly grasped the new techniques of the Industrial Revolution, while others remained almost completely unaffected. These differences formed the basis for a highly complementary pattern of trade wherein underdeveloped nations exported raw materials to the manufacturing nations. The latter in turn came to depend upon the expanding markets of the semideveloped and underdeveloped nations in selling their manufactured goods. This trade pattern was accompanied by relatively large flows of private long-term capital from the manufacturing to the raw-materials nations. These flows increased the production of raw materials and simultaneously strengthened overseas markets in the raw-materials nations. Furthermore, laissez faire was the dominant ideology during this golden age of international trade. Governmental interference with the composition and volume of trade was at a minimum. Each nation accepted any and all internal adjustments which inevitable changes in the structure and terms of trade demanded. The international gold standard—characterized, you will recall (Chapter 43), by gold movements and highly stable rates of exchange—worked automatically and effectively during much of this period to resolve balance of payments disequilibria. The world of the last half of the nineteenth century and the early twentieth century was a closely knit economic unit wherein the volume of trade was large and generally in accord with the principle of comparative advantage. But the Great Depression and World War II brought changes which resulted in the demise of this golden age of international trade.

☐ **World Trade in the Thirties**

The Great Depression of the 1930s severely disrupted the volume and composition of international trade. Nations heavily dependent upon foreign trade found that the Depression caused their overseas markets to collapse, preventing them from earning the foreign monies needed to finance the importation of essential goods. Nations which imported more than they exported witnessed the disappearance of the long-term capital flows which financed this difference as the Depression undermined profit expectations. Furthermore, drastic and uneven changes in the price levels of the various nations rendered existing exchange rates unrealistic and raised serious questions about the terms of trade. It is easy to see why many nations faced severe balance of payments difficulties during the thirties.

In addition to upsetting the international flow of goods and capital and posing exchange rate problems, the Great Depression prompted a myriad of trade controls. Serious domestic unemployment almost invariably gives rise to trade barriers designed to create more employment domestically. An obvious means of bol-

stering domestic employment and production is to increase exports and cut imports. Success in this endeavor expands net exports, which through the multiplier effect promises a magnified expansionary effect upon the domestic economy. In seeking this trade surplus, the nations of the world imposed high tariff barriers, created import quotas and export subsidies, established government controls upon foreign exchange, and devalued their currencies. (Note, for example, in Figure 42-2, the high American tariffs imposed in the early 1930s.) Unfortunately, because the exports of one nation are the imports of another, all nations could not succeed in stimulating their domestic economies by exporting more than they imported. But most tried. And the trade barriers which accompanied these attempts further distorted and choked off the declining flow of international trade.

☐ **World War II: Disruption of Trade**

Following on the heels of the Great Depression, World War II virtually completed the disintegration of world trade. The impact of war upon international trade is manifold:

1 Most obviously, the pattern of trade is altered so that it is in accord with military objectives rather than with comparative advantage. At the outset of World War II, the European belligerents sought to mobilize as many resources as possible—both domestic and foreign—for war goods production. On the one hand, this meant cutting exports, that is, shifting resources from export goods to war goods production. On the other hand, it meant increasing imports to supplement the productive capacity of the domestic economy. The resulting excess of imports over exports posed an obvious balance of payments problem: How could the warring nations, when restricting exports, obtain enough foreign exchange to expand greatly their volume of imports?

2 War almost invariably means inflationary pressures (Chapter 39), and, like depression, inflation affects different nations in dif-

fering degrees. Those nations which experience the greatest amount of inflation find that at existing exchange rates, their goods are less attractive to foreign buyers and, unhappily, that domestic consumers are attracted to foreign goods. Down go that nation's exports and up go its imports. This again contributes to a balance of payments deficit and a shortage of foreign monies.

3 World War II had dramatically different effects upon the productive capacities of nations. The capital facilities of some—particularly Great Britain, France, and Germany— were seriously reduced as the result of physical destruction through invasion, bombings, and the inability to replace depreciated capital during the wartime emergency. Those nations whose capital facilities are seriously impaired by war will want to achieve an excess of imports over exports to supplement domestic productive capacity in the postwar reconstruction period. But how is this trade deficit to be financed?

□ **Postwar Problems**

In short, at the close of World War II, world trade was in a shambles. Old trade patterns were almost completely destroyed, the productive capacity of Europe was very low, the price levels of the various nations had changed in a disjointed fashion as a result of the war, and the Depression had imposed a myriad of restrictions upon the flow of trade. The problem of rebuilding the world economy in the postwar period was clearly a formidable one.

Postwar programs and institutions concerned with the immediate reconstruction of world trade sought to resolve several interrelated problems.

1 The most immediate problem was to achieve economic recovery in war-devastated Europe.

2 The artificial barriers to trade which accompanied and contributed to the disinte-

gration of world trade had to be dismantled in order for trade to expand.

3 It was essential that an international monetary system capable of facilitating an anticipated growing volume of world trade and finance be established.

The postwar liberalization of world trade has been detailed in Chapter 42 and will receive no further comment.

REBUILDING THE EUROPEAN ECONOMY

The major economic problem was all too clear: to rebuild European economies and facilitate their transition to peacetime production. Europe was destitute; it needed crucial goods and services but had little to sell in financing their importation. American capitalism, on the other hand, emerged from the holocaust more vigorous and with a greater productive capacity than when it had entered. Thus, the solution for reconstruction was almost as evident as the immediate problem: American economic aid to the needy nations.

In the immediate two or three years following World War II, the United States extended almost $17 billion in aid to Europe. However, much of this aid was temporary relief, centering upon the provision of clothing, food, and medical services. In fact, American postwar inflation made serious inroads on the purchasing power of these grants and loans. Trade among European nations was stifled by serious balance of payments problems. Drought, crop failures, and material and fuel shortages added to these economic woes. In short, European economic recovery was lagging. On the international political front, Soviet Russia was becoming increasingly aggressive in seeking the worldwide spread of communism. On the domestic political front, there was a growing desire to abandon piecemeal aid programs designed to meet each individual economic and political crisis in favor of a comprehensive and coordinated aid program designed to restore the economic health and the political stability of Europe once and for all.

Out of this background the United States established in 1948 the European Recovery Program (ERP), called the "Marshall Plan" for its progenitor, Secretary of State George Marshall. The fundamental objective was to restore the productive capacity of European industry and agriculture. Related objectives were domestic political stability, the establishment of sound monetary and fiscal systems in the reviving nations of Europe, and the solution of the serious balance of payments problems which hampered trade among the nations of Europe in particular and in the world in general. In the less than four years of its existence, the Marshall Plan channeled well over $10 billion in American aid to Europe, most of which was in the form of outright grants.

Although comprehensive aid programs such as the Marshall Plan elude precise evaluation, most experts agree that ERP was highly successful both economically and politically. In 1951, the average level of industrial production in all participating nations was 55 percent above the 1947 level. By the early 1950s, European economic recovery was accomplished. Though far from completely successful in resolving balance of payments difficulties, considerable progress was made in this area. A very rough indicator of the political success of ERP lies in the fact that after 1948 no European nations succumbed to communism. The political ties of the United States and Western Europe were strengthened immeasurably by the Marshall Plan.

THE BRETTON WOODS MONETARY SYSTEM

It was well recognized at the end of World War II that the reconstruction of world trade would depend upon the establishment of a viable international monetary system. In order to lay the groundwork for such a system, an international conference of Allied nations was held at Bretton Woods, New Hampshire, in 1944. Out of this conference evolved a commitment to an *adjustable-peg system* of exchange rates, sometimes called the Bretton Woods system. Furthermore, the conference created the International Monetary Fund (IMF) to make the new exchange rate system feasible and workable. This international monetary system, emphasizing relatively fixed exchange rates and managed through the IMF, prevailed with modifications until 1971.

□ IMF and Adjustable Pegs

What was the Bretton Woods system? Why was it evolved? What caused its demise? Consider the second question first. During the depressed 1930s, various countries resorted to the practice of altering their exchange rates in the hope of stimulating domestic employment. In particular, many of them *devalued* their currencies. For example, if the United States was faced with growing unemployment, it might devalue the dollar by *increasing* the dollar price of pounds from $2.50 for £1 to, say, $3 for £1. This action would make American goods cheaper to the British and British goods dearer to Americans, increasing American exports and reducing American imports. The resulting increase in the net exports component of aggregate demand would stimulate output and employment in the United States. But the problem was that every nation can play the devaluation game, and most gave it a whirl. The resulting rounds of competitive devaluations benefited no one; on the contrary, they actually contributed to the demoralization of world trade. Nations at Bretton Woods therefore agreed that the postwar monetary system must provide for overall exchange rate stability whereby disruptive currency devaluations could be avoided.

What was the adjustable-peg system of

exchange rates like? First, each member of the IMF was obligated to define its monetary unit in terms of gold (or dollars), thereby establishing par rates of exchange between its currency and the currencies of all other members. Each nation was further obligated to keep its exchange rate essentially stable vis-à-vis any other currency; that is, a nation was allowed to vary its exchange rate only 1 percent above and below its established par value. But how was this obligation to be fulfilled? After all, it would only be by chance that in a particular year any given nation would achieve an equilibrium in its balance of payments. And if they were not somehow countered, payments imbalances would be reflected in changes in the demand for, or supply of, a nation's currency and therefore in fluctuating exchange rates. How could a nation finance temporary payments deficits without having to let its exchange rate depreciate? By two basic means.

1   Stabilization Funds   Each member nation established a stabilization fund, affiliated with its central bank or treasury, which holds supplies of both foreign and domestic monies and gold. These monies and gold are used to augment the supply of, or demand for, any currency as required to avoid or restrict fluctuations in the rate of exchange. For example, if the dollar appreciates in value, the United States government can augment the supply by offering extra dollars for sale. This action restricts the rise in the price of dollars. Conversely, if the dollar depreciates in value, the government can use some of the foreign currencies it has on hand to buy dollars. This bolsters the demand for dollars and limits the decline in the price of the dollar.

2   IMF Credit   The IMF plays a major role in stabilizing exchange rates. Specifically, the IMF is empowered to make short-term loans to nations faced with temporary, or short-run, balance of payments deficits. These loans are made out of currencies and gold con-

tributed by the participating nations on the basis of size of national income, population, and volume of trade. If Great Britain or France, for example, faces a temporary shortage of dollars, it can borrow the needed dollars from the Fund by supplying its own currency as collateral. The dollars so acquired are in the form of a loan, not a grant, and must be repaid with interest in a relatively short period. Presumably in the near future, the borrowing country's trade deficit with the United States will be corrected so that it can obtain the gold or dollars needed to retire its IMF loan.

☐   **Correcting Disequilibria**

While stabilization funds and IMF credit are the primary means of avoiding short-run fluctuations in exchange rates, the adjustable-peg system—as its name implies—provided for the orderly alteration of exchange rates to cope with international disequilibrium stemming from long-run, or fundamental, causes. It was recognized that if a nation's currency is overvalued in relation to other currencies, that nation will encounter severe difficulties in exporting. Hence, it will persistently be faced with a payments deficit. To cope with such situations, the Fund allowed each member nation to alter the value of its currency by 10 percent without explicit permission from the Fund in order to correct a deeply rooted balance of payments deficit. Larger exchange rate changes required the sanction of the Fund's board of directors. By requiring approval of significant rate changes, the Fund attempted to guard against arbitrary and competitive currency devaluation prompted by nations seeking a temporary stimulus to their domestic economies or the solution to a payments deficit.

The objective of the adjustable-peg system was to realize a world monetary system which embraced the best features of both a fixed exchange rate system (such as the old international gold standard) and a system of freely fluctuating exchange rates. Short-run exchange rate stability—pegged exchange rates—stimulates trade and is conducive to the efficient use of world resources. Periodic exchange rate adjustments—adjustment of the pegs—made in an orderly fashion through the IMF, and on the basis of permanent or long-run changes in a country's payments position, provided a mechanism by which international payments disequilibria could be resolved by means other than changes in domestic levels of output and prices.

□ **International Monetary Reserves**

The effective functioning of an essentially fixed exchange rate monetary system, such as the Bretton Woods system, requires the availability of sufficient quantities of international monetary reserves. We have noted that as nations incur short-run payments deficits, they need monetary reserves if exchange rates are to be kept stable while domestic adjustments in output and employment are avoided. No international central bank exists to increase or reduce some sort of world money supply to meet the fluctuating needs of international trade and finance. However, throughout most of the postwar period, gold and certain *key currencies* played the major role as international monetary reserves. The dollar has been the primary key currency, although other currencies—the British pound, the German mark, and the Japanese yen, for example—have functioned in that capacity at various times.

The acceptability of gold bullion as an international medium of exchange was derived from its role under the international gold standard of an earlier era. But why did the dollar become acceptable as money internationally? The answer has historical roots. The United States emerged from World War II as the free world's strongest economy; hence it became the center of international trade and finance. Furthermore, before and during the war the United States accumulated vast amounts of gold, and between 1934 and 1971 it maintained a policy of buying gold from, and selling gold to, foreign monetary authorities at a fixed price of $35 per ounce. Thus the dollar was convertible into gold on demand; the dollar came to be regarded as a substitute for gold and therefore "as good as gold."

But the role of the dollar as a key currency—as a component of international monetary reserves—contained the seeds of a dilemma. Consider the situation as it developed in the 1950s and 1960s. The problem with gold as international money was a quantitative one. The growth of the world's money stock depends upon the amount of newly mined gold, less any amounts hoarded or used for industrial and artistic purposes. Unfortunately, the growth of the gold stock lagged behind the rapidly expanding volume of international trade and finance. Thus the dollar came to occupy an increasingly important role as an international monetary reserve. Question: How do economies of the world acquire dollars as reserves? Answer: As the result of United States balance of payments deficits! As Figure 44-1 reveals, the United States obligingly incurred deficits throughout most of the 1950s and 1960s and into the 1970s. Figure 44-2 indicates that these deficits were financed in part by drawing down American gold reserves. But for the most part United States deficits were financed by growing foreign holdings of American dollars which, remember, were "as good as gold" until 1971.

Figure 44-2 also reveals a problem: As the amount of dollars held by foreigners soared and as our gold reserves dwindled, other nations inevitably began to question whether the dollar was really "as good as gold." The ability of the United States to maintain the convertibility of the dollar into gold became increasingly doubtful, and, therefore, so did the role of the dollar as a key currency. Hence, the dilemma: ". . . to preserve the status of the dollar as a reserve medium, the payments deficit of the United States had to be eliminated; but

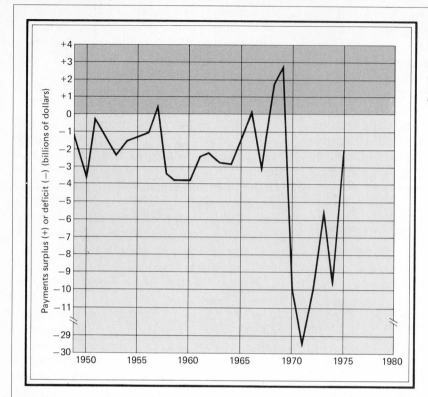

FIGURE 44-1 CHRONIC POST-WAR DEFICITS IN THE U.S. BALANCE OF PAYMENTS

Excepting two or three years, the United States has incurred persistent balance of payments deficits since 1949.

elimination of the deficit would mean a drying up of the source of additional dollar reserves for the system."[1]

UNITED STATES PAYMENTS DEFICITS

Let us pause at this point to examine the causes of our chronic payments deficits and to indicate some potential cures. We shall then consider how the noted dilemma posed by these deficits forced the abandonment of the Bretton Woods monetary system.

[1]Delbert A. Snider, *Introduction to International Economics,* 6th ed. (Homewood, Ill.: Richard D. Irwin, Inc., 1975), p. 358.

☐   **Causes**

A number of interlaced factors have given rise to our payments deficits.

1   Military Expenditures and Economic Aid   American economic grants and loans in the form of both military and economic aid amounted to $3.1 billion in 1976 and were an important contributor to our payments deficit. One might think at first glance that American dollar aid would tend to increase our exports and therefore not contribute to our payments deficit. But it has worked this way only to a limited degree. Some American aid dollars have been spent on American goods, thereby increasing our exports. But other American aid dollars have been spent on, say, German and French goods, ultimately converging on the central banks of these countries

FIGURE 44-2 THE U.S. GOLD STOCK AND FOREIGN DOLLAR CLAIMS SINCE 1950

Chronic balance of payments deficits for over two decades have drained off much of the United States' gold reserves and have resulted in large foreign holdings of dollar claims. (*Federal Reserve Bulletin.*)

expected return on foreign investment has exceeded that on domestic investment, so they have invested abroad. Note in Table 43-1 that net capital outflows were $20.5 billion in 1976.

3 Foreign Productivity Increases The productivity of our major trading partners—the Western European nations and Japan—has increased more rapidly than it has in the United States. This has meant lower production costs and prices for foreign goods as compared to American goods. Our exports have therefore tended to fall and our imports to rise. Rapidly rising foreign productivity has undoubtedly been caused in part by economies of scale associated with the formation of the Common Market (Chapter 42). It may also be attributable to the United States' assumption of a large share of the free world's defense burden, freeing high-level manpower and other crucial resources to the task of modernizing the domestic industries of Japan and Western Europe (Chapter 39). Finally, recall the argument, from Chapter 42, that technology is a highly mobile resource. To a considerable degree the United States' comparative advantage in world markets has had superior technology as its basis. As Western Europe, Japan, and other countries have quickly acquired American techniques and processes—and in many cases improved upon them—their productivity gains began to rival and surpass those of the United States. As a result, their goods have become increasingly competitive in world markets.

4 Domestic Inflation Other things being equal, domestic inflation tends to price American products out of international export markets and simultaneously to make imported goods more attractive. Fortunately for the United States, other things have *not* been equal. Most of our trading partners have also experienced inflation, in some instances more severe than in the United States. Nevertheless, there is no doubt that our rapid inflation of the post-1965 Vietnam war period contrib-

and therefore not being respent on American exports. Thus foreign aid and military spending have entailed dollar outflows not fully matched by dollar inflows resulting from aid-induced expenditures on American exports. In this way, aid and military outlays have contributed to our payments deficit.

2 Private Capital Outflows This outflow of public dollars has been accompanied by substantial outflows of American private capital. Private capital outflows have been expanding since the mid-1950s. Growth in the outflow of long-term capital has occurred in response to the burgeoning profit opportunities available in the more rapidly expanding economies of the world, especially those of Western Europe. Americans have found that the uted substantially to our deteriorating balances of trade and payments.

5 OPEC The United States and many other oil-importing countries experienced a sharp deterioration in their balance of payments positions as a result of the formation of the Organization of Petroleum Exporting Countries (OPEC) and the subsequent increase in oil prices. Recall that the OPEC cartel raised crude oil prices from about $2.10 per barrel in October of 1973 to more than $10 a year later. By 1977 the price per barrel had been pushed well above $13. Given our growing dependence on imported oil, these price increases greatly exacerbated our payments deficits in the 1970s.

☐ **Cures: Basic Measures**

Our discussion of the causes of our balance of payments problem implies the thrust of basic corrective measures. The question is this: How can a chronic balance of payments deficit be corrected within the essentially fixed exchange rate provisions of the Bretton Woods system? The answers include the following steps.

1 Increase American Productivity A basic line of attack is for American producers to intensify their efforts to increase productivity as a means of making American goods more competitive in international markets. This is obviously more easily said than done. It implies the maintenance of full employment and a high level of net investment spending. It suggests increased activity in technological research by both industry and government. It demands farsightedness by labor and management in introducing automation and in eliminating obsolete work rules.

2 Restrict Domestic Inflation Given the causal role of domestic inflation in the United States' payments problem, it is obvious that a more effective use of monetary and fiscal policies to stabilize the price level would strengthen our position in world trade. However, recalling the Phillips Curve (Chapter 18), the vigorous application of monetary and fiscal policies to stabilize prices may engender persistent unemployment and sluggish growth.

3 Redistribute Aid and Defense Burdens Western Europe might well assume a larger share of the costs of the mutual defense effort and of economic aid programs designed to benefit the underdeveloped nations.

4 Surplus Country Obligations Some argue that the responsibility for correcting a payments deficit lies not only with the deficit country, but also with countries which are enjoying surpluses. Thus countries which have a surplus with the United States should remove existing trade barriers to American imports. Similarly, surplus nations should increase their investments in the United States.

☐ **Controls: A Cure?**

A nation with persistent balance of payments deficits is strongly tempted to introduce various controls and restrictions upon its international trade and finance in the hope of "forcing" a payments balance (Chapter 43). In fact, the United States succumbed to that temptation. For example, a deficit nation may raise tariffs or enhance nontariff barriers to trade in the hope of cutting imports relative to exports. President Nixon's imposition, in August 1971, of a 10 percent surcharge on all dutiable imports was a dramatic illustration of such an effort. Furthermore, American foreign aid has been tied to American goods; that is, aid recipients have been obligated to spend aid funds on American goods. Expenditures by government agencies have been subject to "Buy American" provisions. The amount of duty-free goods which American tourists can bring home from overseas was cut, and Congress imposed a special tax on foreign travel.

To reduce the outflow of American capital, Congress in 1963 enacted an "interest equalization tax" to discourage American purchases of foreign stocks and bonds. Restrictions were also imposed upon direct investment abroad by American corporations and upon foreign lending by American financial institutions.

Most of these ad hoc measures have been abandoned. This is fortunate because, as we know (Chapter 42), such controls and restrictions are at odds with our commitment to the free flow of trade and finance; these measures divert the flow and pattern of world trade and investment away from those which are economically desirable. Furthermore, controls and restrictions run the risk of evoking retaliatory responses by other nations. The net result could therefore be a declining volume of trade and the consequent loss of the gains from specialization according to comparative advantage, not to mention serious political divisiveness between the United States and its major trading partners.

☐ Flexible Rates: A New System

Of course, as we know from Chapter 43, there is another option. That is to abandon the essentially fixed exchange rates of the Bretton Woods system in favor of floating exchange rates. It is in this direction that the international monetary system has moved in the 1970s. Let us return to the dilemma mentioned earlier to see precisely how it led to the breakdown of the Bretton Woods monetary system and its replacement by a system involving greater exchange rate flexibility.

■
DEMISE OF THE BRETTON WOODS SYSTEM

The demise of the Bretton Woods system in the early 1970s stemmed from two problems: (1) a reserves or liquidity problem and (2) an adjustment problem. Both these problems were intimately linked to the United States' payments deficits we have just discussed.

☐ The Reserves Problem

Recall the dilemma posed earlier. Gold production in the 1950s and 1960s did not keep pace with the need for additional international monetary reserves; hence, gold became less significant as international money. The dollar, however, became a key currency—in effect, an international money—because of the economic preeminence of the United States and its commitment to convert dollars into gold at a fixed price. But our chronic deficits dramatically increased the amount of dollars held by foreigners and simultaneously reduced our gold reserves (Figure 44-2). The willingness and ability of the United States to maintain its convertibility commitment became increasingly doubtful. Hence, the previously noted dilemma: The United States had to reduce or eliminate its payments deficits to preserve the dollar's status as an international medium of exchange. But success in this endeavor would limit the expansion of international reserves or liquidity and therefore tend to restrict the growth of international trade and finance. This dilemma was central to the reserves or liquidity problem.

☐ The Adjustment Problem

The other basic problem of the Bretton Woods system was that it did not provide an effective means by which a nation could resolve a serious balance of payments deficit. As noted in our discussion of the United States' payments deficits, trading partners may grow apart over time in terms of their productivities, price levels, interest rates, and so forth. This means that fundamental realignments of their exchange rates will be necessary if chronic payments disequilibria are to be avoided. While the Bretton Woods system offered a procedure for orderly currency devaluation to correct a deeply rooted deficit, in reality the system did not work very effectively in this respect. Exchange rate pegs were rarely adjusted, and the system in fact became one of rigid exchange rates. A nation's IMF commitment to stabilize its exchange rate and the availability of loans to help achieve this objective were both conducive to the deferring of exchange rate adjustments. Furthermore, there were also political obstacles to exchange rate realignments. When a nation requested the IMF to adjust the exchange rate pegs so that its money would be worth less vis-à-vis other currencies, its political leaders were in effect confessing their inability to manage domestic economic affairs so that the nation could pay its way in international trade and finance. Conversely, leaders in surplus countries would not be anxious to have their currencies revalued upward because the result would be a fall in net exports and rising domestic unemployment.

Thus, in practice, many deficit nations—including the United States—tended to put off the use of Bretton Woods mechanisms to change their exchange rates in the hope that in time their deficit would somehow correct itself. Typically, the disequilibrium became worse, rather than better, and the use of Bretton Woods adjustment mechanisms became even more distasteful. There was another reason why deficit nations were hesitant to "adjust the peg," that is, to devalue their currencies. In the absence of free markets for foreign exchange, there is no way of knowing by how much the value of a currency should be reduced to correct a "fundamental disequilibrium." Obviously, a devaluation which is too small will not restore equilibrium.

☐ **Shattering of the System**

These problems came to a head in the early 1970s and precipitated the breakdown of the Bretton Woods system. The chronic balance of payments deficits of the United States, which averaged $2 or $3 billion per year in the 1950s and 1960s, increased sharply in the early 1970s (Figure 44-1). Faced with this situation, President Nixon suspended the dollar's convertibility into gold on August 15, 1971. This suspension abrogated the policy to exchange gold for dollars at $35 per ounce, which had existed for thirty-seven years. This new policy severed the link between gold and the international value of the dollar, thereby "floating" the dollar and allowing its value to be determined by market forces. Such profound action was taken on the assumption that, under the basically stable exchange rates of the postwar international monetary system, the dollar had come to be substantially overvalued in relation to the currencies of our major trading partners—Japan and most of the Common Market countries. We know the consequences of devaluation. Exchange rates link the entire price structures of nations. Therefore, a decline in the international value of the dollar means that all American goods will be cheaper to foreigners and, conversely, all foreign goods will be more expensive to Americans. In short, the devaluation of the dollar means that the United States' exports will rise and its imports will fall, tending to correct our payments deficit. More importantly, the floating of the dollar withdrew American support from the old Bretton Woods system of fixed exchange rates and sounded the death knell for that system.

EMERGENCE OF FLOATING RATES

In December of 1971, representatives of ten leading IMF trading nations—the "Group of Ten"—met at the Smithsonian Institution in Washington. The resulting Smithsonian Agreement entailed a new realignment of exchange rates which was designed to correct the prior overvaluation of the dollar. But this new structure of rates was not to persist. The turbulent 1970s (Chapter 18), characterized by rapidly changing economic conditions, seemed to be incompatible with stable exchange rates. In particular, the devaluation of the dollar at the Smithsonian did not bring about the anticipated alleviation of the United States' payments deficit. Therefore, early in 1973 the United States devalued the dollar by 10 percent (raising the official price of gold to $42.22 per ounce). This second devaluation signaled the general abandonment of the realigned system of relatively stable exchange rates negotiated in the Smithsonian Agreement.

☐   The "Managed Float"

The system of exchange rates which has since evolved is not easily described; it can probably best be labeled a system of *managed floating exchange rates*. On the one hand, it is recognized that changing economic conditions among nations require continuing changes in exchange rates to avoid persistent payments deficits or surpluses; exchange rates must be allowed to float. On the other hand, short-term changes in exchange rates—perhaps accentuated by purchases and sales by speculators—can cause frequent and significant exchange rate fluctuations which tend to disrupt the flow of trade and finance. Hence, it is generally agreed that the central banks of the various nations should buy and sell foreign exchange to smooth out these day-to-day fluctuations in rates. In other words, central banks should "manage" or stabilize short-term speculative variations in their exchange rates. These characteristics were formalized by a leading group of IMF nations in 1976. Thus, ideally, the new system will entail not only the needed long-term exchange rate flexibility to correct fundamental payments disequilibria, but also sufficient short-term stability of rates to encourage international trade and finance.

☐   Liquidity and Special Drawing Rights

The shift from the Bretton Woods system of essentially fixed exchange rates to a new system of basically floating rates will presumably help significantly in dealing with "the adjustment problem." That is, a nation expe-

riencing a payments deficit will find its currency depreciating under a floating rate system. Its exports will rise and its imports will fall, tending automatically to adjust its balance of payments toward equilibrium. But what of "the liquidity problem" which played a critical role in the dissolution of the Bretton Woods system?

Recall, first, that under a fixed rate system a nation incurring a payments deficit was required to draw upon its international reserves to cover the deficit. That is, to play the fixed exchange rate game, large quantities of international reserves or liquidity are essential. But with a floating rate system, changing exchange rates automatically tend to correct or ameliorate deficits and thereby lessen the need for reserves. Second, the IMF endorsed in 1967 a plan providing for a new international money called Special Drawing Rights, or simply SDRs. Popularly referred to as "paper gold," SDRs are created at the initiative of the directors of the IMF, but only with the approval of an 85 percent majority of the voting power of Fund participants. SDRs are made available to Fund members in proportion to their IMF quotas and can be used, as gold was once used, to settle payments deficits or satisfy reserve needs.

Special Drawing Rights are created and function in this way. Assume the IMF is authorized to make available, say, $5 billion in SDRs to member nations. Each nation is allocated, not pieces of paper similar to dollars, marks, or pounds, but IMF accounts. Each nation's SDR account, as noted, is in proportion to its IMF quota. In other words, SDRs consist of bookkeeping entries at the IMF, conceptually similar to your demand deposit in a commercial bank. Now assume that Italy, for example, incurs a payments deficit and does not have sufficient quantities of, say, dollars, marks, and yen to cover the deficit. Italy may simply transfer some of its SDR credits to the SDR accounts of the United States, Germany, and Japan to finance its deficit. The basic point is that SDRs constitute an important new source of international monetary reserves.

What backs the SDRs? The answer is simply that they are fiat money. They are international reserves because IMF members have agreed to accept them as such. How are SDRs valued? What are they worth? When first issued in 1970, SDRs were valued in terms of the dollar; one SDR was defined as being worth one dollar. But because of fluctuations (primarily declines) in the value of the dollar and its downgrading as a key currency in the 1970s, the value of the SDR since 1974 has been determined by a weighted average of the international value of the currencies of the sixteen major trading nations. There is safety in numbers: The average international value of this "basket" of sixteen currencies is less likely to fluctuate than might the value of any single currency, for example, the dollar. The stable value of SDRs has contributed to their acceptability as international monetary reserves.

□ **Demonetization of Gold?**

Reform of the international monetary system has also involved the intentional downgrading of the role of gold. Recall (Chapter 14) that close ties between gold and domestic money systems of the various nations were severed long ago. Why? Because there is no particular logic in arbitrarily linking the monetary system to gold or any other commodity; it is much more rational to manage the monetary system so as to accommodate changing levels of economic activity.

What actions has the IMF taken toward the demonetization of gold? First, the creation of SDRs has provided an apparently acceptable replacement for gold as international money. Furthermore, gold has been replaced by SDRs as the official IMF unit of account. Finally, the IMF is in the process of disposing of one-third of its gold holdings. Specifically, one-sixth of its total gold stock is being "restituted," that is, sold back to member nations

in proportion to their IMF quotas. Another one-sixth is being sold at public auction over a four-year period. The profits from this auction are being put in a trust fund to aid the less developed countries. Whether gold will be completely demonetized remains to be seen.

□ **Evaluation and Options**

How well has the managed floating system worked? Although our experience with this system is historically too short for a definitive assessment, the system has both proponents and critics.

Proponents argue that the system has functioned quite well, particularly in view of the diverse and disruptive economic developments of the 1970s. Internationally diverse rates of inflation and growth, shortfalls in agricultural production, varying amounts of unemployment, and the dramatic oil price increases of 1973–1974 were all-important forces which tended to generate substantial international disequilibria. It is contended that flexible rates facilitated international adjustments to these developments, whereas the same events would have put unbearable pressures upon a fixed rate system.

But there is still considerable sentiment in favor of a system characterized by greater exchange rate stability. Those favoring stable rates envision problems with the current system.

1 Reinforcement of Inflation? A controversial criticism of the managed float is that it tends to reinforce a nation's inflationary pressures. Much simplified, the argument is as follows. Assume a nation—the United Kingdom, for example—experiences domestic inflation as the result of, say, inappropriate stabilization policies or cost-push pressures. As a consequence, the British pound will depreciate in value. But this depreciation, by stimulating British exports and diminishing its imports, will increase aggregate demand in Britain and reinforce its inflationary problem. This additional dose of inflation will contribute to the further depreciation of the pound and the process repeats itself. To repeat: this "vicious circle" theory of inflation through exchange rate adjustments is quite new and a source of considerable disagreement among economists.

2 A "Nonsystem"? In the Jamaica Agreement of early 1976, IMF members legitimized the present managed floating system of exchange rates; that is, it was agreed that exchange rates will continue to be flexible and that individual governments may manage the extent of that flexibility. Skeptics feel that the managed float is basically a "nonsystem"; that is, the rules and guidelines circumscribing the behavior of each nation vis-à-vis its exchange rate are not sufficiently clear or constraining to make the system viable in the long run. Bluntly put, the various nations will inevitably be tempted to intervene in foreign exchange markets, not merely to smooth out short-term or speculative fluctuations in the value of their currencies, but to prop up their currency if it is chronically weak or to purposely manipulate the value of their currency to achieve domestic stabilization goals. In short, there is fear that in time there may be more "managing" and less "floating" of exchange rates, and this may be fatal to the present loosely defined system.

Fortunately, there are options beyond either the Bretton Woods system or the managed float which might be capable of capturing the advantages of both exchange rate stability (a large and expanding volume of trade) and exchange rate flexibility (the resolution of balance of payments problems). One much-discussed option is a *crawling-peg* system of exchange rates. Skirting technical details, we can describe the crawling-peg proposal as permission for a nation faced with a chronic payments deficit to adjust the par value of its currency according to some specified formula. For example, if the par value of a currency could be changed by one-quarter of 1 percent each month, the par value of the currency of

the deficit nation could be lowered by 3 percent per year. A similar adjustment could be made in ensuing years if the deficit persisted. The relatively small size of the adjustment per month and per year would preserve short-term exchange rate stability, discourage currency speculation, and be conducive to expanding trade. At the same time, the crawling peg would provide enough flexibility over time to correct persistent payments deficits.

COMPATIBILITY OF DOMESTIC AND INTERNATIONAL POLICIES

Depending upon the particular combination of circumstances facing a nation with respect to domestic conditions and its balance of payments, domestic and international economic policies may be compatible or in conflict. Hence, the thrust of the final section of this chapter is that neither the domestic goal of full employment with reasonable price stability nor the international goal of balance of payments equilibrium should be viewed in isolation. Policies designed to achieve domestic stability will affect the balance of payments, and vice versa. Let us therefore consider briefly various combinations of domestic and international conditions and determine whether appropriate policy in, say, the domestic area is consistent with our balance of payments objectives. Table 44-1 summarizes the four possible cases to be considered.

Suppose the domestic economy is sluggish and characterized by unemployment and slow growth, on the one hand, and that we face a payments deficit, on the other. Appropriate domestic policy would entail an expansionary fiscal policy—more government spending and lower taxes—and an easy money (low interest rate) policy. Unfortunately, these expansionary policies would be inconsistent with the resolution of a payments deficit; indeed, domestic economic expansion is likely to intensify the deficit. Why so? First, recall that rising domestic income will mean an expanding

Table 44-1 COMPATIBILITY AND CONFLICT BETWEEN DOMESTIC AND
INTERNATIONAL ECONOMIC POLICIES

Domestic problem	International (balance of payments) problem	Appropriate domestic policy	Appropriate international policy	Relationship between domestic and international policies
Unemployment	Deficit	Expansionary	Contractionary	Conflicting
Inflation	Deficit	Contractionary	Contractionary	Compatible
Unemployment	Surplus	Expansionary	Expansionary	Compatible
Inflation	Surplus	Contractionary	Expansionary	Conflicting

Source: Adapted from Mordechai E. Kreinin, *International Economics: A Policy Approach,* 2d ed. (New York: Harcourt Brace Jovanovich, Inc., 1975), p. 92.

volume of imports (Table 41-4). Second, given the Phillips Curve and the likelihood of premature inflation, our domestic products will tend to become less and less competitive in world markets, so exports will fall. Third, the decline in interest rates engendered by an easy money policy will prompt outflows of capital to other nations where interest rates are now higher, further contributing to the payments deficit. Incidentally, the situation just described is very similar to that faced by the United States in the early 1960s. The policy decision was made to stimulate the domestic economy by cutting taxes, but this stimulus was at odds with the resolution of our balance of payments disequilibrium.

On the other hand, if the problems are domestic inflation coupled with a payments deficit, there is no policy conflict. On the domestic front, contractionary monetary and fiscal measures are in order. The resulting restraint on income growth will curtail imports, and the halting or diminution of infla-

tion will tend to stimulate exports. Finally, rising interest rates will stop outflows of capital and tend to encourage inflows. The reader should verify that domestic policies to combat inflation are inconsistent with resolving a payments surplus. Similarly, domestic measures to eliminate unemployment are in accord with the correction of a payments surplus.

A final comment: There is an evident and quite understandable propensity for policy makers in the United States to accord priority to domestic stability when that objective conflicts with the realization of a balance of payments equilibrium. On the one hand, the Congress and the Administration recognize that the general public is highly sensitive to the "bread-and-butter" issues of unemployment and inflation. On the other hand, given the fact that international trade is small relative to the size of our domestic economy, according first priority to international equilibrium would be to let the tail wag the dog.

Summary

1 In the 1929–1945 period, the Great Depression and World War II severely disrupted the volume and pattern of world trade. The immediate world economic problem after World War II was to achieve European economic recovery. A large flow of United States aid to Europe through the Marshall Plan contributed to this goal.

2 The post-World War II international monetary system—the Bretton Woods system—was committed to an "adjustable-peg" system of exchange rates. In particular, the International Monetary Fund was created **a.** to make short-term foreign currency loans to help nations meet temporary payments deficits, and **b.** to provide for an orderly adjustment of exchange rates to help correct fundamental payments deficits. As the world's monetary system evolved after the war, gold and certain key currencies—particularly American dollars and British pounds—served as international monetary reserves.

3 Since about 1950 the United States has been faced with large and persistent balance of payments deficits. The growing productivity of Western Europe and Japan, American inflation, large outflows of investment capital, substantial American foreign aid and overseas military expenditures, and, more recently, oil price increases under OPEC have all contributed to these deficits.

4 The use of the dollar as a key currency—as international monetary reserves—in the Bretton Woods system created a dilemma. On the one hand, needed growth in monetary reserves depended upon the persistence of United States payments deficits; on the other hand, these chronic deficits raised doubts as to the continued convertibility of the dollar into gold and therefore as to the status of the dollar as a key currency. Sharp increases in our payments deficit in 1971 forced the abandonment of dollar convertibility into gold, shattering the Bretton Woods system.

5 The new system is one of managed floating exchange rates. Central banks buy and sell foreign currencies to smooth out or "manage" short-term fluctuations, but exchange rates are allowed to float or fluctuate in response to more fundamental changes in a nation's exports and imports.

6 Special Drawing Rights (SDRs) have been successfully introduced by the IMF to provide greater international liquidity. At the same time, the IMF has been moving toward the demonetization of gold.

7 Some economists feel that, given the turbulent economic conditions of the 1970s, the managed floating system has functioned well. Others are more critical, arguing that the system **a.** has an inflationary bias and **b.** may be prone to breakdown because the behavioral guidelines and constraints of the system are poorly defined.

Questions and Study Suggestions

1 Key terms and concepts to remember: Marshall Plan; Bretton Woods system; adjustable pegs; International Monetary Fund (IMF); international monetary reserves; key currencies; SDRs; Smithsonian Agreement; managed floating exchange rates; Jamaica Agreement; crawling-peg system.

2 What factors underlay the disintegration of international trade and finance in the 1930s and 1940s? Explain the impact of each. Describe and evaluate the Marshall Plan.

3 Describe the Bretton Woods monetary system, identifying the role of the IMF and the adjustable-peg system of exchange rates. What constituted international reserves under this system?

4 What have been the major causes of the United States' chronic balance of payments deficits? How did these deficits contribute to the demise of the Bretton Woods system?

5 How do SDRs function as international monetary reserves? Comment on the statement: "The creation of SDRs is part of the IMF's program to demonetize gold."

6 Explain the adjustments which would occur in response to a chronic payments deficit under **a.** the Bretton Woods system and **b.** the managed float.

7 Explain the crawling-peg system of exchange rates. What are the alleged advantages of this system? If you were participating in a revision of the international monetary system, what specific proposals would you offer?

   8   Explain and illustrate:

   a.   "Policies that stimulate the domestic economy tend to cause a trade deficit."

   b.   "A balance of payments deficit imposes severe constraints upon domestic economic policies."

   c.   "Balance of payments equilibrium will quickly result for all nations if their relative prices are in proper relationship to one another. The only systematic means of achieving these proper relationships is through a system of freely fluctuating exchange rates."

   d.   "Monetarily, gold is a barbaric relic of the past which should be given no role in an efficient international monetary system."

Selected References

Economic Report of the President, 1976 (Washington), chap. 4.

Economic Report of the President, 1977 (Washington), chap. 3.

Fried, Edward R., and Philip H. Trezise, "The United States in the World Economy," in Henry Owen and Charles L. Schultz (eds.), *Setting National Priorities: The Next Ten Years* (Washington: The Brookings Institution, 1976).

IMF Survey, current issues.

International Economic Report of the President, 1977 (Washington).

Snider, Delbert A.: *Introduction to International Economics,* 6th ed. (Homewood, Ill.: Richard D. Irwin, Inc., 1975), chaps. 18–22.

Last Word
Multinational Corporations: For Good or Evil?

What have been the effects of the rapid growth of multinational corporations upon our domestic economy? Compare the following labor and business views.

Labor's view: George Meany, President, ALF-CIO:

. . . operations by American [multinational] companies obviously displace United States produced goods in both American markets and world markets. These companies export American technology—some of it developed through the expenditure of Government funds paid by American taxpayers. Their biggest export, of course, is United States jobs. . . .

The multinational firms can juggle their bookkeeping and their prices and their taxes. Their export and import transactions are within the corporation, determined by the executives of the corporation—all for the benefit and profit of the corporation. This is not foreign trade. Surely it is not foreign competition.

The complex operations of multinationals—with the aid of Madison Avenue advertising—have utterly confused the picture of national origin of products. For example, Ford's Pinto has been heralded as the U.S. answer to imported small cars. But the engines are imported from England and Germany, and the standard transmissions are imported from Europe.

This phenomenon is far different from the development of corporations here in America during the last 100 years. The multinational is not simply an American company moving to a new locality where the same laws apply and where it is still within the jurisdiction of Congress and the Government of the United States. This is a runaway corporation, going far beyond our borders. This is a runaway to a country with different laws, different institutions, and different labor and social standards. In most instances, even the name changes. . . .

Ironically, these are the same multinational corporations who have sought to influence U.S. trade legislation in the name of "free trade."

Meanwhile, back in the United States, expansion of large national corporations has been tempered to a degree by Government regulations, standards, and controls. And, in the past few decades, large U.S. corporations have had to meet responsibilities to their employees through labor unions. Moreover, the multinationals' global operations are beyond the reach of present U.S. law or the laws of any single nation.

Business' view: Dr. N. R. Danielian, President, International Economic Policy Association:

The multinational corporations are caught in the contradictions of our policies in defense, aid, and trade. Their alleged sins are now being decried among academicians, certain spokesmen of labor and even in ministerial conferences in Europe. These corporations are accused of exporting jobs; but they seldom receive credit for the jobs they create from exports—as in fact they produce one-fourth of the total U.S. exports with their shipments to their overseas affiliates.

The implication that "runaway" U.S. companies serve the U.S. market with cheap, foreign labor simply is inaccurate in all but a few cases. To take one example: Of the 1,321,000 foreign cars imported during 1970, only 123,299, or 9.3 percent, were made by U.S. subsidiaries abroad. The rest were Volkswagens, Toyotas, Fiats, and the like, all produced by foreign-owned companies. In the case of the 13 million short tons of iron and steel imported during 1970, hardly any could be attributed to American-owned subsidiaries abroad.

If all U.S. investments abroad were suddenly eliminated, the United States would be worse off by nearly $17 billion in its international receipts, two-thirds in exports and one-third in investment income, not including the $1.5 billion income from royalties and fees. As sympathetic as I am to labor's viewpoint in the matter of employment, I sincerely believe that they are whipping the wrong horse in attacking international or multinational corporations. Most of our imports come from foreign-owned enterprises; and if third-country markets could not be supplied by U.S. subsidiaries abroad, they would simply be supplied by foreign competitors. . . .

Many people, who should know better, blame American companies for the recent [international] currency crisis. Multinational corporations are in the business of manufacturing and selling products, not gambling with huge cash reserves. They would not be in business long if they speculated with a magnitude of liquid assets which could shake the foundations of the combined central banks of Europe.

From *Foreign Trade,* Hearings before the Subcommittee on International Trade of the Senate Committee on Finance, 91st Congress, 1st Session, Washington, 1971, pp. 169–171 and 126–127, abridged.

45

The Economic System of Soviet Russia

Soviet-American economic and political relations are in a quite ambivalent state. At the Moscow Summit of May 1972, the two superpowers reached a general accord to the effect that limits should be imposed upon the arms race; both participants explicitly recognized that their resources could be put to more fruitful uses than the realization of higher overkill ratios. Furthermore, as indicated in Chapter 42, important developments have been occurring which point to the possibility of greater trade and economic cooperation between the United States and the Soviet Union. But possible evidence of political détente and hints of expanding economic relations should not conceal the fact that the United States and the U.S.S.R. will continue to be rivals ideologically and economically. Witness the comments by Party Secretary Mikhail A. Suslov a few months after the 1972 summit meeting:[1]

> We Communists have no illusions about the antipopular nature and policy of imperialism. . . . The assertion of the principles of peaceful coexistence in international affairs in no way signifies the weakening of the class struggle . . . or a "conciliation" between socialism and capitalism. . . . Now when the imperialists are increasingly realizing the impossibility of overthrowing socialism by force, this struggle is more frequently being transferred to the spheres of ideology, politics and economics.

[1] As quoted in Paul K. Cook, "The Political Setting," in Joint Economic Committee, *Soviet Economic Prospects for the Seventies* (Washington, 1973), p. 2.

We turn, then, in this final chapter to an analysis of this rival economy. We want to survey its institutions, understand its goals, evaluate its performance, and appreciate the challenge it poses for the West. There are two notable by-products of this endeavor. First, the Soviet economy is a fascinating case study in forced economic growth; the accomplishments and shortcomings of the Soviet system in vigorously pursuing economic growth provide invaluable lessons. Second, by examining an economy at the opposite end of the ideological spectrum, we cannot help but deepen our understanding of the capitalistic system.

INSTITUTIONS OF THE COMMAND ECONOMY

There are two outstanding institutional characteristics of the Soviet economy: (1) state ownership of property resources, and (2) authoritarian central economic planning.

☐ State Ownership

The Soviet constitution of 1936 makes the pervasiveness of public ownership of property resources quite clear:

> **Article IV.** The economic foundation of the U.S.S.R. is the socialist system of economy and the socialist ownership of the instruments and means of production, firmly established as a result of the liquidation of the capitalist system of economy, the abolition of private ownership of the instruments and means of production, and the elimination of the exploitation of man by man.

> **Article V.** Socialist property in the U.S.S.R. exists either in the form of state property (belonging to the whole people) or in the form of cooperative and collective-farm property (property of collective farms, property of cooperative societies).

The Soviet state owns all land, natural resources, transportation and communication facilities, the banking system, and virtually all industry. Most retail and wholesale enterprises and most urban housing are governmentally owned. In agriculture many farms are state-owned; most, however, are government-organized collective farms, that is, essentially cooperatives. The main exception to state ownership is the small plot of land which each collective farm family has set aside for its personal use: "Every household on a collective farm . . . has for its personal use a small plot of household land and, as its personal property, a subsidiary husbandry on the plot, a dwelling house, livestock, poultry, and minor agricultural implements. . . ." And, of course, clothing, household furnishings, and small tools and implements used by craftsmen are privately owned. Workers in rural areas and farmers typically own their homes, as do over one-third of all urban families.

☐ Central Economic Planning

Despite a highly democratic constitution, in practice the government of Soviet Russia is a strong dictatorship. The Communist party, although limited in membership to the most dedicated 4 or 5 percent of the total population, stands unchallenged. Indeed, the party and the government can be regarded as virtually synonymous.

As the constitution makes clear, the Soviet government, through authoritarian economic planning, sets the objectives of the economy and directs resources toward the attainment of these goals:

> **Article XI.** The economic life of the U.S.S.R. is determined and directed by the state national economic plan, with the aim of increasing the public wealth, of steadily raising the material and cultural standards of the working people, and of consolidating the independence of the U.S.S.R. and strengthening its defensive capacity.

In contrast with the decentralized market economy of the United States, that of the Soviet Union is a centralized, "command" economy which functions in terms of a detailed economic plan. The economy of the Soviet Union is government-directed rather than price-directed.

□ **Circumscribed Freedom**

The dominant roles of state ownership and central planning correctly imply that it is not the free decisions of consumers and business-owners which determine the allocation of resources and the composition of total output in the Soviet Union. Yet, subject to the overall restraints imposed by the central planners, consumers and laborers have a degree of free choice.

The concept of consumer sovereignty as we know it does not exist in the Soviet Union. The preferences of individual consumers, as reflected in the size and structure of consumer demand, do *not* determine the volume and composition of consumer goods production in Soviet Russia; this determinination is made by the government. However, consumers are free to spend their money incomes as they see fit on those consumer goods for which the central plan provides.

Similarly, although the Soviet Union has a history of compulsory job assignment, harsh labor codes, and, in the extreme, slave labor, much greater reliance has been put upon free occupational choice in recent years. But again, there are overall restraints imposed by the central plan. The composition of output as determined by the plan establishes the number and kinds of jobs available. Then the government planners set wage rates so as to attract the needed number and types of workers to the various occupations. If the plan assigns great importance to steel and a low priority to shoes, jobs will be plentiful and wage rates established at a relatively high level in the steel industry. Conversely, few jobs will be available and wages will be relatively low in the shoe industry. In short, workers are largely free to change jobs in response to wage differentials;

the differentials, however, are designed and manipulated to bring about an allocation of labor, both geographically and occupationally, which is consistent with the goals of the plan.

CENTRAL PLANNING

Perhaps the most dramatic feature of the Soviet economy is its use of central planning. In the Soviet Union the means of answering the Five Fundamental Questions is central planning. Choices made primarily through the market in the United States economy must be consciously made by bureaucratic decision in the U.S.S.R. The overall character of the Soviet Five- and Seven-year Plans has been succinctly described in these words:[2]

> The Soviet economic plan is a gigantic, comprehensive blueprint that attempts to govern the economic activities and interrelations of all persons and institutions in the U.S.S.R., as well as the economic relations of the U.S.S.R. with other countries. To the extent that the plan actually controls the development of events, all the manifold activities of the Soviet economy are coordinated as if they were parts of one incredibly enormous enterprise directed from the central headquarters in Moscow.

Now let us probe below the surface. What are the goals of the plans? How are the plans constructed and implemented? What problems does central planning entail?

□ **Planning Goals**

The Soviet government—in reality the Communist party—sets the basic objectives for the Russian economy. These objectives have varied somewhat as succeeding Five-year Plans have been formulated, but emphasis has been upon rapid economic growth through the development of heavy industry. The attain-

[2]Harry Schwartz, *Russia's Soviet Economy,* 2d ed. (Englewood Cliffs, N.J.: Prentice-Hall, Inc., 1954), p. 146.

ment of a high level of military strength is a closely correlated goal. Lip service is invariably accorded the goal of a higher standard of living for consumers, but the lower priority assigned to this goal means that it is frequently sacrificed to achieve the objectives of industrial expansion and military strength.

□ Basic Planning Problem: Coordination

It is no simple matter to sweep away the guiding function of the market system, as the Soviet Union has done, and replace it with an effective central plan. After all, we have found that the market system is a powerful organizing force which coordinates millions upon millions of individual decisions by consumers, entrepreneurs, and resource suppliers and fosters a reasonably efficient allocation of resources. Is central planning a satisfactory substitute for the market?

The core of the planning problem is revealed by the input-output table (Table 33-1). Input-output analysis, you will recall, reveals the highly interdependent character of the various industries or sectors of the economy. Each industry employs the outputs of other industries as its inputs; in turn its outputs are inputs to still other firms. This means that a planning decision to increase the production of machinery by, say, 10 percent is not a single, isolated directive, but rather, a decision which implies a myriad of related decisions for fulfillment. For example, in terms of Table 33-1, if planners do not make the related decisions to increase metal output by 6.5 units, fuel by 0.5 units, agricultural products by 1 unit, and to provide an extra 20 units of labor (not to mention additional second-round increases in all these inputs because 2.5 more inputs of machinery are also needed to increase machinery output!), bottlenecks will develop, and the planned increase in machinery output cannot be realized.

Let us look at the matter from a slightly different vantage point: Even if an internally consistent set of decisions—a perfectly coordinated plan—could be constructed by the central planners, the failure of any single industry to fulfill its output target would cause an almost endless chain of adverse repercussions. If iron mines—for want of machinery or labor or transportation inputs—fail to supply the steel industry with the required inputs of iron ore, the steel industry in turn will be unable to fulfill the input needs of the myriad of industries dependent upon steel. All these steel-using industries will be unable to fulfill their planned production goals. And so the bottleneck chain reaction goes on to all those firms which use steel parts or components as inputs.

It must be emphasized that our illustrative input-output table (Table 33-1) is a gross oversimplification of the problem of coordinating a command economy. There are now some 200,000 industrial enterprises producing goods in the Soviet Union. The central planners must see to it that all the resources needed by these enterprises to fulfill their assigned production targets are somehow allocated to them.[3]

> The literally billions of planning decisions that must be made to achieve consistency result in a complex and complete interlocking of macro- and micromanagement. . . . The number of planned interconnections increases more rapidly than the size of the economy, and since 1953 the Soviet economy has doubled in terms of national production. . . . Even with the most sophisticated mathematical techniques and electronic computers, the task of interrelating demands and factor inputs for every possible item by every possible subcategory becomes impossible for the central planners alone.

□ Coordination Techniques

Despite the gargantuan character of the coordination problem, Soviet central planning has worked, and in some respects has func-

[3] Barry M. Richman, *Soviet Management* (Englewood Cliffs, N.J.: Prentice-Hall, Inc., 1965), p. 17.

tioned remarkably well. It is certainly legitimate to inquire: Why? What techniques do Soviet planners employ to achieve the level of coordination sufficient to make central planning workable? The answers lie substantially in the way the plans are constructed and implemented.

1   Planning by Negotiation   Given the overall economic objectives established by the Communist party, it is the task of the State Planning Commission, or *Gosplan,* to construct a detailed economic blueprint designed to bring about the realization of these goals. In formulating a plan, the Gosplan collects voluminous amounts of statistical data from a host of subordinate ministries, each of which is concerned with the operation of certain industries. From these data, a tentative plan is constructed. The projected Five-year Plan is divided into Annual Plans, the latter being more relevant for actual operating purposes. The Annual Plan is then submitted to the various units of the Soviet administrative hierarchy for study, evaluation, and criticism. This criticism, it must be noted, concerns the specific details of the economic plan and not the overall goals which the plan seeks.

Let us illustrate this procedure. Note, first, that there are two obvious organizational alternatives for a planned economy: geographical (regional) and functional (industrial). All enterprises in a given region may be grouped for planning purposes, or all enterprises in a given industry may be grouped for planning regardless of their location. Over time the Soviet Union has used both alternatives and mixtures of the two. Currently the emphasis is upon the industrial approach; thus a number of countrywide ministries—for example, the ministries of construction, machine tools, automobiles, and tractors—are subordinate to Gosplan in the planning hierarchy. The important point is that relevant segments of the overall plan are submitted to the subordinate agencies, which exercise operational control. Thus the Annual Plan is evaluated at the industrywide level, by the trusts and combines—that is, groups of plants which are combined for administrative purposes—and ultimately by the individual plants or enterprises. At each level the plan is analyzed, suggestions are made for revision, and perhaps alterations are proposed in production goals or planned allocations of inputs. These evaluations are passed back up the planning hierarchy to Gosplan. Taking into account those suggestions and criticisms which it feels are worthy, Gosplan then draws up a final plan. When rubber-stamped by the party and the government, this becomes the official Annual Plan.

The point to be emphasized is this: By breaking the overall plan into its component parts and subjecting these detailed segments to considerable critical examination by subministries, combines, and plants, the Gosplan is able to establish a final plan which is more realistic and workable than would otherwise be the case. Soviet planners apparently recognize their limitations in obtaining and digesting masses of detailed information. The "down-and-up" evaluation of the tentative plan by the administrative hierarchy and its subsequent revision is aimed at obtaining on-the-spot knowledge and an understanding of immediate, detailed facts and circumstances which a relatively small group of planners could not otherwise grasp. To the extent that the resulting plan is more realistic and feasible, the chance is less that problems of coordination—in particular, bottlenecks—will arise to jeopardize plan fulfillment.

2   Priority Principle   A second means of making central planning workable is embodied in the priority principle of resource allocation. Not all production goals established by Gosplan are held to be of equal importance. The goals of certain "leading links" sectors or industries (machinery, chemicals, steel) are given high priority; other industries (agriculture, automobiles) in effect are assigned low priorities. Thus, when bottlenecks arise in the actual operation of the national plan, resources or inputs are shifted from low-priority to high-priority sectors of the economy. Coordination and plan fulfillment are sacrificed in low-priority production in order to maintain coordination and fulfill production targets in high-priority sectors. This accounts for the unevenness with which the goals of the various central plans have been fulfilled. Planned increases in housing and consumer goods are typically sacrificed to realize the planned increases in industrial and military goods production.

3 Reserve Stocks To some extent, coordination problems—bottlenecks and the chain reactions they precipitate—can be avoided by drawing upon reserve stocks of various inputs. Inventories, in other words, are used as a cushion or buffer to resolve specific bottlenecks or input deficiencies before they can trigger a serious chain of production shortfalls.

Although all these techniques contribute in varying degrees to the workability of Soviet central planning, they by no means ensure a high degree of efficiency. There is a great amount of evidence gathered from Soviet sources to indicate that bottlenecks do occur with rather alarming regularity. The result is frequent production stoppages and underfulfillment of production plans.[4]

☐ **Executing the Plan: Control Agencies**

Setting up detailed production goals and making some provision for their internal balance are one thing; achieving those objectives may be something else again.

The Soviet government is not inclined to sit back, after each industrial plant and farm has been assigned its production targets, and hope for favorable results. On the contrary, an abundance of control agencies supervises the

carrying out of each plan. Most obvious, of course, is the Gosplan and the various subordinate planning groups affiliated with it. These administrative units keep a running check on the progress of the plan. The Central Committee of the Communist party and a variety of subordinate party organizations function as watchdog agencies by uncovering, reporting, and helping to correct deviations from the plan. The control functions of the infamous secret police are well known. And, too, a less formal type of control is exercised through a much-publicized program of "criticism and self-criticism," whereby the Soviet citizenry is encouraged to register complaints concerning deviations from, and violations of, the plan.

Perhaps the most vital enforcement agency is the state banking system, or *Gosbank*. The Gosbank, with its thousands of branches, supervises the financial aspects of each plant's production activities and in this manner has a running account of each plant's performance. More precisely, this supervision—"control by the ruble"—works something like this: The government establishes prices on all resources and finished products. As a greatly simplified example, the Leningrad Machine Tool Plant may require 1000 tons of steel and 100 workers to produce 5000 units of output per year. If steel costs 60 rubles per ton and each worker is paid 1000 rubles per year, the total cost of the 5000 units of output will be 160,000 rubles. Gosplan then directs the Gosbank to make this amount of credit available to the plant over the course of the year. Now, because all the plant's financial transactions—both receipts and expenditures—must be completed through the use of checks, the Gosbank will have an accurate record (in effect, a running audit) of the plant's progress, or lack thereof, in fulfilling the production targets assigned by the Five-year Plan. Should the plant achieve its assigned output at an expense less than 160,000 rubles, it will have overfulfilled its production goal. Inefficient, wasteful production will cause the plant to exhaust its

[4]Ibid., p. 123.

bank credit before its production goal is reached. Either eventuality will be reflected in the plant's account with the Gosbank.

□ **Incentives**

How are the various economic units motivated toward fulfillment of the Annual Plan? A combination of monetary and nonmonetary incentives, on the one hand, and coercive techniques, on the other, are employed to this end.

Monetary Incentives The Soviet government relies quite heavily upon monetary incentives to obtain the maximum productive effort from labor. In particular, wages are geared to skill and productivity. The resulting wage differentials are considerable. Great emphasis is put upon piecework, more so than in the United States. Probably as much as four-fifths of the Soviet labor force works under a piecework plan of one sort or another. Elaborate systems of bonuses and premiums induce workers to exceed normal production rates. However, in the last two decades there has been a narrowing of wage differentials in the Soviet Union, the impact of which upon incentives is not clear. Keep in mind, too, that Soviet income receivers, though not free to determine the portion of total output which is to take the form of consumer goods, are able to spend their incomes as they wish on the consumer goods which the Gosplan makes available to them. This means that differences in money incomes are generally reflected in real income differentials.

Nonmonetary Incentives A variety of nonmonetary inducements also exist to stimulate labor to greater productivity. A rather comprehensive system of awards and decorations exists to cite exemplary workers. These are closely correlated with material rewards. For example, a "Hero of Socialist Labor" is likely to be accorded certain tax exemptions, monthly bonuses, low rental on state housing, free use of transportation facilities, government-supplied vacations at a Crimean resort, and so forth. The real standard of living of the average Soviet citizen is roughly half that of his American counterpart, so that the value of such benefits is considerable. Much publicity accompanies these awards. A member of the "Order of Lenin" may enjoy fame and prestige comparable to that of a professional baseball player or movie star in the United States. In addition, "socialist competitions" are encouraged by the party, pitting the productive capacities of various groups of workers against one another.

The labor unions to which the vast majority of Soviet workers belong bear little or no resemblance to their American counterparts. In effect, Russian labor unions are essentially functionaries of the state; their basic goals are to encourage a high rate of productivity among their members in carrying out the economic plan, to train new workers, to aid in the solution of labor discipline problems, and to administer the social security system. Wage rates are set by the government; collective bargaining as we know it does not exist; and strikes simply do not occur. Soviet labor unions do, however, prevent undue exploitation of their members by plant managers eager to fulfill their assigned production quotas. They also play an active role in providing recreational and cultural programs for workers.

Coercion Monetary and nonmonetary inducements are duly supplemented by a variety of coercive techniques. Indeed, Article XII of the Soviet constitution of 1936 flatly states, "Work in the U.S.S.R. is a duty and a matter of honor for every able-bodied citizen, in accordance with the principle 'He who does not work, neither shall he eat.'" But labor discipline has at times been very poor: absenteeism, tardiness, and worker indifference are common problems. The rate of labor turnover has also been a major difficulty. Plant managers frequently "pirate" the personnel of one another to ensure a labor force adequate for fulfillment of their output targets. Workers seem very willing to change jobs, however slight the resulting improvement in their standard of living might be.

Soviet authorities have taken action to cope with such problems. Fines, pay reductions, dismissal, eviction from state housing, the freezing of workers to their jobs, and discriminatory treatment with respect to social insurance benefits all hang over the head of the bungling, the lazy, the indifferent, and the overly mobile worker. In extreme cases, "spies" and "wreckers," along with political dissidents, may be subject to the wrath of the secret police and assigned to "correctional labor camps" in Siberia or similarly remote areas. The Last Word section of this chapter is a grim reminder of this aspect of the Soviet economy.

Comparable monetary and nonmonetary inducements and compulsory techniques bear upon plant managers. High salaries, bonuses, awards, and promotion await those who fulfill their production targets. Failure exposes the plant manager to investigation and reassignment to a less palatable position. A good many plant managers are party members and therefore inspired by party doctrines.

□ **Planning and Prices**

Let us now look at the way in which prices have been traditionally used in Soviet planning. Then we shall examine some important microeconomic shortcomings of Soviet planning and some recent reforms designed to meet these problems.

To say that the Soviet system is a command economy rather than a market economy is not to say that prices have no role to play in the centrally planned system. Although Soviet prices are not employed as a guiding mechanism in determining the structure of output, they are used in implementing the production objectives established by the state. *Soviet prices are government-manipulated to aid in the achievement of state-established goals; capitalistic prices, although often sub-ject to serious market imperfections, are more market-oriented and more sensitive to individual wants.*

Actually, the function of prices in the Soviet Union has differed considerably between the production process, on the one hand, and the sale of final products to consumers, on the other. In the first instance, prices are merely accounting devices which facilitate checking the efficiency with which products are manufactured. In the latter case, prices are employed as rationing devices to distribute products to consumers without the use of government rationing.

Producer Prices In producing, say, a television set, a Soviet plant will be faced with certain governmentally established prices for component parts, labor, and other needed resources. And, similarly, the government will determine the price of the final product. Generally speaking, the basic principle in establishing these prices is that a plant or an industry of average efficiency would realize total receipts from its production which will cover its total costs and yield a "planned profit" of 5 to 10 percent. If production is less efficient than that deemed average by the plan, planned profits will not be achieved and losses may result. Greater-than-average efficiency will result in unplanned profits.[5] In short, the prices of resources and components are used as accounting costs to assess the efficiency with which various plants and industries operate. Except for the fact that capitalistic prices are essentially market-determined rather than government-determined, this role of the Soviet price system parallels that of its capitalistic counterpart. But here—for two reasons—the similarity ends.

1 In a capitalistic economy, losses call for

---

[5] For the most part, these profits will accrue to the government as revenue from state-owned enterprises. A part may be used to expand the industry, if such expansion is consistent with the objectives of the plan. Another portion may be shared by the plant's workers and executives as a bonus for their efficiency.

a contraction of output and a release of resources by the affected industry; profits signal industry expansion and the absorption of resources. Not so in the Soviet Union. Expansion and contraction of industry are determined by the government, not the price system. Therefore, a relatively inefficient industry which is considered vital by the state may be expanded despite losses. Similarly, a highly efficient, profit-realizing industry may be purposely contracted by state planning.

2 Despite market imperfections, input prices in a capitalistic system should reflect with some reasonable degree of accuracy the relative scarcity of resources and their value in alternative uses. Thus, to minimize money costs in the production of a product is to minimize real costs, that is, to get a given good produced with a minimum sacrifice of alternative goods (Chapter 26). But in the Soviet Union prices are governmentally determined and therefore do not accurately reflect the relative scarcity of resources. Hence, the minimization of money costs in a Soviet enterprise does not mean that real costs of production are being minimized.

Consumer Prices   Whereas prices in the production process are essentially accounting devices used to gauge plan fulfillment, the prices of finished goods are established to serve as rationing devices. In other words, the government attempts to set consumer goods prices at levels which will clear the market so there will be no persistent shortages or surpluses. As a result, the price of television sets which is used for accounting purposes may vary considerably from the price which is charged consumers who purchase them. The difference typically takes the form of what the Russians call a *turnover tax,* which is very roughly similar to an excise tax.

To illustrate: Suppose the accounting price of a finished television set is 200 rubles. This price is used by the Gosplan in judging the efficiency of the assembly plant. But because of the low priority assigned to consumer

goods, consumer demand in the Soviet Union has persistently exceeded the available supply of many consumer goods. This means that, if shortages and government rationing are to be avoided, the price charged by the state in selling television sets to consumers must be higher than the accounting price. Suppose the government estimates that the consumer price of television sets must be 400 rubles to bring the quantity demanded into balance with the quantity of television sets currently available. This is accomplished by adding a 100 percent turnover tax to television sets. At this price the market will be cleared and government rationing avoided.

Turnover taxes—which, incidentally, are the major source of government revenue in Russia—vary widely among various products. High turnover taxes on particularly scarce goods greatly discourage their consumption and force the amounts demanded into accord with the modest quantities allowed by the plan. Lower rates on abundantly available consumer staples—for example, potatoes and certain other vegetables—encourage their consumption. In general, the greater the relative scarcity of a product, the higher the turnover tax placed upon it. The total prices of such products will necessarily be higher and purchases discouraged. Lower tax rates on more abundant products give them lower relative prices and encourage their consumption. In this way inflation-causing income is taxed away, and the pattern of consumer spending is forced into rough accord with the planned composition of consumer goods output. Furthermore, the use of differential turnover tax rates tends to make *real* income differentials less than *money* income differentials. That is, turnover taxes tend to be higher on "luxury goods" than on "necessities."[6]

---

[6] For an authoritative discussion of Soviet pricing, see Morris Bornstein, "The Soviet Price System" in Morris Bornstein (ed.), *Comparative Economic Systems: Models and Cases* (Homewood, Ill.: Richard D. Irwin, Inc., 1965), pp. 278–309.

RECENT PROBLEMS AND REFORMS

Let us now review some of the operational difficulties of Soviet planning and summarize recent economic reforms designed to resolve these problems.

□ Microeconomic Problems

As the Soviet economy has grown and become more sophisticated and complex, detailed central planning has become more and more difficult and unworkable. Specifically, rather severe microeconomic problems have arisen.

In the first place, lacking a genuine price system to communicate the wants of consumers and producers, central planners have frequently directed enterprises to produce goods for which there is little or no demand. The result is unwanted inventories of unsalable goods. Secondly, the major "success indicator" for Soviet enterprise managers has been the quantity of output; the enterprise's main goal is to fulfill or overfulfill its assigned production target. Production costs and product quality are secondary considerations at best. Indeed, planners have found it very difficult to state a quantitative production target without unintentionally eliciting ridiculous "distortions" in output. Example: If an enterprise manufacturing nails has its production target stated in terms of weight (tons of nails), it will tend to produce all large nails. But if its target is a numerical one (thousands of nails), it will be motivated to produce all small nails! Furthermore, the Soviet press persistently denounces the poor quality of both consumer goods and many producer goods. Least-cost production is virtually impossible in the absence of a system of genuine prices which accurately reflect the relative scarcity of the various resources. Finally, Soviet enterprise managers have been highly resistant to innovation. Managers are more concerned with "bargaining" for realistic production targets and fulfilling their output goals so that they can achieve bonuses. New production processes invariably mean higher and often unrealistic targets, underfulfillment, loss of bonuses.

□ Reforms: Libermanism

The Soviet government responded to these problems by introducing important reforms in the last half of the 1960s. The reforms stem in large measure from the proposals of Professor E. Liberman of Kharkov University. His plan called for the introduction of a modified "profit motive" as the primary success indicator in an enterprise; for greater decentralization of decision making and greater autonomy for enterprise managers; and for some degree of "planning from below."

Under the reforms, enterprises can take orders from customers (retailers or other enterprises) which specify the types (colors, sizes, styles) and amounts of each product. This "planning from below" provides "direct links" to consumer or producer demand and is obviously designed to bring about a better matching of output with the structure of demand. Management also negotiates with other firms for the purchase of needed inputs. Furthermore, the management of each enterprise has restricted authority in setting prices, including rates of pay for its labor force.

The enterprise's major success indicator will no longer be physical output, but rather, "profitability" calculated in relation to the fixed and working capital of the enterprise. The management and labor force of an enterprise will receive bonuses in direct relation to profitability. This reorientation of goals means that enterprises will be penalized for the production of goods which are unsalable because they are of shoddy quality or, in the case of producer goods, because they do not fit the input requirements of purchasing enterprises. That is, enterprises must now be concerned not only with production, but also with the sale of output. Moreover, the new emphasis upon profitability means that greater attention must be paid to production costs.

These reforms have been extensive; it is estimated that over four-fifths of the Soviet Union's industrial production is carried on by enterprises operating under them. And it is clear that the reforms constitute a significant departure from traditional Soviet planning. Nevertheless, it would be incorrect to interpret the reforms as a trend toward capitalism as we know it. The major goals of the Soviet economy and the priorities attached to these goals are still determined by the central planners. It is significant that the plans of all enterprises working under the new system are reviewed by the planning authorities to assure their conformity with overall national goals and priorities.

As a matter of fact, the long-term viability of the Liberman reforms depends upon the ability of the Soviets to resolve certain problems posed by the reforms themselves. One problem stems from the simple fact that the reforms have not been enthusiastically embraced by all members of the Soviet economic and political hierarchy. "Old line" central planners correctly envision their authority and positions of power being eroded by any permanent and widespread decentralization of decision making. A second problem is a technical one: The realization of allocative efficiency depends upon sweeping price reforms which will make Soviet prices more accurately reflect the relative scarcity of inputs. The minimization of the money cost of producing any given output will reflect a minimization of real or opportunity costs only if resource prices are accurate indicators of relative scarcity. It is not at all clear that Soviet planners will be able to achieve, much less maintain over time, a new price structure based upon resource scarcity.

■
SOVIET ECONOMIC GROWTH

In view of our foregoing discussion of the Soviet Union's microeconomic problems, it is fair to say that the system has been quite unsuc-

cessful in realizing the goal of allocative efficiency. But we know there are other measures in terms of which an economy's performance might be judged. The alternative and essentially macroeconomic goal which has been paramount with the Soviet leadership is *rapid* economic growth. Soviet Russia has pursued with great vigor the goal of rapid growth and the political-military strength derived therefrom. These two concepts of efficiency may be in conflict in certain important ways.[7] In particular, because Soviet planning seeks very rapid growth, it results in highly ambitious production targets and the overcommitment of resources. And ambitious targets and overcommitted resources are the source of many of the coordination problems discussed earlier. In any event, we know that the Soviet economy has performed well in terms of the objective of growth. Let us now consider the rate of growth achieved by the Soviet Union, the sources of this growth, and the prospect of its maintenance.

□   **Growth Comparisons**

Authoritative estimates put the Soviet GNP at slightly more than one-half that of the United States. Figure 45-1 shows this relationship and indicates the relative composition of the national outputs of the two nations. Experts also agree that the Soviet growth rate has generally exceeded that of the United States in the post-World War II period as a whole. For the 1948–1974 period the Soviet Union's annual growth rate was 5.9 percent as compared with 3.6 percent for the United States. But there is evidence of convergence in recent years: Soviet annual growth was 4.9 percent in the 1960–1974 period, while the United States enjoyed a 3.8 percent rate. Both economies performed poorly in the first half of

[7]The interested reader should consult Albert O. Hirschman, *The Strategy of Economic Development* (New Haven, Conn.: Yale University Press, 1959).

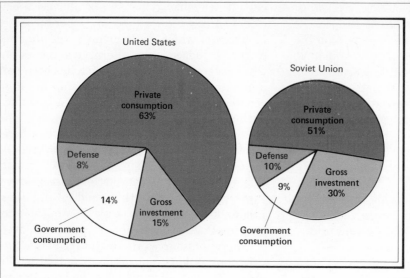

FIGURE 45-1 SIZE AND COMPOSITION OF GNP IN THE UNITED STATES AND THE SOVIET UNION

Soviet Russia's GNP is roughly one-half the size of the United States's GNP. As compared with the United States, the Soviet Union puts relatively greater emphasis on investment goods than on consumer goods. [*Stanley H. Cohn, "Economic Burden of Defense Expenditures," in Joint Economic Committee,* Soviet Economic Prospects for the Seventies (*Washington, 1973*), *p. 151. Data for both countries are for 1969.*]

the 1970s as reflected in a 3.5 percent annual rate for the Soviet Union and a 2 percent rate here at home.[8]

□ **Sources of Soviet Growth**

Let us first pinpoint certain factors which have contributed to the Soviet Union's historically high growth rates.

1 Natural Resource Base The Soviet Union has a generous and varied natural resource base. Although they differ significantly in composition, it is not inaccurate to say that the natural resource endowments of the U.S.S.R. are roughly comparable with those of the United States. The major exception to this generalization is agricultural resources. Most of Russia's most fertile soil lies in regions susceptible to drought and short growing seasons. On the other hand, the Soviet Union is the

world's only major industrial nation which is self-sufficient in energy and likely to remain so in the foreseeable future.

2 Totalitarianism and Allocation Because the Soviet Union is a totalitarian state, the government can and does exercise tight political control over the allocation of resources. That the government has, with little hesitation or reservation, exerted a strong and often brutal "will to develop" is reflected in its efforts to indoctrinate, regiment, push and prod its citizenry, and structure its institutions to the overriding goal of economic growth. The Soviet economy has aptly been described as "totalitarianism harnessed to the task of rapid industrialization and economic growth."[9] To be more specific, we may say that the will to develop has been expressed most explicitly in the high-volume and growth-oriented composition of Soviet investment. The Soviet Union devotes about 30 percent of its total output to

[8] Herbert Block, "Soviet Economic Power Growth— Achievements under Handicaps," in Joint Economic Committee, *Soviet Economy in a New Perspective* (Washington, 1976), p. 268.

[9] Robert W. Campbell, *The Soviet-type Economies,* 3d ed. (Boston: Houghton Mifflin Company, 1974), p. 3.

investment, compared with 15 percent for the United States (Figure 45-1). Furthermore, the composition of Soviet investment has put emphasis upon those industries most crucial to the growth process. Retail and wholesale distributional facilities, for example, have been largely ignored in favor of steel, petroleum, chemicals, and machine tools.

3 Surplus Farm Labor You may recall from Chapter 21 that it is characteristic of underdeveloped countries to have a sizable amount of surplus or underemployed labor in agriculture. This was true of the Soviet Union at the time of the revolution. Under central planning, much of this low-productivity farm labor was shifted to newly created industries, where its productivity was substantially higher. In 1925, 84 percent of the Soviet labor force was in agriculture; currently, about 25 percent are so employed. This reallocation has resulted in significant increases in the Soviet GNP.

4 Technological Gap Rapid expansion in Soviet production has stemmed in good measure from the adoption of the superior technological knowledge pioneered by the Western nations. The Soviet Union has eagerly, unashamedly, and quite effectively borrowed and skillfully applied the superior techniques of other nations. In this manner, the U.S.S.R. has quickly and very inexpensively bridged a long period of research and development activity in many key industries.

5 Full Employment The Soviet economy's growth rate, unlike those of the United States and other capitalistic nations, has benefited in that, since about 1930, Soviet economic planning has virtually eliminated cyclical unemployment. Unlike the United States, the Soviet Union has *not* had to count years of zero or negative growth due to recession in calculating its long-term rate of growth.

□ **Retarding Factors**

Why has the Soviet growth rate diminished? What growth-retarding forces have been at work in the late 1960s and early 1970s?

1 Diversion of Resources A frequently cited reason for the slowing down of Soviet growth is that expanding defense expenditures in the 1960s and 1970s have diverted resources from more growth-effective uses. In particular, growing defense outlays have caused declines in both the quantity and quality of industrial investment. Rising defense expenditures have become an "onerous burden" upon the Soviet economy because of their direct competitiveness with civilian investment and therefore economic growth. Furthermore, the "policy of channeling superior management and the best scientists and engineers into defense research and production denies prime innovative resources to civilian oriented investment"[10] and has adversely affected technological progress and the quality (productivity) of investment in the civilian sector.

The "onerous burden" hypothesis may apply not only to the military, but also to the consuming sector:[11]

> Soviet leaders are finding it increasingly difficult to reject or postpone the satisfaction of consumers' wants. Revolutionary enthusiasm, it is said, no longer is sufficient to make sacrifices of consumer welfare acceptable either to the population at large or to many Communist Party members and leaders. The very sizable improvements that have been made in consumer welfare in recent years have not relieved universal dissatisfaction with living conditions, but rather may have whetted the general appetite for further gains.

[10]Stanley H. Cohn, "General Growth Performance of the Soviet Economy," in Joint Economic Committee, *Economic Performance and the Military Burden in the Soviet Union* (Washington, 1970), p. 12.
[11]Terence E. Byrne, "Recent Trends in the Soviet Economy," in ibid., p. 5.

2   Replacement Investment   A more technical point is that, as the size and age of the Soviet Union's stock of capital increase, replacement investment necessarily increases. That is, a growing proportion of gross investment must be for depreciation, leaving a smaller share as net investment to contribute to growth. Other things being the same, an increasing volume of gross investment is required to maintain a constant rate of growth.

3   Labor Shortage   Whereas much of the Soviet Union's earlier growth was attributable to shifts of surplus labor from agriculture to industry, the Soviet Union is finding it increasingly difficult to make additional labor shifts without significantly imperiling the output of an already troubled agricultural sector. The overall picture in the Soviet Union is one of labor scarcity, and this is particularly so in certain skills and in certain cities and regions. This shortage is partly the consequence of the ambitiousness of the central plans and is undoubtedly aggravated by widespread malutilization of the labor force. It also stems from a slowing down of labor-force growth as the result of declining fertility rates in recent decades. It is interesting that the Soviet Union has occasionally imported workers from Eastern European satellite nations to relieve its labor shortage. The basic point is that the relatively easy means of increasing GNP by employing more labor inputs is less available to the Soviets; they are faced with the more demanding task of expanding their GNP by increasing labor productivity, that is, output per worker.

4   Agricultural Drag   By Western standards Soviet agriculture is something of a monument to inefficiency and now constitutes a drag upon economic growth, engulfing as it does some 25 percent of the labor force. The low productivity of Soviet agriculture is attributable to many factors: the relative scarcity of good land; vagaries in rainfall and length of growing season; the limited use of chemical fertilizers; serious errors in planning and administration; and perhaps most important, the failure to construct an effective incentive system. Given the relatively large size of the agricultural sector, a poor growing season can have highly adverse effects upon the Soviet growth rate. For example, the poor harvest of 1975 was a major factor in pulling that year's growth rate down to 2.5 percent.

5   Planning Problems   As suggested earlier, there are forces at work in the U.S.S.R. which have tended to reduce the relative efficiency of Soviet planning and thereby to retard the growth rate. These planning problems are closely linked to the development of the Soviet economy itself. Early planning under Stalin was not unlike the wartime planning of Western nations: A limited number of key production goals were established, and resources were centrally directed toward the fulfillment of these goals regardless of costs or consumer welfare. But the past success of such "campaign planning" has resulted in an industrially advanced economy. This new, more modern economy is vastly different from that of the earlier period of war-economy planning. The proliferation and realignment of priorities have already been noted. In short, planning techniques which were more-or-less adequate for the Stalinist era of limited production goals are decreasingly relevant and less workable in the more sophisticated economy of the 1970s. With growth the economy, and therefore planning, became decidedly more complex. Neither labor or capital is as relatively abundant as it was a scant decade or so ago. The expansion of a relatively few standard product lines, with a blatant disregard for costs, is relatively simple; production of a much larger variety of products, each of which is more complex, within a context of growing cost-consciousness is quite a different matter. To state the situation quite simply, the Soviet economy has tended to outgrow its planning mechanisms. This fact has posed serious questions concerning the allocative efficiency of the system and its capacity to sustain its growth rate. Evidence of party awareness of planning deficiencies is reflected in the more-or-less continuous restructuring of the production hierarchy.[12]

☐ Future Growth

What of the future? Will the Soviet growth rate persist at comparatively low levels? Or will the rather spectacular rates of the 1950s be reachieved?

There is some agreement that Soviet growth would be accelerated if (1) military production were curtailed and scientific-technical personnel, along with other strategic resources, were reallocated to civilian uses; (2) planning institutions and managerial mechanisms were simplified and improved; and (3) commercial relationships with capitalistic nations were expanded to facilitate the transfer of superior technology to the Soviet Union. On the last point, it is acknowledged that a basic motivation behind growing Soviet trade with the Western economies is to acquire high-technology plants and equipment. "Soviet leaders hope that imported plant and equipment embodying advanced Western technology will permit rapid growth of selected key outputs, raise the productivity of labor and capital, and provide spinoff examples that can spread widely throughout the Soviet economy."[13]

But there are serious obstacles to realizing these three means of growth. Improved economic performance may call for a higher degree of ideological and bureaucratic flexibility than currently prevails in the U.S.S.R.:[14]

Deemphasis of the military and heavy industry run counter to the entrenched interests of important segments of the Soviet elite. Significant changes in planning and management would result in a diffusion or redirection of economic power and control in the Soviet system. Thus the economic role of the Party might be at stake. Changes in relations between the Soviet economy and the non-Communist world might mean renouncing the Stalinist concept of autarky and isolation and joining the international commercial and financial community. Thus, the political costs for improved economic performance might be high, perhaps too high.

It is also recognized that the Soviet planning hierarchy and incentive system are resistant to the technological progress needed by the economy to restore its vitality.

The bureaucratic immobility of the Soviet decision-making mechanism smothers a great deal of the volatility present in a normal market economy. Established procedures regularly grind out standard forms of output, while conventional methods enlarge capital stocks embodying orthodox technology. This stability has, of course, its advantages, but it also means that unfavorable conditions and unsatisfactory performance are hard to remedy. Where new procedures are required in order to produce new forms of output involving altered capital stocks embodying unfamiliar technology, the Soviet system responds poorly. The rewards and penalties that motivate Soviet managers and workers serve admirably to replicate and enlarge the existing economy. These same rewards and penalties act negatively, however, with the effect of protecting the system against changes—even if the needed changes are improvements.[15]

Thus a recent authoritative research study concludes, "The gradual decline in output growth rates since 1958 . . . seems destined to continue in the future. . . . The slacking off of labor-force increments, declining effectiveness

[12]See, for example, Alice C. Gorlin, "Industrial Reorganization: The Associations," in Joint Economic Committee, *Soviet Economy in Perspective,* op. cit., pp. 162–188.

[13]Holland Hunter, M. Mark Earle, Jr., and Richard B. Foster, "Assessment of Alternative Long-Range Soviet Growth Strategies," in Joint Economic Committee, ibid., p. 200.

[14]John P. Hardt, "Summary," in Joint Economic Committee, *Soviet Economic Prospects for the Seventies* (Washington, 1973), p. xvii.

[15]Hunter, op. cit., p. 212.

of capital investment, and other forces underlying the tapering growth of the last 15 years, cast their influence forward into the baseline projection for the coming 15 years as well." The study's basic prediction is that Soviet real GNP will grow at 4.7 percent annually in the last half of the 1970s; at 3.7 percent per year in the 1980–1985 period; and at only 3.3 percent over 1985–1990.[16] *If* these projections turn out to be correct, they will reflect a marked slowdown in Soviet growth. On the other hand, the projected rates are quite comparable to those recently achieved by industrially advanced capitalistic nations (Table 20–2).

■───────────────────────
GENERAL EVALUATION

Our discussion thus far has centered upon central planning and the growth performance which planning has fostered. A more complete evaluation of the Soviet system calls for the consideration of several other accomplishments and shortcomings.

□ Accomplishments

1 Education Though circumscribed by Communist doctrine and shaped in terms of government goals, Soviet Russia has made tremendous strides in increasing the quantity and quality of education. Free public education has been a high-priority goal of the Soviet regime from the outset. Much has also been done to encourage cultural pursuits, again within limits imposed by the party.

2 Economic Security In keeping with socialist tradition, the Soviet Union has developed a quite complete system of social insurance. Medical care is virtually free and disability and sick leave benefits are provided, as are maternity benefits. Rental payments are heavily subsidized and amount to only about 4 or 5 percent of a worker's income. Retirement

pensions are available for industrial workers and have recently been extended to collective farmers. Although the size of benefit payments is not overly generous by American standards, they are sufficient in terms of the Soviet standard of living.

□ Shortcomings

Generally speaking, the major shortcomings of the Soviet system are the offspring of its accomplishments. Two major points merit emphasis.

1 Standard of Living The costs of rapid industrialization and economic growth have been great, and have been borne for the most part by consumers. This is reflected in both the quantity and quality of Soviet consumer goods. Living standards are much lower than in the United States:[17]

> Soviet city life is similar to life in Western cities fifty years ago. People live in crowded apartments, use public transportation, wear drab clothing, and eat a starchy diet. . . . Soviet rural life compares with still earlier European experience, though the presence of large machinery and trucks hampers comparison. The general pattern in both city and country is still "old fashioned," yet elements of modernization run all through it.

Recent improvements in the Soviet standard of living have been significant. For example, during the first eight years of the Brezhnev regime (1965–1972), per capita consumption rose by 5 percent per year, in contrast to 3 percent per year in the Khrushchev era (1956–1964). Unfortunately, the recent overall decline in the Soviet growth rate has had adverse effects upon consumption. In the 1971–1975 period the average annual growth rate for consump-

[16] Ibid., p. 203.

[17] Clair Wilcox, Willis D. Weatherford, Jr., Holland Hunter, and Morton S. Baratz, *Economies of the World Today,* 3d ed. (New York: Harcourt Brace Jovanovich, Inc., 1976), pp. 126–127.

tion has fallen back to about 3 percent. As far as the consumer is concerned, the Soviet Union is far from being a society of abundance.

2   Freedom   The decisions which determine the overall economic, political, social, and cultural environment are made by the Soviet dictatorship. Only within governmentally prescribed limits is individual freedom tolerated. Consumers and wage earners are "free" to choose from the goods and jobs that planners decide to provide. In general, artists and writers must conform to the party line in their creative efforts. The confinement, harassment, and ultimate expulsion of writer Aleksandr Solzhenitsyn vividly illustrate the Soviet system's intolerance of dissident voices.

It must be emphasized that the Soviet Union, viewed in broader perspective, is a dictatorship based ultimately upon coercion, terror, or the effective threat thereof. Though there has been a general relaxation of the tensions which surrounded Stalinist tyranny, the threat of force is omnipresent. Elections are a farce, the press is essentially a propaganda organ of the government, and the role of the secret police in maintaining allegiance and conformity continues to be substantial.[18]

■───────────────────────────

THE CONVERGENCE HYPOTHESIS

Some economists envision a long-term decline in the differences between the capitalistic and communistic systems. Certain fundamental forces, they argue, are at work to promote convergence. The essence of the convergence hypothesis is that as capitalistic and communistic systems evolve, they encounter experiences and problems which induce the adoption of similar institutions and policies. That is, industrialization results in the reallocation of population from rural to urban areas; in greater education and concern for consumer welfare; in greater dependence upon technology and innovation; and so forth. Regardless of ideology, these developments induce behavioral patterns, values, and even institutional changes which make the two types of economies increasingly similar.

Consider the communistic systems. As they develop economically, complex problems arise with respect to allocative efficiency. To deal with such problems, these systems turn more and more to the use of markets and prices. Recall that the Soviet reforms of the 1960s put greater reliance upon the "profitability" of output. And other communistic systems, Yugoslavia, for example, have gone much further than the Soviet Union in upgrading the role of the price system in their economies. Conversely, as capitalistic systems evolve, the public sector becomes increasingly important; government plays a more active role in economic affairs. The provision of social goods and governmental modification of the price system for significant externalities become commonplace. Government also provides a welfare system to temper income inequality and ensure against various personal risks. Finally, government's responsibility to "manage" the economy so as to avoid severe economic instability is well accepted and, more recently, incomes policies have become commonplace. Indeed, some economies of the West—of France, for example—have adopted a loose form of central planning. In short, the argument is that the imperfections of the communistic economies call for a reduced governmental role and increased reliance upon prices and markets, while the shortcomings of capitalistic economies demand less reliance upon the market system and an expanded public sector. The net result is convergence. To promote greater economic efficiency and improve the well-being of their populations, the two systems edge their way toward some common

───────────────────────────

[18] For a short study of the history and strategy of communism, the reader should consult Andrew Gyorgy, *Communism in Perspective* (Boston: Allyn and Bacon, Inc., 1964). Andrei D. Sakharov's *Progress, Coexistence, and Intellectual Freedom* (New York: W. W. Norton & Company, Inc., 1968) is also of great interest. Sakharov, who was largely responsible for the development of Russia's atomic bomb, appeals to the party to democratize the Soviet system.

middle ground between the extremes of laissez faire capitalism and authoritarian central planning.

There may well be an important element of truth to the convergence hypothesis. But differences between the two systems are immense and, in fact, evidence of movement toward convergence may be more apparent than real. For example, some economists point out that the Soviet reforms of the 1960s were designed to strengthen central planning and not to move the economy in the direction of a market system. Furthermore, there is little or no evidence of convergence with respect to certain basic institutional features, such as property ownership. In the Soviet Union, state ownership is not merely a matter of economic ideology, but also a means of political control. That is, to permit the private ownership of farmland and capital would be to diminish political control over a large portion of the Soviet population. There is no evidence that such a dramatic institutional change is in the thinking of the Soviet leadership. Similarly, while the issue of public versus private ownership of large-scale enterprises is open to debate, there is little question on economic grounds that small-scale enterprises should be privately owned. Yet the Soviet Union shows no inclination to move toward private small-scale enterprises. Finally, basic and perhaps insurmountable differences remain between East and West in noneconomic spheres. The nature of the political state, the sources of its power, and the relationship between the individual and the state are viewed in fundamentally different ways in the ideologies of East and West. In brief, there may be forces working toward convergence, but its realization may be far beyond the horizon.

Summary

1 The vivid contrast which the Soviet economy provides to American capitalism, the economic challenge it presents to the Western world, and the rapid economic growth achieved in Soviet Russia are important reasons for studying the Soviet economic system.

2 Virtually complete state ownership of property resources and authoritarian central planning are the outstanding institutional features of the Soviet economy. The major goals of the Five- and Seven-year Plans, as determined by the government, have been rapid industrialization, growth, and military strength.

3 The basic problem of central planners is to achieve coordination or internal consistency in their plans so as to avoid bottlenecks and the chain reaction of production failures which they cause. The evaluation of preliminary plans by the administrative hierarchy, the assignment of priorities to planned goals, and reserve stocks are used to prevent or alleviate coordination problems in the U.S.S.R.

4 Many agencies check upon the actual execution of the Five-year Plans—the planning hierarchy, the Communist party and its numerous officials, and the secret police. The most important of these agencies is the Gosbank, which exerts "control by the ruble."

5 In the production process, governmentally determined prices on resources and components and on finished products serve as accounting devices to evaluate the efficiency of production. In consumer goods markets, prices are adjusted through the turnover tax to ration products to consumers, that is, to balance the amount demanded with available supplies.

6 As the Soviet economy has become more complex, certain microeconomic problems—the production of unwanted goods, a distorted product-mix, and resistance to innovation—have developed. The Liberman reforms of the 1960s, emphasizing profitability of production, "planning from below," and greater decentralization of decision making, have been adopted in response to these problems.

7   Although the Soviet GNP is only one-half as large as that of the United States, the Soviet GNP has grown more rapidly than ours. A generous natural resource base, great emphasis upon capital formation, the transfer of surplus agricultural labor to industry, the adoption of superior production techniques from the West, and the planning away of cyclical unemployment are factors which have contributed to this high growth rate.

8   A number of factors suggest a future decline in the Soviet growth rate: a diversion of resources from growth-inducing uses, the growth of replacement investment, a shortage of industrial labor, the stagnation of agriculture, and mounting planning problems attributable to the increasing complexity of the Soviet economy. Authoritative estimates suggest the Soviet growth rate may fall to about 3.5 percent in the 1980s.

9   In addition to proving the feasibility of central planning and achieving a high growth rate, the Soviet Union has made significant advances in education and has established a comprehensive social security system. On the other hand, the Soviet standard of living is not enviable by Western standards, and freedom is closely circumscribed by party objectives.

Questions and Study Suggestions

1   Key terms and concepts to remember: state ownership; central economic planning; Gosplan; priority principle; Gosbank; "control by the ruble"; turnover tax; Libermanism; convergence hypothesis.

2   Compare the institutional framework of the Soviet economy with that of American capitalism. Contrast the manner in which production is motivated in these two economic systems.

3   "So long as a central planning board, as opposed to society as a whole, sets the economic goals, there can be no freedom of occupational or consumer choice." Explain.

4   Compare the sources of insecurity which face an American and a Soviet steelworker.

5   "It has become increasingly difficult for thoughtful men to find meaningful alternatives posed in the traditional choices between socialism and capitalism, planning and the free market, regulation and laissez faire, for they find their actual choices neither simple nor so grand."[19] Explain and evaluate.

6   How does Soviet planning attempt to cope with the Five Fundamental Questions which all economies must face? Discuss the problem of coordination. What mechanisms do Soviet planners use to avoid and correct problems of coordination? Explain: "Soviet planning problems mainly arise from the fact that the command economy is rooted in the logic of haste."

7   Evaluate carefully the level of efficiency which has been achieved in Soviet economic planning. Discuss the background and character of the Liberman reforms.

8   Compare the size, composition, and rate of growth of the GNPs of the United States and the Soviet Union. What have been the major sources of Soviet economic

[19] Robert A. Dahl and Charles E. Lindblom, *Politics, Economics and Welfare* (New York: Harper & Row, Publishers, Incorporated, 1953), p. 1.

expansion? Do you feel that the Soviet Union will be able to reachieve its past growth performance? Explain.

9 Carefully contrast the role of the price system in Soviet Russia and the United States, distinguishing between resource and product markets. Explain the use of turnover taxes. How is the number of automobiles to be produced determined in American capitalism? In the Soviet Union? How are these decisions implemented in the two economies?

10 Briefly discuss the convergence hypothesis, indicating evidence for and against its validity.

Selected References

Bornstein, Morris, and Daniel R. Fusfeld (eds.): *The Soviet Economy,* 4th ed. (Homewood, Ill.: Richard D. Irwin, Inc., 1974).

Campbell, Robert W.: *The Soviet-type Economies,* 3d ed. (Boston: Houghton Mifflin Company, 1974).

Joint Economic Committee: *Soviet Economy in a New Perspective* (Washington, 1976).

NATO: *Economic Aspects of Life in the USSR* (Brussels: NATO, 1975).

Wilcox, Clair, Willis D. Weatherford, Jr., Holland Hunter, and Morton S. Baratz: *Economies of the World Today,* 3d ed. (New York: Harcourt Brace Jovanovich, Inc., 1976), particularly chap. 5.

Wilczynski, J.: *The Economics of Socialism,* rev. ed. (Chicago: Aldine Publishing Company, 1972).

Last Word
The Testimony of Avraham Shifrin

A refugee from a Soviet prison camp recalls camp conditions, prisoner uprisings, and the important role of prison labor in the economy of the U.S.S.R. Elsewhere in his testimony Mr. Shifrin estimates that there are currently some 5 to 10 million prison laborers in the Soviet Union today.

In 1953, 1954, it was awful conditions in concentration camps. It is hard to explain how bad it was. It was a time when people worked without holidays or any days when they can rest—10, 12, sometimes 15 hours in a day, with one letter to their relatives in the year. One to the year. And without meeting relatives, without any salary, with such bad food that when I came to the concentration camp, I have seen prisoners which have only bones and skin. Each day in our concentration camp, I do not remember a day when it was less than 30, 35 people—less than 35—which died from starvation. People died from scurvy, from pellagra also, a sort of scurvy, and from other diseases, because the body can't work in these conditions when men are so hungry. And that is why people was in such a condition that one day, in Vorkuta, in this district, which you can see on this map up near the polar circle—it was in these days, maybe some millions prisoners in this district—spontaneously, they began to strike. Then they asked some prisoners to speak with the guards, with officers. And they stopped the work in all the coal mines. . . .

This coal mining, it is very important in the U.S.S.R. because industry works on this coal. That is why came to them Khrushchev, Bulganin, Voroshilov, many members of the government, the General Procurator of the U.S.S.R., with members of the Supreme Court, with members of the Supreme Soviet of Ministers. They came to these concentration camps and spoke with these prisoners, but the prisoners answered, "We would work in these coal mines if you would take away these numbers and you would permit us first to live like people; and then you would examine our files again, because we are innocent." And they refused to do this. And these conversations was maybe 20, 25, 30 days in some concentration camps.

Then the government sent bombers and then they sent tanks. They sent troops, and they drowned this uprising in the blood. Thousands and thousands of prisoners was killed. . . .

In Norilsk, there was big uprising. In Norilsk is big mining for molybdenum and uranium and they need uranium in industry. That is why in Norilsk, they tried to speak for weeks; and then these killers sent big guns and tanks and they crushed these people. Thousands of prisoners were killed in Norilsk.

Norilsk is a place in which, before there came prisoners to Norilsk, it was mountains and plain with snow. You could not find there any buildings. Then prisoners build the city for 300,000 or 400,000 people. Now it is a big city. And all this city was built by prisoners. . . .

Building Volga-Don Canal, it was a half million prisoners in the center of the U.S.S.R. Belomorsky Canal here [pointing to map]—also prisoners.

I talked to you about this Omsk refinery [pointing to map]—also built by prisoners. I talked to you about this biggest power station, Bratsk—also prisoners. I can show you here it was in Angarsk [pointing to map] they brought from Germany one of the biggest in Germany refinery, artificial gasoline. And it was here—I have had many friends here—100,000 people for 5 years, they build this synthetic refinery.

They built all the Kolyma gold mines with the hands of prisoners.

You can see on all these places from which they think to send to the United States these rockets, all these missile bases and airfields—all built by prisoners. All the railways in the country—only prisoners. Highways—all prisoners. All lumber cutting—only prisoners. Today, in 1973.

I have seen many times—I have heard, excuse me, please—I have seen twice myself and I have heard many times when prisoners cut their own hands and put them in the cars with lumber. They said to me, "We want that people in the freedom in the West will know who cut this lumber." You know—this lumber goes to free world. When I came to the West and I asked some people which make trade with the U.S.S.R. in this lumber, I asked these people: "It was such cases when came lumber with cut hands?" They answered me, "Yes; it was. . . ."

In all the U.S.S.R., these slaves work without salary, only because prisoners want to live. They work in this industry, in this lumber cutting, in all this country. . . .

I was once in train and Khrushchev was here in the United States, and I was in a special car for prisoners, with guards, with soldiers, and so on. And Khrushchev here in the U.N. made this speech, "I have finished with all the concentration camps in the U.S.S.R.; now we have no prisoners in the U.S.S.R.; we are finished with all the crimes of Stalin." And in a corridor in another stage of this cage stayed an officer. He smoked, smiled, and said to us: "When we come to the station, I will release you because you are not here."

You see, in the U.S.S.R., no one believes the government, because they lie in the eyes of people. People in U.S.S.R. used to all this. I know—I am sure that my father was innocent. I was sure of this when he was arrested. He never was an anti-Soviet man. He was a simple civil engineer. And then came this great purge. He was sent to the prison and died after 10 years. And in 1958, they sent to my mother so little letter, "Your husband, Shifrin, Itzak, was innocent and today he is rehabilitated after death."

Sad. You enjoy here your rights. We also have rights in U.S.S.R. And one of our rights is "after death rehabilitation;" such sad joke in U.S.S.R. you can hear.

Once in such a prisoner railway car, a soldier asked a prisoner, "Why do you sit here in the prison?" And the prisoner answered "I am innocent; for nothing."

"And how many years they gave you?"

The prisoner answered "25 years."

And the soldier said to the prisoner, "Ah, you liar! If men are innocent, they always give only 10 years!"

You understood me?

From *U.S.S.R. Labor Camps,* Hearings before the Subcommittee to Investigate the Administration of the Internal Security Act and Other Internal Security Laws of the Committee on the Judiciary, U.S. Senate, 93d Congress, 1st Session, Washington, 1973, pp. 71–75, abridged.

INDEX

Abdul-Jabbar, Kareem, 83, 647
Ability-to-pay principle of taxation, 158–159
Abraham, William I., 189n.
Abstraction in economics, 5
Accelerationist view of Phillips Curve, 386–388
Accommodating transactions, 894
Acreage allotment programs, 724
Acreage reserve programs, 724
Actual reserves, 317
Adams, Walter, 526n., 576, 590, 612, 697n., 698n., 707n., 786n.
Adjustable-peg system of exchange rates, 907
Administrative lag, 284
Advertising, 584–588
  case against, 586–587
  case for, 585–586
Advisory Commission on Intergovernmental Relations, 740n., 752n., 755n.
"After this, therefore, because of this" fallacy, 16
Agency for International Development (AID), 451
Agglomeration, economies of, 735–737
Aggregate demand, 250
  and growth, 408–410
Aggregate supply, 248–250
Agricultural Adjustment Act of 1933, 723
Agriculture:
  exports, 882
  in Soviet Union, 936
  (See also Farms and farming)
Agriculture and Consumer Protection Act of 1973, 727
Aid to Families with Dependent Children (AFDC) program, 773
Aliber, Robert Z., 370n.
Alienation of workers, 60, 806–807, 840
Allen, Clark Lee, 498
Allocation of resources, 682
  and imperfect competition, 682–683
  and international trade, 860–861
  and pure competition, 550–554
  in radical economics, 840–841

Allocative efficiency:
  and growth, 411, 420–422
  and wage-price controls, 380
Alonso, William, 756n.
American Federation of Labor, 786
American Motors, 529
Ameringer, Oscar, 247
Anderson, William H., 292
Annually balanced budget, 270
Antitrust, 599
  effectiveness of, 712–713
Antitrust laws, 107, 377, 702–704
Apollo program, 827–828
Aronson, J. Richard, 164, 433
Asset, 313
Atomic Energy Commission, 809
Automation, 214
Automobile industry, 208
Autonomous transactions, 893
Average costs, 518
Average fixed cost, 518
Average propensity to consume, 233
Average propensity to save, 233
  and growth, 410
Average revenue, 492
Average tax rate, 153
Average total cost, 519
Average variable cost, 518
Averitt, Robert T., 473

Bach, G. L., 220
Backman, Jules, 588n., 635n.
Baer, George F., 785n.
Bain, Joe S., 142n., 466n., 528, 590, 612, 696n., 826
Baird, Charles W., 473
Baker, Russell, 165, 166n.
Balance of payments, 890–893
  and domestic stabilization policies, 917–918
  of United States, 910–913
Balance sheet of commercial banks, 313–314
Balanced-budget multiplier, 276
Baldwin, Robert E., 867, 868n., 885
Banking system, and money supply, 323–327

Banks, 303–307
  (See also Commercial banks; Federal Reserve Banks)
Baratz, Morton S., 139n., 145, 938n., 942
Barnett, Harold, 431n.
Barriers to entry, 463, 560–563
Barter economy, 54
Base year, 170
Basketball games, demand for, 83–84
Bastiat, Frederic, 886
Becker, Gary, 507
Beckerman, Wilfred, 433
Beer industry, 591
Beman, Lewis, 396n.
Benefit-cost analysis, 115
  limitations of, 117–118
Benefits-received principle of taxation, 158
Bennett, Peter D., 510
Benoit, Emile, 812n., 826
Bernstein, Peter L., 292, 330
Berry, Brian J. L., 733n.
Bias, 14
Bickel, Blaine W., 731
Big business, 141–144
Bilateral monopoly, 467, 642
Bish, Robert L., 757
Black capitalism, 749
Black markets, 487
Blacklisting, 785
Blanchfield, William C., 456
Blaug, M., 650n.
Blinder, Alan S., 292
Block, Herbert, 934n.
Bloom, Gordon F., 642n., 654
Board of Governors of the Federal Reserve System, 304
Boddy, Francis M., 685n.
Bolton, Roger E., 820n.
Bornstein, Morris, 931n., 942
Boulding, Kenneth E., 4n., 21, 82, 102, 145, 175n., 498, 759n., 812n., 826
Bowen, Howard R., 58n., 59, 124n.
Bowen, William G., 650n.
Brady, Gerald P., 711
Break, George F., 164
Brennan, Michael J., 498, 689

Bretton Woods Monetary System, 907–910
Bronfenbrenner, Martin, 848
Brougher, Jack, 884n.
Brown, Lester R., 413
Browning, Edgar K., 764, 765n., 767n.
Brue, Stanley L., 82
Buchwald, Art, 434
Budget restraint, 57, 502
Built-in stabilizers, 218, 260, 277–279
Bureaucracy, inefficiency of, 120–121
Burke, William, 818n.
Burns, Arthur F., 355, 824n., 903
Business cycle, 204–217
Business firms:
  defined, 134
  large-size, 141–144
  legal forms, 135–140
Business unionism, 785
Byrne, Terence E., 935n.

Campagna, Anthony S., 167
Campbell, Robert W., 101n., 934n., 942
Capital, defined, 25
Capital accumulation, 94, 408
  and growth, 408–410
  and interest rate, 664–666
  in underdeveloped countries, 443–445
  (See also Investment)
Capital consumption allowance, 181
Capital gains, 155
Capital goods, 48
  (See also Investment)
Capital-intensive goods, 854
Capital movements, international, 891
Capital-output ratio, 409
Capitalism, mixed, 105
Capitalist ideology, 45
Capricious universe view, 447
Carson, Robert B., 125
Cartels, 599
Cartter, Allan M., 628, 654, 805
Cause and effect, 16
Caves, Richard E., 711, 867
Ceiling prices, 78, 486–487
Celler-Kefauver Antimerger Act of 1950, 704
Central planning, 391–392, 925–932
  (See also Soviet Union)
Chandler, Lester V., 210n., 311, 330, 354
Chase, Richard X., 394
Checkoff, 790
Cheit, Earl F., 145
Chinitz, Benjamin, 738n.
Choice in economics, 86
Churchill, Winston, 824
Circular flow model, 54
  limitations of, 57
Cities (see Urban problems)
Civil Rights Act of 1964, 377, 803
Class struggle, 831
Classical theory of employment, 223–226
  criticism of, 227–231
Clay, Henry, 20n.
Clayton, James L., 810n., 826
Clayton Act of 1914, 470, 703
Cleveland, Frederick W., Jr., 602n., 610n.

Closed shop, 789, 796
Clower, Robert W., 674
Club of Rome, 427
Coal industry, 146–147
Cochran, John A., 311
Cohn, Stanley H., 935n.
Coincidence of wants, 52
Coins, 297
Colberg, Marshall R., 612
Cole, Charles L., 510
Coleman, James S., 650, 651n.
Coleman, John R., 786n.
Collective bargaining:
  grievance procedure, 798
  sample agreement, 793–795
  seniority, 797–798
  wage criterion, 797
  (See also Labor unions)
Collusion, 598, 604
  obstacles to, 599, 602
Command economy, 924
Commercial banks:
  balance sheet of, 313–314
  and money creation, 320–327
Commission on Income Maintenance Programs, 775n.
Committee for Economic Development, 394, 771n.
Common Market, 878
Communism, 39
Communist Manifesto, The, 833
Company unions, 785
Comparative advantage, 49, 854–860
Comparative costs, 50
Compensation of employees, 182
Competition, 94
  defined, 46
  unfair, 562
  (See also Pure competition)
Complementary goods, 67
Conglomerate combination, 134
Conglomerate mergers, 705–706
Congress of Industrial Organizations (CIO), 787
Constant-cost industry, 547
Constant costs, 50
Construction industry, 751
Consumer behavior, theory of, 502–506
Consumer choice under competition, 554
Consumer credit, 344
Consumer protection, 133
Consumer sovereignty, 89, 103–104, 680
Consumption expenditures, 132
Consumption schedule, 231–235
  and average propensity to consume, 233–234
  defined, 231–232
  effect of taxes on, 237–238, 273–274
  and marginal propensity to consume, 234–235
  nonincome determinants, 235–237
  shifts in, 235–238
"Control by the ruble," 928
Convergence hypothesis, 939–940
Cook, Paul K., 923n.
Cooke, Edmund Vance, 675
Corporate capitalism, 835
Corporate income taxes, 154, 160, 182

Corporate profits, 182
  in national income, 670
Corporations:
  advantages and disadvantages of, 137–139
  in West Virginia, 146–147
Correlation, 16
Cost-of-Living Council, 216
Cost-push inflation, 347–348, 374–375
Costs:
  average fixed, 518
  average total, 519
  average variable, 518–519
  defined, 513–515
  of economic growth, 422–424
  explicit and implicit, 514
  fixed, 517
  law of increasing, 31
  in long run, 521–526
  marginal, 519–520
  in short run, 515–521
  total, 518
  variable, and diminishing returns, 517–518
Council of Economic Advisers, 2, 271
Countervailing power, 608–609, 694, 813
Cowens, Dave, 647
Cox, Eli P., 576
Craft unionism, 788
Crawling-peg system of exchange rates, 917
Creditors, 199
Creeping inflation, 202–204
Criminal conspiracy doctrine, 784
Crowding-out effect, 288, 351–352
Cultural factors in growth, 446–447
Cyclical unemployment, 195
Cyclically balanced budget, 270

Dahl, Robert A., 125n., 941n.
Dales, J. H., 746n.
Danielian, N. R., 921
Debt, 236
  private, 287
  public, 285–289
Debtors and inflation, 199
Declining economy, 179
Declining industries, 88
Decreasing-cost industry, 549n.
Deficits, financing, 282
Deflation, 198
Deglomerative forces, 737
de Jouvenel, Bertrand, 767n.
Demand:
  changes in, 66–67
  defined, 62
  derived, 616
  determinants, 64–67
  elasticity of, 478–483
  for farm products, 716
  under imperfect competition, 493
  law of, 62–63, 476, 500–502
  for money, 662–664
    and monetarism, 364–366
  under pure competition, 491
  for resources, 616–619
Demand for money and velocity, 364
Demand curve, 62
  to firm, 491–494

Demand curve:
  kinked, 596–597
  and marginal utility, 506
  monopoly, 563–565
  (*See also* Demand)
Demand deposit multiplier, 325–327
Demand deposits, 297
  (*See also* Money)
Demand-pull inflation, 192, 264, 372–373
Denison, Edward F., 422*n.*
Department of Defense, 809
Depreciation, 181
Derived demand, 89, 616, 680
Dernburg, Thomas F., 189, 246
Descriptive economics, 4
Detente, 819
Devaluation of dollar, 384–385
Dillard, Dudley, 246
Diminishing marginal utility, law of, 501
Diminishing returns, law of, 516
Directing function of prices, 93
Disarmament, 819
Discount rate, 341
Discrimination, 648
  in housing, 751
  and poverty, 769–770
  sex, 799–803
Discriminatory discharge, 785
Diseconomies of scale, 524–525
Disguised unemployment, 27
Disposable income (DI), 185
Distribution of income, 760–765
  (*See also* Income distribution)
Dividends, 182
Division of labor, 49
"Dollar votes," 88
Doomsday models, 426–428
Double counting, 172
Double taxation, 154
Downs, Anthony, 757
Drucker, Peter F., 121*n.*
Dual labor markets, theory of, 839–840
Due, John F., 674
Duesenberry, James S., 330
Dulles, Foster Rhea, 784*n.*
Duncan, Marvin R., 731
Durable goods, 205–206, 236
Durand, John D., 406*n.*

Earle, M. Mark, Jr., 937*n.*
Easterlin. Richard A., 512*n.*
Easy money policy, 335, 343, 345
Ebenstein, William, 59, 145*n.*
Eckstein, Otto, 121*n.*, 125
Eckstein, Peter, 358*n.*
Economic analysis, 4
  and monopolistic competition, 588
Economic costs, 87
  (*See also* Costs)
Economic growth (*see* Growth, economic)
Economic insecurity, 423
Economic integration, 878
Economic planning, 687
  (*See also* Central planning)
Economic policy, 11
Economic profits, 87, 514, 667–670
Economic quackery, 18

Economic rent, 656–661
Economic resources (*see* Resources)
Economic theory, 4
Economic welfare, 682–684
Economics:
  bias and preconceptions, 14–15
  choice in, 86–87
  defined, 1, 27
  dissatisfaction with, 12–13
  and graphic analysis, 6–8
  macro- and micro-, 15–16
  methodology, 3–12
  terminology, 13–14
Economies:
  of agglomeration, 735–737
  of being established, 562
  of scale, 523–524, 529, 560, 593
    internal and external, 735–737
Edgeworth, F. Y., 223*n.*
Education:
  and distribution of income, 761–762
  and wages, 649
  (*See also* Investment, in human capital)
Edwards, Richard C., 127*n.*, 836*n.*, 840*n.*, 843*n.*, 848
Efficiency, economic, 27
Egalitarianism, 150
Ehrlich, Anne H., 427*n.*
Ehrlich, Paul R., 427*n.*
Eilbott, Peter, 279*n.*
Eisenhower, Dwight D., 814
Elasticity of demand:
  concept, 478–482
  determinants of, 482–483
  for resources, 621–622
Elasticity of supply, 484–486
Emerson, M. Jarvin, 757
Emission fees, 746
Employment, 192
  (*See also* Full employment; Unemployment)
Employment Act of 1946, 212, 271
Employment theory, summarized, 349–352
Energy, 430
Engels, Friedrich, 833
Engler, Robert, 835*n.*
Engman, Lewis A., 835*n.*
Entrepreneurial ability, 25
Environment and growth, 150, 425
  (*See also* Pollution)
Equal Rights Amendment, 803
Equalizing differences, 647
Equation of exchange, 372, 385
Equilibrium, 72
  international, 893
  level of NNP, 250–251
  price, 73
  (*See also* General equilibrium)
Equilibrium NNP:
  and government spending, 272–273
  and taxation, 273–274
Etzioni, Amitai, 827
European Economic Community (EEC), 878
European Recovery Program (ERP), 907
Excess capacity in agriculture, 728
Excess reserves, 317, 327, 334

Excess wage settlement tax, 381
Exchange controls, 900
Exchange rates:
  adjustable-peg system, 907–909
  crawling peg system, 917
  flexible or floating, 894–897, 903, 915–916
Excise taxes, 154
Exclusion principle, 112
Exclusive unionism, 640
Expanding industries, 88
Expectations, 17, 67, 236, 241, 243
Expected rate of net profits, 238
Explicit costs, 514
Exploitation of labor, 837
Exports:
  control of, 881
  in national income accounting, 180
  of United States, 852
Externalities, 97, 109
Exxon, 141

Fabricant, Solomon, 413, 634*n.*
Fair Labor Standards Act of 1938, 643
Fair Packaging and Labelling Act, 133
"Fair-return" price, 573
Fallacy:
  of composition, 15–16
  of limited decisions, 122
Farms and farming:
  income, 714–715
  problems, 715–721
  productivity, 716–717
  public policy toward, 721–729
  resource mobility, 718–719
  in Soviet Union, 936
  surpluses, 723
Featherbedding, 789
Federal Deposit Insurance Corporation, 317
Federal Housing Administration (FHA), 750
Federal Reserve Act of 1913, 303
Federal Reserve Bank of Philadelphia, 295*n.*
Federal Reserve Banks:
  balance sheet of, 336–337
  functions of, 307–309
Federal Reserve Notes, 297, 337
Federal Reserve System:
  functions of, 307–309
  structure of, 303–306
Federal Trade Commission, 133, 835
Federal Trade Commission Act of 1914, 703
Fels, Rendigs, 102
Ferguson, C. E., 510
Feudalism, 40
Fiat money, 300
Final goods, 172
Financial intermediaries, 306, 347
Firm, defined, 134
Fiscal drag, 279
Fiscal policy:
  complications, 284–285, 294
  contractionary, 277
  discretionary, 265–277
  expansionary, 277

Fiscal policy:
Keynesian-monetarist debate, 359–361
nondiscretionary, 277–279
Fisher, F. M., 584*n.*
Five Fundamental Questions, 35
Fixed costs, 517
Flood-control project and benefit-cost
analysis, 115–117
Food for Peace program, 451, 725
Food problem, 431
Food stamp program, 725, 773–774
Forbush, Dascomb R., 612
Forecasting, 687
Foreign aid, 451–452
45-degree line, 251
Foster, Richard B., 937*n.*
Franchises, 470
Franklin, Raymond S., 830*n.*
Free trade, 869
Freedom, 95
of choice, 45
and economic system, 122–123
of enterprise, 45
in Soviet Union, 939
and wage-price policies, 381–382
Freely floating exchange rates, 894–897,
903, 915–917
Freeman, Richard B., 418*n.*, 620*n.*, 654,
655*n.*
Frictional unemployment, 194
Fried, Edward R., 920
Friedman, Milton, 79*n.*, 96*n.*, 122*n.*, 356,
357*n.*, 361*n.*, 369, 370*n.*, 386, 779*n.*
Full employment, 27
defined, 195, 390
in Soviet Union, 935
Full Employment and Balanced Growth
Act of 1976, 391
Full-employment budget, 280–281
Full-employment growth model,
409–410
Full production, 27
Functional distribution of income,
128–129, 670–672
Functional finance, 270
Fusfeld, Daniel R., 2*n.*, 758, 759*n.*, 830*n.*,
942

Gains from specialization and trade, 51
Galbraith, John Kenneth, 13*n.*, 21*n.*,
103, 104*n.*, 141*n.*, 209*n.*, 392*n.*,
471*n.*, 473, 474, 608*n.*, 612, 669*n.*,
694*n.*, 695*n.*, 712, 813*n.*, 834*n.*
concept of industrial structure,
474–475
Gambs, Carl M., 311
Gans, Herbert J., 780
GATT, 878
Geneen, Harold S., 635*n.*
General Agreement on Tariffs and
Trade, 878
General equilibrium, 677–681
General Motors, 135, 141
Generalizations in economics, 5
Geneva Round of tariff negotiations,
880
Gentlemen's agreements, 599
George, Henry, 658, 659
Ghettos, problems of, 748–751, 758

Gibbons, James, 21
Gill, Richard T., 413
GNP gap, 196
Goals of American capitalism, 10
Gold, 908, 913
demonetization of, 916
Gold certificates, 336
Gold export point, 899
Gold import point, 899
Gold standard, 898–900, 905
Goldfeld, Stephen M., 311, 330, 354
Goldman, Marshall I., 884*n.*
Goldschmid, Harvey J., 711
Golob, Eugene O., 145*n.*
Gompers, Samuel, 786
Gordon, Robert Aaron, 220
Gorlin, Alice C., 937*n.*
Gosbank, 928
Gosplan, 927
Government:
allocative function of, 108–113
distributive function of, 108
economic functions of, 106, 683
evaluating role of, 114–118
and income distribution, 683–684
radical view of, 126–127
role of, 48
role in economic development,
448–450
stabilization function, 113–114,
272–273
Government purchases, defined, 150, 177
Grabner, John R., Jr., 473
Graham, Frank G., 301*n.*
Graphic expression, 6
Grayson, Henry, 606*n.*
Great Depression, 208–210
and world trade, 905
Green Revolution, 453
Gresham's Law, 331
Grievance procedure, 798
Griliches, Z., 584*n.*
Gross investment, 178–179
Gross national product:
defined, 168
double counting problem, 172
expenditures approach to, 176–180
gap, 196
income approach to, 181–183
inflating and deflating, 169–171
not ideal measure, 173–175
real, 168–171
Gross private domestic investment, 177
Growth, economic, 397–411
and aggregate demand, 408
and agriculture, 721
and allocative efficiency, 411
definitions of, 398
desirability of, 422–426
doomsday models, 426–428
and human values, 423–424
importance of, 398–399
ingredients of, 399–400
and law of diminishing returns,
401–403
and net investment, 178–179
in 1950's, 214
and productivity, 405–406
in Soviet Union, 933–938
in United States, 415–422

Grubel, Herbert G., 902
Gruchy, Allan G., 13*n.*
Guaranteed minimum income, 775
Guiding function of prices, 93
Gurley, John G., 21, 842*n.*
Gwartney, James D., 118*n.*, 125
Gyorgy, Andrew, 939

Hagen, Everett E., 456
Hague, Douglas C., 557, 674
Hamberg, Daniel, 607*n.*
Hansen, Alvin H., 202*n.*, 267, 674
Hansen, Roger D., 439*n.*
Hardin, Clifford M., 442*n.*
Hardt, John P., 937*n.*
Harrington, Michael, 768*n.*, 780
Harshbarger, C. Edward, 731
Hart, Philip, 709
Hathaway, Dale E., 716*n.*, 722*n.*
Haveman, Robert Henry, 125
Hazlitt, Henry, 392*n.*
Heady, Earl O., 731
Heilbroner, Robert L., 2*n.*, 12*n.*, 42, 99*n.*,
102, 209*n.*, 292, 433, 454*n.*
Helfrich, Harold W., Jr., 175*n.*
Heller, Walter W., 2*n.*, 271*n.*, 356, 361*n.*,
369
Helppie, Charles, 21
Henderson, Hubert, 82
Hensman, C. R., 452*n.*
Herriot, Roger A., 162*n.*
Heyne, Paul T., 696*n.*
Hirschman, Albert T., 933*n.*
Hitch, Charles J., 822*n.*, 824*n.*, 826
Hitler, Adolph, 198
Hochman, Harold M., 757
Holt, Robert T., 685*n.*
Homestead Act of 1862, 470
Hoppe, Arthur, 268
Horizontal combination, 134
Hough, Robbin R., 21
Housing, 750
Huff, Darrell, 18*n.*
Human capital, 648–651
Human obsolescence, 423
Human resources, 417–418
Human values and growth, 423–424
Humphrey, Hubert H., 392*n.*
Humphrey, Thomas M., 369, 394, 429*n.*,
674, 867, 875*n.*, 885
Humphrey-Hawkins bill, 391
Hunt, E. K., 837*n.*, 843*n.*, 848
Hunter, Holland, 937*n.*, 938*n.*, 942
Hutchinson, Harry D., 369
Hyde, Francis E., 628, 677*n.*

Ilchman, Warren F., 826
Immobilities, 98
in agriculture, 718
in labor market, 648
Imperfect competition:
and allocative efficiency, 682–683
defined, 467
Imperialism, 832, 841–842, 845, 868
Implicit costs, 514
Import quotas, 870
Imports:
financing of, 888–889

Imports:
of United States, 852
Incentive function, 658
Incentives, 287
and income inequality, 767, 774–775
in Soviet economy, 929–930
Incidence of taxes, 160–161, 489–491
Inclusive unionism, 640–641
Income determination:
by aggregate demand-aggregate supply approach, 248–253
and fiscal policy, 272–276
by leakage-injection approach, 253–255
Income distribution, 97, 174–175, 681, 760–765
changes in, 762–765
determinants of, 130–131
functional, 129, 670–672
inequality, 760–765
causes, 761–762
and monopoly, 571
optimal, 683–684
personal, 129–130, 760–765
and price system, 552–553
and public debt, 288
Income effect, 501
Income inequality, 760–765
in radical economics, 838–840
Income maintenance program, 749
Income policies, 378
Income shares, 670–672
Income tax, 108
Increasing-cost industry, 548
Increasing costs:
and international trade, 859–860
law of, 31–32
Independent goods, 67
Index numbers, 170
India, 43
Indirect business taxes, 181
Industrial Reorganization Act, 709
Industrial reserve army, 831
Industrial unionism, 640–641, 788
Industries:
defined, 134–135
expanding and declining, 88
Inequality:
domestic, 760–765
international, 436–439
(See also Income distribution)
Infant-industry argument for tariffs, 875
Inferior goods, 67
Inflating and deflating GNP, 169
Inflation, 114, 198
and balance of payments, 912
creeping, 202–204
demand-pull, 372–373
in Germany, 301
premature, 373–375
and public debt, 288
redistributive effects, 199–200
and war, 818–819
Inflationary expectations, 388
Inflationary gap, 263, 372
Inflationary psychosis, 203, 216
Infrastructure, 735–736
Ingles, Jerry, 125
Injunction, 784
In-kind transfers, 764

Innovation, 242
Input-output analysis, 684–686
and Soviet economy, 926
Instability and growth, 420
Interest, 182
in national income accounting, 182
on public debt, 286–287
(See also Interest rate; Monetary policy)
Interest rate, 334
and allocation of capital, 666
in classical theory, 224–225
and equilibrium NNP, 664–666
and investment, 238
liquidity preference theory of, 661–666
Interindustry competition, 468, 693
Intermediate goods, 172
International balance of payments (see Balance of payments)
International Development Association (IDA), 452
International disequilibrium, 893
International Finance Corporation (IFC), 452
International Monetary Fund, 907
International reserves, 892
International Telegraph & Telephone Company (ITT), 705
International trade:
America's role, 851–853
barriers to, 870–877
breakdown, 905–906
with communist nations, 882–884
economic effects of, 860–865
financing, 887–889
problems, 904–917
and protectionism, 872–877
theory of, 853–859
and underdeveloped countries, 450
(See also Balance of payments; Comparative advantage; Tariffs)
Interstate Commerce Act of 1887, 700
Inventories, changes in, 255–256
as investment, 177
Investment, 419
capacity-creating aspect, 409
determinants of, 238
gross versus net, 178–179
in human capital, 648–651
and income, 241–242
and income-creating aspect, 409
and income inequality, 766–767
instability of, 242–243
and monetary policy, 348
nonfinancial, 445
planned versus actual saving, 255
in underdeveloped countries, 443–445
variability of, 217
Investment-demand curve, 238–240
and monetary policy, 345–346
shifts in, 240–241
"Invisible hand," 94, 95, 552

Jamaica Agreement, 917
Javits, Jacob K., 824n.
Jencks, Christopher, 651, 764n.
Jewkes, John, 608n.
Job information, 377

Joint Economic Committee (JEC), 271, 717n.
Joint-profit maximization, 598
Jones, Ronald W., 867
Jurisdictional strikes, 789

Kaish, Stanley, 498, 528
Kaplan, A. D. H., 469n., 692n.
Kassarjian, Harold H., 510
Kaysen, C., 584n.
Kendrick, John W., 635n.
Kenen, Peter B., 867, 885
Kennedy, John F., 280
Kennedy Round, 880
Kerner Commission, 748
Kerr, Clark, 672n.
Keynes, John Maynard, 2, 21, 227
Keynesian economics, 226–231
and Phillips Curve, 388–389
political aspects, 357
Killingsworth, Charles C., 786n.
King, Allan G., 628, 654, 805
Kinked-demand curve, 597
Klaasen, Adrian, 102
Klein, John J., 330
Knight, Frank H., 42
Koch, James V., 576, 612, 711
Kohler, Heinz, 689
Korean conflict, 213, 285
Kreinin, Mordechai E., 902, 918
Kreps, Juanita M., 628
Kutscher, Donald E., 415n.

Labor, 25
alienation, 60
Labor force, 417, 421
and Phillips Curve, 388
in underdeveloped countries, 443
Labor-intensive goods, 854
Labor market imbalances, 374
and the military, 816–818
Labor productivity, 508
Labor unions:
history of, 783–792
public policy toward, 787–790
public sector, 792
and wages, 639–645
(See also Collective bargaining; Wages)
Laissez faire capitalism, 39, 226
Lamphear, F. Charles, 757
Lampman, Robert J., 838n.
Land, 25
Land-intensive goods, 854
Land reform, 447
Land rent, 658
Landrum-Griffin Act of 1959, 790
Landsberg, Hans H., 426n., 433
Lange, Oskar, 20n., 21
Law of capitalist accumulation, 831
Law of demand, 8, 62
Law of diminishing marginal utility, 678
Law of diminishing returns, 401–403
Law of increasing costs, 31
Law of supply, 8, 68
Leakages-injections approach to equilibrium NNP, 253–255

Least-cost combination of resources, 90, 623–625
Leeman, Wayne A., 102
Leftwich, Richard H., 501*n.*, 510, 557, 590, 628
Legal prices, 78, 486
Legal reserve deposit, 315
Legal tender, 300
Leiman, Melvin, 59
Leisure, 174
Lekachman, Robert, 13*n.*, 21, 190*n.*, 220, 246
Leontieff, Wassily W., 392*n.*, 684*n.*
Levitan, Sar A., 803*n.*, 805
Levy, John M., 499
Lewis, Arthur W., 445*n.*
Lewis, John L., 788
Liabilities, 314
Libermanism, 932
Limited liability, 138
Lindauer, John, 246
Lindbeck, Assar, 696*n.*, 844*n.*, 845*n.*, 848
Lindblom, Charles E., 125*n.*, 941*n.*
Linder, Staffan B., 424*n.*, 508*n.*, 510
Lindert, Peter H., 369
Liquid assets, 236
Liquidity preference theory, 662
Local finance, 156, 285
  problems of, 753–755
Locational (transport) economies, 735
Long run, 485, 515
Loucks, William N., 59
Lubitz, Raymond, 867, 885
Lucas, Robert E. B., 764*n.*

MacAvoy, Paul W., 701*n.*
McConnell, Campbell R., 654
McDonald, John, 602*n.*
McDougall, Duncan M., 246
MacEwan, Arthur, 127
Machlup, Fritz, 699*n.*
McKean, Roland N., 125, 822*n.*, 824*n.*, 826
McKenna, Joseph P., 42*n.*
McKenzie, Richard B., 188*n.*
McLand, Douglas, 125
McNamara, Robert, 824
Macrae, Norman, 429*n.*, 430*n.*, 431*n.*, 433
Macroeconomics, defined, 15
Maisel, Sherman J., 195*n.*, 354
Makin, John H., 267
Malthus, Thomas R., 404, 429
  and underdeveloped countries, 441
Managed floating exchange rates, 915
Managerial prerogatives, 796
Mangum, Garth, 803*n.*, 805
Mann, H. Michael, 711
Manpower Development and Training Act (MDTA) of 1962, 376
Manpower policy, 376
Mansfield, Edwin, 501*n.*, 510, 557, 628, 711
Margin requirement, 343
Marginal benefit, 109
Marginal cost, 109, 519, 678
Marginal product, 402, 678
  (*See also* Law of diminishing returns)

Marginal productivity theory of resource demand, 615–619
Marginal propensity to consume, 235
Marginal propensity to save, 235
Marginal resource cost, 617
Marginal revenue, 492
Marginal revenue product, 616
Marginal tax rate, 153
Marginal utility, 501
Market economy, 47
Market period, 484
Marshall, Alfred, 22, 223*n.*
Marshall, F. Ray, 628, 654, 803*n.*, 805
Marshall Plan, 212, 907
Marx, Karl, 2, 22, 829, 830, 868
Marxian economics (*see* Radical economics)
Mass-production economies, 142
Mass transit, 743
Material wants, 24
Maurice, S. Charles, 510
Maxwell, James A., 164
Meadows, Dennis L., 427*n.*, 433
Means, Gardiner C., 207*n.*, 698*n.*
Meany, George, 791, 921
Medicaid, 774
Medicare, 774
Medium of exchange, 52
Meier, Gerald M., 456, 868*n.*
Melman, Seymour, 635*n.*, 814*n.*, 821, 826
Meltzer, Jack, 733*n.*
Mergers, 594, 604
Mermelstein, David, 848
Mexico, 457
Meyer, Robert A., 590
Microeconomics, defined, 16
Miernyk, William H., 689
Military-industrial complex:
  allocative aspects, 812–816
  costs, 809–812
  and economic stability, 818–821
  manpower recruitment, 816–818
  size, 809–810
  weapons procurement, 813–814
Mill, John Stuart, 2, 124*n.*, 223*n.*
Miller, Glenn H., Jr., 731
Miller, Herman P., 162*n.*
Miller, James C., III, 816*n.*
Miller, Roger Leroy, 432*n.*
Minimum-wage, 487, 643–644
Mishan, E. J., 423*n.*
Mixed capitalism, 40, 105
Models, economic, 3–9
Monetarism:
  and equation of exchange, 358–359
  political aspects, 357–358
Monetary multiplier, 325–327
Monetary policy, 345–346, 362
  effectiveness, 346–349
  objectives of, 334–335
  qualitative controls, 343–344
  quantitative controls, 337–343
Monetary rule, 361–362
Money:
  and business cycle, 217–218
  creation of, 320–327
  as debt, 299
  defined, 52
  demand for, 662–664
  functions of, 296

Money:
  and prices, 300–302
  value of, 299–302
  (*See also* Monetarism)
Money market, 662
Money supply, 210
Money wages, 632
Monopolistic competition, 578–588
  and advertising, 583–588
  defined, 463–465, 578–579
  demand curve, 580–581
  illustrations, 580
  and profit maximization, 580–582
  "wastes," 582–583
Monopoly:
  and big business, 691–692
  cases for and against, 692–699
  defined, 559–560
  natural, 560–561
  political aspects, 698–699
  public policy toward, 669–709
  pure: and barriers to entry, 560–563
    defined, 559–560
    demand curve, 563–565
    evaluation, 569–572
    price-output adjustments, 565–567
    in professional basketball, 577
    profits, regulation, 572–574
    and technological advance, 571–572
Monopoly capitalism, 832, 835
Monopsonistic competition, 467
Monopsony, 467
  in labor market, 636–637
Monsen, R. Joseph, Jr., 59
Moral suasion, 344
Morgan, Theodore, 203*n.*, 456
Morris, Richard B., 784*n.*
Morse, Chandler, 431*n.*
Mueller, Willard F., 702*n.*
Multinational corporations, 876, 921–922
Multiplier, 218, 256–261
  balanced budget, 276
  characteristics of, 259
  demand-deposit, 325–327
  and international trade, 864–865
  and marginal propensities to consume and save, 259–260
  size of, 261
  and transfer payments, 283
Mundell, Robert A., 42
Musgrave, Peggy B., 125, 163*n.*, 164
Musgrave, Richard A., 125, 163*n.*, 164
Mutual interdependence of firms, 594–595, 603

Nader, Ralph, 133
NASA, 809
National Advisory Commission on Civil Disorders, 748*n.*
National Association of Manufacturers, 124*n.*, 787
National banks, 306
National defense, 152
National Housing Act of 1949, 750
National income, 184
National Labor Relations Act, 788
National Labor Relations Board, 788
"Natural monopolies," 107, 560

Natural resources, 417
  in Soviet Union, 934
  and underdeveloped countries,
    440–441
Near-monies, 298
Negative income tax, 108, 775–777
Negroes:
  economic status, 769
  unemployment, 196–197
Neocolonialism, 452–453
Net exports, 180
  and equilibrium NNP, 862
Net investment, 178–179
  (*See also* Investment)
Net national product, 183
  equilibrium versus full-employment,
    262–264
Net taxes, 278
Net worth, 314
Netzer, Dick, 660*n.*, 743*n.*, 748*n.*, 755*n.*,
  757
New cities concept, 755–756
New Deal, 198
New Economic Policy, 379
Nijhawan, Inder P., 447*n.*
Nixon, Richard M., 216, 384, 913, 914
Noll, Roger G., 83*n.*, 577
Noncompeting groups, 646
Nondurable goods, 205–206
Nonprice competition, 461, 469, 583,
  604–605
Nonproductive transactions, 173
Nontariff barriers to trade, 881
Nonunion shop, 796
Nordhaus, William D., 430*n.*
Normal goods, 66
Normal profit, 87, 514, 667
Norris-La Guardia Act of 1932, 788
Northrup, Herbert R., 642*n.*, 654
Nourse, Hugh O., 757
Novick, David, 823*n.*
Nurkse, Ragnar, 442*n.*

Occupational discrimination, 801–802
Okun, Arthur M., 174*n.*, 272*n.*, 292,
  777*n.*, 780
Okun's Law, 395–396
Old Age, Survivors, Disability, and
    Health Insurance (OASDHI), 772
Oligopoly:
  and barriers to entry, 593–594
  and collusion, 598–599
  defined, 465–466, 592–593
  evaluation, 605–610
  illustrations, 593
  and nonprice competition, 604–605
  price determination under, 592–602
  and profits-payoff table, 602–604
  and technological progress, 606–608
Oligopsony, 467, 637
Olson, Mancur, 426*n.*, 433
OPEC, 216, 217, 351, 385, 453, 881, 912
Open-economy multiplier, 864–865
Open-market operations, 339–341
Open shop, 796
Operational lag, 284
Optimum output, 109
"Other things equal" assumption, 5,
  77

Output effect, 621
Owen, Henry, 920

Paper money, 297
Paradox of thrift, 261
Parity prices, 723
Partial equilibrium, 676
Participatory socialism, 843
Partnership, 136–137
Patent laws, 470, 562, 706–707
Paternalism, 785
Payroll taxes, 154
Peach, W. N., 429*n.*
Peak pricing, 79, 742
Pearson, Donald, 21
Pechman, Joseph A., 164
Pen, Jan, 866*n.*, 867, 885
"Pentagon capitalism," 814
Perlman, Richard, 628
Perrow, Charles, 844*n.*, 846*n.*, 848
Personal consumption expenditures, 176
Personal distribution of income, 129–130
  (*See also* Income distribution;
    Poverty)
Personal income, 184
Personal income tax, 152–154, 160
Personal saving, 132
Personal taxes, 278
Peterson, Wallace C., 246, 267
Petroleum industry as a monopoly, 698
Pfaff, Anita B., 759*n.*
Pfaff, Martin, 759*n.*
Phelps, Edmund S., 125
Phelps-Brown, G. H., 689
Phillips, A. W., 373*n.*
Phillips Curve, 373–376, 918
  and inflationary expectations, 388–389
  stability of, 380, 388–389
Pierson, Frank C., 672*n.*
Pigou, A. C., 223*n.*
Plant, defined, 134
Pohlman, Jerry E., 381*n.*, 394
Policy economics, 9
Political fragmentation of cities,
  711–713, 751–753
Pollution, 79, 110, 743–747
Population:
  and economic growth, 414
  growth of, 149
  and Malthus, 404–405
  optimum, 403–404
  in underdeveloped countries, 441–442
Post hoc, ergo propter hoc fallacy, 16
Poverty, 767–771
  and blacks, 769–770
  in ghettos, 748–750
  welfare state, 771–777
Precautionary demand for money, 662
Preferential hiring, 796
Premature inflation, 193, 264
Price:
  legal, 78, 486–489
  socially optimum, 573
  and wage controls, 211
Price discrimination, 567–569
Price flexibility, 225
Price leadership, 599
Price level, 192
  (*See also* Inflation)

Price rigidity and oligopoly, 596–
  597
Price supports, 923
Price system:
  evaluation of, 95–98, 682–684
  framework of, 85
  and growth, 431
  operation of, 87
  in Soviet Union, 930–932
Primary labor market, 839
Priority principle, 927
Private goods, 112
Producer sovereignty, 103–104
Product differentiation, 464, 579,
  583–584, 600
Product-mix, optimum, 30
Product quality and GNP, 174
Production possibilities curve, 30, 202,
  812, 854
  and diminishing returns, 402
  and growth, 400
Productivity, 405–406, 508, 766
  and income, 130–131
  and resource demand, 620
  slowdown, 634–635
  and wage rates, 375, 632–635
Professional athletics and monopsony,
  637
Professional basketball and monopoly,
  577
Profit maximization for competitive
  firm, 532–550
Profit-maximizing combination of
  resources, 622–623
Profits:
  economic, 514–515
  functions of, 669–670
  and innovation, 668–669
  and investment, 238
  in Marxian economics, 831–832
  and monopoly, 565–566
  normal, 514, 667
  sources, 667–669
  in Soviet economy, 932–933
  and uncertainty, 668–669
Profits-payoff table, 602
Progressive tax, 153, 159
Projector, Dorothy S., 762*n.*
Property tax, 156, 161, 739
  reform of, 754–755
Proportional tax, 159
Proprietors' income, 182
Proprietorship, 136
Protective tariffs, 870
  (*See also* Tariffs)
Public choice, theory of, 118
Public debt, 285–289
  advantages of, 289
  burden of, 287–289
  and growth, 289
  and monetary policy, 289
Public Law, 480, 725
Public sector, failure, 118–121
Public utilities, 560
Pure capitalism, 39
Pure competition:
  defined, 461–462, 531
  and pricing evaluated, 550–554
  profit maximization: in long run,
    544–550

Pure competition:
  profit maximization:
    in short run, 532–544
  and technological advance, 553–554
Pure Food and Drug Act of 1906, 106, 133
Pure monopoly, defined, 462–463
  (*See also* Monopoly)
Pure profit, 87, 667–670
Pursuit-and-escape theory, 672

Qualitative credit controls, 304
Quantitative credit controls, 304

Racial discrimination
  (*see* Discrimination)
Radical economics:
  conception of capitalism, 834–843
  and Karl Marx, 830–833
  methodology, 22, 833–834
  orthodox criticisms of, 843–846
  role of government, 126–127, 835–836
Ranis, Gustav, 456
Rate of exchange, 887
Rate of interest (*see* Interest rate)
Rationing, 487
  of foreign exchange, 900
Rationing function of prices, 74
Rawls, John, 766*n.*
Rayback, Joseph G., 784*n.*
Real estate credit, 344
Real GNP, 169–171
Real wage insurance plan, 381
Real wages, 632
Recession of 1958, 214
Recessionary gap, 262
Reciprocal Trade Agreements Act of 1934, 878
Recognition lag, 284
Rees, Albert, 643*n.*, 645*n.*
Rees, Richard D., 731
Regressive tax, 159, 274*n.*
Regulation:
  dilemma of, 574
  and monopoly, 572–574
  of natural monopolies, 700–702
Regulatory commissions, 107
Reich, Michael, 836*n.*, 840*n.*, 843*n.*, 848
Reid, Samuel Richardson, 145, 711
Rejda, George E., 780
Remittances, 891
Rent, economic, 656–661
  differences in, 660–661
  in national income accounting, 182
Rent controls, 78, 487, 499
Required reserves, 317
Research:
  in agriculture, 716–721
  as barrier to entry, 562
  and growth, 418–419
  under oligopoly, 607–608
  (*See also* Technological advance)
Reserve Bank credit, 342
Reserve ratio, 315, 337
Resource market, 76
Resources:
  allocation of, 108–112, 569–571
  by government, 108–113
  economic, 614–615

Resources:
  economic: demand for, 615–619
    elasticity, 621–622
    least-cost combination, 622–625
    scarcity of, 25–27
Reuss, Henry R., 197*n.*
Reuther, Walter, 791
Revenue sharing, 157, 754
Reynolds, Alan, 294*n.*
Reynolds, Lloyd G., 644*n.*, 654
Ricardo, David, 2
Richardson, J. David, 867, 885
Richman, Barry M., 926*n.*
Right to bequeath, 45
Right-to-work laws, 796
Ritter, Lawrence S., 345*n.*, 354, 361*n.*, 369, 370*n.*
Rivlin, Alice M., 651*n.*, 780
Roberts, Marc J., 426*n.*, 429*n.*, 431*n.*
Robertson, D. H., 311, 312*n.*
Robinson, E. A. G., 528, 576
Robinson-Patman Act of 1936, 703
Rogers, Augustus J., III, 498
Romano, Richard, 59
Root, Franklin R., 902
Rostow, W. W., 413
Rowan, Richard L., 805
"Rule of 70," 202, 399
Ryan, W. J. L., 689

Sakharov, Andrei D., 939
Sales taxes, 154, 155, 161
Samuelson, Paul A., 28*n.*, 123*n.*, 356, 801*n.*
Sanford, Terry, 733*n.*
Saurez, James M., 815*n.*
Savers and inflation, 200
Saving schedule, 233
  effect of taxes on, 273–274
  and marginal propensity to save, 234–235
  nonincome determinants, 235–237
Savings:
  and capital formation, 48–49
  in classical theory, 224
  by consumers, 132
  personal, 185
  relation to income, 231–235
  (*See also* Saving schedule)
Sawers, David, 608*n.*
Say's Law, 223
Scarce resources, 25
Scarcity, 86
Schaap, Dick, 744*n.*
Scherer, F. M., 612, 699*n.*, 707*n.*
School lunch programs, 725
Schultz, Theodore W., 650*n.*
Schultze, Charles L., 824, 920
Schumacher, E. F., 427*n.*, 433
Schumpeter, Joseph A., 469*n.*, 576
Schwartz, Eli, 433
Schwartz, Harry, 925*n.*
Scientific American, 433
Secondary boycotts, 789
Secondary labor market, 839
Secular stagnation, 210
Secular trend, 205
Selective credit controls, 343

Selective service system, 816
Self-interest motive, 45
Seniority, 797
Shaffer, Harry G., 650
Shapiro, Edward, 189, 267
Shaw, George Bernard, 97*n.*, 310*n.*
Sheahan, John, 380*n.*
Sherman, Howard J., 837*n.*, 841*n.*, 843*n.*, 848
Sherman Act of 1890, 107, 470, 702
Shifrin, Avraham, 943
Shifting of taxes, 160–161
Shock effect, 643
Shore, Warren, 773*n.*
Short run, defined, 485, 515
Shultz, George P., 370*n.*, 786*n.*
Sichel, Werner, 358*n.*
Silber, William L., 345*n.*, 354, 361*n.*, 369, 370*n.*
Simon, Julian A., 590
Simons, Henry C., 692*n.*
Single-tax movement, 658
Slichter, Sumner H., 202*n.*
Smith, Adam, 2, 95*n.*, 509*n.*, 869
Smithsonian Agreement, 915
Smoot-Hawley Tariff Act of 1930, 874, 877
Snellings, Aubrey N., 394
Snider, Delbert A., 867, 885, 910*n.*, 920
Social costs, 110
Social goods, 97, 112, 553
Social point of view, 15
Social Security System, 771–777
Social welfare, 173–175
Socialism, 39, 832–833
  participatory, 843
  (*See also* Radical economics)
Soil bank, 724
Solow, Robert M., 425*n.*, 426*n.*
Solzhenitsyn, Aleksandr, 939
Somers, Gerald G., 628
Soth, Lauren, 730*n.*
Soviet Union:
  agriculture, 924, 936
  central planning, 925–932
  composition of output, 934
  economic growth, 933–938
  economic institutions, 924–925
  evaluation of economy, 938–939
  incentives, 929–930
  international trade, 882–884
  and price system, 930–932
  prison labor, 943–944
  reforms, 932–933
  standard of living, 938
  taxation, 931
  technological advance, 935, 937
Special Drawing Rights, 915–916
Special-interest effect, 119
Specialization, 49
  disadvantages of, 52
Speculative demand for money, 365, 663
Spillover benefits, 553, 683
  and output, 110–111
Spillover costs, 553, 683
  and output, 110
Stabilization policies, 113
  and balance of payments, 917–918
  and Phillips Curve, 375–379
Stagnation, 216–217, 381–385, 821

Staley, Eugene, 436*n.*, 446*n.*, 452*n.*
Stanford, Quentin H., 456
State banks, 306
State finance, 155–156, 285
State and Local Fiscal Assistance Act, 157
Static economy, 178
Stein, Herbert, 392*n.*
Stern, Louis W., 473
Stevens, Carl M., 643*n.*
Stevens, Robert Warren, 902
Stigler, George J., 20*n.*, 21, 42*n.*, 528, 557, 689, 690*n.*, 692*n.*
Stillerman, Richard, 608*n.*
Stock, 138
Stock market, 243, 343
  crash of 1929, 209
Stocking, George, 526*n.*
Stonier, Alfred W., 557, 674
Strickland, Allyn D., 711
Strikebreakers, 785
Structural unemployment, 194
Subsidies, 150, 836
  in agriculture, 725–726
Substitutability, 86
  of resources, 622
Substitute goods, 67
Substitution effect, 501, 621
Suburbs, development of, 738–741
Supermultiplier, 262
Supplemental Security Income (SSI), 773
Supply:
  aggregate, 249–250
  defined, 68
  determinants of, 69–70
  elasticity of, 484–486
  law of, 477
Supply of money, and interest rate, 664–666
Supply curve:
  under competition in long run, 547–550
    constant-cost industry, 547–548
    increasing-cost industry, 548–550
  defined, 68
  and marginal cost, 541–542
  and time, 484–486
Supported prices, 78, 487–488
Surplus value, 831
Surpluses, 72
  disposing of, 282
Suslov, Mikhail A., 923
Swagler, Roger M., 145
Sweezy, Paul M., 22*n.*, 833*n.*
Sympathy strikes, 789

Tabb, William K., 830*n.*
Taft-Hartley Act of 1947, 789
Target prices for farm products, 727
Tariffs, 707, 870–872
  arguments against, 869–870
  arguments for, 872–877
  international policies, 877–884
Taussig, F. W., 310*n.*
Tax cut of 1964, 281–282, 285, 361
Tax-exempt securities, 155
Tax loopholes, 154
Tax structure, American, 161

Taxation:
  and consumption schedule, 237
  and equilibrium NNP, 273–274
Taxes:
  average rate, 153
  cut of 1964, 281–282, 285, 361
  excise, 161
  and fiscal policy, 273–274
  incidence, 160–164, 489–491
  income, 152–154
  and level of net national product, 273–274
  local, 156
  marginal rate, 153
  payroll, 154
  personal, 152–153
  progressive, 159
  property, 156, 160
  proportional, 159
  regressive, 159
  sales, 161, 489–491
  shifting, 489–491
  single, 658–659
  state, 155–156
  turnover, 931
  on wage settlements, 381
Taylor, George W., 672*n.*
Technological advance, 48, 418–419
  in agriculture, 716–717
  and market structure, 471
  and the military, 822
  and oligopoly, 607–608
  and pure competition, 553–554
  and resource combinations, 90–91
  in underdeveloped countries, 445–446
Technological determinism, 694, 708
Technology:
  and growth, 429–431
  and international trade, 875–876
  and market structure, 471
  in Soviet Union, 935, 937
  (*See also* Technological advance)
"Technostructure," 695
Telser, Richard G., 588*n.*
Terkel, Studs, 197
Terminology, 13
Terms of trade, 51, 857, 896
Theory of games, 602
Third World, 436
Thompson, Arthur A., Jr., 557
Thompson, George C., 711
Thompson, Wilbur R., 742*n.*, 752*n.*
Thorn, Richard S., 311, 354
Thrift, 236
Thurow, Lester C., 433, 764*n.*, 780
Tight money policy, 335, 343, 345
Till money, 314
Time, value of, 507
Tobin, James, 356
Total cost, 518
Trade Expansion Act of 1962, 880
Trade Reform Act of 1974, 881
Trading possibilities line, 857
Traditional economies, 40
Transactions demand for money, 364, 662
Transfer multiplier, 283
Transfer payments, defined, 150–151, 764

Transformation curve, 30
Transportation problem in cities, 741–743
Treasury deposits, 337
Trebing, Harry M., 145
Trezise, Philip H., 920
Truth in Lending Act, 133
Tuckman, Howard P., 780
Tullock, Gordon, 118*n.*
Turner, John E., 685*n.*
Turnover taxes, 931

Uhler, Robert G., 102
Ulmer, Melville J., 392*n.*, 474, 475*n.*
Underdeveloped countries:
  assistance from advanced nations, 450–453
  attitudes toward growth, 437–438
  government role in growth process, 448–450
  problems of growth, 440–448
Underemployment, 27, 32
Undistributed corporate profits, 182
Unemployment, 27, 32, 114, 442–443
  economic costs of, 195–197
  types of, 194–195
Unemployment compensation, 773
Unfair competition, 562
Union for Radical Political Economics (URPE), 830*n.*
Union shop, 796
Unions, 640–641
  (*See also* Labor unions)
United Automobile Workers, 483
United Mine Workers, 642
United States Department of Commerce, 189, 220
Uppal, J. S., 447*n.*
Urban blight, 739
Urban Mass Transit Act, 743
Urban problems:
  financial, 753–755
  ghettos, 748–751
  political, 739–741, 751–753
  pollution, 743–747
  transportation, 741–743
Urban renewal, 750
Urban sprawl, 738–741
Urbanization, 149
User charges, 742
Utility, 501
Utility-maximizing rule, 503

Value-added, 172
Value judgments, 9
Variable costs, 517
Vault cash, 314
Velocity of money, 347, 363–366
Vertical combination, 134
Veterans' Administration, 750
Vicious circle of underdevelopment, 447–448
Vicious circle theory of inflation, 917
Vietnam, 285, 384
  and inflation, 215
Vitaliano, Donald F., 288*n.*
Volunteer army, 816–818

Wage determination, 635–643
Wage differentials, 645–648
Wage flexibility, 225
Wage-price inflationary spiral, 203
Wage-price policies, 378–381
  controls, 379
  guideposts, 378
Wages:
  defined, 632
  differentials in, 645–648
  general level, 632–635
  and labor markets, 635–643
  minimum, 643–644
  money versus real, 632
  in national income accounting,
    670–671
  and productivity, 375
  and unions, 639–643
Wagner Act of 1935, 788
Wallich, Henry C., 20n., 381n., 392n.
Walton, Clarence C., 602n., 610n.
War industry (*see* Military-industrial
    complex)
Ward, Barbara, 757
Ward, Benjamin, 21

Warren, Russell G., 711
Wastes of monopolistic competition,
    582–583
Watson, Donald S., 528
Wealth, distribution of, 838
Weatherford, Willis D., 938n., 942
Weaver, James H., 848
Webb-Pomerene Act, 706
Weinberger, Caspar W., 781
Weidenbaum, Murray L., 392n., 826
Weiler, E. T., 503n.
Weintraub, Andrew, 433
Weintraub, Sidney, 381n.
Weiss, Leonard W., 526n., 590, 612, 711
Weisskoff, Francine Blau, 801n.
Weisskopf, Thomas A., 836n., 840n.,
    843n., 848
Weisskopf, Walter A., 424n.
Welfare programs, 108
Wentworth, Donald R., 82
West Virginia, and mining corporations,
    146–147
Westerfield, Janice M., 637n.
Weston, J. Fred, 711
Whitaker, Gilbert R., Jr., 612

Whitney, William G., 59
Wilcox, Clair, 575n., 938n., 942
Wilczynski, J., 942
Williams, John D., 602n.
Women:
  economic status of, 800–801
  in the labor market, 799–803
Women's Liberation Movement, 803
Wonnacott, Paul, 367n., 369
Workable competition, 693
World Bank, 451
World trade (*see* International trade)
World War II and world trade, 905–906

Yellow-dog contract, 785
Yntema, Theodore, 483n.

Zagoria, Sam, 792n.
Zero economic growth, 423
Zero population growth, 423

NATIONAL INCOME AND RELATED STATISTICS FOR YEARS, 1954–1976

National income statistics are in billions of current dollars. Details may not add to totals because of rounding.

			1954	1955	1956	1957	1958	1959	1960	1961	1962	196
THE SUM OF	1	Personal consumption expenditures	$235.8	$253.7	$266.0	$280.4	$289.5	$310.8	$324.9	$335.0	$355.2	$374
	2	Gross private domestic investment	52.7	68.4	71.0	69.2	61.9	77.6	76.4	74.3	85.2	90
	3	Government purchases of goods and services	75.8	75.0	79.4	87.1	95.0	97.6	100.3	108.2	118.0	123
	4	Net exports	2.0	2.2	4.3	6.1	2.5	.6	4.4	5.8	5.4	6
EQUALS	5	Gross national product	366.3	399.3	420.7	442.8	448.8	486.5	506.0	523.3	563.8	594
LESS	6	Capital consumption allowances	33.1	35.3	38.9	42.0	44.0	46.1	47.7	49.1	50.5	52.
EQUALS	7	Net national product	333.2	364.0	381.8	400.8	404.8	440.4	458.3	474.2	513.3	542.
LESS	8	Indirect business taxes	34.1	36.0	34.9	38.5	40.8	43.3	46.3	50.0	55.9	59.
EQUALS	9	National income	299.1	328.0	346.9	362.3	364.0	397.1	412.0	424.2	457.4	482.
LESS	10	Social security contributions	10.1	11.5	12.9	14.9	15.2	18.0	21.1	21.9	24.3	27.
	11	Corporate income taxes	17.6	22.0	22.0	21.4	19.0	23.7	22.7	22.8	24.0	26.
	12	Undistributed corporate profits	7.9	12.3	9.9	9.2	7.1	12.4	11.0	10.8	16.5	17.
PLUS	13	Transfer payments	24.6	26.4	28.8	32.5	36.7	39.1	42.5	46.2	48.0	51.
EQUALS	14	Personal income	288.2	308.8	330.9	349.3	359.3	382.1	399.7	414.9	440.7	463.
LESS	15	Personal taxes	32.5	35.4	39.6	42.4	42.2	46.0	50.3	52.0	56.8	60.
EQUALS	16	Disposable income	255.7	273.4	291.3	306.9	317.1	336.1	349.4	362.9	383.9	402.
	17	Real gross national product (in 1972 dollars)	613.7	654.8	668.8	680.9	679.5	720.4	736.8	755.3	799.1	830.
	18	Percent change in real GNP	−1.3	6.7	2.1	1.8	−.2	6.0	2.3	2.5	5.8	4.0
	19	Real GNP per capita	3764	3946	3960	4031	3885	4051	4078	4112	4284	4390

RELATED STATISTICS

		1954	1955	1956	1957	1958	1959	1960	1961	1962	1963
20	Consumer price index (1967 = 100)	80.5	80.2	81.4	84.3	86.6	87.3	88.7	89.6	90.6	91.7
21	Index of industrial production (1967 = 100)	51.9	58.5	61.1	61.9	57.9	64.8	66.2	66.7	72.2	76.5
22	Supply of money (in billions of dollars)	132.3	135.2	136.9	135.9	141.1	143.4	144.2	148.7	150.9	156.5
23	Population (in millions)	163.0	165.9	168.9	172.0	174.9	177.8	180.7	183.7	186.5	189.2
24	Civilian labor force (in millions)	63.6	65.0	65.5	66.9	67.6	68.4	69.6	70.4	70.6	71.8
25	Unemployment (in millions)	3.5	2.9	2.8	2.9	4.6	3.7	3.9	4.7	3.9	4.1
26	Unemployment as a % of the civilian labor force	5.5	4.4	4.1	4.3	6.8	5.5	5.5	6.7	5.5	5.7
27	Total consumer credit outstanding (in billions of dollars)	32.5	38.8	42.3	45.0	45.1	51.5	56.1	58.0	63.8	71.7